International Finance and Open Economy Macroeconomics

SECOND EDITION

International Finance and Open Economy Macroeconomics

SECOND EDITION

Francisco L. Rivera-Batiz

Columbia University

Luis A. Rivera-Batiz

University of California at San Diego

Universitat Pompeu Fabra, Barcelona

MACMILLAN PUBLISHING COMPANY

NEW YORK

Maxwell Macmillan Canada

TORONTO

Maxwell Macmillan International

NEW YORK   OXFORD   SINGAPORE   SYDNEY

Editor: Jill Lectka
Production Supervisor: Helen Wallace
Production Manager: Paul Smolenski
Cover Designer: Russ Maselli

This book was set in Times Roman by Carlisle Communications, Inc., printed and bound by Book Press. The cover was printed by Phoenix.

Macmillan Publishing Company
866 Third Avenue
New York, New York 10022

Macmillan Publishing Company is
part of the Maxwell Communication
Group of Companies

Collier Macmillan Canada, Inc.
1200 Eglinton Avenue East
Suite 200
Don Mills, Ontario M3C 3N1

LIBRARY OF CONGRESS CATALOGING-IN-PUBLICATION DATA
Rivera-Batiz, Francisco L.
    International finance and open economy macroeconomics / Francisco
L. Rivera-Batiz, Luis A. Rivera-Batiz.—2nd ed.
        p.   cm.
    Includes index.
    ISBN 0-02-400581-9
    1. International finance.   2. International economic relations.
3. Macroeconomics.   I. Rivera-Batiz, Luis.   II. Title.
HG3881.R527 1994   92-44656
332'.042—dc20   CIP

Printing: 2 3 4 5 6 7 8   Year: 4 5 6 7 8 9 0 1 2

Preface

We have written this book with the goal of providing a comprehensive but integrated introduction to modern international finance and open economy macroeconomics. With this in mind, we have gathered the most important recent developments in the area—particularly those relating to flexible exchange rates—and the most advanced, frontier-level research in the field. We have simplified this material into a form that is accessible to a wide, general audience. The major common thread running throughout the book is our concern with domestic and international policy issues. This is a policy-oriented textbook. Major policy controversies are thus analyzed in their historical context and in light of the latest theoretical developments in the field.

New to the Second Edition

In addition to the detailed examination of foreign exchange markets, international money markets, and Eurocurrencies that appeared in the first edition, this second edition offers full coverage of the remarkable deregulation and internationalization of banking and finance in the 1980s and 1990s. We also supply a discussion of the growing importance of Japanese finance, the economics of the European integration of 1992, and a comprehensive analysis of exchange rate regimes in developing countries. An up-to-date examination of new instruments in international finance and banking, such as currency futures, options, swaps, and Eurobonds, has been introduced, and new chapters have been added examining the nature and implications of foreign exchange market efficiency, exchange rate risk, expectations, and forecasting.

This book offers an up-to-date discussion of the anatomy of inflation and business cycles in open economies and the related policy issues, the performance of past international monetary regimes such as the gold standard and the gold exchange standard, the why of the collapse of the Bretton Woods system, the economics of managed floating and of central bank intervention in foreign exchange markets, currency target zones and monetary unions, and the changing role and future prospect of gold, the dollar, and other international reserve currencies in world arrangements.

This second edition analyzes in detail the major policy issues confronting the 1990s. One full chapter is devoted to the external debt crisis of the developing countries and its status at the beginning of the 1990s, including a discussion of the latest policy proposals and instruments to deal with it, such as debt buybacks, debt-equity swaps, and debt-for-nature swaps. The European Monetary System and its exchange rate mechanism are also examined in all their complexities, as well as the Maastricht Treaty seeking European monetary unification within the next decade.

Throughout the book, the U.S. economy and recent U.S. economic policymaking are discussed within the context of the growing interdependence prevailing in the world today. We supply a dissection of the possible international repercussions of domestic economic policies and of the costs and benefits of international policy coordination. We also provide an analysis of the process of liberalization and macroeconomic policymaking in Latin

v

America, Eastern Europe, and in the Republics forming part of the former Soviet Union, the current role of the International Monetary Fund in the world economy, the effects of IMF-sponsored macroeconomic adjustment programs in developing countries, the nature of balance-of-payments crises, and the choice of fixed versus flexible exchange rate regimes. By the end of the book the reader should have a thorough understanding of these policy issues, the controversies that have surrounded them, and the available evidence on the matter. Our discussion of recent events in the world economy will also update the reader on the current state of international economic affairs.

International economics is not an easy discipline. There are many alternative economic environments and topic areas to consider in this diverse and growing field. An adequate treatment of the subject must avoid falling into a fragmented approach to the area and instead provide an integrated view of its complexities. This book follows such a route. We start by providing simple frameworks showing basic principles, and then we gradually build a more sophisticated analysis by introducing additional elements into the discussion. The end product is still a highly flexible product that can be easily adapted to the reader's preferences. The more difficult material is left to optional sections or appendixes that can be used by the more knowledgeable reader or set aside without any disruption of continuity.

AUDIENCE AND PREREQUISITES

Our approach is to state the main issues in a down-to-earth manner. No calculus or advanced mathematics is required; only simple algebra is utilized when necessary. A course in introductory economics—and particularly macroeconomics—would be extremely helpful and is recommended by the authors. Those readers with more background will benefit from the rich discussion of recent events and theoretical developments in the area. The abundance of references—and our emphasis in being consistent with the literature—means that the book can be utilized as an initial stepping-stone for advanced study and research in the field. It can thus serve as a handy sourcebook. Working out the problems at the end of the chapter will ensure that understanding of the material has been reached. Adopters of the textbook may obtain a solutions manual for these problems directly from Macmillan.

ACKNOWLEDGMENTS

One may ask what are the main elements in the writing of a textbook. Three key aspects are involved. First must be a supply of comments and suggestions from colleagues and readers of the manuscript. Luckily, in writing the first and second editions of this book, we have been provided with valuable comments. We want to thank Professors Luis Akle (Instituto Tecnológico Autónomo de México), Robert Z. Aliber (Brandeis University), Victor Canto (University of Southern California), Betty Daniel (State University of New York at Albany), Eusebio Diaz (University of Puerto Rico), Steven Husted (University of Pittsburgh), Parul Jain (Rutgers University), Carlos Seiglie (Rutgers University), Marie Thursby (Purdue University), José Viñals (Banco de España), David Findlay (Colby College), Daniel Himarios (University of Texas at Arlington), Alan Isaacs (American University), and Bernard Malamud (University of Nevada at Las Vegas) for their comments at the various stages of our project. Their suggestions and the revisions they suggested make the present version a much improved and polished product compared to the initial drafts.

Scores of undergraduate and graduate students in the Economics Departments at Indiana University, the University of Massachusetts at Amherst, the University of Pennsylvania, Rutgers University, Instituto Tecnológico Autónomo de México, and the Universitat Pompeu Fabra of Barcelona,

Spain, have given us feedback on previous versions of the manuscript. In addition, students at the graduate schools of business at the University of Southern California and the University of Puerto Rico supplied helpful comments. We also successfully tried the second edition with graduate students at the School of International and Public Affairs at Columbia University and at the School of International and Pacific Studies at the University of California at San Diego. Their support is immensely appreciated. We also thank our editor at Macmillan, Jill Lectka for her suggestions, encouragement and, above all, patience during the long march to the completion of the manuscript.

A second requirement for successful book writing is the availability of a supporting staff. We must first express gratitude to our research assistants for bearing with us through many tedious revisions and updating of figures and tables. They were: Susan Despins, Nahla El-Hawli, Priya Ranjan, Debojyoti Sarkar, and José Traslosheros. The efficient word processing, proofreading, and general assistance of Angélica Caraballo, Paula Russell-Hendricks, Sandra Santiago, and Hawthorne Smith made it all really possible.

A third requirement for the writing of a textbook is, of course, a strong background in the field and a familiarity with recent literature and developments in the area. As graduate students at M.I.T. and the University of Chicago, we had the benefit of taking classes from outstanding figures in international economics to whom we owe an intellectual debt: Jagdish N. Bhagwati, Rudiger Dornbusch, Jacob A. Frenkel, Milton Friedman, Arnold Harberger, the late Harry Johnson, Charles P. Kindleberger, Arthur Laffer, Rachel McCulloch, and Paul Samuelson. The more difficult task, however, has been to keep up with a literature that has been growing as fast or even faster than our waistlines. If this book can make current international economics literature accessible to wider audiences and aid in analyzing international economic problems intelligently, its main objective will have been fulfilled.

Francisco L. Rivera-Batiz
Luis A. Rivera-Batiz

Brief Contents

Contents

PART II   The International Financial System

PART III   Introduction to International Macroeconomics

PART IV Income, Trade, and Capital Flows: Fixed and Flexible Exchange Rates

PART V   Inflation, Unemployment, and Economic Policy in the Open Economy

PART **VII**   **Interdependence in the World Economy**

International Finance and Open Economy Macroeconomics

SECOND EDITION

INTRODUCTION

It has become a cliché to say that we live in an interdependent world and that all economies are open—that is, they trade with each other. This means that countries are not self-sufficient. Rather, they specialize in producing and exporting the goods and services in which they enjoy a comparative advantage, while importing the raw materials, equipment, and goods they cannot produce competitively in international markets. International trade has some clear gains. You personally benefit when buying cheap Taiwanese-manufactured shirts and Japanese-made Toyotas or when your company sells more home computers or refrigerators in Europe. There are, however, some constraints imposed by participating in the international trade game: You have to play by the rules, and most of the time—except in cases where countries impose barriers to trade—this means buying or selling your products at terms heavily influenced by international market forces. Free trade implies the crude fact that foreign producers can sell their products in the United States and thus undercut (and take some

consumers away from) American producers selling at higher prices. But it also means that competitive U.S. products can undercut more expensive foreign products in Europe and other world markets. This general interdependence makes the whole world a single market for many commodities, placing constraints on the extent to which prices can diverge across borders.

But how open are economies in the world? U.S. trade with the rest of the world has expanded enormously since World War II. Exports and imports of goods and services have increased drastically over the past five decades, with an average rate of growth of about 6 percent per annum. This expansion is partly accounted for by economic growth—a larger economy—and general inflation, which raise the value of exports and imports. But increased international trade also represents a general trend toward greater openness of the economy. Indeed, the growth of U.S. exports and imports has surpassed that of national income since World War II. This phenomenon is not unique to the

1

United States; it has been characteristic of the world economy. The worldwide aggregate of exports has increased steadily since World War II and currently exceeds $3 trillion per year, notwithstanding the shrinking world trade accompanying global recession during the early 1990s. In an effort to quantify precisely this trend toward greater openness, we will examine various indexes, or measures, of the degree of openness of an economy and apply them to some countries for purposes of comparison.

Measuring the Openness of an Economy

The volume of an economy's international trade is usually measured by the value of its exports, imports, or their sum. In 1991, the United States exported close to $520 billion in goods and services and imported $606 billion, making it the economy with the largest volume of trade. This large volume of trade, however, is mostly attributable to the size of the U.S. economy. It should thus not be deduced that the United States is the economy with the highest degree of openness in the world. In order to correct for size, the degree of openness of an economy is commonly determined by comparing the ratio of international trade in goods and services to the size of the economy, as measured by the value of output produced domestically, called the gross domestic product (GDP). This ratio shows the relative importance of trade in goods and services in the open economy. Table I–1 shows exports and imports relative to GDP for a selected group of countries. In general, it does not matter very much whether exports or imports are used as the numerator because the ratio to GDP is similar with both. However, a substantial difference in the ratios can be observed in countries showing a large excess of imports over exports—such as Israel—or enjoying a huge excess of exports over imports—such as

Table I–1.   Indexes of Openness of the Economy

Country	Exports/GDP (percent)	Imports/GDP (percent)
Argentina	20%	10%
Belgium	69	67
Brazil	7	5
Canada	24	25
Egypt	30	44
France	23	23
Germany	39	32
Hungary	32	28
India	7	8
Israel	30	46
Japan	10	8
Kenya	25	26
Korea, Republic of	29	32
Malta	85	99
Mauritius	64	70
Mexico	19	12
Nigeria	50	22
United Kingdom	23	24
United States	10	11
Venezuela	31	26

Exports and imports represent annual exports and imports of goods and services.

GDP is annual Gross Domestic Product.

The figures for Egypt, Brazil, Nigeria, and Kenya are for 1990; for Argentina and India 1989; for Mexico 1987; the others for 1991.

source: International Monetary Fund, *International Financial Statistics* (Washington, D.C.: IMF, December 1992).

Nigeria. Table I–1 also shows that, roughly speaking, large countries tend to be more self-sufficient than small countries in the sense that they have a lower degree of openness in their external trade in goods. This can be observed by comparing the ratios for the United States and Japan with those for Mauritius and Belgium. There are exceptions. For instance, Burundi, with a population of about five million and a GDP of less than $1.2 billion in 1991, is a small economy with a low export index (equal to 10 percent in 1991).

As measured by the volume of its trade in goods and services relative to GDP, the U.S. economy is indeed relatively closed by world standards. This fact is sometimes quoted to allege that the openness of the U.S. economy is not significant and that, consequently, open economy factors can safely be neglected when analyzing it. Caution should be applied, however, against overstating this case. First of all, even if overall exports and imports constitute a small part of GDP, certain sectors in the economy are markedly dependent on their export sales and on products that are heavily imported. U.S. exports are prominent in agricultural commodities such as wheat (in which more than 80 percent of production is exported), coarse grains (with close to 40 percent of output shipped abroad), cotton, oilseed, paper, and many others. Within the manufacturing sector, U.S. civilian aircraft, construction machinery, oilfield machinery, office and computer equipment, and chemicals are major items of sale abroad. On the other hand, U.S. imports of oil are equal to 40 percent of U.S. oil consumption, and American residents have been purchasing from abroad each year more than $70 billion worth of motor vehicles, $20 billion in apparel and clothing, and $7 billion in footwear. Second, since World War II, U.S. exports and imports have gradually, but significantly, risen relative to GDP. The export-to-GDP ratio has increased from less than 5 percent in the late 1940s to about 10 percent in recent years. The U.S. economy has become increasingly open.

Furthermore, the ratios of exports to GDP and imports to GDP underestimate the economy's degree of openness. This is so because many goods never actually pass through frontiers—that is, they are never exported or imported—but are potentially tradable. This is the case of Chevys and Fords produced and sold domestically. Part of the U.S. automobile production is sold locally and part is exported, but the industry as a whole is an international one, competing with foreign firms both in international markets and locally. When measuring openness, then, it is relevant to consider the importance of *tradable goods,* not just of actually traded goods, such as exports or imports. Although the United States does not allocate a large fraction of its production to exports, and imports as a fraction of GDP are not significant, a large share of U.S. production and consumption consists of goods potentially tradable and subject to direct international competition. Openness, then, is much more prevalent in the United States than is shown by its relatively small import-to-GDP and export-to-GDP ratios.

An adequate measure of openness requires us to determine the relative importance of tradable and *nontraded goods* that are to be interpreted as being *internationally* nontraded goods because they can only be bought and sold in local markets in each country. Whether it is because of their nature or because of high transport costs, high tariffs, or other restrictions on their international trade, these goods and services are not traded in world markets; as a result, they are neither exported nor imported. The most important nontraded goods include building and construction, power generation, and transportation, as well as some manufacturing industries and most services. Their importance in most economies, both developed and developing, can be easily discerned from Table I–2, which shows the share of GDP accounted for by the nontraded goods sector in a selected sample of countries. Nontraded goods in Table I–2 are defined to include wholesale and retail trade; transportation and communication; insurance, real estate, and business services; community, social, and personal services; public administration; and defense. The construction sector has thus been excluded from this measure of nontraded goods, although it is often considered to be one. Its inclusion would increase the shares quoted below by four to seven percentage points. In the case of the United States, the figure is 69 percent, suggesting that tradable goods compose 31 percent of GDP, a far more important figure than indicated by the statistics for exports and imports. The bottom line is that we should beware of treating the

TABLE I–2. **Production of Nontraded Goods as a Fraction of GDP for Selected Countries, 1990**

Country	Percent	Country	Percent
Argentina	53%	Korea, Republic of	46%
Belgium	67	Mexico	59
Brazil	48	Nigeria	25
Egypt	52	Spain	86
France	67	Sweden	63
Germany	62	United Kingdom	62
India	41	United States	69
Italy	63	Uganda	26
Japan	63	Venezuela	48
Kenya	49		

SOURCE: World Bank, *World Development Report* (Oxford: Oxford University Press, 1991).

United States as a closed economy. There are crucial linkages—both direct and indirect—between the United States and the rest of the world that can only be ignored at the cost of a serious distortion. At the same time, it is important to remember that the U.S. economy is not that of a small country heavily dependent on, and completely subject to, the vagaries of international markets; nor is it perfectly integrated into world markets in goods and services.

INTERNATIONAL FACTOR MOVEMENTS AND THE DISTINCTION BETWEEN GNP AND GDP

Openness of the economy means not only that domestic residents can buy and sell products in world markets, but also that they can migrate abroad and produce in foreign countries. Mexican workers, for example, can move to the United States and be employed in the production of fruits and vegetables in the Sunbelt area, while U.S. multinational firms can move their capital to produce in Brazil or Mexico. Openness thus means that productive factors and financial resources can search internationally for the highest return on their services. These international factor movements give rise to a distinction between gross national product (GNP) and gross domestic product (GDP). GNP represents the value of output *produced by domestic residents* and, in a closed economy, corresponds to the value of output *produced domestically,* which is GDP. This correspondence breaks down in an open economy. For instance, consider the case of temporary Turkish migrants employed as guest workers in Germany. Clearly, some of the production generated by Germany (some of its GDP) is from this migrant labor and not from Germany's residents. The income received by Turkish workers in Germany is part of Germany's domestic product but not of its national product. In order to calculate GNP, then, we have to subtract the payments to foreigners from the value of GDP. These payments include foreign-worker wages and salaries, interest and dividends distributed to foreigners, and profits obtained by branches of foreign companies investing domestically. Of course, to be symmetric, we would also have to add to GDP the income received by domestic residents on account of labor or other incomes accruing from their own contributions to production abroad. Symbolically,

$$\text{GNP} = \text{GDP} + R, \qquad (I–2)$$

where R represents net factor income from abroad. A country's GNP exceeds GDP if it is a net provider of services abroad; the country's GNP falls below GDP if it is a net importer of services.

The divergence between GNP and GDP is significant for many countries. For instance, Pakistan receives substantial amounts of income from its workers abroad in Kuwait and Saudi Arabia and has been a net exporter of services, with its GNP generally exceeding GDP by more than 3 percent. A rich, oil-exporting country like Saudi Arabia imports foreign workers, but it receives huge interest payments from its heavy international lending of oil revenues, which more than offsets it.

In 1990, the Saudi GNP exceeded its GDP by close to 4 percent. Examples of countries in which GNP falls short of GDP are Brazil and Costa Rica, countries that became heavy borrowers in the 1970s and 1980s and thus have to incur a substantial debt service burden. In recent years, U.S. GNP and GDP have diverged by about 2 percent or less.

INTERNATIONAL FINANCE

International trade in goods and services is only one aspect of openness. A complete picture of the openness of a country should explicitly consider the economy's international trade in financial assets and its financial openness.

The internationalization of financial markets is one of the major developments of the post-World War II period. The United States has been at the forefront of this multifaceted development. For instance, U.S. multinational corporations' financial dealings and operations extend over dozens of countries, while foreign investors and central banks allocate a vast amount of funds to purchasing U.S. Treasury bills and bonds (representing the short- and long-term debt of the U.S. Treasury). U.S. banks also spread worldwide as bank overseas operations surged beginning in the 1960s. Whereas in 1960 U.S. banks had a total of 124 foreign branches, by 1970 the number was 532, by 1980 it was 799, and by 1990 the number of branches abroad had gone over the 1,000 mark. Associated with this multiplication of the foreign activities of U.S. banks has been a massive growth in their assets. The total assets of the foreign branches of U.S. banks increased from $46.5 billion in 1970 to $397.5 billion in 1980 to $557 billion in 1990. It is a fact that a major share of the earnings—or losses—of the largest American financial institutions—including Citicorp, Chase Manhattan, the Bank of America, and J. P. Morgan—derive from their international operations. The multitude of other, smaller American banks have also augmented their foreign operations in the last decades, and many obtain as much as 20 to 30 percent of their earnings and profits from overseas activities.

The openness of an economy to international trade in financial assets provides its residents with some clear-cut benefits. International capital markets complement domestic financial markets by making available funds with which to finance the projects of local firms and government. They thus provide domestic residents with needed funds not accessible in the local capital markets. In addition, world financial markets allow investors to search for a higher return and minimize risks by engaging in international portfolio diversification. In that way, they provide lenders with investment alternatives not available locally. However, an economy's integration into world financial markets also imposes severe constraints on some of its basic economic variables and on the effectiveness of some of the most crucial national economic policies. As we will repeatedly stress in the ensuing chapters, international capital mobility places stringent boundaries on the extent to which domestic interest rates can diverge from those prevailing in world markets, makes the task of controlling the money supply of an economy under fixed exchange rates very difficult, and can be a source of exchange rate turbulence under flexible exchange rates. In a modern environment, then, international financial markets are essential in determining the macroeconomic behavior of open economies, a major theme of this book.

Macroeconomics studies aggregate phenomena in the economy; it is concerned with issues such as the determination of the level of output and its rate of growth, unemployment, inflation, and interest rates. It is also interested in how government policies can—or cannot—affect the aggregate behavior of the economy. Can expansionary fiscal policy really lift the economy out of a recession? And is it true that when the government steps on the monetary bandwagon inflation picks up? These are problems that macroeconomics tries to answer. It is perhaps unfortunate that macroeconomics is so often cast in a closed-economy context—that is, in a setting where the country's interactions with the rest of the world are ignored. In reality, only the "world" is a closed economy. All national economies, as we have seen, are open, trading with each other at various levels encompassing goods and services, movements of labor and capital, and international finance—that is, trade in financial claims.

OPEN-ECONOMY MACROECONOMICS

The field of open-economy macroeconomics deals with the macroeconomic aspects of economies that trade with each other. As such, it integrates the study of issues involving the balance of payments, exchange rates, foreign trade, and international capital movements into the area of macroeconomics. There are multiple reasons for studying and understanding open-economy macroeconomics. First, openness implies that economies are subject to external events that strongly affect their performance. The United States, for instance, has been the subject of intense import competition from an increasing number of foreign countries in recent years. This has had enormous influence on the stagnation of such pillars of U.S. industrial activity as the steel and automobile industries. Swings in the price of crude oil have also greatly affected the United States and the world economy. Rising oil and gasoline prices have caused our rent payments to increase, our driving sprees to diminish, and our winter room temperature to become rather chilly. It is clear that we live in a closely interdependent world and, consequently, foreign events will influence us deeply.

Another reason for studying open-economy macroeconomics is that openness alters the impact of macroeconomic policies. When domestic variables such as interest rates and prices are closely linked to their foreign counterparts, the issue of whether government policies can truly affect them

is raised. Can monetary policy really affect domestic interest rates in a world of highly interconnected financial markets? Can exchange rate changes alter the international competitiveness of our products or is the latter determined by world market forces? These issues are central to our discussion of open-economy macroeconomics. As consumers, producers, and policymakers, it is crucial to understand how openness affects the role of government policies: Standard closed-economy policy prescriptions seldom stand without modifications or qualifications in the open economy.

THE PLAN OF THIS BOOK

The first part of this book presents a detailed analysis of the foreign exchange market. It covers the traditional material in this area, in addition to recent subjects of interest and research, such as futures and options currency markets. A description of the role played by central banks in foreign exchange markets and of the variety of exchange rate arrangements in the world follows. The European Monetary System, the future of European monetary unification, and various currency regimes in developing countries are also studied. Part II discusses international money and capital markets and the latest evidence on exchange rate forecasting, risk premia, and the efficiency of forward markets. In addition, onshore and offshore banking systems are introduced. Part III describes balance-of-payments accounting and international investment concepts, as well as alternative exchange rate measures, all of them illustrated using actual U.S. data. The remaining chapters in this section introduce national income accounting concepts in an international arena and apply them to the problem of the external debt of developing countries. Parts IV and V present full coverage of the state of the art in open-economy macroeconomics, both under fixed and flexible exchange rates. Part IV introduces the open-economy version of the standard IS-LM macroeconomic analysis. Part V integrates aggregate supply considerations and flexible price macromodeling into an international framework, including a discussion of the so-called rational expectations revolution in macroeconomics, the role of wage contracts and expectations on the effectiveness of macroeconomic policy, real business cycles, and the effects of supply shocks on the open economy.

The asset market approach to the exchange rate and the monetary and asset market approaches to the balance of payments figure prominently in Part V, which integrates international financial theory and macroeconomic analysis in explaining the balance of payments and the exchange rate. Finally, the last part of the book is devoted to the history and evolution of the international monetary system. The book ends with a policy-oriented chapter that presents an up-to-date discussion of interdependence and coordination in, for example, the current regime of managed floating, the European Monetary System, and optimum currency areas.

How To Use This Book

This book is aimed at undergraduate and graduate courses in economics and international affairs as well as M.B.A. courses in international finance and open-economy macroeconomics. Chapters 1 to 12, together with Chapters 19 and 20, comprise a basic one-term course that is fully accessible to undergraduate and graduate students in economics and business administration. The book is quite flexible regarding the subjects to be stressed in particular courses. Undergraduate courses in economics can emphasize open-economy macroeconomics, whereas M.B.A. courses may concentrate on Chapters 1 to 8, 12, and 19, which stress financial subjects. Graduate courses would surely focus on Chapters 13 to 20 in Parts IV, V, and VI, leaving much of the descriptive material as background reference for the students. International affairs courses can concentrate on the international policy issues covered by Chapters 1 to 3, 9 to 15, 21 and 22.

The book's organization also offers wide flexibility with respect to the sequence of subjects because each part can be covered independently. For instance, some instructors may prefer to start with balance-of-payments accounting and open-economy macroeconomics (Part III), studying just the basic international finance concepts required for, or utilized in, the development of the macroanalysis. Others may choose to discuss the monetary and asset market approach to the balance of payments and exchange rates (Chapters 19 and 20) before tackling the Keynesian approach. The book allows this sequence because Chapters 19 and 20 can be read independently of the rest of the book, as well as of each other.

PART I

The Foreign Exchange Market and Exchange Rate Regimes

1. The Foreign Exchange Market
2. Central Banks, Exchange Rate Regimes, and the International Monetary System
3. Foreign Currency Regimes in Developing Countries

The Foreign Exchange Market

In any open economy, it is always possible to observe some domestic residents engaging in international transactions. U.S. car dealers, for example, buy Japanese Toyotas and Nissans, while American computer companies sell pocket calculators to Mexican entrepreneurs. Similarly, some Americans open Swiss bank accounts, while U.S. real estate companies sell houses and condominiums to wealthy Arab sheiks. Most of these international transactions have one special characteristic that distinguishes them from purely domestic transactions: They require the acquisition of a foreign currency on the part of one or more of the participants in the transaction. If a Saudi sheik wants to buy property in the United

States, for example, he will have to sell his riyals in exchange for dollars in order to acquire the property. If an American buys a Toyota and pays the Japanese Toyota dealer in dollars, the latter will have to exchange the dollars for yen in order to have the local currency with which to pay workers and local suppliers. Because most countries have national, sovereign currencies—Germany has the deutsche mark, France the franc, England the pound sterling, Japan the yen—and their residents deal locally in these currencies—the price of food, materials, and domestic securities are all denominated in the local currency—some exchange of currencies is necessary. The foreign exchange market, to put it simply,

11

permits buyers and sellers of currencies to exchange one currency for another. If there were only one world currency, say, Esperanto, there would be no foreign exchange market.

The foreign exchange market is the largest, and one of the fastest-growing, markets in the world. In 1992, foreign exchange trading in the three major financial markets ran at the pace of $623 billion a day, a striking increase over the $430 billion trading volume in 1989. Three financial centers—London, New York, and Tokyo— dominate foreign exchange trading: The daily volume in each of these three markets in April 1992 reached $303 billion, $192 billion, and $128 billion, respectively. All three markets have grown quickly over the last decade, but particularly the Tokyo and New York markets. Foreign exchange trading in New York surged from $5 billion a day in 1977 to $50 billion in 1986 and $303 billion in 1992.[1] This explosion in volume has been accompanied by innovations: new financial instruments, longer trading hours, 24-hour electronic transactions, and international computer and communications networks that tightly link the major foreign exchange markets.

1−1. INTRODUCTION TO THE FOREIGN EXCHANGE MARKET

What precisely do we mean by foreign exchange, and which individuals and institutions participate in the foreign exchange market? The term *foreign exchange,* broadly speaking, includes bank deposits denominated in a foreign currency, foreign currency itself (bills and coins), and other short-term claims on foreigners expressed in foreign currencies. Most foreign exchange transactions, however, involve purchases and sales of bank deposits denominated in foreign currencies.

---

[1]Based on data from joint surveys of the Bank of Tokyo, the Bank of England, and the Federal Reserve Bank of New York for March 1986 and April 1992.

The main participants in the foreign exchange market are retail customers, commercial banks, foreign exchange brokers, and central banks.

1. *Retail customers.* Retail customers buy and/or sell foreign currencies for transaction purposes (to engage in the purchase and/or sale of goods, services, and securities across nationalities) or in order to adjust their portfolios. This increases the amount of a given foreign currency held (buying foreign exchange) or decreases the amount of the foreign currency held (selling foreign exchange). Retail customers usually do not either transact directly with each other or send orders to buy or sell to a centralized market. In the process of exchanging currencies, retail customers transact with commercial banks.

2. *Commercial banks.* The most important institution involved in the operation of the foreign exchange market is the commercial bank, which buys and sells foreign exchange for its clients. In order to carry out these transactions, the banks hold foreign exchange inventories in the form of working balances (deposits) with banks in foreign countries. If a retail customer wants to purchase foreign exchange, the bank withdraws it from its inventory; if the customer sells foreign exchange, the bank's holdings of foreign exchange will increase. Given the continuous flow of purchases and sales of foreign exchange in which commercial banks engage, they sometimes find themselves holding an excess of foreign exchange reserves and at other times having a shortage of foreign exchange. As a result, an active market in foreign exchange has arisen among commercial banks, by means of which banks that are short in foreign exchange buy it from banks wishing to dispose of their excess holdings.

3. *Foreign exchange brokers.* In the United States, banks utilizing the foreign exchange market usually do not transact directly with each other; rather, they interchange currencies (or, more precisely, deposits denominated in different currencies) through foreign exchange brokers, which function as interbank intermediaries. The main function of

the brokers is to bring together banks that are trying to buy foreign exchange with those that are selling. It should be noted that the broker's role, or function, is to arrange a transaction between two parties without at any time actually owning the commodity involved—in this case foreign exchange. In contrast to the commercial bank, the foreign exchange broker does not assume a position in foreign exchange because he or she never owns the foreign exchange being traded. Brokers, then, do not face the risks of exchange rate fluctuations. Commercial banks, on the other hand, in their role as dealers of foreign exchange, own foreign exchange balances and thus bear the risks of their transactions in those currencies.

4. *Central banks.* Foreign exchange brokers may also serve as agents for the economy's central bank—a quasi-public institution in charge of regulating and controlling the economy's banking system—in the bank's foreign exchange dealings. If the Federal Reserve, the U.S. central bank, wants to support the dollar by selling foreign exchange, it will place its sale offer by means of one or more foreign exchange brokers. The actions and role of the central bank in the foreign exchange market depend crucially on the type of exchange rate system or regime under which the country's payments system operates. We discuss central bank intervention in the foreign exchange market in Chapter 2.

The foreign exchange market is the market in which national currencies are traded. As in any other market, a price must exist at which trade can occur. An *exchange rate* is the price of one currency vis-à-vis another. There is, of course, the problem of deciding which of the two currencies is going to be used to express the value of the other. For example, take the case of the pound sterling and the dollar. On September 2, 1992, approximately $2.00 could be traded for £1 in the foreign exchange market. The exchange rate can thus be calculated as either the price of a pound in terms of dollars, which is $2.00 per pound ($/£), or the price of a dollar in terms of pounds, which is £0.50

per dollar (£/$), where 0.50 = 1/2.00. We shall be looking at the exchange rate as the domestic currency price of foreign currency. If we adopt the point of view of the United States as the domestic economy, the exchange rate between any currency and the dollar would be expressed in terms of dollars required to buy the foreign currency. In the dollar-pound sterling case just referred to, the exchange rate would then be $2.00/£.

An increase in the exchange rate between the dollar and the pound sterling (say, from $2.00/£ to $2.50/£) means that the pound sterling has become more expensive in terms of dollars. This implies that the value of the pound has increased because the amount of dollars required to buy a pound has increased. In other words, the pound has *appreciated* (in value) in terms of the dollar. By the same token, the dollar is cheaper in terms of the pound sterling. This means that the dollar has *depreciated* in terms of the pound (from £0.50/$ to £0.40/$). To summarize, and to avoid confusion, the reader should remember that we have defined the exchange rate between a domestic and a foreign currency as the amount of domestic currency needed to buy the foreign currency.[2] If the exchange rate increases, the domestic currency depreciates and the foreign currency appreciates. Similarly, a decrease in the exchange rate implies an appreciation of the domestic currency and a depreciation of the foreign currency.

Figure 1–1 presents the behavior of the exchange rate of the dollar with respect to the British pound, the German deutsche mark (DM), and the Japanese yen (¥) from 1980 to 1993. Note the exchange rate volatility during this time period. Changes in the value of the dollar of more than 20 percent in a year are not uncommon, and

---

[2]In practice, when the dollar price of a foreign currency is low, it is more convenient to express it as its reciprocal—that is, as the foreign currency price of the dollar. Accordingly, one often finds in the literature the yen-dollar exchange rate quoted as, say, ¥ 140 per dollar, rather than as $0.71 per yen. Be aware that uniform conventions regarding exchange rate quotations are not generally followed.

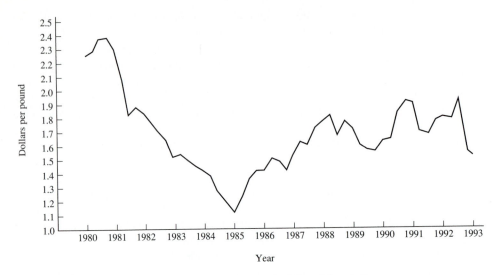

(a) Exchange rate between the dollar and the pound

(b) Exchange rate between the dollar and the deutsche mark

FIGURE 1–1.   Behavior of the Exchange Rate of the Dollar Versus the Pound (£), Deutsche Mark (DM), and Yen (¥), 1980–1993.

disturbances can accumulate to 50 percent, or even 100 percent, in a few years. Figure 1–1 shows that the dollar appreciated significantly against the pound and the deutsche mark between 1980 and 1985 and exhibited a general depreciation afterward, with some turnarounds between 1988 and 1992. By contrast, although there was no overall appreciation of the dollar against the Japanese yen

(c) Exchange rate between the dollar and the yen

FIGURE 1–1 *continued*

from 1980 to early 1985, a dollar depreciation occurred after that time. Clearly, depreciations and appreciations do not necessarily occur simultaneously for all foreign currencies.

Exchange rate changes are a major source of uncertainty in international business. In a world of global investment and trade, the magnitude of fluctuations in currency values can overwhelm other determinants of companies' profits. A discussion of the nature of the risks involved and how to hedge against them, the focus of this chapter, begins with the basic institutional elements of the foreign exchange market.

1–2. SPOT AND FORWARD MARKETS

The foreign exchange market is the largest market in the world, with a daily trading volume often above the $1.0 trillion level, many times the volume on the New York Stock Exchange. Foreign exchange markets can be classified as *spot* markets and *forward* markets. The distinction between spot and forward lies essentially in the type of contract

involved in the exchange of currencies. In spot markets, currencies are bought and sold for immediate delivery and payment; in practice, there may be a one- or two-day delay in delivery. This is the type of transaction that would occur if you were to ask your bank to sell you $250 worth of deutsche marks on the spot. It is not, however, the only type of foreign exchange transaction. The reader may not be familiar with markets for future delivery since most commodities are traded only on spot markets and therefore lack well-developed forward, or futures, markets. For some commodities, however, these markets do exist, along with the usual spot markets. Such is the case with gold, wheat, sugar, pork bellies, and foreign exchange, among others. In forward foreign exchange markets, currencies are bought or sold for future delivery and payment. If today an American buys British pounds thirty-day forward, he or she effectively is making a contract today to buy pounds in thirty days. The seller agrees to deliver and receive payment for the foreign exchange at that date (one month from today) at an exchange rate also specified when the contract is negotiated (today). The main difference between spot and forward contracts, then, is that in a spot market the price at which a currency is traded (the spot exchange rate) is set concurrently with the payment and delivery of the currency (today), whereas in a forward market traders determine the price today (called the forward exchange rate) for future delivery and payment.

Why would anyone engage in contracts to buy or sell currency through the forward exchange market? Consider the following examples. A U.S. compact disk company that wants to purchase British disks in thirty days may also want to ensure the rate at which it is going to buy pounds in the future to pay for them. Otherwise, it will have to pay the spot price for the pound prevailing then, which could be very high. To avoid this exchange risk, and to be able to plan its revenues and costs ahead more accurately, the firm may decide to buy pounds forward, for delivery in thirty days, at the corresponding forward exchange rate quoted today. Suppose, on the other hand, that a British appliance dealer has a contract to buy some Hotpoint refrigerators in thirty days, for which it has to pay in dollars. In this case, the British firm may want to sell a certain number of pounds (in exchange for dollars) in the forward market. This will ensure the firm the rate at which it is going to sell its pounds for dollars in thirty days, when it has to pay for the refrigerators. The importance of the forward market in international finance should not be underestimated. Most customer transactions in foreign exchange involve forward transactions.

Table 1–1 reproduces the foreign exchange rate quotations for May 6, 1992, as published by *The Wall Street Journal*. The first two columns give the quotes as defined in this book, in terms of units of domestic currency ($) required to buy the foreign currency. As can be seen, the spot exchange rate between the dollar and the pound sterling at 3 P.M., U.S. Eastern Standard Time (EST) on Wednesday, May 6th, was 1.7972 dollars per pound ($/£). Similarly, the spot exchange rate for Germany's

mark was 0.6143 dollars per deutsche mark ($/DM). The forward exchange rates for various currencies, depending on the maturity of the forward contract (in days), are also presented. For example, the thirty-day forward exchange rate for the pound sterling was 1.7877 ($/£). This means that a commercial bank, at 3:00 P.M. on that day, would have agreed to sell pounds for delivery in thirty days at the rate of 1.7877 dollars per pound.

The Forward Premium

Table 1–1 shows that forward exchange rate quotes generally differ from spot exchange rates. The difference between the forward and the current spot exchange rates, in proportional terms, is called the forward premium, symbolically represented as follows:

$$\text{Forward premium} = f_M = \frac{F_M - e}{e},$$

where F_M refers to the forward exchange rate for the delivery of a foreign currency M days from today, and e is the current value of the spot exchange rate for that currency. Often, the forward premium is multiplied by 100 to express it in percentage terms. A foreign currency with a positive value of f_M is referred to as being at a forward premium, whereas a negative value is called a forward discount; that is, if there is a premium (discount) on the value of the currency forward relative to the value of the currency spot, more (fewer) dollars will be paid for the delivery of the currency in the future (M days forward) than if delivery were requested today.

Forward contracts can have any maturities, although they are predominantly short term, as reflected in the 30, 90, and 180 day quotes in Table 1–1. Maturities of up to one year are also common. For comparability purposes, it is often convenient to compute forward premiums and discounts on a standardized yearly basis. This annualized form of the forward premium, or dis-

TABLE 1–1. Foreign Exchange Rate Quotations

Wednesday, May 6, 1992

The New York foreign exchange selling rates below apply to trading among banks in amounts of $1 million and more, as quoted at 3 P.M. Eastern time by Bankers Trust Co., Telerate, and other sources. Retail transactions provide fewer units of foreign currency per dollar.

Country	U.S. $ equiv.		Currency per U.S.$	
	Wed.	Tues.	Wed.	Tues.
Argentina (Peso)	1.01	1.01	.99	.99
Australia (Dollar)	.7552	.7582	1.3242	1.3189
Austria (Schilling)	.08725	.08682	11.46	11.52
Bahrain (Dinar)	2.6529	2.6529	.3770	.3770
Belgium (Franc)	.02984	.02970	33.51	33.67
Brazil (Cruzeiro)	.00042	.00041	2364.86	2425.00
Britain (Pound)	1.7972	1.7860	.5564	.5599
30-Day Forward	1.7877	1.7761	.5594	.5630
90-Day Forward	1.7692	1.7588	.5652	.5686
180-Day Forward	1.7449	1.7340	.5731	.5767
Canada (Dollar)	.8357	.8381	1.1966	1.1932
30-Day Forward	.8338	.8361	1.1994	1.1960
90-Day Forward	.8302	.8326	1.2045	1.2010
180-Day Forward	.8247	.8272	1.2126	1.2089
Czechoslovakia (Koruna)				
Commercial rate	.0353607	.0350877	28.2800	28.5000
Chile (Peso)	.002974	.002985	336.29	335.00
China (Renminbi)	.181485	.181485	5.5101	5.5101
Colombia (Peso)	.001775	.001724	563.45	580.00
Denmark (Krone)	.1590	.1580	6.2910	6.3305
Ecuador (Sucre)				
Floating rate	.000743	.000743	1345.01	1345.01
Finland (Markka)	.22609	.22462	4.4230	4.4520
France (Franc)	.18228	.18136	5.4860	5.5140
30-Day Forward	.18132	.18033	5.5152	5.5453
90-Day Forward	.17951	.17859	5.5707	5.5994
180-Day Forward	.17698	.17601	5.6502	5.6815
Germany (Mark)	.6143	.6112	1.6280	1.6362
30-Day Forward	.6110	.6078	1.6366	1.6452
90-Day Forward	.6050	.6022	1.6530	1.6607
180-Day Forward	.5967	.5937	1.6758	1.6843
Greece (Drachma)	.005216	.005198	191.70	192.40
Hong Kong (Dollar)	.12920	.12914	7.7400	7.7435
Hungary (Forint)	.0127796	.0125786	78.2500	79.5000
India (Rupee)	.03527	.03527	28.35	28.35
Indonesia (Rupiah)	.0004954	.0004954	2018.53	2018.53
Ireland (Punt)	1.6387	1.6306	.6102	.6133
Israel (Shekel)	.4209	.4167	2.3758	2.4000
Italy (Lira)	.0008179	.0008138	1222.72	1228.88

continued

TABLE 1–1 *continued*

Country	U.S. $ equiv.		Currency per U.S.$	
	Wed.	Tues.	Wed.	Tues.
Japan (Yen)	.007566	.007522	132.17	132.95
30-Day Forward	.007560	.007516	132.27	133.05
90-Day Forward	.007551	.007508	132.44	133.20
180-Day Forward	.007544	.007502	132.55	133.29
Jordan (Dinar)	1.4852	1.4852	.6733	.6733
Kuwait (Dinar)	3.3898	3.3898	.2950	.2950
Lebanon (Pound)	.000625	.000625	1600.00	1600.00
Malaysia (Ringgit)	.3971	.3979	2.5180	2.5135
Malta (Lira)	3.1596	3.1596	.3165	.3165
Mexico (Peso)				
Floating rate	.0003244	.0003244	3082.50	3082.50
Netherlands (Guilder)	.5458	.5432	1.8323	1.8409
New Zealand (Dollar)	.5385	.5385	1.8570	1.8570
Norway (Krone)	.1574	.1564	6.3545	6.3935
Pakistan (Rupee)	.0401	.0401	24.92	24.92
Peru (New Sol)	.9762	.9524	1.02	1.05
Philippines (Peso)	.03953	.03953	25.30	25.30
Poland (Zloty)	.00007920	.00007692	12627.00	13000.01
Portugal (Escudo)	.007210	.007299	138.70	137.00
Saudi Arabia (Rival)	.26738	.26738	3.7400	3.7400
Singapore (Dollar)	.6059	.6061	1.6505	1.6500
South Africa (Rand)				
Commercial rate	.3497	.3490	2.8593	2.8651
Financial rate	.2950	.2950	3.3900	3.3900
South Korea (Won)	.0013090	.0013090	763.97	763.97
Spain (Peseta)	.009811	.009748	101.93	102.59
Sweden (Krona)	.1704	.1693	5.8680	5.9050
Switzerland (Franc)	.6679	.6648	1.4973	1.5042
30-Day Forward	.6649	.6619	1.5040	1.5109
90-Day Forward	.6596	.6567	1.5160	1.5227
180-Day Forward	.6528	.6497	1.5318	1.5392
Taiwan (Dollar)	.040323	.040000	24.80	25.00
Thailand (Baht)	.03908	.03908	25.59	25.59
Turkey (Lira)	.0001521	.0001504	6576.00	6650.00
United Arab (Dirham)..............	.2723	.2723	3.6725	3.6725
Uruguay (New Peso)				
Financial	.000335	.000335	2983.51	2983.51
Venezuela (Bolivar)				
Floating rate	.01562	.01550	64.03	64.50
SDR	1.37946	1.37681	.72492	.72632
ECU	1.26110	1.25440		

Special Drawing Rights (SDR) are based on exchange rates for the U.S., German, British, French and Japanese currencies. Source: International Monetary Fund.

European Currency Unit (ECU) is based on a basket of community currencies.

SOURCE: *The Wall Street Journal*, May 7, 1992, section C, p. 3. Reprinted by permission of *The Wall Street Journal*, © 1992 Dow Jones & Company, Inc. All rights reserved worldwide.

count, is called a standard premium or discount and is usually expressed as a percentage. It is defined by

Standard forward premium (discount)

$$= \text{SFP}_M = \frac{F_M - e}{e} \cdot \frac{360}{M} \cdot 100,$$

where M is the term to maturity of the forward contract in days.[3] It is known as a premium if it is positive and as a discount if negative. Using the actual exchange rates for one-month ($M = 30$) forward market contracts on May 6, 1992, as quoted by *The Wall Street Journal* (WSJ) and appearing in Table 1–1 under the items called thirty-day forward, the standard forward premiums, or discounts, for the major currencies at that time are:

$$\text{British pound } SFP_{30} = \frac{1.7877 - 1.7972}{1.7972}$$
$$\cdot \frac{360}{30} \cdot 100 = -6.34\%$$

$$\text{Canadian dollar } SFP_{30} = \frac{0.8338 - 0.8357}{0.8357}$$
$$\cdot \frac{360}{30} \cdot 100 = -2.73\%$$

$$\text{French franc } SFP_{30} = \frac{0.18132 - 0.18228}{0.18228} \cdot \frac{360}{30}$$
$$\cdot 100 = -6.32\%$$

$$\text{West German mark } SFP_{30} = \frac{0.6110 - 0.6143}{0.6143}$$
$$\cdot \frac{360}{30} \cdot 100 = -6.45\%$$

$$\text{Japanese yen } SFP_{30} = \frac{0.007560 - 0.007566}{0.007566}$$
$$\cdot \frac{360}{30} \cdot 100 = -0.95\%$$

[3]$(F_M - e)/e \cdot 1/M$ shows the M-day forward premium on a daily basis; $(F_M - e)/e \cdot (1/M)$ 360 then shows it on a yearly basis. Multiply by 100 to express it in percentage terms.

The standard forward premiums for other maturities (e.g., 90 days, 180 days) can be calculated in the same way.

The meaning of the forward premium, that is, why forward and spot exchange rates diverge, will be explained in Section 1–6. For the moment, we return to Table 1–1 to clarify some additional aspects of the foreign exchange market. A look at the small typescript at the top of the display on foreign exchange rate quotations in Table 1–1 shows that the quotations refer to selling prices for *bank transfers* in the United States, as quoted at 3 PM EST (in dollars). Important terms and phrases are italicized throughout this discussion.

The exchange rate quotes in the first column of Table 1–1 refer to quotes for the sale of foreign exchange in the interbank foreign exchange market in New York. These are, then, wholesale quotes, which differ from the rates banks quote at their retail level. In the retail market, banks charge a higher price for the sale of foreign exchange. The additional amount charged compensates the banks for the services they provide at this level. As a consequence, the exchange rates a retail customer faces would exceed those quoted in Table 1–1.

A second aspect of foreign exchange transactions that has to be clarified is that these transactions do not generally involve a physical exchange of currencies across geographic borders. They generally involve only changes in debits and credits at different banks in different countries. The notion of foreign currencies actually being flown across the Atlantic does not make any sense in a highly integrated and developed international economy. Foreign exchange transactions, then, do not have to be carried out through the physical exchange of actual currency.

The main instruments of foreign exchange transactions include electronic and cable bank deposit transfers and bank drafts, bills of exchange, and an array of other short-term instruments expressed in foreign currency, such as international money orders. This wide range of foreign exchange instruments has arisen out of centuries of international trading and is tailored to the varying circumstances and risks faced by traders. The primary instrument traded in foreign exchange markets, and the only one to be discussed here, is the *bank deposit transfer* made by computer-based telecommunications—the electronic transfer. A bank deposit transfer occurs when a seller of foreign currency makes a transfer of deposits from its bank account to the account of the buyer of the currency. For example, suppose that General Electric, which is assumed to accept payments in pounds and has a bank account in London, receives a payment in pounds from a London customer. G.E. now holds excess pound sterling deposits in London and desires to sell them to a New York bank; that is, it wants to sell foreign exchange. Usually, G.E. would electronically communicate with its bank in London to transfer the ownership of, say, £20,000 to the New York bank purchasing the foreign exchange. If G.E. holds an account at this New York bank, the latter can credit G.E.'s account immediately for the corresponding amount of dollars; alternatively, it can issue a cashier's check for the appropriate amount on G.E.'s behalf. The whole process is completed quickly, taking no more than one or two days.

To use another example, suppose that G.E. has to pay a certain amount of pounds to a British supplier of parts and materials. In this case, G.E. has to buy foreign exchange, which it can do through its New York bank. G.E. purchases the necessary pounds from the bank; it orders the bank to debit the corresponding amount of dollar deposits out of its account in New York and to transfer the pounds purchased with those dollars to its bank in London. Then G.E. will advise its London bank to debit its account and provide the London supplier with the appropriate amount of pounds. Again, all these transactions occur very quickly.

Returning to Table 1–1, it should now be clear that the exchange rates quoted apply to bank transfers similar to those just discussed, except that they specifically involve large-scale foreign exchange trading among banks so that both the buyer and the seller are banks.

The foreign exchange market is a truly international market. Commercial banks in different financial centers are interconnected by a fast communications system involving telex and computer links, as well as telephone lines. Exchange rate quotes from different financial centers can be obtained immediately at the touch of a telex terminal or through a telephone call. Because of this close interconnection, a demand for dollars in London by a British firm importing goods from the United States can easily be transmitted into a supply of sterling in New York City. The main financial centers—including New York, London, Tokyo, Singapore, Frankfurt, and Zurich—are all really part of one international market for foreign exchange. In most of these large financial centers, virtually any currency can be bought or sold quickly. The reason is that these centers have attracted banks from throughout the world, either through branches or through working relationships with major banks in the centers. To have access to foreign exchange, though, does not require being in a large financial center. Local banks can provide foreign exchange by purchasing it from major banks.

Returning to Table 1–1, it can now be seen that the statement that the quotes were for 3:00 P.M. EST does not at all imply that the foreign exchange market closed at that hour. The foreign exchange market never—or almost never—closes: At any given time, foreign currencies can be found somewhere in the many financial centers around the world. When New York banks close at the end of the day, it is morning in Tokyo, and as the evening progresses in New York City, morning arrives in London. Thus, foreign exchange trading can move from place to place while the New York market is closed. The current trend toward extended banking hours and longer trading days in the financial markets confirms the twenty-four-hour nature of the currency trading business.

1–3. TRACING A TYPICAL FOREIGN EXCHANGE TRANSACTION

How does a typical foreign exchange transaction take place? We now follow through the main actions involved in one such typical transaction. Suppose that Acme Importers has to pay £1 million to Royal Exporters, Ltd. in London. The foreign exchange transaction begins when Acme's international financial manager calls the international banking department of, say, Goodbuck Bank. The bank receives the call in its foreign exchange division, where orders to buy and sell foreign exchange from both retail customers and correspondent banks are taken. Here, the bank has several foreign exchange traders who are usually linked by telephone, cable, and computers to major customers, brokers, and domestic and foreign correspondents.

The first thing Acme's manager wants from the bank is the current price of the pound sterling, that is, the (spot) exchange rate between the dollar and the pound. The manager would probably receive an answer consisting of two different exchange rates, say 1.5000 and 1.4985. What this means is that the bank will sell pounds at the price of $1.5000 per pound and that it will buy pounds at the price of $1.4985 per pound.[4] In order to profit from buying and selling foreign exchange, commercial banks buy the foreign exchange at a certain price and sell it at a higher price. Otherwise, they would not engage in the activity. The percentage difference between the bank's buy (bid) and sell (ask, or offer) prices for any given currency is known as the *spread,* or *trading margin,* which is generally on the order of about 0.1 percent. In this particular case, we have the following spread:

$$\text{Spread} = \frac{P_A - P_B}{P_A} \times 100$$

$$= \frac{1.5000 - 1.4985}{1.5000} \times 100$$

$$= 0.1\%,$$

where P_A represents the ask (sell) price and P_B means the bid (buy) price; we multiply by 100 in order to express the spread as a percentage. The spread for any given currency is affected by the amount of currency traded (the smaller the quantities, the greater the margin); the size of the financial center (if in a major international center, such as New York or London, the margin is smaller); the turbulence, or price variability, of the currency (the larger the turbulence, the greater the margin); the thinness of the currency market (if it is the New Zealand dollar, the margin is larger); and the type of instrument traded (e.g., bank notes and bank drafts require a larger margin).[5] This means that, depending on the type of dealer with whom the transaction is being made and the type of transaction undertaken, different prices may be quoted for the sale or purchase of foreign currencies. Noticing these differences can save the traveler money. For instance, suppose that you are traveling in Paris and decide to charge the cost of an expensive gourmet meal to your credit card. The French restaurant charges the credit card company for the cost of the meal in French francs. The company then converts the francs into dollars and bills you back home in dollars. Now, the exchange rate at which the credit card company converts foreign currency into dollars is usually different from the one you would obtain if you had purchased francs and paid for your Parisian cuisine extravaganza in cash. It may thus pay to check these things out.

---

[4]The gap between $1.5000 and $1.4985 is 0.15 cents. This difference will generally be referred to as being 15 basis points, with each point corresponding to 1/100 cents, or 0.01 cents.

[5]For an analysis of the relative importance of these factors in determining bid-ask spreads, see P. Boothe, "Exchange Rate Risk and the Bid-Ask Spread: A Seven Country Comparison," *Economic Inquiry* (July 1988); and D. Glassman, "Exchange Rate Risk and Transactions Costs: Evidence from Bid-Ask Spreads," *Journal of International Money and Finance* (December 1987).

The average of the bid and ask quotes is called the midpoint, or middle, exchange rate. In our terminology, the middle exchange rate between the pound and the dollar is $e(\$/£) = (P_A + P_B)/2$. Often, when the exchange rate in a particular market is referred to, it is likely that it is the middle exchange rate. Based on our example, the middle exchange rate for the pound quoted by Goodbuck is $1.49925.

The foreign exchange market spread measures the amount that a customer pays if she or he simultaneously buys and sells a foreign currency. In our dollar-pound example, if Acme were to buy one pound and then immediately sell it to the bank, the net cost of these two transactions would be 0.0015 dollars, which in percentage terms is equal to 0.1 percent (note that 0.0015 divided by 1.5000 is equal to 0.001). The cost of each transaction—the cost of either buying or selling the foreign currency—is then one-half of the spread, or 0.00075 dollars per pound; expressed in percentage terms, this is equal to 0.05 percent. It is thus possible to use the difference between bid and ask prices as a measure of transaction costs in the foreign exchange market.[6]

As already mentioned, the primary instrument traded in the foreign exchange market is the bank transfer. It is precisely one of these transfers that Acme wishes to make to Royal. After receiving the quote on the spot exchange rate, Acme's financial manager asks to make a transfer of £1 million from its own account to be deposited in Royal's account at Barclays Bank in London. This concludes the transaction between the bank and its customer, but it does not end the foreign exchange transaction.

After Acme hangs up, one of Goodbuck's foreign exchange traders examines the bank's current *position statement* in terms of the pound. A bank's

position statement in a foreign currency shows the bank's assets and liabilities denominated in that foreign currency. Because the bank may hold some pound-denominated deposits in a London branch or at a London correspondent, these appear as assets in the position statement. On the other hand, the bank may owe foreign exchange to customers, appearing as a liability in the position statement. Goodbuck's transaction with Acme, regarding Acme's payment to Royal, generates a liability in Goodbuck's position statement. A bank's *closed,* or *balanced,* position—as related to its position statement—occurs when assets denominated in a given foreign currency, arising from foreign exchange purchases over time, match the amount of the liabilities denominated in that currency arising from the bank's foreign exchange sales. Otherwise, a bank is said to have an open position in the currency. A positive open position means that assets denominated in a given currency exceed liabilities in that currency. It is often referred to as being long in a currency. Conversely, a bank (or any trader, for that matter) is short in a currency if it registers a negative balance on its position statement; that is, its liabilities exceed its assets denominated in the given foreign currency.

Goodbuck's foreign exchange trader observes the bank's current position statement and then proceeds in the following manner. Suppose that the bank is long on the pound, as it would be if it had £1 million available as deposits in its account at a London branch or correspondent bank. Goodbuck's foreign exchange trader, or his or her clerical staff, will proceed to communicate with the London bank and order it to debit Goodbuck's account on the amount of £1 million and credit it to the account of Royal Exporters at Barclays.[7] If,

---

[6]If we denote the customers' transaction costs of purchasing a pound by t, in proportional terms, the purchase price of a pound in terms of dollars (inclusive of the transactions costs) is given by $P_A = e(\$/£)(1 + t)$, where $e(\$/£)$ is the middle exchange rate. In our example $t = 0.0005$ and $e(\$/£) = 1.49925$.

[7]The communication between Goodbuck and Barclays usually occurs through the interbank electronic message service provided by the Society for Worldwide International Financial Telecommunications (SWIFT). This computer-based satellite communications network, based in Brussels, links the major banks selling foreign exchange in the world, providing them with immediate transfer of information.

however, Goodbuck has a short position on the pound, the foreign exchange trader will try to purchase the £1 million by placing calls to other banks. If that fails, the trader will place an order to buy £1 million through a foreign exchange broker in New York.

Major trading centers, such as New York and London, have a small number of foreign exchange brokers. Their number varies, but in most cases you can count them on the fingers of your hands. The main work of a broker is to exchange currencies among the major commercial banks dealing in foreign exchange. Brokers charge only a small margin to carry out any transaction (approximately $0.001 per pound sold) because of the large quantities with which they deal. They compete keenly with each other, sometimes by means of rate cutting but more often through a melee of nonprice mechanisms—providing selected customers with inside information, better-quality services, and personal gifts. One bank trader claimed that one Christmas he received more than $1,000 worth of presents from brokers. Another recalled that when his wife had a child, a broker called him at the hospital and offered to pay the hospital bill!

In our specific foreign exchange example, suppose that Goodbuck is short £1 million. One of Goodbuck's foreign exchange traders will then call a broker, placing an order to buy £1 million. The broker may then either quote the rate at which he or she has offers to sell pounds or, if there are none, may put the trader on hold. The broker will then proceed to call the other major banks in New York that deal in foreign exchange and get their offers to sell pounds (their ask prices). He or she will then inform Goodbuck's trader of the existing ask prices and, if the trader accepts, as is usually the case, the transaction is concluded. In some cases, the trader may not accept the ask prices in the New York market and will proceed to place bids for the purchase of pounds in other financial centers. Whenever an agreement to purchase pounds occurs, the foreign exchange trader proceeds to inform each bank of the other party's

name, charging a fee to each of them for its services. The bank agreeing to sell pounds to Goodbuck will then immediately deposit the £1 million purchased on Goodbuck's account at a London branch or correspondent.[8] Goodbuck's foreign exchange trader then asks the London bank to transfer the deposit to Royal's account, concluding the transaction.

1–4. SPATIAL AND TRIANGULAR ARBITRAGE

Although the foreign exchange market is spatially dispersed across major cities and countries, it is unified by keen competition among the highly sophisticated market participants. These participants operate with the most modern information and communications network and face low transaction costs, usually well below 1 percent of the value of transactions. A powerful force keeping exchange rate quotations in different places in line with each other is the search on the part of market participants for foreign exchange arbitrage opportunities.

Arbitrage is the simultaneous purchase and sale of a commodity or asset in different markets with the purpose of obtaining a sure profit from the differential between the buying and selling price. For instance, if the dollar-pound sterling exchange rate is $2.00 per pound in London when it is only $1.50 in New York, it is possible to buy pounds in

---

[8]The dollar payment for the pound sterling purchased by Goodbuck from the other bank is usually settled through the Clearing House Interbank Payments System (CHIPS). This is a computer-based system located in New York through which foreign exchange trading among banks is cleared. If, for instance, Citibank is the bank selling £1 million to Goodbuck, the foreign exchange trader at Goodbuck will access the CHIPS computer and enter its own code, Citibank's code, and the payment in dollars to be made to Citibank. On the other side, Citibank's trader will enter its code, that of Goodbuck, and the amount of dollars to be received from Goodbuck. CHIPS keeps track and informs more than 150 member banks of their more than $425 billion daily foreign exchange transactions.

New York and simultaneously sell them in London, obtaining a net gain of 50 cents (minus the very small transaction costs) for each pound purchased and sold. Of course, spatial arbitrage opportunities of this sort—entailing the purchase and sale of a given currency in different locations—would be quickly eliminated as investors rushed to profit from them, pulling together the New York and London exchange rate quotations, as is usually observed in practice. That spatial arbitrage opportunities are quickly eliminated is attributable to the market's low transaction costs and high operational efficiency. Such opportunities also reflect that exchange rate quotations in different locations are widely available, and traders are efficient in using this information to exploit profit opportunities.

A more complicated arbitrage operation is three point, or triangular, arbitrage. Suppose that New York's dollar-pound sterling and dollar-deutsche mark exchange rates are $2.00 and $0.50, respectively, while the deutsche mark is worth one-fifth of a pound (£0.20) in Germany. Under these conditions, it can be shown that there are effectively two different dollar-deutsche mark exchange rates in the market. The first one is the dollar-deutsche mark rate quoted in New York, by means of which 1 DM can be purchased for $0.50, referred to as the direct exchange rate. A second exchange rate, called a cross-exchange rate, can be obtained by acquiring deutsche marks indirectly—by first exchanging dollars for pounds and then using those pounds to buy deutsche marks. Because each deutsche mark costs one-fifth of a pound (£0.20) and each pound is equivalent to $2.00, the dollar-deutsche mark cross-exchange rate is, then, $0.40 per DM. Obviously, deutsche marks acquired directly in New York are more expensive than those obtained through the cross-exchange rate, or

$$\$0.50/DM = e(\$/DM) > e(\$/£)e(£/DM)$$
$$= \$0.40/DM,$$

where $e(\$/DM)$ represents the direct dollar-deutsche mark exchange rate; $e(\$/£)$ is the dollar-pound sterling direct exchange rate; and so forth. Triangular arbitrage profits can then be easily obtained. For instance, each pound bought in the United States at $2.00 per pound sterling can be exchanged for marks in Germany at 5 DM per pound. If those deutsche marks were then sold in the United States at the rate of $2.50 for each 5 DM sold, there would be a net profit of $0.50 each time the operation was undertaken. This would be a sure profit, at least in principle, because simultaneously buying and selling currencies entails no open positions in particular currencies. Note again, however, that if foreign exchange market traders make efficient use of the information available, triangular arbitrage profits should quickly disappear. The forces of triangular arbitrage insure the consistency between direct and cross-exchange rates, or

$$e(\$/DM) = e(\$/£)e(£/DM). \qquad (1\text{-}1)$$

In summary, neither spatial nor triangular arbitrage should yield profits in a market in which information is cheaply available and efficiently used by participants in the market.

In practice, exchange rates in different locations are closely related, and direct and cross-exchange rates are approximately consistent with each other. The relations tend to break down, however, during periods of great turbulence, or volatility, in foreign exchange markets. This suggests that the degree of risk entailed in trading currencies soars in turbulent periods, or that turbulence increases transaction costs. Transaction costs create a wedge between direct and cross-exchange rates (measured with middle rates). The explanation is that the cross-exchange rate involves two transactions—in our example, buying pounds with dollars and then selling pounds to buy deutsche marks—while the direct rate involves only one transaction (buying the marks directly).

The deviations from triangular arbitrage due to transactions costs are usually small. Estimates of transaction costs in the trading of industrial currencies arrive at very small figures, usually less than 0.1 percent. This is consistent with evidence from bid-ask spreads in the foreign exchange market. On the other hand, when considering the currencies of many developing countries, substantial deviations can be detected from the triangular arbitrage parity condition. This does not necessarily mean that foreign exchange markets in developing countries are not efficient. In some countries, the deviations from triangular arbitrage parity can be explained by high transactions costs linked to high exchange rate volatility. In these cases, commercial banks charge more to trade the currency in order to cover for the greater risks they take in holding the currencies. Still, in many countries, deviations from triangular arbitrage parity can not be explained by transactions costs. In these countries, local authorities restrict and sometimes directly control the foreign exchange market. The forces of arbitrage cannot operate in the presence of so-called exchange controls that block or restrict the transactions required by arbitrage operations. Under those circumstances, consistency of exchange rates should not be expected across locations or between direct and cross-exchange rates.[9]

We have examined arbitrage operations undertaken by selling and purchasing currency in spot foreign exchange markets. In most industrialized countries, opportunities for profit from arbitrage disappear rapidly as the consequence of the actions of bank foreign exchange traders. Hence,

most firms do not frequently engage in such operations. Instead, among nonbanks, more habitual types of foreign exchange market operations involve hedging and speculation.

1–5. THE FORWARD MARKET IN FOREIGN EXCHANGE: HEDGING AND SPECULATION

The forward market is the market in foreign exchange contracts that provides deliveries of currencies at a future time. Similarly to spot market traders, forward market traders deal neither directly with each other nor through a centralized market; rather, each usually deals with a commercial bank. To discuss the details and nature of the forward market, let us refer to our earlier example involving the foreign exchange transaction of a U.S. firm called Acme that had to pay in pounds to a London firm called Royal Exporters, Ltd. It was assumed that Acme had to pay Royal instantly—so that Acme ordered pounds on the spot.

It is often the case, however, that a firm will know that it will have to pay a certain amount in a foreign currency before the actual payment has to be made. For example, Acme may make a contract specifying the amount of pounds to be paid in three months for the import of some equipment from Royal at that time. Acme is now open to substantial exchange rate risk because during those three months the dollar may depreciate relative to the pound (a depreciation of the dollar is an increase in the dollar price of foreign exchange). Such a development would force Acme to spend a larger amount of dollars to satisfy its import commitment. Acme can avoid this risk by purchasing the pounds in the forward market, for delivery in ninety days, at a price specified today. At the end of the ninety-day wait, Acme pays for the pounds at the prespecified price in dollars and uses the pound proceeds to pay for the imports. This procedure, which permits Acme to know in advance the exact amount of dollars it will need to

---

[9]In fact, the International Monetary Fund (IMF), an international organization monitoring world monetary arrangements (discussed in the next chapter) uses deviations from the triangular arbitrage parity condition in determining which countries have effectively adopted exchange controls in their currency trading. A deviation of cross and direct exchange rates of more than 1 percent is considered by the IMF to constitute evidence of governmental interference with foreign exchange trading and of the existence of exchange controls.

settle the deal with Royal, is called *hedging,* or *covering.* It refers to a transaction that occurs in order to close an open position in a given currency. In this case, Acme, before covering, had a negative open position on the pound, in the sense that it had a commitment to pay a given amount of pounds at a certain date. (A positive open position indicates an excess of pounds, and it could have arisen if Acme had been holding pounds or if it had been expecting to receive pound payments in ninety days.) After Acme covers itself by purchasing pounds forward, its negative position is closed, or eliminated. Acme still has a ninety-day commitment to pay pounds, but this liability is offset by a pound-denominated asset—the forward contract. It also matures in ninety days and eliminates the risk arising from possible changes in the dollar-pound sterling exchange rate. This example suggests a basic function of forward markets: They allow traders to insure themselves against exchange rate uncertainties and thereby facilitate international trade.

Notice that there has to be a counterpart to Acme's forward purchase of pounds. Who is the seller of those pounds? The immediate seller would be a commercial bank, as in the spot market. But remember that the bank only acts as an intermediary between Acme and an ultimate seller. This ultimate seller of forward pounds may be another hedger, like Acme, but with a position just opposite Acme's. Suppose, for example, that an American firm has invested in three-month British securities, which it wants to convert back into dollars after the end of the three months. The investor may decide to sell the pound proceeds forward in order to assure itself of the rate at which the pounds are to be converted back into dollars after the three months. This is precisely the counterpart to Acme's purchase of forward pounds. We see, then, that depending on their special circumstances, some hedgers enter the forward market as buyers and others as sellers of foreign exchange. The forward market permits them to get together and engage in mutually beneficial transactions. In its presence, both the seller and the buyer of forward

exchange are able to insure against the exchange rate uncertainty present in their transactions.

Another type of investor may be providing the forward contract bought by Acme. This is the speculator, who attempts to profit from changes in exchange rates. Depending on their expectations, speculators may enter the forward market either as sellers or as buyers of forward exchange. An example of the mechanics of speculation through forward markets follows. You, the reader, will be a fictitious speculator investing in the forward exchange market.

Let us assume that the three-month forward rate for the pound is $2.10 per pound, and that the current spot rate is $2.00 per pound. We will also assume that, based on a subjective evaluation of future possibilities, you expect the spot rate to remain at $2.00 per pound three months from today. If these expectations were to be realized, then you, as a speculator, could profit by selling pounds forward at the current forward rate of $2.10 per pound. Why? If the spot rate remains at $2.00 per pound three months from today, you can buy pounds spot then (at $2.00 per pound) to satisfy the commitment you have made to deliver pounds in three months. However, the forward contract has specified that the sale of pounds is to be made at $2.10 per pound, so that you would obtain a profit of $0.10 per pound sold forward. In general, then, a speculator deliberately makes a commitment to sell pounds forward, assuming an open position in pounds, on the expectation that some profits can be earned from it. Observe, however, that the speculator's expectations could turn out to be incorrect, as they would in our example if the spot exchange rate did not stay constant at $2.00 per pound but increased over the following three months to, say, $2.50 per pound. In this case, you would be forced to buy pounds spot at $2.50 per pound at that time, in order to deliver the pounds you have agreed to sell three months forward at $2.10 per pound. You would lose $0.40 per pound sold forward.

Speculation in foreign exchange markets is constantly being undertaken by individuals, firms, banks, and even governments. Some highly successful investment firms, such as Soros Fund Management, Tudor Investment, Caxton Corporation, and Moore Capital Management, have obtained a significant share of their profits from currency speculation. Indeed, according to *Financial World Magazine,* four of the six highest paid people in Wall Street in 1991 were heavy traders in currencies. Often, however, investors will not openly admit that they have engaged in speculative activities. Commercial banks obtain a large share of their profits from foreign exchange trading. Citicorp alone received $709 million in income from currency trading in 1991. Yet, banks will often link those profits to their arbitrage operations or fee-for-service activities, not speculation. Speculation is more visible when it results in large losses. On March 19, 1991, *The New York Times* reported that the British food and liquor firm Allied-Lyons (whose products include Mister Donut, Baskin Robbins, and Lowenbrau beer) had just suffered a $285 million foreign exchange loss; it was speculated that the loss resulted from foreign exchange exposures not easily explained by hedging activities.

In conclusion, the speculator assumes a risky position and faces the risk of exchange rate uncertainty. As a consequence, whenever speculators provide the forward contracts desired by hedgers, the forward market serves as a mechanism for transferring risk from hedgers to speculators. Both will be satisfied with their transaction because the hedgers are able to reduce their exchange rate risk, and the speculators hope to profit from the transaction.

1−6. Forecasting Exchange Rates: Forward Markets and Foreign Exchange Advisory Services

The previous section examined a case in which speculation on the basis of differences between the exchange rate anticipated to prevail in the future

($2.00 per pound) and the forward exchange rate ($2.10 per pound) could be expected to provide substantial profits. This looks quite easy so far, but be aware that it is not. Generally, the forward exchange rate tends to reflect the spot exchange rate that most investors anticipate will prevail at the point of maturity of the forward contract. This means that when an anticipated future exchange rate differs from the forward rate, you are leaning against the wind in the sense that your expectations differ from those of most participants in the market.

Why does the forward exchange rate tend to reflect the expected future spot exchange rate? This topic will be discussed in more detail in Chapter 6. At this point we will provide only a heuristic explanation. Suppose we take our earlier example in which it was assumed that your expectation of the future exchange rate differs from the forward rate. If you have based your estimate or expectation of the future spot rate on public information and knowledge, as well as on well-known forecasts about the future of the U.S. and British economies, you could expect that most other investors and speculators would arrive at an estimate of the future spot exchange rate similar to yours. Let us assume, then, that most investors have the same expectations you do and that, as a consequence, they expect the spot exchange rate between the dollar and pound to remain constant over the next three months, at $2.00 per pound. This approach implies, by our earlier calculations, that all these investors could expect to profit by selling pounds three months forward. As a result, there would be a massive increase in the sale of pounds in the three-month forward market. The exchange rate on three-month forward pounds (the price of forward pounds in terms of dollars) would then decline below $2.10 in response to the increased supply of forward pounds. This decrease in the forward exchange rate would continue until it moved close to the expected exchange rate ($2.00 per pound). At that point, most investors would stop drawing contracts to sell pounds forward because they could not expect to realize any more profits once the forward exchange rate moved close to the expected exchange rate. When expected profits are eliminated, the forward exchange rate will tend to reflect the expected exchange rate on the part of most investors in the market.

What is suggested here is that a forward premium for a given currency (over a given contract period, M) implies that most investors expect the currency to appreciate with respect to the dollar over the period of the contract (because $F_M > e$). Similarly, if the currency is at a forward discount, the currency is expected to depreciate vis-à-vis the dollar (because $F_M < e$). In conclusion, a forward premium for a given currency reflects the expected rate of appreciation of that currency relative to the dollar, and a forward discount the expected rate of depreciation of the currency vis-à-vis the dollar over the period of the contract. (At this point, you might find it useful to return to Table 1–1 and specify what this discussion suggests about the market's assessments of the future exchange rates of the U.S. dollar against the Canadian dollar, French franc, and so forth.)

If, as we assumed above, your expectation about the future exchange rate is different from the forward rate, you would be leaning against most investors' expectations of what the future exchange rate is going to be. You would thus be trying to beat the market by guessing better than other investors. Can you do that? As a matter of chance, you can do it at various points in your lifetime if you keep trying. The real question, however, is whether you could systematically assemble a more accurate forecast of future exchange rate changes than that of the consensus of market participants as embodied in the forward exchange rate. This question is a controversial one in international finance and relates to the question of whether foreign exchange markets are efficient. A market is considered informationally efficient if prices fully reflect available information.[10]

---

[10]For a recent survey on foreign exchange market efficiency, see R. Levich, "Is the Foreign Exchange Market Efficient?," *Oxford Review of Economic Policy* (October 1989).

In this context, market efficiency implies that forward exchange rates reflect all available information relevant for future exchange rate determination and will therefore yield as accurate a prediction of future spot exchange rate changes as any available. We will investigate this issue in detail in Chapter 6. Suffice it to say here that the balance of the evidence on the matter indicates that the forward exchange rate (the forward premium) can be looked at as being the most accessible, yet highly unbeatable, forecast of future exchange rates. This does not mean that the forward exchange rate provides a relatively good forecast of future currency values, only that it seems to give as good a prediction as those made by foreign exchange traders and market-based advisory services. In fact, the forward rate does not give a particularly accurate forecast of future spot exchange rates. Figure 1–2 shows forward exchange rates for three-month delivery of pounds and the corresponding spot exchange rates prevailing at the time of maturity of the forward contract. As can be observed, the forward rate is not a highly accurate predictor of future spot exchange rates, repeatedly being in error by as much as 10 percent or more. This failure of forward rates to predict future exchange rates is the result of the extreme volatility and unpredictability of the dollar-pound sterling exchange rate during the period.

The inaccurate predictions of the forward market have induced many investors to use the services of foreign exchange advisory services, which offer forecasts and make recommendations as to which currency to hold. Because foreign exchange advisors are generally highly knowledgeable experts on foreign markets who derive their income from these activities, they can be expected to provide informed advice. The question arises as to whether they can systematically beat the market. If they can, this might imply that the forward exchange market is not efficient in fully reflecting available information.

The evidence suggests that most foreign exchange advisory services indeed do not actually do

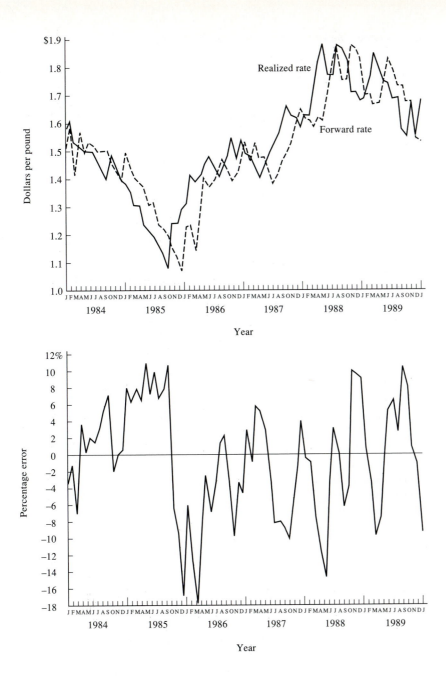

FIGURE 1–2. The Inaccuracy of the Forward Exchange Rate in Predicting Future Exchange Rates. The error is given by: error = (forward rate−realized rate)/realized rate. It is annualized and expressed in percentage form by multiplying by 100. The forward rate is the rate on ninety-day delivery of sterling. The realized rate is the spot rate prevailing at the maturity of the forward contract.

SOURCE: *The Wall Street Journal*, various issues.

better than the forward market in predicting future exchange rates, but that some have a consistently superior performance difficult to attach to chance.[11] This means that a speculative investment strategy following the advisor's forecasts would yield positive profits. The interpretation of this result is ambiguous, however. On the one hand, it can be taken to imply that experts can systematically beat the market. On the other, in order to benefit from foreign exchange advisors' forecasts, open positions would have to be held in certain currencies. The profits obtained may then just reflect a compensation for the risk taken by the investor in holding risky open positions. The notion that profits in foreign exchange markets can merely be a compensation for risk taking—and not evidence of superior performance on a risk-adjusted basis—is illustrated by the following example.

Suppose that the thirty-day forward exchange rate on the pound is equal to $1.50 per pound and that holding open positions in pounds is very risky for you, perhaps because of the relatively high uncertainty about future exchange rate changes. In such a situation, assume also that you require $0.04 per pound held in compensation for the heart-stopping and stomach-upsetting effects of the additional risks involved in holding open positions in pounds. Suppose, then, that your foreign exchange advisor—whose forecast has been right on average in the past—gives you a forecast of $1.46 on the dollar-pound sterling exchange rate to prevail in thirty days. On this basis, you agree to sell pounds thirty days forward at $1.50 per pound, which could be expected to yield $0.04 per pound

(because the spot rate you expect to prevail thirty days from now is $1.46). Assuming that, this time, the advisor's expectation was exactly right and a dollar-pound sterling exchange rate of $1.46 actually prevails in thirty days, you would then make a profit of $0.04 per pound. Such a profit, however, is merely equal to the amount required to compensate you for the risks taken in holding an open position in pounds. In other words, the risk-adjusted profit obtained from the advisor's service would be zero, in accord with market efficiency, even if the advisor's forecasts do better than the forward market and yield profits on average.[12] The source of ambiguity in the interpretation of this and other empirical evidence regarding market efficiency is the fact that the studies are really testing the joint hypothesis that markets are efficient *and* that compensation for exchange risk—the so-called exchange risk premium—is absent. This is referred to as the joint hypothesis problem in testing market efficiency. A rejection of the forward premium as the "best" predictor of future exchange rate changes can either mean that the forward exchange market is inefficient or that risk premia cannot be ignored, or both—or perhaps neither, if the tests used are not well constructed.

In conclusion, the solution to the difficulties of testing market efficiency has not been achieved yet; this is a subject of active current research, the details of which are presented in Chapter 6. The evidence available suggests, however, that the forward exchange rate (the forward premium) might still be looked at as being the most accessible, yet highly unbeatable, forecast of future exchange rates. The inaccuracy of the forward exchange rate in predicting future spot exchange rate changes should thus not be taken to mean that it could be easily beaten by other forecasts; it is connected to the general unpredictability of future

---

[11]See R. M. Levich, "Evaluation of Exchange Rate Forecasts," in R. Z. Aliber, ed., *The Handbook of International Financial Management* (Homewood, Ill.: Dow Jones-Irwin, 1989); D. Blake, M. Beenstock, and V. Brasse, "The Performance of UK Exchange Rate Forecasters," *Economic Journal* (December 1986); and R. M. Levich, "Analyzing the Accuracy of Foreign Exchange Advisory Services: Theory and Evidence," in R. Levich and C. Wihlborg, eds., *Exchange Risk and Exposure* (Lexington, Mass.: D.C. Heath, 1980).

[12]For more details, see J. Bilson, "The Evaluation and Use of Foreign Exchange Rate Forecasting Services," in R. J. Herring, ed., *Managing Foreign Exchange Risk* (New York: Cambridge University Press, 1983), pp. 149–179.

exchange rates, something to which all forecasts are subject.

It may appear that engaging in speculation through the forward market is very simple. Actually, if a speculator were to try to engage in a contract to buy or sell pounds thirty days forward, the commercial bank with which he or she deals would either refuse to offer the contract or probably set a high *margin requirement*. The margin requirement is a request that the client deposit an amount, say, 20 percent, of the total value of the forward transaction as a partial guarantee in case of default. In order to satisfy the margin requirements, the speculator has to set aside part of his or her capital. Credit worthiness and good financial standing are also essential for an individual or institution to engage in transactions through the forward market. This answers the reasonable question: Given the possibility that speculation will lead to losses, what protects banks from contract defaults on the part of speculators? High margin requirements and customer screening insure banks against this risk.

More than two decades ago, the Nobel Prize winning economist Milton Friedman attempted to engage in forward currency transactions for speculative purposes. To his dismay, banks discouraged him. Friedman's answer to the banks' denial was to promote an alternative to the forward market that would be open to all, including speculators. The so-called futures markets, discussed next, represent such an alternative.

1–7. FUTURES TRANSACTIONS AND THEIR ROLE IN THE FOREIGN EXCHANGE MARKET

Futures markets are centralized markets for the future delivery and payment of a commodity or an asset. These markets have existed in the United States ever since the Chicago Board of Trade, the country's oldest and largest futures exchange, came into existence in the mid-1800s. For more than a century, futures markets dealt only in contracts for the future delivery of homogeneous commodities like sugar, gold, and coffee. In the 1970s, however, futures markets were the object of a profound transformation.

In 1972, the International Monetary Market (IMM) of the Chicago Mercantile Exchange—the so-called Merc, one of the leading commodities futures exchanges in the United States—began trading in currency futures. *Currency futures markets* are centralized markets for the future delivery and payment of currencies. As a financial innovation, the introduction of currency futures has been hailed as one of the major financial innovations in decades. The establishment of the IMM opened the way for the introduction of a wide array of other futures contracts and markets. The number of futures markets as well as the range of currencies traded have proliferated worldwide since the establishment of the IMM. Currency futures trading is now available at the London International Financial Futures Exchange (LIFFE), MidAmerica Commodity Exchange, Singapore International Monetary Exchange (SIMEX), Sydney Futures Exchange, and others. Close links have developed among these markets. Trading in SIMEX, for instance, is closely linked to trading in the IMM. An agreement exists by which individuals can trade in Singapore when the Chicago Merc is closed, with those transactions being recognized by the IMM. A similar linkage has been developed by the Chicago Merc and Japan as part of an electronic trading system, called Globex, that allows trading after business hours. This system complements pit trading during regular IMM trading hours and permits transactions to be made after hours through computers.

Both forward and futures foreign exchange markets offer contracts for the future delivery or payment of currencies. There are, however, major differences between the two types of markets. At an institutional level, forward contracts are offered by commercial banks and, as discussed in the previous section, banks will supply quotes on their forward purchases or sales of foreign currency.

Futures contracts, on the other hand, are offered through an organized, centralized exchange, such as the IMM. How futures currency prices can be obtained and how futures trading actually takes place are the focus of Table 1–2.

Table 1–2 shows *The Wall Street Journal*'s price quotations for futures traded in the IMM. At first sight, futures price quotations may appear

esoteric. As shown, the IMM provides futures for only a limited number of currencies. Let us look closely at the figures on the British pound. All the quotations refer to contracts of a standard size of £62,500 for delivery at the specific dates stated, which are the third Wednesday of the months of September, December, March, and June. The IMM allows only a limited range for the choice of

TABLE 1–2. Foreign Exchange Futures in the International Monetary Market, May 6, 1992

FUTURES PRICES

	Open	High	Low	Settle	Change		Lifetime High	Lifetime Low	Open Interest
JAPAN YEN (IMM)—12.5 million yen; $ per yen (.00)									
June	.7537	.7563	.7531	.7560	+	.0044	.8125	.7015	55,162
Sept	.7528	.7550	.7522	.7547	+	.0043	.8080	.7265	3,504
Dec	.....	.....	.....	.7546	+	.0041	.8045	.7410	1,821
Mr93	.....	.....	.....	.7555	+	.0040	.8005	.7445	2,132
Est vol 14,950; vol Tues 9,769; open int 62,619, +152.									
DEUTSCHEMARK (IMM)—125,000 marks; $ per mark									
June	.6075	.6111	.6069	.6105	+	.0035	.6490	.5322	67,662
Sept	.5990	.6021	.5983	.6019	+	.0035	.6400	.5685	3,429
Dec	.5920	.5945	.5919	.5944	+	.0035	.6106	.5645	5,129
Mr93	.....	.....	.....	.5883	+	.0035	.6100	.5724	522
Est vol 40,995; vol Tues 34,788; open int 76,742, +605.									
CANADIAN DOLLAR (IMM)—100,000 d/rs.; $ per Can $									
June	.8346	.8347	.8324	.8337	−	.0020	.8820	.8263	17,504
Sept	.8291	.8291	.8268	.8282	−	.0020	.8774	.8191	1,210
Dec	.8220	.8225	.8215	.8232	−	.0020	.8740	.8130	667
Mr93	.....	.....	.....	.8187	−	.0020	.8712	.8115	275
Est vol 5,908; vol Tues 3,682; open int 19,664, +37.									
BRITISH POUND (IMM)—62,500 pds.; $ per pound									
June	1.7750	1.7876	1.7742	1.7862	+	.0122	1.8346	1.6410	31,921
Sept	1.7494	1.7620	1.7484	1.7604	+	.0120	1.8066	1.6490	2,107
Dec	1.7320	1.7370	1.7320	1.7378	+	.0118	1.7370	1.6280	455
Est vol 12,496; vol Tues 10,653; open int 34,483, +991.									
SWISS FRANC (IMM)—125,000 francs; $ per franc									
June	.6599	.6653	.6595	.6642	+	.0033	.7328	.6405	34,805
Sept	.6529	.6575	.6520	.6567	+	.0031	.7265	.6335	1,703
Est Vol 19,444; vol Tues 18,299; open int 36,583, −1,405.									
AUSTRALIAN DOLLAR (IMM)– 100,000 dirs.; $ per A.$									
June	.7553	.7553	.7526	.7532	−	.0025	.7670	.7274	2,441
Est vol 248; vol Tues 99; open int 2,540, +18.									

delivery dates because in terms of volume, the IMM is a small market compared to, for example, the commercial banks' forward market. It thus tries to avoid the excessive thinning and the corresponding price instability that would arise in the event of a much larger choice of maturity dates for a given currency. The IMM contracts differ from forward contracts in that the latter specify the delivery dates of the currency in terms of days after the contract is drawn (say, ninety days), rather than as specific dates in the future.

Customers can buy or sell futures in the IMM by placing their orders with firms that have access to it. These firms employ individuals who are members of the IMM and are permitted to trade on the floor. Customer orders are then placed on the floor in accordance with the customer's instructions, with biddings and offers being literally shouted in (this is the hectic pit trading system that is often shown on TV and that most people associate with stock and commodity exchanges). A trade occurs when the price at which some seller is willing to sell is matched by the bid price indicated by some other customer(s). These trading prices are recorded almost instantly and used to obtain the prices quoted in Table 1−2 as opening, highest, lowest, and settlement prices for the day (settlement price is a representative price established for the end of the day).

Table 1−2 also provides information on the change in the settlement price from the previous day and about the lifetime high and low prices for a contract. Trading in contracts for a given delivery date may begin up to eighteen months and last up to a week before that date. This period is the lifetime of the contract. The highest and lowest prices that have prevailed during the lifetime of the contract can thus be computed, all the way from the initial moment of trading up to the present. These are the so-called lifetime high and low prices quoted in Table 1−2.

The last number observed in any given column in Table 1−2 refers to *open interest*. Open interest is the number of contracts outstanding and not already liquidated (canceled) by an offsetting contract (or by delivery of the commodity). A customer can cancel any contract (say, a purchase of foreign exchange for March delivery) just by taking an opposite position (say, a sale of foreign exchange for delivery in March). The IMM's clearinghouse then clears these offsetting positions, liquidating the contracts and paying (or collecting from) the customer any difference between the purchase and sale prices.

The last line for each currency in Table 1−2 exhibits figures for the daily trading volume for that currency. This volume measures the extent of the currency trading during the day and should not be confused with open interest, which is the stock of contracts outstanding (nonliquidated) in the currency. Open interest can decline from one day to another, even if the volume of trading during the day is positive. Daily volume partly reflects new contracts that are added to augment open interest. However, because of the liquidation of contracts, daily volume also reflects trading taken by customers to offset existing positions, which reduce open interest.

An example of the gains that can be obtained through the futures market is provided by the events that took place between 1989 and 1990: The pound sterling rose from a value of about $1.50 in June 1989 to a value of $1.70 six months later. An individual could have agreed on September 1, 1989, to buy pounds for delivery in March 1990 at a price of $1.5170 per pound. By late February, however, the price of a pound to be delivered in March had risen to $1.6844. If the individual had liquidated his or her futures contract to buy pounds, the gain would have been $0.1674 per pound purchased (the difference between the sale price of $1.6844 and the purchase price of $1.5170). In fact, most futures contracts are liquidated in this way, rather than actually delivered. The ease with which any contract can be liquidated at any time simply by engaging in an opposite transaction provides significant liquidity. It is possible to realize a large gain and then get out of the market at any time. If losses are accumulating, further losses can be avoided at any given time by liquidating the account.

Cross-Rate Trading in Futures Markets

Traditionally, futures markets in the United States have only offered contracts that allow speculators to bet on changes in the value of the dollar vis-à-vis a limited set of foreign currencies. Speculating on the value of one foreign currency versus another must be done indirectly by means of triangular trading, which is to engage in contracts to purchase or sell two or more foreign currencies versus the dollar. As noted in our discussion of arbitrage, "triangular" operations have higher transaction costs than those directly involving the trade of foreign currencies. There is, therefore, an incentive to introduce *cross-rate trading*—the direct trading of foreign currencies. In the past, the futures exchanges considered the potential extent of cross-rate trading to be insufficiently large to merit its introduction. In recent years, however, the growth of direct foreign currency trading has boomed. Currently, about 40 percent of all world currency trades do not involve the dollar, and the percentage is growing. Several U.S. futures exchanges are planning to introduce *cross-rate futures,* which would allow speculators to bet on changes in the value of one foreign currency versus another without having to use the dollar as an intermediary. The IMM, for instance, introduced in 1991 cross-rate currency futures for the mark-pound, yen-mark, Swiss franc-mark, yen-pound, Swiss franc-pound, and yen-Swiss franc.

1−8. DIFFERENCES BETWEEN FORWARD AND FUTURES MARKETS

Although they are sometimes used interchangeably, there are many differences between a forward and a futures contract. A *forward* foreign exchange contract occurs between a bank and an individual or firm. It usually involves the identity of the individual or company in an essential way and may require specific arrangements and negotiations between the bank and the person or officers involved. The bank may in fact refuse to deal with particular persons or firms—remember the commercial banks that refused to deal with Friedman, a well-known economist. By contrast, a transaction in the *futures* foreign exchange market occurs through an organized, centralized exchange—such as the IMM—that deals in standardized contracts. Instead of the more personal bank-client relationship, the contracts offered by the exchanges are open to anyone, including the speculators, so long as they obey the law and follow the standardized rules governing futures trading.

This difference in the interaction between participants in futures and forward markets is linked to the fact that in futures markets the exchange's clearinghouse acts as a third party that guarantees the performance of all contracts originating in the exchange. A buyer of currency for future delivery can thus be sure that the contract will be honored even if some sellers of currency futures default. The identity of the ultimate seller or buyer of the futures contract loses importance because the exchange itself (and its financial standing) guarantees the contracts. This contrasts with the bilateral trade between a bank and its client, in which the bank is not insured against the possibility that the client may default, and vice-versa. To the bank, the financial standing, credit worthiness, and identity of its client are crucial as a guarantee that the contract will be honored. The transaction frequently involves arrangements and negotiations between the bank and the person involved.

Commercial banks protect themselves from customer default on forward contracts mainly by engaging in client screening and relying on the credit worthiness of the customer for reassurance that forward contracts will be honored. How do futures exchanges cover against customer default? To protect themselves, futures exchanges impose minimum margin requirements on all contracts. These margins represent an amount of money that the investor must maintain at the clearinghouse as a kind of deposit that the futures exchange can use to insure that the investor will honor its contracts even if losses occur. Both buyers and sellers in the foreign currency futures market are required to sustain margins, which do not necessarily have to be in cash (sometimes Treasury bills are used). Margin requirements can be adjusted by the exchange in response to increased volatility or turbulence. For instance, margins in the Chicago Mercantile Exchange were raised—sometimes tripled—after the stock market crash of October 1987. Late in 1990, the Merc again raised margin requirements in response to the uncertainty surrounding the impending Gulf War.

Margin requirements are monitored by the futures exchange's clearinghouse, which establishes the accounts where the margin deposits are held. The clearinghouse has a number of recordkeeping functions (keeping track of the members of the exchange) and provides a guarantee against default on the part of buyers and sellers of futures contracts. The clearinghouse is usually organized as a nonprofit, incorporated association. It is also often a separate legal entity from the exchange. This is done so that the exchange can avoid direct liability on claims resulting from the default insurance supplied to customers by the exchange. Sometimes, however, the clearinghouse is set up as a division within the exchange.

To increase the likelihood that futures contracts will be honored, clearinghouses adopt the practice of *marking to market*—of computing any daily gains or losses in the value of the futures contract and adding or subtracting them to or from the investor's margin account. The gains are immediately credited to the account and the investor can withdraw them. For instance, if an investor engages in a futures contract to buy pounds in March at $1.50 per pound and the price of those March futures surges to $1.75 tomorrow, the value of the contract rises by $0.25 per pound (because the investor could liquidate the contract by selling pounds and receiving the difference between the $1.50 purchase price and the $1.75 selling price). This gain of $0.25 per pound would be credited to the investor's margin account and could be with-

drawn in cash. Similarly, daily losses are immediately debited to the margin account; if cumulative losses reduce the amount in the margin account below a certain maintenance level, the investor is asked to replenish it.[13] The practice of marking to market creates a key difference between forward and futures markets. The reason is that marking to market allows you to receive immediately any profits you make from speculation in the futures market. In the forward market, by contrast, if you guess correctly about the future value of a currency and you profit from a forward contract, the profits are obtained when the contract matures in the future, not before. In the same vein, if, as it happens, you lose a certain amount of money by speculating, under a futures contract you must pay some of these losses to the clearinghouse before the expiration of the futures contract; with a forward contract, your losses would be realized when the forward contract expires, which is when you have agreed to buy or sell currency forward.

The presence of margins tends to make futures transactions relatively unattractive for hedging transactions: Commercial banks, depending on their knowledge and previous contact with a customer, set zero or very low margin requirements on this type of transaction. As a result, most hedging transactions are usually made through the forward markets operated by commercial banks. Speculators, on the other hand, use the futures markets more frequently because commercial banks often reject or impose high margins on speculative transactions. In fact, the futures markets have practically become a market of speculative transactions in foreign exchange.

The standardization, impersonality, and dependability of futures contracts make them much more liquid than forward contracts. This has given rise

---

[13]The foregoing is a highly simplified explanation of the way that margin accounts and related procedures work. For the nitty gritty of margin accounts and resettlement procedures, see Chapter 3 in D. Duffie, *Futures Markets* (Englewood Cliffs, N.J.: Prentice Hall, 1989).

to the statement that "a futures contract is to a forward contract as payment in currency is to payment by check."[14] This liquidity is enhanced by the fact that futures contracts can be liquidated at any time, and any profit (or loss) from changes in exchange rates can be realized before the contract expires.

1–9. TRADING IN FOREIGN CURRENCY OPTIONS

In forward and futures contracts, the buyer and sellers promise either to deliver or accept delivery of a certain amount of foreign currency at some time in the future. This allows a company to hedge against exchange rate risk whenever the future timing and amount of the currency transaction is known with certainty. However, if the investor does not know with accuracy whether the future foreign exchange transaction will be required, forward and futures contracts may not be helpful instruments. Suppose, for example, that Eastman Kodak Inc. has bid for a contract to supply a London firm with £1 million worth of VCR cameras. The British company is considering bids from several firms and has made assurances that it will decide among them within thirty days, at which time it will make the payment of £1 million to the selected supplier. If Kodak knew that it would be the chosen company and that the British firm would pay in exactly thirty days, it could agree to sell £1 million in the thirty-day forward market and it would fully hedge against the risk involved in possible dollar-pound exchange rate changes within the thirty-day period. In reality, however, Kodak does not know whether it will be the selected firm or precisely when the British decision will be made in the thirty-day interval. If the forward contract to sell pounds in thirty days is made by Kodak's international division, but it is later discovered that Kodak is not to be the chosen supplier, the corporation would be obligated to buy £1 million at that time in order to fulfill the existing contract to sell £1 million forward. By engaging in the forward contract without knowing for certain whether the prospective receipt of pounds was going to occur, Kodak in effect *increased* its exposure to exchange rate risk.

A preferable strategy for Kodak would have been to purchase a thirty-day option to sell £1 million in thirty days. A *foreign currency option* is a contract giving the buyer or holder the opportunity or right—but not the obligation—to buy or sell a given amount of foreign currency at a preagreed exchange rate for a specified period of time. Major banks such as Citibank and Bank of America offer custom-tailored currency options on transactions of $1 million or more to corporate customers. In addition to this so-called over-the-counter market, trading in standardized currency options was introduced by the Philadelphia Stock Exchange in December 1982 and soon after by the IMM and other exchanges in the United States, Canada, and Europe. Trading in options has grown rapidly, and currently more than $3 billion worth of business is transacted daily in the organized markets.

Table 1–3, taken from *The Wall Street Journal,* provides details on currency options trading on the Philadelphia Exchange for May 6, 1992. As is also the case in futures markets, organized exchanges try to offer wide choices to investors; at the same time, however, they limit the variety of contracts available—by maturity and by the preset exchange rate—to avoid the volatility associated with thin markets. Just how thin these markets are can be seen in the large number of items with the letters *r* and *s* in Table 1–3: the letter *r* means that the contract was not traded that day and the letter *s* implies that the option was not offered at all.

The price quotes in Table 1–3 can be perplexing for the newcomer. Consider the figures for the British pound (one of the several "underlying" currencies for which options are available). Note

---

[14]Lester Telser and Harlow Higinbotham, "Organized Futures Markets: Costs and Benefits," *Journal of Political Economy* (October 1977), p. 696.

that there are two sets of figures on the British pound. The first set consists of quotes for *European-style* options and the second for *American-style* options. An American-style option can be exercised at any time between the date the option is written and its maturity or expiration date. The European-style option can be exercised only at the time of expiration. We will concentrate our attention on the American-style option quotes, for which trading is more extensive.

TABLE 1–3. **Currency Options in the Philadelphia Exchange, May 6, 1992**

OPTIONS
PHILADELPHIA EXCHANGE

Option & Underlying	Strike Price	Calls—Last			Puts—Last		
		May	Jun	Sep	May	Jun	Sep
50,000 Australian Dollars-cents per unit.							
ADollr	75	r	0.86	r	r	r	r
75.82 .	76	0.14	r	r	r	r	r
31,250 British Pounds-European Style.							
BPound ..	177½	1.50	2.15	r	r	r	r
178.56 .	180	0.79	1.52	r	r	r	r
31,250 British Pounds-cents per unit.							
BPound ..	170	r	r	9.15	r	0.22	r
178.56 .	172½	5.85	5.95	r	r	r	r
178.56 .	175	4.42	4.60	r	0.13	0.95	r
178.56 .	177½	2.15	2.45	r	0.60	2.38	r
178.56 .	180	r	r	r	2.12	r	r
178.56 .	182½	0.25	r	r	r	r	r
50,000 Canadian Dollars-European Style.							
CDollar ...	83	r	0.78	r	r	r	r
50,000 Canadian Dollars-cents per unit.							
CDollr	83½	0.27	r	r	0.28	r	r
83.89 .	88	r	r	r	r	r	5.12
250,000 French Francs- 10ths of a cent per unit.							
FFranc	16½	r	r	r	r	0.06	r
181.21 .	18	r	2.66	r	r	r	r
181.21 .	18½	r	0.80	r	r	r	r
1,000,000 GermanMark-JapaneseYen cross.							
GMk-JYn	81	0.44	0.71	r	0.41	1.08	r
62,500 German Marks-European Style.							
DMark ...	51	r	0.29	r	r	r	r
61.07 .	58½	r	r	s	r	0.13	s
61.07 .	60	1.14	r	r	r	0.45	r
61.07 .	60½	0.75	r	s	r	r	s
61.07 .	61	r	r	1.16	r	r	r
61.07 .	61½	0.21	0.53	s	r	r	s
61.07 .	62½	r	0.26	s	r	r	s
61.07 .	63	r	r	0.54	r	r	r

continued

TABLE 1–3 *continued*

62,500 German Marks-cents per unit.

	Strike						
DMark ...	55	r	r	r	r	r	0.19
61.07	57	r	4.38	r	r	0.03	r
61.07 ..	58	r	r	3.19	r	0.08	r
61.07 ..	58½	r	r	s	r	0.13	s
61.07 ..	59	r	r	r	r	0.22	1.08
61.07 ..	59½	1.75	r	s	0.04	0.28	s
61.07 ..	60	1.21	1.37	r	0.09	0.44	1.50
61.07 ..	60½	1.02	1.02	s	0.16	r	s
61.07 ..	61	0.65	0.81	1.20	0.32	0.82	2.00
61.07 ..	61½	0.33	0.65	s	r	1.08	s
61.07 ..	62	0.17	0.36	r	r	r	r
61.07 ..	62½	r	0.27	s	r	1.90	s
61.07 ..	64	r	0.06	r	r	r	r

6,250,000 Japanese Yen-100ths of a cent per unit.

	Strike						
JYen	74	1.58	r	r	r	0.30	r
75.14 ..	74½	r	r	s	r	0.43	s
75.14 ..	75	0.81	0.99	1.69	r	r	1.48
75.14 ..	75½	0.41	0.74	s	r	0.88	s
75.14 ..	76	0.24	0.53	r	0.67	r	r
75.14 ..	77	r	0.30	r	r	r	r
75.14 ..	78½	r	0.09	s	r	r	s

6,250,000 Japanese Yen-European Style.

	Strike						
JYen	73	r	r	r	r	0.11	r
75.14 ..	75½	r	0.83	s	r	r	s
75.14 ..	77	r	0.31	r	r	r	r

62,500 Swiss Francs-European Style.

	Strike						
SFranc	65	r	r	r	0.07	0.46	r
66.42 ..	65½	r	r	s	0.15	r	s
66.42 ..	66	r	r	r	0.31	0.86	r
66.42 ..	67	r	0.45	r	r	r	r
66.42 ..	67½	0.09	r	s	r	r	s
66.42 ..	68½	r	0.15	s	r	r	s
66.42 ..	69	0.02	r	r	r	r	r

62,500 Swiss Francs-cents per unit.

	Strike						
SFranc	64	r	r	r	r	0.22	r
66.42 ..	65	r	r	r	0.05	0.52	1.48
66.42 ..	65½	r	r	s	0.12	r	s
66.42 ..	66	r	r	r	0.38	r	r
66.42 ..	66½	0.53	r	s	r	r	s
66.42 ..	67	0.16	0.60	r	r	r	r
66.42 ..	68	r	0.38	0.79	r	r	r

Total Call Vol	20,547				Call	Open	int	308,335
Total Put Vol	13,154				Put	Open	int	509,943

All the pound option price quotes are for standard contracts of £31,250. The first column for the British pound in Table 1–3 consists of identical quotes for 178.56 under the heading "Option and Underlying." These show the spot price of a pound in cents. This indicates that, at the close of trading, the spot price on one pound was 178.56 cents, or $1.7856. The second column shows the *strike,* or *exercise,* price, which is the prespecified exchange rate at which the option can be exercised—that is, the guaranteed price at which you have the option to buy or sell the currency. These prices are set by the exchange at 2.5-cent gaps between each other and are kept close to—above and below—the spot exchange rate. On May 6, *The Wall Street Journal* provides seven strike price quotes for pound options, ranging from $1.7000 to $1.8250.

The remaining columns in Table 1–3 are labeled calls and puts. The *call option* gives the right to buy the foreign currency—pounds in this case—at the given strike price; the *put option* gives the opportunity to sell the foreign currency at the strike price. The maturities of the call or put options are listed in the column headings. As with other exchanges, the Philadelphia Exchange trades in a limited set of maturities, which include the three consecutive months following the current date and the nearest three months on a quarterly basis. At the beginning of May, these maturity dates were May, June, July, September, December, and March (the day of maturity of option contracts is on the Saturday before the third Wednesday of the month). *The Wall Street Journal* provides quotes only for May, June, and September.

The price quote for the purchase of a call or put option, the option's *premium,* is expressed in cents per foreign currency unit (cents per pound in our example). Therefore, to compute the price of a contract, the premium quote is multiplied by the amount of foreign currency in a given contract. For instance, the standard size of a pound contract is £31,250. The price of a May call option with a strike price of 175.0 is then equal to its premium, 4.42 cents per pound multiplied by £31,250, for a total of $1,381.25 per contract.

An option contract has two parties: the investor, also called the holder or buyer of the contract, and the *writer,* also called the offeror or seller of the contract. Consider a call option (an option to buy). The investor is the person purchasing the option to buy foreign currency. The writer is the opposite side in the contract and must stand ready to honor the contract by selling the stipulated amount of foreign currency at its strike price if the investor decides to exercise his or her call option. The investor in a put option (an option to sell) acquires the right to sell foreign exchange, and the writer stands ready to buy the given foreign currency at the strike price if the investor exercises the put option. The options exchange organization guarantees these transactions, imposing margin requirements on option writers to insure settlement.

What Makes Options Different from Futures and Forward Contracts?

Options have an insurance content that makes them different from forward and futures markets. It allows the investor trading foreign currency to profit from favorable changes in exchange rates while insuring that the cost of the currency will not rise above a certain level. The call option permits those purchasing foreign exchange to gain from increases in the price of foreign currency; the put option allows those selling foreign currency to benefit from reductions in its price. In both cases, if exchange rate shifts are unfavorable, the investor is insured against the losses because the option can be exercised at its strike price. The premium paid on the option can also be seen as an insurance premium—the price the investor pays in order to avoid the potential losses associated with unfavorable currency value swings.

To understand the comparative advantage of an option contract compared to a futures contract, consider the following exercise, using figures for the British pound. Suppose that, because of the need to insure the dollar cost of a September 1992 trip to the United Kingdom, you decide, on May 6, 1992, to contemplate buying £62,500 for September

1992 delivery in the futures market. From the figures in Tables 1–2 and 1–3, the contemporary (May 6, 1992) spot exchange rate was $1.7856, and the exchange rate for September 1992 delivery in the IMM futures market was $1.7604. This means that, in May, you could have engaged in a futures contract to purchase £62,500 for September delivery with an exchange rate of $1.7604, at a cost of $110,025.00 (plus a fee and the cost of a margin requirement, which we will ignore). Suppose, however, that the spot price of a pound declines between May and July from $1.7856 to $1.5402. This means that if you had waited until July, you would have obtained a lower price for the purchase of pounds ($1.5402) when compared to the one guaranteed—and now forced upon you—by the futures contract ($1.7604).

As an alternative, an option allows you to have the opportunity of benefiting from such favorable changes in exchange rates while assuring a preset future exchange rate if no favorable exchange rate changes occur. If, instead of buying the September futures contract, you had purchased a September option, you would have had the opportunity of not exercising your futures contract by allowing the option to expire, and you would have then been able to purchase the pounds at $1.5402 in July. Of course, if the exchange rate between the dollar and the pound had risen to $1.870 by July, you could in this case still have exercised your futures option and been guaranteed a September purchase of pounds at $1.7500.

The differences between options and futures or forward contracts can be clarified by considering the value of an option at the time the contract expires, compared to the value of a comparable futures (forward) contract at expiration. In the ensuing discussion, we will momentarily ignore some of the details of these contracts—the option's premium, margin requirements, and marking to market—all of which would be taken into account in a full comparison of the costs and benefits of the alternative instruments.

Consider a futures contract to buy pounds with an exercise price of $1.50 and a call option with the same strike price as the futures exercise price, so that they can be compared to each other. The value of the futures contract at expiration is the spot price of the currency at that time minus the exercise price of the futures contract. This represents the gain (or loss) to the investor buying pounds at $1.50 and selling them back into dollars at the spot exchange rate. How much money the investor makes or loses depends on the spot price of a pound at expiration. If the spot price exceeds the exercise price, the investor can make a profit and the value of the contract is positive. If the spot price is less than the exercise price, the investor loses and the value of the contract is negative.

In Figure 1–3(a), the value profile of a futures contract to buy pounds is shown in relation to the spot price at expiration. The vertical axis in Figure 1–3(a) represents the value of the futures contract at the expiration date, and the horizontal axis represents the spot price of pounds at expiration. The value profile of the futures contract slopes upward: it is negative when the spot price at expiration is below the exercise price, $1.50, and positive when the spot price exceeds $1.50. If, for instance, the spot price at expiration turns out to be equal to $2.00, the investor will buy pounds through the futures contract at $1.50 and sell them at $2.00, making 50 cents, a value of $0.50 for the futures contract. On the other hand, if the spot price at maturity turns out to be equal to $1.00, the investor would buy pounds at $1.50, selling them at $1.00, losing 50 cents, a value of −$0.50 for the futures contract.

The value of a call option at expiration is the difference between the spot price of the currency at that time and the strike price. This value depends on the spot exchange rate. If the spot price of a pound at expiration exceeds the strike price at which the investor can exercise his or her option, the investor gains by exercising the option (by buying pounds at $1.50 and selling them at the higher spot price) and the value of the option is

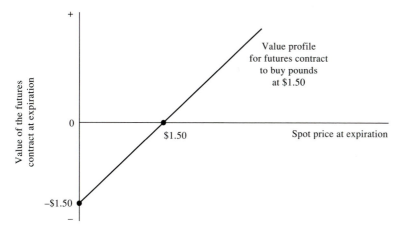

(a) Value profile of a futures contract to buy pounds at expiration

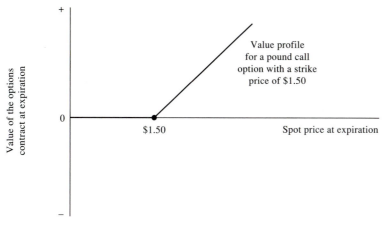

(b) Value profile of a call option at expiration

FIGURE 1–3. Value Profiles of a Futures Contract to Buy Pounds and a Call Option on the Pound

positive. However, if the difference between the spot price and the strike price at maturity is negative, the option generates losses. In this case, the investor will not exercise the option and its value is zero. Figure 1–3(b) presents the value profile of a call option, relating the value of the option to the spot price of a pound at expiration.

The profile lies along the horizontal axis up to the strike price of $1.50 (below $1.50 the value of the option is zero) and slopes upward at higher spot prices.

The differences in the value profiles of futures and options contracts depicted in Figure 1–3 illustrate the economic difference between the two types of contracts. The futures contract offers the possibility of gain if the spot price turns out to exceed the exercise price, but it also entails the risk of large losses if the spot price lies below the $1.50 exercise price. With the call option, there are possibilities of gain, just as with the futures contract; however, if the spot price turns out to be below the strike price, the option does not have to be exercised and the investor does not suffer the losses undertaken under the futures contract. Compared with the futures contract, the call option insures against the risk of downward movements in the spot rate.

The insurance benefits provided by options are not without cost for the investor. The price premium of the option partly represents what investors are willing to pay for the option's insurance benefits. What determines the prices of options is discussed in the next section.

Options on Futures Contracts

In addition to options on currencies, the IMM offers *options on futures contracts*. An option on a futures contract differs from a traditional options contract in that the underlying security is not a spot currency but a futures contract on that currency. Table 1–4 shows the IMM's futures options prices for May 6, 1992, as quoted by *The Wall Street Journal*. An option on a futures contract allows the buyer of the contract to have the choice of whether or not to fulfill a futures contract. The underlying futures contracts for which options are available mature on a quarterly basis (March, June, September, and December). For each futures contract maturity, the IMM offers monthly options. This means that for a September futures contract, options will be traded that expire in July, August, and September. The terminology in Table 1–4 is as in Table 1–3 with calls and puts as defined earlier and "settle" indicating the price at which the contract closed that day. From the figures in the table, the price of a $1.750 British pound September futures call option contract ex-

piring in June was 4.38 cents per pound, or $2,737.50 (equal to the standard size of the contract, £62,500, times the premium paid for the contract, 4.38 cents).

1–10. PRICING CURRENCY OPTIONS

There are a number of regularities that can be determined from Tables 1–3 and 1–4 regarding the price premia for options. Consider first the prices of calls of a given maturity, such as those for May pounds in Table 1–3. Going down the column, the option price premia are quoted in order of rising strike prices. It can be clearly seen that the premia drop as the strike price increases—from 5.85 cents per pound for a strike price of 172.50 all the way down to 0.25 cents for a 182.50 strike price. The same pattern holds for all other call options in Tables 1–3 and 1–4: strike prices and call option prices are inversely related. On the other hand, looking at the premia paid for put options in Table 1–3, it is obvious that strike prices and put option prices are directly related to each other. What explains these relationships?

For call options, the explanation is that the higher the strike price, the lower the *intrinsic value* of the option. The intrinsic value of the call option is equal to the dollar amount that would be gained if the option is exercised and the foreign currency immediately sold at its spot price. Measured in cents per pound purchased, the intrinsic value is equal to the difference between the spot exchange rate and the strike price (to find the intrinsic value for the overall contract, multiply by the size of the contract). If the difference between the spot exchange rate and the strike price is positive, the option is said to be *in the money;* and if the differential is negative, the option is *out of the money;* and if the differential is exactly equal to zero, the option is *at the money.* In Table 1–3, the intrinsic value of a May pound option with a strike price of 172.50 is equal to 6.06 cents per pound (the differential between the spot exchange rate and the strike price), or $1,893.75 per contract (6.06 cents per pound times £31,250, the size of the contract). This option was thus "in the money." For a May call option with a strike price of 175, the intrinsic value quoted is 3.56 cents per pound and the option was thus also "in the money." On the other hand, a May call option with strike price of 182.5 had an intrinsic value approximately

TABLE 1–4. **Futures Options in the International Monetary Market, May 6, 1992**

CURRENCY

JAPANESE YEN (IMM)

12,500,000 yen; cents per 100 yen

Strike	Calls—Settle			Puts—Settle		
Price	May	Jun	Jly	May	Jun	Jly
7450	1.13	1.42	1.59	0.04	0.33	0.63
7500	0.67	1.07	1.29	0.08	0.48	0.82
7550	0.32	0.79	1.07	0.23	0.70	....
7600	0.14	0.57	0.80	0.55	0.98	....
7650	0.05	0.40	0.62	0.96	1.31	....
7700	0.03	0.28	0.47	1.44	1.69	....

Est. vol. 9,193;

Tues vol. 1,594 calls; 2,761 puts

Op. int. Tues 45,526 calls; 49,249 puts

DEUTSCHEMARK (IMM)

125,000 marks; cents per mark

Strike	Calls—Settle			Puts—Settle		
Price	May	Jun	Jly	May	Jun	Jly
6000	1.10	1.37	1.12	0.05	0.33	0.93
6050	0.66	1.04	0.88	0.11	0.49	1.19
6100	0.32	0.76	0.69	0.27	0.71	....
6150	0.13	0.53	0.53	0.58	0.98	....
6200	0.06	0.36	0.40	1.01	1.31	....
6250	0.02	0.24	....	....	1.68	....

Est. vol. 25,041;

Tues vol. 11,197 calls; 6,326 puts

Op. int. Tues 94,539 calls; 117,630 puts

CANADIAN DOLLAR (IMM)

100,000 Can.$, cents per Can.$

Strike	Calls—Settle			Puts—Settle		
Price	May	Jun	Jly	May	Jun	Jly
8250	....	1.03	....	0.01	0.17	....
8300	0.42	0.67	0.54	0.05	0.30	0.72
8350	0.10	0.41	0.35	0.23	0.54	....
8400	0.02	0.21	0.22	0.65	0.84	1.39
8450	.0000	0.10	....	1.13	1.23	....
8500	.0000	0.05	0.08	....	1.67	....

Est. vol. 2,107;

Tues vol. 479 calls; 115 puts

Op. int. Tues 11,747 calls; 13,959 puts

continued

TABLE 1–4 *continued*

BRITISH POUND (IMM)
62,500 pounds; cents per pound

Strike	Calls—Settle			Puts—Settle		
Price	May	Jun	Jly	May	Jun	Jly
1725	6.12	6.42	4.98	0.004	0.36	1.46
1750	3.68	4.38	3.44	0.06	0.78	2.40
1775	1.46	2.72	2.24	0.36	1.60	....
1800	0.30	1.46	1.38	1.70	2.86	....
1825	0.06	0.74	....	3.94	4.62	....
1850	0.004	0.34	0.46	....	6.70	....

Est. vol. 3,835;
Tues vol. 734 calls; 1,372 puts
Op. int. Tues 14,495 calls; 15,444 puts

SWISS FRANC (IMM)
125,000 francs; cents per franc

Strike	Calls—Settle			Puts—Settle		
Price	May	Jun	Jly	May	Jun	Jly
6550	0.99	1.35	1.18	0.07	0.43	1.01
6600	0.57	1.03	0.96	0.15	0.61	....
6650	0.27	0.77	0.76	0.35	0.85	....
6700	0.12	0.56	0.59	0.70	1.14	....
6750	0.06	0.40	0.46	1.14	1.48	....
6800	0.01	0.27	0.35	1.59	1.84	....

Est. vol. 3,161;
Tues vol. 1,878 calls; 730 puts
Op. int. Tues 18,514 calls; 17,787 puts

SOURCE: *The Wall Street Journal,* May 7, 1992, section C, p. 13. Reprinted by permission of *The Wall Street Journal,* © 1992 Dow Jones & Company, Inc. All rights reserved worldwide.

imately equal to –3.94 cents per pound and it was thus "out of the money."

Other things constant, the higher the strike price of a call option, the lower its value and, therefore, the lower the price premium at which it is sold. However, even if the option is at the money or out of the money—that is, if there is no gain from exercising it immediately—the option could have a positive value. The reason is that the spot exchange rate may rise between today and the time the option expires. This means that there is a possibility that the option will have a high intrinsic value in the future. As long as investors are willing to pay for the chance that this may occur, the at-the-money or out-of-money options can still have a *time value* and, thus, a positive price premium. In Table 1–3, the May call option on the pound with 182.50 strike price was out of the money; its price thus mostly reflects the time value of that option. The time value is largely determined by market expectations about the future value of the currency: The more prevalent the belief that the spot exchange rate of the foreign currency will rise in the future, the larger the time value of the option. In addition, time value is related to the time to maturity of the option: The closer the option is to maturity, the less likely that spot exchange rates will change and the less significant time value will become. In fact, at the time of maturity, the time value of the option would be zero. Finally, the greater the volatility of the exchange rate, the larger the expected returns from possible future exchange rate changes and the higher the time value of the currency.[15]

An example of how time value may stimulate demand for out-of-the-money call options emerged in the months preceding the United Nations deadline for Iraq to withdraw from Kuwait by January 15, 1991. It was the opinion of many speculators at the time that, because Japan is so heavily dependent on oil from the Gulf region, if war were to break out the yen would sharply drop in value.[16] They consequently raised the demand for out-of-the-money call options on the yen—options that otherwise would have appeared to be worthless at the time. Their expectation was that, even though the yen call options' strike price exceeded the spot exchange rate prevailing before the deadline, the spot price of a yen in dollars would shoot up after a war started, making the call option highly profitable. With the time value of these—and other—call options rising, premiums on them also went up. Trading in the options exchanges boomed in the prewar period. At the Philadelphia Stock Exchange there was an average of approximately 65,000 currency options a day traded in the week preceding the U.N. deadline, far above the 40,500-a-day average for 1990.[17] The principles involved in the pricing of calls also apply to puts. In *selling* foreign currency, however,

the higher the strike price of the currency, the larger the intrinsic value of the option and the greater its premium.

Pricing models attempting to measure the intrinsic and time values of options have a long history.[18] Given the many parameters involved in these models—and their complex intertemporal and stochastic components—we will not present them here.[19]

Summary

1. The foreign exchange market is the market in which national currencies are traded. Its basic function is to provide the means of payment required for the smooth operation of international transactions. As in any market, a price must exist at which trade occurs; the exchange rate is the price of one currency in terms of another.

2. In this book, we look at the exchange rate as the domestic currency price of a foreign currency. Adopting a U.S. vantage point, we quote exchange rates in terms of the dollars required to buy foreign currency.

3. An increase in an exchange rate means that the domestic currency price of a foreign currency increases; that is, the foreign currency becomes more expensive in terms of domestic money. This is referred to as a domestic currency depreciation. Similarly, a reduction in a given exchange rate means that the

---

[15]See I. H. Giddy, "The Foreign Exchange Option as a Hedging Tool," in J. M. Stern and D. H. Chew, eds., *New Developments in International Finance* (New York: Basil Blackwell, 1988), pp. 83–93.

[16]Baruch Deutsch, a vice-president in foreign exchange at Shearson Lehman in New York, stated in *The Wall Street Journal* that "Some people are using options to speculate on the yen, betting that the yen's value will decline if there's a war." (Quoted by J. Taylor, "Speculators Make Big Option Play on U.N. Deadline," *The Wall Street Journal,* January 14, 1991, Section C, p. 1.

[17]See C. Cumberbatch, "Traders are Choosing Currency Options As Crisis in Mideast Enters Crucial Week," *The Wall Street Journal,* January 14, 1991.

[18]The classic in this literature is F. Black and M. Scholes, "The Pricing of Options and Corporate Liabilities," *Journal of Political Economy,* (May-June 1973). The pricing of currency options has been discussed by M. B. Garman and S. W. Kohlhagen in "Foreign Currency Option Values," *Journal of International Money and Finance* (December 1983), 231–237; and J. O. Grabbe in *International Financial Markets* (Amsterdam: Elsevier Publishing Co., 1991).

[19]There are advanced texts and a number of widely available computer programs used to calculate them. See, for instance, Chapter 8 in D. Duffie, *Futures Markets* (Englewood Cliffs, N.J.: Prentice Hall, 1989).

foreign currency becomes relatively cheaper or that the domestic currency appreciates (increases) in value.

4. Foreign exchange markets can be differentiated into two types: spot and forward. In spot markets, currencies are bought and sold for immediate delivery and payment; in forward (futures) markets, contracts are provided for the delivery of currencies at some future date. The crucial difference between the spot and forward markets is that in a spot transaction the price at which a currency is traded (the spot exchange rate) is set concurrently with the payment and delivery of a currency; in forward markets, traders determine the price today (the forward exchange rate) for future delivery and payment. The forward market is used by investors to cover their open positions in foreign currencies and thus hedge against unpredictable exchange rate fluctuations. Open positions in a given currency mean that the value of assets and liabilities denominated in that currency does not match. In order to close (or cover) the position, investors must hold equal assets and liabilities denominated in the same currency.

5. The forward exchange rate tends to reflect the spot exchange rate that most participants in the market anticipate will prevail at the point of maturity of the forward contract. Even though the forward rate does not generally predict actual future exchange rates with any degree of accuracy, it still provides the most accessible and yet highly unbeatable forecast of future exchange rates. The inaccuracy of the forward exchange rate in predicting future spot rates is connected to the general unpredictability of future exchange rates, something to which all forecasts are subject.

6. The proportional difference between the forward and the current spot exchange rates of domestic currency against a foreign currency is called the forward premium on that Foreign currency. A positive forward premium means

that the foreign currency is worth more, in terms of domestic currency, for future than for current delivery. A positive forward premium tends to reflect an expected depreciation of domestic currency against the foreign currency. When negative, the forward premium (referred to as being at a discount) suggests that participants in the exchange market anticipate the domestic currency will appreciate relative to the foreign currency.

7. Futures markets are centralized markets for the delivery and payment of a commodity or asset. Futures currency markets differ from forward markets in that futures markets are centralized and offer standardized contracts, which are more liquid than forward contracts. Also, futures markets credit or debit gains and losses in the value of contracts daily, a practice called marking to market; in forward markets, any accumulated gains or losses from the contract can be credited or debited by the investor only when the contract expires.

8. A currency option is a contract giving the buyer or holder the opportunity or right—but not the obligation—to buy or sell a given amount of foreign currency at a pre-agreed exchange rate (called strike price) for a specified period of time. A call option gives the right to buy the foreign currency at the given strike price, whereas a put option gives the right to sell the foreign currency at the strike price. The price of the option is called the premium and is what the writer (or offeror) of the option receives as reward for accepting the commitment to sell or buy foreign currency if the option is exercised. When compared to forward or futures contracts, options provide holders with a certain degree of insurance against unfavorable exchange rate changes.

Problems

1. Describe the process through which someone living in a small town can make a payment in

deutsche marks. How does a local bank obtain the foreign exchange? Explain the mechanics involved.

2. Find *The Wall Street Journal*'s foreign exchange rate quotes for today, and calculate the ninety-day forward market premiums of the pound sterling, deutsche mark, and French franc against the U.S. dollar. How do these forward premiums (discounts) compare with those determined from Table 1–1? What do they suggest about the market's assessment of the future behavior of the exchange rates examined?

3. Using *The Wall Street Journal*'s daily quotes, find today's implicit or cross deutsche mark-pound sterling exchange rate. Then check a British financial periodical to determine the actual exchange rate between the deutsche mark and pound sterling in England for the corresponding date. Are these two quotes strictly comparable?

4. The foreign exchange market expanded by close to 50 percent over the period of 1989 through 1992. What explains this massive growth?

5. Reviewing a number of recent studies supplied by economists Kenneth Froot of Harvard University, Robert Shiller of Yale, and Stephen Taylor of Lancaster University, the magazine *The Economist* [December 5, 1992, pp. 21–23] concludes that "the possibility of making long-term profits by playing the foreign exchange markets or by picking stocks can no longer be ruled out." What does this imply about foreign exchange market efficiency?

6. During September 1992, world foreign exchange markets underwent one of their most tumultuous periods in recent years, caused by a crisis in the European exchange markets (the next chapter will discuss the nature of this crisis). During this time period, some of the larger U.S. commercial banks (such as Citicorp, Chemical, Bankers Trust, and BankAmerica) reportedly increased their foreign exchange earnings by over 50 percent. What explains the "excess" profits earned by banks on their foreign exchange trading during this time period? (Hints: How does market turmoil affect the foreign exchange market spread? Do you think speculative activity increased during the crisis?)

7. Consider the following statement about traders in currency options markets: "Aggressive traders welcome volatility, or what they call implied, volatility, the expectation that sudden price changes are likely in the near future." (J. Fuerbringer, "In Options Trading, Volatility Is a Virtue," *The New York Times,* January 26, 1992, Section F. p. 5). Why would options traders "enjoy" increased exchange rate volatility?

8. The following are bid-ask quotes for the purchase or sale of a U.S. dollar in London on January 30, 1991, in terms of Canadian dollars (i.e., in Canadian dollars required to purchase or sell a U.S. dollar in London). Calculate the bid-ask spreads for the U.S. dollar in terms of Canadian dollars. Why do you think bid-ask spreads rise in the forward exchange market?

	Bid price of a U.S. dollar	Ask price of a U.S. dollar
	(in Canadian dollars per U.S. dollar)	
Spot	1.1605	1.1615
Forward, one-month	1.1640	1.1653
Forward, three months	1.1707	1.1722

SOURCE: *The Financial Times,* January 31, 1991, p. 31.

9. Using the June figures for futures contracts in Table 1–2, compute the (approximate) thirty-day premiums on the Japanese yen, the West German mark, and the British pound. Should these premia coincide with the premia in the forward market for contracts with equal maturity? What would be the role of arbitrage in

keeping futures and forward exchange rates unified?

10. In Table 1−3, describe which Swiss Franc options are "in the money," "at the money," and "out of the money."

11. Using Table 1−3, calculate the intrinsic values of June call options for the British pound and the West German mark. Compute the time value of those options that are "out of the money." Assuming that forward exchange rates reflect market expectations of future exchange rates, what do the pound and mark forward exchange rates in Table 1−1 say about the time values you have just calculated?

12. What factors determine the price of a put currency option? How do you define the intrinsic value and the time value of a put option? Explain using the quotes presented in Table 1−3.

13. An M.B.A. student who just completed a finance course states that "a forward contract and a portfolio consisting of a long call and a short put position, with both options having the forward rate as their strike price, are equivalent." Do you agree?

14. A *straddle* is a combination of call and put options with the same exercise price. Why do many currency speculators prefer straddles to either call or put options in times of great uncertainty about the future (such as during the period preceding the Gulf War)? What is the cost of a straddle relative to a simple put or call?

15. Explain the difference between a financial option and a traditional option.

CHAPTER 2

Central Banks, Exchange Rate Regimes, and the International Monetary System

Chapter 1 discussed the mechanics of how foreign exchange markets operate, emphasizing the different ways in which individuals, firms, and commercial banks transact in those markets. We now begin a detailed analysis of the role that governments play in foreign exchange markets.

Sovereign states establish the legal framework in which a country's international transactions take place. A key element of this framework is the exchange rate regime: the rules that determine how the private sector buys and sells foreign currencies. Exchange rate regimes vary remarkably from one country to another, and they may change over time. In the United States, the monetary authorities allow the free exchange of currencies, although an effort is made to influence the value of the dollar through purchases and sales of currencies in the free market. In many developing countries, on the other hand, transactions in foreign currency are much more regulated. In Bolivia, for example, exporters are obliged to sell to the state, at an exchange rate fixed by the government, the foreign currencies they receive from exports. In Mexico, the government of President José Lopez Portillo nationalized the banking system in September 1982 and took direct control over most foreign currency transactions, a move subsequently reversed by President Carlos Salinas de-Gortari.

It is the purpose of this chapter and the next one to survey the various exchange rate regimes currently adopted throughout the world. In this chapter we discuss the mechanics of how governments determine exchange rates under each regime and the basic economic consequences of such government intervention. We also provide a brief history of the international monetary system and an analysis of the current state of international monetary arrangements, including a detailed examination of the European Monetary System (EMS). The following chapter is concerned with the exchange rate regimes of developing countries.

2−1. CENTRAL BANKS AND EXCHANGE RATE REGIMES: AN INTRODUCTION

The domestic institution in charge of managing exchange rates is usually the central bank, although other authorities might be involved (such as the Department of the Treasury in the United States). Central banks, like the Federal Reserve System in the United States or the Bank of England in Great Britain, are government or quasi-government banks that regulate a nation's banking system and manage its monetary affairs. Central banks differ in the way they intervene in foreign exchange markets, but generally their intention is to influence or to fix exchange rates. This agenda is not easy, and when exchange rate policies fail, the people at the top of the central bank and other related institutions are quickly replaced. A graphic example of the pressures suffered by central bankers comes from Germany at the end of World War I. Following Germany's defeat in that war, a rapid

increase in prices (hyperinflation) was accompanied by an accelerated rise in the dollar price of the mark (Germany's currency). In 1919, the value of the dollar was around 14 marks. By November 20, 1923, the exchange rate had gone up to four trillion marks per dollar. On that day, the president of the Reichsbank, the German central bank at the time, died of a heart attack.

The intervention of central banks in the foreign exchange market is related to the exchange rate regime under which a nation is governed. We differentiate among three basic types of exchange rate regimes. Different historical versions of each regime exist, but countries and periods can generally be classified in terms of combinations or permutations of the basic types.

A *freely flexible* (or *free-floating*) *exchange rate regime* exists whenever exchange rates (currency prices) are freely determined by the demand and supply of currencies by private parties. This regime assumes the absence of any systematic government intervention in the foreign exchange market. The exchange rate moves freely in response to market forces.

Under a *fixed* (or *pegged*) *exchange rate regime,* the government intervenes in foreign exchange markets through its central bank in an effort to maintain the exchange rate vis-à-vis different currencies within narrowly prescribed limits. The central bank in this regime will buy and sell currencies in order to limit the variations of the exchange rate. To carry out its foreign exchange operations, the central bank will then hold inventories (or *international reserves*) of foreign exchange. The central value of the exchange rate, around which the government maintains narrow limits, is called a peg for the currency. The Haitian gourde, for example, was officially pegged to the U.S. dollar at an exchange rate, or peg, of $0.20 per gourde from 1907 to 1991—a remarkable example of a fixed exchange rate. Observe that exchange rates must exist between any given national currency and all other foreign currencies traded in foreign exchange markets. A currency can then be floating in value with respect to some foreign currencies and fixed in value with respect to others. Argentina's peso, for instance, fluctuates in value with respect to the French franc but is officially pegged to the dollar.

A third type of foreign exchange regime is the *managed,* or *controlled, floating exchange rate regime.* In contrast to the free-floating regime, a controlled-floating regime exists when government intervenes in the foreign exchange market in order to influence the exchange rate but does not commit itself to maintaining a certain fixed exchange rate or some narrow limits around it. The central bank "gets its hands dirty" by manipulating the marketplace for foreign exchange; however, it does not intervene to fix the price of foreign exchange as it would in a system of fixed exchange rates.

In order to visualize more clearly the difference between fixed and floating exchange rate regimes, it is useful to think of the market for foreign exchange in terms of traditional supply-and-demand curves.[1] The private sector's demand for foreign exchange arises from the needs of domestic residents to acquire foreign currencies. These needs may derive from many sources. The prices of foreign goods and assets are denominated in foreign currency and to buy them requires the purchase of foreign exchange. This gives rise to a

demand for foreign exchange. In addition, the demand of the private sector for foreign exchange may not come from immediate transaction needs. It may come from currency diversification decisions made by economic agents (mainly corporations and banks) holding deposits denominated in various currencies to maximize expected returns and to minimize the risk of holding foreign exchange. A rumor that a currency may depreciate (i.e., a "weak" currency) may generate diversions of deposits away from that currency and into "strong" currencies, a phenomenon called currency substitution.

The private sector's demand curve for foreign exchange is represented in Figure 2–1 by the downward-sloping *DD* curve. In order to simplify the exposition, it is assumed that there are only two currencies under consideration: a domestic currency and a foreign currency. The price of the foreign currency in terms of domestic currency is, then, the exchange rate *e*. The demand curve for foreign exchange shows the quantity demanded of foreign exchange as a function of the exchange rate. It is downward sloping on the assumption that, as the price of foreign exchange increases, the quantity demanded will show a decline. How can we rationalize this assumption? Suppose, for example, that domestic (U.S.) residents are buying

[1]The supply-and-demand analysis we are about to pursue constitutes a partial equilibrium analysis, in the sense that it concentrates on one particular market—the foreign exchange market—and ignores the simultaneous interrelationships between all markets in the economy. It would be inconsistent with some general equilibrium theories of exchange rate determination. For a specific case in which this analysis is consistent with some general equilibrium considerations, see R. Dornbusch, "Exchange Rates and Fiscal Policy in a Popular Model of International Trade," *American Economic Review* (December 1975). The reader should be aware, then, that the analysis presented in this section is not applicable to every situation and is only valid under special assumptions. Subsequent chapters will treat complete, general equilibrium theories in full detail. See also, P. Kouri, "Balance of Payments and the Foreign Exchange Market: A Dynamic Partial Equilibrium Model," in J. S. Bhandari and B. H. Putnam, eds., *Economic Interdependence and Flexible Exchange Rates* (Cambridge, Mass.: The MIT Press, 1983).

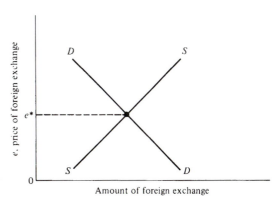

FIGURE 2–1. Equilibrium Under Flexible Exchange Rates

British rock compact disks. If the price quoted by the British suppliers is £4.0 and the exchange rate is $2.50 per pound, the price of one disk in U.S. dollars is $10.00. Some rock fans are then willing to pay the price, buying the compact disks and creating a given demand for pounds. Suppose now that the exchange rate between the dollar and the pound increases to $3.00 per pound. If the British suppliers keep their price at £4.0, the price of a disk in terms of dollars will now be $12.00. As a consequence, the number of rock compact disks demanded will tend to decline; at a fixed price of disks in pounds, this decline will result in a reduction in the total amount of pounds that U.S. residents wish to spend on British disks. This represents a decrease in the quantity demanded of foreign exchange. An increase in the exchange rate, e, then induces a reduction in the quantity demanded of foreign exchange by the private sector.

The supply of foreign exchange by the private sector arises from the desires of foreign residents to acquire domestic currency. In order to do so, they have to sell their own currencies, creating the supply of foreign exchange. As such, the supply of foreign exchange is implicitly a demand for domestic currency. Foreigners may wish to acquire domestic currency for transaction purposes (to buy domestic goods, services, and assets—the prices of which are denominated in domestic currency) or for currency diversification purposes (e.g., to hold domestic currency in the expectation of a depreciation of the foreign currency).

The private sector supply curve of foreign exchange is represented in Figure 2–1 by the upward-sloping SS curve. This curve shows the quantity supplied of foreign exchange as a function of the exchange rate. The upward slope of the supply curve assumes that, as the price of foreign exchange increases, the quantity supplied of foreign exchange increases. How can we rationalize this assumption? Suppose that a domestic producer of jazz compact disks can sell any desired amount of disks at a price of £4.0 in the British market. At

that price, and with an exchange rate equal to $2.5 per pound, the domestic currency price of a compact disk sold in England would be $10.00. Given this price, the domestic producer may decide to sell—that is, to export—a certain number of jazz disks to England. The British buyers of these compact disks will then sell their pounds to acquire U.S. dollars with which to pay for the disks, generating a supply of pounds in the foreign exchange market. What happens now if the exchange rate increases to $3.00 per pound sterling? At this new exchange rate, and assuming that jazz disks can still be sold at a price of £4.0 each, the dollar receipts from selling a compact disk in England would increase to $12.00 (£4.00 × $3.00/£). Given this new, higher dollar price, the U.S. producer would find it profitable to increase its exports of jazz disks. As foreign residents buy these disks, they sell pounds to acquire U.S. dollars with which to buy them, and the supply of pounds increases; that is, as the exchange rate, e, increases, the quantity supplied of foreign exchange increases.[2]

Freely Flexible Exchange Rates

Under freely flexible exchange rates the private demand and supply of foreign exchange must be equal in order to have equilibrium in the market. Obviously, government authorities could buy or sell foreign exchange if they wish. Our definition

[2]This process assumes that the exporter is small in the British market for compact disks in the sense that it can sell all the disks it wants to at the given market price; an alternative assumption is that our exporter can only sell more disks by decreasing the price in pounds. In this case, we have an ambiguity: As the exchange rate increases, the quantity of compact disks exported increases, but at a lower price in pounds. As a result, the total supply of pounds could either increase or decrease. This suggests that the supply curve could slope upward or downward. We do not examine the latter because our purpose in utilizing the supply-demand framework in Figure 1–2 lies only in its usefulness as a tool in describing the main differences between fixed and flexible exchange rate regimes, and not as a rigorous formal analysis of the determination of exchange rates, which it is not.

of the freely flexible exchange rate system, however, assumes that under this regime government interventions in the foreign exchange market are unsystematic and negligible in determining the exchange rate. As a consequence, they can be safely ignored.

The exchange rate at which the demand and supply of foreign exchange are equal is the equilibrium exchange rate e^*, determined in Figure 2–1 by the intersection of the DD and SS curves. At that point, algebraically,

$$D(e^*; D_0) = S(e^*; S_0), \qquad (2–1)$$

where D represents the demand for foreign exchange and S is the supply of foreign exchange. Note that we represent the demand for foreign exchange as a function of the exchange rate, e, and of D_0, where D_0 represents a number of other variables affecting D, assumed fixed in deriving the demand curve DD. Similarly, the supply of foreign exchange depends not only on the exchange rate but also on other variables, represented here by S_0. In deriving the supply curve, we *assume* these variables to be fixed. The variables that may affect S_0 and D_0 include interest rates, income levels, and expectations about future

events. Changes in these variables will tend to shift the demand or supply curves of foreign exchange and will thus change the equilibrium exchange rate. Because we have not yet explained how all these variables affect the DD and SS curves, we have not fully specified the analytics behind the determination of the exchange rate e^*. Such an analysis will appear in Chapters 13, 15, and 19. In any case, whatever the factors affecting the demand and supply of foreign exchange, the equilibrium exchange rate under a regime of flexible exchange rates would be determined by the equality shown in Equation 2–1.

Fixed Exchange Rates

The foreign exchange market equilibrium under a fixed exchange rate regime is portrayed in Figure 2–2, where we show our usual DD and SS curves. Figure 2–2(a) assumes that the government is pegging the exchange rate at a level equal to $\underline{e}$, which is below the private sector equilibrium exchange rate e^*. In general, governments will permit some variation of e within a small band around its peg $\underline{e}$. For the sake of simplicity, our diagrammatic analysis assumes that the exchange rate is absolutely fixed at $\underline{e}$, with no band around

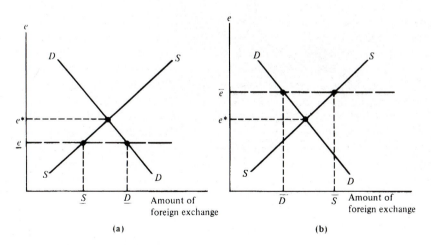

FIGURE 2–2. Pegging the Exchange Rate

it. At that fixed exchange rate, there is an excess demand for foreign exchange on the part of the private sector. This excess demand is represented by the horizontal distance between the private demand-and-supply curves for foreign exchange, which is numerically equal to $\underline{D} - \underline{S}$. At the given exchange rate, demanders of foreign exchange wish to buy more than what suppliers are willing to offer. This excess demand for foreign exchange is filled by the central bank, which sells foreign exchange to the private sector in order to prevent the exchange rate from moving above the level of the peg at $\underline{e}$. This means that, during the period of concern, the central bank loses (sells) an amount of international reserves (foreign exchange) equal to $\underline{D} - \underline{S}$. Under a regime of fixed exchange rates, the central bank must hold international reserves to maintain exchange rates at peg levels.

Suppose that the exchange rate is pegged at a level equal to $\bar{e}$, which is higher than the equilibrium exchange rate e^*, as shown in Figure 2–2(b). At that exchange rate, there would be an excess supply of foreign exchange on the part of the private sector, as quantity supplied, $\bar{S}$, exceeds quantity demanded, $\bar{D}$. At the given peg, suppliers of foreign exchange wish to supply more than the demanders of foreign exchange wish to demand. This excess supply of foreign exchange by the private sector is purchased by the central bank, as it tries to prevent the exchange rate from dropping below the peg at $\bar{e}$. This example shows that the fixed exchange rate regime, as compared with the flexible exchange rate regime, is one in which the government intervenes to set the price in the market. As in any other market in which the government fixes prices, there will generally be discrepancies between the private sector's demand and supply. In this case, the central bank fills these gaps by buying or selling foreign exchange reserves. By contrast, under a freely flexible exchange rate regime, the government does not intervene in the market so that the private sector's demand and supply for foreign exchange will be equal in equilibrium. Therefore, with floating

rates, the central bank does not have to buy or sell foreign exchange reserves; in theory, it does not have to hold any at all.

In short, under fixed exchange rates, shifts in the private sector's demand-and-supply curves of foreign exchange produce changes in the amount of foreign exchange reserves. This differs from the situation under freely flexible exchange rates, in which the opposite holds: Shifts in the private sector's demand-and-supply curves of foreign exchange produce changes in the exchange rate but do not affect the amount of foreign exchange reserves. In general, however, central banks do intervene in foreign exchange markets, even if they are not committed to a regime of fixed exchange rates. This is, of course, the managed floating regime mentioned earlier. Under managed floating, shifts in private demand and supply trigger central bank intervention; therefore, both variations in exchange rates and changes in the levels of international reserves will be observed. Hence, this regime can be viewed as a mix of fixed and floating regimes.

When a country systematically sustains an exchange rate parity below the equilibrium exchange rate, foreign currency is kept cheaper than in equilibrium. In this case—illustrated in Figure 2–2(a)—we say that the domestic currency is *overvalued:* Its value in terms of foreign currency is set above equilibrium. On the other hand, if the exchange rate parity established by the central bank is above the equilibrium exchange rate—as shown in Figure 2–2(b)—we say that the domestic currency is *undervalued:* Its value in terms of foreign currency is below equilibrium. To understand this, remember that there is a negative relationship between the exchange rate—conventionally defined as the domestic currency price of foreign currency—and the value of domestic currency in terms of foreign money. In the United States, when we use the conventional definition of an exchange rate, we are thinking in terms of the dollar price of foreign currency. When the exchange rate goes up, foreign currency becomes more expensive. This means that the cost of buying foreign money increases and the value of a dollar in terms of acquiring foreign currency thus declines. Hence, there is an inverse relationship between the level of the exchange rate and the value of the dollar in terms of foreign currency. When the exchange rate is set below its equilibrium level (fixed at a level that is "too low"), the value of the dollar is above equilibrium and the dollar is thus overvalued. The opposite holds if the exchange rate is fixed at a level above equilibrium; in this case, the value of the dollar is above equilibrium and the dollar is undervalued. For instance, suppose that the equilibrium exchange rate is $1.00 per pound and the current exchange rate is $2.00 per pound. Then the equilibrium value of a dollar is 1 pound but its current value is half a pound. In other words, the dollar is currently undervalued.

The determination of whether, and by how much, a currency is undervalued or overvalued is not as simple as it may seem. The reason is that the equilibrium exchange rate must be known. However, if there is no free market in the economy, only the official rate, e or $\bar{e}$, is observed. The equilibrium exchange rate has to be estimated. In terms of Figures 2–2(a) and 2–2(b), this requires that the supply-and-demand curves for foreign currencies be estimated. This can be a very complicated statistical task because the curves DD and SS are not fixed entities but are in constant flux, shifting up and down in response to economic fluctuations. However, unless the central bank lets the exchange rate fluctuate freely (which means abandoning the fixed exchange rate regime), there is no alternative way of knowing by how much the currency is overvalued or undervalued.[3]

---

[3]As we will see in Chapter 3, black markets may provide some information about free-market equilibrium exchange rates. Other measurements of currency over- and undervaluation (exchange rate misalignment) are examined by S. Edwards in *Exchange Rate Misalignment in Developing Countries* (Baltimore: Johns Hopkins University Press, 1988).

Parity Adjustments Under Fixed Exchange Rates

Under fixed exchange rates, central banks systematically intervene to fix the exchange rate around a certain peg value. Nothing prevents them, however, from changing the parity value at which they buy or sell foreign currency. For instance, in many developing countries, parities at any given time are pegged relative to the dollar but are altered periodically. Sometimes they are altered following a list of pre-announced exchange rate changes established by the government in so-called *tablitas* ("little tables" in Spanish). This system, in which the exchange rate is adjusted little by little, every certain period of time, represents a *crawling peg* regime.

What factors make governments alter parity levels? The fixing of currency values follows a variety of political and economic considerations that will be discussed in later chapters. At this point, it is the immediate factors that may force officials to change parity levels that we will focus on. Let us consider the case of the overvalued currency illustrated in Figure 2–2(a). In this situation, the central bank fixes an exchange rate below equilibrium and is obliged to sell dollars equal to $D - S$ in every time period. As a result, if the private supply of and demand for foreign exchange do not change, the central bank will eventually suffer a severe reduction of its international reserves. If the government runs out of reserves, a so-called exchange crisis will occur, in which the central bank can no longer sustain its foreign currency sales to the public and is forced to impose controls on foreign transactions or close the foreign exchange market. Because these actions could seriously disrupt the country's international commerce, the government may wish to avoid such a calamity by increasing the exchange rate parity. In the example depicted by Figure 2–2(a), the exchange rate could be adjusted from e to $e*$, which would stop the central bank's loss of dollar reserves.

If an exchange rate peg is increased, the price of foreign currency in terms of domestic currency is increased and the domestic currency is said to be *devalued*. If the exchange rate peg is decreased, the domestic currency price of foreign currency is decreased and the domestic currency is said to be *revalued*. Note that a devaluation corresponds to a depreciation of the domestic currency, and a revaluation corresponds to an appreciation of the currency. The different terminology arises from the different exchange rate regimes. Devaluation and revaluation refer to adjustments in fixed exchange rate regimes. Depreciation and appreciation, on the other hand, refer to changes in the exchange rate under a system of flexible exchange rates. The pound sterling, for example, was devalued in November 1967 from a long-standing $2.80/£ to $2.40/£. This means that monetary authorities in England decided to change the peg of the pound vis-à-vis the dollar. On the other hand, in the second half of 1992, the pound sterling steadily depreciated vis-à-vis the dollar, from $2.00 (in September) to $1.55 (in December). This means that the value of the pound sterling decreased, as determined in the foreign exchange markets. The difference between devaluation (revaluation) and depreciation (appreciation) is terminological; the terms are often used interchangeably.

In developing countries, the use of currency devaluation is a policy decision that is considered very carefully before its implementation. The fact is that the public often views devaluation as a sign of weakness in the government and/or its economic policies.[4] Devaluations make imports more expensive in local currency, pushing domestic prices upward. Hence, there are groups within the economy—such as labor unions facing an infla-

tionary erosion in the purchasing power of their contractual wages—that are affected negatively by the devaluation and may create an intensive public and private lobby against it. In some cases, the reluctance to engage in currency devaluation is so strong that the policy is explicitly prohibited by the country's constitution (as was once the case in Honduras). Currency devaluations indeed dramatically increase the political vulnerability of the regime using them. It is estimated that a devaluation—or the policies and problems that accompany it (or follow it)—approximately double the probability that a government will be deposed. It also triples the probability that the finance minister responsible for the devaluation loses his or her job.[5]

If a government sustains a persistent loss of foreign exchange reserves, as illustrated in Figure 2–2(a), but avoids the use of devaluation as a means of correction, it most likely will have to impose *exchange controls* to avoid a foreign exchange crisis. Exchange controls include government measures restricting the convertibility of domestic currency into foreign currency. These mainly involve the imposition of a system of permissions or licenses, required for any person to acquire foreign currency and the creation of *multiple exchange rates*. A regime of multiple exchange rates exists when monetary authorities establish two or more exchange rates for a given foreign currency. Each exchange rate is assigned to a particular group of international transactions. For instance, exchange rates assigned to financial transactions entailing the purchase of foreign assets are frequently different from those applied to imports.

The objective of exchange controls is to reduce or ration the demand for foreign exchange and to curtail—or stop—the drainage of foreign currency reserves from the central bank. However, the data

---

[4]It is so important that, in reporting exchange rate instability in Argentina in early 1991, *The Financial Times* of London—January 30, 1991, section 1, page 3—noted "The exchange rate is Argentina's most sensitive political and economic indicator."

[5]See R. N. Cooper, "Currency Devaluation in Developing Countries," in G. Ranis, ed., *Government and Economic Development* (New Haven: Yale University Press, 1971).

show that exchange controls can only delay the use of currency devaluation. They usually cannot prevent the eventual devaluation of an overvalued currency: The economic problems and distortions created by exchange controls become too severe for the government to handle in the long run. These problems include bureaucratic delays, corruption in the granting of licenses and permits, a general deterioration of international trade flows due to the limited access of traders to foreign exchange, and the high costs of policing the controls in order to avoid the development of black markets and illegal international transactions. When devaluations are finally carried out, exchange controls are often relaxed, which provides an immediate boost to imports and foreign trade.[6] There is no assurance, however, that the controls will not be reimposed subsequently.[7]

A clear example of the use of exchange controls as a policy to avoid devaluations in the presence of losses of foreign exchange reserves is that of Central American economies during the early 1980s. As economists P. L. Brock and D. Melendez remark: "At the beginning of the 1980s, maintaining fixed exchange rates in Central America had become a symbol of economic stability and was considered an important component of regional monetary integration."[8] During the same period, five Central American countries (Costa Rica, El Salvador, Guatemala, Honduras, and Nicaragua) suffered sustained losses of international reserves. As a result, between 1981 and 1984, all of them established a series of exchange controls. Although devaluations were delayed, the currency convertibility restrictions resulted in substantial costs for the Central American countries by eliminating most of the multilateral trade among them.[9] In spite of the exchange controls, all the countries—except Honduras—had officially devalued their currencies by the end of 1986. Even Guatemala, whose official exchange rate had been 1 quetzal per dollar for sixty-five years, had to devalue in 1986, after establishing numerous exchange controls and a system of multiple exchange rates.

2–2. The International Monetary System: An Introduction

The history of the international monetary system shows a pattern of shifts between a number of variants and combinations of fixed and flexible exchange rate regimes. In the late nineteenth century and up to 1914, the *gold standard* predominated in the international monetary system. A gold standard can be classified as a fixed exchange rate regime. Any country participating in the system would peg its currency to gold at a mint parity. This meant that dollar bills, for example, had a value in gold and could be exchanged for gold through the nation's monetary authorities. The official exchange rate between any two currencies then had to equal the ratio of their mint parities.

---

[6]This is the picture obtained by evidence based on thirty-nine episodes of devaluation, in the period 1960 to 1982, studied by S. Edwards. See his *Real Exchange Rates, Devaluation, and Adjustment: Exchange Rate Policy in Developing Countries* (Cambridge, Mass.: The MIT Press, 1989).

[7]There are countries that have taken the opposite route by using devaluation as an occasion to enhance exchange controls. For example, it appears that Brazil's 1957 devaluation reduced its short-run drain of foreign exchange reserves by being combined with strong protective measures against imports; on the other hand, other Brazilian devaluations in the 1960s were combined with export promotion policies, rather than import-substitution strategies. For a thorough discussion of the issues involved when devaluation is carried out in the presence of exchange controls, see D. Papageorgiou, M. Michaely, and A. K. Choksi, eds., *Liberalizing Foreign Trade* (Oxford: Basil Blackwell, 1991); and A. Krueger, *Liberalization Attempts and Consequences* (New York: Ballinger, 1978).

[8]P. L. Brock and D. Melendez, "Exchange Controls and the Breakdown of Central American Trade in the 1980s", in P. L. Brock, M. B. Conolly, and C. Gonzalez-Vega, eds., *Latin American Debt and Adjustment* (New York: Praeger, 1989), p. 181.

[9]Ibid., p. 182.

The U.S. dollar had a mint parity equivalent to $20.67 per ounce of gold, and the mint parity of the pound sterling was about £4.25 per ounce of gold; then the dollar-pound sterling official exchange rate was equal to $4.87 per pound sterling (a small margin of variation was allowed around this exchange rate).

The onset of World War I in 1914 led to the breakdown of the gold standard. During the interwar years, the international monetary system experienced disarray, with the major industrial countries swinging between periods of flexible exchange rate regimes (as in the period 1919 to 1925 and from 1933 to 1934) and periods of return to the gold standard. In 1944, representatives from the major industrial nations met in Bretton Woods, New Hampshire, and agreed to constrain their countries' actions in order to develop a more consistent and less variable international monetary system. The International Monetary Fund (IMF)—a country membership organization—was then created as an international agency coordinating and operating the agreements of what became known as the Bretton Woods System. The Bretton Woods agreements imposed a set of rules, or constraints, mainly oriented toward restricting the freedom of the member countries to change their exchange rate parities. It differed from the gold standard in that most exchange rates were pegged in terms of the dollar, which was used as a vehicle currency—a medium of transaction and a means of obtaining other currencies—and served as an international reserve asset. The dollar also had the role of intervention currency, being the currency that central banks bought and sold to support their currencies. Gold still maintained an important role in the system in the sense that it continued to serve as a means of settling international transactions and because the United States stood ready to exchange gold for dollars at the fixed price of $35.00 per ounce. For this reason, the Bretton Woods system is usually referred to as a gold exchange standard.

The Bretton Woods system was in operation in the 1950s and 1960s, although some countries did not enter into the agreement and were able to maintain independent flexible exchange rate regimes, as Canada had from 1950 to 1962. In the 1960s, Bretton Woods began to experience difficulties. A glut of U.S. dollars and a shortage of gold gradually eroded confidence in the dollar and its convertibility into gold at a fixed price. An attempt was thus made to create a new international reserve asset that would supplement gold and the U.S. dollar. The outcome was the creation by the IMF in 1969 of *Special Drawing Rights* (SDRs), which central banks can use to settle transactions among themselves and with the IMF.[10]

The creation of SDRs, as well as many other patch-up arrangements, did not prevent further difficulties. In 1971, another major crisis in the international monetary system occurred as most European countries and Japan permitted their currencies to float freely with respect to the U.S. dollar. Even though this flexibility was short-lived (lasting from August to December 1971), and parities and pegs were re-established for a while longer, since 1973 the currencies of most of the industrial countries have been free to fluctuate vis-à-vis the dollar. Central banks, however, have intervened quite frequently in the foreign exchange market; thus, the current international monetary arrangement of the United States vis-à-vis other industrial countries can be categorized as a managed floating regime.[11]

Actually, and perhaps paradoxically, central bank intervention by industrial countries in the

---

[10]SDRs are allocated to member countries according to a formula that depends on such factors as the economic size of the country. The value of an SDR was originally set to equal that of the dollar. Since the emergence of floating exchange rates in 1973, however, it has been based on a basket of major currencies that currently include the U.S. dollar, the British pound sterling, the French franc, the Japanese yen, and the West German mark.

[11]Care must be taken in applying this statement to specific countries and periods. Some countries intervene more frequently and heavily than others, and even the same country shifts from periods of heavy to periods of light intervention in foreign exchange markets.

dollar market under the current system has been much greater than under Bretton Woods. In fact, there has been *coordinated intervention,* in which a group of central banks pursue joint exchange rate policies. An important example of coordinated intervention occurred on September 21, 1985, when monetary authorities from France, Germany, Great Britain, Japan, and the United States (the so-called Group of Five, or G–5) met at the Plaza Hotel in New York City. They announced that they were jointly intervening in foreign exchange markets to induce a dollar depreciation. It was their belief that the dramatic dollar appreciation of the early 1980s (see Figure 1–1) had resulted in an overvalued dollar and that coordinated central bank intervention had to be undertaken to bring down the value of the dollar to equilibrium, or "fundamentals."

Joint exchange rate policy among the G–5 has continued following the Plaza Agreement and has included additional countries, such as Canada. For instance, at a meeting in Paris on February 22, 1987, the monetary authorities of the G–5 countries and Canada pledged to continue intervention in order to stabilize their exchange rates around the levels prevailing then. The rationale used by central banks to justify intervention in the foreign exchange markets is that they intervene to smooth out fluctuations in exchange rates. Some empirical evidence tends to indicate, however, that government intervention in foreign exchange markets may have increased, rather than decreased, the turbulence in the market in recent years.[12]

The definitive breakdown of the Bretton Woods regime in March 1973 represented a fundamental shift from a system of adjustable pegs to one of wider flexibility in the management of exchange rates. This change in international monetary arrangements was officially sanctioned in 1978 when the IMF's Articles of Agreement were amended to take into account the exchange rate flexibility that had already become a fact of life half a decade before. The amended articles allowed a large degree of freedom to countries in choosing their exchange rate regime. Currencies could float or be pegged to the dollar, the SDR, or other currencies. In effect, the present international monetary regime—as it has worked since 1973—has become a hybrid, amalgamated system that, because of its free-for-all nature, has led some to refer to it as a nonsystem.[13] Perhaps the best illustration of the hybrid character of the present international monetary regime is the exchange rate arrangements of the EMS, discussed in the next section.

2–3. Economic Integration and the European Monetary System: Some Background

As introduced in March 1979, the main goals of the European Monetary System (EMS) are to promote monetary cooperation and exchange rate stability among European Community (EC) countries. The EMS involves a joint, or cooperative, currency float in which participating countries agree to peg their currencies to each other and to let their currencies float vis-à-vis those of nonparticipating countries. In effect, a participating country has a pegged exchange rate regime vis-à-vis other participating countries and a flexible exchange rate regime against nonparticipating countries. The exchange rate of the French franc, for instance, fluctuates with respect to the U.S. dollar but is pegged to the German mark.

---

[12]See M. D. Bordo and A. J. Schwartz, "What Has Foreign Exchange Market Intervention Since the Plaza Agreement Accomplished?" *Open Economies Review* (1990). See also, M. Obstfeld, "The Effectiveness of Foreign Exchange Intervention: Recent Experience," in W.H. Branson et. al., eds., *International Policy Coordination and Exchange Rate Fluctuations* (Chicago: University of Chicago Press, 1990). Evidence on the effects of government intervention in exchange markets can be found in Chapters 14 and 15.

[13]See K. W. Dam, *The Rules of the Game: Reform and Evolution in the International Monetary System* (Chicago: University of Chicago Press, 1982), p. 2.

The EMS has also given birth to a new international currency, the European Currency Unit (ECU), used as a unit of account and for a variety of transactions in the European Community. The ECU is not a so-called hard currency that circulates among the public, but it plays an important international financial role. European Community budgets are quoted in ECUs, just as U.S. government budgets are quoted in dollars. ECUs are also used by the Community as an international reserve asset drawn upon when there is a need to intervene in foreign exchange markets, just as the Federal Reserve in the United States uses dollars to intervene in foreign exchange markets. Even more importantly, the exchange rate pegs at which EMS members must fix their exchange rates are quoted in ECUs.

The EMS replaced the so-called snake agreement developed during the twilight of the Bretton Woods regime. The Smithsonian Agreement of December 1971 had established a realignment of exchange rates among the United States, the major European countries, and Japan (the so-called Group of Ten, or G–10) after the earlier months of generalized floating. The exchange rate arrangement among the European countries that emerged out of the agreement and through negotiations in the following months was one in which (1) the bilateral exchange rates of the European currencies involved would be maintained within close margins (the so-called snake), while (2) the exchange rates against the dollar would be maintained within twice those margins (the so-called tunnel). The resulting regime was referred to as the snake in the tunnel; its membership dwindled as European countries abandoned their pegging margins vis-à-vis the U.S. dollar or other European currencies (the United Kingdom and Ireland abandoned the snake by mid-1972, Italy in 1973).

The EMS represented a move back toward a history of close exchange rate monitoring and monetary integration on the part of the European Economic Community (EEC). Established by the Treaty of Rome in 1957, the EEC originally consisted of Belgium, France, Luxembourg, the Netherlands, Italy, and West Germany. It now also includes Britain, Denmark, and Ireland (which all joined in 1973), Greece (which joined in 1981), and Portugal and Spain (which joined in 1986). In 1990, East Germany joined the community through its unification with West Germany. The creation of the EEC had the ultimate goal of encouraging economic integration. The immediate task undertaken on this account was to reduce the many barriers that existed on the flow of trade among EEC nations, with the ultimate goal of creating a customs union. A customs union establishes preferential trading arrangements among member countries while maintaining common trade policies against the rest of the world. One major step in this direction was the introduction of the Common Agricultural Policy (CAP) on December 31, 1961; it eliminated agricultural trade barriers within the EEC and imposed a common barrier to the importation of some agricultural products from outside.

Another major step was achieved in March 1985 when the European Council of Ministers, whose members include the chiefs of state and government of the twelve constituents of the EEC, agreed to dismantle existing barriers to the flow of trade in goods, services, and capital within the Community. This major economic integration initiative, which was formalized under the Single European Act of 1987, is referred to as the Europe 1992 project. It established a deadline of December 31, 1992, for the dismantling of trade barriers and the creation of a single internal European market. The "single market" went into effect on Friday, January 1, 1993, as planned.[14]

[14]The 1992 initiative has generated a new growth industry among book writers. Some popular books on the subject include N. Colchester and D. Buchan, *Europower: The Essential Guide to Europe's Economic Transformation in 1992* (New York: Random House, 1990); A. Roney, *The European Community Fact Book: A Question and Answer Guide to 1992* (Chicago: Longman Financial Services, 1990); and D. Burstein, *Euroquake* (New York: Simon and Schuster, 1991). For a scholarly discussion of the effects of 1992, see F. Rivera-Batiz and R. Ginsberg, "European Regional Economic Integration:
(continued)

These moves toward economic integration are of immense significance for the United States: The EEC is the United States' largest trading partner and a major ally in international relations. As Carla Hills, the U.S. trade representative at the time, told Congress in Washington in July 1989: "No other market is as important for American exporters or our investors as is the market of the European Community."[15] Indeed, the integration initiative would create an entity of 345 million people with a combined GNP of over $4.2 trillion, the largest trading bloc in the world. Although it is widely believed that Europe 1992 will have long-lasting positive effects on European growth, there is more disagreement about the likely effects outside Europe.[16] President George Bush, on a visit to Leiden in mid-July, 1989, said: "A stronger Europe, a more united Europe, is good for my country. And it is a development to be welcomed, a natural evolution within an alliance, the product of true partnership, forty years in the making." Although this is the predominant view among many experts, there are others who see the initiative toward internal economic integration as also leading to greater protectionism against non-European countries, a so-called Fortress Europe. These fears are partly based on the experience with the Common Agricultural Policy (CAP) the

EEC established in 1961 to protect a wide array of agricultural commodities from import competition. Over the years, the CAP has been a bastion of protectionism, and some experts fear the EEC may be equally protectionist when it sets common commercial policies against the rest of the world. The mere creation of a huge trading block that can have significant effects on world trade by engaging in joint, European policy inspires fears of international economic instability and disarray.[17]

The momentum behind the 1992 initiative pulled other areas into the integration movement and has generated renewed discussion and policy moves toward the creation of a European monetary union. A *monetary union* represents a group of countries that fix their exchange rates vis-à-vis each other and abdicate the active use of domestic monetary policy, leaving such tasks to a central organization or fund that coordinates the monetary actions of the union's members. The extreme example of a monetary union would be a *common currency area,* in which states or countries arrange to utilize a common currency. In this case, the exchange rates among the area's members are permanently fixed; at the same time, monetary policy is under the control of a joint, coordinating monetary agency or bank.

The United States represents, in effect, a common currency area because it satisfies both of these characteristics: there is one currency, the dollar, and this currency is created under the authority of a joint, coordinating agency, the Federal Reserve system. The Federal Reserve is not composed of a single entity but consists of a system of twelve branches akin to regional central banks. It is also not popularly known that each of

---

An Introduction," *Regional Science and Urban Economics* (Summer 1993).

[15]As quoted by *The Trenton Times,* July 16, 1989, Business Section, p. 1.

[16]Integration expands any member country's flows of goods, ideas, and technology with other members. This is generally associated with increased innovation, technological change, and economic growth [see R. Baldwin, "The Growth Effects of 1992," *Economic Policy* (October 1989); and L. A. Rivera-Batiz and P. M. Romer, "Economic Integration with Endogenous Technological Change," *Quarterly Journal of Economics* (May 1991)]. The expansion of the European internal market as a result of the 1992 initiative also allows the exploitation of economies of scale and can be expected to raise output in Europe by perhaps as much as 6.5 percent. This conclusion was reached in 1988 by a commission chaired by P. Cecchini [see M. Emerson et al., *The Economics of 1992: The EC Commission's Assessment of the Economic Effects of Completing the Internal Market* (Oxford: Oxford University Press, 1988)].

[17]These fears were voiced in a report issued in April 1991 by the General Agreement on Tariffs and Trade (GATT). The GATT was established in 1947 and represents a set of rules and regulations governing international trade policies. The GATT monitors trade policies through an organization headquartered in Geneva. For a discussion of the possible impacts of regional trading blocks on world trade, see J. N. Bhagwati, *The World Trading System at Risk* (Princeton, N.J.: Princeton University Press, 1991).

the twelve district banks issues its own currency notes and that the dollar bills issued by each bank are physically different from each other.[18] This means that if the twelve district Federal Reserve banks were to operate independently—each of them deciding by how much to change the supply of its own dollar A, dollar B, and so on—and if the exchange rates between the twelve different dollars could fluctuate, a system of floating exchange rates could be created within the United States. The fact that the Federal Reserve Board, which controls the system of twelve district "central" banks, is the single authority in charge of issuing all twelve versions of the dollar—and is willing to buy and sell them for each other at one rate— makes the United States a common currency union.[19]

The EMS is currently far from being a common currency area and its exchange rate mechanism for EEC currencies can best be described as an adjustable peg regime of the Bretton Woods type. Still, it does include some features that constitute a signif-

icant move toward monetary union. For instance, even though each EEC country has complete autonomy in domestic monetary affairs, the European Monetary Cooperation Fund—the EEC's counterpart of the IMF during Bretton Woods— serves the function of a joint central monetary organization in the EMS. In addition, even though each country has retained use of its own currency, exchange rates among them are indeed pegged (within a band) and the community has shown increased resistance to change the pegs.

The vigorous progress of the Europe 1992 single internal market initiative has jump-started the move to shift current European monetary arrangements more in line with monetary unification. Although plans for a monetary union in the Europe 1992 drive to integration had a slow start (and did not constitute part of the original discussions in 1985 and 1986) this was slowly reversed. The ex-Chancellor of Germany, Helmut Schmidt, for instance, complained: "Whoever heard of a single market with eleven currencies?" The ball started rolling on this issue in April 1989, when Jacques Delors, president of the EEC's executive body, the European Commission, unveiled a report—now referred to as the Delors Report—recommending that the EEC follow a set of stages oriented toward the eventual creation of a single European Community currency and a centralized monetary decision-making authority fashioned after a central bank or a so-called European System of Central Banks. The report received widespread praise and, at a meeting in Madrid in July 1989, the last country opposing such plans, the United Kingdom, under Margaret Thatcher, decided to reconsider its no-negotiation stand. The way was thus cleared for a serious discussion on timetables for monetary unification.

At a meeting in Maastricht in December 1991, the twelve members of the community designed a new treaty that would revise the Treaty of Rome and start the process of political and monetary reforms needed for possible monetary unification by the end of the century. A set of four stages was

---

[18]Indeed, the dollar bills you may be holding in your wallet are likely to have been issued in different parts of the country. Although dollar bills all look alike (they are green and black with similar markings stating that they are Federal Reserve Notes from the United States of America), they are not exactly the same. Each is identified in several ways as to which district bank issued it: on the front left is a circle with the district bank's name (such as the Federal Reserve Bank of New York) printed on it; inside the circle is a bold, black letter representing the Federal Reserve district of origin (A for the first district, B for the second, etc.); the first character of the serial number is the district's letter (A, B, etc.); and the district's number (1, 2, etc.) is printed four times on the front of the bill.

[19]For discussions of how the U.S. currency union can serve as a model for European initiatives on this matter, see B. Eichengreen, "Designing a Central Bank for Europe: A Cautionary Tale from the Early Years of the Federal Reserve System," in M. Canzoneri, V. Grilli and P. Masson, eds., *Establishing a Central Bank* (Cambridge: Cambridge University Press, 1992); W. E. Weber, "America's Own Fixed-Exchange Model," *The Wall Street Journal*, April 26, 1990; and R. F. Graboyes, "A Yankee Recipe for a EuroFed Omelet," *Federal Reserve Bank of Richmond Economic Review* (July-August 1990).

discussed. The first stage would last until the end of 1993 and would involve (1) strengthening the current EMS by adding any remaining EEC currencies into the system and (2) ratification of the treaty by members. The second stage would start on January 1, 1994, with the creation of a European Monetary Institute that would begin to assume control of the EEC's monetary affairs. This embryo Eurocentral bank would pool the Community's international reserves and engage in foreign exchange market intervention to support the EMS's fixed exchange rate system. Stage three would commence five years later, establishing a European Central Bank, or European System of Central Banks, and setting the legal background for fixing exchange rates permanently within the Community—possibly within the context of a single currency—by the year 2000.

Differences among countries have emerged regarding the Maastricht Treaty in terms of both timing and substance. Delors, for instance, has supported the use of the current ECU as the single European currency of the next century. The British administration, by contrast, under Prime Minister John Major, favors the creation of a new currency, the so-called hard ECU, jointly with the establishment of the European System of Central Banks.[20]

2-4. THE EXCHANGE RATE MECHANISM OF THE EUROPEAN COMMUNITY

The EMS's exchange rate mechanism (ERM) establishes a set of exchange rate pegs among the EEC currencies forming part of the mechanism. There are also some fixed margins (target zones) around the pegs, inside which the values for these currencies must be kept. To determine the exchange rate peg between two currencies, the Community fixes the values of the currencies relative to the ECU. These *ECU central rates* are set for each currency in the exchange rate mechanism, and they are expressed as the price of one ECU in terms of the currency. As of August 20, 1992, there were ten ECU central rates for the European Community currencies participating in the exchange rate mechanism: the German mark, French franc, British pound, Italian lira, Dutch guilder, Belgian/Luxembourg franc, Danish krone, Spanish peseta, Portuguese escudo, and Irish pound.[21] The British pound, for example, had a central rate equal to £0.696904 per ECU, whereas the rate for the German mark was equal to DM2.00586 per ECU. Note that, although Greece had joined the Community, the Greek drachma was not part of the exchange rate mechanism (because its participation in the ERM was delayed to ease its adjustment to Community integration).

The ratio of any given two central rates is the *bilateral central rate;* it represents the exchange rate peg, or parity, among the two currencies. For example, the bilateral central exchange rate between the German mark and the pound sterling in August 1992 was equal to DM2.95 per pound (determined from DM2.05586/£0.696904). The set of bilateral rates among EC countries is referred to as the Community's *parity grid.* The margins around the parities are set at 2.25 percent above or below the central rates, so that the exchange rate between any two currencies can fluctuate only inside a narrow 4.5 percent band. There are three

---

[20]A thorough discussion of the Maastricht Treaty is provided by M. Fratianni, J. Von Hagen, and C. Waller, "The Maastrich Way to EMU," *Princeton Essays in International Finance,* no. 187 (June 1992).

[21]During the second week of September 1992, the EMS suffered one of its major crises when the governments of Great Britain and Italy decided to abandon the ERM in order to let the British pound and the Italian lira float in value vis-à-vis other European currencies. Thus only eight currencies remained in the ERM. Although Italy and Great Britain said the suspension was to be temporary, the crisis raised serious questions about the stability of the EMS and its propensity for crises. (Chapter 22 examines the economics of foreign exchange crises under target zones and fixed exchange rate systems.) For expositional simplicity, the discussion in this chapter will proceed as if Italy and the U.K. were still part of the EMS, as they were on August 20, 1992.

TABLE **2–1.**   **European Currency Unit Rates**

Currency	ECU Central Rate (in units of the currency)	Actual Price of an ECU (in units of the currency)
German mark (DM)	2.05586	2.03364
French franc (FFr)	6.89509	6.90316
British pound (£)	0.696904	0.723002
Italian lira (L)	1538.24	1545.84
Dutch guilder (G)	2.31643	2.29237
Belgian franc (BFr)	42.4032	41.8873
Spanish peseta (Pta)	133.631	130.633
Danish krone (DKr)	7.84195	7.85173
Irish pound (I£)	0.767417	0.765539
Portuguese escudo (Esc)	178.735	177.238

SOURCE: *The Financial Times,* August 21, 1992, p. 32.

exceptions: the Spanish peseta, the British pound, and the Portuguese escudo can fluctuate within a 6.00 percent zone on each side.

Table 2–1 depicts the ECU central rates and the actual rates on August 20, 1992, for the ten currencies members of the exchange rate mechanism at that time. As noted earlier, the British pound has a central rate equal to £0.696904 per ECU, whereas the rate for the German mark is equal to DM2.00586 per ECU, with a bilateral central exchange rate between the German mark and the sterling equal to DM2.95 per pound (DM2.05586/£0.696904). The actual mark-pound exchange rate is given by the ratio of the actual ECU rates for the mark and the pound on August 20, 1992; it was equal to DM2.81 per pound (from DM2.03364/£0.723002). The deviation of the actual from the central parity exchange rate on August 20, 1992, was then equivalent to −4.74 percent (calculated from [2.81 − 2.95]/2.95 = −0.0474, multiplied by 100 to be expressed as a percentage). Thus the price of a pound in marks was 4.74 percent below its central parity value on August 20: within the 6.00 percent deviation from parity allowed by the exchange rate mechanism to the sterling exchange rate, but dangerously close to the limit. Note that, for Germans holding marks, buying a pound on

August 20, 1992 was cheaper than if the exchange rate had been at its central parity. In other words, the German mark was a strong currency relative to the pound, while the latter was relatively weak compared to the mark.

Under the exchange rate mechanism, each central bank intervenes in foreign exchange markets in order to prevent currency values from moving beyond the 2.25 or 6.00 percent margins, depending on the currency. The intervention is compulsory when the exchange rate between two currencies reaches their bilateral margin—that is, when it diverges by exactly 2.25 or 6.00 percent. This so-called *marginal intervention* is carried out by both central banks involved. There is no obligation to intervene before the exchange rate reaches its margins. Most often, however, central bank intervention will occur before marginal intervention is required. Such *intramarginal intervention* is carried out by the central bank issuing the relatively weak currency. In the preceding sterling-mark example, when the exchange rate of the pound-mark had passed the "threshold of divergence" relative to the central rate, the Bank of England intervened in currency markets by buying pounds using marks in order to raise the price of the pound vis-à-vis the mark. The intervention of the Bank of England was

TABLE 2–2. Dates of Realignments of the EMS and the French Franc-German Mark Rate, 1979–1990

Period of a Given Fixed Parity for the Franc-Mark Rate	Dates	French Franc-Deutsche Mark Exchange Rate (francs per deutsche mark)
I	March 13, 1979	2.30950
II	September 24, 1979	2.35568
	November 30, 1979	2.35568
	March 23, 1981	2.35568
III	October 5, 1981	2.56212
	February 22, 1982	2.56212
IV	June 14, 1982	2.83396
V	March 21, 1983	3.06648
	July 22, 1985	3.06648
VI	April 7, 1986	3.25617
	August 4, 1986	3.25617
VII	January 11, 1987	3.35386
	January 5, 1990	3.35386
	September 12, 1992	3.35386
	September 16, 1992	3.35386
	November 22, 1992	3.35386

not successful. On September 16, the British government gave up and decided to temporarily abandon the ERM and let the pound float freely versus the mark and the other EMS currencies.

The EMS is a system of pegged, but adjustable, exchange rates in which the central parity grid can be altered. In this sense, the exchange rate mechanism is a Bretton Woods-type system. However, the way in which realignments of the exchange rate mechanism's central parity grid are made diverges from how exchange rate adjustments were made during Bretton Woods. In the latter, currency values were often changed unilaterally by one country without consultation with others. Under the EMS in its current form, realignments of the parity grid are a collective decision of the EEC's members subject to intense negotiation. In general, country authorities have to intervene in foreign exchange markets to keep exchange rates within their bands. They are also urged by the EEC to

adopt policy actions—such as monetary growth changes or interest rate adjustments—that are expected to induce exchange rates to move toward currency parity levels. If these measures fail, currency value realignments may be considered.[22]

By the end of 1992, there had been fifteen realignments of the parity grid since the inception of the EMS in 1979. The last one occurred on November 22, 1992. These realignments have not always involved the major currencies. As the list in Table 2–2 shows, of the fifteen realignments since 1979 only six have involved changes in the value of

[22]For excellent surveys of the economics of the EMS, see H. Ungerer et al., *The European Monetary System: Developments and Perspectives,* IMF Occasional Paper no. 73 (1990); F. Giavazzi and A. Giovannini, *Limiting Exchange Rate Flexibility: The European Monetary System* (Cambridge, Mass.: The MIT Press, 1989); and H. Ungerer, O. Mayer and P. Young, *The European Monetary System: Recent Developments,* IMF Occasional Paper no. 48 (1986).

the French franc versus the mark. Although recent realignments in the EMS have been accompanied by feverish speculation, this pattern was not typical in the past. The new pattern has been due in part to "timely" realignments that changed the target zone while leaving market rates unchanged. Such "discrete" readjustments alter both the target zone and the market exchange rate.

The difference between these two types of realignments is shown in Figure 2–3. Here we see the behavior of the French franc-German mark exchange rate and the EMS band within which that rate has fluctuated. The six realignments of the franc-mark exchange rate are illustrated by Roman numerals. Note that the first realignment in September 1979 did not lead to immediate exchange rate changes: The target zone before and after the parity change overlapped, leaving room for the franc-mark rate to fluctuate very closely to the range in which it was fluctuating before the realignment. By contrast, the parity change made in October 1981 led to a major, discrete jump of exchange rates: the EMS band shown by region III does not overlap with region II because it is associated with a discrete increase.

Such jumps in franc-mark exchange rates reflect periods in which the franc became grossly overvalued. With long-delayed franc devaluations being anticipated by speculators, the latter would purchase marks en masse with francs, in the expectation that the mark would rise in value relative to the franc when realignment was finally undertaken. This was clearly the case in the early years of the Mitterand administration, when such speculation forced the French government to impose a whole variety of exchange controls. In terms of the value of all the EMS currencies in the 1980s, it is estimated that 70 percent of the exchange rate mechanism parity changes were timely.[23]

[23]See M. J. Artis, "The European Monetary System," in A. M. El-Agraa, ed., *Economics of the European Community* (New York: St. Martin's, 1990); and P. B. Kenen, *Managing Exchange Rates* (London: Routledge, 1988).

2–5. THE EUROPEAN CURRENCY UNIT AND THE EMS

Although the countries participating in the exchange rate mechanism have fixed pegs versus each other, they engage in a joint currency float against the U.S. dollar. That is, even though each country's central exchange rate is fixed vis-à-vis the ECU, the ECU itself floats against the U.S. dollar. What determines the exchange rate between the dollar and the ECU?

As noted in the preceding section, the ECU is used as a unit of account within the EEC, particularly as the means through which currency pegs are established. In addition, the ECU is utilized in transactions among central banks and has been growing as a currency of denomination of international bond issues, bank loans and deposits, and even European travelers' checks.

To specify how much an ECU is worth in terms of dollars, the ECU must be seen as a composite currency—that is, a currency composed of other currencies. Currently, the ECU is made up of a basket of the twelve European currencies. The EEC determines how much of each currency goes into one ECU. The amounts—effective after September 1989—are given in the first column of Table 2–3. For instance, there are 6.885 pesetas and 0.6242 German marks in one ECU.

So, to determine the dollar cost of an ECU, we must add up the value of each European currency component of the ECU in terms of dollars. As an example, in column 2 of Table 2–3, we depict the exchange rates between the corresponding EEC currencies and the dollar for January 10, 1991. The price of a Spanish peseta in dollars was equal to 0.0104, a German mark cost $0.6607, a pound was equal to $1.902, and so on. If we multiply the amount of each currency in an ECU—column 1— by the cost of each of these currencies in dollars— column 2—we obtain the value of each component of the ECU in dollars. The results are depicted in column 3. If we add these dollar components of the

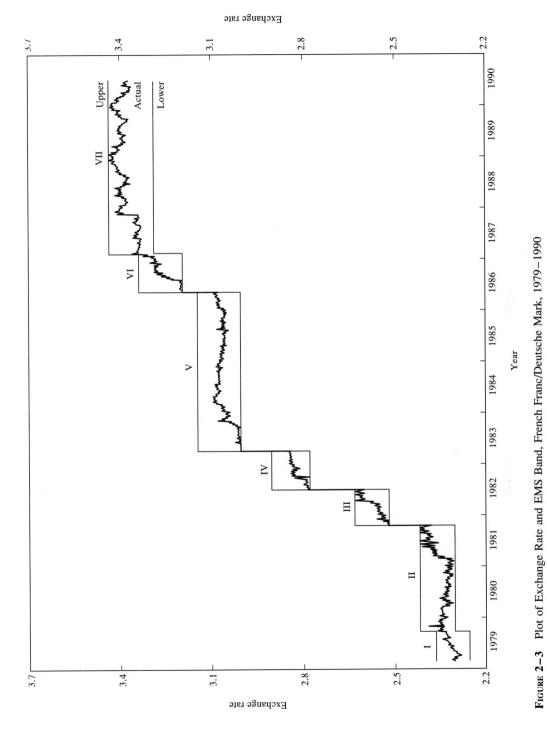

Figure 2–3 Plot of Exchange Rate and EMS Band, French Franc/Deutsche Mark, 1979–1990

SOURCE: H. J. Edison and G. Kaminsky, "Target Zones, Intervention, and Exchange Rate Volatility, France 1979–1990" (University of California at San Diego, March 1991); mimeo.

67

TABLE 2–3. **What Is an ECU and How Much Is It Worth in Dollars?**

Currency	Amount of the Currency in One ECU	Exchange Rate of the Currency in Dollars	Value of the Currency's ECU Component in $	Weight of Each Currency in the ECU
	(1)	(2)	(3) = (1) × (2)	(4)
German mark (DM)	0.6242	0.6607	0.4127	30.8
French franc (FFr)	1.332	0.1942	0.2587	19.3
British pound (£)	0.08784	1.90250	0.1671	12.5
Italian lira (L)	151.8	0.000877	0.1331	9.9
Netherland guilder (G)	0.2198	0.5848	0.1285	9.6
Belgian franc (BFr)	3.301	0.032	0.1056	7.9
Luxembourg franc (LFr)	0.130	0.0167	0.0021	0.2
Spanish peseta (Pta)	6.885	0.0104	0.0716	5.4
Danish krone (DKr)	0.1976	0.1711	0.0338	2.5
Irish pound (I£)	0.008552	1.7415	0.0148	1.1
Greek drachma (Dr)	1.440	0.00328	0.0047	0.4
Portuguese escudo (ESC)	1.393	0.00384	0.0053	0.4
			1.3380	100.0

The currency composition of the ECU has been valid since September 21, 1989. The exchange rates between the dollar and European currencies are for bid rates for January 10, 1991, as quoted by *The Financial Times,* January 11, 1991, p. 34.

SOURCE: Composition of the ECU: R. J. Mehnert, *User's Guide to the ECU* (London: Graham & Trotman, 1992), p. 59.

ECU, we obtain the total value of one ECU in dollars. As we can see, on January 10, 1991, the value of one ECU was equal to $1.338.

The fluctuations of the ECU-dollar exchange rate between 1979 and 1993 are depicted in Figure 2–4. The wide variation exhibited in the figure indicates the great degree of flexibility exhibited by the joint EEC float versus the dollar. There is currently no explicit joint EMS policy on central bank intervention in the dollar market. Each country intervenes according to its interests, although the effects of dollar market interventions on intra-EMS exchange rates are usually carefully considered. It has been pointed out, however, that there is an implicit dollar intervention policy in the EMS, associated with the active role played by the Bundesbank in the dollar market.[24] That Bundesbank dollar intervention may have significant effects on the relationship between the currencies participating in the exchange rate mechanism and the dollar is related to the prominent role of the deutsche mark within the ERM, reflected in the relatively large weight that the deutsche mark has within the ECU, as discussed next.

The amount of each EEC currency that goes into an ECU is decided on by EEC finance ministers and can be altered if they so wish. The numbers in column 1 in Table 2–3 have been in

[24]See H. Ungerer, "The European Monetary System and the International Monetary System," *Journal of Common Market Studies* (March 1989).

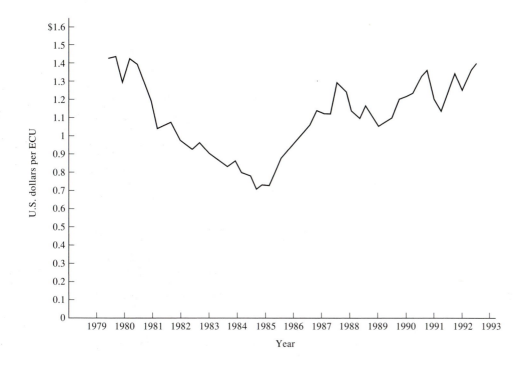

FIGURE 2–4. Exchange Rate of the ECU Against the U.S. Dollar

SOURCE: *International Financial Statistics* (Washington, D.C.: International Monetary Fund) various issues.

force since September 21, 1989, when the currency amounts were changed to incorporate the peseta and escudo into the ECU. The amounts have been chosen to give each currency a weight that is roughly related to the relative size and economic strength of the country within the EEC. The relative weight of each currency in the ECU on January 10, 1991, can be determined from Table 2–3 by dividing the dollar value of each ECU currency component by the total dollar value of the ECU. The resulting weights are presented in column 4.[25] Note that the deutsche mark has the

highest weight, just below one-third of the total. This weight gives the German currency a major influence on the ECU and has given rise to the view that the EMS is effectively a "Deutsche-Mark Standard." Other EEC countries peg their currencies to the deutsche mark (via pegging to the ECU), with the Bundesbank and the mark acting very much in the same dominant way that the

[25]Because the relative dollar values of the European currencies will vary over time, the relative weights will also change,

although the variations are comparatively minor. For an analytical discussion of the weighing scheme of the ECU, see H. J. Edison, "Is the ECU an Optimal Currency Basket?," in R. M. Levich and A. Sommariva, eds., *The ECU Market: Current Developments and Future Prospects of the European Currency Unit* (Lexington, Mass.: D. C. Heath, 1987).

United States and the dollar functioned in the Bretton Woods system.[26]

Although the relative economic size of Germany and the strength of the mark as a currency do give that country substantial independence in terms of its policymaking within the EMS, there is also evidence of extensive cooperation between the Bundesbank and other EEC central banks in coordinating key decisions involving the Community's monetary affairs.[27] It is also not clear what the extent is to which other countries in the EEC bear the burden of economic adjustment in sustaining the EMS parity grid. The questions of German dominance within the Community and whether the EMS operates in an "asymmetric" way are clearly controversial and bound to remain in the public eye for years to come.

In spite of the significant role of the ECU as a unit of account within the EEC, the private use of the currency has been slow to grow. A few years ago, surveys found that very few individuals had even heard of the ECU and thought that it was a board game or a tropical fruit. Discussions of its possible future as a single European currency have greatly enhanced its visibility. A recent European Commission poll found that 60 percent of people surveyed would welcome the ECU as the eventual European currency. The greater interest in the ECU parallels a growth in its use by the private sector. The currency unit is currently the third largest currency of denomination for bond issues, and there are thriving spot and forward markets on the ECU, ECU options and futures contracts, and ECU syndicated loans, among many other financial instruments. However, although at one time Belgium issued coins denominated in ECUs and travelers checks can be purchased in ECUs, the currency has not been used much as a means of transactions among individuals. Given the current plans for monetary unification, the European Commission is pursuing ways to encourage such use.[28]

The next section discusses the factors determining the use of a currency in international transactions.

2–6. INTERNATIONAL AND VEHICLE CURRENCIES IN THE WORLD ECONOMY

Although most countries have a national currency that is used for local transactions, few have moneys that are utilized by residents of other countries for their transactions. It would be odd, for instance, to see the Nicaraguan córdoba being used to pay for restaurant dinners in Chicago. By contrast, it is fairly common in Latin America and other countries to see store owners or restaurants willing—and sometimes more than willing—to accept dollars as payment. This means that the dollar is an *international currency,* a currency adopted by non-U.S. residents in their transactions. In this section, the factors influencing why a given currency becomes an international currency are explained.

The British pound sterling dominated the early decades of this century as an international currency. Storekeepers in Teheran, Buenos Aires, Amsterdam, and places all over the world accepted sterling as payment as if it were local currency. It was possible for Phineas Fogg, Jules Verne's character in *Around the World in Eighty Days,* to pay his expenses with Bank of England notes. After World War II, however, the dollar rapidly became the dominant international currency, a role it has

---

[26]For academic and journalistic statements of this view, see F. Giavazzi and A. Giovannini, "Models of the EMS: Is Europe a Greater Deutsche Mark Area?" in R. Bryant and R. Portes, eds., *Global Macroeconomics: Policy Conflicts and Cooperation* (London: Macmillan, 1987); and G. Melloan, "Say Hello to the Deutsche-Mark Standard," *The Wall Street Journal,* October 15, 1990, p. A17.

[27]See the data provided by M. Fratianni and J. Von Hagen, "German Dominance in the EMS: The Empirical Evidence," *Open Economies Review* (January 1990), 67–87.

[28]See R. S. Masera, "An Increasing Role for the ECU": A Character in Search of a Script," *Princeton Essays in International Finance,* no. 167 (June 1987).

sustained. The U.S. dollar today circulates in a wide array of countries. In Argentina alone, estimates are that between $5 billion and $7 billion freely circulate; the U.S. government calculates that the amount of dollars in Poland (called lettuce by the Polish) in 1988 was $5 billion. Dollars are also used for transactions (legally, or illegally through black markets) in countries as dispersed geographically as Peru, Israel, Mexico, the former Soviet Union, and the Dominican Republic. The holding of dollars—referred to as dollarization—reached such magnitude in the Soviet Union in the late 1980s that, in 1990 and 1991, the Soviet authorities had to rapidly introduce legislation intended to discourage such transactions and to increase the use of the ruble (the Soviet Union's national currency) as a means of transaction. Overall, as much as $180 billion or so may be circulating outside of the United States. This calculation was made by the Federal Reserve Board, based on the fact that the difference between the existing supply of dollars and estimates of the demand for dollars by U.S. residents is equal to about $180 billion. This "missing money" is believed to be in the hands of foreign residents.

A country issuing an international currency profits from its use because of *seigniorage,* which is defined as a government's power to generate revenues by means of its right to issue money. The gains from seigniorage are equal to the difference between what the money costs to print and the value of the currency. It costs very little to print a dollar bill: only two and a half cents. Suppose, then, that the U.S. government pays $100,000 for one thousand boxes of imports of fruits from Central America, and that this $100,000 remains in Central America to be used there by individuals. The U.S. government thereby profits by about $97,500 from the transaction (in the form of a large supply of fruit) because it costs only $2,500 to print the money. So long as Latin American residents are willing to hold dollars for their own use (whether for local transactions or stashed away in mattresses), the United States receives substan-

tial gains from issuing those dollars. One way to visualize these gains is to think of the profits that American Express could make were it to sell traveler's checks that were never cashed.[29]

What makes a currency an international one? A currency has three main functions: as a medium of exchange, a unit of account, and a store of value. Consider the latter first. An international currency may be used because its value is relatively stable compared to other currencies. Such is the case, for instance, of the dollar in some Latin American countries, where hyperinflation erodes the value of national money. An international currency may also be utilized because it is used as a unit of account, either for invoicing merchandise trade or for denominating financial transactions. Oil prices, for instance, are always quoted in dollars, and trade in oil is invoiced in dollars. The ECU and SDR are significant as international currencies partly because they are used as units of account by the European Community and the International Monetary Fund (although, in fact, as we noted earlier, ECUs and SDRs are not "hard" currencies that circulate among the public).

A third reason a currency may become international is because it is a convenient money to use globally as a medium of exchange. The relatively low transaction costs of using dollars as compared to other moneys in foreign exchange markets make it the most popular *vehicle currency* in the world today. A vehicle currency is a national currency used by nonresidents in their international transactions. The dollar is highly popular in the international transactions of both central banks and private participants in world trade and finance.

Central banks around the world hold dollars in the form of international reserves. Countries under a pegged exchange rate system must, of course, hold inventories of foreign exchange because, under this regime, central banks are committed to

[29]The real value of seigniorage is affected by a number of factors, including the impact of an increase in the supply of currency on prices. This issue will be considered in Chapter 20.

TABLE 2–4. **Composition of Official Holdings of Foreign Exchange,
1975–1989 (percentage)**

Currency	1975	1980	1985	1989
U.S. dollar	79.4%	68.6%	64.9%	60.2%
Deutsche mark	6.3	14.9	15.2	19.3
Japanese yen	0.5	4.4	8.0	7.9
British pound sterling	3.9	2.9	3.0	2.7
French franc	1.2	1.7	0.9	1.3
Swiss franc	1.6	3.2	2.3	1.7
Netherland guilder	0.6	1.3	1.0	1.1
Unspecified currencies	6.5	3.0	4.6	5.7

SOURCE: *IMF Annual Report, 1990.* The 1989 figures are IMF staff estimates, as quoted in G. S. Tavlas and Y. Ozeki, "The Japanese Yen As an International Currency," IMF Working Paper no. WP/91/2 (January 1991), p. 46.

buying or selling foreign currencies to the public at given exchange rates. Central banks, however, do not have holdings of every conceivable foreign currency used in international trade. Rather, they own international reserves mainly in the form of vehicle currencies (dollars, SDRs, ECUs) and international reserve assets such as gold. These international reserves are then used as intermediaries in order to, for instance, buy relatively rare foreign currencies. To purchase Greek drachmas, the Banco de Mexico (Mexico's central bank) would sell some of its dollar reserves for drachmas in foreign exchange markets.

For countries under fixed exchange rates, international reserves are what cash balances are to a household. They constitute widely acceptable means of payment and serve to settle international transactions. They provide liquidity—that is, funds in a form that can be easily spent or exchanged for goods or other assets at low transaction costs and with no capital losses.

The popularity of the dollar as an international reserve has been, to a great extent, the result of its great liquidity.[30] Almost every conceivable cur-

rency can be easily exchanged into dollars. Thus, it is easier for the central bank of Mexico to use dollars to acquire drachmas than to try to buy drachmas directly with Mexican pesos (which would be a rather exotic transaction). The low transaction costs of trading dollars in foreign exchange markets can be linked to the great volume of the dollar market and the economies of scale that this generates.[31]

The significant role of the dollar as a vehicle currency is reflected in the figures shown in Table 2–4. The table exhibits the share of the dollar—and other currencies—in official (monetary authorities) holdings of foreign exchange in the world for selected years. Central banks may hold foreign currency reserves in many forms, not only in the currency itself (dollar notes), but also as demand deposits (dollar deposits) and other liquid assets (such as U.S. government Treasury bills).

The numbers in Table 2–4 indicate that the dollar remains the world's major vehicle currency, accounting for 60.2 percent of official foreign exchange holdings. Two currencies do appear to

---

[30]For a discussion of the determinants of the currency composition of central bank reserves, see M. P. Dooley, J. Saúl Lizondo and D. J. Mathieson, "The Currency Composition of Foreign Exchange Reserves," *IMF Staff Papers* (June 1989).

[31]See S. W. Black, "Transactions Costs and Vehicle Currencies," *Journal of International Money and Finance* (December 1991), and P. Krugman, "Vehicle Currencies and the Structure of International Exchange," *Journal of Money, Credit and Banking* (August 1980).

have magnified their role as vehicle currencies since 1975: the German mark and the Japanese yen. The deutsche mark, in particular, has tripled its share in world reserves. This increase reflects the growing role of the mark in the international monetary system through the expanding role of Germany in world trade and finance, the relatively low and stable German inflation rate (which makes the mark a safe currency to hold), the importance of the mark within the EMS, and the use of the mark by the Federal Reserve as an intervention currency (to intervene in foreign exchange markets).[32]

2–7. CENTRAL BANKS AND THE DEMAND FOR INTERNATIONAL RESERVES

Table 2–5 presents data for selected years on the international reserves of groups of countries. Note that, overall, since 1973, international reserves have increased faster than in previous periods.

The rise in the price of gold accounted for a large chunk of the increase in the value of international reserves in the 1970s and 1980s. From the original $35 per ounce sustained by the United States under the Bretton Woods system, to a price presently fluctuating at around $400.00, the rise has implied a massive explosion in the value of gold reserves. Even at constant gold prices, however, international reserves have grown, having quadrupled just over the period from 1969 to 1979.

How can the rise rather than the decline of international reserves after 1973 be explained? What factors determine the demand for international reserves by a central bank? Countries under pegged exchange rates hold inventories of foreign exchange because they are committed to buying or selling foreign currencies to the public at given exchange rates. As noted earlier, to these countries, international reserves are what cash balances

are to a household: They constitute widely acceptable means of payment and serve to settle transactions with the rest of the world. The analogy between a household and a country suggests some of the possible factors influencing central bank demands for reserves.[33]

In the same way that a household holds cash as a precautionary measure against the need to make sudden payments not matched by income, the demand for international reserves is influenced by the variability of the economy's international payments and receipts. The higher (or lower) the variability, the larger (or smaller) the optimal precautionary amount of international reserves in the central bank. In addition, just as individuals hold cash for transaction purposes, a country can hold reserves for the same reason. The higher the degree of openness of the economy, the larger the volume of transactions with the rest of the world and the larger the level of reserves required to sustain such transactions. A relatively closed economy, on the other hand, could get away with holding a relatively small proportion of reserves. A final major factor affecting the demand for international reserves is the economy's level of income, which reflects the size of the country and influences, in a positive way, the absolute amount of reserves demanded.

The sustained increase in the demand for international reserves observed in the post-Bretton Woods era is partly explained by the increased openness, real income, and variability of international payments and receipts faced by most countries during the period. It also embodies the fact that, although there was a substantial degree of exchange rate flexibility after 1973, most developing countries and many developed economies continue

---

[32]See G. S. Tavlas, "International Currencies: The Rise of the Deutsche Mark," *Finance and Development* (September 1990).

[33]For a discussion of the factors affecting the optimal level of international reserves, see J. Frenkel, "International Liquidity and Monetary Control," in G. von Furstenberg, ed., *International Money and Credit: The Policy Roles* (Washington, D.C.: IMF, 1983); and B. J. Cohen, "International Reserves and Liquidity," in P. B. Kenen, ed., *International Trade and Finance: Frontiers for Research* (New York: Cambridge University Press, 1975).

TABLE 2–5. International Reserves for Selected Years, 1952–1991 (in millions of SDRs, end of period)

Area and Country	1952	1962	1972	1982	1988	1989	1990	1991 Nov	1991 Dec
All countries	49,388	62,851	147,323	361,452	576,103	624,146	670,780	695,275	n.d.
Industrial countries[1]	39,280	53,502	113,362	214,014	381,104	410,113	441,924	428,867	n.d.
United States	24,714	17,220	12,112	29,918	36,471	57,525	59,958	55,225	55,770
Canada	1,944	2,561	5,572	3,428	12,037	12,781	13,060	13,017	11,816
Australia	920	1,168	5,656	6,053	10,383	10,763	11,710	12,250	11,837
Japan	1,101	2,021	16,916	22,001	72,727	64,735	56,027	52,179	51,224
New Zealand	183	251	767	577	2,108	2,303	2,902	2,391	n.d.
Austria	116	1,081	2,505	5,544	6,215	7,266	7,305	7,944	7,924
Belgium	1,133	1,753	3,564	4,757	8,113	9,250	9,599	n.d.	n.d.
Denmark	150	256	787	2,111	8,057	4,925	7,502	5,372	5,234
Finland	132	237	664	1,420	4,801	3,959	6,849	3,690	n.d.
France	686	4,049	9,224	17,850	21,713	21,592	28,716	24,969	n.d.
Germany	960	6,958	21,908	43,909	46,824	49,527	51,060	47,879	46,996
Greece	94	287	950	916	2,808	2,572	2,517	3,910	3,857
Iceland	8	32	78	133	218	258	308	248	316
Ireland	318	359	1,038	2,390	3,793	3,100	3,684	3,913	4,017
Italy	722	4,068	5,605	15,108	28,131	37,884	46,565	40,044	36,365
Netherlands	953	1,943	4,407	10,723	13,483	14,100	13,827	13,874	13,980
Norway	164	304	1,220	6,272	9,901	10,531	10,819	9,193	9,292
Portugal	603	680	2,129	1,179	4,372	8,135	10,736	14,701	n.d.
Spain	134	1,045	4,618	7,450	28,041	32,104	36,555	46,336	46,562
Sweden	504	802	1,453	3,397	6,523	7,487	12,856	10,643	n.d.
Switzerland	1,667	2,919	6,961	16,930	20,900	22,148	23,456	21,987	23,191
United Kingdom	1,956	3,308	5,201	11,904	33,438	27,121	25,864	29,963	29,948
Developing countries: Total[2]	9,648	9,349	33,961	147,438	195,000	214,033	228,856	266,407	n.d.
By area:									
Africa	1,786	2,110	3,962	7,731	7,815	9,460	11,935	13,337	n.d.
Asia[3]	3,793	2,772	8,129	44,476	112,162	121,690	128,826	153,279	n.d.
Europe	269	381	3,345	5,571	10,013	14,931	15,641	15,316	n.d.
Middle East	1,183	1,805	9,436	64,094	41,644	42,288	38,011	42,327	n.d.
Western Hemisphere	2,616	2,282	9,089	25,566	23,366	25,664	34,443	42,148	n.d.
Memo.									
Oil-exporting countries	1,699	2,030	9,956	67,163	42,993	44,363	43,930	48,446	n.d.
Non-oil developing countries[3]	7,949	7,319	24,005	80,275	152,006	169,670	184,926	217,961	n.d.

Note: International reserves is comprised of monetary authorities' holdings of gold (at SDR 35 per ounce), special drawing rights (SDRs), reserve positions in the International Monetary Fund, and foreign exchange. Data exclude U.S.S.R., other Eastern European countries, and Cuba (after 1960).

U.S. dollars per SDR (end of period) are 1952 and 1962—1.00000; 1972—1.08571; 1982—1.10311; 1988—1.34570; 1989—1.31416; November 1991—1.38072; and December 1991—1.43043.

[1]Includes data for Luxembourg.

[2]Includes data for Taiwan Province of China.

[3]As of this Report, data include Czechoslovakia.

SOURCE: *Economic Report of the President,* Washington, D.C.: U.S. Government Printing Office, February 1992, p. 417.

tinue to use pegged exchange rates—against each other or against the dollar—requiring international reserves in their foreign exchange operations. It further reflects the managed nature of the post-1973 float against the dollar and the fact that discretionary central bank intervention requires holdings of international reserves with which to carry the intervention. For the G–5 countries, plus Canada and Italy (the G–7), reserves are used in central bank foreign currency operations and are partly linked to the monetary authorities' exchange rate policy.

Summary

1. A free-floating exchange rate regime exists whenever exchange rates are freely determined by the supply and demand of currencies by private parties. It presumes the absence of government intervention in the foreign exchange market. Changes in the private demand and supply of foreign exchange can then alter exchange rates but not the country's international reserves.

2. Under a fixed (or pegged) exchange rate regime, the government, through its central bank, intervenes in foreign exchange markets in order to maintain the exchange rate against different currencies within prescribed limits. To carry out its foreign exchange operations, the central bank holds inventories of foreign exchange, referred to as international reserves. Changes in the private demand and supply of foreign exchange will then alter the level of the country's international reserves.

3. A controlled, or managed, floating exchange rate regime exists when governments intervene in foreign exchange markets to influence the exchange rate but do not commit themselves to maintaining a fixed exchange rate. Depending on central bank intervention, changes in the private demand and supply of foreign exchange might then be associated with changes in exchange rates and/or changes in international reserves.

4. Under a freely floating or managed-floating system, when the price of foreign exchange increases (decreases) the domestic or local currency is said to have depreciated (appreciated) in value. Under a fixed exchange rate regime, when the central bank increases (reduces) the exchange rate, the domestic currency is said to have suffered a devaluation (revaluation).

5. The Bretton Woods system (1947 to 1971) was an adjustable peg regime in which currency values were pegged in terms of the U.S. dollar. The dollar served as intervention currency, the currency central banks bought and sold to keep their exchange rates fixed. The United States, in turn, stood ready to exchange gold for dollars at the fixed price of $35.00 per ounce. For this reason, the Bretton Woods system is referred to as the gold exchange standard.

6. Since 1973 the international monetary system has become an amalgamation of pegged and floating regimes. The currencies of the United States, Canada, Japan, and other major industrial countries fluctuate among themselves and with respect to the currencies of the EMS members. The countries participating in the EMS exchange rate mechanism keep their exchange rates pegged among themselves while they engage in a joint currency float against the U.S. dollar and other currencies. Many developing countries continue to peg their currency values in terms of the dollar, French franc, or other major currencies or basket of currencies.

7. Paradoxically, central bank intervention by industrial countries in the dollar market has been much greater than under Bretton Woods. In fact, there has been coordinated intervention in which a group of central banks pursue joint exchange rate policies. An important example of coordinated intervention occurred on September 21, 1985, when monetary authorities from France, Germany, Great Britain, Japan, and the United States (the so-called

Group of Five, or G–5) met at the Plaza Hotel in New York City and announced that they were jointly intervening in foreign exchange markets to induce a dollar depreciation. Joint exchange rate policy among the G–5 (G–7 at the present time) has continued.

8. The EMS was introduced in March 1979 to promote economic cooperation and exchange rate stability among EEC countries. The EEC currently consists of twelve countries: Belgium, Britain, Denmark, France, Greece, Ireland, Luxembourg, the Netherlands, Italy, Portugal, Spain, and Germany. The EMS involves a joint, or cooperative, currency float in which participating countries agree to peg their currencies to each other and to let their moneys float via-à-vis those of nonparticipating countries.

9. The EMS's exchange rate mechanism (ERM) pegs EEC members' currency values with respect to the European Currency Unit (ECU). The ECU is a composite currency, defined in terms of a basket that includes the currencies of the EMS member countries. The peg system establishes central values of the currencies with respect to the ECU and a target zone around the implied bilateral exchange rates between any two currencies. Central bank intervention to keep exchange rates within the margins of the target zone is compulsory when the exchange rate between two currencies reaches their bilateral margins. Realignments of the currency pegs are undertaken through consultation and negotiation among EMS participants.

10. A vehicle currency is a national currency used by nonresidents in their international transactions. The dollar is the most significant vehicle currency in the world today, followed by the German mark and the Japanese yen.

11. The sustained increase in the demand for international reserves observed in the post-Bretton Woods era can be explained by the continued adoption of pegged exchange rates

by many countries and by massive central bank intervention in foreign exchange markets on the part of economies under managed floating. Central banks have also found a need to increase their international reserves as a result of the increased openness, growing real income, and greater variability of receipts and payments faced by most countries since 1973; all of these factors augment the demand for international reserves.

Problems

1. You are told that the private demand for British pounds can be represented by the following equation:

$$Q_D = 10 - 3e,$$

where Q_D represents the quantity demanded of pounds (in millions), and e represents the exchange rate of the dollar against the pound. You are also given the private supply curve of pounds, which is represented by

$$Q_s = 5 + 2e,$$

where Q_s is the quantity supplied by pounds (in millions).

(a) Suppose that the United States and Britain are under a system of flexible exchange rates. What would be the equilibrium exchange rate during the period of concern? How many pounds (in millions) would be traded during this period?

(b) Given the situation in part (a), suppose now that the Federal Reserve Board in the United States decides to intervene in the foreign exchange market by purchasing £3 million. What would be the effects of this operation on the dollar per pound exchange rate? (Provide a numerical answer and illustrate it diagrammatically.) Assuming that the Fed's actions are a once-only event, would the intervention have a lasting effect on the exchange rate? Explain your answer.

(c) Imagine that the United States and Britain were under a system of fixed exchange rates and that the exchange rate was given at $2.00/£. What would be the U.S. central bank's gain (loss) of foreign exchange reserves, given the private supply-and-demand curves of part (a) and assuming that the United States is the country in charge of foreign exchange market intervention? Explain your answer.

2. Do you expect forward markets to develop in a fixed exchange rate system? What is the role of the forward market in that system?

3. Countries under pegged exchange rates tend to have forward exchange rates that diverge from the peg. For instance during the period before the August 1976 devaluation of the Mexican peso in terms of the U.S. dollar, the peso was consistently quoted at a discount on the forward market. This means that, if the forward rate were taken as the predictor of future exchange rates clear, consistent errors would result, except perhaps when the country changes its peg value. Does this mean that the forward rate cannot be looked at as a predictor of future exchange rates in a fixed exchange rate regime? How do you interpret the forward rate in this case? This issue is referred to as the peso problem in the literature.

4. The exchange rate of the French franc against the West German mark in April 1982 was pegged at 0.39 DM per French franc, with a 2.25 percent margin of variation allowed by the European Monetary System around that value. A quote for the ninety-day forward rate at the time was 0.38 DM per French franc. What does this suggest about the market's assessment regarding the prospects of a change in the bilateral French franc-deutsche mark exchange rate at that time? (Hint: Does the forward rate fall within or outside the band?)

5. Determine the actual and central exchange rates between the deutsche mark and the French franc at the time you are reading this. What is the percentage deviation of the actual exchange rate from the central rate? Which currency is the weaker currency, the franc or the mark? (Figures on central and actual exchange rates for the exchange rate mechanism currencies can be calculated from figures supplied by the Companies and Markets section of *The Financial Times*.)

6. Using the EC currency amounts embodied in an ECU, determine the value of one ECU in dollars at the time you are reading this. (Daily exchange rates between the dollar and European currencies can be found in *The Wall Street Journal, The New York Times, The Financial Times,* and a number of periodicals.) Has the ECU appreciated or depreciated in value versus the dollar, compared to the $1.338 value determined from Table 2–4?

7. The EMS's exchange rate mechanism establishes that the actual exchange rate between the Italian lira and the German mark may not deviate more than 2.25 percent from the established bilateral central rate. In fact, however, the maximum divergence of the actual and the bilateral rates is less that 2.25 percent. Explain why. [Hint: The maximum divergence can be calculated using the formula: $(1 - \text{official weight}) \times 2.25$; this formula is used because the ECU is partly composed of the lira.]

CHAPTER 3

Foreign Currency Regimes in Developing Countries

The first direct contact of individuals outside developing countries with the intricacies of economic life in these nations is often through the foreign exchange market. Whether as tourists engaged in visits to Cancún, Malaysia, or Martinique, or in business trips to New Delhi, Manila, or Rio de Janeiro, the first major transaction of visitors in these locations is to exchange dollars for local currencies. Exchange rate regimes in developing countries can be extremely complex, and sometimes outright exotic, as the following discussion will make clear.

Despite the great flexibility observed in the value of the dollar relative to the currencies of industrial economies since the early 1970s, many developing countries have continued to adopt, to some extent or another, regimes of adjustable pegs versus the U.S. dollar. At the time of writing, this is the case in much of Latin America and in a variety of other countries, such as Angola, the Bahamas, Ethiopia, Grenada, Iraq, Syria, and Yemen. At the same time, many African countries have pegged their currencies to the French franc (such as Cameroon, Congo, the Ivory Coast, Mali, and Senegal). There are also countries that have pegged their currencies against major trading partners: Lesotho, for instance, to the South African rand, Bhutan to the Indian rupee, Kiribati to the Australian dollar, and the Republic of Georgia to the Russian ruble. Some others, like Iran, Libya, and Rwanda, have pegged their currencies to the SDR. Finally, a large number of countries—including Algeria, Bangladesh, Hungary, Mauritius, Morocco, Nepal, Tanzania, and Zimbabwe—have pegged their currencies to a selected basket of foreign currencies.

Moving against a tradition of fixed exchange rates, the 1980s have witnessed the shift of many developing countries to regimes allowing greater exchange rate flexibility. Currently, the use in some way or another of floating rates can be seen in countries as diverse as Albania, the People's Republic of China, India, Jamaica, Korea, Lebanon, Lithuania, Mexico, Vietnam, and Zaire. The increased reliability on floating exchange rates does not preclude countries from also using fixed exchange rates. Some combine fixed and floating rates in what can only be described as hybrid systems—using fixed rates for some international transactions and floating rates for others.

3–1. EXCHANGE RATE REGIMES IN LATIN AMERICA

The best way to understand currency regimes in developing countries is to use actual examples, and for this there is no better region than Latin America. The variety of regimes in Latin American countries is flabbergasting. Not only do we see the use of fixed, floating, and hybrid systems, but, to make things more complicated, the governments' use of these exchange rate regimes can vary through time. For instance, in the 1980s and early 1990s, Argentina introduced at least one major overhaul of its exchange rate system on an average of every two years. Even the currencies used can change with some frequency. Argentina, for instance, switched its currency from the peso to the austral in 1985 and back to the peso in 1992, and Brazil has changed its currency several times since 1980, first from the cruzeiro to the cruzado and then to the new cruzado and finally back to the cruzeiro again. In the early 1990s, both Nicaragua and Peru were involved in changing their currencies, Nicaragua from the cordoba to a gold cordoba (introduced in 1990) and Peru from the sol to the inti in 1985 and then to the sol nuevo (new sol) in January 1991. In the transition periods, new and old

currencies circulate simultaneously. To make things worse, residents in many Latin American countries often use U.S. dollars in addition to local currency in their transactions. This dollarization makes some countries, in effect, multiple-currency economies. In Argentina, for example, it is estimated that 5 billion U.S. dollars circulate inside the country alongside the peso.

Table 3–1 provides quotes for the exchange rates of a selected sample of Latin American currencies versus the dollar for June 1989 and January 1990. The first two columns present quotes for *official exchange rates,* which include all those controlled or fixed by government authorities, arbitrarily or following rules that change over time. Among them is the currency of Honduras, the lempira (La), which was fixed arbitrarily at La 2.00 (per dollar) until January 1990; the colon of Costa Rica, for which the government had multiple exchange rates that applied to different international transactions; and the Mexican peso, which until November 1991 was fixed through a crawling peg regime, with the Banco de Mexico (the Mexican central bank) devaluing the peso relative to the dollar at a periodic rate over time.

A second category of quotes is shown in columns 3 and 4 of Table 3–1. These are floating exchange rates that change in reaction to demand and supply in the foreign exchange market. These quotes can be *free market rates,* which are for markets that are legally sanctioned, and/or *black market rates,* which are established in illegal or parallel foreign exchange markets. The free markets can operate without any type of governmental influence. More commonly, they are subject to various kinds of intervention, such as when the central bank tries to influence the market rate through sales or purchases of foreign currencies. In some countries, free markets are not sanctioned by the government. Everyone is legally bound to exchange currencies by transacting with the local monetary authorities, at official exchange rates. Frequently, the government also imposes exchange controls that ration the amount of foreign

TABLE 3–1. **Exchange Rate Quotes for Latin American Currencies (price of U.S. dollar in local currency)**

Country and Currency Name	Official Market		Free or Black Market	
	1/20/1989	1/26/1990	1/20/1989	1/26/1990
Argentina (austral)	13.7	652.5	16	1,810
Bolivia (boliviano)			2.5	3.02
Brazil (nuevo cruzado)	1.0	16.5	1.4	38.0
Colombia (peso)	340.0	444.0	332.0	447.0
Chile (peso)	250.9	297.0*	267.0	311.0
Costa Rica (colon)	20.0, 79.2*	20.0, 85.5*	84.5	94.0
Cuba (peso)	0.8	0.8	6.0	6.0
Ecuador (sucre)	418.0**	667.5	540.0	697.0
El Salvador (colon)	5.0**	5.0**	5.8	6.7
Guatemala (quetzal)	1.0, 2.7**	1.0, 3.6**	2.7*	3.6*
Honduras (lempira)	2.0	2.0	2.7	3.5
Nicaragua (cordoba)	2,000**	46,380**	5,500	55,720
Mexico (peso)	2,264	2,676	2,281	2,721
Panama (balboa, dolar)	1.0	1.0		
Paraguay (guarani)	400, 550**		1,065	1,245
Peru (intis)	700, 125***	6,211	1,750	12,700
Republica Dominicana (peso)			6.4	8.4
Uruguay (nuevo peso)			402.0	849.0
Venezuela (bolivar)	14.5**		36.2	43.4

*Banking rate ** Commercial rate *** Financial rate
In some cases, the official exchange rate is an average of a set of multiple exchange rates.

SOURCES: *Latin American Economic Report* (January 30, 1990); and IMF, *International Financial Statistics* (July 1990).

currency—dollars, for example—that can be purchased from the authorities. Under these circumstances, parallel or black markets have developed, through which both individuals and commercial firms acquire foreign exchange illegally or "unofficially."

For a number of countries, the parallel market constitutes a vital segment of the foreign exchange system. As a result, although some governments actively prosecute participants in the black market, other governments have adopted an attitude of indifference, transforming the market into "gray" or "brown." In the Dominican Republic, the black market has freely operated for many years, and even the governmental authorities have employed its services extensively. In Guatemala, the post offices are used as general facilities for the *cambistas* (the traders in the black market). Lima, Peru, has thousands of *cambistas* that cross the city every day with their pocket calculators and bunches of bills, looking for business. The black market in Peru grew with the expansion of international trade in coca and the payments in dollars made by international cocaine dealers to the Peruvian coca producers. A large part of these dollars are changed into the local Peruvian currency through the black market. Recognizing the difficulties involved in controlling these transactions, the Peruvian government legalized the black market in 1988.

Note that for many countries, Table 3–1 exhibits both official and free market rates. Indeed, throughout much of the developing world, *dual* or *two-tiered* exchange rate regimes prevail in which there are two exchange rates: an official rate fixed by the government, at which certain international transactions have to be carried out (usually commercial transactions involving merchandise goods), and a free market rate, at which all the other international transactions take place. In the case of Mexico, Table 3–1 shows that the official exchange rate for pesos by the end of January 1990 was 2,671 per dollar. That was the exchange rate directly controlled by the Banco de Mexico and the one used by the great majority of the Mexican business sector in its international trade. This official rate was periodically changed: in 1989 and 1990, the Banco de Mexico was using a system of mini-devaluations, increasing the controlled exchange rate by 30 pesos per dollar every month. Alongside the official market, the government allowed a number of exchange houses and banks in the border region with the United States to exchange pesos freely for dollars. As cited in Table 3–1, the free market exchange rate by the end of January 1990 was 2,698 pesos per dollar. Although this rate was freely determined by supply and demand, the Banco de Mexico intervened sporadically—buying or selling dollars—to influence its value. During 1987, for example, the Banco de Mexico frantically bought pesos (and sold dollars) in the free market, trying to avoid a depreciation of the peso in that market. By mid-November 1987, however, the Mexican authorities decided to stop the intervention in order to avoid a major depletion of reserves. As a result, the free market exchange rate went up immediately from 1,715 to 2,700 pesos per dollar.

The following sections study in detail several of the particular exchange rate systems that exist in developing countries and that are reflected in the Latin American cases in Table 3–1. These are multiple exchange rates, dual exchange rate systems, and black currency markets.

3–2. MULTIPLE EXCHANGE RATE SYSTEMS

Most developing countries use or have used systems of multiple exchange rates. A regime of multiple exchange rates exists when monetary authorities establish two or more rates for a given foreign currency. Each exchange rate is assigned to a particular group of international transactions. The government then establishes which transactions require which exchange rates but does not necessarily fix arbitrarily all currency values; it is common to allow some of the rates to float.

To understand how a system of multiple exchange rates works, consider the extreme case of Argentina under General Juan Domingo Perón (whose first administration lasted from 1946 to 1955). Table 3–2 shows the various Argentinean peso exchange rates versus the dollar for October 1949. The first column displays the central bank's dollar buying rates while the second column depicts the central bank's dollar selling rates. Of the six rows of quotes in the table, the first four (preferential A and B, special and basic) were fixed by the government; the last two (auction and free) floated according to demand and supply, although under the supervision of the government.

Let us first consider the central bank's selling rates in Table 3–2. These are the rates at which dollars were sold to Argentineans purchasing or importing U.S. goods, services, or assets. The fourth row quotes the basic rate of 6.0857 pesos per dollar used as the basis for setting other exchange rates; it was utilized by most of the importers of merchandise goods. The preferential exchange rates allowed importers of certain goods to buy dollars at a lower price. For example, the preferential selling rate A (applying to importers of coal, coke, and petroleum products) was 3.7313 pesos per dollar, a price significantly lower than the basic selling rate. This constituted a subsidy

TABLE 3–2.   **Multiple Exchange Rates in Argentina, 1949 (pesos per dollar)**

Exchange Rate Category	Buying Rate	Selling Rate
1. Preferential A	4.8321	3.7313
2. Preferential B	5.7286	5.3714
3. Special	7.1964	
4. Basic	3.3582	6.0857
5. Auction		fluctuating
6. Free	9.0000	9.0200

International transactions allocated to each category:

Buying Rates (rates at which the government would buy dollars):

Preferential A: wool, hides, vegetable oil, oil cakes, tallow, meat extract, some prepared meats, poultry, live animals, and minerals (except tungsten).

Preferential B: combed wool, cheese, butter, casein, powdered milk, quebracho extract, pork, eggs, pulses, shark-liver oil, and glycerine.

Special: leather goods, footwear, selected textiles, salted meats, ground bones, fresh fruits, tripe, gelatin, stearin, tung oil, tungsten, and mica.

Basic: beef, mutton, wheat, corn, barley, rye, and oilseeds.

Free: receipts from all nonmerchandise transactions.

Selling Rates (rates at which the government would sell dollars):

Preferential A: coal, coke, petroleum, and petroleum by-products.

Preferential B: raw materials and articles of popular consumption.

Basic: articles whose import is considered less essential.

Auction: imports of permissible luxury goods.

Free: remittances for all nonmerchandise transactions.

SOURCE: Based on E. R. Schlesinger, "Multiple Exchange Rates and Economic Development," *Princeton Studies in International Finance* (Princeton, N.J.: Princeton University Press, 1952), p. 63.

on these imports, which were products the government considered to be of basic need to the population and thus worthy of subsidy, relative to other, less essential products.

In addition to the basic and preferential exchange rates, two additional selling rates existed. These two rates were allowed to float, one by means of an auction and the other through a free market. The free market was used by individuals involved in any nonmerchandise transaction. An Argentinean acquisition of financial assets in the United States, for example, would have required the purchase of dollars at a price of 9.020 pesos per dollar. This free exchange rate floated on a day-to-day basis according to supply and demand. The central bank, however, intervened in the market by buying or selling dollars to restrain sudden jumps in the market rate. Observe that the free exchange rate was 50 percent higher than the basic. The government was thus implicitly imposing a tax on external financial transactions relative to commercial transactions.

The remaining item in Table 3–2, row 5, states that there was an auction exchange rate that was "fluctuating." *Foreign exchange auction markets are utilized by central banks to sell a limited* amount of dollars to buyers who submit bids for them. In some cases, participants in the auction are restricted to a certain group of importers. In Argentina in 1949, the import of luxury products was completely controlled by the government on the basis of permits. Those individuals or firms that had obtained a license to import luxuries then had to acquire the foreign currency by submitting bids in the auction market.

In the auction system, the central bank chooses the amount of dollars to sell and the minimum (base) price at which bids will be taken. The importers submit their bids and the quantity of dollars they want to buy. The authorities then go down the list of bids, accepting the highest ones and calculating the equilibrium bid, which is the highest bid that exhausts the quantity of dollars offered in the auction. All those bids above the equilibrium are accepted, and the final results of the auction—including the equilibrium bid and the number of successful bids—are publicly announced. The exchange rate finally charged to the participants in the auction—the bid submitted originally by each importer, or the equilibrium bid (the so-called market exchange rate)—depends on the type of auction the government uses. Under a *dutch auction,* each importer receives foreign currency according to the bid that he or she submits to the auction. Under a *marginal price auction,* all the importers buy their foreign exchange at the equilibrium market rate. Countries that have used dutch auctions in the foreign exchange market in the last few years are Bolivia, Ghana, Jamaica, and Zambia. Marginal price auctions have been used in Guinea, Nigeria, and Uganda.

Note that in a dutch auction a participant may end up paying a much higher price for the foreign currency than the equilibrium price. This results in government profits that exceed those in a comparable marginal price auction. By engaging in price discrimination, the government maximizes its monopoly power in the foreign exchange market, extracting the highest possible profit from the importers. Note, however, that a dutch auction, like any other system engaging in price discrimi-

nation, can generate profits only in the absence of black markets. The well-known proliferation of black markets in developing countries diminishes the profitability of these auctions; it is difficult to force importers to pay a price higher than the equilibrium because they will be induced to use the black market instead of participating in the auction. This causes a leakage of activity from the auction market to the black market, reducing the government's profits.[1]

An example of the limits that black, or parallel, markets impose on the exchange rates settled in a dutch auction is the one provided by the Bolsín, Bolivia's exchange rate auction system. The Bolsín was established on August 29, 1985, as part of a new economic policy program that also legalized the unofficial foreign exchange market. The Bolsín operates as a dutch auction in which the government sells foreign exchange holdings obtained from exporters.[2] A five-person committee from the Banco Central de Bolivia decides on both the base price and the quantity of dollars to be sold on each auction day. Because the parallel market is legally available to anyone, the expected price of a dollar in the parallel market after the auction serves as a ceiling for auction bid prices. How much below the parallel market rate the equilibrium auction rate is settled depends on the relative supply of dollars in the auction relative to the parallel market. For the Bolsín, the equilibrium exchange rate has indeed remained below the parallel market rate, with the two diverging very little from each other (one percentage point on average).[3]

[1]For more details, see P. T. Quirk, et al., "Floating Exchange Rates in Developing Countries: Experience with Auction and Interbank Markets," IMF Occasional Paper no. 53 (May 1987).

[2]The Bolivian government requires that all exporters sell their foreign currency proceeds to the central bank. The government buys the foreign exchange from the exporters at the prevailing Bolsín rate.

[3]For a discussion of the Bolsín and its role in exchange rate policymaking, see K. Dominguez, "Do Exchange Rate Auctions Work? An Examination of the Bolivian Experience," National Bureau of Economic Research, Working Paper No. 3683 (April 1991).

Although the Bolsín is the premiere example of an auction foreign exchange market at the time of writing, another well-known auction market experiment is operating in Russia. The Russian currency auction, which occurs on a semi-weekly basis in Moscow, sets the value of the ruble. Established in 1992 as a temporary mechanism to let the market determine the "equilibrium" value of the ruble, the auction has established ever-declining values for the ruble in terms of the dollar. Between mid-August 1992 and January 30, 1993, for instance, the ruble's value in the auction fell from 160 rubles per dollar to 568 to the dollar. Critics of the economic reforms of President Boris Yeltsin opposed the use of a market-determined exchange rate, pressuring instead for the return to a fixed exchange rate system.

We return now to Table 3–2 and the case of Argentina in 1949 to discuss the central bank's dollar buying rates. The prices at which Argentinean exporters were required to exchange their dollar receipts for pesos through the central bank are stated in the first column of the table. Row 4 shows the basic rate of 3.3582 pesos per dollar, which was applied to certain agricultural and livestock exports—among them, beef mutton, and wheat. The authorities bought dollars from exporters of these goods at the basic rate. As in the case of imports, the government had some preferential exchange rates for certain exports. The preferential rate B, for example, allowed the exporters of a number of basic foodstuffs to exchange dollars for pesos at 5.7286 pesos per dollar, a rate much higher than the basic. The special exchange rate—applying to other export products—was even more generous, providing twice the number of pesos for each dollar than the basic rate. Finally, the free exchange rate applied to all transactions other than merchandise.

Just as multiple dollar selling rates reflected a structure of subsidies to certain imports (e.g., goods that fulfill basic needs) in comparison to others (e.g., luxuries), the structure of the buying rates was oriented toward the protection of certain

export industries and the taxing of others. As Table 3–2 indicates, the exchange rate structure in Argentina worked mainly to protect manufacturing relative to traditional agricultural exporters. The basic rate, which offered the most adverse exchange rate for commercial transactions, applied to the exporters of beef, wheat, and corn, among others—all traditional agricultural products. The special rate—offering the most favorable exchange rate in terms of commercial products—applied to the shoe and textile industries, as well as to other major manufacturers. Overall, by installing a system of multiple exchange rates, the Argentine government established a structure of economic incentives that promoted manufacturing production against traditional agricultural exports. In this context, a system of multiple exchange rates does not differ from the imposition of a system of tariffs or taxes that protect certain industries and tax others.

The relative magnitude of protection or taxation to a particular domestic industry implicit in a system of multiple exchange rates can be measured through the use of *relative exchange rates,* which are calculated in the following way. Suppose that there are four commercial (merchandise) exchange rates at which the government *buys* dollars—as in the case depicted by the first column of rates in Table 3–2—symbolized by $e_1, e_2, e_3,$ and e_4. If we define the average exchange rate as $e = (e_1 + e_2 + e_3 + e_4)/4$, the degree of protection or taxation of a particular industry is indicated roughly by the relative exchange rate: e_i/e, where e_i is one of the four exchange rates, depending on the industry being considered. Industries with a relative exchange rate that exceeds a value of 1 are being implicitly subsidized, relative to the average, whereas those with a relative rate below 1 are taxed. For example, in Table 3–2, the exporters using the basic exchange rate had a relative rate equal to $3.3582/5.2788 = 0.64$ (where 5.2788 pesos per dollar is the average commercial rate). These figures indicate that the agricultural and livestock producers using the basic rate, such as wheat and beef exporters, were being subject to substantial taxation by the Argentine government.[4]

The structure of taxes and subsidies often responds to forces that are political in nature and may not reflect any economic rationality. The hierarchy of relative rates may only show the relative lobbying power of different groups of exporters and importers in the country and may not align with the comparative advantage of the country or the economic incentives required to promote efficiency and productivity. For instance, the system of multiple exchange rates prevailing in Argentina for many years resulted in the heavy taxation of agriculture, discouraging investments in that sector. This resulted in a serious misallocation of resources: land, one of Argentina's richest natural resources, became underutilized. The economic costs were at times substantial, as the following quote from MIT economist Rudiger Dornbusch emphasizes: "One of the clearest examples of the costs created by the distortions of an excessive number of multiple exchange rates took place in Argentina during 1973. In that year, both the international and the domestic price of wheat reached record levels. The world price was the highest in history, the domestic price the lowest. The outcome was as can be expected: Led by low prices, the Argentine producers did not produce much wheat and so Argentina missed the opportunity to export a competitive commodity at a good price."[5]

The fact that a system of multiple exchange rates can function as a regime of taxes on imported products implies that it is a policy that discriminates against the countries that sell or export those products. The IMF discourages the use of international discrimination policies and disapproves the adoption of multiple exchange rates by member countries. The IMF will approve their use only under extraordinary conditions—as in the case of balance-of-payments crises—and then only temporarily and rarely for periods of time longer than one year.

The IMF's articles of agreement[6] consider as multiple exchange rate policies all those for which (1) there are differences of more than 2 percent between any two buying rates for a foreign currency; (2) there is a difference of more than 2 percent between any two selling rates for a foreign currency; (3) there is a gap of more than 2 percent between buying and selling rates for a foreign currency, and (4) there is a deviation of more than 1 percent from the triangular arbitrage parity.[7]

In spite of the distortions created by multiple exchange rates, and the IMF's disapproval of these policies, many governments are tempted to use

---

[4]In analyzing export and import taxes and subsidies, intermediate goods must be taken into account—that is, goods used to produce other goods (such as automobile parts). Subsidies on the import of intermediate goods in fact constitute a subsidy to those final goods industries using the intermediate products. For details on how to define rates of protection that take into account the structure of taxes and subsidies on intermediate products—the so-called effective rates of protection—see R. Dornbusch, "Multiple Exchange Rates for Commercial Transactions," in S. Edwards and L. Ahmed, eds., *Economic Adjustment and Exchange Rates in Developing Countries* (Chicago: University of Chicago Press, 1986), pp. 143–165.

[5]Ibid., pp. 161–162.

[6]As discussed in the IMF's *Annual Report on Exchange Rate Arrangements and Exchange Restrictions* (Washington, D.C.: IMF, 1981), pp. 23, 36.

[7]Deviations from triangular arbitrage parity can be used as an estimate of transactions costs in the foreign exchange market. For a Latin American country whose currency is the peso, the triangular arbitrage condition states that

$$e(\text{pesos}/\$)/e(\text{pesos}/£)e(£/\$) = 1,$$

where $e(\text{pesos}/\$)$ is the exchange rate between the peso and the dollar, $e(\text{pesos}/£)$ is the exchange rate between the peso and the pound sterling, and $e(£/\$)$ is the exchange rate between the dollar and the pound. As explained in Chapter 1, deviations from triangular arbitrage can be used as estimates of transactions costs in the foreign exchange market. Estimates of the cost of buying and selling a foreign currency based on deviations from the triangular arbitrage parity condition are by far lower than 1 percent. As a consequence, according to the IMF, if deviations from triangular arbitrage exceed 1 percent, it can be assumed that this deviation cannot be explained by transaction costs and that a system of multiple exchange rates exists that generates the deviation.

them to generate revenues they could not generate otherwise. In contrast to industrialized economies, developing countries often have difficulties collecting income and property taxes. This is partly because of the lack of adequate funding for tax collection and for the prosecution of tax evaders. Sometimes a large part of the population lives in areas where, for geographical reasons, it is virtually impossible to collect taxes. External trade transactions, on the other hand, occur mainly through surface, marine, or air transport lines that are not numerous and are much easier for the authorities to intercept. With better supervision of the flow of international merchandise, governments in many developing countries find it more convenient to utilize tariffs and multiple exchange rates as an important source of income for their operations. Taxes on international transactions constitute about 75 percent of all tax revenues in Uganda, 40 percent in Burma, 45 percent in Honduras, 37 percent in Bangladesh, 36 percent in Ethiopia, 27 percent in El Salvador, and 23 percent in Costa Rica.[8]

The revenue a government generates by operating a system of multiple exchange rates depends on the buying and selling rates established by the authorities and on the quantity of foreign currency the public sells and buys. If, for example, the central bank's selling rate for dollars is e_1 (say in pesos per dollar), applying to imports for which the volume of transactions is M (in pesos), and if there is a buying rate for dollars, e_2, that applies to exports whose value is E (in pesos), the government's net revenues, RE, are

$$RE = e_1 M - e_2 E.$$

Given the value of imports and exports in local currency (that is, for given M and E), the government can raise its net revenues by imposing a

selling rate that exceeds the buying rate. On the other hand, a selling rate that is below the buying rate can generate negative net revenues if the value of imports is close to the value of exports.

In the case of Argentina, it is estimated that the system of multiple exchange rates generated just below $308 million per year between 1946 and 1948, which represents 3.7 percent of Argentina's GDP in those years. From 1949 to 1955, the estimated revenues from Argentina's exchange rate system were approximately equal to 0.9 percent of the country's GDP.[9]

3–3. DUAL EXCHANGE RATES

A special case of multiple exchange rates is adopted by monetary authorities whose main interest is to set different exchange rates for two types of transactions: commercial (involving trade in goods) and financial (involving trade in assets, such as stocks and bonds). Those exchange rate regimes for which financial transactions are channeled into a foreign exchange market that is different from the market for commercial (nonfinancial) transactions are called *dual exchange rate systems*. In these regimes, the exchange rate in the financial market is usually floating (although there might still be some form of government intervention in the market), whereas the commercial exchange rate is officially fixed by the monetary authorities. This is the system followed by Argentina in Table 3–2. In it, the free rates are precisely floating rates that apply to every financial transaction; the other exchange rates (except for the auction rate) are for commercial transactions, all fixed by the government.

Dual exchange rate systems are generally established by countries that wish to isolate the ex-

---

[8]These figures are for 1988, based on the data presented in the IMF's *Government Finance Statistics,* (Washington, D.C.: IMF, 1990).

[9]Fundación de Investigaciones Economicas Latinoamericanas (FIEL), *El Control de Cambios en la Argentina: Liberación Cambiaria y Crecimiento* (Buenos Aires: Ediciones Manantial, 1989), pp. 69, 74.

change rate used for commercial transactions from the unpredictable fluctuations associated with speculative international financial flows. The system is an alternative to an economywide floating exchange system, in which commercial transactions are also carried out at an exchange rate that may vary constantly in response to sudden shifts in supply and demand caused by speculation. It is also an alternative to a unified fixed exchange rate regime, in which a massive outflow of speculative capital could potentially eliminate the official reserves of the central bank and precipitate a costly exchange crisis.[10]

Although in principle a dual exchange rate system could provide a greater degree of stability to the commercial foreign exchange market than other exchange rate systems, in practice the regime suffers from certain problems.[11] First, there is a danger that the commercial exchange rate will be fixed at an artificially low level (resulting in an overvaluation of the domestic currency). In fact, dual exchange rates are often established by governments whose goal in setting up the system is to avoid (or at least delay) domestic currency devaluation. This overvaluation cheapens foreign currencies and encourages domestic imports at the expense of exports. Although perhaps politically attractive, such a move curtails the ability of the country to export competitive products in world markets.

Another basic problem of dual exchange rate systems is that they work only if the foreign exchange markets can be effectively segmented. That requires a large amount of government control over foreign exchange transactions. All the foreign exchange transactions in the Argentina example in Table 3–2 took place through the government, which was in complete charge of the purchase and sale of foreign currency. In cases where the private sector is the one involved in currency trading, government control is more difficult and requires a special degree of supervision. Even when the government can closely monitor foreign exchange markets, transactions will leak from the official market to the free market through fraudulent means—such as *underinvoicing* exports and *overinvoicing* imports. These practices are more common when the financial exchange rate is much higher than the commercial rate because of the great profits that can be obtained in such a situation, as explained next.

How do transactions leak from one market to another through underinvoicing exports and overinvoicing imports?[12] Let us suppose that a wheat exporter in country X (using dual exchange rates) receives $1 million as a payment for a shipment to the United States. This exporter can (fraudulently) create a bill of $800,000 for its exports. The $800,000 would then be changed at the commercial rate, but the other $200,000—which is invisible to the government because it does not appear on the bill—could be changed for domestic currency at the free market rate.[13] If the free market exchange rate is high relative to the commercial rate, the exporter can make a substantial profit. For

---

[10]The properties of dual exchange rates in insulating trade transactions from speculative capital flows are discussed in J. S. Lizondo, "Exchange Rate Differential and Balance of Payments Under Dual Exchange Markets," *Journal of Development Economics* (June 1987); R. Flood and N. Marion, "The Transmission of Disturbances Under Alternative Exchange Rate Regimes," *Quarterly Journal of Economics* (February 1982); R. Dornbusch, "The Theory of Flexible Exchange Rate Regimes and Macroeconomic Policy," *Scandinavian Journal of Economics* (May 1976); and M. Fleming, "Dual Exchange Markets and other Remedies for Disruptive Capital Flows," *IMF Staff Papers* (March 1974).

[11]The macroeconomic consequences of dual exchange rate systems have been surveyed by S. Collins, "Multiple Exchange Rates, Capital Controls and Commercial Policy," in R. Dornbusch and C. Helmers, eds., *The Open Economy: Tools for Policymakers in Developing Countries* (Oxford: Oxford University Press, 1985), pp. 128–164.

[12]For a more detailed discussion of these practices, see J. N. Bhagwati, ed., *Illegal Transactions in International Trade* (Amsterdam: North Holland Publishing Company, 1982).

[13]As an alternative, the exporter can deposit the $200,000 in a U.S. bank, which would represent capital flight out of the country. Capital flight is a major phenomenon in developing countries and will be examined in chapters 5 and 12.

example, if the domestic currency is the peso and the commercial rate is 2.00 pesos per dollar, with the financial rate equal to 4.00 pesos per dollar, the gain from selling in the free market instead of the official market would be 400,000 pesos ($200,000 multiplied by 2 pesos, which is the gap between the official and the free market rates).

In the following example, profits are made by overinvoicing imports. If an importer of computers in country X has to pay $1 million to a supplier in the United States, she or he could falsify the bill so that the payment appears as $1.2 million. Although the importer has to pay $1 million abroad, there is an extra $200,000 acquired at the commercial rate. If the commercial exchange rate is lower than the financial rate, the importer can sell the $200,000 in the free market, gaining 400,000 pesos (buying $200,000 at the commercial exchange rate of 2.00 pesos per dollar and selling them at the financial rate of 4.00 pesos per dollar).

Strong evidence suggests that underinvoicing exports and overinvoicing imports is widespread in countries with dual exchange rate systems in which the gap between the free and official exchange rates is large. It is estimated that, by the beginning of 1986, the overinvoicing of imports in Venezuela was about $150 million a month. In Malaysia, the underinvoicing of exports between 1976 and 1984 was estimated at about $10 billion, and in Nigeria in 1979 the overbilling reached $4 billion.[14]

The leakage of transactions from one foreign exchange market to another implied by these and other illegal or fraudulent transactions represents a cost to the central bank, which loses foreign exchange reserves and revenues in this process.

(The profits made by the importers and exporters who carry out the over and underinvoicing are at the expense of the government.) We can conclude that dual exchange systems will not work effectively when there is a large and persistent gap between the free and official rates.[15] As Dornbusch has noted: "The official dual exchange rate is more efficient if there is a close link to the free market rate. This way, the system can isolate the economy from sudden financial disturbances; but the rate must be altered when there are fundamental macroeconomic changes."[16]

The problems of dual exchange markets are reflected in the experience that Mexico had with such systems in the 1980s. Mexico's use of a dual exchange rate system can be traced back to August 6, 1982, when the country's central bank—running out of foreign exchange reserves in the face of massive capital outflows associated with anticipated peso devaluations—instituted a stabilization plan with dual exchange rates as a key component. The dual exchange rate system was mainly the result of the central bank's immediate desire to prevent speculative capital outflows from reducing its foreign exchange reserves. It was hoped that allowing the financial rate to float would lead capital outflows to increase the demand for dollars in the financial market and to a depreciation of the peso in that market, but that it would leave the central bank's foreign exchange reserves unchanged. In addition, it was hoped that the peso depreciation, being circumscribed to the financial peso, would not affect international trade

---

[14]I. Walter, *The Secret Money Market: Inside the Dark World of Tax Evasion, Financial Fraud, Insider Trading, Money Laundering and Capital Flight* (New York: Basic Books, 1990), p. 62. For a detailed discussion of fraudulent schemes involving exchange controls and multiple exchange rates in Latin America, see P. N. Miranda, *La Agonía del Dinero: Los Grandes Fraudes Financieros en América Latina* (Caracas: Editorial Metropolis, 1990).

[15]The impact of leakages on the effectiveness of dual exchange rate systems has been examined by J. S. Bhandari and C. A. Vegh, "Dual Exchange Markets Under Incomplete Separation," *IMF Staff Papers* (March 1990); P. Guidotti, "Insulation Properties Under Dual Exchange Rates," *Canadian Journal of Economics* (November 1988); and A. Lanyi, "Separate Exchange Markets for Capital and Current Transactions," *IMF Staff Papers* (November 1975).

[16]R. Dornbusch, "Special Exchange Rates for Capital Account Transactions," *The World Bank Economic Review* (September 1986), 28.

TABLE 3–3.   Black Market Premiums for the Dollar, 1986

Black Market Premiums/Discounts for the U.S. Dollar
(based on official or effective rates at the end of December 1986)

Iceland	−4%	Mexico	6%	Costa Rica	31%	Guatemala	270%
Italy	−2	Kenya	7	Hungary	34	Romania	294
France	−1	Bermuda	8	Botswana	39	Poland	343
Australia	1 −	India	8	Somalia	62	Iraq	347
Malaysia	1 −	Taiwan	8	Peru	63	German Dem. Rep.	500
New Zealand	1 −	Chinese People's Rep.	9	Argentina	67	U.S.S.R.	512
Spain	1 −	Bahamas, The	10	Zimbabwe	70	Iran	977
Ireland	1	Colombia	11	El Salvador	82	Nigeria	1,316
Jordan	3	Indonesia	11	Brazil	111	Vietnam	1,588
Sri Lanka	3	Chile	14	Egypt	164	Cuba	3,520
Israel	4	Jamaica	18	Bangladesh	218	Mozambique	4,807
Guinea	5	Yugoslavia	20	Afghanistan	219	Lao P. D. Republic	5,850
Zaire	5	Lesotho	24	Algeria	246	Angola	6,083
Greece	6	South Africa	24	Bulgaria	253	Nicaragua	7,186

SOURCE: P. P. Cowitt, *World Currency Yearbook, 1986–1987* (Brooklyn, N.Y.: International Currency Analysis, 1989).

transactions, which were subject to the preferential rate controlled by the government. That rate was being devalued over time through a crawling peg, but at a much lower rate than the financial rate was depreciating.

The system of dual rates imposed in Mexico after 1982 failed to stop the drain of foreign exchange rate reserves from the central bank and did not prevent major currency devaluations of the controlled rate from being eventually carried out.[17] One reason for the loss of foreign exchange rate reserves is that the central bank continued to intervene in the financial foreign exchange market so as to prevent sharp depreciations of the peso in that market. This forced the central bank to sell dollars in the free market, sometimes at a hectic pace. In October and November 1987, the Banco de Mexico sold $800 million in the free market,

[17]For detailed evidence on the performance of Mexico's dual exchange rate system, see G. Kaminsky, "Dual Exchange Rates: The Mexican Experience 1982–1987," working paper, Department of Economics, University of California at San Diego (October 1990).

trying to prevent further peso depreciation. In response to this and other problems, the Mexican government modified its dual exchange rate regime in December 1987. The action sharply devalued the peso in the controlled market and introduced mini-devaluations that kept the controlled rate closer to the free market. Subsequently, in November 1991, the Mexican government ended the regulations and controls that sustained a dual exchange market and allowed the unified exchange rate to be market-determined.

3–4. THE ECONOMICS OF BLACK AND PARALLEL CURRENCY MARKETS

Table 3–1 represents how widespread parallel and/or black markets are in developing countries. How are exchange rates determined in these markets and how do they relate to the official, legally sanctioned markets? Table 3–3 shows the premium of the dollar's black market exchange rate relative to the official rate (expressed in percentage terms) for a group of countries, most of them developing countries, at the end of 1986. The dollar premium is positive when the black market price of a dollar exceeds the official price. Note that for most countries the premium was more than 10 percent. The premium was particularly high in East Germany and in the Soviet Union (countries which have disappeared or disintegrated since 1986) where it was equal to 500 percent, but these numbers were small compared to the 3,520 percent and 7,186 percent premiums exhibited by the Cuban peso and the Nicaraguan córdoba, respectively. At the other extreme, there were some premiums that were negative (meaning that there was a discount on the dollar), as in the cases of Iceland and Italy. What explains whether the premium is positive or negative?

Black markets emerge in situations where the exchange rate established in the official foreign exchange market does not generate an equilibrium with equality of demand and supply. Figure 3–1 reproduces Figure 2–2(a), showing a domestic currency overvaluation. As we saw earlier, this means that there is an excess demand for foreign exchange equal to $D_0 - S_0$ at the official exchange rate e_0. This excess demand could be satisfied by the central bank, which could sell dollars in the amount $D_0 - S_0$. Often, however, the central bank is short of dollars and decides not to supply any dollar reserves to the market. The dollar supply in the market is then equal to the privately generated quantity supplied, S_0. In this case, there will be some individuals in the economy who will have their demands for foreign currency unfulfilled. The black market emerges to satisfy those demands.

For expositional simplicity, let us assume that the black market is not subject to legal prosecution and that it therefore operates freely, as a free parallel market. Let us also make the simplifying assumption that participants in the foreign exchange market are similar to each other and that therefore each of them wishes to acquire some additional dollars at the exchange rate e_0. Let us consider first how to determine the supply of foreign exchange in the black market, using Figure 3–1. If the black market exchange rate is below or

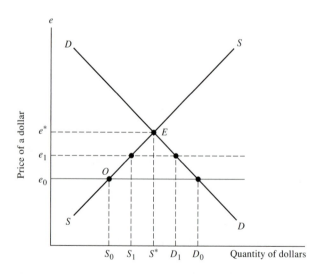

Figure 3–1. Determination of Official and Black Market Exchange Rates

equal to e_0, there would be no supply of foreign exchange forthcoming to that market because the central bank is willing to buy all the dollars that individuals wish to sell at a price e_0. However, if the exchange rate in the black market is equal to e_1, this would elicit some additional supply of foreign exchange, as given by S_1 in Figure 3–1. The quantity of foreign exchange supplied to the black market would then be equal to $S_1 - S_0$. Higher exchange rates would increase the quantity supplied even further, as given by the supply curve *SS*. The supply curve in the black market is therefore equal to *OES*, with its origin at point *O*.

At the black market exchange rate e_1 there would be an excess demand for dollars equal to $D_1 - S_0$ because the quantity supplied in the black market, equal to $S_1 - S_0$, is still less than the quantity demanded at that exchange rate. Competition for the scarce dollars being offered in the market would bid up the black market rate, in turn eliciting additional dollar supplies. The equilibrium in the black market would occur at point *E*, where the demand for and supply of black market dollars are equal. The total quantity of dollars sold in the economy is equal to S^*, which would be the total quantity supplied if the market were free. The equilibrium exchange rate is e^*, which would also be the exchange rate if the foreign exchange market were a free market.

The fact that the black market allows individuals to purchase foreign currency that otherwise would not be available suggests that it serves as a mechanism improving market efficiency. The additional foreign exchange is bound to increase international trade, resulting in greater economic activity. This is a result that may extend to black or "informal" markets in general. As Peruvian writer Mario Vargas Llosa notes: "The 'informal economy' is usually thought of as a problem: clandestine, unregistered . . . [where] black-marketeers are brigands. . . . That kind of thinking . . . is totally erroneous. In countries like Peru, the problem is not the black market but the state itself. The informal economy is the people's spontaneous and creative response to the state's incapacity to satisfy basic needs. . . ."[18]

The black market also can provide valuable information about how the official exchange rate and the equilibrium exchange rate compare with each other. When the black market rate is equal to the rate that would prevail if markets were allowed to clear, it provides an indicator of the equilibrium exchange rate and, consequently, of how overvalued the official exchange rate is. In fact, the black market exchange rate is often used as a predictor of the imminence of an official currency devaluation and of the likely magnitude of that devaluation. The devaluation of the Honduran lempira in January 1990 shows how the black market rate is seen by many—including monetary authorities in developing countries—as a predictor of future exchange rates. When President Callejas of Honduras took office in January 1990, he actually adopted the parallel market rate as the new official exchange rate applied to most international transactions. This implied a lempira devaluation of more than 50 percent, from 2.0 lempiras per dollar to 4.4 lempiras per dollar.

There are a number of pitfalls in using the black market exchange rate as the equilibrium rate that would prevail if exchange rates were to be allowed to fluctuate freely. First of all, the black market rate is highly sensitive to the shifting expectations and speculation of participants in the market. Those expectations are often based on news and information about the future of the local economy. For instance, news that the government may be planning highly inflationary policies may send local residents into a frenzy of dollar buying to get rid of the local currency, whose value inflation would shrink. The black market cost of the dollar would surge upward. This means that black market rates are determined by current and expected future government policies. Because a change in

[18]From the foreword to Hernando de Soto, *The Other Path: The Invisible Revolution in the Third World* (New York: Harper & Row, 1989), pp. xiii–xiv.

those policies may alter the black market rate, governments should not think of the black market rate as the exact rate to which the official rate should be adjusted in currency reforms (which are usually associated with major policy reforms).

The stance of local authorities regarding parallel markets ranges from benign neglect to active prosecution. In some countries, government toleration of the black market can change rapidly. In general, whenever exchange controls and multiple exchange rates are imposed, black markets tend to proliferate and their premia stand in the public light as a reminder of the degree of overvaluation of the official exchange rate (or exchange rates). Under these conditions, governments may crack down on black market traders. Active prosecution and strong penalties artificially raise the black market premium by making those activities riskier and reducing the supply of foreign exchange to that market. This makes the black market exchange rate an even less accurate indicator of the equilibrium, free market rate.

Figure 3–2 shows the consequences of government prosecution of black market traders on the black market exchange rate. It shows the demand for and supply of foreign exchange in an unrestricted black market by means of the DD_N and $e_0 S_N$ curves, with their intersection at point E corresponding to point E in Figure 3–1. As established earlier, the black market exchange rate in this case corresponds to the equilibrium exchange rate, e^*. The outcome of active prosecution and punishment of black market traders is to shift the supply curve from $e_0 S_N$ to $e_0 S_R$. The result is a reduction in the quantity traded in the market and an increase in the exchange rate to e_R. Because the black market rate now exceeds the equilibrium rate, the former becomes an inaccurate measure of the latter; the gap between the two grows with the virulence with which the government enforces black market restrictions.[19]

The Argentinian case provides a clear illustration of how black market exchange rates react in

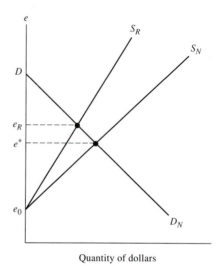

FIGURE 3–2. Determination of Exchange Rates in a Restricted Black Market

response to changes in economic policy and the imposition of exchange controls. The black market in Argentina has been officially acknowledged for decades. In contrast to the informal, sidewalk-style nature of the market in some countries, Argentina's houses of exchange have often operated from long-standing, established locations. Shifts in Argentina's government policies toward the foreign exchange markets, however, can alter attitudes toward the black market very quickly. Figure 3–3 displays the history of the dollar black market premium in Argentina from 1928 until 1990, relating it to the various exchange rate regimes adopted in that country. Note the large number of shifts in regime over the years. Argentina's instability can be traced to the nineteenth century and is clearly in line with the following statement made in 1899: "The Argentines alter their currency almost as frequently as they change presidents . . . no people on the world take a keener interest in currency experiments than the Argentines."[20]

---

[19]Evidence on this issue is provided by H. Huizinga, "Law Enforcement and the Black Market Exchange Rate," *Journal of International Money and Finance* (December 1991).

[20]As quoted by R. Dornbusch and J. C. de Pablo, "Debt and Macroeconomic Instability in Argentina," in J. Sachs, ed., *Developing Country Debt and the World Economy* (Chicago: University of Chicago Press, 1989), p. 39.

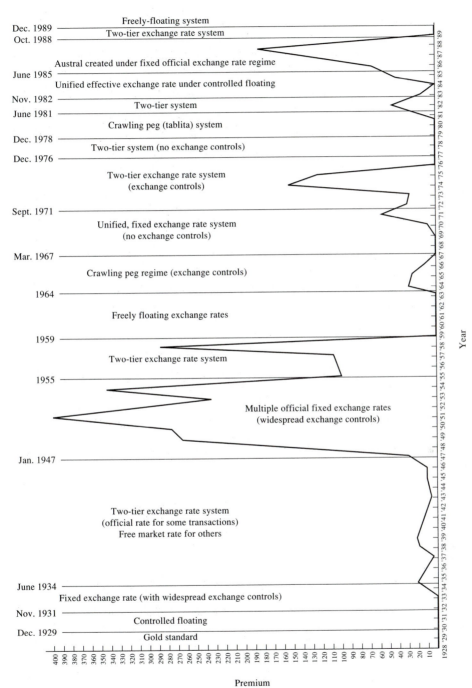

FIGURE 3–3. The Dollar Black Market Premium in Argentina, 1928–1990

SOURCE: R. Dornbusch and J. C. de Pablo, "Debt and Macroeconomic Instability in Argentina," in J. Sachs, ed., *Developing Country Debt and the World Economy* (Chicago: University of Chicago Press, 1989); and Fundación de Investigaciones Economicas (FIEL), *El Control de Cambios en la Argentina: Liberación Cambiaria y Crecimiento* (Buenos Aires: Ediciones Manantial, 1989).

93

The data in Figure 3–3 show that periods of exchange controls, such as the one in the late 1940s under General Perón (who was president from 1946 until September 1955), caused the black market premium to explode. Similarly, periods of active government prosecution of black market traders have also raised the premium. In 1985, the Argentine government imposed a wide range of exchange controls. The black market thus became a threat to the government's foreign exchange policies, and police action was undertaken. Sweeping raids were conducted that left the black market scattered and limited in scope. The black market premium rose to more than 40 percent. As a result, illegal trading in dollars moved from Buenos Aires to Montevideo, Uruguay, where Argentineans would travel to exchange pesos for dollars. Figure 3–3 reflects the growth of the black market premium during 1985 and afterwards.

3–5. LIBERALIZATION AND EXCHANGE RATE UNIFICATION: RECENT TRENDS

The last two decades have witnessed a dramatic shift toward the elimination of exchange controls and the liberalization of foreign exchange transactions in the industrialized world. West Germany eliminated a great deal of its controls as early as 1973 and 1974. The United Kingdom eliminated its most significant exchange controls at the beginning of Margaret Thatcher's administration in 1979 and completed the deregulation initiative in the ensuing years. The Japanese government relaxed many of its exchange controls between 1982 and 1984 and continues to do so. More recently, on January 1, 1991, France completed the removal of all of its controls on foreign exchange, some of which had been in place for forty-four years. This move was shared by other European countries involved in the 1992 initiative toward economic integration: The European Community gave Greece, Ireland, Portugal, and Spain until the end

of 1992 to eliminate any remaining exchange controls.

In developing countries, the process of deregulation of foreign exchange transactions picked up momentum during the 1980s. The two key manifestations of this process—greater currency market unification and the elimination of exchange controls—tend to occur together. The *unification* of currency markets involves the elimination of multiple exchange rates and the alignment of official and free-market rates. The latter is sometimes carried out through major devaluations that immediately shift the official rate closer to the free market rate. Then, over time, a crawling peg regime is used that keeps the official rate close to the free market rate. Alternatively, some countries unify their exchange rate systems by abandoning fixed exchange rates altogether, letting official rates float. Currency market unification is not effectively completed, however, unless there is a decline in the black market or an alignment of black market and official exchange rates. This is accomplished by the elimination of exchange controls (such as import licensing schemes), the legalization of black market trading, or the imposition of a realistic official rate that causes the black market to decline.

Unification and exchange market liberalization are not without problems. Indeed, most unifications are followed by a substantial increase in inflation. Partly, such inflation is a one-shot event caused by the currency depreciation that is required to align overvalued official exchange rates with free market rates: The depreciation sharply increases the prices of imports, resulting in domestic inflation. A more lasting impact on inflation can be traced to the elimination of exchange controls. As we discussed earlier, multiple exchange rates can be used by governments to generate revenues. When the system is eliminated, the resulting loss of income may force governments to print money in order to finance budget deficits. The expansion of the money supply may raise inflation. The government of Sierra Leone, for instance, unified its exchange rate in June 1986, letting its currency, the leone, float. Associated with this move was an inflation rate that rose from an annual average of 70 percent in the three years before the float to more than 200 percent after the unification.[21] It is imperative, then, that moves toward liberalization be joined with fiscal reforms that curtail the need of the government to finance budget deficits by "printing money." Successful liberalizations, such as that engaged by Bolivia in the mid-1980s, were implemented jointly with fiscal reform.[22]

The increased liberalization of foreign exchange markets has been accompanied by a heavier reliance on market-determined exchange rates. Although these moves began in the industrial world in the early 1970s, they picked up in the developing world in the mid-1980s. Before 1983, only a few instances of extended periods of floating had existed in the developing world. As Figure 3–3 depicts, Argentina had several such periods, Mexico had them in 1976 and 1977, Costa Rica in 1981, and Chile in 1982. Since then, long-term unified floating exchange rate systems have been adopted by Bolivia, Chile, Uganda, Jamaica, Zaire, the Philippines, the Dominican Republic, Gambia, Guinea, Sierra Leone, Nigeria, Venezuela, and others. Some countries—such as Mexico—have introduced systems that are close to (and for all effective purposes work like) unified exchange rate regimes. The presence of more flexible and market-determined exchange rates has in turn led to the development and growth of forward foreign exchange markets in developing

countries. In many cases, the forward contracts are offered by government institutions and not by the private financial sector. Even when there are private forward markets, the government often imposes restrictions, such as limits on the maturity of the contracts. Still, the growth of forward markets is an important innovation in developing countries.[23]

The economic reforms occurring in Eastern Europe and in the countries of the former Soviet Union include perhaps the strongest and most difficult attempts to liberalize foreign exchange transactions in the world today.[24] For the residents in some of these countries, their currencies up to the early 1990s were not *convertible* at all. Individuals could not use their currencies to purchase or sell any foreign currencies. In fact, under central planning, the absence of markets implied that currencies were often only partially convertible internally, meaning that rubles or other currencies could be used to freely purchase only a limited set of local goods and services.

In the early 1990s, a number of Eastern European countries and former Soviet republics began the process of developing market economies, and currency convertibility became a major goal of the liberalization movement. In Poland, the zloty was

[21]For a discussion of this issue, see P. R. Agenor, "Parallel Currency Markets in Developing Countries: Theory, Evidence and Policy Implications," *Princeton Essays in International Finance* (November 1992); and B. Pinto, "Black Market Premia, Exchange Rate Unification and Inflation in Sub-Saharan Africa," *The World Bank Economic Review* (September 1989), 321–338.

[22]See J. Sachs, "The Bolivian Hyperinflation and Stabilization," *American Economic Review* (May 1987); and J. A. Morales and J. Sachs, "Bolivia's Economic Crisis," in J. Sachs, ed., *Developing Country Debt and Economic Performance* (Chicago: University of Chicago Press, 1990).

[23]Unregulated forward exchange rates, provided by commercial banks, exist in Argentina, Brazil, Chile, Indonesia, Jordan, Korea, Malaysia, Nigeria, the Philippines, Singapore, South Africa, Sri Lanka, Thailand, the United Arab Emirates, Uruguay, and Zaire. Regulated forward markets exist in Bangladesh, the People's Republic of China, India, Kenya, Malta, Mexico, Pakistan, and Zimbabwe. For details on forward markets in developing countries, see P. J. Quirk and V. Schoofs, "Forward Foreign Exchange Markets in LDCs," *Finance and Development* (September 1988).

[24]For a description of recent currency reforms in Eastern Europe and the former Soviet republics, see J. Williamson, ed., *Trade and Payments After Soviet Disintegration* (Washington, D.C.: Institute for International Economics, 1992); E. M. Claassen, ed., *Exchange Rate Policies in Developing and Post-Socialist Countries* (San Francisco: International Center for Economic Growth, 1991); and J. Williamson, ed., *Currency Convertibility in Eastern Europe* (Washington, D.C., Institute for International Economics, 1991).

made convertible in January 1990, which allowed individuals and firms to exchange currencies for the purchase or sale of foreign goods and services. The value of the zloty was fixed against the dollar at 9,500 zlotys to the dollar. The National Bank of Poland agreed to buy or sell dollars at that price to licensed banks, which were then allowed to exchange currencies with the public. In essence, the convertibility of the zloty to the dollar was achieved through a system of pegged exchange rates. Other countries have followed this route, such as Estonia, which created an independent central bank and pegged its newly-created currency, the kroon, against the deutsche mark in June 1992.

Russia adopted a floating exchange rate mechanism in setting the value of the ruble against the dollar. Its other former republics, such as Armenia, Belarus, Georgia, Kyrgystan, and Moldova, which trade heavily with Russia, continued to use the Russian ruble as a major currency and/or have adopted currencies that are pegged to the ruble as of September 1992.

Summary

1. Exchange rate systems in developing countries are often characterized by the presence of a variety of exchange rates, each applying to a different set of transactions. These regimes are called multiple exchange rate systems. Multiple exchange rates can be official exchange rates, directly controlled or fixed by the government, or free market ones, determined by private demand and supply (with perhaps some occasional government influence). Floating rates can also be determined in black or "unofficial" markets.

2. As defined by the IMF, multiple exchange rate regimes occur when more than one rate exists for buying or selling a currency, or when the buying and selling rates diverge by more than 2 percent (a smaller divergence between buying and selling rates serves to cover the costs of realizing foreign exchange operations and does not imply the presence of multiple rates).

3. Multiple exchange rates are used by governments in developing countries as a device to collect revenues. Revenues are generated when a central bank sells foreign exchange to importers at a price (the central bank selling rate) that substantially exceeds the price at which it buys foreign exchange from exporters (the central bank buying rate).

4. Multiple exchange rates are also used by authorities in developing countries to subsidize or tax particular industries or sectors in the economy. A relatively high selling rate to importers of particular items acts like a tax imposed on those items. A low buying rate to particular exporters acts like a tax on those exports.

5. Dual exchange rate regimes exist when there is one foreign currency market for financial transactions and a different one for commercial transactions. Usually, the financial market exchange rate is allowed to float while the commercial rate is an officially pegged rate (sometimes following a crawling peg). The rationale for dual markets is to let the financial exchange rate adjust to speculative financial transactions and capital flows while keeping commercial transactions insulated from that instability. The proper operation of this regime requires that the two markets be effectively segmented and that no intermarket leakage occur.

6. In dual exchange rate systems, when the officially set commercial exchange rate is well below the financial rate, an incentive arises to underinvoice exports in order to exchange the undeclared export revenues in the parallel market. There is also an incentive to overinvoice imports.

7. Black market exchange rates are set in illegal or unofficial markets that proliferate in developing countries. Black markets emerge in

situations where the exchange rate established in the official market does not generate an equilibrium with equality between the private supply and demand. The prices of foreign currencies in black markets are almost always greater than official exchange rates.

8. Black market rates can be used as a rough estimate of what the equilibrium exchange rate is in economies with pegged exchange rates. However, when the illegal markets are prosecuted by the government, black market rates generally will be above the equilibrium rate. Also, black market rates reflect expectations of future government policies and probabilistic anticipations of currency devaluations. Unanticipated policy reforms that act to stabilize inflation rates in the future can reduce black market rates over time; existing black market rates thus provide overestimates of what the post-reform equilibrium exchange rate would be.

9. Exchange rate unification refers to the reduction in the number of exchange rates in existence and the realignment of official and free market (black or parallel) rates. Liberalization programs relax exchange controls and deregulate foreign trade transactions.

10. Exchange controls limit and regulate the private sector's use of the foreign exchange market to realize external transactions and may become very costly for economies using them.

Problems

1. The black market dollar premium for the cruzeiro in Brazil has been shown to have a seasonal pattern, declining sharply in the early months of the year. Can you explain why?

2. Show diagrammatically how, in equilibrium, a black market exchange rate can lie below the official exchange rate.

3. In February 1984, Venezuela had a system of multiple exchange rates. Given the following rates at which the Venezuelan government

sold dollars, calculate relative exchange rates for each category and determine the relative degree of taxation or subsidization of each type of product.

Multiple Exchange Rates in Venezuela, February 1984

4.3 bolivares per dollar:	fixed rate applying to essential imports including wheat and milk
6.0 bolivares per dollar:	fixed rate, applying to imported raw materials and other inputs
7.5 bolivares per dollar:	basic fixed rate, applying to most other imports of goods and services
13.2 bolivares per dollar:	average floating rate applying to nonessential imports (such as alcohol)

SOURCE: S. Collins, "Multiple Exchange Rates, Capital Controls, and Commercial Policy," in R. Dornbusch and C. Helmers, *The Open Economy: Tools for Policymakers in Developing Countries* (Oxford: Oxford University Press, 1988), pp. 129, 133.

---

4. In an article written in 1991, Russian economists Andrei Kazmin and Andrei Tsimailo suggested, among other things, that the countries of the former Soviet Union could be well-served by imposing a system of dual exchange rates, with official and market rates co-existing during an undetermined period of transition [see A. Kazmin and A. Tsimailo, "Toward the Convertible Ruble: The Case for a Parallel Currency," in J. Williamson, ed., *Currency Convertibility in Eastern Europe* (Washington, D.C.: Institute for International Economics, 1991)]. What are the advantages and disadvantages of a dual exchange rate system? Would you agree with Kazmin and Tsimailo that the former Soviet states' optimum policy is to use a dual exchange market?

5. As Table 3–1 shows, at the end of 1989, Peru had in place a system of multiple exchange

rates. Reflecting on such a system, economists Felipe Larraín and Jeffrey Sachs advised the government to establish a unified exchange rate, stating, "To achieve short-term stabilization and long-term development goals, Peru must have a coherent, stable exchange rate system. In particular, it needs a single, convertible, stable rate." [See F. Larraín and J. Sachs with M. Palomino, "Exchange Rate and Monetary Policy," in C. E. Paredes and J. D. Sachs, eds., *Peru's Path to Recovery: A Plan for Economic Stabilization and Growth* (Washington, D.C.: The Brookings Institution, 1991), p. 255.] What are the advantages and disadvantages of shifting from a multiple exchange rate system to a unified exchange rate?

6. Exchange rate systems are changed with amazing frequency. In order to determine what has happened to some of the exchange rate regimes discussed in this chapter, check financial papers and other publications (such as the *World Currency Review* and the IMF's *International Financial Statistics*) to specify the current regimes used by: Argentina, Bolivia, Lithuania, Mexico, Peru, Poland, Russia, Slovakia, Sweden, and Venezuela.

7. Consider the fiscal effects of a dual exchange rate system where black market and official exchange rates coexist: (a) Does a black market premium represent a tax on exports or a tax on imports? (b) In evaluating the fiscal effects of this dual system, what role is played by the so-called equilibrium exchange rate?

8. Suppose that the exchange market for dollars in a small Latin American country, X, can be represented by the following demand and supply equations:

$$Q_D = 10 - 3_e,$$
$$Q_S = 5 + 2_e,$$

where Q_D represents the quantity demanded of dollars by the private sector in country X's foreign exchange market (measured in millions), e represents the exchange rate between the local currency—the peso—and the dollar (expressed in pesos per dollar), and Q_S denotes the quantity of dollars supplied by the private sector (in millions).

(a) Suppose that the government has a fixed exchange rate system, with the exchange rate set at $0.50 per peso. Strict controls govern the foreign exchange market, and all transactions (purchases and sales of dollars) occur through the central bank. What would be the equilibrium amount of dollars that the central bank of country X will sell to the private sector in each time period?

(b) Due to a shortage of foreign reserves, the government of country X decides to sell an amount of dollars equal to that supplied by the private sector at the official exchange rate of $0.50. What would be the amount of dollars that the central bank would sell in this case? How many dollars would the private sector wish to buy? Suppose that a black market emerges. If the government lets the black market operate freely without enforcing penalties, what would be the exchange rate in the black market?

PART II

The International Financial System

International Money and Capital Markets

Chapters 1, 2, and 3 introduced the mechanics behind the operation of world foreign exchange markets, stressing that the basic function of those markets is to provide the means of payment required for the smooth operation of international transactions. With this purpose, agents engaging in international transactions purchase foreign currencies and transferable or checkable deposits denominated in foreign currencies. However, foreign exchange is not generally acquired for its own sake, to be held indefinitely. Just as tourists acquire foreign currency in order to spend it abroad—and have little use for the spare foreign coins left over after their travels—most foreign exchange is acquired in order to be transferred to someone else, either as payment for goods and services purchased or to be invested in interest-yielding foreign financial assets. When foreign exchange is acquired in order to engage in international transactions involving the purchases of goods and services, it is said that international trade in goods and services has taken place. When international transactions involve the purchase or sale of financial assets, they are referred to as international financial transactions.

The arena of international finance is an unusually broad and dynamic one, encompassing such disparate activities as those of cocaine drug lords smuggling dollars into the United States for money-laundering purposes, OPEC members choosing in which location and in which foreign assets to invest their wealth, and major Japanese banks setting up foreign branches at a rate faster than the appearance of new international finance textbooks. Chapters 4 through 8 will examine systematically the nature of these transactions and the key variables behind them. The discussion will focus first on the operation of international markets for short-term financial instruments and then move to analyze longer-term markets. The rest of the book will address the broader range of issues relating to the role played by international financial markets in the macroeconomy.

4–1. INTRODUCTION TO CAPITAL AND MONEY MARKETS

Financial markets are commonly classified into capital and money markets. *Capital markets* deal in financial claims having a maturity longer than one year, usually referred to as long-term claims. Such claims include stocks (which represent ownership claims and bear no maturity dates), bonds, and long-term loans, among others. *Money markets,* on the other hand, deal in short-term claims, with maturities of less than one year.[1] These include marketable government securities (like Treasury bills, which are available in thirty-day, six-month, and other short-term maturities), large-denomination certificates of deposit (CDs) issued by banks, commercial paper (representing short-term corporate debt), and many others. In spite of

[1]*Maturity,* as used here, refers to the remaining term to maturity of a financial instrument. Accordingly, if the instrument has an *original* term to maturity longer than one year (say, ten years), but its *remaining* term is less than one year (say, six months), it is considered a money market claim. By implication, Treasury notes or bills, and bonds and other claims with original medium-term and long-term maturity are transformed into money market instruments when their remaining time to maturity becomes less than one year. For an extensive discussion of money market instruments and the money market in general, see M. L. Stigum, *The Money Market* (Homewood, Ill.: Dow Jones-Irwin, 1987).

the wide range of money market instruments, which vary according to the type of issuing institution, term to maturity, and other factors, they share some basic traits: they are short-term assets that can be bought and sold quickly at low transaction costs (i.e., they are liquid). For these reasons, they are a convenient investment outlet, especially for funds available only for short periods of time. Because of their liquidity, money market assets are regarded as close substitutes for money and are often referred to as near moneys.

The money market is a highly competitive market, with information about the interest rates available on alternative instruments readily within reach of a telephone line. The rates being offered by major money markets can be followed easily by reading their quotes in the daily newspapers. There is also a broad diversity of investors participating in the money market, ranging from individuals and government institutions to large corporations, all of which can choose from a whole menu of domestic money market instruments. They can also choose to invest in money market instruments abroad—that is, go international. The decision may be made, for example, to buy Swiss franc-denominated certificates of deposit (CDs) issued by a Swiss bank, dollar CDs issued by the same Swiss bank (called Eurodollar deposits), U.K. Treasury bills, or commercial paper issued by a Canadian multinational company.

The decision to "go international" poses some problems that do not arise in domestic investment. For instance, when investments in sterling-denominated assets (say, U.K. Treasury bills or sterling-denominated CDs) are made, how do you protect yourself against a sudden depreciation of the pound sterling? In addition, how do you compare rates of return between dollar and sterling-denominated CDs? For instance, Table 4–1 shows the interest rates on three-month Treasury bills for a sample of countries. Interest rates can be seen to vary widely from country to country. The 9.65 percent interest rate on U.K. Treasury bills greatly exceeds the 3.14 percent interest rate on U.S. Trea-

TABLE 4–1. Interest Rates in a Sample of Countries, August 1992 (Treasury bill rates, period average, yearly percentage)

Country	Interest Rate
United States	3.14%
Canada	4.87
Belgium	6.25
Italy	14.00*
Netherlands	3.20
Spain	12.58
Sweden	13.26
United Kingdom	9.65
Australia	5.78
Brazil	1,623.00
Lesotho	14.91*
Jamaica	32.16
Japan	2.15*
Mexico	16.49
New Zealand	6.65
Germany	9.01
South Africa	16.00*
Venezuela	35.39

*Data for June 1992.

Figures for Belgium, Brazil, Canada, Japan, and Venezuela are for deposit interest rates.

SOURCE: IMF, *International Financial Statistics* (December 1992).

sury bills. Does this mean that on August 1992 it was more profitable to invest in the United Kingdom than in the United States? What about the 1,623.00 percent interest rate in Brazil? Does it really reflect an exorbitantly high rate of return of investment on the cruzeiro?

The information needed to answer these questions—the particular procedures and problems of investing in international money and capital markets—can be found in this and the following two chapters. This chapter begins with a discussion of the idiosyncrasies inherent in comparing rates of return involving assets denominated in different currencies, concentrating on investments that minimize risks (hedged or covered investments). Also discussed are the last decade's re-

markable liberalization of financial markets and the process of capital market integration that has irrevocably transformed the world of finance into international finance. Chapter 5 examines the role played by exchange risk and portfolio diversification on international investing; Chapter 6 then surveys the existing evidence on exchange rate forecasting, the formation of exchange rate expectations, and the efficiency of foreign exchange markets. Chapter 7 describes the recent global banking and finance revolution that has given rise to the increased penetration of foreign banks into domestic (*onshore*) banking systems, as in the case of Japanese banks opening branches in the United States. Chapter 8 traces the growth of the *offshore* banking and finance industry, which involves the trading of financial assets denominated in a particular currency but issued or located in different national jurisdictions, such as dollar certificates of deposit offered by London banks (Eurodollars) or yendenominated bonds issued by Swiss banks (Euroyen bonds, or Eurobonds).

4–2. INVESTING ON A COVERED BASIS

We now focus on the problems associated with investing in assets denominated in different currencies. International investing can be as fascinating and profitable as it can be discouraging and woeful. The intricacies of covering, arbitrage, and speculation absorb the minds of financial managers and executives just as much as they perplex newcomers. Still, the present sophistication of high international finance requires taking a hard look at the elements of international investing.

For a U.S.-based investor, purchasing assets denominated in foreign currencies means that, for a certain period of time, the investor's wealth is potentially subject to the whims of exchange rates and the negative impact these may have on the dollar value of his or her investments. In order to avoid this *exchange risk,* international financial managers often engage in *covered* foreign investments—that is, investments in which the forward exchange market has been used to cover foreign currency proceeds from possible exchange rate changes. This chapter examines in detail the mechanics of these covered foreign investments and how they compare with investments denominated in local currency (dollars in the case of a U.S.-based investor). Chapter 5 will examine the issues surrounding *uncovered* foreign investments—that is, investments whose foreign currency proceeds are not covered in the forward market.

Suppose that you are the international financial manager of a large American corporation that has investment funds available for one year and is interested in obtaining the highest return subject to the least possible risk. The international finance division in which you work is considering the choice between investing in American and British one-year Treasury bills. Both U.S. and U.K. Treasury bills are among the safest assets available in the market (because of their negligible default risk, which means that both the amount invested and the attached interest are default free). You are asked to determine whether the corporation should invest in U.K. or U.S. Treasury bills and are told that the advice provided must be top-notch; otherwise, heads will roll. What would your advice be? In which asset should the company invest?

If the corporation were to invest in U.S. Treasury bills, it would receive $R_{U.S.}$ dollars back after one year, per dollar invested, where

$$R_{U.S.} = 1 + i, \qquad (4\text{--}1)$$

with i representing the one-year interest yield on U.S. Treasury bills. In other words, after one year, the firm would receive back the dollar invested plus its interest return.

The alternative investment involves U.K. Treasury bills, which yield an interest return equal to i^*. Each pound bought and invested in U.K. Treasury bills then generates $1 + i^*$ pounds one year in the future. Because corporate funds are going to be shifted back to dollars (picturesquely

described as the firm's "preferred habitat"), a problem arises when you think about investing in U.K. Treasury bills. If pound-denominated assets are purchased today and the pound depreciates relative to the dollar during the year, the firm may end up with fewer dollars than it started with, even if the yields on U.K. Treasury bills are very high.

The exchange risk involved in the chance that the value of the currency in which the assets held are denominated will fluctuate can be substantial; it means that exchange rate fluctuations can completely offset any interest advantage offered by a given foreign currency-denominated asset. It must thus be realized that a strategy that involves buying pounds, investing in one-year U.K. Treasury bills, waiting until they mature, and exchanging the pound proceeds for dollars is risky: It involves exchange risk. Although buying U.K. Treasury bills avoids default risk, this merely means that the amount of *pounds* to be received at the end of the year is without risk, but the *dollar* equivalent of those pounds is still subject to exchange risk. Because your assumed financial objectives involve minimizing risks, how do you proceed in order to avoid exchange risk? As discussed in Chapter 1, it is precisely this type of risk that the forward market can insure against. In order to be fully covered, you should sell pounds forward by an amount corresponding to the proceeds of your U.K. Treasury bill investment (including both the pounds invested and the interest to be received on them). This covered investment strategy, then, involves the following simultaneous steps:

1. Buy pounds in the spot market. At a spot exchange rate of e dollars per pound, you obtain $1/e$ pounds for each dollar invested.
2. Invest the pounds obtained in the spot market in one-year U.K. Treasury bills. This will give you $(1/e)(1 + i^*)$ pounds at the end of one year (per dollar invested).
3. Sell forward the future pound proceeds from the investment. At a forward exchange rate of F dollars per pound, for each pound you sell

for delivery one year hence, you will receive F dollars at that time; because you will have $(1 + i^*)/e$ pounds available to transfer back to dollars, you receive one year from now $[(1 + i^*)/e]F$ dollars.

The proceeds from the covered investment strategy, in terms of the dollars you end up with after a period of one year—per dollar initially invested abroad—are represented by $R_{\text{U.K.}}$ and given by

$$R_{\text{U.K.}} = \frac{F}{e}(1 + i^*),\qquad (4\text{--}2)$$

where F and e represent the U.S. dollar-pound sterling forward and spot exchange rates. Note that this covered investment strategy avoids both default and exchange risk. This was achieved, first, by investing in a very safe asset with negligible default risk and, second, by selling forward the future pound proceeds so that exchange risk is eliminated.

We have examined two alternative investment strategies, both of which lack default and exchange risk: Equation 4–1 represents the dollar proceeds from an investment in U.S. Treasury bills; Equation 4–2 represents the dollar proceeds from an alternative covered investment in U.K. Treasury bills. Which is the superior investment strategy? A complete answer to this question requires us to account for a host of elements, including an analysis of the transaction costs involved, applicable taxes, and forward market margin requirements. To highlight the essentials of the discussion, however, we shall abstract from these issues momentarily.

When investment alternatives are similar in terms of the explicit objective to minimize risk, a maximizing investor would choose whichever investment provides a higher dollar return after one year. As long as $R_{\text{U.S.}} > R_{\text{U.K.}}$, you should invest in the United States; if $R_{\text{U.S.}} < R_{\text{U.K.}}$, you should invest in the United Kingdom. Note that if $R_{\text{U.S.}} = R_{\text{U.K.}}$, there is no clear incentive to choose one alternative over the other. The existence of

incentives to invest in one or the other country is therefore measured by the differential between $R_{\text{U.K.}}$ and $R_{\text{U.S.}}$—the *covered interest differential* (*CD*):

$$CD = R_{\text{U.K.}} - R_{\text{U.S.}} \qquad (4\text{--}3)$$

$$= \frac{F}{e}(1 + i^*) - (1 + i).$$

A positive value of CD is referred to as a covered differential in favor of the U.K.—that is, there would be incentives to invest in the United Kingdom relative to the United States. A negative value of CD is referred to as a covered differential in favor of the United States because there are incentives to invest in the United States. Subjecting Equation 4–3 to some approximation and manipulation, we easily derive a simple expression that highlights the essential elements involved in evaluating competing investment strategies, with the following result:[2]

$$CD = \frac{F - e}{e} + i^* - i \qquad (4\text{--}4)$$

$$= f + i^* - i,$$

where the symbol f denotes $(F - e)/e$.

[2]The derivation of Equation 4–4 is

$$CD = \frac{F}{e}(1 + i^*) - (1 + i)$$

$$= \left(\frac{F}{e} - 1\right) - i + \frac{e}{e}i^* - \frac{e}{e}i^* + \frac{F}{e}i^*$$

$$= \frac{F - e}{e} - i + i^* + \frac{F - e}{e}i^*$$

$$= \frac{F - e}{e} - i + i^*,$$

where the last equality is only an approximation because it ignores the term $[(F - e)/e]i^*$. This term represents the foreign exchange gain or loss on the interest received from investing abroad; because it is usually a product of two fractions, it yields a very small number. As a matter of fact, for sufficiently (infinitesimally) small investment periods, the term becomes negligible and can be ignored.

Equation 4–4 presents a convenient form of the covered interest differential, expressing in a simple way the sources of the returns associated with different investment strategies and facilitating their evaluation. We will examine it in some detail to discern its economic significance. The first two terms, $f + i^*$, represent the return from engaging in a *covered* investment in U.K. Treasury bills. To visualize this, recall that the covered investment strategy involving U.K. Treasury bills consists of three *simultaneous* transactions: (1) buy pounds, (2) invest in U.K. Treasury bills, and (3) sell forward the pound proceeds. The return from this investment strategy can then be broken down into two basic components: One component arises from the second transaction, which just represents the interest earned on the investment in U.K. Treasury bills, i^*, the so-called interest gain; the other component, $f = (F - e)/e$, arises from the first and third transactions and reflects the return—or loss—from purchasing pounds spot and simultaneously selling pounds forward, the so-called exchange gain—or loss. This return (loss) is equal to the difference between the price at which the forward pounds are sold (the forward exchange rate, F) and the price at which spot pounds can currently be bought (the spot exchange rate, e). Expressed in percentage terms, this exchange gain (loss) is precisely equal to $f = (F - e)/e$, which, as we saw in Chapter 1, is the *forward premium*, or *discount* on the pound. The third and final term in Equation 4–4 represents the gain from investing in U.S. Treasury bills, i. Because U.S. Treasury bills are denominated in dollars and are not involved in any international transactions, they require no forward covering; for that reason, the exchange cost of investing in the United States is zero.

The first two terms in Equation 4–4 represent the return obtained from covered investments in U.K. Treasury bills. The interest rate, i, denotes the return on U.S. Treasury bills. It is therefore clear that the covered interest differential, CD, represents the difference between the returns on these two investments.

Consider the following hypothetical example involving a current spot exchange rate for the pound of $e = \$2.00$ per pound, a one-year forward rate of $F = \$1.90$ per pound, a yearly interest rate on U.K. Treasury bills equal to $i^* = 0.12$, and a one-year return on U.S. Treasury bills of $i = 0.10$. In this case, the first component of the rate of return on U.K. investments is the 12 percent rate of interest. The second component involves the gain or loss from having to purchase pounds spot and selling them forward to cover the foreign investment. In the present example, this second component is equal to

$$f = \frac{F - e}{e}$$
$$= \frac{1.90 - 2.00}{2.00}$$
$$= -0.05.$$

The negative value (−0.05) of f obtained implies pounds are at a discount in the forward market, meaning that pounds can only be sold for one-year delivery at a price *lower* than that at which pounds spot can currently be bought (\$1.90 per pound as compared with \$2.00 per pound). This reduces the attractiveness of investing in pound-denominated assets because part of the interest return is, in a sense, used up in the forward covering transactions.

Because the return on covered investments in U.K. Treasury bills is the sum of the interest earned and the forward premium (discount)—that is, $f + i^*$—the return in the present example is equal to 0.07 (because $f = -0.05$ and $i^* = 0.12$). In other words, the one-year return on covered investing in U.K. Treasury bills is 7 percent. Given that the one-year return on U.S. Treasury bills is assumed to be equal to $i = 0.10$ (or 10 percent), the rate of return on U.K. Treasury bills as calculated is clearly smaller. There is, thus, an incentive to invest in U.S. Treasury bills. This is exactly what Equation 4–4 tells us. By substituting the specific values for f, i^*, and i used in our example, the covered interest differential in this case would be given by

$$CD = f + i^* - i$$
$$= -0.05 + 0.12 - 0.10$$
$$= -0.03.$$

A covered interest differential in favor of the U.S. (negative CD) thus exists.

The concept of a covered interest differential involves comparing the returns of two assets that are similar or equivalent in their risk characteristics. After we find such alternative investment strategies providing the same risk characteristics, our choice is obvious: We select the one with the highest return. Observe, however, that choosing the investment strategy with the highest return does not imply that we should choose the investment with the highest interest rate. The appropriate comparison is between the returns from different investment strategies after we cover to eliminate the exchange risk. As a matter of fact, in our numerical example involving U.S. Treasury bills and covered U.K. Treasury bills, the highest return was provided by the U.S. investment (10 percent relative to the 7 percent provided by the covered U.K. investment). Still, the investment offering the highest rate of interest was the U.K. Treasury bill, which earned 12 percent compared with the 10 percent provided by U.S. Treasury bills. The reason for the difference in favoring the U.S. Treasury bills in spite of the interest rate differential favoring the U.K. Treasury bills is that the *covered* interest differential favors the former. In order to cover the U.K. investments, we would have to sell forward pounds at a discount, which yields an exchange loss large enough to offset the interest rate gain from U.K. investments. As a consequence, the U.K. Treasury bills become an inferior investment strategy. The international investor must guard against investing just on the basis of the relative interest rates (yields) available on comparable instruments in different countries.

4–3. THE COVERED INTEREST PARITY CONDITION

We now move beyond the simple analysis of covered investment strategies toward an examination of the market forces governing international interest rate linkages. We will look first at the main ideas behind the so-called *covered interest parity condition,* which establishes a rigid connection between international interest rate differentials and forward premia. Later on, we shall look at actual data on covered interest differentials to test whether the covered parity condition holds.

By applying some economic reasoning, we can easily transform our discussion of covered investment strategies in the previous section into a theory of international money market equilibrium, establishing how international interest rates relate. In order to carry out this task initially at the maximum level of simplicity, we continue to ignore transaction costs, taxes, and the like.

Note, first, that as long as the covered interest differential is different from zero, there will be incentives for the movement of funds from one country to another because profits can be made from such an undertaking. Equilibrium is defined as a situation in which there are no profit opportunities to be made from the movement of funds across borders. In other words, there are no unexploited opportunities for profit in the simple act of moving funds across borders. This implies that, in equilibrium, the covered interest differential, CD, is zero, or, from Equation 4–4, $f + i^* = i$. Rearranging this, we find that[3]

$$f = \frac{F - e}{e} = i - i^*. \qquad (4\text{–}5)$$

[3]For simplicity, Equation 4–5 states the equality of the forward premium and the interest rate differential, even though (from the derivation of Equation 4–4) in general it is only an approximate equality. The precise equilibrium condition is derived by setting $CD = 0$ in Footnote 2:

(*continued*)

That is, the forward premium, *f*, must be equal to the interest rate differential, $i - i^*$. This is what is known as the covered interest rate parity condition, often called the (covered) interest parity theorem.

The interest parity condition is basically a statement about the law of one price, which asserts that a single price should prevail all over the market for any given commodity. In international money markets, the analogy to the law of one price is that securities or assets with the same characteristics (e.g., the same risks and liquidity) should yield the same return in equilibrium. In other words, interest rates should be in *line,* or in *parity,* with each other. If U.S. investments and covered U.K. investments are similar in terms of risk and other characteristics, we would expect them to yield the same return.

From a slightly different perspective, the interest parity condition can also be interpreted as representing the absence of profits to be made from undertaking the operation of interest arbitrage in international money markets. Interest arbitrage is best understood by considering a situation in which the covered returns from U.K. T-bill investments exceed the cost of borrowing in the United States—that is, $i^* + [(F - e)/e] - i > 0$. Smart investors could then borrow in the United States and invest in the United Kingdom, which yields a sure profit with no commitment of personal funds, because the operation is credit financed. Furthermore, the amount of profit is only limited by the borrowings the arbitrageurs manage to obtain. Obviously, from this viewpoint, covered interest differentials should quickly disappear as hordes of arbitrageurs jump on the bandwagon of easy profits. A zero-profits-from-arbitrage equilibrium condition thus ensues.

$$CD = 0 = \frac{F - e}{e} - i + i^* + \frac{F - e}{e} i^*$$

$$= \frac{F - e}{e}(1 + i^*) + i^* - 1,$$

which yields $f = [(F - e)/e] = [(i - i^*)/(1 + i^*)]$.

The equality between the forward premium and the interest rate differential in equilibrium is represented graphically in Figure 4–1 by line *IP*. Point *A,* for instance, shows that, in equilibrium, a 5 percent forward premium on the pound sterling (a discount on the dollar) would have to be associated with a 5 percent equilibrium interest rate differential favoring dollar assets. In the event that the forward premium on the pound were to exceed the interest differential—such as at point *B,* where a 5 percent forward premium is coupled with a 4 percent interest differential favoring U.S. investments—this would suggest that profits could be made by investing in sterling-denominated assets. Such a situation was defined earlier as being inconsistent with financial equilibrium within the present framework. Conversely, if the forward premium on the pound were less than the interest differential—as at point *C* in Figure 4–1, where a 5 percent forward premium is associated with a 6 percent interest differential in favor of U.S. investments—profits could be made by shifting funds to the United States. Again, this would be inconsistent with equilibrium. Interest parity, then, is represented by points along the line *IP,* where $f = (F - e)/e = i - i^*$.

The covered interest parity establishes an equilibrium relationship between a set of interdependent economic variables but does not specify their individual equilibrium values. In a more specific context, what we want to know is exactly how the variables composing the covered interest parity equation (interest rates and spot and forward exchange rates) move to their equilibrium values to maintain interest parity. This is the subject of the open economy macroeconomics chapters (Chapter 15 in particular), in which it will be shown how the general equilibrium values of *F, e, i,* and *i** are established to maintain the condition in Equation 4–5.

At first glance, Equation 4–5 looks like an innocuous and perhaps obvious condition. In our discussion, however, we have neglected a host of real-world complications (such as transaction

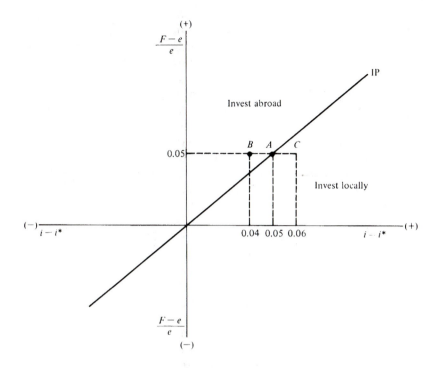

FIGURE 4−1. Covered Interest Parity Line

costs) that might preclude the condition in Equation 4−5 from holding. The empirical validity of Equation 4−5 and whether interest parity actually holds in financial markets are addressed in the following sections.

4−4. DEVIATIONS FROM COVERED INTEREST PARITY

Figure 4−2 shows the interest differential between U.S. and U.K. Treasury bills from 1983 to 1988, as well as the corresponding forward premium, or discount, on the pound sterling versus the U.S. dollar during those years. Deviations from the covered interest parity condition do occur and appear to persist; at some points covered interest differentials differ from zero by a margin of more

than 2 percent. This was the case late in 1988, when the deviation from a zero covered differential slightly exceeded 2.7 percent. Going further back in time to the 1970s, deviations of more than 5 percent can be seen. Why these divergences from covered interest parity?

A variety of factors may preclude covered interest parity from holding, such as:

1. Transaction costs
2. Costs of gathering and processing information
3. Government intervention and regulation
4. Financial constraints and capital market imperfections
5. Noncomparability of assets

We will now discuss in detail how each of these factors influences deviations from covered interest parity. We begin by examining transaction costs.

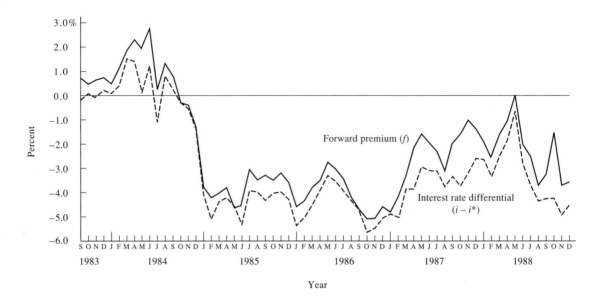

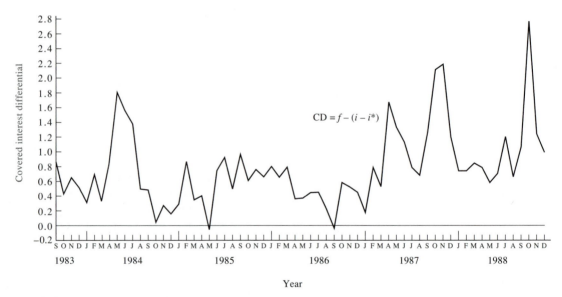

Figure 4–2.   Interest Rate Differential, Forward Premium, and Covered Interest Differential Between the United States and the United Kingdom. The forward premium, *f,* is the ninety-day forward premium on the pound vis-à-vis the U.S. dollar; the interest rates *i* and *i** are the three-month U.S. and U.K. Treasury bill rates, respectively. All variables have been annualized and expressed in percentage form.

Transaction Costs

There are basically two elements in the cost of transactions: the cost of transacting in the foreign exchange markets (spot and forward) and the cost of transacting in the securities markets (domestic and foreign). Consider, for example, the transactions involved when a U.S. resident holding cash initially engages in covered foreign investments— that is, in capital outflows. In this case, the transactions involved are the purchase of foreign currency (spot), the purchase of foreign securities, and the sale of foreign currency (forward).[4] Each of these transactions involves transaction costs and reduces the net revenues from investing abroad. Investing at home (locally), however, requires only one transaction—the purchase of domestic securities. As a result, investments in domestic assets require a smaller number of transactions and tend to involve lower transaction costs than investments in foreign currency-denominated assets. The implication is that an individual or institution holding dollars will invest in assets denominated in foreign currency only if there is a covered interest differential favoring foreign assets large enough to offset the higher transaction costs involved. In the presence of transaction costs, then, the interest gain from investing abroad relative to investing domestically must offset not only any exchange loss arising from covering the investment, but also the higher transaction costs they require.

The additional transaction costs of a covered foreign investment arise from the need to buy and sell foreign currency.[5] The cost of this round-trip currency transaction consists of two elements: the ask-bid spread and the brokerage fee. As noted in Chapter 3, the ask-bid spread represents the difference between quotes supplied by commercial banks to sell and buy foreign currency. By selling at a price higher than it buys, the banks provide for the overhead costs of the transactions (telephone and computer charges, salaries, etc.) and a profit. This is, of course, paid by the investor, whose returns from investing abroad are diminished. Because the spread varies by type of currency, for example, the cost of transacting in foreign exchange also varies.

In addition to the ask-bid spread, some customers may face brokerage fees. This might be the case, for instance, when the covered investments are made by a commercial bank that is short in the currency and has to purchase the required foreign currency spot from another commercial bank. Although the bank's foreign exchange traders may initially seek direct quotes from some other banks, they may also have to seek the aid of a foreign exchange broker in order to obtain the foreign currency. In that case, the broker will charge some fees for his or her services, which adds to the foreign exchange transaction costs of the commercial bank.

How important are these transaction costs in determining deviations from interest parity between U.S. and U.K. Treasury bills? Not too much. The available evidence suggests that, on average, less than 30 percent of the discrepancies from covered interest parity between U.S. and U.K. T-bills can be explained by transaction costs

---

[4]An additional cost is incurred if the securities are sold before they mature. This would be the case, for instance, when a 180-day Treasury bill is purchased and then sold in sixty days, before maturity.

[5]This assumes that the investor wishes to transfer his or her foreign currency returns back into dollars. However, the investor may not wish to convert back. This may be the case of a corporation that is going to use the proceeds of its investments to pay for some purchases of foreign goods in the future. Because the company has to pay in foreign currency for the purchases of those goods, it will in fact wish to hold foreign

currency at the end of the investment period. Because there is no need to transfer the foreign currency back into dollars, the transaction costs of covered interest arbitrage in this context— called one-way interest arbitrage—are lower than those for the two-way arbitrage on which we have focused. [See M. Bahmani-Oskooee and S. Das, "Transaction Costs and the Interest Parity Theorem," *Journal of Political Economy* (August 1985), 793–799; and A. V. Deardorff, "One-Way Arbitrage and Its Implications for the Foreign Exchange Markets," *Journal of Political Economy* (April 1979), 351–364].

(assuming that investors hold cash initially; if they were holding U.S. securities, the percentage explained by transaction costs increases, but minimally).[6] However, this percentage rises when periods of great turbulence in foreign exchange markets are considered. Many studies find that deviations from covered interest parity increase in such periods partly because commercial banks charge higher bid-ask spreads to incorporate the increased risk they take in trading currencies.[7]

The conclusion that, on average, transaction costs cannot explain major deviations from interest parity between the U.S. and the U.K. is what can be expected from a casual look at the foreign exchange and securities markets. The foreign exchange market, for example, involves such a huge volume of transactions that the resultant economies of scale, taken in conjunction with the relatively small number of currencies and instruments traded, give rise to high transacting efficiency and, hence, small costs. As a matter of fact, the banks and other large-scale institutions that constitute the core of the international money market face transaction costs frequently below one-tenth of 1 percent, a negligible amount.[8] Other factors also

affect the low costs of foreign exchange transactions, such as the lack of government intervention. Most contracts in the foreign exchange markets of industrialized countries are made initially through simple—although legally binding—verbal agreements, and they do not necessitate filling out forms or otherwise satisfying constraining government requirements and regulations.

Costs of Gathering and Processing Information

A second factor generating divergencies from interest parity involves the costs of gathering and processing information. In deriving the interest rate parity condition, it was implicitly assumed that the investor had free access to all necessary information about interest and exchange rates and that this information could be processed in a timely fashion in order to profit from investment opportunities. Information costs will introduce a gap between the returns made in different countries, depending on the differential availability and price of information. Nevertheless, information costs may not affect the parity condition significantly because the data-processing and telecommunications technological revolution has made information very cheap. It simply does not cost much to acquire and process information from all of the world's markets very rapidly. This is especially true of banks and large organizations, which are the day-to-day participants in the market.

Government Intervention and Regulation

Government intervention and regulation is a third factor influencing capital flows and generating deviations from covered interest parity. Government intervention comes in all forms and devices—among them, regulation of financial transactions, exchange controls restricting foreign exchange transactions, and differential tax treatment of various types of income. A common form of government intervention involves domestic in-

---

[6]See F. McCormick, "Covered Interest Arbitrage: Unexploited Profits? Comment," *Journal of Political Economy* (April 1979); and J. Frenkel and R. Levich, "Covered Interest Arbitrage: Unexploited Profits?" *Journal of Political Economy* (April 1975).

[7] This is found by M. P. Taylor, "Covered Interest Arbitrage and Market Turbulence," *Economic Journal* (June 1989), 376–391; and J. Frenkel and R. Levich, "Transaction Costs and Interest Arbitrage: Tranquil Versus Turbulent Periods," *Journal of Political Economy* (December 1977), 1207–1224.

[8]See R. Z. Aliber "Transaction Costs in the Foreign Exchange Market," unpublished manuscript (1984). Alternative estimates of transaction costs range from less than 0.1 percent to more than 1 percent of the value of the transaction. Be aware that there is no unique measure of transaction costs in foreign exchange markets. As discussed in Chapter 1, these vary according to the type of transaction, the specific currencies being traded, and the amount exchanged. For instance, transaction costs are higher for individuals and commercial firms engaging in international trade than for large international banks. The lower costs faced by banks, however, are particularly relevant for interest parity because banks are a predominant force in international money markets and interest arbitrage.

terest rate ceilings, which prevent domestic interest rates from rising above a certain level. Such regulations tend to create a gap between domestic and foreign rates of return and are thus frequently associated with covered differentials in favor of foreign currencies. The massive capital outflows such differentials would encourage are then avoided through the imposition of exchange controls; exchange controls limit purchases of foreign exchange and consequently restrict investment abroad. In this way, government intervention sustains deviations from covered interest parity.[9]

Differential taxation can also explain deviations from covered interest parity. For instance, before 1986, U.S. tax laws considered interest income as ordinary income for tax purposes. Foreign exchange gains obtained from covering transactions, on the other hand, were catalogued under the separate category of asset capital gains and taxed at the capital gains tax rate. Because the capital gains rate (about 20 percent) was far lower than the income tax bracket applying to a large corporation (about 50 percent), a corporate taxpayer would prefer to receive its income in the form of capital gains. This tended to generate deviations from covered interest parity. Consider the case of a U.S. corporation that was evaluating whether to invest in U.S. or Canadian assets. If the Canadian dollar was at a forward premium with respect to the U.S. dollar, this meant that part of the returns from covered Canadian investments would be obtained in the form of foreign exchange (currency) gains, taxable at the lower capital gains rate. Because all of the domestic interest gains are taxable at the higher corporate income tax rate, the American corporation would prefer to invest in Canadian securities, even if Canadian covered yields are lower than U.S. yields, as long as the tax benefit is sufficiently high. The U.S. Tax Reform

Law of 1986 introduced massive—and often complicated—changes in U.S. tax rules on international transactions. Foreign exchange gains or losses obtained from transactions in forward and futures markets are under sections 988 and 1256 of the law and most of them are now taxed as ordinary income or expense rather than capital gains or losses. The new regulations, however, are complicated and at times fuzzy; this has allowed some exchange gains or losses to remain subject to the capital gains tax rates.[10]

In conclusion, international rates of returns are significantly affected by tax rate considerations. When the relevant taxes are explicitly considered, deviations from covered interest parity may very well be consistent with equilibrium in international money markets, with the relatively low covered returns observed in one country being offset by tax benefits.

Financial Constraints and Capital Market Imperfections

The presence of margin requirements forces investors to set aside some funds when engaging in forward market transactions. As explained in Chapter 1, these margin requirements help ensure that investors satisfy their commitments in the forward market. At the same time, they impose an additional cost because the funds set aside cannot be optimally invested in interest-yielding assets. A covered interest differential in favor of foreign assets would not then be necessarily associated with unexploited profits, since it might be offset by the cost of margin requirements associated with covered foreign investments. As a result, and

---

[9]Evidence on this issue is supplied by: R.C. Marston, "Interest differentials under Bretton Woods and the Post-Bretton Woods Float: The Effects of Capital Controls and Exchange Risk," in M.D. Bordo and B. Eichengreen, eds., *A Retrospective on the Bretton Woods System* (Chicago: University of Chicago Press, 1993).

[10]For details on the subject of U.S. tax regulations governing foreign-source incomes and losses, see H. S. Engle and M. T. Campbell, "Foreign Currency and U.S. Income Taxes," in R. Z. Aliber, ed., *The Handbook of International Financial Management* (Homewood, Ill.: Dow Jones-Irwin, 1989), pp. 594–637. See M. D. Levi, "Taxation and 'Abnormal' International Capital Flows," *Journal of Political Economy* (June 1977), for an explanation of theintricacies of U.S. and Canadian tax laws at the time.

similar to transaction costs, forward market margin requirements give rise to a neutral band around the covered parity line.

Other factors may also work by preventing or restricting the entry of investment funds into areas with favorable covered differentials. The unavailability of liquid funds for investment purposes, for instance, may prevent traders from exploiting potential profit opportunities. The management of many commercial banks do impose limits on the amounts that foreign exchange and money market traders can use in their covered arbitrage operations with other banks. Once the "credit" limit facing the trader is filled, no further business can be conducted until the relevant outstanding liabilities mature. This, in effect, creates a preference for interest arbitrage in shorter maturities because credit limits are filled for shorter time periods. This allows the bank arbitrageurs to have funds with which to take advantage of any sudden profit opportunities. The implication is that covered interest arbitrage is not as extensive in long-term maturities, which may explain the puzzle that there appear to be wider deviations from covered interest parity when longer maturities are considered.[11]

Capital market imperfections may result in excess profits for those enjoying monopoly power. These will then be associated with persistent deviations from covered interest parity. Among major industrial countries, however, imperfections in the capital market and the availability of investment funds are expected to be relatively unimportant because (1) there is a large amount of funds available to investors both in national markets and through the Eurocurrency market (to be discussed in Chapter 8) ready to be shifted to the most profitable and/or less risky venture, and (2) given the size of both the securities and the foreign exchange markets in these countries, any investor is very small and, consequently, cannot influence

---

[11]See R. MacDonald and M. P. Taylor, "Interest Parity: Some New Evidence," *Bulletin of Economic Research* (October 1989), 255–274.

or manipulate prices to any significant extent. Of most markets, both the foreign exchange and the securities markets of industrial countries are among the most perfectly competitive. This is not the case in many developing economies. Both financial markets and foreign exchange markets remain relatively inefficient in a large part of the developing world. Although this is sometimes related to the low volume and thinness of markets in these countries, it is to a greater extent the result of tight government controls and regulation, as was explained in Chapter 3.

Noncomparability of Assets

The empirical evidence available suggests that the factors discussed to this point leave substantial unexplained deviations from covered interest parity. As it turns out, there is indeed a crucial source of measured deviations from interest parity that we have not yet mentioned. To introduce this factor, let us recall that when the covered parity condition was derived, it was made explicit that the rates of interest, i and i^*, should be for comparable domestic and foreign assets. This means they must be in the same category in regard to liquidity, maturity, and risk class, among others. A major source of measured deviations from covered parity arises precisely because of the differences among the assets being compared. Risk factors such as default and political risk are particularly significant in generating differences among otherwise identical assets.

Default risk represents the chance that the issuer of the asset under consideration will not satisfy all its commitments—such as not being able to pay interest or repay the principal on time or even at all. Of course, the higher the default risk of an asset, the higher the interest rate it would have to offer in order to compensate investors for the associated risk bearing. Consequently, a covered interest differential in favor of a given asset may just reflect the higher default risk class of that asset relative to the one with which it is being compared, and not any unexploited profit opportunities. To evaluate whether the covered interest parity condition holds, care must then be taken to ensure that the assets compared are strictly similar in terms of their default-risk category. If, for instance, the assets are relatively safe, such as U.K. and U.S. Treasury bills, the default risk problem is not important. By contrast, when comparing CDs issued by U.S. banks relative to those issued by foreign banks, the relative default risks involved must be carefully evaluated; the judgment as to whether there is any covered differential in returns among them should be based on risk-adjusted interest rates.

Even in the absence of issuer's default risk, political risk is unavoidable in a world of sovereign countries. In the next section, we discuss political risk, which is essential for correctly interpreting observed deviations from covered interest parity.

4–5. POLITICAL RISK AND INTERNATIONAL MONEY MARKETS

Political risks are those arising from the exercise of political sovereignty by the government of a given country. As such, they are linked to the political jurisdiction under which the assets are issued or held. Perhaps the first thing that comes to mind when political risks are mentioned is the possibility of outright expropriation, such as when U.S. assets abroad are nationalized, or the threat of an asset freeze, as when the Carter administration froze Iranian assets in the United States in 1979.[12]

Although expropriations and freezes are a widely talked-about form of government intervention, political risks need not reflect any dramatic political events. Rather, investors need only be concerned about whether the pertinent authorities will impose exchange controls between the date on which a foreign investment is made and the date of expected repatriation. Exchange controls are intended to impede or restrict foreign exchange transactions and block the transfer of funds across borders through legal sanctions. As a result of the imposition of exchange controls, many an investor has been stuck with foreign assets denominated in foreign currency that cannot be repatriated.[13] Changes in tax legislation and the restrictive regulation of internal financial transactions are still other sources of uncertainty related to political events.

Political risks arising from the possibility of expropriation, asset freeze, exchange controls, and other forms of government intervention and regulation cannot generally be eliminated in a world of sovereign countries because each reserves the right to engage in any of them. The extent to which firms are actually subject to these risks, however, varies widely from one country to another. Consequently, varying degrees of risk are associated with different political jurisdictions. It is clearly not a matter of indifference whether our assets are located in the United States, Kuwait, Switzerland, Britain, or Serbia.

How can investors protect themselves against political risk? The most obvious response is to

---

[12]The freeze meant that Iranian deposits held in the United States or with U.S. banks abroad could not be used to pay debts or be exchanged for other assets; the value of the assets frozen amounted to more than $12 billion. More recent freezes were imposed by President George Bush against Panamanian assets in the United States during the 1989 conflict with General Manuel Noriega, and by a group of countries against Iraq in August 1990 (according to the Bank for International Settlements, in 1990 Iraq had a total of $2.9 billion deposited in about eleven Western countries).

[13]Such was the case of many Americans who had invested in Mexico in the very early 1980s, attracted by interest rates of 25 and 30 percent on Mexican certificates of deposit. When the Mexican government took over the banking system in 1982, it imposed strict exchange controls, outlawing the export of U.S. dollars and devaluing the peso. Some American investors ended up losing hundreds of thousands of dollars in this debacle; a group of them sued the Mexican banks from which they had bought the CDs, but the Ninth U.S. Circuit Court of Appeals agreed to dismiss the lawsuits on the basis that the investors' losses were part of the risk they took when they opted to seek the high rates of return.

diversify by investing in many countries and to avoid investing in those countries that pose a serious threat or risk to financial transactions. Indeed, it is a crucial prerequisite for the development of any financial center not to impose undue restrictions on its guest investors and to prevent fears of restrictive government regulations or of major impediments to financial transactions. Multinational corporations hedge against political risk by purchasing political risk insurance. They spend hundreds of millions of dollars annually in political risk premiums, usually paid to government insurance plans like the U.S. government's Overseas Private Investment Corporation (OPIC). OPIC offers insurance against currency inconvertibility, expropriations, wars, and other adverse insurable events. Still, some residual political risk is unavoidable. The best an investor can hope for is to acquire or purchase reliable information and data regarding the political climate and potential risks of alternative locations or jurisdictions. Indeed, a whole array of political risk-assessment firms has arisen to provide such services to investors.

The implications of political risk for the analysis of international money market equilibrium are clear. Because political risks vary across political jurisdictions, assets such as CDs issued by New York and London banks are not strictly comparable. Similarly, U.S. and U.K. Treasury bills are not strictly comparable because they are, again, issued in financial centers that differ in political risk. This means that the traditional covered interest parity comparison involving dollar assets and foreign currency-denominated assets is not strictly valid. Covered interest rate differentials in favor of some asset may just imply that the asset carries political risk and bears a compensatory premium to attract investors.

In the face of political risks, how can a valid test of the covered interest parity condition be devised? The trick is to compare assets issued in the same political jurisdiction but denominated in different currencies.[14] This would be the case if dollar-denominated and sterling-denominated CDs were purchased in London or some other financial center. Such deposits are available through the Eurocurrency market. A Eurocurrency deposit is a deposit denominated in a currency different from the currency of the financial center in which the deposit is held. Eurodollars, for example, are dollar deposits held outside the United States (offshore), such as dollar deposits in London, Zurich, or Paris. The Eurocurrency market is a huge one. It encompasses bank deposits and loans, Eurobonds (bonds denominated in a currency different from the currency of the financial center in which the bond is issued, such as Euroyen bonds), and a variety of other financial instruments. The details on the growth of the Eurocurrency market will be discussed in detail in our discussion of the global nature of banking in Chapter 8.

Comparing the returns on Eurocurrency deposits in a particular location permits a comparison of assets similar in political risk but differing in terms of the currency in which they are denominated. The available evidence based on this comparison for the major industrialized country currencies indicates that political risk presently accounts for most of the observed gaps between the forward premium and interest differentials remaining after taking into account transaction costs. If dollar-denominated deposits and sterling-denominated deposits are compared in a given financial center, say, Paris, the discrepancies found between forward premia and interest rate differentials are much smaller than when U.S. dollar-denominated and U.K. sterling-denominated deposits are compared. The minor discrepancies from covered interest parity remaining can then be accounted for by transaction costs.[15] These results suggest that

---

[14]The importance of political risk can also be examined by comparing the returns offered by assets denominated in the same currency but located in different financial centers, such as the interest rates on dollar-denominated CDs offered in New York, London, and Paris. A full discussion of such comparisons is presented in Chapter 8, on the Eurodollar market.

[15]See R. Z. Aliber, "The Interest Rate Parity Theorem: A Reinterpretation," *Journal of Political Economy* (November-December 1973); and F. McCormick, "Covered Interest Arbitrage: Unexploited Profits? Comment," *Journal of Political*

(continued)

political risks are a crucial factor in international money markets and are indispensable to a correct analysis of international investments.

In summary, the available data on Eurocurrency interest rates indicate that once political risk and transaction costs are adjusted for, the covered interest rate parity condition does tend to hold approximately among the major industrialized countries. There is, thus, evidence that the covered parity condition is a key equilibrium relationship in international money markets. As such, it will be basic to our analysis in the rest of this book. Three obvious, but easily forgotten, points need to be stressed here. First, there are substantial observed deviations from covered interest parity when no adjustment is made for transaction costs and political risks. Second, the preceding analysis is concerned only with widely traded international money market instruments. Because of the latter qualification, it should be clear that international rate of return equalization does not apply to sheltered or nontraded assets—that is, to assets that are domestic and not significantly traded internationally, such as housing equity.[16] Our analysis does not imply that the rates of return on all local assets are linked to foreign rates of return in a rigid manner. It only suggests that there is a tendency for internationally traded assets to conform to the covered parity condition, once the latter is adjusted for transaction costs and political risk. Finally, barriers to capital flows and exchange controls, which can generate major deviations from covered interest parity, need to be factored in.

Economy (April 1979). It must be emphasized that, to measure unexploited profit opportunities in the real world accurately, the quotes used to measure exchange rates and interest rates must coincide in time. On this issue, see M. P. Taylor, "Covered Interest Parity: A High-Frequency, High-Quality Data Study," *Economica* (November 1987).

[16]As a matter of fact, claims on houses, such as mortgages and equity ownership, are traded internationally because foreigners participate in the mortgage market and buy domestic houses. Nevertheless, these assets, and particularly housing equity ownership, lack the liquidity and the low information costs of the assets more heavily traded in international money markets.

4–6. CURRENCY SWAPS AND COVERED INTEREST PARITY

The previous section established that deviations from covered interest parity using Eurocurrency data for industrialized country currencies are almost nil. This will not surprise anyone familiar with the forward trading techniques of banks. The reason is that banks quote forward rates among themselves, using the covered parity condition and Eurocurrency interest rates.

Forward transactions between banks and commercial customers are usually called outright forward transactions. The terminology emphasizes that the transaction is one involving only the forward market, such as a sale of pounds thirty-days forward made by the British bank Barclays to an American firm in London. On the other hand, forward market transactions among commercial banks mostly take the form of *currency swap* transactions. A swap contract involves the sale of a foreign currency spot with the agreement that the currency will be repurchased sometime in the future. For instance, Barclays may agree to sell a certain amount of pounds to Citibank and, at the same time, agree to repurchase the pounds for dollars at some time in the future. Barclays will then quote to Citibank its *swap rate,* which is the difference between the prices at which Barclays is willing to sell pounds on the spot and buy pounds in the future. Note that the prices at which Barclays is willing to repurchase pounds in the future is conceptually a forward exchange rate; the swap rate is, therefore, the difference between the forward exchange rate, F, and the spot rate, e, between the dollar and the pound.

Banks set swap rates in accordance with covered interest parity. Algebraically, using Equation 4–5, the swap rate is identically equal to

$$F - e = e(i - i^*),$$

where F is the forward rate, denoting the price at which one bank will buy back foreign currency in the future from another bank. In order to set the swap rate, bank traders are constantly looking at spot rates as well as Eurocurrency rates, which they use in place of i and i^*. This procedure implicitly sets the forward rate, F, at a level equal to

$$F = e + e(i - i^*). \qquad (4\text{–}6)$$

It is in this sense that commercial banks use covered interest parity in setting the forward rates implicit in their interbank swap transactions.[17]

Most of the interbank trade involving the future purchase and sale of currencies occurs in swaps. The latter account for close to 30 percent of the total turnover in the interbank foreign exchange market; outright forward transactions make up only 6 percent of the total. However, the interbank market is a spot-dominated market: Spot market transactions account for 64 percent of all transactions.

The interbank market in currency swap contracts represents a small part of a broader market in currency and interest rate swaps. As has been explained, a currency swap is an exchange of assets or liabilities denominated in one currency for assets or liabilities issued in another. An *interest rate swap* involves the exchange of fixed interest rate assets or liabilities for floating interest rate assets or liabilities. Currency swaps were the first innovation in the swap market and they are, therefore, the oldest of swaps. They became popular in Great Britain as a way of avoiding the exchange and capital controls in that country in the 1970s.

For an example of how currency swaps between firms work, consider the case of a British firm seeking $1 million to finance an expansion of its subsidiary operating in New York City. The firm could purchase the dollars directly, through the foreign exchange market. In the 1970s, however, the Bank of England had foreign exchange regulations that forced any British firm to pay an

expensive premium over market rates when buying dollars. To avoid this effective tax on the purchase of dollars, the British firm would order its New York subsidiary to seek an American firm with which to make a currency swap. The currency swap allowed the U.K. firm to obtain dollars without using the foreign exchange market directly. The swap works like this: The subsidiary issues $1 million worth of bonds to the U.S. company.[18] The British subsidiary thus receives $1 million from this issue. In exchange, the British company agrees to provide sterling financing to the subsidiary of the American company in the United Kingdom. It does so by buying sterling-denominated bonds issued by the American firm's subsidiary abroad. This transaction package is equivalent to an exchange of dollars for sterling without directly using the spot foreign exchange market.

Throughout the maturity of the bonds, the British subsidiary would make coupon interest-rate payments in dollars to the American firm, and the American subsidiary in London would make coupon interest payments in pounds to the British firm. When the bonds matured, the British subsidiary in the U.S. would pay back its obligation in dollars, while its parent company in London paid back its sterling bonds. The amounts of these repayments in dollars and sterling are known in advance. As in the case of forward contracts, when maturity comes, the British company would be converting a certain amount of dollars for a known

---

[17]An empirical analysis of covered interest parity using swap rates is presented by K. Clinton, "Transactions Costs and Covered Interest Arbitrage: Theory and Evidence," *Journal of Political Economy* (April 1988), 358–370.

[18]A bond is a long-term debt instrument. It represents "debt" in the sense that the buyer or holder of the bond actually lends the face value of the bond to the bond issuer. The conditions, or terms, of the loan made by the holder of the bond to the issuer are called the bond indenture. Their main provisions include the amount of the loan (the face value, or principal), a rate of interest (bonds are issued with a specified "coupon," or interest rate, set contractually for the life of the bond), a schedule or form of interest payments (interest on most bonds is paid every six months), and term of repayment (the maturity of the bond, the term of time until the principal is repaid). For details on the bond market, see New York Institute of Finance, *How the Bond Market Works* (New York: NYIF Corp., 1988).

amount of sterling. Hence, from the point of view of the British firm, the dollar payments and sterling receipts at maturity are equivalent to a forward sale of dollars. As we consider the sequence of operations, we see that the British firm effectively accomplished a spot purchase of dollars combined with a forward dollar sale. The transaction is thus a currency swap. Swaps are mutually beneficial for the firms involved. In the example just examined, the British firm found a way to acquire dollars without purchasing them through the controlled foreign exchange market; the American firm, in turn, also benefited from the swap because foreign-owned firms often encounter difficulties finding access to local financing abroad.[19]

The emergence of currency swaps highlights the creativity of international finance in the presence of restrictive government regulations, as well as the ultimate futility of such restrictions. The next section looks at the global trend toward the liberalization of financial markets in the last decade.

4–7. WORLD FINANCIAL LIBERALIZATION IN THE 1980s AND 1990s

Nothing has been more striking in revealing the integration of world financial markets in recent years than the simultaneous drop of equity prices in stock markets throughout the world during the so-called stock market crash of October 1987. The closing prices quoted on the New York Stock Exchange that day were closely linked to opening prices in Tokyo three hours later, and the Tokyo closing prices in turn sharply influenced the subsequent opening prices on the London Stock Mar-

ket. The structure of closing stock prices in London then sharply affected the opening prices on the New York exchange the following day. In a short period of time, under nervous worldwide observation, equity price indexes in every industrial country had declined between 20 and 30 percent.

The globalization of finance is reflected in the fact that, currently, one out of every seven equity trades involves a foreign party on one side or another. In the United States, 10 percent of all trading in equity takes place outside the country. This internationalization of finance has accelerated in recent years; in the period from 1984 to 1990, gross cross-border equity flows increased from approximately $300 billion per year to about $1.7 trillion.[20] It is the purpose of this section to document the marked liberalization of domestic and international financial markets that has resulted in the remarkable extent of global finance we observe today. Because Japanese cross-border investments have been the fastest growing during the last decade, we will present the case of Japanese financial liberalization in detail in section 4–8.

Table 4–2 shows the covered interest rate differentials for a sample of twenty-five countries. The differentials are displayed as we calculated them in Equation 4–4. They show the covered rate of return (annualized, in percentage form) in a particular country minus the Eurodollar rate of return (annualized, in percentage form). Negative (positive) covered differentials indicate that rates of return in the country are below (above) the Eurodollar rates of return. These may be explained by transactions costs if the differentials are below 1 percent (a conservative upper bound on transactions costs) or 0.5 percent (a more accurate upper bound on transactions costs among industrialized countries). Negative covered differentials that

[19]For a discussion of currency and interest rate swaps, see B. Solnik, *International Investments* (Reading, Mass.: Addison-Wesley, 1991), chap. 6; and J. Orlin Grabbe, *International Financial Markets* (Amsterdam: Elsevier Publishing Company, 1991), chap. 19. The World Bank has used currency swaps often in its financial activities; for details on these, see D. Bock and C. I. Wallich, *Currency Swaps: A Borrowing Technique in a Public Policy Context,* World Bank Staff Working Paper no. 640 (Washington, D.C.: World Bank, 1984).

[20]Figures cited by Richard Breeden of the U.S. Securities and Exchange Commission as quoted in L. Tesar in I. Werner, "Home Bias and the Globalization of Securities Markets," National Bureau of Economic Research, Working Paper No. 4218 (November 1992), p. 1.

TABLE 4–2. **Covered Interest Rate Differentials for a Sample of 25 Countries**

Group of Countries	Mean Covered Interest Differential
Australia	−0.75
Austria	0.13
Bahrain	−2.15
Belgium	0.12
Canada	−0.10
Denmark	−3.53
France	−1.74
Germany	0.35
Greece	−9.39
Hong Kong	0.13
Ireland	−0.79
Italy	−0.40
Japan	0.09
Malaysia	−1.46
Mexico	−16.47
Netherlands	0.21
New Zealand	−1.63
Norway	−1.03
Portugal	−7.93
Singapore	−0.30
South Africa	−1.07
Spain	−2.40
Sweden	−0.23
Switzerland	0.42
United Kingdom	−0.14

SOURCE: J. A. Frankel, "Quantifying International Capital Mobility in the 1980s," National Bureau of Economic Research Working Paper no. 2856 (February 1989), Table 6.

exceed in absolute value 1 or 0.5 percent are likely to be the result of governmental controls preventing the outflow of capital from the country being considered. Positive covered interest differentials indicate barriers to capital inflows or, alternatively, the presence of political risk in the country being considered.

The covered interest rate differentials in Table 4–2 are the average for each country from September 1982 to April 1988. Many of the less developed countries in the sample—like Mexico

and Greece—had covered interest differentials that could not be explained by transactions costs; they reflect the presence of barriers to capital flows (such as those present in the highly regulated structure of the nationalized Mexican banking system in this time period). By contrast, most European countries—such as Germany, Italy, and the United Kingdom—have covered interest differentials that can be explained by transaction costs. This is associated with a major liberalizing movement in Europe to allow greater freedom of cross-border financial capital. However, some European countries, like France and Spain, can be seen to have large covered interest rate differentials throughout the 1980s. The next section explains these differences.

The European Experience with Financial Liberalization

Europe's move toward greater openness in financial markets has involved a two-pronged attack. First, a number of reforms were introduced on the initiative of particular countries, as in the case of the United Kingdom. In addition, in 1992 the European Community as a unit solidified its stance on financial market restrictions by eliminating all controls on capital flows within the EC. The Europe 1992 program resulted in the dismantling of a variety of exchange controls and restrictions on capital flows.

This section surveys the European financial liberalization reform movement, focusing, for reasons of space, on a limited set of countries that were selected as representative of the great diversity of economic environments and regulatory reform in Europe. We begin with the British experience.

The experience of the United Kingdom with restrictions on capital flows dates back to the pre-1973 Bretton Woods regime, in which the restrictions were used to prevent major drains of foreign exchange reserves from the Bank of England. They remained in place in the 1970s and were finally eliminated in 1979 by the Thatcher administration.

The principal controls abolished in 1979 were of two types.[21] First, the government limited the holding by U.K. residents of foreign currency deposits to "working balances." This meant that, in spite of a growing Eurocurrency market located in London that offered currency deposits of all kinds at comparatively high interest rates, British residents were barred from acquiring Eurocurrency; only foreign residents could own Eurodollar or Euromark deposits in London. British residents were also restricted from investing abroad. The limitations stated that purchases of foreign currency for investment purposes by U.K. residents could only be made by selling any foreign securities they already owned or from foreign currency borrowing. This created, in effect, a dual currency market—international commercial transactions occurred at an official exchange rate, and a parallel, "investment currency" market traded the limited supplies of foreign exchange available for foreign investment purposes. In the latter market, the dollar was more expensive than its official value. The large premium relative to the official rate often reached the 30 to 50 percent range.

The restrictions on the flow of capital out of the sterling-denominated market created a surplus of investment funds in the United Kingdom and rates of returns that were below those in other countries or in other currencies. The fact that such a negative covered differential existed suggests that there were incentives to invest outside the country; however, because of the capital controls, funds could not flow across borders to exploit the differences in rates of return. Figure 4–3 shows the covered interest rate differential between investments in three-month sterling-denominated U.K. assets (onshore) and the three-month Eurodollar

(offshore) interest rate in London. The graph displays the covered differential as it is stated in Equation 4–4, which represents the rate of return on sterling-denominated U.K. assets minus the rate of return in Eurodollar assets. Algebraically, the plot shows $CD = f + i^* - i$, where i is the Eurodollar interest rate; i^* is the onshore, sterling-denominated interest rate; and f is the forward premium as defined earlier. Because the two assets are located in London they are both subject to identical political risk: The source of deviations from covered interest parity must then be mostly from the controls on capital outflows.

As can be seen from Figure 4–3, in the 1970s, the covered interest rate differential was systematically negative, with the rates of return on sterling assets sometimes substantially below the rates of return on Eurodollars. Only when the liberalization of financial markets occurred in 1979 did the covered interest differential move temporarily in favor of London and then decline toward zero. Deviations from covered interest parity are not significantly different from zero in the 1980s and 1990s, reflecting the great degree of capital mobility now facing the United Kingdom.

Another country that had substantial controls on capital outflows until recently was Italy. Until 1987, Italian residents were essentially barred from financial investments abroad. A zero-interest deposit requirement was imposed equal to 50 percent of the value of the foreign investment being made. This represented a huge tax that in effective terms destroyed the profitability of any legal foreign investments made by Italian residents, even if the investments had very high interest rates compared to Italian assets. Indeed, an analysis of covered interest rate differentials between lira-denominated and Eurodollar investments shows substantial deviations in favor of Eurodollar investments during this period.[22]

---

[21]We focus on the restrictions imposed on British residents. For a full discussion of the U.K. experience with exchange controls and their elimination, see M. J. Artis and M. P. Taylor, "International Financial Stability and the Regulation of Capital Flows," in G. Bird, ed., *The International Financial Regime* (London: Surrey University Press, 1990), pp. 163–196. The material in the text draws heavily from this article.

[22]See F. Giavazzi and A. Giovannini, *Limiting Exchange Rate Flexibility: The European Monetary System* (Cambridge, Mass.: MIT Press, 1989), chap. 7; and S. Micossi and S. Rossi, *(continued)*

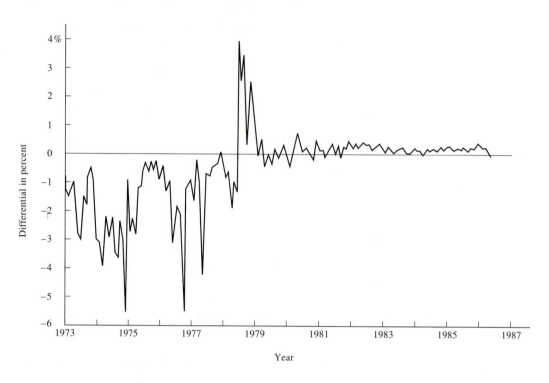

FIGURE 4–3.   Departures from Covered Interest Parity, United Kingdom, Before and After Deregulation in 1979

SOURCE: M. J. Artis and M. P. Taylor, "International Financial Stability and the Regulation of Capital Flows," in G. Bird, ed., *The International Financial Regime* (London: Surrey University Press, 1990), p. 179. Reprinted with permission.

The Italian restrictions on capital outflows were eliminated in May 1987, along with a number of other capital and exchange controls dismantled in recent years as part of the EC's 1992 program.

France also has a long history of exchange controls dating back to 1939. The most recent set of restrictions was imposed by President François Mitterand at the beginning of his term in 1981, as a result of massive capital flight linked to speculation about the policies that his Socialist government would impose. The system imposed by Mit-

terand was one in which a French resident could purchase foreign assets only from another French citizen. This, in effect, froze the total stock of foreign assets owned by French residents. The system was eliminated in the French liberalization of 1986, and all other remaining exchange controls were dismantled by January 1991, as part of the Europe 1992 initiative.[23]

The Belgian system of exchange controls, in place until very recently, is reminiscent of the exchange rate regimes imposed by developing countries discussed in Chapter 3. Belgium had a

"Restrictions on International Capital Flows: The Case of Italy," in I. Gordon and A. P. Thirlwall, eds., *European Factor Mobility: Trends and Consequences* (New York: St Martin's Press, 1989).

[23]For an analysis of the French liberalization process, see C. Wyplosz, "Capital Movement Liberalization: A French Perspective," *European Economy* (1986).

dual exchange market. In this regime, transactions in goods with the rest of the world had to go through the official market, which followed the rules established by the Exchange Rate Arrangement of the EMS. Financial transactions, however, had to go through a parallel market whose exchange rate was free floating. This meant that Belgian residents were free to make foreign investments, but to acquire foreign currency they had to go through the financial foreign exchange market. The financial prices of foreign exchange (in local currency) were usually relatively close to the official market rates, except during periods of EMS realignments.[24] As part of the liberalization associated with the Europe 1992 program, Belgium eliminated its dual exchange market in 1990.

In contrast to the European countries surveyed so far, German residents have not been subject to restrictions on foreign investments since the late 1950s. Some regulations existed limiting capital flows into that country, but these were also eliminated in the 1970s. By 1981, capital could flow into Germany without restrictions. In the case of Spain, controls on long-term capital flows began to be dismantled with the entry of that country into the EEC in 1986; the Spanish government substantially restricted short-term capital inflows in the late 1980s. These controls were associated with the growing presence of foreign capital in the country, attracted by the booming Spanish economy of the late 1980s (the boom extended into the early 1990s). The controls were short-lived. Spain dismantled them as part of the European 1992 financial integration process.[25]

4–8. JAPANESE FINANCIAL POWER AND WORLD CAPITAL MARKETS

Japan is the world's largest foreign investor. By the end of 1988, Japanese investors held $431 billion worth of foreign securities, compared with $157 billion in foreign securities held by U.S. investors, $176 billion by Germany, and $267 billion by the United Kingdom. A large part of Japanese investment is in the United States: more than 40 percent of Japan's net purchases of foreign securities were U.S. securities.[26] This is clearly visible in the substantial fraction of U.S. Treasury bonds that is sold to Japanese investors. In 1986, the "Big Four" Japanese securities firms—Nomura, Daiwa, Nikko, and Yamaichi—bought as much as 80 percent of new U.S. Treasury bonds at a bond auction; by the end of the 1980s, however, the yearly average was closer to 33 percent, and declining. It is also evident in the stock exchanges; the New York Stock Exchange is soaked with Japanese finance: two-thirds of Japan's total net foreign equity purchases have gone into the U.S.

This massive participation in world financial markets is partly related to the massive wealth that Japan has accumulated. By some estimates, Japan became wealthier than the United States in 1987: the value of Japan's holdings of stocks, bonds, deposits, insurance, production facilities, housing, land and inventories equaled $43.7 trillion, exceeding the $36.2 trillion worth of assets owned by U.S. residents.[27] This type of calculation should be taken with a grain of salt, however. International comparisons of wealth and income are not straightforward because there are differences in prices that make purchasing

---

[24]The relatively small gap in exchange rates can be explained by the presence of substantial leaks between the two markets, as discussed in Chapter 2; see D. Gros, "Dual Exchange Rates in the Presence of Incomplete Market Separation," *IMF Staff Papers* (September 1988).

[25]For a discussion of Spain's experience with financial liberalization, see J. Viñals, "Spain and the 'EC cum 1992' Shock," in C. Bliss and J. Braga de Macedo, *Unity with Diversity in the European Economy: The Community's Southern Frontier* (Cambridge: Cambridge University Press, 1990), pp. 145–234.

[26]For details on Japanese investments in foreign capital markets, see *World Financial Markets* (November 10, 1989).

[27]These numbers were reported by Japan's top economic daily, *Nihon Keizai Shimbun*, using figures from the U.S. Federal Reserve Board and Japan's Economic Planning Agency. See K. Phillips, *The Politics of Rich and Poor: Wealth and the American Electorate in the Reagan Aftermath* (New York: Random House, 1990), p. 117.

power in one country different from that in another. Converting figures from one currency to another may hide such differences in purchasing power and distort the comparison. In addition, Japan, experienced a great devaluation in both stock prices and land prices in the early 1990s. As a consequence, the value of Japan's wealth shrank considerably.

Japanese wealth was not totally responsible for the country's growing participation in global markets. In the 1970s and early 1980s, Japan's foreign investments were minimal compared to its wealth.[28] In 1983, for instance, nonofficial Japanese holdings of foreign securities were smaller than the United Kingdom's and about half the size of those of the United States (as noted earlier, by 1988 the holdings had risen to twice the U.S. stock of foreign investments). A central factor behind the explosion of Japanese foreign financial expansion in the 1980s was the revolutionary liberalization of Japanese restrictions over its financial system in the late 1970s and 1980s. Those changes are described next.[29]

Restrictions on Capital Inflows

In 1979, Japan had an extensive network of barriers to capital inflows and outflows. With respect to capital inflows, foreigners were not permitted to purchase many types of Japanese assets. The reasons for the controls varied. A common one was that the Japanese government feared that flows of capital into Japan would raise the demand for the yen, increasing the price of the currency in foreign exchange markets. The yen had substantially appreciated in value over the late 1970s, and the concern was that a further yen appreciation would result in a lower competitiveness for Japanese products in world markets.[30] The government reacted by preventing any significant capital inflows. In 1979, however, the yen depreciated against the dollar. In that year, the Japanese authorities quickly dismantled their controls on capital inflows, allowing foreigners to buy a wide array of Japanese securities, including yen-denominated bonds, yen-denominated *gensaki,* and yen-denominated CDs.[31] Capital inflows were liberalized further under the 1980 Foreign Exchange and Trade Control Law, which eliminated the requirement that foreigners obtain government approval for their investments in Japan.

Some restrictions on inflows remained in the form of limits on investments in many industries. These irked officials of the Reagan administration, who had been actively seeking the liberalization of restrictions on imports of foreign goods into Japan. The elimination of restrictions on the import of capital seemed to fit well with that administration's interest in "opening up" Japanese markets to foreigners, and they pressured Japanese officials on this account. After intense negotiation, a liberalization agreement was issued in November 1983 by Treasury Secretary Donald Regan and Japanese Finance Minister Noburu Takeshita. Most remaining restrictions on capital flows into Japan were

---

[28]For an examination of this and other issues regarding Japan's financial markets, see J. Frankel, "Japanese Finance in the 1980s: A Survey," in P. Krugman, ed., *Trade with Japan: Has the Door Opened Wider?* (Chicago: University of Chicago Press, 1991).

[29]A scholarly examination of Japanese finance is available in E. J. Elton and M. J. Gruber, *Japanese Capital Markets* (New York: Harper & Row, 1990) and J.A. Frankel, "Japanese Finance in the 1980s: A Survey," in P. Krugman, ed., *Trade with Japan: Has the Door Opened Wider?* (Chicago: University of Chicago Press, 1991). The number of popular books on Japanese finance has grown fast. A sample includes D. Burstein, *Yen! Japan's New Financial Empire and Its Threat to America* (New York: Simon & Schuster, 1988); and A. Viner, *Inside Japanese Financial Markets* (Homewood, Ill.: Dow Jones-Irwin, 1988).

[30]For a long-term analysis of yen exchange rates, see J. R. Lothian, "A History of Yen Exchange Rates," in W. T. Ziemba, W. Bailey, and Y. Hamao, eds., *Japanese Financial Market Research* (Amsterdam: Elsevier, 1991).

[31]The *gensaki* is a so-called repurchase agreement in which an investor agrees to purchase (or sell) an authorized bond for a specified duration under the agreement that the bond will be resold (repurchased) at an agreed-upon price. The differential between the sale and purchase prices establishes the rate of return, or yield, on the *gensaki.*

dismantled at that time, and unrestricted acquisition of all types of Japanese securities by Japanese nonresidents became possible, except for equity investments in certain areas.[32]

Restrictions on Capital Outflows

Restrictions on the investments of Japanese residents abroad existed throughout the 1960s and 1970s and were mostly eliminated by the early 1980s. Prior to 1970, Japanese residents were prohibited from purchasing foreign securities. That year the Ministry of Finance eliminated the restriction and the Asian Development Bank (an international development bank similar to the World Bank, headquartered in Manila) immediately offered ¥6 billion in yen-denominated bonds for sale to Japanese residents. Yen-denominated bonds floated in Japan by nonresidents seeking sources of finance in that country are called Samurai bonds. Selected regulations on investments abroad remained throughout the 1970s and were dismantled in 1980 under the landmark new Foreign Exchange and Foreign Trade Control Law (the old law, enacted in 1949 after World War II, heavily restricted cross-border trading and had been gradually liberalized over the years).

The process of liberalization described here has resulted in the intense integration of Japan's financial system with the outside world.[33] It underlies the upsurge of Japanese investments in the United States and elsewhere, which has received so much press attention. Alongside Japan's increased openness to international capital flows, there has been a movement of liberalization in the domestic financial system. Interest rates, for instance, had been highly regulated up to the 1970s. A slow process of liberalization in the late 1970s and throughout the 1980s led to a dismantling of interest rate ceilings. Currently, controls on interest rates remain only in certain areas, such as small, short-term deposits.[34] Other areas of financial regulation exist, but at levels comparable to those in other industrialized countries. Section 65 of Japan's Securities Exchange Act of 1948 prohibits banks from dealing in securities in a way similar to the separation of the banking and securities industries that the Glass-Steagall Act (also known as the Banking Act of 1933) imposed in the United States. This protects securities firms, such as Nomura, but it has created great opposition from the Japanese banking industry. Just as in the United States, banking lobbyists in Japan have been gathering force in their drive to reduce barriers between the securities and banking industries. So far, however, their progress has been limited: the Japanese securities industry is quite powerful and highly concentrated (the Big Four account for about 44 percent of all stocks transactions and 41 percent of all bond transactions). Indeed, the Big Four are not only the most powerful financial firms in Japan but they also rank among the world's leading, most profitable financial institutions. They are members of the New York Stock Exchange and of the select and prestigious group of primary dealers of Treasury securities that deal directly with the U.S. Treasury.

---

[32]For a discussion of the November 1983 agreement, see J. Frankel, *The Yen/Dollar Agreement: Liberalizing Japanese Capital Markets* (Washington, D.C.: Institute for International Economics, 1984).

[33]This is evident from the data in Table 4–2 and has been confirmed by many studies documenting the disappearance of the wide deviations from covered interest parity observed in the 1970s and early 1980s; see V. Vance Roley, "U.S. Money Supply Announcements and Covered Interest Parity," *Journal of International Money and Finance* (March 1987), 57–70; R. A. Feldman, *Japanese Financial Markets: Deficits, Dilemmas and Deregulation* (Cambridge, Mass.: The MIT Press, 1986); and I. Otani and S. Tiwari, "Capital Controls and Interest Rate Parity: The Japanese Experience, 1978–1981," *IMF Staff Papers* (December 1981).

[34]The economic and political details of the liberalization of Japan's domestic financial system are discussed by F. McCall Rosenbluth, *Financial Politics in Contemporary Japan* (Ithaca, N.Y.: Cornell University Press, 1989); H. Ueno, "Deregulation and Reorganization of Japan's Financial System," *Japanese Economic Studies* (Spring, 1988); and Y. Suzuki, ed. *The Japanese Financial System* (Oxford: Clarendon Press, 1987).

Summary

1. International money markets are the markets in which short-term claims are traded among countries.

2. Investing in foreign, vis-à-vis domestic, assets gives rise to exchange risk—that is, the risk involved in the chance that the value of the currency in which assets are denominated will fluctuate unpredictably. Investors can insure against such fluctuations by covering in the forward market.

3. The returns on covered foreign investments have two components: the nominal interest rate on the foreign assets purchased, i^*, and the gain (or loss) from purchasing foreign currency spot and selling it forward. The latter corresponds to the forward premium (or discount) on the foreign currency, f, and is referred to as exchange gain (or loss).

4. Because covering foreign investments results in possible exchange gains (or losses) aside from interest gains, when determining whether to invest in covered investments abroad or in domestic investments—with the same risk attached to each—the investment strategy with the highest return should be the choice, although it may not necessarily be the one with the highest interest rate.

5. The difference between the return on covered foreign investments and the return on domestic investments is called a covered interest differential, CD. If the nominal interest return on domestic assets is i, then $CD = i^* + f - i$. A positive (or negative) value of CD is referred to as a covered differential in favor of (or against) the foreign country; it suggests there are incentives to invest abroad (or domestically) relative to incentives to invest domestically (or abroad).

6. Equilibrium in international money markets will occur when covered differentials are equal to zero, representing the absence of unexploited profit opportunities in the movement of funds across borders. This implies that the forward premium on a foreign currency must be equal to the interest rate differential between domestic assets and the assets denominated in the foreign currency—that is, if $CD = 0$, then $f = i - i^*$. This is the covered interest parity condition.

7. Significant deviations from the covered interest parity condition can be observed. Such factors as transaction costs, costs of gathering and processing information, government regulation, financial constraints, and capital market imperfections all explain some of these deviations, but not nearly all.

8. Noncomparability of assets, especially political risk differentials, is a significant factor generating measured deviations from covered parity. Political risks arise from the exercise of political sovereignty by the government of a given country and might involve the possibility of asset expropriations or freezes and the unexpected imposition of exchange controls and other government regulations. A covered interest rate differential in favor of some asset might just imply that the asset carries political risk and bears a compensatory premium to attract investors.

9. In the absence of extensive government regulation, the covered interest parity condition tends to hold approximately, once adjustments are made for political risk and transaction costs.

10. A currency swap contract involves the sale of a foreign currency spot with the agreement that the currency will be repurchased sometime in the future. Most interbank trade involving the purchase and sale of currencies occurs in swaps. Banks use the covered interest parity condition in setting the forward rates implicit in their interbank swap transactions.

11. The last two decades have witnessed a major liberalization of international financial flows in the industrialized world and in some developing countries. This is reflected in declining

covered interest differentials. Among developing countries, however, serious barriers to capital flows remain.

12. The Japanese economy underwent a remarkable degree of financial liberalization in the 1970s and 1980s. This deregulation has resulted in the globalization of Japanese investments: Japan is the world's largest foreign investor.

Problems

1. Suppose that the U.S. dollar-pound sterling exchange rate equals $1.60/£, while the one-year forward rate is $1.64. The yields on one-year U.S. and U.K. Treasury bills are 9 and 8 percent, respectively. Calculate the covered interest differential, using the exact formula and the approximation represented by Equation 4–4. What is the difference between the two calculations? On the basis of these results, which country would you expect to face capital outflows? Capital inflows?

2. Using the data provided in Problem 1, suppose that an American investor is considering covered investments in U.K. Treasury bills that can be financed by borrowing at the U.S. prime rate of 10 percent. Would that investor be able to obtain net profits from his or her covered operations? Suppose that in addition to the borrowing costs, this investor also faces transaction costs that further reduce the gains from investing abroad by 0.75 percent. Would there now be net gains or losses from engaging in covered interest arbitrage? Explain your answer. Use approximations in this exercise, if you wish.

3. Consider the case of a British investor holding pounds initially and evaluating whether to invest in U.K. Treasury bills or in covered U.S. Treasury bills. Using the definitions presented in the text discussion—that is, F is the forward exchange rate of the sterling in dollars, e is the spot exchange rate in dollars per pound, i is the U.S. interest rate, and i^* is the U.K. interest rate—determine the U.K. returns and the covered U.S. returns per pound invested by the British investor. Show that, if U.S. and U.K. returns are equal, the covered interest parity condition derived in the text would again be obtained.

4. Consider a U.S. firm deciding whether to invest pounds locally or to undertake covered investments in Canada. Suppose that the Canadian dollar is worth $0.80, the one-year forward exchange rate is $0.84, and the U.S. and Canadian annual interest rates are 14 and 7 percent, respectively. The applicable tax rate on the corporation's income is 50 percent, while that on the firm's capital gains is 25 percent. Compute the post-tax returns on local (U.S.) investments (per U.S. dollar invested). Compute the post-tax returns on covered Canadian investments (per U.S. dollar invested). Which alternative investment yields the highest post-tax return? Would there be any difference if the investments being considered were thirty-day rather than yearly investments? (Hint: Are there any differences in the tax rates applicable to short-term and long-term capital gains?)

5. Suppose that you are working for Microprocessors Inc., an American computer firm that has to make a payment of $1 million worth of deutsche marks in one year. The firm has the $1 million in cash today and you are asked by your boss to compute the best way to invest this money in the coming year. Compare the rates of return per dollar invested in deutsche marks and in dollars, taking into account the fact that the $1 million has to be paid one year from today, in marks. State the covered interest parity condition in this case (involving one-way arbitrage).

CHAPTER 5

Exchange Rate Risk and Uncovered International Investments

Chapter 4 analyzed covered, or hedged, international investments, allowing us to show in full view the connection between forward exchange premia and interest rate differentials. This chapter moves on to examine uncovered, or unhedged, international investments. Uncovered investments involve taking open positions in foreign currencies; as a result, they are subject to—exposed to—the effects of exchange rate movements on their returns. This *exposure* to foreign exchange rate changes must be clearly understood: appar-

ently profitable foreign investments may actually not be so once the effects of exchange rate changes are taken into account. A depreciation of the currency in which assets are denominated, for example, can completely offset any advantageous yields they might offer.

The basic nature and dangers of widespread exposure to foreign exchange rate changes were made crystal clear to international money markets when, between June and October 1974, two major multinational banks, the Franklin National Bank of

New York and Bankhaus I. D. Herstatt of Germany, went under because of losses suffered from their open positions in foreign currencies. Franklin National, at that time the twenty-third largest bank in the United States, had an outstanding foreign exchange exposure of nearly $2 billion. Herstatt's was equal to $200 million. This massive exposure, combined with unanticipated exchange rate fluctuations, resulted in massive foreign exchange losses and subsequent bank failure. Less drastic and more frequent examples of exchange-related losses can be found in the day-to-day operations of participants in international money markets, whether bank traders, corporate executives, or individual investors.

But just as there are major losers from foreign exchange exposure, there are also those who have profited substantially. For instance, after the October 19, 1987 stock market crash, the largest U.S. financial institutions entered into foreign currency trading strategies based on speculation that the dollar would decline in value as a result of the crash. The bet turned out to be correct, and the profits of the nation's biggest banks boomed in the fourth quarter of 1987; Bankers Trust of New York, for instance, made $337 million in profits from its foreign exchange operations in that quarter, compared to $71.3 million in the third quarter. In September 1992, a month characterized by unusual turmoil in European currency markets, estimates are that speculators and commercial bank foreign exchange traders made profits of between $4 billion and $6 billion by betting against the ability of European central banks to prevent depreciations of the British pound, Italian lira, and Spanish peseta in that month. The expectations of the foreign exchange traders were realized because the currencies in question were indeed eventually devalued. One rumor has it that Citicorp's traders alone may have made $200 million in just one week during September 1992.[1]

This is the first of two chapters studying the economics of risk and return in international finance. This chapter examines the nature of the possible gains and losses from uncovered investments and its implications regarding the linkages among national interest rates. To shed light on these issues, the concepts of inflation risk, exchange risk, and international diversification are introduced, concepts at the core of the modern theory of international finance. Chapter 6 focuses on the formation of exchange rate expectations and the complexities of forecasting exchange rates. The available evidence on the extent to which forward exchange rates reflect anticipated future exchange rates is also considered.

5−1. INTEREST RATES, EXCHANGE RATE EXPECTATIONS, AND UNCOVERED INTEREST PARITY

The analysis of uncovered investments can best be introduced by abstracting initially from risk considerations. We can pretend that the investors under consideration are risk-neutral, in the sense that they have neither an aversion nor any preference toward risk taking and therefore base their investment decisions on factors other than risk. We will return to examine the questions of exchange risk and the plight of the risk-averse investor later in this chapter.

Suppose that a U.S. investor is considering whether to engage in uncovered foreign investments or to invest in comparable (i.e., same maturity) domestic assets. The rate of return on domestic assets is given by the domestic interest rate, i. On the other hand, the rate of return that the investor can anticipate to obtain from foreign

---

[1]As quoted by *The Wall Street Journal,* section C, p. 1, October 1, 1992. Commercial banks and corporations usually do not admit publicly that they engage in foreign exchange market speculation. Because of that, speculation is often referred to as being undertaken by the "gnomes" of Zurich. See R. Z. Aliber, *The International Money Game* (New York: Basic Books, 1988), chap. 4.

assets is composed of two parts: the foreign rate, i^*, and the expected rate of foreign currency appreciation—which is also the expected rate of domestic currency depreciation, x.

To visualize this, consider the following example involving dollar and pound-denominated assets. Suppose that the spot exchange rate between the dollar and the pound is given by $e = \$2.0/£$. If the one-year interest rate in the United Kingdom is 5 percent and you invest $200.00 (£100) in a pound-denominated asset, at the end of one year, you would then receive £105 (100 of principal plus 5 interest). In order to compare this return with what could be earned on a U.S. asset, however, you have to convert the pounds into U.S. dollars. If you expect the exchange rate to remain unchanged at its current spot level of $e = \$2.0/£$, the pound proceeds would be converted into $210.00 (£105 multiplied by $2.0/£). There would then be a 5 percent return on the U.K. investment. However, suppose instead that a variety of information sources has pointed to a depreciation of the dollar against the pound by 3 percent over the next year. This suggests that the exchange rate at which you can expect to convert pounds back to dollars in one year is $\bar{e} = \$2.06/£$. As a result, the dollar proceeds from the U.K. investment would be $216.30 (2.06 × 105). These proceeds correspond to about an 8 percent increase above the original investment of $200.00 and represent the sum of the 5 percent interest gain plus the 3 percent anticipated foreign exchange gain connected to the expected depreciation of the dollar. The implication is that the anticipated return on uncovered foreign assets involves the sum of the nominal interest rate abroad, i^*, plus the anticipated rate of depreciation of domestic currency, $x = (\bar{e} - e)/e$. The symbol $\bar{e}$ represents the expected exchange rate (in dollars per unit of foreign currency) anticipated to prevail when the investments mature.

As long as the rate of return on domestic investments exceeds the expected rate of return on foreign assets—risk considerations aside—the investor will shift funds toward domestic assets. Similarly, whenever expected foreign returns exceed domestic

returns, funds will be shifted abroad. Incentives for the movement of funds across borders are then absent only when domestic and foreign assets have equal expected returns. In other words, equilibrium in international financial markets suggests that differences in the expected returns obtainable from domestic currency-denominated investments and similar foreign currency-denominated investments will be arbitraged away and therefore cannot be sustained in any systematic way. Equality of rates of return then implies

$$i = i^* + x, \qquad (5\text{--}1)$$

where i and i^* represent domestic and foreign interest rates on comparable assets, and $x = (\bar{e} - e)/e$ is the anticipated rate of depreciation of the domestic currency.[2]

[2]Equation 5–1 involves a small approximation. To visualize this, consider the following example involving one-year investments. For each dollar invested in domestic assets, the return after one year would be given by $(1 + i)$, where i is the domestic rate of interest (annual). The return on foreign investment, on the other hand, is $(1 + i^*)\bar{e}/e$ per dollar invested. The latter is determined by the fact that each dollar will yield $1/e$ units of foreign currency, which, when invested abroad for one year, provide a return of $(1 + i^*)/e$ in foreign currency. When it is exchanged back into dollars, the anticipated dollar return from the foreign investment would be given by $(1 + i^*)\bar{e}/e$, where $\bar{e}$ is the exchange rate (in dollars per unit of foreign currency) which is anticipated to prevail one year in the future. In equilibrium, the expected return abroad must equal the domestic return, or $(1 + i) = (1 + i^*)\bar{e}/e$, which implies that $i = i^* + x + i^*x$, where $x = (\bar{e} - e)/e$ is the anticipated rate of change of the domestic currency during the next year.

The derivation of this last formula is similar to the one for interest parity in Chapter 4. Observe that Equation 5–1 is only an approximation because it neglects the term i^*x. This last term represents the anticipated foreign exchange gain or loss on the interest received from investing abroad; because it is usually the product of two small fractions, it yields a very small number. Its insignificance was seen in the U.S.–U.K. investment example in which the approximation involved in Equation 5–1 meant that the $216.30 return on the $200 invested abroad was approximately, but not exactly, an 8 percent return (the sum of the foreign interest rate, i^*, plus the anticipated exchange gain). The minor difference is accounted for by the term under discussion. However, for a sufficiently small investment period, the term becomes negligible and can be ignored.

Equation 5–1 is called the *uncovered interest parity* condition. It can be transformed into

$$i - i^* = x, \qquad (5–1a)$$

indicating that interest rate differentials among comparable assets denominated in different currencies represent anticipated exchange rate movements. Assets denominated in currencies that are expected to depreciate will have higher interest rates in order to compensate for the expected (currency) loss associated with the anticipated currency depreciation. If, for example, the foreign interest rate, i^*, is equal to 5 percent and there is an anticipated depreciation of the domestic currency, x, of 3 percent, then Equation 5–1(a) implies that the domestic interest rate, i, would have to equal 8 percent. There would thus be an interest differential in favor of domestic assets to compensate asset holders for their anticipated foreign exchange loss associated with the expected domestic currency depreciation.

5–2. PITFALLS IN THE TESTING OF UNCOVERED INTEREST PARITY

The discussion in Section 5–1 suggests that interest rate differentials are associated with anticipated exchange rate movements. What is the evidence for this? Are interest rate differentials between domestic and foreign assets equal to anticipated rates of depreciation of the domestic currency? In order to answer these questions, a measure of anticipated exchange rate changes must first be found—a very difficult task, as we will see.

As a starting point, hypothesize that people have perfect foresight and can correspondingly accurately predict exchange rate movements. In this case, anticipated exchange rate changes would be measured by the actual exchange rate movements that occur over time. The uncovered interest parity condition could then be tested by examining how closely interest rate differentials and actual exchange rate changes move together. An interest

rate differential in favor of domestic assets would be associated with domestic currency depreciation; a differential in favor of foreign assets would be linked to domestic currency appreciation.

Figure 5–1 shows this experiment for the case of U.S.-U.K. Treasury bills and U.S. dollar-pound sterling exchange rate changes. As observed, interest rate differentials fail to predict actual exchange rate changes accurately. In 1981 and 1982, for instance, the U.S. dollar generally appreciated in value relative to the pound. Still, over these two years, U.S. interest rates, i, generally remained above U.K. interest rates, i^*. According to the uncovered interest parity condition, an interest differential favoring the United States would be linked to an anticipated dollar depreciation. Similar results can also be found for more recent time periods and for other countries. What explains these prediction errors?

One basic reason for the failure of interest rate differentials to predict actual exchange rate changes is that people simply cannot be expected to have perfect foresight. A substantial part of exchange rate movements is completely unanticipated—and, hence, unpredictable. This unpredictability arises from the fact that exchange rates respond to changes in a variety of economic variables that cannot be perfectly anticipated. Loosely speaking, and as was noted in Chapter 2, in a floating exchange rate regime the exchange rate will adjust to changes in the demand and supply of domestic and foreign currency associated with international trade in goods, services, and assets. Factors that affect these transactions—such as changes in relative foreign and domestic asset supplies, income growth, and fluctuations in inflation—will all influence the exchange rate. Because it is generally impossible to forecast accurately how these factors change over time (try forecasting what the inflation rate will be next year and then compare it with the actual outcome!), there will clearly be a substantial degree of uncertainty as to the behavior of future exchange rates.

Actual exchange rate changes thus consist of a systematic component, which is predictable, and a

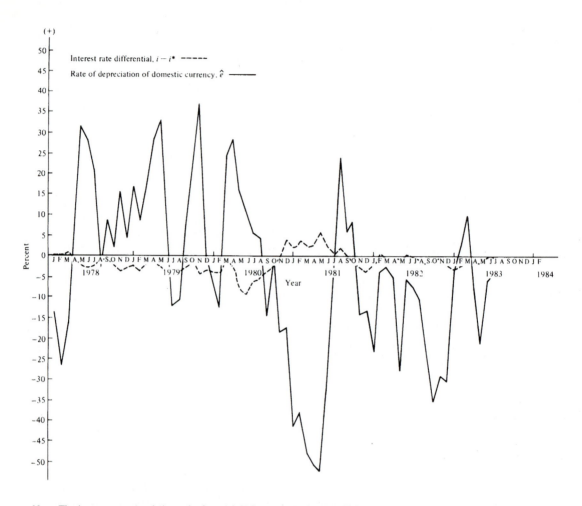

Note: The interest rates i and i^* are the 3-month U.S. and U.K. Treasury bill rates, respectively; the rate of domestic currency depreciation is the actual rate of depreciation of the dollar vis-à-vis the pound over the 3-month period corresponding to that of the Treasury bills considered. All variables have been annualized and expressed in percentage form.

FIGURE 5–1. Do Interest Rate Differentials Forecast Actual Exchange Rate Movements?

random component, which is unpredictable. Symbolically, this idea can be expressed as

$$\hat{e} = x + \hat{e}_u \qquad (5\text{--}2)$$

In this equation, $\hat{e}$ represents actual proportional exchange rates changes—that is, at time t, $\hat{e}_t = (e_{t+1} - e_t)/e_t$, where e_t is the exchange rate at time

t and e_{t+1} is the exchange rate one period later. By the same token, $x_t = (\bar{e}_{t+1} - e_t)/e_t$ is the anticipated domestic currency depreciation at time t, where $\bar{e}_{t+1}$ is the exchange rate anticipated to prevail at time $t + 1$. Finally, $\hat{e}_u$ denotes unanticipated exchange rate movements expressed in proportional terms—that is, at time t, $\hat{e}_{ut} = (e_{t+1} - \bar{e}_{t+1})/e_t$.

In this situation, it is apparent that even if interest differentials do coincide with anticipated currency depreciations—as given by uncovered interest parity—they will not necessarily be closely associated with actual currency depreciations. Using the uncovered interest parity condition, $x = i - i^*$, as expressed by Equation 5–1(a), to substitute for the anticipated rate of depreciation of domestic currency in Equation 5–2, yields

$$\hat{e} = (i - i^*) + \hat{e}_u, \qquad (5\text{–}3)$$

which clearly shows how actual proportional exchange rate changes, $\hat{e}$, and interest differentials, $i - i^*$, diverge by the presence of unanticipated exchange rate movements, $\hat{e}_u$, even if uncovered parity holds. In conclusion, in order to test adequately whether uncovered interest parity holds, it is necessary to be able to measure anticipated exchange rate changes. The use of actual exchange rate changes as a measure of anticipated currency value changes is incorrect because there is a substantial degree of uncertainty in future exchange rate movements; participants in money markets can thus not be expected to be endowed with perfect foresight. We are then back to the problem of measuring anticipated exchange rate movements.

To anticipate what the exchange rate will be at a certain moment in the future, participants in international financial markets often use the forward exchange rate for the delivery of currency at that time. As we discussed in Chapter 1, the forward premium can be visualized as a predictor of exchange rate changes; hence, it can be used as a proxy for the anticipated rate of depreciation of the domestic currency. Symbolically,

$$f = \frac{F - e}{e} = \frac{\bar{e} - e}{e} = x, \qquad (5\text{–}4)$$

where f represents the forward premium, e is the current (spot) exchange rate, and $\bar{e}$ represents the anticipated future exchange rate. Equation 5–4 states that a possible proxy for the anticipated rate

of change of the domestic currency value over a given period is the corresponding forward premium. Thus, if the forward premium accurately represents the expected rate of change of the domestic currency value, uncovered interest parity $i - i^* = x$ reduces to the covered interest parity condition $i - i^* = f$ because, as we saw in Chapter 4, once transaction costs and political risk are adjusted for, the covered parity condition $i - i^* = f$ does tend to hold. The suggestion is then that the uncovered parity condition would hold as well—an inference, however, that is highly misleading.

The forward premium does not necessarily present an accurate picture of the anticipated rate of domestic currency depreciation because it also reflects the existence of a risk premium, which we have so far ignored in this discussion. The following sections examine the nature of this risk premium.

5–3. REAL RATES OF RETURN AND INFLATION RISK

Up to this point, investors have been assumed to be risk-neutral—that is, indifferent to the riskiness of different assets. More generally, however, individuals are sensitive to differences in risk. In particular, the traditional assumption made in financial economics is that investors tend to be risk-averse. People are risk-averse when their preferences are such that they have an inherent dislike for uncertainty and have to be compensated with higher returns in order to bear greater levels of risk. The relative attractiveness of foreign assets when compared to domestic assets thus depends not only on their expected returns, but also on their riskiness vis-à-vis their domestic counterparts. Foreign assets with expected returns equal to domestic assets, but entailing much greater variability, may not be as attractive as domestic assets.

There are many sources of differences in risk between domestic and foreign assets. One important source of relative riskiness is associated with differences in the default assessment of foreign relative to domestic assets; another is political risk, related to the likelihood that assets in a particular country may be confiscated. Assuming, however, that foreign and domestic investments with the same default and political risk characteristics are being compared, are there any particular differences in risk associated with uncovered foreign investments relative to domestic investments? The answer to this question is a resounding yes, and the particular risk involved is called foreign exchange risk or simply *exchange risk*. The following discussion is intended to clarify the role played by exchange risk in the portfolio decisions of the international investor.

Defining Real Rates of Return

The first thing to understand in determining the nature of foreign exchange risk is that investors are concerned with the *real* interest rate offered by an asset. The (domestic) *nominal* interest rate is the rate of return of any given interest-bearing asset in terms of domestic currency. For example, if you invest $100.00 in a U.S. certificate of deposit and earn $5.00 after a period of one year, the nominal interest rate is equal to 5 percent because that is the amount of U.S. dollars you net at the end of the year as a proportion of the original investment.

The (domestic) *real interest rate,* on the other hand, is the rate of return on any given asset in terms of its purchasing power in domestic goods. For instance, if during the year that you invest that $100.00, the prices of goods in the economy increase by 5 percent, the real interest rate would be equal to zero. The nominal gain in interest of 5 percent keeps pace just exactly with the 5 percent loss of purchasing power during the year. As a result, the $105.00 you have at the end of the year is worth, in terms of domestic goods, as much as the $100.00 was worth one year before. The real rate of return on the asset was reduced to zero by inflation.

Using symbols, the real rate of return on domestic assets, r, is equal to the domestic nominal interest rate, i, adjusted by the rate of inflation, $\hat{P}$, or

$$r = i - \hat{P}. \tag{5-5}$$

For example, if the nominal annual rate of return on domestic assets is equal to $i = 5\%$ and the annual domestic inflation is $\hat{P} = 3\%$, the real rate of return on holding domestic assets would be 2 percent ($r = 5\% - 3\%$).

In addition to evaluating the real return on domestic assets, the international investor will also evaluate the real return obtained by holding foreign assets uncovered. This return is composed of three parts. First there is the nominal interest rate on the foreign assets, i^*, which is a return denominated in foreign currency. Then there is the gain or loss obtained from the purchase and sale of foreign currency at the start and end, respectively, of the foreign investment period. This return arises from the appreciation (or depreciation) of the foreign currency in the period in which foreign assets were held uncovered; it is represented by the proportional rate of increase of the exchange rate, $\hat{e}$. The sum of the nominal foreign interest rate and the foreign exchange gain (loss) is equal to the return on the uncovered foreign investment in terms of domestic money (i.e., dollars). If domestic inflation, $\hat{P}$, is adjusted for, the real rate of return on the holding of uncovered foreign assets, r^*, is obtained. Symbolically,

$$r^* = i^* + \hat{e} - \hat{P}. \tag{5-6}$$

If, for example, the foreign annual nominal interest rate is $i^* = 10\%$, the domestic currency depreciates by $\hat{e} = 5\%$ during the year the foreign assets are held, and the domestic inflation rate for that period is $\hat{P} = 3\%$, the real rate of return on holding foreign assets uncovered is $r^* = 10\% + 5\% - 3\% = 12\%$. Note that in adjusting for inflation, the foreign uncovered rate of return is adjusted by the rate of *domestic* inflation (and not the foreign inflation $\hat{P}*$). The reason is that domestic investors generally use their investment returns to enjoy greater consumption. On the assumption that domestic investors reside domestically (technically called their local habitat) and do not intend to emigrate within the investment period, they will spend their interest income on goods whose overall prices are given by the domestic price index. Because the rate of increase of domestic prices is domestic inflation, it represents the loss of purchasing power facing domestic investors.

Anticipated Real Returns

In evaluating the real rates of return in Equations 5–5 and 5–6, note that nobody knows exactly what the domestic inflation rate will be in the future. Therefore, real interest rates cannot be completely determined beforehand. An estimate, or forecast, of what the inflation rate will be can be made, however, in order to calculate the *expected real* interest rate, $\bar{r}$. The expected real interest rate is the ex-ante rate of return that is anticipated by the investor. Symbolically, the anticipated (ex-ante) real rate of return on domestic assets is

$$\bar{r} = i - \pi, \qquad (5\text{–}7)$$

where π is the expected rate of inflation in the economy.

Equation 5–7 is commonly called the Fisher equation in honor of the economist Irving Fisher, who stressed its importance in monetary economics. If the nominal annual rate of return on domestic assets is $i = 5\%$ and domestic inflation is anticipated to be 1 percent over the next year, then, from the Fisher equation, the real rate of return that you can expect, ex ante, to receive from holding domestic assets in one year would be $\bar{r} = 4\%$ (equal to 5% minus 1%). Observe that, insofar as you fail to predict future inflation accurately, this ex ante real rate will generally differ

from the actual real rate of return realized by the investor. For instance, if, in our example, the actual inflation rate turns out to be $\hat{P} = 5\%$ in the next year instead of the $\pi = 1\%$ that was anticipated, the (realized) real rate of interest would be $r = 0\%$, while the (ex-ante) expected real rate was $\bar{r} = 4\%$. Because you failed to forecast inflation accurately, you end up holding an asset with a real return of 0 percent instead of the higher anticipated real yield of 4 percent. The implication is that, in the presence of uncertainty regarding rates of inflation—that is, in the presence of *inflation risk*—real rates of return on domestic assets cannot be perfectly anticipated and will generally be unpredictable. Domestic assets thus provide an unpredictable real return.

The real rate of return on uncovered foreign investments will also be subject to uncertainty both because future domestic inflation is not known precisely and because future currency values cannot be predicted accurately in advance when exchange rates are fluctuating. (Recall Equation 5–6, which represents the real return on uncovered foreign investments.) As a result, in assessing the returns on foreign investments, investors must forecast how inflation and the exchange rate will behave. The ex ante (expected) real return on uncovered foreign investments, $\bar{r}*$, can then be defined by

$$\bar{r}* = i* + x - \pi, \qquad (5\text{–}8)$$

where x denotes, as before, the anticipated rate of depreciation of domestic currency and π the expected rate of domestic inflation. Equation 5–8 simply states that the ex ante real return on uncovered foreign assets is equal to the nominal interest gain plus the anticipated foreign exchange gain adjusted by the anticipated domestic rate of inflation.

In general, both inflation and exchange rates are unpredictable and, therefore, foreign real rates of return, $r* = i* + \hat{e} - \hat{P}$, will be uncertain. It should be stressed, however, that a priori presumptions that uncovered foreign investments are more uncertain than domestic real returns are to be avoided. The variabilities of domestic inflation and of the exchange rate are not necessarily additive. Because these variables can be positively correlated (associated) with each other, the variability of exchange rate changes minus domestic inflation, $\hat{e} - \hat{P}$, may be lower than the variability of domestic inflation, $\hat{P}$. This would make the real returns on uncovered foreign investments less variable than those of domestic investments. The next section examines this issue in more detail.

5–4. RELATIVE INFLATION RISK, EXCHANGE RISK, AND CAPITAL FLIGHT

That the real return on uncovered foreign investments can be less uncertain than that of domestic investments is not always well appreciated. Frequently the reason is because of an overemphasis on the exchange rate fluctuations to which uncovered investments are subject—that is, the inaccuracy of anticipated exchange rate changes—and a failure to recognize the inflation risk from which domestic assets suffer.

To understand how uncovered foreign investments might entail less uncertain real returns than domestic assets, let us return to compare equations 5–5 ($r = i - \hat{P}$) and 5–6 ($r^* = i^* + \hat{e} - \hat{P}$). As observed in Equation 5–5, the unpredictability of domestic real returns is associated with unanticipated domestic inflation, while the unpredictability of the real return on uncovered foreign assets is connected to inflation *and* exchange rate variability. Superficially, this might be taken to suggest that uncovered foreign investments are generally more uncertain than domestic assets: After all they are subject to the whims of the foreign exchange market. This is misleading. It is easy to visualize how uncovered foreign investments can yield less uncertain real returns than domestic investments. Note that if the rate of domestic currency depreciation and domestic in-

flation move together, in the same direction, the effect of each of these on foreign real returns would tend to offset each other. This would leave the variability of the term $\hat{e} - \hat{P}$ in Equation 5–6 with a smaller degree of variability than that of $\hat{P}$ or $\hat{e}$ alone. For example, in the extreme case where the rate of depreciation (or appreciation) of the domestic currency, $\hat{e}$, is exactly matched by domestic inflation, $\hat{P}$, the real return on uncovered foreign investments would remain unchanged—in spite of the fluctuation in the exchange rate—and thus would be perfectly predictable. Algebraically, because the term $\hat{e} - \hat{P}$ would always be equal to zero (no matter how uncertain the exchange rate changes are, they would always be matched by an equal change in domestic inflation), the real return on uncovered foreign investments, r^*, will coincide with the nominal interest rate, i^*, which is a determinate return, known exante.

Observe that, in this case, the domestic real interest rate still fluctuates unpredictably because of the uncertain domestic inflation. Domestic assets would then be relatively uncertain, as compared to the uncovered foreign investments, which would be safe. By moving funds abroad in this situation, the investor could hedge against domestic inflation risk. This point has not escaped the attention of citizens in countries with highly unpredictable inflation relative to U.S. inflation. They frequently shift their funds to dollar-denominated assets in the United States precisely because of this, a phenomenon called *capital flight*.[3]

When a resident of Mexico leaves his or her wealth in Mexican peso-denominated assets, there

---

[3]The terminological difference between capital flight and general capital outflows is subtle, and sometimes the two terms are used interchangeably. In the present context, we adopt the definition used by Donald R. Lessard and John Williamson, to the effect that "capital flight is 'money that runs away' or 'Flees' [due to] . . . the level of domestic risk perceived by some or all residents," in *Capital Flight: The Problem and Policy Responses* (Washington, D.C.: Institute for International Economics, 1987), pp. 2–3. Capital outflows associated with high relative domestic inflation risk certainly fall into this category.

is the possibility that the peso returns will be completely eroded by unanticipatedly high inflation. If, on the other hand, Mexican inflation were always to be associated with the same proportional depreciation of the peso (an appreciation of the dollar), the investor could insure against the uncertainty about Mexican inflation by investing in dollar-denominated assets. If Mexican inflation turns out to be unanticipatedly high, the Mexican peso will fall in value in the same proportion vis-à-vis the dollar; or, what is the same, the value of the dollar will rise relative to the peso in the same proportion. By holding dollar-denominated assets, the Mexican resident gains from the increased value of the dollar because when he or she shifts funds back into Mexico each dollar will be exchangable for a larger amount of pesos. This gain then compensates for the reduced purchasing power of the peso caused by the unexpectedly high Mexican inflation. Real returns in this case would then be completely unaffected by the Mexican inflation. In other words, foreign investments serve as a hedge against the uncertain inflation that might be suffered at home.[4]

The example takes the extreme case in which domestic inflation and the proportional rate of depreciation of the domestic currency (the rate of appreciation of the foreign currency) are always equal. Although this will not generally be the case, there is considerable evidence of instances in which prices and exchange rates do tend to move in the same direction. This phenomenon was true of Brazil, as presented in Table 5–1. This table shows the monthly rate of depreciation of the new cruzado vis-à-vis the dollar in 1989 and January 1990 and compares it to the rate of inflation in the same month. The depreciation of the new cruzado (Brazil's currency at the

TABLE 5–1. The Positive Correlation Between Brazilian Inflation and New Cruzado Depreciation Versus the Dollar

Month		Brazilian Inflation Rate	Rate of New Cruzado Depreciation
1990	January	56.1%	56.1%
1989	December	53.5	54.2
	November	41.4	41.0
	October	37.6	37.6
	September	36.0	35.5
	August	29.3	29.4
	July	28.8	42.6
	June	24.8	31.7
	May	9.9	11.7
	April	7.3	3.2
	March	6.1	0.0

$$\text{Inflation} = \frac{P_t - P_{t-1}}{P_{t-1}},$$

$$\text{Rate of Depreciation} = \frac{e_t - e_{t-1}}{e_{t-1}},$$

where P_{t-1} is the consumer price index at time $t - 1$, P_t is the consumer price index at time t, e_{t-1} is the exchange rate at the end of month $t - 1$, and e_t is the exchange rate at the end of month t.

SOURCE: Wharton Econometric Forecasting Associates Group, *Latin America Monthly Economic Report* (February 1990).

time) was positively associated with Brazilian inflation. In some months the relationship was very close, as in January 1990, when inflation was 56.1 percent and the peso depreciation versus the dollar was 56.1 percent. In other months the association between the two variables was somewhat looser.[5]

---

[4]For an analysis and evidence showing how relative inflation risk may explain capital flight in Latin America in the 1970s and 1980s, see J. Cuddington, "Capital Flight: Estimates, Issues and Explanations," *Princeton Studies in International Finance,* No. 58 (December 1986); and F. Rivera-Batiz, "Modeling Capital Flight from Latin America: A Portfolio Balance Approach," in W. G. Vogt and M. H. Mickle, eds., *Modeling and Simulation* (Pittsburgh: University of Pittsburgh and Instrument Society of America, 1986).

[5]The question arises as to why, if domestic-currency denominated assets are riskier than foreign-currency denominated assets, the domestic interest rate cannot adjust in such a way as to eliminate the incentive to move funds abroad. One factor is the presence of controls over interest rates. These controls impede domestic interest rates from rising under conditions of high inflation or increased domestic risks. Even when domestic interest rates can adjust, the gains from portfolio diversification will lead to capital flight.

It is possible to conclude that, in order to say something definite about the uncertainty of uncovered foreign investments relative to domestic assets, the degree of association, or *correlation,* between exchange rate movements and price changes must be known. The following section provides a brief introduction to the issues involved.

5–5. PURCHASING POWER PARITY AND THE CORRELATION BETWEEN EXCHANGE RATES AND PRICES

One of the best-known and most debated relationships in international economics has been and remains the so-called purchasing power parity (PPP) doctrine. It establishes a connection between exchange rates and differences among domestic and foreign price levels.[6] In its simplest form, the hypothesis starts by postulating that domestic prices, P, and foreign prices, $P*$, are connected by the following relationship, also often referred to as the law of one price:

$$P = eP*, \qquad (5–9)$$

where e is the exchange rate (say, dollars per unit of foreign currency). If, for example, the price of an automobile in the United Kingdom is $P* = $ £5,000 and the dollar-pound exchange rate is $e = \$2.00$ per pound, Equation 5–9 suggests that the price of an auto in the United States would be $P = \$10,000$. No matter where you purchase the car—the United States or the United Kingdom—once you convert into the same currency the price will be the same (hence the name purchasing power parity).

---

[6]The purchasing power doctrine has a long historical tradition in international economics. Its intellectual origins can be traced to the writings of David Ricardo and J. Wheatley in the early nineteenth century and to Gustav Cassell, C. Bresciani-Turroni, and others in the early twentieth century. We will examine PPP in detail as a theory of exchange rate determination in Chapters 16 and 19.

The PPP relationship is often justified by observing that if it did not hold, profits could be made by the simple movement of goods across borders. For instance, in our earlier example, if autos were actually to cost $P = \$12,000$ in the United States, anyone could potentially make $2,000 in profits by shipping U.K. automobiles—which cost $10,000—into the United States and selling them for $12,000. The result would be a massive shipment of autos into the United States, as profit-minded entrepreneurs sought to obtain the $2,000 per car. However, the increased supply of autos flooding the U.S. market would reduce U.S. auto prices. So long as the prices in the United States remained above those in the United Kingdom, the arbitrage would continue and the flood of autos into the United States would keep U.S. auto prices going down until they were aligned with the dollar price of U.K. autos. At that point, the profits from shipping more autos from the United Kingdom to the United States would become zero and the arbitrage would end. The equilibrium outcome in the market would thus be PPP. This example suggests that, in an open economy, unfettered market forces would pull domestic prices, P, into alignment with foreign prices converted into domestic currency, $eP*$, as given by Equation 5–9.

It must be stressed, though, that the presence of transportation costs, government barriers to trade—such as customs duties and import quotas—and other factors can prevent the law of one price from holding. The PPP relationship can be generalized to encompass situations in which the law of one price does not hold precisely, but international prices will still exhibit a stable relationship to each other. The generalized version is expressed by the equation $P = \alpha eP*$, where α represents the stable gap between the dollar price of domestic and foreign goods. For a stable α, domestic and international prices do not equalize exactly, but P and $eP*$ are proportional to each other. It then becomes clear that proportional changes in foreign prices (foreign inflation), $\hat{P}*$, and proportional changes in the exchange rate, $\hat{e}$, will have to be matched by equal proportional changes in domestic prices (domestic inflation), $\hat{P}$. For instance, if foreign inflation runs at 3 percent and foreign currency appreciates by 5 percent, domestic prices must increase by 8 percent to keep prices in a stable relationship. This relationship between price and exchange rate changes is called the *relative version* of PPP, to distinguish it from the law of one price, which is also often referred to as the *absolute version* of PPP.

The relative version can be expressed algebraically by taking the proportional changes in Equation 5–9, which yields

$$\hat{P} = \hat{e} + \hat{P}*, \qquad (5\text{--}10)$$

with $\hat{P}$, $\hat{e}$, and $\hat{P}*$ representing—as before—domestic inflation, the rate of domestic currency depreciation, and foreign inflation, respectively—all specified over the same, given time period.

Equation 5–10 can be transformed to show

$$\hat{e} = \hat{P} - \hat{P}*, \qquad (5\text{--}11)$$

which illustrates the basic connection between exchange rate changes and inflation rates implied by PPP: high domestic inflation relative to foreign inflation is associated with a domestic currency depreciation. If, for example, U.S. inflation were to equal 12 percent, $\hat{P} = 12\%$, over a certain period of time, and U.K. inflation were to equal 2 percent, $\hat{P}* = 2\%$, over that same time period, then according to PPP the dollar-pound exchange rate would have to rise by $\hat{e} = \hat{P} - \hat{P}* = 10\%$.

The connection between proportional exchange rate movements and inflation levels determined by the PPP relationship in Equation 5–11, $\hat{e} = \hat{P} - \hat{P}*$, can be substituted into the expression for the real return on uncovered foreign investment given by Equation 5–6, $r* = i* + \hat{e} - \hat{P}$, to yield

$$r* = i* - \hat{P}*. \qquad (5\text{--}6a)$$

In other words, with PPP, the real rate of return on uncovered foreign investments becomes equal to the foreign real interest rate—that is, the foreign nominal interest rate adjusted for foreign inflation. The unpredictability of foreign inflation—that is, foreign inflation risk—will then be associated with the uncertainty of real returns on uncovered foreign investments. Because the uncertainty in domestic real returns is linked to domestic inflation risk—see Equation 5–5: $r = i - \hat{P}$—differences in the riskiness of foreign relative to domestic investments will be related to differences in foreign and domestic inflation risk. In the extreme case in which foreign inflation risk is absent but domestic inflation risk is uncertain, uncovered foreign investments will then be a less risky investment compared to domestic assets.

5–6. DIVERSIFICATION AND THE DETERMINANTS OF ASSET RISK

It has been shown that differences in inflation risk among countries tend to generate differences in the variability attached to the real returns of domestic and uncovered foreign investments.[7] Within this context, risk-averse investors will

---

[7]In addition, once deviations from PPP are allowed for, further divergences in uncertainty will arise between the holding of domestic and uncovered foreign assets in the form of *real exchange rate risk*. Deviations from PPP imply that Equation 5–11, $\hat{e} = \hat{P} - \hat{P}*$, does not hold exactly, but rather that $\hat{e} = \hat{P} - \hat{P}* + u$, where u represents unpredictable deviations from PPP. Substitution of this relationship into the definition of the real interest rate on uncovered foreign investments in Equation 5–6 yields $r* = i* - \hat{P}* + u$. In the absence of deviations from PPP (with $u = 0$) it is foreign inflation risk that makes real returns on uncovered investments uncertain. On the other hand, unpredictable deviations from PPP will also affect the uncertainty of the real return on uncovered investments, as reflected by the variability of the u term. The term *real exchange rate risk* comes from the fact that u represents proportional changes in the real exchange rate, $e_r = (eP*)/P$.

generally diversify their asset holdings—that is, their portfolio. Just as you would avoid "placing all your eggs in the same basket," asset holders will diversify their portfolios in order to reduce the risks attached to only one type of asset. In our context, holding domestic and foreign-currency denominated assets can serve the important function of reducing investors' portfolio risk below what they would bear if they could only hold domestic assets.

For investors that diversify internationally—hold domestic and foreign assets—assessing the effects of uncovered foreign investments on the risk of their portfolio becomes crucial. If, for instance, adding the uncovered foreign investment results in an increase in the overall risk of the investors' portfolio, the investor must be compensated for this increased risk. Risk-averse investors will require a risk premium to compensate them for the increased risk of their uncovered undertakings. If, on the other hand, investors are already holding highly risky portfolios and the uncovered foreign investments reduce the portfolio's overall riskiness, the foreign investments will then be associated with a negative risk premium (a discount), in the sense that the investors will be willing to pay a certain amount to obtain the reduced portfolio risk.

The magnitude of the exchange risk premium, or discount, attached to acquiring assets uncovered in a particular currency will depend on the extent to which the foreign investments increase or reduce the overall risk of the investors' portfolio.[8]

This is related, first of all, to how much the foreign real returns are correlated with the returns of the investors' portfolio. Suppose, for instance, you are holding only two assets: domestic assets and those of country X. If the real returns on uncovered investments in the currency of country X rise when domestic real returns drop, then holding the foreign assets reduces the variability of the investors' portfolio and, therefore, they would have a risk discount attached. The greater the negative covariance between the returns on the foreign and domestic assets—that is, the greater the extent to which their variations offset each other—the lower the variability of the investors' portfolio and, consequently, the larger the risk discount on the foreign assets.

In this two-asset case, the determinants of a foreign asset's risk premium can be decomposed into three factors.[9] The first is the covariance between domestic and foreign returns. The second, determining the magnitude of the risk premium (discount), is related to the variability of the real returns of the foreign compared to domestic assets. The greater the variability of the foreign assets' real returns compared to domestic investments, the more investors have to be compensated to hold them and the larger the risk premium. Similarly, the lower the relative variability of the foreign assets' returns, the smaller the risk premium (or the higher the risk discount) that will be attached to them. The third factor influencing risk premia is the degree of risk aversion—that is, the magnitude of the investors' compensation in order for them to take any given additional amount of risk. Other

---

[8]There are two approaches to the determinants of the exchange risk premium. The first approach follows traditional mean-variance finance theory applied to an international finance and open-economy macroeconomics context and is often referred to as portfolio balance approach. It has been discussed by R. Dornbusch, "Exchange Rate Risk and the Macroeconomics of Exchange Rate Determination," in R. Hawkings, R. M. Levich, and C. Wihlborg, eds., *The Internationalization of Financial Markets and National Economic Policy* (Greenwich, Conn.: JAI Press, 1983); and W. H. Branson and D. Henderson, "The Specification and the Influence of Asset Markets," in R. W. Jones and P. B. Kenen, eds., *Handbook of International Economics,* vol. 2 (Amsterdam: North Holland, 1985). The second approach is based on a general equilibrium approach to asset markets. It has been formulated by R. Lucas, "Interest

Rates and Currency Prices in a Two-Country World," *Journal of Monetary Economics* (November 1982); and R. J. Hodrick and S. Srivastava, "An Investigation of Risk and Return in Forward Foreign Exchange," *Journal of International Money and Finance* (March 1984). Although the two approaches obtain similar results regarding the relevance of covariances, relative variances, and risk aversion in determining the risk premium, they do differ in the assumptions used to derive those results and the nature of the underlying uncertainty facing consumers or investors.

[9]See Dornbusch, ibid.

things constant, the greater the degree of risk aversion, the larger the premium that will be attached to investments that are relatively risky: Investors request higher compensation for taking those risks.[10]

In summary, whether a particular foreign-currency denominated investment bears a risk premium, or discount, depends on whether it adds or subtracts from the risk of the investors' portfolio of assets. Because the nature of the risk premium (or discount) involves the increased (reduced) riskiness associated with uncovered foreign investments, it is usually referred to as a foreign exchange risk premium (discount), or simply as an exchange risk premium. The consequences of the exchange risk premium in analyzing uncovered interest parity—and related issues—are examined in the next section.

5–7. THE EXCHANGE RISK PREMIUM AND DEVIATIONS OF THE FORWARD PREMIUM FROM THE ANTICIPATED RATE OF DOMESTIC CURRENCY DEPRECIATION

The existence of an *exchange risk premium* (or discount) deeply influences forward market equilibrium and thus the determination of the forward premium. Because they bear different risks, there will generally be a discrepancy between the return on uncovered foreign investments, $i^* + x$, and the return from covered foreign investments, $i^* + f$. If the uncovered investments increase (reduce) portfolio risks, the expected returns on the uncovered foreign investments will have to be higher (lower)

than returns from covered investments by the amount of the risk premium (discount), to compensate risk-averse investors for increased (reduced) risk taking. Note that the interest gains are the same for both uncovered and covered investments because both have received the foreign interest rate, i^*. The differential in expected returns between the two associated with risk premia thus gives rise to a divergence between x and f—that is, between the expected exchange gain from holding foreign assets uncovered (equal to the anticipated rate of depreciation of the domestic currency, x) and the exchange gain from holding foreign assets covered (equal to the forward premium, f).

The presence of a risk premium creates a wedge between x and f, implying that financial market equilibrium will occur at a point where the anticipated rate of appreciation of foreign currency, x, exceeds (or is exceeded by) the forward premium, f, by the amount of the risk premium (discount). Symbolically, this relation is represented by

$$x = f + R, \qquad (5\text{–}12)$$

where R represents the risk premium, or discount, attached to the acquisition of foreign assets in the absence of covering.

The foreign exchange risk premium is positive if foreign investments increase investors' portfolio risk. In that case, the expected exchange gain from uncovered foreign investments, x, must exceed the exchange gain from covered investments, f, by the risk premium R to compensate (risk-averse) investors for their increased risk taking. For instance, if the foreign currency has a 2 percent risk premium attached, the anticipated appreciation of the foreign currency would have to exceed the forward market exchange gain by 2 percent in order to compensate for the excess risk in holding the foreign currency uncovered.

A negative value of R, on the other hand, means that uncovered foreign investments reduce the investors' portfolio risk. As a result, the exchange

---

[10]Note that when investors can acquire assets denominated in a variety of foreign currencies, random exchange rate movements that can be diversified away by holding many of these currencies—so that negative and positive disturbances to real returns offset each other—do not offer any exchange risk in an economic sense. It is so-called *systematic,* or nondiversifiable, fluctuations—fluctuations that cannot be diversified away by holding many currencies—that matter in terms of generating exchange risk (that is, systematic exchange risk) and that are, therefore, relevant for portfolio decisions.

gain from covered investments, *f,* will be larger than the anticipated exchange gain from uncovered foreign investments, *x,* by the risk discount. Finally, if the foreign investments do not add or subtract from investor portfolio risk, the exchange risk premium, *R,* will be zero and the forward premium will equal the anticipated rate of depreciation of the domestic currency.

The existence of a foreign exchange risk premium, or discount, means that forward premia and anticipated rates of domestic currency depreciation will not be equal; as a result, the first cannot be used as a proxy for the second. The validity of covered interest parity thus cannot be used to infer the validity of uncovered interest parity. The problem in comparing the two is easily visualized by substituting *f* from Equation 5–12, $x = f + R$, into the covered parity condition $i - i^* = f$, which results in

$$i - i^* = f = x - R. \qquad (5\text{–}13)$$

Equation 5–13 implies that uncovered interest parity, $i - i^* = x$, is not a general condition in a risky world; that is, deviations from uncovered parity may be associated with the existence of a risk premium, or discount. Note that, given the domestic interest rate, *i,* and the larger the value of the risk premium, *R,* the higher the foreign interest rate, *i*,* would have to be to compensate for the higher risks of uncovered investments. Interest rate differentials may thus reflect expected exchange rate changes (through *x*) or risk premia (or discounts) on foreign assets (through *R*).

It is, of course, possible that the risk premium is relatively small anyway, and that interest rate differentials and the forward premium are still approximately equal to the anticipated rate of foreign currency appreciation (domestic currency depreciation). The behavior and magnitude of foreign exchange risk premia, or discounts, has been an area of intense research in international finance for a few years now. The available empirical evidence has yielded many results uncovering the

nature of exchange risk premia. At the same time, various competitive approaches have emerged, jolting the subject into dispute and controversy. The next chapter provides an introduction to the issues involved in specifying risk premia and in testing Equations 5–12 and 13.

Summary

1. The uncovered interest rate parity condition states the equality of the interest rate differential between domestic and foreign assets and the expected rate of depreciation of domestic currency. Because expectations are unobservable, this condition is not directly testable.

2. Interest rate differentials are not accurate predictors of exchange rate changes. The gap between interest rate differentials and exchange rate changes frequently rises to more than 10 percent on a quarterly basis, or to 50 percent if the gap is annualized.

3. Investors are concerned with the real rates of return on assets. The realized real rate of return on domestic interest-bearing assets is the nominal interest rate minus the domestic inflation rate. The real rate of return on uncovered foreign investments is the foreign interest rate plus the proportional rate of change of the exchange rate minus the domestic inflation rate. The anticipated, or ex ante, real rates of return are calculated in a similar manner but utilize anticipated inflation and expected exchange rate changes. For domestic assets, the ex ante real interest rate is equal to the nominal interest rate minus the anticipated inflation, called the Fisher equation.

4. In determining the variability of domestic real returns, the domestic inflation risk attached to these investments must be considered. The variability of the real return on uncovered foreign investments is related to the variability of exchange rates, as well as to the variability of domestic inflation. The variance of uncovered returns, however, can be lower than that of com-

parable domestic investments if exchange rates and prices are positively correlated.

5. The law of one price, also called the absolute version of purchasing power parity (PPP), states that domestic prices will equal foreign prices when the latter are converted into domestic currency. It is hypothesized that the forces of arbitrage will align prices in different countries to satisfy the law of one price. The relative version of PPP states that the domestic inflation rate equals the sum of the rate of depreciation of domestic currency and foreign inflation. Relative purchasing power parity establishes a positive correlation between exchange rate changes and domestic inflation (given the level of foreign inflation).

6. Domestic and foreign inflation risk—that is, the unpredictability of inflation—as well as real exchange rate risk are associated with the variability attached to the real returns of domestic and foreign investments. Investors respond to these risks by diversifying their portfolios and by capital flight out of countries with highly variable inflation.

7. The presence of an exchange risk premium invalidates the uncovered interest parity as a general condition of international money markets. In general, domestic minus foreign interest rate differentials correspond to the anticipated rate of appreciation of the foreign currency minus the risk premium on the foreign currency. Covered and uncovered interest parity conditions coincide only if the risk premium is zero.

8. The exchange risk premium on a foreign currency depends on the co-variability between the real returns on foreign and domestic currency-denominated assets, their relative variability, and the degree of investors' risk aversion.

Problems

1. You are told that the annual interest rate of U.S. Treasury bills is 12 percent, while that of Canadian Treasury bills is 6 percent. The U.S.-Canadian dollar exchange rate at the time is equal to 0.80 U.S. dollars per Canadian dollar. Assuming that the uncovered interest parity condition holds, what do you think is the market's assessment of the U.S.-Canadian dollar exchange rate one year in the future? Do you see any problems with this calculation? Explain your answer.

2. Suppose that both covered interest parity and the relative version of PPP hold exactly. Domestic inflation runs at 10 percent and domestic currency is depreciating at the rate of 5 percent. Both are expected to continue changing at the current rates. The domestic nominal interest is 8 percent. What are the values of the foreign nominal and real interest rates? Do nominal and real interest rates equalize internationally? Why or why not?

3. In many Latin American economies, local residents hold dollars. Often, local banks do not accept dollar deposits and, therefore, the person does not earn any interest on his or her dollar holdings. Still, the phenomenon—called currency substitution—is very widespread. Adopt the perspective of a local resident in Mexico who expects the peso to depreciate by 20 percent versus the dollar (in our terminology: $x = 0.20$, where x is the expected rate of peso depreciation versus the dollar). If the local interest rate in Mexico available to the Mexican investor is 18 percent ($i^* = 0.18$), would it pay that resident to invest in acquiring dollars, even if he or she cannot take them out of Mexico and cannot earn interest on them? (Assume that local residents can freely acquire dollars through black markets.)

4. Based on a survey you have made of the expectations of international finance professors, you find that this group anticipates that the dollar will depreciate versus the yen by 20 percent in the next year ($x = 0.20$). From some banks, you calculate that the one-year forward premium on the yen is negative (there

is a discount on the yen) and it is equal to 5 percent ($f = 0.05$). Assuming that you compare assets with the same default and political risk characteristics, what can you infer from your data about the exchange risk premium (or discount) on yen-denominated assets?

5. During late January 1993, there were growing expectations in European financial markets that the Irish punt would be devalued in the ERM. In fact, the front page of *The Financial Times* on January 29, 1993 had as one of its headlines: "Fears grow for punt devaluation." Assuming increased expectations of punt depreciation (and holding other things constant), would you have expected financial capital to flow into or out of Ireland during this time period? What consequences could these capital flows have on the ERM? (Hint: the Irish punt was indeed devalued.)

CHAPTER 6

Exchange Rate Forecasting, Risk Premia, and Forward Market Efficiency

Chapter 5 specified the role played by exchange risk in the determination of interest rate differentials between domestic and foreign assets. It also established that exchange risk premia, or discounts, generate a wedge between anticipated exchange rate changes and forward premia, possibly making the latter an inaccurate indicator of market expectations about future currency values. In this chapter, we look at the evidence available on the significance of risk premia in international finance. The formation of exchange rate expectations is intimately linked to this topic; thus, we will examine how actual participants in foreign exchange markets forecast exchange rates. We use this data to determine the extent to which forward exchange rates reflect anticipated future exchange rates. This is a major issue in international finance, as the forward premium is seen and used by many as an easily available, inexpensive way of getting a forecast of future currency values. We also look at how optimal exchange rate forecasts are made and whether the behavior of forward and spot exchange rates is consistent with this type of forecasting.

6–1. THE RISK PREMIUM AND THE WEDGE BETWEEN THE FORWARD PREMIUM AND ANTICIPATED EXCHANGE RATE CHANGES

The existence of an exchange risk premium (or discount) creates a wedge between the anticipated rate of currency appreciation of a foreign currency and the forward premium on that currency. Symbolically, this relation is represented by

$$x = f + R, \qquad (6-1)$$

where x is the anticipated rate of foreign currency appreciation (equal to the rate of domestic currency depreciation), f is the forward premium on the foreign currency, and R represents the risk premium, or discount, attached to the acquisition of foreign assets in the absence of covering. As established in Chapter 5, financial market equilibrium will lead to the equality in Equation 6–1— that is, to the point where the anticipated rate of appreciation of foreign currency, x, exceeds (or is exceeded by) the forward premium, f, by the amount of the risk premium (discount), R.

The exchange risk premium is positive if foreign investments increase investors' portfolio risk. In this situation, the expected exchange gain from unhedged foreign investments, x, must exceed the exchange gain from hedged investments, f, by the exchange risk premium, R, to compensate (risk-averse) investors for their higher risk bearing. For example, if the foreign currency is bearing a 5 percent risk premium, the anticipated appreciation of the foreign currency would

have to exceed the forward market exchange gain by 5 percent to compensate the asset holder for the excess risk involved in acquiring the foreign currency uncovered.

A negative value of the exchange risk premium, R, on the other hand, means that acquiring unhedged foreign assets reduces the investors' portfolio risk. Therefore, the exchange gain from covered or hedged investments, f, will exceed the anticipated exchange gain from uncovered or unhedged foreign investments, x, by the risk discount. Finally, it is possible that the foreign investments do not add or subtract from investor portfolio risk, in which case the exchange risk premium, R, will be zero and the forward premium will equal the anticipated rate of depreciation of the domestic currency.

If a foreign exchange risk premium, or discount, is found to be significantly different from zero, this means that forward premia and anticipated rates of domestic currency depreciation will not be equal; as a result, the first cannot be used as a proxy for the second. In order to assess how much the forward premium deviates from the anticipated rate of currency depreciation and the significance of the risk premium in explaining such deviations, one must first understand how exchange rate expectations are specified or measured. There are two approaches to this: the *survey-based* approach and the *rational-expectations-based* approach. The survey-based approach uses the actual exchange rate expectations of experts involved in financial markets, as supplied by financial service firms that survey those individuals. The rational-expectations-based approach, on the other hand, does not look directly at survey measures of exchange rate expectations in evaluating Equation 6–1, but assumes that investors in the market follow the expectational implications of the so-called rational expectations hypothesis. The next section discusses the survey-based approach. The rational-expectations-based approach will be discussed in Sections 6–4 and 6–5.

6−2. SURVEY-BASED EXCHANGE RATE EXPECTATIONS AND ESTIMATES OF THE RISK AND FORWARD PREMIUMS

The survey-based approach uses data on the reported forecasts of individuals and experts involved in the foreign exchange market (such as foreign exchange advisory services, bank traders, financial analysts, and monetary officials). The forecasts are collected from data gathered by an array of services. *The Economist,* for example, has published its *Economist Financial Report* since 1981; it periodically reports the results of a survey of the three-month, six-month, and twelve-month expectations (forecasts) of future dollar exchange rates made by fourteen leading international banks. Money Market Services (MMS) of California publishes another set of exchange rate expectations of a sample of thirty professional services. Godwins of London conducts surveys of about fifty leading investment managers, and the Japan Center for International Finance (JCIF), a private institution affiliated with Japan's Ministry of Finance, surveys forty-four market participants in Tokyo regarding the dollar-yen exchange rate.[1]

Survey data on exchange rate expectations can be used directly in Equation 6−1, in combination with the forward premium, to determine, as a residual, the risk premium. Symbolically, the risk premium, R, is equal to the gap between the anticipated appreciation of the foreign currency and the forward market premium,

$$R = x - f. \qquad (6-2)$$

In order to supply an estimate of R, we obtain an estimate of x from survey data; the value of f can

be calculated from actual data on forward and spot exchange rates for the time periods corresponding to the survey-based exchange rate forecasts.

Table 6−1 shows the decomposition of the forward premium (discount, if negative) in terms of the anticipated rate of currency depreciation and the risk premium for a variety of currencies and time periods. Consider, for example, the first row in Table 6−1. The row considers MMS-based data involving expectations of the dollar-pound exchange rate one month in the future. It indicates that from October 1984 to February 1986, the pound was expected to depreciate (the dollar was expected to appreciate versus the pound) by 11.91 percent ($x = -11.91$), corresponding to a forward discount of 3.85 percent ($f = -3.85\%$) and a risk discount of 8.06 percent on holding uncovered pound-denominated assets ($R = -8.06\%$). The suggestion is that, although the pound was anticipated to depreciate sharply versus the dollar during this time—by 11.91 percent—the forward discount was comparatively small—only 3.85 percent—because of a high risk premium on holding U.S. assets relative to uncovered U.K. assets (i.e., the pound entailed a risk discount).

Looking at the overall pattern for the various forecasts in Table 5−2, note that the yen was anticipated to appreciate relative to the dollar (thus, the dollar was expected to depreciate—that is, x is positive). The pound sterling was sometimes anticipated to depreciate and at other times to appreciate versus the dollar. The forward premium followed the direction of exchange rate expectations, with the currencies that were expected to appreciate versus the dollar also having a positive forward premium. In this sense, then, the forward exchange rate does reflect, but only partially, the participants' expected exchange rate movements.

The quantitative link between the forward premium on a foreign currency and its anticipated rate of appreciation is tenuous because of the presence of substantial risk premia. Furthermore, the link

[1] For more details on these surveys (and an excellent review of the studies based on them), see S. Takagi, "Exchange Rate Expectations: A Survey of Survey Studies," *IMF Staff Papers* (March 1991).

TABLE 6–1. **The Relationship Between the Forward Premium on Foreign Currencies Versus the Dollar, Expected Exchange Rate Changes, and the Risk Premium**

Data	Currency	Horizon	Dollar Expected Depreciation (expected appreciation if negative)	Forward Premium (on the listed currency)	Imputed Risk Premium (on the listed currency)
			x	f	$(R = x - f)$
MMS[a]					
10/84–2/86	Pound	1 month	−11.91	−3.85	−8.06
	Mark		−2.26	3.23	−5.49
	Yen		2.29	1.68	1.31
1/83–10/84	Pound	3 month	4.46	0.37	4.09
	Mark		8.33	4.68	3.65
	Yen		8.68	3.85	4.83
Economist[a]					
6/81–12/85	Pound	3 month	3.66	−0.06	3.72
		6 month	4.19	0.14	4.05
		12 month	3.38	0.36	3.02
	Mark	3 month	11.84	4.36	7.48
		6 month	12.39	4.35	8.04
		12 month	10.67	4.24	6.43
	Yen	3 month	12.66	4.67	7.99
		6 month	12.94	4.74	8.20
		12 month	10.67	4.66	6.01
Godwin[b]					
1/81–7/85	Pound	12 month	−6.41	−0.79	−5.62
JCIF					
5/85–2/87	Yen	3 month	5.00	1.52	3.48
		6 month	−0.40	1.64	−2.04
2/87–7/89	Yen	3 month	9.20	3.64	5.56
		6 month	5.20	3.64	1.54

Note: The figures are for average annualized logarithmic changes in basis points (close to percentage changes).

[a]The source for these numbers is J. Frankel and K. A. Froot, "Using Survey Data to Test Propositions Regarding Exchange Rate Expectations," *American Economic Review* (March 1987).

[b]The source for these numbers is M. P. Taylor, "Expectations, Risk and Uncertainty in the Foreign Exchange Market: Some Results Based on Survey Data," *Manchester School of Economics and Social Studies* (June 1989).

SOURCE: S. Takagi, "Exchange Rate Expectations: A Survey of Survey Studies," *IMF Staff Papers* (March 1991), table 3.

between f and x is complicated by the fact that risk premia appear to vary significantly over time and with the term over which forecasts are made. For instance, consider the data from the JCIF survey of dollar-yen exchange rate expectations from May 1985 through February 1987 and February 1987 through July 1989. Looking at the figures based on expectations six months into the future, the yen risk premium is negative in the 1985–1987 period—equal to $R = -2.04\%$—but it becomes positive in the 1987–1989 period, shifting to $R = 1.54\%$. The MMS survey indicates similar shifts over time.

An issue that arises when utilizing survey data to measure exchange rate expectations is that, by using the average expectation among survey participants, we give the impression that there is a consensus among market traders regarding expected exchange rates; nothing could be farther from the truth. The surveys indicate that there is a great range of variation in, both, exchange rate expectations and in the way that the individuals sampled make those expectations. In the next section we examine this issue in detail.

6–3. HETEROGENEITY OF EXPECTATIONS: CHARTISTS VERSUS FUNDAMENTALISTS IN THE FOREIGN EXCHANGE MARKET

Evidence from survey data suggests that there are two different types of exchange rate forecasters: chartists and fundamentalists. This section describes the methods utilized by these two types of market speculators and traders and examines their role in the foreign exchange market.

Chartists and Adaptive Expectations Mechanisms

Chartists are individuals who use so-called chart, or technical, analysis in forming exchange rate expectations. Chart analysis consists of looking at the recent behavior of exchange rates in the market

to construct charts that can then be used to extrapolate the future behavior of the exchange rate. Usually, chartists are engaged in short-run forecasting, making forecasts about exchange rates in the very near future.[2] Although they use a variety of forecasting techniques, chartists tend to rely heavily on so-called adaptive expectations mechanisms. There are many forms of adaptive expectations mechanisms. We will illustrate one particular case.

The basic concept behind the adaptive expectations mechanism is that individuals use information relating to past forecasting errors to revise expectations. We will look at how past forecast errors are used to determine the anticipated exchange rate change, x_t, made at time t about the exchange rate to prevail at some future time, $t + 1$.[3] The chartist, or technical analyst, will form expectations about the future by looking at past forecasts and comparing them with actual exchange rate changes. For instance, suppose that the technical analyst made a certain forecast in a past period, $t - 1$, about what the exchange rate would be at time t. Let us denote this past, expected exchange rate change between times $t - 1$ and t, by

$$x_{t-1} = E_A\left[\left(\frac{e_t - e_{t-1}}{e_{t-1}}\right) \mid t - 1\right]. \quad (6-3)$$

This expression can be read as "the expected exchange rate change between $t - 1$ and t," where $(e_t - e_{t-1})/e_{t-1}$ represents the exchange rate change between the time period $t - 1$ and period t

---

[2]See H. Allen and M. P. Taylor, "Charts, Noise and Fundamentals in the London Foreign Exchange Market," *The Economic Journal* (Supplement, 1990).

[3]The terminology here gets slightly cumbersome, but it is absolutely necessary. The time period over which the expectation is made (the time at which the expectation is being formed *and* the future time for which the forecast is made) must be clear. The type of expectation being formed (whether it is adaptive or not) should also be noted.

(expressed in proportional terms), and the symbol E denotes the expectation made by the investor or analyst about this exchange rate change. The subscript A in the symbol E_A means that the expectation is formed adaptively; we use a bar followed by $t - 1$ to signify that the expectation is formed at the time period $t - 1$.

If the actual exchange rate change from period $t - 1$ to period t is denoted by $\hat{e}_{t-1}$, the analyst will compare it to x_{t-1}. He or she will then set the expected exchange rate change at time t about the future exchange rate at time $t + 1$ according to the gap between the past expectation and the actual exchange rate change. We will denote the analyst's expected exchange rate to occur from period t to the future time period $t + 1$ by

$$x_t = E_A\left[\left(\frac{e_{t+1} - e_t}{e_t}\right)\mid t\right], \qquad (6-4)$$

where $(e_{t+1} - e_t)/e_t$ is the exchange rate change from period t to period $t + 1$, E is the expectation the analyst makes of that future exchange rate change, the subscript A is again used to denote the fact that the expectation is being formed adaptively, and the t after the vertical bar shows that the expectation is being formed at time t.

The adaptive expectations formation mechanism means that the analyst will form his or her future expectation, x_t, according to

$$x_t - x_{t-1} = \phi\,(\hat{e}_{t-1} - x_{t-1}), \qquad (6-5)$$

where ϕ represents a positive coefficient between zero and 1 to be interpreted momentarily.

Equation 6–5 states that if the actual exchange rate movement, $\hat{e}$, observed in a given time period turns out to be above the exchange rate change, x, that had been previously anticipated for that period (if $\hat{e}_{t-1} - x_{t-1}$ is positive), the expected exchange rate change for the subsequent period is revised upward ($x_t - x_{t-1}$ is positive). The parameter ϕ

indicates by how much the expected exchange rate change is adjusted in response to past mistakes. For example, if ϕ is very small (close to zero), expectations are not adjusted in any significant way and x_t remains close to x_{t-1}. On the other hand, if ϕ is close to 1, the expected exchange rate change from t to $t + 1$ is revised to almost equal the most recently observed exchange rate change, $\hat{e}_{t-1}$. When $\phi = 1$, $x_t = \hat{e}_{t-1}$, and in this case the present expectation, x_t, will not relate at all to the past expectation, x_{t-1}.

From Equation 6–5, the exact expression for the expected exchange rate change from t to $t + 1$ is given by

$$x_t = E_A[\hat{e}_t \mid t] \qquad (6-6)$$
$$= (1 - \phi)\, x_{t-1} + \phi\hat{e}_{t-1}.$$

This equation states that, when an investor follows the adaptive expectations mechanism, the exchange rate change expected to prevail from the period t to $t + 1$ is a weighted average of the exchange rate change that was expected to prevail from $t - 1$ to t, x_{t-1}, and the actual exchange rate change from $t - 1$ to t, $\hat{e}_{t-1}$.

Note that adaptive expectational behavior can be consistently off target. Its historical, or backward-looking, nature makes for a slow reaction to sudden change. Consider the following example:

Suppose that OPEC is meeting next week but the outcome of their deliberations is a formality; everyone knows that they will announce a doubling of oil prices. Surely economists will be predicting higher inflation from the moment at which news of the prospective oil price increase first becomes available. Yet the hypothesis of Adaptive Expectations asserts that individuals raise inflation expectations only after higher inflation has gradually fed into the past data from which they extrapolate. Adjustment of expectations is very sluggish. Using such a rule, individuals would make systematic mistakes, underpredicting the actual inflation rate for many periods after the oil price rise. It is not plausible that individuals would take no action to amend the basis of their forecasting rule under such circumstances.[4]

Because chartists ignore public information that is usually deemed relevant for forecasting purposes, they are frequently attacked as mechanistic forecasters who bypass basic economic and financial relations. This criticism is addressed next.

Fundamentalists and Purchasing Power Parity

In contrast to chartists, fundamentalists do not mechanically look at past exchange rates in predicting future exchange rates. Instead, individuals form expectations on the basis of a model that they believe determines the fundamental, long-run exchange rate in the market. Although there are different models that fundamentalists can use to form their long-run expectations, one that is frequently used incorporates the notion of PPP as a guide to assess exchange rate movements.

The assumption made by fundamentalists using PPP is that, although deviations from PPP do occur frequently over the short run, the arbitrage forces that keep domestic and foreign prices linked to each other through PPP will eventually predominate so that exchange rate movements will tend to mirror relative inflation rates. Therefore, PPP fundamentalists calculate the exchange rate movements that would be consistent with the relative version of PPP over time and use them as forecasts of exchange rate changes. The relative version of PPP states that exchange rate changes in a certain time period, t (when expressed in proportional terms), are equal to the difference between domestic inflation and the inflation in the foreign country whose currency value is being examined. Symbolically, PPP implies that

$$\hat{e}_t = \hat{P}_t - \hat{P}^*_t \qquad (6-7)$$

where $\hat{e}_t$ is the exchange rate change from time $t-1$ to time t, $\hat{P}_t$ is the domestic inflation rate during $t-1$ to t, and $\hat{P}^*_t$ is the foreign inflation.[5] The expected exchange rate change from t to $t+1$ is therefore

$$x_t = E_F[\hat{e}_t \mid t] = \pi_t - \pi^*_t, \qquad (6-8)$$

where $x_t = E_F[\hat{e}_t \mid t]$ is the PPP fundamentalists' expected exchange rate change from t to $t+1$ (with all symbols used as before and with the subscript F denoting that the expectations are being formed by fundamentalists), π_t is the expected domestic inflation from t to $t+1$, and π^*_t is the expected foreign inflation. Of course, the fundamentalist must forecast domestic and foreign inflation rates to utilize the PPP relationship.

Heterogeneity of Expectations

In our discussion in Section 6–2, we assumed that there was a particular "market" exchange rate expectation that represented the typical or average expectation in the foreign exchange market. However, the presence of two distinct groups of agents has been uncovered: chartists, who form an expectation on the basis of extrapolations of recent trends (so-called bandwagon expectations) and fundamentalists, who construct an expectation on the basis of what their models of exchange rate determination indicate the long-run exchange rate should be (so-called fundamentals). What would then be the "market" expectation about future exchange rates? One approach is to take an average of the chartists' and fundamentalists' anticipations of exchange rates movements, with each forecast weighted by the proportion of agents in the economy that are either chartists or

---

[4]From D. K. H. Begg, *The Rational Expectations Revolution in Macroeconomics: Theories and Evidence* (Baltimore: Johns Hopkins University Press, 1982), p. 26.

[5]Equation 6–8 attaches an explicit time context to Equation 5–11 in chapter 5: $\hat{e} = \hat{P} - \hat{P}^*$.

fundamentalists.[6] If we symbolize chartists' expected exchange rate changes by x_A and fundamentalists' expected exchange rate changes by x_F, the market forecast of exchange rate movements, x_m, is

$$x_m = \lambda x_F + (1 - \lambda)x_A$$
$$= \lambda E_F[\hat{e}_t | t] + (1 - \lambda)E_A[\hat{e}_t | t],$$

where λ is equal to the proportion of market participants who use fundamentals to determine exchange rates, so that $1 - \lambda$ represents the proportion of the market that forms chartists' expectations. The question is, then, what determines the parameter ϕ—that is, what is the proportion of the market that consists of fundamentalists relative to chartists?

Ever since Milton Friedman's seminal work, the key factor in determining the relative presence or absence of different groups of speculators in a market is deemed to be the extent to which on average they win or lose money.[7] According to Friedman, traders with systematically incorrect expectations—who have become known as *noise traders*—will not survive in a competitive market because on average they will be making losses as a result of their systematic expectational errors. Applying this concept to the foreign exchange market, economists J. A. Frankel and K. A. Froot argue: "If the fundamentalists sell the dollar short and keep losing money, while the chartists go long and keep gaining, in the long run the fundamentalists will go bankrupt and there will only be chartists in the marketplace."[8] However, this de-

pends on the relative wealth of the traders: it may take a long time for the group making systematic errors to disappear if they dominate the market in terms of initially being very wealthy.[9] In addition, in keeping with W. C. Fields's dictum that "there is a sucker born every moment," it is not impossible that a group of noise traders could be sustained in the market for a long period of time, being constantly refreshed with new "suckers." There is also the possibility that, by taking greater risks, a group of noise traders will still have larger expected profits in the long run or learn to become successful traders in the process.[10]

One example of shifts in the relative weights of chartists relative to fundamentalists in the foreign exchange market occurred during the sustained appreciation of the dollar in the early 1980s. Recent evidence using survey-based expectations suggests that between 1981 and 1985, the formation of exchange rate expectations shifted dramatically away from fundamentalists and toward chartists.[11] This shift apparently occurred as a result of the continuing errors made by fundamentalists at the time. According to PPP, the dollar should not have appreciated as much as it did during the period; there was every indication that, if PPP were to hold, the dollar would depreciate. Still, the dollar persistently appreciated in value, making the fundamentalists' expectations systematically

---

[6]This approach is the one adopted by J. A. Frankel and K. A. Froot, "Chartists, Fundamentalists and the Demand for Dollars," in T. Courakis and M. Taylor, *Policy Issues for Interdependent Economies* (Oxford: Oxford University Press, 1990); see also C. Goodhart, "The Foreign Exchange Market: A Random Walk with a Dragging Anchor," *Economica* (November 1988).

[7]See M. Friedman, "The Case for Flexible Exchange Rates," in *Essays in Positive Economics* (Chicago: University of Chicago Press, 1953).

[8]J. A. Frankel and K. A. Froot, "Explaining the Demand for Dollars: International Rates of Return, and the Expectations of

Chartists and Fundamentalists," in P. L. Paarlberg and R. G. Chambers, eds., *Macroeconomics, Agriculture and Exchange Rates* (Boulder, Colo.: Westview Press, 1988).

[9]A point formalized by S. Figlewski, "Market 'Efficiency' in a Market with Heterogeneous Information," *Journal of Political Economy* (August 1979).

[10]See J. B. DeLong et al., "The Survival of Noise Traders in Financial Markets," *Journal of Business* (January 1991); and R. J. Shiller, "Stock Prices and Social Dynamics," in *Market Volatility* (Cambridge, Mass.: The MIT Press, 1989).

[11]See J. A. Frankel and K. A. Froot, "Chartists, Fundamentalists, and Trading in the Foreign Exchange Market," *American Economic Review* (May 1990); and K. A. Froot and T. Ito, "On the Consistency of Short-Run and Long-Run Exchange Rate Expectations," *Journal of International Money and Finance* (December 1989).

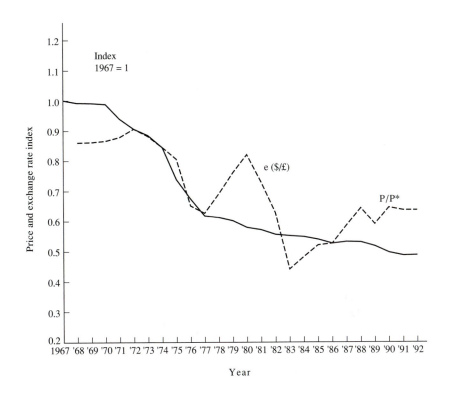

FIGURE 6–1. The Failure of Purchasing Power Parity: The Exchange Rate of the Dollar Versus the Pound and Relative U.S. and U.K. Prices, 1969–1992

P and P* are the consumer price indexes for the United States and the United Kingdom, respectively. The exchange rate is the bilateral exchange rate between the dollar and the pound sterling (in dollars per pound).

SOURCE: *Economic Report of the President* (Washington, D.C.: U.S. Government Printing Office, 1992).

incorrect. At the same time, the chartists, who were predicting continuing appreciation of the dollar as extrapolated from the immediate past, turned out to be systematically correct in their expectations. As a consequence, those following fundamentals shrank as a fraction of total traders in the foreign exchange market.

The complete failure of PPP to explain exchange rate changes in the late 1970s and the first half of the 1980s is explicitly seen in Figure 6–1, where we depict the dollar-pound exchange rate and the

ratio of prices in the United States, $P_{U.S.}$ to prices in the United Kingdom, $P_{U.K.}$. If PPP were to hold, the two series would move together. Although deviations from PPP can be clearly seen from the start of floating exchange rates in 1973 to 1978, the two series did tend to move together during these years. After that time, the doctrine completely broke down, which demolished its forecasting record.

This is reflected in the data presented in Table 6–2, where we show the techniques used by foreign exchange forecasting firms (fundamentals

TABLE 6–2.   **Techniques Used by Forecasting Services**

Year	No. of Services Surveyed[a]	No. Using Technical Models	No. Using Fundamentals	No. Using Both Models
1978	23	3	19	0
1981	13	1	11	0
1983	11	8	1	1
1984	13	9	0	2
1985	24	15	5	3
1986	34	20	8	4
1987	31	16	6	5
1988	31	18	7	6

[a]The source for these numbers is *Euromoney,* the August issues for each year cited in the table. When a forecasting firm offers more than one service, each is counted separately. Some services did not indicate the nature of their technique.

SOURCE: J. Frankel and K. A. Froot, "Exchange Rate Forecasting Techniques, Survey Data, and Implications for the Foreign Exchange Market," National Bureau of Economic Research Working Paper no. 3470 (October 1990).

versus technical models or chartism), as reported in surveys carried out by *Euromoney* magazine. Note that between 1978 and 1985 the number of foreign exchange advisory services using fundamentals to forecast exchange rates dropped dramatically. In 1978, nineteen out of twenty-three foreign exchange advisory services described themselves as relying exclusively on fundamentals for their forecasts; in 1983, however, only one firm out of eleven reported using only fundamentals (the rest used either charts or a combination of charts and fundamentals).

6–4. RATIONAL EXPECTATIONS, EXCHANGE RATE FORECASTING, AND THE EMPIRICAL EVIDENCE ON RISK PREMIA AND THE FORWARD MARKET

Although survey-based data appear to provide a direct line to the exchange rate expectations of actual participants in foreign exchange markets, they do have some shortcomings. In particular, many economists are suspicious about whether the respondents of surveys will truthfully reveal their expectations. As University of Chicago economist Robert Hodrick has noted concerning the surveys conducted by Money Market Services and similar organizations: "Consider the incentive problem of a trader who possesses private information that he has used to construct a portfolio of positions based on the deviations of his expectations from the current forward rates. When MMS calls him for his expectations, will he reveal his information, or will he lie and quote something like the forward rate?"[12]

When reliable data on expectations are not available, we are forced to use a proxy for the unobserved expectations. One way to obtain an estimate of investors' anticipations is to use optimal forecasts as proxies. If people determine their expectations as optimal forecasts, given the information they have available, all we have to do is to try to find out what is the best forecasting method at hand.

[12]R. Hodrick, *The Empirical Evidence on the Efficiency of Forward and Futures Foreign Exchange Markets* (Chur, Switzerland: Harwood Academic Publishers, 1987).

Presumably, this will approximate the unobserved anticipations. The idea that investors use the information they have available to formulate optimal forecasts is related to the notion that expectations are not formed inconsistently and in ignorance, blatantly ignoring available information, but are made in an informed, rational way.

The next section studies the implications of rational expectations, comparing it to the adaptive expectations mechanism discussed earlier in reference to chart, or technical, analysis.

Rational Expectations and Its Implications

The problem of expectations formation arises in almost any human activity—purchasing a car, going camping for the weekend, or purchasing uncovered U.K. Treasury bills. Whether you are evaluating the price of a car, the weather, or the value of the British pound, you have to base your actions on expectations about how these variables will change. The study of the formation of expectations examines how individuals determine their forecasts of the behavior of relevant economic variables.

There are many different alternative perspectives on how individuals form expectations. At this point, simply note that there are two basic types of expectations formation that have been widely examined in the international finance and open-economy macroeconomics literature. The first regards the *adaptive expectations* mechanism first emphasized by Phillip Cagan of Columbia University, and Marc Nerlove of Northwestern University in the 1950s. The second is the *rational expectations* approach, associated with the names of Indiana's John Muth, University of Chicago's Robert Lucas and Thomas Sargent, University of Minnesota's Neil Wallace, Harvard's Robert Barro, and others.

We studied an example of adaptive expectations when discussing chartism. To reiterate, the adaptive expectations formation mechanism assumes that individuals form expectations on the basis of mechanical extrapolations of past and present values of a variable. This is often what we do when relevant information for the future behavior of a certain variable is hard to obtain or to discern. In this situation it becomes easier to make predictions on the basis of given rules concerning present and past values of the variable at stake. Such is the case of the person who looks out the window and assumes that the afternoon weather will be more or less what it was in the morning.

As opposed to a person who relies on more or less arbitrary rules or hunches in deciding about the future, an individual following rational expectations looks around for information and makes decisions on the basis of that information. In contrast to adaptive expectations adjustments, the person who forms rational expectations will immediately embody new information into his or her decisions. If new information suggests that the rules this person uses are no longer valid, he or she will modify them immediately, even before actually observing them fail. This is the person who calls the weather bureau for a forecast and relies on all available current information to determine the expected weather.

The starting point of rational expectations behavior, then, is that people incorporate all the relevant systematic information they have available in forming their expectations of a given variable. The rational expectation of a given variable, X, can thus be expressed as

$$X_R = E_R[X_{t+1}|I_t], \qquad (6\text{--}9)$$

where $E_R[X_{t+1}|I_t]$ symbolizes the fact that X_R is defined as the value that the variable X is expected to have at time $t + 1$, given all the information available at time t, which is denoted by I_t.

We will refer to the rational expectation of the exchange rate change from t to $t + 1$ by x_R, which is given by

$$x_{Rt} = E_R[\hat{e}_t|I_t]. \qquad (6\text{--}10)$$

The errors made by rational expectations forecasting are obtained by comparing the rational expectation forecast of exchange rate movements with the actual exchange rate changes. Symbolically, the forecast errors are

$$\hat{e}_{ut} = x_{Rt} - \hat{e}_t, \tag{6-11}$$

where $\hat{e}_{ut}$ represents an error term reflecting the unanticipated component of the exchange rate movement from t to $t + 1$. Under rational expectations, forecasting errors are unsystematic. They arise from unanticipated, random disturbances about which an individual has no information on which to base a prediction. This property will be very useful momentarily.

To visualize how the rational expectations hypothesis can be used to test for the presence of a risk premium, we will substitute the expression for the anticipated rate of currency depreciation in Equation 6–1, $x = f + R$, into Equation 6–11. This yields

$$\hat{e}_t = x_{Rt} + \hat{e}_{ut} \tag{6-12}$$
$$= f_t + R_t + \hat{e}_{ut},$$

where $\hat{e}_t = (e_{t+1} - e_t)/e_t$ is the actual currency depreciation occurring between period t and period $t + 1$, R_t is the foreign currency risk premium during this period, f_t is the forward premium, and $\hat{e}_{ut}$ denotes the unanticipated exchange rate change occurring from period t to period $t + 1$. The first line of Equation 6–12 only states that actual exchange rate changes can be broken down into an anticipated component, x_{Rt}, and an unanticipated component, $\hat{e}_{ut}$, where the anticipated component is equal to the forward premium plus the risk premium.

What are the implications we can derive from the rational expectations assumption? Recall that under rational expectations, forecasting errors are unsystematic; they arise from unanticipated, random disturbances about which an individual has no information on which to base a prediction. This translates into various properties for Equation 6–12 and its error term $\hat{e}_{ut}$. These are

1. Given that the forecast errors made when expectations are rational are unsystematic, the error term would, on average, be equal to zero because it represents random disturbances affecting the exchange rate. If we take a series of forecast errors, we should expect to obtain some overestimates and some underestimates of exchange rate changes, but not systematic errors on the upward or on the downward side. For instance, the following sequence of forecast errors $\hat{e}_{ut}$: $-3, -2.5, -4, -1.0, -7, 0.05, -4, -3$, and so on, entails errors that have an average value of -3. This would most likely be inconsistent with rational expectations.[13] The rational forecaster realizes that he or she is making systematic mistakes and that expectations should be adjusted to suppress the mistakes.

2. The absence of systematic forecasting errors implies that, *on average,* the rational expectation x_R will be equal to the actual exchange rate movement, $\hat{e}$. Although the expectation will generally be off target, sometimes exceeding and sometimes being below the actual exchange rate movement, the random pluses and minuses will offset each other, leaving the rational expectation on the mark, on average.

[13] Another implication is that it is unlikely (but it is always probabilistically possible) that we observe $\hat{e}_{ut}$ sequences that repeat this type of pattern: $-1, -1, -1, 1, 1, 1$. This sequence pattern satisfies the criterion that, *on average,* forecast errors are zero. However, these errors are systematic in a more subtle way. If you know that the forecast errors follow this pattern, after you see the first "1" coming in, you know it will repeat itself twice more. A rational expectations forecaster would adjust his or her expectations in a way that eliminates any forecasting pattern in which future errors can be predicted from past observations of mistakes. Rational expectations means that present forecast errors cannot be predicted from past mistakes. Technically, this requirement is expressed as "forecast errors should be serially uncorrelated." Serial correlation of errors occurs when a time series of forecast errors shows a pattern of correlation or association between present and past mistakes.

Technically, a forecast, or an estimate, that is, on the average, right on target, is said to be an *unbiased* forecast, or estimator. Therefore, X_R is an *unbiased* estimator, or forecast, of exchange rate movements. In terms of Equation 6–12, this has two specific implications. First, if rational expectations hold, then—on average—the sum $f + R$ will be on target when forecasting exchange rate movements. Second, if the risk premium is zero or negligible, the forward premium itself should be an unbiased predictor of exchange rate movements.

What does the evidence show? Do the data indicate that the forward premium is an unbiased estimate of exchange rate changes? What is the empirical significance of the risk premium? The next section examines these issues.

6–5. FORWARD AND RISK PREMIA IN THE FORECASTING OF EXCHANGE RATE MOVEMENTS

This section examines the lack of bias in forward premia and the role of risk premia in foreign exchange markets. Equation 6–12 is the basis for the analysis. To determine the role of forward and risk premia, consider a general exchange rate equation such as

$$\hat{e}_t = a_0 + a_1 f_t + a_2 R_t + \text{error}_t \quad (6\text{–}13)$$

and test whether the a_0, a_1, and a_2 coefficients that best fit the data in the sample period analyzed are as postulated by the hypotheses embodied in Equation 6–12: $a_0 = 0$ (because Equation 6–12 has no constant term), $a_1 = 1$, and $a_2 = 1$. We begin by analyzing cases in which the risk premium is not significant; the term involving the risk premium disappears and the forward premium becomes an unbiased estimator of exchange rate changes.

Is the Forward Premium an Unbiased Forecast of Future Exchange Rates?

To determine whether the forward premium is an unbiased estimator of future exchange rate changes, it must be shown to be consistent with the data. In order to do that, the general equation 6–13 must be modified, such as

$$\hat{e}_t = a_0 + a_1 f_t + \text{error}_t, \quad (6\text{–}14)$$

and whether the a_0 and a_1 coefficients that best fit the data in the sample period analyzed are as postulated by the unbiased forward premium hypothesis: $a_0 = 0$ and $a_1 = 1$ must be tested.

A large number of studies exists on this issue, covering a wide range of currencies and time periods. The weight of the evidence is that the unbiased forward premium hypothesis is not supported by the data. When estimated using figures for the dollar-pound, dollar-mark, and dollar-yen spot and forward exchange rates, both coefficients, a_0 and a_1, are different from those postulated by the hypothesis.[14]

The failure of the unbiased forward premium to hold up under empirical scrutiny leads to a questioning of the preconditions or assumptions under which the unbiased result is obtained. As noted earlier, the forward rate is an unbiased predictor of the future exchange rate under the joint hypothesis that there is a zero risk premium and that foreign exchange market traders form rational expectations about future exchange rates. Therefore, one explanation for the lack of empirical support regarding unbiased forward premia is that there is a nonzero risk premium (or discount) that generates a systematic deviation of the forward premium from average exchange rate changes. In terms of Equation 6–12, R is different from zero. In fact,

[14]See the surveys by Hodrick, op. cit., and R. Baillie and P. McMahon, *The Foreign Exchange Market: Theory and Econometric Evidence* (Cambridge: Cambridge University Press, 1989).

studies that have adopted the equation $\hat{e}_t = a_0 + a_1 f_t + \text{error}_t$ to test the unbiasedness hypothesis often find estimates of a_0 that are different from zero. This suggests the presence of a risk premium, although—by construction—such a risk premium is being assumed to be constant over time (a_0 is a constant).

Testing for the Presence of a Risk Premium

In order to test for the presence of a time-varying risk premium, a general equation, Equation 6–13—rather than 6–14—must be tested to examine its consistency with the data. This means that the general equation used in the estimation is

$$\hat{e}_t = a_0 + a_1 f_t + a_2 R_t + \text{error}_t,$$

where, in addition to $a_0 = 0$ and $a_1 = 1$, the hypothesis to be tested is that the coefficient a_2 is equal to 1.

Unfortunately, estimating this equation requires that the statistician have some data available on what the risk premium, R, is for the foreign assets being examined. As can be implied from our earlier discussion, the exchange risk premium is related not only to the variability of domestic and foreign real rates of return, but also to the co-variability (correlation) between these returns, and the degree of risk aversion for agents in the economy. A substantial amount of recent research has been carried out estimating some of these variables from available data and using them to test versions of Equation 6–13. Just as in the case of the survey studies examined previously, the results support the idea that the risk premium is varying over time.[15] Because the relative riskiness of assets and their associated risk premia change

over time, a currency bearing a risk premium this year might be at a discount in two years, making the estimation of risk premia extremely difficult. Specifying the determinants of time-varying risk premia in actual data and their role in explaining deviations from uncovered interest parity represents a complex econometric problem that presently commands the serious effort of some of the most capable researchers in the field.[16]

6–6. FORECASTING ERRORS AND THE MEASUREMENT OF MARKET EFFICIENCY

The lack of bias in the forward premium in forecasting exchange rate movements can be interpreted in terms of the presence of risk premia. An alternate way to interpret the failure of the forward premium to be an unbiased forecast of future exchange rates is that the assumption of rational expectations does not reflect the expectations formation mechanism of individuals involved in the foreign exchange market. According to one version of this view, the reason for the forward premium bias is not the presence of a risk premium but the irrationality of exchange rate expectations. Also, the heterogeneity of market traders signifies that there is not a unique anticipation that

equilibrium approach—and this is reflected in its measurement. A typical study using the portfolio balance approach is J. Frankel, "In Search of the Exchange Risk Premium: A Six Currency Test Assuming Mean-Variance Optimization," *Journal of International Money and Finance* (December 1982); a typical study using the general equilibrium approach is R. J. Hodrick and S. Srivastava, "An Investigation of Risk and Return in Forward Foreign Exchange," *Journal of International Money and Finance* (January 1984).

[16]See G. Kaminsky and R. Peruga, "Can a Time-varying Risk Premium Explain Excess Returns in the Forward Market for Foreign Exchange?" *Journal of International Economics* (February 1990); A. Giovannini and P. Jorion, "The Time Variation of Risk and Return in the Foreign Exchange and Stock Markets," *The Journal of Finance* (June 1989); and F. Diebold and P. Pauly, "Endogenous Risk in a Portfolio Balance/Rational Expectations Model of the Deutschemark-Dollar Rate," *European Economic Review* (January 1988).

[15]For a survey of these studies, see R. Meese, "Empirical Assessment of Foreign Currency Risk Premiums," in C. C. Stone, ed., *Financial Risk: Theory, Evidence and Implications* (Boston: Kluwer Academic Publishers, 1989). As noted earlier, there are two alternative approaches to the determinants of the risk premium—the portfolio balance approach and the general

rules in the market. Some forecasters gain and others lose, while some among them might be losing systematically (to exit eventually as a result of cumulative losses).

Some authors have thus tried to evaluate and test the rational expectations hypothesis by focusing on the various statistical properties of the forecast errors when the forward rate is used as a predictor. This has been of considerable interest, partly because of its bearing on the question of *market efficiency.* A market is efficient if prices fully reflect all publicly available information at any given time. In the present context, the forward market is efficient if the forward exchange rate (the price determined in the forward market) fully reflects all available information relevant for future exchange rate determination. Market efficiency is an issue that has a long tradition in the finance literature (mostly relating to the efficiency of the stock market). It was picked up with vigor as a topic of research by international finance economists who were investigating the directly related question of whether a violation of rational expectations explains the forecasting bias of the forward premium.

The hypothesis that agents in the foreign exchange market form rational expectations—and that the forward market incorporates information efficiently—can be tested directly by examining some of its additional implications. For instance, consider Equation 6–12, which we now restate:

$$\hat{e}_t = x_t + \hat{e}_{ut}$$
$$= f_t + R_t + \hat{e}_{ut}.$$

Assume that the risk premium is zero. Then, the difference between the actual rate of currency depreciation and the forward premium—that is, the forecasting error made by the forward premium (or the unanticipated exchange rate change)—is

$$\hat{e}_{ut} = \hat{e}_t - f_t, \qquad (6-15)$$

where rational expectations imply that these forecasting errors are random, reflecting new information available to individuals in the market. This means that the forecasting error at any given time t, $\hat{e}_{ut}$, should not be correlated with the error at time $t + 1$, $\hat{e}_{ut+1}$.

The hypothesis that the forward premium's forecasting errors at any given time are not correlated with past errors has been amply examined; however, in spite of some early evidence supporting it, many studies do not corroborate the hypothesis.[17] The data indicate that the forecast errors in Equation 6–15 are correlated over time—that is, they are *serially correlated.* In fact, the pattern of correlation is very clear in certain periods: a positive error in any given time period tends to be correlated with a larger positive error in the following time period, and so on; similarly, negative errors are followed by larger negative errors, and so on.

Nevertheless, the implication of this evidence regarding the rationality of expectations and market efficiency is plagued by the joint assumption that the risk premium will be equal to zero. In the presence of a time-varying risk premium, we can expect that the forecast errors from Equation 6–15 would generally be correlated over time, even under rational expectations. With a time-varying risk premium, the variance of the errors (i.e., the average of the squared fluctuations around their mean value) would not be constant—a phenomenon referred to as *heteroskedasticity.* Heteroskedasticity can be visualized by considering the case of turbulent and tranquil periods in relation to exchange rate volatility. The variance of the errors would be greater in periods of unpredictability than in periods of tranquility. The heteroskedastic nature of exchange rate movements and their forecast errors is now well established empirically.

[17]See L. P. Hansen and R. J. Hodrick, "Risk-Averse Speculation in the Forward Foreign Exchange Market: An Econometric Analysis of Linear Models," in J. Frenkel, ed., *Exchange Rates and International Macroeconomics* (Chicago: University of Chicago Press, 1983); and J. F. O. Bilson, "The Speculative Efficiency Hypothesis," *Journal of Business* (July 1981).

The presence of heteroscedasticity has given rise to the development of new statistical procedures to analyze the foreign exchange market.[18]

6–7. LEARNING AND THE FORMATION OF EXPECTATIONS

Rational expectations emphasizes the idea that individuals do not persist in making systematic forecasting errors, that predictions about the future should be "free of systematic and easily correctable biases."[19] However, it is consistent with rational expectations to recognize that individuals may have to learn about their economic environment—and acquire information—over a certain period of time in order to be able to eliminate systematic forecasting errors. In the meantime, while the learning occurs, systematic prediction biases would indeed be observed. This would be especially significant in situations where economic environments change suddenly and by surprise. It may take agents in the economy a while to learn about the new

regime, during which time they could be expected to make mistakes systematically.[20] Similarly, it is not expected that new information would be incorporated immediately into exchange rate expectations and, thus, forward exchange rates. Rather, new information has to be collected and digested by traders who expect to profit from its use and dissemination, a process that takes time.[21]

A learning model has been utilized by economist Karen K. Lewis to explain the systematic failure of the forward premium to predict future dollar exchange rates in the early 1980s. For instance, during that period of dollar strengthening, dollar-mark forward exchange rates were consistently above the actual exchange rate at time of maturity. In other words, the dollar was appreciating in value, but the forward market appeared to be suggesting instead that the dollar would depreciate, and it was consistently wrong in its prediction.

Now, the sustained appreciation of the dollar vis-à-vis the German mark between 1980 and 1985 was associated with a sharp turn in the U.S. monetary policy regime. In October 1979, the Federal Reserve announced new procedures for the operation of monetary policy—a shift that resulted in wider fluctuations of interest rates. Associated with the new policy was the entrance of Paul Volcker as chairman of the Federal Reserve Board and the imposition of an anti-inflationary monetary policy. Lewis has argued that individuals in the foreign exchange market had to learn the new policy regime and, as a result, they made systematic errors. She finds that this learning could account for as much as one-half of

---

[18]The intertemporal structure of exchange rates and the variance of the error term have been fashioned after so-called Auto Regressive Conditional Heteroskedastic (ARCH) models. An autoregressive specification provides a model of the complex association between a variable and its past values (autoregression). Conditional heteroskedasticity refers to the fact that the variance of the error term changes from period to period and is hence conditional on the date. See R. J. Hodrick, "Risk, Uncertainty and Exchange Rates," *Journal of Monetary Economics* (May 1989); R. T. Baillie and T. Bollerslev, "The Message in Daily Exchange Rates: A Conditional Variance Tale," *Journal of Business and Economics Statistics* (November 1988); and I. Domowitz and C. Hakkio, "Conditional Variance and the Risk Premium in the Foreign Exchange Market," *Journal of International Economic* (September 1985). Using equations similar to the ones we have presented, R. Cumby and M. Obstfeld found that forecast errors are heteroskedastic. See "International Interest-Rate and Price-Level Linkages Under Flexible Exchange Rates," in J. F. O. Bilson and J. Frenkel, eds., *Exchange Rates: Theory and Practice* (Chicago: University of Chicago Press, 1984).

[19]R. E. Lucas, "Understanding Business Cycles," in K. Brunner and A. H. Meltzer, eds., *Stabilization in the Domestic and International Economy* (Amsterdam: North Holland, 1977), p. 224.

[20]For a discussion of recent developments in the economics of learning and expectations formations, see J. B. Bullard, "Learning, Rational Expectations and Policy: A Summary of Recent Research," *Review, Federal Reserve Bank of St. Louis* (January-February 1991); and A. Marcet and T. Sargent, "The Fate of Systems with Adaptive Expectations," *American Economic Review* (May 1988).

[21]For a discussion of the range of issues relating to the incorporation of information into expectations formations and financial market prices, see S. Grossman, *The Informational Role of Prices* (Cambridge, Mass.: The MIT Press, 1989).

the errors involving the forward premium in predicting the dollar-mark exchange rates from October 1979 to 1984.[22]

Large (discrete) shifts in economic policy regimes are associated with major economic changes whose timing, credibility, and continuance are uncertain and can thus induce substantial expectational errors both after and *before* the policy shift occurs. Shifts in economic policy regimes can generate expectational errors before they are implemented because individuals will be trying to forecast when and how the new policy will be implemented. When the market expects a major policy change that does not materialize for an extended period of time, forecasting errors will occur that appear to be systematic in nature. It is true, though, that these forecasting errors are consistent with rational expectations—that is, the expectations are still being formed rationally, based on all the information publicly available; it just happens to be the case that the information available about the timing and extent of the policy change is by nature incomplete, generating the persistent errors.

In terms of the forward exchange rate, the implication is that, in the presence of potentially large changes in economic policy, the forward rate could generate persistent forecasting errors, even though rational expectations still hold. This is referred to as the peso problem in the literature.[23] The reason for the terminology is that countries that have operated under pegged exchange rates, such as Mexico, tend to have forward exchange rates that persistently diverge from that peg. For instance, in the period before the August 1976 devaluation of the Mexican peso in terms of the U.S. dollar, the peso was consistently quoted at a discount in the forward market. This means that if the forward rate were taken as a predictor of the future exchange rate, clear, consistent errors would be committed, except perhaps when the country changed its peg value. Because the governments of many countries sometimes find ever ingenious ways of delaying currency devaluations, the forward rate could be in error for extended periods of time. This seems inconsistent with forward market efficiency. However, this conclusion does not follow. The problem lies in that, under a pegged exchange rate regime, the forward premium would not predict by how much the exchange rate will change from day to day or from month to month (it cannot because the exchange rate is fixed and does not change from day to day); rather, the forward premium reflects the *probability* that a devaluation will occur within the horizon established by the forward contract. As a result, even though a simple look at the data seems to suggest that market efficiency should be rejected, a sophisticated analysis reveals that the rejection of informational efficiency may not be guaranteed.

Summary

1. The exchange risk premium generates a wedge between the forward premium and expected exchange rate changes. Only when the risk premium is not significantly different from zero should the forward premium be considered as forecasting future exchange rate changes.

2. Survey-based expectations suggest that there is a substantial, time-varying risk premium. This means that the value of the forward premium does not correspond to what the market anticipates the exchange rate will do in the future. However, the forward premium still tends to have the same sign as the expected exchange rate change of experts and participants in the foreign exchange market.

---

[22]See K. K. Lewis, "Can Learning Affect Exchange Rate Behavior? The Case of the Dollar in the Early 1980s," *Journal of Monetary Economics* (February 1989).

[23]See K. K. Lewis, "Was There a 'Peso Problem' in the U.S. Term Structure of Interest Rates: 1979–1982?" National Bureau of Economic Research Working Paper no. 3282 (March 1990); W. S. Krasker, "The 'Peso Problem' in Testing the Efficiency of Forward Exchange Markets," *Journal of Monetary Economics* (April 1980). For an early treatment of this problem, see K. Rogoff, "Essays on Expectations and Exchange Rate Volatility," Ph.D. diss., MIT, 1979.

3. Surveys of foreign exchange market participants suggest that there are two types of participants holding alternative expectations formation mechanisms: chartists and fundamentalists. Chartists use charts, or technical analysis, to forecast exchange rates. One example of the expectations formation mechanism underlying chartists is adaptive expectations. Under adaptive expectations, individuals form expectations on the basis of mechanically adjusting past forecast errors in the direction of the actual values of the variable being predicted. Fundamentalists have models of what the future equilibrium (fundamental) value of the exchange rate should be and form expectations on that basis. Some fundamentalists use PPP to forecast exchange rates.

4. The "market" expectation of future exchange rate changes is a weighted average of the expectations of chartists and fundamentalists, with the weight of each determined by the relative proportion of investors forming expectations by each type of mechanism. Recent evidence suggests that, in the 1980s, many participants in foreign exchange markets shifted from using fundamentals to using chartism, partly as a result of the systematic failure of exchange rate models, such as PPP, to predict future exchange rate changes.

5. Under rational expectations and no risk premium, the forward premium will be an unbiased estimator of future exchange rate movements. However, the available evidence suggests that the forward premium is not an unbiased forecast. This means that either rational expectations do not hold in the foreign exchange market or that there is a variable exchange risk premium. Current empirical studies have yet to resolve this issue.

6. Because new economic environments require some learning and experience to be understood, exchange rate expectations can be systematically wrong over time, even if investors are forming rational expectations. A large share of the systematic errors committed by the forward premium in the early 1980s can be traced to what was the need to understand the monetary policy regime shifts that took place before and during that period.

7. In the presence of unknown future policy regime shifts, optimal forecasts can be systematically wrong. This has become known as the "peso problem." It suggests that the forward premium can be a biased predictor of future exchange rates and still be a rational forecast, so long as the available information about major future policy shifts is unreliable.

Problems

1. It was one of the points of this chapter that investing in a country with high interest rates relative to domestic rates may not turn out to be such a good idea because the country's currency could depreciate in value, absorbing the potential interest gains. Yet, some economists have found that the following strategy does seem to generate, on average, some sustained profits to investors: "When interest rates rise in other countries, put your money there and take your chances on the currency falling. On the other hand, if rates in the foreign country fall relative to domestic rates, keep your money here," [see R. H. Thaler and K. A. Froot, "Exchange," in R. H. Thaler, ed., *The Winner's Curse: Paradoxes and Anomalies of Economic Life* (New York: The Free Press, 1992), pp. 182–183]. Could you explain this result? What does it suggest about foreign exchange market efficiency? [Hint: Use Equation 6–14 and the fact that a_1 is generally observed to be less than one.

2. On the basis of the discussion in this chapter, would you conclude that the foreign exchange market is an informationally efficient market?

CHAPTER 7

Onshore Banking in International Perspective

Our foray into the international financial system ends with two chapters, 7 and 8, whose focus is banking. The world banking industry has been revolutionized over the last two decades. Its activities have been globalized, creating a truly worldwide market for bank services and deposits. This internationalization operates through two distinct channels linked to the differentiation between so-called *onshore* and *offshore* banking systems.

The *onshore banking system* of any given country consists of the domestic banking activities conducted in local currency. In the United States, these activities comprise those of all banks located within its borders that offer dollar deposits and loans. Onshore banking is not entirely the turf of

locally owned firms. For instance, many banks operating in the United States are foreign owned and offer dollar deposits and loans in direct competition with those that are American owned. When a Japanese bank in Los Angeles lends $2 million to an American firm in California, this is as much a part of the onshore banking system as a Citibank loan to a corporation in New York City. In this respect, the activities of Japanese, Canadian, and other foreign-owned banks in the United States are in the same category as those of the Bank of America or Chase Manhattan: By locating themselves in the United States, foreign-owned banks have joined the U.S. banking system. A similar situation applies to the increasing cross-national penetration of banking systems in Europe under the recent European Community drive to integrate its financial markets by 1992. When German banks operate in London and accept sterling deposits and make sterling loans, they are subject to British law and participate in the onshore sterling system. The onshore banking system is, thus, internationalized by the entry of foreign firms that compete directly with domestic-owned firms for local customers.

Banks can also participate in the *offshore banking system*. The offshore banking system is composed of deposits, loans, and bonds denominated in a currency, say dollars, but issued outside the country where the currency is legal tender, say the United States. Dollar-denominated deposits outside the boundaries of the United States—called Eurodollars—have proliferated since the 1970s. Numerous American, European, and Japanese banks have entered the Eurodollar market, making it one of the most dynamic and active components of the international banking network. The deutsche mark, the yen, and other currencies are now also widely offered as deposits or loans outside their domestic markets. These offshore, external, or "Euro," markets—offering Eurodollar, Eurosterling, and Euroyen deposits, loans, and bonds—are not separate from onshore banking: They both complement and substitute for the activities undertaken by the onshore system.

The next two chapters examine the structure of onshore and offshore banking. This chapter focuses on the major onshore systems—in the United States, Japan, and Europe—as well as those of emerging economies, looking at how international forces affect them. Chapter 8 explores offshore banking and the Eurodollar market.

7–1. INTERNATIONAL BANKING: SOME BACKGROUND

Banks are financial intermediaries—that is, they are institutions that mediate between lenders and borrowers. There are two crucial types of banking

activities: commercial banking and investment banking. *Commercial banking* involves borrowing from customers—issuing checking or other types of deposit accounts in exchange—and using the money to lend to corporations, individuals, or the government, through loans or by purchasing securities or other assets. *Investment banking,* on the other hand, does not itself involve in the business of lending; it acts on behalf of firms that want to borrow, by serving as an agent or underwriter for the securities those firms issue. When the investment banker *underwrites* securities, he or she purchases them from the issuing corporation or institution and sells them to dealers and investors. Profit comes from the spread between the selling (public offering) price and the buying price. Because the investment bank must purchase and hold the securities before it sells them—which could involve large sums of money—it must commit a certain amount of funds as working capital; it also takes risks in the process. To share this burden, investment bankers will often form a *syndicate* to finance the acquisition and sale of large volumes of securities. Alternatively, the banker may act as an *agent* of the borrowing firm, acting only to sell its securities without actually buying them and then charging the firm a commission on the sales.

In the United States, historically, banks performed both investment and commercial banking activities. During the nineteenth century, American banks were feverishly underwriting U.S. private and government securities linked to the massive external borrowing that helped finance wars, canals, railroads, warehouses, and a number of industrial ventures. The investment funds came mostly from Europe. As British, French, Dutch, and German capital poured into America, U.S. banking grew with it. The beginnings of modern international investment banking were embodied in the ventures of J. P. Morgan, J. and W. Seligman, Lehman Brothers, and Goldman Sachs, all of which had heavy business underwriting securities for American railroads, states, and municipalities and selling them to European investors. For instance, when the railroad magnate William H.

Vanderbilt decided to sell 250,000 shares of his New York Central railroad stock in 1879, he went to J. P. Morgan in New York, who organized a syndicate that purchased the shares from Vanderbilt at $120 per share and sold them in London at $130 a share.[1] The attraction of these American securities for foreign investors was their high relative yields. These meaty returns, however, were subject to high risk; many European borrowers were burned by loan defaults on the part of U.S. borrowers, such as when canal companies failed in the 1840s and state and local governments defaulted in the 1870s.

A similar experience held for investors in other countries on the American continent. The growth of loan flows from Europe to Central and South America in the nineteenth century was halted by widespread debt crises and defaults in the 1820s and 1870s. In fact, the first world debt crisis occurred in the 1870s when fifteen nations—including not only Latin American countries (such as Peru, Honduras, and Paraguay), but other major debtors (such as Egypt and Turkey)—suspended payments on debt to European nations worth almost £300 million.[2] The characteristics of the 1870s debt crisis provide valuable lessons in understanding the present external debt problems suffered by developing countries. Although significant differences exist by country, a large share of

the unpaid external debt of the 1870s was undertaken to finance overambitious government investment projects intended to develop mining and agricultural production as well as to construct infrastructure (railroads and shipping). For instance, in Peru, the external borrowing was linked to the expansion of guano, a natural fertilizer. Guano was in great demand in Europe at the time, and Peru had a virtual monopoly over its production. On the basis of the great potential of guano, the Peruvian state engaged in massive borrowing from British and French sources (among others) to finance a wide array of projects. By the early 1870s, Peru had become the Latin American nation with the largest foreign debt. Some of these ventures were truly spectacular, even by today's standards. For example, Peru's export production occurred—as it remains today—mostly on the coast, where Lima, the seat of the government, is located (guano also was mostly available from a tiny archipelago a few miles off the coast). In order to integrate the mountainous Andean region with the coastal area, the government decided to construct several railroads. Massive loans were undertaken to build bridges and tunnels across towering mountains. Although Peru can today claim the highest railway on earth—at more than 15,000 feet above sea level—the cost of the venture was enormous both in terms of money and in lives (thousands died in the construction of these engineering feats). When combined with declining guano revenues in the 1870s, the Peruvian government essentially became bankrupt; in January 1876, it abruptly stopped payments on its external debt. It did not resume payments for a decade, and the European investors and bankers who had aggressively supplied the loans were seriously burned.

By the beginning of the 1900s, the dominant role European banking had played in the Americas during the previous century was beginning to be challenged by U.S. financial capital. The rapid industrial growth of the United States in the second half of the nineteenth century had resulted in an accelerated accumulation of capital. Between

[1]S. L. Hayes and P. M. Hubbard, *Investment Banking: A Tale of Three Cities* (Boston: Harvard Business School Press, 1990), p. 18. International lending and securities trading during this period were obviously much slower than today. However, financial markets displayed a remarkable degree of openness and integration, with information on securities prices rapidly circulated and with widespread cross-border trading. The rise of capital market integration in the eighteenth century is discussed by L. Neal in *The Rise of Financial Capitalism: International Capital Markets in the Age of Reason* (Cambridge: Cambridge University Press, 1990).

[2]A detailed description of the international lending activities of European banks in Latin America and of the debt crises of the nineteenth century is supplied by C. Marichal in *A Century of Debt Crises in Latin America: From Independence to the Great Depression, 1820–1930* (Princeton, N.J.: Princeton University Press, 1989).

1860 and 1890, the total assets of financial intermediaries in the country multiplied six times.[3] U.S. bankers were supplying funds to the rest of the world. Nearly 250 foreign loans, totaling more than $1 billion, were arranged in the United States between 1900 and 1913.[4] This was still a comparatively small number by international standards because the City of London was lending more than that amount abroad in a single year. However, this was not to last. U.S. foreign lending accelerated during World War I. Wall Street became the center of international finance when London and other European financial markets were burdened with closings related to the war. American banking was instrumental in the financing of that war and, by its end, the Allies owed $10 billion in war debts to the U.S. government. Great Britain, the world's biggest lender five years earlier, was now heavily in debt to the United States.

The international business of American banks continued to boom in the 1920s. Some of this expansion was undertaken under the umbrella of the 1919 *Edge Act*. The act allowed U.S. national banks to establish special corporations through which an array of international banking activities could be pursued, including acquisitions of foreign banks and investment banking in other countries. These Edge Act corporations (as they became known) continue to exist and allow U.S. banks to supply an array of services abroad in which regular foreign branches of domestic banks are not permitted to engage.[5]

The foreign penetration of U.S. banking in the 1920s is reflected in the growth of the National City Bank of New York (later to become Citibank). National City Bank set up its first foreign branch in 1914; by 1926 it had eighty-four foreign branches. This expansion was associated with a move into Latin America, where, with the exception of Mexico, U.S. investments had been small compared to European lending. In total, U.S. bankers sold approximately $2 billion in Latin American bonds to American investors between 1922 and 1928. New York bankers aggressively competed and sought business in Brazil, Cuba, Colombia, Peru, and other countries. When combined with the increased U.S. political influence associated with these investment flows, the process became known as dollar diplomacy.[6]

The Great Crash of the New York Stock Exchange on October 24, 1929, and the Great Depression of the 1930s brought international finance to a halt. The drop in worldwide economic activity and international trade, and the consequent defaults on domestic and foreign loans and securities, resulted in a widespread loss of confidence in the banking system. Runs on local banks from customers seeking to withdraw their deposits from potentially (but not necessarily) insolvent banks resulted in a rash of bank closings and collapses that affected not only troubled institutions but many solvent ones. In the four years between 1930 and 1933, 9,096 banks failed, fully 36 percent of the number that had existed at the beginning of 1930. Many governments reacted by imposing an array of regulations on both the domestic and foreign operations of banks. Exchange controls were imposed in Britain, France, and numerous other countries to prevent local capital from being invested abroad. Some of those controls were not eliminated until the late 1970s and 1980s.

In the United States, the government responded to the collapse of the banking industry by instituting a major overhaul of the banking regulatory system. The reforms were embodied in the bank-

---

[3]For an analysis of U.S. economic growth in this period, see G. M. Walton and H. Rockoff, *History of the American Economy* (New York: Harcourt, 1990), chap. 17.

[4]R. C. Smith, *The Global Bankers* (New York: Dutton, 1989), p. 18.

[5]See K. Cooper and D. R. Frazer, *Banking Deregulation and the New Competition in Financial Services* (Cambridge: Ballinger, 1986), chap. 3.

[6]A discussion of the economic and political power of U.S. investments in Latin America is available in B. Stallings, *Banker to the Third World: U.S. Portfolio Investment in Latin America: 1900–1986* (Berkeley: University of California Press, 1987).

ing acts of 1933 and 1935; the acts shaped the American banking industry as we know it today. The reforms imposed a set of restrictions on banks—including the separation of commercial from investment banking and the elimination of bank competition across state lines—and created new institutions (such as the federal insurance of bank deposits, under the flag of the Federal Deposit Insurance Corporation [FDIC]) intended to provide a safety net under the banking system. The new regulatory framework supplied stability to U.S. banking: There has not been a single systemwide run on banks since the 1930s.

The debacle embodied by the Great Depression led to widespread default and to major losses for both the borrowing countries and the American banks and investors that did a lot of the lending.[7] World War II also resulted in a major breakdown of international financial markets. By the 1960s and 1970s, however, U.S. banking abroad was climbing new heights, with Citibank, the Bank of America, and other commercial banks operating extensive international operations. Partly, international banking was growing through offshore business, which will be discussed in Chapter 8. Another important development was the renewed U.S. lending to developing countries, which had been growing since the end of World War II but was booming in the late 1970s.

In 1977, U.S. banks had $46.9 billion in claims on non-OPEC developing countries. By June 1982, this amount had more than doubled. Argentina, Brazil, and Mexico alone owed $52.4 billion to U.S. banks in June 1982. It was later in 1982 that it became crystal clear that, as a result of a conjunction of internal and external events—

including a contraction of export earnings associated with world recession and higher interest payments linked to climbing world interest rates—many heavily indebted developing countries were no longer able to pay even the interest on their loans. The new debt crisis erupted in full view in August 1982 when the government of Mexico—running out of funds with which to service loan payments—stopped servicing its external debt. A number of other countries—including Peru and Brazil—engaged in similar disruptions of external debt payments in the 1980s; a rash of others have been involved in continuous reschedulings and renegotiations of their debts ever since. This topic will be discussed in detail in Chapter 12.

The emergence of the developing country debt crisis coincided with the appearance of a number of U.S. bank failures. The fall of Continental Illinois in 1985 and of Dallas's First Republic Bankcorp and MCorp in 1988 and 1989 (in the face of bad loans resulting from the effects of the then low energy prices in the Texas economy) were the tip of the iceberg in a glacier of coming difficulties. As illustrated by Table 7–1, bank failures surged from a low number of ten failures a year in the 1970s up to 172 per year in the late 1980s. The number of banks appearing on the "problem list" exploded from approximately two hundred in 1980 to almost fifteen hundred in 1988 (although these failures should not be exaggerated: There were more than fourteen thousand banks in the U.S. at the time). In 1988, more than two hundred banks failed, and the FDIC reported its first operating loss in its history. As bank failures continued to accumulate, the FDIC financial position deteriorated and its financial capacity to pay depositors in failed banks suffered to the point of exhaustion.

The nonperformance of a significant part of the loan portfolio of American banks involved in developing-country lending affected their profitability in the 1980s. On the other hand, only the largest American banks have been involved in

---

[7]It is estimated that, in spite of readjustments and reschedulings, defaulted loans in the interwar period resulted in a loss of 75 percent of the interest due to American investors. See B. Eichengreen and R. Portes, "After the Deluge: Default, Negotiation and Readjustment During the Interwar Years," in B. Eichengreen and P. H. Lindert, eds., *The International Debt Crisis in Historical Perspective* (Cambridge, Mass.: The MIT Press, 1989), p. 40.

TABLE 7–1.   U.S. Commercial Bank Failures in the Twentieth Century

Time Period	Total No. Closed	Annual Average No. Closed	No. of Banks Beginning of Period
All Institutions			
1910–1919	849	85	25,151
1920–1929	5,882	588	30,909
1930–1933	9,106	2,277	24,273
Insured Institutions			
1934–1939	400	67	14,144
1940–1949	115	12	13,442
1950–1959	46	5	13,446
1960–1969	58	6	13,126
1970–1979	80	8	13,511
1980–1984	190	38	14,434
1985–1988	689	172	14,405

Note: "Banks closed" comprise all banks that suspended operations as the result of financial difficulties. After 1933, the numbers refer to all FDIC-insured banks.

SOURCE: D. M. Jaffee, "Symposium on Federal Deposit Insurance for S&L Institutions," *Journal of Economic Perspectives* (Fall 1989), Table 1, p. 4. Reprinted with permission.

substantial lending to heavily indebted countries. Other factors must thus explain the financial difficulties of the many smaller commercial banks that constitute the majority of recent bank failures. One influence has been the greater competition faced by American banks both domestically and abroad. The 1991 *Economic Report of the President* observed: "U.S. banks are facing greater competition from foreign banks at home, while only a few U.S. banks are significantly increasing their business overseas."[8] Some experts have suggested that current regulatory structures hinder U.S. banking as compared to foreign banks and have clamored for their modification and, sometimes, elimination.[9] The next sections examine the increased competition faced by U.S. banking and the current regulatory issues affecting it.

7–2. EXPANDING INTERNATIONAL COMPETITION IN FINANCIAL SERVICES

A widely discussed recent trend in international banking is the dramatic growth of Japanese vis-à-vis American and European banking. The preeminence of American banking in the time when Bank of America, Chase Manhattan Bank, and Citicorp were the three largest banks in the world has collapsed. By the early 1990s, between seven and ten of the largest banks worldwide were Japanese, and among American banks only Citicorp made the top-twenty list. The rise of Japanese banking reflects the rapid growth of Japan's indus-

[8]*Economic Report of the President* (Washington, D.C.: U.S. Government Printing Office, 1991), p. 164.

[9]C. A. Glassman, "U.S. Financial Institutions in a World Market," in C. A. Glassman et al., *Regulating the New Financial Services Industry* (Washington, D.C.: Center for National

Policy Press, 1988); and R. E. Litan, *What Should Banks Do?* (Washington, D.C.: Brookings Institution, 1987).

trial might, its growing wealth, and its financial internationalization in the 1980s and 1990s.[10]

Table 7–2 presents the top fifteen banks in the world in terms of assets.[11] Note the absence of American banks and the dominance of Japanese banks. Seven of the fifteen biggest banks are Japanese. The largest among them, such as Dai-ichi Kangyo Bank, Sumitomo Bank, and Fuji Bank, had assets close to $400 billion each, almost duplicating the size of Citicorp, the largest U.S. bank and the only American bank on the top-twenty list (ranked eighteen in 1991). Just fifteen or twenty years earlier, the picture looked very different. In 1969, seven out of the ten largest banks were American. None was Japanese. In 1974, the Bank of America, the Chase Manhattan Bank, and Citicorp were the three largest banks in the world, and the list of the ten largest banks was dominated by U.S.-owned banks, followed by French, British, and West German banks. By the late 1980s, Japan had pushed aside the traditional powers. Its share in the total assets of the largest ten banks had risen from less than 10 percent in the early 1970s to between 90 and 100 percent in the late 1980s.

[10]For a comprehensive examination of the evolving international financial system that focuses on the United States, Japan, and the United Kingdom, see D. M. Meerschwam, *Breaking Financial Boundaries. Global Capital, National Deregulation, and Financial Services Firms* (Boston: Harvard Business School Press, 1991); see also J. A. Frieden, *Banking on the World: The Politics of International Finance* (New York: Basil Blackwell, 1987).

[11]The financial structure of a commercial bank can be described in terms of its assets, liabilities, and equity. Its liabilities consist of deposit accounts issued to customers, as well as the amount of borrowing from the central bank and other sources. A bank's assets consist of its precautionary cash reserves (in the form of currency and reserves at the central bank, used to pay depositors when they withdraw funds), investments such as loans and bonds, and other assets such as the bank's premises. The bank's liabilities (its deposits) provide funds used by the institution to finance its asset acquisitions (its loans). Finally, bank equity, or net worth, is the difference between the total value of the bank's assets and its total liabilities. It represents the capital that the bank's owners would accumulate if they were to sell the institution.

TABLE 7–2. The Top Fifteen Banks Worldwide

1990 Rank	Name of Bank	Country
1.	Dai-ichi Kangyo Bank	Japan
2.	Mitsui Taiyo Kobe Bank	Japan
3.	Sumitomo Bank	Japan
4.	Mitsubishi Bank	Japan
5.	Fuji Bank	Japan
6.	Sanwa Bank	Japan
7.	Credit Agricole	France
8.	Banque Nationale de Paris	France
9.	Credit Lyonnais	France
10.	Industrial Bank of Japan	Japan
11.	Barclays	Britain
12.	Deutsche Bank	Germany
13.	Tokai Bank	Japan
14.	National Westminster Bank	Britain
15.	Abn-Amro Holding	Netherlands

Ranking is based on dollar value of total assets.

SOURCE: S. Lohr, "For Lagging American Banks, Survival Means Consolidation," *The New York Times,* July 21, 1991, Section E, p. 5.

The relative decline of American banks can be illustrated by reviewing the experience of Bank of America, the largest bank worldwide throughout most of the 1970s. The history of Bank of America's ranking, as determined from total bank assets, shows a drop from first or second place in the 1960s, 1970s, and early 1980s, down to fourth place in 1984, followed by a free fall to the forty-first place in 1988. Chase Manhattan had a similar experience when by 1987 it had fallen to the thirty-third place.[12]

[12]Systematic data on banks for past decades can be found in the periodicals *Euromoney, American Banker,* and *The Banker.* The changing nature of global banking has been discussed by H. de Carmoy, *Global Banking Strategy: Financial Markets and Industrial Decay.* (Cambridge, Mass.: Basil Blackwell, 1990). The rise and fall of Bank of America worldwide has been described by M. Johnston, *Roller Coaster: The Bank of America and the Future of American Banking* (New York: Ticknor & Fields, 1990).

It should be stressed that evaluating changes in the relative economic size and leadership of banks is very tricky. For instance, the ratings just examined were based on bank assets. The rankings change when banks are classified by the value of their equity. In 1990, the equity position of Citicorp exceeded that of most Japanese banks in the top-fifteen list and came close to that of the three largest banks.[13] In addition, the large increase in Japanese bank assets measured in dollars—as reported in Table 7–2—is partly explained by the rising value of the yen vis-à-vis the dollar. (The dollar value of foreign bank assets depends on the exchange rates used to convert assets denominated in foreign currencies into dollars.)

The figures on banking assets in Table 7–2 include those assets acquired through investments and loans made in the domestic market as well as the foreign loans and investments made by banks. The rise of Japanese banking reflected in Table 7–2 is largely the result of the increased size of Japan's domestic banking system. However, it also reflects the increasing internationalization of Japanese banking by expansion into the onshore systems in other countries, as well as increased participation in offshore banking. Foreign assets amount to about 40 percent of Japanese banking assets. The assets of the overseas branches of Japanese banks had already passed the $1,000 billion mark in 1987.[14] The Sumitomo Bank, for instance, is well established in the United States and has subsidiaries in London, Switzerland, and

Asia. By the early 1990s, Union Bank (controlled by the Bank of Tokyo), Bank of California (Mitsubishi Bank), Sanwa, and Sumitomo were among the top ten banks in California and held about 25 percent of the banking assets in the state. However, the state's bank leaders were still American banks such as Bank of America, Security Pacific, and Wells Fargo.

As reflected in the growing presence of Japanese banks, foreign banking in the United States has generated increased competition with American banks. At the end of 1989, the foreign share of U.S. banking assets was 20.4 percent. Similarly, the importance of foreign banking has been rising in Europe, although it varies wildly by country. As measured by the share of foreign assets in the banking sector, foreign penetration of domestic banking in Europe in 1987 varied from 3 percent in Italy, 4 percent in Germany, 17 percent in France, 60 percent in the United Kingdom, and 90 percent in Luxembourg. The extent of foreign banking activity is still low in Japan. Although there were about seventy foreign banks operating in Japan in the mid-1980s, their share was a mere 3 percent of the loan market.[15]

Table 7–3 presents a schematic description of the types of foreign-owned banking institutions found in the United States. They consist of subsidiaries of foreign banks, foreign-owned banks not owned by other banks (commercial banks, in Table 7–3), agencies and branches of foreign banks, and international banking facilities (IBFs).[16] Clearly,

---

[13]Even evaluating the equity of a bank is complicated. The equity values reported on the banks' balance sheet are book values, reflecting the prices at which assets were purchased by the bank. This will not necessarily be the current, or market, value of its assets. In 1990, the market value of Citicorp was about $3.5 billion; the market values of Sumitomo Bank, Deutsche Bank, and Union Bank of Switzerland were $41 billion, $15 billion, and $10.25 billion, respectively. See F. G. Rohatyn, "These Are Wars We Have to Win," *The GAO Journal* (Winter 1990–1991).

[14]See "Principal Accounts of Overseas Branches of Japanese Banks," year-end, 1981 through 1987, *Japan Financial Statistics,* Federation of Bankers Associations of Japan, 1989, p. 26.

[15]See C. de Boissieu, "The French Banking Sector in the Light of European Financial Integration," in J. Dermine, ed., *European Banking in the 1990s* (Cambridge, Mass.: Basil Blackwell, 1990), p. 199; and L. Pauly, *Opening Financial Markets: Banking Politics on the Pacific Rim* (Ithaca, N.Y.: Cornell University Press, 1988).

[16]IBFs accept deposits from foreign residents. Because these are dollar-denominated accounts, IBFs are technically part of the domestic banking system. In practice, however, they were set up to compete with Eurodollar accounts held by foreign residents outside the United States. For this reason we will defer discussing them until we examine Euromarkets in Chapter 8.

TABLE 7–3. **Types of Foreign-Owned Banking Institutions**

Commercial Bank
- Chartered in the U.S. as a bank.
- Owned by foreign individuals, firms or banks.
- Same capital and insurance requirements as a domestically owned bank.
- Same regulations as other domestically chartered banks.
- May offer full range of banking services.
- May provide both retail and wholesale banking services.

Subsidiary Bank
- Owned and operated as a U.S. subsidiary of a foreign commercial bank.
- Subsidiaries are chartered in the U.S. as a bank.
- Incorporated as a separate entity from the foreign parent.
- Same capital and insurance requirements as a domestically owned bank.
- Same regulations as domestic banks.
- May offer full range of banking services.
- May provide both retail and wholesale banking services.
- May be funded by parent bank or affiliated institutions.

Agency of a Foreign Bank
- Offers only limited banking services.
- Cannot accept deposits, but may accept "credit balances."
- Concentrates on trade-financing and money market services.
- May be funded with borrowings from parent or affiliates.

Branch of a Foreign Bank
- Has full banking powers.
- Can accept deposits.
- Provides many trade-financing and money market services.
- May be funded with borrowings from parent or affiliates.

International Banking Facility (IBF)
- Not a separate entity, but a set of accounts on the books of the bank, agency, or branch.
- May accept deposits from and extend credit to foreign residents, parent, and other IBFs.
- Not subject to U.S. reserve requirements or interest rate ceilings.

SOURCE: G. C. Zimmerman, "The Growing Presence of Japanese Banks in California," Federal Reserve Bank of San Francisco, *Review* (Summer 1989), p. 5.

there is a wide variety of foreign activity in the U.S. onshore banking system. This foreign presence has generated some concerns among some sectors of the American public which fear that the U.S. is rapidly becoming "owned" by foreigners [see, for instance: Martin and Susan Tolchin, *Our Security: The Erosion of America's Assets* (New York: Alfred A. Knopf, 1992)]. This is an issue that we will discuss in detail in Chapters 9 and 10. Suffice it to say here that there has been some exaggeration of the extent to which foreign investments in the banking industry of the U.S. have risen over the 1980s and 1990s. The case of California—a state characterized by a high concentration of foreign-owned banks—shows that, contrary to popular perceptions, the extent of foreign banking remained

stable throughout the 1980s. It stayed at about 30 percent of the state's total banking assets throughout the decade. The higher visibility of foreign banking was basically a consequence of the purchase of foreign-owned banks by the Japanese, which came to dominate among other foreign nationalities.

The increased competition faced by American commercial banks both in the onshore system and worldwide has generated cries from the industry that U.S. regulations hamper their competitiveness. It is argued that the elimination or modification of regulatory structures would aid in raising the profitability of domestic operations and enhance the ability of the banks to compete internationally. The next sections examine the regulatory issues involving banking.

7–3. THE GLASS-STEAGALL ACT AND THE REGULATION OF U.S. BANKING

The experience of the Great Depression led to a basic restructuring of the U.S. banking system under a set of reforms implemented during the administration of President Franklin D. Roosevelt. The Banking Reform Act of March 1933, also called the Glass-Steagall Act, was the main law determining the new system that would govern the business of banking for years to come.

Among its key provisions, the Glass-Steagall Act forbid commercial banks from investing in corporate stocks and bonds. Thus, the asset side of U.S. banks' balance sheets today show items such as bank's cash reserves,[17] loans granted to a variety of borrowers, bonds, and other assets, such as bank's premises, but no stocks or ownership claims on firms. Only government bonds, but not corporate bonds, can appear as assets. The reason for this is that the Glass-Steagall Act prohibited banks from investing in stocks and bonds issued by corporations. In the aftermath of the 1929 stock market crash and the wave of corporate bankruptcies in the early 1930s, banks investing in stocks came to be viewed as extremely risky and as having been key in generating the banking crisis of the period. The purpose of forbidding banks from acquiring corporate stocks and bonds was to enhance the safety of bank assets and to reduce bank instability.

A second key consequence of the Glass-Steagall Act was the separation of investment and commercial banking activities. Before the new laws, banks could pursue commercial loans while being active participants in the issuance of new domestic or foreign stock and bonds. In fact, about a third of all corporate securities issued in the late 1920s were underwritten by banks in one way or another. In response to reports that losses associated with the holding and underwriting of securities by banks had been critical in some bank failures, the Banking Act of 1933 limited the underwriting activities of banks to state and local government bonds; it permitted banks to serve only as dealers for government and not for corporate securities. Again, this prohibition was intended as a safety mechanism that would prevent the spillover of troubles in securities markets into the banking system.

A third set of reforms instituted in the 1930s involved the institution of federal deposit insurance. The FDIC was established to insure bank deposit accounts up to a certain ceiling, which at the present time is $100,000 per account. The goal of federal deposit insurance was to discourage bank runs. In the past, when a bank failed, depositors were not insured and could lose all their money. This, of course, meant that any rumors or hints of banking institutions in trouble (even if unfounded) would lead customers to withdraw their bank deposits to prevent losses if the bank failed. Banks that were otherwise in sound condition could face liquidity deficiencies or even insolvency as a result of a depletion of deposits associated with a lack of confidence in the banking system. The possibility of bank panics presented a systemic risk that surrounded the banking system as a whole. Federal deposit insurance was intended to deal with this problem.

Other important provisions of the banking reform laws had the explicit intention of reducing competition among banks in order to prevent the closings associated with such competition. Banks were prohibited from paying interest on demand deposits, ceilings were imposed on interest paid on time deposits, and competition across state borders

---

[17]Not all of the money deposited in banks is invested in income-generating assets. Commercial banks hold precautionary reserves in the form of currency and coin (called cash in vaults) and as deposits at the central bank. The latter form part of minimum reserve requirements that the central bank imposes on commercial banks and that vary by type of deposit (for instance, in April 1992, the Federal Reserve Board imposed a 10 percent reserve requirement on transactions accounts, which include demand deposits). Commercial banks thus have liabilities in the form of bank deposits and assets in the form of loans, securities, and cash.

was limited through restrictions on interstate banking and branching.

The regulatory structure set by the banking reforms of the 1930s did provide a stable banking environment. Although banks continued to fail in the 1930s, the 315 banks failures between 1934 and 1939 compared favorably with the nine thousand between 1930 and 1933. On average, about six banks closed per year between 1945 and 1980. However, the regulations have come under increasing attack. Over the last thirty years many of them have been circumvented, modified, or eliminated (for instance, ceilings on interest rates were eliminated in the 1980s). The issue was recently inflamed by the rash of bank failures that surfaced in the late 1980s and early 1990s. What is the role played by the regulatory framework inherited from the Glass-Steagall era on current commercial banking problems? The next section examines this issue.

7–4. DEREGULATION AND THE INCREASED COMPETITIVENESS OF AMERICAN BANKING

The recent tribulations of American commercial banks have given way to a flurry of reform-oriented activity centered on raising commercial banks' profitability without augmenting their risk taking to levels that would endanger the public's overall confidence in the banking system. The reform effort seeks to eliminate many of the remaining Glass-Steagall restrictions.

One of those restrictions relates to the separation of commercial from investment banking activities. The exclusion of commercial banking from the securities business began to break down in the 1960s as a result of financial innovation and deregulation. Investment bankers began to compete directly with commercial banks with the development of money market funds. These funds invest in short-term securities such as Treasury bills and pay an interest rate called the money market interest rate. Money market funds allow the penalty-free transfer of funds in a way similar to a bank checking account. Because money market securities are safe, bear interest, and are easily transferable, they compete with commercial bank deposits and take business away from the banking system. The development of money market funds effectively represented an encroachment by securities firms into the commercial bank deposit business. Commercial banks responded to this increased competition by expanding into securities business through bank holding companies. The bank holding company is a corporation that owns the bank as well as other corporations. Bank holding companies—but not the commercial bank forming part of the holding company—can offer investment and brokerage services. In effect, banks are circumventing the spirit of the Glass-Steagall regulations.

In spite of the ability of commercial banks to innovate their way out of regulations, the restrictions on the joining of investment and commercial activities do not allow U.S. commercial banks to offer full-scale, or "universal," services to customers and curtail commercial banking competitiveness. This is particularly significant because, as a result of the massive appearance of securities in world finance in the last decade, the securities underwriting and trading business is currently one of the most profitable among financial activities, especially compared to bank loans.[18] Another area in which the reform of banking law is being examined to enhance U.S. bank competitiveness consists of the existing limits on banking and branching across state lines. Although the latter have been liberalized or circumvented over the years, the remaining restrictions impede the exploitation of economies of scale in banking.

The extent to which regulatory restrictions on commercial banks should be eliminated and the balance kept between the interests of increased

[18]For a discussion of securities and other recent trends in financial markets, see R. M. Levich, "Financial Innovations in International Financial Markets," in M. Feldstein, ed., *The United States in the World Economy* (Chicago: University of Chicago Press, 1988).

competitiveness and sustaining the public's confidence in the system's safety is a matter that will receive considerable discussion in the future. The debate can benefit from the recent experience of the savings and loan industry.[19]

The savings and loan (S&L) industry was already in crisis in the early 1980s. Traditionally, S&Ls issued savings accounts (whose deposit interest rates were subject to regulated ceilings) and used those deposits to make long-term, fixed-rate mortgage loans. As the name indicates, *fixed-rate* loans have a fixed interest rate attached to them over the maturity of the loan (*floating-rate* loans have interest rates that vary, perhaps yearly, depending on prevailing interest rates). The 1970s saw a general increase in interest rates. In order for the S&Ls to keep and attract depositors, deposit interest rates had to be raised. In addition, the stock of existing fixed-rate loans held by S&Ls earned the lower interest rates that had prevailed in earlier years. The result was a decline in profitability and in the economic net worth, or capital, of the institutions.

The reaction of the government to the S&L problems in the late 1970s was to try to promote their relative competitiveness by eliminating ceilings on deposit interest rates, relaxing restrictions on the type of lending permitted (they could then engage in consumer, business, and commercial real estate lending), and allowing them to engage in nontraditional spheres. In spite of the deregulation, the S&Ls still collapsed; the problems finally erupted with a wave of S&L insolvencies in the late 1980s. The insurer of S&Ls, the Federal Savings and Loans Insurance Corporation (FSLIC), found itself running out of money even after raising insurance premiums. In 1989, the Financial Institutions Reform, Recovery and Enforcement Act (FIRREA) paved the way for a massive

bailout of the S&Ls insurance agencies. The cost of the operation has been estimated at $300 billion to $500 billion.[20] FIRREA closed more than five hundred insolvent S&Ls and eliminated FSLIC and transferred its functions—including the insurance function—to the FDIC. It also increased the insurance premiums charged by the FDIC to banks in an unsuccessful attempt to replenish the insurance funds. However, by inheriting the duties of the failed insurer of the S&Ls, the FDIC fell into deep trouble itself.

The S&L industry was in difficulty in the early 1980s, and the deregulation process does not appear to have helped. Some observers have actually argued that deregulation aggravated the crisis. Their reasoning is that, given the low levels of net worth of many S&Ls owners, they had little to lose by engaging in risky investments that could yield fast, high returns: "If the S&L becomes insolvent, the owners will eventually be forced to surrender ownership, and any remaining assets of the S&L will be used to pay off depositors. In such cases, some owners might decide that risky investments are worth the gamble, for if the investments are profitable enough to return the institution to economic health, the owners retain the net worth of the S&L. If the investment fails, the deposit insurer will repay any losses on insured deposits. The closer an institution comes to insolvency, the more rewards become one-sided: Heads, the S&L owners win; tails, the deposit insurer loses."[21] The rash of failed real estate and other investments made by some S&Ls in the 1980s attests to this phenomenon.

---

[19]For academic and journalistic discussions of the S&L crisis, see respectively L. J. White, *The S&L Debacle: Public Policy Lessons for Bank and Thrift Legislation* (Oxford: Oxford University Press, 1991); and J. Ring Adams, *The Big Fix: Inside the S&L Scandal* (New York: Wiley, 1991).

[20]When the S&L crisis surfaced in earnest in the late 1980s, between six hundred and eight hundred thrift institutions, about a quarter of the nations' savings and loan associations, were insolvent. See J. L. Pierce, *The Future of Banking* (New Haven, Conn.: Yale University Press, 1991), p. 77; and E. J. Kane, *The S&L Insurance Mess: How Did It Happen?* (Washington, D.C.: Urban Institute, 1989). The reform of federal deposit insurance is addressed in a symposium published in the *Journal of Economic Perspectives* (Fall 1989).

[21]*Economic Report of the President,* (Washington, D.C.: U.S. Government Printing Office, 1991), p. 172.

The federal insurance problem faced by S&Ls is also one bank reform legislators are encountering. The latter have to contend with a number of troubled commercial banks seeking greater freedom to engage in activities that may increase their risk taking. A number of plans has been advanced to deal with the FDIC financial problems and to improve the implementation of the federal deposit insurance system itself. Some proposals have sought to reduce the amount of deposits insured. Another popular proposal is the introduction of risk-based insurance premiums. Under this proposal, banks that make unsafe investments would be subject to correspondingly higher risk premiums by the FDIC. This presumably would reduce the incentive to engage in high risk taking by placing a greater insurance cost on it. In addition, higher premiums would provide funds to the insurance agency. The proposal is not without its problems, which are related to the difficulties involved in the risk-taking assessment activities of overburdened regulators.

The issue of bank reform is one of great importance for the health of the U.S. banking system and for its ability to compete in evolving global financial markets. Financial centers compete strenuously to attract banking business and to produce financial services at low costs. This competition forces markets that become relatively overburdened with regulation to deregulate or otherwise lose business. However, deregulation must be considered carefully. As the S&L case illustrates, deregulation may or may not increase the long-term health of the American banking industry.[22]

[22]Recent proposals for reforming bank regulations are examined by F. Mishkin, "An Evaluation of the Treasury Plan for Banking Reform," *Journal of Economic Perspectives* (Winter 1992). For a discussion of the relative competitiveness of U.S. financial institutions, see T. H. Hanley, "Domestic and International Bank Stock Investing: A Global Approach," Salomon Brothers Inc. Research Department (March 1988); and R. B. Cohen, "The Foreign Challenge to U.S. Commercial Banks," in T. Noyelle, ed., *New York's Financial Markets: The Challenges of Globalization* (Boulder, Colo.: Westview Press, 1989).

7–5. KEIRETSU, BANKS, AND DEREGULATION IN JAPAN

The increasing worldwide significance of Japanese finance will be a fact of life in the coming decades, just as British finance was in the nineteenth century and U.S. financial power was early in the twentieth. This section looks at the Japanese banking industry and the factors behind its recent expansion.

There are many key economic factors behind the rise of the Japanese banking giants noted earlier. Among those factors is, first, that country's high savings rate and accumulation of wealth, which created a massive local deposit base. Second is the process of liberalization in the Japanese financial markets that, in the 1970s and 1980s, made possible the competitive expansion of Japanese banking abroad. Third is bank mergers, which vastly increased the size of Japanese banks. For instance, in April 1990, two of Japan's largest commercial banks, the Mitsui and Taiyo Kobe banks, merged to form one of the world's largest banking groups, the Mitsui-Taiyo Kobe, with about six hundred branches in Japan and twenty-five foreign offices. The merger was realized under the auspices of the country's Ministry of Finance. It is questionable whether bank regulators in the United States would have allowed this type of merger; U.S. regulators have been sternly antitrust and have fought concentration in the banking industry for decades.

Some Background on Japanese Banking

The Japanese banking (and financial) system has traditionally been tightly controlled by the Finance Ministry and the Bank of Japan (the country's central bank).[23] The high degree of regulation and

[23]For discussions of Japanese finance, see Y. Suzuki, ed., *The Japanese Financial System* (New York: Clarendon, 1987); A. Viner, *Inside Japanese Financial Markets* (Homewood, Ill.: Dow Jones-Irwin, 1988); R. Feldman, *Japanese Financial Markets: Deficits, Dilemmas and Deregulation* (Cambridge,
(continued)

government intervention has led to the unusual experience in which not a single bank has failed since World War II. Various traits differentiate the Japanese system from that in the United States. First, interest rate controls have proliferated for decades. Second, foreigners have been excluded or restricted through a variety of mechanisms, protecting local interests from foreign competition. Third, banks are functionally compartmentalized. There are banks that specialize in corporate lending, in pension fund management, and in regional banking. Fourth, contrary to the U.S. experience, Japanese banks are allowed to hold stocks. Group financial institutions can hold up to 5 percent of a firm's outstanding shares. Also, Japanese banks are not subject to the restrictions on real estate investments that apply to U.S. banks. U.S. banks lend for real estate purposes; Japanese banks both lend and invest in that market. Finally, Japanese banks and financial institutions are the central elements of the *keiretsu,* or "industrial group," system that characterizes the Japanese economy. The term *keiretsu* comes from the words *kei* and *retsu* that mean "faction" or "group" and "arranged in order," respectively. The close interactions among the group's members make for very different banking and industrial systems in Japan and the United States.

Large segments of the Japanese economy are dominated by a system of huge industrial groups whose modern form originated in the 1950s. The six largest industrial groups are Mitsubishi, Mitsui, Sumitomo, Fuji, Dai-ichi Kangyo, and Sanwa. These bank-led groups bring together banks and other financial institutions, such as insurance companies and manufacturing firms. The Mitsubishi group, for instance, is formed by Mitsubishi Bank, Mitsubishi Trust Bank, Meiji Life Insurance, Tokyo Fire and Marine Insurance, and many manufacturing firms. About half of Japan's largest

two hundred firms are members of one of these groups.

A close relationship between a bank and its client firms emerges from this system. The bank provides a substantial part of debt financing for member firms. It also owns equity in the firm and frequently places bank employees in its client firms' management positions. Because the groups incorporate many manufacturing firms that buy and sell to each other, a close relationship develops between a firm, its bank, many of its suppliers, and even customers. These ties are strengthened when firms in a group hold shares in other firms within the group (cross-share investing). Analysts have argued that this system reduces information costs, contributes to relax liquidity constraints promoting investment, and helps the recovery of firms that fall into financial distress, reducing the cost of that distress.[24] For instance, when Mazda fell into financial problems after 1972, Sumitomo Bank helped restructure the company and put it on its feet again. The industrial group ties are deemed a key element in this rescue operation.

Deregulation in Japan

The traditionally highly regulated Japanese financial system has been gradually decontrolled since the 1980s. The Banking Act of 1982 partially reversed the strict separation between banking and securities that had ruled since the establishment of the Securities and Exchange Act at the time of U.S. occupation. Article 65 of that law established an American-style separation between the banking and securities industries. The 1982 law permits

---

Mass.: MIT Press, 1986); J. Horne, *Japanese Financial Markets* (London: Allen & Unwin, 1985); and T. Cargill and S. Royama, *The Transition of Japanese Finance and Monetary Policy in Comparative Perspective with the United States* (Stanford, Calif.: Hoover Institute Press, 1977).

[24]A comparison of the U.S. and Japanese financial systems is provided by S. D. Prowse in "Institutional Investment Patterns and Corporate Financial Behavior in the United States and Japan," *Journal of Financial Economics,* (October 1990). The role of banks and *keiretsu* in corporate behavior is discussed by T. Hoshi, A. Kashyap, and D. Scharfstein, "Bank Monitoring and Investment: Evidence from the Changing Structure of Japanese Corporate Banking Relationships," in R. Glenn Hubbard, ed., *Information, Investment, and Capital Markets* (Chicago: University of Chicago Press, 1990).

banks to sell government bonds as well as to hold them in their own portfolios. Major banks currently deal in government bonds.

Securities firms have also benefited from deregulation that permits entry into areas previously reserved for banks. For instance, in June 1985, securities firms were allowed to participate in the secondary market for CDs. At the same time, the securities industry continues to be protected from bank competition. For example, the highly profitable retail brokerage business remains strictly off limits to banks. The reluctance to permit the entry of banks and securities companies into each other's activities is related to the country's industrial structure. The problems involved are most prominent in the case of banks engaging in the securities business. Given the close interaction and extensive information flows between the banks and industrial companies, it will be very difficult for the banks to avoid conflict of interests and access to inside information about firms. The securities selling and underwriting activities of banks could be easily abused or distorted under these conditions.[25]

Interest rate liberalization has proceeded in stages. In April 1985, interest rates on money market certificates of ¥ 50 million or more were deregulated. This move was followed in October of that year by the deregulation of interest rates on bank time deposits of Y1 billion or more and with a maturity exceeding three years and two months. It was not until 1989 that deregulation freed interest rates on "small" money market certificates of ¥ 3 million or more (approximately $220,000 at the exchange rates prevailing at the time). Interest rates received by small savers and investors continue to be controlled.

Other liberalization measures taken in the 1980s included allowing local and foreign banks to sell Euroyen CDs. These yen-denominated CDs are issued outside Japan, are payable to the bearer (that is, the owner is anonymous), and are tradable

in a secondary market. This move boosted the Euroyen deposit market, to be discussed in Chapter 8. Also, selected foreign banks were allowed to enter the vast Japanese pension fund management business, the largest in the world.

The Japanese experience shows a clear, gradual movement toward deregulation and a slowly evolving financial opening. In the early 1990s, however, the decontrol of banking activities was nowhere near completion, and a financial opening was, to a large extent, merely symbolic in some areas. Opening has meant freeing the ability of Japanese firms to operate abroad, but it has not yet resulted in greater competition from foreign firms in Japan's domestic markets.

7—6. EUROPEAN BANKING AND THE FINANCIAL INTEGRATION OF 1992

In 1985, the European Commission—the body of representatives of the European Community's member countries that initiates its policy initiatives—proposed a plan to create a unified internal European market by 1992. A key aspect of the economic integration initiative concerned financial integration. However, the integration of capital markets involved in the Europe 1992 project encountered serious problems with the banking system.[26] The main challenge involved how to make the local legal autonomy of each country's banking system consistent with a unified communitywide market. Banking laws and regulations differ substantially across countries. Also, the relaxation of restrictions on capital flows and of limits imposed by local authorities to the entry of foreign-owned firms had to be achieved to develop a free internal market.

The principle followed in creating the single market was to allow legal autonomy to governments while harmonizing certain aspects of the member countries' laws and eliminating restrictions

---

[25]So-called universal (full-service) banks in Europe are also subject to these same problems when they sell the securities of companies in which they have an ownership interest.

[26]For a detailed survey of banking in Europe, see J. Dermine, *European Banking in the 1990s* (Cambridge, Mass.: Basil Blackwell, 1990).

that impacted adversely on nonlocal firms. For this reason, although financial opening has evolved, a truly unified market with full financial integration has not been achieved.

As was examined in earlier chapters, the European integration process can be traced back to the 1957 Treaty of Rome, but banking and financial integration did not advance until decades later. The First Banking Directive of 1977 left in the hands of local authorities the faculty to approve the request from foreign banks to operate locally. Local authorities retained full supervisory powers over operations in their territory. Restrictions on capital flows and on the establishment of banking facilities in other countries also impeded integration; however, their effects have gradually diminished, as many have been dismantled, particularly in relation to the Europe 1992 project. The Second Banking Directive of 1988 took the integration process a long step forward. It established a single banking license and the principle that all financial institutions operating in one country will automatically be able to operate in all member countries (principle of mutual recognition). Under this directive, controls on solvency and broad exposure were assigned to the home country of the financial institution; other controls were assigned to the host country in which the bank would actually operate.

The process of building a single financial market has affected the market structure of European banking. That industry has traditionally been highly concentrated, as compared with the United States and Japan. For instance, the number of banks belonging to the French Bankers Association has varied, hovering at about four hundred since 1950. In the United States, about as many *new* banks have been created in a single year (the number of U.S. commercial banks has fluctuated at around 14,000 since 1934, and there are more than 3,000 savings banks). The largest nine banks in France accounted for 90 percent of total bank deposits in 1987. The United Kingdom, Belgium, Ireland, Luxembourg, Portugal, Greece, Denmark, and the Netherlands also exhibit high concentra-

tion in the banking industry.[27] Only Italy, Germany, and Spain exhibit levels of concentrations in banking that come close to the low concentration in the United States and Japan.

The financial opening in Europe has promoted the cross-penetration of banking. This has led to a rash of mergers, as banks have moved to operate on a European scale. For instance, Deutsche Bank acquired Bank of America operations in Italy. Two major Spanish banks, Banco de Bilbao and Banco de Vizcaya, merged in order to be better able to survive the incoming wave of large foreign banks expected as a result of the opening of the internal market. The greater competition among banks within the EEC is bound to have a deep impact in some countries, such as Italy and France, with their state-owned banking.

An area in which European banking has traditionally differed from that in the United States is the insurance of bank deposits. The coverage of deposit insurance in Europe is more limited than in the United States, and the insurance systems, because they are not well advertised, are sometimes unknown to depositors. For instance, in the United Kingdom, the Deposit Protection Fund protects 75 percent of sterling deposits up to £20,000 (it was only £10,000 before 1987). The maximum amount a depositor can receive in the case of bank failure is thus £15.000 (75 percent of £20,000), as compared to $100,000 in the United States.

The harmonization of the banking laws of European Community countries has been advocated to avoid the potential capital flight that may occur

---

[27]See A. Steinherr and P. Gilbert, "The Impact of Freeing Trade in Financial Services and Capital Movements on the European Banking Industry," Center for European Policy Studies, Financial Markets Unit, Research Report no. 1 (January 1989). For comparative data on banking concentration, reserve requirements, and other banking variables, see F. Bruni, "Banking and Financial Regulation Towards 1992: The Italian Case," in Dermine, op. cit. For a comprehensive discussion of the market structure issues surrounding European banking regulation, see X. Vives, "Banking Competition and European Integration," in A. Giovannini and C. Mayer, eds., *European Financial Integration* (Cambridge: Cambridge University Press, 1991).

out of those locations featuring limited deposit insurance, high reserve requirements on bank deposits, and high taxes. However, harmonization remains an elusive goal. For instance, the harmonization of the various insurance systems within the EC has been widely discussed but not yet solved. A similar situation exists with reserve requirements. In 1988, reserve requirements on bank deposits ranged from nil in Belgium and Denmark to 0.5 percent in the United Kingdom, to about 10 percent in Germany, all the way up to 25 percent in Italy (where bank reserves are remunerated). Another area in which harmonization is relevant is the payment of withholding taxes. Some government income tax authorities withhold taxes on interest income before the interest payments are received. Withholding tax rates thus affect the attractiveness of the interest-bearing investments of financial centers. A small withholding tax is especially attractive when there is no requirement to report interest income to the authorities. In 1988–1989, all European Community countries except Luxembourg either had a withholding tax on interest income received by residents (for instance, 25 percent in the United Kingdom and Belgium) or required that this income be reported to the authorities. However, nonresidents did not pay withholding taxes in Denmark, Luxembourg, and the Netherlands; by contrast, in Belgium and the United Kingdom, there was a 25 percent tax for both residents and nonresidents.[28]

7–7. Financial Repression, Liberalization, and Economic Growth

Financial market liberalization has not been restricted to industrialized countries. It has also been adopted by some developing countries as an integral part of their economic development strategies. The shift from the economics of financial regulation or repression to a world of financial market liberalization in Asia and Latin America provides a historical comparison between the performance of two alternative orders. *Financial repression* occurs when authorities impose controls over interest rates, encumber financial returns with high taxes, establish limits on the credit allocations of financial institutions, and engage in other forms of intervention that distort financial decisions.[29] Financial repression has characterized most Latin American economies for decades, although liberalization was implemented in some countries in the 1970s and 1980s. Asian countries have also followed the path from repression toward liberalization, although the trend generally began earlier.

In the definition of financial repression, the emphasis must be placed on the impact of government policies in generating *substantial distortion* of financial decision making. Controls on interest rates do not necessarily entail significant financial repression. For instance, until the deregulation of the 1980s, Japanese interest rates had been controlled for decades. However, the low inflation rates experienced by that country meant that interest rates remained generally positive.

Table 7–4 displays the behavior of interest rates and inflation in the major financial markets from 1953 to 1982. The discount rate is the rate charged by the central bank on its loans to commercial banks. The call money rate is a short-term interest rate, and the Treasury bill (TB) yield represents the return on short-term government securities. Note that, if you subtract inflation from these interest rates, the resulting real interest rate was generally positive in all markets throughout

---

[28]For data on the tax treatment of interest, dividends, and capital gains, see A. Giovannini and J. R. Hines, "Capital Flight and Tax Competition," in Giovannini and Mayer, ibid., and R. Levich, "The Euromarkets After 1992," in Dermine, ed., *European Banking in the 1990s* (Cambridge, Mass.: Basil Blackwell, 1990).

[29]For an overview of financial repression and liberalization strategies, see M. J. Fry, *Money, Interest, and Banking in Economic Development* (Baltimore: Johns Hopkins University Press, 1988). R. McKinnon analyzes the recent experience in Asia and Latin America in *The Order of Economic Liberalization: Financial Control in the Transition to a Market Economy* (Baltimore: Johns Hopkins University Press, 1991).

time—with the exception of the period between 1973 and 1977. This result was independent of whether the wholesale price index (WPI) or the consumer price index (CPI) was used to measure inflation (both indices are depicted in Table 7–4).[30]

The history of the real interest rate in the industrial countries shown by Table 7–4 contrasts drastically with the case of Latin American nations. In many Latin American countries, interest rates have been endemically set at levels near or below the rate of inflation. This entails significant economic effects. The prevalence of negative real interest rates leads to distorted financial decisions. In those circumstances, creditors are effectively receiving less than what they lend in real terms. For this reason, they will seek alternative outlets for investable funds. Bank depositors will shun the banking system, and its intermediation function will be negatively affected, with a consequent contraction in the flow of loanable funds. The economy's financial deepening, as measured by the ratio of total savings and demand deposits as a proportion of GNP, shrinks and remains at a low value.[31] In these circumstances, lenders that lack access to the collapsing banking system are forced to obtain credit in informal markets at a high cost.

Financial repression has been prevalent in Latin America. Between 1960 and 1980, Argentina and Chile experienced annual inflation rates ranging from 20 percent to more than 200 percent. Brazil's inflation averaged more than 30 percent a year in this period, and Colombia and Peru had inflation rates of more than 20 percent. The combination of interest rate controls and high inflation produced negative real interest rates and a stagnant financial sector. The ratio of savings and demand deposits to GNP generally stayed between 0.14 and 0.22 (but went down to 0.01 in Chile under the high-inflation conditions prevailing in the mid-1970s).

The experience of Taiwan illustrates the fact that continuous growth in financial deepening can occur in the presence of positive real interest rates (even though the banking system may be subject to some degree of financial repression). Real interest rates received by savers and paid by borrowers in Taiwan have generally been positive and high. From 1956 to 1962, the average real interest rate on savings deposit was 8.6 percent; from 1963 to 1973 it was 6.7 percent; and in 1984 it was equal to 6.3 percent.[32] This structure of relatively high real interest rates supported an enormous increase in financial deepening. The ratio of total savings and demand deposits to GNP steadily increased from 0.10 in 1955 to 0.75 in 1980. This reflects a financial expansion that took Taiwan close to the financial deepening levels of countries like Germany and Singapore (but still lagging far behind the 1.40 ratio of deposits to GNP in Japan in 1980).

Although it is clear that financial repression restricts financial deepening, its economic effects are controversial. The experience of rapidly growing countries in Asia and Europe suggests a positive relationship between greater financial deepening and growth (although it is not clear what causes what). Countries like Germany, Japan, Korea, Taiwan, and Singapore were rapidly growing

---

[30]These real interest rates represent ex post real interest rates, defined as the nominal interest rate minus the actual inflation rate prevailing during the maturity of the investment. These are different from ex ante interest rates, equal to the nominal rate minus expected inflation, as defined in Chapter 5. Financial decisions are based on the basis of ex ante real interest rates, but ex post real interest rates can be used as an indicator of the ex ante rates. The value of the real interest rate depends on which inflation measure is used. For instance, between 1958 and 1964, the Japanese CPI exceeded the WPI by more than 4 percent.

[31]See E. S. Shaw, *Financial Deepening in Economic Development* (New York: Oxford University Press, 1973); and R. I. McKinnon, *Money and Capital in Economic Development* (Washington, D.C.: Brookings Institution, 1973).

[32]The real interest rate here is the ex post real interest rate, equal to the nominal interest rate on savings account deposits minus the corresponding inflation rate in consumer prices. See R. I. McKinnon, "Financial Liberalization and Economic Development: A Reassessment of Interest-Rate Policies in Asia and Latin America," *Oxford Review of Economic Policy* (Winter 1989).

TABLE 7–4. **History of Interest Rates and Inflation in Major World Financial Markets, 1952–1982**

	Official Discount Rates, Deposit Rates, and Money Market Rates (annual average, percent)					
	1953–57	*1958–62*	*1963–67*	*1968–72*	*1973–77*	*1978–82*
Japan						
Discount rate	6.9%	7.1%	5.9%	5.4%	7.1%	5.6%
Call money rate	8.7	9.6	7.4	7.0	8.6	7.1
Deposit rate[a]	5.1	5.3	5.0	5.0	6.0	5.2
WPI rate of change	1.1	−1.0	1.4	1.3	11.4	5.1
CPI rate of change	3.1	3.6	5.6	5.9	13.1	4.6
United States						
Discount rate	2.4	3.1	4.2	5.2	6.5	11.0
TB rate	2.1	2.7	4.0	5.4	6.2	10.7
Deposit rate[b]	2.6	3.2	5.0	5.0	5.5	5.7
WPI rate of change	1.0	0.3	1.1	3.6	10.4	9.1
CPI rate of change	1.2	1.5	2.0	4.6	7.7	9.8
United Kingdom						
Discount rate	4.7	4.7	6.4	7.2	11.4	14.5[c]
TB rate	3.5	4.4	5.2	6.6	9.9	12.2
Deposit rate[d]	2.8	2.7	4.4	4.9	8.2	11.2
WPI rate of change	1.7	1.4	2.3	5.8	17.9	11.4
CPI rate of change	2.9	2.2	3.3	6.6	16.3	12.0
Germany						
Discount rate	3.8	3.4	3.6	4.7	4.6	5.8
Call money rate	3.7	4.0	3.8	5.3	6.3	7.7
Deposit rate[e]	3.5	2.9	3.1	5.4	6.0	6.8
WPI rate of change	−0.5	0.5	0.9	2.6	6.2	5.4
CPI rate of change	0.9	2.0	2.7	3.5	5.7	5.8

[a]The interest rate on six-month deposits.

[b]The interest rate on time deposits less than U.S. $100,000 (maximum). From 1953 to 1967, the maximum rate on deposits of more than one year.

[c]1978–80. The Bank of England stopped announcing the minimum lending rate—that is, the discount rate.

[d]The interest rate on deposits account repayable at seven days' notice (maximum).

[e]The interest rate on three-month deposits (maximum).

SOURCE: Based on R. I. McKinnon "Financial Liberalization and Economic Development: A Reassessment of Interest-Rate Policies in Asia and Latin America," *Oxford Review of Economic Policy* (Winter 1989), Table 4, p. 36.

countries in which the ratio of deposits to GNP multiplied as much as twice (in Japan) or even seven times (in Taiwan) between 1950 and 1980. On the other hand, countries like Argentina, Brazil, Chile, Colombia, India, the Philippines, Sri Lanka, and Turkey had slow-growth economies that did not deepen financially from 1960 to 1980, generally keeping a ratio of deposits to GNP below 30 percent (an exception was India's 38 percent ratio in 1980). However, in recent research, economists Rudiger Dornbusch and Alejandro Reynoso were unable to find a significant relationship between per capita income growth and increased financial deepening for a sample of eighty-four developing countries between 1965 and 1985.[33] In a sense, the interaction between the financial sector and economic growth is a complex one that depends on a multitude of accompanying factors and is mined by pitfalls. The divergent experiences in the financial liberalization of Latin America and Asia, to be discussed next, illustrate the pitfalls of mechanically relating liberalization and greater growth.

Latin American Liberalization: Good-bye Financial Repression, Hello Financial Crash[34]

The fast pace of the financial liberalization experiments of the Southern Cone Latin American countries—Argentina, Chile, and Uruguay—in the 1970s contrasts with the slow-paced deregulation of the newly industrializing Asian countries. The instability associated with financial deregulation in these countries has given rise to serious questions about the strategy. At the same time, the Asian experience shows that well-implemented liberalization is consistent with stability.

Financial liberalization has had two components in Latin America.[35] The first is the elimination of ceilings on interest rates. The second is an increased financial opening to the world by freeing international financial transactions from restrictions. The actual implementation of these changes

in the Southern Cone has been fast and drastic, but most importantly it has occurred in the presence of distorted economic policymaking in other spheres. Whether it is the existence of high, unstable inflationary environments, overvalued exchange rates, lack of regulation of the banking system, or all of these, the financial liberalizations in Latin America have been undertaken under conditions that stimulate either massive capital flight from the economy (intended to avoid local inflationary taxes or domestic inflation risk) or otherwise huge capital inflows (attracted by unbelievably high real interest rates). The result of the reforms under these conditions has been financial disaster.

In Chile, interest rate ceilings were removed in 1976 in the midst of three-digit inflation. Although government budget deficits were suppressed and disinflation followed, the consumer price index was still rising by 40 percent in 1979 and 30 percent in 1980.[36] Nominal interest rates were even higher. Real interest rates on peso loans declined from 64 percent in 1976 to 17 percent and 12 percent in 1979 and 1980, respectively; however, they remained far above real interest rates on dollar-denominated loans. As a consequence, foreign capital flowed toward Chile. The explanation of the high real interest rates is still bothersome. Economist Arnold Harberger of the University of Chicago has focused on the high demands for credit: "The internal source of difficulty in Chile was a proliferation of bad loans within the banking system. The rolling over of these loans, capitalizing interest along the way, created what I call a 'false' demand for credit, which, when added to the demand that would normally be viable, allowed real interest rates to reach unprecedented (and, to many, incredible)

[33]R. Dornbusch and A. Reynoso, "Financial Factors in Economic Development," *American Economic Review* (May 1989). See, however, McKinnon, op. cit.

[34]This apt description is the title of a much-cited article by the late Carlos Diaz Alejandro: "Good-Bye Financial Repression, Hello Financial Crash," *Journal of Development Economics* (September-October, 1985).

[35]Latin American liberalization is examined in V. Corbo and J. de Melo, "Lessons from the Southern Cone Policy Reforms," *The World Bank Research Observer* (July 1987).

[36]With the credibility of the policy still in question in 1979, the government proceeded to fix the exchange rate as an anti-inflation device. Inflation receded in 1979 and 1980, to be reignited in 1981–1982. The Chilean program is examined by S. Edwards and A. Cox-Edwards in *Monetarism and Liberalization. The Chilean Experiment* (Cambridge, Mass.: Ballinger, 1985).

levels."[37] Under very loose supervision on the part of the authorities, the flood of foreign funds into the country resulted in a surge of unsafe loans. The crisis exploded in 1982 when the financial system crashed and the government intervened with a massive bailout. The Chilean government absorbed and guaranteed the debt that the local banks could not repay. This move transformed a private sector banking debacle into a public sector external debt problem. The episode is widely deemed a failed liberalization occurring under lax government supervision and inauspicious economic events.

The cases of Argentina and Uruguay differ in significant respects. Rather than creating capital inflows, as in Chile, financial liberalization in these countries was associated with the flight of private capital in gigantic proportions. High inflation and an overvalued exchange rate meant that capital controls played the role of keeping funds from flowing out of the country. Again, the lesson is that financial liberalization that is not backed by a stable, non-distorted economy and a credible government policy regime can be counterproductive.

In the 1980s and early 1990s, deregulation and financial opening have returned with stronger force in Latin America. Proceeding at a slower pace and with greater understanding of past policy mistakes, the current wave of financial liberalization offers hope. In the Mexican case, it successfully supported economic recovery in the late 1980s and early 1990s.

Financial Deregulation in Asia

The process of financial reform in Asia that had proceeded gradually since the 1970s, took on force in the 1980s and 1990s. Deposit and lending rates,

already deregulated in Singapore (1975) and Malaysia (1978), were deregulated in Korea (1988), Taiwan (1989), the Philippines (in 1983, for lending rates), and Indonesia (1983, for state banks, and earlier for private banks). Some state-owned banks have been privatized in Korea (1988) and Taiwan (1989). New banks, including foreign banks or their branches, have been permitted to operate in Indonesia (1988), Thailand (1988), and Taiwan (1986). In addition, foreign exchange controls have been relaxed and new markets have been opened in CDs and other instruments.[38]

As opposed to the financial instability—the litany of foreign debt, bankruptcies, and capital flight—associated with some of the better-known financial liberalization experiments in Latin America, Asian reform has resulted in the orderly accumulation of assets in the financial sector. Continuous growth has been maintained since the early 1980s in Korea, Taiwan, Hong Kong, and Singapore. Healthy growth has also characterized the member countries of the Association of Southeast Asian Nations (ASEAN)—Thailand, Malaysia, Indonesia, and the Philippines—although in the case of the Philippines, political instability prevented economic growth from being renewed until after 1987.

On the other hand, Asian financial liberalization has not been free of complications. The Korean liberalization of 1964 represented an eminently successful economic reform program in the long term. Yet, it was plagued by problems similar to—although of a lower magnitude—those we encountered in the Latin American experiments. Korea's program consisted of trade and exchange rate reform (liberalization of imports, currency unification, and a large, once-and-for-all devaluation) coupled with a major change in the financial and fiscal system. Controlled interest rates were increased to levels that yielded positive real

[37]A. C. Harberger, "Lessons for Debtor Country Managers and Policy Makers," in G. W. Smith and J. Cuddington, eds., *International Debt and the Developing Countries* (Washington, D.C.: World Bank, 1985). See also, A. C. Harberger "Welfare Consequences of Capital Inflows," in A. M. Choksi and D. Papageorgiou, eds., *Economic Liberalization in Developing Countries* (New York: Basil Blackwell, 1986), and the comments by L. Ahamed and R. Dornbusch in the same volume.

[38]See Bank of Japan, "Financial Reform in Asian Economies," Special Paper no. 189, Research and Statistics Department (May 1990). The appendix in that paper contains a detailed listing and chronology of reform measures in Asia.

interest rates. The results were dramatic. Domestic prices stabilized by 1965, and the economy initiated a long-lasting path toward economic progress. However, short-term financial inflows flooded the economy in 1966, leading to financial destabilization and inflation. Once again, the experience shows the delicate nature of the path toward deregulation and openness.

The Order of Liberalization of Capital Flows and International Trade

The implementation of liberalization programs is a complex issue. Should international financial flows and trade in goods and services be liberalized at the same time? In many instances, bureaucratic and other constraints do not permit the simultaneous liberalization of everything. Which one should be liberalized first? When financial flows are liberalized while some goods remain protected from foreign competition, capital may flow toward the protected goods sectors. If the protected sectors are inefficient industries that cannot withstand foreign competition, the capital inflows may in fact result in the expansion of inefficient production. This argument suggests freer trade in goods should precede financial opening.

The experience of Latin American nations suggests that opening the economy to internationally mobile, short-term financial flows when the reform is not supported by a stable economy can generate substantial instability. For this reason, many analysts have suggested that short-term financial flows should be restricted during the transition to a freer trade regime.[39]

A further argument for controls on international capital flows can be made in the case of trade liberalizations that are temporary or that lack credibility (that is, that are not expected to survive). For instance, consider tariff reductions that are expected to be reversed. Given the anticipation of an increase in tariffs, consumers have an incentive to accumulate durable goods while the tariff is at a low level, perhaps incurring large storage costs in the process. This costly accumulation of durable goods is financed through external borrowing. Controls over capital movements can be beneficial because they will restrict costly borrowing for the purposes of accumulating inventories.[40]

Summary

1. The onshore banking system of any given country consists of the domestic banking activities conducted in local currency. The onshore system is not totally the turf of locally owned banks: Foreign banks can operate in the onshore system, subject to the rules for domestic banks or under special regulation. The offshore banking system is composed of deposits, loans, and bonds denominated in a currency but issued outside the boundaries of the country where the currency is legal tender.

2. In the nineteenth century, British and European lending dominated American banking. By the 1920s, though, the United States was lending to Great Britain and U.S. banks had hegemony in Latin American lending. The Great Crash of 1929, the Great Depression, and World War II seriously curtailed the expansion of international banking. In the 1960s and 1970s, U.S. banking regained its earlier momentum. In the late 1970s, American banks were heavily and aggressively lending to developing countries. By 1982, it was clear that many of these countries would not be able to

[39]See R. I. McKinnon, "The Order of Liberalization: Lessons from Chile and Argentina," in K. Brunner and A. Meltzer, eds., *Economic Policy in a World of Change* (Amsterdam: North Holland, 1982); S. Edwards, "The Order of Liberalization of the Current and Capital Accounts of the Balance of Payments," in A. M. Choksi and D. Papageorgiou, eds., *Economic Liberalization in Developing Countries* (Cambridge, Mass.: Basil Blackwell, 1986); and S. Edwards, "The Sequencing of Economic Reform: Analytical Issues and Lessons from Latin America," *The World Economy* (March 1990).

[40]These points are elaborated in G. Calvo, "Costly Trade Liberalizations: Durable Goods and Capital Mobility," *IMF Staff Papers* (September 1988).

repay their debts. The nonperformance of developing country loans constituted a significant shock to U.S. bank profitability.

3. The worldwide expansion of Japanese banking has supplanted the predominant position that U.S. and British banking held in previous centuries. Foreign bank participation is significant in the United Kingdom, Germany, and in some U.S. states, such as California and New York, but it is not a worldwide phenomenon.

4. The Banking Act of 1933, also called the Glass-Steagall Act, introduced federal deposit insurance, established a separation between commercial and investment banking activities, and prohibited commercial banks from holding corporate stocks. The structure established by this banking reform stabilized American banking in the 1930s and determined its present structure. After forty years of stabilized banking, the late 1980s and early 1990s saw a wave of commercial bank failures that has pushed the Glass-Steagall regime into deep crisis. By the early 1990s, the Federal Deposit Insurance Corporation (FDIC) was in financial difficulty. Bank reform efforts in the 1990s are oriented toward restoring bank competitiveness.

5. Large segments of the Japanese economy are dominated by a system of bank-led industrial groups (*keiretsu*). About half of the country's largest firms are members of these groups, which consist of banks and other financial institutions joined with an array of manufacturing firms. The close relationships between banks and industrial-firm members of the same group include bank financing, cross-share investing, and interlocking directorates. Analysts have argued that this system reduces information costs, contributes to relaxing liquidity constraints on firms (thus promoting investment), and helps the recovery of firms that fall into financial distress.

6. Since the early 1980s, Japan has taken a set of financial liberalization measures, including the elimination of long-standing controls over interest rates on large- and medium-sized deposits. More recent measures make it easier for foreign firms to enter into the Japanese financial markets.

7. The integration of European financial markets by 1992 opened local banking systems to entry by firms from other European countries. The principle followed in creating the single market was to allow legal regulatory autonomy to national governments but to eliminate the restrictions that impact adversely on European banks seeking to locate anyplace within the internal market. The harmonization of bank deposit reserve requirements, deposit insurance systems, tax laws, and other regulations has not yet been undertaken. For this reason, although increased integration of banking has occurred, a truly single market has not been achieved.

8. Financial repression occurs when authorities impose controls over interest rates, subject financial returns to high taxes, establish limits on the credit allocation of financial institutions, and engage in other forms of intervention that distort financial decision making. Financial repression has resulted in negative real interest rates on bank deposits in many countries. As a result, funds leave the banking system, and the economy's financial deepening—as measured by the ratio of total deposits to GNP—remains at low levels (from 0.10 to 0.30).

9. The experience of Asia and Latin America suggests that successful financial liberalization has been accomplished within a stable, credible domestic economic environment that is free of distorting inflationary and exchange rate policies. The order in which the financial and the trade sectors are liberalized, the accompanying macroeconomic policies, and the extent and efficiency of government supervision of financial institutions are some factors that affect the outcome of financial liberalization.

Problems

1. The growing foreign bank presence in the United States has led some policymakers to seek increased regulation of foreign banks operating in the U.S. On December 19, 1991 the Congress enacted the Foreign Bank Supervision Enhancement Act, which substantially increased the supervisory and regulatory role of the Federal Reserve over U.S. activities of foreign banks. What are the benefits and costs of increased regulatory constraints over the operations of foreign banks in the United States?

2. Compare the contemporary banking systems of the United States, the major European countries, and Japan. Describe the depositors' protection system, reserve requirements, the segmentation of investment and commercial banking, and capital requirements imposed by the authorities on banks. Given the ongoing reforms in these countries, research your answer to this question.

3. Examine the overall state of savings and loan institutions. How does it compare with the situation described in the text? Are there any major new policy initiatives since the book was written?

4. Analyze the evolving financial integration of Europe. Has the widely predicted wave of bank mergers materialized? How has the integration led to changes in the banking systems of individual countries?

5. Consider a country that is launching a major trade liberalization program. A group of major international donors decides to make the transition smoother by granting vast amounts of foreign aid. What are the financial effects of foreign aid in these circumstances? How will the foreign aid program affect the transition toward free trade? An instance of liberalization with foreign aid is that of Egypt in the 1970s. What does that experience suggest?

6. The government of a highly interventionist country is considering financial and trade liberalization. The question arises as to whether liberalization should be completed rapidly and fully or be realized gradually. Which factors would you consider in analyzing this problem? (This question concerns the speed of the transition toward a liberalized trade regime.)

7. In April 1993, Mr. Ernesto Hernandez-Cata, deputy director of the IMF's division dealing with the former Soviet Union, suggested that there was a need for Russian interest rates to rise from 100 percent to a level above the 1,000 percent inflation rate [as quoted in *The Financial Times* (April 30, 1993), p. 6]. Given the experiences of countries in Asia and Latin America with financial liberalization, would you agree with Mr. Hernandez-Cata? What other suggestions would you present to Russian policymakers in this regard?

CHAPTER 8

Eurocurrencies and Euromarkets: The Offshore Banking System

Chapter 7 dealt with the onshore banking system, which offers domestic currency deposits and domestic currency loans. This chapter focuses on offshore banking. The offshore banking system is composed of deposits, loans, and other instruments denominated in a currency, say dollars, but issued outside the country where the currency is legal tender. We move on, so to speak, from an examination of the market for dollar certificates of deposit (CDs) in New York to an exploration of the market for dollar CDs in London and the linkages between the New York and London banking systems. This shift of attention extends the scope of the analysis in a major way because it incorporates an important development in financial markets since the 1960s—the remarkable growth of the Eurodollar market.

Eurodollars are dollar deposits held outside the United States (offshore), such as dollar deposits in London, Zurich, or Paris. The development of a large and active market for these Euro- or offshore dollar deposits has added a new dimension to international financial management. A multinational corporation holding investable dollar funds can now place them in New York, London, or elsewhere. This means that financial executives are required to undertake decisions regarding both the currency of denomination and the location of assets. This chapter examines the reasons for the development of the Euromarkets. It looks at their main institutional and economic aspects and their practical implications for both investors and borrowers.

The globalization of banking in the 1980s and 1990s has meant that dollar-denominated deposits now proliferate outside the boundaries of the United States and that an active and sophisticated market in them has surged. American, European, and Japanese banks have entered the Eurodollar system, becoming main players in its multiple activities. However, the deutsche mark, the yen, and other currencies also have spilled over, outside of their domestic markets, and become widely used abroad. Taken together, these offshore, external, or Eurocurrency markets—such as the Eurodollar, the Eurosterling, and the Euroyen markets—constitute a closely knit network competing with domestic banking systems and among themselves. They can influence the impact of government policies and provide an alternative market for investable funds. When financial secrecy is offered as a special benefit, they also open a channel for tax evasion, money laundering, and similar activities.

The significance of the offshore, external, or Eurocurrency markets is not confined to bank deposits. For instance, a large market in dollar-denominated loans made by banks outside the United States is easily accessible to corporations and governments. This Eurodollar loan market provides a source of dollar funds alternative to the domestic U.S. financial market. It has assumed a particularly significant role in meeting the financial needs of the public sector in many developing countries. Also, the development of Eurobond markets and other offshore sources of funds has internationalized the credit markets. Table 8–1 depicts the relative magnitude of the loan, bond, and other activities of the Eurocurrency market. Note the overall growth of these activities, particularly of the Eurobond item (which expanded from $20.4 billion in 1980 to over $200 billion in 1990), and the relative stagnation of the loan category. This chapter examines these patterns in detail.

8–1. Eurocurrencies, Eurodollars, and Money

A Eurocurrency deposit is a deposit denominated in a currency that is different from the currency of the financial center in which the deposit is held.

TABLE 8–1. Activities of the Eurodollar Market, 1980–1986 (in billions of dollars)

	1980	1981	1982	1983	1984	1985	1986
Bank loans[a]	$ 81.0	$144.4	$ 96.0	$ 73.5	$108.5	$110.3	$ 82.8
Eurobonds	20.4	31.3	50.3	50.1	81.7	135.4	187.0
Equity-related bonds				8.0	10.9	11.5	22.3
Other facilities[b]					11.4	32.3	70.8
Total	101.4	175.7	146.3	131.6	212.5	289.5	362.9

[a]Credits extended by commercial banks to nonbanks wholly or in part out of Eurocurrency funds.

[b]Mainly commercial paper programs.

SOURCE: IMF, *International Capital Markets* (January 1988).

Deutsche mark deposits in London banks or in Luxembourg are Eurocurrencies, as are sterling deposits in Paris. The term *Eurocurrency* is misleading, however, because what is usually referred to as a Eurocurrency deposit may not necessarily involve deposits in Europe at all. For instance, what is traditionally called a Eurodollar is a dollar deposit held outside the United States, regardless of whether it is held in a European, Asian, or Caribbean bank. Therefore, dollar deposits in Asian financial centers such as Hong Kong and Singapore are, paradoxically, Eurodollars. The terminology can be confusing: It derives from the historical evolution of the Eurocurrency market in the 1950s and 1960s as a primarily European one, acquiring its present worldwide scope during the 1970s. The prefix *Euro-* has been retained despite its lack of accuracy. In fact, the terms *external,* or *offshore,* deposits are more precise because they connote more accurately the idea of dollar deposits located outside the United States, sterling deposits outside Britain, and so on. By the same token, Eurocurrency loans refer to external (offshore) loans in general and are not necessarily obtained from European banks.

The Eurodeposit market is composed essentially of time deposits, with maturities varying from one week or less (overnight deposits are common) to about three years.[1] Similarly, Euroloans extend over the short-term and medium-term maturity range. The vast majority of both Eurodeposits and loans, however, are concentrated at the short end of the maturity spectrum, with most maturities being earlier than six months. The Eurocurrency market should thus be envisioned as forming part of the international money market. As such, the London dollar market interacts and competes with the U.S. dollar money market, as well as with the U.K.

pound-sterling money market and the German and Swiss money markets.

Should Eurocurrencies then be considered to be money—that is, should Eurodollars be counted as part of the U.S. money supply? The answer to this controversial question hinges on how broad a concept of money is to be adopted. Inasmuch as the offshore system offers only short-term time deposits (in large part, CDs), it is basically a market in near-monies—that is, it deals mainly with short-term liquid instruments very similar to money but not usually included in a narrow definition or concept of money. Eurodollar deposits rarely consist of demand deposits (checking accounts) and therefore would be excluded from a narrow definition of money consisting of currency and checking deposits. The distinction is admittedly somewhat arbitrary; in fact, Eurodollars should be included in broad concepts of the U.S. money supply. Actually, the Federal Reserve Board of the United States, in its recent definitions of money, has included some components of Eurodollar deposits as forming part of what it has called M2 and M3. What should be stressed is thus that what distinguishes the Eurodeposit money market from domestic money markets is not so much the type of financial instruments traded, but the fact that they are externally traded.

8–2. AN INTRODUCTION TO EXTERNAL FINANCIAL MARKETS

Commercial banks constitute the core of the Eurocurrency market. Accordingly, in examining the banking system of the United States or any other economy having a Eurocurrency, it becomes critical to remember the distinction between the domestic and external banking systems made in Chapter 7. The U.S. banking system is an extensive network including thousands of banks operating all over the country. It embraces all dollar deposits accepted and loans made by domestic

---

[1] For details on Euromarket instruments, currencies, and other issues, see E. Sarver, *The Eurocurrency Market Handbook* (New York: Prentice Hall and New York Institute of Finance, 1988).

banks and by domestic branches or subsidiaries of foreign banks operating in the United States.[2] The dollar external banking system, on the other hand, consists of dollar deposits held in—and loans obtained from—the whole array of foreign banks and foreign branches and subsidiaries of U.S. banks that participates in the Eurodollar market. These banks accept Eurodollar deposits, which they then lend to such borrowers as large multinational corporations and governments in developing countries. The dollar external banking system is dominated by the activities of foreign branches and subsidiaries of major U.S. banks (e.g., Bank of America, Chase, and Citibank) whose tentacles extend worldwide. These are joined by the major Japanese, British, German, and Swiss banks—among many other so-called *Eurobanks*—that issue external dollar deposits and make external dollar loans. These banking activities effectively create a banking system that operates outside the boundaries of the domestic banking system—that is, an external banking system.

One of the key points to remember about Eurobanks, however, is that they are not independent banks specializing in the issuance of external deposits and loans; they are, rather, a part (branches or subsidiaries) of major national banks that have the issuance of external deposits and loans as only one of their many activities. For instance, Eurobanking is just one activity among many others for an American bank office in London. Because the bank might be issuing deposits and

loans in pounds sterling, this also suggests that banks are frequently simultaneously a part of the British domestic banking system and of the U.S. external (Eurodollar) banking system.

Eurobanking operations are concentrated in a limited number of financial centers that attract external transactions in various Eurocurrencies. The most active Eurocurrency center is located in London. The City of London, the traditional name of London's financial district, features a rich international banking tradition and enjoys a supportive regulatory environment; it has attracted banks from many nationalities that engage mostly in Eurodollar transactions but also transact in the main Eurocurrencies and in sterling. Although the London market remains the center of the Eurocurrency market, its traditional historical predominance has been declining in relative terms as a consequence of the rapid deployment of alternative centers. For example, the North American Eurocurrency Market, which includes Euromarket dealings channeled mainly through the Bahamas and Cayman Islands, has been closing in on London's activity; by some measures, in fact, its size may be more than two-thirds that of London's. An Asian dollar market centered in Singapore and Hong Kong has also grown rapidly, operating mainly as a regional market servicing the Far East. Other major financial centers with significant Eurocurrency dealings are located in Switzerland, Luxembourg, Panama, and Bahrain. Note that New York (or Chicago, or any other U.S. financial center) is not on the list. This is because U.S. monetary authorities have used various means to discourage the issuance in the United States of deposits denominated in currencies other than the dollar; the amounts are therefore insignificant. Until 1990, U.S. banks were not allowed to offer accounts in foreign currency. This is now permitted, and Citibank, Bank of America, and other banks offer interest-bearing foreign currency accounts that are covered up to $100,000 by federal deposit insurance (accounts in foreign countries and Eurodeposits are not covered by federal insurance).

---

[2]The distinction between a branch and a subsidiary is a legal one. A U.S. subsidiary of a foreign company is incorporated in the United States and has a legal identity apart from that of the parent company. A U.S. branch of a foreign company is not incorporated in the United States and is considered to be an extension of the parent company. A similar distinction applies to foreign branches and subsidiaries of U.S. firms. The U.S. branches and subsidiaries of foreign-owned banks account for approximately 15 percent of U.S. banking assets and have a visible presence in major U.S. cities, as a walk through New York's or Chicago's financial districts will quickly reveal. A wide range of nationalities is represented in U.S. banking, including Israel's Bank Leumi, Japan's Mitsubishi Bank, the United Kingdom's Barclays, and many others.

Who uses the Eurocurrency market? Eurobanking activities are a segment of the wholesale international money market. The vast majority of Eurocurrency transactions fall in the above $1 million value range, frequently reaching the hundreds of millions (or even billion) dollar value. Accordingly, the customers of Eurobanks are almost exclusively large organizations, including non-Eurobank institutions such as multinational corporations, governments, and international organizations, as well as Eurobanks themselves.[3] Multinational corporations form a large and active part of the Eurodeposit market, as they search for the highest rate of return and move liquid funds around to maximize interest receipts. Actually, hundreds of millions of dollars in corporate funds lie deposited in Eurobanks, in the form of CDs. As borrowers, large multinational corporations—by virtue of their size and credit reputation—can obtain access to external credit with a minimum of documentation or investigation by the banks, and at quite attractive prime rates.[4]

The competitive interest rates offered by Eurodeposits, on the other hand, have also attracted government funds. Central banks, in particular, maintain a substantial share of their countries' international reserves in the form of high-yielding Eurodeposit holdings. Government borrowing in the Euroloan market is also substantial; it includes the dramatic rise of Eurobank loans to developing countries in the 1970s and early 1980s, which was followed by a debt crisis in these countries, a subject to which we will return later, in Chapter 12. International institutions such as the World Bank also borrow in the Eurocurrency market and lend the proceeds to developing countries. Finally, a substantial share of Eurobanking activities is in fact interbank, in which banks trade among themselves, lending and borrowing.

The interbank market constitutes a major part of Eurobanking activities. In fact, most transactions in the London market are wholesale interbank transactions. By means of the interbank lending market, a Eurobank holding surplus funds, and with no commercial customers immediately available, can lend its excess reserves to other Eurobanks with clients (borrowers) available but no loanable funds at the moment. The interest rates charged by Eurobanks lending through the interbank market are referred to as *interbank offered rates*. The widely publicized London interbank offered rate (LIBOR) is an average of interbank-offered rates often used as a basis for setting non-Eurobank customer lending rates. The latter are usually above the LIBOR, and the margin between the two is referred to as the Eurolending *spread*. The size of the spread is dependent on the creditworthiness of the borrowers and may vary over time.

The symbiotic relationship between Eurobanks implied by interbank lending gives rise to a question of interpretation regarding the size of the Eurocurrency market. The interbank network generates Eurodeposits when banks enjoying surplus funds deposit them with another Eurobank. Interbank depositing constitutes a transfer of funds from one bank to another within the same network and does not increase the capacity of the Eurobanking system to lend to commercial customers. What the interbank market does is to allow Eurobanks to achieve a more efficient use of existing funds by making them immediately available where they are needed the most.

Because the size of the Eurocurrency market is frequently measured by including all Eurodeposits—both non-Eurobank and interbank deposits—this measure, referred to as a *gross* measure of the Eurocurrency market, must be distinguished from the so-called *net* measure, which excludes interbank deposits. The measure—net or gross—used depends on the purpose for which the calculations of size are being carried out. The interbank market is a very active and important part of Euromarket trading; if a measure

---

[3]The Eurocurrency market is, however, easily accessible to affluent individuals and to small firms.

[4]The prime rate is the interest rate charged by banks for short-term loans to corporations and other creditors with high financial standing.

of the overall activity of the Eurocurrency market is desired, the gross measure is more appropriate. A net measure, on the other hand, is more useful if the capacity of Eurobanks as a whole to create deposits and credit vis-à-vis the nonbank public is being measured. This distinction should be kept in mind when figures provided on the size of the Eurocurrency market are being assessed, such as those presented next, in Section 8–3.

Banking is internationalized when banks enter the onshore systems of foreign countries as well as when they participate in the offshore banking system. These two parallel banking systems operate under different rules and actively compete with each other. Section 8–3 studies the offshore sys-tems, focusing on the most important among them—that is, the Eurodollar markets.

8–3. HOW EUROCURRENCY DEPOSITS ARE CREATED

The growth of Eurocurrency deposits ever since the early 1960s has been astonishing. This explosion can be clearly seen in the data presented in Table 8–2. These figures show both the gross and net measures of the size of the Eurocurrency market. Whereas in 1973 gross Eurocurrency deposits totaled about $315 billion, by the end of 1983 they were more than $2,000 billion and

TABLE 8–2. **Growth in the Size of the Eurocurrency Market (in billions of dollars)**

Year	Gross Size	Net Size	Eurodollars as a Percentage of Gross	US Money Stock (M2)
1973	$ 315	$ 160	74%	$ 861
1974	395	220	76	908
1975	485	255	78	1,023
1976	595	320	80	1,164
1977	740	390	76	1,287
1978	950	495	74	1,389
1979	1,235	590	72	1,500
1980	1,525	730	75	1,633
1981	1,954	1,018	79	1,796
1982	2,168	1,152	80	1,954
1983	2,278	1,237	81	2,185
1984	2,386	1,277	82	2,363
1985	2,846	1,480	75	2,563
1986	3,683	1,833	72	2,808
1988	4,561	2,227	67	2,966
1992 (June)	5,774	-	-	4,167

SOURCES: Morgan Guaranty Trust, *World Financial Markets,* various issues; *Economic Report of the President,* 1989, table B–67. Bank for International Settlements, *International Banking and Financial Market Developments,* November 1992, p. 4; *Economic Report of the President,* 1993, Table B–65. Based on R. M. Levich, "The Euromarkets After 1992," in J. Dermine, ed., *European Banking in the 1990s* (Oxford: Basil Blackwell, 1990), p. 378. Reprinted with permission.

soared to over $5,700 billion in 1992. This growth has been associated with the increased importance of international financial activity. The external deposits of the major currencies constitute most of Eurocurrency deposits. Eurodollar deposits represent most of the Eurocurrency market, with as much as 70 percent of gross liabilities in Eurocurrencies in recent years. Other Eurocurrency deposits, however, grew substantially in the 1980s and early 1990s.

The basic reasons for the growth of external deposits will be examined in Section 8–4. At this point, we will try to answer the more elementary question of how Eurocurrency deposits are actually created. Consider the example of an American firm called Acme, which decides to transfer $1 million out of the account it holds at Goodbuck Bank (in the United States) to a Eurodollar account at Barclays of London.

The first step in the process occurs when Acme draws a $1-million check on its account at Goodbuck payable to Barclays. Barclays then deposits the $1 million received from Acme in its own account at Goodbuck (assuming, for the sake of this example, that Barclays holds some deposits at Goodbuck, which means Goodbuck is a *correspondent bank* to Barclays). The following changes occur in terms of the participants in the transaction, Acme and the two banks, where traditional *T* accounts have been used to show the changes in each participant's financial statements:

Acme

Change in Assets		Change in Liabilities	
(in millions of dollars)			
Deposits			
Goodbuck	−$1		
(New York)			
Barclays	+$1		
(London)			

Barclays (London)

Change in Assets		Change in Liabilities	
(in millions of dollars)			
Reserves		Deposits	
Goodbuck	+$1	Acme	+$1
(New York)			

Goodbuck (New York)

Change in Assets		Change in Liabilities	
(in millions of dollars)			
		Deposits	
		Acme	−$1
		Barclays	+$1
		(London)	

The transfer of dollars by Acme out of the U.S.-based Goodbuck to the Eurobank Barclays does not decrease the dollars deposited in the U.S. banking system. All that is involved is a bookkeeping operation that does not require either an actual physical movement of dollars or the $1 million to leave the U.S. banking system.[5] What the transfer of funds does is to give Barclays claim, or right of ownership, to the domestic deposits previously held by Acme. Total deposits at Goodbuck are not affected; only the ownership

[5]This point has been forcefully argued by Milton Friedman in "The Eurodollar Market: Some First Principles," *Morgan Guaranty Survey,* 4–I4 (October 1969). That the physical transfer of dollars abroad is not required for Eurodollar deposits to be created is not often realized by investors. For example, in his book *The Money Lenders* (New York: Viking, 1981), A. Sampson states that he was told by a lawyer that some of his clients often demand insurance against possible losses arising in the event of a Cuban invasion of the Bahamas and the corresponding potential nationalization of assets located there. "I have to explain," the lawyer says, "that Castro wouldn't find any Eurodollars in the safe. They're all really held in New York or London" (p. 228).

of its deposit liabilities has changed.[6] Note, however, that U.S. deposits held by the public do decrease as Acme shifts its funds toward the Eurodollar market. What happens to Barclays? Its total deposit liabilities are increased—that is, a Eurodollar deposit has been created. However, the process does not necessarily end here. Because Barclays' dollar reserves—in the form of deposits at Goodbuck—have simultaneously increased, Barclays can loan or invest part of the newly acquired funds.

Suppose, then, that Barclays lends its dollars to Bozo, Inc., a firm that makes cosmetics for clowns. Bozo then goes out and deposits its dollars at Ballantine Bank (in London). Ballantine in turn holds its reserves in the form of dollar deposits at Goodbuck (in New York). What has happened, in terms of our T accounts? The changes are as follows:

Barclays (London)

Change in Assets		Change in Liabilities
(in millions of dollars)		
Reserves		
Goodbuck (New York)	−$1	
Loans and Investments		
Loan to Bozo	+$1	

Ballantine (London)

Change in Assets		Change in Liabilities	
(in millions of dollars)			
Reserves		*Deposits*	
Goodbuck (New York)	+$1	Bozo	+$1

[6]What if Goodbuck is not a correspondent bank to Barclays? The answer is that Goodbuck's total deposits will indeed be affected; that is, they will go down by the amount of Acme's withdrawal. Nevertheless, as long as Barclays maintains its reserves in another U.S. bank, deposits in the U.S. (onshore) banking system as a whole will not be affected.

Goodbuck (New York)

Change in Assets	Change in Liabilities
	(in millions of dollars)
	Deposits
	Barclays (London) −$1
	Ballantine (London) +$1

As can be observed, the total dollar deposits in New York (at Goodbuck) have not changed. But the total Eurocurrency deposits have increased from $1 million to $2 million because Acme's deposits at Barclays are still outstanding, as are Bozo's deposits at Ballantine. This creation of dollars outside the United States is called the *multiple* (or *multiplier*) expansion of Eurodollars since Acme's original $1-million deposit at Barclays generates new, additional deposits as Barclays concedes loans to Bozo. Note, however, that the expansion of Eurodollar deposits does not have to stop at $2 million. As seen from Ballantine's T account in the preceding example, this bank now has extra reserves to lend. As long as some of the proceeds of such a loan are deposited back into Ballantine, Barclays, or any other Eurobank, the total amount of Eurodollars would again increase (up to $3 million, if Ballantine were to lend all its reserves).

The implication is that the multiple expansion of Eurodollars could be infinite. Although it is a theoretical possibility, this outcome would be highly unlikely. The reason is that our example is based on two unrealistic assumptions. First, we assumed that Barclays lends all its newly acquired dollar reserves ($1 million to Bozo) and that Ballantine does exactly the same. Second, we supposed that Bozo deposited all its loan proceeds into another Eurobank (Ballantine) and that Ballantine's borrower also deposited all its loan proceeds into another Eurobank. These are unrealistic assumptions. If, for example, Barclays believes that it must have some reserves—in the form of, say, deposits at other banks—in order to meet any withdrawals from its accounts, it will lend Bozo less than $1 million. In the event that the bank believes it needs 10 percent of those deposits as reserves (a reserve-to-deposit ratio of 0.10), it will lend only $900,000 and hold $100,000 as reserves. When Bozo—or whichever firm receives the final proceeds of the loan when spent—deposits all its funds in Ballantine, total Eurodeposits would increase by $1.9 million (the sum of Acme's $1 million plus Bozo's $900,000 outstanding), which is less than $2 million. But this is not all. If Bozo is an important multinational company, it would probably deposit only a fraction of its loan in Europe. It would deposit the rest directly in the United States, in which case those dollars would leave the Eurodollar system (i.e., they would leak out of the system). If Bozo deposits 80 percent of its funds at some bank in New York and the rest (20 percent) at Ballantine (in London), Eurodollars would increase by only $1,180,000 (which is the sum of Acme's $1 million plus the 20 percent of Bozo's loan receipts of $900,000 redeposited in the Euromarket). In conclusion, the multiple expansion of Eurodollars—given a transfer of funds out of the United States—can be expected to decrease with increases in bank-reserve-to-deposit ratios and with increases in the leakages out of the Eurodollar system.

What is the empirical evidence on this matter as it relates to the actual operation of Eurocurrency markets? A quantitative approach to this question must pinpoint precisely the connections between the multiplier expansion of Eurodeposits and actual reserve-to-deposit ratios and Eurodollar leakages. As shown in the appendix to this chapter, the evidence indicates that a shift of deposits from the domestic to the external banking system results in a total dollar deposit increase of about 1.22 times the original shift. This number provides us with the *Eurodollar multiplier* effect of a shift in deposits from the domestic to the external banking system. It means that any million-dollar shift of deposits from the United States to the Eurodollar market would increase total dollar deposits by $1,220,000 (this figure consists of the original

dollars deposited in the Euromarket plus $220,000 of additional deposits created through the multiplier expansion mechanism). The implication is that the major component in the creation of Eurodollar deposits is the original shift in deposits from domestic to external markets and not so much the multiple expansion of these deposits once they are in the Eurocurrency system. The actual shifts of funds that have occurred from the United States to external banking facilities are explained in the next section.

8–4. THE ECONOMIC RATIONALE OF EUROCURRENCY MARKETS

The Eurocurrency market started out as, and is still predominantly, a Eurodollar market. The origin of the term *Eurodollar* is assigned to the defunct Soviet Union. In the late 1950s and early 1960s, a number of Soviet-bloc countries found themselves holding a large stock of dollars, a result of their trade in gold and commodities with both the United States and other European countries. At the time, however, there was a strong anti-Soviet and anti-Communist sentiment in the United States. As a result, the Soviets were afraid of investing their dollars in U.S. assets because of the possibility that they could be seized by the U.S. government. The Soviets consequently decided to deposit their funds in France, in a bank whose cable and telex address was EURO-BANK. In time, the dollars deposited in that bank were referred to as Eurodollars, from which all offshore dollars later gathered their name. Whether or not this is the actual etymology of the name *Eurodollar*, it illustrates dramatically a basic trait of Eurocurrency markets: In large part they are outside the range of national government intervention and regulation. This single fact provides a basic underlying rationale for the growth of the Eurocurrency market overall and a common thread across the large number of empirical regularities, particular financial procedures and practices, and histories of the various Eurocurrencies. Although its importance will be emphasized here within the context of the Eurodollar market, it clearly extends to other Eurocurrencies as well.

The key immediate reason for the growth of the Eurodollar market in the 1960s was the ability of Eurobanks to offer higher interest rates on deposits and lower interest rates on loans than were being offered by banks in the domestic system. In so doing, they were able to lure customers—both depositors and borrowers—from domestic commercial banks. That Eurobanks were able to sustain a persistently lower loan-deposit interest rate differential was specifically the result of the presence and imposition of a variety of U.S. government regulations at the time. One of those policies was the Interest Equalization Tax (IET) introduced by the United States in July 1963. The IET taxed foreign borrowings in the United States and had the intention of reducing the acquisition of dollars by foreigners; this imposition emerged from the fear of a dollar glut in the hands of foreign residents. As a result of the imposition of the IET, the foreign branches of U.S. banks immediately started to float dollar-denominated bonds, or *Eurobonds,* which could carry lower interest than that available in the suddenly more expensive New York credit market. Foreign borrowers jumped at the opportunity. The real effect of the IET and of other capital controls imposed in its aftermath—such as voluntary credit restraints—was that instead of the foreigners following the dollar into the United States, the dollar followed the foreigners by going abroad. The number of U.S. bank foreign branches and subsidiaries ballooned after this period. At the end of 1964, only eleven banks had established branches abroad; by the end of 1974, when the restrictions were repealed, there were close to 130 banks with a total of 737 foreign branches.

The shift in international banking toward the Eurodollar system was given a second boost by the invocation of Regulation Q by the Federal Reserve in 1966 to prevent domestic interest rates from rising. Regulation Q imposed a ceiling on how high domestic deposit rates, including interest rates on CDs, could rise. With their ability to attract deposits severely curtailed, U.S banks proceeded to counteract the credit crunch by raising their interest rates on Euro-CDs. The higher Eurodollar interest rates attracted the escaping corporate funds to their branches and subsidiaries abroad. The Eurobanks could then lend to their U.S.-based parent banks, providing the latter with a much-needed source of funds that was not otherwise available. Note that these international banking operations are not especially cumbersome to manage. In fact, all they involve are changes of bookkeeping entries in bank records, allocating credits and debits among the parent company and their foreign branches and/or subsidiaries. This discussion should thus make clear the importance that the integration of the external and domestic banking systems has had in the development of the Eurodollar market. The close relationship between domestic parent banks and their Eurodollar branches and/or subsidiaries means that their decision making cannot be separated—either regarding to whom they lend or the interest rates they set. In any case, the effect of Regulation Q was to provide a further incentive for the growth of the Eurodollar market in the late 1960s and early 1970s.

In addition to controls on interest rates, other government regulations on U.S. banking gave Eurobanks a competitive edge over domestic banks. For instance, the U.S. Federal Reserve Board requires that all depository institutions (commercial banks, savings and loans, credit unions, and others) hold a ratio of noninterest-yielding reserves to total deposits equal to 10 percent for transaction accounts of more than $46.8 million and 3 percent for transaction accounts of less than $46.8 million. These reserve requirements were set in 1992 and represent a reduction compared to earlier reserve requirements of more than 16 percent. Eurobanks are not subject to U.S. reserve requirements; consequently, they can hold their reserves in the form of interest-bearing deposits at other banks. They can also hold a smaller fraction of their assets in the form of reserves, resulting in a larger amount of interest-yielding investments. Eurobanks can also avoid the requirement faced by U.S. domestic banks regarding the purchase of deposit insurance from the government, which raises costs for banks located in the United States and yields a relative advantage to Eurobanks. In effect, these regulations amount to a tax imposed by the government on domestic banks. By setting up Eurobank branches and subsidiaries, U.S.-based banks are able to avoid the implicit taxation associated with being located in the United States.[7]

The main government regulations associated with the growth of the Eurodollar market in the 1960s and early 1970s have been partly phased out, particularly those relating to interest rate controls. The late 1970s and the 1980s became a period of heavy deregulation of the U.S. domestic banking industry, although reserve and deposit insurance requirements have been maintained. Still, as shown in Figure 8–1, Eurodollar loan-deposit interest rate differentials have to date generally remained below those in domestic banks. Furthermore, the growth of the Euromarket has continued unabated. What explains this sustained expansion of the Eurodollar market? One major explanation is associated with investors' changing perceptions of the political risk attached to the Eurodollar market, as we will now explain.

The expansion of multinational business and finance during the 1960s and 1970s, as well as the

growth of petroleum-derived revenues in the hands of Arab countries after the oil-price hikes of the 1970s, gave rise to a substantial pool of investment funds seeking placement in international financial markets. In the 1980s and early 1990s, the rise of Japanese foreign investments and banking provided a further source of new funds. The Eurodollar market has served well as a haven for these funds. This is partly the result of the flexibility Eurodollars allow the firm or individual engaged in international transactions. When funds are urgently needed to complete a deal late in the day in Hong Kong, an investor just cannot wait until its New York bank opens the next day. A worldwide network of dollar deposits thus makes multinational business more efficient. In addition, investors—whether Arab sheiks or multinational conglomerates—generally seek to diversify their portfolios to maximize returns with a minimum of risk. That is, they try to avoid placing all their eggs in the same basket. Toward that end, they hold a range of assets denominated in different currencies and located in various countries. Eurodollar deposits have become a major component in the portfolios of international investors.

In general, dollar deposits abroad are subject to a number of risks not generally faced if domestic deposits are held. The possibility of exchange controls blocking the withdrawal of funds from Eurobanks, the potential imposition of taxes on the repatriation of Eurodollars, and even the chance of severe regulation of Eurobank activities—something many countries have flirted with—create an environment subject to substantial political risk as compared with domestic deposits. To compensate investors for their increased risk taking, Eurodeposits generally offer higher interest rates than domestic deposits. These higher deposit rates—and the associated lower loan-deposit interest differential—can be sustained through the competitive edge and flexibility Eurobanks can attain relative to domestic banks. In this way, they can attract funds even when they bear higher political risks.

---

[7]Tax avoidance has been a major motivating factor in setting up foreign branches and subsidiaries, not only in terms of avoiding the implicit tax of government regulations, but also with regard to circumventing explicit domestic taxes. Domestic banks often search for foreign locations with low corporate income tax rates in order to legally shift income gains to those locations and reduce tax brackets. Similarly, investors seek to deposit their income in low-tax areas, shifting their funds to Eurobanks located in such areas. Switzerland has been particularly successful in attracting deposits. Within the legal jurisdiction of the United States, the Commonwealth of Puerto Rico has attracted dollar deposits on the basis of federal income tax exemption.

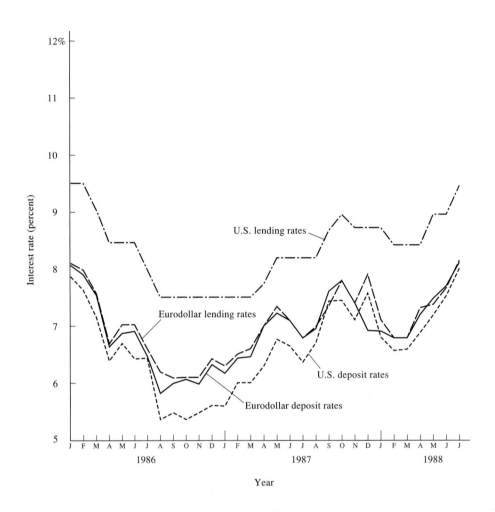

FIGURE 8–1.   U.S. and Eurodollar Interest Rates, 1986–1988

The perception of the political risks associated with Eurodollar deposits relative to onshore deposits has, however, changed over time. As a matter of fact, the growth of Eurodollars in the 1970s and 1980s can be associated with a general reduction in the perceived political risk of holding Eurodollars. This increased confidence made Eurodollars relatively attractive to many investors, especially at the higher deposit interest rates they offered. Of course, a substantial number of investors maintained their domestic deposits in fear of the still high comparative risks involved in investing abroad; however, the relative growth of the Euromarket can certainly be associated with the reduction of perceived political risks over time.[8] A

[8]For more details on the association of shifting risk and the growth of the Eurodollar market, see R. Z. Aliber, "The Integration of Offshore and Domestic Banking Systems," *Journal of Monetary Economics* (October 1980). Note that shifting perceptions on the political risk of domestic currency holdings in anticipation of possible government controls on domestic financial transactions can also influence the relative-

(continued)

partial reversal of this trend between 1981 and 1984 related to the difficulties of many developing countries in repaying their debts to Eurobanks. The so-called debt crisis of the 1980s cast a dark cloud on the continued health of Eurobanks and Eurolending and might have been a factor in the stagnation of Eurocurrency market growth between 1981 and 1984. After that time the market experienced a strong rebound (see Table 8–2), although lending activities have been sluggish in recuperating. The subject of Eurolending will be addressed next.

8–5. EXTERNAL FINANCIAL INTERMEDIATION

One of the major functions of the Eurocurrency market is to funnel funds, mostly Eurodollars, from lending countries to borrowing countries. The United States and several oil-exporting countries have figured prominently as net lenders of Eurodollar funds; the republics forming part of the former Soviet Union, Eastern European countries, and developing countries in general have predominated as net borrowers. In bringing together lenders and borrowers, the Eurodollar market performs a global financial intermediation task, a task whose scope and delicate nature are best appreciated by looking at its history.

The dramatic oil-price hikes of the 1970s were associated with a massive redistribution of wealth from oil-importing to oil-exporting countries. In the period from 1974 to 1981, for instance, members of the Organization of Petroleum Exporting Countries (OPEC) increased their wealth by an average of $50 billion per year.[9] Associated with this transfer of wealth were ballooning oil bills faced by the oil-importing countries. The oil-import bill of non-oil-producing developing countries alone increased from $10 billion in 1973 to $120 billion in 1980. As a result, there were great fears at the time that the failure of oil-importing countries to foot the bills for their oil purchases would result in a collapse of the international monetary system. The collapse did not materialize, a reflection of the ability of the international financial community to match the dollar revenues of the OPEC giants with the demands for financing required by the oil-importing countries. This so-called recycling of oil-related (petro) dollars from the oil czars to the oil paupers was substantially realized precisely through the Eurodollar market. Because of the existence of Eurodollars, for example, a country such as Brazil could arrange within a regulation-free environment to obtain multimillion-dollar loans from a consortium of American, German, and Japanese banks and thereby finance its oil imports.

By financing their huge import bills, Eurolending allowed developing countries to sustain their levels of consumption and investment. Eurodollars thus aided in supporting Brazil's ambitious development projects, the red-ink deficits of government corporations in Mexico (such as Petroleos Mexicanos), and the privatization of enterprises previously nationalized by Salvador Allende's government in Chile. This dynamic lending activity paved the way for the debt problems of the 1980s, during which the difficulties of developing countries in repaying their debts finally made the headlines.

---

attractiveness of Eurocurrencies. For instance, widespread capital controls were imposed in Germany from 1970 to 1974 to impede the inflow of funds into German bank deposits. This led to a general anticipation that further controls would be imposed. As a result, to compensate investors in Germany for their higher political risk, the West German mark deposit interest rate rose relative to the Euromark deposit rate. See M. P. Dooley and P. Isard, "Capital Controls, Political Risk and Deviations from Covered Interest Parity," *Journal of Political Economy* (April 1980).

[9]The price of oil (Saudi quotes) increased from $1.30 per barrel in 1970 to $33.50 in 1982. Associated with this general increase in oil prices were the sharp oil price shocks of 1973—when crude petroleum rose from $2.75 to $12.50 a barrel—and 1979, when oil prices more than doubled. These price increases were possible largely because of OPEC's tight control over oil prices. The 1973 and 1979 shocks, however, were precipitated by major political events taking place in the Middle East.

The debt of developing countries to the West's banking system has risen above the $1.7-trillion mark. Mexico and Brazil alone owe more than $100 billion each to Western banks. In addition, the countries of the former Soviet Union and East European countries jointly owe more than $100 billion. The debt problem of the 1980s arose from the inability of many developing countries to finance their loan repayments, either principal or interest. The response of the heavily indebted economies initially was to attempt to continue their borrowing in order to finance the payments on previous debts, to seek the aid of international organizations such as the IMF, or, when default loomed, to renegotiate or reschedule their debts. Debt rescheduling usually involves a stretching of the maturities attached to loans. Some countries had to stop temporarily payments on principal and interest on their external debt. In some cases, the countries have arbitrarily constrained their external debt payments—as did Peru, which limited its repayments to 10 percent of its exports. More recently, the move has been toward debt reduction, which we will discuss in Chapter 12.

The developing country debt problem is particularly chilling for the Eurobanks, which, as a result of their earlier lending practices, find themselves holding a vast amount of morose and prospectively defaulted debts. Indeed, since the debt crisis erupted in full in 1982, Eurobank lending contracted and has only very recently gathered back some momentum (see the figures in Table 8–1, showing how Eurolending was almost halved in 1982 and 1983). The wide exposure on the part of Eurobanks to developing country debt has caused much public concern. There is the fear that a default by one or more major developing country borrowers could trigger a sudden withdrawal of funds from the Euromarket and cause a string of Eurobanks to go under, with disastrous repercussions for the international financial system. To what extent are these worries valid?

Such fears, although legitimate, are somewhat exaggerated. What needs to be understood is the integrated character of domestic and external banking. That Eurobanks are branches and subsidiaries of domestic banks means that the parent banks back them up in the event of any serious difficulties. As a matter of fact, those Eurobanks that are *branches* of domestic banks cannot fail independently of their parent companies. (Even though *subsidiaries* could, in principle, fail independently of their associated domestic banks, in fact they don't because the latter back them up by absorbing losses and/or providing them with liquid funds to continue operations.) The implication is that unless the failure of their foreign branches and subsidiaries is connected to a failure of domestic banks, short-term difficulties on the part of Eurobanks would not disturb the market for long. Consequently, for an international crisis to be associated with Eurobanking activities requires that governments and monetary authorities stand still and allow the failure of their major commercial banks—an unlikely possibility.[10] In any case, by the early 1990s, banks had made adjustments in their books and capital position to be able to absorb any losses that might be forthcoming from the loans to developing countries.

The case of the failure of the Franklin National and I. D. Herstatt banks in mid-1974 provides a clear example of the issues involved. Both banks had borrowed heavily from Eurobanks. As a consequence, the announcement of Herstatt's closing and Franklin National's losses resulted in fears of Eurobank failures and in a sudden withdrawal of deposits from Eurocurrency markets. The overall size of the London market fell temporarily as a result. The associated instability generated a rapid response from the central bank governors of the Group of Ten countries and Switzerland, indicating their willingness to intervene in the event of a crisis. In September 1974 they reported:

---

[10]For a discussion of the many issues relating to international public policies to ensure stability of the international financial system in the presence of a crisis, see R. Portes and A. K. Swoboda, eds., *Threats to Financial Stability* (Cambridge, Mass.: Cambridge University Press, 1987).

At their regular meeting in Basle on 9th September, the governors also had an exchange of views on the problem of the lender of last resort in Euromarkets. They recognized that it would not be practical to lay down in advance rules and procedures for the provision of temporary liquidity. But they were satisfied that means are available for that purpose and will be used if and when necessary.[11]

After this move, and by early 1975, the Eurocurrency market returned to stability. Thus, given that Eurobanks are closely connected to domestic banks, and because it is unlikely that central banks will allow major domestic bank failures to occur without their intervention, a Eurobank-related international monetary crisis does not seem imminent.

Another stabilizing force involves the variety of financial practices Eurobanks have developed to minimize their risk exposure. Even though Eurobanks are often visualized as taking excessive risks because they are unregulated, the Eurocurrency market has been at the forefront of financial innovations intended to deal with exposure to risky ventures. The technique of *syndicated credit* is a feature that allows a group (syndicate) of banks to pool funds for the concession of very large loans. By providing only part of the financing, the risks of default on the loan are spread among the participating banks. Because the banks frequently are from different nations, the default risk is effectively spread among countries, reducing the prospect of a crisis in the event that default actually occurs.

From the bankers' perspective, another stabilizing factor in the Eurodollar market is the maturity structure of its deposits and loans. Table 8–3 breaks down Eurobank claims (Euroloans) and liabilities (Eurodeposits). The striking features of the figures shown are that (1) most of the claims

and liabilities are short-term, and (2) the maturity structure for deposits and loans does not differ that much. The close matching of the maturities of deposits and loans in the Eurocurrency market forms the basis of a crucial difference from domestic banks. The latter usually accept short-term deposits and invest in long-term loans and assets. As a result, Eurobanks are not subject to the risk that domestic banks often face of having interest rates rise while holding old, low-yielding long-term loans. Euroloans are due on a short-term basis and can be reissued at rates commensurate with prevailing interest rates. These adjustable, short-term interest rates allow Eurobanks to shift the risk associated with interest rate variability to the borrower.

Even though Euroloans are effectively made on a short-term basis, long-term and medium-term lending engaging Eurobank participation in syndicated credit (Eurocredit) is a frequent undertaking. In effect, the banks commit themselves to reissue—that is, roll over—a succession of short-term loans over the term to maturity of the medium-term or long-term loan. The institutional procedure used is to agree beforehand on the long-term duration of the loan and on the interest rate spread to be charged above the prevailing LIBOR—which is partially determined by an assessment of the risk attached to the long-term loan. Once the duration of the long-term lending and the spread are specified, an agreement is made on a short-term period, during which the interest charged remains fixed. Each time the loan is rolled over, however, the interest rate is adjusted to equal the prevailing LIBOR plus the fixed spread. Spreads are not altered during the time in which the long-term loan agreement is in effect; however, if a loan has to be renegotiated, spreads will frequently change, depending on reassessments of credit worthiness. For instance, Brazil generally borrowed in Euromarkets for years at a spread equal to a small fraction above LIBOR. Once Eurobanks recognized that country's mounting debt problems in 1980, the spreads quickly rose to 2 percent.

---

[11]As quoted by R. B. Johnston, *The Economics of the Euromarket: History, Theory and Policy* (New York: St. Martin's, 1982), p. 30. The Group of Ten includes Belgium, Britain, Canada, France, Italy, Japan, the Netherlands, Sweden, the United States, and Germany. Switzerland has a limited membership.

TABLE 8–3. **Maturity Structure of Eurocurrency Claims and Liabilities**
[all U.K.-based Eurobanks (percent of total)]

	Claims					Liabilities				
	March 1974	Feb. 1977	Feb. 1980	Feb. 1984	Jan. 1987	March 1974	Feb. 1977	Feb. 1980	Feb. 1984	Jan. 1987
Total business										
Less than 8 days	18.3%	17.0%	16.9%	16.5%	18.3%	21.5%	22.6%	21.9%	22.8%	24.0%
8 days–1 month	19.6	13.2	16.0	15.7	17.5	21.0	17.0	19.4	20.1	22.3
1 month–3 months	22.6	22.0	23.0	23.4	21.9	26.4	26.9	28.1	28.1	25.7
3 months–6 months	16.9	15.8	15.8	14.0	12.1	19.7	18.7	18.4	17.7	13.8
6 months–1 year	7.7	8.0	7.0	6.4	5.4	7.6	8.1	7.3	6.2	4.8
1 year–3 years	5.0	9.8	6.7	7.2	5.9	2.2	4.8	3.2	2.6	2.9
3 years and over	9.9	14.2	14.6	16.8	18.9	3.4	1.9	1.7	2.5	6.5
Nonbank business										
Less than 8 days	8.2	4.5	8.9	7.1	12.0	31.7	35.8	31.7	35.1	38.2
8 days–1 month	13.0	5.7	8.6	9.0	11.0	19.7	22.1	21.6	21.2	24.0
1 month–3 months	19.7	11.4	11.2	12.2	13.7	20.8	21.4	23.9	21.7	18.2
3 months–6 months	14.9	9.4	8.2	8.0	9.3	13.3	12.1	12.9	12.3	6.9
6 months–1 year	6.3	8.3	6.0	6.5	6.1	7.7	4.9	5.7	4.9	2.7
1 year–3 years	10.7	20.5	13.4	16.5	13.1	2.7	1.7	2.0	1.5	2.0
3 years and over	27.2	40.2	43.7	40.7	34.8	4.1	2.0	2.2	3.3	8.0

SOURCES: Bank of England, *Sterling Business Analysed by Maturity and Sector* (March 1987); Bank of England, *Maturity Analysis by Sector of Liabilities and Claims in Foreign Currencies* (March 1987). Reprinted with permission from M. K. Lewis and K. T. Davis, *Domestic and International Banking* (Cambridge, Mass.: The MIT Press, 1987), p. 306.

In conclusion, a wide variety of safeguards exists. They run from the financial mechanisms installed by the Eurobanks themselves up to the level of central bank support, suggesting that fears of a Eurodollar-induced international monetary crisis are largely unfounded.

8–6. EUROBONDS AND GLOBAL INVESTMENT BANKING

After 1984, a new source of external financial intermediation—the Eurobond market—acquired increasing significance. Eurobonds are bonds denominated in one country's currency but issued in markets outside that country.[12] Dollar-denominated bonds issued in London and yen-denominated bonds issued outside Japan are Eurobonds. The leading centers in this market are London, New York, and Tokyo, which means that the term *externally issued bonds* is more accurate since Eurobonds do not have to be issued in Europe.[13]

Is there any advantage in using these markets? For many firms, Eurobond issues can be highly advantageous compared to other financial sources of funds. For instance, a Euroyen issue can be completed about a week after receiving the approval of Japan's Ministry of Finance; an issue by a non-Japanese company in Japan (Samurai bond) can take two or three months. Also, there is frequently more competition and better terms in the Euroyen market as compared to the Samurai market.

The Eurobond market, developed in the early 1960s, has experienced sustained growth. The expansion accelerated after 1984, when the U.S. government eliminated the 30 percent withholding tax on interest paid by U.S. bond issuers to nonresidents (withholding accelerates tax collections to the detriment of the taxpayer and reduces the attractiveness of the financial instruments subject to it). This move was intended to encourage U.S. corporations to borrow through the issue of Eurobonds. U.S. residents were also permitted to issue bearer bonds to foreigners. Bearer bonds are payable to whoever holds them and are not registered in the name of a particular individual. Because the identity of the holder is not revealed, the financial privacy and secrecy of these bonds induces many investors to buy them.

In 1984 and 1985, the Japanese also liberalized the Euroyen bond markets and opened the Japanese bond market to foreigners. Non-Japanese corporations were permitted to issue Euroyen bonds and non-Japanese firms could be the lead underwriters in Euroyen issues. (Samurais continued to require a Japanese lead manager.)[14] The

---

[12]A bond represents medium- and long-term credit financing to the issuing agent—a government, corporation, or international institution. The debt is repaid to the bond holder over a defined period and bears an interest rate that is usually fixed but can also be adjustable. Domestic bonds are issued in the borrower's home currency and are sold in the borrower's country of origin to domestic and foreign investors. Notice that what distinguishes a Eurobond from a domestic bond is that with the Eurobond, the currency of denomination (say, the yen) and the country of issue (outside Japan) do not match. When a foreign firm issues yen-denominated bonds in Japan, it is called a foreign bond issue (these are the famous Samurai bonds that U.S. firms have been issuing). Notice that the currency of denomination and the country where it is issued coincide in the case of foreign issues. The only thing that distinguishes a foreign bond issue from a domestic issue is the residence of the issuer.

[13]For analysis and data on Eurobond markets, see S. L. Hayes and P. M. Hubbard, *Investment Banking: A Tale of Three Cities,* (Boston: Harvard Business School Press, 1990); and P. Gallant, *The Eurobond Market* (New York: New York Institute of Finance, 1988).

[14]In order to issue Euroyen bonds, Japanese companies must obtain approval from the Finance Ministry. The ministry requires a good credit rating and conditions of financial strength in order to approve a company. Borrowers do not place new bond issues themselves but hire a group of firms that specialize in marketing securities. The underwriting syndicate is the group of firms that sells the bonds issued by a borrower. The lead underwriter, or lead manager, is the principal underwriter in a bond issue. (The term *underwriter* comes from the signature in the contracts for the marketing of new bond issues.)

Euroyen market was also liberalized for Japanese firms. Until that time, Japanese banks and companies had been restricted from participating in it. Furthermore, a 20 percent withholding tax on interest paid by Japanese companies on bonds sold outside Japan to non-Japanese residents was eliminated in 1985. The 20 percent withholding tax had effectively prevented the issue of Euroyen bonds by Japanese firms. The liberalization measures encouraged the expansion of an Euroyen bond market. These and further liberalization measures (in Germany and Italy) gave an impetus to the Eurobond market after 1984. The $700 billion in Eurobonds outstanding in 1986 made that market the largest international capital market in the world. It reached an annual value of new issues of $212 billion in 1989. However, the Eurobond market is still small in comparison with domestic bond markets. The size of the externally issued bond markets is about a tenth of the size of domestic bond markets in major countries.

The Eurobond market is a market of corporations, especially American, Japanese and British, of governments, and of supranational borrowers such as the World Bank. The market provides large-scale financing: The average value of a new bond issue was $80 million in 1988. Eurobond issues are usually unsecured (that is, there is no required collateral), in contrast to the security requirements facing most domestic bond issues. Various developing countries' governments were active participants in this market until the debt crisis limited credit from this source. In the case of Mexico, credit flows stopped completely in the period immediately following 1982, when Mexico ceased servicing its debt on a regular basis.

The Eurobond markets are similar to Eurodeposit and Euroloan markets in that they are largely unregulated external markets. Also, the holder of an Eurobond is frequently anonymous. Secrecy is accomplished by not registering the instrument and making it payable to the bearer. This means that whoever holds an Eurobond can receive interest and debt repayments independently of his or her identity. Eurobond markets also differ from

Eurodeposits and Euroloan markets in significant ways. First, Eurobonds provide medium- and long-term financing, as opposed to the short-term effective maturities of Euroloans. In other words, Eurobond markets are a segment of the world capital markets, whereas the Eurodeposit and Euroloans markets are part of the international money markets. Second, the role of commercial banks is different in each market. Commercial banks frequently act as investment bankers when bonds are issued. However, investment bankers in Eurobonds are not limited to commercial banks like Morgan Guaranty and Deutsche Bank, which are major participants in the market. Securities firms like Merrill Lynch International, Salomon Brothers, Goldman Sachs, and Credit Suisse First Boston Ltd. (an affiliate of First Boston Inc.) are also major investment bankers. Investment bankers act as intermediaries when new bonds are issued, selling the issue and charging a price for the marketing services rendered. Investment bankers usually adopt the following procedure: They buy the whole issue of new bonds, guaranteeing a price to the issuer, and then proceed to sell the bonds to interested investors. The bonds are only held in the investment bankers' portfolio for the time required to sell them. As such, investment bankers are a marketing intermediary rather than a lender like commercial banks in the Euroloan markets. Because bond issues are large-scale operations measured in the dozens of millions of dollars, a single investment banker does not undertake the operation alone. A group of investment bankers—called a syndicate—gets together and allocates the new issue among themselves, to be sold to investors. After an issue is sold, the investment banking function has been completed. At this point, a secondary market in the Eurobond emerges in which investors can sell their holdings. (The market for the initial issue is called the primary market in this context.)[15]

---

[15]See I. Walter and R. C. Smith, *Investment Banking in Europe. Restructuring for the 1990s* (Cambridge, Mass.: Basil Blackwell, 1989).

The Eurobond markets are presently fully global. They are led by London, New York, and Tokyo but are active in many countries. Investment banking syndicates are multinational as is the pool of investors. Investment bankers such as New York's Goldman Sachs, Salomon Brothers, and others have active branches in Europe and Asia, including the previously closed Japanese market. The borrowing countries extend worldwide, and more than ten currencies of denomination are used. The development of the Euroyen bond market in the 1980s contributed to the internationalization of the yen. Euroyen bonds accounted for more than 20 percent of Eurobond issues in the late 1980s, surpassed only by the U.S. dollar as the currency of denomination.

8–7. OFFSHORE MARKETS AND THE EFFECTIVENESS OF MONETARY CONTROL

The Eurodollar market has been accused of generating all sorts of maladies. It has been blamed for world inflation, implicated in speculative behavior destabilizing the value of the dollar, and singled out as undermining government control over the economy. These charges presuppose the notion that the Eurodollar market has substantial macroeconomic significance—that is, that it plays a strong role in the overall behavior of national economies. This section examines the macroeconomic implications of the Eurodollar market, stressing the issues bearing on the ability of policymakers to attain public policy goals.

We have seen how the Eurodollar market operates as a kind of monetary haven—that is, a jurisdiction in which banks are subject to minimal regulation. The close integration of Eurobanking with domestic banks implies that, by shifting activities among their domestic and foreign locations, banks can avoid the controls and regulations imposed by national monetary authorities. This severely constrains the ability of the latter to execute policies. For instance, consider the case of reserve requirements. As noted earlier, depositary

institutions in the United States are subject to the requirement that they hold non-interest-bearing reserves against deposits. These reserve requirements were imposed to insure the liquidity of domestic banks in the presence of an unexpected large withdrawal of deposits. Because they are crucial in influencing the amount of loanable funds available to banks, reserve requirements also affect the ability of domestic central banks to control credit and the money supply in the economy. With the presence of Eurobanks, however, domestic banks can, in effect, reduce their reserve requirement burden by shifting deposits to the unregulated offshore banking system, which is not subject to the same requirements. Given that national monetary authorities can control only domestic reserve requirements, they cannot effectively influence the reserve-to-deposit ratios that banks hold. What is worse, central banks might even find themselves unable to calculate accurately the effective reserve-to-deposit ratios held by banks because the relative amounts of Eurodeposits and domestic deposits vary unpredictably from week to week.

It is easy to understand why domestic policymakers are so concerned about the Eurocurrency market: Its existence and affinity to domestic banking severely undermine the effectiveness of monetary authorities to regulate and control domestic banks and their credit activities. Even though, as we saw earlier, the Eurodollar market does not lead to a massive, frenzied expansion of dollar deposits, it makes the dollar money supply more difficult to manage and adjust.[16] This means the efforts of central bank policies become more uncertain and the economy even more difficult to steer. Restrictive domestic monetary policy, for instance, might fail in curtailing credit because, in the face of any upward pressures on domestic

---

[16]That this is so must appease the fears of those who, mistakenly, believe that the Eurodollar market can give rise to an explosion of the supply of dollars in the world and, therefore, to rampant world inflation. The low inflation rates in the early 1990s, in spite of substantial Eurodollar growth, should allay their fears.

interest rates, domestic banks could shift funds from the Eurodollar to the domestic market. Such action would result in increased credit and prevent domestic interest rates from rising relative to rates abroad. The short-term capital flows associated with the integration of domestic and external money markets mean that local interest rates become closely linked to Euromarket rates and cannot significantly diverge from them. Government control of the economy is thus undermined. The sting of this fact on policymakers has resulted in renewed calls for regulation of the offshore banking system.

8–8. THE REGULATION OF EUROMARKET ACTIVITIES

Domestic banking systems have traditionally been subject to various forms of regulatory constraints intended to promote a stable monetary environment. Reserve requirements, for instance, limit deposit expansion, while mandatory deposit insurance serves to protect depositors against bank bankruptcies, and so on. That a significant segment of the world banking system—the Eurocurrency market—remains largely unregulated has been the source of much public concern. As a matter of fact, it is bewildering to some that the Eurocurrency market has been able to operate under a minimal-regulation environment for so long. This situation is perplexing indeed because there is reasonable consensus among policymakers regarding the need for some regulation. Nevertheless, a look at the alternative means by which regulations might be introduced clearly reveals the reasons for their absence. Suppose, for example, that the United States places regulatory trappings on its Eurobanks in the form of restrictive reserve and deposit insurance requirements.[17] This action on

the part of U.S. authorities would not affect foreign Eurobanks, which are outside the reach of U.S. regulatory constraints. Hence, a major part of the Eurodollar market would remain effectively uncontrolled. The main impact of U.S. regulatory measures would be to increase the costs of U.S. banks, reduce their competitive edge, and shift clients toward foreign banks. It is thus apparent why U.S. authorities have not taken such actions. Alternatively, U.S. authorities can attempt to limit U.S. residents' transactions with Eurobanks by means of exchange controls and other restrictions on capital mobility. Although these restrictions may keep a New York firm from purchasing Eurocertificates of deposit or obtaining Eurodollar loans, foreign subsidiaries of U.S firms could still use the Euromarket freely. And, of course, U.S. government supervision does not extend at all to foreign residents and foreign banks. In conclusion, the possibility of a unilateral introduction of effective controls on the part of any single country over the Euromarket system is questionable.

An alternative route in regulating the Euromarket is through the initiative of the financial centers in which Eurobank activities locate. The impracticality of this route, however, is obvious from the fact that attempts to regulate Euromarket activity in a given financial center will simply shift funds to less rigidly regulated regions. Actually, there is keen competition among countries for Eurobanking business. Some of these countries, such as Panama, developed a booming Eurobanking sector, generating wel-

---

[17]The most obvious way of eliminating the loopholes from government intervention provided by offshore markets is to establish uniform requirements for both domestic and Eurobanks. Imposing reserve and deposit insurance requirements

on Eurodeposits is a way to establish uniformity. The outright extension of regulation to offshore banking, however, implies an overall increase in government regulation of the economy and has therefore been opposed by some. An alternative suggestion has been to attain uniformity of regulatory constraints by coupling increased Euromarket regulation—say, the establishment of reserve requirements—with reduced domestic regulation—such as reduced reserve requirements on domestic banks. See R. Z. Aliber, "Monetary Aspects of Offshore Markets," *Columbia Journal of World Business* (Fall 1979).

comed employment and income. From the point of view of individual countries, the major incentives are toward attracting Eurobanking business, not discouraging it.

The Swiss financial market represents one of the most successful stories of the use of regulation—or, rather, lack of regulation—as a tool for international financial center competition. As a consequence of it, Switzerland, a small country of 6.5 million people, has become one of the top banking centers worldwide. The cornerstone of Swiss banking, and its competitive advantage in attracting banking business, hinges on the veil of secrecy surrounding its deposit activity. Swiss law allows numbered accounts that hide the depositor's identity. Secrecy has traditionally been protected through explicit regulation that imposes penalties on bank officials revealing clients' names. For this reason, the popular perception is that Swiss bank accounts are owned by a large number of tax-evading millionaires, corrupt presidents, and big-time criminals trying to avoid the law and tax authorities. While this perception may be correct or not, some recent changes in Swiss laws have altered Swiss secrecy in many respects. Responding to pressure from foreign countries, the Swiss have frozen the accounts of such former dictators as Haiti's Jean Claude Duvalier, the Philippines' Ferdinand Marcos, Panama's Manuel Antonio Noriega, and Romania's Nicolae Ceausescu. In August 1990, money laundering was made a crime in Switzerland, and in May 1991, banking authorities abolished the Form B bank accounts that allowed lawyers and other agents to deposit money without identifying their clients. The purpose of these measures is that all account holders must be identified. The names of all depositors will then be known to a small number of bank officials who are required to disclose those names in cases of criminal investigations. Still, this disclosure requirement does not mean the death of Swiss banking secrecy. Tax-related investigations abroad do not affect banking secrecy because tax fraud in

foreign countries is not recognized as a crime in Switzerland.[18]

Another example of deregulation of financial restrictions to stimulate domestic banking competitiveness in global markets has occurred in the United States. Since 1981, the Federal Reserve has allowed banking offices located in the United States to set up international banking facilities (IBFs), which are free of deposit reserve requirements and interest ceilings on deposits and loans made to foreigners. Because they deal only with foreign customers, IBFs are essentially an entrepôt business—they accept deposits and lend to foreigners but do not compete with domestic banking activities. The establishment of IBFs reveals the Federal Reserve's clear recognition that when other countries maintain Eurobusiness, an individual country gains nothing by restrictive measures. Only multilateral measures on the part of all the major countries involved assure effective regulation. That such measures may actually be imposed in the future cannot be ruled out, however, given the heightened fears and worries about the performance of domestic and international banking in the face of crises in developing country lending, the savings and loan crisis, and so forth.

In this chapter we have discussed in detail the basic aspects of the Eurocurrency markets, which play a central role in promoting international capital flows and in integrating domestic and international financial markets. We have not specified the precise influence of the Eurodollar market on U.S. international transactions and on the economy's macroeconomic performance. To do so first requires a discussion of the principles involved in measuring transactions with the rest of the

---

[18]See A. Riding, "New Rule Reduces Swiss Banking Secrecy," *The New York Times,* May 6, 1991, p. C1. Swiss banking is discussed in M. A. Jones, *Swiss Bank Accounts: A Personal Guide to Ownership, Benefits, and Use* (Blue Ridge Summit, Pa.: Liberty House, 1990). Another battle of pressures has arisen between the U.S. and Panama concerning bank secrecy in that Central American republic; Panama has not yet converted to the gospel of financial disclosure.

world—that is, of the balance of payments accounts—which is the task of Chapter 9.

Summary

1. The Eurocurrency market comprises deposits and loans denominated in currencies that differ from that of the financial center where the deposits are held or loans are made. A gross measure of the Eurocurrency market includes all Eurodeposits, whereas a net measure excludes interbank deposits.

2. The central role of the Eurocurrency market has been to promote capital flows and to integrate domestic and international financial markets. One of its major functions has been to funnel funds from lending to borrowing countries. In particular, the recycling of petrodollars and Japanese financial wealth has been carried out to a large extent through the Eurodollar market.

3. Eurodollar deposits can be created by transferring funds out of the United States. This results in a multiple expansion of Eurodollars, depending on bank reserve holdings and leakages out of the Eurodollar system. The major component in the creation of Eurodollar deposits seems to be the original shift in deposits from domestic to external markets, rather than the multiplier expansion of these deposits.

4. Eurobanks are not independent entities that specialize in accepting Eurodeposits and issuing Euroloans. They are, rather, foreign branches and subsidiaries of national banks whose Eurobanking operations are just one among multiple bank activities. Eurobanking activities are a segment of the wholesale international money market because they overwhelmingly involve large transactions in short-term Eurodeposits and Euroloans.

5. An interbank offered rate is the short-term lending rate Eurobanks charge other banks in the interbank market. Euroloan rates are frequently at a spread of 1 to 2 percent above the London interbank offered rate (LIBOR).

6. A major factor behind the development of Eurocurrency markets has been the minimal regulation of Eurobanks as compared with domestic banks. This factor, combined with the integration of Eurobanking into domestic banking, undermines the ability of monetary authorities to regulate and control effectively domestic banks and their credit activities.

7. Even though Eurobanks are often envisioned as taking excessive risks because of their unregulated nature, the Eurocurrency market has been at the forefront of financial innovations intended to deal with exposure to risky ventures.

8. Medium-term Euroloans are frequently rolled over and interest rates are readjusted periodically (say, every six months) to reflect changes in market interest rates (LIBOR). The spread remains fixed during the term of the loan, however.

9. The marked growth of the Eurocurrency market in the 1960s and 1970s slowed down between 1983 and 1984. This phenomenon was associated with the dark cloud that the so-called debt crisis of the 1980s cast over the continued health of Eurobanks and Eurolending. Since the mid-1980s, the Eurocurrency market has rebounded to record growth rates.

Problems

1. Contrast Eurobanks and domestic banks in terms of the maturity transformation they carry out, the degree of government regulation to which they are subject, the reserve-to-deposit ratios chosen, and the spread between lending and borrowing rates.

2. Why do Eurodollars rarely consist of demand deposits?

3. Are the liabilities of foreign-owned banks operating in the United States included in Federal Reserve Board concepts of the money supply, say M2? Why? Are these liabilities Eurodollars? Are offshore deposits included in M1? In M2?

4. "As long as they renounce or are unable to regulate Euromarkets, domestic authorities will be incapable of affecting credit conditions in Euromarkets." Evaluate this statement.

5. The U.S. banking system experienced substantial deregulation in the 1980s and 1990s. For instance, a gradual phase out of interest rate controls on U.S. deposits was completed by 1986. Discuss the impact that this deregulation process had on the Eurodollar market.

6. Suppose that there is a general increase in interest rates. How would such a disturbance affect the relative competitiveness of Eurobanks vis-à-vis U.S. onshore banks? Would you expect the Eurodollar market to expand or contract?

7. Suppose that a large Euromarket borrower, say a country like Brazil, defaults on its Euroloan repayment commitments. Can that create a massive Eurobanking and international monetary crisis? Explain why or why not, and then specify possible alternative scenarios regarding the effects of a major debt default on the international financial system and the Eurocurrency market.

8. Define the following concepts and indicate their relationship to the Eurocurrency market: (a) Floating rate loans and notes; (b) LUXIBOR; (c) Eurobonds; (d) Edge Act.

Appendix: The Eurodollar Multiplier

This appendix develops the Eurodollar multiplier approach to the analysis of deposit expansion in the Eurodollar market. The multiplier approach specifies algebraically the Eurodollar market expansionary capacity (i.e., its ability to create deposits) and the effect of Eurobank reserves and deposit leakages out of the Eurodollar system on this capacity. This quantitative approach provides empirical estimates of how large the expansionary capacity of the Eurodollar market actually is.

To begin with, the total supply of dollars in the hands of the nonbank public, $M^\$$, is defined as

$$M^\$ = M^{\text{U.S.}} + ED - RE, \qquad (A\text{--}1)$$

where $M^{\text{U.S.}}$ represents the U.S. supply of dollars (a measure of the U.S. money supply, which includes currency and coins plus demand deposits located in the United States), and ED denotes Eurodollar deposits. Note that if we were to add the U.S. dollar supply and Eurodollar deposits, $M^{\text{U.S.}} + ED$, we would obtain the world supply of dollars. However, when Eurobanks deposit their reserves in U.S. banks there would be double counting of some dollar deposits. On the assumption that all Eurobank reserves, RE, are held in the form of deposits at U.S. banks, these would have to be netted out to obtain the world dollar supply in the hands of the public. This is why RE is subtracted in Equation A–1.

As mentioned earlier, Eurodeposits are not subject to legal reserve requirements. Still, banks will voluntarily hold some reserves against Eurodeposits as a precautionary measure. The reserves, RE, that banks choose to hold as a proportion of Eurodollar deposits, ED, can be represented by

$$RE = reED, \qquad (A\text{--}2)$$

where $re = RE/ED$ represents the bank's reserve:deposit ratio. As noted before, re is an important variable in determining the multiplier expansion of Eurodollars. The second factor our textual analysis posits as crucial in understanding Eurodollar creation is Eurodeposit leakages. Leakages arise from the fact that individuals do not keep all their deposits in the Euromarket but rather allocate them among both the domestic and offshore banking systems. For the sake of simplicity, we assume that Eurodollar deposits, *ED,* are related to the total supply of dollars in the hands of the public, $M^\$$, in the following linear fashion:

$$ED = \alpha + \epsilon M^\$, \qquad (A\text{–}3)$$

where α denotes the preferences for Eurodollar deposits on the part of the public (i.e., the higher α is, the more Eurodollar deposits the nonbank public will hold), and ϵ represents that fraction of every additional dollar available to the public that is deposited in the Eurodollar market. The smaller ϵ is, the larger the leakages from the Eurodollar market are, in the sense that individuals will deposit only a small fraction of their additional dollars in the Euromarket.

Equation A–2 represents the needs that Eurobanks have to hold reserves on their Eurodollar deposits, while Equation A–3 expresses the demand for Eurodollar deposits on the part of the public. How do these two basic relationships affect the Eurodollar market capacity to expand? By substituting Equations A–2 and A–3 into A–1, we obtain the following formula, specifying the determination of $M^\$$:

$$M^\$ = M^{U.S.} - RE + ED$$
$$= M^{U.S.} - (re - 1)ED$$
$$= M^{U.S.} + (1 - re)\,\alpha$$
$$+ (1 - re)\,\epsilon\,M^\$$$

which, solving for $M^\$$, yields

$$M^\$ = \frac{M^{U.S} + \alpha\,(1 - re)}{1 - \epsilon\,(1 - re)} \qquad (A\text{–}4)$$
$$= \mu\,[M^{U.S.} + \alpha\,(1 - re)]$$

where $\mu \equiv 1/[1 - \epsilon(1 - re)] > 1$ is the so-called Eurodollar money multiplier. The value of the multiplier increases with the value of ϵ—which is inversely related to Eurodollar leakages—and de-

creases with the value of *re,* which is the reserve:deposit ratio. Observe that given the multiplier, μ, Equation A–4 tells us that the world supply of dollars in the hands of the public can increase from two sources: a rising U.S. supply of dollars (i.e., increases in the U.S. money supply, $M^{U.S.}$), or a shift in the preferences of the public toward depositing additional amounts of Eurodollars and reducing domestic deposits (i.e., an increase in the α parameter).

The effect of a given change in the U.S. money supply, $\Delta M^{U.S.}$, on the total world supply of dollars is derived by taking changes in Equation A–4, with the following result:

$$\Delta M^\$ = \mu\Delta M^{U.S.}$$

Observe that because the Eurodollar multiplier μ is greater than 1, any given increase in the U.S. money supply is magnified into a larger increase in the world supply of dollars. The extent of this multiplier effect is dependent on the value of μ, which, as we saw earlier, depends on the values of the *re* and ϵ coefficients. The value of *re,* the reserve:deposit ratio held by Eurobanks, has been estimated to be between 0.01 and 0.05, whereas the value of ϵ, the fraction redeposited into the Eurodollar market out of any of the additional dollars supplied, is usually regarded as being smaller than 0.20.[A1] Assuming that *re* = 0.02 *and* ϵ = 0.20, and substituting into Equation A–4, we obtain

$$\Delta M^\$ = \frac{1}{0.804}\,\Delta M^{U.S.} \cong 1.24\,\Delta M^{U.S.},$$

that is, an increase in the domestic supply of dollars increases the total dollar supply (through the Eurodollar market) by 24 percent more than the domestic increase. This relatively minor expansionary effect suggests that the fears of many

---

[A1]For further details, See R.I. McKinnon, *Money in International Exchange* (New York: Oxford University Press, 1979).

authorities as to the explosive deposit expansionary capacity of the Eurodollar market is perhaps mistaken. The present analysis implies that each additional dollar in the U.S. money supply generates only an additional $0.24 in terms of Eurodollars.

The influence of a shift in deposits from domestic to Eurodeposits can be represented by a positive change in the coefficient $\alpha(\Delta\alpha > 0)$, or

$$\Delta M^\$ = \mu(1 - re)\Delta\alpha,$$

which is positive because $\mu > 0$ and $re < 1$. With the approximate actual values of μ and re given earlier ($\mu = 1.24$ and $re = 0.02$), we obtain

$$\frac{\Delta M^\$}{\Delta\alpha} = (1.24)(0.98) = 1.22.$$

This means that a shift of $1.00 from the domestic to the Eurodollar banking system generates $1.22 in additional dollars. Correspondingly, there is only a marginal expansionary capacity of the Eurodollar market above the creation of dollars arising from the direct shift of the dollar deposit abroad.

PART III

Introduction to International Macroeconomics

A Broad Picture of the Open Economy: International Transactions and the Balance-of-Payments Accounts

In an open economy, domestic residents can engage in a variety of international transactions involving the purchase or sale of goods, services, and assets. For example, U.S. residents buy Japanese TV sets and U.S. airplane manufacturers sell commercial jets to European airlines. Similarly, vineyards in California purchase the services of Mexican temporary workers, while American engineers sell their services to Saudi Arabia. At the same time, U.S. investors are purchasing Swiss bank accounts and U.S. corporations are raising funds by selling stocks to foreign investors. It is these transactions that the balance of payments intends to register. More formally, a given country's *balance of payments* records all the economic transactions that have taken place in a given period between the country's residents and the rest of the world. This chapter takes a close look at the statistical presentation of the U.S. balance of payments. An examination of these data will acquaint us with the many links existing between the United States and the rest of the world. Before embarking on this task, however, we must make some basic guiding remarks regarding the notion of residency and the mechanics of international transactions accounting.

9–1. U.S. INTERNATIONAL TRANSACTIONS: THE STATISTICAL PRESENTATION

Because U.S. international transactions involve transactions between U.S. residents and the rest of the world, the first thing to clarify is the notion of a U.S. resident. The concept of a resident is intended to encompass individuals, institutions, and the government. Thus, when we speak of the transactions of U.S. residents, we refer not only to the transactions of individual Americans but also of U.S. firms and the U.S. government at all levels. What designates a U.S. resident is sometimes difficult to determine. As a result, the following—somewhat arbitrary, but necessary—rules of thumb are adopted in U.S. international transactions statistics. Tourists, diplomats, military personnel, and temporary migrant workers are all regarded to be residents of the country from which they come. For example, the expenditures of Japanese tourists in purchasing U.S. goods are regarded as U.S. exports because they involve U.S. sales to foreign residents (the tourists). Similarly, the expenditures of U.S. tourists abroad are treated as imports in the U.S. balance of payments because they involve purchases of foreign goods by U.S. residents. The income received by Mexican temporary migrants working on U.S. farms would also be catalogued as an import. It represents a purchase of foreign services by domestic residents and is therefore an international transaction appearing under the service item in the accounts. There are, however, enormous difficulties in accurately measuring such international transactions. For instance, nobody really knows exactly how many foreign temporary workers, legal plus illegal, there are in the United States or, for that matter, how much they earn.

Determining the residence of multinational firms is another tricky problem. How do you assign residence to a firm located in a number of countries? The convention followed in U.S. international statistics is to treat foreign affiliates of U.S. (parent) firms as residents of the country in which they are located.[1] As a result, transactions between the parent company in the United States and a foreign affiliate are recorded as transactions between a U.S. firm and a foreign resident. Similarly, when a Japanese firm located in the United States imports parts and raw materials from its parent company in Japan, these are recorded as purchases of foreign goods by a U.S. resident.

The basic rule of balance-of-payments accounting is that any transaction giving rise to a receipt from the rest of the world is considered a *credit* and appears as a positive item in the account; any transaction giving rise to a payment to the rest of the world is a *debit* and appears as a negative item. The way these concepts are used in balance-of-payments accounting is best envisioned through the use of a so-called T account, which records a transaction's credit and debit items. A stereotype of the use of a T account is shown in Table 9–1,

TABLE 9–1. **T Account for a Balance-of-Payments Transaction**

Credits (+)		Debits (−)	
Exports		Increase in U.S. Assets Abroad	
Automobiles	$20,000	Deposits at a London Bank	$20,000

[1] Foreign affiliates of U.S. firms can be broken down into foreign subsidiaries and branches according to their legal status. The foreign subsidiary is legally incorporated in the country where it operates, whereas the branch is considered an extension of the parent company and is not incorporated abroad. Even though, for purposes of international transactions accounting, both foreign subsidiaries and branches of U.S. firms are considered foreign residents, for tax purposes the subsidiary is considered a foreign resident (a foreign corporation), and the branch is considered a domestic resident (part of a domestic corporation).

which illustrates a transaction involving $20,000 worth of U.S. exports of automobiles to a British customer who pays with a check drawn on his account at a London bank. For simplicity, we assume the U.S. exporter and the British importer hold Eurodollar accounts at the same London bank and that the transaction is completed by a deposit transfer from the importer to the U.S. exporter.

The T account records credits (positive items) on its left-hand side and debits (negative items) on its right-hand side. Exports of automobiles giving rise to receipts of $20,000 are recorded on the left-hand side of the T account in Table 9–1. The American exporter's purchase of $20,000 worth of foreign assets in the form of a London bank account, on the other hand, is recorded as a debit item on the right side. In general, our international sales, whether in the form of goods, services, or

assets, are regarded as credits. Conversely, our international purchases, whether they are in the form of goods, services, or assets, are regarded as debits. In order to avoid confusion, think of the acquisition of the preceding deposit at the London bank as the purchase of a foreign asset, which is a debit. Finally, note that Table 9–1 illustrates the basic convention of double-entry bookkeeping, by means of which any transaction gives rise to both a credit and a debit of the same value.

Table 9–2 presents the U.S. balance of payments for 1991. It is taken from the September 1992 issue of the *Survey of Current Business* and is based on data gathered and published by the Bureau of Economic Analysis, an agency of the U.S. Department of Commerce. Note that the table includes data on U.S. international transactions in goods, services, investment income, transfers, and

TABLE 9–2. Summary of U.S. International Transactions, 1991 (in millions of dollars)

Transaction	1991
Exports of goods, services, and investment income	$ 704,914
Merchandise goods, excluding military	415,962
Services and military goods	163,637
Income receipts on investments	125,315
Imports of goods, services, and investment income	−716,624
Merchandise goods, excluding military	−489,398
Services and military goods	−118,341
Income payments on investments	−108,886
Unilateral transfers, net	8,028
U.S. assets abroad, net [increase/capital outflow (−)]	−62,220
U.S. official reserve assets, net	5,763
U.S. government assets, other than official reserve assets, net	3,397
U.S. private assets, net	−71,379
Foreign assets in the United States, net [increase/capital inflow (+)]	66,980
Foreign official assets, net	18,407
Other foreign assets, net	48,573
Allocations of special drawing rights	0
Statistical discrepancy	−1,078

SOURCE: U.S. Department of Commerce, *Survey of Current Business* (September 1992).

assets. Each of these items is discussed subsequently in detail.

Exports of Goods, Services, and Investment Income

The first item in the international transactions table is "Exports of goods, services, and investment income," the value of which is registered as a credit item because exports represent sales to foreigners and thus give rise to receipts from the rest of the world.[2] As observed, the value of U.S. exports of goods, services, and investment income in 1991 was $704.9 billion, composed of $416.0 billion worth of merchandise exports, $163.6 billion of service exports, and $125.3 billion of investment income receipts. The value of merchandise exports is estimated from data received by the Department of Commerce from U.S. customs agents. All exported (and imported) commercial merchandise must be legally registered through customs, which is in charge of assessing tariffs and other levies on the merchandise. As a result, merchandise exports (and imports) are among the most accurate items reported in balance-of-payments accounts. They are also the most frequently reported items, available on a monthly basis.

Exports of services include receipts from transportation services provided to foreigners, expenditures of visitors in the United States, receipts from royalties, license fees, and the provision of technical services to foreign residents, and other service exports. Transactions in services are much more difficult to measure than transactions in goods, even though the Department of Commerce and other government agencies keep tabs on them through surveys and questionnaires. Appropriately enough, these transactions are usually referred to as *invisibles*. In addition to the categories already mentioned, the Department of Commerce includes

military transactions—such as U.S. sales of military equipment to foreign countries—in the category of service exports. For example, in the third and fourth quarters of 1990, the United States delivered $1.2 billion worth of military equipment to Saudi Arabia in response to the Iraqi invasion of Kuwait; these were recorded under service exports in the 1990 balance of payments accounts.

The category referred to as exports of investment income encompasses the receipts of income on U.S. assets abroad—that is, the income received by U.S. residents, both private and government, from their investments in foreign countries.[3] This appears as a credit in the balance of payments because it gives rise to receipts from the rest of the world. Items included are interest payments made by foreigners to U.S. residents, dividend receipts from foreign investments, the share of the retained earnings of foreign subsidiaries of U.S. firms corresponding to U.S. residents, the earnings of foreign branches of U.S. firms,[4] and receipts from U.S. government assets abroad, such as interest paid by foreign governments on their debts to the U.S. government.

Imports of Goods, Services, and Investment Income

The second major item in the U.S. international transactions table regards "Imports of goods, services, and investment income." Their value ap-

---

[2]The reader may also find it convenient to refer to Appendix Table 9–A1, at the end of this chapter. It provides a detailed breakdown of the general categories included in Table 9–2.

[3]The U.S. Department of Commerce has traditionally placed investment income receipts alongside exports of goods and services in its presentation of U.S. international transactions. In fact, until 1990, the Department of Commerce considered receipts on investment income as part of service exports. Beginning in June 1990, services were separated from investment income, as is reflected in our presentation. For the technical details of this redefinition, see R. E. Nicholson, "U.S. International Transactions, First Quarter 1989," *Survey of Current Business* (June 1990).

[4]Earnings of foreign branches and of foreign subsidiaries are considered to accrue to the U.S. parent company, even if they are not actually received. For instance, the undistributed profits of foreign affiliates are included as a U.S. receipt, in spite of not actually being remitted to the parent company.

pears as a debit item representing purchases from foreigners and give rise to payments to the rest of the world. As displayed in Table 9–2, the value of these items in 1991 was $716.6 billion, made up of $489.4 billion in merchandise, $118.3 billion in service imports, and $108.9 billion worth of investment income payments to the rest of the world. The purchase of foreign goods and services by domestic residents can be broken down into the same categories as the sales of domestic goods and services. They will include items such as imports of merchandise goods, U.S. military expenses abroad, U.S. tourist expenses in foreign countries, and royalties and license fees paid to foreigners. For example, a significant import item in the third and fourth quarters of 1990 was U.S. direct defense expenses abroad. These expenses rose in those quarters to a total of $9.2 billion as a result of U.S. armed forces involvement in the Persian Gulf.

Imports of investment income represent income payments on foreign assets in the United States—that is, they measure the income that foreign residents earn on their investments in the United States. This appears as a debit in the balance of payments because it gives rise to a payment from U.S. residents to the rest of the world. Items included are, for example, interest payments made by U.S. borrowers—both private and government—to foreign lenders, and capital gains received by foreigners from their investments in the United States.

Unilateral Transfers

The next major item in the balance of payments is net *unilateral transfers*. It refers to international transactions that do not involve an explicit exchange of goods, assets, or services. Included are U.S. government grants, such as foreign aid provided by U.S. foreign assistance programs and food donations under the Public Law 480 program. Pension checks received by retired Americans residing abroad are also considered unilateral transfers since the retiree does not provide any

current services in exchange for them. A final category includes private unilateral transfers, such as gifts made to foreigners. Unilateral transfers made to foreigners appear as a debit in the balance of payments because they represent payments to the rest of the world. The United States has traditionally been a net supplier of foreign aid. As a result, the unilateral transfers item in the U.S. balance of payments is generally negative. However, in 1991 the unilateral transfers item in the balance of payments was positive and equal to $8.0 billion. During the first two quarters of 1991, the United States received close to $26 billion in cash contributions from coalition partners in Operation Desert Storm. These contributions constituted a credit in the balance of payments and made the net balance of unilateral transfers positive during 1991.

U.S. Assets Abroad

A fourth major category in the balance of payments regards "U.S. assets abroad," which represent the net purchases of foreign assets by domestic residents in the given time period.[5] As Table 9–2 indicates, in 1991, U.S. residents increased their holdings of foreign assets by an amount equal to $62.2 billion. This number appears as a debit in the balance of payments because the purchase of foreign assets gives rise to a payment to the rest of the world. Purchases of foreign assets consist of the following categories: increases in "U.S. official reserve assets," which represent increases in the holdings of international reserves by the

---

[5]The purchase of foreign assets refers to an acquisition of claims on foreigners—that is, a purchase of assets issued abroad. These include, for example, the purchases of stocks and bonds issued by Japanese companies or the purchase of Mexican real estate. Notice that the term *foreign assets* has a different meaning when used by U.S. balance-of-payments statistics in referring to "Foreign assets in the United States." The meaning of the term *foreign asset* in this latter context refers to domestic assets *owned by foreigners* rather than to *claims of foreigners*.

central bank;[6] increases in "U.S. government as-sets," which include such transactions as new loans made by the U.S. government to foreign countries; and increases in "U.S. assets abroad," representing the private sector's net purchases of foreign assets, such as direct private investment abroad, portfolio investment in foreign assets, and private loans to foreigners.[7] Note that, just as with any other transaction involving increases in U.S. assets abroad, loans made by U.S. residents to foreigners represent a debit in the balance of payments. This debit can be understood by envi-sioning a new loan as involving the acquisition on the part of the lender of an IOU, a promissory note by the borrower to repay a certain amount later on. Upon agreeing to the IOU, the domestic lender makes a payment to the foreign borrower for the

amount of the loan. Because it gives rise to a payment to foreigners, the acquisition of an IOU is then recorded with a negative sign in the balance-of-payments accounts.[8]

In summary, net increases (or decreases) in U.S. holdings of foreign assets appear as a debit (or credit) in the U.S. balance of payments under the U.S. assets abroad category. Since increases in U.S. assets abroad represent a payment on the part of the United States, they are usually referred to as *capital outflows*. A useful way to remember that capital outflows are a debit in the balance of payments is to envision the purchase of a foreign asset as an import of assets, just as purchases of foreign goods represent imports of goods. Imports (whether of goods or assets) give rise to payments to foreigners and are thus balance-of-payments debits.

Foreign Assets in the United States

Returning to Table 9–2, we see that the next item in the balance of payments is "Foreign assets in the United States," which represent the net sales of domestic assets made by U.S. residents to foreign residents in the given time period. U.S. residents sold foreigners a (net) amount of domestic assets worth $67 billion in 1991. This amount appears as a credit in the balance of payments because the sale of domestic assets to foreigners gives rise to receipts from the rest of the world. It also repre-sents an inflow of funds into the country and is thus usually referred to as a *capital inflow.* To remember that capital inflows appear as a credit item in the balance of payments, the sale of a

---

[6]Such as acquisitions of gold, SDRs, and foreign currencies, and increases in the U.S. reserve position in the IMF.

[7]The distinction between direct investment and portfolio investment is sometimes subtle and arbitrary; however, the general concept to remember is that direct investment is intended to comprise investments involving a certain degree of control (by the investor) over the use of the funds invested, whereas portfolio investment lacks such control. Thus, a clear-cut case of direct investment abroad occurs when a domestic resident buys foreign real estate (land or houses), whose ownership is clearly in control of the asset holder. Portfolio investment occurs when a domestic resident buys either foreign short-term securities or bonds, which do not have attached to them any claim on foreign control or ownership of the enter-prise. There are less clear cases, however. For instance, what happens when you buy stocks in a foreign enterprise? Is this direct investment or portfolio investment? The stocks give you a nominal claim over the decisions of the enterprise, but to be regarded as direct foreign investment a line has to be drawn as to whether you really have any effective control over the use of your funds. The balance-of-payments conventions here are not completely unambiguous and vary from country to country and from time period to time period. The U.S. Department of Commerce currently considers direct investment a purchase by a U.S. resident of equity in a foreign enterprise in which he or she owns 10 percent or more of the voting securities. In the preceding example, had you already owned, say, 20 percent of the voting securities of the enterprise in which you have purchased stocks, your purchase of stocks would be considered direct foreign investment.

[8]The subsequent repayment of the amount loaned (the principal) by the foreigner represents a decrease in U.S. assets abroad and a receipt for the United States in the future. It will be recorded as a credit (with a positive sign) in the U.S. assets abroad account at that time. As mentioned earlier, the interest on the loan is recorded as a receipt of investment income on the part of the United States (income receipts on U.S. assets abroad) and enters in the "exports of goods, services, and investment income" category.

domestic asset to a foreign resident can be thought of as an export of assets, just as sale of domestic goods to foreigners represent exports of goods. Exports (whether of goods or assets) give rise to receipts from foreigners and are thus credits in the balance of payments. Sales of domestic assets to foreigners can be broken down into two categories: those made to foreign central banks, in the form of increases in *foreign official assets in the United States* (such as a purchase of certificates of deposit or Treasury bills by the Bank of England), and asset sales to other foreign residents, catalogued as increases in "Other foreign assets in the United States" and including direct investment, portfolio investment by foreigners in the United States, and foreign loans to domestic residents.

The transactions recorded in the "U.S. assets abroad" and "Foreign assets in the United States" categories of the balance of payments involve *net* asset flows, which register a net change in each entry in a given time period (one year in the case of Table 9–2). The $62.2-billion figure for "U.S. Assets Abroad" refers then to the amount of U.S. imports of securities and other claims on foreigners, net of U.S. sales of these items, in 1991, as opposed to *gross* flows, which register the total volume of transactions involving purchases of foreign assets and do not subtract the sales of foreign assets in the given time period. Similarly, the $67-billion figure given for "Foreign Assets in the U.S." refers to all foreign purchases of domestic assets, net of the sales of domestic assets owned by foreigners, in 1991. Since these figures are on the net flow of assets, they do not give us any sense of the actual volume of international transactions involving trade in assets.[9] For exam-

ple, a single U.S. securities dealer often engages in more than $50 million (and perhaps up to more than $200 million) worth of *daily* international transactions in securities and money market instruments denominated in U.S. and foreign currencies.

Allocation of SDRs and Statistical Discrepancy

The last two major items in the balance of payments are the allocation of *special drawing rights* (SDRs) and the *statistical discrepancy*. SDRs are a type of international reserve asset created and distributed to member countries by the IMF. The allocation of SDRs measures the amount of SDRs allocated to the United States by the IMF over the year. These payments represent receipts for the United States and appear as a credit in the balance of payments. In 1990, there were no allocations of SDRs.

The statistical discrepancy ensures that the items in the balance of payments add up to zero. Consequently, it is a residual category that counteracts the net balance of all the other positive and negative items in the accounts. Why is it that adding all items in the balance of payments must necessarily give a value of zero? The answer lies in the double-entry bookkeeping in balance-of-payments accounting. Its principle is simple: Any international transaction should be recorded as involving both a credit and a debit of equal size. For example, the transaction involving a sale of Japanese-made automobiles to the United States obviously represents an import of goods, which appears as a debit in the balance of payments. It also gives rise, however, to a payment for the same amount by the American purchaser to the Japanese manufacturer, which involves an export of some kind of U.S. asset or claim on the U.S. and is, thus, a credit. If the auto imports are worth $1 million and the payment occurs, for instance, in the form of a bank transfer, the foreign assets in the U.S. item

---

[9]To visualize the difference between gross transactions and net asset flows, consider a large U.S. corporation that invests $100 million abroad (say, in the Eurodollar market) for three months (say, from March to June) but does not roll this over in June. The operation clearly involves a substantial financial transaction but does not appear in the U.S. balance of payments because it nets out and cancels before the end of the year.

in the balance of payments would increase by $1 million. The imports-of-goods debit should thus be exactly offset by the foreign assets in the U.S. credit, leaving a net balance of zero. A statistical discrepancy arises, however, because of measurement errors and the physical inability of recording instantaneously all international transactions. As a result, a difference will always be observed between the totals of *recorded* credits and debits in the balance-of-payments accounts. The statistical discrepancy item makes sure all items add up to zero; it therefore reflects the extent of unrecorded transactions and measurement errors in the balance of payments.

The statistical discrepancy tends to fluctuate from year to year, but it has shown extraordinary volatility in recent years—soaring from a value of −$1.5 billion in 1969 to $73 billion in 1990 and back down to −$1.1 in 1991. It is widely believed that the statistical discrepancy mostly represents *unrecorded* services such as tourist expenditures and capital flows. A positive value of the statistical discrepancy, then, represents either unrecorded exports of services or unrecorded capital inflows—that is, unrecorded exports of U.S. assets to foreigners. For instance, in the preceding example, the U.S. importer may delay payment to its Japanese supplier. As a result, the import of goods is recorded, but the export of U.S. assets or claims on the United States (the capital inflow) goes unrecorded. The underreporting of capital inflows also arises from the inherent problems involved in accurately accounting for volatile funds rapidly transferred among financial centers. The problems are especially difficult when intentional deception is confronted—whether it is related to tax avoidance, money-laundering activities originating in the underground cocaine trade, or other illegal undertakings.

An area in which the Commerce Department and the relevant agencies have received considerable criticism for their data-collection activities is direct foreign investment in the United States.

The Commerce Department does currently engage in surveys of U.S. affiliates of foreign companies, but it is often alleged that there is significant noncompliance and a number of inconsistencies in the data.[10] Unrecorded foreign direct investment in the United States represents unreported capital inflows and provides yet another indication that the statistical discrepancy may represent unreported capital flows. On the other hand, the presence of major gaps and systematic biases in the collection of data in other categories is becoming very clear. In 1989, for instance, estimates of U.S. international trade in services for several previous years were substantially revised as the outcome of a long-term project between the Commerce Department and a number of private service-sector companies.[11] The project involved improved data collection on travel and tourism as well as the implementation of surveys on several difficult-to-estimate areas, such as the expenditures of foreign students in the United States (as well as U.S. students abroad) and exports versus imports of legal, accounting, and other professional and technical services. In these areas, the Commerce Department discovered that U.S. exports of services were severely undercounted. In 1988, for instance, the study found $23 billion more exports than previously reported and $11.6 billion more imports, leaving a net balance of $11.4 billion in unrecorded exports for 1988. Combined with other estimates, the Commerce Department estimates that about $20 billion a year may have gone undetected in the late 1980s.

---

[10]See E. M. Graham and P. R. Krugman, *Foreign Direct Investment in the United States* (Washington, D.C.: Institute for International Economics, 1989), Appendix A.

[11]See A. Y. Kester and R. E. Baldwin, eds., *Behind the Numbers: U.S. Trade in the World Economy* (Washington, D.C.: National Academy Press, 1992), pp. 8–9; and H. Murad, "U.S. International Transactions, Revised Estimates for 1976–1991," U.S. Department of Commerce, *Survey of Current Business* (June 1992).

9–2. BALANCE-OF-PAYMENTS CONCEPTS: SUMMARIZING THE INTERNATIONAL EXPERIENCE

The items in the international transactions table always sum to zero because of the double-entry bookkeeping in its accounting. As a consequence, the overall balance of payments is always zero. What is it, then, that economists refer to when they speak of balance-of-payments surpluses or deficits? Clearly, the numbers quoted must have some meaning because, over the years, they have been blamed for inflation, unemployment, high interest rates, and almost any economic (and sometimes political and social) calamity. They must also provide information of concern to policymakers; otherwise, President John F. Kennedy would not have equated a balance-of-payments deficit with nuclear war.[12]

The balance of payments can be broken down into several (sub)balances or accounts. Each of these (sub)balances measures the international trade of the economy in a broad class of transactions. The concepts of surplus and deficit apply to these particular accounts. An account is said to be in *surplus* when credits exceed debits on that account—that is, when receipts outstrip payments. A particular balance shows a *deficit* when receipts fall short of payments on the items comprised by the account. We now examine some specific balances with the aid of Table 9–3, which provides a summary statement of how balance-of-payments subaccounts are calculated. Appendix Table 9–A2 provides additional figures for selected years.

The Trade Balance

Perhaps the most publicized account in the balance of payments is the merchandise trade balance, which summarizes the net trade in (merchandise)

goods of the economy with the rest of the world. It is measured by the economy's exports minus the imports of merchandise goods from the rest of the world. For the United States in 1991, the merchandise trade balance, or just *trade balance,* was equal to −$73.4 billion. The negative sign means that merchandise imports exceeded merchandise exports by the given amount. As a result, there was a so-called trade-balance-account deficit: The payments from all international transactions involving exchanges of physical (nonmilitary) goods with the rest of the world exceeded the receipts.

The trade balance provides a summary of the economy's performance and trade patterns as reflected through its trade in goods. Figure 9–1 illustrates how the U.S. trade balance has behaved in the recent past. The pattern is clear: The trade surpluses of the 1950s and 1960s gave way to huge deficits in the 1970s, 1980s, and early 1990s. Note, however, the significant ups and downs that the balance has suffered over the years. Even though the recent trend is toward larger deficits, there have been extended periods of reduced deficits. Indeed, the trade balance deficit peaked in 1987 with a $159.5 billion deficit and has exhibited a declining trend since.

What factors account for the overall shifting pattern of U.S. trade? Why does the trade balance fluctuate up and down so much over the short run? These are questions we will address in the next few chapters. For the moment, we will simply state that the trade balance is affected by a whole array of factors, including exchange rate changes, monetary and fiscal policies, domestic economic growth, income changes abroad, unexpected supply shocks, and the economy's international competitiveness. This last factor has received special attention in the United States in recent years because of the increasing competition U.S.-manufactured products have suffered at the hands of those produced by Canada, Western Europe, Japan, and the newly industrialized countries (NICs), such as Brazil, Korea, and Taiwan. In the early 1970s, for example, the trade deficits

---

[12]A. M. Schlesinger, *A Thousand Days* (Boston: Houghton-Mifflin, 1965), p. 654.

TABLE 9–3. **Summary Calculation of Balance-of-Payments Subaccounts in the United States, 1991 (in billions of dollars)**

Current account balance (CAB)		$ −3.7
Trade balance	−73.4	
Capital account balance		−18.9
Reported capital account	−17.8	
Statistical discrepancy	−1.1	
Allocation of SDRs		0.0
Official reserve settlements (ORS) balance		−22.6
(Decrease in) U.S. official reserve assets		5.8
(Increase in) foreign official assets in the U.S.		16.8
Overall balance of payments		0.0

SOURCE: U.S. Department of Commerce, *Survey of Current Business* (September 1992). The survey is reproduced in the appendix at the end of this chapter as Table 9–A1. The precise figure for the reported capital account balance is obtained by adding lines 39, 43, 53, and 56 of Table 9–A1. The ORS balance can be calculated as (the negative of) the sum of lines 34, 50, 54, and 55, which register the items below the line—involving official reserve assets. Note that in the calculation of the ORS balance we exclude some foreign official assets in the United States (line 53) that are not regarded as international reserves by foreign monetary authorities. Observe also that the statistical discrepancy has been incorporated into the capital account on the assumption that it represents unrecorded capital flows.

emerged with Japan ($1.4-billion deficit in 1973), West Germany ($2.6-billion deficit in 1973), and Canada ($2.6-billion deficit in 1973). By 1983, the U.S. trade deficit with Japan alone had grown to $19.6 billion and by 1990 it had ballooned to $41.8 billion. The increasing import competition from other NICs in textiles, steel, chemicals, and a variety of other products was also felt in the 1980s, not only by the United States but also by other developed economies. The plight of the declining traded goods industries, which once formed the pillars of the U.S. trade balance surplus, is typified by the U.S. steel industry. Between 1959 and 1969, U.S. exports of steel mill products increased at an average pace of 11.2 percent annually; between 1969 and 1978, the rate of decline of exports averaged 8.6 percent annually. The reasons for the decline and fall of the steel industry have been found in a number of factors: relatively high real labor costs (among the top of the industrial wage scale in the United States); the obsolescence of the technology used compared

with that used by the Japanese, Brazilians, and other newcomers; and increases in the prices of raw materials and the cost of transportation, among others.[13]

Another factor that can account for some of the broadening of U.S. trade balance deficits has been

[13]For a detailed examination of the sources of the problems of the U.S. steel industry, see J. P. Hoerr, *And the Wolf Finally Came: The Decline of the American Steel Industry* (Pittsburgh: University of Pittsburgh Press, 1988). One of the traditional reactions of the U.S. government to the steel industry's problems has been to impose protectionist policies, such as voluntary export restraints. VERs are agreements between the United States and steel-exporting countries (such as Japan) that set quotas on the amount of U.S. steel imports for a certain period. For a discussion of protectionism in the steel industry, particularly in the 1980s, see W. T. Hogan, "Protectionism in the Steel Industry: A Historical Perspective," in D. Salvatore, ed., *The New Protectionist Threat to World Welfare* (Amsterdam: North Holland, 1987); and D. G. Tarr, "Costs and Benefits to the United States of the 1985 Steel Import Quota Program," in R. Sato and P. Wachtel, eds., *Trade Friction and Economic Policy: Problems and Prospects for Japan and the United States* (Cambridge: Cambridge University Press, 1987).

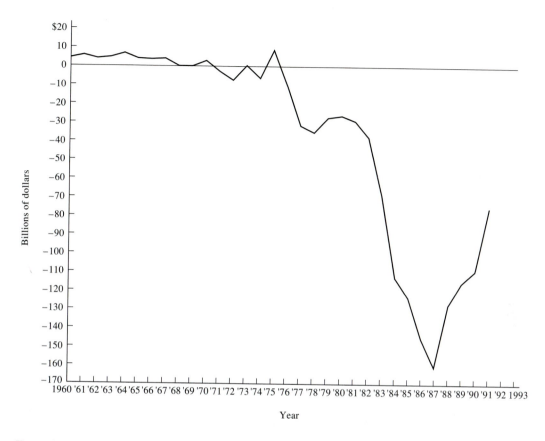

FIGURE 9–1. The U.S. Trade Balance

SOURCE: U.S. Department of Commerce, *Survey of Current Business* (September 1992).

increased oil prices. The price of a barrel of crude oil rose in the 1970s and early 1980s from (on average) $2.60 in 1972 to $13 in 1978 and $29 in 1983. The impact was a burgeoning U.S. oil import bill. In 1973, the value of U.S. crude oil imports was equal to about $8.4 billion. By 1981, it was at a high of $79.4 billion, almost a tenfold increase in fewer than ten years. In the mid- and late 1980s, though, the price of crude oil fell; by the end of 1989 it was at about $17, and the U.S. oil import bill dropped to $51 billion. Then, in 1990, the price of oil exploded as a result of Iraq's invasion of Kuwait and the ensuing crisis in the Persian Gulf. In the fourth quarter of 1990, the price of crude oil averaged $28.47 a barrel. Associated with the higher oil prices was a huge oil-import bill, which rose to $62.1 billion in 1990, the highest level since 1981.

Although the oil-price shocks of 1973 to 1974, 1979 to 1980, and 1990 to 1991 had an evident impact on the U.S. economy, the effects on the trade balance should not be exaggerated. First of all, oil prices tumbled both after 1983 and after the quick victory of the Coalition forces in the Persian Gulf in 1991; such temporary oil-price increases are unlikely to have a substantial impact on the trade balance over the long-run. Second, and most important, even though oil-price shocks have the effect of increasing oil-import bills, their significance in determining the overall trade balance is not so clear. For instance, right after the oil-price hikes, the balance of trade of many oil-importing countries has turned out to be in surplus.

The Balance on Services

A second account that can be calculated from the balance of payments is the *balance on services.* This balance measures the net trade in services of domestic residents with the rest of the world. It is calculated by subtracting imports of services from the value of exports of services. In the case of the United States for 1991, the balance on services was equal to $45.3 billion. This was determined by subtracting $118.3 billion worth of imports of services from $163.6 billion worth of exports of services. This meant that, in 1991, there was a surplus in the balance on services (a net export of services): the payments from such transactions exceeded the receipts.

While we saw earlier that there was a 1991 U.S. trade balance deficit, the services balance exhibited a surplus, which has generally been the case since the early 1970s. Figure 9–2 depicts the balance on services from 1960 to the present. Observe that the trend of this balance has been positive and that in 1990 and 1991 there were record levels of net exports of services. Currently, the United States is a strong net exporter of financial, educational, business, professional, and technical services. In addition, American residents are major recipients of royalties and license fees; in 1991, there was a $14 billion excess of receipts over payments from royalties and license fees.

The Balance on Investment Income

The balance on investment income is equal to the income received by domestic residents from their investments in foreign countries minus the income paid to foreign residents from their domestic in-

vestments. In the United States in 1991, the balance on investment income was equal to $16.4 billion. This means that, in 1991, there was a surplus: The $125.3 billion that American residents received in income from their assets abroad exceeded the $108.9 billion in income payments made to foreigners who had assets in the United States. Figure 9–3 displays the U.S. balance on investment income from 1960 to 1991. Traditionally, the United States had a large, growing investment income balance. In 1973, for instance, the investment balance was equal to $12 billion, and by 1984 it was more than $31 billion. In the late 1980s, however, the balance dropped significantly. By 1987, it was down to $10.9 billion.

What caused this recent decline in the investment income balance? A look at the figures on exports and imports of investment income reveals that the income received by U.S. residents from their investments abroad did not decline. From 1981 to 1991, income from U.S. assets abroad increased from $86 billion to $125.3 billion. However, the income paid to foreigners with assets in the United States rose at a faster pace. In 1981, the latter was equal to $53.6 billion, whereas in 1991 it mushroomed to $108.9 billion. The generally rising pace of the income received by foreigners from their assets in the United States is related to the growing volume of those assets, a controversial topic we will discuss in Chapter 10.

The Balance on Goods, Services, and Investment Income

A fourth balance often calculated from the balance-of-payments accounts is the balance on goods, services, and investment income. This balance represents the net exports in goods, services, and investment income of a country with the rest of the world. It is determined by subtracting the imports of goods, services, and investment income from the value of exports of these items. In the case of the United States in 1991, the balance on goods, services, and investment income was equal

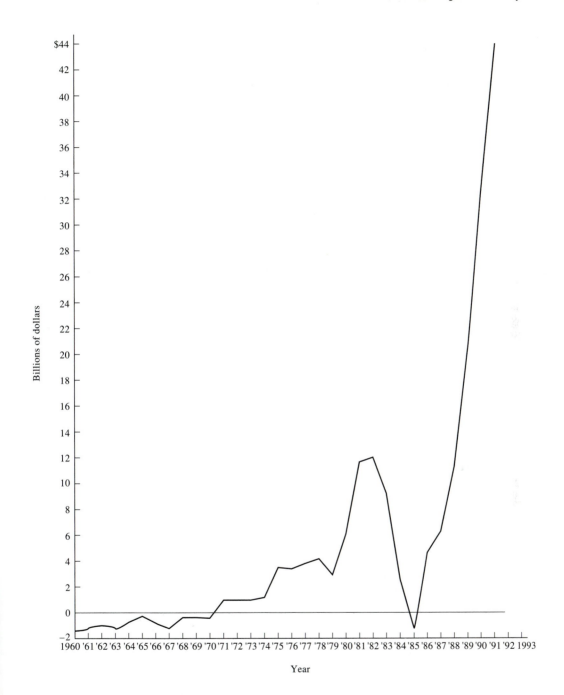

FIGURE 9-2.   The U.S. Balance on Services

SOURCE: U.S. Department of Commerce, *Survey of Current Business* (September 1992).

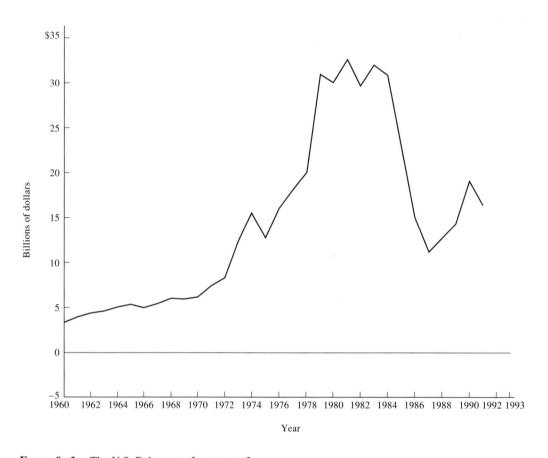

FIGURE 9–3.   The U.S. Balance on Investment Income

SOURCE: U.S. Department of Commerce, *Survey of Current Business* (September 1992).

to −$11.7 billion. It was calculated by subtracting $716.6 billion worth of imports of goods, services, and investment income from $704.9 billion worth of exports of these items. This deficit reflects the fact that, although there was a surplus in the service and investment income balances, the trade deficit more than offset them in 1991.

The Current Account Balance

A fifth account usually calculated from the international transactions table is the *current account balance* (CAB). The CAB measures the econo-

my's trade in goods and services with the rest of the world, taking into account unilateral transfers. Table 9–3 shows that the CAB for the United States was equal to −$3.7 billion in 1991. This amount represents a deficit in the CAB; the economy's payments exceeded the receipts from its international trade in goods, services, and investment income, taking into account the payments made by the United States to the rest of the world through unilateral transfers. Note that the only major set of international transactions not included in the CAB involves international trade in assets. Thus, except for statistical discrepancies, a CAB deficit (surplus) must be financed (offset) by a surplus (deficit) in the balance of the economy's international trade in assets. Otherwise, the balance of payments would not add up to zero.

The CAB corresponds to the net acquisition of foreign assets by the country as a whole. This situation can be clearly visualized by drawing an analogy between the case of a household and that of an economy or a country. A household holds receipts from its sales of goods and services in the form of salaries, interest earned, yard-sale receipts, and so on, as well as from transfers received from other households, such as gifts from friends. It also makes payments for the purchases of goods and services and for transfers to other people, such as charitable donations. The balance on these purchases and sales of goods and services, plus the net transfers made, is for a household what the CAB is for a country. The household faces the equivalent of a CAB surplus when its receipts exceed its payments on goods, services, and transfers transactions. It faces the equivalent of a CAB deficit when its payments exceed its receipts from these transactions. Consider the first case in more detail. An excess of receipts over payments in the CAB must give rise to some corresponding (offsetting) transactions involving increases in asset holdings. The household, for example, may lend, buy some stocks and bonds, or increase its holdings of certificates of deposit, currency, or bank deposits. All these transactions are analogous to the international transactions of a country under a CAB surplus; the economy may lend abroad or buy some foreign stocks and bonds, or the country's central bank may increase its holdings of foreign currencies. The same analogy between a household and a country can also be made for the case of a deficit in the CAB. In this situation, the household would have to borrow from other households or reduce its cash holdings and bank deposits in order to finance the excess of payments over receipts. Similarly, a country facing a CAB deficit has to finance it by borrowing from other countries; selling some of its stocks, bonds, and other financial assets; or reducing its holdings of foreign currencies (its official reserve assets).

In summary, the CAB measures the net acquisition of foreign assets—the net foreign investment—by the country as a whole. A surplus in the CAB implies that the country is increasing its holdings of foreign assets or lending funds abroad and so it is acquiring net claims on foreigners. A deficit, on the other hand, means that the country is selling assets to foreigners or borrowing funds from abroad.

The U.S. CAB has undergone major transformations over the years. For long periods in the nineteenth century, the United States was a CAB-deficit country, acquiring foreign debt and accepting foreign investment while it developed its industrial base. The CAB deficits were thus associated with the country's economic growth drive—which should warn against unqualifyingly labeling CAB deficits as a bad thing. The experience of the U.S. CAB in the 1950s and 1960s was one of persistent surpluses, which financed a boom of U.S. investment abroad. Since then, the CAB has fluctuated, sometimes being in deficit and sometimes in surplus. However, as Figure 9–4 shows, the 1980s saw the emergence of a growing U.S. CAB deficit. This deficit was greatly reduced in the late 1980s and early 1990s.

The U.S. CAB deficit has worried many experts and policymakers who fear that the United States is accumulating a potentially unmanageable debt burden. Note that the behavior of the CAB deficit is closely linked to that of the trade balance deficit, depicted in Figure 9–1. Is the U.S. trade balance deficit reversible in a short period of time? Economist Barry Eichengreen at the University of California at Berkeley, has gathered historical evidence suggesting that trade balance deficits have been rapidly eliminated in a number of industrialized countries in the past.[14] In most cases, however, shrinking the deficits has required major,

[14]B. J. Eichengreen, "Trade Deficits in the Long Run," in A. E. Burger, ed., *U.S. Trade Deficit: Causes, Consequences and Cures* (Boston: Kluwer Academic Publishers, 1989).

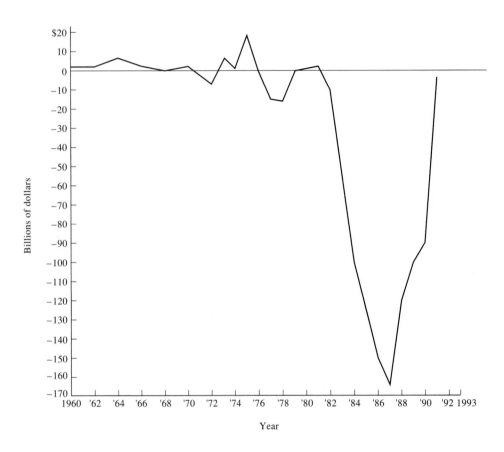

FIGURE 9-4. The U.S. Current Account Balance (CAB)

SOURCE: U.S. Department of Commerce, *Survey of Current Business* (September 1992).

prolonged recessions. Just as individuals refrain from purchasing various goods and services when their income drops, reductions in domestic economic activity result in a contraction of purchases of foreign goods and services (i.e., imports decline). However, the lower output and employment associated with economic recession not only have negative social consequences but are unpalatable to politicians intent on sustaining their own popularity. The real question, then, is whether there are cases where trade deficits have been reduced without a sizable recession. Eichengreen's answer is "not too many," though he does find some few cases—Canada after 1912, Japan after 1924, and Britain after 1951. In these instances, the deficit was quickly reduced either because favorable shifts in world market conditions occurred that lifted export prices (and thus export earnings), or because the debt associated with the CAB deficit was used to finance investments that increased long-run growth in exports. In the case of the U.S., assuming no benefit from a lucky rise in export prices, has the CAB deficit been associated with investments oriented to increase long-run growth? The answer to this question is to be found in the discussion in Chapter 10.

The Capital Account Balance

All international asset transactions, excluding the ones made by monetary authorities in those assets that serve as official international reserves, are grouped into the *capital* account.[15] The capital account thus registers, among others, our purchases of foreign stocks and bonds, and U.S. bank lending to foreign corporations and government agencies. The investments of foreign corporations in U.S. Treasury bills and CDs are also included in the capital account, but foreign central bank purchases of those assets are not because they involve the official international reserves of those countries.

The U.S. capital account was −$18.9 billion in 1991. This represented a net acquisition of foreign assets by Americans over and above the purchase of U.S. assets by foreigners. As shown in Table 9–3, the capital account is obtained by adding the statistical discrepancy to the value of the capital account derived from the actual data reported by individual transactors—which we call the reported capital account and amounted to −$17.8 billion in 1991. The reason the reported capital account needs to be supplemented by adding the statistical discrepancy is that a significant amount of U.S. international capital market transactions are difficult to measure and/or are underreported. The statistical discrepancy is widely regarded as reflecting such unreported asset transactions. Consequently, in order to obtain a more accurate measure of the actual capital account—one that includes reported and unreported transactions—the statistical discrepancy is frequently added to the other items in the account.

For instance, and as we noted earlier, it is widely believed that the −$1.1 billion statistical discrepancy in the 1991 U.S. balance of payments largely represents unrecorded sales of U.S. assets by foreigners (net capital outflows). When this amount is added to the −$17.8 billion reported capital account, the capital account becomes equal to a −$18.9 billion deficit. The divergence between the capital account as obtained from reported data and that obtained on the assumption that the statistical discrepancy represents capital flows is not at all negligible.

Figure 9–5 traces the behavior of the capital account balance since 1960. The reported U.S. capital account deficit shifted from deficit to surplus in 1982, but the overall (i.e., reported plus unreported) capital account balance was already in surplus in the late 1970s. This behavior reflected an increasing tendency for foreign residents to invest in the United States. Most of these increased foreign assets are in the form of liabilities of U.S. banks (such as CDs), U.S. Treasury securities, and direct foreign investments in the United States. It is interesting to observe that, in the 1980s, foreigners accounted for about 20 percent—and in some years more than 50 percent—of the increase in the total public debt privately held (this dropped in the 1990s; in 1990, foreign purchases of Treasury securities were down to 11 percent of the $272 billion in Treasury securities issued to finance the U.S. government's budget deficit). Another rising category of capital flows into the United States is direct investment.

What caused the U.S. capital account surpluses in the 1980s? What has given rise to the capital account deficits of the early 1990s? Figure 9–5 displays the substantial ups and downs of the capital account over the years. What causes this short-term volatility? These are questions that will be addressed in the following chapters. Here we will only mention that the capital account is strongly influenced by interest rates, exchange rate

---

[15]This means that transactions in U.S. official reserve assets—the U.S. monetary gold stock, Federal Reserve and Treasury holdings of foreign currencies, and others—are not included in the capital account. Also excluded are those transactions involving foreign official assets in the United States. Because the U.S. dollar is an international money, widely accepted as a means of international payments, foreign central banks hold dollar-denominated assets in the United States, such as U.S. Treasury bills and CDs issued by New York banks. These foreign official assets in the United States help settle international transactions and are regarded as equivalent to international reserves by foreign central banks.

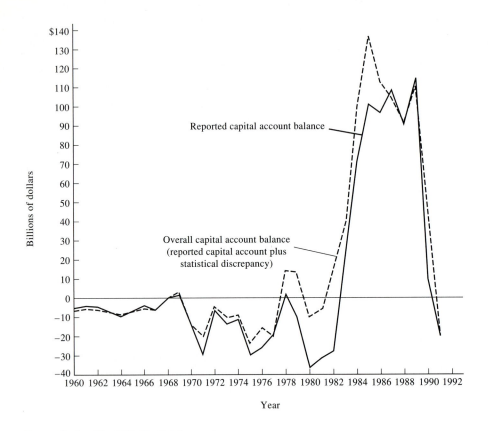

FIGURE 9–5. The U.S. Capital Account

SOURCE: U.S. Department of Commerce, *Survey of Current Business* (September 1992).

expectations, risk perceptions, and a number of other variables that determine the movement of funds across borders.

The capital account is an aggregate of international transactions involving a wide variety of financial instruments. As a result, it is often apparent that the balance-of-payments statistics of a given country distinguish between different conceptual types of asset transactions, such as short-term versus long-term or liquid versus illiquid, and calculate capital account subbalances made on these distinctions. Indeed, the U.S. Department of Commerce used to calculate a variety of payments balances, each of which grouped a different subset of assets. Since 1976, however, Commerce has

stopped presenting these calculations in published statistics.[16] Still, there are some vestiges. For instance, the differentiation between short-term

[16]For a detailed discussion of the reasons behind the changes in the presentation of U.S. balance-of-payments statistics, see "Report of the Advisory Committee on the Presentation of Balance of Payments Statistics," *Survey of Current Business* (June 1976). See also "The Presentation of the U.S. Balance of Payments: A Symposium," *Princeton Essays in International Finance,* no. 123 (1977). A thorough discussion of some particular balances, such as liquidity and basic balances, that have fallen into disuse under the present floating exchange rate system can be found in C. P. Kindleberger, "Measuring Equilibrium in the Balance of Payments," *Journal of Political Economy* (November/December 1969).

and long-term assets is still present in the detailed presentation of the U.S. international transactions table, in Appendix Table 9–A1. (Both the IMF and the World Bank also continue to follow this differentiation in their presentation of balance-of-payments statistics.) What is the basis for this distinction?

Assets whose contractual maturity is less than a year are considered short-term assets, while all others are considered long-term. According to this definition, six-month CDs are classified as short-term assets, whereas three-year bonds are considered long-term assets. The basic goal of this distinction is to differentiate capital flows according to their volatility—that is, according to the investors' horizon regarding the period over which they intend to hold an asset. Identifying investments as volatile and nonvolatile requires caution, however. First, some long-term capital flows, such as the transactions of U.S. firms with foreign affiliates, are empirically quite volatile. Second, it is apparent that assets having a short term to maturity are frequently intended to be held as a long-term investment. For instance, a firm investing in six-month CDs that are automatically rolled over five times in a row is not making a very different investment than when it purchases an instrument that has a contractual maturity of three years. Still, the sequence of six-month CDs would be catalogued as short-term investments, whereas the purchase of three-year instruments would be regarded as long-term investments. The crux of the problem is that whether a capital flow is intended to be short-term or long-term does not necessarily depend on the contractual maturity of the instrument used. You can generally sell assets with long-term maturities before they are due and roll over assets with short maturities for long periods of time. A final ambiguity regarding short-term versus long-term capital flows is related to the distinction between the original, or contractual, maturity and the remaining term to maturity of an asset. An asset with a contractual maturity of ten years issued nine and one-half years ago is, in effect, a six-month short-term security with regard

to its remaining term to maturity—six months. Because the U.S. Department of Commerce has classified short-term versus long-term assets in terms of their original maturity, however, such an asset would be classified as long-term.

For all these reasons, the distinction between short-term and long-term capital flows has not been thoroughly pursued recently by the Department of Commerce. Some asset transactions are still catalogued as short-term and long-term, however.

The Official Reserve Settlements Balance

The *official reserve settlements (ORS) balance* records—that is, places above the line—the net balance on all the economy's international transactions except those engaged in by domestic and foreign central banks in changing the assets they consider their official international reserves. Accordingly, the balance adds the current account, the capital account (including the statistical discrepancy), and the allocation of SDRs. Table 9–3 shows the calculation of the U.S. ORS balance for 1991, which gives a value of −$22.6 billion. Note that the ORS balance must correspond to the economy's asset transactions left out of the capital account, which takes the form of changes in U.S official reserve assets and/or foreign official assets in the United States. As Table 9–3 indicates, U.S. official reserve assets declined by $5.8 billion in 1991. This reduction represents a sale by the Federal Reserve of its international reserve assets, such as foreign currencies, and is catalogued as a credit (with a positive sign) in the balance of payments. Table 9–3 also exhibits a $16.8-billion increase in the U.S. assets that foreign central banks consider official international reserves. Recall that increases in the holdings of U.S. assets by foreign central banks represent a sale, or export, of domestic assets to foreigners and are catalogued as a credit in the balance of payments. Consequently, the 1991 U.S. ORS balance deficit corresponds to an increase of $22.6 billion in foreign official holdings of U.S. assets combined with a reduction of $5.8 billion in U.S. official reserve assets. These changes in official reserve assets build up a credit in the balance of payments that offsets the ORS deficit, thereby keeping the overall balance of payments equal to zero.

The ORS balance can be used to measure the intervention of monetary authorities in foreign exchange markets. How is central bank intervention in foreign currency markets reflected in the ORS balance? Up to now we have not clearly specified which central banks do the intervention in foreign exchange markets. Most countries have their own responsibility for supporting their fixed exchange rate, and their central banks must correspondingly engage in the intervention. For instance, if there were an excess demand (shortage) for foreign exchange, the domestic central bank would supply the needed foreign currency at the fixed price the bank is committed to support. This is reflected in the balance of payments as a decrease in the domestic central bank's level of official reserves and corresponds to an ORS deficit. Similarly, if the domestic central bank faces an excess supply of foreign exchange arising from the settling of private transactions at a fixed exchange rate, it would purchase it, in which case an ORS surplus would occur. In conclusion, when the domestic central bank is in charge of fixing the exchange rate, domestic official reserves will be affected by intervention in the foreign exchange market. As a result, the ORS balance will correspond closely to changes in domestic official reserve assets.

The case of U.S. intervention in foreign exchange markets is more particular, however, because the United States is a *reserve currency country.* A reserve currency is a currency widely held by central banks around the world in the form of international reserves. About 60 percent of the world's official reserves of foreign exchange are in the form of U.S. dollar-denominated assets. Japanese yen, Swiss francs, and West German marks have been used increasingly over the years but not nearly as much as the dollar. With the dollar being

the major world reserve money, a number of countries fix their currencies against it and then use their dollar holdings to maintain that fixed rate. As a consequence, the United States has not had full responsibility for maintaining its exchange rate fixed against other countries' currencies. Thus, most of the action has been left to the countries that fix their rates against the dollar. In this situation, foreign central banks intervene in foreign exchange markets by buying and selling their own holdings of dollar-denominated assets. The consequence is that foreign exchange market intervention is carried out through changes in both U.S. official reserve assets and foreign official assets in the United States.[17] So the U.S. ORS balance involves both types of transactions and not just the official reserve transactions of the U.S. monetary authorities. For instance, if foreign commercial banks hold an excess supply of foreign currencies that they want to exchange for dollars, either the Federal Reserve can buy the foreign currencies, thereby increasing its official reserve assets, or foreign central banks can sell the dollars, decreasing their official reserve assets in the United States.

Figure 9–6 depicts the behavior of the U.S. ORS, as well as the change in U.S. official reserve assets. The diagram clearly displays several phenomena. First, the ORS has not been eliminated since the dollar started floating versus the currencies of other major industrialized countries in the early 1970s. In fact, the ORS has been much greater and more volatile during floating. This behavior partly reflects the great degree of central bank intervention oriented to influence exchange rates, which makes the regime a *managed* floating

---

[17]Often, foreign central banks will hold dollar-denominated deposits outside the United States. If a central bank's intervention occurs by means of reductions in, say, its London-based U.S. dollar deposits, this transaction would not be recorded at all either in the U.S. balance of payments or in the ORS. The ORS balance does not provide a complete measure of foreign central bank intervention to stabilize exchange rates against the dollar.

one. A second observation that can be made from Figure 9–6 is the clear divergence between the ORS and changes in U.S. official reserves. This divergence illustrates how heavily foreign central banks use the dollar in their transactions. European central banks, particularly the German Bundesbank, have intervened substantially in recent years, by buying or selling dollars, in order to influence the value of their currencies vis-à-vis the dollar. This intervention is reflected in Figure 9–6.

There is one major problem in associating the ORS balance with central bank intervention in the foreign exchange market to fix or manipulate the exchange rate. In many cases, central banks will autonomously change the level of their international reserves holdings, and not in response or accommodation to the demands and supplies of

private actors in the economy. For instance, when a foreign central bank decides to reduce its holdings of deutsche mark reserves and to place the proceeds in higher-yielding U.S. Treasury bills, it is increasing its official assets in the United States but it is not intervening to fix or manipulate the exchange rate in the foreign exchange market. The foreign central bank is just responding autonomously to economic incentives. Thus, the positive item under changes in foreign official assets in the 1991 U.S. balance of payments may not just result from the intervention of foreign central banks to keep their exchange rates vis-à-vis the dollar from declining—it may have partly resulted from shifts in the portfolios of foreign central banks that were seeking dollars as a safe haven during uncertainty surrounding the Persian Gulf crisis that year. In

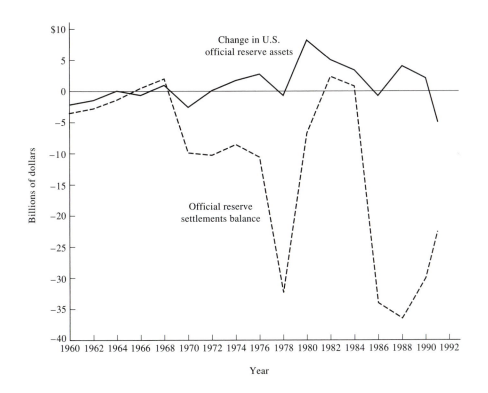

FIGURE 9–6.   The U.S. Official Reserve Settlements (ORS) Balance

SOURCE: U.S. Department of Commerce, *Survey of Current Business* (September 1992).

this situation, the ORS cannot be unequivocally associated with official intervention in foreign exchange markets.

A particularly important historical case in point is the behavior of the U.S. ORS balance in the 1950s and 1960s. Figure 9–6 shows the values of the U.S. ORS balance in the recent past (dashed line). The mostly negative values during the 1960s and early 1970s give the appearance that in this period the United States was losing an inordinate amount of foreign exchange reserves to sustain its exchange rate fixed (by selling its holdings of foreign exchange reserves to satisfy the excess of the private sector's payments over receipts). As a matter of fact, from 1954 to 1974, the United States only lost $7 billion worth of reserves out of an initial $23 billion. The minor changes in U.S. official reserves are represented by the solid line in Figure 9–6. Clearly, the U.S. ORS deficits were financed primarily through the acquisition of dollars and dollar-denominated assets by foreign central banks. Their willingness to hoard these dollar assets as international reserves made possible the relatively small loss of U.S. official reserves over the period. (The loss actually took the form of reductions in the gold holdings of the Federal Reserve.) More specifically, many analysts have argued that the persistent ORS deficits of the 1960s furnished the world with needed liquidity by providing foreign central banks with holdings of liquid dollars. It is implied that the ORS deficits reflected a strong dollar broadly used and demanded by foreign monetary authorities, as opposed to a weak dollar that had to be supported through central bank dollar purchases. Of course, this situation had changed by the early 1970s when pressures against the dollar developed, resulting in its devaluation and the breakdown of the Bretton-Woods system.

Summary

1. A country's balance of payments records all its economic transactions in a given period between its residents and the rest of the world.

   The basic rule of balance-of-payments accounting is that any transaction giving rise to a receipt from (payment to) the rest of the world is a credit (debit) and appears as a positive (negative) item in the account.

2. Double-entry bookkeeping conventions mean that the overall balance of payments is always zero. However, the balance of payments can be subdivided into several (sub)balances or accounts, which will be in surplus or deficit, depending on whether each represents an excess or deficiency of receipts over payments on that account.

3. The current account registers the economy's international trade in goods, services, and investment income, as well as its transfers to or from other countries. A surplus in the current account balance (CAB) means that receipts exceed payments from transactions in goods, services, and investment income, plus transfers received exceed payments in those items to foreigners. The contrary is true for a deficit on current account. The trade balance measures exports minus imports of merchandise.

4. The capital account registers all asset transactions except those involving the monetary authorities' international reserves. A capital account surplus or deficit arises depending on whether the receipts from the sales of assets registered by the capital account have exceeded or fall short of purchases of those assets.

5. The sum of the current and the capital accounts (plus the allocation of SDRs) is called the official reserve settlements (ORS) balance. This balance can be used, although imperfectly, to measure the intervention of monetary authorities in foreign exchange markets; it is particularly meaningful in an economy under a fixed exchange rate regime. Its calculation loses interest under freely floating regimes when the monetary authorities let the exchange rate fluctuate and follow a hands-off policy with respect to foreign exchange markets. Under a managed floating system, in which the exchange rate is allowed

to fluctuate but monetary authorities still intervene in foreign exchange markets in order to smooth out fluctuations in exchange rates, the ORS balance remains a useful concept to calculate.

Problems

1. Using the most recent data available in the *Survey of Current Business,* compute the U.S. trade balance, CAB, and all the concepts summarized in Table 9–3. (Recalculate Table 9–3.)

2. Indicate which entry in the U.S. balance-of-payments accounts is to be credited and debited for each of the following transactions, illustrated through the use of T accounts.

   (a) A businessperson visiting the United States lures a New York cab driver into accepting ¥11,000 for a ride in the Big Apple. The cab driver exchanges the yen for $90.00 through his or her bank.

   (b) A German distributor buys $20 million in high-tech equipment from IBM in the United States. It pays by means of a bank transfer from its Los Angeles bank.

   (c) The U.S. government ships $1 million worth of grain, cheese, and butter as food aid to Bangladesh.

   (d) A U.S. investor purchases $1 million in Japanese securities. Payment is made by a check drawn on his or her account in a New York bank.

   (e) A subsidiary of a German multinational firm operating in the U.S. invests part of its retained earnings in American securities.

   (f) A conservative political action committee (PAC) receives a gift of $100,000 in a check drawn on the Swiss account of a free-enterprise advocate.

   (g) After some negotiation, the U.S. government agrees to lend $200 million to a Latin American country. Payment takes place through an increase in that government's account at the New York Federal Reserve Bank.

   (h) Each author of this book receives $2,000 in royalties from its foreign edition. Because of a foreign exchange crisis abroad, the money is delivered in foreign currency. The authors decide to take a vacation and spend all the royalties abroad, bringing back $200 worth of gifts.

   (i) (1) A U.S. automobile manufacturer exports $1 million worth of cars. The foreign importer signs a bill of exchange for the value of the goods.

      (2) The U.S. exporter discounts the bill of exchange with Chase Manhattan Bank, which in turn keeps the bill until maturity. (Assume a 10 percent discount on the bill.)

      (3) On the bill's maturity ninety days later, Chase accepts payment for it in dollars, in the form of a check drawn on the importer's Citibank account. The interest accrued on the bill is $50,000.

   (j) A consortium of American banks lends $100,000 to a developing country. The country immediately spends one-half the loan in U.S. oil-drilling equipment. The rest is invested in ninety-day CDs issued by Chicago banks.

3. Compute the net effect of the preceding transactions on the trade balance, the CAB, and the ORS balance of the United States.

4. The last decade has seen a substantial increase in the volume of direct foreign investment in the United States. Evidence suggests that Japanese firms located in the U.S. purchase a large share of their parts and materials from the parent companies in Japan with which they are affiliated. Are these purchases catalogued as U.S. imports? Explain your answer.

5. Indicate how the U.S. balance-of-payments accounts and the size of the Eurodollar market are affected by the following transactions:

   (a) An American corporation moves $10 million out of CDs in New York to invest them in Eurodollar CDs issued by Barclays in London.

(b) Barclays disposes of $10 million through the interbank market. The funds are loaned to an American firm abroad, which exchanges the $10 million for deutsche marks to purchase German money market instruments.

6. The growth of the Eurocurrency market, and particularly of Eurodollar deposits, is frequently attributed to U.S. balance-of-payments deficits and the corresponding accumulation of dollar balances abroad. Evaluate this statement.

7. Would you expect to find a difference in the structure of the balance-of-payments accounts (e.g., the value of the trade balance and capital account) of countries in different stages of their development? What do the historical data suggest regarding stages in the balance of payments?

8. The following items are the recorded international transactions of a developing country called Banania with the rest of the world during 1992:

Foreign aid received by Banania's government from abroad was equal to $5 billion.

Imports of grain were equal to $20 billion.

Profits of U.S. multinationals operating in Banania were equal to $5 billion.

Lending by U.S. banks to the government of Banania totaled $20 billion.

Exports of bananas were equal to $10 billion.

Purchases of Florida real estate by wealthy Bananians were equal to $15 billion.

Banania's central bank sold $3 billion worth of international reserves in an effort to influence the exchange rate between the dollar and Banania's currency.

How much was the trade balance for Banania in 1992? What was the value of the current account balance? Was the reported capital account for this country in 1992 in deficit or in surplus? How much was the official reserve settlements balance? Was there a statistical discrepancy in Banania's balance of payments accounts?

9. From an accounting viewpoint, a current account balance surplus for one country is a current account balance surplus for the rest of the world. Therefore, in principle, the sum of the current account balances of all countries in the world should add up to zero. Yet, the IMF has calculated the presence of a huge world current account deficit [see *Report on the World Current Account Discrepancy* (Washington, D.C.: International Monetary Fund, 1987), pp. 8–9]. Assuming that there is currently no trade between humans and aliens from outer space, what else could explain this excess of world debits over credits on current account?

TABLE 9–A1. U.S. International Transactions

Line	(Credits +; debits −)[1]	1960	1970	1980	1982	1984	1985	1986	1987	1988	1989	1990	1991
1	Exports of goods, services, and income	30,556	68,387	344,440	361,436	391,435	380,051	398,583	445,216	550,323	629,468	680,890	704,914
2	Merchandise, adjusted, excluding military[2]	19,650	42,469	224,250	211,157	219,926	215,915	223,344	250,208	320,230	361,697	388,705	415,962
3	Services[3]	6,290	14,171	47,584	64,079	71,094	73,026	86,241	98,434	110,636	127,080	148,638	163,637
4	Transfers under U.S. military agency sales contracts[4]	2,030	4,214	9,029	12,572	9,969	8,718	8,549	11,106	9,289	8,526	9,833	10,691
5	Travel	919	2,331	10,588	12,393	[17]17,320	17,920	20,529	23,718	29,665	36,571	43,418	48,757
6	Passenger fares	175	544	2,591	3,174	[17]4,058	4,382	5,545	6,966	8,925	10,525	15,140	15,627
7	Other transportation	1,607	3,125	11,618	12,317	13,809	14,674	15,784	17,334	19,456	21,095	22,942	23,625
8	Royalties and license fees[5]	837	2,331	7,085	5,603	6,098	6,550	7,927	9,914	11,802	13,064	16,470	17,799
9	Other private services[5]	570	1,294	6,276	17,444	19,126	19,904	[17]27,312	28,869	30,835	36,711	40,166	46,444
10	U.S. Government miscellaneous services	153	332	398	576	714	878	595	526	664	587	668	693
11	Income receipts on U.S. assets abroad	4,616	11,748	72,606	86,200	100,415	91,110	88,998	96,574	119,456	140,692	143,547	125,315
12	Direct investment receipts	3,621	8,169	37,146	[17]23,922	30,581	29,630	30,850	38,080	50,436	54,490	55,428	49,221
13	Other private receipts	646	2,671	32,898	58,160	[17]64,607	55,981	51,735	53,183	62,318	80,567	77,612	67,990
14	U.S. Government receipts	349	907	2,562	4,118	5,227	5,499	6,413	5,311	6,703	5,635	10,508	8,104
15	Imports of goods, services, and income	−23,670	−59,901	−333,774	−355,804	−469,647	−478,821	−521,937	−585,637	−652,109	−705,005	−738,401	−716,624
16	Merchandise, adjusted, excluding military[2]	−14,758	−39,866	−249,750	−247,642	−332,418	−338,088	−368,425	−409,765	−447,189	−477,365	−497,558	−489,398
17	Services[3]	−7,674	−14,520	−41,491	−51,749	−67,657	−72,859	−79,892	−90,243	−97,930	−101,314	−116,583	−118,341
18	Direct defense expenditures	−3,087	−4,855	−10,851	−12,460	−12,516	−13,108	−13,730	−14,918	−15,643	−15,364	−17,651	−16,215
19	Travel	−1,750	−3,980	−10,397	−12,394	[17]−22,913	−24,558	−25,913	−29,310	−32,114	−33,418	−37,349	−36,958
20	Passenger fares	−513	−1,215	−3,607	−4,772	[17]−5,724	−6,484	−6,554	−7,318	−7,768	−8,258	−10,608	−10,636
21	Other transportation	−1,402	−2,843	−11,790	−11,710	−14,843	−15,643	−16,715	−17,788	−19,534	−20,664	−23,401	−23,297
22	Royalties and license fees[5]	−74	−224	−724	−795	−1,164	−1,165	−1,392	−1,844	−2,585	−2,602	−3,133	−3,984
23	Other private services[5]	−593	−827	−2,909	−8,159	−8,963	−10,166	[17]−13,901	−17,172	−18,365	−19,137	−22,522	−25,154
24	U.S. Government miscellaneous services	−254	−576	−1,214	−1,460	−1,534	−1,735	−1,686	−1,893	−1,921	−1,871	−1,919	−2,097
25	Income payments on foreign assets in the United States	−1,238	−5,515	−42,532	−56,412	−69,572	−67,875	−73,620	−85,629	−106,991	−126,326	−124,261	−108,886
26	Direct investment payments	−394	−875	−8,635	[17]−1,943	−8,723	−7,213	−7,058	−7,425	−11,693	−6,643	−1,083	3,675
27	Other private payments	−511	−3,617	−21,214	−35,187	−39,694	−37,689	−42,491	−52,913	−65,133	−83,827	−85,308	−73,575
28	U.S. Government payments	−332	−1,024	−12,684	−19,282	−21,155	−22,972	−24,071	−25,291	−30,164	−35,856	−37,870	−38,986
29	Unilateral transfers, net	−4,062	−6,156	−8,349	−17,075	−20,612	−22,950	−24,176	−23,052	−24,869	−25,606	−32,916	8,028
30	U.S. Government grants[4]	−3,367	−4,449	−5,486	−6,087	−8,696	−11,268	−11,867	−10,287	−10,506	−10,773	−17,597	24,487
31	U.S. Government pensions and other transfers	−273	−611	−1,818	−2,251	−2,159	−2,138	−2,197	−2,221	−2,501	−2,517	−2,945	−3,462
32	Private remittances and other transfers[6]	−423	−1,096	−1,044	[17]−8,738	−9,756	−9,545	−10,112	−10,544	−11,863	−12,316	−12,374	−12,996

continued

TABLE 9–A1 *continued*

Line	(Credits +; debits –)[1]	1960	1970	1980	1982	1984	1985	1986	1987	1988	1989	1990	1991
33	U.S. assets abroad, net (increase/capital outflow (–))[1]	–4,099	–9,337	–86,967	–122,335	–29,224	–34,069	–91,069	–62,402	–92,708	–114,944	–56,321	–62,220
34	U.S. official reserve assets, net[7]	2,145	2,481	–8,155	–4,965	–3,131	–3,858	312	9,149	–3,912	–25,293	–2,158	5,763
35	Gold	1,703	787	—	—	—	—	—	—	—	—	—	—
36	Special drawing rights	—	–851	–16	–1,371	–979	–897	–246	–509	127	–535	–192	–177
37	Reserve position in the International Monetary Fund	442	389	–1,667	–2,552	–995	908	1,501	2,070	1,025	471	731	–367
38	Foreign currencies	—	2,156	–6,472	–1,041	–1,156	–3,869	–942	–7,588	–5,064	–25,229	–2,697	6,307
39	U.S. Government assets, other than official reserve assets, net	–1,100	–1,589	–5,162	–6,131	–5,489	–2,821	–2,022	1,006	2,967	1,271	2,304	3,397
40	U.S. credits and other long-term assets	–1,214	–3,293	–9,860	–10,063	–9,599	–7,657	–9,084	–6,506	–7,680	–5,580	–8,417	–12,123
41	Repayments on U.S. credits and other long-term assets[8]	642	1,721	4,456	4,292	4,490	4,719	6,089	7,625	10,370	6,725	10,853	16,522
42	U.S. foreign currency holdings and U.S. short-term assets, net	–528	–16	242	–360	–379	117	973	–113	277	126	–131	–1,002
43	U.S. private assets, net	–5,144	–10,229	–73,651	–111,239	–20,605	–27,391	–89,360	–72,556	–91,762	–90,922	–56,467	–71,379
44	Direct investment	–2,940	–7,590	–19,222	[17]991	–10,948	–13,401	–17,090	–27,181	–15,448	–28,995	–32,694	–27,135
45	Foreign securities	–663	–1,076	–3,568	–7,983	–4,756	–7,481	–4,271	–5,251	–7,846	–22,070	–28,765	–45,017
46	U.S. claims on unaffiliated foreigners reported by U.S. nonbanking concerns	–394	–596	–4,023	6,823	6,226	–5,186	–8,024	1,995	–12,146	11,398	–2,477	5,526
47	U.S. claims reported by U.S. banks, not included elsewhere	–1,148	–967	–46,838	–111,070	–11,127	–1,323	–59,975	–42,119	–56,322	–51,255	7,469	–4,753
48	Foreign assets in the United States, net (increase/capital inflow (+))	2,294	6,359	58,112	92,418	102,010	130,966	223,191	229,972	219,489	213,693	99,379	66,980
49	Foreign official assets in the United States, net	1,473	6,908	15,497	3,593	3,140	–1,119	35,648	45,387	39,758	8,489	33,908	18,407
50	U.S. Government securities	655	9,439	11,895	5,085	4,703	–1,139	33,150	44,802	43,050	1,532	30,243	17,116
51	U.S. Treasury securities[9]	655	9,411	9,708	5,779	4,690	–838	34,364	43,238	41,741	149	29,576	15,815
52	Other[10]	—	28	2,187	–694	13	–301	–1,214	1,564	1,309	1,383	667	1,301
53	Other U.S. Government liabilities[11]	215	–456	615	605	739	844	2,195	–2,326	–467	146	1,866	1,600
54	U.S. liabilities reported by U.S. banks, not included elsewhere	603	–2,075	–159	–1,747	555	645	1,187	3,918	–319	4,976	3,385	–1,668
55	Other foreign official assets[12]	—	—	3,145	–350	–2,857	–1,469	–884	–1,007	–2,506	1,835	–1,586	1,359
56	Other foreign assets in the U.S., net	821	–550	42,615	88,826	98,870	132,084	187,543	184,585	179,731	205,204	65,471	48,573
57	Direct investment	315	1,464	16,918	[17]12,464	24,748	20,010	35,623	58,219	57,278	67,872	45,137	11,497
58	U.S. Treasury securities	–364	81	[16]2,645	[16]7,027	23,001	20,433	3,809	–7,643	20,239	29,618	–2,534	16,241

59	U.S. securities other than U.S. Treasury securities	282	2,189	5,457	6,085	12,568	50,962	70,969	42,120	26,353	38,767	1,592	34,918
60	U.S. liabilities to unaffiliated foreigners reported by U.S. nonbanking concerns	-90	2,014	6,852	-2,383	4,704	-366	-2,641	2,863	5,626	5,565	4,906	-405
61	U.S. liabilities reported by U.S. banks, not included elsewhere	678	-6,298	10,743	65,633	33,849	41,045	79,783	89,026	70,235	63,382	16,370	-13,678
62	Allocations of special drawing rights	—	867	1,152	—	—	—	—	—	—	—	—	—
63	Statistical discrepancy (sum of above items with sign reversed)	-1,019	-219	25,386	41,359	26,038	24,825	15,407	-4,096	-126	2,394	47,370	-1,078
	Memoranda:												
64	Balance on merchandise trade (lines 2 and 16)	4,892	2,603	-25,500	-36,485	-112,492	-122,173	-145,081	-159,557	-126,959	-115,668	-108,853	-73,436
65	Balance on services (lines 3 and 17)	-1,385	-349	6,093	12,329	3,437	167	6,350	8,191	12,707	25,766	32,055	45,296
66	Balance on investment income (lines 11 and 25)	3,379	6,233	30,073	29,788	30,843	23,235	15,378	10,945	12,466	14,366	19,287	16,429
67	Balance on goods, services, and income (lines 1 and 15 or lines 64, 65, and 66)[13]	6,886	8,486	10,666	5,632	-78,212	-98,771	-123,354	-140,421	-101,787	-75,537	-57,511	-11,710
68	Unilateral transfers, net (line 29)	-4,062	-6,156	-8,349	-17,075	-20,612	-22,950	-24,176	-23,052	-24,869	-25,606	-32,916	8,028
69	Balance on current account (lines 1, 15, and 29 or lines 67 and 68)[13]	2,824	2,331	2,317	-11,443	-98,824	-121,721	-147,529	-163,474	-126,656	-101,143	-90,428	-3,682

[1] Credits, +: Exports of goods and services; unilateral transfers to United States; capital inflows (increase in foreign assets (U.S. liabilities) or decrease in U.S. assets); decrease in U.S. official reserve assets; increase in foreign official assets in the United States. Debits, −: Imports of goods and services; unilateral transfers to foreigners; capital outflows (decrease in foreign assets (U.S. liabilities) or increase in U.S. assets); increase in U.S. official reserve assets; decrease in foreign official assets in the United States.

[2] Excludes exports of goods under U.S. military agency sales contracts identified in Census export documents, excludes imports of goods under direct defense expenditures identified in Census import documents, and reflects various other adjustments (for valuation, coverage, and timing) of Census statistics to balance of payments basis.

[3] Includes some goods: Mainly military equipment in line 4; major equipment, other materials, supplies, and petroleum products purchased abroad by U.S. military agencies in line 18; and fuels purchased by airline and steamship operators in lines 7 and 21.

[4] Includes transfers of goods and services under U.S. military grant programs.

[5] Beginning in 1982, line 8 and line 22 are redefined to include only net receipts and payments for the use or sale of intangible property rights. Other services are reclassified to lines 9 and 23.

[6] Affiliated and unaffiliated transactions, previously shown separately, have been combined.

[7] For all areas, amounts outstanding December 31, 1990, were as follows in millions of dollars: Line 34, 83,316; line 35, 11,058; line 36, 10,989; line 37, 9,076; line 38, 52,193. Data are preliminary.

[8] Includes sales of foreign obligations to foreigners.

[9] Consists of bills, certificates, marketable bonds and notes, and nonmarketable convertible and nonconvertible bonds and notes.

[10] Consists of U.S. Treasury and Export-Import Bank obligations, not included elsewhere, and of debt securities of U.S. Government corporations and agencies.

[11] Includes, primarily, U.S. Government liabilities associated with military agency sales contracts and other transactions arranged with or through foreign official agencies.

[12] Consists of investments in U.S. corporate stocks and in debt securities of private corporations and State and local governments.

[13] Conceptually, the sum of lines 49 and 62 is equal to "net foreign investment" in the national income and product accounts (NIPA's). However, the foreign transactions account in the NIPA's (a) includes adjustments to the international transactions accounts for the treatment of gold, (b) excludes capital gains and losses of U.S. parent companies from the NIPA's measure of income receipts from direct investment abroad, and from the corresponding income payments on direct investment in the United States, (c) includes an adjustment for the different geographical treatment of transactions with U.S. territories and Puerto Rico, and (d) includes services furnished without payment by financial intermediaries, except life insurance carriers and private noninsured pension plans. In addition, for NIPA purposes, U.S. Government interest payments to foreigners are excluded from "net exports of goods and services" but included with transfers in "net foreign investment." A reconciliation of the balance on goods and services from the international accounts and the NIPA net exports appears in the "Reconciliation and Other Special Tables" section in this issue of the SURVEY OF CURRENT BUSINESS. A reconciliation of the other foreign transactions in the two sets of accounts appears in Table 4.5 of the full set of NIPA tables (published annually in the July issue of the SURVEY).

SOURCE: U.S. Department of Commerce, *Survey of Current Business* (September 1992).

TABLE 9–A2. Balance-of-Payments Subaccounts: Selected Years (in billions of dollars)

	1974	1976	1978	1980	1982	1984	1986	1988	1990	1991
Current account balance (CAB)	$ 2.0	$ 4.2	$–15.4	$ 2.3	$–11.4	$–99.0	$–147.5	$–126.7	$–90.4	$ –3.7
Capital account balance[a]	–10.7	–14.7	–15.1	–10.3	13.5	99.5	113.7	89.6	60.6	–18.9
Allocation of SDRs[b]	—	—	—	1.2	—	—	—	—	—	—
Official reserve settlements (ORS) balance	–8.7	–10.5	–30.5	–6.8	2.1	0.5	–33.8	–37.1	–29.8	–22.6

[a]Includes the sum of the reported capital account plus the statistical discrepancy.
[b]For completeness, we include the allocation of SDRs, although it has not been a significant item in U.S. balance-of-payments accounts in the recent past.

SOURCE: U.S. Department of Commerce, *Survey of Current Business* (September 1992).

CHAPTER 10

Measuring Interdependence: The International Investment Position of a Country and Exchange Rate Concepts

This chapter continues our presentation of concepts relating to the measurement of international transactions. Two popular indicators of a country's international economic status (seen frequently in the press and in public policy statements) are its *net investment position*, the net balance of its foreign assets and liabilities, and its *external competitiveness*, a measure of how competitive domestic products are in terms of price when compared to foreign goods. Both of these concepts are overall indicators of an economy's interactions with the rest of the world, and both are of considerable concern to the public and to policymakers. Thus, we read in the press that "the United States has become the world's greatest debtor nation," or that "U.S. products have lost their competitiveness in world markets."

There are many misconceptions in the use of these indicators, and it is the purpose of this chapter to study carefully their measurement and meaning. We start by describing and assessing a country's net international investment position and its economic implications. We then specify the various exchange rate concepts required to seriously define the concept of "competitiveness."

10–1. THE U.S.'s INTERNATIONAL INVESTMENT POSITION: INTRODUCTION

International investments have taken on increasing significance for the United States since World War II. Commerce Department figures suggest that U.S. investments abroad have expanded enormously, exceeding by far the growth of GNP. Expressed as a proportion of GNP, the external assets of the United States represented 7 percent in 1952, swelling to 34.6 percent by the end of 1991. These developments have not passed unnoticed. The magnitude and riskiness of U.S. bank assets in the form of loans to developing countries is just one aspect that has attracted public attention. Not only have U.S. external assets risen dramatically, but foreign assets in the United States have increased as well. As a proportion of GNP, U.S. external liabilities increased from 6 percent in 1952 to 39.3 percent by the end of 1991. This largely represents U.S. bank liabilities to foreigners, such as CDs purchased by foreign central banks and corporations. However, a more visible and controversial item has been foreign direct investment in the United States. The latter has grown substantially in the last twenty years. Estimates are that, from 1981 to the end of 1991, the stock of direct foreign investments in the U.S. (valued at current cost) more than tripled, from $160 billion to just over $487 billion.

The upward trend of foreign investment in the U.S. has been observed with great concern by many Americans, as exemplified by the common cries by some journalists and politicians that "foreigners are buying the U.S." Indeed, a number of U.S. firms

producing goods and services of everyday consumption are foreign owned. Columbia Pictures, Grand Union, Libby's fruits and vegetables, Keebler cookies, Baskin-Robbins ice cream, Alka Seltzer, Carnation, Stouffer cakes, *The New York Post, The Village Voice,* and many others are owned by foreign interests (including Macmillan Publishing Company, which was bought by the British Maxwell Communications Corp). The visibility of some of the recent Japanese investments (such as the purchase of Columbia Pictures by Sony) has instilled particular fear in the average American. The nervousness this issue generates can be summed up by a story that has the president falling into a deep sleep and waking up four years later to be told by an adviser that unemployment was at zero, inflation was at zero, and the budget deficit was at zero. "Great news" says the president. "By the way, I'd love a cup of coffee. How much is one these days?" "Oh," answers the adviser, "about 50 yen."[1]

Many of the stereotypes about direct foreign investment and the general topic of external indebtedness have been greatly exaggerated and often just plain wrong. The following sections study the issue carefully, looking at the nature of the data used to assess a country's international investment position and the economic issues surrounding the role played by direct foreign investment in the U.S. economy.

10–2. AN ECONOMY'S INTERNATIONAL INVESTMENT POSITION: MEASUREMENT

A comprehensive presentation of U.S. assets and liabilities vis-à-vis the rest of the world is given in Table 10–1, which shows the *international investment position statement* of the United States for selected years. The international investment position is the country's international investment balance sheet; it shows the composition of the stock

---

[1] This story was delivered by correspondent Jeff Greenfield in the opening segment of *Nightline,* on ABC News, December 13, 1989.

Table 10-1. International Investment Position of the United States at Year End, 1977–1991 (in millions of dollars)

Line	Type of investment	1977[P]	1978[r]	1979[r]	1980[r]	1981[r]	1982[r]	1983[r]	1984[r]	1985[r]	1986[r]	1987[r]	1988[r]	1989[r]	1990[r]	1991[P]
	Net international investment position of the United States:															
1	With direct investment positions at current cost (line 3 less line 24)	190,548	228,421	342,929	392,547	374,254	378,933	337,376	232,852	138,950	18,735	−26,630	−183,715	−312,286	−294,836	−361,503
2	With direct investment positions at market value (line 4 less line 25)	—	—	—	—	—	264,774	267,553	175,910	142,205	109,146	54,240	−37,988	−158,782	−272,027	−381,835
3	U.S. assets abroad: With direct investment at current cost (lines 5+10+15)	519,032	627,261	792,908	936,275	1,004,162	1,119,178	1,169,162	1,177,532	1,252,535	1,410,190	1,564,748	1,654,582	1,794,727	1,884,199	1,960,301
4	With direct investment at market value (lines 5+10+16)		—	—	—	—	958,577	1,068,263	1,081,766	1,244,460	1,507,734	1,648,367	1,817,494	2,049,801	1,977,053	2,107,041
5	U.S. official reserve assets	53,376	69,450	143,260	171,412	124,568	143,445	123,110	105,040	117,930	139,875	162,370	144,179	168,714	174,664	159,223
6	Gold[1]	45,781	62,471	135,476	155,816	105,644	120,635	100,484	81,202	85,834	102,428	127,648	107,434	105,164	102,406	92,561
7	Special drawing rights	2,629	1,558	2,724	2,610	4,096	5,250	5,025	5,641	7,293	8,395	10,283	9,637	9,951	10,989	11,240
8	Reserve position in the International Monetary Fund	4,946	1,047	1,253	2,852	5,054	7,348	11,312	11,541	11,947	11,730	11,349	9,745	9,048	9,076	9,488
9	Foreign currencies	20	4,374	3,807	10,134	9,774	10,212	6,289	6,656	12,856	17,322	13,090	17,363	44,551	52,193	45,934
10	U.S. Government assets, other than official reserve assets	48,567	53,187	57,419	63,865	68,774	74,682	79,626	84,971	87,752	89,637	88,880	85,860	84,553	82,230	78,729
11	U.S. credits and other long-term assets[2]	47,749	52,252	56,477	62,023	67,201	72,884	77,814	82,883	85,814	88,710	88,099	85,388	84,225	81,787	77,355
12	Repayable in dollars	45,154	49,817	54,085	59,799	64,959	70,948	75,991	81,103	84,087	87,112	86,486	83,923	82,743	80,462	76,129
13	Other[3]	2,595	2,435	2,392	2,224	2,242	1,936	1,823	1,780	1,727	1,598	1,613	1,465	1,482	1,325	1,226
14	U.S. foreign currency holdings and U.S. short-term assets	818	935	942	1,842	1,573	1,798	1,812	2,088	1,938	927	781	472	328	443	1,374
15	U.S. private assets: With direct investment at current cost (lines 17+19+22+23)	417,089	504,624	592,229	700,998	810,820	901,051	966,426	987,521	1,046,853	1,180,678	1,313,498	1,424,543	1,541,460	1,627,305	1,722,349
16	With direct investment at market value (lines 18+19+22+23)	—	—	—	—	—	740,450	865,527	891,755	1,038,778	1,278,222	1,397,117	1,587,455	1,796,534	1,720,159	1,869,089
17	Direct investment abroad: At current cost[4][5]	252,832	291,039	343,940	396,249	412,418	387,239	371,667	361,588	387,183	421,167	493,341	515,702	552,822	623,587	655,260
18	At market value[6]	—	—	—	—	—	226,638	270,768	265,822	379,108	518,711	576,960	678,614	807,896	716,441	802,000
19	Foreign securities	49,439	53,384	56,769	62,454	62,142	74,046	84,723	88,804	114,670	145,878	164,717	183,061	220,865	241,748	305,886
20	Bonds	39,329	42,148	41,966	43,524	45,675	56,604	58,569	62,810	73,655	82,880	95,091	97,071	101,004	131,715	147,612
21	Corporate stocks	10,110	11,236	14,803	18,930	16,467	17,442	26,154	25,994	41,015	62,998	69,626	85,990	119,861	110,033	158,274

continued

TABLE 10-1 *continued*

Line	Type of investment	1977[r]	1978[r]	1979[r]	1980[r]	1981[r]	1982[r]	1983[r]	1984[r]	1985[r]	1986[r]	1987[r]	1988[r]	1989[r]	1990[r]	1991[p]
22	U.S. claims on unaffiliated foreigners reported by U.S. nonbanking concerns[7]	22,256	29,385	34,491	38,429	42,752	35,188	75,531	91,498	97,637	106,295	105,983	117,744	106,052	109,821	104,447
23	U.S. claims reported by U.S. banks, not included elsewhere[8]	92,562	130,816	157,029	203,866	293,508	404,578	434,505	445,631	447,363	507,338	549,457	608,036	661,721	652,149	656,756
	Foreign assets in the United States:															
24	With direct investment at current cost (lines 26+33)	328,484	398,840	449,979	543,728	629,908	740,245	831,786	944,680	1,113,585	1,391,455	1,591,378	1,838,297	2,017,013	2,179,035	2,321,804
25	With direct investment at market value (lines 26+34)	—	—	—	—	—	693,803	800,710	905,856	1,102,255	1,398,588	1,594,127	1,855,482	2,208,583	2,249,080	2,488,876
26	Foreign official assets in the United States	140,867	173,057	159,852	176,062	180,425	189,109	194,468	199,678	202,482	241,226	283,058	322,036	337,277	371,101	396,607
27	U.S. Government securities	105,386	128,511	106,640	118,189	125,130	132,587	136,987	144,665	145,063	178,916	220,548	260,934	265,708	296,971	318,018
28	U.S. Treasury securities[9]	101,092	123,991	101,748	111,336	117,004	124,929	129,716	138,168	138,438	173,310	213,713	252,962	256,137	286,702	305,888
29	Other[9]	4,294	4,520	4,892	6,853	8,126	7,658	7,271	6,497	6,625	5,606	6,835	7,972	9,571	10,269	12,130
30	Other U.S. Government liabilities[10]	10,260	12,749	12,749	13,367	13,029	13,639	14,231	14,959	15,803	17,993	15,667	15,200	15,346	17,212	18,812
31	U.S. liabilities reported by U.S. banks, not included elsewhere	18,004	23,327	30,540	30,381	26,737	24,989	25,534	26,090	26,734	27,920	31,838	31,520	36,495	39,880	38,361
32	Other foreign official assets[9]	7,217	8,470	9,923	14,125	15,529	17,894	17,716	13,964	14,882	16,397	15,005	14,382	19,728	17,038	21,416
	Other foreign assets in the United States:															
33	With direct investment at current cost (lines 35+37+41+42)	187,617	225,783	290,127	367,666	449,483	551,136	637,318	745,002	911,103	1,150,229	1,308,320	1,516,261	1,769,736	1,807,934	1,925,197
34	With direct investment at market value (lines 36+37+41+42)	—	—	—	—	—	504,694	606,242	706,178	899,773	1,157,362	1,311,069	1,533,446	1,871,306	1,877,979	2,092,269
	Direct investment in the United States:															
35	At current cost[5][11]	56,715	69,581	88,335	125,944	159,926	176,870	184,394	211,201	231,326	265,833	313,451	374,345	433,164	466,515	487,022
36	At market value[12]						130,428	153,318	172,377	219,996	272,966	316,200	391,530	534,734	536,560	654,094
37	U.S. Treasury securities[9]	7,562	8,910	14,210	16,113	18,505	25,758	33,846	62,121	87,954	96,078	82,588	100,877	134,488	130,716	154,665
38	U.S. securities other than U.S. Treasury securities[9]	51,235	53,554	58,587	74,114	75,085	92,988	113,811	128,477	207,868	309,803	341,732	392,292	484,418	471,888	559,655
39	Corporate and other bonds[9]	11,456	11,457	10,269	9,545	10,694	16,709	17,454	32,421	82,290	140,863	166,089	191,314	223,830	240,713	277,013
40	Corporate stocks[9]	39,779	42,097	48,318	64,569	64,391	76,279	96,357	96,056	125,578	168,940	175,643	200,978	260,588	231,175	282,642

		11,921	16,019	18,669	30,426	30,606	27,532	26,937	31,024	29,458	26,902	29,818	35,003	40,549	45,379	43,761
41	U.S. liabilities to unaffiliated foreigners reported by U.S. nonbanking concerns[13]															
42	U.S. liabilities reported by U.S. banks, not included elsewhere[8]	60,184	77,719	110,326	121,069	165,361	227,988	278,330	312,179	354,497	451,613	540,731	613,744	677,117	693,436	680,094

r Revised.

p Preliminary.

[1] U.S. official gold stock valued at market price.

[2] Also includes paid-in capital subscriptions to international financial institutions and outstanding amounts of miscellaneous claims that have been settled through international agreements to be payable to the U.S. Government over periods in excess of 1 year. Excludes World War I debts that are not being serviced.

[3] Includes indebtedness that the borrower may contractually, or at its option, repay with its currency, or with a third country's currency, or by delivery of materials or transfer of services.

[4] Estimates for 1982 forward are linked to both the 1982 and 1989 U.S. Department of Commerce benchmark surveys. Estimates for 1977–1981 are linked to both the 1977 and 1982 Commerce benchmark surveys.

[5] Estimates from 1977 forward reflect new 1987 base-year price indexes for tangible assets, which replace the 1982 base-year price indexes previously used in the national income and product accounts (NIPA's).

[6] Estimates are linked to both the 1982 and 1989 U.S. Department of Commerce benchmark surveys.

[7] Breaks in series reflect the following: in 1978, expanded reporting coverage by U.S. compilers and the introduction of Canadian-source data; in 1982, an increase in reporters' exemption levels; in 1983, the introduction of United Kingdom-source data; and in 1984, the introduction of Federal Reserve Board data for the Bahamas and British West Indies (Cayman Islands).

[8] Breaks in the series reflect the following: in 1978, expanded coverage of bank holding companies and of brokers' and security dealers' reporting of liabilities; in 1981, expanded coverage of brokers' and security dealers' reporting of claims; in 1977 and 1982, an increase in reporters' exemption levels; and in 1986, an increase in liabilities of nonbanking concerns held in bank custody.

[9] Estimates include results of 1978 and 1984 portfolio benchmark surveys conducted by the U.S. Department of the Treasury. Beginning with the 1978 benchmark, marketable Treasury bonds are valued at market price; previously, they were valued at acquisition price.

[10] Primarily U.S. Government liabilities associated with military sales contracts and other transactions arranged with or through foreign official agencies.

[11] Estimates for 1980 forward are linked to both the 1980 and 1987 U.S. Department of Commerce benchmark surveys. Estimates for 1977–1979 are linked to both the 1974 and 1980 Commerce benchmark surveys.

[12] Estimates for 1982 forward are linked to both the 1980 and 1987 U.S. Department of Commerce benchmark surveys.

[13] Breaks in the series reflect the following: in 1978, expanded reporting coverage; and in 1982, an increase in reporters' exemption levels.

NOTE.—Revised area tables for 1977–91 are available upon request from the Balance of Payments Division (BE-58), Bureau of Economic Analysis, U.S. Department of Commerce, Washington, DC 20230.

SOURCE: U.S. Department of Commerce, *Survey of Current Business* (Washington, D.C.: U.S. Government Printing Office, June 1992), p. 49.

of external assets and liabilities accumulated by a country's residents up to a certain date. Note that the international investment position measures a country's stock of foreign claims and liabilities at a certain point in time. In this way it differs from the balance-of-payments accounts discussed in Chapter 9. Balance-of-payments accounts record changes or flows in the foreign claims and liabilities of a country in a given time period. As a matter of fact, the flows or changes in asset holdings measured by the balance of payments will be reflected as changes in a country's stock of assets and liabilities.

Table 10–1 highlights some basic aspects of the United States' international financial condition. It illustrates the breadth and diversity of U.S. financial relations with the rest of the world. It also shows the great expansion of foreign asset holdings over time, especially during the last decade. This is partly explained by a growing world economy, but it predominantly reflects the liberalization and globalization of world financial markets and the consequent increased acquisition and sale of assets across borders.

We will explain the items in Table 10–1 in some detail, but care must be exercised in using the numbers in the table. The international investment position of the United States is computed by the Bureau of Economic Analysis (BEA) of the U.S. Department of Commerce, which publishes its estimates in the *Survey of Current Business* (June issues). The figures it supplies represent the dollar *values* of U.S. assets abroad and those of foreign assets in the United States.

There are, however, several alternative ways of valuing assets. For instance, the value of a Japanese direct foreign investment made in California in 1990 could be valued at the historical, book-value prices at which the investment was made. Alternatively, the foreign investment could be valued at the current cost of replacing plant, equipment, and other tangible assets. There is also the choice of using the current stock market value

of owner's equity so that you obtain a measure of the market assessment of the investment today.

Because asset prices change significantly, these three ways of valuing assets can yield very different numbers. The Commerce Department presents estimates of direct investments using all three types of valuation, although the calculations of the international investment position of the United States include only the current cost and market value alternatives. Based on the latter two alternatives, the Commerce Department calculates two measures of the net international investment position of the United States, as is reflected in Table 10–1. Let us proceed to discuss the various items of Table 10–1 in detail.

U.S. Assets Abroad

The category of U.S. assets abroad consists of U.S. claims on foreigners and includes U.S. official reserve assets, other assets held by the U.S. government, and foreign assets held by U.S. private residents (U.S. private assets). As displayed in Table 10–1, the most prominent of these is the latter, whose main components are direct foreign investment and claims on foreigners reported by banks.

U.S. direct foreign investment has traditionally been a significant component of U.S. external assets, as well as a source of considerable controversy abroad. Direct foreign investment provides the investor with a concomitant degree of control over the use of the funds invested. This is a financial concept involving financial control of assets located abroad and is not necessarily related to physical investment abroad. For example, when a foreign subsidiary of a U.S. firm acquires equipment that it financed by means of a foreign bank loan, the transaction involves physical investment abroad but does not represent U.S. direct investment because U.S. residents are not acquiring claims on foreigners with a controlling interest; in fact, there is no acquisition of any foreign asset at all. Similarly, when a U.S. firm acquires a controlling interest in a foreign firm by purchasing stocks, this does not involve physical investment abroad at all; however, it is catalogued as direct investment. In a nutshell, direct foreign investment is not physical investment abroad; for our purposes here, the two concepts are not equivalent.

The second major current component of U.S. assets abroad involves claims reported by banks. These claims represented a relatively minor part of U.S. claims on foreigners until the 1970s, when they skyrocketed. A significant part of these bank claims consisted of loans made by U.S. banks to foreign countries. By June 1982, non-East Bloc developing countries owed more than $125 billion to U.S. banks. This ballooning developing country debt became difficult to repay. In September 1982, a crisis situation erupted when the Mexican government announced its inability to make scheduled payments on its external debt. The debt crisis of the developing countries was one of the key international economic maladies of the 1980s and continues to be so in the 1990s. We will examine the issues behind it in Chapter 12.

The figures on bank claims include only assets and liabilities of banking offices in the United States. Loans made by Eurobanks—that is, external branches and subsidiaries of U.S. banks—are not included as U.S. assets abroad because Eurobanks are treated as foreign residents. Only the lending by the home office to its affiliated Eurobanks appears as an asset reported by U.S. banks, not the lending made by the Eurobank itself. The data on the U.S. international investment position essentially neglect the substantial lending made by external branches and subsidiaries of U.S. banks through the Eurodollar market.

The remaining components of U.S. private assets abroad are (1) foreign securities, excluding those that provide some controlling interest, which are catalogued as direct foreign investment, and (2) nonbank claims on unaffiliated foreigners. With respect to this second category, recall that all reported bank claims are already catalogued and that the claims of nonbank residents on affiliated foreigners, such as those relating to the intercompany accounts of a multinational firm, are also already catalogued under direct foreign investment. Nonbank claims on unaffiliated foreigners consist of items such as loans made, say, by a U.S. firm to a foreign (unaffiliated) importer.

Foreign Assets in the United States

Foreign assets in the United States consist of the liabilities of U.S. residents to foreigners. Included are foreign official assets in the United States and other foreign assets, such as direct foreign investment, in the United States. Foreign official assets in the United States include CDs as well as U.S. Treasury securities owned by foreign central banks. As observed in Table 10–1, official assets are a major component of foreign assets in the United States, reflecting the demand for dollar-denominated assets by foreign central banks and the role of the U.S. dollar as an international reserve asset. The presentation of other foreign assets in the United States follows basically the same pattern as that of private U.S. assets abroad, but through the liabilities side.

Observe how private foreign direct investment in the United States has grown in the 1980s and 1990s. The next section examines this phenomenon in more detail.

10–3. DIRECT FOREIGN INVESTMENT IN THE UNITED STATES

MIT economist Paul Krugman has predicted that "the political issue of the 1990s is going to be the foreign invasion of the United States."[2] The general

---

[2]As cited by K. Phillips, *The Politics of Rich and Poor: Wealth and the American Electorate in the Reagan Aftermath* (New York: Random House, 1990), pp. 122–123.

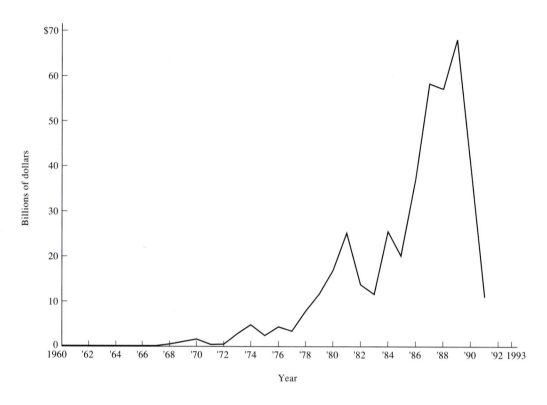

FIGURE 10–1.   Direct Foreign Investment in the United States

SOURCE: U.S. Department of Commerce, *Survey of Current Business* (September 1992).

upward pattern of direct foreign investment in the United States in the 1980s is depicted by Figure 10–1. In 1981, for the first time in the post-World War II period, direct foreign investment in the United States increased more than U.S. direct investment abroad, a trend that continued throughout the 1980s. In 1991, however, U.S. direct investments abroad increased more than foreign investments in the United States. This change resulted from the combination of greatly reduced foreign investments in the United States (a drop from $45.1 billion in 1990 to $11.5 billion in 1991) and a close to record-high increase in U.S. investment abroad in the same year ($27.1 billion).

   The growth of foreign investment in the United States has been observed with great concern by many Americans, generating fears that "foreigners will own the nation."[3] Direct foreign investment generally involves some degree of control over the use of the funds invested and creates the image of foreigners owning and controlling the businesses

---

[3]The Iowa legislature in 1980 went so far as to enact a law that absolutely prohibits foreigners from buying farmland in the state. This was in reaction to some real estate investments apparently made by OPEC investors in the state. Other restrictions controlling foreign direct investment have been imposed at various times, although many of them have been reversed and eliminated in the last decade. For popular descriptions of the rise of foreign investments in the U.S. and policy initiatives related to it, see M. Tolchin and S. Tolchin, *Buying into America: How Foreign Money Is Changing the Face of Our Nation* (New York: The New York Times Books, 1988).

in which local residents work, eat, and reside. The apprehension about direct foreign investment is reflected in the results of a *Wall Street Journal/NBC News* poll carried out in June 1990. In response to the question: "Do you think the amount of Japanese companies' investment in the United States is too much, about the right amount, or too little?" close to 70 percent of respondents in the United States answered, "Too much."[4]

Although these fears are not completely without foundation, painting with a broad brush and making unfounded generalizations should be avoided in this area. It is true that the *growth* of foreign investment in the U.S. in recent years has been very significant. These foreign investments have led to particular areas of the U.S. economy where foreign-owned firms do constitute a significant share of economic activity. Foreign companies control approximately 70 percent of the tire industry in the United States, one-half of the consumer electronics industry, almost one-half of the film and recording industry, and one-third of the chemical industry. Foreign ownership in banking is also influential (as was discussed in Chapter 6).[5]

To avoid losing perspective on the subject, however, let us stress that foreign-owned firms still compose a small fraction of the overall economic activity in the United States. For instance, in 1987, U.S. affiliates of foreign companies accounted for only 4.3 percent of all the U.S.-business gross product.[6] The comparable figures for the manufacturing sector were higher, equal to

10.5 percent. In terms of employment, foreign affiliates accounted for only 8.5 percent of all manufacturing in the United States. Concerns over "foreigners controlling the U.S. economy" are thus premature. Only continued high rates of growth of foreign direct investment in the United States could potentially generate such an outcome, and then perhaps only in the distant future.

The role played by Japan as a component of direct investment in the United States is also exaggerated. In spite of the high profile of some of the Japanese investments and their high rate of growth in some specific sectors, the portion of the stock of foreign direct investment in the United States owned by the Japanese is still comparatively small, although rising. Table 10–2 depicts the share of the value of total foreign investment in the United States accounted for by the major investing countries. Japan's share grew in the 1980s, but by the end of 1991 it was still equal to a relatively small 21.3 percent. The United Kingdom is the largest direct investor in the United

[4]As reported by U. C. Lehner and A. Murray, "Selling of America to Japanese Touches Some Very Raw Nerves," *The Wall Street Journal*, June 19, 1990, p. C1.

[5]For a discussion of these figures—and their sources and implications—see the debate by L. D'Andrea Tyson and R. B. Reich, "Should Foreign Ownership Matter to Us?" *The American Prospect* (Winter 1991); see also, N. J. Glickman and D. P. Woodward, *The New Competitors: How Foreign Investors Are Changing the U.S. Economy* (New York: Basic Books, 1989).

[6]J. H. Lowe, "Gross Product of U.S. Affiliates of Foreign Companies, 1977–87," *Survey of Current Business* (June 1990).

TABLE 10–2. Country Shares of Direct Foreign Investment in the United States, 1985 and 1991; by Rank

Country	Percentage Share of Total Direct Investment in the United States	
	1985	1991
United Kingdom	23.6%	26.0%
Japan	10.5	21.3
Netherlands	20.0	15.7
Canada	9.2	7.3
Germany	8.0	6.9
France	3.6	5.5
Switzerland	5.8	4.3
Netherlands Antilles	5.7	1.9
Others	13.6	11.1
Total	100.0	100.0

SOURCE: U.S. Department of Commerce, *Survey of Current Business* (June 1992), p. 57.

States, accounting for close to 26 percent of the total. In terms of U.S. employment, Japan's presence in the United States remains below that of Great Britain, Canada, West Germany, and the Netherlands. As economists Edward Graham and Paul Krugman recently concluded: "The rise of DFI [direct foreign investment] in the United States is not an essentially Japanese phenomenon. . . . From 1977 to 1987, the number of workers employed by U.S. affiliates of foreign firms increased by 1.6 million, but only 200,000 of these employees were in Japanese-controlled firms."[7]

An additional issue involves whether fears about the foreign ownership of domestic production facilities are reasonable. Critics of direct foreign investments in the United States argue that foreign companies differ significantly in their behavior relative to U.S.-owned firms in ways that reduce U.S. economic welfare. In particular, it is argued that foreign firms provide relatively little labor compensation relative to U.S.-owned firms (either by providing fewer jobs or lower wages or both), import most of their parts and supplies from abroad (causing the U.S. trade balance to deteriorate), provide relatively few positive externalities to the U.S. economy (because research and development—R&D—activities are kept at home rather than brought to the United States), and pose serious threats to national security.[8]

Some of these criticisms of direct investments in the United States are not supported by the data. Detailed studies of the labor compensation of foreign firms in the United States do not generally find significant differences between them and U.S.-owned firms in the same sector or industry.[9] Similarly, studies of established multinational firms indicate that these firms do not concentrate their R&D activities at home.[10] In fact, foreign direct investment may generate positive externalities or spillovers by making available new technology, introducing improved management techniques, and stimulating the domestic production of specialized business services, all of which may benefit local producers as well.[11] On the other hand, there is substantial evidence that foreign-owned—especially Japanese—firms do have a greater proportion of their inputs imported from abroad.[12] However, to determine whether such imports cause the U.S. trade balance to deteriorate, the fact that foreign multinationals often are replacing exports to the United States when establishing their production facilities in America must also be entered into the equation. It is thus not clear at all whether foreign investment in the United States explains part of the growth of the U.S. trade deficit in the 1970s and 1980s. Finally, with respect to security issues, it is clear that foreign ownership of domestic production facilities involving sensitive defense-related products can be a national security threat. This was the ground for the provisions of the Omnibus Trade and Competitiveness Act of 1988. By means of this act, the president can now prevent foreign acquisition of a U.S. firm if the transaction threatens national security. However, in the absence

[7]E. M. Graham and P. R. Krugman, *Foreign Direct Investment in the United States* (Washington, D.C.: Institute for International Economics, 1989).

[8]For a journalistic presentation of some of these views, see D. Frantz and C. Collins, *Selling Out: How We Are Letting Japan Buy Our Land, Our Industries, Our Financial Institutions, and Our Future* (Chicago: Contemporary Books, 1989); and P. Choate, *Agents of Influence: How Japan's Lobbyists in the United States Manipulate America's Political and Economic System* (New York: Knopf, 1990).

[9]See J. S. Leonard, "Working for Foreign Masters: Wages and Employment in Foreign Direct Investment in the U.S." (Berkeley: University of California, 1987). (Mimeo.)

[10]J. Cantwell, *Technological Innovation and Multinational Corporations* (Oxford: Basil Blackwell, 1989).

[11]There is a recent but growing literature specifying and estimating the positive external effects that trade and investment generate; see R. J. Caballero and R. K. Lyons, "The Role of External Economies in U.S. Manufacturing," National Bureau of Economic Research Working Paper no. 3033 (July 1989); and F. Rivera-Batiz and L. Rivera-Batiz, "The Effects of Direct Foreign Investment in the Presence of Increasing Returns Due to Specialization," *Journal of Development Economics* (November 1990).

[12]See M. E. Kreinin, "How Closed Is Japan's Market: Additional Evidence?" *World Economy* (December 1988).

of an immediate danger of war, the costs of subsidizing inefficient domestic producers must be weighed against the security risk of those who are currently American allies.

10–4. FACTORS LINKED TO THE RISE OF DIRECT FOREIGN INVESTMENT IN THE UNITED STATES

A number of factors have been postulated to explain the rise of direct foreign investment in the United States since the 1970s. At the top of the list is the rising competitiveness of foreign firms relative to U.S. producers, measured in terms of technological and managerial advantages over American suppliers.[13] According to this perspective, foreign firms, particularly Japanese producers, have increasingly moved closer and surpassed U.S. producers both in technology and managerial skills. This has allowed them to compete effectively with local American producers, and the recent explosion of foreign investments in the U.S. is one reflection of this rising foreign competitiveness. A similar phenomenon has been observed in Europe regarding the growth of Japanese direct investments there. As economists Stefano Micossi and Gianfranco Viesti conclude: "The main reason underlying the dramatic increase in Japanese direct investment is Japan's organizational-technological lead in particular industries."[14]

From the perspective of the foreign producer, however, there must be an advantage to *locating* in

the United States over just producing abroad and exporting the product to America. In some sectors—such as the banking, insurance, hotel, and transportation industries—the nature of the good or service being provided requires being located in the country where the product is sold. For these (internationally) nontraded goods and service sectors, foreign producers must locate in the United States in order to compete for a share of the U.S. market. In order to compete in the hotel industry in New York City, for example, foreign firms must acquire hotels there. However, for goods that are traded in world markets, there must be an advantage to the foreign firm shifting its production location to the United States, as opposed to just exporting the commodity and leaving its facilities abroad.

According to surveys of Japanese multinational firms, one of the key motives for locating production facilities in the United States has been the desire to avoid import restrictions imposed by the U.S. authorities. This seems to be a significant factor tilting the balance in favor of location in the United States for foreign producers that already have a certain technological or managerial advantage that would allow them to compete effectively with the American firms already operating inside the U.S. market. Such appears to be the case in the automobile and electronics sectors. For instance, consider the color television industry in the late 1970s and 1980s. Before 1977, the U.S. imported approximately 3.5 million television sets a year from Japan's major electronics manufacturers. Then, in 1977, these manufacturers were charged with dumping; import restrictions (voluntary export restraints) were established to protect U.S. suppliers. Before import restrictions, only Sony and Matsushita were producing color television sets in the United States. Afterward, five other Japanese electronics firms shifted their television manufacturing activities to the United States. From 1977 to 1980, Japanese production of color television sets in the United States had grown from slightly over one million units to more than 3.2 million units, generating employment estimated at

---

[13]See R. McCulloch, "Japanese Investment in the United States," in D. B. Audretsch and M. P. Claudon, eds., *The Internationalization of U.S. Markets* (New York: New York University Press, 1989); and E. M. Graham and P. Krugman, *Foreign Direct Investment in the United States* (Washington, D.C.: Institute for International Economics, 1989).

[14]S. Micossi and G. Viesti, "Japanese Direct Manufacturing Investment in Europe," in L. A. Einters and A. Venables, *European Integration: Trade and Industry* (Cambridge: Cambridge University Press, 1991); see also, J. H. Dunning, *Japanese Participation in British Industry* (Beckenham: Croom Helm, 1986).

over 500,000;[15] by 1987, Japanese firms were producing six million color TV sets in the United States (while importing only 1.6 million units). Ironically, at the time of writing, there is only one American-owned firm producing color television sets in the United States (Zenith).

Another explanation links foreign direct investment in the United States to expected future protectionism. The argument is that direct investment is made to avoid trade fiction with the United States and thus to defuse protectionist sentiment. For example, by replacing exports to the U.S. with local production, a Japanese firm can reduce the U.S.-Japan trade gap in its industry, reducing the likelihood that the United States will impose import restrictions in the future. Although direct investment on its own may not be cost-effective, the expected benefits from the defusion of protectionism may more than compensate.[16]

Exchange rate movements have been another variable that economists have linked to direct investment flows into the United States. As Figure 10–1 indicates, the pattern of expansion of foreign direct investment in the U.S. has a long history and cannot easily be associated with upward or downward movements in exchange rates. However, a tendency can be noted for dollar depreciations to be associated with greater foreign direct investment. For instance, in the late 1970s and then in the late 1980s, the dollar depreciated rapidly and direct foreign investment in the nation expanded.[17]

One mechanism through which exchange rate changes affect the magnitude of direct investment flows is related to the sectoral shifts with which such exchange rate movements are associated.[18] To understand this point it is important to realize that the greatest share of foreign direct investment in the United States is in internationally traded goods sectors (manufacturing, mining, and petroleum products), as opposed to nontraded goods (such as construction, real estate, and insurance). Fully 50 percent of foreign direct investment in the U.S. falls in the manufacturing sector alone. A dollar depreciation—to the extent that it increases U.S. relative competitiveness—will lead to a shift in production from nontraded goods to internationally traded goods. As traded goods sectors such as manufacturing expand, so will the foreign-owned firms that proliferate in these sectors, leading to a growth of direct foreign investment.[19]

---

were being implemented. The effects of the new tax law on direct foreign investment are ambiguous, but some estimates indicate that the net impact has been to stimulate direct investment. For analyses of the relative role played by exchange rate changes, U.S. and foreign taxation, and other variables in direct foreign investment, see J. Slemrod, "Tax Effects on Foreign Investment in the United States: Evidence from a Cross-Country Comparison," in A. Razin and J. Slemrod, eds., *Taxation in the Global Economy* (Chicago, University of Chicago Press, 1990); E. J. Ray, "The Determinants of Direct Foreign Investment in the United States, 1979–1985," in R. C. Feenstra, ed., *Trade Policies for International Competitiveness* (Chicago: University of Chicago Press, 1989); and R. E. Caves, "Exchange Rate Movements and Foreign Direct Investment in the United States," in D. B. Audretsch and M. P. Claudon, eds., *The Internationalization of U.S. Markets* (New York: New York University Press, 1989).

[18]As developed by E. M. Graham and P. Krugman, *Foreign Direct Investment in the United States* (Washington, D.C.: Institute for International Economics, 1989); other mechanisms have been examined by K. A. Froot, "Multinational Corporations, Exchange Rates, and Direct Investment," in W. H. Branson, J. A. Frenkel, and M. Goldstein, eds., *International Policy Coordination and Exchange Rate Fluctuations* (Chicago: University of Chicago Press, 1990); and K. Froot and J. Stein, "Exchange Rates and Foreign Direct Investment: An Imperfect Capital Markets Approach," National Bureau of Economic Research Working Paper no. 2914 (1989).

[19]See Graham and Krugman, op. cit. p. 36.

---

[15]See T. Shishido, "Capital Transfers from Japan to the United States: A Means to Avoid Trade Friction," in R. Sato and J. Nelson, eds., *Beyond Trade Friction Japan–U.S. Economic Relations* (Cambridge: Cambridge University Press, 1989).

[16]This *quid pro quo* foreign investment has been explored by J. N. Bhagwati, R. Brecher, and E. Dinopoulos in "Quid Pro Quo Direct Foreign Investment," *Journal of Development Economics* (October, 1987).

[17]This relationship is not particularly strong and could be spuriously related to other changes that occurred in the same period as the depreciations. For instance, the dollar depreciation of the late 1980s occurred at the same time that a number of changes established by the U.S. tax code reform of 1986

The apparent acceleration of direct foreign investment in the United States when the dollar depreciates has given rise to the hypothesis that U.S. assets are being sold at basement prices in a gigantic "fire sale." To take this issue seriously, though, requires documentation as to whether the assets that are being sold to foreigners are really undervalued—that is, are being sold at bargain prices. Such could be the case if the dollar were to depreciate to a level below its equilibrium value—that is, if the dollar became undervalued. Then, foreign currency would be artificially high in value—relative to the equilibrium level—and the foreigners acquiring U.S. assets would indeed obtain great bargains. The problem here is to show that indeed the dollar is undervalued: not an easy matter because equilibrium exchange rates—if they diverge from actual exchange rates—are not observed and must be estimated on the basis of factors determining fundamental or long-run currency values. Economists disagree about what determines equilibrium exchange rates, and an unambiguous measure is not likely to be achieved. Consequently, although the relationship between exchange rate changes and direct investment is not in question, the "fire sale" effect is.[20]

10–5. THE NET INTERNATIONAL INVESTMENT POSITION OF THE UNITED STATES

Previous sections have described in detail the various items in a country's international investment position particularly the direct investment category. Now we proceed to study the overall picture of an economy's international investment position.

[20]As Paul Krugman notes referring to the "bargain basement" argument: "If U.S. assets are such a good buy, then why is it that their prices do not get bid up? And if it is now so attractive to invest in the United States, should not the desire to keep investing here drive up the value of the dollar?" in P. Krugman, "The J-Curve, the Fire Sale and the Hard Landing," *American Economic Review* (May 1989).

A country's *net international investment position* is the difference between the sum of the value of its assets abroad and the sum of the value of all foreign assets in the country. A positive value of this position means that the country's accumulated investments abroad exceed what foreigners' have accumulated domestically. A negative position shows that accumulated foreign investments in the domestic economy exceed domestic investments abroad, suggesting that the country overall has a net liability to foreigners.

The first two rows in Table 10–1 show the net international investment position of the United States from 1977 to 1991, calculated with direct investment valued at current cost and market value, respectively. The position was positive in the 1970s and early 1980s but has declined drastically since 1981. According to the Commerce Department estimates in Table 10–1, the U.S. net investment position (with direct investment at market value) became negative in 1988, and by the end of 1991 it was equal to –$381.8 billion. This pattern is not related to a reduction in U.S. assets abroad because, as Table 10–1 indicates, the trend for this item has been positive. What has happened instead is that foreign assets in the United States grew much faster in the 1980s than U.S. assets abroad. For instance, foreign holdings of U.S. corporate and other (non-government) bonds grew from $16.7 billion in 1982 to $277 billion by the end of 1991, averaging an astounding 173 percent increase *a year*. By contrast, U.S. private holdings of foreign bonds rose at the more moderate rate of 18 percent a year. Similarly, direct foreign investment in the United States grew at an average annual rate of 19 percent from 1982 to 1991, while U.S. direct investment abroad increased by only 7.7 percent a year.

Is the United States the World's Greatest Debtor?

The massive negative U.S. net investment position has created a worldwide unison of voices claiming that the U.S. has become the "world's greatest debtor," placing the nation with that group of developing countries usually referred to as heavily indebted. Is this vision correct?

First of all, it is simply not correct to interpret a negative net investment position with "indebtedness." The term *indebtedness* refers to an increase in debt, not equity. A substantial fraction of the international trade of the United States with the rest of the world, however, is in equity, as represented by foreign purchases of U.S. stocks. Therefore, the net investment position of the United States is not really a measure of the nation's "indebtedness."

Second, although the figures on the U.S. net investment position supplied by the Commerce Department illustrate very well the trends that are occurring, they have to be taken with a grain of salt when considering the exact magnitude of the numbers involved. As was noted earlier, there are different types of asset valuation methods, which can result in wildly different estimates of the values of foreign and domestic assets. As a consequence, the net investment position can vary greatly depending on the direct investment valuation method used.[21]

This fact is reflected in the first two rows of Table 10-1. Consider, for instance, the figures for 1987. Using the current cost valuation of direct investment, the net international investment position of the United States was negative (-$26.6 billion). But, utilizing the market value method of valuing direct investment, the net international investment position was positive ($54.2 billion). Alternatively, if one had used the historical cost measure of valuation for direct investment, the net international investment position for 1987 would have showed a massive net indebtedness (-$387.3 billion).[22]

It can be concluded, however, that whatever the numbers used, since 1981 foreign assets in the United States have grown faster than U.S. assets abroad. The exact magnitude of this trend, however, varies according to the method of valuing assets.

10-6. FINANCIAL OPENNESS AND THE SHARE OF FOREIGN ASSETS HELD BY INVESTORS

The U.S. international investment position shows the diversity of U.S. international financial relations. Yet, it provides an incomplete picture of the economy's financial openness because it records only assets that are actually traded internationally. The spectrum of assets that are potentially tradable in international markets is far greater than those that are actually traded. Furthermore, the international investment position only records the stocks of assets accumulated by United States and foreign residents up to a certain point. It does not measure the year-to-year trade in assets—that is, capital flows—recorded by the balance-of-payments statement. Just as the level of water in a pond stays more or less fixed in spite of the inflow and outflow of water, the stock of assets held and the international investment position may stay more or less fixed in the face of massive capital flows in and out of the economy. However, the openness of the domestic financial system is also reflected by those capital flows, which are critically associated with the integration of the economy to world financial markets.

Despite the evident growing openness of world financial markets, individuals still hold nearly all of their wealth in domestic assets. This is what University of Chicago economist Kenneth R. French and MIT's James M. Poterba found in their estimates of cross-border equity holdings (such as stocks) for investors in the United States, the United Kingdom, and Japan.[23] They concluded

---

[21]This issue has been noted by R. Eisner and P. J. Pieper, "The World's Greatest Debtor Nation?" *The North American Review of Economics and Finance* (Spring 1990); and M. Ulan and W. G. Dewald, "The U.S. Net International Investment Position," in J. A. Dorn and W. A. Niskanen, eds., *Dollars, Deficits and Trade* (Boston: Kluwer Academic Publishers, 1989).

[22]As calculated by the Commerce Department and reported in *Economic Report of the President* (Washington, D.C.: U.S. Government Printing Office, February 1991), p. 401.

[23]K. R. French and J. M. Poterba, "Investor Diversification and International Equity Markets," National Bureau of Economic Research Working Paper no. 3609 (January 1991).

that 93.9 percent of the portfolios of U.S. investors, is held in U.S. equities and only a small proportion in Japanese and U.K. equities. For Japanese investors, the extent of local equity holdings is even more drastic—equal to 98.1 percent of the portfolio, with U.S. and U.K. holdings equal to small fractions. Investors in the United Kingdom hold the smallest component of domestic equities in their portfolios: 82 percent.

What explains the finding that portfolio investors tend to prefer their own equity market? French and Poterba calculate that there are apparent unexploited gains from international diversification and that some other costs must exist that make investors prefer domestic assets. Clearly, the great degree of liberalization of foreign exchange, money, and capital markets discussed in previous chapters—and reflected in the figures provided here—suggests that barriers to cross-country financial flows cannot be a major factor. An alternative hypothesis is that investors attach "extra risk" to foreign investments because they lack knowledge of the foreign markets, their institutions, and their firms. However, new instruments have emerged with ways to trade these risks, and it seems likely that cross-country equity investments will rise over time.[24]

10-7. EXCHANGE RATE CONCEPTS AND MEASUREMENTS

Up to this point, openness of the economy has been examined by observing the wide array of its international trade in goods, services, and assets, as well as the extent of trade in each of these categories, as recorded by the balance of payments. An economy's interactions with the rest of the world, however, are not only directly reflected in the *quantities* of the various items traded internationally, but also through the *prices* of those items. The prices of many of the basic items in our daily life are crucially affected, and often determined, by situations in foreign or world markets. The price of oil is an obvious example, but the prices of such a variety of products as automobiles, stereos, refrigerators, grain, sugar, coffee, the clothes you are wearing, and the makeup on your face are all heavily influenced by events in international markets and by the prices of competitive products available abroad. In order to compare domestic prices with foreign prices, conversion into the same currency has to be made. Exchange rates represent the terms at which currencies can be converted into each other. This section and the next one examine the basic concepts and problems in the measurement of exchange rates and their interpretation.

Effective Exchange Rates

The exchange rate between any two given currencies, called a *bilateral exchange rate* in the present context, measures the cost of that currency in foreign exchange markets. If the price of a deutsche mark in foreign exchange markets is 40 cents, the exchange rate between the two currencies is $e_{DM} = \$0.40/DM$. When the exchange rate increases, the cost in dollars of acquiring foreign currency increases. For instance, if the exchange rate between the dollar and the deutsche mark increases to $e_{DM} = \$0.50/DM$, the cost of purchasing a deustche mark increases by 10 cents. This implies that the amount of deutsche marks we can purchase with any given amount of dollars declines. In other words, the value of the dollar declines against the deutsche mark, that is, the dollar becomes weaker.[25] A revaluation, or appreciation, of the dollar represents an increase in its value, popularly referred to as a stronger dollar relative to the mark in foreign exchange markets.

---

[24]See, for instance, C. Bonser-Neal et al., "International Investment Restrictions and Closed End Country Fund Prices," *Journal of Finance* (June 1990).

[25]Remember that, as the exchange has been defined, dollar depreciations are associated with increases in the exchange rate, e_{DM}.

Making overall statements about whether a currency is weak or strong in foreign exchange markets on the basis of exchange rate changes is a very tricky business. For example, in 1989, the U.S. dollar appreciated substantially in terms of the pound and the Japanese yen. Indeed, from January to September 1989, the dollar appreciated 17.5 percent with respect to the yen and 16.1 percent against the pound. The so-called rising dollar became a topic of public discussion in financial circles. Beside the fact that this phenomenon turned out to be short-lived, with the dollar depreciating against these currencies in 1990, a close look at the facts shows that focusing on a few currencies resulted in an exaggerated view of the dollar's decline. For instance, although the dollar did also appreciate against the German mark in the first half of 1989, this was sharply reversed in the second half, leaving no clear upward trend during the year. In addition, in 1989 the dollar depreciated in terms of various other currencies such as the Canadian dollar, the currency of the United States' main trading partner. The overall position of a currency in foreign exchange markets can be distorted by focusing unduly on a small number of currencies.

This example illustrates a general characteristic of exchange rate movements: A general depreciation or appreciation of a currency vis-à-vis other currencies is not generally observed; rather, a simultaneous depreciation with respect to some currencies and an appreciation with respect to others is usually the case. It is convenient to develop an index or summary measure of how a currency fares, on average, in foreign exchange markets. Such an index is called an *effective exchange rate;* it is different from the usual exchange rates, such as the dollar-yen rate, which, as noted earlier, are called bilateral exchange rates. An effective exchange rate stands in the same relationship to bilateral exchange rates as a price index to the prices of individual commodities: An effective exchange rate is nothing more than an average of bilateral exchange rates.

There are currently more than one hundred different national currencies. This means that we can compute more than one hundred different bilateral exchange rates, each involving the dollar and a different foreign currency. Of course, it would be burdensome and superfluous to include all these in constructing an effective exchange rate index for the dollar. The first step in constructing an effective exchange rate index involves selecting a representative group of currencies to be included in the index. The group of currencies to be included must be in some way involved in the country's international trade. For the United States, it makes little sense to include a currency such as the Maltese pound because there are minimal trade connections between the United States and Malta. The currencies of Canada, the Federal Republic of Germany, and Japan, however, would clearly have to be included in the effective exchange rate index.

Once the currencies to be included in the effective exchange rate are determined, how to compute the index must be decided—that is, how to calculate an average of the various exchange rates. Different weights are assigned to different components of the average, depending on their relative importance. In the case of the U.S. effective exchange rate, the obvious weighing scheme is to give more weight to the currencies of those countries with which U.S. international trade is most significant. More weight should be given to countries that trade heavily with the United States and less weight to countries with which trade is moderate. Because Canada is the United States' main trade partner, the Canadian dollar would be assigned a larger weight than the currencies of Germany or Japan. An effective exchange rate index in which a currency's weight is assigned on the basis of the extent of its bilateral trade with the United States is called a *bilateral trade-weighted* index. In practice, there are various variants of bilateral trade-weighted indexes, depending on whether trade is measured on the basis of imports, exports, or total trade (i.e., exports plus imports).

One basic problem with a bilateral trade-weighted effective exchange rate index is that it gives inordinate importance to the currencies of the country's major trading partners. First, the share of a given country in U.S. trade does not necessarily measure its real importance in terms of the influence it has on U.S. external trade. For example, U.S. exports and imports to Germany may be much more sensitive to changes in the dollar-deutsche mark exchange rate than Canadian trade would be to a U.S.-Canadian dollar exchange rate change. In this case, an increase in the dollar-deutsche mark rate may signify a relatively more important event than an increase in the U.S.-Canadian dollar exchange rate—in terms of its effects on the U.S. balance of trade and the overall economy. The deutsche mark would be assigned a relatively higher weight, even if the share of U.S. trade with Germany is smaller than with Canada. Such an index is calculated by the IMF and is called the *multilateral exchange rate model index* (MERM), attributable to the name of the model of the economy used by the IMF to determine the relative responsiveness of U.S. exports and imports to changes in various exchange rates.[26]

Another reason bilateral trade-weighted effective exchange rates may overstate the importance of trade partners is that the real significance of a country's currency is often more closely related to the country's participation in world trade and not necessarily to participation in U.S. trade. Those countries that trade heavily in world markets, and not necessarily with the United States alone, will be more involved in competing with U.S. products abroad. It is changes in the exchange rates of their currencies that will be of crucial importance to U.S. trade abroad, as well as to its economy. More weight should then be given to these currencies.

Under this weighing scheme, the Canadian dollar would receive a smaller weight than the deutsche mark or yen: Even though Canada's trade with the United States is indeed very heavy, the Canadian share of world trade is much smaller than Germany's or Japan's. An effective exchange rate index that assigns weights to a country's currency on the basis of the importance of that country's trade in global or world trade, as opposed to its importance in U.S. trade, is interchangeably called a multilateral, world, or global trade-weighted effective exchange rate index. An index of this type is published by the Federal Reserve Board and published monthly in the *Federal Reserve Bulletin*.

Effective exchange rates are index numbers, expressed in terms of a base year assigned a value of 100. A value of 200 for the U.S. dollar index means that the average price of foreign exchange has doubled in comparison to the base year; overall, the dollar has depreciated. A value of 50 means that, generally, foreign currencies have become cheaper in terms of the dollar—that is, the dollar has appreciated. Column 1 in Table 10–3 exhibits the behavior of the effective exchange rate index for the U.S. dollar from March 1973 to 1992 (based on the multilateral trade-weighted index computed by the Federal Reserve Board). Actually, the dollar was relatively stable in the 1960s; it depreciated about 15 percent between 1971 and 1973 and has fluctuated around its 1973 level ever since. A pattern that stands out is that the effective exchange rate of the U.S. dollar has fluctuated greatly in the floating exchange rate period, an experience that contrasts with the stability in the 1960s under the Bretton Woods regime. The gyrations of the effective exchange rate were wild in the 1980s, and they continue to be so. Between 1980 and 1985, the dollar had a sharply declining effective exchange rate. Then, from 1986 to 1988, it underwent an effective depreciation. Since then, the currency has not had a clear trend up and down, but it has fluctuated furiously. The dollar appreciation of 1989 depicted in Table 10–3 is far

[26]Estimating the responsiveness of exports and imports to various exchange rate changes is a difficult task. For this purpose, the IMF has developed a statistical model of international trade in many respects similar to the one developed in parts IV and V of this book.

TABLE 10–3.   U.S. Dollar Effective Exchange Rates, 1973–1992

Year	Nominal Effective Exchange Rate *e* (1)	Ratio of World to U.S. Consumer Price Index *P*/P* (2)	Real Effective Exchange Rate (3) = (1) × (2) (3)
1992	115.3	1.040	119.9
1991	111.3	1.038	115.6
1990	112.2	1.036	116.3
1989	101.4	1.047	106.2
1988	107.9	1.053	113.6
1987	103.2	1.070	110.4
1986	89.1	1.086	96.8
1985	69.9	1.084	75.8
1984	72.3	1.076	77.8
1983	79.8	1.070	85.4
1982	85.8	1.043	89.5
1981	96.7	1.025	99.1
1980	114.4	1.031	117.9
1979	113.5	1.056	120.3
1978	108.2	1.098	118.8
1977	96.7	1.112	107.5
1976	94.6	1.089	102.9
1975	101.5	1.049	106.5
1974	98.6	1.022	100.8
1973 (March)	100.0	1.000	100.0

Note: A multilateral trade-weighted exchange rate index is used with the base period of March 1973, as computed by the Federal Reserve System.

To avoid confusion, the reader may note that effective exchange rates are frequently reported as the inverse of the way we have computed them.

SOURCE: *Economic Report of the President* (Washington, D.C.: U.S. Government Printing Office, January 1993).

smaller when compared with the sharp appreciations against specific currencies, such as the close to 20 percent depreciation against the Japanese yen during that period.

In summary, a wide menu of alternative effective exchange rate indexes is published by different organizations, depending on the basket of currencies included in the index and the weight-assignment scheme—whether bilateral, global, or MERM. However measured, the usefulness of an effective exchange rate index hinges on its allowing us to evaluate a currency's value vis-à-vis other currencies in a multicurrency world. Especially in a system of flexible exchange rates, in which a variety of currencies will be fluctuating up and down, it is often extremely useful to have such a summary measure. It tells us how the currency has fared overall in foreign exchange markets. The information provided can be combined with the data presented by the balance of payments, to provide us with a clearer view of the economy's interrelationships with the rest of the world.

10−8. EXCHANGE RATES, PRICES, AND EXTERNAL COMPETITIVENESS

One aspect that can be illuminated by the effective exchange rate is how the country's competitiveness changes vis-à-vis the rest of the world. To understand this, it must first be realized that, other things equal, a depreciation of the dollar vis-à-vis any given foreign currency tends to make U.S. products more competitive relative to those of the foreign country. For instance, a depreciation of the dollar in terms of the deutsche mark from $0.40 to $0.50/DM means that a German Volkswagen priced at DM20,000 will increase its dollar price from $8,000 to $10,000. If the prices of comparable U.S. automobiles (say, Chevys) remain unchanged, U.S. cars would then become relatively more competitive than German cars. Given that, in general, we will find the dollar depreciating with respect to some currencies and appreciating vis-à-vis others, the effective exchange rate provides a summary index of how U.S. goods have fared overall, relative to foreign goods in terms of price competitiveness. An increase in the effective exchange rate would mean that, overall, the dollar price of foreign currencies has increased, making U.S. products generally more competitive relative to foreign goods. Caution is required, however, in associating changes in effective exchange rates with changes in the overall price competitiveness of U.S. goods relative to foreign goods. The reason is that the prices of domestic goods will not necessarily stay fixed when the exchange rate changes and could very well increase substantially. In the dollar-deutsche mark example, the prices of Chevys in the United States may go up in response to the switch in demand toward U.S. cars. In addition, foreign prices could also be changing; for example, foreign exporters of Volkswagens may decide to lower the deutsche mark price of their autos. Consequently, in order to illuminate the question of changes in the relative competitiveness of U.S. products, exchange rate changes must be adjusted for price changes.

Nominal and Real Exchange Rates

A key distinction to bear in mind, now and throughout the rest of this book, is between nominal and real exchange rates. A *nominal exchange rate* states the home currency price of foreign exchange. The usual bilateral exchange rates, such as the U.S. dollar price of sterling, are nominal exchange rates. Similarly, effective exchange rates, being an average of nominal exchange rates, are also nominal rates. A *real exchange rate* is a price-adjusted nominal exchange rate. Specifically, the relationship between a nominal exchange rate, e, and a real exchange rate, e_r, can be expressed algebraically by

$$e_r = eP^*/P,$$

where P^* and P represent relevant indexes of foreign and domestic prices, respectively.[27] As observed, the real exchange rate is equal to the nominal exchange rate adjusted by the ratio of foreign to domestic prices.

What can real exchange rates tell us? As noted in the last section, a full measure of the competitiveness of U.S. products relative to foreign products must take into account not only changes in nominal exchange rates, but price changes as well. This is exactly what the real exchange rate does. Consequently, the real exchange rate can be used to illuminate how U.S. goods are faring relative to foreign goods in terms of their price competitiveness.

---

[27]Various alternative indices of prices and costs are commonly used to calculate effective exchange rates, such as consumer prices, wholesale prices, and labor costs; for more details, see J. A. Rosensweig, "Constructing and Using Exchange Rate Indexes," *Economic Review of Federal Reserve Bank of Atlanta* (Summer 1987).

To discern this more clearly, consider the real exchange rate between the U.S. dollar and the British pound. As the expression for e tells us, the real exchange rate is basically the ratio of the term eP^* to the term P. The symbol P^* in this example stands for the price level in the United Kingdom, which is the average price of a basket of goods in the United Kingdom expressed in pounds. However, because e denotes the exchange rate of the U.S. dollar vis-à-vis the British pound, expressed in dollars per pound, then eP^* represents the price of a basket of goods in the United Kingdom expressed in terms of dollars. Of course, P in the present case is the U.S. price level expressed in dollars. As a result, the ratio eP^*/P essentially denotes the ratio of the prices of British and American goods, both expressed in dollars. In other words, the real exchange rate between the dollar and the pound basically shows how the prices of British goods compare with the prices of U.S. goods when expressed in terms of dollars. An increase in the real exchange rate would imply that U.S. goods become more price competitive relative to British goods, and a reduction of the real exchange rate would imply that British goods have become relatively more competitive. Observe how crucial it is to adjust exchange rate changes for price changes when calculating its effects on the relative competitiveness of U.S. goods relative to foreign goods. For example, if the dollar-pound nominal exchange rate were devalued by 20 percent (an increase in e), but the U.S. price level increased at the same time by 20 percent, with the British price level remaining more or less fixed, the dollar-pound real exchange rate would remain unchanged. In other words, U.S. price competitiveness relative to Great Britain would not be altered. The devaluation makes British goods absolutely more expensive in terms of dollars; however, because U.S. prices have also increased by the same proportion, no net effect would be observed in terms of their relative price. If, for example, a dollar devaluation were to increase the prices of U.K. records by $2.00, but at the same

time U.S.-made records were to increase in price by $2.00 as well, no real change in the relative competitiveness of the two products would be observed.

In general, we are interested in obtaining some measure of competitiveness for the United States vis-à-vis its main trading partners, rather than just against a particular country such as the United Kingdom. In other words, we are interested in obtaining a real effective exchange rate index. In order to derive a real from a nominal effective exchange rate, we adjust the latter by means of an appropriate price index for the United States' main trading partners divided by a U.S. price index. In terms of the algebraic expression for e_r used earlier, e would now be the nominal effective exchange rate, P^* would be an index of foreign prices, and P would be an index of U.S. prices.

Column 3 in Table 10–3 displays the behavior of the real effective exchange rate for the U.S. dollar from 1973 to 1992, obtained by adjusting the nominal effective rates in column 1 by means of consumer price indexes. Two important observations can be made from Table 10–3. First, real effective exchange rates exhibit substantial yearly fluctuations, frequently exceeding 10 percent. Second, although no clear trend is observed for the period as a whole, two distinct patterns can be identified for the 1980s: the real appreciation of the dollar from 1979 to 1985 and the subsequent sharp real depreciation after 1985.

The nominal and the real effective exchange rates of the dollar roughly moved together in the 1970s and 1980s, but this is not a general characteristic. Nominal and real exchange rates frequently move in different directions. A case in point is that of the British pound between 1973 and 1979, a period in which the pound experienced a nominal depreciation and a real appreciation at the same time. This divergent behavior of the two indexes arose because U.K. inflation relative to that of its trade partners exceeded the nominal depreciation of the sterling. As a result, the United Kingdom lost price competitiveness relative to its trade partners while its currency was depreciating.

Summary

1. A country's international investment position statement is the economy's international investment balance sheet: It shows the composition of the stock of external assets and liabilities accumulated by a country's residents up to a certain date. It differs from the balance-of-payments accounts in recording *stocks* of foreign claims and liabilities rather than changes, or *flows.*

2. The increase both in U.S. assets abroad and foreign assets in the United States has been remarkable, especially in the last decade. This increase is partly explained by a growing world economy, but it predominantly reflects the many steps taken to liberalize world financial markets and the consequent increased acquisition and sale of assets across borders.

3. Although not the most significant in terms of magnitude, one of the most visible items in the United States' international investment position is direct foreign investment. The growth of direct foreign investment in America has generated great fears of a "foreign invasion." We find that these fears are greatly exaggerated and unjustified at this time. For instance, the portion of the total stock of assets in the U.S. economy owned by foreigners is small. In terms of employment, foreign affiliates have accounted in recent years for less than 10 percent of all manufacturing employment in the United States. Japan's role in the alleged foreign invasion has also been exaggerated. By the end of 1989, Japan's share of foreign direct investment in the United States was only 17.4 percent. This percentage has been rising rapidly, however, and it does hide substantial investments in particular sectors.

4. A number of factors has influenced direct foreign investment in the United States. Underlying the investment is the rising competitiveness of foreign firms relative to U.S. producers, measured in terms of technological and managerial advantages over American suppliers. In addition, a number of factors has stimulated foreign producers to shift their location to the United States, as opposed to exporting their products there. These include U.S. restrictions on imports (actual and anticipated), exchange rate movements, and changes in tax codes.

5. A country's net international investment position is the difference between the sum of the value of its assets abroad and the sum of the value of all foreign assets in the country. It is a summary measure of the net claims (or liabilities) of a country's residents on the rest of the world.

6. Estimates supplied by the U.S. Commerce Department suggest that the United States has had a negative international investment position since 1985. These estimates, however, are partly based on the book value of some assets. Book values are measured in terms of the prices at the time the transactions occurred, rather than the prices that prevailed in the period considered. The latter gives rise instead to market values. Adjustments of the Commerce Department estimates using market values continue to show a negative trend for the U.S. net international investment position; however, the position does not appear to have become negative as quickly, only reaching that landmark in 1988.

7. An effective exchange rate is an average of various bilateral exchange rates. It is used as an index, or summary, measure of how a currency fares, on average, in foreign exchange markets in a multicurrency world.

8. A real effective exchange rate is a price-adjusted effective exchange rate frequently used as an index of the competitiveness of a country's goods relative to those of other countries.

Problems

1. Using the latest data on the international investment position statement of the United States (from the June issue of the Commerce Department's *Survey of Current Business*), update the net international investment position of the United States and the net position on *direct* investment. Are there any changes from the trends noted in the text?

2. Foreigners are forbidden to acquire control over U.S. airlines, broadcast companies, and nuclear power plants. Some have recently suggested that the United States eliminate some of these restrictions, such as those involving airlines. Do you agree or disagree?

3. The magnitude of Japanese investment in the EEC accelerated in the last few years before the end of 1992. Some have argued that this occurred in anticipation of the Europe 1992 project. With your knowledge of Europe 1992, developed from previous chapters, why did the Japanese accelerate their European investments before the end of 1992?

4. Collect data on (a) the nominal exchange rate of the dollar versus the pound from 1980 to the present, and (b) the U.S. and U.K. consumer and wholesale price indices (these can be obtained from the IMF's *International Financial Statistics*). Compute the real exchange rate between the dollar and the pound for these years, adjusting the nominal exchange rate by using first the ratio of consumer prices and, second, the ratio of wholesale prices. Is there any difference between the two calculations? Explain your answer.

5. In a recent article, United Nations economists Persephone Economou and David Gold discuss the dramatic rise in the 1980s of Japan as a source of direct investment in Asia. According to them, "The rise in the value of the yen after 1985 was a major stimulant to Japanese foreign direct investment in Asia." [From: P. Economou and D. Gold, "Japan and Foreign Direct Investment," *International Economic Insights* (November/December 1992), p. 41.] What is the rationale for this statement? Do you agree or disagree with it?

6. Compute Canada–U.S. real exchange rates between 1985 and 1991 using the following data showing the Canadian nominal exchange rate vis-à-vis the U.S. dollar (in Canadian dollars per U.S. dollar) and consumer prices in Canada and the United States:

Year	Nominal Exchange Rate	Canadian Consumer Price Index	U.S. Consumer Price Index
1985	1.3655	100.0	100.0
1986	1.3895	104.2	101.9
1987	1.3260	108.7	105.7
1988	1.2307	113.1	109.9
1989	1.1840	118.7	115.2
1990	1.1668	124.4	121.4
1991	1.1457	131.4	126.6

SOURCE: International Monetary Fund, *International Financial Statistics* (December 1992). The base year for price data is 1985 = 100.

CHAPTER 11

National Income Accounting and the Open Economy

The last two chapters showed how the economy's transactions with the rest of the world are measured. Open-economy macroeconomics goes one step further: it studies the links between international transactions and the economy's key aggregate, macroeconomic variables. The national income and product accounts (NIPA) are involved in measuring the components of the economy's aggregate income and output. Such items as consumption spending, savings, investment, and budget deficits are all recorded by these accounts. This chapter studies the national income and product accounts (NIPA) and integrates balance-of-payments concepts with NIPA accounting. This will give us the overall picture of how the external sector is linked to the national economy.

The national income and product accounts are a rat's maze of intricacies and terminological complexities. Government expenditures, for instance, are determined from budgets that can be cleverly manipulated by politicians and administrators to hide negative trends in government finances. Even when full disclosure is available, there are many levels of government to deal with (local, state, and federal) and major differences in the timing of data (government budgets are fiscal-year budgets, whereas the national accounts follow the calendar year). Expenditures related to consumption and investment are also plagued not only by data-collection difficulties, but by basic terminological issues such as what constitutes investment (are educational expenditures investment spending?)

and how the depreciation of plant and equipment is to be measured. This complexity is compounded by the major differences in how governments collect and present the national income accounts. What in some countries is considered part of investment in others represents consumption. Thus care must be taken in assessing NIPA data. In this chapter we will note the ambiguities and problems associated with particular measurements and their interpretation. We hope to make the reader wiser when evaluating the often wild—and conflicting—statements made in the press about U.S. income, savings, investment, and the current account balance.

The first part of the chapter goes over the basic national income accounting identities and how the CAB fits into them. We then study the accounting relationships linking savings, investment, budget deficits, and the CAB. We apply this to the U.S. current account and budget deficits—the so-called twin deficits—in the 1980s and to the national income accounts of Japan and Germany. We also discuss the controversy regarding the recent downward trend of U.S. savings and its implications.

11−1. NATIONAL INCOME ACCOUNTS IN THE OPEN ECONOMY

The basic national income accounting concept is the national income, or GNP, identity. It breaks down GNP—the value of all the (final) goods and services produced by a country's residents in a given period—into various spending categories. In an open economy, the goods produced by a country's residents can be purchased by foreign and domestic residents. This is in sharp contrast to a closed economy—one that has no trade connections with the rest of the world. The expenditures of foreign residents on domestic goods and services are our exports, symbolized by X_N.[1] What

makes up the purchases of domestic goods and services on the part of domestic residents? The expenditures of our residents on domestic products are given by the total aggregate amount that we spend—referred to as domestic absorption and denoted here by A_N—minus our spending on foreign goods and services—that is, domestic imports, symbolized by M_N.

Expressed algebraically, the value of national output (GNP), denoted by Y_N, is accounted for by the sum of domestic and foreign expenditures on domestic goods and services, or

$$Y_N = (A_N - M_N) + X_N$$
$$= A_N + X_N - M_N,$$

where $X_N - M_N$ is the net value of exports minus imports of goods, services, and investment income.

The total expenditures of domestic residents—aggregated into the absorption term A_N—include a variety of items that can be catalogued as private consumption expenditures, C_N, private investment expenditures, I_N, and government expenditures, G_N. In other words, domestic expenditures include our purchases of vegetables, Coca Cola, and meat; the expenditures of firms and investors on new machines, new buildings, and the accumulation of inventories; and government outlays on missiles, paper, and stamps. The total spending of domestic residents is thus given by

$$A_N = C_N + I_N + G_N.$$

If we net imports out of domestic absorption, the residual then represents that part of the total spending by local residents that falls exclusively on domestic goods. Symbolically, this component is given by

$$A_N - M_N = C_N + I_N + G_N - M_N.$$

[1]The subscript N with a variable is used in this book to indicate that the variable is expressed in nominal terms. A nominal variable is measured in terms of currency, such as dollars in the United States, as opposed to real variables, which refer to physical quantities of goods, such as bushels of wheat.

Substituting into the expression for the value of national output (GNP), Y_N, then yields:

$$Y_N = A_N + X_N - M_N$$
$$= C_N + I_N + G_N + X_N - M_N. \qquad (11-1)$$

Equation 11–1 shows the basic accounting identity in an open economy. If the various categories—production, consumption, investment, and so forth—were defined and measured appropriately, Equation 11–1 would always hold exactly. This is because the equation represents an accounting definition: The spending items are defined such that they can account for all the domestic output measured on the left-hand side. Sometimes, broad definitions are necessary to cover all possible uses of national output. For instance, unsold goods are classified as an investment expenditure made by firms in the form of inventory accumulation; they are thus catalogued under the investment category in the national accounts.

The identity stated in Equation 11–1 can be used to show how the spending categories accounting for domestic output in the open economy compare with their closed-economy counterparts. In a closed economy, the basic national income identity states that the value of domestic output must equal absorption—that is, $Y_N = A_N$. The reason is that, in the absence of foreign trade, aggregate spending on domestic goods and services must be identical to the aggregate spending of domestic residents (i.e., absorption). In an open economy, this does not have to be so. Foreign trade implies that some spending on domestic goods comes from foreign sources (e.g., the Japanese buying American refrigerators) and that a part of domestic spending falls on foreign goods (e.g., Americans buying imported automobiles). In order to derive aggregate spending on *domestic goods and services* from the aggregate spending of *domestic residents* (absorption), we must add to absorption the foreign spending on domestic goods and services (exports) and then subtract the spend-

ing of domestic residents on foreign goods and services (imports). That is what the expression on the right-hand side of Equation 11–1 shows.

The GNP, or national income identity, can be rearranged to yield

$$X_N - M_N = Y_N - A_N, \qquad (11-2)$$

which expresses the balance on goods and services as the gap between national income and domestic absorption. Note that, in the absence of unilateral transfers, the balance on goods and services corresponds to the CAB.[2] Thus, ignoring unilateral transfers,

$$CAB = Y_N - A_N, \qquad (11-3)$$

which tells us that the CAB is identically equal to the difference between national income and domestic absorption. A CAB deficit ($CAB < 0$) implies an excess of the spending of domestic residents over their income, whereas a surplus ($CAB > 0$) means an excess of income over spending. The insights of this formulation of the current account in terms of aggregate categories in national income accounts, rather than as a relationship between the country's credits and debits in its international transactions accounts, were coherently formulated by MIT's Sidney Alexander in 1952 and labeled the absorption approach to the

---

[2]We are defining the balance on goods and services here to include investment income so that CAB is identical to the balance on goods and services plus unilateral transfers. However, strictly speaking, in the terminology of the U.S. balance of payments, the CAB is the balance on goods, services, *and investment income* plus unilateral transfers. If we were to exclude investment income from the balance on goods and services, then Equation 11–3 would establish the equality of the balance on goods and services to the gap between GDP and absorption. The present discussion also disregards the distinctions between GNP and national income arising from the need to adjust for investment depreciation and indirect taxes. In a more detailed presentation, we would have to subtract both of these from GNP to obtain national income.

current account (or the balance of payments).[3] The absorption approach analyzes the CAB by examining the economic factors determining the gap between income and absorption. Its influence on the thinking of both international monetary economists and policy makers in the post-World War II period has been immense, as we will see later, in Parts IV and V of this book.

How does the income-minus-absorption view of the CAB fit into that derived from the balance-of-payments accounts—which identifies a CAB surplus with a net accumulation of foreign assets by domestic residents? Just as we as individuals use an excess of income over spending to acquire assets, whether in the form of bank deposits or as stocks and bonds, a country uses an overall excess of income over spending to accumulate foreign assets, such as foreign currencies or foreign stocks and bonds. Accordingly, the interpretation of a CAB surplus as the excess of income over spending of domestic residents is clearly the same as that of net accumulation of foreign assets (our net foreign investment). Similarly, an excess of spending over income is associated with a net decumulation of foreign assets or, alternatively, with increased liabilities to foreigners; the excess of spending over income has to be financed, whether by selling stocks and bonds or by borrowing. Consequently, the view of a CAB deficit as an excess of spending by domestic residents over their income is equivalent to viewing it as a net decumulation of foreign assets or, alternatively, as an accumulation of liabilities to foreigners.

If we consider that the CAB represents the net acquisition of foreign assets, can we validly identify it with changes in domestic wealth so that a CAB surplus would be associated with increasing

domestic wealth and a CAB deficit with decreasing wealth? The answer is no—we generally cannot identify the CAB with changes in wealth. To clarify the issue, consider a situation of current account deficit. Because this situation represents a net decumulation of *foreign* assets by the country as a whole, it tends to reduce domestic residents' asset holdings. Nevertheless, domestic residents can also increase their total wealth through accumulation of *domestic* assets.

A CAB deficit does not necessarily connote shrinking wealth if domestic assets are being accumulated at the same time, as would be the case in a growing economy that invests in both physical and human capital. Within this context, a CAB deficit suggests that the country is selling or mortgaging part of the newly created assets. It cannot be deduced that the country's total wealth is decreasing. As a matter of fact, a CAB deficit might imply that the country is borrowing abroad to complement its own resources in order to invest and import the machines and equipment necessary for economic growth. In this situation, the CAB deficit is associated with growth—not contraction—of domestic wealth in the form of domestic capital accumulation and increased claims on it. There is, thus, no necessary connection between changes in domestic wealth and CAB deficits.

11–2. SAVINGS, INVESTMENT, AND THE CURRENT ACCOUNT BALANCE

The representation of the current account as the difference between income and expenditure as derived in the last section—and as depicted by Equation 11–3—can provide us with additional insights when we disaggregate spending into its constituents. There are various ways to proceed, but one popular approach is to break down domestic absorption into consumption and investment categories. This is not a straightforward approach because government spending on goods and services

---

[3]Professor Alexander coined the terminology of absorption. Another key contributor to the development of this macroeconomic approach to the open economy was Nobel prize winner James Meade in his book *The Balance of Payments* (London: Oxford University Press, 1951).

includes both the investment and consumption expenditures of the general government.[4] That is,

$$G_N = C_N{}^G + I_N{}^G, \qquad (11\text{–}4)$$

where $C_N{}^G$ is government consumption spending (expenditures on defense, education, health, and social security, among others), and $I_N{}^G$ is government investment spending (expenditures on fixed capital formation, such as purchases of machinery, equipment, and buildings). Note that the distinction between government investment and consumption spending is somewhat arbitrary because spending on education could be envisioned as a type of investment (human capital formation).

Substituting the decomposition of government spending in Equation 11–4 into Equation 11–1 yields

$$
\begin{aligned}
CAB &= Y_N - (C_N + I_N + C_N{}^G + I_N{}^G) \\
&= (Y_N - C_N - C_N{}^G) - (I_N + I_N{}^G) \\
&= \text{Gross National Savings} \\
&\quad - \text{Gross National Investment,}
\end{aligned}
\qquad (11\text{–}5)
$$

where gross national savings is equal to the difference between GNP and total consumption (including both private and governmental consumption), while gross national investment is equal to the investment spending of domestic residents, by both the private and government sectors.

---

[4]As noted in the introduction, national income accounting methods differ across countries. The U.S. national income accounts catalogues government investment spending (general government purchases of physical plant and equipment) as part of government purchases of goods and services, G_N, a tradition we have followed. In other countries, however, the authorities commonly separate public from private investment, lumping government and private investment expenditures into the investment category. In this case, the item "government purchases of goods and services" refers to government consumption expenditures. We recommend that in examining the national accounts of any government, caution be exercised to avoid major differences in definitions and the use of terms.

Equation 11–5 states that a CAB deficit (a negative CAB) is equal to an excess of gross national investment over savings. What is the interpretation of this accounting identity? When a country's residents invest more than they are saving in any particular year, there must be external borrowing to finance the excess of investment over savings. But, as noted earlier, net external borrowing on the part of domestic residents represents a CAB deficit of equal magnitude. The NIPA view of a CAB deficit as the excess of savings over investment thus coincides with the balance-of-payments perspective of a CAB as involving net external borrowing or increased liabilities to foreigners. Similarly, when a country's residents save more than what they are investing domestically in any given year, they will accumulate foreign bonds or stocks, or engage in net lending abroad. A current account surplus is thus equivalent to "net foreign investment" by domestic residents.

Most of the figures reported in this chapter are expressed as a fraction of GNP—that is, the variable is divided by GNP when reporting it. The reason is that, in analyzing changes in economic variables over time, meaningful comparisons can often be carried out only if the size of the economy is adjusted for changes. For instance, the total value of gross national savings in the United States in 1980 was equal to $520 billion, whereas in 1988 it was equal to $722 billion. This massive increase in national savings appears to suggest that U.S. residents were saving more out of their income during that time. On the other hand, the U.S. economy grew in these years and, therefore, there were more people and businesses in the country. Could the increase in savings be explained by the fact that there was an increase in the size of the U.S. economy, rather than show any increase in the savings that the average U.S. resident took out of his or her income? Because GNP is closely related to the size of the economy, one divides by GNP to adjust for changes in the size of the economy over time. In this example, GNP grew from $2,732 billion in 1980 to $4,851 billion in 1988. Dividing national savings by GNP shows that, as a fraction of GNP, national savings actually declined from 0.190 (equal to 520/2,732) in 1980 to 0.149 (equal to 722/4851) in 1988. This means that savings grew more slowly than GNP in the decade of the 1980s and, therefore, the savings *rate* of U.S. residents declined. This decline in the U.S. savings rate represents an important phenomenon that will be examined later in this chapter.

Because of the generally growing U.S. economy, relying on changes in the absolute magnitude of variables hides important real phenomena, and we will adjust whenever necessary by dividing by GNP or GDP. For example, in terms of Equation 11–5, if we divide both sides of the equation by GNP, Y_N, then

$$CAB/Y_N = \text{Gross National Savings}/Y_N$$
$$- \text{Gross National Investment}/Y_N. \qquad (11-5a)$$

In Equation 11–5a, the current account divided by GNP is equal to the national savings rate (national savings divided by GNP) minus the national investment rate (national investment divided by GNP).

The interpretation of the CAB as the gap between savings and investment is important in specifying any potential difficulties a country may face if its external debt grows. The accumulation of persistent current account deficits over time may lead to a burgeoning external debt. The economic implications of this can vary, depending on the type of domestic spending the debt is financing. The NIPA accounting identity helps identify the spending categories associated with the growth of external debt. According to Equation 11–5, persistent CAB deficits are associated with a systematic shortfall of savings below investment. This gap may arrive by means of two main routes: through sustained and rising investment expenditures with relatively fixed savings, or through decreased savings—expansions of consumption

relative to income—with relatively fixed investment spending. (There could, of course, also be a combination of increased investment and reduced savings.) The first possibility implies that countries borrow in order to accumulate capital with which to increase future income; the second possibility implies that countries borrow to finance current consumption expenditures that have no clear-cut effect on economic growth or future income. Accordingly, the first possibility seems less likely to give rise to problems involving the repayment of the debt. As long as the investment projects undertaken are profitable, increased future income streams should provide enough funds for repayment of the principal plus interest. Borrowing for consumption purposes, however, does not provide such a clear-cut future repayment potential. It seems likely to require a reduction of consumption sometime in the future by means of which funds can be obtained to pay for the debt without crippling reductions in domestic wealth.

The economic difficulties that can be associated with the financing of large, persistent CAB deficits may help explain a controversial finding by Harvard economist Martin Feldstein and his collaborators, Charles Horioka and Philippe Bacchetta. Feldstein, Horioka, and Bacchetta have studied the relationship between national savings and national investment for a group, or sample, of twenty-three industrialized countries in the 1960s, 1970s, and 1980s.[5] To their surprise, they have found that national savings and investment rates are closely linked in these countries: Higher savings rates tend to be matched by higher investment rates. This is what is depicted in Figure 11–1, which plots the combination of average national saving and investment rates between 1960 and 1986 for a sample

[5] See M. Feldstein and P. Bacchetta, ''National Saving and International Investment,'' in B. Douglas Bernheim and J. B. Shoven, eds., *National Saving and Economic Performance* (Chicago: University of Chicago Press, 1991); and M. Feldstein and C. Horioka, ''Domestic Savings and International Capital Flows,'' *Economic Journal* (June 1980).

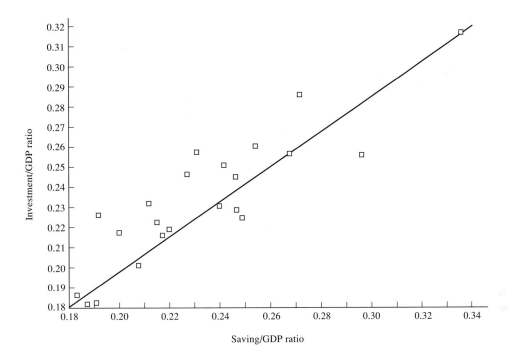

FIGURE 11–1.   The Link Between Savings and Investment Rates in 23 OECD
Countries

SOURCE: R. Dornbusch, "Comment on Feldstein and Bacchetta," in B. D. Bernheim and J. B.
Shoven, eds., *National Saving and Economic Performance* (Chicago: University of Chicago Press,
1991), p. 221. Reprinted with permission.

of 23 industrialized countries. Points lying along
the diagonal of the box in Figure 11–1 indicate
countries for which national savings and investment rates were equal. Observe how closely most
nations lie to the diagonal, suggesting a close correlation (association) between national savings and
investment rates.

In their initial study of this puzzle, Feldstein and
Horioka suggested that their findings could indicate the presence of substantial barriers to the
mobility of capital across the industrialized countries being studied. Indeed, the data indicate that,
on a net basis, domestic residents in these countries had essentially financed their investments out
of their own savings, without requiring any net

external financing. As the national income accounting identities imply—as expressed by Equation 11–5—if national savings and national investment rates are roughly equal to each other, the
current account balance will be close to zero. This
means that there is no reliance on net external
lending or borrowing on the part of the economy
as a whole: The investments made by domestic
residents are matched by their own savings.[6]

[6] See D. Y. Wong, "What Do Saving-Investment Relation-
ships Tell Us About International Capital Mobility?" *Journal
of International Money and Finance* (March 1990); and M. J.
Dooley, J. Frankel, and D. Mathieson, "International Capital
Mobility: What Do Saving-Investment Correlations Tell Us?"
IMF Staff Papers (September 1987).

The Feldstein-Horioka conjecture that their data could imply the presence of substantial barriers to capital flows among industrialized countries was very controversial. It stood in contrast to many studies—based on deviations from covered interest parity, for instance—that suggested that the industrialized countries have been subject to a relatively high degree of capital mobility and capital market openness (see our discussion of such studies in Chapter 4). The conjecture, however, is subject to criticism. First of all, in the original study, Feldstein and Horioka used data for the 1960s and 1970s. When data for the 1980s are considered—provided by Feldstein and Bacchetta—the tendency for national investment and savings

rates in the industrialized countries to be equal diminishes. Figure 11−2(a) and (b) plots the combination of national savings and investment rates for the United States in the 1970s and 1980s. Although in the 1970s the points lie very close to the diagonal—supporting the Feldstein-Horioka results—the relationship breaks down in the 1980s. This could be interpreted as evidence that countries have been better able to finance increased investment from external sources, thus suggesting increased international capital market liberalization. Confirming such an interpretation is the fact that, although in some countries there appears to have been a great degree of freedom to shift capital across borders in the 1970s, many industrialized countries—such as

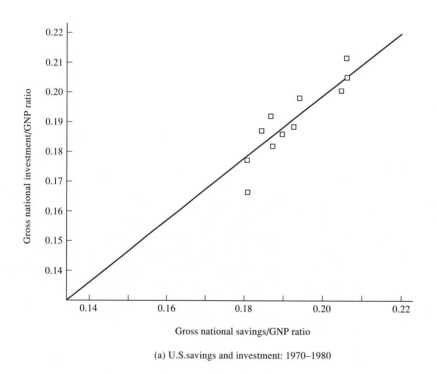

(a) U.S. savings and investment: 1970–1980

FIGURE 11−2. The Link Between Savings and Investment Rates in the United States, 1960–1990

SOURCE: Based on data from *Economic Report of the President,* 1990 (Washington, D.C.: U.S. Government Printing Office, February 1991).

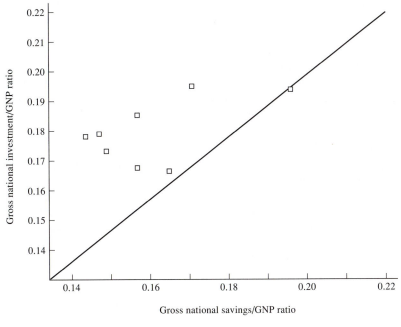

(b) U.S. savings and investment: 1981–1988

FIGURE 11-2 *continued*

the United Kingdom and Japan—engaged in great liberalization moves in the late 1970s and 1980s (a matter documented in Chapter 4).

There is another reason to doubt the Feldstein-Horioka conjecture: The fact that, *on a net basis,* residents of industrialized countries finance higher investment rates by raising their own savings without borrowing externally should not be taken to imply that barriers exist to borrow abroad. We emphasize "on a net basis" because what the Feldstein-Horioka evidence indicates is not that there is very little external borrowing and lending among the industrialized countries, but only that the net balance of this lending and borrowing is close to zero. The data are thus not inconsistent with substantial international capital flows, so long as these flows tend to add up to zero. In fact, two-way capital flows (such as when

there are, simultaneously, U.S. investments in the United Kingdom and U.K. investments in the U.S.) abounded from the 1960s to the 1980s. This suggests a relatively large—and increasing—degree of freedom in capital flows, a matter that interest parity conditions have tended to reflect.[7]

If the close link between national savings and investment rates in industrialized countries does not indicate lack of international capital mobility, what does it reflect? One explanation is that domestic residents in industrialized countries do

---

[7] On this issue, see J. A. Frankel, "International Capital Mobility and Crowding Out in the U.S. Economy: Imperfect Integration of Financial Markets or of Goods Markets?" in R. W. Hafer, ed., *How Open Is the U.S. Economy?* (Lexington, Mass.: D. C. Heath, 1986).

not find it optimal or desirable to raise or further accumulate their current levels of external debt. They thus do not wish to engage in any major, sustained current account imbalances. This puts strict limits on how much national savings can diverge from investment. The behavior here may come from the private or public sectors. Governments, for instance, may become more frugal in their external borrowing if the private sector begins to borrow heavily from abroad. Similarly, the private sector may reduce its external borrowing if the public sector's external debt grows.[8] These links between private and public sector behavior are explored more fully later in this chapter and in Part IV of this book. The next section lays out the national income and product accounting concepts for such analysis.

11–3. THE GOVERNMENT SECTOR, THE PRIVATE SECTOR, AND THE CURRENT ACCOUNT

One key shortcoming of analyzing external borrowing by focusing on the aggregate investment and savings behavior of domestic residents is that it ignores the issues that relate to the breaking down of these aggregates into their public and private components. The role played by the government in accounting for a CAB deficit is easily discerned through a slight modification of the right-hand side of Equation 11–3, by incorporating taxes, TX_N, and transfer payments, TR_N (transfer payments represent government subsidies and grants given to domestic residents, such as welfare payments). This implies that

$$CAB = (Y_N + TR_N - TX_N - C_N - I_N)$$
$$+ (TX_N - TR_N - G_N)$$
$$= (S_N - I_N) + (TX_N - TR_N - G_N), \quad (11-6)$$

where $S_N = Y_N + TR_N - TX_N - C_N$ represents private savings, which is the excess of disposable income, $Y_N + TR_N - TX_N$, over private consumption, C_N. Note that the term $(TX_N - TR_N - G_N)$ represents the excess of the government's receipts (in the form of tax revenues) over its disbursements (which include transfers to individuals plus general government expenditures) and is generally referred to as the government budget surplus.

Equation 11–6 tells us that the current account balance can be associated with a gap between private savings and private investment, $S_N - I_N$, and/or a gap between domestic taxes and government transfers and expenditures, $TX_N - TR_N - G_N$. Note that the latter is the so-called government budget surplus (if positive) or budget deficit (if negative). How do we interpret Equation 11–6? Consider first the private savings-investment gap, and let us assume for the moment that the government budget is balanced ($TX_N = G_N + TR_N$). In this case, Equation 11–6 shows that, if the economy faces a current account surplus, then the savings of domestic private residents exceed their investments by the amount of the current account surplus. Why? Note that the excess of private domestic savings over domestic investment is invested abroad and represents a net accumulation of foreign assets. This accumulation of foreign assets corresponds—from a balance-of-payments perspective—to the economy's CAB surplus. Therefore, Equation 11–6 is just another way of visualizing the earlier-noted association between an accumulation of net foreign assets—net foreign investment—and the CAB. Similarly, according to Equation 11–6, if the government budget is balanced, a CAB deficit is associated with a shortfall of private savings relative to private domestic investment. To finance this excess of private investment over saving, domestic residents either increase liabilities to foreigners in the form of net borrowing from the rest of the world or, equivalently, engage in a net decumulation of foreign assets. Either way, from a balance-of-payments perspective, the net magnitude of these transactions is identical to the CAB.

[8]See L. Summers, "Tax Policy and International Competitiveness," in J. Frenkel, ed., *International Aspects of Fiscal Policy* (Chicago: University of Chicago Press, 1988).

The second component of the current account balance according to Equation 11–6 is the government budget surplus, representing the excess of tax revenues over government disbursements. If the economy's private savings are equal to private investment, a current account deficit will be associated with a government budget deficit. The interpretation is that the government sector is borrowing abroad to finance an excess of its expenditures over its income (tax revenues can be seen as representing the government's income). This foreign borrowing is the counterpart of the current account deficit. Similarly, a budget surplus would correspond to a current account surplus.

11–4. ACCOUNTING FOR THE U.S. CURRENT ACCOUNT BALANCE DEFICIT

The U.S. CAB deteriorated sharply in the 1980s (evidence of which was supplied in Chapter 9). This section shows the factors that account for the deterioration using NIPA concepts.

The mammoth task of estimating the items in the national income accounts of the United States is in the hands of the Bureau of Economic Analysis (BEA) of the U.S. Department of Commerce. The BEA relies on a number of other government agencies, surveys, and projections to compute the consumption, investment, government spending, and export and import figures that are publicly released and published regularly in the *Survey of Current Business*. As with any estimates, these numbers are subject to measurement error. We must also stress that the estimates of the value of exports, imports, and other international transactions in the national income accounts are not necessarily identical to those obtained from the balance-of-payments accounts. This is the result not only of differences in the basic data sources utilized by the two sets of accounts but also of the timing, recording, definition, and valuation of transactions. The end result is that the numbers for the CAB reported in this section are not necessarily the same as those reported in Chapter 9,

although they generally are close and tend to follow the same trends and direction over time.

The Current Account, Total Savings, and Total Investment

We begin by studying the U.S. CAB as the difference between gross national savings and gross national investment, as given by Equation 11–5. Table 11–1 shows the actual figures for the United States from 1970 to 1988. Concentrating on the 1980s, observe the now-familiar growth of the CAB deficit: As a percentage of GNP, the CAB

TABLE 11–1. U.S. Current Account Balance, Gross National Savings, and Gross National Investment, 1970–1988

Year	CAB/GNP	Savings/GNP	Investment/GNP
1970	0.004	0.181	0.177
1975	0.014	0.181	0.167
1976	0.005	0.187	0.182
1977	−0.004	0.194	0.198
1978	−0.005	0.206	0.211
1979	0.001	0.206	0.205
1980	0.004	0.190	0.186
1981	0.003	0.196	0.193
1982	−0.001	0.165	0.166
1983	−0.010	0.157	0.167
1984	−0.024	0.171	0.195
1985	−0.028	0.157	0.185
1986	−0.032	0.147	0.179
1987	−0.034	0.144	0.178
1988	−0.024	0.149	0.173

CAB: Current account balance is derived from national income accounts data.

Savings: Gross national savings is equal to the difference between national disposable income and the consumption spending of domestic residents (both private and government).

Investment: Gross capital formation of domestic residents (both private and government).

GNP: Gross national product.

SOURCE: *National Accounts Statistics: Main Aggregates and Detailed Tables: 1988* (New York: United Nations, 1990).

declines from a surplus of 0.4 percent in 1980 to a deficit of 3.4 percent in 1987. The CAB deficit has declined in recent years from its high in 1987 (it was down to 2.4 percent in 1988, 1.9 percent in 1989, and 1.6 percent in 1990).

According to Equation 11–5, a deteriorating CAB can be associated either with lower gross national savings or higher gross domestic investment, or both. Looking at the figures in Table 11–1, it is apparent that the deteriorating U.S. CAB in the 1980s was associated with a persistent drop in gross national savings. In 1981, savings were equal to 19.6 percent of GNP; by 1988, they were down to 14.9 percent. On the other hand, there is no clear upward movement in the investment rate in the 1980s. Rising domestic invest-

ment was not the culprit behind the deteriorating CAB. If anything, there appears to be a negative trend in investment compared to the late 1970s, especially after 1984.

How does the United States compare with other countries in accounting for current account imbalances in the 1980s? Because the U.S. had a mostly negative CAB, for comparison we take two countries that had current account surpluses: Japan and Germany. In Table 11–2 we depict the Japanese and German CABs—as a fraction of the GNP—and how they break down into the savings-investment gap. Both countries experienced persistent CAB surpluses, with CAB deficits making cameo appearances mainly between 1979 and 1980, when oil-price hikes substantially raised the import

TABLE 11–2. Current Account, Savings, and Investment: Japan and Germany

	Japan			Germany		
Year	CAB/GNP	Savings/GNP	Investment/GNP	CAB/GNP	Savings/GNP	Investment/GNP
1970	0.010	0.401	0.391	0.005	0.281	0.276
1975	−0.001	0.327	0.328	0.011	0.209	0.198
1976	0.006	0.325	0.319	0.008	0.224	0.216
1977	0.015	0.324	0.309	0.008	0.218	0.210
1978	0.017	0.326	0.309	0.014	0.225	0.211
1979	−0.008	0.316	0.324	−0.008	0.226	0.234
1980	−0.011	0.312	0.323	−0.018	0.217	0.235
1981	0.005	0.317	0.312	−0.008	0.201	0.209
1982	0.007	0.308	0.301	0.006	0.203	0.197
1983	0.018	0.301	0.283	0.007	0.210	0.203
1984	0.029	0.311	0.282	0.013	0.217	0.204
1985	0.037	0.321	0.284	0.026	0.221	0.195
1986	0.043	0.323	0.280	0.044	0.239	0.195
1987	0.037	0.326	0.289	0.040	0.236	0.196
1988	0.030	0.340	0.310	0.041	0.245	0.204

CAB: Current account balance is derived from national income accounts data.

Savings: Gross national savings is equal to the difference between national disposable income and the consumption spending of domestic residents (both private and government).

Investment: Gross capital formation of domestic residents (both private and government).

GNP: Gross national product.

SOURCE: *National Accounts Statistics: Main Aggregates and Detailed Tables: 1988* (New York: United Nations, 1990).

bills of both countries. These deficits were reversed in the early 1980s, and by 1986 both countries had significant CAB surpluses: Germany had a surplus equal to 4.4 percent of its GNP and for Japan it was 4.3 percent.

As in the case of the United States, gross national savings rates in Germany and Japan declined in the early 1980s. After 1983, however, there was a marked shift, with both Germany and Japan exhibiting sharply rising savings rates. This contrasts with the United States, where the gross national savings rate continued to exhibit a downward trend. What explains these differences in savings behavior? One possible hypothesis is that government behavior in the two countries diverged beginning in the early 1980s, with the U.S. government increasing its expenditures in a way that reduced its gross national savings. An alternative approach is that the private sector's behavior changed, with U.S. private savings declining in the 1980s. We next examine these two hypotheses.

11–5. EMERGENCE OF THE AMERICAN TWIN DEFICITS

As depicted by Equation 11–6, a deteriorating CAB can be the result of a drop in private savings relative to private investment and/or by a growing government budget deficit. Table 11–3 breaks down the current account deficit of the United States in the 1980s into its private-sector and governmental components. All the figures are expressed as a fraction of the GNP to correct for size. Note that the government budget deficit figures are

TABLE 11–3.   Emergence of the U.S. Twin Deficits

Year	$\dfrac{CAB}{GNP}$	Budget Surplus $\dfrac{}{GNP}$	$\dfrac{(S_N - I_N)^*}{GNP}$	$\dfrac{S_N}{GNP}$	$\dfrac{I_N}{GNP}$	Statistical Discrepancy $\dfrac{}{GNP}$
1980	0.004	−0.012	0.016	0.175	0.160	0.001
1981	0.003	−0.001	0.004	0.180	0.169	−0.007
1982	−0.001	−0.036	0.035	0.176	0.141	0.000
1983	−0.010	−0.038	0.028	0.174	0.147	0.001
1984	−0.024	−0.028	0.004	0.178	0.176	0.002
1985	−0.028	−0.033	0.005	0.166	0.160	−0.001
1986	−0.032	−0.034	0.002	0.158	0.156	0.000
1987	−0.034	−0.023	−0.011	0.147	0.155	−0.003
1988	−0.024	−0.018	−0.006	0.154	0.153	−0.005
1989	−0.019	−0.017	−0.002	0.150	0.148	−0.004
1990	−0.016	−0.024	0.008	0.144	0.136	0.000

*Includes the statistical discrepancy.

CAB: Current account balance is derived from national income accounts data.

S_N: Private savings is equal to the difference between national disposable income and the consumption spending of private domestic residents.

I_N: Gross private capital formation.

GNP: Gross national product.

SOURCE: *Economic Report of the President, 1990* (Washington, D.C.: U.S. Government Printing Office, February 1991).

for the "general government" budget deficit. This represents the net budget deficit of all governmental jurisdictions, including federal, state, and local government. Often, figures quoted as "the budget deficit" include only the federal government budget deficit. To incorporate all governmental revenues and expenditures, we must consider those of state and local governments in addition to those at the federal level.[9] This is significant because, in the 1980s, just as the federal budget deficit increased, state and local government budgets moved into surplus. For instance, in 1990, the federal government had a budget deficit equal to $161.3 billion, while state and local governments had an overall budget *surplus* equal to $35.4 billion. The overall government budget deficit was equal to $125.9 billion, which is the figure used in calculating the numbers in Table 11−3. Using the federal budget deficit in computing U.S. government budget deficits would have substantially distorted the overall government deficit, making it appear larger than it actually was.[10]

According to the figures in Table 11−3, the government budget deficit in the United States, as a fraction of the GNP, rose from 0.1 percent in 1981 to 2.4 percent in 1990. Figure 11−3 shows how this deterioration of the budget deficit accompanied the worsening of the U.S. current account deficit. The association between the budget and current account

deficits in the 1980s, however, is tainted by significant deviations. For instance, Figure 11−3 shows that the budget deficit declined between 1983 and 1984; yet, the current account continued to deteriorate during those years. In the same vein, the budget deficit widened between 1989 and 1990, but the current account deficit shrank.

That larger budget deficits are not necessarily linked to higher current account deficits is suggested by Equation 11−6: If private savings goes up—and/or private investment declines—in response to greater budget deficits, this can offset the overall impact of that deficit on the current account. Are there any reasons to expect budget deficits to cause higher private savings? According to the so-called Ricardian approach to budget deficits, the answer is yes. The idea, first articulated by David Ricardo in the early 1800s and revitalized in recent years by Harvard economist Robert J. Barro, is as follows: Suppose the government cuts taxes this year and keeps its expenditures constant. This will lead to an increased budget deficit that must be financed. Assume that the government borrows from the public by issuing public debt (Treasury bills). This will allow the government to pay its current bills in the presence of the tax cut. However, the amount of money that the public sector has borrowed must be repaid in the future (plus interest). The government will have to raise taxes in the future to pay back the principal and interest on the debt it has engaged today. According to the Ricardian approach, this future increase in taxes is foreseen by households. Knowing that their future disposable income will be reduced because of the impending increase in taxes, households reduce their consumption spending and raise their savings to be able to smooth out the expected reduction in income. Because higher budget deficits will lead to increased private savings, "the current account balance would not respond to an increase in the budget deficit."[11]

---

[9]This point is forcefully made by R. Eisner "The Deficits and Us and Our Grandchildren," in J. M. Rock, ed., *Debt and the Twin Deficits Debate* (Mountain View, CA.: Mayfield Publishing Company, 1991), p. 82.

[10]Although the United States and other major industrialized countries supply ample information on state and local governments, this is not often the case with other countries. As a consequence, many publications compute only federal or central government budget data. The World Bank, in its annual presentation of world data on budget deficits, notes that "the inadequate coverage of state, provincial, and local governments has dictated the use of central government data only. This may seriously understate or distort the role of government, especially in large countries, where lower levels of government are important" [See World Bank, *World Tables 1992* (Baltimore: Johns Hopkins University Press, 1992), p. xii].

[11] R. Barro, "The Ricardian Model of Budget Deficits," in J. M. Rock, ed., op. cit., p. 146.

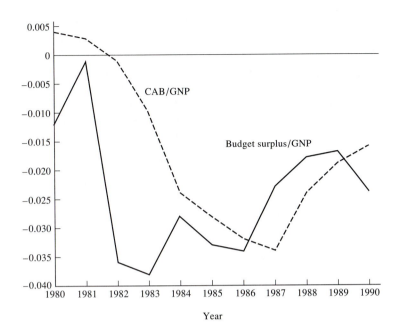

FIGURE 11–3.   The Association Between Budget Deficits and the Current Account Balance Deficits in the United States in the 1980s

SOURCE: Based on data from *Economic Report of the President, 1990* (Washington, D.C.: U.S. Government Printing Office, February 1991).

The implication that U.S. budget deficits and CAB deficits are unrelated to each other has many critics. First of all, the conclusion is obtained on the assumption that individuals raise their savings in anticipation of the future tax hikes needed to finance current budget deficits. However, this presumes that the government will not react to the deficit by slashing expenditures rather than raising taxes. Although it is true that cuts in government spending are politically difficult, they are not inconceivable: It was, for instance, the original policy of the Reagan administration in the early 1980s to engage both in tax cuts and government austerity. If individuals expect the public sector to generate its own budget surpluses through future cuts in spending, they will have no incentive to augment their savings. In this case, budget deficits will be closely linked to current account deficits, even under the Ricardian approach.[12]

A number of objections have also been raised against the Ricardian framework itself. In particular, the approach relies on the assumption that a higher budget deficit is associated with an impending increase in future taxes. However, the timing of the future taxes is uncertain. No one knows precisely when the government will decide to raise taxes in order to pay off its debts. In fact, the government could potentially borrow for a long time in order to avoid a politically costly tax hike. However, if the tax increase is far in the future, it

[12] See M. Obstfeld, "U.S. International Capital Flows: A Comment," *Carnegie-Rochester Conference on Public Policy* (Amsterdam: North Holland, 1989), p. 292.

may be imposed after the current generation has died. If the future taxes are to be paid by future generations in some distant future, individuals in the current generation would not have to save to pay them. The increased budget deficit would *not* be offset by higher private savings.[13] Proponents of the Ricardian approach have responded to this argument by noting that, even if future taxes are imposed on later generations, individuals may still increase their savings in order to help their descendants pay the higher taxes. These *intergenerational transfers* could occur in a number of ways, such as inheritance bequests.

So long as private savings decline when budget deficits rise, the twin deficits will not be closely linked and significant deviations will occur. A number of studies has been undertaken in recent years of the association between budget deficits and the CAB. With respect to the 1980s, the results coincide with those obtained by analyzing the numbers in Table 11–3 and Figure 11–3: higher U.S. government budget deficits are generally linked to greater U.S. current account deficits. For instance, Stanford University economist B. Douglas Bernheim concludes that his "analysis of U.S. time series suggests that a $1.00 increase in government budget deficits leads to roughly a $0.30 rise in the current account deficit."[14] This result, however, depends on the time period considered and the country. In the case of the United States, the connection between budget and current account deficits appeared to be weaker before the emergence of the current regime of floating exchange

rates.[15] In other industrialized countries, such as Japan, there appears to be no connection between budget deficits and the CAB. In Canada, the CAB and the government budget balance moved in opposite directions between 1973 and 1985, with larger budget deficits being linked to higher CAB *surpluses;* as in the Ricardian approach, Canadian private savings increased during this time.[16]

The link between budget and current account deficits in the 1980s implies that a significant amount of the U.S. external borrowing in these years was undertaken to finance the government's budget deficit. This has given rise to fears that, as the U.S. public debt rises, repayment of principal plus interest may become more and more difficult. In 1992, the government's interest payments constituted $200 billion, or close to 15 percent of its outlays in that year (up from 10 percent in 1981). Should the mounting U.S. government debt be of concern to us?

In answering this question, the first thing to realize is that, historically speaking, the U.S. public debt is not abnormally high. In the 1940s and 1950s, the U.S. public debt—expressed as a ratio of GNP—was much higher than it is today (in those years, the public debt was associated with the World War II military buildup). Figure 11–4 depicts the U.S. debt to GNP ratio since 1918. Note that, although rising, the ratio in the 1980s was not unusually high by historical standards. Furthermore, in an international comparison, the U.S. public debt in the late 1980s was not significantly different from that in other industrialized

[13] On the basis of this—and other—criticisms, B. Douglas Bernheim assails the Ricardian approach: "While the Ricardian exercise is an interesting thought experiment, it is predicated upon extreme and unrealistic assumptions. Those who recommend this framework as a guide to actual policy formulation offer a prescription for disaster" [See B. D. Bernheim, "A Neoclassical Perspective on Budget Deficits," *Journal of Economic Perspectives* (Spring 1989), p. 56].

[14] B. D. Bernheim, "Budget Deficits and the Balance of Trade," in L. H. Summers, ed., *Tax Policy and the Economy* (Cambridge, Mass.: The MIT Press, 1988), p. 2.

[15] See B. Eichengreen, "Trade Deficits in the Long Run," in A. E. Burger, ed., *U.S. Trade Deficit: Causes, Consequences and Cures* (Boston: Kluwer Academic Publishers, 1989). Some authors have found no significant connection between budget deficits and the CAB when incorporating a broad historical period and a number of countries; see P. Evans, "Do Budget Deficits Affect the Current Account?" (August 1988) Economics Department, Ohio State University (mimeo.); and W. A. Niskanen, "The Uneasy Relation Between the Budget and Trade Deficits," *Cato Journal* (Fall 1988).

[16] C. Carroll Summers and L. H. Summers, "Why Have Private Savings Rates in the United States and Canada Diverged?" *Journal of Monetary Economics* (September 1987).

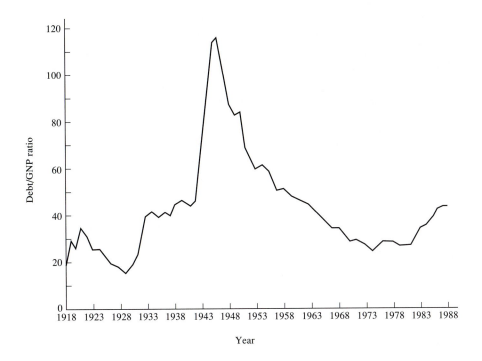

FIGURE 11–4. U.S. Debt/GNP Ratio

SOURCE: R. Dornbusch and J. M. Poterba, "Debt and Deficits in the 1990s," in J. H. Makin,
N. J. Ornstein, and Z. Zlowe, eds., *Balancing Act: Debt, Deficits and Taxes* (Washington, D.C.:
American Enterprise Institute, 1990), p. 3. Reprinted with permission.

economies. The overall public-debt-to-GNP ratio in 1988 was 58.7 percent in Europe (including a 126.5 percent ratio in Denmark and 118.6 percent in Ireland) and 68.3 percent in Japan.[17] For the United States, the public-debt/GNP ratio in 1988 was equal to 51.5 percent—lower than the average among other Organization for Economic Cooperation and Development (OECD) economies. The situation is, thus, far from being one of crisis.

On the other hand, concern should be expressed about the continuous growth of the debt. Partly, it is the result of U.S. government spending having been mostly in the form of consumption spending, such as defense expenditures on tanks and missiles. In the 1980s, fully 75 percent of federal government expenditures were defense related. Net investment by the federal government actually declined in the 1980s. In real terms (adjusted for inflation), investment spending from 1980 to 1984 was 25 percent less than from 1975 to 1979.[18]

[17]The figures quoted here are for the gross public debt, as opposed to net public debt, which reduces the public debt to take into account the government's assets. The two measures provide similar international comparisons.

[18]See R. Dornbusch and J. M. Poterba, "Debt and Deficits in the 1990s," in J. H. Makin, N. J. Ornstein, and Z. Zlowe, eds., *Balancing Act: Debt, Deficits, and Taxes* (Washington, D.C.: American Enterprise Institute, 1990). There has also been a drop in the amount of public capital per worker since 1971. Preoccupation with deteriorating public infrastructure (such as bridges and roads) has been growing; see J. Tatom, "Should Government Spending on Capital Goods be Raised?" *Federal Reserve Bank of St. Louis Review* (March–April 1991); and A. H. Munnell, "Is There a Shortfall in Public Capital Investment? An Overview," *New England Economic Review* (May–June 1991).

Studies examining the sources of economic growth find that public consumption spending is inversely related—and public investment positively related—to economic growth.[19] The lack of government investment means that borrowing is not being used to finance increased productive capacity and will not therefore provide a solid basis for future repayment of the debt. Future government budget surpluses will be needed to raise the net revenues to repay the public debt. Budget surpluses can be generated through higher tax revenues and/or lower government spending. Considerable skepticism can be expressed about the likelihood of cuts in government spending rates: The fact is that there has been an upward trend in public expenditures, even when tax cuts were implemented by the Reagan administration in the early 1980s. This means that the ballooning public debt of recent years will most likely be financed through higher tax rates in the future.[20] However, as the debt grows, so does the future tax burden—and the larger the drainage in the standard of living of current and future generations to pay for these taxes.[21] As has been noted

before, governments often rely on inflation as a means to tax their subjects when income and other conventional taxes are politically infeasible. This is especially so in the case of the United States as a result of the large share of the U.S. public debt owed to foreigners. This creates an incentive for the government to inflate the economy: The inflation reduces the real value of the liabilities to foreigners, reducing the tax burden on domestic residents.[22]

Whether the source of revenues is through an inflation tax, higher income taxes, or other taxes, the continued growth of external debt raises the specter of possible sharp future drops in standards of living. Under these circumstances, some concern over the persistence of budget deficits is justified.

11–6. Private Savings, Private Investment, and the Current Account

That part of the CAB that is not explained by budget deficits must be accounted for by the gap between private savings and investment. Table 11–3 shows how private savings and investment behaved in the U.S. in the 1980s and in 1990. There is a clear negative trend in the difference between private savings and investment; the gap drops from 3.5 percent of the GNP in 1982 to −1.8 percent of the GNP in 1988.[23] This reduction in $S_N - I_N$ can be seen more clearly in Figure 11–5, which plots the gap between private savings and investment with the CAB. The drop in the U.S. CAB is seen to be associated with a reduction in private savings minus investment.

---

[19]R. Barro, "A Cross-Country Study of Growth, Saving and Government," in B. Douglas Bernheim and J. B. Shoven, eds., *National Saving and Economic Performance* (Chicago: University of Chicago Press, 1991).

[20]Raising taxes, however, does not insure deficit reduction. As economist and Nobel Prize winner Milton Friedman argues: "Higher taxes will not eliminate the deficit. They will, after a brief delay, simply increase spending. Taxes have been going up for fifty years without any apparent success in eliminating deficits. That experience suggests Congress will spend whatever the tax system yields plus the highest deficit the public will accept." ["Why the Twin Deficits Are a Blessing," (*The Wall Street Journal,* December 14, 1988), p. A16]. For a thorough examination of the links between tax changes, government spending, and the deficit, see G. M. von Furstenberg, "Taxes: A License to Spend or a Late Charge?" in R. G. Penner, ed., *The Great Fiscal Experiment* (Washington, D.C.: Urban Institute, 1991).

[21]For a calculation of the intergenerational distribution of the burden of U.S. fiscal policy in the 1980s, see A. W. Throop, "Fiscal Policy in the Reagan Years: A Burden on Future Generations?" *Federal Reserve Bank of San Francisco Economic Review* (Winter 1991). A popular survey of the causes and consequences of U.S. fiscal policy in the 1980s is provided by B. Friedman, *Day of Reckoning: The Consequences of*

American Economic Policy Under Reagan and After (New York: Random House, 1988).

[22]An analytical exposition of this point is made by H. Bohn, "Time Consistency of Monetary Policy in the Open Economy," *Journal of International Economics* (February 1991).

[23]The gap between savings and investment includes a statistical discrepancy. The statistical discrepancy arises from the inherent difficulties in measuring items in the GNP identity, particularly savings.

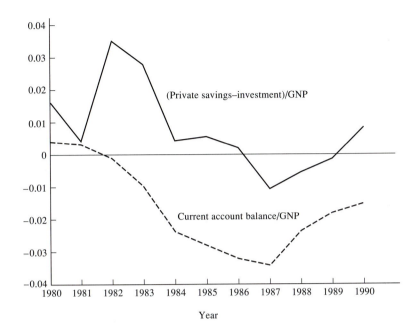

Note: Both the current account balance and the gap between private savings and investment are expressed as a fraction of GNP. The figures for private savings and investment are for gross national savings and investment.

FIGURE 11–5. The Gap Between U.S. Private Savings and Investment and the U.S. Current Account in the 1980s

SOURCE: *Economic Report of the President, 1990* (Washington, D.C.: U.S. Government Printing Office, February 1991).

A shrinking gap between private savings and investment can be the result of a rise in investment, a drop in savings, or both. In the case of the United States, it was private savings that exhibited a downward trend in the 1980s. Private investment certainly did not exhibit an upward trend in this time period, and after 1985 it tended to *decline*. Such a reduction improves rather than worsens the CAB.[24] On the other hand, as depicted by Table 11–3, gross private savings declined from a high of 18 percent of the GNP in 1981 to a low of 14.4 percent in 1990.

The drop of the private savings rate in the United States in the 1980s has been a matter of concern for many experts and policymakers who believe it can have two serious negative consequences. First,

[24]The surge of investment in the United States in some of the years between 1980 and 1985 has been tied to the 1981 Reagan administration tax cuts; according to this view, the rise of the CAB deficit during that period reflected the behavior of investment; see H. W. Sinn, "American Economic Policy and the International Debt Crisis," John M. Ohlin Discussion Paper, Woodrow Wilson School of Public Affairs, Princeton University (October 1990).

at given investment rates, the decline in private savings means greater foreign indebtedness. As we have just shown, the drop in the U.S. private savings rate in the 1980s was indeed partly reflected in higher current account deficits and in the greater external debt these represent. With the United States already becoming the world's largest debtor, there is concern about the rising interest costs of such debt and the nation's ability to repay it eventually. Second, if the lower private savings rates are to be sustained over time without a deterioration of the current account deficit, the implication is that investment rates will have to decline. However, lower investment rates are associated with reduced capital accumulation and, consequently, dwindling economic growth and lower standards of living in the future.

The concern over these scenarios is reflected in the following quote by economist B. Douglas Bernheim: "The United States has become a nation of consumers. During the last decade, Americans maintained high standards of living in part by neglecting the need to provide for their collective future. This cannot continue forever. Inadequate rates of saving have begun to threaten the very foundations of economic prosperity. Before the final bill comes due, Congress and the president must take decisive steps to limit excessive national consumption."[25] The matter is compounded when the private savings rate in the United States is compared with savings rates in other industrialized countries. As economist Martin Feldstein has noted: "The United States has long had one of the lowest saving rates in the world.... The low rate of savings means that the United States has a lower rate of income and possibly a substantially lower level of income growth than would otherwise be possible."[26]

Why did the U.S. private savings rate decline in the 1980s? According to the most popular theory of savings, the *life cycle theory,* the fraction of their income that individuals save varies according to the person's "life cycle." In general, young people save very little as they tend to borrow in order to finance their education and to buy a house, an automobile, and all sorts of consumer durables. As the individual ages, he or she starts to save a higher fraction of income in order to accumulate funds with which to finance consumption after retirement. But when individuals become much older, there is again very little saving—rather, they dissave, using the previously accumulated savings to finance consumption in old age. The aggregate savings rate depends, then, on the population's age structure. The greater the fraction of young and old in the population, the lower the savings rate. In the United States, the years following World War II saw a large number of births. That generation—which became known as the "baby boom" generation—moved into its thirties and forties in the late 1970s and in the 1980s. This represents a high-spending, low-saving period in the life cycle (it represents the peak years in home buying, for example). It was to be expected, then, that the U.S. savings rate would drop in the late 1970s and 1980s. And, as the baby-boomers continue to age, the U.S. private savings rate can be anticipated to rise in the following decades. According to this perspective, the recent drop in the U.S. private savings rate is only a temporary phenomenon that should be reversed in the following decades. As the baby-boomers continue to age, their higher savings rate should be reflected in improved CABs.

The evidence assessing the life-cycle approach suggests that this paradigm cannot completely explain the sustained drop in private savings in the 1980s.[27] Other factors that have been postulated to

[25] B. Douglas Bernheim, *The Vanishing Nest Egg: Reflections on Saving in America* (New York: Priority Press, 1991), p. 1.

[26] M. Feldstein, "Tax Policies for the 1990s: Personal Saving, Investment and Corporate Debt," National Bureau of Economic Research Working Paper no. 2837 (February 1989), p. 4.

[27] See A. J. Auerbach and L. J. Kotlikoff, "Demographics, Fiscal Policy, and U.S. Saving in the 1980s and Beyond," National Bureau of Economic Research Working Paper no. 3150 (October 1989); and J. K. Hill, "Demographics and the

complement it include changes in U.S. personal and business tax policies, which have tended to discourage private savings; the rise in real interest rates in the 1980s, which raised the wealth of older people, inducing them to reduce their savings rate; and the shift in psychological perceptions involved in the decline of Depression-era individuals with conservative spending habits.[28] In response to these hypotheses, a number of government policies has been recommended by economists to stimulate personal and business savings in the 1990s, among which are reductions in capital gains taxes and the restoration of independent retirement accounts (IRAs).[29]

As measured in the national income and product accounts, U.S. gross private savings rates have generally been below those in other industrialized countries in the recent past. These differences tend to remain even when savings rates are adjusted to correct for problems related to the conceptual measurement of gross savings.[30] For instance, gross savings can be broken down into two components: net national savings and depreciation. Depreciation is that part of savings that is set aside to replenish the economy's capital stock—as a

result of the continuous wear and tear associated with production. Net national savings then equals that part of savings that represents new additions to the capital stock owned by domestic residents. Net national savings rates are often preferred as indicators of the wealth-enhancing capacity of savings. If two economies, X and Y, for example, have identical gross savings rates, but country X has a very high rate of depreciation (perhaps because its capital stock is older), country Y will have a higher net savings rate and will augment its capital stock at a higher rate than country X.

On the other hand, the measurement of depreciation is no easy matter, and some prefer to use the gross savings rate to avoid any biases from the faulty measurement of how much capital wears down. Differences in how authorities in different countries measure depreciation can create havoc in comparing net savings rates. This is the case, for instance, when net savings rates in Japan and the United States are compared. In Japan's NIPA, depreciation is valued at book, or acquisition, value—the cost of replacing the worn-out capital at the value the capital had when it was purchased. In the U.S. system, on the other hand, depreciation is valued at replacement costs, which measures the cost of the worn-out capital at the current, market cost of replacing it. Because prices rise over time, depreciation at book value is lower than depreciation at market value. This means that net savings rates in Japan tend to be higher than those in the United States just because of the differences in valuing depreciation in the countries' NIPAs.

University of Pennsylvania economist Fumio Hayashi has adjusted net savings in Japan to coincide with the measurement of net savings in the United States. His results are presented in Figure 11–6, which shows both the adjusted and unadjusted Japanese and U.S. net national savings rates. The data suggest that, although Japanese savings rates exceeded U.S. savings rates in the sample period, since 1975 the gap between the two has diminished and in 1979 the U.S. net savings rate *exceeded* Japan's. These data are consistent

Trade Balance," *Federal Reserve Bank of Dallas Economic Review* (September 1989).

[28]See S. F. Venti and D. A. Wise, "The Saving Effect of Tax-Deferred Retirements Accounts: Evidence from SIPP," in B. Douglas Bernheim and J. B. Shoven, eds., *National Saving and Economic Performance* (Chicago: University of Chicago Press, 1991); E. Sheshinski and V. Tanzi, "An Explanation of the Behavior of Personal Savings in the United States in Recent Years," National Bureau of Economic Research Working Paper no. 3040 (July 1989); and B. Douglas Bernheim, *The Vanishing Nest Egg: Reflections on Saving in America* (New York: Priority Press, 1991).

[29] See the various articles in M. Kosters, ed., *Personal Saving, Consumption, and Tax Policy* (Washington D.C.: American Enterprise Institute, 1992) and C. E. Walker et. al., eds., *The U.S. Savings Challenge: Policy Options for Productivity and Growth* (Boulder, Colo.: Westview Press, 1990).

[30] This is documented by C. Y. Horiba, "Why Is Japan's Household Saving Rate So High? A Literature Survey," *Journal of the Japanese and International Economies* (January 1990), table 1.

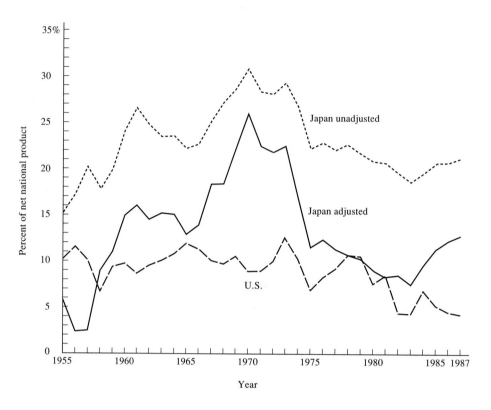

FIGURE 11–6.   Comparing Savings Rates in the United States and Japan

SOURCE: F. Hayashi, "Japan's Savings Rate: New Data and Reflections," National Bureau of Economic Research Working Paper no. 3205 (December 1989), fig. 1.

with the view that high Japanese savings rates have been a temporary phenomenon linked to Japan's desire to rebuild its economic capacity after World War II. Professor Hayashi suggests that his results may point to a convergence of savings rates in the future.[31] However, the noticeable divergence in the trend of the savings rates in the 1980s—with the U.S. rate declining and the Japanese rate increasing—appears to run against

that hypothesis. In any case, these figures point to the many difficulties involved in using NIPAs to compare savings rates across nations.[32]

Summary

1. The National Income and Product Accounts (NIPA) are involved in measuring the components of an economy's aggregate income and

---

[31] F. Hayashi, "Japan's Savings Rate: New Data and Reflections," National Bureau of Economic Research Working Paper no. 3205 (December 1989), fig. 1.

[32] For a thorough discussion of the many problems involved in measuring savings, see W. E. Cullison, "Is Saving Too Low in the United States?" *Federal Reserve Bank of Richmond Economic Review* (May–June 1990).

output. The basic national income accounting concept is the national income or GNP identity; it breaks down GNP—the value of all the final goods and services produced by a country's residents in a given period—into various spending categories.

2. Domestic absorption represents all the expenditures of domestic residents. The CAB is equal to the difference between income and domestic absorption.

3. The CAB can also be seen as the difference between gross national savings and gross national investment—or, alternatively, as the sum of the government budget surplus and the difference between private savings and private investment.

4. Economists M. Feldstein and C. Horioka found that higher national savings rates were closely matched by higher investment rates for a sample of OECD countries between 1980 and 1986. They explained this result as suggesting the presence of restrictions on the mobility of capital in those countries. Recent studies by Feldstein and P. Bacchetta and others suggest that this conclusion is no longer warranted.

5. The U.S. CAB deficit deteriorated drastically in the 1980s. During the same period, there were increased budget deficits and reduced private savings rates.

6. According to the Ricardian approach to budget deficits, increased budget deficits should not cause higher CAB deficits. Higher budget deficits will raise private savings rates, as households reduce consumption in order to pay for the expected future taxes that will be required to finance the public debt.

7. The public debt of the United States has increased sharply since the early 1980s. However, the current debt-GNP ratios are not unusual by historical standards and remain below those in other industrialized economies.

8. Gross private savings in the United States declined from a high of 18 percent of the GNP in 1981 to a low of 14.4 percent in 1990.

According to the life-cycle theory of savings, the drop in savings can be explained by demographics. Savings tend to be the lowest during the midlife years. The aging of the so-called baby-boomers into their thirties and forties in the late 1970s and 1980s should thus have been reflected in lower savings rate. Other explanations for the drop in U.S. private savings rates include changes in U.S. personal and business tax policies and shifts in psychological perceptions linked to the reduced presence of depression-era individuals with conservative spending habits.

Problems

1. In the text, it was established that the CAB is equal to the difference between gross national savings minus gross national investment. Show that the balance on goods and services is equal to gross domestic investment minus gross domestic savings, where gross domestic investment is the sum of the private and public investment spending of domestic residents and gross domestic savings is equal to the excess of GDP over the consumption spending of domestic residents (assume that unilateral transfers are equal to zero).

2. Suppose that the U.S. government decides to reduce the capital gains tax. How would you expect this policy change to affect the CAB? Explain your answer.

3. Suppose that in response to growing concerns by some economists, President Clinton decides to raise income taxes in order to eliminate completely the U.S. government budget deficit. Would this improve the U.S. CAB? What would the Ricardian approach suggest? Explain your answer.

4. Do you think the Feldstein-Horioka observation that rising savings rates have matched rising investment rates in the OECD countries holds for South Korea? Explain why and supply data to support your conclusion.

5. The table to the right provides figures for the NIPAs of Mexico for 1980 and 1982. On the basis of these figures, answer the following questions:

(a) Did the Mexican CAB, as a fraction of the GNP, deteriorate between 1980 and 1982?

(b) Break the CAB down into savings minus investment (as a fraction of the GNP, as given by Equation 11–5). Are there any changes from 1980 to 1982?

(c) Break the CAB down into its budget surplus and private savings-private investment components (as fractions of the GNP, as depicted in Table 11–3). Are there any changes in these components between 1980 and 1982?

(d) How did the CAB and its components in Mexico compare with those in the United States?

6. Consider the following statement made by University of Virginia historian Mark Thomas about the U.S. trade deficit: "Perhaps the simplest lesson to be drawn from history . . . is that the trade deficit is not more than the surface manifestation of more elemental economic forces. In the nineteenth century, it was the pull of American opportunity for foreign capital that generated deficits; today, it is the combination of low savings and unbalanced budgets that is at work." [From: M. Thomas, "Who's Afraid of the Big Bad Trade Deficit?" in D. N. McCloskey, ed., *Second Thoughts: Myths and Morals of U.S. Economic History* (Oxford: Oxford University Press, 1993), p. 95]. Do you agree or disagree with this statement? Explain.

Mexico's National Income Accounts
(in millions of Mexican pesos)

	1980	1982
Gross National Product (GNP)	4,341	380,544
Absorption (A_N)	4,572	388,459
Private Consumption (C_N)	2,909	267,876
Private Investment (I_N)	854	13,763
Government Spending (G_N)	809	106,820
Current Account Balance (CAB_N)	−231	−7,915

Mexican Government Consolidated Budget

	1980	1982
Government Revenue (TX_N)	675	68,588
Government Spending (G_N)	809	106,820
Government Consumption ($C_N{}^G$)	449	39,876
Government Investment ($I_N{}^G$)	360	66,944
Government Budget Balance ($TX_N - G_N$)	−1,454	−38,232

SOURCE: World Bank, *World Tables: 1989–1990 Edition* (Baltimore: Johns Hopkins University Press, 1990).

CHAPTER 12

The External Debt Crisis of Developing Countries

On August 13, 1982, the government of Mexico announced that it could not continue to pay the interest and principal on its $80 billion external debt; at the same time, it requested a $3-billion loan that would enable it to continue its debt payments. The event marked the beginning of a deep debt crisis that spread like a forest fire across a large number of Latin American countries, most African countries, and various East European and Asian economies. One by one, difficulties in making external debt payments led countries to lose access to private international financial markets, especially commercial bank lending. The large financial inflows that many developing coun-

tries benefited from in the 1970s and early 1980s—and that marked the massive growth of Eurolending—had dried up, giving rise instead to a decade of net capital outflows. As late as 1991, none of the heavily indebted countries was able to obtain new loans from commercial banks on the same basis as before the debt crisis. Credit was still available, but it was granted with many strings attached and under close monitoring by lenders.

The impact of the debt crisis on the countries involved has been enormous. The collapse of economic conditions in many debtor countries lasted throughout the decade and extended into the early 1990s. Standards of living reverted to the levels of the 1970s and 1960s in Argentina, Chile, Venezuela, Nicaragua, and other places. Brazil faced stagnation and widespread despair after decades of superior growth within Latin America. Popular desperation with diving standards of living led to economic turmoil and political change. The fall of entrenched dictatorships and the movement toward democracy in Latin America in the 1980s and 1990s represent to a great extent a reaction to the debt crisis and the government policies associated with it.[1] Similar pressures and a movement toward democratization surfaced in Africa, affecting Socialist Ethiopia and other nations. Even the collapse of Communist-styled socialism in countries like Poland can be related to the economic difficulties associated with the heavy burden of external debt.

This chapter analyzes the genesis and nature of the debt crisis, its consequences, and the responses of borrowers and lenders. The discussion attempts to provide answers to the following questions: Why did the crisis emerge so abruptly and unexpectedly, and what was the relative role played by external events and domestic policies in bringing it about? Why is it that the crisis does not seem to have been properly anticipated by financial markets, and why did banks expose themselves so deeply by overlending? Why did it last so long? What has been done about it in terms of government policies in both borrowing and lending countries? These problems are approached in a comparative way, contrasting the similarities and differences among the various heavily indebted developing countries.

---

[1]Political scientist Paul Drake of the University of California, San Diego, finds that democracies have more flexibility than authoritarian regimes in dealing with the economic adjustments required by the debt crisis. Indeed, the 1980s saw a shift from seven democracies and thirteen dictatorships to seventeen democracies and three dictatorships in Latin America; see P. Drake, "Debt and Democracy in Latin America," in B. Stallings and R. Kaufman, eds., *Debt and Democracy in Latin America* (Boulder, Colo.: Westview Press, 1989); see also S. Haggard and R. Kaufman, "Economic Adjustment and the Prospects for Democracy," in *The Politics of Economic Adjustment* (Princeton: Princeton University Press, 1992).

12–1. THE EXTENT OF THE DEBT PROBLEM

External debt refers to all the fixed-income foreign claims to which a debtor nation is subject. For most developing countries, external debt is largely bank debt because bond indebtedness is not used as frequently as a source of financing. The total external debt of developing countries surged from a total of $560 billion in 1980 to more than $800 billion in 1983 and more than $1.6 trillion in 1992. Table 12–1 shows the levels of external debt of the most heavily indebted developing countries, as computed by the World Bank. In 1991, the three developing countries with the largest debt volumes were Brazil ($116.5 billion), Mexico ($101.7 billion), and Indonesia ($73.7 billion). Table 12–1 also shows that three of the top six megaborrowers are in Latin America. Indeed, Latin America has a much higher absolute level of debt than other regions, as indicated in Table 12–2, part A, where the volume of external debt is broken down geographically. The $439.7 billion in Latin American debt at the end of 1991 was more than twice that in sub-Saharan Africa, and more than three times that in South Asia.

The picture that emerges from the data, then, points toward Latin America as the major developing country debtor, which some observers attribute to the huge borrowing engaged in by Latin American countries as compared to other nations. This is indeed the view one gets from the press, which reports incessant Latin debt negotiations and renegotiations, whether by Mexico, Brazil, or Peru. There is no question that, in terms of difficulties in making external debt payments, Latin America has been a region of incomparable crisis in the 1980s and early 1990s. However, two important observations must be made. First, as Table 12–2, part A shows, in the 1980s, Latin American debt grew more slowly than in other regions. From 1980 to 1991, its debt rose by 81 percent, while in South Asia the debt grew by 217 percent, in North Africa and the Middle East by

TABLE 12–1. **External Debt Indicators for the Developing Countries with Largest Indebtedness 1991 (in billions of dollars)**

Country	Total Debt Outstanding	Debt/GNP (percent)
Brazil	$116.5	29%
Mexico	101.7	37
Indonesia	73.7	66
India	71.6	29
Former Soviet Union	67.2	—
Argentina	63.7	49
China	60.8	16
Poland	52.5	61
Turkey	50.3	48
Egypt	40.6	130
Republic of Korea	40.5	14
Thailand	35.8	39
Nigeria	34.5	109
Venezuela	34.4	65
Philippines	31.9	70
Algeria	28.6	70
Panama	22.9	130
Malaysia	21.4	48
Morocco	21.2	80
Peru	20.7	43
Ivory Coast	18.8	223
Syrian Arab Republic	16.8	—
Sudan	15.9	222
Nicaragua	10.5	728

SOURCE: World Bank, *World Debt Tables: 1992–93* (Washington, D.C.: World Bank, December 1992), Tables A.VI.3 and A.VI.4, pp. 132–135.

121 percent, in East Asia and the Pacific by 203 percent, in Africa south of the Sahara by 216 percent, and for Europe and the Mediterranean by 226 percent. Second, once debt figures are examined in a careful and comparative way, Latin America does not appear to be unusual compared to other developing countries. When comparing economic conditions across countries, one should beware of using absolute levels of debt since such a measure does not take into account variations in the size of the economies involved. A country can have a large amount of debt just because it is a large country,

with a large GNP or population, even though its debt is small in relation to GNP or in per capita terms. To correct for size, economists calculate debt-GNP ratios or per capita levels of debt.

Adjusting for size significantly alters the picture as to which countries are the most heavily indebted. As Table 12, part B shows, debt-GNP ratios in Latin America are not unusually high by world standards. In 1980, just before the onset of the crisis, Latin American countries had, on average, a debt-GNP that was similar to that in North Africa and the Middle East; the ratio was not that

TABLE 12–2.   **Measuring External Indebtedness, by Geographical Region (in billions of dollars)**

Year	Sub-Saharan Africa	East Asia and Pacific	Europe and Central Asia	North Africa and Middle East	Latin America and Caribbean	South Asia
A. Absolute Levels of Debt						
1980	$ 56.2	$ 88.6	$ 80.7	$ 66.3	$242.5	$ 38.1
1983	79.8	139.0	95.5	76.4	361.0	55.0
1985	98.8	166.1	157.6	109.6	390.1	68.3
1987	142.8	202.6	204.7	141.9	445.8	92.6
1989	153.9	204.8	219.4	149.3	422.7	103.7
1991	178.0	268.7	263.4	146.7	439.7	120.9
B. Debt/GNP (percent)						
1980	29.2%	16.9%	27.6%	33.1%	35.1%	17.3%
1983	43.4	24.8	37.3	32.8	58.6	21.7
1985	56.1	29.3	19.5	32.8	61.3	24.7
1987	97.4	32.6	21.2	47.3	64.9	28.4
1989	103.0	23.4	22.4	55.6	47.8	29.1
1991	109.6	28.2	26.1	57.9	41.4	34.3

SOURCE: World Bank, *World Debt Tables, 1992–93* (Washington, D.C.: World Bank, December 1992), Summary Tables, pp. 160–187.

much greater than that for the Sub-Saharan Africa region and for the debtors in Europe and the Mediterranean region. Debt-GNP ratios generally went up in the developing world until 1987, reflecting the sluggishness of those countries to surpass the crisis. Since 1987, Latin American countries have reduced their debt/GNP ratios, but the rest of the developing world has not. In 1991, as Table 12–2(B) shows, the degree of indebtedness (measured by debt/GNP) in Africa and the Middle East was the greatest worldwide. The debt-GNP ratio for Latin America and the Caribbean was not unusually high by global standards.

The significance of correcting for size in evaluating degree of indebtedness is also evident when debt-GNP figures are computed for the heavily indebted developing countries listed in Table 12–1. The calculation is depicted in the second column of that table. Once size is adjusted for, the nations with the highest debt-GNP ratio are not Brazil or Mexico but Nicaragua, Ivory Coast, Egypt, Sudan, and Panama. For each of the latter, total external debt surpasses the value of GNP. Note that this is a different group from that yielded by the rankings based on absolute levels of debt. Brazil and Mexico are the two nations with the highest total debt outstanding in the sample, yet Brazil's debt/GNP value (29 percent) is among the lowest in the sample, and so is Mexico's.

Our analysis makes clear that countries in Latin America and the Caribbean do not have unusually high indebtedness ratios when compared to other developing nations. Yet, a significant part of Latin America is involved in a debt imbroglio, with some countries struggling even to pay for the interest on its external debt. What explains the Latin American debt crisis? In order to clarify the nature of the debt problem, the next section identifies some key traits of debtor countries.

TABLE 12–3. **Interest Payments/GNP, Developing Countries (percent)**

Year	Sub-Saharan Africa	East Asia and Pacific	Europe and Central Asia	North Africa and Middle East	Latin America and Caribbean	South Asia
1980	1.7%	1.5%	2.2%	2.1%	3.5%	0.6%
1983	2.2	2.0	2.8	2.1	5.6	0.9
1985	2.7	2.2	1.4	1.5	5.5	1.0
1987	2.5	2.1	1.3	1.6	4.1	1.2
1989	3.0	1.7	1.4	2.4	2.9	1.3
1991	3.2	1.7	1.4	2.4	2.5	1.3

SOURCE: World Bank, *World Debt Tables, 1992–93* (Washington, D.C.: World Bank, December 1992), Summary Tables, pp. 160–187.

12–2. WHAT IS THE MARK OF A DEBT-RIDDEN COUNTRY?

What determines which countries face and which do not face a crippling debt problem? Why are so many Latin American countries in the list of severely-indebted middle-income countries?[2] Answers to these questions help pinpoint the real sources of the debt crisis.

Interest Rates, Debt Service, and the Debt Crisis

Table 12–3 shows the interest payments developing countries pay on their external debt, expressed as a fraction of GNP and broken down by region. Consider the figures for 1980 and 1983, which represent the period when the debt crisis first exploded. Two facts stand out: Latin America has the highest fraction of GNP dedicated to paying interest on its debt and, between 1980 and 1983, this fraction climbed from 3.5 to 5.6 percent.

The interest/GNP figures for Latin America in Table 12–3 are significant because the rise of

interest payments on the debt was directly linked to the failure of many of the heavily indebted developing countries to *service* their external debt. Debt service refers to loan amortization and payments of the interest on the loans. Loan amortization is the disbursements made by the borrower to repay the loans. A loan is in *default* when the borrower does not make the payments specified in the loan contract. Defaulting borrowers frequently repay their loans in full, but with a delay. *Repudiation* arises if the borrower refuses to pay and ceases to recognize the lender's claim. When debt commitments are repudiated, the borrowing country asserts that it does not intend to pay the loan, even after a delay. Although default usually leads to negotiations with the lender that are intended to allow the borrower to get some time to pay off its debts, repudiation is an extreme measure. It closes off the borrower's access to further credit by the lender, and it may shut it out of the entire international financial community.[3] Defaults have permeated the debt crisis of the 1980s and 1990s, but no repudiation has occurred yet.

The rise of the interest payments made by Latin American countries on their debts between 1980

[2]The World Bank distinguishes among severely indebted low-income and middle-income countries. The severely indebted low-income countries (SILICs), are dominated by Sub-Saharan countries. See World Bank, *World Debt Tables: 1992–93* (Washington, D.C.: World Bank, 1992), p. 155.

[3]For a discussion of defaults and repudiations of U.S. state debts in the 1840s, see W. B. English, "When America Defaulted: American State Debts in the 1840s," Department of Economics University of Pennsylvania (January 1991) (mimeo.).

and 1983 was a heavy burden that some countries were unable to handle. The debt crisis is closely related to the inability of these borrowing countries to service their debts. What explains the rise of interest payments? Figure 12–1 provides a graphic answer to this question. It shows the behavior of the London Interbank Offered Rate (LIBOR) in the 1970s and 1980s. As was noted in Chapter 8, on Eurocurrency markets, LIBOR is the interest rate that commercial banks use as a basis in setting interest rates on developing country loans. Interest rates on these loans are given by LIBOR plus a certain percentage—called the spread—which varies according to various factors, including the riskiness of the loan. Interest rates on

developing country loans are often floating-rate loans—that is, loans whose interest rate is adjusted at certain intervals (e.g., three months or a year). If LIBOR increases, the borrower will face higher interest payments. Figure 12–1 documents the surge of the six-month LIBOR from an average of 9.2 percent in 1978 to 18.3 percent in the third quarter of 1981. This increase resulted in a substantial magnification of the interest payments that developing countries had to pay on their debts.

The rise in interest rates explains the difficulties that debtor countries faced in servicing their debts in the early 1980s. However, why were Latin American countries more adversely affected than other developing countries? Why was the interest/GNP

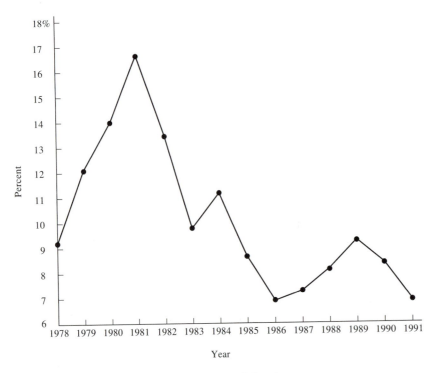

Note: The interest rate is on 3-month interbank deposits.

FIGURE 12–1.   The London Interbank Offered Rate (LIBOR), 1978–1991*

SOURCE: International Monetary Fund, *International Financial Statistics,* various issues.

ratio of 5.6 percent faced by Latin America and the Caribbean in 1983 more than twice that of developing countries in most other regions? One key element in the explanation is that loans to these economies were granted mostly by the private sector, with relatively limited participation by so-called official lenders. Private creditors or lenders include, among others, commercial banks and individuals or companies holding bonds issued by the debtor country. *Official credit* is granted by governments and international lending organizations such as the IMF. Official lending can be classified as either multilateral or bilateral, according to the type of creditor. Multilateral lending is supplied by multilateral organizations such as the IMF and the World Bank, which represent a group of member countries. Bilateral credit is granted by individual governments, such as the U.S. government, when they engage in lending to selected nations bilaterally—that is, on a one-to-one basis.

Latin America's external debt is owed primarily to the private sector (commercial banks); in other regions, however, especially in Asia and Africa, the external debt is owed mostly to official creditors. The share of external debt owed to official creditors in Latin America was 17.7 percent in 1980 and 29.6 percent in 1989. By contrast, in 1980, 55 percent of the African and Middle Eastern debt was owed to official creditors, and in 1989 the figure was close to 70 percent. In South Asia, 89.8 percent of the external debt was owed to official creditors in 1980 and 72.5 percent in 1989. Within the developing world, Latin American countries, on average, were by far the most immersed in borrowing from private banks.

Why did Latin countries rely so much on private banks compared to other regions, such as Asia and Africa? Part of the answer lies in the relatively high income levels of Latin American economies by developing country standards. Official loans are one way that governments of industrialized countries and multilateral institutions seek to provide aid to very poor economies. However, most Latin American countries are not in the poorest category. In 1990, according to figures provided by the World Bank, there were no Latin American countries with a GNP per capita lower than $590, but it was that low for thirty-five African and Asian countries.[4] A second factor behind the comparative lack of official credit received by Latin American countries lies in the fact that industrialized countries' lending often follows the lenders' foreign policy priorities. In the case of the United States, evident foreign policy interests have led to the supply of vast amounts of official credit to Middle Eastern and East European countries.

Credits obtained from official sources differ from commercial bank loans in various respects. First, official credits are frequently granted at concessional interest rates—that is, at interest rates below the prevailing market rate. This is explained by the previously noted fact that many official loans are offered to low-income countries. They thus have a development-assistance component to them that is reflected in the lower interest rates. Second, official credits tend to be fixed-rate loans (as compared to the floating-rate loans offered by private banks) and have longer and more flexible amortization periods than private-sector loans. Official loans are thus comparatively sheltered from the whims of short-run market interest-rate fluctuations, such as the marked rise of world interest rates in the 1970s and early 1980s. Finally, official debtors have been known to react in a remarkably flexible way toward debtor countries in situations of financial distress. For instance, in March 1991, Western governments decided to cut substantially the debt that Poland owed them. This negotiated measure released financial pressures and took Poland out of the "top five" group of debtors. In May 1991, Egypt also received debt concessions and reductions. Official creditors agreed to write off more than $10 billion out of the more than $20 billion of debt then owed to the United States and

---

[4]World Bank, *World Development Report, 1992* (Oxford: Oxford University Press, 1992).

the other governments that were allies in the 1990–1991 conflict with Iraq.[5]

In contrast to the sometimes benign experience of some debtor countries with official credit, Latin America's predominantly private-sector loans were deeply affected by the surge of market interest rates in the late 1970s and early 1980s. The interest-rate hike resulted in massive increases in the interest payments of Latin American countries when compared to developing nations more dependent on official debt. This helps explain why the 1982 debt crisis was predominantly a Latin American problem.

Inward Orientation, Trade Regimes, and the Ability to Export

A second factor that helps to explain why some countries fell into a debt crisis in the 1980s while others did not involves policymaker differences regarding international trade. Three main types of trade policy can be observed among developing countries: inward-oriented, natural-resource exports-oriented, and industrial-exports-oriented. Inward-oriented trade regimes, or *import-substitution regimes,* are countries in which the government has encouraged the production of goods that compete with imports. The goal is to reduce the consumption of foreign goods and improve the CAB by producing import substitutes domestically. To do this, the government imposes a whole array of policies—such as tariffs and quotas—to discourage imports. In general, inward-

oriented policies favoring increased domestic production of import substitutes act to discourage the production of exports by shifting resources from export-producing industries to import-substituting sectors. Import substitution regimes can thus seriously undermine a country's export base.

Natural-resource exports-oriented regimes, by contrast, seek to exploit natural resources and to raise the nation's export of raw materials such as oil, copper, and tin. Such a policy however, does not necessarily mean that the economy's export base becomes more solid. It is now well known that countries that have expanded their export of natural resources have simultaneously weakened their exports of manufactured goods. Economists refer to this problem as the Dutch disease, after the squeeze placed on traditional export sectors of the Dutch economy by the rapid development of its natural gas industry. (The exact mechanisms explaining how increased exports of natural resources result in reduced exports of manufactured goods will be discussed in the next chapter. Suffice it to point out here that exports of natural resources pull resources out of other sectors, including manufactured goods, thus reducing their output.) Another problem of resource-oriented regimes is that the exploitation of many of their resources requires formidable capital expenditures. These investments have been almost invariably undertaken by governments and have resulted in substantial public debt.

The third type of trade regime, *manufacturing-exports-oriented regimes,* have not generally involved the economy in huge governmental natural resource projects or in policies blocking international trade; rather, they have aimed at liberalizing international transactions in goods and, if anything, promoted exports of manufactured goods.

Of the three trade regimes just considered, only the industrial-exports-oriented regime was able to provide a solid basis to sustain the increased interest burden faced by heavily indebted countries in the 1980s. In order to avoid falling into further external debt, the debtor countries had to be able

---

[5]In Poland, debt reduction was partly intended to facilitate market-oriented economic reforms and the country's reinsertion into the world trade system. The concessions to Egypt, on the other hand, were a response to that country's support of the U.S.-led coalition of nations in the 1991 Persian Gulf War. The debt relief was to compensate Egypt for losses from tourist spending, Suez Canal revenues, and remittances from two million Egyptians working in Kuwait and Iraq before the conflict emerged. See S. Greenhouse, "Half of Egypt's $20.2 Billion Debt Being Forgiven by U.S. and Allies," *The New York Times,* May 27, 1991.

to finance higher interest payments on the debt by sustaining larger trade-balance surpluses. In order to augment the trade balance, either exports of goods and services had to increase, imports decrease, or both. Imports of goods and services are directly related to domestic economic activity (when domestic income declines, individuals and businesses curtail their consumption of foreign goods and services). Reducing imports is thus concomitant with recession, and it represents a painful and politically difficult policy. The reduction in imports can be ameliorated through higher export earnings, but in countries with inward-oriented strategies, exports represent a relatively small proportion of GNP and cannot therefore serve as an engine for improving the trade balance significantly. At the same time, the export earnings of countries following natural-resource-based strategies are dependent on the prices of raw materials in world markets. In the 1980s, many of those prices deteriorated, making it impossible for natural-resource exports-oriented countries to sustain higher export earnings. Only outward-oriented countries with strong manufactured exports were able to navigate through the 1980s without a crisis: Even though they faced higher interest payments on their debts, the solidity of their export base allowed them more flexibility in generating the trade surpluses required to finance the growing interest payments.[6]

The research carried out by a team of economists under the direction of Harvard University's Jeffrey D. Sachs finds that the external trade regimes followed by Latin American countries had much to do with their crises. As Sachs concludes: "All of the Latin American countries are judged to be moderately or extremely inward oriented, except for Brazil during the 1970s, which was designated by the World Bank as moderately outward oriented. No Latin American country showed an important rise in the share of manufactured exports in GNP during the 1970s."[7] This conclusion is reflected in the high ratios of debt to exports exhibited in Latin American economies. The ratio of a country's debt relative to its exports earnings is an important indicator of a country's ability to sustain higher external debt payments without a major crisis. Given the debt, the higher the export earnings, the larger the country's ability to earn the foreign exchange necessary to finance increased debt payments. Indeed, if debt-exports ratios are calculated for heavily indebted countries on the eve of the debt crisis in 1981, a high degree of association is found between these ratios and the country's ability to avoid debt crisis in the 1980s. For instance, in 1981, South Korea was a heavily indebted country with a debt-GNP ratio that exceeded Mexico's and Brazil's. Yet, South Korea survived the 1980s without a crisis, while both Brazil and Mexico had to stop payments on their debts. It is telling that the debt-exports ratio for South Korea in 1981 (in percentage terms) was equal to 122.1 percent while the corresponding figures for Brazil and Mexico were 296.3 percent and 257.5 percent, respectively. More generally, for crisis-free countries, debt-exports ratios are usually less than 100 percent. Debt-stricken nations tend to have debts equivalent to twice to four times the level of their exports.

The Uses and Misuses of External Debt: Consumption Versus Investment

A third set of factors that have been postulated to explain the debt crisis surrounds the uses of the funds borrowed by developing countries. Some economists have stressed that the loans were used for consumption purposes and were not invested properly. It is argued that the borrowed money was

---

[6]The role of trade policies in determining differences in the economic behavior of developing countries in East Asia and Latin America has been emphasized by Sachs in "Developing Country Debt," in M. Feldstein, ed., *International Economic Cooperation* (Chicago: University of Chicago Press, 1988).

[7]Introduction in J. D. Sachs, ed., *Developing Country Debt and Economic Performance,* vol. 2 (Chicago: University of Chicago Press, 1990), p. 11.

not put to good use, having been wasted in conspicuous consumption by public officials, bribes, corruption, excessive hiring of government employees, and in purchasing military equipment. Presumably, if the funds had been invested wisely, countries would have been able to repay them.

Although misuse of funds obtained from external debt loans can be detected in some countries, the issue should not be overemphasized.[8] No one visiting Latin America could fail to see the proliferating structures reflecting massive investments in oil-production facilities and hydroelectric and mining projects, for example. The extent to which developing country loans were used for investment purposes is, therefore, an empirical question to be examined carefully on the basis of the facts. One problem is the lack of comprehensive, carefully collected data on consumption and investment in developing countries. The figures supplied here are provided by governments to international organizations like the IMF and the World Bank. Many developing-country governments, however, do not have the institutional capabilities to monitor the use of fiscal revenues accurately or to estimate private sector consumption and investment with confidence. In fact, in some of these economies the underground, informal sector accounts for a great part of economic activity. By definition, the activities of the informal sector are not recorded by the government. There are also difficulties determining the accounts of public enterprises, which are often kept separate from those of the general government. Given these caveats, we proceed to examine the issue of investment rates in Latin America.

Table 12−4 presents the investment rates (gross domestic investment/GNP) for a group of Latin American debtors, developing countries in general, and economies in the OECD, as computed from World Bank data.[9] Note first of all the

variability of the investment rates both by countries and by regions. This suggests that, in examining the nature of the debt crisis, the substantial differences existing among the various countries be taken into account. Therefore general trends cannot be relied on exclusively in seeking to explain the origins of debt in particular countries. For instance, within Latin America, Uruguay has had chronically low investment rates while Venezuela has sustained world-high investment rates equal to more than 40 percent of its GDP. Overall, and especially since the mid-1970s, Latin American countries have had investment rates that exceed those of the OECD and are above average for developing countries in general. Table 12−4 indicates that African and South Asian countries have been the countries exhibiting comparatively low investment rates. For instance, in 1974, the investment rate in South Asia was equal to 16.1 percent, while in Latin America and the Caribbean it was equal to 22.1 percent.[10] Investment rates in Latin America were near or over 20 percent before the debt crisis emerged. Presumably, the increased productive capacity associated with these investments should have yielded payoffs that would have provided the resources to repay loan commitments.[11] If many Latin American countries had relatively high investment rates, what explains then the debt crisis that exploded in 1982?

One explanation is that, although productive capacity was increased, investments failed to generate long-run growth because (1) a substantial

---

[8]For a description of some of the rackets, see R. T. Naylor, *Hot Money and the Politics of Debt* (New York: Linden/Simon & Schuster, 1987).

[9]OECD countries include European Community members, Japan, and the United States.

[10]The point that investment rates in Latin America have been high by world standards was originally made by J. D. Sachs, "The Current Account and Macroeconomic Adjustment in the 1970s," *Brookings Papers on Economic Activity* (1981).

[11]The Latin external debt was associated with CAB deficits that indicated a shortfall of domestic savings relative to investment. Savings rates in Latin America, however, have not been low by world standards. For instance, in the 1970s, South Asia had gross savings rates below 20 percent, while in Latin America they were generally above 20 percent. The CAB deficits were accounted for by the fact that, in spite of comparatively high savings rates, investment rates were even greater.

TABLE 12–4. **Investment Rates in Selected Countries and Regions, 1970–1990**

	1970	1972	1974	1976	1978	1980	1982	1984	1986	1988	1990
1. Selected Latin American Countries											
Argentina	21.6	20.8	19.3	26.8	24.4	22.2	15.9	11.3	8.8	16.4	11.9
Bolivia	23.8	29.6	21.4	28.3	24.0	14.8	13.8	7.2	7.9	11.9	13.5
Brazil	20.5	21.2	25.4	23.1	23.0	23.3	21.0	15.3	19.2	21.8	—
Chile	16.5	12.2	21.2	12.8	17.8	21.0	11.3	13.6	14.6	17.0	19.4
Mexico	21.3	19.0	21.8	21.0	22.3	27.2	22.9	19.9	18.3	20.6	14.4
Peru	15.5	15.2	25.9	21.9	19.4	27.5	31.3	22.2	22.4	25.7	20.6
Uruguay	11.5	11.8	11.5	14.8	16.0	17.3	14.4	9.9	8.2	9.8	—
Venezuela	32.9	33.2	26.1	36.2	43.9	26.4	27.7	17.5	20.9	28.0	15.9
2. Developing Countries: By Region											
Sub-Saharan Africa	15.1	17.5	17.5	23.1	21.1	19.9	17.3	10.8	15.1	15.6	15.5
South Asia	16.3	15.9	17.9	19.4	21.0	22.0	22.5	21.2	22.7	22.5	21.2
East Asia and Pacific	26.5	25.5	27.6	27.1	30.8	30.4	29.0	29.7	32.3	33.6	—
Latin America and Caribbean	21.3	20.5	23.1	23.6	24.5	24.3	21.7	16.8	17.7	20.9	—
Middle East and North Africa	19.3	21.3	23.0	29.3	26.9	29.0	22.5	23.5	26.5	24.5	—
3. High Income OECD Countries											
EEC	22.3	21.9	24.0	23.4	22.1	23.0	20.0	19.7	19.4	20.9	—
Japan	37.6	34.9	37.6	32.1	31.0	32.3	30.1	28.3	28.0	31.1	—
United States	12.0	15.5	15.7	15.5	18.4	16.0	14.4	17.9	15.7	15.3	15.1

Investment Rate = Gross Domestic Investment/GDP

Figures for European developing countries are not presented because investment rates for the Socialist countries in this group were not available.

SOURCE: World Bank, *World Tables 1991* (Baltimore: Johns Hopkins University Press, 1991).

share of the funds was invested in inefficient import-substituting industries that required sustained protection and subsidization to survive (they could not provide a solid basis for self-sustained economic growth, and were limited to supplying a limited domestic market); and (2) investments in the exploitation of natural resources and in the export of raw materials failed to yield the expected rates of return as a result of drops in the prices of these products in world markets, a phenomenon we will discuss shortly.

A problem encountered in analyzing the impact of external borrowing by focusing on aggregate investment in the economy is that it ignores the issues relating to the disaggregation of this aggregate into its public and private components. The next section examines the role played by the public sector in the debt crisis.

12–3. BUDGET DEFICITS AND THE PUBLIC EXTERNAL DEBT

Public external borrowing has been an increasingly important source of revenues for the governments of developing countries and has consistently

TABLE 12–5. **Budget Deficits in Heavily Indebted Developing Countries, 1978–1988 (as a percent of GDP)**

	1978	1979	1980	1981	1982	1983	1984	1985	1986	1987	1988
Overall* surplus(+) or Deficit(−)	−2.6%	−1.6%	−2.1%	−5.4%	−7.4%	−4.2%	−2.7%	−2.8%	−4.0%	−5.0%	−3.8%
Primary surplus(+) or Deficit(−)	−1.7	−0.9	−1.3	−4.4	−2.7	1.0	2.4	2.5	1.0	0.1	1.4

* Overall surplus or deficit on the fiscal accounts of the consolidated public sector.

Note: Heavily indebted countries included in this sample are Argentina, Bolivia, Brazil, Chile, Colombia, Ivory Coast, Ecuador, Mexico, Morocco, Peru, the Philippines, Uruguay, Venezuela and Yugoslavia.

SOURCE: Based on P. Guidotti and M. S. Kumar, "Domestic Public Debt of Externally Indebted Countries," *IMF Occasional Paper* no. 80 (June 1991), table 11.

comprised a growing part of their external borrowing. In 1970, 57 percent of the stock of all Latin external debt was public or publicly guaranteed; by 1992 the corresponding figure was 93 percent.[12] Public debt is even more significant in African and Middle Eastern countries, where the percentage of the debt engaged by the public sector—or publicly guaranteed—has been above 95 since the 1970s. This public external borrowing is directly related to the expansion of government budget deficits in the 1970s and 1980s. Table 12–5 depicts the budget deficits of heavily indebted developing countries, as a percentage of GDP, from 1978 to 1988. Note the rapid growth of

the deficits from 1979 to 1982: In three years, the average deficit in these countries grew from 1.6 percent of their GDP to 7.4 percent. Observe also that, although there was deficit reduction after the crisis, the overall public sector deficits have remained way above 1979 levels.

The implication so far is that, although investment rates in heavily indebted countries have been relatively high, the investments have been carried out to a great extent by the government. What special problems are associated with public sector—as compared to private sector—investment? The case of Mexico illustrates the problems linked to government investment.[13] Public investment in Mexico increased in the late 1970s and exploded between 1980 and 1982. A large share of the government's investments was in the exploitation and export of oil resources, massive deposits of which had been confirmed in the 1970s. As a result, government budget

[12]Publically guaranteed debt represents private sector debt that the government is committed to assume if the private sector defaults. It is often lumped with public debt because it represents a potential liability for the government. Indeed, there are many instances of governments taking over debt on which the private sector has defaulted. In Argentina in 1980, a financial crisis led to a rash of major bank failures forcing the authorities to assume billions of dollars of debt. In Chile between 1981 and 1983, the government again intervened in the midst of a financial crisis, taking over the debts of failed financial institutions; in this case, though, the debt was not originally publically guaranteed. See S. Edwards and A. Cox Edwards, *Monetarism and Liberalization: The Chilean Experience* (Cambridge: Ballinger, 1987), p. 80.

[13]For a recent discussion of Mexico's economic policymaking, see N. Lustig, *Mexico: The Remaking of an Economy* (Washington, D.C.: The Brookings Institution, 1992). For a more general discussion of the relationships between the public sector and the debt crisis, see F. Larrain and M. Selowsky, *The Public Sector and the Latin American Crisis* (San Francisco: ICS Press, 1991).

deficits started to climb. From a magnitude of 6.7 percent of the GDP in 1978, the budget deficit increased to more than 15 percent of the GDP by 1982.[14]

Concern over Mexico's growing budget deficits surfaced in the early 1980s, heightened and compounded by a shifting environment in world financial markets. In contrast to the relatively low interest rates of the early 1970s, the 1980s brought about rising interest rates. Consequently, the government's new borrowing and the refinancing of maturing debt through short-term borrowing had to be undertaken at relatively high interest rates. Debt service payments increased dramatically, and the Mexican government's liquidity problems started to look quite bleak. When these combined with less-than-expected oil revenues (facing sagging demand in world markets, Mexico was forced to slash oil prices by $4.00 per barrel in early 1981), persistent current account deficits, and recession, rumors and speculation arose about the government's financial situation and the likelihood of a devaluation. The massive capital flight induced by the expected devaluation led to unsustainable losses of international reserves. In February 1982, the Mexican government allowed the peso to float, which resulted in a 40 percent effective peso devaluation. The episode culminated in the nationalization of the Mexican banking sector in September 1982.

The Mexican case clearly illustrates what can go wrong when government spending goes out of control, even when it is associated with increased investment. We presented Mexico's gross national investment rates in Table 12–4. These investment rates include both public and private investment and hide a fundamental shift in the composition of investment from the private to the public sector in Mexico between 1978 and 1982. The public sector investment component rose markedly during this period, from 24.4 percent of all investment in 1978 to 86.7 percent in 1982. There was, thus, a clear association between the rise of government investment spending and the reduction in private domestic investment—that is, public sector growth led to a *crowding out* of the private sector.

The fact that in some developing countries increased public investment has been linked to reduced private domestic investment is reflected in the paradox of a public sector that *borrows* abroad to finance its investments while the local private sector invests abroad—or *lends* to the rest of the world—the excess of its savings over domestic investment. In this situation, growing external debt does not mean greater availability of resources for investment purposes in a country. It means that the external debt largely finances the private sector's capital flight, substituting for—instead of adding to—private sector investment. Capital flight played a critical role in the onset of not only the Mexican debt crisis, but the Argentinean and Venezuelan crises, as well.[15]

According to economist John Cuddington's estimates, Argentina had $15 billion in capital flight between 1980 and 1981 alone.[16] Mexico and

---

[14]There is a great variation in the experiences of Latin countries with public debt. Although in Mexico budget deficits were linked to higher public investment, in the Dominican Republic the opposite occurred: From 1975 until the crisis outburst of 1982, the share of total investment accounted for by the government declined. The Dominican debt crisis of the 1980s was associated with burgeoning budget deficits that financed consumption expenditures. See J. T. Cuddington and C. Asilis, "Fiscal Policy, the Current Account and the External Debt Problem in the Dominican Republic," *Journal of Latin American Studies* (1990).

[15]For a discussion of Argentina, see C. A. Rodriguez, "Argentina's Foreign Debt: Origins and Alternatives," in S. Edwards and F. Larrain, eds., *Debt, Adjustment and Recovery* (Cambridge, Mass.: Basil Blackwell, 1989); and R. Dornbusch, "Overborrowing: Three Case Studies," in R. Dornbusch, *Dollars, Debts and Deficits* (Cambridge, Mass.: The MIT Press, 1987). The case of Venezuela is discussed by R. Hausman, *External Shocks and Macroeconomic Adjustment* (Caracas: Central Bank of Venezuela, 1990).

[16]See J. T. Cuddington, "Capital Flight: Estimates, Issues, and Explanations," *Princeton Studies in International Finance* (December 1986); see also J. Williamson and D. R. Lessard, *Capital Flight: The Problem and Policy Responses* (Washington, D.C.: Institute for International Economics, 1987).

Venezuela lost more than $20 billion each in capital flight between 1980 and 1982. On the other hand, we must not overemphasize the role of capital flight. For instance, many Latin American countries, including Chile, did not experience this phenomenon to any major extent in the 1980s.

The association between capital flight and external debt in some developing countries is clear, but the line of causation can run from external debt causing capital flight, to capital flight causing external debt. For instance, in Argentina, Mexico, and other nations suffering from massive capital flight, there is evidence that some of the capital outflows were motivated by anticipated exchange rate changes not directly linked to external debt developments. Rather, inappropriate exchange rate policies led to grossly overvalued exchange rates that investors anticipated would have to be raised in the near future. The expected devaluations, as well as the greater uncertainty about future government policies, led investors to perceive local assets as being highly risky investments offering low expected real rates of return. Seeking more profitable and less risky opportunities, they shifted their assets abroad. Capital flight then forced central banks to sell large quantities of foreign currency reserves that were financed through external borrowing. The augmented public debt precipitated the crisis. Many developing countries, such as Mexico, underwent large currency depreciations after the crisis was imminent, too late to avoid it.

Capital flight can be the cause of—instead of being caused by—high public external indebtedness. When governments increase their debts, local investors anticipate that the government will impose future taxes on their assets to finance growing budget deficits. Expectations about future taxes—plus the increased riskiness of holding domestic assets in the face of uncertain government policies—led private investors in Latin America to move their capital out of their countries into "safe havens" abroad, such as the United States. The capital outflows, in turn, forced local central banks committed to fixed exchange rates to lose huge

amounts of foreign currency reserves. The central banks then borrowed abroad to finance their sales of foreign exchange, exacerbating public-sector borrowing and the governments' inability to pay back their external debt. This, in turn, augmented the loss of private sector confidence on government policies and fueled further capital flight.[17]

This section has shown that capital flight has been intimately linked to the debt crisis in some Latin American economies. The question arises: If capital flight anticipated or preceded the onset of the debt crisis, why were local investors in Latin America able to recognize the government's problems and the forthcoming crisis while foreign lenders did not seem to have anticipated it? Furthermore, when one looks at international financial market indicators, why is it that there does not appear to have been a clue in those markets in 1981 or early 1982 that the debt crisis was imminent? These paradoxes are addressed next.

12–4. COMMERCIAL BANK EXPOSURE TO DEVELOPING COUNTRY DEBT: THE ROAD FROM LOAN PUSHING TO DEBT WRITE-OFFS

The debt crisis presents various paradoxes. Perhaps the most surprising element of such a far-reaching and long-lasting quagmire is that it does

---

[17]This cascade of events is started by increased public spending. Some recent research in political economy has examined the determination of government expenditures in an economy in which political groups use spending and tax policies to shift income distribution in favor of their constituency. This literature points to political instability as generating the economic policy uncertainty that stimulates capital flight. See A. Alesina and G. Tabellini, "External Debt, Capital Flight and Political Risk," National Bureau of Economic Research Working Paper no. 2610 (June 1988). For earlier discussions of the interplay of public debt and capital flight, see A. Ize and G. Ortiz, "Fiscal Rigidities, Public Debt and Capital Flight," *IMF Staff Papers* (June 1987); and J. Eaton, "Public Debt Guarantees and Private Capital Flight," *World Bank Economic Review* (May 1987).

not appear to have been properly anticipated by financial markets.

Figure 12–2 shows the Mexican bond price in New York as a percentage of the price of a U.S. bond with identical characteristics but free of default risk. The extent of the shortfall below the 100 percent mark represents the degree of risk of the Mexican bonds: The greater that risk relative to the risk-free U.S. bonds, the lower the relative market price of the Mexican bonds. Asset holders will require a lower price to compensate them for the greater risk they assume when acquiring the

Mexican bonds. Figure 12–2 indicates that the Mexican bonds were trading at near 100 percent of the U.S. price in 1981 and at about 90 percent in early 1982. This suggests that investors in the bond market at that time were still relatively confident that Mexican bonds would not be defaulted upon. They thus attached relatively little risk to holding Mexican bonds, and the price of these bonds was close to the price of risk-free U.S. bonds. Matters suddenly changed in mid-1982, when the crisis was imminent. Mexican bond prices experienced a sharp fall, going down to

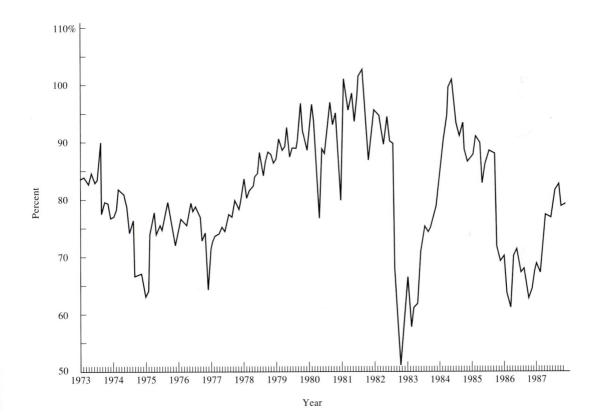

FIGURE 12–2. The Mexican Bond Price in New York, 1973–1988 (percentage of risk-free U.S. bond price)

SOURCE: R. Dornbusch, "Mexico: Stabilization, Debt and Growth," *Economic Policy* (October 1989), p. 243.

about 50 percent of the U.S. price by August of that year. By that time, commercial banks had stopped lending to Mexico, which then fell into arrears.[18]

Further evidence from the lending side supports the view that the timing and extent of the crisis were not properly anticipated. For instance, commercial banks failed to respond to the increased likelihood of default, which should have led them to raise the interest rate charged on developing country loans. UCLA economist Sebastian Edwards has studied the interest rates set by banks lending to those developing countries that eventually experienced debt crisis. He finds that, as late as 1980, the interest rates did not reflect any perception on the part of the banks that there was a significant likelihood of default.[19] Actually, the spread between the interest rate charged to borrowing countries and the LIBOR in London (a measure of commercial bank assessment of countries' default risk), had been declining for many of them. According to Professor Edwards's calculations, based on these spreads, the default probabilities implicitly assigned by the banks to their loans *declined* between 1976 and 1980 for Argentina, Mexico, and Uruguay.

Even in the period immediately preceding the crisis, commercial banks were not exactly reluctant lenders. They were funneling funds to developing countries at the pace of $40 billion to more than $50 billion annually between 1980 and 1982. This lending behavior contrasts with that of the post-1982 period. The response of the banks to the cessation of debt service by some countries was to contract their credit severely. Net lending was maintained below $5 billion annually throughout the late 1980s. It went down to a mere $700,000 in 1987. A large number of countries were practically excluded from commercial bank lending. As MIT's economist Rudiger Dornbusch notes for Mexico: "Bank lending came to an end in the first half of 1982. The last loan floated was a jumbo

loan of $2.5 billion in May–June. . . . With no new credits available to roll over the maturing principal and fund the interest payments, Mexico was illiquid. The old bankers' adage was borne out again: 'It is not speed that kills, it is the sudden stop!' "[20]

When borrowing countries stopped their debt service, the major U.S. banks were hit hard. In 1982 the exposure of the nine major American banks to developing-country debt—that is, the value of bank asset portfolios consisting of loans made to these countries—was $83.4 billion. The loans exceeded the value of the banks' equity by a factor of two or three. A massive loan default would have thrown them into bankruptcy. This situation continued throughout the 1980s. In 1987, BankAmerica, Chase Manhattan, Citicorp, Chemical Bank, and Manufacturers Hanover had a combined $37.6 billion invested in their developing-country loan portfolios.

Why did the banks fail to anticipate the crisis? Why did they become so overexposed? First, to understand the issue it must be recognized that, although locals knew of—and some indicators suggested—the presence of potential problems in some countries, there were no signals before 1980 that the investments made by so many borrowing countries were failing or about to fail. The prices of the commodities in which developing countries had invested were generally rising, and their export earnings were growing at least as fast as the debt. Debt-export ratios in 1980 were similar to those prevailing in 1973, well before debt accumulation started in earnest. The fact is that lending matched export growth up until 1980. Nobody predicted at that time that interest rates would mount to 18 percent levels a few months ahead (as dramatically depicted in Figure 12–1). The same situation applies to the economic downturn in the United States and the world economy between 1980 and 1982—the steepest since the Great Depression of the 1930s: it was an unanticipated event. It was difficult from the vantage point of the late 1970s to imagine a collapse in developing

---

[18]Arrears represent any debt, loan payment, or bond interest that is due but unpaid.

[19]See S. Edwards, "LDC's Foreign Borrowing and Default Risk: An Empirical Investigation, 1976–1980," *American Economic Review* (September 1984).

[20]R. Dornbusch, "Mexico: Stabilization, Debt and Growth," *Economic Policy* (October 1989), p. 243.

countries' export earnings. However, that was precisely what happened.

The world depression of 1980 and 1981 is usually blamed on the rapid oil-price increases of 1979, on U.S. government policies in 1979 and 1980, and on the contemporaneous surge of interest rates. The combination demolished the scenario behind banks' exuberant lending policies. Developing country exports declined in dollar terms, and the debt mounted as countries repaid old debts by engaging in new short-term borrowing at higher interest rates. Consequently, debt-export ratios surged rapidly. By 1982, they had climbed to almost 300 percent in Latin America and the Caribbean. The setting for the debt crisis was now complete.

If the unanticipated events of the early 1980s are blamed for throwing developing countries into crisis, then the lending policies of commercial banks toward these countries do not appear to be irrational. Given the trends in prices and output, and the—albeit imperfect—information available to bank managers and loan officers in the 1970s, the expectations were that the borrowing countries would not fall into economic difficulties. Some economists, however, believe that the aggressive bank lending policies of the late 1970s and early 1980s, often referred to as "loan pushing," attached too little weight to the likelihood that some major random disturbance could disturb the developing economies. According to business economists Jack Guttentag and Richard Herring, bank managers "have sometimes behaved . . . as if the probability of a major shock affecting their international loan portfolios were zero."[21] They give the name "disaster myopia" to this phenomenon. It is particularly difficult to understand the active bank lending activity to developing countries between 1980 and 1982. From this perspective, just as S&L institutions in the

United States engaged in sometimes outrageously risky (and sometimes outrageously fraudulent) use of their funds in the 1980s, banks went beyond what was prudent risk taking in lending to developing countries in the late 1970s and early 1980s.

The explanation for commercial bank overexposure to developing country debt is partly related to the incentives that banks had to take risks. A large portion of the lending to developing countries was undertaken by Eurobanks that were organized as subsidiaries of American banks and banks of other nationalities. As we saw in Chapter 8, Eurobanks operate in a lax regulatory environment. In particular, they were not subject to extensive supervision and monitoring, and they faced few sanctions if they failed. Because Eurodeposits were not insured, the parent bank faced no liability if its Eurobranch were to fall in default to its depositors. This situation encouraged overexposure to risky loans. Paradoxically, as discussed in Chapter 7, risk taking was also encouraged by the presence of U.S. (onshore) bank deposit insurance. Through such insurance the U.S. government assures depositors that, in the case of bank failure, official authorities will assume any unpaid bank deposits (up to a certain limit). Insured deposits means that commercial banks are partially immune to the costs of bank failure. In this situation, risk taking by banks will not affect the safety of their deposits. Incentives were there for banks to take risky investments—not only in developing countries, but also locally. The crisis of the S&L industry and the wave of U.S. bank failures in the 1980s and 1990s has been linked to a surge of nonperforming real estate loans whose parentage is similar to the loans responsible for the external debt crisis.[22]

Commercial banks responded to the proliferation of nonperforming external loans by trying to

[21]J. Guttentag and R. J. Herring, *The Current Crisis in International Lending* (Washington, D.C.: Brookings Institution, 1985), p. 2. See also J. Guttentag and R. J. Herring, "Disaster Myopia in International Banking," *Princeton Essays in International Finance* (September 1986); and W. Darity and B. Horn, *The Loan Pushers: The Role of Commercial Banks in the International Debt Crisis* (Cambridge: Ballinger, 1988).

[22]The regulatory aspects of U.S. onshore banking were discussed in Chapter 7. A nontechnical review of the issues and events surrounding the U.S. banking system in the 1980s and 1990s—including the external debt aspects—is found in L. L. Bryan, *Bankrupt: Restoring the Health and Profitability of Our Banking System* (New York: HarperCollins, 1991), part I.

avoid borrower's open default by all means. Unpaid interest was added to the amounts owed, augmenting them. At the same time, bankers were slow to adjust the value of nonperforming external loans in their portfolios. Loan write-downs would have reduced bank equity and thrown greater doubts on their financial solidity.[23] Instead, banks engaged in "provisioning"—that is, in setting aside some reserves in safe and liquid, but low-interest, assets that could be used in the event of default. (Provisioning reduces the profitability of banks because it involves setting aside funds into low-yielding investments.)[24] The general recognition that loan downgrading had not been appropriately accounted for by banks led U.S. government regulators to intervene. In 1990, the Inter-Agency Country Exposure Review Committee, composed of the Federal Reserve Board, the FDIC, and the comptroller of the currency, ordered banks to take write-offs on loans to developing countries. On regulators' orders, Brazil's $11 billion exposure was written off by 20 percent for the first time, and Argentina's write-offs were increased by 20 percent. In April 1991, required write-downs increased an additional 20 percent for Brazil and 10 percent for Argentina. As a consequence, total required adjustments had mounted to 40 percent and 70 percent for Brazil and Argentina, respec-

tively, by mid-1991.[25] Banks' continued adjustments of both the values of external loans in their portfolios and the reserves on potentially unrecoverable loans, coupled with the series of debt agreements that have been engaged in between lenders and borrowers to prevent default, have built up a solid buffer against default uncertainty.

12–5. DEALING WITH THE DEBT CRISIS

Table 12–6 depicts changes in per-capita GNP in the 1980s. The decade-long depression in developing countries was the deepest since the Great Depression. In 1991, most developing countries were unable to surpass their per capita income levels of the late 1970s. A generalized lack of economic recovery in heavily indebted countries keeps the debt crisis a Damocles sword over debtors and creditors alike. Why has the crisis been so strong and long-lasting? Some attribute the slow recovery to the way official creditors and private banks have managed the crisis. Others blame the debtor countries for not implementing adequate policies to deal with debt. This section examines the actions and policies that the major actors in the debt theater—banks, official creditors, and the debtor countries—have undertaken since 1982 to deal with the debt crisis.

Debt Rescheduling and the Paris Club

In 1982, commercial banks responded to the inability of debtors to service their debts by engaging in *rescheduling* negotiations. Debt rescheduling means that the debt payments due by a country on a particular date are negotiated to be postponed. When debt is rescheduled, the principal payments due are delayed and interest is charged on the unpaid principal amounts. By rolling over matur-

---

[23]The reluctance to write down nonperforming loans, however, did not prevent a fall in bank's price-to-earnings ratios (stock prices in relation to reported earnings) after 1982. Financial markets were thus able to assess the downgrading in loans even if this was not reflected in financial statements and reported earnings. See J. H. Makin, "The Third World Debt Crisis and the American Banking System," *The American Enterprise Institute Economist* (May 1987).

[24]One of the first major banks to establish a substantial provision against possible losses on developing country debt was Citicorp, which on May 19, 1987, announced it would reserve $3 billion on this account. See J. Guttentag and R. J. Herring, "Accounting for Losses on Sovereign Debt," *Princeton Essays in International Finance* (May 1989); and G. Bird, "Loan-Loss Provisions and Third-World Debt," *Princeton Essays in International Finance* (November 1989).

[25]As reported by P. Truell, "Banks Must Take More Write-Downs on Certain Loans," *The Wall Street Journal*, April 22, 1991.

TABLE 12–6. Changes in Gross National Product per Capita in the 1980s, by Region (in dollars)

| Year | Developing Countries | | | | | | OECD Countries |
	Sub-Saharan Africa	East Asia and Pacific	Europe	North Africa and Middle East	Latin America and Caribbean	South Asia	
1981	$570	$430	—	$2170	$2140	$260	$11,180
1982	550	440	2450	2450	2100	270	11,130
1983	500	440	2260	2500	1890	270	11,110
1984	450	450	2150	2390	1790	270	11,480
1985	450	440	2040	2340	1730	280	11,830
1986	390	430	2170	2250	1700	280	12,710
1987	350	440	2560	2130	1720	300	14,390
1988	340	480	2760	1960	1780	320	17,100
1989	340	540	2710	1860	1920	330	18,840
1990	340	590	2250	1820	2140	330	20,250

SOURCE: World Bank, *World Tables, 1992* (Baltimore: Johns Hopkins University Press, 1992), table 1, pp. 2–5.

ing debt, reschedulings effectively convert short-term debt into longer-term debt but do not increase the principal owed and do not entail new lending. Reschedulings proliferated after 1982 as a result of the endemic nonservicing among debtor countries.

Because each creditor prefers to be repaid and to let the debtor reschedule its loans with other creditors, no bank is motivated to reschedule unless other creditors also do so. Coordinated action is thus called for. The banks involved with a particular problem debtor often engage in joint action when negotiating reschedulings. For instance, in the aftermath of Mexico's default in 1982, a bank advisory committee was organized to manage the crisis. The advisory committee included the largest lenders but acted on behalf of all creditors, coordinating their response to nonservicing. The same type of mechanism has been in place more recently with banks providing new lending to problem debtors: they often engage in *concerted lending*. This type of arrangement is necessary because each creditor prefers that other lenders augment their commitments, as opposed to increasing its own lending. Concerted lending

specifies that each bank contribute new funds in proportion to its loan exposure at a given time. This arrangement allows banks to coordinate the provision of new credit to distressed debtors even if individual banks would like to reduce their exposure and would not lend alone.

The debtors in crisis in 1982 and 1983 had received significant loans from official sources during their borrowing frenzy. Debt reschedulings were thus carried out by official lenders in addition to commercial banks. Most reschedulings by official creditors have been sponsored by the so-called Paris Club. The Paris Club was formed back in 1956 as a forum for negotiations between debtors and government creditors. There is no set "membership" in this club; it consists of debtor and creditor governments that get together in Paris to conduct debt negotiations. The meetings are traditionally chaired by a high-ranking official of the French treasury. Participation is limited to governments and international organizations, with no commercial bank attendance. The Paris Club has served as the coordinating backbone for a large number of rescheduling negotiations since 1956.

Negotiations are based on the principle of the symmetric treatment of creditors—that is, all creditors are treated equally.

The Paris Club reschedulings are closely linked to separate negotiations carried out by the IMF with debtors. An IMF agreement with the debtor country is usually required by creditor governments when they approve Paris Club rescheduling agreements. The IMF package is regarded as serving to assure creditors that the rescheduling negotiations will be effective in propping up debt repayments. The next section discusses the role played by IMF lending in the debt crisis.

The International Monetary Fund and Conditionality

The IMF has been a major source of financing for countries in severe balance-of-payments and external debt difficulties since its creation; however, in the 1980s, this role acquired gigantic importance. The IMF will lend to an ailing debtor country, but only under certain arrangements. Under the typical "standby" arrangement between the IMF and a debtor country, the IMF will supply a line of credit under a specific set of conditions, referred to as *IMF conditionality*.[26] The conditions are formalized in a Letter of Intent negotiated between the country's government and IMF staff. The letter usually stipulates an array of reforms the country must follow in order to stabilize its economy (*a stabilization program*). The IMF, of course, sustains close surveillance of the country's affairs

after the line of credit is granted. A country's noncompliance with the stipulated conditions means immediate suspension of fund withdrawals from its line of credit.

The policies that countries must follow under IMF conditionality vary. In most cases they involve measures directed at "getting the house in order," to improve the balance of payments (stop losses of international reserves by the country's central bank) and insure the resumption and/or maintenance of full external debt service. This involves controlling government budget deficits and introducing exchange rate realignments, which in countries with overvalued currencies means devaluation. To control budget deficits, harsh austerity measures are imposed to curtail public spending, tax rates are increased, government subsidies are eliminated, and prices charged by public enterprises are raised. These measures frequently create wide public protests in the countries imposing them. The elimination of public subsidies and controls leads to increases in the prices of many goods and services of everyday use, such as public transportation and electricity. Cuts in government spending result in public-sector layoffs and/or reductions in wages. The economies are thus thrown into recession and unemployment, with angry resentment on the part of the public.

Because of their "shock-treatment" nature, IMF stabilization programs are not only very unpopular among the public suffering its consequences, but also are controversial in terms of their eventual outcome. There are many economists that question whether the policies used by IMF conditionality really promote long-run economic growth.[27] Later in this book we will examine the macroeconomics of these programs. Suffice it to say here that IMF programs are often more than just austerity pro-

---

[26] Funds approved by the IMF to a debtor country are not necessarily *disbursed*. A loan is considered disbursed when it is used by the borrower. In some cases, the creditor and debtor agree to a *standby* loan, by which the creditor commits itself to have the funds available on the borrower's demand. This is the nature of the so-called standby loans granted by the IMF to member countries in support of stabilization programs. This credit is not considered disbursed until the money is actually claimed by the borrower. The credit that has been approved but not disbursed is not included in published external debt statistics because the borrower might decide not to claim and use it.

[27] See T. Killick et al., "The IMF: Case for a Change of Emphasis," in R. E. Feinberg and V. Kallab, eds., *Adjustment Crisis in the Third World* (New Brunswick, N.J.: Transaction Books, 1984).

grams. They consist of a complex array of policies, some of which may not be consistent with long-run growth but others certainly are. Furthermore, the fund's programs have sometimes served as catalysts for the elimination of burdensome economic policies that may have stalled sustainable economic development for decades in many countries.[28]

The IMF, by intervening with heavily indebted countries both through its lending and its coordinating activities with private banks and creditor governments, fulfilled a crisis-management function that most likely averted widespread debt default and repudiation.[29] At the same time, IMF staff may have failed to recognize the staying power of the crisis and the fact that it was not a short-term problem involving the inability of some countries to sustain debt servicing in the face of higher interest rates. As UCLA's Edwards has noted: "In early 1983 the Fund Staff, like most observers, saw the crisis as a temporary liquidity problem only affecting a handful of countries. In fact during 1983 and 1984 the Fund had high expectations for a quick and relatively painless resolution of the problem. . . . Things, however, did not work as expected and in the following years the Fund came to recognize that it had badly underestimated the magnitude of the problem."[30]

Muddling Through and the 1985 Baker Plan

The continuation and severity of the debt crisis through 1985 led to a number of proposals and plans by a variety of governments, individuals, and institutions. Cuba's Fidel Castro proposed that debtors get together in an organization to bargain on equal terms with their creditors. Some Latin American politicians openly asserted the need to repudiate the debt. In the United States, the Reagan administration had been flirting with a number of proposals. Then, in October 1985, at a meeting in Seoul, then Secretary of the Treasury James Baker made the proposals that became known as the Baker Plan.

The Baker Plan represented a muddling-through approach to the debt crisis that essentially recommended a continuation of what had been done until then. The plan was based on (1) debt rescheduling and renegotiation between commercial banks and debtor governments, (2) increased lending on the part of the World Bank and IMF coupled with the use of IMF-styled conditionality, and (3) promotion of market-oriented reform—such as the privatization of public enterprises—geared to reducing government regulatory burden in developing countries.

The Baker Plan was the main initiative ventured by the Reagan administration and was widely discussed but not formally implemented. It became a sort of reference plan as debt reschedulings kept a steady pace and country after country was forced to abide by IMF conditionality and adopt World Bank's Structural Adjustment Programs[31]

---

[28]A thorough discussion of IMF conditionality and stabilization policies in developing countries is provided in L. Taylor, *Varieties of Stabilization Experience* (Oxford: Clarendon, 1988); and J. Williamson, ed., *IMF Conditionality* (Washington, D.C.: Institute for International Economics, 1983).

[29]From yet another point of view, IMF lending has been criticized for being destabilizing and counterproductive in resolving the debt problems of developing countries. The argument is that IMF lending generates a moral hazard in providing bailouts to countries that have engaged in economic mismanagement, reducing the incentives for them to remain solvent and keep their house in order. See R. Vaubel, "The Moral Hazard of IMF Lending," *The World Economy* (January 1984).

[30]S. Edwards, "The International Monetary Fund and the Developing Countries: A Critical Evaluation," National Bureau of Economic Research Working Paper no. 2909 (March 1989), p. 33.

[31]The World Bank traditionally engaged in development lending to developing countries—that is, lending specifically targeted to particular development projects, such as the building of dams and technical assistance. In the 1980s, however, the World Bank in effect engaged in lending intended to ease balance-of-payments difficulties in many heavily indebted countries. These Structural Adjustment Loans have been provided to governments undertaking measures to promote net exports. For more details, see S. Please, "The World Bank Lending for Structural Adjustment," in R. E. Feinberg and V.

(continued)

as part of increased lending agreements. Renegotiation of the debt took place on a country-by-country basis as conditions varied, depending on the economy in distress. In a sense, although the Baker Plan was never officially adopted, countries partially implemented many of the proposals informally.

By the late 1980s most debtors had engaged in adjustment policies that had converted their trade balances into surpluses, but CABs remained negative as a result of the huge payments on external debt (leading to highly negative investment income balances).[32] This is clearly depicted by the data in Table 12–7, which shows the balance on goods and services (as defined in Chapter 9) and the CAB of the severely indebted countries: In spite of surpluses in the balance on goods and services, most of these countries still had significant CAB deficits in 1989. Interest payments on external debt are also reflected in public sector finances. A large share of the government revenues in developing countries are spent precisely on financing interest payments on the public debt. To measure the role played by interest payments on the budget, economists calculate a so-called *primary budget deficit,* which is the balance of all government revenues and expenditures *except* interest payments. The primary budget deficit for heavily indebted developing countries is presented in Table 12–5. As can be seen, this deficit shifted into a surplus in 1983. This implies that the public sector in the heavily indebted countries would have had budget surpluses after 1983, were it not for the interest payments on the debt.

In spite of costly adjustment policies that led to the immiserization of much of their population, developing countries have had to continue borrowing in order to repay their loan interest and principal. Furthermore, any financial gains have been committed in advance to be used toward debt repayments and payments of interest in arrears. This situation, in which the payments on a massive debt absorb so much of a country's resources that the country cannot pull itself out of the crisis, is called the debt overhang problem. It makes it very difficult for heavily indebted countries to get out of the "hole" they fell into when the debt crisis exploded in 1982.

Table 12–8 displays the net transfer of resources that flowed between international financial markets and the public sector of highly indebted countries in the late 1980s. These *net resource transfers* represent the amount of new money developing countries received from banks net of the amortization and interest payments the countries made to the banks. The fact that the figures in Table 12–8 are all negative suggests that there was a net outflow of resources from developing countries in these years: The governments were paying more to the banks than they were receiving from them in new loans. However, the new lending received by the countries in Table 12–8 was being used to pay the interest on the old debt. This means that on a net basis the countries were accumulating debt, not reducing it. This experience is typical of many debtors and is a major factor behind the strength and length of the debt crisis.[33] The combination of accumulating debt

Kallab, eds., *Adjustment Crisis in the Third World* (New Brunswick, Transaction Books, 1984).

[32] A survey of the adjustments undertaken by indebted countries in response to the debt crisis is supplied by J. Williamson, ed., *Latin American Adjustment: How Much Has Happened?* (Washington, D.C.: Institute for International Economics, 1990); M. Bruno, S. Fischer, E. Helpman, N. Liviatan and L. Meridor, eds., *Lessons of Economic Stabilization and Its Aftermath* (Cambridge, Mass.: The MIT Press, 1991), and R. N. Cooper, *Economic Stabilization and Debt in Developing Countries* (Cambridge, Mass.: The MIT Press, 1992).

[33] Historical analysis pinpoints many periods in which developing countries engaged in massive external borrowing that led to defaults and the suspension of debt service. In contrast to the current crisis, the evidence tends to indicate that defaults led to negotiations that resulted in favorable debt reductions (debt forgiveness or debt relief). The negotiations were usually timely and allowed a relatively quick resumption of lending activities. (The developing country debt crisis of the 1930s was slow to generate new lending, but this may have been related to the general breakdown of international trade and finance during the Great Depression.) See B. Eichengreen and P. H. Lindert,

TABLE 12–7. **Trade and Current Account Balances (CABs) of the Severely Indebted Developing Countries (as a percentage of GDP)**

	Trade Balance		Current Account Balance	
Country	1981	1989	1981	1989
Argentina	−0.4%	3.7%	−8.2%	−2.2%
Bolivia	−2.1	−3.7	−13.5	−8.8
Brazil	−0.4	3.2	−4.4	0.2
Chile	−10.3	3.2	−14.7	−4.3
Congo	−18.1	−9.1	−25.3	−5.6
Costa Rica	−4.9	−3.9	−15.6	−9.6
Côte d'Ivoire	−7.1	2.8	−16.9	−11.2
Ecuador	1.0	−2.0	−7.3	−6.1
Egypt	−15.4	−16.7	−10.1	−8.5
Honduras	−6.4	−1.6	−11.6	−6.8
Hungary	−1.0	3.4	−2.3*	−2.0
Mexico	−2.5	0.9	−6.4	−2.8
Morocco	−14.6	−5.5	−12.7	−4.7
Nicaragua	−19.6	−34.6	−26.6	−23.8**
Nigeria	−3.4	8.4	−6.4	−0.9
Peru	−5.9	2.4	−7.5	1.2
Philippines	−5.4	−1.0	−5.8	−4.1
Poland	−2.1	0.0	−8.0	−2.7
Senegal	−21.0	−4.6	−25.9	−8.5
Uruguay	−3.9	5.8	−4.1	1.7
Venezuela	4.9	13.7	5.2	5.7

* Data for 1982
** Data for 1987

SOURCE: World Bank, *World Tables 1991* (Baltimore: Johns Hopkins University Press, 1991), Country Tables, pp. 63–668.

with a net drain of resources is a deadly mix for a troubled, stagnant economy: To raise debt payments, investment rates decline (Table 12–4 documents the drop of the investment rates of heavily indebted countries) and the economy tends to fall into a deeper and deeper abyss.

eds., *The International Debt Crisis in Historical Perspective* (Cambridge, Mass.: The MIT Press, 1989); and A. Fishlow, "Lessons from the Past: Capital Markets During the 19th Century and the Interwar Period," *International Organization* (1985).

The debt overhang problem made painfully clear that continued debt rescheduling and IMF conditionality would not be enough to turn heavily indebted countries toward long-term economic growth. As noted earlier, the IMF as well as many other creditors and governments did not envision the extent of the crisis. By continuing their muddling-through approach, they may have delayed the implementation of debt-reduction schemes and other, longer-term approaches to the debt crisis. Some critics thus assign a large share of the blame for the length of the debt crisis to the actions taken by pri-

TABLE 12–8.   **Net Resource Transfers from International Financial Markets to Selected Public-Sector Borrowers, 1985–1987 (in billions of dollars)**

Country	1985	1986	1987
Argentina	$ −0.5	$ −2.2	$ −2.6
Brazil	−4.2	−5.0	−1.9
Chile	−0.2	−0.8	−0.8
Mexico	−7.4	−5.4	−2.1
Venezuela	−2.0	−2.8	−2.7
17 highly indebted countries	−18.2	−18.2	−12.8

SOURCE: J. D. Sachs, "New Approaches to the Latin American Debt Crisis," *Princeton Essays in International Finance* (July 1989), table 4.

vate banks, the IMF, and other official institutions.[34] Economic analyst Jude Wanniski of the firm Polyconomics trenchantly presents his view of the muddling-through approach from the vantage point of 1989: "The recent Venezuela riots left three hundred dead that can be counted as IMF victims. Peru, ravaged by the IMF formula, has been steadily pushed into the arms of the drug trade; smothered by taxes and confetti currency, its economy is kept afloat by cocaine cash crops. Argentina is in tatters, Brazil a basket case after years of sipping IMF cocktails, and Mexico is bravely fighting off yet another push by the IMF and its friends in the U.S. Treasury to force a peso devaluation."[35]

The ever-growing difficulties of implementing IMF programs in the presence of persistently high external debt payments has resulted in rising non-compliance and program enforcement difficulties. Politically, many debtor governments find themselves unable to sustain policies that keep draining economic resources from their countries and into foreign banks. On this basis, IMF conditionality has become very controversial. However, all the

blame for the decade-long stagnation of debtor countries cannot be placed on IMF conditionality and muddling through. Other factors were involved, which the next section examines.

12–6. WHY DID THE DEBT CRISIS HIT SO HARD AND LAST SO LONG?

Why do we have such a long-term collapse of the debtor nations? One of the key factors throwing debtor nations into crisis was the climb of interest rates in the late 1970s and 1980s. Yet, as Figure 12–1 showed, LIBOR did go down in the mid-1980s and stayed below 10 percent for the rest of the decade. Shouldn't this imply that the debt-servicing troubles of developing countries should have eased?

The Rising Real Interest Rate

Figure 12–3 depicts the behavior of the LIBOR rate adjusted for inflation—that is, the real interest rate. As was discussed in Chapter 6, it is the real interest rate that should be used in measuring the real cost of borrowing money. Note how the real interest rate climbs from −3.0 percent in 1975 to 9.0 percent by 1982. Since then, there has been a drop in real interest rates, but at no time have they dropped to the levels of

---

[34]See C. Payer, *Lent and Lost: Foreign Credit and Third World Development* (London: Zed Books, 1991) for the point of view of a long-time critic of the IMF and the World Bank.

[35]J. Wanniski "Another Round of IMF Poison," *The Wall Street Journal,* March 20, 1989.

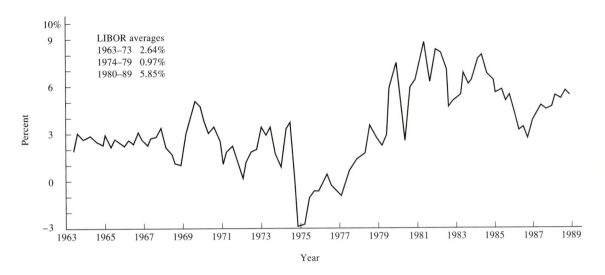

Note: The real interest rate is calculated as the London Interbank offered rate (LIBOR) minus the U.S. GDP deflator.

FIGURE 12–3. Dollar Real Interest Rates, 1963–1989

SOURCE: World Bank, *World Development Report* (Baltimore: Johns Hopkins University Press, 1990), p. 16.

the mid-1970s. On average, between 1963 and 1973, the real interest rate was equal to 2.64 percent. Between 1974 and 1979, the real rate dropped to 0.97 percent and in the 1980s it was equal to 5.85 percent.

Why the differences between the behavior of nominal and real interest rates? The reason is that in the 1970s the rate of inflation either exceeded or stayed close to the nominal interest rate, keeping it low or even negative. Indeed, in real terms, it was costing developing countries very little (if anything) to borrow dollars. It is therefore understandable that they borrowed so extensively, even if today—with the benefit of hindsight—the strategy looks distressingly myopic. In the 1980s, dollar nominal interest rates skyrocketed. Although the dollar inflation rate also increased, it was not by as much, leading to the much higher real rates. The increase in real interest rates on dollar-denominated assets from the 1970s to the 1980s is

then another factor explaining why the crisis endured for so long.

While the sustained, higher real interest rates on dollar assets were crucial in preventing borrowers of dollars from easing their debt service burden, other factors also harmed developing countries throughout the 1980s. The financial systems of many of them fell into disarray. In some cases, interest rates on assets denominated in the domestic currency increased dramatically, giving a shock to investment and contributing to the economic debacle. In other instances, surging inflation led to highly negative interest rates and financial disintermediation. IMF-sponsored reforms often did not help in reestablishing confidence and interest rate stability because their short-term focus prevented investors from believing that government policies would not be reversed in the near future. The general instability of real rates in developing countries contributed to a worsening of capital flight problems in many countries in the 1980s. As of 1987, the amount of financial capital exported by local residents exceeded the long-term government debt in Argentina, Bolivia, Colombia, Ecuador, Mexico, Nigeria, the Philippines, Uruguay, and Venezuela. This indicates that a key element in financial recovery hinges on creating conditions to bring capital back into domestic use. How to accomplish this is subject to various views (see the discussion in Chapter 7, Section 7-7). On the one hand, excessively regulated financial markets do not yield a return on assets that can compensate adequately for the large financial risks encountered in developing countries. On the other hand, financial deregulation in the presence of lax government supervision, high domestic risk, and expected devaluations can touch off capital flight because they open the door for moving capital investments abroad. It is clear, in either case, that continuing capital flight acted as a retardant to economic recovery in troubled countries.

Commodity Prices and Terms of Trade Deterioration

Yet another factor that contributed to a continuing economic malaise in indebted developing countries in the 1980s was adverse changes in terms of trade. The terms of trade are equal to the price of exports divided by the price of imports. In the 1980s, the prices of exports in world markets tumbled for many heavily indebted countries. The reason is that their exports were concentrated in primary commodities and the prices of these generally dropped in those years. Some examples should highlight the problem.[36] Consider the oil industry. Average oil prices fell from $35.5 per barrel in 1980 down to $14.5 per barrel in 1986. This 60 percent fall in nominal prices represents an even larger decline if it is deflated to take the

[36]The data on commodities prices used here are from *Primary Commodities: Market Developments and Outlook* (Washington, D.C.: International Monetary Fund, July 1990).

inflation rate into account. Figure 12–4 depicts the behavior of the real price of oil (the price of oil divided by the general price index) from 1970 to the first quarter of 1990; it shows the steep increase in the 1970s and the precipitous decline in the 1980s. (The price of oil rose temporarily to more than $30 in 1990 as a result of the Iraqi invasion of Kuwait, but it again dropped precipitously after the defeat of Iraq in the first quarter of 1991.) Note, though, that real oil prices did not fall much until after 1985. The price of oil only fell from $35.5 to $31.4 between 1980 and 1982—not a significant reduction by commodity price standards. It is thus difficult to attribute the *onset* of the debt crisis in oil-exporting countries like Mexico to such a fall. However, the general slump in prices in the 1980s, particularly the sharp drop after 1985 can explain the absence of an economic recovery in oil-producing countries.

Venezuela, Libya, Mexico, and Ecuador were major oil exporters hit by the tumbling oil prices. The heavy concentration of their exports in oil magnified the effects of these price falls. Oil generates about 90 percent of Venezuela's and 95 percent of Libya's foreign exchange earnings. Libyan GNP per capita dropped 40 percent between 1980 and 1987, bringing the oil-led boom of the 1970s to a sharp end. Venezuela's economy experienced a similar collapse. Oil generated more than 50 percent of Mexico's exports in the early 1980s. While this share has since declined, it still fluctuated between 25 and 35 percent between 1987 and 1990. Mexico's long-lasting recession in the 1980s reflected the path of oil prices.

The prices of copper, bauxite (which accounts for about 60 percent of the export values of the West African nation of Guinea), and other minerals and metals exported by developing countries also fell substantially in the 1980s. Copper fell from $1.00 a pound in 1980, to 69 cents in 1982 and 62 cents in 1986. The low price in 1982 is considered to be one of the key factors behind the Chilean economic collapse from 1982 to 1987 and that of the East Asian country of Papua New

(a) Petroleum prices (index of spot petroleum prices: 1980 = 100)

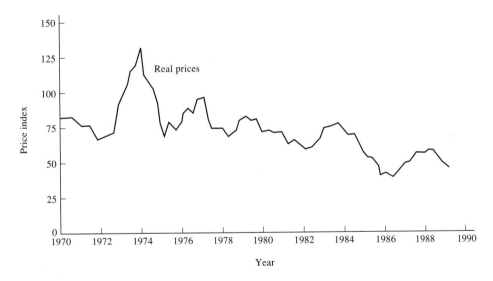

(b) Prices of nonfuel primary commodities (index of prices: 1980 = 100)

FIGURE 12–4. Prices of Primary Commodities, 1970–1990

SOURCE: International Monetary Fund, *Primary Commodities: Market Developments and Outlook* (July 1990), p. 2.

Guinea in the same period. (Copper exports constituted about 50 percent of Chile's exports and a third of Papua New Guinea's in the 1980s.) Tin constitutes about a fourth of Bolivia's export values. Its prices declined gradually from $7.00 per pound in 1979 to $5.23 in 1985 and then took a dive to $2.94 by 1986. Since then, the price has fluctuated, experiencing a weak recovery to about $4.00 per pound and then falling back to less than $3.00 in 1990.

The litany of tumbling prices of developing countries' exports carries over to many agricultural products. Sugar sold in world free markets went from 29 cents a pound in 1980, to 8 cents in 1982 and 4 cents in 1986. Coffee prices drifted downward, from $1.54 per pound (for coffee from Mexico and Central America) in 1980 to $1.12 in 1987 and $0.83 by 1990. This kind of a drop also had a hard impact on El Salvador (60 percent of its exports are coffee sales), Colombia, Brazil, and other coffee exporters. Not all agricultural prices fell during the debt crisis. Some agricultural and meat products experienced periods of price increases in the 1980s. As Figure 12–5 (b) depicts, however, on an overall basis, nonfuel primary commodity prices dropped (in real terms) in the 1980s.

12–7. THE BRADY PLAN AND DEBT REDUCTION

The Brady Plan, proposed by then U.S. Treasury Secretary Nicholas Brady in March 1989, intended to deal with the debt overhang problem.[37] While recognizing the need to continue the Baker Plan's focus on continued economic reform and adjustment in developing countries, it shifted the emphasis toward debt-reduction schemes.

[37]For the text of Brady's remarks introducing the plan, see N. Brady, "Third World Debt" in R. Dornbusch, J. Makin, and D. Zlowe, eds., *Alternative Solutions to Developing Country Debt Problems* (Washington, D.C.: American Enterprise Institute, 1989), pp. 115–121.

The idea of debt reduction has gathered some momentum in recent years, and most of the parties involved—including the IMF, private banks, and governments—have been involved in some way or another in debt relief. Reductions in debt have included both market-based reductions involving private bank loans as well as official-sector debt relief. There have been some major market-based debt-relief activities in Bolivia, Chile, Mexico, and other debtor countries. Large official debt reductions have been obtained through debt forgiveness in Poland and Egypt.

Market-based debt reduction schemes operate through the use of the so-called secondary market in debt. We begin this section by discussing this secondary market. In later sections we will describe in more detail the mechanisms through which debt reductions occur. An appendix to this chapter supplies a thorough discussion of the mechanics of the debt-reduction schemes, complete with examples.

The Secondary Market in Developing Country Debt

Secondary markets for external debt were developed in 1983 to provide an outlet for depreciated loans in bank's portfolios and to increase the liquidity of external debt assets. Through these markets, banks can sell their developing country loans or swap them (exchange one loan for another loan, for cash or equity). The bank can thus rid itself of the loan, reducing its exposure to developing country debt. On the other hand, the loans are sold at a discount, meaning that, for every dollar of face value of the loan the bank sells, it gets only a fraction of a dollar from the purchaser. For instance, if the price quoted is 40 cents on the dollar, a bank can sell a loan of $100 million in the secondary market for $40 million in cash or in some other financial instrument. In selling the loan at such a price, the bank is acknowledging that the loan carries the significant probability of nonpayment. The price of a loan in the secondary market will vary according to the riskiness and credit worthiness of the borrower to whom the loan was originally made. The less risky the loan, the more likely its full value will be recuperated, and the closer its price is going to be to one dollar. On the other hand, if the country owing the money represented by the loan is not creditworthy, the secondary market price will go down. If the loan is not expected to be repaid at all, its price would be zero (the bank would not be able to sell it at any price because it is worthless).

Table 12–9 reports the secondary market prices of the external debt of a sample of developing countries from 1986 to 1990. The discount below 100 cents provides a rough measure of the probability of default of those assets. Mexican and Argentinean debt, quoted at more than 60 cents in 1986, was trading at 40 and 10 cents to the dollar, respectively, in early 1990. Brazilian debt went down from 77 cents in early 1986 to about 30 cents in early 1990. Similar downfalls in secondary market prices characterize all countries in the sample. The 60-something prices for the best performers in 1990, Chile and Colombia, were unimpressive, compared to the prices prevailing in 1986 in the midst of the debt crisis. These figures clearly illustrate the remarkably poor international financial standing of Latin American countries after a decade of exclusion from credit.

Debt-Reduction Schemes: Buybacks

Debt reductions can be accomplished through (1) debt buybacks or (2) asset swaps, such as debt-for-equity and debt-for-debt swaps.[38] Through these mechanisms, a developing country can exchange debt that it owes to private banks in exchange for cash, equity, or another type of debt. We discuss each mechanism next, as well as some variations on them, such as debt-for-nature swaps.

---

[38]For a clear discussion of these concepts and specific examples, see P. Krugman, "Market-Based Approaches to Debt Reduction," in ibid, pp. 43–63. Asset swaps such as debt-for-equity and debt-for-debt should not be confused with the currency swaps discussed in Chapter 3.

A *debt buyback* entails entering the secondary market to buy debt that is trading at prices below face value. The purpose is to wipe out debt by buying it at discount prices in the secondary market. Debt buybacks can be internally or externally financed. In an *internally,* or *self-financed, buyback,* the debtor country provides its own cash for the purchase of secondary debt. Because large debtors facing large discounts in the secondary market are in financial trouble and face liquidity constraints, substantial cash buybacks are not a realistic alternative in most cases. An *externally financed buyback* depends on funds provided by an international organization or a donor country. When it is financed by third parties (that is, the financing is not provided by the creditor itself), this type of buyback is called a third-party buyback. Notice that debt forgiveness can be looked at as a special case of an externally financed buyback in which the buyback is financed by the creditors themselves.

Debt-buybacks look like a bargain for a debtor country because, although some resources have to be spent in repurchasing the debt, the loans are sold at a heavy discount, and retiring the debt from the books improves the country's financial soundness and capacity to grow. This is deceptive. At the margin, there are reasons to expect that the buyback may not actually provide a net gain to the debtor at all. In other words, for the developing country, the cost of purchasing the debt may exceed its benefits. Why?

When a country buys its own debt in the secondary market, it purchases it at a big discount relative to its book value, but the debt's current value is its market value, which is represented by the secondary market price. When a developing country pays 20 cents per dollar of its old debt, it is not purchasing a bargain: The banks are not expecting to recover the full book value of the loan, but only 20 cents per dollar of the original loan. The debtor country is paying for what the loans are actually worth, not less (and no more either).

This is not the whole story. Developing countries may effectively lose from engaging in debt

TABLE 12–9. Secondary Market Prices, Developing Country Debt, 1986–1990 (in percent of a dollar)

Year	Argentina	Bolivia	Brazil	Chile	Colombia	Costa Rica	Ecuador	Mexico	Nicaragua	Panama	Peru	Philippines	Poland	Venezuela
1990														
February	10.75%	11.50%	32.50%	64%	64%	19.50%	14.75%	40%	4%	17.50%	6.25%	48.50%	14.25%	36.50%
1989														
December	12.25	11.50	23.50	60.50	65	19	15	36	3	18	6.25	50.50	17.75	35.50
October	16	13.50	21.75	59.75	68.25	19.50	15.50	36.75	3	12.50	5.50	44.25	30.75	38.75
August	15	13.50	31.50	64.50	62.50	16	15.50	43.25	3	11.25	4.50	50.37	38.37	39.37
June	13.75	11	31	63	57.30	13	13	40	3	11	4	49	37.25	37
April	17.25	11	37.75	59.50	54	13.25	12.25	42.75	3	10	4	47.50	39.25	39
February	17.50	11	27	56	50.50	12	12	33.15	3	14	4.50	36	32.50	27
1988														
December	21.5	11	39.50	59	57	13	12.50	41.50	4	17	5	47.75	34.25	38
October	22.50	11	46.50	59	65	12	16.50	46.75	5	20	5	51	38	46.50
August	22.50	11	46.50	60	66.50	12	21	46.50	5.50	22	6	52.50	39	50
June	24.50	11	51.75	60.75	66	12.50	26	51.50	5	23.50	8	52.50	41	55
April	29	11	50	59	65	15	27	51	5	20	8	50	42	55
February	30	11	46	61	65	15	34	48	5	27	8	50	42	54
1987														
December	36	10	46	53	63	15	34	50	5	35	8	50	42	58
October	36	10	42	52	74	25	33	51	5	45	8	53	42	50
August	42	10	43	59	80	29	35	48	5	52	8	66	42	59
June	52	12	60	68.50	83	35	49	56	5	65	13	69	42	71
April	59	12	63	69	84	36	55	58	5	67	15	71	42	73.50
February	63.50	10	71	68.50	84	36	63.50	58	5	67	18	71	42	73.50
1986														
December	64	9	74	68.50	84	36	65	56	5	67	21	71	43	73.50
October	65	8	75	68.50	64	36	65	57	5	67	22	71	43	74.50
August	66	8	75	68.50	83	36	65	58	5	67	22	—	43	75
June	65.75	7.75	75	68.50	83	36	64	58	5	70	22	—	44	76
April	65.75	7.75	77	67.50	83	36	64	58	5	70	22	—	45	77.50
February	66	7.75	76.50	69	83	36	69	64	8.25	73	22	—	45	78

SOURCE: Based on quotes cited in the magazine *Latin Finance*, April 1990, p. 15.

318

buybacks. The reason is that the price of secondary debt changes when a debt buyback is undertaken. Consider a self-financed buyback and let us examine how it affects the price of debt in the secondary market. The secondary market price of debt reflects the probability of repayment of that debt. The lower the probability, the lower the secondary market price. The usually low price of Latin debt in the secondary markets in recent years means that repayment of the loans is considered unlikely. When a chunk of existing debt is bought, the remaining debt becomes less risky: With some debt retired, the debtor country has more financial flexibility with which to pay for the remaining debt. Hence, the price of the country's debt in the secondary markets rises. However, if holders of secondary debt anticipate that this price increase will occur as a consequence of the buyback, they will not wait to see what happens after the buyback occurs. They will be unwilling to sell their debt to the developing country at the low, existing price—a price that reflects the risk situation before the buyback. Rather, they will immediately ask for a higher price, which represents the improved risk rating of the country when it engages in the buyback. Thus, the country will be forced to pay the higher price. This represents an additional cost of the buyback to the developing country. It is a transfer to the private banks, which are the ones that really gain on a net basis from the operation. This suggests that, in order to benefit from debt buybacks, countries conducting them might have to seek, in addition, debt concessions from the banks holding the debt. In this way, the countries would share in the gains of the buybacks with the private banks.

Debt buybacks do not have to be self-financed. Third-party buybacks involve cases in which a third party—a government or an institution—provides funds to a developing country so that it can buy its own debt. In addition, secondary debt can be forgiven or retired by creditors. The implication of the analysis just carried out is that third-party buybacks and debt forgiving entail costs that partially offset the attached gift of resources. The reason is that the secondary debt

prices rise, thus increasing the cost of the debt to the developing country. The Bolivian buyback of March 1988, based on donated resources, exemplifies this point and is discussed next.

In March 1988, Bolivia engaged in a buyback of $34 million in secondary bank debt, illustrating how a country might lose from a buyback.[39] The price of Bolivian debt was 6 cents to the dollar in August 1986, just before the buyback was proposed in September 1986. At 6 cents per dollar, the $670 million that the country owed to banks was valued at $40.2 million in the secondary market. After the repurchase was completed in March 1988, the country had $362 million in debt that was valued at 11 cents on the dollar in April of that year, or $39.8 million. The net reduction in the market value of the debt over this time period was only $0.4 million, obtained at a cost of $34 million. The $34 million reduced the face value of Bolivia's debt by $308 million ($670 − $362), at an average cost of 9.06 cents to the dollar rather than 6 cents to the dollar. Stanford economist Jeremy Bulow and Princeton's Kenneth Rogoff suggest that the price increase was largely the result of the buyback. Data on the secondary market bid prices for fifteen highly indebted countries shows that these dropped between August 1986 and April 1988 for all except Bolivia. (This is confirmed in our Table 12–9, which shows secondary prices.) Bulow and Rogoff attribute the increase in the price of Bolivia's debt to the buyback.[40]

---

[39]The 1988 Bolivian buyback is discussed in J. Bulow and K. Rogoff, "The Buyback Boondogle," *Brookings Papers on Economic Activity*, no. 2 (Washington, D.C.: Brookings Institution, 1988). Because the $34 million represented donations, there was no net loss from the transaction for Bolivia.

[40]The evidence could be interpreted differently, however. Secondary market prices had reached 10 cents on the dollar in 1987, a year before the buyout was completed. The increase in the price of secondary debt might not have been related to the buyback or to any expectations generated by it; it may simply have been a result of the economy's recovery from depressed hyperinflationary conditions, which occurred between the time the buyback was proposed in September 1986 and its completion in March 1988. For an analysis of secondary market prices, *(continued)*

Debt-Equity Swaps

Debt-equity swaps differ from debt buybacks in that debt bought at discounted prices in the secondary market is paid for by equity claims rather than cash. In 1985, Chile began a debt-equity swap program that served as the model for Mexico, Argentina, Brazil, Nigeria, and others. Since that time, more than $10 billion in debt has been swept out through this mechanism.[41] Debt-for-equity swaps have been part of privatization programs in Argentina and Mexico. For instance, in Argentina, debt was exchanged for investments in the privatized telephone and airline companies.

The debt-for-equity swap typically works like this. The country finds a multinational corporation willing to buy secondary debt and to sell it back to the debtor country in exchange for the country's money. The money given by the country is then invested by the multinational in local equity shares or placed in the debtor economy through direct investments. The net result of the operation is to exchange outstanding debt for equity shares that do not entail repayment or interest-payment commitments. Notice that this mechanism can have inflationary effects if the country's central bank issues local currency to the multinational firm. Also, although swaps have been hailed as generating new capital flows to countries in severe need of such inflows, the mere fact that a swap is accompanied by a capital inflow does not mean that this is in excess of what would have been realized if the swap had not occurred.[42]

A debt-to-debt swap is simply an exchange of one type of debt for another of a different type—that is, with different terms or maturities. For instance, outstanding debt can be exchanged for debt that is more senior, meaning that it is to be paid in full before payments on the existing debt are made. Because senior debt has priority, there will be situations in which the senior debt receives payments but not the lower-priority debt. This harms the old creditors. Lenders thus traditionally object to the issuance of new debt that has a higher priority than outstanding claims on borrowers. This prevents de-facto expropriations by new-debt issues. The arrangement is often prohibited or limited in loan agreements.

The Mexican debt swap of 1988 illustrates the problems with debt reduction through confiscation of the existing debtors' position. The Mexican plan, announced in December 1987, retired old bank debt by issuing bonds and using the proceeds to buy secondary debt at a discount of about 50 percent. This operation combines a debt-to-bond swap with a cash buyback. The interest on the twenty-year bonds, but not the principal, was guaranteed by U.S. Treasury obligations held by the Mexican authorities. This guarantee was intended to make the bonds a senior debt instrument in comparison to the existing bank debt, and thus to command a lower discount than the existing debt. And it did so because $3.67 billion of the bank debt was retired with $2.56 billion of newly issued bonds. However, this was not all that happened. The bonds carried a higher interest rate than that prevailing for bank reschedulings and did not entail a true net benefit. This outcome can be interpreted as showing that the Mexican government failed to establish a credible claim that the new bonds would be senior to existing debt.[43]

see S. Ozler and H. Huizinga, "Bank Exposure, Capital and Secondary Market Discounts on Developing Country Debt", National Bureau of Economic Research, Working Paper no. 3961 (March 1992).

[41] See World Bank, *World Debt Tables, 1990–91* (Washington, D.C.: The World Bank, 1991), p. 46.

[42] Debt-equity swaps are discussed by F. Larrain and A. Velasco in "Can Swaps Solve the Debt Crisis? Lessons from the Chilean Experience," *Princeton Studies in International Finance* (November 1990); and S. Edwards, "Capital Flows, Foreign Direct Investment, and Debt-Equity Swaps in Developing Countries," National Bureau of Economic Research Working Paper no. 3497 (October 1990).

[43] The Mexican debt deal is examined in J. Williamson, *Voluntary Approaches to Debt Reduction* (Washington, D.C.: Institute for International Economics, 1988); and S. Van Wijnbergen, "Mexico and the Brady Plan," *Economic Policy* (February 1991).

Debt-for-Nature and Other Types of Swaps

Other variations on debt swaps are debt-for-nature swaps, debt-for-trade swaps (Peru and Yugoslavia), debt-for-scholarship swaps (Ecuador), and debt-for-health swaps. Bolivia, Ecuador, Costa Rica, and the Dominican Republic have conducted various versions of debt-for-nature swaps. This type of swap exchanges external debt for the debtor country's commitment to invest domestic currency funds in protecting or improving a previously approved domestic natural resource. Projects financed by swaps have involved environmental protection of areas with a rich biological life, ecological conservation, and indigenous communities. The importance of debt-for-nature swaps has been small compared with buybacks and other types of swaps. In Latin America more than $90 million dollars in debt had been redeemed through this mechanism by the end of 1990. The dollar cost of these operations only mounted to about $14 million because the debt of the countries involved was selling at big discounts when the swaps took place.

A debt-for-nature swap operation entails the following steps:

1. Participating foreign governments or institutions, such as a conservation organization, buy at a discount a financial instrument or note representing a portion of the country's external debt.

2. The dollar-denominated note is transferred to the debtor country government. This transfer liquidates the debtor's external commitment. The debtor government pays for the note by means either of domestic currency or the issuing of a domestic currency-denominated promissory note. The cash or promissory note is then dedicated to a previously agreed conservation project.

The devaluation of debt-for-nature swaps is complicated by the fact that they usually involve a negotiated element that is difficult to assess in advance. The dollar-denominated note representing the foreign debt is bought at a discount below its face value. However, when it is transferred to the debtor's central bank in exchange for local cash or a domestic currency-denominated asset, the discount obtained on the purchase is not necessarily transferred to the debtor country. In Latin American debt-for-nature swaps conducted between 1987 and 1990, the conversion of foreign-currency debt into local-currency debt entailed an average discount of 41 percent rather than the 85 percent at which the debt was purchased in the first place.[44] In other words, buyers paid 15 cents/$ in face value, but then sold the instrument to the debtor country at the higher price of 59 cents/$ of face value. Depending on how expensive this conversion is, the debtor country can win or lose in the transaction.

Alternative Approaches to the Debt Crisis

Despite the growing popularity of debt-reduction schemes and major debt-relief efforts on the part of creditor governments, there are some scholars who recommend caution. There is, first of all, a moral-hazard problem in that debt relief allows governments that have mismanaged the use of their borrowed funds to "get away with it." Debt relief thus provides an incentive for them to continue to mismanage, in the expectation that if another crisis emerges their debts will again be forgiven by their creditors.[45] The basic difference between private-sector and sovereign debt (debt owed by sovereign states) is that in the latter there is no collateral that creditors can acquire in the

---

[44]U.N. Commission for Latin America and the Caribbean (ECLAC), "Debt-for-Nature Swaps in Latin America," *CEPAL News* (May 1991).

[45]This argument has been made by W. H. Buiter and T. N. Srinivasan, "Rewarding the Profligate and Punishing the Prudent and Poor: Some Recent Proposals for Debt Relief," in P. King, ed., *International Economics and International Economic Policy: A Reader* (New York: McGraw-Hill, 1990).

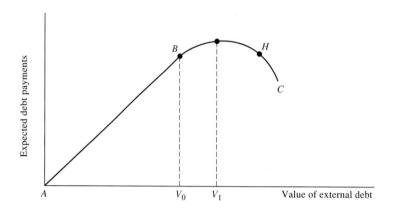

FIGURE **12–5.**   The Debt Laffer Curve

event of default.[46] Repayment of sovereign debt is therefore a decision made by governments after they weigh the local political costs of raising the revenues required by debt service against the costs of breaking off normal relations with international financial markets in case of default. If debt relief is prevalent, the costs of default decline, making the reemergence of problem debt more likely.

Debt-reduction schemes work on two premises: (1) that developing countries are not likely to be able to repay all their debts, so that creditors should forgive that part of the debt that is unlikely to be paid; and (2) that the debt overhang stifles long-run growth in the debtor nations. These two premises have been subject to criticism from some economists. Consider the first one. Some take argument with the assumption that developing countries—especially natural-resource rich countries like Venezuela or Mexico—would not be able to service their debts over the long haul. Even if they are not likely to service all their debts now, so long as there is a possibility—even if relatively small—that they will be able to do so in the future, it would not be in the interests of creditors to

forgive the debts. Indeed, the rapid (though temporary) rise of the price of oil in 1990 made it clear that oil-exporting developing countries could get a huge bonanza that would enable them to repay a larger fraction of their debts to private banks. The banks would thus be unwise to forgive debts for which there was still the potential for repayment.

The second premise of proponents of debt reduction is that reducing the debt overhang will raise the probability that the remaining debt will be paid by stimulating economic growth, benefiting both debtors and creditors. It is therefore argued that it is possible for debt reduction to raise the expected payments from the debt, if the likelihood that the remaining debt will be paid is much greater. This possibility is depicted in Figure 12–5. The horizontal axis in this figure represents the nominal value of developing country debt and the vertical axis shows the expected payments from the debt.[47] The segment AB shows how higher debt is associated with equal increases in expected payments when the debt is relatively

---

[46]See D. Cohen, *Private Lending to Sovereign States* (Cambridge, Mass.: The MIT Press, 1991).

[47]For more details on this diagram, see P. Krugman, "Developing Countries in the World Economy," *Daedalus* (Winter 1989).

small: both rise in the same proportion because, at low levels of debt, banks can expect full repayment from debtors. At debt levels above V_0, however, there is a positive probability that the country will not be able to completely repay its debts. The curve BC then shows how the expected debt payments behave in response to higher and higher levels of indebtedness. Note that at very high levels of debt, above V_1, increased indebtedness reduces the expected repayments on the overall debt. After a point, debt becomes so big that economic growth in the country is hampered and perverse incentive effects surface that reduce expected payments in absolute terms. Various factors can give way to these perverse incentive effects. Large debt accumulation implies large repayments and greater taxes to finance them. Greater taxes reduce incentives to invest and to engage in productive effort, reducing economic growth and the country's ability to pay.[48] Also, excessively high debt leads to conflict between debtors and creditors, as well as among various groups within the domestic economy. These conflicts lead to lower expected debt repayments. This means that, at a point like H, debt reduction would actually increase expected debt payments; both debtors and creditors would benefit from it (the creditors benefit because expected repayments increase and the debtors win because of increased growth). Proponents of debt relief believe that this is the case for at least some heavily indebted countries.

It all depends, however, on where the heavily indebted countries are along curve AC, a curve that has become known as *debt Laffer curve*.[49] Opponents of debt relief think that most of the severely indebted countries are not in the downward-sloping region of the debt Laffer curve. Their argument is that these countries do not have levels of debt large enough for the growth-stifling effects noted earlier to occur.[50]

Even if we assume that reducing debt overhang will help developing countries, a second problem is whether debt-reduction schemes as implemented under the Brady Plan actually help developing countries. Some argue that, despite the appearance that debt-reduction schemes actually benefit the debtor countries, they can in fact provide very little gain. This was shown very clearly in the previous section: Buybacks and other market-based debt reductions may just funnel funds from the pockets of taxpayers in industrialized countries (ultimately financing the buybacks) to the coffers of private banks.[51] On the other hand, mechanisms can be developed that would distribute any possible gains from debt reduction to both creditors and debtors (see the appendix for details).

Whatever the outcome of debt-reduction policies, many severely indebted countries have reacted to their crises by trying new economic policies, hoping to stimulate long-run economic growth and reduce fiscal deficits. A large number of governments have embraced the use of free markets and the elimination of government restrictions on domestic and international trade. For instance, shortly after his inauguration in July 1989, Argentina's President Carlos Menem introduced new policies to induce greater openness toward international trade, privatization of state-owned enterprises, and increased market orientation. They reversed decades of inwardly oriented development and strong interference with market mechanisms. Some variant of market-oriented reforms has been followed by Mexico, Venezuela,

---

[48]See I. Diwan and D. Rodrik, "External Debt, Adjustment, and Burden Sharing: A Unified Framework, *Princeton Studies in International Finance* (November 1992).

[49]In honor of Arthur B. Laffer, the economist who immortalized the paradoxical idea that reducing taxes may raise a government's tax revenues.

[50]See J. Eaton, "Debt Relief and the International Enforcement of Loan Contracts," *Journal of Economic Perspectives* (Winter 1990).

[51]See J. Bulow and K. Rogoff, "Cleaning Up Third World Debt Without Getting Taken to the Cleaners," *Journal of Economic Perspectives* (Winter 1990).

Poland, Turkey, and other debtor countries.[52] The outcome of these reforms remains to be seen. Market-oriented programs have been associated with the renewal of sustained growth in Chile, Mauritius after 1984, and Mexico after 1988. However, the new market orientation has not yet eradicated political turbulence and economic instability. Attempts to implement the programs have evoked great resistance and have not often yielded quick progress.

From a 1993 vantage point, it could be argued that the worst of the developing country debt crisis is over. In many of the indebted countries, debt/GNP or debt/exports ratios have gone down substantially over the last few years. The exposure of American banks to developing country debt has also declined drastically. In fact, a large share of the debt owed by the heavily indebted developing countries in 1982 has been paid over the last decade. For instance, in terms of the present value of the debt, estimates are that Argentina paid 40 percent of its debt from 1983 to 1989, Mexico 62 percent, Brazil 38 percent, Nigeria 30 percent, and Venezuela 75 percent.[53]

In spite of the overall release from the grip of the debt crisis, a greater number of indebted countries, particularly the low-income countries, face grim economic conditions. Among many African and Asian countries, external debt continues to rise and standards of living to deteriorate. Similar conditions hold among the former Soviet Republics and East European economies. We can only conclude that the issues discussed in this chapter will remain in the forefront of the international agenda long into the 1990s.

[52]For a discussion of the economic reforms followed by developing countries in recent years, see World Bank, *World Development Report* (New York: Oxford University Press, 1991); and L. B. Krause and K. Kihwan, eds., *Liberalization in the Process of Economic Development* (Berkeley: University of California Press, 1991).

[53]As computed by D. Cohen, "The Debt Crisis: A Postmortem," in O. J. Blanchard and S. Fischer, eds., *NBER Macroeconomics Annual 1992* (Cambridge, Mass.: The MIT Press, 1992), pp. 70–71.

Summary

1. The debt crisis of developing countries took full force after the government of Mexico announced in August 1982 that it would be unable to continue servicing (paying interest and amortization payments on) its debt. By 1986, a large number of Latin American and African countries had joined the class of countries not servicing their external debt. As late as 1991, none of the heavily indebted countries was able to obtain credit on a normal basis in international financial markets.

2. Creditors confronted the widespread nonservicing of debt by engaging in concerted actions entailing the provision of new lending and by rescheduling nonserviced debt payments. Concerted lending arrangements involve a group of creditors that get together to make credit available to debtors usually under a series of conditions. The Paris Club of creditor countries has been the major channel for creditor countries' concerted actions in rescheduling debts. Debt rescheduling means that debt repayment is negotiated to be postponed. Interest is charged on the amounts owed, but the principal is not increased; for this reason, debt rescheduling can be seen as a mechanism to convert short-term debt into longer-term debt.

3. The IMF has played a major role in the crisis. It served as a lender of last resort through its own lending activities. The IMF supplies funds to indebted countries by means of "standby" arrangements. These provide lines of credit to the borrowing countries, but only under a set of conditions referred to as IMF conditionality.

4. Although there is no unique profile for debtor countries, troubled debtors are frequently characterized by a variety of the following traits, when compared to less strained debtors: large debts to private creditors relative to that owed to official lenders; high debt-to-exports ratios; unprofitable investments and unsound

financial strategies that do not provide buffers to face economic slowdowns; high government deficits; and capital flight and overvalued exchange rates.

5. The strength and length of the debt crisis is related to a series of factors that slowed down the recovery. The adverse short-term effects of IMF-sponsored austerity programs have been coupled with extended isolation from financial markets to produce a delay in recovery in some countries. Negative resource transfers coupled with positive net flows of public and publicly guaranteed external debt have caused protracted financial strain. Substantially higher real interest rates on dollar-denominated assets in the 1980s harmed debtors, while the dislocation of internal financial markets entailed unstable domestic rates that led to capital flight. Capital flight meant that new lending to developing countries went to finance capital outflows. To make matters worse, adverse terms of trade changes hit hard on a large number of developing countries, accentuating the crisis.

6. Debt relief has taken the form of concerted new lending, reschedulings, forgiving of debt, and various forms of debt buybacks and swaps. A debt buyback entails entering the secondary market to buy debt that is trading at prices below the face value. Debt buybacks can be financed by the debtor, by the creditors (forgiving), and by third parties. Debt-equity swaps differ from debt buybacks in that debt bought in the secondary market is ultimately paid for by equity claims rather than cash. A debt-to-debt swap is the exchange of one type of debt for another with different maturity or terms.

7. Debt buybacks look like bargains, but they are deceptive. Because the secondary price reflects the likelihood of repayment, they are adjusted upward as a result of the buyback; this increases the cost of the operation to the debtor and yields a gain to the creditors.

8. The debt Laffer curve shows the relationship between the value of developing country debt and expected payments on that debt. It shows that, at high levels of debt, further increases in debt result in a reduction of expected payments. This is so because the high debt has a number of effects that constrain economic growth in the debtor country, reducing its ability and willingness to pay.

Problems

1. Using the national income accounting equations developed in Chapter 11, show how changes in private investment, national savings, and government budget deficits could augment or reduce the external debt of a developing country.

2. On the basis of the discussion and data presented in this chapter, do you think that the Feldstein-Horioka result explained in Chapter 10 holds for developing countries? If it does not hold, what makes the situation in these countries different from that of industrialized countries in this respect?

3. Is the following statement correct or incorrect: "Even if a country is in the rising portion of the debt Laffer curve, it would benefit from a reduction in debt." Explain your answer.

4. Using data from the World Bank's latest *World Development Report,* examine whether, currently, the savings rates of the heavily indebted countries in Table 12–1 exceed those of the United States and Japan. (Hint: Find the statistical Appendix table on the structure of production, which gives data on gross domestic savings rates.) Then assess the following statement: "The heavily indebted developing countries have been overconsuming in recent years—relative to industrialized nations—which is why they have difficulties servicing their debts."

5. Calculate the current debt-GNP and debt-exports ratios for the United States. Are they higher or lower than for the countries in Table 12–1?

6. Is the following statement correct or incorrect: "Debt-nature swaps are a scam that provides gains to private banks, not developing countries." Explain your answer.

7. Recently, the city of Burlington, Connecticut, defaulted on its debts. What are the differences between this default and those of developing countries?

8. "Unless financed by third parties, debt buybacks represent a transfer from debtors to creditors." Discuss.

9. "Debtors will benefit from debt-to-debt swaps only if the swaps confiscate the position of the creditors and reduce the value of the creditors' debt." Discuss.

APPENDIX: THE MECHANICS OF DEBT REDUCTION AND THE DEBT LAFFER CURVE

This section describes the analytics of debt buybacks and swaps, utilizing simple, stylized numerical examples to pinpoint the basic principles.[A1] For this purpose, consider a country owing $100 billion and suppose that there is only a 40 percent probability that the debt will be paid in full. There is, thus, a 60 percent probability that things will go wrong and that the country will not be able to pay its debt in full. If the latter occurs, we assume that the country is able (or willing) to pay only $20 billion of its $100 billion debt. Under these conditions, creditors' expected receipts are the weighted average of the $100 billion received, with probability 0.40 and the $20 billion received with probability 0.60, or

Creditor's expected receipts before buyback
$$= (0.40)\$100 + (0.60)\$20$$
$$= \$52.$$

The $52 billion market value of the debt falls below the $100 billion face value because of the possibil-

ity of default. Investors anticipate a 0.40 probability for the best conditions (or good state) that would lead to full repayment. However, there is a 0.60 probability that the worst conditions (or bad state) will occur, which entail default and receipt of only a fifth of the amount lent. In this example, an investor would expect to receive $52 billion on average.

The secondary market for debt reflects the expected payments to investors. The secondary price of debt is determined on the basis of the investors' estimates of the probabilities of full and partial repayment. If investors value debt on the basis of their expected receipts, and if the secondary market accurately reflects the probabilities and values of repayments, we can compute the price of secondary debt simply as the expected receipts per dollar invested. In our example, the secondary price would be 52 cents to the dollar—that is, the debt trades at a discount of 48 percent of par. The high discount is the result of the high likelihood of default (a 60 percent probability) and the small amount anticipated to be received in the event of default (only $20 billion out of $100 billion).

The Effects of a Debt Buyback Financed by Third Parties

The simplest case of a debt buyback is the one financed by third parties, also called debt financed by donation. We will illustrate a buyback that is large enough to make the remaining outstanding

---

[A1]For more details on market-based debt reduction, see P. Krugman, "Market-Based Approaches to Debt Reduction," in R. Dornbusch, J. Makin, and D. Zlowe, eds., *Alternative Solutions to Developing-Country Debt Problems* (Washington, D.C.: American Enterprise Institute, 1989); I. Diwan and S. Claessens, "Market-Based Debt Reductions," in I. Diwan and M. Husain, eds., *Dealing with the Debt Crisis* (Washington, D.C.: World Bank, 1989); and P. Krugman, "Market-Based Debt-Reduction Schemes," in J. A. Frenkel, M. P. Dooley, and P. Wickham, eds., *Analytical Issues in Debt* (Washington, D.C.: IMF, 1989).

debt riskless. Going back to our previous example, a buyback of $80 billion will reduce outstanding debt to $20 billion. Because that is what the debtor country can pay under the worst conditions, the remaining $20-billion debt becomes free of default risk. The buyback thus causes the secondary price to increase from 52 cents to the dollar to a no-discount value of $1.00.

What is the cost of the buyback operation to the country purchasing the debt? It would seem that the cost is $41.6 billion ($80 billion purchased at 52 cents/$ of debt). This is misleading because once the buyback is announced, the price of secondary debt will rise and the country will not be able to buy it at the 48 percent initial discount. Existing investors will anticipate that, after the buyback, the price of the debt will go up to 100 percent of par value. No investor will be willing to sell unless it receives the post-buyback price, which is 100 percent of par value. At a price of $1.00, the cost of the debt is $80 billion.

Our analysis suggests that the $80-billion buyback operation will not be a bargain but rather a full $80-billion cost operation conducted with no discount. The costs of a swap with donation are really borne by the third parties financing the operation which is financing the developing country buyback. Who gets the benefits of the operation? It is clear that the creditors benefit from the revaluation of the debt from $52 billion to $100 billion. This price revaluation entails a $48 billion gain to the creditors. However, the operation cost was $80 billion. Thus, the question is still who gets the remaining $32 billion.

It is the debtors who gain the remaining $32 billion from the buyback. In order to visualize why the debtor country's benefit is $32 billion, consider the country's post-buyback commitments. First, notice that there is no difference in the amounts that the country would pay in the event that things go wrong (bad state). In this case, the debtor would pay $20 billion both before and after the buyback. The only difference is that, before the buyback, the $20 billion meant that only a fifth of the debt amount could be paid, whereas after the

buyback the $20 billion is enough to pay in full the reduced volume of debt. Consider now the eventuality that the debtor country falls into good times (good state). In this case, the country pays the full amount of its debts. But because the debt is now only $20 billion, payments are reduced from $100 billion to $20 billion—that is, by $80 billion. This represents a gain for the debtor country if the country falls into good times. How much is the expected value of this gain? The probability of falling into good times is 40 percent; therefore, the expected gain to the debtor country, in terms of reduced expected payments, is (0.40) ($80 billion) = $32 billion.

The Effects of Internally Financed Debt Buybacks

We have obtained the surprising result that most of the gain from a third-party financed buyback is obtained by the creditors. The financial gains of creditors and debtors, of course, depend on the specific example being considered; however, the point remains that the price-revaluation effect shifts the benefits toward creditors (see the preceding problems section for cases of other situations in which this holds). The analysis also suggests that a debt buyback entirely financed by the debtor should result in a net financial loss to them. To see how this can happen, just consider the previous example and assume that the buyback is paid by the debtor. The $80-billion cost of the buyback is now borne by the debtor country itself. This $80-billion cost and the $32-billion benefit net out to a $48-billion loss, which corresponds to the creditors gain. This example shows the fallacy of the notion of a debt buyback as a bargain. The revaluation of the debt that the buyback causes means that the buyer is financing a price increase rather than getting a bargain. When a third party pays for the operation, there is still a gain to the debtor on account of the reduced debt burden. If the debtor has to pay for the operation itself, the gains disappear when the costs of the operation are netted out.

The analysis of a debt buyback financed by the debtor has a tricky side that makes ambiguous our results concerning the benefits to debtors. Suppose that the $80 billion used to finance the buyback are taken out of money that was going to be used to pay off the creditors. This is a likely situation when the debtor is in a tight financial squeeze. In the extreme case in which all the money used in the buyback comes from what the creditors would otherwise get, it is easy to see that the debtors gain at the expense of the creditors. In practice, the gains to debtors and creditors depend on the origin of the funds used to finance the buyback, and no general result can be obtained.

The Analytics of Debt Swaps

We have discussed the mechanics of externally and internally financed debt buybacks. Another popular debt-reduction mechanism is the debt swap—that is, exchanging existing debt for a different type of debt. It should be clear that the effects of a debt swap are a function of the type of debt being exchanged for the existing debt. There are three possible cases, depending on whether the old or the new debt has precedence in repayment. When the old debt has a higher priority, in the sense that it is paid in full before the new debt is repaid, the old creditors are protected from the addition to the pool of creditors. On this account, the value of the old debt is unaffected by the increase in total debt. A similar situation arises if the new and the old debt have the same priority in the repayment queue. The swap then just involves exchanging a type of debt with the same type of debt with no net financial effect.

The effect of the buyback when the new debt is senior to existing debt, in the sense that newly issued debt has a higher priority for repayment, is more complicated to analyze because the old lenders' position is effectively expropriated as a result of the operation. Consider now our previous example and suppose that a debt-retirement operation occurs in which the new debt gets all the payments in the case of default. In other words, new senior debt is issued with a value of $20 billion. Because this is the most the country can pay in the case of deteriorating conditions (bad state), the old creditors will get nothing if things become worse. The old lenders' debt will then be reduced in value as a result of the operation.

In order to compute the loss in the value of the old debt, notice that, although under a bad state the old creditors can expect to get nothing back, they still receive full payment in the good state. Expected repayments to the old lenders out of each dollar owed is then equal to the probability of the good state multiplied by the full payment received under those conditions—that is $(0.40)\$1.00 = \$0.40$ cents/$ owed. The price of the old debt will thus fall from 52 cents to 40 cents, as a result of the swap of senior for existing debt. Note that, at that price, the issuing of $20 billion of new debt can buy $\$20/0.4 = \$50$ billion of the old debt. Hence, the swap will involve the exchange of $20 billion of new debt for $50 billion of old debt, and total debt would be reduced by $30 billion.

What are the gains and losses from the swap operation? Old creditors lose $12 billion—that is, 12 cents per each of the $100 billion owed them. These debtors find that their position has been partially confiscated by the swap. The gain goes to the debtors. This can be seen by noting that the debtor's expected repayments before the swap were $52 billion, computed as $(0.40)\$100$ billion $+ (0.60)\$20$ billion. Post–swap expected payments equal $40 billion, computed as $(0.40)\$70$ billion $+ (0.60)\$20$ billion $= \$40$ billion.

PART IV

Income, Trade, and Capital Flows: Fixed and Flexible Exchange Rates

CHAPTER **13**

The Determination of Output, Exchange Rates, and the Trade Balance

This chapter is the first of three providing an introduction to the macroeconomics of an open economy under fixed and flexible exchange rate regimes. Our main goal is to analyze the determinants of key macroeconomic variables such as national output and employment, the trade balance, interest rates, and capital flows. We are particularly interested in the role of the balance of payments in bringing about macroeconomic adjustment under fixed exchange rates, and the corresponding role of exchange rate changes under floating exchange rates.

Ever since the early 1970s, there has been a marked increase in the flexibility of exchange rates as compared to previous decades. Before 1973, few countries had allowed their currencies to float over extended periods of time. Among the industrial countries, the only one having an extended experience with flexible exchange rates was Canada, which let its exchange rate float between 1950 and 1962 and then again after 1970. Since 1973, most industrial countries have faced an environment of considerable exchange rate flexibility. This situation is clearly expressed in Figure 13–1, which shows the exchange rate of the dollar against the British pound, the Japanese yen, and the deutsche mark.

The currency fluctuations since 1973 dwarf the changes that occurred before. In Britain, for example, only an extended, bitter dispute led, in 1967, to a 14 percent pound devaluation, which at the time was considered a major event. By comparison, from late 1980 to January 1984, the dollar price of the pound fell by more than half relative to the dollar. Sharp, short-term movements have become the rule in the behavior of dollar values vis-à-vis other industrial country currencies. For example, from September 1992 to January 1993, the dollar rose by close to 30 percent in value vis-à-vis the British pound. What factors affect exchange rates in a flexible exchange rate regime? Why is it that exchange rates have been so turbulent—that is, so variable—in recent years?

With these questions in mind, our discussion in this chapter begins with economies under flexible exchange rates. Our goal is to identify not only the factors influencing exchange rates, but also how currency values themselves affect output, the trade balance, and other variables. Chapter 14 shifts gears to study economies under fixed exchange rates. We focus on how macroeconomic mechanisms under pegged exchange rate regimes differ from those under flexible exchange rates. Chapter 15 gets back to a discussion of floating rates to explain exchange rate dynamics and the brusque ups and downs that are observed in currency values. We specify some of the major hypotheses about the short-run behavior of nominal and real exchange rates, output, and the trade balance, and

the crucial role played by expectations in this regard.

Our analysis is policy-oriented. We seek to establish the influences of government policies—in the form of fiscal and monetary policies—in an open economy and how these diverge from closed economies. For instance, Yale's Nobel Prize winning economist James Tobin has argued that U.S. authorities should engage in antirecessionary monetary policy, expanding the money supply in conditions of growing unemployment such as was the case in the United States in the early 1990s. He suggests that the dollar will depreciate in value in response to expansionary monetary policy, and "dollar depreciation is good medicine for a country suffering from a recession and trade deficit. It stimulates exports and slows imports."[1] Other economists are skeptical of the notion that exchange rate changes have any significant impact on international trade or domestic output, especially in recent years. MIT's Paul Krugman observes that "one of the most puzzling, and therefore one of the most important, aspects of the floating rates of the 1980s has been that huge swings in exchange rates have had only muted effects on anything real . . . the remarkable thing is not how much effect exchange rate changes have had but how little."[2] By the end of the following three chapters, we expect the reader to have an introductory framework of analysis within which the relationship between the trade balance and exchange rates can be examined.

This chapter is concerned with setting up the analytical model that has been called "the workhorse of traditional open-economy macroeconomics."[3] This framework was developed by economists Robert Mundell of Columbia University and Marcus Fleming of the IMF and is commonly

---

[1] J. Tobin, "Bring the Dollar Down," *The New York Times,* March 24, 1991, Section A, p. 27.

[2] P. Krugman, *Exchange Rate Instability* (Cambridge, Mass.: The MIT Press, 1989), p. 36.

[3] J. A. Frenkel and A. Razin, "The Mundell-Fleming Model: A Quarter-Century Later," *IMF Staff Papers* (December 1987). p. 568.

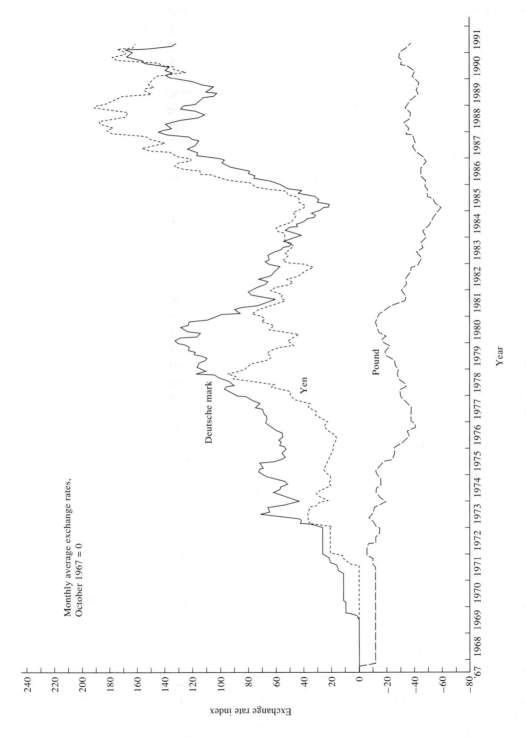

FIGURE 13–1. Behavior of Selected Dollar Exchange Rates, 1967–1991.

SOURCE: *OECD Economic Outlook* (July 1991).

referred to as the Mundell-Fleming model.[4] The fundamental basis of the approach is to apply a simple Keynesian view to examine the open economy (13–1). In the next section we begin our discussion by describing the nature of the Keynesian approach and its modeling of the goods markets. In later sections we examine the assets markets and the role played by capital mobility and the exchange rate in determining macroeconomic equilibrium. We then study the effects of economic policies.

13−1. AGGREGATE DEMAND AND INTERNATIONAL TRADE

Two of the key variables in macroeconomics are the price level and the output of domestic goods (two other variables are directly derived from these: inflation, which represents changes in the price level, and economic growth, which reflects increases in output). We know from introductory microeconomics that price and output in a market are determined by the interaction of demand and supply. Diagrammatically, we are all familiar with the determination of equilibrium price and production in a perfectly competitive market by the intersection of a downward-sloping demand curve and an upward-sloping supply curve. A similar conceptual framework can be applied in a macroeconomic context. Macroeconomics uses the concepts of *aggregate demand* and *aggregate supply* to determine the price level and output of domestic goods. Diagrammatically, the intersection of a downward-sloping aggregate demand curve and an upward-sloping aggregate supply curve specify the economy's equilibrium price level and production. There are, however, key differences between the microeconomic and macroeconomic concepts of

demand and supply. Macroeconomics deals with the aggregate outcomes of many markets, including various goods and asset markets; the theory behind the concepts of aggregate demand and aggregate supply is more complex than in microeconomics. It is useful, therefore, to begin within a simplified setting.

The simple Keynesian approach used in the present discussion is such a setting. Consider the market for domestic goods—that is, the market for goods produced domestically. The Keynesian framework assumes that the prices of domestic goods are rigid and that firms producing these goods can supply all the output that is demanded of them at the given prices. In a demand-supply setting, the assumption is that the aggregate supply curve of domestic goods is perfectly horizontal. Because sales are constrained only by the level of demand, it is the level of aggregate demand for domestic goods—that is, desired spending on domestic goods—that determines an economy's output. Diagrammatically, given a horizontal supply curve, changes in output are directly linked to shifts in demand.

This framework can be applied to economies suffering from severe unemployment and recession. In these economies, firms have excess capacity and could expand production at will, when so requested by customers. However, prolonged output expansions would be expected to move firms close to full employment; in that case, increased production would become more costly and firms would request higher prices when taking new orders. The Keynesian framework in this chapter may thus best be seen to apply in a short-run situation.[5] Remember Keynes's concern with

---

[4]R. Mundell, "Capital Mobility and Stabilization Policy Under Fixed and Flexible Exchange Rates," *Canadian Journal of Economics and Political Science* (November 1963); and J. M. Fleming, "Domestic Financial Policies Under Fixed and Under Floating Exchange Rates," *IMF Staff Papers* (November 1962).

[5]The Keynesian assumption of short-run price rigidity has been amply studied. Firms, for instance, often find it costly to alter posted prices because that involves changing catalogs and printing new information for customers (these are referred to as menu costs because of their association with the costs that restaurants face printing new menus). Firms also engage in contracts that fix the prices offered to customers in the short run. For the theory of and evidence on price rigidities, see N. G. Mankiw and D. Romer, eds., *New Keynesian Economics:*
(continued)

short-run phenomena, expressed in his famous dictum: "In the long run, we are all dead." The study of situations in which unemployment and underutilization of the economy's productive capacity are prevalent was one of the main motivations behind Keynes's 1936 masterpiece, *The General Theory of Employment, Interest, and Money,* published just when the impact of the Great Depression was being felt all over the world.

Within a simple Keynesian context, domestic output is determined by the aggregate demand for domestic goods. What factors influence aggregate demand? The first step in answering this question is to recall the national income accounting identities (summarized here but discussed in detail in Chapter 11). The basic national income accounting concept is the national income, or GNP, identity. It breaks down GNP—the value of all the final goods and services produced by a country's residents in a given period—into various spending categories. To specify these categories, first note the obvious fact that, in an open economy, the goods produced by a country's residents can be purchased by both foreign and domestic residents. The expenditures of foreign residents on domestic goods and services are our exports, symbolized by X_N (the subscript N denotes that the variable is measured in nominal terms). The expenditure of domestic residents on domestic products can be seen as a residual, equal to the total aggregate amount that domestic residents spend—referred to as absorption, A_N—minus the domestic spending on foreign goods and services, which represents imports, M_N. Symbolically, if we use Y_N as the symbol for total spending on domestic goods, then, adding its foreign and domestic spending:

$$Y_N = X_N + (A_N - M_N)$$
$$= A_N + (X_N - M_N) \qquad (13\text{--}1)$$
$$= A_N + T_N,$$

where $X_N - M_N$ is the net value of exports minus imports of goods and services, which, for expositional convenience, we will assume corresponds to the trade balance, T_N (the trade balance only includes trade in merchandise goods).

Equation 13–1 states that spending on domestic goods is equal to absorption plus the trade balance. Since in a Keynesian context output is determined by aggregate demand, the implication of Equation 13–1 is that domestic output will be influenced by domestic absorption and the trade balance. What are the determinants of absorption and the trade balance? Before answering this question, we must briefly digress to deal with another important issue.

Nominal and Real Variables

Up to this point, most variables in this book have been expressed in nominal terms, that is, in terms of their currency values (i.e., the dollar for the United States). It will be convenient, from this point on, to express variables in real terms, that is, in terms of physical units of domestic output. Since a nominal variable involves a quantity multiplied by a price, if we wish to transform it into a real variable (which involves only a quantity), we have to deflate it, that is, divide by an appropriate price. The real values of absorption, A, and the trade balance, T, can be obtained from their nominal values, A_N and T_N, by dividing by the price of domestic goods.[6]

To clarify the steps involved in transforming nominal variables into real variables in the open economy, consider the definition of the trade balance in nominal terms:

$$T_N = X_N - M_N$$
$$= PM^* - eP^*M. \qquad (13\text{--}2)$$

[6]We follow the standard simplifying assumption of open economy Keynesian analysis, which is that the country be specialized in producing exportables, part of which are consumed and part of which are exported. The price of domestic goods will then be the price of these goods, that is, the price of exports. If the country produces both exportables and importables, then the price of domestic goods is an index of the prices of both of these categories of goods; that is, it includes the prices of both exports and imports.

Imperfect Competition and Sticky Prices (Cambridge, Mass.: The MIT Press, 1991).

Note that M^* denotes the physical quantity of domestic goods exported (say, U.S.-produced Hotpoint appliances), which, when multiplied by the price of domestic goods, P, becomes the value of exports, PM^*. The variable M depicts the physical amount of foreign goods (say, Japanese-produced Toyotas) imported. When M is multiplied by the price of foreign goods in foreign currency, P^*, and then converted into domestic currency using the prevailing exchange rate, e (say, dollars per Japanese yen), it becomes the value of imports expressed in domestic currency (in dollars, for the case of the United States). The equality in Equation 13–2 therefore involves export and import categories expressed in domestic currency.

To express the trade balance in real terms, we divide both sides of Equation 13–2 by the domestic price level, P. The result is:

$$T = \frac{T_N}{P} = M^* - \frac{eP^*}{P} M$$
$$= M^* - qM, \qquad (13\text{--}3)$$

where $q = eP^*/P$ represents the relative price of imports in terms of domestic goods which allows us to convert quantities of foreign goods (M) into their equivalent in domestic goods (qM). The variable q, that is, the price of goods produced abroad (i.e., the price of imports) relative to that of domestic goods (i.e., the price of exports), is a central variable in our analysis of an open economy and is a particular version of the concept of real exchange rate (price-level-adjusted exchange rate) defined in Chapter 10. Note that q is defined as the ratio of the price of imports to the price of domestic goods, both measured in domestic currency. Since P^* is the price of goods produced abroad measured in foreign currency (pounds sterling per unit of British imports), and e is the exchange rate (measured in dollars per pound sterling), eP^* represents the price of imports in domestic currency (dollars per unit of British imports). By dividing this foreign price, eP^*, by

the price of domestic goods, P (which is always measured in domestic currency), we obtain q.

An increase in q means that imports become more expensive relative to domestic goods, improving domestic competitiveness in international goods markets. A reduction of q, by contrast, means that domestic goods become relatively expensive as compared with foreign goods, worsening the competitiveness of domestic goods in international markets.

In a nutshell, q measures the relative price of foreign goods in terms of domestic goods. Its use in Equation 13–3 is required in order to avoid adding apples and oranges—or Hotpoint appliances and Toyotas—when domestic exports and imports involve different commodities. By multiplying the volume of imports, M, by their relative price in terms of domestic goods, q, we express them in terms of domestic output. The qM can be subtracted from the exports of domestic goods, M^*, to determine the economy's trade balance, T, expressed in real terms.

Adjustments would also have to be made in transforming nominal absorption, expressed in domestic currency, A_N, into real absorption, A.

Exports, Imports, and the Determinants of International Trade

What are the determinants of the trade balance? The trade balance represents the difference between domestic exports and the value of imports. Domestic exports correspond to the foreign demand for domestic goods and, as with demand relationship, depend on relative prices and foreign income. Symbolically, domestic exports, M^*, can be represented by

$$M^* = M^*(q, Y^*), \qquad (13\text{--}4)$$

where q is the relative price of foreign goods in terms of domestic goods and Y^* is foreign real income. Note that as the relative price of foreign goods increases (as q goes up), foreign residents will switch their spending out of foreign and into domestic goods, with a consequent positive effect on domestic exports. Similarly, as foreign income increases (as Y* rises), some of that income will be spent on domestic goods and domestic exports, M*, will expand.

Domestic imports, M, correspond to the quantity demanded of foreign goods by domestic residents and are influenced by the relative price of foreign goods, q, and domestic real income, Y, or

$$M = M(q,Y), \qquad (13–5)$$

An increase in the relative price of foreign goods (i.e., a rise in q) results in a switch of domestic demand away from the relatively more expensive foreign goods and toward domestic goods. This switch reduces domestic imports (M declines). A rise in domestic income (i.e., an increase in Y), on the other hand, is associated with higher imports (i.e., a higher M) because some of the additional income will be spent on foreign goods.

Substitution of the expressions for the demand for exports and imports shown by equations 13–4 and 13–5, respectively, into the trade balance equation in 13–3 yields

$$T = M^*(q,Y^*) - qM(q,Y)$$
$$= T(q, Y^*, Y)$$
$$= \bar{T}(Y^*) - mY + \phi q, \qquad (13–6)$$

where the last row depicts the three basic determinants of the trade balance: foreign and domestic income plus the real exchange rate. The first component of the trade balance, $\bar{T}$, depends on foreign income, Y*, which is assumed to be exogenously determined, an assumption to be relaxed later in this book. Note that higher levels of foreign income shift upward the demand for domestic goods, increasing exports and improving the trade balance. This means that $\bar{T}$ rises when Y* increases. The second term in Equation 13–6 reflects the influence of domestic income on the

trade balance and is equal to mY, where m is the marginal propensity to import, defined as that fraction of the value of additional income spent on imports. Higher levels of domestic income raise imports and reduce the trade balance. The third term in Equation 13–6 reflects how the trade balance is affected by the real exchange rate, q. The parameter φ shows the impact of a given change in the real exchange rate on the trade balance. Note that φ can be positive or negative. If φ is positive, an increase in the real exchange rate would be linked to an improvement in the trade balance; if φ is negative, higher real exchange rates would deteriorate the trade balance. Because the nominal exchange rate enters directly into Equation 13–6 through q = eP*/P, the impact of exchange rate changes on the trade balance relates to the sign and magnitude of φ, a question to which we turn next.

The Effects of Exchange Rates on the Trade Balance: The Marshall-Lerner Condition

The issue of the links between exchange rate changes and the trade balance has been a controversial one. Some economists believe that the huge trade deficit accumulated by the United States in the 1980s was the legacy of the sustained appreciation of the dollar in the early years of that decade, which caused a substantial real exchange rate reduction. Others disagree completely, noting that there is no clear statistical evidence connecting exchange rate changes and the trade balance.

What can we say so far about this controversy? A close look at the first line of Equation 13–6 will confirm that the effect of exchange rate changes on the trade balance is ambiguous—that is, it can be positive, negative, or zero. Note first that the trade balance is influenced by the real exchange rate, q, not the nominal exchange rate, e. The reason is that the trade balance depends on the demands for domestic goods relative to foreign goods, and these demands depend on relative prices—that is,

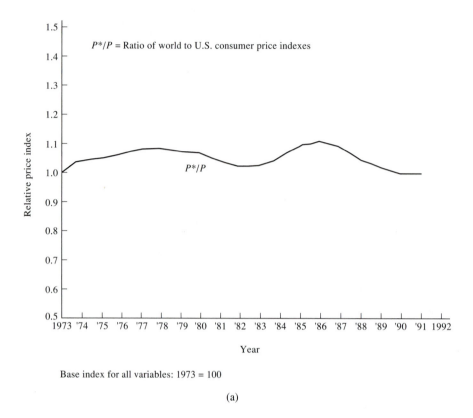

$P*/P$ = Ratio of world to U.S. consumer price indexes

Base index for all variables: 1973 = 100

(a)

FIGURE **13–2.** The Relationship Between Nominal and Real Exchange Rates, 1973–1991

SOURCE: *Economic Report of the President* (Washington, D.C.: U.S. Government Printing Office, 1992).

on how foreign goods compare in price relative to domestic goods. This means that changes in nominal exchange rates can influence the trade balance only insofar as they change real exchange rates. Could changes in nominal exchange rates fail to affect the real exchange rate? The answer is yes, if domestic and foreign currency prices—P and $P*$—adjust so that when e varies, $P*/P$ simultaneously moves in the opposite direction. Then, changes in nominal exchange rates would be offset by compensating shifts in $P*/P$, leaving the real exchange rate, $eP*/P$, unaltered. For instance, if a domestic currency depreciation—an increase in

e—causes an increase in domestic prices, P, of equal proportion, then $q = eP*/P$ would not change.

The simple Keynesian approach discussed in this chapter assumes that price levels are sticky in local currency. It thus implies that nominal and real exchange rates are closely connected to each other. In terms of our terminology, if P and $P*$ are assumed to be fixed, then $P*/P$ is rigid, and changes in the exchange rate, e, are directly related to real exchange rate adjustments, $q = eP*/P$. Is this assumption justified? Some evidence tends to support the Keynesian approach. Figure 13–2(a)

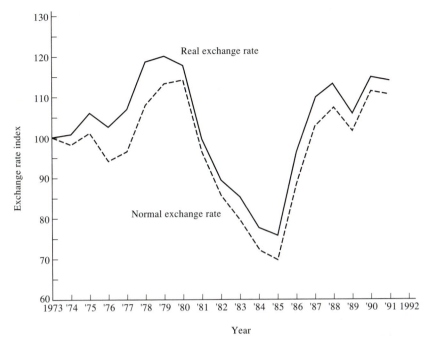

Year

Note: Nominal exchange rate = e = Federal Reserve Board multilateral trade-weighted exchange rate index. Real exchange rate = eP*/P

Base index for all variables: 1973 = 100

(b)

FIGURE 13–2 *continued*

shows that P*/P has been remarkably stable for the United States in recent years. The implication is clear, as exhibited in Figure 13–2b: nominal and real exchange rates move together.

Assuming that nominal and real exchange rates do move together, the mechanisms through which changes in real exchange rates affect the trade balance can be seen by returning to the first row of Equation 13–6. To simplify things, let us consider the effects of changes in the real exchange rate, q, *ceteris paribus*—assuming other variables are constant. In the present case, we assume that domestic and foreign income, Y and Y*, are fixed. We can then rewrite the first row of Equation 13–6 to read

$$T = M^*(q, \bar{Y}^*) - qM(q, \bar{Y}), \qquad (13\text{--}7)$$

where the bar over the variable Y means that we are keeping it fixed for purposes of this discussion. A domestic currency depreciation increases the relative price of imports in terms of exports, q, which tends to raise exports (i.e., M* increases) and decrease imports (i.e., M declines). The reason is that as q increases, domestic goods become cheaper relative to foreign goods, so both foreign and domestic residents tend to buy more domestic goods. This effect tends to improve the trade balance. The net effect of the depreciation on the trade balance is not clear, however, because an increase in q raises the amount that has to be paid per unit of imports. As a result, and as can be more easily seen from Equation 13–7, even though physical imports, M, decline, the total cost of imports in terms of the amount of domestic goods that have to be paid for them (qM) may increase. This may more than offset the increase in the volume of exports, M^*. Nevertheless, the more responsive the physical amounts of exports and imports are to the depreciation, the more likely it is that there will be a direct improvement in the trade balance. In this situation, the increase in exports, M^*, and the decline in imports, M, dominate the rise in q, with a net improvement in the trade balance.

The responsiveness of the demand for domestic exports and imports to a domestic currency depreciation is measured by so-called price elasticities of demand for domestic exports and imports. The price elasticity of demand for domestic exports, η^*, measures the percentage change in exports due to a 1 percent change in the relative price of foreign goods in terms of domestic goods. That is,

$$\eta^* = \frac{\Delta M^*/M^*}{\Delta q/q} = \frac{\Delta M}{\Delta q} \cdot \frac{q}{M}.$$

The higher η^* is, the more responsive exports are to a change in q. The price elasticity of demand for domestic imports, η, on the other hand, measures the (negative of the) percentage change in imports due to a 1 percent change in the price of foreign goods relative to domestic goods. Symbolically,

$$\eta = -\frac{\Delta M/M}{\Delta q/q} = -\frac{\Delta M}{\Delta q} \cdot \frac{q}{M}.$$

Note that because $\Delta M/\Delta q < 0$—that is, a rise in the relative price of foreign goods reduces imports—the elasticity, η, is positive. It is standard to express elasticities as a positive number. The higher η is, the more responsive imports are to a change in q.

As explained before, the higher the price elasticities of demand for domestic exports and imports, η^* and η, respectively, the more likely it is

that an increase in the exchange rate will have positive effects on the trade balance. The exact condition for a positive impact of a domestic currency depreciation on the trade balance is given by

$$\eta^* + \eta > 1. \tag{13–8}$$

The inequality in Equation 13–8 is the so-called *Marshall-Lerner condition*. It states that the direct effect of a domestic currency depreciation on the trade balance will be positive when the sum of the price elasticities of demand for domestic exports and imports exceeds 1. If we assume that the Marshall-Lerner condition holds, an exchange rate increase will improve the trade balance at any given level of income.[7] Stating this result in terms

---

[7]The direct effects of a domestic currency depreciation on the trade balance, holding foreign and domestic income constant, can be found by expressing Equation 13–7 in terms of changes (keeping Y and Y^* constant):

$$\Delta T = \Delta M^* - q\Delta M - M\Delta q,$$

where ΔM^* represents the change in exports resulting from the depreciation, $q\Delta M$ shows the change in imports (expressed in terms of domestic goods), and $M\Delta q$ denotes the change in the cost of imports connected to a change in the relative price of foreign goods, q. Expressing ΔT explicitly as the change in the trade balance arising from a change in q, and assuming, for simplicity, that the currency depreciates from a starting point of balanced trade ($M^* = qM$), then

$$\begin{aligned}
\frac{\Delta T}{\Delta q} &= \frac{\Delta M^*}{\Delta q} - q\frac{\Delta M}{\Delta q} - M\frac{\Delta q}{\Delta q} \\
&= \frac{M^*}{q}\left(\frac{\Delta M^*}{\Delta q} \cdot \frac{q}{M^*} - \frac{\Delta M}{\Delta q} \cdot \frac{q}{M} - 1\right) \\
&= \frac{M^*}{q}(\eta^* + \eta - 1)
\end{aligned}$$

or, more conveniently:

$$\Delta T = M^*(\eta^* + \eta - 1)\frac{\Delta q}{q} = M^*(\eta^* + \eta - 1)\hat{e},$$

where $\hat{e} = \Delta e/e = \Delta q/q$ is easily derived by recalling that because $q = eP^*/P$, with p and p^* exogenous, then $\Delta q =$

of Equation 13–6: the parameter ϕ is positive if the Marshall-Lerner condition is satisfied.[8] For instance, suppose that the price elasticity of demand for imports is equal to 0.5 and the price elasticity of demand for exports is equal to 1.2. In this case, the Marshall-Lerner condition is satisfied (because the sum of 0.5 and 1.2 is 1.7, which exceeds 1) and the parameter ϕ is positive. This result indicates that an increase in the exchange rate—holding other things constant—would improve the trade balance. On the other hand, were the elasticity of demand for imports to be 0.5 and the elasticity of demand for exports 0.2 (meaning that the demands for exports and imports are not very sensitive to changes in real exchange rates), the Marshall-Lerner condition would not be satisfied and the parameter ϕ would be negative. This result would suggest an *inverse* relationship between the exchange rate and the trade balance.

For expositional simplicity, our ensuing analysis will assume that the Marshall-Lerner condition holds (symbolically, the parameter ϕ in Equation 13–6 is assumed to be positive). Later in the chapter we will look at the evidence for whether the condition is satisfied.

Consumption, Investment, and the Determinants of Absorption

What are the determinants of domestic absorption? Absorption is the aggregate spending of domestic residents and includes consumption, investment, and government spending components (see the

discussion in Chapter 11). Each component is influenced by a whole range of variables, both economic and noneconomic, but the discussion at this point will concentrate on some basic determinants. Government spending, for instance, is assumed to be exogenous, at a level equal to $\bar{G}$, although in later chapters we will examine the political forces influencing government expenditures.

Consider consumption spending, C. Consumption depends mostly on income, Y, and we postulate the following linear relationship (function) between income and consumption:

$$C = C_o + aY.$$

The term C_o refers to *autonomous consumption—* the amount of consumption that does not depend on domestic income. The positive parameter a is equal to the marginal propensity to consume, which is that fraction of additional income spent on consumption by domestic residents. The parameter a is positive on the assumption that, as domestic income increases, domestic residents consume more. It is also less than 1, meaning that out of any additional dollar of income only a fraction is consumed. The rest is saved. Because additional income is either consumed or saved,[9] the marginal propensity to save, s, and the marginal propensity to consume, c, must add up to 1: $s + a = 1$.

Absorption is also responsive to domestic interest rates because of the influence of interest rates on investment spending. Investment spending is intended to increase (or maintain) the domestic capital stock. To finance the acquisition of capital, however, the firm (or household) has to borrow (or tie up) a certain amount of funds. The cost of these funds is the interest rate that has to be paid (or

---

$(p^*/p)\Delta e$, and dividing both sides by q: $\Delta q/q = \Delta e/e$. Note that $\Delta T > 0$ only if $\eta^* + \eta - 1 > 0$, which is the condition stated in Equation 13–8.

[8]We can determine the exact algebraic expression for ϕ using the derivations in Footnote 7. Taking changes in Equation 13–6, if income and other variables are held constant, the change in the trade balance, ΔT, associated with a change in the real exchange rate, Δq, is $\Delta T = \phi \Delta q$, or

$$\Delta T/\Delta q = \phi = (M^*/q)(\eta^* + \eta - 1),$$

where we have used the results obtained in Footnote 7.

[9]The simplified framework presented in this section assumes that investment and government expenditures do not vary with income. This implies that additional income is spent exclusively on consumption; hence, the marginal propensity to spend is equal to the marginal propensity to consume.

given up) for their use. Therefore, if the interest rate increases, the cost of purchasing new capital will rise and investment spending can be expected to decline. This effect is particularly important with respect to residential investment.

On the basis of these considerations, investment spending, I, is explicitly made a function of domestic interest rates:

$$I = I(i)$$
$$= I_o - bi,$$

where I_0 represents autonomous investment (that part of investment that is exogenous, or independent of both domestic income and the interest rate), and b is a positive parameter representing the responsiveness of investment with respect to the domestic interest rate, i. Note that $\Delta I / \Delta i = -b$, which is negative; in other words, the higher the rate of interest, the more firms (and households) have to pay to finance their investments, with the result that investment spending decreases.[10]

In summary, absorption is the sum of consumption, investment, and government spending, which, based on the algebraic expressions just stated, is represented by

$$A = C + I + \bar{G}$$
$$= C_o + aY + I_o - bi + \bar{G}$$
$$= \bar{A} + aY - bi, \qquad (13-9)$$

where $\bar{A} = C_o + I_o + \bar{G}$ represents autonomous absorption, that part of domestic absorption that does not depend on income or on interest rates. Note that $\bar{A}$ depends on the level of government expenditures, autonomous investment, and autonomous consumption—all of which are assumed to be independent of domestic income and the interest

rate. In addition, because the only component of absorption that is assumed to depend on the interest rate is investment, the responsiveness of absorption to the interest rate corresponds to the responsiveness of investment to the interest rate, b. The influence of income on absorption is related to the impact of additional income on consumption expenditures, as reflected by the marginal propensity to consume, a.

13-2. THE GOODS MARKET EQUILIBRIUM CONDITION AND THE *IS* CURVE

The Keynesian goods market equilibrium condition expressed in real terms states that domestic output, Y, is determined by the aggregate demand for domestic goods, which is equal in turn to absorption, A, plus the trade balance, T. Therefore, in equilibrium[11]

$$Y = A + T. \qquad (13-10)$$

---

[10]The interest rate relevant for the investment decision is the real interest rate, which is equal to the nominal interest rate adjusted for the rate of inflation. In the present framework, however, the real interest rate coincides with the nominal interest rate, since prices are assumed to be rigid.

[11]The equality in Equation 13–10 represents a goods market equilibrium relationship and it is *not* an identity (as it would be in a national income accounting framework). The reason is that the aggregate demand variables used in Equation 13–10, such as consumption and investment, involve specific behavioral relationships of economic agents and all represent *planned* spending levels. This means that $A + T$ depicts the aggregate demand for domestic goods that households, firms, government authorities and foreigners *plan* to spend. Usually, we do not expect to see a substantial gap between actual and planned government and consumer spending. In the case of firms, however, planned spending differs from actual spending whenever they find themselves carrying out unplanned investment in the form of unsold goods, which occurs quite frequently. If they do, the equality in Equation 13–10 would not be satisfied because there would be an excess of production over planned spending (firms would be accumulating unwanted inventories), and the economy would be out of equilibrium. The equality stated in Equation 13–10, then, does not always necessarily hold, as an identity must. It holds only when equilibrium is attained. When planned aggregate spending on domestic goods equals the aggregate supply of domestic goods, households and firms find themselves buying and selling the amount of goods they planned and there is equilibrium in the goods market.

Absorption, the aggregate spending of domestic residents, includes consumption, investment, and government expenditures and depends on income, the interest rate, and some exogenous parameters, as given by Equation 13–9. The trade balance is the difference between domestic exports and imports and is related to domestic income, the real exchange rate, and some exogenous parameters, as expressed by Equation 13–6.

Equations 13–6 and 13–9 can be substituted into the goods market equilibrium condition to yield

$$Y = A + T$$
$$= \bar{A} + aY - bi + \bar{T} - mY + \phi q. \quad (13\text{–}11)$$

By simplifying, we obtain

$$Y(1 - a + m) = \bar{A} - bi + \bar{T} + \phi q$$

or

$$Y = \alpha (\bar{A} - bi + \bar{T} + \phi q), \quad (13\text{–}12)$$

where

$$\alpha \equiv \frac{1}{1 - a + m} = \frac{1}{s + m}$$

is the so-called open economy Keynesian income multiplier. This multiplier can be easily calculated if the specific values of the marginal propensities to save and import in the economy are known. Suppose, for example, that the marginal propensity to save is equal to 0.2 and that the marginal propensity to import is equal to 0.3. In this case,

$$\alpha = \frac{1}{s + m} = \frac{1}{0.2 + 0.3} = 2.0,$$

which is the value of the multiplier for an economy with $s = 0.2$ and $m = 0.3$. The implication is that any net change in the spending categories

inside the parentheses on the right-hand side of Equation 13–12 would have a magnified effect on domestic income; the precise amount of this magnified effect depends on the precise value of the open-economy income multiplier. How different economic disturbances and economic policies affect the spending categories in Equation 13–12 will be discussed later in this chapter.

Equation 13–12 expresses the relationship between the level of domestic income, Y, and the interest rate, i, that keeps the domestic goods market in equilibrium at any given level of the exchange rate, e, and in the absence of disturbances affecting autonomous spending $(\bar{A}, \bar{T})$ or prices (P^* and P). Note that an increase in the interest rate reduces domestic investment; as a consequence, it decreases aggregate demand, requiring a reduction in domestic output (and real income) to maintain the goods market equilibrium. This negative relationship between domestic income and the interest rate is reflected in the negative slope of the so-called *IS* curve. The *IS* curve depicts the combinations of the interest rate and income that keep the domestic goods market in equilibrium. This graphic representation of Equation 13–12 is shown in Figure 13–3.

Two variables of key interest are assumed constant in deriving the *IS* curve: the relative price of foreign goods in terms of domestic goods, q, and the level of government spending, $\bar{G}$. An increase

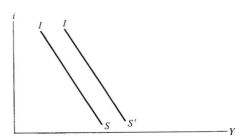

FIGURE 13–3. The *IS* Curve: Goods Market Equilibrium

in government spending at a given level of the interest rate and the real exchange rate will tend to raise aggregate demand (by increasing $\bar{A}$) and, therefore, domestic income by means of a multiplier effect. An increase in q, such as that brought about by a domestic currency depreciation, will shift demand away from foreign and toward domestic goods. This raises the aggregate demand for domestic goods and tends to increase domestic income. Both changes, an increase in $\bar{G}$ and an increase in q, shift the IS curve upward, as represented in Figure 13–3 by the rightward shift of the IS curve to IS'. By contrast, a domestic currency appreciation would—everything else constant—shift the IS curve to the left by inducing a switch in spending away from domestic and toward foreign goods, reducing the demand for domestic goods at a given level of the interest rate.

In analyzing shifts of the IS curve, it is important to remember the following rules: (1) Any factor that increases aggregate demand shifts the IS curve to the right through its positive income-multiplier effect, and (2) any factor that reduces aggregate demand shifts the IS curve to the left by means of a negative multiplier effect.

In summary, points along the IS curve represent different alternatives or possible pairs of income and interest rates consistent with goods market equilibrium. To be able to select one of these pairs as the economy's equilibrium, the assets markets, to which we now turn, must be considered.

13–3. INTRODUCTION TO THE ASSETS MARKETS

This section develops a concise presentation of the basic analytics of assets market equilibrium.[12] The assets markets are the markets in which money,

bonds, stocks, real estate, and other forms of wealth or stores of value are exchanged. Asset claims can be traded within borders, as when a New Yorker purchases Treasury bills from Merrill Lynch, or they can be traded across borders, such as when an Italian movie star buys some real estate in California. The volume and variety of assets being traded within and across borders are enormous. To simplify matters, we will consider the presence of only two types of assets: bonds and money. In addition, we will assume that residents of any given country hold only their own currency. We thus ignore *currency substitution,* which would occur if domestic residents were to hold foreign currency or if foreigners were to hold domestic money. Currency substitution is a significant phenomenon and we will return to discuss it in Chapter 19.

In our simplified framework, two types of assets are held by domestic residents: bonds and domestic money. Domestic money does not yield any interest, but it serves as a store of value and as a means of transaction. At any given moment in time, the nominal money supply is fixed, although it may change over time. We represent this fixed money supply existing at any given moment in time by M^S. This implies that the real money supply would be M^S/P, where P is the price of domestic goods (exports), as defined earlier. If P is rigid, as in the Keynesian model used in this chapter, a fixed nominal supply of money implies a fixed real supply of money.[13] The (real) supply of bonds, which are interest-yielding assets, is also assumed to be fixed. Expressed in terms of domestic goods, the stock of bonds in the economy is represented by V^S. Total (real) wealth in the economy is then given by

$$\frac{\hat{W}}{P} = \frac{M^S}{P} + V^S, \qquad (13\text{–}13)$$

---

[12]For a detailed discussion of the material in this section, see R. Dornbusch and S. Fischer, *Macroeconomics,* 5th ed. (New York: McGraw-Hill, 1990), chap. 4; and A. Abel and B. Bernanke *Macroeconomics* (Reading, Mass.: Addison-Wesley, 1992), chap. 4. These books should serve as a good background for the discussion carried out in the following chapters.

[13]Note that, following the literature, we express real variables in terms of export goods, even though, strictly speaking, a variable such as the money supply should be deflated by a price index that includes imports.

where $\hat{W}$ is the nominal wealth in the economy (i.e., wealth measured in dollars).

Domestic residents face a wealth constraint, in the sense that the aggregate value of bonds and money that they decide to hold (the amount they demand of money and bonds) cannot exceed their wealth. Because no one will throw away wealth, the demand for money and bonds will equal the supply of wealth in the economy—that is,

$$\frac{W}{P} = L^D + V^D, \qquad (13\text{–}14)$$

where L^D is the real demand for money (in terms of domestic goods) and V^D is the real demand for bonds.

Equating the expressions in Equations 13–13 and 13–14, we obtain

$$\frac{M^S}{P} + V^S = L^D + V^D$$

or

$$\left(L^D - \frac{M^S}{P}\right) + (V^D - V^S) = 0. \quad (13\text{–}15)$$

This implies that, as long as the money market is in equilibrium (i.e., as long as $L^D = M^S/P$), the bond market will also be in equilibrium ($V^D = V^S$). This result, usually referred to as Walras's law, justifies that we concentrate our attention on analyzing equilibrium in only one of the markets (either the bond or the money market). We choose the money market, which we will now analyze in detail.

The money market equilibrium would occur when

$$L^D = \frac{M^S}{P}, \qquad (13\text{–}16)$$

that is, when the demand for money is equal to its supply. On what variables does the demand for money depend? The real demand for money is given by

$$L^D = L\,(i, Y). \qquad (13\text{–}17)$$

We assume that real money demand, L^D, is a decreasing function of the interest rate, i, and an increasing function of real income in the economy, Y. Note that, as the interest rate goes up, the opportunity cost of holding money increases. Domestic residents then increase the proportion of their wealth invested in bonds relative to money (i.e., they shift funds out of money and into bonds). The positive effect of income on money demand is attributable to the fact that people hold money to finance their spending transactions; as income increases, people engage in more transactions, and money demand rises.

The demand-for-money function in Equation 13–17 can be linearized to

$$L^D = kY - hi, \qquad (13\text{–}18)$$

where k is a positive parameter representing the positive response of money demand to income, and h is a positive parameter that represents the responsiveness of money demand to the interest rate. Other variables affect the demand for money—domestic wealth and the development of the financial system, among others—but are held constant for purposes of this analysis.

The money supply is considered to be under the influence of monetary authorities in economies under flexible exchange rates. (We will delay studying the complications of the money supply process under fixed exchange rates until the next chapter.) We thus assume that M^S is an exogenous variable, determined by governmental and/or central bank policies. Expansionary monetary policy is associated with an increased money supply, whereas contractionary monetary policy involves a reduction in monetary holdings.

13–4. Assets Market (Money Market) Equilibria: The *LM* Curve

According to Walras's law, we can concentrate our analysis of assets market equilibria by looking explicitly only at the money market. Equilibrium in the money market occurs when money supply equals money demand. Algebraically, using Equations 13–16 and 13–18, we obtain

$$\frac{M^S}{P} = L^D(i, Y) = kY - hi. \quad (13\text{–}19)$$

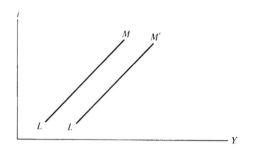

Figure 13–4. The *LM* Curve: Assets Market Equilibrium

Because the price of domestic goods, P, is rigid, there are only two endogenous variables in Equation 13–19: i and Y; M^S, k, and h are exogenous parameters.

By solving Equation 13–19 for the interest rate, it is transformed into

$$i = \frac{1}{h}\left(kY - \frac{M^S}{P}\right). \quad (13\text{–}20)$$

Equation 13–20 expresses the relationship between income and the interest rate that keeps the money market in equilibrium. Note that the implied relationship between income and interest rates is positive. An increase in domestic income raises the demand for money; given the money supply, the interest rate (the opportunity cost of money) must increase to clear the market.

Representing the interest rate on the vertical axis and domestic real income on the horizontal axis, Figure 13–4 plots money market equilibrium as a positively sloped locus, the *LM* curve. The *LM* curve shows the alternative combinations of the interest rate and real income that keep the money market in equilibrium and is drawn for a given level of the money supply, M_o. In algebraic terms,

$$i = \frac{1}{h}\left(kY - \frac{M_o}{P}\right). \quad (13\text{–}21)$$

The impact of changes in the money supply on the money market can be seen from Equation 13–21. For instance, an increase in the money supply, say from M_0 to M_1, gives rise to an excess supply of money, requiring a market-clearing reduction in the interest rate at any given level of income. This is shown in Figure 13–4 by means of the shift of the *LM* curve to *LM'*. Do not confuse *shifts* of the *LM* curve and *movements along* the *LM* curve itself. Shifts of the *LM* curve occur when a change in some variable affecting the money market (e.g., the money supply) alters the interest rate consistent with money market equilibrium, *at a given level of income*. Movements along the *LM* curve reflect the fact that alternative levels of income require different interest rates for money market equilibrium to occur, *ceteris paribus*—keeping all other variables affecting the market constant.

In summary, points along the *LM* curve represent different alternative or possible pairs of income and interest rates consistent with money market equilibrium. To be able to select one of these pairs as the economy's equilibrium, the goods and money markets must be considered both simultaneously. In addition, there is a third equilibrium condition that must be satisfied. This third condition states that the economy must have balance-of-payments equilibrium, as discussed in the next section on flexible exchange rates and the balance of payments.

13−5. FLEXIBLE EXCHANGE RATES AND THE BALANCE OF PAYMENTS

This section specifies the role played by the balance of payments in the analysis of economies under flexible exchange rates. It may prove useful at this point to leaf through Chapter 9 again to refresh your understanding of the balance-of-payments concepts. We supply here a very brief review.

The balance of payments catalogues all of the transactions of a country's residents with the rest of the world. These include transactions giving rise to payments to foreign residents—recorded as a negative item in the balance-of-payments accounts (such as when a U.S. resident imports Japanese cars from abroad)—and transactions that generate receipts from foreigners—recorded with a positive sign in the balance-of-payments accounts (as when a Japanese resident buys a CD at Citibank in New York).

There are many different ways to catalogue the transactions recorded by the balance of payments. One key set of transactions includes international trade in goods, services, investment income, and unilateral payments. The net balance of receipts and payments on these transactions is called the current account balance (CAB). If the CAB is negative—that is, in deficit—the economy has an excess of payments over receipts in its international trade in goods, services investment income plus unilateral transfers; if the CAB is positive, or in surplus, there is an excess of receipts over payments on these items.

A second category of transactions involves international trade in financial assets, including domestic sales of bonds and real estate to foreigners, and domestic purchases of foreign stocks and bonds, for example. The net balance of receipts and payments on these transactions is called the capital account balance. If the capital account balance is negative, or in deficit, the implication is that there is an excess of payments relative to receipts with respect to the economy's interna-

tional trade in financial assets, referred to as a capital outflow. If the capital account is positive, or in surplus, there is an excess of receipts over payments in the economy's international trade in financial assets, referred to as a capital inflow.

When economists refer to a balance-of-payments surplus or deficit, they are usually referring to whether the sum of the capital and current accounts is in surplus or deficit. (Other concepts exist and are discussed in Chapter 14.) A balance-of-payments surplus occurs, for instance, if the current and capital accounts are positive; balance-of-payments deficits may result from deficits in the current and capital accounts.

Suppose that there is a balance-of-payments deficit. The deficit indicates that the overall balance of the receipts and payments of the economy's international trade in goods, services, financial assets, and unilateral transfers is negative. In a nutshell, domestic residents are making more payments to foreigners than foreigners are making to us. Who finances this excess of payments over receipts? For instance, who supplies the foreign currency that is required to make these net payments to foreigners?

Consider economies under fixed exchange rates, in which central banks are committed to buying and selling foreign currencies on demand at a given exchange rate. For these purposes they hold official reserve assets in the form of foreign exchange inventories. When there is a balance-of-payments deficit, the "excess" payments made to foreign residents implied by that deficit are accounted for by changes in the official reserve assets of central banks. For instance, in the United States under the Bretton Woods system, the Federal Reserve could have supplied the required foreign exchange, reducing the Fed's official reserve assets. Alternatively, foreign residents could have sold their "excess" receipts in dollars to foreign central banks in exchange for their own currencies. In this case, foreign central banks end up increasing the dollars that they hold in U.S. banks as international reserves, which in U.S.

balance-of-payments terminology represents an increase in foreign official reserve assets in the United States. But the sum of the changes in U.S. official reserve assets and in foreign official reserve assets in the United States is called the *official reserve settlements balance* (ORS). A balance-of-payments deficit thus corresponds to a deficit in the ORS. A surplus in the balance of payments represents increases in domestic official reserve assets and/or reductions in foreign official reserve assets in the United States; it is therefore a surplus in the ORS.

For expositional convenience, we will abstract from considering unilateral transfers as well as the service and investment income accounts of the balance of payments. In this case, the current account corresponds to the trade balance and the balance of payments is then equal to the sum of the trade balance and the capital account. Symbolically,

$$B = T + K, \qquad (13\text{–}22)$$

where T is the trade balance and K is the capital account balance.[14]

In economies under fixed exchange rates, persistent balance-of-payments deficits and surpluses are seen with great concern by the public and policymakers. Central banks cannot continuously finance a balance-of-payments deficit without running out of foreign exchange reserves. The depletion of these reserves would then imply an inability of the government to intervene in foreign exchange markets and to maintain its commitment to fixed exchange rates. This might force a devaluation and/or a foreign exchange crisis, leading perhaps to a severe dislocation of the economy's foreign trade and financial sectors. As a consequence, persistent balance-of-payments deficits are usually seen as a state of affairs to be avoided. If a country faces a persistent balance-of-payments

[14]The statistical discrepancy is assumed to be part of the capital account; allocations of SDRs are ignored in this analysis.

surplus, on the other hand, it will systematically be acquiring foreign exchange reserves. These accumulated reserves represent funds that could otherwise be used to buy and consume goods currently, again a situation that is avoided by policymakers.

Under flexible exchange rates, monetary authorities do not face a "balance-of-payments problem," in the sense that they are not obliged to intervene in foreign exchange markets and thus do not have to worry about losing or gaining international reserves. As a matter of fact, in a world of *freely floating* exchange rates, in which central banks completely refrain from intervening in foreign exchange markets, there would be no changes at all in the international reserve holdings of central banks. In this situation, the balance of payments of the economy will be equal to zero. With central banks keeping their hands off foreign exchange markets, any excess demand or supply in the market would have to clear by itself. Therefore, the balance-of-payments deficits or surpluses that emerge under fixed exchange rates are no longer the outcome; under freely floating exchange rates, the exchange rate would adjust to guarantee external payments balance. In other words, the economy's international transactions recorded by the trade account, T, and capital account, K, will balance to zero. Symbolically,

$$B = T + K = 0, \qquad (13\text{–}23)$$

stating that balance-of-payments deficits or surpluses disappear under flexible exchange rates.

Suppose, for the sake of the argument, that the U.S. economy is initially at balanced payments and that there is a sudden surge of capital outflows as investors—perhaps because of an increase in interest rates abroad or because of reduced domestic interest rates—seek to sell dollars to purchase more attractive foreign assets. Under fixed exchange rates, these increased capital outflows (net purchases of foreign assets) would—other things being equal—generate a balance-of-payments deficit. But suppose that, as is the case under a freely fluctuating exchange rate regime, central banks do not intervene in foreign exchange markets. How then is the balance-of-payments deficit that would arise under fixed exchange rates eliminated? Everything else being constant, the excess supply of dollars associated with the capital outflows indicates that some investors trying to dispose of dollars would not be able to do so at the original exchange rate. In order to attract buyers, they have to accept a lower price for their dollars in terms of foreign currencies. That is, the dollar depreciates in foreign exchange markets. The increased exchange rate of the dollar vis-à-vis foreign currencies (in dollars per foreign currency) will then tend to eliminate the excess supply of dollars arising from the sudden capital outflow. The exchange rate would adjust—all else being constant—to eliminate the balance-of-payments deficit that would otherwise arise at a given exchange rate. The precise mechanisms involved in the interaction of exchange rate changes with balance-of-payments adjustments will be discussed in more detail in the next sections. Suffice it to say that an increase in the exchange rate tends to shift demand toward domestic goods and away from foreign goods, thus improving the trade balance. This acts to eliminate the payments deficit that would arise if the exchange rate were fixed. Similarly, factors that could generate a balance-of-payments surplus under fixed exchange rates—such as a surge of capital inflows or increased exports—tend to induce a currency appreciation under flexible exchange rates, ensuring that the surplus is eliminated.

13–6. PERFECT CAPITAL MOBILITY AND BALANCE-OF-PAYMENTS EQUILIBRIUM

What are the determinants of the balance of payments? Since the balance of payments is equal to the sum of the trade balance and capital accounts, the determinants of these two in turn influence the

balance of payments. Previously, we concluded that the key variables affecting the trade balance are domestic income, Y, and the real exchange rate, q. If we denote the dependence of the trade balance on the real exchange rate and domestic income by $T(q,Y)$, the balance of payments, B, is then given by

$$B = T(q, Y) + K(i - i^*), \qquad (13-24)$$

where the capital account is represented by K, with a capital account surplus—a positive value of K—associated with net capital inflows and a deficit—a negative K—with net capital outflows.

Equation 13–24 relates the capital account to the differential between the domestic interest rate, i, and the world interest rate, i*. In this chapter, we will assume that the economy is a small one in world financial markets, meaning that its financial transactions cannot in any way affect the world interest rate. This means that i* is an exogenous variable. This leaves the domestic interest rate as the key variable determining the capital account.[15]

How exactly does the domestic interest rate influence the capital account? One extreme case is that of *perfect capital mobility,* which refers to an environment of highly integrated capital markets, with investors rapidly obtaining information about interest rates in different countries and engaging in portfolio adjustments among national assets instantaneously and with minimal transaction costs. In this situation, the domestic economy can, at any time, borrow all it wants (sell all the bonds it wants) and lend all it wants (buy all the bonds it desires) at the prevailing world interest rate, i^*.

[15]There are other important factors influencing the capital account involving exchange risk, political risk, exchange rate expectations, etc.: factors considered in Chapters 4–6. For the present, we will assume that domestic and foreign bonds share the same characteristics in terms of liquidity, maturity, default risk, political risk, exchange risk, and so on. These assumptions greatly simplify the present discussion, although some of them are relaxed and discussed in great detail in later chapters.

Accordingly, the capital account is perfectly elastic (responsive) with respect to changes in the domestic interest rate relative to the world rate: Capital inflows and outflows emerge without requiring changes in domestic interest rates (or involving instead only negligible changes in interest rates). Any rise in the domestic interest rate above the world rate would tend to induce a massive capital inflow immediately into the economy, as investors shift out of foreign bonds and into the more profitable domestic bonds. A decrease in the domestic interest rate below the world rate, on the other hand, would induce a massive capital outflow, as investors shift out of domestic and into more profitable foreign bonds.

A less extreme case compared to perfect capital mobility is *imperfect capital mobility.* Imperfect capital mobility arises when the domestic economy has to raise its interest rate in order to attract foreign funds or to lower it in order to make domestic funds more attractive to borrowers. In this situation, if the country wants to increase its borrowing (lending) it has to increase (decrease) its interest rate i, above (below) the given world level, i^*. In addition, and in contrast to the case of perfect capital mobility, deviations in the domestic interest rate from the world interest rate will not generate massive capital flows; rather, they will induce only a certain finite flow, which will unfold gradually over time. Imperfect capital mobility can arise when domestic capital markets are not well integrated with world capital markets or when investors can adjust their portfolios only slowly, over time. In these cases, changes in the domestic interest rate above or below the interest rate abroad produce sluggish changes in portfolio composition and capital flows therefore take place gradually over time. The instantaneous adjustments possible under perfect capital mobility are impossible here.

In summary, changes in interest rates give rise to changes in the desired amounts and/or location of stocks of various types of assets. These then give rise to capital movements geared toward eliminating the gaps between the desired and actual stocks of assets. How long it takes to complete stock adjustments depends on the speed at which actual and desired stocks can be brought into equality. Under perfect capital mobility, the speed of adjustment is infinite: You can adjust your portfolio instantaneously just by engaging in telephone calls. Under imperfect capital mobility, the capital account responds to changes in interest rates, but to a lesser extent than in the case of perfect capital mobility. Given the world interest rate, an increase (or decrease) in the domestic interest rate will attract a certain inflow (or outflow) of funds over time; however, it will not create a massive flood (or exodus) of funds, as with perfect capital mobility. The capital account will be positively, but not infinitely, elastic with respect to the domestic interest rate.

The modern industrial economy is subject to a relatively high degree of financial integration with other countries. We live in a world where information about foreign interest rates, exchange rates, and so on, is widely available at a low cost by reaching for a phone or a computer terminal. We thus initiate our discussion of flexible exchange rates under the context of perfect capital mobility. This means that domestic investors can borrow or lend freely and instantaneously at the world interest rate, i^*, and foreigners can similarly lend and borrow in domestic capital markets at the domestic interest rate, i. Arbitrage between domestic and world capital markets then guarantees an alignment of domestic and world interest rates.[16] This is represented symbolically by the condition that, in equilibrium, is $i = i^*$.

---

[16]In general, under perfect capital mobility, the domestic interest rate will not be linked just to the world interest rate, but will also reflect the expected rate of depreciation of the domestic currency. Assuming static expectations, however, the expected rate of depreciation is equal to zero, leading to the equality of domestic and foreign interest rates stated in the text. The topic of exchange rate expectations and their influence on the economy will be discussed in Chapter 15.

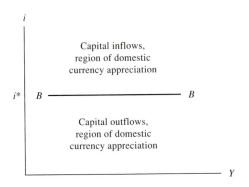

FIGURE 13–5. Capital Flows and Balance-of-Payments Equilibrium

In terms of Figure 13–5, perfect capital mobility imposes the constraint that balanced payments occur along the BB curve, which is drawn at a vertical distance equal to the world interest rate, i^*. The underlying reason for this constraint lies in the fact that, under perfect capital mobility, the capital account is extremely sensitive to deviations of the domestic interest rate from the world interest rate. When the domestic interest rate increases above the world level (when $i > i^*$), there is a huge inflow of foreign funds into the economy. This generates a massive capital account surplus that would move the balance of payments into surplus at a given exchange rate. In terms of Figure 13–5, the region above the BB curve—for which $i > i^*$—represents a region of balance-of-payments surpluses. By contrast, if the domestic interest rate were to fall below the world rate, massive capital outflows would move both the capital account and the balance of payments into deficit. The region below the BB curve thus represents balance-of-payments deficits. Only when the economy lies along the BB curve will balanced payments be obtained.

Note that, as will be discussed in the next section, under flexible exchange rates currency values would adjust to eliminate balance-of-payments surpluses or deficits. For instance, in the

region above the BB curve massive capital inflows would result in an increase in the supply of foreign currency (as investors shift from foreign into domestic bonds) at the original exchange rate. The increased supply of foreign exchange would then reduce the price of foreign currency; that is, the exchange rate would decrease or domestic currency would appreciate in value. But, in the region below the BB curve, massive capital outflows would augment the demand for foreign exchange (as investors shift from domestic into foreign bonds). The latter tends to raise the price of foreign currency; that is, there would be an increase in the exchange rate or a domestic currency depreciation.

13.7. DETERMINING EQUILIBRIUM OUTPUT AND THE EXCHANGE RATE

The equilibrium of the economy under perfect capital mobility occurs when there is simultaneous equilibrium in the goods and assets markets, as well as in the balance of payments. According to Figure 13–6(a), the equilibrium of the economy occurs at point E, which shows the intersection of the IS and LM curves along the BB curve at an equilibrium level of output equal to $\overline{Y}$.

One of the key properties of output determination under flexible exchange rates and perfect capital mobility is that, algebraically, domestic output is completely specified by the money market equilibrium condition. To visualize this important result, let us set $i = i^*$, as established by perfect capital mobility, in the money market equilibrium condition (Equation 13–19), yielding

$$\frac{M^S}{P} = kY - hi^*. \qquad (13\text{–}19a)$$

With the money supply fixed by the monetary authorities, with domestic prices rigid over the present short-run context, and with i^* the exogenously–given world interest rate, Equation 13–19a com-

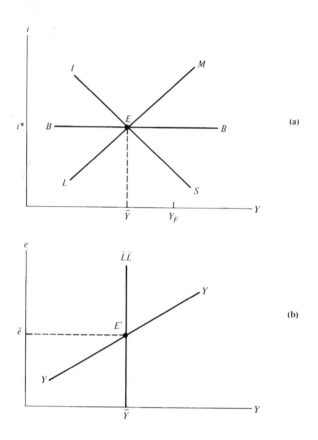

FIGURE 13–6. Determination of Equilibrium Output and the Exchange Rate

pletely determines the equilibrium level of income in the economy. Solving for that equilibrium level of income, we obtain

$$\bar{Y} = \frac{M^S}{kP} + \frac{h}{k}i^*. \qquad (13–19b)$$

Equation 13–19b shows the striking result that the equilibrium level of income, $\bar{Y}$, can be completely determined by the knowledge of three variables, M^S, P, and i^*. Combined with the world interest rate, i^*, M^S and P fully specify the equilibrium at point E. Still, note that neither Equation 13–19b nor Figure 13–6(a) tells us the equilibrium level of the exchange rate.

Figure 13–6(b) shows the determination of the exchange rate under perfect capital mobility. The vertical $\bar{L}\bar{L}$ curve represents all combinations of the exchange rate and income that keep the money market in equilibrium. From Equation 13–19b, it can be seen that the money market equilibrium specifies a level of income, $\bar{Y}$, which is not directly affected at all by the exchange rate, e. Money market equilibrium is consequently represented by the vertical line $\bar{L}\bar{L}$, resting at a level of income $\bar{Y}$ in Figure 13–6(b).

The YY line, on the other hand, depicts all combinations of the exchange rate and income keeping the goods market in equilibrium. It is derived by observing that, with $i = i^*$, Equation 13–12 becomes

$$Y = \alpha(\bar{A} + \bar{T} + \phi q - bi^*),$$

which denotes a positive relationship between the exchange rate and income. An increase in the nominal exchange rate, e, raises the real exchange rate, q, switching demand from foreign to domestic goods, requiring an increased output to maintain goods market equilibrium. A domestic currency appreciation, on the other hand, switches demand out of domestic goods and requires a reduction of domestic output. This positive connection between exchange rates and income in sustaining goods market equilibrium is what curve *YY* depicts. The equilibrium exchange rate is specified by the condition that the goods market clear at a level of income ($\bar{Y}$) consistent with equilibrium in the money market. In terms of Figure 13–6(b), this occurs at the intersection of the *YY* and $\bar{L}\bar{L}$ loci at point E', with a corresponding exchange rate equal to $\bar{e}$.

Having established the factors determining equilibrium output and the exchange rate, in the following sections we will examine the effects of various economic disturbances and investigate how the economy behaves in its adjustment toward a new equilibrium. We start with the impact of a fiscal policy disturbance.

13–8. The Ineffectiveness of Fiscal Policy Under Flexible Exchange Rates

One of the main ideas of Keynesian economics is that the economy's short-run equilibrium level of output can settle below full employment; unemployment and recession can remain a stubborn and ugly feature of a laissez-faire economy. Government policy intervention is then believed to be instrumental in moving the economy out of recession, with increased government spending having

a leading role in that recovery. The purpose of this section is to examine the effects of an increase in government spending on the economy's equilibrium and to determine whether, under flexible exchange rates, such an increase can indeed stimulate output growth. The answer, as we will see, is in the negative.

Figure 13–7 analyzes the impact of increased autonomous expenditures on the economy. Initial equilibrium is shown by points E and E', with output and the exchange rate equal to $\bar{Y}$ and e_o, respectively. An expansion of government spending raises aggregate demand for domestic goods and tends to shift the *IS* curve upward, from IS_o to IS' in Figure 13–7(a). This results in upward pressures on domestic interest rates, generating incipient capital inflows as investors shift their portfolios toward the relatively more attractive domestic assets. These capital inflows surface as an excess supply of foreign exchange, as foreigners attempt to dispose of their foreign money to acquire domestic assets. The result is a reduction in the price of foreign currencies, or, in other words, a domestic currency *appreciation*. This appreciation, however, induces a switch of aggregate demand out of domestic goods, deteriorating the current account balance and shifting the *IS* curve back to its original position at IS_o in Figure 13–7(a).

As long as there is any pressure on the domestic interest rate to remain above the world rate, capital inflows will continue to appreciate domestic currency and reduce aggregate demand. The *IS* curve will therefore stop shifting back only when it reaches the original equilibrium at point E, where it intersects the *LM* curve precisely at the world interest rate, i^*. In other words, a fiscal expansion in the present context has no effects on the equilibrium level of output of the economy, which remains at $\bar{Y}$. The increased aggregate demand brought about by the rise in government spending is exactly compensated by the reduction in aggregate demand associated with the domestic currency appreciation, the deterioration of the price competitiveness of domestic goods in world markets, and the consequent reduction of net domestic exports. In effect, the increase in government expenditures *crowds out* the private sector of the economy producing goods for export. Only the composition, but not the total level of output, is altered by the fiscal intervention.[17]

A better understanding of these results is obtained by examining the effects of a fiscal disturbance on the exchange rate determination diagram in Figure 13–7(b). The increased government expenditures raise aggregate demand at any given level of the exchange rate, shifting the YY locus to Y'Y'. The effects of this change at the original exchange rate would be to increase income, as represented by point G'. The higher income raises money demand and, at a given level of the money supply, requires a market-clearing rise in the inter-

est rate. The upward pressure on domestic interest rates induces domestic currency to appreciate, as depicted by the movement from point G' to F' in Figure 13–7(b). The equilibrium of the economy thus moves to point F', with a reduction of the exchange rate from e_0 to $\bar{e}$, but no change in output, which remains at $\overline{Y}$. Geometrically, as long as the $\overline{L}\,\overline{L}$ curve in Figure 13–7(b) remains unaltered, output will also remain unchanged. Fiscal intervention cannot then be called upon to bring about an economic recovery.

The same conclusions apply to the effects of other real disturbances. A real disturbance refers to any policy measure or exogenous disturbance that does not alter money demand or money supply—as opposed to nominal disturbances, which originate in the money market. For instance, commercial policy in the form of protection against imports is a real disturbance; given the preceding analysis, it would have no lasting effects on output and would only be associated with an exchange rate appreciation. This is an important point, considering the currently popular view that the U.S. trade deficit is caused by unfair competition with Japan and that the United States should "get tough" with Japan by imposing greater tariffs or other barriers to Japanese imports. Given floating dollar values, increased U.S. protectionism may not help much in reducing the U.S. trade deficit. Indeed, this is the conclusion that is obtained by economists Warwick McKibbin and Jeffrey Sacks in a recent analysis based on a sophisticated, dynamic version of the Mundell-Fleming approach.[18]

---

[17]This strong conclusion was obtained by Robert A. Mundell and Marcus Fleming in the early 1960s and is at the crux of the so-called Mundell-Fleming model. Note that the increased government expenditures must be financed. There are three possible sources of government finance: taxation, government borrowing, and money creation (i.e., printing money to pay for expenses). In the present analysis, it is assumed that the increase in government spending affects only the *IS* curve. This is more likely to be so if the increased spending is financed by an emission of government bonds. The emission of bonds does not affect the domestic money supply because the money obtained by the government in selling the bonds returns to the public as the government spends it. From this source, then, the *LM* curve is not directly affected by the changes in government spending. By contrast, if the government finances its increased expenditures by money creation, then both the *IS* and *LM* curves would be affected. The effects of increased government spending also depend on how the private sector reacts to the policy change. For instance, government and private spending may be close substitutes, as in the case of a school lunch program that may result in reduced private spending on food, offsetting the program's aggregate-demand effects. Consumers may also reduce their spending if the higher government expenditures are associated with increased present or expected future taxes to finance them. For a rigorous analysis of the issues relating to the reaction of the private sector to fiscal policy, see R. J. Barro, *Macroeconomics* (New York: Wiley, 1990), chaps. 12–14.

[18]See W. McKibbin and J. Sacks, *Global Linkages: Macroeconomic Interdependence and Cooperation in the World Economy* (Washington, D.C.: Brookings Institution, 1991). The issue of the impotence of commercial policy under flexible exchange rates was forcefully stated by R. Mundell in "Flexible Exchange Rates and Employment Policy," in *International Economics* (New York: Macmillan, 1968), chap. 17. Note that if account is taken of the distortionary effects tariffs have in increasing the relative cost of imports, protective commercial policy may, in effect, reduce domestic real income.

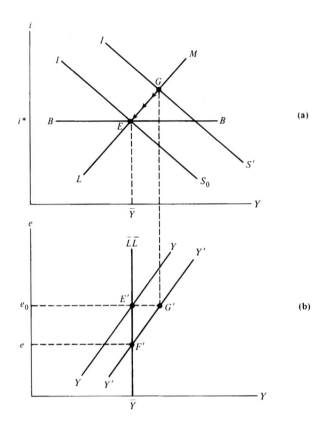

FIGURE 13–7.   Ineffectiveness of Fiscal Policy Under Flexible Exchange Rates

Another real disturbance to the economy giving rise to the phenomena discussed in this section would be a sudden exogenous increase in domestic exports, such as may arise from an income boom abroad that spreads into an increase in demand for domestic goods. This boom has no lasting effect on the domestic trade balance or on domestic output. The implications of this analysis for the operation of actual economies under flexible exchange rates is examined in the following section, in which the effects of North Sea oil exports on the U.K. economy are discussed.

13–9. THE EXCHANGE RATE AND INTERNATIONAL COMPETITIVENESS: OIL AND DE-INDUSTRIALIZATION IN THE UNITED KINGDOM

The massive increase of oil production in the United Kingdom in the 1970s and 1980s associated with the exploitation of North Sea reserves represented a significant real disturbance in the British economy. Its effects serve well to illustrate the issues involved in the impact of real disturbances

bances on open economies under flexible exchange rates. The case of Britain is particularly interesting because it represents an example of a country that, discovering it is richly endowed with energy resources, proceeds to a drastic exploitation of those resources and, at the same time, undergoes a protracted decline in economic activity. The analysis in this section will try to provide an answer—not necessarily the only one—to this paradox, emphasizing its open-economy ramifications.

At a glance, it seems perfectly reasonable to assert that the effects of increased oil production on domestic income would be positive and that the impact of an increase in oil exports (or a reduction in oil imports) would be to improve the trade balance. However, not everything that glitters is gold (or, in the present case, black gold), and only a casual look at the issue may be immensely misleading. Our discussion in the preceding section, showing that an exogenous increase in domestic exports may not have any significant positive effects on either income or the trade balance, should make us realize that, in a complex modern industrial economy, the effects of economic disturbances may diverge substantially from what they appear to be. For this reason, we must look carefully at the overall impact of increased oil production on the economy, and not just at its apparent expansionary effects. A closer look shows that a sudden expansion of oil production and exports may not be the blessing it appears to be.

The increased domestic income initially associated with a hike in oil production would raise money demand and, with a fixed money supply, would place upward pressures on domestic interest rates. Foreign capital would then flow into the economy, reducing the exchange rate; but the appreciation would hurt the international competitiveness of domestic goods by making them relatively expensive vis-à-vis foreign goods. The production of exports and import-competing manufactured goods will then decline, offsetting the positive impact of the increased oil exports. In other words, increased oil production crowds out the production of manufac-

tured export and import-competing products, not necessarily causing a net increase in domestic output. This phenomenon, in which an energy-sector boom leads to de-industrialization in the form of a decline in the production of the economy's traditional export and import-competing goods is the so-called Dutch disease.[19]

In the case of the United Kingdom, the association between the increased production of North Sea oil and gas in the late 1970s and the decline of the manufacturing sector is striking, as reflected by the data shown in Figure 13–8. This figure plots the behavior of the share of North Sea oil and gas in the United Kingdom's GDP and the share of manufacturing in it over time. Even though major discoveries of oil and gas reserves in the North Sea date back to the 1960s and early 1970s, the first year in which substantial quantities of North Sea oil were forthcoming was 1976. The following years saw rapidly rising production and widespread expectations that exploitation of reserves would continue to increase rapidly.[20] The growth of North Sea oil and gas production and the decline of manufacturing in this period is apparent from Figure 13–8.

Our analysis emphasizes an appreciation of domestic currency as the major link in the de-industrialization effects of an oil boom. Figure 13–9 shows the sharp appreciation of the pound vis-à-vis the currencies of the U.K.'s main trading partners in the late 1970s and up to 1981. This can be closely

[19]An early economic analysis of issues relating to the Dutch disease was carried out by J. P. Neary, "Booming Sector and De-Industrialization in a Small Open Economy," *Economic Journal* (1982). Applications to the cases of the Netherlands, United Kingdom, Australia, and other countries have been made in J. P. Neary and S. Van Wijnbergen, eds., *Natural Resources and the Macroeconomy* (Oxford: Basil Blackwell, 1986). A recent discussion of oil-producing economies is presented by G. Heal and G. Chichilnisky, *Oil and the International Economy* (Oxford: Clarendon, 1991), chap. 7.

[20]For details on the development of North Sea oil production and its macroeconomic impact, see R. E. Rowthorn and J. R. Wells, *De-Industrialization and Foreign Trade* (Cambridge: Cambridge University Press, 1987), chap. 12.

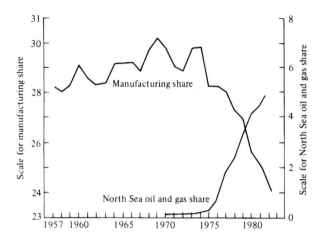

FIGURE 13–8. Oil and De-industrialization in the United Kingdom. The figures are the shares of manufacturing and North Sea oil and gas in U.K. GDP at 1975 factor cost.

SOURCES: Central Statistical Office, United Kingdom, *Annual Abstract of Statistics* (1983); and U.K. Department of Energy, *Digest of U.K. Energy Statistics* (1980).

associated with a sharp deterioration in the international competitiveness of British manufactured exports during this time and this sector's dismal performance, reflected in Figure 13–8.

The consequence of these developments was the absence of any realized boom in U.K. GDP as a result of the expansion of North Sea oil production. The British economy moved into sharp recession in the late 1970s and remained so during the early 1980s. We must stress, however, that even though the North Sea oil-induced de-industrialization certainly had its effect, the recession of the British economy in the late 1970s and early 1980s was brought about by a combination of factors, including a reduction in money-supply (Ml) growth at the time. The effective appreciation of the pound sterling and the deterioration of the manufacturing sector can also be linked to the monetary restrictionist regime.[21] Why this is so

will be discussed in Section 13–11, which is concerned with the effects of monetary policy in economies under flexible exchange rates.

13–10. INSULATION AND INTERDEPENDENCE UNDER FLOATING EXCHANGE RATES

The inability of an exogenous increase in domestic exports to lead to economic expansion under flexible exchange rates and perfect capital mobility

---

[21]Studies of the U.K. economy during this time suggest that North Sea oil may account for close to half of the real

appreciation of the pound in 1979 and 1980. See C. Bean, "The Impact of North Sea Oil," in R. Dornbusch and R. Layard, eds., *The Performance of the British Economy* (Oxford: Clarendon Press, 1987). Whether monetary policy was too tight in the early years of the Thatcher administration is a matter of controversy. See C. Bean and J. Symons, "Ten Years of Mrs. T.," in O. Blanchard and S. Fischer, eds., *NBER Macroeconomics Annual: 1990* (Cambridge, Mass.: The MIT Press, 1989), pp. 15–21.

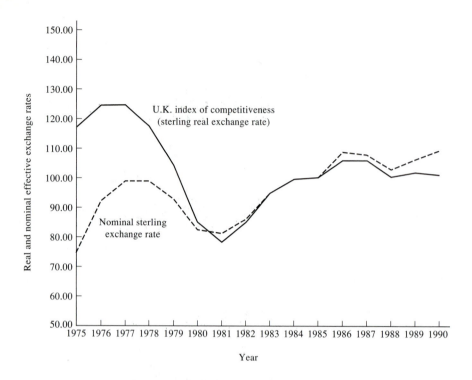

Note: The nominal exchange rate for the sterling is an effective exchange rate based on an index of the exchange rates of seventeen trade partners; the U.K. index of competitiveness is the real exchange rate, which is the effective exchange rate multiplied by the ratio of an index of relative costs; 1985 = 100 for both variables.

FIGURE 13–9.   Sterling Exchange Rate and U.K. Export Competitiveness, 1975–1990

SOURCE: International Monetary Fund, *International Financial Statistics Yearbook* (Washington, D.C.: IMF, 1991).

suggests a basic ineffectiveness of export-led recoveries in such economies. Expansion in one country, spilling over into increased demand for goods of other countries does not increase the overall exports or income of the other countries. It appreciates their currencies, offsetting the initial boom in demand for their products. In other words, an income expansion in one country is not transmitted into higher income in other countries

under exchange rate flexibility. Domestic authorities should not count on foreign recovery as a sure way out of recession and unemployment.

The underlying analytical explanation of this result is the earlier-noted connection between the determination of domestic income and the money market equilibrium condition (Equation 13–19b). Any country's real income is determined by its real money supply, interest rates, and other money demand parameters. If these are fixed, an exogenous increase in the foreign demand for a country's goods cannot have any impact on its output and must be associated with offsetting effects on aggregate demand, as described in the previous section. Graphically, the analysis of the impact of an increase in foreign income, Y^*, on the economy is identical to that in Figure 13–7.

Note that the knife here cuts both ways: Just as an income boom abroad is not transmitted locally, a recession would not be transmitted either. A reduction of foreign income would indeed spill over into reduced demand for domestic exports, at given exchange rates. This reduced aggregate demand, however, places downward pressures on domestic interest rates. As a consequence, capital flows out, generating a currency depreciation that switches demand back toward domestic goods. Only when the initial (foreign-income related) reduction in exports is offset by an (exchange rate depreciation-induced) improvement of the trade balance will adjustments stop. A country's recession is therefore not transmitted internationally. In this sense, an economy under flexible exchange rates and perfect capital mobility has macroeconomic independence from business cycles in the rest of the world. This insulation from external disturbances makes the behavior of countries operating under a flexible exchange rate regime diametrically different from the way they would behave under fixed exchange rates. In the latter case, business cycles are transmitted internationally, giving rise to the saying that "When one country sneezes, the others catch cold." (We will discuss this point in Chapter 14.)

Coordinated Aggregate Demand Disturbances and Interdependence Under Flexible Exchange Rates

The insulation provided by floating exchange rates from foreign autonomous spending disturbances hinges on the critical assumption that the disturbance originates in a single country abroad and is not a global one. A coordinated expansion by a group of foreign countries or disturbances in large, major foreign countries would be able to impinge on domestic output and employment. For instance, if all European countries except The Netherlands pursue expansionary aggregate demand policies—through, say, increased government expenditures—this will tend to raise each expanding country's interest rate, inducing the world interest rate to rise. Under perfect capital mobility, however, a rise in the world interest rate above its Dutch counterpart would generate massive capital flight out of the Netherlands, a sharp depreciation of the Dutch guilder, and output expansion in that country. It is, consequently, quite possible to have international transmission of disturbances under fluctuating exchange rates.[22] A foreign income disturbance associated with changes in world interest rates will generally be transmitted domestically. A coordinated fiscal expansion in Europe might thus aid in pulling the U.S. economy out of recession, and vice-versa. Note that the channel of transmission of the foreign aggregate demand disturbance originates in changes in the world interest rate and involves exchange rate changes as a key link.

In conclusion, floating exchange rates insulate an economy from foreign spending disturbances when these involve single, uncoordinated actions with no impact on world interest rates. If the foreign disturbance is simultaneously engaged by major foreign countries, it will be transmitted domestically through its effects on world interest rates. However, without an effect on world interest rates, fiscal policy in one country tends to have no impact on the income of either the country imposing it or on any other foreign country.

---

[22]For further details, see R. Dornbusch and P. Krugman, "Flexible Exchange Rates in the Short Run," *Brookings Papers on Economic Activity* (1976), particularly pp. 543–548; and P. Minford, "Do Floating Exchange Rates Insulate?" in R. MacDonald and M. P. Taylor, eds., *Exchange Rates and Open Economy Macroeconomics* (Oxford: Basil Blackwell, 1989).

13–11. MONETARY POLICY UNDER FLEXIBLE EXCHANGE RATES

The central role of money market equilibrium in determining output in an economy under flexible exchange rates and perfect capital mobility suggests that monetary policy in such an environment may be particularly effective. This indeed is what is shown in this section.

Suppose that the central bank expands the money supply. What are the effects of this disturbance? The analysis is carried out in Figure 13–10, in which the initial equilibrium is assumed to occur at points E and E', with corresponding levels of in-

come and the exchange rate equal to Y_o and e_o, respectively.

An expansion of the money supply directly affects the money market by generating an excess supply of money at the original income and exchange rate. This puts downward pressure on the domestic interest rate. Geometrically, the increased money supply would shift the LM curve to the right: At any given level of income, the domestic interest rate would have to be lower to absorb the excess supply of money. This shift of the LM curve is represented in Figure 13–10a by its move toward $L'M'$. As a result of the downward pressure on domestic interest rates, however, the

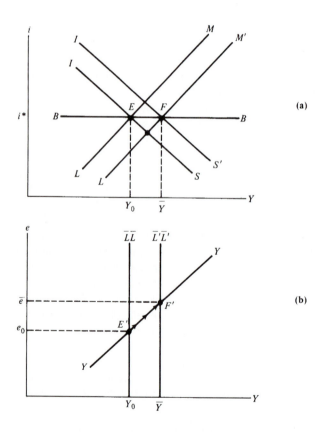

(a)

(b)

FIGURE 13–10. Monetary Policy Under Perfect Capital Mobility

economy would face massive capital outflows as investors would switch toward the relatively more attractive foreign assets. At a fixed exchange rate, these outflows would result in an excess demand for foreign currency in exchange markets as domestic investors dispose of their domestic money to acquire foreign assets. The result is an increase in the price of foreign currency or, in other words, an increase in the exchange rate.

This depreciation, in turn, shifts aggregate demand toward domestic goods by increasing the relative price of foreign goods in terms of domestic goods. This is shown in Figure 13–10(a) by the rightward shift of the *IS* curve. The outcome is a rise of domestic income, which induces the demand for money to increase and partially releases the downward pressure on the domestic interest rate. As long as there is any pressure on the domestic interest rate to remain below the world rate, capital outflows will induce domestic currency to depreciate and income to increase. Therefore, the *IS* curve will stop shifting rightward only when it reaches point *F,* where it intersects the *L'M'* curve at the world interest rate, i^*. Point *F* is thus the new equilibrium of the economy. The result of the monetary expansion is to increase output by inducing a domestic currency depreciation. Notice that the expansionary effects of an increased money stock on the economy are spearheaded here, not by reductions in interest rates, such as in a closed economy—interest rates here remain fixed at i^*—but by an expansion of the domestic exports sector, connected to a domestic currency depreciation.

Figure 13–10(b) displays the exchange rate increase associated with a monetary expansion. The shift of the $\overline{L}\,\overline{L}$ curve to $\overline{L}\,'\overline{L}'$ is related to the increase in income consistent with monetary equilibrium, from Y_o to $\overline{Y}$, as is algebraically specified by Equation 13–19b. The economy's equilibrium in Figure 13–10(b) then shifts from point E' to F', and the exchange rates rises from e_o to $\overline{e}$.

In conclusion, monetary policy under flexible exchange rates can be highly effective in influenc-

ing output over the short run, particularly if the environment is one of perfect capital mobility. Within this context, *expansionary* monetary policy can be instrumental in leading recovery in an economy suffering from severe recession. Contractionary monetary policy, on the other hand, would have the opposite effect: It would effectively worsen the recession.

Competitive Depreciations and Policy Conflict in the World Economy

In examining the effects of expansionary monetary policy on the domestic economy, we have thus far assumed that foreign countries behave passively, accepting without protest the effects that the associated *appreciation* of their currencies vis-à-vis the domestic currency have on their economies. However, a currency appreciation has exactly the opposite effects of a depreciation. By switching expenditure toward domestic goods, a foreign currency appreciation reduces the demand for goods, worsening the foreign trade balance and reducing foreign output. Expansionary monetary policy in this context is therefore a *beggar-thy-neighbor policy:* It increases domestic output at the expense of the output of the country's trading partners. Foreign authorities may then react by expanding their own money supply and depreciating their currencies vis-à-vis the currency of the country originally following the expansionary monetary policy. Such a change would offset the original policy action; if large enough, it could turn things around by switching demand toward foreign goods and away from domestic goods. Domestic authorities might then retaliate by depreciating domestic currency even further, and so on.

These *competitive depreciations* followed by countries seeking domestic expansion at the expense of their trading partners point to a potential source of exchange rate instability. They also suggest the possibility that large, influential countries could successfully manipulate real exchange rates in their favor at the expense of others. Some economists have thus suggested that countries coordinate their policies to avoid conflicts of this sort. Economist W. Max Corden, for instance, has proposed that policymakers coordinate their economic policies to avoid large sudden swings in real exchange rates. There are, however, both a number of obstacles to engaging in international policy coordination and detractors of the idea. Harvard economist Martin Feldstein, for example, has stated: "I believe that many of the claimed advantages of cooperation and coordination are wrong; that there are substantial risks and disadvantages to the types of coordination that are envisioned, and that an emphasis on international coordination can distract attention from the necessary changes in economic policy."[23] Our analysis in this section makes it clear that there are some possible benefits to be derived from coordination; later chapters will investigate some of the difficulties.[24]

13–12. THE ECONOMY'S EQUILIBRIUM AND IMPERFECT CAPITAL MOBILITY

This section considers the behavior of an economy in which the degree of capital mobility is less than perfect. In this type of setting, collectively referred to as imperfect capital mobility, a rise in the domestic interest rate attracts capital inflows, but to a lesser degree than under perfect capital mobility. This means that domestic investors cannot borrow or lend all of the amount they wish to at the world interest rate. A rise in the domestic

interest rate above the world rate is required to attract a higher amount of foreign funds; a lowering of the rate leads domestic residents to lend abroad. The resulting positive relationship between the capital account and domestic interest rates is algebraically depicted by

$$K = \beta i \qquad (13\text{--}25)$$

where β is a positive parameter representing the sensitivity of the capital account to changes in the domestic interest rate relative to the world interest rate.[25]

The analytics of imperfect capital mobility entail some basic modification of our earlier framework. In particular, the domestic interest rate will no longer be constrained to equal the world interest rate, as in the case of perfect capital mobility discussed in previous sections. A rise in domestic interest rates above world rates generates capital flows, but not in such massive amounts as to require a return to the world rate. Similarly, a reduction in domestic interest rates below world rates will result in capital outflows, but not to such an extent as to require the domestic interest rate to return to the world level. Intercountry interest rate differentials arise naturally under imperfect capital mobility.

Consider first the goods market equilibrium condition, $Y = A + T$. As noted before, under freely flexible exchange rates, the balance of payments will equal zero. As a result, the capital and trade-balance accounts must offset each other in adding up to zero. Symbolically, $T = -K$.

---

[23]M. Feldstein, "Distinguished Lecture on Economics in Government: Thinking About International Economic Coordination," *Journal of Economic Perspectives* (Spring 1988).

[24]For a comprehensive survey of the arguments for and against economic policy coordination, see J. A. Frenkel, M. Goldstein, and P. R. Masson, "The Rationale for, and Effects of, International Economic Policy Coordination," in W. H. Branson, J. A. Frenkel, and M. Goldstein, eds., *International Policy Coordination and Exchange Rate Fluctuations* (Chicago: University of Chicago Press, 1990).

[25]As a matter of fact, the capital account expression in Equation (13–25) should be a function of the interest rate differential between domestic and foreign bonds $i - i^*$. For simplicity, we are assuming that i^* is fixed and have thus deleted it from Equation 13–25. In addition, observe that capital flows arising from portfolio adjustments tend to disappear over time, as desired changes in portfolio composition are realized. The capital flows represented by Equation 13–25 should then be interpreted as occurring over the short run.

Substituting this relationship into the goods market equilibrium condition yields

$$Y = A + T$$
$$= A(Y, i, G) - K$$
$$= \bar{A} + aY - bi - \beta i, \qquad (13-26)$$

where the functional relationship $A(Y, i, G)$ is used to emphasize that absorption is related to domestic income, the domestic interest rate, and government spending (among other variables). To derive Equation 13–26, use has been made of the linearized absorption expression

$$A = \bar{A} + aY - bi.$$

Equation 13–26 can be simplified to yield

$$Y = \bar{\alpha}[\bar{A} - (b + \beta)i], \qquad (13-27)$$

where the parameter $\bar{\alpha} = 1/(1 - a) = 1/s$ is the reciprocal of the marginal propensity to save. Equation 13–27 shows the combinations of domestic interest rates and income that keep the goods market and the balance of payments in equilibrium, given some fixed parameters. It represents a modified *IS* curve that takes into account the adjustments of the exchange rate required to move the balance of payments to equal zero. Algebraically, Equation 13–27 represents not only the goods market equilibrium condition, $Y = A + T$, but also the balanced payments condition, $T = -K$. The diagrammatic representation of this joint goods-market, balance-of-payments equilibrium condition is given by the downward-sloping *XX* curve in Figure 13–11.

To visualize the negative relationship between domestic interest rates and output depicted by the curve *XX*, suppose that there is a reduction in the domestic interest rate below the world rate. This stimulates investment and raises the equilibrium level of output. In addition, the reduction in domestic interest rates causes capital outflows and a consequent deterioration of the capital account.

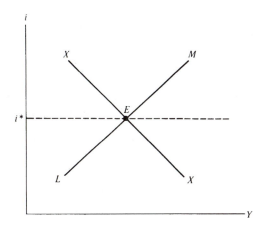

FIGURE 13–11. The Economy's Equilibrium with Imperfect Capital Mobility

Domestic currency then depreciates, improving the trade balance and equilibrating the balance of payments. This exchange rate depreciation also tends to raise domestic output. The implication is that changes in domestic interest rates will be associated with opposite changes in output to maintain goods-market and balance-of-payments equilibrium. Observe that the slope of the *XX* curve will depend, among other factors, on the degree of capital mobility the economy faces. The higher the degree of capital mobility (the larger the β coefficient), the flatter the *XX* curve will be. This occurs because the higher the degree of capital mobility, the larger the capital outflows that result from a given reduction in domestic interest rates, thus requiring a larger depreciation of the exchange rate to maintain balanced payments. Hence, the increase in output is larger. If the degree of capital mobility is low, however, the *XX* curve will be steeper; in this case, a reduction of domestic interest rates will induce minor capital outflows with negligible effects on the exchange rate and output.

The money market equilibrium condition remains as represented by Equation 13–13, shown diagrammatically by the *LM* curve in Figure 13–11. Goods, money, and balance-of-payments equilibrium then occur at point *E* in Figure 13–11, where the *XX* and *LM* curves intersect. This is the combination of domestic output and interest rates consistent with the general equilibrium of goods, assets, and foreign exchange markets. For expository reasons, the equilibrium domestic interest rate in Figure 13–11 is shown to coincide with the world interest rate. In general, however, under imperfect capital mobility, domestic and world interest rates do not have to equalize.

Figure 13–12 illustrates the effects of an expansionary monetary policy. Such an expansion shifts the *LM* curve to the right. In contrast to the case of perfect capital mobility, the economy's equilibrium after the shock occurs with higher output, as well as with a lower interest rate, as shown by point *F* in Figure 13–12. Under perfect capital mobility, the new equilibrium would occur at point *H,* with the domestic interest rate perfectly aligned with the world interest rate, and with an increment in output larger than the one obtained in the case of imperfect capital mobility. The reason for the dampened effect of monetary

policy under imperfect capital mobility lies in the fact that the currency depreciation required to eliminate balance-of-payments disequilibria under imperfect capital mobility will be smaller than in the case of perfect capital mobility, increasing output by a smaller proportion.

What are the effects of fiscal policy under conditions of imperfect capital mobility? As in the case of perfect capital mobility, an increase in government spending shifts the *IS* curve to the right, inducing a rise in domestic interest rates above world levels. In contrast to the case of perfect capital mobility, however, aggregate demand will not revert to the level prevailing before the rise in government spending. Rather, the domestic equilibrium interest rate will rise above the world rate and the level of domestic output above its initial value. Diagrammatically, in terms of Figure 13–13, these changes in the *IS* curve are embodied in the *XX* curve: the rise in government expenditures shifts the *XX* curve to the right to *X'X',* increasing both the equilibrium level of income and the interest rate.

Under imperfect capital mobility, increased government spending could depreciate or appreciate domestic currency. The explanation lies in that increased fiscal expenditures raise income and deteriorate the trade balance but raise interest rates, attracting capital inflows, and improving the capital account. The net effect on the balance of payments depends on the relative importance of the marginal propensity to import and the sensitivity of capital flows to interest rates. If there is a large degree of capital mobility, the balance of payments will improve and the exchange rate will decline to sustain external balance. If the marginal propensity to import is relatively high, the balance of payments will deteriorate, inducing a domestic currency depreciation (which imparts an additional stimulus to income).

These results are significant for analyzing the foreign repercussions of domestic economic policies. If, for instance, a U.S. fiscal expansion results in an appreciation of the dollar vis-à-vis the yen,

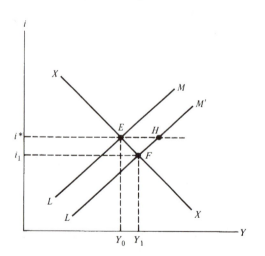

FIGURE 13–12. Effects of Monetary Policy Under Imperfect Capital Mobility

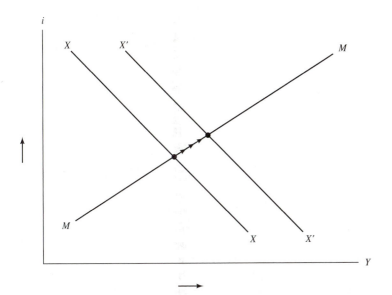

FIGURE 13–13. Effects of Fiscal Policy Under Imperfect Capital Mobility

the enhanced price competitiveness of Japanese products in the United States would expand Japanese exports relative to what they would otherwise be. On the other hand, if the increased U.S. government spending causes a depreciation of the dollar relative to the yen, Japanese exports to the U.S. would decline. These results may explain why studies examining how fiscal policies are transmitted among countries find significant differences in how some countries influence others, depending on the structure of their economies. University of California (Berkeley) economist Jeffrey Frankel notes that some of the large econometric models used to simulate the international impact of fiscal policies can "exhibit an assymmetry: Fiscal expansion in the United States appreciates its currency but— whether because of lower capital mobility . . . or other factors—fiscal expansion in Europe or Japan depreciates their currencies."[26]

[26]J. Frankel, "Ambiguous Policy Multipliers in Theory and in Empirical Models," in R. C. Bryant, D. W. Henderson, G.

13–13. ANATOMY OF EXCHANGE RATE ADJUSTMENT AND CAPITAL MOBILITY

This chapter has provided an introduction to the economics of flexible exchange rates, emphasizing the determination of output and the exchange rate and the role played by the degree of capital mobility. To round out the discussion, it may be useful to summarize the basic principles that have been—and have not been—established regarding the determination and behavior of the exchange rate.

In an economy under flexible exchange rates, the exchange rate adjusts to ensure the elimination of balance-of-payments disequilibria. Symbolically, exchange rate changes would ultimately guarantee that the sum of the trade balance and capital accounts add up to zero:

Holtham, P. Hooper and S. A. Symansky, eds., *Empirical Macroeconomics for Interdependent Economies* (Washington, D.C.: Brookings Institution, 1988), p. 18.

$$B = T(q, Y) + K(i)$$
$$= \bar{T} + \phi q - mY + \beta i = 0, \quad (13\text{-}28)$$

derived by substituting Equation 13–6 and 13–25 into Equation 13–23. It is clear from Equation 13–28 that the nature of balance-of-payments disequilibrium depends on the degree of capital mobility in the economy. In the absence of capital mobility, for instance, balance-of-payments surpluses or deficits will coincide with trade-balance surpluses or deficits. This case can be symbolized in Equation 13–28 by setting $\beta = 0$, in which case $K(i) = \beta i = 0$, and the balance-of-payments accounts become a record of international transactions in goods.

The case in which the exchange rate adjusts to ensure the immediate elimination of trade-balance disequilibria, with capital flows having no role in exchange rate adjustment, formed the basis for much of the economic analysis of flexible exchange rates up until the late 1950s. Although indeed a special case by present standards, the development of economic analysis along those lines should not be surprising. The world of high-capital market integration and rapid portfolio adjustment observed in most industrial countries today is a relatively recent event by post-World War II standards. At least up until the 1950s most short-term capital flows between countries were heavily regulated by governments; as a result, they turned out to be relatively minor, as compared with the value of international trade in goods and services. The theory of flexible exchange rates developed in those years thus understandably emphasized the role of the trade balance in exchange rate adjustment. The focus of concern was on whether (and how) exchange rate changes would guarantee the elimination of balance-of-trade disequilibria. The fear was that a flexible exchange rate regime could be inherently unstable if Marshall–Lerner elasticities conditions were not satisfied and exchange rate depreciation did not improve, but rather worsened, the trade balance. The finding that, in some instances, the values of the elasticities of demand for exports

and imports were lower than those required for the fulfillment of the Marshall–Lerner condition led to the influential school of "elasticity pessimism" after World War II. It was frequently associated with "flexibility pessimism"—the belief that a flexible exchange rate regime was inherently unstable and, thus, unfeasible.[27]

In the 1960s and 1970s, however, increasing financial liberalization, the growth of multinational business and international portfolio finance, and to topple it all, the massive recycling of OPEC oil revenues and the expansion of Eurocurrency banking all combined to generate an environment of high mobility of financial capital. As a result, international economic analysis—spearheaded by the contributions of Mundell and Fleming discussed earlier in this chapter—proceeded to incorporate the assumption of perfect capital mobility into its breadth. The consequence was a shift in emphasis toward the effects of short-term capital movements on the adjustment of the exchange rate. In terms of Equation 13–25, the capital mobility parameter (measuring the responsiveness of capital flows to changes in the domestic interest rate relative to foreign rates) was assumed to be very large. In this situation, slight pressures on domestic interest rates generate massive (actual or threatened) capital flows that induce the exchange rate to adjust. The capital account became a predominant factor in explaining exchange rate changes.

It is within this historical and analytical context that our discussion should be viewed. The important conclusion to be remembered is that the behavior of the exchange rate is closely linked to the degree of capital mobility in the economy. The higher that degree, the more capital account be-

[27]See R. A. Mundell, "The Great Exchange Rate Controversy: Trade Balances and the International Monetary System," in C. Fred Bergsten, ed., *International Adjustment and Financing: The Lessons of 1985–1991* (Washington, D.C.: Institute for International Economics, 1991) for a discussion of the issues that surrounded this controversy at the time.

havior and short-run capital movements should be looked at to explain exchange rate adjustments, particularly within the short-run milieu with which this chapter has been concerned.[28]

The inescapable reality of high capital mobility facing most industrial economies today has generated fears and pessimism regarding the operation of a flexible exchange rate regime different from those of the flexibility pessimists of earlier vintage. The boogeyman of flexible exchange rates in the 1980s and 1990s is destabilizing short-term speculative capital movements and widespread exchange rate turbulence, rather than trade elasticities. These fears have been fueled by the performance of the current regime of floating exchange rates under which most industrial economies operate. Considerable exchange rate variability has indeed characterized the international scene since the breakdown of the Bretton Woods system in the early 1970s. What factors are associated with this variability? Our analysis in this chapter sets the stage for an eventual answer to this question. The main problem is that, to focus on the introductory analytics of flexible exchange rates with a minimum of complexity, we have had to make the assumption of a static economic environment in which individuals do not anticipate disturbances. The continuous changes surfacing not only in exchange rate behavior, but also in economic policies and a range of other economic and noneconomic variables, should make us aware of the need to take into account flux and its influence on the behavior of agents in the economy. It is the purpose of Chapter 15 to begin this effort by analyzing exchange rate dynamics and the role of expectations formation—particularly exchange rate expectations—on the operation of economies under flexible exchange rates. Before undertaking

this task, we will examine the macroeconomics of fixed exchange rates in the next chapter.

SUMMARY

1. The Mundell-Fleming model is the "workhorse" of open-economy macroeconomics. The fundamental basis of this framework is to apply a simple Keynesian approach to examine the open economy. The strategy is to extend the basic *IS–LM* macroeconomic paradigm to examine economies under fixed and flexible exchange rates. The *IS–LM* framework takes into account the interaction of goods and money markets in determining equilibrium levels of income and interest rates in the economy. Its open-economy counterpart stresses the crucial impact of the balance of payments and exchange rate changes in economic adjustment.

2. The simple Keynesian *IS–LM* framework assumes that the prices of domestic goods are rigid and that firms producing these goods can supply all the output demanded of them at the given prices. In this case, the equilibrium level of domestic output is determined by the level of aggregate demand for domestic goods.

3. Aggregate demand for domestic goods is equal to domestic absorption plus the trade balance (ignoring trade in services and investment income). Shifts in aggregate demand are determined by variables affecting absorption and the trade balance.

4. The key variables affecting the trade balance are domestic income and the real exchange rate. In a Keynesian framework, price levels are sticky in local currency. This implies that nominal and real exchange rates are directly connected to each other. The recent evidence for the United States tends to support the Keynesian view: During the floating exchange rate regime, nominal and real exchange rates have moved together.

[28]Over the long run, the trade balance may have an important role in exchange rate adjustment, even if there is perfect capital mobility. This basic point, associated with the wealth-adjustment role of trade imbalances, will be discussed in detail in Chapter 19 within the context of the assets market approach to exchange rate determination.

5. A domestic currency depreciation does not necessarily improve the trade balance. The less responsive exports and imports are to changes in the real exchange rate, the less likely that a currency depreciation will improve the balance of trade; on the other hand, if exports and imports are very sensitive to shifts in real exchange rates, then the trade balance will improve. In a Keynesian context, if the sum of the price elasticities of demand for exports and imports is greater than 1, a currency depreciation will improve the trade balance. This is called the Marshall–Lerner condition.

6. Absorption spending can be broken down into consumption, investment, and government spending. Government expenditures are considered to be exogenous (as determined by the political process); consumption is closely related to income; and investment is influenced by interest rates. Absorption is, therefore, determined by income, interest rates, and an autonomous component that does not depend on income and interest rates (and that includes government spending).

7. The goods market equilibrium condition establishes a negative relationship between income and interest rates that is graphically depicted by the *IS* curve (as interest rates rise, investment spending and income decline). Shifts in the *IS* curve can be generated by fiscal policy changes and exchange rate adjustments, among other variables. The simple Keynesian income multiplier shows by how much net changes in spending categories would alter output at a given interest rate. To be able to select one of the income and interest rate combinations depicted by the *IS* curve as the economy's equilibrium requires analysis of the assets markets.

8. Discussion of the assets markets can concentrate on the money market (a result of Walras's law). Money market equilibrium occurs when money supply equals money demand; this condition establishes a positive relationship between income and interest rates: As income increases, money demand rises and to clear the market an increase in the price (opportunity cost) of money is required; the interest rate must rise. The combinations of income and interest rates that keep the money market in equilibrium are graphically depicted by the *LM* curve. Shifts in the *LM* curve can originate in money supply changes.

9. In an economy under freely floating currency values, the exchange rate adjusts to eliminate the balance-of-payments surpluses or deficits that would emerge under fixed exchange rates. When economists refer to a balance-of-payments surplus or deficit they usually refer to whether the sum of the capital and CAB is in surplus or deficit. This balance-of-payments concept corresponds to the official reserve settlements balance.

10. Under perfect capital mobility, which describes an environment of highly integrated capital markets, the domestic economy can, at any time, borrow and lend all it wants to at the prevailing world interest rate; foreigners can similarly lend and borrow in domestic capital markets at the domestic interest rate. Arbitrage between domestic and world capital markets then guarantees an alignment of domestic and world interest rates. The condition of perfect capital mobility imposes the constraint that balanced payments occur at the world interest rate. Diagrammatically, the equilibrium of the economy must lie along a balance-of-payments equilibrium curve, *BB*, that is horizontal at the world interest rate.

11. The equilibrium of the economy under perfect capital mobility occurs when there is simultaneous equilibrium in the goods and assets markets as well as in the balance of payments. This occurs at the intersection of the *IS, LM,* and *BB* curves.

12. Under perfect capital mobility, fiscal policy measures adopted by a single, small country are not effective in changing output. An increase in government expenditures, for example, would raise aggregate demand for domes-

tic goods and place upward pressures on domestic interest rates. This induces financial capital to flow into the economy, leading to an appreciation of the exchange rate and switching demand away from domestic goods. This aggregate demand reduction would offset the direct expansionary effects of increased government spending.

13. Under flexible exchange rates, the impact of real disturbances on output is very limited. A real disturbance refers to any policy measure or exogenous disturbance that does not alter money demand or money supply, as opposed to nominal disturbances, which originate in the money market. Commercial policy is a real disturbance and, according to the Mundell-Fleming framework, it has no lasting effects on output, being associated instead with domestic currency appreciation.

14. Although on the surface increased oil exports, associated with the discovery and exploitation of oil reserves, appears to be a disturbance that should make an economy increase its output, matters can be much more complicated. In fact, economies with increased oil exports often suffer from collapsing manufacturing sectors, a phenomenon called the Dutch disease. The Mundell-Fleming framework predicts that an exogenous increase in exports will, other things being equal, result in an appreciation of domestic currency that reduces the output and exports of manufactured goods.

15. Monetary policy is highly effective in influencing output under perfect capital mobility. An increase in the money supply, for example, places downward pressure on domestic interest rates, inducing incipient capital outflows and depreciating domestic currency. This depreciation switches demand toward domestic goods and is expansionary. At the same time, because the domestic currency depreciation amounts to a foreign currency appreciation, higher domestic money growth may adversely affect output abroad. In this sense, monetary

policy can be a beggar-thy-neighbor policy under flexible exchange rates.

16. Under imperfect capital mobility, both monetary and fiscal policies will influence domestic output, with the effectiveness of fiscal policy inversely related to the degree of capital mobility in the economy.

17. Flexible exchange rates insulate the economy from isolated foreign autonomous spending disturbances, but not from a general coordinated disturbance by a group of foreign countries. A coordinated fiscal policy initiative by a group of major countries abroad affects world interest rates and is transmitted worldwide. Within this context, expansionary fiscal policy simultaneously engaged in by major countries will stimulate income growth in the world economy.

PROBLEMS

1. Flexivia is a small industrial country operating under flexible exchange rates and perfect capital mobility (with a world interest rate equal to $i^* = 0.10$). The economy's money supply is 400 billion flexivians (Flexivia's currency, which freely floats in value against other currencies), and the price of Flexivia's products is $P = 1$ flexivian. Assume that the real money demand in Flexivia, L^D, has been estimated to be

$$L^D = 0.25Y - 4000i,$$

which is measured in terms of Flexivian goods. Find the equilibrium level of output of the economy. What would be the impact on output of an increase in the money supply of 50 billion flexivians? Provide numerical answers.

2. The government of a country facing perfect capital mobility imposes a tariff on imports, distributing the tariff revenues back to the public in the form of tax rebates. Find the effects of the tariff on the level of income and the exchange rate using *IS–LM* curves. Explain the economics behind your results.

3. This problem is concerned with the determination of the exchange rate under perfect capital mobility.
   (a) Using the aggregate demand equation 13–12, solve for the exchange rate as a function of the level of income; that is, find a formula for the curve YY under perfect capital mobility. (Hint: Recall that $q = (eP^*/P)$ and ϕ a positive parameter.)
   (b) Determine the equilibrium exchange rate as a function of exogenous variables. (Hint: Substitute the equilibrium level of income in Equation 13–19b into the exchange rate expression obtained in Part a.)
   (c) What is the effect on the equilibrium level of income and the exchange rate of an exogenous increase in the world interest rate, i^*? Illustrate graphically and algebraically which factors determine the magnitude of the impact of this disturbance on output and the exchange rate.

4. Consider the imperfect capital mobility setup described in the text.
   (a) Solve for the level of income as a function of exogenous variables. (Hint: Use the expression for the interest rate obtained from Equation 13–21 to substitute into Equation 13–27.)
   (b) Determine and illustrate by means of IS–LM curves the impact of a change in government spending on income. What happens to this impact when the degree of capital mobility increases? When it decreases? Why?

5. Consider a country with no capital mobility and flexible exchange rates.
   (a) Solve for the exchange rate that clears the trade balance as a function of the level of income, Y. (Assume that the trade balance is in the form $T = \bar{T} + \phi q - my$, where ϕ is a positive constant and $q = (eP^*/P)$.)
   (b) Solve for the level of income as a function of all exogenous variables. (Hint: Substitute the value of e deter-mined in Part a into the aggregate demand Equation 13–12.) In what way does the multiplier differ from all other open-economy multipliers computed in the previous three chapters?
   (c) Suppose that there is an exogenous increase in the demand for the country's exports. Determine algebraically the effect on the exchange rate and on income. Illustrate your answer geometrically by means of the open-economy IS–LM diagram. (Hint: Assume that T_o increases.)
   (d) Suppose that government spending on domestic goods increases. Determine algebraically and illustrate graphically the effects on output and the exchange rate.
   (e) Compare the results from parts c and d here. Why do they differ qualitatively even if both disturbances initially increase desired spending on domestic goods? What principle does this exercise illustrate regarding the impact of internal and external real disturbances under flexible exchange rates and capital immobility?

6. Short-run import and export elasticities are smaller than their longer-run counterparts. This gives rise to the possibility that a domestic currency depreciation may deteriorate the trade balance in the short run. What does this suggest about the short-run effectiveness of monetary policy on output and employment under flexible exchange rates?

7. Within a framework of perfect capital mobility and flexible exchange rates, what effects does a domestic monetary expansion have on the country's foreign trade partners? Could the effects of the domestic policy, if any, be undone by foreign authorities? How?

8. In the early 1980s, the Reagan administration engaged in a tax-cut experiment. Assuming that the money supply and government spending stay unchanged (so that the tax cut generates a budget deficit that is financed through increased borrowing):

(a) What impact would a tax cut have on output, the exchange rate, and the CAB? (Hint: Recalculate the economy's equilibrium with the following modifications:

$$L^D = kY_D - hi$$

$$Y_D = Y - \text{Tax}$$

$$\text{Tax} = tY$$

$$\bar{T} = T - mY_D + \phi q$$

$$\bar{A} = A + aY_D - bi$$

$$Y = A + T,$$

with all variables as defined before, and with Y_D representing disposable income, and Tax denoting the tax revenues received by the government. Assume that the tax cut takes place in the form of a reduction in t, the average and marginal tax rate.

(b) What problems do you see with this Keynesian analysis of the impact of a tax cut? Explain your answer. (Hint: Do consumers take into account in their decision making the effects of possible future tax increases?)

9. In the early 1990s, the Clinton administration undertook a plan to raise taxes with the intention of reducing the rapidly growing U.S. budget deficit. On the basis of your answer to problem 8, what impact would such a tax hike have on output, the exchange rate and the CAB?

CHAPTER **14**

Balance-of-Payments Adjustments and the Macroeconomics of Fixed Exchange Rate Regimes

This chapter is concerned with the determination of income, interest rates, and the balance of payments in economies operating under fixed exchange rates.

Although the United States, Japan, and an array of other countries presently have a regime of floating exchange rates, many economies have adopted systems with considerable exchange rate rigidity. Table 14–1 shows the variety of fixed and flexible exchange rate arrangements currently in place in the world. Many countries, such as Sweden and the Bahamas, have fixed exchange rates, with currencies pegged in value to the dollar, the French franc, the ECU, and so forth. Other countries have exchange rates with limited flexibility. Such is the case with the European Community (EC), whose European Monetary System (EMS) currently limits exchange rate fluctuations among member countries within narrow bands. In addition, member countries of the European Community have agreed to pursue monetary union by the year 2000. Monetary union implies the adoption of a common currency among participating countries, the ultimate form of fixed exchange rates. Countries forming part of the EC would be de facto under fixed exchange rates among themselves if unification were to be achieved.

We start by discussing the major differences in the money supply process of economies under fixed and flexible exchange rates. Although under floating exchange rates control of the money supply is to a great extent in the hands of governmental or quasi-governmental monetary authorities, under fixed exchange rates this assumption cannot automatically be made. In fact, for economies under fixed exchange rates, monetary authorities sometimes face extreme difficulties controlling the money supply. We will also be considering additional systemic differences between fixed and flexible exchange rate regimes, including a discussion of differences in economic policymaking.

14–1. The Balance of Payments and the Money Supply Process Under Fixed Exchange Rates

In a closed economy, a central bank can in principle determine the money supply, and might easily do so given stability in the behavior of banks and individuals towards holding money. In an open economy under fixed exchange rates, however, the money supply is not only influenced by the central bank but also by the country's *balance of payments*—that is, by the actions of domestic and foreign residents in trading with the rest of the world. This point is perhaps the most crucial one in this chapter, and we will therefore explain it in detail.

The Money Supply in the Open Economy

This section develops a simple, yet essential, approach to the determination of the money supply in an open economy. The discussion is brief in institutional detail, emphasizing instead the open-economy aspects of the money supply process. This approach presents a more comprehensive and encompassing view of the money supply process than is usually carried out within the context of a closed economy. It will explain many of the divergences of our results from those traditionally derived in introductory (closed-economy) macroeconomics textbooks. We will also examine the differences in money supply determination in economies under fixed and flexible exchange rates.

A wide range of measures is used by monetary authorities and economists regarding the definition of the money supply. We assume that the nominal money supply is composed of currency in the hands of the nonbanking public and demand deposits. Symbolically,

$$M^S = C^P + DD, \qquad (14\text{–}1)$$

TABLE 14–1. **World Exchange Rate Arrangements as of September 30, 1992**

		Currency pegged to			
U.S. Dollar	*French Franc*	*Russian Ruble*	*Other Currency*	*SDR*	*Other Composite*[a]
Angola	Benin	Armenia	Bhutan (Indian Rupee)	Iran., I. R. of	Algeria
Antigua and Barbuda	Burkina Faso	Belarus	Estonia (deutsche mark)	Libya	Austria
Argentina	Cameroon	Georgia	Kiribati (Australian dollar)	Myanmar	Bangladesh
Bahamas, The	C. African Rep.	Kyrgyzstan		Rwanda	Botswana
Barbados	Chad	Moldova		Seychelles	Burundi
Belize	Comoros		Lesotho (South African Rand)		Cape Verde
Djibouti	Congo		Namibia (South African Rand)		Cyprus
Dominica	Côte d'Ivoire				Czechoslovakia
Ecuador	Equatorial Guinea		Swaziland (South African Rand)		Fiji
Ethiopia	Gabon				Hungary
Grenada	Mali				Iceland
Iraq	Niger				Jordan
Liberia	Senegal				Kenya
Marshall Islands	Togo				Kuwait
Mongolia					Malawi
Nicaragua					Malaysia
Oman					Malta
Panama					Mauritania
St. Kitts & Nevis					Mauritius
St. Lucia					Morocco
St. Vincent and the Grenadines					Nepal
Suriname					Norway
Syrian Arab Rep.					Papua New Guinea
Trinidad and Tobago					Solomon Islands
Yemen, Republic of					Sweden
Yugoslavia					Tanzania
					Thailand
					Tonga
					Vanuatu
					Western Samoa
					Zimbabwe

Note: The currency of Cambodia is excluded; no current information is available. For members with dual or multiple exchange markets, the arrangement shown is that in the major market.

[a]Comprises currencies which are pegged to various "baskets" of currencies of the members' own choice, as distinct from the SDR basket.

TABLE 14–1   *continued*

Flexibility Limited in Terms of a Single Currency or Group of Currencies		*More Flexible*		
Single Currency[b]	*Cooperative Arrangements[c]*	*Adjusted According to a Set of Indicators[d]*	*Other Managed Floating*	*Independently Floating*
Bahrain	Belgium	Chile	China, P.R.	Afghanistan	Nigeria
Qatar	Denmark	Colombia	Egypt	Albania	Paraguay
Saudi Arabia	France	Madagascar	Greece	Australia	Peru
United Arab Emirates	Germany	Zambia	Guinea	Bolivia	Philippines
	Ireland		Guinea-Bissau	Brazil	Romania
	Luxembourg		India	Bulgaria	Russia
	Netherlands		Indonesia	Canada	Sierra Leone
	Portugal		Israel	Costa Rica	South Africa
	Spain		Korea	Dominican Rep.	Sudan
			Lao P.D. Rep	El Salvador	Switzerland
			Maldives	Finland	Uganda
			Mexico	Gambia, The	Ukraine
			Pakistan	Ghana	United Kingdom
			Poland	Guatemala	United States
			Sao Tome and Principe	Guyana	Venezuela
				Haiti	Zaïre
			Singapore	Honduras	
			Somalia	Italy	
			Sri Lanka	Jamaica	
			Tunisia	Japan	
			Turkey		
				Latvia	
			Uruguay	Lebanon	
			Viet Nam	Lithuania	
				Mozambique	
				New Zealand	

[b]Exchange rates of all currencies have shown limited flexibility in terms of the U.S. dollar.
[c]Refers to the cooperative arrangement maintained under the European Monetary System.
[d]Includes exchange arrangements under which the exchange rate is adjusted at relatively frequent intervals on the basis of indicators determined by the respective member countries.

SOURCE: *International Financial Statistics* (December 1992).

where M^S is, the money supply, C^P refers to currency (coins and dollar notes) in the hands of the public, and DD is demand deposits plus other checking deposits. This definition of the money supply corresponds closely to what is called in U.S. banking jargon M1, as defined by the Federal Reserve Board.[1] In October 1992, the amount of currency in public hands in the United States was $288 billion and the amount of demand and other checking deposits was roughly $719 billion. The U.S. money supply, in terms of our definition, was thus equal to $1,007 billion. There are, of course, other measures of the money supply, depending on how much liquidity the concept of money used is chosen to have.[2]

The Monetary Base and the Money Supply Multiplier

What is the role of the economy's central bank—the Federal Reserve Bank in the United States—in the money supply process? The central bank affects the domestic money supply by influencing high-powered money or, as it is often called, the monetary base. The monetary base, H, is defined as

$$H = C^P + RE \qquad (14\text{--}2)$$

where C^P refers to the value of currency in the hands of the public and RE refers to the reserves held by commercial banks and other depository

---

[1]In addition to currency, demand deposits, and other checkable deposits, M1 also includes some forms of travelers checks in the definition of the money supply, which we have included as part of checking deposits in our figures.

[2]For example, short-term liquid assets, such as savings accounts and short-term time deposits, are sometimes considered money. They are included in the definition of the so-called M2 by the Federal Reserve Board. Note also that C^P includes only cash in the hands of the nonbank public and excludes cash in bank vaults. In the presence of shifts in individual money holdings among checkable, and time and savings deposits, narrow definitions of money become unstable and unreliable as barometers of monetary policy. For a discussion of this issue, see B. Higgins, "Implications of Recent M2 Behavior," *Federal Reserve of Kansas City Economic Review* (Third Quarter, 1992).

institutions. (Reserves are held in the form of deposits at the central bank and in the form of cash in the banks' vaults.) In October 1992, the monetary base was equal to $316 billion, broken down into $288 billion in currency held by the public and $28 billion as bank reserves.

The monetary base is closely linked to the money supply, and it is through this link that the central bank influences the money supply. But how are the monetary base and the money supply related? We will show that in the simple framework adopted here, the monetary base is proportional to the money supply, symbolically represented as

$$M^S = \mu H,$$

where μ is a constant; thus, changes in the monetary base will affect the money supply proportionally. We will then specify how the central bank affects the monetary base. In addition, we will show that, in economies under fixed exchange rate, monetary base is also affected by the balance of payments.

The first step in discovering the link between the monetary base and the money supply is to discuss two key parameters involved in the determination of the money supply: the reserve-deposit ratio and the currency-deposit ratio. The currency-deposit ratio, cu, is defined as

$$cu = \frac{C^P}{DD},$$

where C^P represents currency in the hands of the public and DD represents demand deposits. This parameter reflects the public's preferences in allocating its money holdings between currency and demand deposits. The larger the cu is, the larger the amount of currency the public decides to hold relative to holdings of demand deposits in commercial banks. Using our earlier figures for October 1992, we find that the currency-deposit ratio at that time was $cu = 0.40$ ($288 billion divided by $719 billion).

The reserve-deposit ratio, *re*, is defined as

$$re = \frac{RE}{DD},$$

where *RE* represents bank reserves and *DD* represents demand deposits. This ratio is chosen by commercial banks so that they can maintain enough reserves to finance withdrawals by their customers and to satisfy the reserve requirements set by the central bank. Commercial banks hold these reserves as cash-in-vault and as deposits at the central bank. An increase in *re* means that banks would decide to hold more reserves for each dollar of deposits they receive from their customers; a decrease in *re*, on the other hand, denotes a reduced reserve-deposit ratio. In October 1992, the reserve-deposit ratio was approximately *re* = 0.04 because banks were holding $28 billion as reserves out of a volume of demand deposits equal to $719 billion.

We can now easily derive an expression showing the relationship between the money supply and the monetary base. For this purpose, we take *cu* and *re* as constants.[3] Dividing Equation 14–1 by 14–2, we obtain

$$\frac{M^S}{H} = \frac{C^P + DD}{C^P + RE}.$$

To make this equation more illuminating, we divide both the numerator and the denominator on the right-hand side by *DD*. The result is

[3]In general, however, *cu* and *re* will not be fixed constants but stable functions of some parameters. For example, *cu* depends on how confident depositors are in the banking system, and *re* is affected by interest rates, the so-called discount rate, and reserve requirements. The discussion here is just intended to illustrate the role of openness of the economy in the determination of the money supply. The general case, with full discussion of these and other institutional details is given by K. Brunner, "Money Supply Process and Monetary Policy in an Open Economy," in M. Connolly and A. Swoboda, eds., *International Trade and Money* (Toronto: University of Toronto Press, 1973). See also, S. E. Weiner, "The Changing Role of Reserve Requirements in Monetary Policy," *Federal Reserve Bank of Kansas City Economic Review* (Fourth Quarter, 1992).

$$\frac{M^S}{H} = \frac{(C^P/DD) + (DD/DD)}{(C^P/DD) + (RE/DD)} = \frac{cu + 1}{cu + re},$$

where we have substituted for the definitions of *cu* and *re* described above. A simple rearrangement then yields

$$M^S = \left[\frac{cu + 1}{cu + re}\right] H = \mu H, \qquad (14\text{--}3)$$

where $\mu = (cu + 1)/(cu + re)$ is the so-called money supply multiplier, which tells us by how much the money supply would increase if the monetary base were to increase by one dollar. Note that $\mu > 1$ because the reserve-deposit ratio, *re*, is less than 1. As a consequence, any given change in the monetary base will lead to a multiple increase in the money supply. This result explains why μ is called a multiplier, and why *H* is also called high-powered money. For the case of the United States in about October 1992, a rough estimate of the money supply multiplier can be obtained using the previously calculated values of 0.04 for *re* and 0.40 for *cu*. Substituting these into the definition of the multiplier implies that

$$\mu = 3.18 = \frac{0.40 + 1.00}{0.40 + 0.04}.$$

For any dollar increment in the monetary base, the U.S. money supply (M1) would increase by $3.18. What is the economic mechanism behind this multiple expansion of money arising from a given change in the monetary base?

When commercial banks accept deposits, their reserves increase by a corresponding amount. Since, as mentioned earlier, banks hold only a fraction of their deposits as reserves (in the form of precautionary cash-in-vault and deposits at the central bank), they will proceed to lend their excess reserves. Those funds that are lent by any given bank are then spent by the borrowers. The recipients of these funds in turn will deposit some of them back into the banking system, depending on how much currency vis-à-vis demand deposits they want to hold. The funds that are actually deposited lead to an increase in the volume of deposits for the banking system as a whole since the initial deposits (on the basis of which loans were made) are still outstanding. The implication is that a dollar deposited in a given bank can lead to a multiplier expansion of deposits in the overall banking system.

The size of this multiplier effect clearly depends on the size of μ and therefore on the parameters *re* and *cu*. Note from Equation 14−3 that an increase in the reserve-deposit ratio, *re*, tends to decrease the money supply multiplier, μ. A larger reserve-deposit ratio implies that, for each dollar of deposits, banks hold a larger fraction as reserves and thus lend a smaller fraction. As a consequence, for any given value of the monetary base and the currency-deposit ratio, bank deposit creation would be smaller.

Similarly, an increase in the currency-deposit ratio, *cu*, will result in a decrease in the multiplier. The explanation, which is not really obvious by just looking at Equation 14−3, is as follows. A larger *cu* means that a larger amount of currency leaks out of the banking system as currency held by the public. Out of any given amount of high-powered money, banks are left with less reserves. This reduction in reserves implies that the deposits created by the banking system will decline by an even larger amount because $re = RE/DD < 1$, so that each dollar of reserves supports more than one dollar of deposits. Thus, even though an increase in *cu* induces an increase in the currency component of the money supply, the demand deposits component will decline even more, and so the net effect on the money supply is negative. In other words, at given levels of the monetary base and the reserve-deposit ratio, increases in the currency-deposit ratio will tend to reduce the money multiplier.

To summarize, note that increases in *cu* and *re* tend to decrease the multiplier because both imply that a higher proportion of funds in the economy will leak out of the credit-creating portion of the banking system's portfolio.

Given the value of the money multiplier, Equation 14−3 shows the proportional relationship between the monetary base, *H,* and the money supply, M^S. Note that the monetary base represents the total amount of money potentially available to commercial banks as reserves and, thus, it serves as a basis for the creation of bank deposits. The larger the monetary base, given *cu* and *re,* the larger the volume of deposits in the banking system of the country.

Having determined how the monetary base affects the money supply, let us now proceed to analyze the factors influencing the base.

Central Banks, the Balance of Payments, and the Money Supply

Even though in a closed economy the monetary base is determined by the actions of the central bank, in an open economy it is determined by the actions of the central bank *and* by the balance of payments. To clarify these issues, let us now take a closer look at the monetary base and its relationship to the central bank's financial statement (i.e., balance sheet). The simplified balance sheet of a hypothetical central bank is shown in Table 14−2.

High-powered money is created when the central bank acquires assets in the form of *international reserves* (foreign exchange and gold) and *central bank credit* (loans, discounts, and government bonds). The central bank pays for these assets by issuing checks on itself. These checks are deposited in commercial banks and end up in the form of currency and commercial (member) bank deposits at the central bank. Algebraically,

$$IR + CBC = C^P + RE = H, \quad (14\text{--}4)$$

where *IR* represents international reserves, *CBC* is central bank credit, and C^P and *RE* refer to currency and commercial bank reserves, as before. The implication is that the monetary base, *H,* can be looked at from both the assets side (as *IR* + *CBC*) and the liabilities side (as C^P + *RE*) of the central bank balance sheet.

TABLE 14–2. **Simplified Central Bank Balance Sheet (in billions of dollars)**

Assets		Liabilities		
International reserves	$100	Currency		$240
		Cash in vaults	20	
		Currency in the hands of the public	220	
Central bank credit	200	Commercial bank deposits at the central bank		60
Monetary base	300	Monetary base		300

Note: In general, the government's consolidated monetary account, which includes other institutions (such as the Treasury) in addition to the central bank, should be examined. Furthermore, a complete central bank balance sheet would include an item adding up all other assets (such as building and equipment) on the assets side, and a net worth item as a residual on the liabilities side. International reserves and net foreign assets, which are equal to international reserves net of the central bank's liabilities to foreign central banks, would also have to be differentiated. The latter are in the form of foreign official deposits held at the domestic central bank and generally compose a relatively minor item on the central bank's balance sheet.

The next step is to analyze how changes in the different components of this balance sheet occur. We start with the central bank credit component and how it can change—that is, how central bank credit is created. Central bank credit refers to the securities held by the central bank (such as Treasury bills), loans and discounts made by the central bank (such as an overnight loan made to Morgan Guaranty), and various other credit assets of the central bank. Credit creation occurs if the central bank increases its holdings of any of these assets. Let us take the example of a central bank purchase of securities in the open market (an *open market operation*). What is the exact process and impact of central bank credit creation on the bank's balance sheet?

The first step occurs when the central bank pays for the securities by issuing a check on itself. The seller of the securities bought by the central bank then deposits this check in his private bank. The bank may do one of two things. It may decide to convert the check into cash. In this case, the increase in the securities held by the central bank (on the assets side of the balance sheet) has as a counterpart an increase in currency (on the liabilities side). We illustrate this operation through the use of the T account represented in Table 14–3,

showing the changes in the central bank's balance sheet on the assumption that the bank buys $20 million in bonds. (Table 14–3 is based on the assumption that the bank in question converts its check into cash.) Alternatively, the commercial bank may deposit the check in its account at the central bank. This will increase commercial bank deposits at the central bank. In terms of a T account, see Table 14–4 for the changes in the balance sheet.

Observe that in both cases (Tables 14–3 and 14–4), the monetary base, H, increases by the same amount ($20 million). All else being constant, changes in central bank credit will tend to alter the monetary base and therefore the money supply, as reflected by Equation 14–3.

The economy's balance-of-payments situation can also affect the monetary base. The nature of this connection will be examined shortly. First we must clarify which balance-of-payments concept is to be used in our analysis. This is a vital question because, as discussed in Chapter 9, there are various possible concepts of the balance of payments, depending on which items are placed above and below the line. The balance-of-payments concept that best captures the net effect of international transactions on the money supply, and that is thus

TABLE 14–3.   Effects of an Open-Market Purchase on the Central Bank Balance Sheet (in millions of dollars)

Change in Assets		Change in Liabilities	
International reserves	$ 0	Currency in vaults	$ +20
Central bank credit	+20	Commercial bank deposits	0
Monetary base	+20	Monetary base	+20

TABLE 14–4.   Effects of an Open-Market Purchase on the Central Bank Balance Sheet (in millions of dollars)

Change in Assets		Change in Liabilities	
International reserves	$ 0	Currency	$ 0
Central bank credit	+20	Commercial bank deposits	+20
Monetary base	+20	Monetary base	+20

the most useful in the discussion of the money supply process in economies under fixed exchange rates, is called the *money account* of the balance of payments. It is defined as the changes in the international reserves of the *domestic* central bank (or, more generally, as the changes in the central bank's net foreign assets). A money account balance-of-payments surplus then corresponds to an accumulation of international reserves on the part of the central bank. A deficit involves a reduction in international reserves.

Note that the money account does not exactly correspond to any of the balance-of-payments concepts discussed in Chapter 9. It does not, for example, correspond exactly to the official reserve settlements (ORS) balance. The reason is that the ORS measures changes in the international reserves of both domestic and foreign central banks. For instance, an ORS balance-of-payments deficit associated with increased foreign official deposits at a New York commercial bank does not affect the international reserves held by the Federal Reserve and would thus be associated with a zero money account deficit. It does not affect the monetary base

either. Intuitively, the ORS deficit results in a transfer of commercial bank deposits from U.S. residents to foreign central banks. Although this changes the ownership of the deposits, it does not affect the monetary base or total demand deposits.

For a reserve currency country like the United States, which accepts a substantial amount of foreign official deposits in its commercial banking system, this distinction between the money account and the ORS balance is not negligible and should not be taken lightly. For other countries, however, the difference between the money account and the ORS does not amount to much and can be safely ignored. We now proceed to examine the connections between the money supply process and the balance of payments, as defined.

Suppose that the economy is in a situation of balance-of-payments deficit. As previously explained in Chapter 2, under a system of fixed exchange rates, the deficit represents an excess demand for foreign exchange on the part of the private sector. The central bank satisfies this excess demand by providing (selling) the appropriate amount of foreign exchange to the private sector.

**TABLE 14–5.   Effects of a Drain of International Reserves on the Central Bank
Balance Sheet (in millions of dollars)**

Change in Assets		*Change in Liabilities*	
International reserves	$–$20	Currency	$ 0
Central bank credit	0	Commercial bank deposits	–$20
Monetary base	–$20	Monetary base	–$20

Exactly how does this central bank foreign exchange market intervention occur? Usually, the central bank will sell foreign exchange to commercial banks (which then sell it to customers). In this case, the central bank debits the commercial bank accounts at the Fed in payment for the foreign exchange sold. Therefore, the external payments deficit appears in the central bank's balance sheet as a reduction in commercial bank deposits at the central bank (through the liabilities side) and as a reduction in the bank's international reserve holdings (through the assets side). Table 14–5 displays a T account illustrating how the central bank's balance sheet is affected by a balance-of-payments deficit of $20 million; the deficit surfaces as a $20-million decrease in the monetary base. This implies that the payments deficit reduces the money supply by an amount determined by the money multiplier as established in Equation 14–3.

In the case of a balance-of-payments surplus, the private sector will face an excess supply of foreign exchange. Under fixed exchange rates, the central bank will then buy this excess supply and will pay the private sector—for their sales of foreign exchange—by drawing a check on itself. This type of operation is very similar to an open-market purchase of bonds by the central bank. The central bank thus acquires international reserves (as reflected on the assets side of the balance sheet) at the same time that currency and/or commercial bank deposits increase (as reflected on the liabilities side). The implication is that a payments surplus increases the monetary base and, therefore, expands the money supply in the economy.

Fixed Exchange Rates and the Control of the Money Supply

It may be wise to stop for a moment to review the preceding discussion, as well as its implications. We have shown that the money supply in the economy is basically determined by the monetary base (high-powered money), given the preferences of banks and individuals (as represented by the reserve-deposit and currency-deposit ratios). This relationship between the monetary base and the money supply is represented by the money market multiplier, assumed to be fixed in our simplified framework. Clearly, those factors affecting the monetary base will essentially determine the money supply. In an open economy under fixed exchange rates, the two basic factors tending to influence the monetary base are central bank actions, which affect credit creation in the economy, and the economy's balance-of-payments situation, which alters the central bank's international reserve holdings. The impact effect of increases (or decreases) in credit creation is to raise (or reduce) the monetary base and thus the money supply, *ceteris paribus*. Balance-of-payments deficits (or surpluses), by contrast, tend to reduce (or increase) the central bank's international reserve holdings and to decrease (or increase) the monetary base and the money supply.

The most important conclusion so far regards the difference that exists between an analysis of the money supply process geared toward a closed economy compared with one that is oriented toward an open economy. In the closed economy case it can plausibly be assumed that high-powered money, or some version of it in more sophisticated analyses, can be directly manipulated by the central bank. This means that monetary policy (e.g., an open-market operation) is well defined in terms of how it affects the monetary base (and the money supply). An expansionary (or contractionary) open-market operation can be defined as being associated directly with an increase (or decrease) in the monetary base and thus the money supply. In an open economy under fixed exchange rates, however, this direct association between monetary policy in the form of credit creation by the central bank and changes in the monetary base (and the money supply) cannot be made. In this case, control of the monetary base is not completely in the hands of the central bank because of its links to balance-of-payments disequilibria.

High-powered money, H, looked at from the assets side of the central bank's balance sheet, is composed of international reserves, IR, and central bank credit, CBC, or

$$H = IR + CBC. \qquad (14-5)$$

Expressing Equation 14–5 in terms of changes,

$$\Delta H = \Delta IR + \Delta CBC, \qquad (14-6)$$

which expresses algebraically what we have already discussed: Changes in the monetary base, ΔH, can arise from changes in central bank credit, ΔCBC, *and* changes in the international reserves of the central bank, ΔIR. The implication is that the central bank can manipulate or directly control only one component of high-powered money: central bank credit. The second component (international reserves) cannot be directly controlled by the central bank because, in an economy under fixed exchange rates, it depends essentially on the economy's balance-of-payments situation. The balance of payments is endogenous to the economy; that is, it is determined by the decisions of the private sector in buying domestic and foreign goods and securities, which depend on basic economic variables such as income and export and import prices.

As a consequence, the influence of the central bank on the monetary base is very difficult, or impossible, to isolate. What the monetary authorities clearly affect in the economy is credit creation, through their purchases or sales of bonds in the open market. The effects of changes in central bank credit on the monetary base, and therefore on the money supply, are ambiguous and depend on how credit creation affects the balance of payments. This can be seen by expressing Equation 14–3 in terms of changes and then substituting Equation 14–6, yielding

$$\Delta M^S = \mu \Delta H = \mu(\Delta IR + \Delta CBC), \qquad (14-7)$$

which represents a general equation specifying changes in the money supply in an open economy.

In order to determine how the central bank affects the money supply, then, it is necessary to determine how credit creation affects international reserves. The link between these two will be examined in depth in the following sections. Because the balance of payments is endogenous to the economy, however, a complete and integrated analysis of the determinants of the balance of payments and of the assets and goods markets is necessary. That is the topic to which we now turn.

14–2. Balance-of-Payments Equilibrium and the Degree of Capital Mobility

Countries that are not able to borrow in international financial markets (whether because of low credit ratings or other factors) are forced to finance current account balance (CAB) deficits through losses of international reserves. In such cases, CAB deficits become balance-of-payments deficits. More generally, however, the access to international financial capital represented by an economy's capital account suggests that current account balance deficits do not necessarily have to be associated with losses of international reserves but can be financed by net capital inflows—that is, by net borrowing from abroad. Table 14–6 shows the balance-of-payments accounts of the non-oil-developing countries for recent years. The figures depict how the huge current account deficits of the developing countries in the 1980s and early 1990s were financed by net financial capital inflows, with their overall holdings of international reserves increasing rather than declining. In the presence of international capital mobility, there is no necessary connection between losses (or gains) of international reserves and current account deficits (or surpluses).

Access to international financial markets offers some clear-cut benefits by providing additional sources of financing and investment possibilities to the domestic economy. But openness to international capital movements can impose some severe constraints on the behavior of the economy and on the effectiveness of domestic economic policies. Many a central bank has found its foreign exchange reserves rapidly depleted in the face of sudden, massive capital outflows. Also, monetary authorities often find it extremely difficult to control basic economic variables in the presence of international capital mobility over even short periods of time. It is therefore of the utmost importance to examine international capital movements, their determinants, and their influence on the economy.

Given an economy's international trade in goods and assets, the balance of payments, B, is represented by

$$B = T(q, Y) + K(i), \qquad (14–8)$$

where the service and investment income accounts are ignored for the sake of expositional simplicity. Note that the trade balance, T, is assumed to depend (as in Chapter 13) on the relative price of foreign goods in terms of domestic goods, q, and on domestic income, Y. The capital account is represented by K, with a capital account surplus—a positive value of K—associated with net capital inflows and a deficit—a negative value of K—with net capital outflows. We continue to assume

TABLE 14–6. **Financing Current Account Deficits: The Non-Oil Developing Countries (in billions of U.S. dollars)**

Account	1983	1984	1985	1986	1987	1988	1989	1990	1991
Current account balance (CAB)	$-48.4	$-20.3	$-28.9	$-47.3	$ 0.6	$-26.2	$-35.6	$-42.5	$-94.4
Capital account balance[a] (net capital inflows)	58.0	37.8	45.7	53.1	53.4	26.2	59.6	82.6	109.7
Changes in official reserves (positive represents a gain in reserves)	9.6	17.5	16.8	5.8	52.8	—	24.0	40.1	15.3

[a]Includes all international asset transactions except those involving official reserves; net errors and omissions and net credit from the IMF are included as part of the capital account.

SOURCE: International Monetary Fund, *World Economic Outlook* (October 1991), p. 132.

that domestic and foreign bonds share the same characteristics in terms of liquidity and maturity. In addition, the exchange rate is assumed to be, and expected to remain, fixed; there are no anticipated exchange rate changes. (These assumptions will be relaxed in later chapters.)

The capital account in Equation 14–8 is shown to depend on the domestic interest rate, i. Given the world interest rate, as the domestic interest rate rises, more capital is attracted to the domestic economy; therefore, an improvement in the capital account occurs. The response of the capital account to domestic interest rate changes (given the world interest rate) depends on the degree of capital mobility in the economy. Under conditions of perfect capital mobility, the interest elasticity of the capital account is infinite. Massive capital flows are generated by infinitesimal deviations of the domestic interest rate from the world interest rate, i^*. By contrast, imperfect capital mobility is associated with a less dramatic responsiveness of capital flows to interest rate changes.

What are the implications for the balance of payments of the presence of alternative degrees of capital mobility and interest elasticity of the capital account in the economy?

From Equation 14–9, balance-of-payments equilibrium (zero surpluses or deficits) is achieved when

$$B = T(q, Y) + K(i) = 0. \qquad (14\text{–}9)$$

This balance-of-payments equilibrium condition is illustrated in Figure 14–1 for varying degrees of capital mobility. For an economy facing no capital mobility (no international trade in financial assets), the capital account is always identically equal to zero so that $B = T(q, Y)$, which does not depend on the interest rate. The balance-of-payments equilibrium locus is thus represented by the vertical line $T = 0$. For an economy under imperfect capital mobility, however, the balance-of-payments equilibrium locus is represented by the upward-sloping $B = 0$ locus in Figure 14–1.

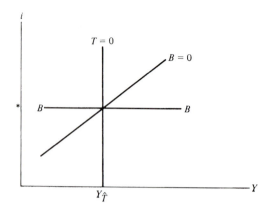

FIGURE 14–1. Capital Flows and Balance-of-Payments Equilibrium

Why does the $B = 0$ locus slope upward? Consider, for the sake of the argument, a situation in which the economy is in balanced payments and balanced trade initially. Suppose, now, that domestic income increases. At any given level of the interest rate, as income increases, imports surge and the trade balance deteriorates. As a consequence, the economy moves into a payments and trade account deficit. In order to correct the payments deficit (assuming a fixed exchange rate), the domestic interest rate would then have to rise. As the domestic interest rate increases, domestic bonds become more attractive relative to foreign bonds and a capital inflow occurs. This capital inflow moves the capital account into a surplus ($K > 0$) and tends to improve the balance of payments. For any given degree of capital mobility, there will then be an increase in the domestic interest rate sufficiently large to induce the capital inflows required to finance the trade deficit (eliminate the balance-of-payments deficit) created by the increase in income. Hence, as domestic income increases, balanced payments can be maintained through an appropriate rise in the domestic interest rate, and the balance-of-payments equilibrium locus in the case of imperfect capital mobility must be upward sloping.

This result is precisely what the $B = 0$ locus in Figure 14–1 illustrates. Note that, moving along the points in that curve, any trade balance deficit ($T<0$) is financed by external borrowing or by foreign financial investments in the domestic economy—that is, by purchases of domestic assets by foreigners ($K>0$). Therefore, no external payments or money account deficit develops. Similarly, any trade surplus ($T>0$) is offset by external lending or domestic purchases of foreign assets ($K<0$), so that no net inflow of money or international reserves results ($B = 0$).

A final case to consider is perfect capital mobility. In an economy facing perfect capital mobility, balance-of-payments equilibrium can occur only if the economy is on the perfectly horizontal BB locus shown in Figure 14–1. Why? Consider an economy with balanced external payments. Suppose now that domestic income increases. As a result, imports increase and the trade balance worsens, which deteriorates the balance of payments. In the case of imperfect capital mobility, a given increase in the domestic interest rate would be required to raise the capital inflows necessary to "finance" the trade deficit—that is, to move the economy back into a payments balance. In the case of perfect capital mobility, however, the domestic interest rate does not have to increase—or has to increase by a very small or an infinitesimal amount—because any amount of funds necessary to finance the trade deficit is available in the world capital markets at the world interest rate, i^*. If the domestic interest rate had to increase at all (to attract a capital inflow), it would only be by a small, negligible amount. Geometrically, then, the BB locus must be perfectly horizontal, placed at a vertical distance given by i^*, the world interest rate, which is the interest rate that the economy under perfect capital mobility has to take as given. Note also that, moving to the right along the BB locus, the economy's trade balance deteriorates: As income increases, imports tend to rise, *ceteris paribus*. The worsening

trade deficit is, of course, financed by a capital account surplus.

In economies under fixed exchange rates, the balance of payments equilibrium condition enters macroeconomic analysis because the balance of payments directly influences the money supply. The endogeneity of the money supply in a regime of fixed exchange rates can be expected to have serious implications for the implementation and impact of monetary policy. How do the monetary adjustments associated with balance-of-payments surpluses or deficits affect the determination of macroeconomic equilibrium? We begin our discussion of these issues in the next section.

14–3. SHORT-RUN AND FULL EQUILIBRIUM UNDER FIXED EXCHANGE RATES

In this section we discuss the determination of equilibrium in the goods and assets markets in an economy under fixed exchange rates.

First, the goods market equilibrium condition is stated by the equality of the output of domestic goods, Y, with the aggregate demand for domestic goods, which is the sum of absorption and the trade balance

$$Y = A + \bar{T} = \bar{A} + aY - bi + \bar{T} - mY + \phi q,$$

where $A = \bar{A} + aY - bi$ and $T = \bar{T} - mY + \phi q$, with $\bar{A}$ denoting autonomous absorption (representing that part of absorption that is independent of income and interest rates and that includes government expenditures, $\bar{G}$), i is the domestic interest rate, q is the real exchange rate, $\bar{T}$ is the autonomous trade balance (that component of the trade balance that is independent of income and the real exchange rate), b is a parameter reflecting the sensitivity of investment spending with respect to the interest rate, and ϕ shows the particular effects of real exchange rates on the trade balance

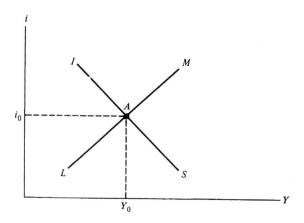

FIGURE 14–2.   Short-Run Equilibrium in the Goods and Assets Markets

(positive on the assumption that the Marshall-Lerner condition is satisfied).[4]

Solving for income yields

$$Y = \alpha(\bar{A} + \bar{T} - bi + \phi q), \qquad (14\text{–}10)$$

where $\alpha = 1/(s + m)$ is the open-economy Keynesian multiplier.

The goods market equilibrium condition algebraically stated in Equation 14–10 can be represented geometrically by the now familiar *IS* curve shown in Figure 14–2. Note that under fixed exchange rates, if P and P^* are exogenously given, as they are in the Keynesian analysis, then the real exchange rate, q, is under the control of domestic policymakers. A domestic currency devaluation— an increase in the exchange rate, e—would be associated with a real exchange rate increase; similarly, a domestic currency revaluation (a reduction of the exchange rate, e, would be linked to a decrease in the real exchange rate. These real exchange rate changes shift the IS curve.

[4]For more details, see the discussion relating to Equation 13–12.

Assets market equilibrium can be represented by money market equilibrium, which obtains when the demand for money equals the money supply given at any moment in time. Algebraically,

$$\frac{M_0}{P} = L^D(i, Y), = kY - hi, \qquad (14\text{–}11)$$

with M_0 equal to the money supply, P is the fixed price of domestic goods and $L^D(i, Y)$ represents the money demand function, with the parameters k and h denoting the responsiveness of money demand to income and the interest rate. (For more details, see our analysis surrounding Equation 13–19 in Chapter 13, which remains unchanged in the present context.) The money market equilibrium condition in Equation 14–11 is depicted by the upward-sloping *LM* curve in Figure 14–2. Note that the *LM* curve represents the combinations of domestic interest rates and income that clear the money market, *given the level of the money supply.* Changes in the money supply would shift the *LM* curve. Because under fixed exchange rates the money supply is an endogenous variable, reacting to the economy's balance-of-payments situation, the *LM* curve will also shift in response to the balance of payments.

Short-Run Equilibrium in the Goods and Assets Markets

Up to this point, we have independently derived a set of pairs of income and interest rates that keep the money market in equilibrium (given the money supply and other parameters) and a set of pairs of interest rates and income that keep the goods market in equilibrium (given the level of government spending, the exchange rate, and other parameters). Short-run equilibrium in the goods and assets markets is obtained when both the money and the goods markets are in simultaneous or general equilibrium, given the various parameters assumed constant during the period of analysis. This implies that the short-run equilibrium levels of the interest rate and income in the economy must be such that both the goods and money markets are in equilibrium simultaneously.

The short-run equilibrium of the economy occurs on the basis of a given level of the money supply, which is assumed to be fixed during the time period of concern. Clearly, the domestic stock of money will be changing over time in response to the country's balance-of-payments situation. If the country is in deficit, the central bank will be losing international reserves. As a result, the monetary base and, consequently, the money supply, will be decreasing. Similarly, if the country has a surplus in the balance of payments, the domestic money supply will be rising. Only if the economy is in balance-of-payments equilibrium (i.e., the balance of payments is equal to zero) will there be no change in the money supply (assuming, as we do throughout this section, that the central bank does not alter domestic credit). In that case, and if there are no other changes in government policy parameters (such as government spending or the exchange rate), the economy will also be in *full equilibrium*. Full equilibrium exists, then, when there is external balance and money holders are neither adding to nor subtracting from their money balances.[5]

[5] The concept of full equilibrium is seldom used in introductory macroeconomics textbooks because endogeneity of the

Let us now proceed to characterize the economy's short-run equilibrium (assuming a fixed money supply). In a later section we will analyze the adjustment process toward full equilibrium by examining how the balance of payments affects the domestic money supply and output over time.

Short-run equilibrium in the economy is depicted graphically by point A in Figure 14–2, which represents the intersection of the IS and LM loci. Point A shows the combination of the interest rate and income, i_0 and Y_0, respectively, at which the goods and money markets are in simultaneous equilibrium in the short run. At those levels, the demand for domestic goods is equal to its supply, as specified by the fact that point A lies along the IS curve. The given supply of money in the short run (M_0) is also equal to the demand for money, so that the money market is also in equilibrium as represented by the fact that point A lies along the LM curve. Note that because the money market is in short-run equilibrium, the bond market will also

money supply through the influence of the balance of payments is rarely taken into account. It is a concept widely used in open-economy macroeconomics, however. It should be noticed that in an economy under fixed exchange rates the distinction between short-run equilibrium (which occurs on the basis of a given money supply at any moment in time) and full equilibrium (which occurs when the money supply is not changing in response to the balance of payments) is essential. For a discussion of the various problems of defining equilibrium in an open economy, see A. Swoboda, "Monetary Approaches to Balance of Payments Theory," in E. Claasen and P. Salin, eds., *Recent Issues in International Monetary Economics* (Amsterdam: North Holland, 1976), especially pp. 9–16. An advanced analysis of the economic dynamics involved in short-run and full equilibrium is carried out by A. Stevenson, V. Muscatelli, and M. Gregory in *Macroeconomic Theory and Stabilization Policy* (Totowa, New Jersey: Barnes and Noble, 1988), chap. 7. As a final note, we should mention that our concept of full equilibrium is often referred to as long-run equilibrium. We prefer the terminology *full equilibrium* in order to associate the concept of long-run equilibrium to longer-run economic adjustments that are ignored in the present, simplified Keynesian framework. These involve changes in prices, the gradual recovery of the economy toward full employment, wealth adjustments, and so on. These aspects will be treated in later chapters.

be in short-run equilibrium; thus, the assets market, in general, is in short-run equilibrium at point A in Figure 14-2.

The next section supplies an algebraic description of the economy's equilibrium. It may be skipped by readers who are less interested in the algebraic underpinnings of short-run macroeconomic equilibrium.

Short-Run Equilibrium: An Algebraic Treatment

The economy's short-run equilibrium, depicted by the intersection of the *IS* and *LM* curves, can also be described algebraically. The procedure solves the equations representing the goods and money market equilibrium conditions simultaneously for the equilibrium interest rate and income, expressing these as functions of exogenous variables. Restating equations 14-10 and 14-11, we find that the money and goods market equilibrium conditions are

$$i = \frac{1}{h}\left(kY - \frac{M_0}{P}\right) \tag{14-11a}$$

$$Y = \bar{A} + \bar{T} + aY - mY - bi + \phi q. \tag{14-10a}$$

To solve these two equations simultaneously, we proceed by substituting the value of the interest rate given by Equation 14-11a into Equation 14-10a, obtaining

$$Y = \bar{A} + \bar{T} + aY - mY - b\left[\frac{1}{h}\left(kY - \frac{M_0}{P}\right)\right] + \phi q,$$

and, simplifying, by moving all terms involving domestic income to the left-hand side:

$$Y\left(1 - a + m + \frac{bk}{h}\right) = \bar{A} + \bar{T}$$

$$+ \frac{b}{h}\frac{M_0}{P} + \phi q. \tag{14-12}$$

By defining $\gamma = b/h$, and simplifying Equation 14-12 a bit further, we obtain

$$Y_0 = \frac{1}{s + m + \gamma k}\left(\bar{A} + \bar{T} + \gamma\frac{M_0}{P} + \phi q\right)$$

$$= \tilde{\alpha}\left(\bar{A} + \bar{T} + \gamma\frac{M_0}{P} + \phi q\right)$$

$$= \tilde{\alpha}(\bar{A} + \bar{T}) + \tilde{\alpha}\gamma\frac{M_0}{P} + \tilde{\alpha}\phi q, \tag{14-13}$$

where $\tilde{\alpha} = 1/(s + m + \gamma k)$. The solution, Y_o, depicts the level of income that clears both the money and goods markets in the short run as a function of the exogenous variables in the system. The latter are foreign income (which influences $\bar{T}$) the money supply (which affects M_0/P), the level of government spending (which affects $\bar{A}$, the exchange rate (which affects q), the price of domestic goods (which affects M_0/P and also q, through its effects on the relative price of foreign to domestic goods), and the behavioral parameters of the economy, such as the marginal propensity to import, m, and the interest sensitivity of the demand for money, h. Changes in any of these exogenous variables can alter the equilibrium level of domestic income, Y_0, at least in the short-run context we are concerned with in this section. Such changes will also tend to alter the equilibrium level of the interest rate. The algebraic value of the short-run equilibrium interest rate can be easily derived by substituting the expression for income in Equation 14-13 into Equation 14-11a.

As mentioned at the beginning of this section, short-run equilibrium is defined as the equilibrium of the economy given a level of the money supply. Clearly, if there is an imbalance, or disequilibrium, in the balance of payments, the domestic money supply will change, and the short-run equilibrium must change as well. Thus, there will be an adjustment process of the economy toward a full equilibrium in which external payments are balanced, with the money stock achieving a state of rest, or equilibrium.

How do changes in the money supply affect short-run equilibrium as portrayed in Figure 14–2? How does the adjustment from a short run to a full equilibrium occur? The answers to these questions are discussed in the next section.

Full Equilibrium in the Goods and Assets Markets

Suppose that we observe a given economy in short-run equilibrium, such as that described by point A in Figure 14–2. If the economy has a balance-of-payments deficit at that point, there will be an excess demand for foreign exchange on the part of the private sector at the given, fixed exchange rate. This excess demand for foreign exchange is satisfied by the central bank, which sells some of its holdings of international reserves to the private sector. As a result, the balance-of-payments deficit induces a reduction in the monetary base and a consequent decrease in the money supply. If the economy has a balance-of-payments surplus, there is an excess supply of foreign exchange held by the private sector that must be purchased by the central bank. The gain in international reserves implies a rise of the monetary base, which leads to a consequent increase in the money supply. Symbolically, from Equation 14–7 it is easily seen that

$$\Delta M^S = \mu \Delta H = \mu \Delta IR, \qquad (14\text{–}14)$$

where ΔM^S represents the change in the money supply, μ is the money market multiplier, ΔH is the change in the economy's monetary base, and ΔIR represents the change in international reserves over time. On the assumption that the central bank does not alter domestic credit (a crucial assumption, as we shall see later), the change in the monetary base must equal the change in the central

bank's international reserve holdings; that is, from Equation 14–6, $\Delta H = \Delta IR$. This means that a short-run equilibrium sustaining a balance-of-payments deficit and losses of international reserves leads to a decline in the money supply and a leftward shift of the LM curve. A balance-of-payments surplus, on the other hand, must shift the LM curve to the right.

In order to examine the adjustment of an economy from short-run to full equilibrium, it must first be known whether the economy is experiencing a balance-of-payments deficit or surplus. Diagrammatically, we must be able to determine whether a point such as A, showing a certain short-run equilibrium in Figure 14–2, represents a point of balance-of-payments deficit or surplus. To visualize this, we must determine a locus showing the balance-of-payments equilibrium ($B = 0$) of the economy in diagrammatic form. This is precisely what is depicted by the loci in Figure 14–1. Depending on the degree of capital mobility, balance-of-payments equilibrium is represented by the BB curve (perfect capital mobility), $T = 0$ curve (zero capital mobility), and $B = 0$ curve (imperfect capital mobility).

Consider the case of zero-perfect capital mobility as an example. In this situation, the economy does not engage in any international trade in assets; therefore, balanced payments is represented by balanced trade. Using our expression for the trade balance (see the discussion at the beginning of Section 14–3):

$$B = T = \bar{T} - mY + \phi q = 0,$$

with all variables as defined before. This equation can be manipulated to show that the balance of payments will be in equilibrium at that level of income, referred to as Y_T, where

$$Y_T = \frac{\bar{T} + \phi q}{m}. \qquad (14\text{–}15)$$

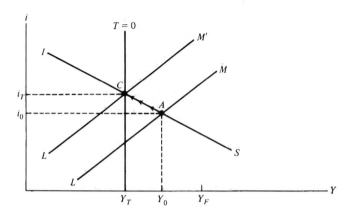

FIGURE 14–3.   The Short-Run and Full Equilibria of the Economy with Zero Capital Mobility

Only at a level of income equal to Y_T will there be equilibrium in the trade balance. At a lower level of income, $Y < Y_T$, there is a smaller amount of imports and the trade balance moves into surplus; if $Y > Y_T$, imports increase above the level necessary to maintain a trade balance, moving the balance of trade into a deficit. Consequently, balance-of-payments equilibrium can be represented by a vertical line at Y_T, as shown in Figure 14–1. Balance-of-payments equilibrium is independent of the interest rate because there are no capital flows.

In Figure 14–3, we have transferred the economy's short-run equilibrium shown in Figure 14–2 to Figure 14–1 under zero capital mobility. The purpose is to show whether the short-run equilibrium at point A represents a balance-of-payments deficit or surplus. In this particular case, the short-run equilibrium is to the right of the balanced payments locus, representing a balance-of-payments deficit.[6] That is,

[6]Diagrammatically, the economy's balance of payments can be represented by the horizontal distance of the short-run equilibrium point from the $T = 0$ locus. In Figure 14–3, the payments deficit is directly related to the horizontal distance between point A and the $T = 0$ line.

$$B = T = \bar{T} - mY < 0.$$

The reason for the deficit lies in the fact that the short-run equilibrium level of income Y_0 implies an amount of imports too large to support balanced external payments. Accordingly, the question we wish to answer is how the short-run equilibrium represented by point A changes over time.

A payments deficit leads to a reduction of the domestic money supply over time, as long as the central bank does not alter domestic credit over that period. The money supply will stop shrinking when the balance-of-payments disequilibrium is eliminated, which occurs only when the external payments deficit is zero. At that point, the central bank no longer loses international reserves and, therefore, the monetary base (and the money supply) stops shrinking. Symbolically, if balance-of-payments equilibrium is attained,

$$\Delta M^S = \mu \Delta H = \mu \Delta IR = 0. \quad (14\text{–}14a)$$

Equation 14–14a represents the full equilibrium condition for the economy. How can we illustrate this condition graphically? In terms of Figure 14–3, the short-run equilibrium at point A will move to the northwest, as the LM curve shifts to the left, in response to the external payments deficit. Full equilibrium is the point at which the deficit is eliminated. This would occur at point C, where the IS and LM curves intersect just precisely at that level of domestic income that would maintain balance-of-payments equilibrium. At that point, the domestic money supply would stop changing and the economy would attain full equilibrium at a level of income equal to Y_T and an interest rate equal to i_T. The monetary contraction entailed in the process of adjustment toward full equilibrium involves rising interest rates and a reduction in income and imports, which is what eliminates the trade deficit.

Our analysis suggests that there is an automatic adjustment process in the economy that tends to eliminate the balance-of-payments deficit. The private sector, through its own laissez-faire actions, would eradicate it over time. A similar type of adjustment can be shown to exist if the economy is at a balance-of-payments surplus. The surplus tends to raise the domestic money supply (as the central bank gains international reserves), increasing domestic income and leading to a consequent rise in imports. The latter then tends to reduce the payments surplus. This adjustment process ends only when the external payments disequilibrium is completely eliminated.

14−4. STERILIZATION OPERATIONS

We can now easily visualize that a balance-of-payments deficit or surplus can only be temporary, as long as the central bank does not intervene to maintain the payments disequilibrium. The central bank has an incentive to intervene, however, in order to prevent the adjustment toward external balance from occurring. The reason? External balance is realized only through a process involving a protracted recession. This is a cruel choice, in the sense that external balance is attained only at the cost of reducing domestic output and employment. Naturally, certain governments would have an incentive to interfere with the market mechanism in order to prevent this balance-of-payments adjustment through recession from occurring. Historically, the result of this recognition of high employment as a primary goal of economic policy (with priority over the goal of external balance, whenever they are in conflict) has resulted in government intervention geared toward preventing the automatic adjustment process of the balance of payments from occurring. This government-induced general breakdown of the automatic mechanism of balance-of-payments adjustment in the world economy has been labeled the international disequilibrium system by Professor Robert Mundell of Columbia University.[7] The question that arises is: How might a central bank intervene to keep the economy from adjusting to an external payments disequilibrium? It can intervene by means of what are called sterilization operations.

Sterilization operations are carried out by the central bank in order to neutralize (sterilize) the effects that its intervention in foreign exchange markets has on the monetary base. Under a regime of fixed exchange rates, the central bank's actions in the foreign exchange market are linked to the country's balance-of-payments surplus or deficit. For example, in the case of a deficit, the central bank has to sell its foreign exchange reserves to the public. As a consequence, the monetary base tends to decline. In this situation, if the central bank wants to sterilize the effects of the deficit on the monetary base, it has to increase domestic credit creation by exactly the same amount. A typical sterilization operation in this case would then be a purchase of bonds by the central bank in the open market. The purchase would have to be of an amount equal to the loss of international

---

[7]See R. Mundell, "The International Disequilibrium System," in his *International Economics* (New York: Macmillan, 1968), chap. 15.

reserves induced by the balance-of-payments deficit. Symbolically, a constant monetary base means

$$\Delta H = \Delta IR + \Delta CBC = 0$$

or, alternatively,

$$\Delta CBC = -\Delta IR. \qquad (14\text{--}6a)$$

In other words, the increase in central bank credit, ΔCBC, must be equal in value, but opposite in sign, to the loss in international reserves, ΔIR, generated by the deficit in the balance-of-payments account. If there were a balance-of-payments surplus in the economy, on the other hand, a typical sterilization operation would be an open-market sale of bonds by the central bank. This counteracts the gain in reserves.

The effects of sterilization operations can be illustrated graphically. Looking back at Figure 14–3, what sterilization operations would do is keep the economy at its short-run equilibrium at point A and prevent it from moving to its full equilibrium at point C. That is, the central bank would prevent the operation of the automatic adjustment mechanism of the balance of payments. By sterilizing the effects of the deficit on the monetary base, it effectively prevents any changes in the domestic money supply. Symbolically,

$$\Delta M^S = \mu \Delta H = \mu(\Delta IR + \Delta CBC) = 0,$$

where the reduction in international reserves over any given period of time is exactly offset by an equal increase in the credit creation of the central bank ($\Delta IR = -\Delta CBC$). With a fixed money supply, the LM curve remains unchanged and unresponsive to the payments deficit. The economy then remains at point A with the balance of payments in deficit, artificially sustained by the central bank and its sterilization operations.[8]

The only way in which sterilization operations can be carried out over an extended period of time, in the presence of a persistent external payments disequilibrium, is if the central bank's holdings of international reserves and bonds are large enough. Suppose, for example, that the economy faces a persistent payments deficit. If the central bank chooses to sterilize, it will have to sell foreign exchange reserves continually because the payments deficit is kept alive by the sterilization. Experiencing dwindling reserves, the central bank would either have to stop sterilizing or else abandon foreign exchange intervention in support of the fixed exchange rate. In the case of countries with persistent balance-of-payments surpluses, on the other hand, the monetary authorities would have to maintain a continuous sale of bonds in the open market to keep the monetary base fixed. Only countries with substantial central bank bond holdings would be able to maintain such intervention.

A final point to recognize with respect to sterilization is that these operations are used by monetary authorities in order to prevent a country's external payments situation from affecting internal monetary and credit conditions. Under conditions of perfect capital mobility, however, sterilization may not be able to fulfill its mission. The next section describes the equilibrium of the economy under perfect capital mobility.

14–5. MACROECONOMIC EQUILIBRIUM UNDER PERFECT CAPITAL MOBILITY

Most economies are highly integrated to international capital markets and engage in substantial trade in financial assets. It is thus important to

---

[8]This situation, where a short-run equilibrium is maintained by government intervention over the automatic adjustment

mechanism of the economy, has been called quasi-equilibrium by A. K. Swoboda is his well-known article, "Equilibrium, Quasi-Equilibrium and Macroeconomic Policy Under Fixed Exchange Rates," *The Quarterly Journal of Economics* (February 1972).

study the consequences of perfect capital mobility for macroeconomic equilibrium. In this section, we discuss the basic determination of equilibrium in the goods and assets markets under conditions of perfect capital mobility. In later sections we consider the effects of economic policies, including the impact of monetary, fiscal, and exchange rate policies and sterilization.

In a situation in which the domestic economy faces perfect capital mobility, the following condition must be satisfied

$$i = i^*, \qquad (14-16)$$

stating the equality of domestic and world interest rates. The balance-of-payments equilibrium condition is then given by Equation 14–9, subject to this constraint. Geometrically, balance-of-payments equilibrium occurs when the economy is along the horizontal *BB* locus illustrated in Figure 14–1, whose vertical height is given by the world interest rate, i^*. Points above the *BB* locus represent balance-of-payments surpluses. This can be realized by noting that if the domestic interest rate were to be above its world level, there would be a massive capital inflow into the economy. This would induce a huge increase in the capital account and move the economy into a payments surplus. A similar argument can be used to show that points below the *BB* locus represent balance-of-payments deficits.

The equilibrium of an economy under fixed exchange rates and perfect capital mobility occurs at the point at which there is goods and money market equilibrium as well as balanced payments. This is depicted by point A in Figure 14–4. This equilibrium corresponds to both short-run and full equilibrium, as defined in previous sections. The explanation is the following. In Section 14–3, we analyzed an economy that did not engage in any international trade in financial assets. In that case, the economy's short-run equilibrium was consistent with payments disequilibrium. In the absence of sterilization, and depending on the loss or gain

in international reserves, the short-run equilibrium shifted over time in response to the implied changes in the money supply. This adjustment process stopped when full equilibrium was attained, at balanced trade. The speed of adjustment depended mainly on the size of the trade deficit in the short run. The larger the trade deficit, the larger the effect on the domestic money supply and, therefore, the faster the adjustments in the economy.

Under perfect capital mobility, an economy's adjustment process in short-run equilibrium but payments disequilibrium is very fast—perhaps instantaneous—because international capital flows allow the economy's money supply to adjust immediately to its full equilibrium level. Consider, for example, a hypothetical case in which the economy's short-run equilibrium interest rate is above its full-equilibrium level. In that event, the domestic interest rate would be out of line with the world interest rate and a balance-of-payments disequilibrium would exist. Massive inflows of funds would occur in response to the differential between the domestic interest rate and the world rate. Such massive capital inflows would generate huge payments surpluses, changing the domestic money supply precipitously. The adjustments in the domestic economy can therefore be quite large and occur over a very short period of time. As a consequence, within the context of perfect capital mobility, the short-run and full-equilibrium distinctions are not necessary. With negligible adjustment and information costs, investors adjust their portfolios quite quickly; any purchase or sale of bonds in the world market would finance any payments surplus or deficit, moving the money supply to its full-equilibrium level instantaneously. In this situation, full equilibrium can be attained in the short run.

It should be stressed that the fact the economy can attain balanced payments (full equilibrium) quickly by means of changes in portfolio composition (by buying or selling bonds) does not preclude other economic forces from operating and shifting its full equilibrium over time. The Keynesian framework employed here ignores some long-run aspects of the adjustment process in the economy. First, wages and prices can be expected to adjust over time in response to deviations of employment from its full-employment level. These long-run changes in wages and prices will be discussed in Chapter 16. Then a second set of adjustments takes place over the long run. These involve changes in the level of domestic wealth by means of capital accumulation (decumulation) and/or through the accumulation (decumulation) of monetary and financial assets by domestic residents. These wealth adjustments are set aside in the present discussion but will be examined in Chapter 20.

The equilibrium of an open economy under fixed exchange rates and perfect capital mobility is graphically portrayed by point A in Figure 14–4, where the IS, LM, and BB loci intersect. At that point, the economy is in equilibrium in the goods and assets markets, as well as in the balance of payments. Note that the equilibrium domestic interest rate, i, coincides with the world interest rate, i^*; otherwise, massive capital flows will emerge, inducing the domestic interest rate to return immediately to the world level.

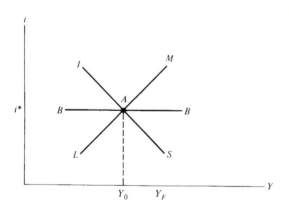

FIGURE 14–4. Equilibrium Under Perfect Capital Mobility

Economic policymaking could shift the equilibrium at point A. There are two possible objectives that come to mind in determining policy intervention in economies under fixed exchange rates: *internal balance* and *external balance*. The goal of internal balance is the attainment of full employment. Unemployment implies that the economy produces below its potential capacity; in that sense it is wasteful. Unemployment also carries a concomitant net welfare loss suffered by those individuals who are involuntarily unemployed. As a consequence, most governments consider internal balance a priority goal.

External balance means that there is no surplus or deficit in the balance of payments. Why should there be any concern for external balance? First, monetary authorities under fixed exchange rates avoid sustained balance-of-payments deficits because they cannot be financed for long without running out of foreign exchange reserves or borrowing extensively. Second, persistent balance-of-payments surpluses involve the accumulation of "excess" foreign exchange reserves that could be used by the government for other purposes. Again, governments are reluctant to accumulate such payments surpluses.

As was stressed earlier, with perfect capital mobility the domestic economy can always finance a trade deficit (or surplus) by means of capital inflows (or outflows) at the given world interest rate. Simple interchanges of bonds and money can alter the domestic money supply and adjust it to full equilibrium, with the economy moving instantaneously to balanced payments. This means that external balance can be immediately attained through the private international capital markets. Within the Keynesian framework followed in this chapter, the private sector would tend to move the economy to external balance but not to internal balance. Point A in Figure 14–4, for instance, shows an equilibrium level of domestic income, Y_0, below the full-employment level, Y_F, with no inherent tendency for the economy to move toward internal balance. Accordingly, there is scope for government intervention in achieving internal balance jointly with external balance. The next sections examine the various effects of government policies. Let us begin with monetary policy.

14–6. THE INEFFECTIVENESS OF MONETARY POLICY UNDER PERFECT CAPITAL MOBILITY

In this section we analyze the effects of monetary policy on the economy's equilibrium. Suppose, for example, that there is a once-and-for-all increase in the central bank's holdings of bonds. Potentially, this would increase the money supply, reduce domestic interest rates, and spur investment and output. In terms of Figure 14–5, the *LM* curve would shift to *LM'* and a new equilibrium would arise at point *C*, with increased output and lower domestic interest rates. The problem, however, is that point *C* is not an equilibrium point. If the domestic interest rate were to decrease below *i**, a massive capital outflow would occur, moving the capital account and the balance of payments into deficit. Furthermore, as domestic income increases (from point *A* to point *C*), imports increase and the trade balance deteriorates, which also tends to worsen the balance of payments.

The balance-of-payments deficit at point *C* implies an excess of the private demand for foreign exchange over its supply as investors try to acquire foreign exchange with which to buy the more profitable foreign financial assets. The central bank satisfies this excess private demand for foreign exchange by selling some of its holdings of foreign exchange reserves. The money supply will then decrease in response to the loss in international reserves. Diagrammatically, the *LM'* curve would have to shift back toward the initial *LM* curve. Clearly, the outflow of capital would continue as long as the domestic interest rate tends to be below the world level. As a consequence, the adjustment process of the economy, which occurs instantaneously under perfect capital mobility, stops only when there are no pressures on domestic interest rates to decrease below the world interest rate.[9] But, at that point, the payments deficit is eliminated. The domestic money supply thus returns to the level that existed before the government engaged in the open-market purchase of bonds. In other words, in an economy under fixed exchange rates and perfect capital mobility, *monetary policy is completely ineffective* in influencing the economy's equilibrium. This result is exactly the opposite to the one obtained in Chapter 13 under flexible exchange rates, making this conclusion a quite powerful one.

[9]As an expository device in our arguments, the domestic interest rate differs from the world rate for a split second, after which it moves back to the world level. An alternative way of viewing the effects of monetary policy (or lack of them) is to observe what domestic residents do when the money supply increases, assuming that they face a given world interest rate. If we suppose that investors are initially at portfolio equilibrium, when the central bank raises domestic credit, domestic investors will find themselves holding excess money balances. Therefore, in order to move their portfolio composition back to an optimum, they will then invest the excess money balances. They do this by buying foreign bonds, at the given world interest rate, which requires the acquisition of foreign exchange from the central bank. In the process, the central bank loses international reserves and the domestic money supply decreases back to its original level. Credit creation by the central bank simply gives rise to an offsetting operation by the private sector, in the form of a purchase of foreign bonds.

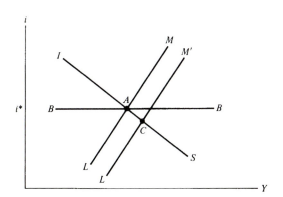

FIGURE 14–5. Effects of Monetary Expansion Under Perfect Capital Mobility

What central bank credit creation can be observed to do is just to change the composition of the asset structure of the central bank portfolio by increasing its holdings of bonds and decreasing foreign exchange reserves. The overall change in the monetary base, ΔH, is, however, equal to zero. Because changes in the monetary base can be broken down into changes in central bank credit and changes in international reserves (see Equation 14–6), then:

$$\Delta H = \Delta CBC + \Delta IR = 0.$$

An increase in central bank credit, $\Delta CBC > 0$, would lead to offsetting capital flows, reducing international reserves, $\Delta IR < 0$, by the same amount as the initial increase in central bank credit ($\Delta CBC = -\Delta IR$). This inability of monetary policy to affect the economy's equilibrium can be better understood once we realize that the effectiveness of monetary policy depends basically on how it alters domestic interest rates. Under a regime of fixed exchange rates with perfect capital mobility, domestic monetary authorities would not be able to affect the domestic interest rate, which has to align with the interest rate given by world capital markets. What happens, then, is that the increase in central bank credit generates an excess supply of money—at the given world interest rate—that tends to push down the domestic interest rate. This downward pressure on the domestic interest rate induces capital outflows, reducing the domestic money supply and eliminating the excess supply of money created initially. On the assumption of perfect capital mobility, all of these adjustments take place instantaneously.

In conclusion, in the case of perfect capital mobility, monetary policy is not able to influence the domestic money supply, even over the short run. It is therefore improper to define monetary policy in terms of changes in the domestic money supply. Monetary policy is correctly defined in this case in terms of credit creation by the central bank. We cannot overemphasize that the availability of some instruments of monetary policy does not imply that the central bank has control of the domestic money supply or that monetary policy is effective in achieving some government goal, such as stabilizing income.

14–7. FISCAL POLICY AND ITS FULL EFFECTIVENESS UNDER PERFECT CAPITAL MOBILITY

The next government policy we analyze is fiscal policy. Consider, as an illustration, the effects of an increase in the level of government spending on domestic goods (financed by, say, an issuance of government bonds). First of all, by increasing government spending, aggregate demand for domestic goods rises; this tends to increase domestic income. As a result, money demand increases, credit becomes tighter, and upward pressure on interest rates builds. This is reflected in Figure 14–6 by the upward shift of the IS curve to IS', which would give rise to a domestic interest rate above the world interest rate, as shown by point C. This situation, however, is not an equilibrium for the economy because it represents a balance-of-payments surplus. If the domestic interest rate were to increase above the world level, i^*, massive capital inflows would result, moving the capital account and the balance of payments into a huge surplus. This payments surplus occurs in spite of the fact that at point C the trade balance has worsened. Even though the movement from point A to point C is associated with increased income and imports and, therefore, a worsened trade deficit, it also implies an increase in the interest rate and a massive surplus in the capital account. The capital account surplus would always dominate the trade balance deficit under perfect capital mobility, leaving a surplus in the overall balance of payments.

The external payments surplus at point C means that, at that point, there would be an excess of the private supply of foreign exchange over its demand as investors sell foreign exchange to acquire domestic currency and buy domestic financial as-

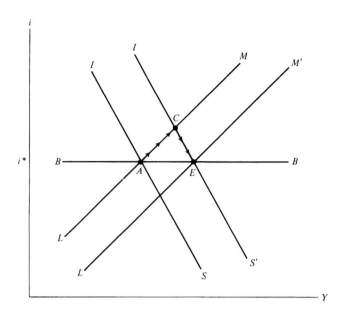

FIGURE 14–6.   Effectiveness of Fiscal Policy Under Perfect Capital Mobility

sets. The central bank acquires this foreign exchange as reserves and, hence, the domestic money supply rises. This increase would be represented in Figure 14–6 by a rightward shift of the *LM* curve, such as that from *LM* to *LM'*. Notice that, insofar as domestic interest rates exceed their world counterparts, capital inflows would persist and the *LM* curve would continue to shift to the right. This process continues until the full equilibrium following the increase in government spending is reached at point *E*. Note that point *E* is attained in the short run because the speed of the adjustment process under perfect capital mobility is very fast.

The new equilibrium at point *E* represents an increase in domestic output and a worsened trade deficit—because income and imports have increased—financed by an improved capital account. The domestic interest rate would remain at the level it was before the fiscal expansion (at *i**). We can conclude, then, that expansionary fiscal policy is quite effective in increasing the real income of an economy under fixed exchange rates

and perfect capital mobility. The economic reasoning behind this result lies in the tendency of the initial spurt of income associated with the increased government spending to create a credit tightness—which, under perfect capital mobility, instead of raising domestic interest rates, induces capital inflows, increasing the domestic money supply and generating further increases in income. In contrast to the traditional crowding-out effect of government spending on private investment, in this situation interest rates do not increase; they remain at their world level and there is thus no negative impact on domestic investment. This makes fiscal policy especially effective in moving the economy toward internal balance.

The quantitative effect of fiscal policy on output under fixed exchange rates is determined from Equation 14–10. Substituting the equality of the domestic and world interest rates under perfect capital mobility into Equation 14–10 yields

$$Y = \alpha(\bar{A} + \bar{T} - bi^* + \phi q).$$

Taking changes in this equation, we obtain

$$\Delta Y = \alpha(\Delta \bar{A} + \Delta \bar{T} - b\Delta i^* + \phi \Delta q), \qquad (14-17)$$

where Δ symbolically denotes change in a variable. Equation 14–17 illustrates the effect of various disturbances and economic policy changes on the full-equilibrium output of the economy. Note first of all that changes in central bank credit do not enter directly into Equation 14–17. This reflects the conclusions in the previous section to the effect that monetary policy is ineffective in raising output under fixed exchange rates. By contrast, a rise in world interest rates would reduce domestic income because it would curtail domestic investment. In addition, a rise in the real exchange rate would augment domestic output (an issue discussed in detail in the next section), and an exogenous expansion of exports $\Delta \bar{T} > 0$) would also raise equilibrium production.

Increased government expenditures would directly raise autonomous absorption ($\Delta \bar{A} > 0$). Assuming that there are no other disturbances, then, from Equation 14–17

$$\Delta Y = \alpha \Delta \bar{A}.$$

This means that every dollar increase in fiscal expenditures has a multiplier effect on output that is given by the Keynesian multiplier $\alpha = 1/(s + m)$. If the marginal propensity to save, s, is equal to 0.25 and the marginal propensity to import is 0.25, then the multiplier is $\alpha = 2.00$ and every dollar spent by the government on domestic goods and services would have a two-dollar effect on output.

The Keynesian conclusion that expansionary fiscal policy increases output while raising the international reserves of the central bank must be taken with a grain of salt. It is the outcome of a short-run analysis that ignores many of the complications arising in economies adopting such policies. Indeed, the evidence supplied by econo-

mists Sebastian Edwards and Peter Montiel from a sample of developing countries is that balance-of-payments difficulties (persistent losses of international reserves) have been preceded by *expansionary*, not contractionary, fiscal policies.[10] Why? One of the shortcomings of the short-run analysis is that it ignores the growing debt service payments faced by governments engaging in external borrowing linked to increased fiscal expenditures. These interest payments to foreigners constitute a negative item in the service account of the balance of payments and have consequences similar to those an exogenous increase in imports would have in the analysis. An exogenous rise in imports would, other things being equal, reduce the autonomous trade balance, $\bar{T}$, shift the IS curve to the left, and induce an equilibrium loss of international reserves as well as an output contraction. Both of these forces counteract the initial impact of the increased government spending discussed earlier. In addition, extended government borrowing, with an associated explosion of public debt to GNP and/or public debt to exports ratios, increases the likelihood that the debt will not be repaid and raises the interest rate the government must pay on additional borrowing. This *country risk premium* adds to the cost of debt servicing and is further associated with losses of international reserves and domestic output contraction.[11]

---

[10]See S. Edwards and P. J. Montiel, "Devaluation Crises and the Macroeconomics of Postponed Adjustment in Developing Countries," *IMF Staff Papers* (December 1989).

[11]The losses of foreign exchange reserves may be the result of private capital flight linked to the uncertainty generated by deteriorating government finances. This is analyzed by J. Eaton and M. Gersovitz in "Country Risk and the Organization of International Capital Transfer," in G. Calvo, R. Findlay, P. Kouri, and J. Braga de Macedo, eds., *Debt, Stabilization and Development* (Oxford: Basil Blackwell, 1989). We will examine this issue in detail in Chapter 20.

14-8. THE IMPACT OF CURRENCY DEVALUATION

Countries suffering from persistent losses in international reserves often rely on currency devaluation as a measure of last resort to avoid a balance-of-payments crisis. This section provides the details of the Keynesian analysis of devaluation.

A domestic currency devaluation, an increase in *e,* changes domestic economic variables by affecting the relative price of imports in terms of exports. If the exchange rate increases, the relative price of imports in terms of exports rises ($q = eP^*/P$ increases), a result of the Keynesian assumption that P and P^* are fixed. For example, adopting a Mexican perspective, a devaluation of the peso increases the peso price of Mexican imports (i.e., given the dollar price of, say, American Oldsmobiles sold to Mexico, a devaluation of the peso will increase the peso price of the automobiles); thus, more units of Mexican exports will have to be given up in order to buy one unit of imports (e.g., an Oldsmobile).[12]

On the assumption that the Marshall-Lerner condition is satisfied, a currency devaluation will raise the real exchange rate, *q,* and improve the trade balance. This will exert a positive impact on aggregate demand, shifting the *IS* curve to the right. The upward pressure on interest rates then attracts capital inflows that raise the domestic money supply and induce the *LM* curve also to shift to the right. The equilibrium impact of the policy is an increase in output and a gain in international reserves. Diagrammatically, then, the consequences of devaluation are similar to those depicted in Figure 14-6 for expansionary fiscal policy.

Devaluation, Income, and the Trade Balance: An Algebraic Analysis

The quantitative effects of currency devaluation on income and the trade balance can be determined from Equation 14-17. Suppose that a domestic currency devaluation raises the real exchange rate by Δq. Then, assuming that there are no changes in $\bar{A}, \bar{T}$, and i^*, Equation 14-17 suggests that domestic production would be changed by this much:[13]

$$\Delta Y = \alpha\phi\Delta q. \qquad (14-18)$$

We are saying a devaluation has a positive effect on domestic income whose value depends on (1) the magnitude of the real exchange rate impact of the devaluation, Δq, (2) the open-economy Keynesian multiplier, symbolized by α, and (3) the value of the parameter ϕ. The parameter ϕ reflects how changes in real exchange rates affect the trade balance, holding other things constant. As determined in Chapter 13, the value of ϕ—and therefore the magnitude of the impact of devaluation on output—is related to the demand elasticities for exports and imports, η and η^*. The reason is that devaluation works its effect on income by means of an expenditure-switching effect, making foreign goods relatively expensive and shifting the expenditures of foreign and local residents toward domestic goods. The larger the demand elasticities for imports and exports, the stronger the impact of devaluation on income.

---

[12]In a more general setting, a devaluation would also induce changes in the prices of foreign and domestic goods, making the analysis more complicated. Our discussion in Chapter 16 examines this important issue in detail.

[13]The exact expression for the effect of a devaluation on income is obtained by using our results in Chapter 13 (Footnote 7) showing that $\phi = (M^*/q)(\eta^* + \eta - 1)$, where M^* represents the quantity of domestic goods exported. Equation 14-18 then implies that $\Delta Y = \alpha M^*(\eta^* + \eta - 1)\Delta q/q$. In deriving this expression, it is assumed that the economy devalues from a starting point of external balance. As a result, the effects of a devaluation under conditions of trade deficit will not correspond exactly to those based on this expression. We leave for the Problems section at the end of this chapter the complications introduced when a country devalues from a position of trade deficit.

The next step is to determine the effects of a devaluation on the trade balance. The trade balance is given by

$$T = \bar{T} + \phi q - mY.$$

Assuming that the autonomous trade balance (which depends on foreign income and other exogenous variables) is fixed, then changes in the trade balance, ΔT, are represented by

$$\Delta T = \phi \Delta q - m \Delta Y. \qquad (14\text{--}19)$$

Equation 14–25 suggests that a currency devaluation has direct, positive effects on the trade balance (as given by the first term on the right-hand side of the equation); however, because it also generates an increase in income, it will raise imports and have an induced negative impact on the trade balance (as is indicated by the second term on the right-hand side of the equation). Is it possible that a devaluation may actually worsen the trade balance because of its expansionary effects on income and thus on imports? To answer this question, we substitute the change in income, ΔY, associated with a currency devaluation, as given by Equation 14–18, into Equation 14–19. This yields

$$\begin{aligned} \Delta T &= \phi \Delta q - m \alpha \phi \Delta q \\ &= s \alpha \phi \Delta q, \end{aligned} \qquad (14\text{--}20)$$

which is positive on the assumption that the Marshall-Lerner condition is satisfied.[14] That is, a devaluation unambiguously improves the trade balance, even after considering the negative effects of increased income on it. The reason can be obtained through the use of our now-familiar aggregate demand equation: $Y = A + T$, which can also be expressed as

$$T = Y - A. \qquad (14\text{--}21)$$

Equation 14–21 shows that the trade balance is equal to the excess of income over absorption. A devaluation has been assumed to have no direct effect on absorption. (Remember that absorption is equal to the sum of a component that is exogenous and depends on government spending, $\bar{A}$; a part that depends on income, mY; and a component that is dependent on the interest rate, $i = i^*$.) At the same time, a currency devaluation tends to increase income, which in turn raises absorption. The increase in absorption, however, is smaller than the increase in income because the marginal propensity to spend is less than 1. This means that $Y - A$ must increase in response to the devaluation. In order to maintain equilibrium, $Y - A = T$; thus, the trade balance, T, *must* improve, even after we consider the induced income effects.

The direct effect of a devaluation on the trade balance, which we associate with the parameter ϕ and the first term in Equation 14–19, involves the Marshall-Lerner condition as an integral part and is at the crux of the so-called elasticities approach to the balance of payments, developed independently by economists C. F. Bickerdike, L. Metzler, and J. Robinson. On the other hand, the perspective that, to affect the trade balance, a devaluation must reduce absorption relative to income—as stated by Equation 14–21—is referred to as the absorption approach. At first, when MIT economist Sidney Alexander (among others) developed the absorption approach, it was thought that the framework was at odds with the elasticities approach. Cornell University economist S. C. Tsiang and the University of Chicago's Harry Johnson, as well as others, later realized that both approaches can be integrated quite nicely. This integration is implicit in our discussion in this section, as reflected by Equations 14–18 and 14–20.

Devaluation, Absorption, and the Laursen-Metzler-Harberger Effect

Up to this point, we have examined the effects of devaluation on the assumption that domestic ab-

---

[14]In deriving Equation 14–20, we have used the relationship: $1 - m\alpha = 1 - m(s + m) = s/(s + m)$. Using the value of ϕ stated in Footnote 13, the exact expression for the impact of a currency devaluation on the trade balance is $\Delta T = s \alpha M^*(\eta^* + \eta - 1)\Delta q/q$.

sorption, A, is not affected by changes in the relative price of foreign goods in terms of domestic goods, q. As the discussion in relation to Equation 14–10 makes clear, absorption is assumed to depend on exogenously determined autonomous absorption, domestic income, and the interest rate—but not on relative prices. In our analysis of devaluation, this meant that although the trade balance responded directly to a rising q, absorption did not. This might be a reasonable assumption, but it does not generally hold. A devaluation makes imports relatively more expensive in terms of domestic goods. Therefore, the purchasing power of domestic residents declines: Any given amount of domestic output is now able to purchase a smaller amount of foreign goods. This effect is usually referred to as a domestic-terms-of-trade deterioration. The *terms of trade* are defined as the ratio of the price of exports in domestic currency, P, to the price of imports in domestic currency, eP^*, and is just the reciprocal of q.

A decrease in the purchasing power of domestic goods, with our assumption that spending *in terms of domestic goods* remain unchanged, must then imply that there is a reduction in the real spending of domestic residents—that is, a decline in their standard of living. As the unwillingness of oil-importing countries to allow their standard of living to decrease in the face of oil-price increases in the 1970s tended to indicate, at least over short periods of time, we could very well expect that domestic residents will try to maintain their standard of living (i.e., real spending) as a relative constant, even in the face of increased import prices. A completely legitimate alternative to our earlier assumption, then, is that domestic residents keep their real expenditure constant whenever they face a reduction in purchasing power. In this case, a devaluation leads to an increase in absorption (i.e., an increase in expenditure measured in terms of domestic goods) in order to offset the decrease in purchasing power of domestic output. This positive effect of devaluation on absorption has been called the Laursen-Metzler-Harberger effect.[15] We have seen that the effect arises when-

ever domestic residents try to maintain their standard of living in the face of changes in the purchasing power of their income.

The implication of the Laursen-Metzler-Harberger effect is that devaluation may actually worsen the trade balance. The associated deterioration of the terms of trade induces domestic residents to reduce their savings in order to sustain their real standard of living. There is, therefore, an increase of absorption relative to income that, as Equation 14–21 illustrates, worsens the trade balance.

Studies evaluating the Laursen-Metzler effect conclude that a temporary deterioration of the terms of trade, such as that faced by the oil-importing countries during the Iraq-Kuwait crisis of 1990 and 1991, leads to a temporary worsening of the trade balance in the short run, but to long-run trade balance improvements. It is thus important, in examining the effects of devaluation, whether the terms-of-trade deterioration is expected to be temporary or permanent by agents in the economy. If the decline of the terms of trade associated with currency devaluation is expected to be temporary, the policy may be ineffective in improving the trade balance.[16]

The fact that devaluation tends to reduce the domestic standard of living and may deteriorate

---

[15]This effect is named in honor of economists S. Laursen and L. Metzler, who analyzed it in "Flexible Exchange Rates and the Theory of Employment," *Review of Economics and Statistics* (November 1950); and A. Harberger, who examined it in "Currency Depreciation, Income and the Trade Balance," *Journal of Political Economy* (1950). For a particularly illuminating (but advanced) exposition of this effect, see R. Dornbusch, *Open Economy Macroeconomics* (New York: Basic Books, 1980), pp. 78–81.

[16]The role of temporary versus permanent shifts in the terms of trade, and the role of anticipated versus unanticipated disturbances on this, has been investigated by M. Obstfeld, "Aggregate Spending and the Terms of Trade: Is There a Laursen-Metzler Effect?" *Quarterly Journal of Economics* (May 1982); T. Persson and L. E. O. Svensson, "Current Account Dynamics and the Terms of Trade: The Harberger-Laursen-Metzler Effect Two Generations Later," *Journal of Political Economy* (February 1985); and M. Gavin, "Structural Adjustment to a Term of Trade Disturbance: The Real Exchange Rate, Stock Prices, and the Current Account," *Journal of International Economics* (May 1990).

the trade balance in the short run should alert us to the fact that the adjustments brought about by devaluation are not without cost and might be quite painful. Even when the economy's competitiveness is improved and a surge of exports and production eventually occurs, these results cannot be obtained without the sacrifices generally implied by worsening terms of trade. This is one of the reasons why, in spite of its frequent use, devaluation is a decision that is very carefully considered before it is implemented.

Evidence on the Impact of Devaluation: The J-Curve Effect

The chief means through which a devaluation works in increasing domestic production is by improving the trade balance. The previous section, however, has raised questions about a possible negative impact of devaluation on the trade balance in the short run. What has experience shown us about the effects of devaluation on trade?

In spite of the popular belief that devaluation improves the trade balance, in practice there appears to be a rather intricate relationship between them. Indeed, a worsening of the trade balance is often observed over the period of time immediately following a devaluation. Eventually, however, an improvement in the trade balance does seem to come about. This type of pattern is referred to as the J-curve effect, depicted by the curve in Figure 14–7, which shows the change in the trade balance induced by a given devaluation plotted against time. This curve illustrates the initial worsening of the trade balance in response to a devaluation and the subsequent swing toward a positive effect over time. Because the shape of the curve is that of a J, the rationale for the terminology is clear.

The time lag involved in the improvement of the trade balance to a devaluation varies significantly from country to country. For example, IMF economist Jacques Artus found that the historical 1967 devaluation of the pound had an adverse effect on the trade balance of the United Kingdom only

during the first half of 1968, eventually turning into an improvement of about £940 million ($2,501 million) by 1971.[17] The variety of possible time profiles of the effects of devaluation in different countries has been studied by Sebastian Edwards. He surveyed the effects of thirty-nine devaluations carried out by developing countries in the 1960s through the 1980s on trade, the CAB, output, and other variables. He found that in 41 percent of the cases he studied, a devaluation reduced a country's CAB–GDP ratio in the first year after the devaluation (relative to its value one year before devaluation). In many of these cases, however, the devaluation had improved the CAB after three years had elapsed.[18] More evidence on the lack of improvement in the trade balance in response to devaluation is provided by Andrew K. Rose of the University of California at Berkeley. Professor Rose used a sophisticated version of Equation 14–19 in finding empirical estimates of ϕ (showing the impact of changes in the real exchange rate on the trade balance) for a sample of thirty countries, covering data on devaluations between 1970 and 1988. His results indicate a negative effect of devaluation on the trade balance in fourteen out of the thirty countries he examined. He concluded that "a depreciation of the real exchange rate is not strongly associated with a significant improvement in the trade balance."[19]

---

[17]See J. Artus, "The 1967 Devaluation of the Pound Sterling," *IMF Staff Papers* (November 1975). Others have characterized the initial deterioration of the trade balance as having persisted throughout 1968.

[18]S. Edwards, *Real Exchange Rates, Devaluation and Adjustment: Exchange Rate Policy in Developing Countries* (Cambridge, Mass.: MIT Press, 1989), pp. 280–281. See also, D. Himarios, "Do Devaluations Improve the Trade Balance?" *Economic Inquiry* (January 1989).

[19]A. K. Rose, "Exchange Rates and the Trade Balance: Some Evidence from Developing Countries," *Economics Letters* (November 1990), 275. See also, D. K. Backus, P. Kehoe and F. Kydland, "Dynamics of the Trade Balance and the Terms of Trade," National Bureau of Economic Research Working Paper No. 4242 (December 1992).

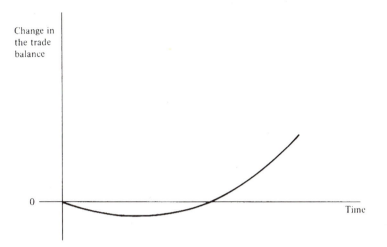

FIGURE 14–7. The J-Curve Effect of a Devaluation

In conclusion, even though some studies suggest that devaluation has a positive effect on the trade balance at some point, it appears that in many cases the impact is only a modest, or negative, one in the period immediately following the devaluation. What determines this behavior of the trade balance in response to devaluation? That is, what explains the J-curve effect?

Explaining the J-Curve Effect

Whether a devaluation improves or worsens the trade balance is closely connected to the question of whether the Marshall-Lerner condition is satisfied. The condition states that an increase in the relative price of imports will improve the trade balance only if the sum of the price elasticities of imports and exports is larger than 1. It appears, however, that over the short run, the value of these elasticities is rather small. In other words, the evidence tends to indicate that, over short periods of time, both exports and imports are quite unresponsive to changes in relative prices. This is because consumers and producers generally adjust

slowly to the devaluation. There are various reasons for this. First, there is a *consumer-response lag:* It takes time for buyers to recognize a changed competitive situation, and this delay can be expected to be longer in international than in domestic trade because of language differences and distance obstacles. In addition, pre-existing contracts might not permit adjustments in quantities purchased over the immediate short run. Second, there is a *production-response lag:* It takes time for new business connections to be formed and new orders to be placed; even if buyers can be found rapidly, the contracting of new equipment, raw materials, building capacity, and so on, to increase production could require a substantial amount of time.[20]

That the adjustment of exports and imports to devaluation occurs only slowly over time has been found in many studies. For example, in a sample of

[20]For instance, in countries producing raw materials, the output of exports is often limited by the inability to raise extraction levels significantly over the short run. See T. Gylfason and M. Radetzki, "Does Devaluation Make Sense in the Least Developed Countries?" *Economic Development and Cultural Change* (October 1989).

thirteen industrial countries, Helen B. Junz and Rudolf R. Rhomberg found the responses of exports of manufactured goods to a change in relative prices to spread over a period of about five years, with only 50 percent of the full effect occurring in the first three years. Others have found similar results for both imports and exports, although the time span involved is frequently found to be shorter.[21] This evidence provides much of the explanation for why the trade balance fails to respond positively (and often worsens) in the period immediately following devaluation. With quantities of exports and imports relatively unchanged, the devaluation would have little positive effect on the trade balance and may worsen it by increasing the value of imports (through increases in import prices). Of course, over longer periods of time, the amounts of exports and imports would respond to relative price changes and the effects on the trade balance would tend to be positive.

The fact that devaluation might worsen the trade balance over the period immediately following the currency devaluation suggests that the actual impact of exchange rate increases over the short run might be contractionary rather than expansionary. Indeed, a range of studies has found devaluation to have short-run contractionary effects. For example, Harvard's Richard N. Cooper finds this experience common in developing countries, sometimes lasting a few months and, not infrequently, sometimes lasting longer than a year.[22] In a more recent study, Edwards observed contractionary effects in the first year after devaluation in a sample of twelve developing countries.[23] On the other

side of the argument, some economists have argued that the association of output reductions with devaluation might be spurious. Steven Kamin of the Federal Reserve Board has noted that in many developing countries, deep recessions appear in the year before a devaluation is carried out. As a result, the output contraction after the devaluation may be the remainder of a recessionary process that started *before* the devaluation.[24] To conclude, although the evidence might be mixed on this issue, policymakers must act cautiously in using currency devaluation as a policy tool.

14−9. INTERDEPENDENCE AND THE INTERNATIONAL TRANSMISSION OF AGGREGATE DEMAND DISTURBANCES

Up to this point, our emphasis has been on determining a given economy's macroeconomic equilibrium and how it is affected by domestic disturbances, assuming that foreign variables (foreign income and foreign prices) remain unchanged. Here we extend the discussion to determine how changes in foreign income alter domestic equilibrium.

Spillover Effects and Interdependence Under Fixed Exchange Rates

In an interdependent world, disturbances affecting income in one country can have significant effects on other countries. As a result, an economy can be subject to major dislocations associated with eco-

---

[21]H. B. Junz and R. R. Rhomberg, "Price Competitiveness in Export Trade Among Industrial Countries," *American Economic Review* (May 1973); and T. Gylfason, "The Effects of Exchange Rate Changes on the Balance of Trade in Ten Industrial Countries," *IMF Staff Papers* (October 1978).

[22]R. N. Cooper, "Devaluation and Aggregate Demand in Aid-Receiving Countries," in J. N. Bhagwati et al., eds., *Trade, Balance of Payments and Growth* (Amsterdam: North Holland, 1971).

[23]S. Edwards, "Are Devaluations Contractionary?" *Review of Economics and Statistics* (August 1986). Data concentrating

on particular countries is now widely available; for example, evidence on contractionary effects in the case of Jamaica has been provided by L. Barbone and F. Rivera-Batiz in "Foreign Capital and the Contractionary Impact of Currency Devaluation, with an Application to Jamaica," *Journal of Development Economics* (February 1986). For an extensive survey of the literature on this topic, see J. S. Lizondo and P. Montiel, "Contractionary Devaluation in Developing Countries: An Analytical Overview," *IMF Staff Papers* (March 1989).

[24]S. B. Kamin, "Devaluation, External Balance and Macroeconomic Performance: A Look at the Numbers," *Princeton Studies in International Finance* (August 1988).

nomic events abroad. For instance, by reducing foreign demand for domestic goods (our exports), a recession and unemployment abroad can *spill over* or be transmitted into recession and unemployment in the domestic economy. How is our earlier framework extended to incorporate the analysis of these foreign income disturbances on domestic output?[25]

Our earlier discussion assumed foreign income, Y^*, to be fixed, submerging its influence on domestic exports into the autonomous trade balance, $\bar{T}$, The effects of foreign income on domestic exports can then be taken into account by breaking down the autonomous trade balance, $\bar{T}$, into two components: One component, T_0, representing that part of the trade balance that is not influenced by foreign (or domestic) income, and another component, m^*Y^*, accounting for the influence of foreign income on domestic exports. Symbolically, this breakdown is represented by

$$\bar{T} = T_0 + m^*Y^*, \qquad (14-22)$$

where m^* is the marginal propensity to import domestic goods by foreign residents.[26] The term m^*Y^* can tell us what part of their additional income foreigners spend on domestic goods, which represents domestic exports. If we assume that everything else is constant, a change in foreign income, ΔY^*, will influence the autonomous trade balance by $\Delta\bar{T}=m^*\Delta Y^*$. This expression can be substituted into Equation 14–17 to determine the influence of changes in foreign income on domestic income:

$$\Delta Y = \alpha m^*\Delta Y^*, \qquad (14-23)$$

where other variables are assumed constant, so that $\Delta\bar{A} = 0$, $\Delta i^* = 0$ and $\Delta q = 0$. Equation 14–23 is usually expressed in proportional terms by dividing both sides by domestic income, yielding

$$\hat{Y} \equiv \frac{\Delta Y}{Y} = \alpha m^* \frac{Y^*}{Y}\frac{\Delta Y^*}{Y^*}$$
$$= \alpha m^* \frac{Y^*}{Y}\hat{Y}^* \qquad (14-24)$$

where $\hat{Y}\equiv\Delta Y/Y$ and $\hat{Y}^*\equiv\Delta Y^*/Y^*$ represent the proportional rates of change of domestic and foreign income.

Equation 14–24 highlights the major factors determining the influence of a foreign income disturbance on domestic income. The first factor is the foreign marginal propensity to import, m^*, which is associated with the economy's degree of openness. If the economy is relatively closed so that foreign residents do not spend on domestic goods to any significant extent, then m^* becomes close to zero, and foreign income growth will have minimal influence on domestic growth. If foreign residents spend a large fraction of their income on domestic goods, any given reduction in foreign growth will bring about a substantial drop in demand for domestic goods and therefore a sharp domestic recession.

A second factor influencing the magnitude of spillover effects is the economic size of the foreign trading partners relative to the size of the domestic economy. This is measured by the ratio of foreign to domestic income, Y^*/Y, in Equation 14–24. If foreign income and, therefore, the foreign demand for domestic goods represents a negligible fraction of domestic income, a foreign recession will have a minor effect on domestic growth. The larger the relative size of the foreign economy, on the other hand, the greater the impact of foreign disturbances on domestic growth.

Finally, the size of the domestic income multiplier, α, will influence the effects of foreign disturbances on domestic growth. The larger (or smaller) the multiplier, the stronger (or weaker) the transmission of a foreign recession into the domestic economy.

[25]For the detailed mechanics of interdependence within a Keynesian framework of the open economy, see J. A. Frenkel and A. Razin, *Fiscal Policies and the World Economy* (Cambridge, Mass.: The MIT Press, 1987), pt II; and R. Dornbusch, *Open Economy Macroeconomics,* op. cit., chap. 3, pp. 43–56.

[26]It is assumed that foreign income, Y^*, is measured in terms of domestic goods, to insure consistency of units.

Repercussion Effects and the Income Multiplier

Spillover effects point to the global nature of income determination in regimes of fixed exchange rates. To illustrate the issues further, let us consider the hypothetical situation of a world in which the industrialized countries fix their exchange rates vis-à-vis each other. Suppose a fiscal expansion results in a U.S. economic boom. As income grows, U.S. imports will swell because some of the additional spending falls into purchases of foreign goods and services. Because higher domestic imports correspond to an increase in foreign, say European, exports to the United States, the U.S. income expansion generates an export-led production and income expansion abroad. In other words, the U.S. boom is transmitted to Europe as Americans spend more on European goods.

The matter does not end there, though. The induced expansion of European income can be expected to increase European spending on U.S. goods, feeding back into the U.S. economy in the form of increased exports to Europe and therefore increased U.S. production and income. The process involves a *repercussion effect* of the initial U.S. autonomous spending expansion on the U.S. economy. This repercussion effect is positive in the sense that it serves to expand U.S. income further. Our discussion of economic policy in previous sections ignored repercussion effects by assuming an exogenously given foreign income. It is apparent, however, that in interdependent economies, foreign income can be affected by domestic disturbances. Because the repercussion effects amplify the expansionary impact of a rise in domestic autonomous spending (or enhance the contractionary effects of a spending reduction), the income multiplier taking into account repercussion effects is generally larger than the one derived earlier, which ignored repercussions. The precise algebraic expression for the multiplier in this context is derived in the appendix to this chapter.

Under fixed exchange rates, autonomous disturbances in one country are transmitted internationally, giving rise to the saying "When one country sneezes, the others catch cold." This result is diametrically different from the transmission mechanism in economies under flexible exchange rates. In the latter case, under perfect capital mobility, economies are insulated from foreign business cycles. Only changes in world interest rates would supply a mechanism for the international transmission of autonomous disturbances.

Evidence of interdependence under fixed exchange rate regimes is available from the Bretton Woods era. More recently, economists have investigated the same issue by using simulations of how the current world economy would react to various disturbances if there were fixed exchange rates instead of the current managed floating regime. Table 14–7 shows the results of a recent study by economists Warwick J. McKibbin and Jeffrey D. Sachs estimating the spillover effects of expansionary fiscal policies in the OECD.[27] Assuming that countries other than the United States intervene in foreign exchange markets to fix their exchange rates versus the dollar, Professors McKibbin and Sachs carried out an examination of the impact *on the United States and Japan* of a fiscal expansion in the rest of the OECD. The increase in government expenditures examined was equal to 1 percent of the GNP in the OECD countries engaging in the fiscal expansion (with the increased spending financed through higher public debt). The results reported in Table 14–7 show how increased autonomous spending in the OECD countries involved in the policy disturbance would raise income in those countries but would also spill over into economic expansion in Japan and the United States. At the same time, the trade balance of the economies engaging in expansionary fiscal policy would deteriorate (because their income and thus imports rise) and the balance of trade

---

[27]Remember that the OECD consists of the United States, Japan, Germany, France, Italy, the United Kingdom, Canada, Austria, Belgium-Luxembourg, Denmark, Finland, Greece, Iceland, Ireland, the Netherlands, Norway, Portugal, Spain, Sweden, Switzerland, Turkey, Australia, and New Zealand.

TABLE 14–7. **Spillover Effects and the International Transmission of Fiscal Policies Under Fixed Exchange Rates**

Economies	First Year	Second Year	Third Year
U.S. economy			
Real GNP, Y	0.1%	0.5%	0.6%
Trade balance, T (% of GNP)	0.3%	0.4%	0.6%
Money supply, M^S	0.0%	0.0%	0.0%
Japanese economy			
Real GNP, Y	0.6%	0.9%	0.8%
Trade balance, T (% of GNP)	0.2%	0.4%	0.5%
Money supply, M^S	0.2%	0.6%	0.9%
Rest of the OECD			
Real GNP, Y	4.7%	4.5%	3.2%
Trade balance, T (% of GNP)	−0.3%	−0.4%	−0.5%
Money supply, M^S	1.7%	4.2%	6.2%

SOURCE: W. J. McKibbin and J. D. Sachs, "Coordination of Monetary and Fiscal Policies in the Industrial Economies," in J. A. Frenkel, ed., *International Aspects of Fiscal Policies* (Chicago: University of Chicago Press, 1988), p. 85.

of their trading partners—Japan and the United States—would improve (the expansion of income and spending in the rest of the OECD would raise demand for U.S. goods). There is, finally, growth of the money supply in Japan and in the other OECD countries. (These countries fix their exchange rates versus the dollar and their money supply is endogenous; their increased income raises money demand, which will then be associated with money supply growth through the accumulation of international reserves.) There are, however, wide differences in the precise, quantitative effects of the disturbance on Japan and the United States. These divergences are connected to the differences in the magnitude of spillover and repercussion effects for each particular country linked to variations in marginal propensities to import, relative size of the economies involved, and the like.

Policy Coordination and Conflict in the World Economy

A major conclusion of the analysis in this section is that, within a context of Keynesian recession and unemployment, raising domestic autonomous

spending is not only associated with domestic recovery, but it also tends to spur foreign income growth. As a matter of fact, if all countries involved were to raise their own autonomous expenditures, the result would be a stronger income expansion than if each country alone were to pursue its expansionary objectives. It is therefore apparent that expansionary autonomous spending policies do not result in policy conflict; a joint expansion of autonomous spending would heighten each country's expansionary efforts rather than hinder them.

One curious aspect of a simultaneous global expansion of income, bringing to the fore the nature of interdependence, regards its effects on the trade balance. An increase in domestic income raises imports and thereby worsens the trade balance. What happens when all countries concerned tj;5expand their income? Would the trade balance of all these countries deteriorate? Emphatically not. Because one country's imports are another country's exports, the sum of the trade balances of all countries trading with each other must add up to zero; that is, the global trade balance deficit is equal to zero. When there is joint economic expansion for all countries concerned, those countries growing above the average tend to have trade deficits, while those whose income grows at a rate below the average will have trade balance surpluses. The deficits of the faster-growing countries then balance the surpluses of the slower-growing countries, producing a zero global trade balance.

The positive effects of autonomous spending policies of one country on other countries under fixed exchange rates do not extend to exchange rate policy. A domestic currency devaluation represents a foreign currency revaluation; just as it switches demand toward domestic goods, it also switches demand away from foreign goods. Any improvement in the domestic trade balance and output is thus obtained at the expense of foreign country income. Devaluation is thus often referred to as a beggar-thy-neighbor policy.

Foreign authorities may react against a revaluation of their currencies by countering with their own currency devaluations. These *competitive devaluations* make the analysis of devaluation more complicated than when the policy is imposed unilaterally. The expansion of production resulting from devaluation would vary by country. With a variety of economies following nominal currency devaluations against each other, countries that engage in greater devaluations may gain vis-à-vis those that adopt smaller devaluations. This is indeed what Professors Barry Eichengreen and Jeffrey Sachs find best describes the world situation during the competitive devaluations observed in the Great Depression in the 1930s. They find a clear positive relationship between economic recovery between 1929 and 1935 and the magnitude of the currency depreciation of the country during that time. Economies such as France, the Netherlands, and Belgium had lower rates of currency devaluation in the aftermath of the Great Crash but by 1935 had failed to recover to 1929 levels of industrial production. By contrast, the United Kingdom, Denmark, and the Scandinavian countries deval-

ued at an early date, and grew much more rapidly.[28]

The competitive devaluations followed by countries seeking domestic expansion at the expense of their trading partners point to a basic weakness of a system in which currency devaluation is a policy that is easy to execute. In situations of global recession and unemployment, domestic policymakers in each country might have an incentive to export the problems to foreign economies, thereby engaging in competitive devaluations. As a matter of fact, the competitive devaluations in the 1930s were closely linked to the experience of worldwide economic collapse in the Great Depression years. The general instability and uncertainty associated with the competitive devaluations of the 1930s gave impetus to the more rigorous restrictions imposed by the IMF on the use of devaluation as a macroeconomic adjustment policy under the Bretton Woods regime.[29]

14−10. STERILIZATION OPERATIONS AND PERFECT CAPITAL MOBILITY

Sterilization operations refer to operations carried out by the economy's central bank to neutralize (sterilize) the effect that its intervention in foreign exchange markets has on the monetary base (see Section 14−4). The basic conclusion of this section

---

[28]B. Eichengreen and J. D. Sachs, "Exchange Rates and Economic Recovery in the 1930s," in B. Eichengreen, ed., *Elusive Stability: Essays in the History of International Finance, 1919–1939* (Cambridge: Cambridge University Press, 1990).

[29]Although competitive devaluations may reduce world trade by generating instability and uncertainty, they could also allow recovery from recession if they are accompanied by other policies. For instance, suppose that all countries engaging in competitive devaluations raise their central bank credit. If the credit expansions are sufficiently large, the increase in the world money supply would ease world credit conditions and reduce world interest rates. Lower interest rates would then tend to raise output in each country by stimulating investment.

is that sterilization operations are not viable under fixed exchange rates and perfect capital mobility.

Consider the following example, which assumes that the economy is initially at balanced payments and that the central bank is committed to sterilization policies in the face of any payments disequilibria.

Suppose, then, that government spending suddenly declines, entailing a negative multiplier effect on income. As a result, transactions demands for money would decrease, generating an excess money supply that places downward pressure on domestic interest rates. There would then be a massive capital outflow as investors shift out of the now relatively unattractive domestic bonds. A balance-of-payments deficit would arise. The deficit, of course, implies a loss in the central bank's holdings of international reserves. If the central bank does not sterilize, this reduction in reserves would tend to reduce the domestic money supply until the excess money supply is eliminated and the downward pressure on domestic interest rates ends.

Suppose, however, that the authorities, through sterilization operations, buy an amount of bonds in the open market equal to the loss of international reserves. In this case, the downward pressure on domestic interest rates would be sustained because the domestic money supply is not allowed to adjust in response to the payments deficit. In other words, the excess money supply would still exist. Given the downward pressure on domestic interest rates, massive capital outflows would continue to occur. To maintain its sterilization operations, and as long as it remains committed to maintaining a fixed exchange rate, the central bank would continuously have to sell a massive amount of foreign exchange reserves. No matter how large the holdings of these reserves are, however, the central bank would not be able to support its sterilization operations to any significant extent in the face of the massive capital outflows that would occur under perfect capital mobility. International reserves would be quickly depleted and a devalua-

tion would become necessary. Something must give, and it must be either the sterilization operations or the central bank's pegging of the exchange rate. Sterilization policies and fixed exchange rates are, in this context, inconsistent.

14–11. IMPERFECT CAPITAL MOBILITY AND MONETARY POLICY

Up to this point, we have concentrated our attention on the economic plight of an economy under perfect capital mobility. It is time to relax this assumption. The major alternative yet to be analyzed is the case of imperfect capital mobility, to which we now turn.

The equilibrium of an economy facing imperfect capital mobility is represented by means of our standard *IS–LM* diagram, with the only caveat being that the balance-of-payments equilibrium locus is now the upward-sloping $B = 0$ locus. We illustrate an initial equilibrium of the economy by means of point A in Figure 14–8. At point A, the economy is in balanced payments as well as in goods and money market equilibrium. What are the effects of monetary and fiscal policies in this context?

An expansionary monetary policy, say a central bank open-market purchase of bonds, tends to shift the *LM* curve to the right, as represented in Figure 14–8 by the shift to *LM'*. The equilibrium of the economy would then move to point C, with an increase in income and a decline in domestic interest rates, both of which tend to worsen the balance of payments. This means that point C represents only a short-run equilibrium for the economy. The balance-of-payments deficit would lead, over time, to a decrease in the domestic money supply, which would shift the *LM'* curve upward, back toward its initial position. Over longer periods of time, then, monetary policy would be ineffective and the full equilibrium of the economy would be back at point A in Figure 14–8. Only if the central bank engages in sterilization operations will a point

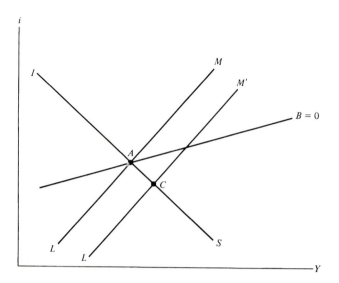

FIGURE 14–8. Monetary Policy Under Imperfect Capital Mobility

like C be maintained over time. With imperfect capital mobility, sterilization is a feasible policy in the short run, although over the longer run the central bank runs the risk of running out of foreign exchange reserves.

That monetary policy tends to be ineffective under fixed exchange rates after all the monetary adjustments induced by the balance of payments have taken place is a result that can be obtained no matter what the degree of capital mobility. This can be understood by noticing that whatever the degree of capital mobility is—that is, no matter what the shape of the $B = 0$ curve is—the LM curve will always move back to the point determined by the intersection of the IS and $B = 0$ curves, as illustrated by point A in Figure 14–8. It is apparent, then, that monetary authorities under fixed exchange rates might face great difficulty in controlling the money supply and that the role of monetary policy in affecting output in this regime might be quite limited, especially over the long run. What is the evidence on these issues?

14–12. CAN WE CONTROL THE MONEY SUPPLY? OFFSETTING CAPITAL FLOWS AND MONETARY POLICY

International capital mobility places stringent boundaries on how much domestic interest rates can diverge from those that prevail in world markets; it also makes very difficult the task of controlling the money supply of an economy under fixed exchange rates. An expansionary monetary policy in the form of an open-market purchase of Treasury bills, for example, increases the central bank credit component of the monetary base but (*ceteris paribus*) places downward pressures on domestic interest rates and induces capital outflows that reduce the monetary base's international reserves component. Capital outflows can thus offset the effects of an open-market operation on the money supply. In its most extreme form, capital outflows would be of the same amount as the initial increase in central bank credit. This is the case in which central bank credit expansion is *fully offset.* The only net effect of the operation is then to alter the central bank's portfolio composition (increased credit but reduced international reserves) and domestic residents' portfolios (reduced holdings of domestic Treasury bills but increased holdings of foreign securities). There would be no change in the domestic money supply and, *ceteris paribus,* no change in domestic interest rates away from their world levels.

A critical question concerns how fast the offset can be completed. If portfolio adjustments can be made very rapidly, no constraints exist on the extent to which capital movements can flow in and out of an economy; consequently, offsetting capital flows can occur freely and quickly, perhaps instantaneously. When transactions costs, information lags, and government controls—such as capital controls—prevent these rapid adjustments from happening, the full offset of open-market operations would then take longer to complete, as described in Section 14–4.

What evidence exists regarding offsetting capital flows? What do the data say on the effectiveness of open-market operations in affecting the monetary base in actual economies under fixed exchange rates? In Figure 14–9 we have plotted how the two components of the monetary base (domestic credit and international reserves) in Mexico changed in the 1970s. A general negative correlation can be seen between changes in central bank credit and changes in international reserves, but they clearly do not appear to offset each other completely. The question that thus arises is by exactly how much are changes in central bank credit offset by capital flows in this and other cases?

Most empirical studies start by postulating the following equation:

$$K_N = K_0 - b\Delta CBC, \qquad (14\text{–}25)$$

where K_N is defined as total capital flows ($K_N > 0$ if a capital inflow); K_0 represents those capital flows not directly related to domestic credit

creation; ΔCBC is central bank credit creation, and b is a parameter called the *offset coefficient.* The offset coefficient measures how much of a given change in domestic credit is offset by capital flows over a given period of time (holding everything else constant). When $b = 1$, there is a full offset of open-market operations by capital flows during the time period analyzed. When $b = 0$, there is no offset, and changes in central bank credit are not found to be offset at all by capital flows.

The evidence regarding the offset coefficient gives a wide range of results, depending on the country considered, the time period examined, and the empirical procedures used. The best-known results are those provided by P. Kouri and M. Porter on Germany, Australia, Italy, and the Netherlands in the 1960s. They found the quarterly offset coefficients to vary from $b = 0.43$ for Italy to $b = 0.77$ for Germany.[30] In other words, it appears that 43 to 77 percent of the changes in central bank credit were offset by international capital flows during a quarter. A similar range of estimates is provided by a multitude of other studies done for the same and other countries.[31] Thus, the conclusion from these studies is that changes in central bank credit do not tend to be associated with completely offsetting capital flows—at least over short periods of time—but that for some countries the offset coefficient may indeed be relatively close to $b = 1$.

One of the main problems with these studies, however, is that they ignore the role of sterilization policies in controlling the effects of balance-of-payments deficits on the domestic money supply. For countries that engage in sterilization, changes in central bank credit are not exogenously given;

[30]See P. K. Kouri and M. G. Porter, "International Capital Flows and Portfolio Equilibrium," *Journal of Political Economy* (May 1974).

[31]Such as L. Girton and D. Roper, "A Monetary Model of Exchange Market Pressure Applied to the Postwar Canadian Experience," *American Economic Review* (September 1977).

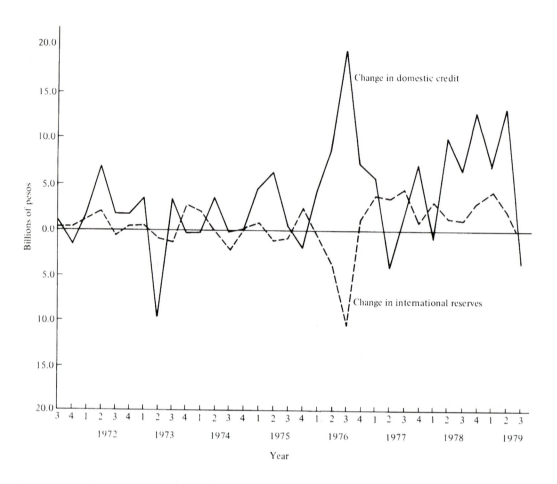

FIGURE 14–9. Central Bank of Mexico: Changes in Domestic Credit and International Reserves in the 1970s.

SOURCE: R. Cumby and M. Obstfeld, "Capital Mobility and the Scope for Sterilization: Mexico in the 1970s," in P. Aspe Armella, R. Dornbusch, and M. Obstfeld, eds., *Financial Policies and the World Capital Market: The Problem of Latin American Countries* (Chicago: The University of Chicago Press, 1983), p. 249.

they respond to the economy's balance-of-payments situation—the central bank's losses or gains in reserves. For example, the central bank may pursue the following behavior with regard to its open-market operations:

$$\Delta CBC = (\Delta CBC)_0 + \gamma K_N N, \quad (14\text{--}26)$$

where $(\Delta CBC)_0$ refers to factors influencing the central bank's credit creation decisions other than observed capital flows, K_N is the capital account ($K_N > 0$ if capital inflows), and γ is a negative parameter called the *sterilization coefficient*. The sterilization coefficient measures how much of a given capital inflow is sterilized by the central bank through countervailing open-market operations. If $\gamma = -1$, the central bank tries to sterilize completely the effects of capital inflows on the monetary base; if $\gamma = 0$, no sterilization occurs and the actions of the central bank follow other goals, as represented by $(\Delta CBC)_0$. When γ is between 0 and -1, some sterilization operations occur but do not completely neutralize capital flows.

When the central bank engages in sterilization operations, as represented by Equation 14–26—called a *reaction function*—the estimates of offset coefficients must be interpreted very carefully. Estimates of offset coefficients may not just be measuring the offsetting capital flows arising from changes in central bank credit—through Equation 14–25—but also the correlation between (spontaneous) capital flows and changes in central bank credit arising from sterilization—as given by Equation 14–26. For example, suppose that, all of a sudden, capital outflows occur from the U.K., say, because British investors abruptly decide to buy more German bonds. This move induces the Bank of England to engage in expansionary open-market operations in order to sterilize the outflows. In this situation, capital outflows and increases in central bank credit will be associated; of course, however, we do not want to attribute these capital flows to the credit creation because in fact the opposite is true. We must thus use the adequate statistical procedures to isolate the offsetting capital flows generated by a given change in central bank credit from those (spontaneous) capital flows giving rise to sterilization.[32]

In general, these studies have found substantial sterilization operations in both developing countries and in more industrialized economies. For Germany, sterilization coefficient estimates[33] tend to be insignificantly different from $\gamma = -1$. For other European countries, some of the sterilization coefficient estimates are smaller in absolute value. For instance, Italian economists C. Mastropasqua, S. Micossi, and R. Rinaldi find sterilization coefficients equal to -0.3 for Italy and -0.4 for France.[34] In combination, these results have been taken to suggest that Europe is a greater deutsche mark area; that is, within the European EMS, Germany acts as a "center country," controlling its own money supply more tightly while other countries let their money supply adjust to changes in international reserves, accommodating to Germany's monetary policies. This development is, of course, a matter of considerable controversy, both in theory and evidence.[35]

The significance of sterilization in many countries also implies offset coefficients much smaller than those obtained by the earlier studies. Maurice Obstfeld of the University of California at Berkeley, for example, finds the German quarterly offset coefficient in the 1960s to be about 0.10, much smaller than the 0.77 found by Kouri and Porter.[36] Similarly, in a study of Mexico, Obstfeld found

---

[32]These are called simultaneous equation methods. In the present context, the problem arises because of the simultaneity between Equations 14–25 and 14–26. Changes in central bank credit generate offsetting capital flows—through Equation 14–25—but capital flows induce the central bank to change central bank credit through sterilization, from Equation 14–26.

[33]See M. Obstfeld, "Exchange Rates, Sterilization and the Sterilization Problem," *European Economic Review* (February 1983); and N. Roubini, "Sterilization Policies, Offsetting Capital Movements and Exchange Rate Intervention Policies in the EMS." Ph.D. diss., Harvard University, 1988, chap. 4.

[34]C. Mastropasqua, S. Micossi, and R. Rinaldi, "Interventions, Sterilization and Monetary Policy in European Monetary System Countries, 1979–87," in F. Giavazzi, S. Micossi, and M. Miller, eds., *The European Monetary System* (Cambridge: Cambridge University Press, 1988).

[35]A discussion of some of the issues in this regard is supplied by F. Giavazzi and A. Giovannini, *Limiting Exchange Rate Flexibility: The European Monetary System* (Cambridge, Mass.: MIT Press, 1989), chap. 4.

[36]M. Obstfeld, "Sterilization and Offsetting Capital Movements: Evidence from West Germany, 1960–70," National Bureau of Economic Research Working Paper no. 494 (1980). See also, R. Herring and R. Marston, *National Monetary Policies and International Financial Markets* (Amsterdam: North-Holland, 1977).

the offset coefficient to be in the range of $b = 0.31$ to 0.37 on a quarterly basis.[37] These results tend to indicate that, for the countries considered, national monetary authorities do appear to have widespread ability to control their money supplies over short periods of time (i.e., on a quarterly basis).

The next natural question refers to the longer-run effects of changes in central bank credit. Even if there is very little offset of open-market operations by means of capital flows over the short run, the value of the offset coefficient over the long run may still be equal to 1. In his paper on Mexico in the 1970s, Obstfeld finds that, including all portfolio adjustments made over time in response to an open-market operation, the long-run offset coefficient is equal to 0.50. This is larger than the short-run coefficient of 0.31 noted earlier, but it still leaves open an influential role for monetary policy, even over the long run.

Another conclusion that can be derived from these studies is that sterilization operations can be successfully engaged in over short periods of time because capital flows do not generally appear to move massively in or out of the economy in response to changes in domestic interest rates.[38] It also seems that most industrial countries are permitted some leeway over control of domestic interest rates. The main constraining force on monetary policy then lies in the fact that capital

flows do occur; over time, wide divergences of domestic interest rates from world levels lead to persistent losses (or gains) in international reserves. Given that foreign exchange inventories are depletable, there are some clear long-run constraints on the influence of domestic monetary authorities on the money supply and domestic interest rates.

14–13. FISCAL POLICY AND THE DEGREE OF CAPITAL MOBILITY

We now show that, under imperfect capital mobility, expansionary fiscal policy can stimulate output and employment but raises interest rates and inhibits investment. An increase in government spending financed, say, by government borrowing raises the demand for domestic goods, shifting the *IS* curve upward to *IS'* in Figure 14–10. The economy's equilibrium then switches from point *A* to point *B*, resulting in higher income and interest rates. Is point *B* a point of balance-of-payments deficit or surplus? Note that because income increases, this tends to worsen the balance of payments by deteriorating the trade balance. But there is also an increase in interest rates, which tends to improve the balance of payments by improving the capital account. Which of these effects dominates? Clearly, it will depend on the relative strength of each effect, which is influenced by the degree of capital mobility (determining how much the capital account improves in response to a given increase in domestic interest rates) as well as by the marginal propensity to import (which determines by how much imports increase and the trade balance deteriorates in response to an increase in income). If the latter is high relative to the former, the trade balance deterioration dominates the capital account improvement and the balance of payments will worsen overall. The opposite holds if the marginal propensity to import is small relative to the degree of capital mobility.

---

[37]M. Obstfeld, "Capital Mobility and the Scope for Sterilization: Mexico in the 1970s." In P. Aspe Armella, R. Dornbusch, and M. Obstfeld, eds., *Financial Policies and the World Capital Market: The Problem of Latin American Countries* (Chicago: University of Chicago Press, 1983).

[38]A clear exception arises when expectations regarding a potential currency devaluation generate a sudden run on the currency. In these cases, to be examined in Chapter 20, the central bank may not be able to cope with the growing capital outflows. This may result in an eventual balance-of-payments crisis or a retreat from support of a fixed exchange rate. Such was the case preceding the British abandonment of the ERM in 1992. Frantic foreign exchange market intervention by the U.K. and other countries to prevent a pound devaluation in the period preceding the crisis amounted to £10 billion.

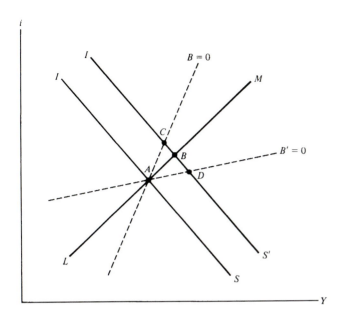

FIGURE 14–10. Fiscal Policy Under Imperfect Capital Mobility

These cases are illustrated in Figure 14–10 by noting that if the balance-of-payments equilibrium locus is represented by the steeply sloped $B = 0$ curve (depicting a relatively low degree of capital mobility compared with the marginal propensity to import), then the short-run equilibrium point, B, lies below the $B = 0$ curve and there is a balance-of-payments deficit. If the balance-of-payments equilibrium locus is the gently sloped $B' = 0$ curve (representing a relatively high degree of capital mobility compared with the marginal propensity to import), then point B would be a point of balance-of-payments surplus.

The full equilibrium effects of expansionary fiscal policy vary according to whether short-term equilibrium entails a balance-of-payments deficit or surplus.

When a balance-of-payments deficit arises (corresponding to the steeply sloped $B = 0$ line), the money supply will decrease over time, inducing income to decrease (until a point such as C in Figure 14–10 is attained), which partially offsets the initial boom. In the case in which a balance-of-payments surplus arises (corresponding to the gently sloped $B' = 0$ locus), the money supply will increase, generating an additional income expansion over time (until a point such as point D in Figure 14–10 is attained). Note that the positive connection between the degree of capital mobility and the effectiveness of fiscal policy in affecting domestic output is consistent with our earlier results. For instance, in the case of perfect capital mobility discussed earlier in this chapter, we found that fiscal policy had its full effectiveness. This would arise if the $B' = 0$ curve in Figure 14–10 were perfectly horizontal.

We have now analyzed the effects of monetary and fiscal policies under imperfect capital mobility in both the short run and in full equilibrium. In the forthcoming sections, we restrict ourselves to the short-run horizon within which most policymakers act. We set aside the modifications entailed by the longer-run monetary adjustments of the economy (it might thus be assumed that the policymakers systematically sterilize the effects of the balance of payments on the money supply).

14–14. The Monetary-Fiscal Policy Mix

It is the purpose of this section to show that, within the context of imperfect capital mobility, the government can attain the goals of internal balance (full employment) and external balance (balanced payments) through the exclusive use of monetary and fiscal policies. There is no need to use additional policies, such as devaluation or tariffs. This result does not hold under the capital immobility case discussed in Section 14–3. As we shall see, with zero capital mobility both expenditure-switching and expenditure-changing policies are required to move an economy with, say, unemployment and payments deficit toward internal and external balance. Because monetary and fiscal policies are both

expenditure-changing policies, there is a need for an additional policy, such as exchange rate policy, which could act as an expenditure-switching policy. First we proceed to examine the situation under capital mobility.

Figure 14–11 shows the upward-sloping balance of payments equilibrium locus $B = 0$ under imperfect capital mobility. Notice that if the equilibrium of the economy lies along the $B = 0$ curve there would be external balance. If the equilibrium is to the right of $B = 0$ instead, a balance-of-payments deficit prevails, and if it lies to the left, the economy is in surplus. Figure 14–11 also shows the level of domestic output associated with full employment, which corresponds to the vertical line at output Y_F. If the equilibrium of the economy lies on this curve, there would be internal balance; if it lies to the right, the economy would be in a situation of overemployment, and if to the left, it would face unemployment.

Through the use of Figure 14–11, we can catalog how a given equilibrium of the economy fares with respect to the government's goals. If the economy

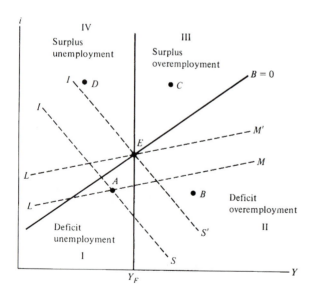

Figure 14–11.   The Fiscal-Monetary Policy Mix

is in region I, at a point like *A*, for example, it would suffer a payments deficit and unemployment. If the equilibrium were to take place in region II, at a point like *B*, it would imply overemployment and deficit, and correspondingly for regions III and IV. Clearly, the desired point in terms of the government's goals is point *E*, where both internal and external balance are obtained. The exact combination of policies required to attain that point depends on the initial position of the economy.

Suppose that the economy's *IS* and *LM* curves intersect at point *A*, with a consequent balance-of-payments deficit and unemployment. Observe that, in this case, expansionary fiscal policy (such as that shifting the *IS* curve to *IS'*) and contractionary monetary policy (such as that shifting the *LM* curve to *LM'*) would move the economy to balanced payments and full employment at point *E*. An appropriate combination of fiscal and monetary policies is therefore sufficient to attain internal and external balance. The same conclusion can be derived for economies whose equilibrium lies in quadrants II, III, and IV.

The sufficiency of monetary and fiscal policies to attain internal and external balance does not hold under capital immobility. With no international trade in assets, the balance of payments coincides with the trade balance, in which case there is indeed a need for both expenditure-switching and expenditure-changing policies: Trade balance equilibrium requires an expenditure-switching policy to twist spending away from foreign and toward domestic goods. In the presence of international capital movements, however, balanced payments do not coincide with balanced trade because of the presence of the capital account. As a consequence, any policy that serves to switch demand away from foreign and toward domestic assets can be employed to improve the balance of payments by affecting the capital account. By changing interest rates, monetary or fiscal policy can influence the capital account, and consequently the balance of payments, without the need for an expenditure-switching policy. In terms of the *IS–LM* paradigm, instead of there being only one single level of in-

come at which balanced payments could be attained (Y_T in Section 14–3), there is now a set of combinations of interest rates and income consistent with balanced payments. Accordingly, one of these combinations involves the full-employment level of income, Y_F. The two instruments of monetary and fiscal policy can then be used to attain this exact combination of interest rates and income at which both balanced payments and full employment would be obtained (point *E* in Figure 14–11).[39]

14–15. Shortcomings of the Monetary-Fiscal Policy Mix

This section states the various shortcomings of a policy mix consisting of only monetary and fiscal policies. Up to this point, the discussion has been carried out on the assumption that the government desires to attain external balance, defined as zero balance of payments. The implication is that the country is indifferent with respect to the composition of the balance of payments as long as it is balanced. Balanced payments with a capital account deficit (and a trade balance surplus) is assumed to be valued by the policymakers in the economy in equal terms as balanced payments with a capital account surplus (and a trade deficit). In general, however, a country is not indifferent with respect to the composition of its balance of payments. Even if balanced payments are sustained, persistent capital account surpluses are often considered to be a negative burden on the economy. The reason is that a persistent capital account surplus implies sustained capital inflows. There is, therefore, a persistent net external borrowing on the part of the economy as a whole and the country's debts to the rest of the world

---

[39]The policy mix approach to the attainment of internal and external balance was developed by Robert Mundell in an influential series of articles that were published in his book *International Economics*, op. cit.

would climb. If the economy is borrowing in order to accumulate capital, the economy's productive capacity would increase over time, raising, in turn, its ability to repay the debt. If the borrowing is for current consumption purposes, however, the capital account surplus just implies that the economy is substituting future consumption for present consumption. Future consumption would thus have to decline in order for the debt to be repaid. Furthermore, the accumulation of debt through persistent capital account surpluses would imply a huge interest payments burden. Over time, this burden could absorb a substantial amount of the economy's productive activities. Because of these factors, a major policy objective in some economies is not balanced payments as such but balanced trade.

When the goals of policymakers are *balanced trade* and full employment, the policy mix of monetary and fiscal policies breaks apart. In an economy facing a trade deficit, for example, it is necessary now to use an expenditure-switching policy, which could swing demand away from foreign goods and improve the trade balance. Neither monetary nor fiscal policies are expenditure-switching policies because they only change the level of spending on domestic and foreign goods; that is, they are expenditure-changing policies. The implication is that the analysis carried out in the previous section as to the need to use only expenditure-changing policies to attain internal and trade balance simultaneously does not apply here. The policy mix for an economy with unemployment and a trade balance deficit would prescribe the use of devaluation as an expenditure-switching mechanism, combined with monetary and/or fiscal policies as an expenditure-changing mechanism. These policies could then move the economy toward both internal and trade balance.

In addition, a goal of balanced payments implicitly assumes that the central bank desires its holdings of international reserves to remain unchanged. It should be recognized, however, that this is an ad hoc assumption and that the preferences and requirements of the central bank in determining an optimal level (or rate of change) of international reserves have not yet been adequately considered. Given the commitment of the central bank to pegging exchange rates, it may then be an important goal of the central bank to attain or maintain a target level of international reserves. Balance-of-payments equilibrium at a low level of reserves (below the target level), for example, may generate speculative financial transactions and may not be consistent with a stable exchange rate regime. Furthermore, an increasing level of international reserves may be the adequate policy for a growing economy with ever-increasing transactions with the rest of the world. This implies that, before stating the goals of the policymakers, central bank preferences and the determination of its desired level of international reserves must be analyzed in detail.

The monetary-fiscal policy mix also neglects the effects of the mix on the composition of aggregate demand in the economy. It assumes, first, that domestic residents are indifferent to the size of the private sector relative to the government sector and, second, that the authorities are indifferent to the size of the investment component in aggregate demand relative to the consumption component. In general, however, domestic government authorities will have specific goals regarding the relative size of the investment component of aggregate demand, depending on their preferences toward economic growth. Furthermore, domestic residents will usually also have some preferences toward the relative size of the government sector vis-à-vis the private sector. It is not clear, then, that a policy of contractionary monetary policy and expansionary fiscal policy oriented toward eliminating a payments deficit and unemployment would be attractive to both domestic residents and policymakers. This policy mix generally induces an increase in domestic interest rates, which reduces investment and increases the size of the government sector vis-à-vis the private sector. Both of these may be unattractive side effects of the mix.

Another problem with the monetary-fiscal policy mix is that it neglects the lags involved in policy formulation and implementation. It usually takes a longer period of time for fiscal legislation to pass through the legal-legislative process than it takes monetary policy to pass through the decision-making process of the central bank authorities. If this is so, the policy mix concept breaks apart again (at least in the context of short-run policy making) because fiscal policy would not be available as a functional policy. The problems do not end here, however. There also are lags in terms of the impact of both fiscal and monetary policies. The policymaker lacks knowledge not only about the magnitude of the impact of its policies, but also about the lag with which these policies act on the economy. Consequently, in a continually changing environment, the policy mix may destabilize the economy and move it away from, rather than toward, internal and external balance. It is easy to visualize a situation in which a policy takes so long to operate that, when it does, it is no longer necessary and is perhaps counterproductive.

A related problem of the policy mix is that it assumes monetary and fiscal policies are independent of each other. In many countries, however, fiscal policy is financed in large part through monetary expansion—that is, by printing money. In this situation the two policy instruments are dependent, so that a given level of public spending implies a particular change in the domestic money supply. If fiscal policy is used, say, to attain the goal of internal balance, then monetary policy is not free to change in accord with the requirements of the goal of external balance. For any operational purposes, the two policy instruments—monetary and fiscal policy—have collapsed into one, and the economy remains one instrument short.[40]

[40]The present analysis draws upon M. V. N. Whitman, "Policies for Internal and External Balance," *Princeton Special Papers in International Economics* (December 1970), pp. 7–8.

Summary

1. The *IS–LM* framework under fixed exchange rates takes into account the interaction of the goods and money markets with the external payments situation of the economy in determining equilibrium output, employment, and interest rates.

2. The money supply process in an open economy is generally distinct from that in a closed economy. The reason is that the monetary base is composed not only of central bank credit creation, but of the central bank's holdings of international reserves as well. Under fixed exchange rates, balance-of-payments deficits (or surpluses) tend to decrease (increase) the domestic money supply by decreasing (or increasing) foreign exchange reserves and, thus, the monetary base. In this case, the central bank can influence central bank credit in the economy but not necessarily the monetary base or the money supply.

3. Short-run equilibrium in the goods and assets markets is obtained when both the goods and money markets are in equilibrium, on the basis of a given level of the money supply. The economy's balance-of-payments situation affects short-run equilibrium by changing the money supply. The economy will attain full equilibrium in the sense that the money supply will be fully adjusted and will stop changing when external payments are balanced.

4. An economy under fixed exchange rates faces an automatic adjustment mechanism that tends to move the economy toward balanced payments (external balance). This adjustment process is a monetary one in the sense that it moves the economy toward full equilibrium by adjusting the domestic money supply through the balance of payments. Sometimes, however, this adjustment toward balanced payments involves a protracted recession, which some government authorities find untenable. As a consequence, they intervene to

prevent the operation of the automatic adjustment mechanism. They do this by sterilizing the influence of the balance of payments on the monetary base through the use of offsetting open-market operations. These sterilization operations, however, keep the economy at a payments disequilibrium and may be impossible to sustain over extended periods of time if the central bank does not have enough holdings of securities or foreign exchange reserves.

5. Even though the economy, left to its own devices and without government intervention, can be expected to move toward external balance automatically, within the Keynesian context of this chapter there is no automatic adjustment mechanism moving the economy toward full employment. Thus, there is room for policy intervention with the purpose of moving the economy toward both external and internal balance.

6. Macroeconomic equilibrium and the effects of government policies on output, the trade balance, and the like, generally differ according to the degree of capital mobility.

7. Under perfect capital mobility, the economy will adjust instantaneously toward external balance (balanced payments) because trade deficits or surpluses can always be immediately financed by borrowing or lending at fixed interest rates in the world capital markets and because portfolio adjustments occur immediately. This implies that the full-equilibrium level of the money supply can be attained rapidly.

8. Monetary policy has no effects at all on the equilibrium levels of income, interest rates, the balance of payments, or the trade balance under perfect capital mobility. The only effect of an open-market operation is to change the composition of the central bank's portfolio because a purchase (sale) of bonds will imply an equal loss (gain) of international reserves. On the other hand, fiscal policy is highly effective in altering equilibrium income and

employment because it does not crowd out investment.

9. Exchange rate (devaluation) and commercial policies can be used to alter equilibrium output. By switching demand away from foreign and toward domestic goods, a domestic currency devaluation would increase domestic output while improving the trade balance. This result requires that the sum of the price elasticities of the demand for domestic imports and exports be greater than 1—that is, the Marshall-Lerner condition must be satisfied. Experience has demonstrated that, over the short run, these elasticities might be quite small and that devaluation might worsen the trade balance and have a contractionary effect on output. The so-called *J*-curve effect alludes to the initial deterioration but eventual improvement of the trade balance in response to a devaluation.

10. In an interdependent world, domestic disturbances will spill over into foreign economies. Changes in one country's income and employment will therefore be transmitted abroad. The degree of influence of a foreign income disturbance on domestic income depends on the foreign marginal propensity to import, the economic size of the foreign relative to the domestic economy, and the magnitude of the Keynesian income multiplier.

11. With interdependence, an increase in domestic autonomous spending will spill over into foreign income expansion. Because some of the increased foreign spending will fall on domestic goods, spillovers result in further expansionary repercussions on domestic income.

12. In contrast to expansionary autonomous spending policies, which have positive repercussions abroad, a devaluation raises domestic production by improving the domestic trade balance; it thereby worsens the trade balance of the rest of the world and contracts foreign production. Devaluation is therefore often categorized as a beggar-thy-neighbor policy.

13. Under imperfect capital mobility, domestic interest rates will diverge from world interest rates, inducing capital inflows or outflows, depending on whether they are higher or lower than the world rates. In this context, an expansionary monetary policy generates a rise in income and a decrease in interest rates over the short run. Both lead to a payments deficit, which, if the central bank does not sterilize, induces, in turn, a gradual reduction of the money supply back toward its original level, diluting its initial effects on the economy.

14. Fiscal policy, in the form of increased government expenditure, affects positively both the short-run level of income and the interest rate under imperfect capital mobility. As these two effects have opposite consequences for the balance of payments, either a surplus or a deficit may develop over the short run, depending on how large the degree of capital mobility is relative to the marginal propensity to import. Over the longer run, monetary adjustments tend to move the economy toward balanced payments.

15. A mix of monetary and fiscal policies can succeed in attaining the goals of internal balance and balanced payments in the short run. An expenditure-switching policy is required, however, to attain the goals of balanced trade and full employment.

Problems

1. Explain in detail the precise mechanics involved in the process by which a balance-of-payments surplus surfaces as a money supply increase in an economy under fixed exchange rates. Using T accounts, describe how the central bank's balance sheet is affected.

2. You are given the following data regarding a Latin American country with a banking system similar to that of the United States (all figures in pesos, the currency of the country concerned):

   Currency = 50 billion
   Demand deposits = 160 billion
   Bank reserves = 20 billion

   (a) Define and calculate the following:
   1. the monetary base
   2. the money supply
   3. the money multiplier
   (b) Suppose that in the month of April the country's central bank gains international reserves by an amount equal to 10 billion pesos. Assuming central bank credit remains unchanged, what will be the impact of the gain in reserves on the monetary base and the money supply?
   (c) The government wants to keep the money supply unchanged in spite of the gain of reserves. In what offsetting operation could it engage? For all of these questions, provide numerical answers and explain how they are obtained.

3. Consider a country whose central bank holds international reserves in the form of U.S. dollars and gold, and suppose that the price of gold doubles. How does this affect the level of the country's international reserves? How would the doubling in the price of gold affect the country's money supply?

4. In September 1992, a crisis of the EMS led Britain and Italy to abandon the ERM. One of the factors explaining the crisis was the rise of interest rates in Germany relative to other economies. Assuming that the German interest rate corresponds to the world interest rate within the EEC, how would a rise in the German interest rate affect other EEC economies, such as that of the U.K.? In particular, how would output, trade, the capital account, and central bank foreign exchange reserves be altered? (You can assume the presence of perfect capital mobility.)

5. A developing country, X, in Central America has lost access to international financial markets as a result of a bloody military coup, a subsequent violent civil war, and the angry

threats of expropriation and nationalization on the part of the military *junta*. Examine the effects of a domestic currency devaluation in this economy, using diagrammatic and algebraic analysis. (Hint: Assume zero capital mobility.) What will be the impact of the devaluation on the following:

(a) Short-run equilibrium levels of output, trade balance, and interest rates.

(b) Full equilibrium output, trade balance, and interest rates. Could devaluation be used by itself to attain the goals of internal and external balance? Explain why or why not.

(c) Suppose that the country's central bank decides to monetize the capital gains on its international reserves accruing from the devaluation. Examine the effects of this action on the short-run and full equilibria of the economy. Does the devaluation in the present situation necessarily improve the trade balance in the short run? Illustrate by means of an *IS–LM* diagram.

6. Using *IS–LM–BB* curve analysis under perfect capital mobility, specify the effects on domestic income of

(a) an exogenous increase in domestic exports

(b) an increase in the world interest rate Determine the algebraic expressions to show how these disturbances affect domestic output.

7. Consider an economy under perfect capital mobility. Suppose that you are given the following expressions for absorption, A, the trade balance, T, and the world interest rate, i*:

$$A = \bar{A} + aY - bi = 480 + 0.75Y - 900i$$

$$T = \bar{T} - mY + \phi q = 30 - 0.25Y + 2q$$

$$i* = 0.10\ (10\%)$$

$$q = 10\ (indexed\ variable),$$

with variables measured in billions of domestic output. The economy is perfectly integrated into world capital markets.

(a) What is the equilibrium level of output in the economy (in numerical terms)? Is the balance of trade in surplus or deficit? What about the balance of payments?

(b) Suppose that there is an exogenous increase in the foreign demand for domestic exports, which is reflected in an autonomous trade balance increase of 50 billion. What is the effect on

(1) the equilibrium level of output in the economy?

(2) the balance of trade, the capital account, and the balance of payments?

(c) Consider the impact of an exogenous reduction in government spending of 50 billion. What would be the effect on

(1) the equilibrium level of output in the economy?

(2) the value of exports, imports, the trade balance, and the capital account?

Explain the economic reasoning behind your answers. Do you think the effects of government spending cuts, as you have analyzed them here, would apply to the particular case of cuts in school lunch programs? What additional considerations have to be taken into account?

8. In the previous question, assume that the domestic real money demand function has been estimated to be

$$L^D = 0.20Y - 3000i$$

Each unit of domestic output has a domestic currency price of $P = \$1.00$.

(a) What is the economy's equilibrium money supply (in billions of dollars)?

(b) Consider the impact of a reduction in government spending of $50 billion. What would be the effect of this reduction on the domestic money supply?

Provide numerical answers. Explain your results.

9. You are advising Tropalia, a large tropical country that currently has a balance of trade equal to zero but is facing a high rate of unemployment. You are told that the economy is under a system of fixed exchange rates under perfect capital mobility, and you are given the following information:
   (1) The marginal propensity to import is 0.1.
   (2) The marginal propensity to save is 0.2.
   (3) The price elasticity of demand for imports is equal to 2.1.
   (4) The price elasticity of demand for Banania's exports is 1.8.
   (5) Domestic exports (which equal the value of imports) are 50 million.

   Suppose that the government decides to devalue the tropalian (Tropalia's currency) by 10 percent. What would be the impact on the balance of trade and on equilibrium income? Give a numerical answer and explain it. (Hint: Use the algebraic expressions in Section 14–8.)

10. Consider two interdependent economies, the domestic one being the same as that described in Problem 7. You are also provided with the following information regarding the foreign economy:
    (1) The foreign marginal propensity to save is 0.04.
    (2) The foreign marginal propensity to import is 0.04.
    (a) What is the value of the domestic open-economy Keynesian multiplier in this case—that is, with repercussion effects? How does it compare with the multiplier determined in Problem 7?
    (b) Suppose that there is an exogenous reduction in government spending on domestic goods of 50 billion. What would be the effect on
       (1) the equilibrium level of domestic income?

(2) the value of domestic exports, imports, and the trade balance? Compare your results with those obtained in Problem 7(c). (Hint: Use the Appendix.)

11. Domestic absorption can be disaggregated in alternative ways. One way is to emphasize its consumption, investment, and government components, as in the text. Another is to break it down into

$$A_N = D_N + G_N + M_N,$$

where D_N denotes the value of private domestic resident spending on domestic goods, G_N is government spending, and M_N is the value of imports. Interpret this expression for domestic absorption, assuming that government expenditures fall only on domestic goods. Then express absorption in real terms—that is, in terms of domestic goods. Does the relative price of foreign goods in terms of domestic goods, q, enter into the resulting expression showing real absorption?

12. Show the direct effect of a devaluation on the trade balance (at a fixed level of income), assuming that the economy is initially in a trade deficit. (Hint: Derive the counterpart to the expression for ΔT in Footnote 7 in Chapter 13. Assuming that domestic exports, M^*, are only a fraction of domestic imports, qM,— that is, $M^* = \theta qM$, where $0 < \theta < 1$). Does the Marshall-Lerner condition still hold? Explain your answer.

13. A government facing external payments deficits, unemployment, and budget deficits adopts the advice of a committee recommending the imposition of a tariff on imports. The experts report that this policy represents the best of all worlds because it improves the trade balance, stimulates the economy, and provides revenues to the government. Analyze the macroeconomic effects of a tariff on imports within the Keynesian framework described in this chapter.

What are the effects on the domestic economy? How are foreign countries affected? What are

the global effects of many countries following such a protectionist route?

APPENDIX: THE OPEN-ECONOMY MULTIPLIER WITH REPERCUSSIONS

This appendix discusses the interactions between the domestic economy and the rest of the world. The trade balance in the domestic economy is given by

$$T = \bar{T} - mY + \phi q.$$

Substituting Equation 14–22 in the text into this equation yields

$$T = T_o + m^*Y^* - mY + \phi q. \qquad (14\text{A}-1)$$

Note that the domestic trade balance deficit (surplus) must be equal (but in opposite sign) to the trade balance surplus (deficit) of the rest of the world—that is $T = -T^*$, where T^* is the foreign trade balance.

Equilibrium in the domestic goods market is

$$Y = A + T = \bar{A} + aY + T_o + m^*Y^*$$
$$- mY + \phi q, \qquad (14\text{A}-2)$$

where we have made use of Equation 14A–1. Equilibrium in the foreign goods market is

$$Y^* = A^* + T^*$$
$$= \bar{A}^* + a^*Y^* - T_o - m^*Y^*$$
$$+ mY - \phi q, \qquad (14\text{A}-3)$$

where A^* is foreign absorption, $\bar{A}^*$ is autonomous foreign absorption, and a^* is the foreign marginal propensity to spend. By solving Equation 14A–3, we can determine the equilibrium level of income abroad:

$$Y^* = \alpha^*\bar{A}^* - \alpha^*T_o$$
$$+ \alpha^*mY - \alpha^*\phi q, \qquad (14\text{A}-4)$$

where $\alpha^* = 1/(s^* + m^*)$ is the foreign income multiplier ($s^* \equiv 1 - a^*$). Substituting the value of Y^* in Equation A–4 into Equation A–2 and simplifying, we now obtain

$$Y = \hat{\alpha}(\bar{A} + m^*\alpha^*\bar{A}^*$$
$$+ s^*\alpha^*T_o + s^*\alpha^*\phi q), \qquad (14\text{A}-5)$$

where $\hat{\alpha} \equiv 1/(s + m - \alpha^*m^*m)$ is the Keynesian income multiplier with repercussion effects. This multiplier measures the impact of a change in autonomous spending on domestic income taking into account repercussions. Equation A–5 also shows how a domestic currency devaluation affects domestic income in the presence of repercussions.

CHAPTER 15

Expectations, Exchange Rate Dynamics, and Economic Policy

When the major European countries, Japan, and the United States abandoned the Bretton Woods regime of fixed exchange rates and allowed their currencies to float vis-à-vis the dollar in the 1970s, they implicitly accepted the vicissitudes of living in a world of fluctuating currency values. However, the sharp and wide movements of exchange rates observed during the float have surpassed any of the expectations of academics and policymakers. As an example, between May 1990 and January 1991, the dollar depreciated relative to the mark by more than 15 percent; then, from February to June 1991, the dollar sharply rose in value by 27 percent, and between June to September it dropped by 6 percent. This chapter explains the choppy behavior of currency values in a regime of floating exchange rates. It focuses on the role played by exchange rate expectations in the dynamic behavior of economies with floating currency values.

In a world of fluctuating exchange rates, future currency values become essential in determining the costs of and benefits from international investments. The capital account records these investments and it is, consequently, highly sensitive to expected exchange rate changes. Rumors that a currency will depreciate in the future may ignite massive capital outflows, drastically worsening the capital account. Under a regime of fixed exchange rates, such changes would tend to generate balance-of-payments deficits, massive losses of international reserves and—if persistent—may lead to a balance-of-payments crisis. Under flexible exchange rates, no balance-of-payments crises arise because exchange rate adjustments insure the elimination of any balance-of-payments deficits. Still, exchange rate expectations can feed massive short-term capital flows and generate a relentless speculative attack on a currency's value. This chapter examines the role of exchange rate expectations in determining the level and turbulence of exchange rates, interest rate differentials among countries, and the response of the economy to macroeconomic disturbances.

15−1. Exchange Rate Expectations and Interest Rates

The introduction of exchange rate expectations forces into the open the fact that interest rates do not always equalize internationally; that is, it demonstrates that the equality $i = i*$ is not an ever-holding condition, even under perfect capital mobility. If domestic currency is expected to depreciate, the domestic interest rate, i, rises above the world interest rate, $i*$, to compensate investors in domestic assets for the anticipated capital gains they forego by holding assets denominated in domestic rather than foreign currency. An expected appreciation of the domestic currency, on the other hand, will be associated with lower domestic interest rates in order to offset the anticipated capital gains from holding domestic cur-

rency instead of foreign currency. In a nutshell, equalization of net expected rates of return among comparable domestic and foreign assets implies

$$i = i* + x, \qquad (15–1)$$

where i is the domestic interest rate, $i*$ is the world interest rate, and x is the expected rate of depreciation of the domestic currency, all over a given time period.[1] If, for instance, the world interest rate is equal to 5 percent and the expected rate of depreciation of domestic currency is equal to 2 percent, Equation 15−1 implies a domestic interest rate equal to 7 percent. The higher domestic interest rate compared with the world rate serves to compensate holders of domestic assets for the expected (currency) loss arising from the expected depreciation.

What factors give rise to expected exchange rate changes? To answer this question, we must know how individuals form expectations about the future value of economic variables. The following discussion assumes rational expectations formation. This means that individuals gather and process all relevant information about economic variables and their interrelationships and use these facts efficiently in predicting the effects of economic disturbances.[2] For instance, when the government formulates a reversal in economic policy, investors will immediately calculate the effects of such policies on the exchange rate, interest rates, and other relevant economic variables. On this account, they form rational expectations about the future behavior of the economy. Clearly, to determine how economic disturbances, such as policy changes, affect the economy over time requires knowledge of how the economy reacts to such

---

[1] Equation 15−1 is referred to as the uncovered interest parity condition. As examined in chapts. 5 and 6, in order for Equation 15−1 to hold, risk considerations must be set aside. The discussion in this chapter will disregard the influence of risk and exchange risk premia on exchange rate determination, a topic to be discussed in Chapter 19.

[2] A thorough discussion of rational expectations appears in Chapter 6.

disturbances. In forming expectations, then, investors need to understand such dynamic adjustments. Rational expectations formation appears to be an adequate description of situations in which individuals actively search for and process information regarding the future of the economy. This is certainly the case of corporate treasurers, bankers, and international investors regarding exchange rates. The day-to-day life of the foreign exchange trader or the international financial manager is a constant search for leads and hints that may provide relevant information about the future levels of various exchange rates. Failure to gather and interpret adequately important news on the matter can be disastrous.

15−2. ECONOMIC DYNAMICS AND THE GOODS AND ASSETS MARKETS

There are two basic concepts required to understand the dynamic adjustment of an economy in the present context. First, organized assets markets tend to clear relatively quickly, as compared to goods markets; and, second, a sudden excess demand for (or supply of) domestic goods tends to give rise to increases (or reductions) in domestic output, but only gradually over time. The first concept regards the relative speed at which assets and goods markets clear. Transactions in assets markets, such as portfolio adjustments between money and bonds and between domestic and foreign assets, can be made rapidly and with ease by means of modern communications and the close integration of national capital markets with the world financial community. Interest rates and exchange rates also tend to adjust rapidly, changing with a disheartening speed in response to new information on economic and noneconomic events. These rapid adjustments ensure that assets market equilibrium, in terms of the equality of demand and supply of given stocks of assets, is attained very rapidly, often instantaneously. It is thus appropriate to assume that the money market continuously, or almost con-

tinuously, clears. The same cannot generally be said, however, of goods markets.

Output response to changes in economic variables occurs sluggishly over time. For instance, available evidence tends to suggest that export growth in response to a currency depreciation takes place slowly because of lags in the recognition of relative price changes, production lags, and so forth. The analysis by economists William Helkie and Peter Hooper of the Federal Reserve Board finds that the elasticity of U.S. exports with respect to relative price changes is equal to only 0.28 over three quarters, or approximately one-third of the full adjustment elasticity over two years, which is 0.83.[3] Other authors find alternative and variable lengths for the delay in the response of exports to currency depreciation.[4]

The response of investment spending to changes in interest rates also shows a laggard behavior: Investment adjusts at a slow pace, and the timing here is in terms of months or years, not hours, days, or weeks.[5] Furthermore, goods market prices

---

[3]W. L. Helkie and P. Hooper, "An Empirical Analysis of the External Deficit, 1980−86," in R. C. Bryant, G. Holtham, and P. Hooper, eds., *External Deficits and the Dollar: The Pit and the Pendulum* (Washington, D.C.: Brookings Institution, 1988), table 2−5. This elasticity represents the percentage increase in the quantity of exports in the stated period of time, given a 1 percent increase in the price of foreign goods relative to domestic goods (in the terminology of the last two chapters, $\eta = 0.28$ over a period of three quarters).

[4]According to the estimates of J. Rosenzweig and P. Koch, it may take as long as eight months for export volumes to rise after a dollar depreciation, with the export growth gradually occurring in the following sixteen months. See J. Rosenzweig and P. Koch, "The U.S. Dollar and the Delayed J-Curve," *Federal Reserve Bank of Atlanta Economic Review* (August 1988); see also R. Dornbusch and P. Krugman, "Flexible Exchange Rates in the Short-Run," *Brookings Papers on Economic Activity* (1976); and our discussion of the J-curve effect in Chapter 14.

[5]One of the problems in predicting the impact of policy shifts on investment spending is precisely the uncertainty involved in the laggard response of investment to changes in real interest rates and other variables. See P. K. Clark, "Investment in the 1970s: Theory, Performance, and Prediction,"

(continued)

in the short run tend to adjust sluggishly, especially in the downward direction and under recessionary conditions, a situation stylized in the present Keynesian analysis by assuming that goods market prices are indeed fixed.

The conclusion is that assets markets can be assumed to clear continuously, whereas goods markets may be presumed to adjust slowly and possibly to remain out of equilibrium, in disequilibrium, for extended periods of time. The output response to an excess demand or supply of domestic goods thus extends over a period of time, resulting in a sluggish movement of the economy toward equilibrium. The details of these adjustments will be examined in the following sections.

15–3. EXCHANGE RATE EXPECTATIONS, DISEQUILIBRIUM DYNAMICS, AND ADJUSTMENT TOWARD FULL EQUILIBRIUM

This section focuses on the dynamic adjustment toward equilibrium in economies under flexible exchange rates, perfect capital mobility, and sluggish output response. The equilibrium established by the Mundell–Fleming framework developed in Chapter 13 will be labeled full equilibrium to convey the notion that it is the equilibrium toward which the economy moves *after all the disequilibrium adjustments* arising from sluggish output response are over.[6] When full equilibrium is at-

Brookings Papers on Economic Activity (1979), and C. W. Bischoff, E. C. Kokkelenberg, and R. A. Terregrosa, "Tax Policy and Business Fixed Investment During the Reagan Era," in A. P. Sahu and R. L. Tracey, eds., *The Economic Legacy of the Reagan Years* (New York: Praeger, 1991).

[6]Our concept of full equilibrium is referred to as long-run Mundell–Fleming equilibrium by Rudiger Dornbusch in "Exchange Rate Expectations and Monetary Policy," *Journal of International Economics* (August 1976). We prefer the terminology of full equilibrium in order to associate long-run adjustments strictly with price adjustments. The Mundell-Fleming framework assumes that prices are fixed within the time context considered.

tained, no further changes in economic variables are expected to occur, in the absence of disturbances. In particular, the exchange rate would not be expected to change, implying that $x = 0$ and suggesting that domestic and world interest rates will equalize, that is, $i = i^*$.

Figure 15–1, which corresponds to Figure 13–6(b) in Chapter 13, depicts the full equilibrium of the economy at point E. The upward-sloping YY curve represents the positive connection existing between the exchange rate and domestic output in maintaining the goods market equilibrium. An increase in the exchange rate, e, by increasing the relative price of foreign goods, raises the demand for domestic goods and requires an increase in domestic output, Y, in order to clear the goods market. The $\overline{LL}$ curve, on the other hand, represents the equality of money demand and supply at full equilibrium. The reason for the perfectly vertical nature of the $\overline{LL}$ curve is best understood by looking at the money market condition at full equilibrium (at $i = i^*$),

$$\frac{M^s}{P} = L^D(i^*, Y), \qquad (15\text{–}2)$$

which is independent of the exchange rate. Given the money supply, the price level, and the world interest rate, Equation 15–2 determines a level of output, $\overline{Y}$, consistent with assets market clearing at full equilibrium. Assuming no disturbances, point E shows equilibrium in both goods and assets markets. It thus represents the economy's full equilibrium and determines accordingly a *full equilibrium exchange rate* equal to $\overline{e}$ and a full equilibrium income equal to $\overline{Y}$. The exchange rate $\overline{e}$ prevails when goods market disequilibria in the economy are eliminated. It is the exchange rate toward which individuals believe the economy would move over time if left undisturbed. How is full equilibrium attained? In other words, what is the dynamic behavior of the economy in disequilibrium?

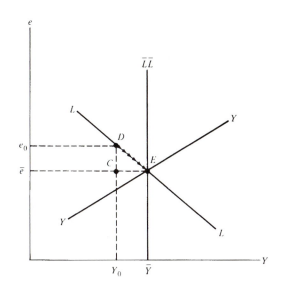

FIGURE 15-1. Disequilibrium Adjustment of the Economy

Disequilibrium Dynamics in the Open Economy

Consider a reduction in income from its full equilibrium level, $\overline{Y}$, to Y_0. Algebraically, from the money market equilibrium condition

$$\frac{M^s}{P} = L^D(i, Y), \qquad (15\text{–}3)$$

we see that a reduction in income, Y, decreases money demand relative to the given real money supply, M^s/P, which places downward pressure on domestic interest rates to maintain equilibrium in the money market. The downward pressure on domestic interest rates would then generate incipient capital outflows and depreciate domestic currency.

In short, a reduction of domestic income below its full-equilibrium level is associated with a jump in the exchange rate above its full-equilibrium value. This is represented by point D in Figure

15–1, where the reduction of income from $\overline{Y}$ to Y_0 is associated with an increase in the exchange rate from $\overline{e}$ to e_0. Note that as long as the current spot exchange rate is above the full equilibrium rate, $\overline{e}$, and as long as individuals recognize that the structure of the economy is such that the exchange rate will eventually return to its full-equilibrium value, an expected appreciation of the domestic currency emerges at point D. Symbolically, at that point, $x < 0$. Even though the reduction in income from $\overline{Y}$ to Y_0 immediately *increases* the exchange rate up to e_0, individuals still expect the exchange rate to decline over time to its longer-term, full-equilibrium value, $\overline{e}$. Just how much the currency is anticipated to appreciate is examined next.

As mentioned earlier, we assume that individuals form rational expectations of future variables in the economy. Accordingly, x represents the rational expectation of the rate of depreciation of domestic currency, which can be expressed as

$$x = \theta\!\left(\frac{\overline{e} - e}{e}\right), \qquad (15\text{–}4)$$

where e is the current spot exchange rate, $\overline{e}$ is the long-run equilibrium exchange rate, and θ is a positive number representing that fraction of the gap between the current and full-equilibrium exchange rate that is expected to be eliminated in any given time period.[7] Note that as long as the full-equilibrium exchange rate is below the current exchange rate ($\overline{e} < e$), there will be an expected appreciation of the domestic currency ($x < 0$), as agents in the economy realize that the exchange rate will eventually decline toward its full-equilibrium

---

[7]Even though Equation 15–4 appears ad hoc, it can be rigorously shown to hold in the type of setting we are considering. The proof is not of particular interest here and can be obtained from R. Dornbusch, "Expectations and Exchange Rate Dynamics," *Journal of Political Economy* (December 1976); or from the simplified version in P. De Grauwe, *International Money: Postwar Trends and Theories* (Oxford: Clarendon, 1989).

value. Such is the case at point D, where the expected rate of appreciation of the domestic currency over the next time period is given by

$$x = \theta \left(\frac{\bar{e} - e_0}{e_0} \right) < 0.$$

If, on the other hand, the full-equilibrium exchange rate were to be above the current value of the exchange rate (if $\bar{e} > e$), individuals would then expect the exchange rate to rise—that is, the currency to depreciate over time ($x > 0$). Only when the current spot exchange rate is equal to the full-equilibrium exchange rate (when $\bar{e} = e$) will there be no further expected exchange rate changes.

Substituting the expression for the expected rate of depreciation of domestic currency in Equation 15–4 into Equation 15–3 yields the following expression for the *money market equilibrium condition in the short run:*

$$\frac{M^s}{P} = L^D(i, Y)$$

$$= L^D(i^* + x, Y) \qquad (15\text{--}3a)$$

$$= L^D \left[i^* + \theta \left(\frac{\bar{e} - e}{e} \right), Y \right].$$

Equation 15–3(a) shows a connection between domestic income and the exchange rate, given the level of the money supply, the domestic price level, the world interest rate, and the equilibrium exchange rate. It therefore, provides the combinations of domestic income and the exchange rate that keep the money market in short-run equilibrium. This is the algebraic counterpart of the curve LL in Figure 15–1. The LL curve slopes downward, indicating that Equation 15–3(a) exhibits a *negative* relationship between domestic income and the exchange rate. Note that point D lies along LL because it is a point of short-run assets market

equilibrium, with Equation 15–3(a) at this point represented by

$$\frac{M^s}{P} = L \left[i^* + \theta \left(\frac{\bar{e} - e_0}{e_0} \right), Y_0 \right].$$

The reduction in income from $\bar{Y}$ to Y_0 is associated with an increase in the exchange rate from $\bar{e}$ to e_o in maintaining short-run money market equilibrium.

Points along the LL curve represent points of short-run assets market equilibrium, but not generally of goods market equilibrium. Point D is clearly not a goods market equilibrium point because—although it satisfies *assets* market equilibrium—it is off the YY curve; accordingly, it is not one of the combinations of income and the exchange rate that maintains goods market equilibrium. At point D there is an *excess demand* for domestic goods because the increased exchange rate shifts demand toward domestic goods by increasing the price of foreign goods relative to domestic goods. This excess demand can generate an increase in output, but only after the domestic exports sector has had enough time to expand production. Over time, the economy would move away from point D (which represents only a *short-run* equilibrium point in the asset markets) and toward the longer-run equilibrium at point E. This adjustment from the goods market disequilibrium existing at point D to full equilibrium at point E always occurs with the assets market clearing—that is, with money demand equal to money supply, as given by Equation 15–3(a). Consequently, it is shown in Figure 15–1 by the pointed arrows lying along the short-run assets market equilibrium locus, LL.

This section has examined how the economy adjusts over time in response to a movement out of full equilibrium—that is, the disequilibrium dynamics of the economy. The next step is to determine which particular factors may disturb full equilibrium and exactly how the economy adjusts to them. The following section examines the impact of monetary shocks—in the form of an unanticipated increase in the domestic money supply—on the economy, and the resulting exchange rate dynamics.

15−4. UNANTICIPATED SHOCKS AND EXCHANGE RATE OVERSHOOTING

One of the most remarkable features of the world experience with flexible exchange rates from the 1970s to the 1990s has been the relatively large and abrupt exchange rate movements suffered by the currencies of major industrial countries. These fluctuations have perplexed many of the proponents of flexible exchange rates, which expected a more tranquil—and less turbulent—exchange rate behavior. What factors can explain the volatility of currency values in the recent past? It is the purpose of the following sections to present a first view of the analytics of exchange rate dynamics over the short run. In particular, an attempt is made to provide an explanation for the observed association between exogenous economic disturbances—such as monetary shocks—and rapid and drastic movements in the exchange rate. This section begins by analyzing the effects of an unanticipated monetary shock, in the form of an unexpected increase in the money supply.

Figure 15–2 shows the initial full equilibrium of the economy at point E, with a level of output equal to Y_0 and an exchange rate of e_0. It is at point E that the initial goods and money market loci, YY and $\overline{L}\,\overline{L}$, intersect. Suppose, however, that there is a sudden, unanticipated increase in the domestic money supply—say because of a central bank purchase of bonds in the open market. Note that the disturbance generates changes in the full-equilibrium values of income and the exchange rate. The increased money supply places downward pressures on domestic interest rates, depreci-

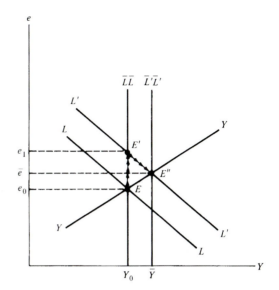

FIGURE 15−2.   Unanticipated Monetary Shocks and Exchange Rate Dynamics

ating domestic currency and shifting demand toward domestic goods, which requires output to increase when full equilibrium is reached. The full response of the economy to the money supply expansion is represented by the shift of the full-equilibrium money market locus from $\overline{L}\,\overline{L}$ to $\overline{L}'\,\overline{L}'$, implying a switch of the full equilibrium point from E to E''. The new full equilibrium levels of output and the exchange rate are $\overline{Y}$ and $\overline{e}$, respectively.

Even though point E'' represents the new equilibrium toward which the economy will move over time, this full equilibrium cannot be expected to be reached immediately because of the sluggishness with which domestic output will expand. Accordingly, the short-run behavior of the economy has to be specified. Over the time period immediately after the unanticipated monetary expansion, output can be expected to remain more or less at its initial level, Y_0. The monetary disturbance, however, generates immediate exchange rate and domestic interest rate changes that combine to eliminate the excess supply of money existing at the initial point E. In diagrammatic terms, the immediate adjustment of the economy would be from point E to point E'. Point E' lies along the $L'L'$ curve, which is the short-run money market equilibrium locus, as derived in the previous section. The result of the money supply expansion would thus be an immediate increase in the exchange rate from e_o to e_1. This represents the exchange rate change required to clear the money market in response to the monetary disturbance, given the initial level of output, Y_0. Note that the exchange rate depreciation will induce a switch of demand toward domestic goods and, at the initial level of output, will result in an excess demand for domestic goods. Point E' represents a point of short-run assets market equilibrium but of goods market *disequilibrium*. This is reflected in the fact that point E' lies along the $L'L'$ curve, the short-run money market equilibrium locus, but is above the YY curve, the goods market equilibrium curve. Of course, over time, the domestic export sector will expand in response to the domestic currency depreciation and the output of domestic goods will gradually adjust to match the increased demand. The economy will accordingly move along the $L'L'$ curve toward point E''. This full-equilibrium point differs from the short-run equilibrium at point E' in that it represents the equilibrium of the economy in *both* the goods and assets markets. Graphically, point E'' lies along both the $L'L'$ and YY curves. Because the goods market adjusts toward equilibrium sluggishly, full equilibrium at E'' is attained only after an extended period, with the economy immediately moving to point E' instead.

The behavior of the exchange rate in response to the money supply expansion is illustrated in Figure 15–3. At time t_0, the exchange rate is equal to e_0; in response to the monetary shock, it adjusts immediately to e_1 and then gradually moves to its new, long-run equilibrium value, $\bar{e}$. This pattern, in which the short-run response of the exchange rate

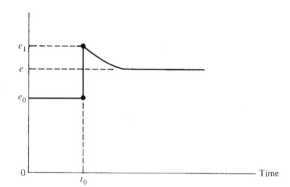

FIGURE 15–3. Overshooting of the Exchange Rate in Response to an Unanticipated Monetary Expansion

to a given disturbance exceeds the change that would occur if the economy's full equilibrium were attained immediately is referred to as *overshooting* of the exchange rate.[8] As depicted in Figure 15–3, it represents an exchange rate adjustment that is rather choppy and abrupt, first increasing above its full-equilibrium level and then gradually decreasing toward that level. It is thus suggestive of the exchange rate movements frequently observed recently in the experience of industrial countries with floating exchange rates.

As long as economic agents recognize the overshooting response of the exchange rate to an unanticipated money supply disturbance, they will anticipate domestic currency appreciation. In other words, even though domestic currency immediately depreciates in value in response to the money-supply expansion, individuals expect it to

---

[8]The concept of exchange rate overshooting was formally developed by Rudiger Dornbusch in his article, "Expectations and Exchange Rate Dynamics," *Journal of Political Economy* (December 1976). For further extensions of Dornbusch's framework, see W. H. Buiter, *International Macroeconomics* (Oxford: Clarendon, 1990); and K. Alec Chrystal, "Overshooting Models of the Exchange Rate," in D. Greenaway, ed., *Current Issues in Macroeconomics* (New York: St. Martin's, 1989).

appreciate over time. This is apparent in Figure 15–3. An individual watching the behavior of the exchange rate immediately after the disturbance at time t_0 would see a drastic exchange rate increase. At the same time, what goes up comes down and, if the exchange rate follows the behavior depicted in Figure 15–3, the investor knows that the exchange rate will be declining in the future toward its lower, full-equilibrium value, $\bar{e}$. That is, over the adjustment period toward full equilibrium, there is an expected currency appreciation, $x < 0$.

The apparent consistency of the present framework with the recent experience of industrial countries with floating rates, leads us to inquire about which specific factors contribute to generating the exchange rate overshooting. First, note that if the economy were to move to its long-run equilibrium immediately—that is, if domestic output could be increased without any time lags—the behavior of the exchange rate would exhibit no overshooting. The increased money supply would immediately induce capital outflows, depreciate domestic currency, and increase output. In terms of Figure 15–2, the economy would move immediately from point E to E''. This is the same type of adjustment implied by the Mundell–Fleming framework discussed in Chapter 13. The unanticipated monetary shock generates immediate adjustments, leaving no room for exchange rate overshooting or any other type of sophisticated exchange rate dynamics. In the present framework, overshooting in the exchange rate is closely related to the assumption that assets markets clear quickly relative to goods markets. This is embodied by the fixity of output over the immediate short run versus the full flexibility of the exchange rate and domestic interest rates. With output fixed, the unanticipated money supply increase requires a reduction of the domestic interest rate to maintain money market equilibrium. Given world interest rates, domestic interest rates can decline only if an expected domestic currency appreciation develops. From the uncovered interest parity condition, $i = i^* + x$, domestic interest rates decline if x

becomes negative. This implies that, to maintain money market equilibrium over the short run, the exchange rate will have to move above its full-equilibrium level, giving rise to an expected domestic currency appreciation, a reduction in domestic interest rates, and an increase in money demand that matches the money supply expansion. This is the nature of the overshooting of the exchange rate in the present framework: It is required in order for assets market equilibrium (money market equilibrium) to be sustained in the short run.

The role of exchange rate expectations on macroeconomic adjustment and exchange rate behavior is evident from our discussion so far. But, as we examined in Chapters 1, 5 and 6, exchange rate expectations are also connected to the behavior of the forward foreign exchange market. It is the purpose of the following sections to analyze the dynamic behavior of exchange rate expectations and the forward exchange rate.

15–5. THE FORWARD FOREIGN EXCHANGE MARKET UNDER FLOATING EXCHANGE RATES

Forward exchange rates and, hence, the forward premium are closely linked to the expectations that participants in the foreign exchange market hold about future currency values. Presently, we will assume that the forward premium is equal to the expected rate of depreciation of the domestic currency.[9] In this case, the forward premium becomes an indicator of the currency depreciation expected to occur during the term of the forward contract. Algebraically, the equality of the forward

---

[9]A divergence of the forward premium from the expected rate of domestic currency depreciation can arise within the context of an uncertain world. Essential in explaining these deviations is the presence of risk aversion on the part of investors and of a risk premium in the determination of the forward premium. These issues were examined in Chapters 5 and 6 and will reappear in Chapter 19.

premium for a given maturity, f, with the expected rate of depreciation of the domestic currency for that maturity, x, is given by

$$f = x.$$

A thirty-day forward premium on the pound, for example, means that the pound is expected to increase in value relative to the dollar—or, in other words, there is an expected depreciation of the dollar. If, for instance, the thirty-day forward premium on the pound is $f = 0.10$, this suggests that participants in the foreign exchange market expect the dollar to depreciate in value by 10 percent over the one month of the forward contract—that is, $x = f = 0.10$. By the same token, a forward discount on the pound (a negative value of f) would imply that there is an expected appreciation of the value of the dollar.

Merely knowing that the forward premium is equal to the expected rate of depreciation of domestic currency does not provide us with an answer to the question of how the forward premium is determined: We have yet to specify the factors affecting the expected rate of domestic currency depreciation. In Section 15–3, we discussed how expected exchange rate changes are determined, relating them to deviations of the full-equilibrium exchange rate, $\bar{e}$, from the current spot exchange rate, e. This expectation-formation relationship was stylized by Equation 15–4, which shows how, when the full-equilibrium exchange rate exceeds (or is exceeded by) the spot exchange rate, an expected domestic currency depreciation (or appreciation) arises—a natural consequence of anticipating an eventual adjustment of the economy to full equilibrium.

Equating the expression for the expected rate of domestic currency depreciation in Equation 15–4 with the forward premium yields

$$f = x = \theta \left(\frac{\bar{e} - e}{e} \right), \qquad (15\text{–}5)$$

where θ is a positive parameter that shows by how much participants in the foreign exchange market expect the exchange rate to increase (or decrease) over the term of the forward contract. For instance, if the full-equilibrium exchange rate is $\bar{e} = 3.00$, the current spot exchange rate is $e = 2.00$, and individuals expect the difference between the full-equilibrium and the current exchange rate to diminish by 20 percent in the next month (implying $\theta = 0.20$), the (one-month) forward premium is equal to

$$f = 0.20 \left(\frac{3.00 - 2.00}{2.00} \right).$$
$$= (0.20)(0.5) = 0.10$$

The pound will thus be at a 10 percent forward premium, meaning that the one-month forward exchange rate exceeds the spot exchange rate by 10 percent. Because individuals expect a 10 percent increase of the exchange rate during the one-month life of the forward contract, arbitrage will insure the equality of this expected rate of domestic currency depreciation with the forward premium, as described in Chapter 1.

The relationship between the forward premium and the current and full-equilibrium exchange rates indicated by Equation 15–5 can be easily transformed to provide a clearer picture of the factors influencing the forward exchange rate in the present framework. Using the definition of the forward premium and combining it with Equation 15–5, we obtain

$$f = \frac{F - e}{e} = \theta \left(\frac{\bar{e} - e}{e} \right), \qquad (15\text{–}5a)$$

with F equal to the forward exchange rate. Because the exchange rate in the denominator of each side of Equation 15–5(a) cancels out, a simple modification of it provides us with the following expression for the forward exchange rate:

$$F = \theta \bar{e} + (1 - \theta)e. \qquad (15\text{–}6)$$

Equation 15−6 expresses the forward rate as a weighted average of the full-equilibrium exchange rate, $\bar{e}$, and the current spot exchange rate, e, with the weights equal to the parameter θ and the related fraction $(1 - \theta)$. For instance, if $\theta = 0.20$, the current exchange rate between the dollar and the pound is $e = \$2.00/\pounds$, and the full-equilibrium exchange rate is $\bar{e} = \$3.00/\pounds$; then the one-month forward exchange rate will equal $F = \$2.20/\pounds$, obtained from

$$F = (0.2)\,(\$3.00/\pounds) + (0.8)\,(\$2.00/\pounds)$$
$$= \$2.20/\pounds.$$

Notice that the greater the extent to which individuals expect the exchange rate to adjust toward its long-run level during the term of the forward contract (the closer θ is to 1), the closer F will be to the full-equilibrium exchange rate. As a matter of fact, if individuals expect the exchange rate to adjust fully toward $\bar{e}$ in the thirty days covered by the forward contract, then $\theta = 1$ and, from Equation 15−6, $F = \bar{e}$, (the forward exchange rate equals the long-run exchange rate). More generally, because the presence of rigidities prevents the immediate attainment of full equilibrium, we can assume that individuals expect only part of the exchange rate adjustment to occur over the term of the forward contract. Actually, if the economy adjusts very slowly, individuals may expect no perceptible change toward equilibrium to occur within the next thirty days. In this case, the parameter θ is close to zero and, from Equation 15−6, the forward exchange rate approximates the current spot exchange rate, e; that is, because individuals expect no significant change in the economy over the next thirty days, they will expect the exchange rate to remain unchanged. This expectation is reflected in the forward exchange rate. Again, this is an extreme case and we can assume that, in general, θ will be larger than zero. The forward exchange rate is, therefore, related to both the current exchange rate and the full-equilibrium exchange rate, with the relative importance of each of these in influencing the forward rate determined by how fast individuals expect the economy to adjust over time. The faster the expected adjustment toward full equilibrium, the larger the weight carried by the full-equilibrium exchange rate in determining the forward rate. The slower the adjustment toward full equilibrium, the larger the influence of the current exchange rate on the forward rate.

The interaction between the forward, spot, and full-equilibrium exchange rates is best illustrated by examining how they are affected by economic disturbances. This is discussed in Section 15−6.

15−6. THE DYNAMICS OF THE FORWARD EXCHANGE RATE

Figure 15−4 shows the behavior of the 180−day forward exchange rate between the dollar and the pound sterling from 1989 to 1992 and compares it with the path of the contemporaneous dollar–pound spot exchange rate in that period. Two striking observations can be discerned from the data. First, the forward exchange rate appears to be subject to substantial volatility during the period and, second, spot and forward exchange rates generally tend to move together in the same direction. What explains these two patterns of behavior of forward rates in the recent experience with floating exchange rates? This section investigates forward exchange rate dynamics, examining the role of unanticipated disturbances on those dynamics. We illustrate by taking the case of an unexpected money supply expansion.

Let us return to the analytics of an unanticipated money supply disturbance, as described previously through the use of Figure 15−2. Prior to the monetary expansion, the economy rests at point E and agents expect the exchange rate to remain at its prevailing level, e_o. The spot and full-equilibrium exchange rates coincide and the forward exchange rate is consequently equal to both. Symbolically, at point E,

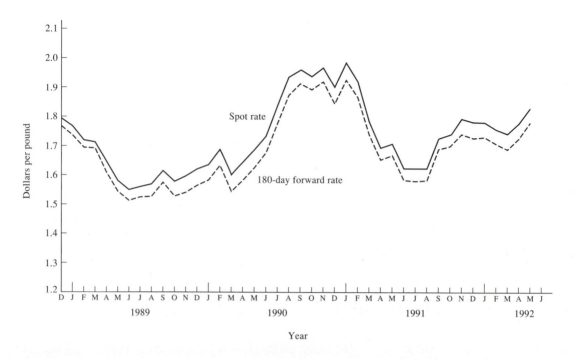

FIGURE 15–4.   180–Day Forward Exchange Rate and Contemporaneous Spot Rate for the Pound Sterling, 1989–1992.

SOURCE: Monthly data from *The Wall Street Journal,* end-of-month quotes.

$$F_0 = e_0 = \bar{e}_0,$$

with F_0 representing the forward exchange rate prevailing before the unanticipated monetary disturbance and $\bar{e}_0$ the initial full-equilibrium exchange rate. Now, an unanticipated money supply expansion leads to a sudden upward movement of the spot exchange rate, as represented by the switch of equilibrium in the economy from point E to point E'. As explained previously, the spot exchange rate overshoots its full-equilibrium level, $\bar{e}$, moving upward to e_1.

What happens to the forward exchange rate? The increased money supply raises the exchange rate individuals in the economy expect to prevail in future periods, compared with the initial exchange rate, e_0. Because the expected exchange

rate is reflected in the forward exchange rate, the latter increases in response to the monetary disturbance. From Equation 15–6, immediately after the monetary shock (with the economy at point E'), the forward exchange rate rises to

$$F_1 = \theta \bar{e} + (1 - \theta) e_1. \qquad (15\text{–}6a)$$

Because both $\bar{e}$ and e_1 are higher than the initial exchange rate, the forward exchange rate will jump above its initial value ($F_1 > F_0$). Note, however, that the forward rate does not increase by the same amount as the long-run equilibrium exchange rate. Instead, following the spot exchange rate, the forward exchange rate overshoots its full-equilibrium value. The full-equilibrium forward exchange rate is determined by the full equilibrium at point E''. At that point, the economy's output would have fully expanded to match the increased demand for domestic goods arising from the monetary expansion. When the economy reaches point E'', the spot exchange rate will equal the full-equilibrium exchange rate and, consequently, both will equal the forward exchange rate. Full equilibrium, however, is attained only after an extended period of time. Meanwhile, the forward exchange rate will remain *above* its full-equilibrium value.

The reason for the overshooting of the forward exchange rate lies in the overshooting of the spot exchange rate. Because the current spot exchange rate overshoots its full-equilibrium value, and given that the economy attains full equilibrium only after an extended period of time—presumably longer than the, say, one-month term of the forward contracts—individuals will expect the exchange rate to remain above its full equilibrium for some time to come. With the forward exchange rate reflecting the foreign exchange market's expected exchange rate at the time of expiration of the forward contract (say, one month in the future), its value immediately after the monetary disturbance will then exceed the full-equilibrium exchange rate.

In a framework in which asset markets clear relatively quickly compared with goods markets, the immediate response of the forward exchange rate to an unanticipated monetary disturbance is to increase suddenly and drastically, overshooting its longer-run value. This choppy and abrupt forward exchange rate adjustment is consistent with the behavior of forward rates in the recent floating exchange rate regime. In addition, we have found that the movement of the forward exchange rate follows closely that of the spot exchange rate, rapidly depreciating at first and then appreciating toward its long-run equilibrium value. The joint movements of spot and forward rates are again suggestive of the recent behavior of the exchange rates of major currencies, as typified by Figure 15–4. In conclusion, it is apparent that the present framework explains well the most striking regularities observed in the recent experience with floating currency values. This feature has made it a very popular framework of analysis of economic events under flexible exchange rates.

15–7. ECONOMIC POLICY, INTEREST RATES, AND EXCHANGE RATE ADJUSTMENT: THE U.S. DOLLAR IN THE 1980s AND EARLY 1990s

This section provides an overview of the main issues we have discussed within a real-world context. The case taken to illustrate them is that of the U.S. dollar in the 1980s and early 1990s. Figure 15–5 shows the behavior of the value of the dollar since 1980. There are three clearly defined periods: (1) from the beginning of 1980 through the first quarter of 1985, when the dollar sharply appreciated in value; (2) from the second quarter of 1985 to the first quarter of 1987, when the dollar depreciated quickly back to the levels it was early on in the decade; and (3) the period from the second quarter of 1987 through 1992, during which the dollar continued to fluctuate in value but within a narrower range than its earlier swings. It is the purpose of this section to supply some explanations for these exchange rate fluctuations, particularly in relation to the overshooting model described in this chapter and the basic Mundell-Fleming framework developed in Chapter 13. Other explanations can be postulated and will be discussed in Chapter 19.

Contractionary Monetary Policy, Expansionary Fiscal Policy, and the Dollar

The general appreciation of the dollar in the first half of the 1980s can be accounted for by two major policy events. The first was the emergence of the tight monetary policies followed by the Federal Reserve after 1979 under the chairmanship of Paul Volcker. This policy regime represented a sharp

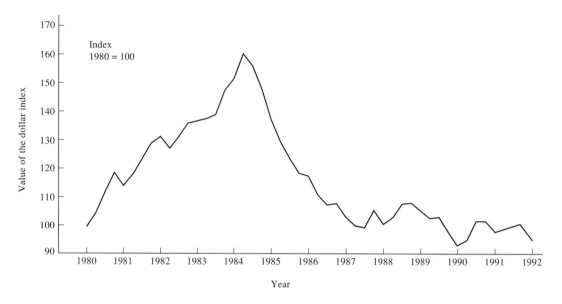

Note: The data for the value of the dollar is based on the multilateral exchange rate model index used by the International Monetary Fund, taken from selected issues of *International Financial Statistics*. The value of the dollar index is equal to the reciprocal of the effective exchange rate index as defined in this book (see Chapter 10, Section 7).

FIGURE **15–5.** The Value of the Dollar, 1980–1991

turnaround from policies followed during the Carter administration, which had sustained relatively high rates of monetary growth. The tightening of monetary policy under Volcker was intended to represent a commitment to controlling inflation. The behavior of the U.S. economy from 1980 through 1982 follows closely that predicted earlier in this chapter as arising in the presence of unanticipated contractionary monetary policy. The effects were a sharp rise in U.S interest rates, growing capital inflows, and an immediate appreciation of the dollar. The economy also gradually moved into a sharp recession, with unemployment climbing from an average of 5.9 percent in 1978 and 1979 to 7.4 percent in 1980, 8.3 percent in 1981, and 10.7 percent in 1982. Given the gradual adjustment of output to the monetary policy disturbance, and fol-

lowing our analysis of exchange rate dynamics in Section 15–4, one can postulate that the sharp appreciation of the dollar in this period represented a case of exchange rate overshooting.[10] It can be argued that the monetary contraction induced the dollar exchange rate to move below its long-run equilibrium value. With the economy adjusting sluggishly toward its new equilibrium, the exchange rate remained below its longer-term value over the short run.

Although the overshooting model provides a possible explanation for the appreciation of the

[10]Such an association has been made by R. Dornbusch and J. Frankel, "The Flexible Exchange Rate System: Experience and Alternatives," in S. Borner, ed., *International Finance and Trade in a Polycentric World* (London: Macmillan, 1988).

dollar from 1980 to 1982, the continued increase in the dollar effective exchange rate all the way through February 1985 is difficult to account for in this framework. According to the model, unanticipated contractionary monetary policy leads to a sharp currency appreciation that is then followed by a *depreciation* and a gradual expansion of production. In the case of the dollar, U.S. economic activity did recover after 1982, but the currency continued to appreciate. One clue to answering this puzzle can be found in the behavior of interest rates. Between 1982 and 1984, U.S. interest rates were generally above foreign interest rates. If we associate an interest rate differential in favor of the dollar with an expected rate of depreciation of this currency, its positive tendency would imply a sustained expected depreciation.[11] However, as Figure 15–5 shows, the dollar did not depreciate during this period; it actually appreciated, leaving a discrepancy between its expected depreciation and its actual behavior. In other words, it is possible that an unanticipated appreciation of the dollar recurred over and over in the early 1980s. This behavior was most likely connected to an unexpectedly staunch commitment to monetary tightness on the part of the Federal Reserve. A sustained unanticipated monetary contraction tends to maintain high U.S. interest rates and gives rise to a continued appreciation of the dollar. The recurrence of these monetary shocks over time and the stubborn expectation that the monetary tightness was about to be reversed might have sustained the appreciation of the dollar until early in 1984. However, after this time period, even the interest rate data begins to be inconsistent with the overshooting hypothesis: After the second quarter of 1984, the differential between U.S. and world interest rates tends to diminish and begins to

favor foreign assets, even though the dollar continues to appreciate in value.

An alternative explanation for the appreciation of the dollar after 1982 has been emphasized by Professor William Branson of Princeton University. Going back to a version of the Mundell-Fleming model, he suggested that it was not monetary policy but the fiscal policy changes made by the Reagan administration that caused the dollar appreciation during that time. Through a combination of income tax cuts and increased expenditures associated with a buildup of the military arsenal, the beginning of the Reagan administration marked the start of a dramatic growth of the U.S. budget deficit. As Branson summarizes: "The combined federal, state, and local deficit was roughly zero at the beginning of 1981. It expanded to a peak of $167 billion in the bottom of the recession in the fourth quarter of 1982 and then shrank in the recovery. But the shift in the federal budget position left the total budget deficit at $155 billion at the end of 1985, after three years of recovery."[12] The consequences of expansionary fiscal policy were examined in Chapter 13. The Mundell-Fleming model predicts that increased government spending will generate capital inflows, appreciate domestic currency, and crowd out private economic activity by reducing net exports. In terms of these variables, the behavior of the America economy followed the Mundell-Fleming prescription.[13]

---

[11]For the pitfalls of such an association, see Chapter 5. For the present purposes, the general, directional coincidence of the two variables is sufficient to establish the argument; it does not rely on a strict equality of the differential with the expected depreciation.

[12]W. H. Branson, "Sources of Misalignment in the 1980s," in R. C. Marston, ed., *Misalignment of Exchange Rates: Effects on Trade and Industry* (Chicago: University of Chicago Press, 1988), p. 13. Normally, with unchanged income tax rates, economic expansion is associated with increased income and higher tax revenues, which reduce the budget deficit.

[13]Harvard economist Martin Feldstein has argued that contemporaneous and anticipated budget deficits were the culprit behind the dollar appreciation (see his article, "The Budget Deficit and the Dollar," in S. Fischer, ed., *NBER Macroeconomics Annual 1986* (Cambridge, Mass.: The MIT Press, 1986). However, the links between budget deficits and exchange rates depend on the source of the fiscal deficit (whether
(continued)

There are alternative views on the failure of the dollar to depreciate to any significant extent in 1984 and early 1985. One regards the possibility of speculative effects embodied in so-called exchange rate bubbles, to be discussed next.

The Dollar Overvaluation and Exchange Rate Bubbles

A situation in which a given economic variable progressively or cumulatively deviates from the path consistent with its fundamental, long-run value is called a bubble.[14] In the foreign exchange market, a *bubble* may cause the currency to remain *overvalued* or *undervalued*—that is, to remain above or below its fundamental long-run value for extended periods of time. What gives rise to exchange rate bubbles? The most frequent explanation is provided by the existence of extraneous beliefs or misperceptions about the future exchange rate that gradually become prevalent or progressively catch up with investors in the foreign exchange market. For example, unfounded rumors may generate a belief that the dollar will

soon change drastically in value. As these extraneous beliefs catch up with investors in the foreign exchange market, in much the same way that fads and fashions spread, they will strongly influence exchange rate expectations and, as a result, the behavior of the exchange rate. Note that, in the same way as fashions change and misperceptions are found to be incorrect, eventually the bubble will recede or burst and the exchange rate will return to its fundamental value—but it might take an extended period of time for the speculative effects to be eliminated.

A second explanation for bubbles does not rely on individuals holding false beliefs or making consistently incorrect future evaluations. Instead, it holds that individuals form rational expectations about the future, basing their anticipations on all the information currently available about the fundamental determinants of future exchange rates and about the structure of the foreign exchange market. The bubble is explained in the following terms: Once a specific economic disturbance, such as a contractionary monetary policy, generates changes in the exchange rate in a given direction—say, a currency appreciation—and if individuals are not certain about the exact magnitude of the movement in that direction, they will expect, with some probability, that the movement will continue. As long as the probability is high, and with no other forces or disturbances occurring, the result will be a continuing appreciation. As new investors enter the market with an expectation that the original exchange rate movement will continue, the movement will become self-sustained, originating a persistent exchange rate deviation from its long-run, fundamental value. For example, if increasing numbers of investors and speculators get on the bandwagon of an expected dollar appreciation, the consequent sustained capital inflows will maintain the exchange rate appreciation. Note that the bubble here is a rational bubble: Participants in the market are not relying on any extraneous beliefs in predicting that the original disturbance will give rise to an exchange rate movement. They just do not know exactly by how much the move-

---

it is reduced taxes or increased government spending), how agents in the economy see the current and future burden of the debt associated with this deficit, and other intervening variables such as risk premia (see the comments by R. Dornbusch and A. C. Stockman on the Feldstein paper in the NBER volume). For instance, the increased debt associated with large budget deficits could compromise the credibility of a government's anti-inflation program, generating expectations of future monetary expansion and an anticipated currency depreciation. The expected depreciation, in turn, can be self-fulfilling if it induces a run on the domestic currency. For a discussion of the various issues surrounding the connections between currency values and budget deficits, see A. C. Stockman, "Exchange Rates, the Current Account and Monetary Policy," in W. S. Haraf and T. D. Willett, eds., *Monetary Policy for a Volatile Global Economy* (Washington, D.C.: American Enterprise Institute, 1990); and A. W. Throop, "Reagan Fiscal Policy and the Dollar," *Federal Reserve Bank of San Francisco Weekly Letter* (March 1989).

[14]Some economists use the term *sunspots,* in addition to bubbles, to specify the fact that such phenomena are dependent on events that are totally exogenous to the market.

ment will be and, consequently, assign a probability that the bubble will continue and also a probability that the bubble will collapse or crash toward the long-run fundamental exchange rate. This type of behavior may be applied to the appreciation of the dollar in the first half of the 1980s.[15]

A third type of bubble behavior is related to the presence of heterogeneity in the formation of expectations among foreign exchange market participants. As was examined in Chapter 6, some evidence exists to suggest the presence of two types of participants in the foreign exchange market: fundamentalists and chartists. Fundamentalists form expectations about the future exchange rate on the basis of the best available information on the fundamental variables influencing exchange rates. Given the model developed in this chapter, fundamentalists would have predicted that, given an initial overshooting of the exchange rate in response to the contractionary monetary policy followed by the Federal Reserve in the early 1980s, the dollar should have depreciated in 1984 and 1985. Chartists, on the other hand, relying strictly on rules, form adaptive expectations that trace the future behavior of currency values to current and past values. In the case of the dollar, once the currency started to appreciate in 1980 and 1981, chartists were expecting the currency to continue appreciating. According to Berkeley economists

Jeffrey Frankel and Kenneth Froot, a speculative bubble was associated with the appreciation of the dollar between 1981 and 1985, linked to an increase in the relative weight of chartists relative to fundamentalists in the group of forecasters in the foreign exchange market.[16] Because chartists expected the dollar to continue appreciating, their increased role in the market induced the demand for dollars to rise and fueled the continuing, self-fulfilling appreciation. At the same time, fundamentalists, who were expecting the dollar to depreciate, found themselves in a minority among market analysts. Why did fundamentalists shrink in importance? According to Frankel, the explanation is related to the continued failure of fundamentalists to predict the sustained appreciation of the dollar, a failure that made them less accurate in their forecasts compared to the chartists.

There is some evidence indicating the presence of bubbles in the stock market as well as in the foreign exchange market.[17] However, formal testing for the presence of bubbles is not an easy matter. As economists Robert Flood, Peter Garber, and Robert Hodrick have argued, in order to determine whether exchange rates diverge from fundamentals, an accurate model of the fundamental determinants of exchange rates is needed.[18] At the present time, however, exchange rate models—whether the Mundell–Fleming model, the overshooting approach, purchasing power parity, or

---

[15]Although it is apparent that a bubble could explain the persistent appreciation of the dollar in the early 1980s, it is not exactly obvious how it explains the also persistent interest rate differential in favor of U.S. assets. Note, however, that a rational speculator will anticipate the possibility of a crash, meaning that he or she knows that this is a risky business and will require compensation for that risk taking. A positive interest rate differential in favor of the United States in the early 1980s may then just represent this compensation for risk bearing. Recall from Chapters 5 and 6 that the domestic interest rate is influenced by the world interest rate, the expected rate of depreciation of the domestic currency, and an exchange risk premium. The bubble and the associated risk of its bursting at any moment give rise to a positive exchange risk premium on the dollar, thus possibly explaining the interest differential in favor of the United States.

[16]J. A. Frankel and K. A. Froot, "Chartists, Fundamentalists and the Demand for Dollars," in A. S. Courakis and M. P. Taylor, eds., *Private Behavior and Government Policy in Interdependent Economies* (Oxford: Clarendon, 1990).

[17]See E. N. White, "The Stock Market Boom and the Crash of 1929 Revisited," *Journal of Economic Perspectives* (Spring 1990); W. T. Woo, "Some Evidence of Speculative Bubbles in the Foreign Exchange Markets," *Journal of Money, Credit and Banking* (November 1987); and R. Meese, "Testing for Bubbles in Exchange Markets: The Case of Sparkling Rates," *Journal of Political Economy* (April 1986).

[18]In R. P. Flood and R. J. Hodrick, "Testing for Speculative Bubbles," *Journal of Economic Perspectives* (Spring 1990); and P. M. Garber, "The Dollar as a Bubble," in P. A. Petri and S. Gerlach, eds., *The Economics of the Dollar Cycle* (Cambridge, Mass.: The MIT Press, 1990).

those to be discussed in Chapter 19—have been highly inaccurate in predicting short-run exchange rate changes. We have just seen how the overshooting model itself failed to predict the sustained appreciation of the dollar from 1984 to 1985. As a consequence, there will always be difficulties in determining whether evidence of a bubble implies that exchange rates did in effect deviate from fundamentals or it means that the researcher had an inaccurate model of fundamentals, a model that deviates from the fundamental currency values as set in actual foreign exchange markets.

The presence of bubbles underlies the fact that the exchange rate does not always necessarily adjust toward its long-run value but often deviates and remains persistently away from it. The implications of this result are best summarized by Rudiger Dornbusch:

> Why should we be concerned about such deviations? The obvious reason is that given the path of policy variables an exchange rate bubble will have real effects on competitiveness, inflation, and employment. It represents a macro-shock that, if possible, we would want to offset. The possibility of rational bubbles is important to recognize because it represents a fundamental departure from the view that markets do things right, all the time.[19]

This statement is particularly important because it sets the stage for one possible interpretation of the sharp depreciation of the dollar after 1985. We turn to the next section to examine this topic.

15–8. FOREIGN EXCHANGE MARKET INTERVENTION AND THE DEPRECIATION OF THE DOLLAR AFTER 1985

The long-awaited depreciation of the dollar began in February of 1985 and continued through 1988. Since that time, the dollar has had swings in value,

but not to the great extent that it did in the 1980s.

Just as the appreciation of the dollar in the first half of the 1980s had been initiated by sharp turns in U.S. economic policymaking at the Federal Reserve and the Treasury in 1979 and 1980, the start of the dollar depreciation was also marked by a significant change: January 1985 was the inaugural month of the second Reagan administration, and in terms of policymaking there was a new Secretary of the Treasury, James Baker.

James Baker replaced Donald Regan, who had been a staunch supporter of leaving foreign exchange markets alone—independent of government hands, except perhaps in periods of market "disorder." This policy was reflected in the minimal extent of foreign exchange market intervention during the first Reagan administration. Although preoccupation with the dollar appreciation in those years ran high in some quarters of the administration—particularly with the Council of Economic Advisors, then headed by Martin Feldstein—Mr. Regan resisted pressures to intervene. In fact, it has been suggested that Regan believed that a "strong" dollar reflected the strength of the American economy and was not a major cause for worry.

Baker was not as ideologically biased against foreign exchange market intervention as Regan was. Indeed, during the January confirmation hearings, he "explicitly showed signs of the departure with respect to exchange rate policy, stating at one point that the Treasury's previous stance against intervention was 'obviously something that should be looked at'...."[20] A more direct signal that the economic policy regime at the Treasury was changing was given at a meeting of G-5 finance ministers and central bank governors (from the group of France, Germany, Japan, the United Kingdom, and the United States) in London on January 17, 1985. At this meeting, Baker agreed to engage in a coordinated intervention with the others in an effort to dampen the appreciation of

---

[19]R. Dornbusch, "Equilibrium and Disequilibrium Exchange Rates," National Bureau of Economic Research, Working Paper no. 983 (September 1982), p. 16.

[20]J. Frankel, "The Making of Exchange Rate Policy in the 1980s," National Bureau of Economic Research Working Paper no. 3539 (December 1990), p. 19.

the dollar. Although the intervention by the U.S. itself was minimal, the German monetary authorities intervened heavily, selling large amounts of dollars in February and March. Some have argued that this intervention burst the bubble that had been sustaining the dollar appreciation. Other economists, however, have emphasized that shifting fundamentals were really behind the depreciation (in the form of more relaxed monetary policy and concern for reducing the budget deficit). Whatever the case, coordinated intervention in foreign exchange markets among the G-5 continued and was formalized in a meeting of these countries at the Plaza Hotel in New York City on September 22, 1985. At this gathering, the group agreed to try to depreciate the dollar by 10 to 12 percent over the near term and to cooperate over the long term in sustaining an appreciation of nondollar currencies. When the agreement—referred to now as the Plaza Agreement—was announced, the exchange rate of the dollar immediately increased by more than 4 percent against the mark and the yen. The G-5 group was later expanded to include Canada and Italy, and became the G-7.

In assessing the role played by intervention in foreign exchange markets on the depreciation of the dollar since 1985, we must first determine how foreign exchange market intervention affects exchange rates.[21] We examine this issue next.

Sterilized Versus Nonsterilized Intervention

Central bank intervention in foreign exchange markets can be of two types: *sterilized* and *nonsterilized*. Sterilized intervention occurs when the central bank buys or sells foreign exchange reserves but does not allow these changes in reserves to affect the domestic money supply. It does this by engaging in offsetting changes of domestic credit through open-market operations. Nonsterilized intervention, on the other hand, means that the central bank allows its purchases and sales of foreign exchange to alter the domestic money supply. In general, nonsterilized intervention tends to be more effective than sterilized intervention in influencing exchange rates because it is associated with changes in the domestic money supply.

We can relate these concepts to our earlier discussion by recalling the money-supply process in open economies, as specified by our analysis in Chapter 14, Section 14–1. Restating Equation 14–7,

$$\Delta M^S = \mu \Delta H = \mu(\Delta IR + \Delta CBC),$$

which states that changes in the domestic money supply are connected to changes in the monetary base, ΔH, which are related in turn to changes in the international reserves of the central bank, ΔIR, and/or changes in central bank credit, ΔCBC, given the money supply multiplier, μ.

Our analysis of monetary policy earlier in the chapter assumed that authorities were not engaged in foreign exchange market intervention, so that $\Delta IR = 0$. In this case, the central bank can control the money supply by changing its credit. It is clear, though, that in an economy under floating exchange rates, policymakers can also influence the money supply by buying or selling international reserves. Assuming that the central bank holds its credit constant ($\Delta CBC = 0$), if the authorities buy international reserves ($\Delta IR > 0$), they pay by issuing checks on themselves and raise the money supply ($\Delta M^S > 0$). On the other hand, if the central bank sells foreign exchange reserves, this reduces the money supply. Both of these cases represent nonsterilized intervention operations because the authorities allow their official intervention to alter the domestic money supply. They are thus similar to monetary policy in their impact. For

---

[21]A survey of exchange rate policy in the United States and in the other G-7 countries is available in K. Dominguez and J. Frankel, *The Effects of Foreign Exchange Intervention* (Washington, D.C.: Institute for International Economics (IIE), 1993), I. M. Destler and C. Randall Henning, *Dollar Politics: Exchange Rate Policymaking in the United States* (Washington, D.C.: IIE, 1989); and Y. Funabashi, *Managing the Dollar: From the Plaza to the Louvre* (Washington, D.C.: IIE, 1988).

instance, a nonsterilized purchase of foreign currencies in exchange markets raises the domestic money supply and depreciates domestic currency. If the intervention is unanticipated, it will have an overshooting effect on the exchange rate. On the other hand, a sale of foreign exchange reserves reduces the monetary stock and will appreciate domestic currency.

In the case of sterilized intervention, the monetary authorities engage in open-market operations that counteract the influence of the intervention on the money supply. Algebraically, with sterilized intervention:

$$\Delta M^S = \mu\Delta H = \mu(\Delta IR + \Delta CBC) = 0,$$

because

$$\Delta H = \Delta IR + \Delta CBC = 0$$

or, alternatively,

$$\Delta CBC = -\Delta IR.$$

For instance, in the case of a sterilized sale of foreign exchange reserves, the central bank would purchase bonds in the open market, issuing checks on itself and supplying credit to the economy. The reduction in international reserves over any given period of time is exactly offset by an equal increase in the credit creation of the central bank ($\Delta IR = -\Delta CBC$). With a fixed money supply, the *LM* curve remains unchanged and unresponsive to the intervention. The economy thus also tends to remain unchanged.

Because sterilized intervention does not alter the economy's money supply, how would it affect exchange rates? This is a particularly important question because the United States has tended to engage in sterilized intervention over the years. As Harvard economist Kathryn Dominguez reports: "It is known that daily intervention by the Federal Reserve Bank of New York is fully and automatically sterilized: the foreign exchange trading room immediately reports its dollar sales to the open market trading room, which then buys that many

fewer bonds, so that the daily money supply is precisely what it would have been if no intervention had occurred."[22]

Sterilized intervention can alter exchange rates by means of a so-called expectations, or signaling, effect. This effect stems from the role of intervention in conveying information to market participants. When the public learns that a central bank is intervening to support a currency, its expectations about the value of that currency can be altered. The announcement of the intervention signals to the public the authorities' intentions concerning the future value of the currency. It can thus change the public's expectations with respect to the likelihood of future potential interventions. Suppose, for instance, that the government suddenly announces that it is committed to reducing the value of domestic currency. At the same time, a sterilized purchase of foreign currencies is engaged in by the central bank. The sterilized intervention does not affect the money supply, and it would therefore have no real effects on the economy. However, it is possible that the public will take the sterilized purchase of international reserves as a signal that the authorities will in fact engage in a *future* nonsterilized purchase of foreign currencies in order to depreciate domestic currency values. This expectation of a future increase in the money supply does have real effects and leads to an immediate increase in the exchange rate, as is established in the next section.

---

[22]K. Dominguez, "The Informational Role of Official Foreign Exchange Market Intervention Operations: An Empirical Investigation" (mimeo.), John F. Kennedy School of Government, Harvard University, 1988. The Federal Reserve Bank of New York is in charge of carrying out foreign exchange market operations. The mechanics of how U.S. monetary authorities intervene has been discussed by D. S. Batten and M. Ott, "What Can Central Banks Do About the Value of the Dollar?" *Review of the Federal Reserve Bank of St. Louis* (May 1984); and A. B. Balbach, "The Mechanics of Intervention in Exchange Markets," *Review of the Federal Reserve Bank of St. Louis* (February 1978).

Anticipated Economic Disturbances and Exchange Rate Dynamics

This section is concerned with the effects of anticipated economic disturbances on the economy's equilibrium. In particular, it discusses the channels by which an anticipated monetary expansion impinges on the economy even before it actually takes place.

Suppose that the Federal Reserve Board announces today that it will increase the money supply by a certain amount two weeks from today. What would be the response of the exchange rate to such an announcement? With the money supply scheduled to increase in two weeks, individuals will immediately anticipate an exchange rate increase. The forthcoming domestic currency depreciation tends to reduce expected returns on domestic assets, at any given level of the domestic interest rate, generating capital outflows that would immediately depreciate the spot exchange rate. In other words, even though the money supply has not yet actually increased, the expectation of the money-supply hike immediately increases the exchange rate. Of course, this currency depreciation would tend to raise the demand for domestic goods and would have an expansionary effect on domestic output. Some of the increased output might then be forthcoming even before the monetary expansion actually takes place. We can thus conclude that anticipated monetary policy will usually generate immediate changes in the economy; economic adjustment to the disturbance starts even before the expected or announced change actually occurs.[23]

The economic effects generated by anticipated disturbances are not necessarily positive and may, in effect, be very distressing. Suppose, for instance, that there is a sudden expectation among foreign exchange market participants that the dollar will appreciate vis-à-vis the pound in the future. This will immediately lead to speculative capital flows into the United States, reducing the spot exchange rate between the dollar and the sterling. This dollar appreciation will then result in a loss of competitiveness of U.S. goods in international markets, a switch in demand away from U.S. products, and a reduction in domestic output and employment.

Reiterating, we note that exchange rate expectations have, in general, important short-run macroeconomic consequences, some of which are not necessarily a blessing. A classic example of this proposition relates to the short-run effects of an anticipated real disturbance in the economy in the form of a discovery of oil deposits. This was the case in the U.K. North Sea oil-deposit discoveries of the 1970s. The realization in 1976 that massive exploitation of these reserves would be undertaken in the near future fueled anticipations that the U.K.'s net oil exports would increase in the years ahead, leading in turn to immediate effects on the value of the pound and on the economy in general.

The effects of an oil discovery on exchange rates and the economy overall depend on how the future oil exports are anticipated to affect the economy at that time. In Section 9 of Chapter 13, we examined the possible effects of an exogenous increase in the net exports of an economy and applied it to the specific case of the U.K.'s North Sea oil exports. As shown, the increased oil exports could be expected to lead to an appreciation of the pound sterling. However, an expected currency appreciation would lead to immediate capital inflows into the United Kingdom and an appreciation of the pound. Even though the extraction and exportation of the discovered oil would not occur for some time, the anticipation of such exports immediately appreciates domestic currency, with consequent deleterious effects on output and employment. Therefore, even though, it

---

[23]For an advanced exposition of the effects of anticipated monetary policy, see H. Genberg and A. K. Swoboda, "Policy and Current Account Determination Under Floating Exchange Rates," *IMF Staff Papers* (March 1989); and C. Wilson, "Anticipated Shocks and Exchange Rate Dynamics," *Journal of Political Economy* (June 1979).

would appear, superficially, that the oil discoveries would have a positive effect on the economy by sparking hopes of economic expansion, they actually might become counterproductive in the short run and have a recessionary impact instead. The behavior of the U.K. economy during the period in which it became evident massive exploitation of the North Sea oil discoveries would occur is consistent with these conclusions, being associated with a sharp appreciation of the pound and a deepening economic recession.

Another major source of anticipated disturbances involves the expectations generated by foreign exchange market intervention. As noted earlier, sterilized intervention can have real effects on the economy if it alters the expectations of agents in the economy. Suppose, then, that a sterilized purchase of foreign currencies by the central bank—combined with an announcement that the authorities are committed to lowering the value of domestic currency—generates an expectation that the central bank will expand the money supply in the future. According to the discussion in this section, this will immediately generate a currency depreciation. The policy announcement is thus effective in lowering the value of the currency. The next section expands on the signaling effect involved in foreign exchange market intervention.

Foreign Exchange Market Intervention, Signaling, and Currency Values

The presumption that central bank intervention has a signaling effect depends on two basic ideas. The first is the notion that central bankers have information about future policies that the private sector lacks. In the technical jargon of finance, the central bankers have inside information about their own policy plans. They also have an interest, at least in some cases, in communicating to the public information about their intended course of action. Consumers and investors welcome any signal about future policies because they must anticipate government policies in order to make appropriate

spending decisions. The second idea is that the central bankers have an interest in communicating accurate information to the public about their future policies. The truthful revelation of policy intentions and goals through intervention is the basic requirement for the signaling effect to be valid and useful for consumers and investors. Lack of credibility on government actions would invalidate intervention as a signaling device.

The signaling effect also crucially depends on the public recognizing the intervention. Because data on intervention are secret, authorities can choose to announce the intervention, and its magnitude, in order to maximize its expectational effect. A secret intervention that is not detected by the public will fail to have a signaling effect. The distinction between undetected and publicly announced interventions is thus crucial.

Notice that the impact of the expectations, or signaling, effect does not depend on the magnitude of the current intervention.[24] The important factor is how well the current intervention is able to convey information about the government's intended future policies. In the same manner, the expectation effect can operate whether the intervention is sterilized or not. The mechanism does not depend on the intervention affecting the current money supply. In that sense, exchange market

---

[24]Some analysts claim that the scale of intervention operations is simply too small to yield a significant impact. For instance, in the late 1980s, the U.S. money supply amounted to more than $3,000 billion. According to Harvard economist Kathryn Dominguez, the average scale of the coordinated interventions operations involving the dollar between January 1985 and December 1987 ranged between 200 and $300 million. These numbers represent less than 0.01 percent of the U.S. money supply. The magnitudes of daily intervention operations are small even in relation to daily flows of foreign exchange. For instance, daily trading in New York alone frequently exceeds $100 billion. Daily trading in New York, London, and Tokyo exceeds $400 billion. These figures have led economist Martin Feldstein to conclude that the impact of the coordinated intervention of 1985 by the G-5 on the value of the dollar was minimal: "New Evidence on the Effects of Exchange Rate Intervention," National Bureau of Economic Research Working Paper no. 2796 (October 1986).

intervention is a rather unique policy instrument: In theory, intervention is able to affect expectations about future monetary policies without altering the current money supply. As long as the intervention conveys inside information about future policies in a credible way, current and future exchange rates will be affected.[25]

How can we measure this expectations effect? Is it significant? The evidence is still scarce. The reason is that data on the timing and extent of intervention are jealously protected by monetary authorities. The researchers that work in this area are the selected few that can get access to government files. This access is usually quite limited, and the researchers are not allowed to publicize the data that authorities make available to them. Because daily intervention data are not public, empirical findings cannot be corroborated by other researchers and the results presented must be accepted at face value. This is one of the most secretive areas of research in economics and business.

In a recent article, Kathryn Dominguez and Jeffrey Frankel conclude that "a typical $100 million of 'secret' intervention has an effect of less than 0.1 percent on the exchange rate, but that the effect of intervention can be as large as an additional 4 percent."[26] To have a lasting impact, though, the signaling effect requires that the government back its announcements and intervention with the appropriate monetary and fiscal policies.

Otherwise, the expectation effect will be short lived, as the public will lose their credibility on governments' announcements.[27] A second factor that influences the impact of intervention is whether it is coordinated by a group of countries or undertaken by a country on its own. We discuss the role of coordinated intervention next.

Coordinated Versus Unilateral Intervention

Coordinated intervention occurs when countries agree to follow a cooperative intervention mechanism. The fact that a group of countries support the operation can enhance its credibility and strengthen its signaling effect. An example will illustrate the point. In 1986, the monetary authorities of various countries undertook intervention operations. However, the operations were not consistent and acted to offset each other. As a result, they did not achieve any impact on exchange rates. A clear policy of cooperative intervention will not only avoid the problem of central banks acting at cross purposes, but also will enhance the credibility of the intervention operations.

In principle, coordinated intervention can be sterilized or nonsterilized. In practice, most of the coordination operations by the G–7 group have been largely sterilized. Dominguez has examined the effects of the coordinated sterilized central bank intervention characterizing the period between 1985 and 1987. She concluded that some of the operations, such as the Plaza Agreement operations, were effective.[28]

---

[25]In principle, announcements about future policies can convey information without requiring actual exchange market intervention. See J. C. Stein, "Cheap Talk and the Fed: A Theory of Imprecise Policy Announcements," in *American Economic Review* (March 1989). Kathryn Dominguez reports that sterilized intervention by the Federal Reserve "in certain periods is a leading indicator of future (unanticipated) Fed monetary policy" in "The Informational Role of Official Foreign Exchange Intervention Operations: An Empirical Investigation" (mimeo.), John F. Kennedy School of Government, Harvard University, 1988.

[26]K. Dominguez and J. Frankel, "Does Foreign Exchange Intervention Matter? Disentangling the Portfolio and Expectations Effect for the Mark," National Bureau of Economic Research Working Paper no. 3299 (October 1990).

[27]See M. Obstfeld, "The Effectiveness of Foreign Exchange Intervention: Recent Experience, 1985–1988," in W. H. Branson, J. Frenkel, and M. Goldstein, eds., *International Policy Coordination and Exchange Rate Fluctuations* (Chicago: University of Chicago Press, 1990); and R. C. Marston, "Exchange Rate Policy Reconsidered," in M. Feldstein, ed., *International Economic Cooperation* (Chicago: University of Chicago Press, 1988).

[28]K. Dominguez, "The Informational Role of Official Foreign Exchange Intervention Operations: An Empirical Investigation," op. cit.

15-9. OFFICIAL INTERVENTION AND MANAGED FLOATING

The floating exchange rate arrangement followed by the major industrialized countries in recent years has been characterized by the active intervention of central banks in foreign exchange markets. The regime is thus clearly managed floating. This is exemplified by, but not restricted to, the coordinated actions of the G–7 group.

What rationale do central banks have for intervening in foreign exchange markets? The answer most frequently given, as reflected for instance in the Plaza Agreement and other actions of the G–5 and G–7 groups, is that intervention is called for in order to smooth-out "excessive" fluctuations in exchange rates in order to avoid the effects of these fluctuations on domestic economic activity. There are three basic links in this argument for intervention. First, it is asserted that exchange rate turbulence can be excessive, setting the basis for possible intervention. Second, it is assumed that these exchange rate fluctuations can have substantial effects on economic activity and are therefore an important economic problem. Finally, it is believed that central banks can, in practice, smooth out excessive turbulence through the purchase and sale of foreign exchange reserves. These three issues are examined next.

Has Exchange Rate Turbulence Been Excessive?

The wide gyrations of exchange rates described in this chapter have given rise to claims that exchange rate changes have been excessive and that central bank intervention in foreign exchange markets is required to smooth them out. However, how much can be considered excessive? In other words, what constitutes an excessive exchange rate change?

Exchange rate variability has many sources. Changes in fundamental economic variables, such as real income growth and inflation rates, will alter the fundamental equilibrium values of exchange rates and generate exchange rate variability. The rising U.S. rate of inflation relative to European inflation in the late 1960s and early 1970s, for instance, required an increase in the equilibrium exchange rate of the dollar against most European currencies. During the last years of Bretton Woods, then, the dollar was overvalued—that is, above its fundamental equilibrium value. The float of 1971, and then that of 1973, effectively devalued the dollar, moving it toward its equilibrium value at the time. Exchange rate variability can therefore arise from changes in the *equilibrium* value of exchange rates, a simple result of the fact that we live in a dynamic world in which fundamental economic variables are constantly changing.

On the other hand, exchange rate changes may be of the *disequilibrium* type, where the exchange rate deviates from its fundamental equilibrium value. As we have repeatedly noted, expectations about the future exert a major influence on exchange rates. Generally, speculation in foreign exchange markets can be of the *stabilizing* type, accelerating required equilibrium exchange rate changes or smoothing out adjustment in that direction. However, *destabilizing speculation,* which moves exchange rates away from their fundamental, equilibrium values, has been a recurrent source of worry for many supporters of floating exchange rates. It is feared that destabilizing speculation has caused exchange rate movements to be excessive and should be offset by government intervention in the foreign exchange market. [29]

[29]The debate on the theoretical and actual significance of stabilizing and destabilizing speculation under flexible exchange rates has a long history. Scandinavian economist Ragnar Nurkse argued strongly against floating exchange rate regimes precisely on the basis of destabilizing speculation: *International Currency Experience* (Princeton, N.J.: Princeton University Press, 1946). Milton Friedman, on the other hand, has emphasized the role of stabilizing speculation: "The Case for Flexible Exchange Rates," *Essays in Positive Economics* (Chicago: University of Chicago Press, 1953).

What factors are associated with destabilizing speculation; that is, what type of speculative phenomena can generate deviations of exchange rates from their fundamental, equilibrium values?[30] One situation is connected to the presence of speculative bubbles, in which investors get caught in the bandwagon of speculating against, or in favor of, a currency, keeping the exchange rate moving away from its fundamental value. It might also arise from the effects of extraneous (unsubstantiated) exchange rate expectations on exchange rates. By inducing a run on domestic currency, expectations of domestic currency depreciation will be associated with an immediate exchange rate depreciation, even if the expectations are based on unsubstantiated rumors or beliefs that do not actually occur and are, therefore, completely reversed ex post. Examples of both of these phenomena have been observed.[31]

The possibility that speculative influences on exchange rates might lead to excessive exchange rate movements in the sense of cumulative deviations from fundamental, equilibrium exchange rates does not automatically call for intervention. The question of how significant these deviations are in influencing the economy must first be answered—that is, do deviations of exchange rates from their fundamental, equilibrium value have any negative impact on the economy?

Exchange Rate Variability and Real Economic Activity

A major channel through which exchange rate variability can affect economic activity is by altering real exchange rates. Real exchange rates are equal to nominal exchange rates weighted by the ratio of foreign to domestic prices and can be used to measure the relative price of foreign goods in terms of domestic goods. Rising real exchange rates can be associated with increased price competitiveness of domestic products relative to foreign products and declining real exchange rates with worsening domestic competitiveness. As a result, if fluctuations in nominal exchange rates are connected to changes in real exchange rates, they will have a crucial effect on domestic net exports, production, employment, and so forth. As we have noted earlier, the flexibility of nominal exchange rates from the 1970s to the 1990s has generally revealed an association between swings in real and nominal exchange rates. The basic reason is that nominal exchange rates adjust more rapidly than goods market prices, which change sluggishly. Accordingly, nominal and real exchange rate turbulence are closely related.

One of the traditional arguments against flexible exchange rates as a regime is that the presumably greater real exchange rate (or terms of trade) uncertainty present in that system discourages international commerce. Even though the evidence is not conclusive, and world trade definitely did not stagnate in the post-1973 period, recent work suggests that real exchange rate uncertainty has had a negative impact on international trade among several industrial countries.[32] Deviations of

---

[30]An alternative question often asked in this regard is whether speculators will stabilize the exchange rate when the foreign exchange market is rendered unstable because of the failure of the Marshall-Lerner condition to hold or because of any factors generating a *J*-curve response of the trade balance to exchange rate changes. See W. Witte, "Another Case of Profitable Destabilizing Speculation," *Journal of International Economics* (February, 1973); and R. Driskill and S. McCafferty, "Spot and Forward Rates in a Stochastic Model of the Foreign Exchange Market," *Journal of International Economics* (May 1982).

[31]MIT economist Paul Krugman has noted two likely episodes of destabilizing speculation: the 1984–1985 appreciation of the dollar (discussed earlier in this chapter) and the surge of the dollar from April to June 1989. See P. Krugman, "The Case for Stabilizing Exchange Rates," *Oxford Review of Economic Policy* (February 1989).

[32]See D. Cushman, "U.S. Bilateral Trade Flows and Exchange Risk During the Floating Period," *Journal of International Economics* (May 1988); P. De Grauwe and B. de Bellefroid, "Long-Run Exchange Rate Variability and International Trade," in S. W. Arndt and J. David Richardson, eds., *Real-Financial Linkages Among Open Economies* (Cambridge, Mass.: The MIT Press, 1987); and D. Cushman, "Has Exchange Risk Depressed International Trade? The Impact of Third-Country Exchange Risk," *Journal of International Money and Finance* (November 1986).

exchange rates from their fundamental, equilibrium levels then imply real economic activity is similarly disturbed away from equilibrium. If we assume that excessive exchange rate changes do arise, given the potentially disruptive effects of such changes on real economic activity, is it desirable for the central bank to intervene in an effort to smooth them out?

Can Intervention Smooth Out Exchange Rate Fluctuations?

Central bank intervention geared toward smoothing out excessive exchange rate fluctuations takes the form of leaning against the wind. When domestic currency starts to depreciate, the central bank will buy domestic currency and sell international reserves to prevent the currency's value from declining further. Consequently, when the currency starts to appreciate, the central bank will sell domestic currency (and purchase foreign exchange) with the intention of preventing further rises in value. The obvious question that arises— and a tough one, for that matter—is how the central bank determines when to intervene. If the intention of the authorities is to limit disequilibrium movements in exchange rates, how do they distinguish between equilibrium and disequilibrium movements? This problem is crucial, as errors made by mistakenly intervening to prevent changes in the fundamental level of the exchange rate might result in delays of such equilibrium adjustments and can be quite costly both for the central bank and for society.

The problems involved in central bank intervention when the authorities lack knowledge of the source of a disturbance to the exchange rate (i.e., when they do not know whether it represents a destabilizing speculative movement or a change in the equilibrium exchange rate) are illustrated by Figure 15–6. Two disturbances are depicted—one, a bubble, is purely speculative and destabilizing, occurring at time t_0. The second one, representing an equilibrium change in the fundamental level of

the exchange rate from its initial value of $\bar{e} = \$1.50/£$ to $\bar{\bar{e}} = \$2.00$, occurs at time t_1. It is assumed the United States is intervening in the market in order to smooth out fluctuations in the dollar–pound exchange rate. The behavior of the exchange rate in the absence of central bank intervention would be the one illustrated by means of the continuous tracing in the diagram. If the central bank had perfect information about the sources of disturbance to the exchange rate, it could choose to intervene only during the first, destabilizing disturbance at time t_0. In general, however, there is no clear-cut, foolproof way of determining on the spot whether a certain exchange rate movement represents a change of the fundamental, equilibrium value of the exchange rate or it is a destabilizing speculative disturbance. As a result, having no way to select among them, it is assumed the U.S. authorities intervene in both instances. During the speculative disturbance, the central bank prevents the bubble from deviating the exchange rate upward to $e_0 = \$2.25$, instead bursting it apart and inducing a rapid movement back toward the initial equilibrium level of the exchange rate. The dotted line indicates how the exchange rate would behave in the presence of intervention.

In the case where the disturbance involves a permanent increase of the equilibrium exchange rate from $\bar{e} = \$1.50$ to $\bar{\bar{e}} = \$2.00$, occurring at time t_1, intervention will prevent the currency from depreciating. The U.S. authorities would support the dollar, keeping the exchange rate at a level, say, equal to $e_1 = \$1.60$. The central bank can do this by selling pounds in exchange for dollars in foreign exchange markets. Given the equilibrium nature of the disturbance at t_1, however, the upward pressure on the exchange rate will continue and the U.S. authorities would have to maintain their dollar support operations. Usually, in a situation such as this, the authorities will eventually give up defending the currency and allow the exchange rate to increase. Figure 15–6 shows this to occur at time t_2. During the period in

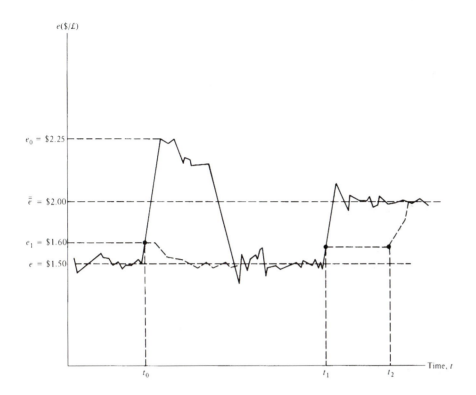

FIGURE 15–6.   The Problems of Central Bank Intervention

which the central bank has intervened to avoid the domestic currency depreciation, however, the exchange rate has been prevented from adjusting to its higher equilibrium level, generating socially costly, government-induced deviations from equilibrium.

Foreign exchange market intervention can stabilize or destabilize the exchange rate, depending on the source of the disturbance. Stabilizing intervention usually provides a revenue gain to monetary authorities; destabilizing intervention will result in losses. This can be explained using the cases illustrated in Figure 15–6. Central banks will frequently sell a substantial portion of their international reserves during their operations supporting a depreciating currency. They correspondingly

replenish their reserves at some point. Now, consider first a stabilizing intervention, such as that occurring at t_0. In that situation, the domestic authorities sell pounds at an exchange rate of $e_1 = \$1.60$, in order to burst open the exchange rate bubble. Immediately after the situation settles down, the central bank will replenish its lost international reserves and will therefore buy pounds at the prevailing exchange rate, which would be about $\bar{e} = \$1.50$. In other words, the central bank, in its sale and purchase of foreign exchange, has made a profit of approximately $\$0.10/£$. Consider, on the other hand, the case of destabilizing intervention, such as would occur at time t_1 in Figure 15–6. In this case, the central bank sells pounds at the rate of $\$1.60$ in the period between t_1 and t_2, losing a certain portion of its pound-sterling reserves in the process. When the authorities abandon the intervention, the exchange rate jumps upward to approximately $2.00. This is the rate at which the central bank would have to replenish its reserves of sterling. The result is a loss of close to $0.40/£ sold and purchased.

In summary, as Milton Friedman has remarked:

> It would do little harm for a government agency to speculate in the exchange market provided it held to the objective of smoothing out temporary fluctuations and not interfering with fundamental adjustments. And there should be a simple criterion of success—whether the agency makes or loses money.[33]

The available evidence on whether the intervention carried out by the central banks of industrial countries during the managed floating regime has been profitable suggests that some central banks made profits in some periods and in others lost from their intervention in foreign exchange markets.[34]

The present analysis is consistent with the view that there is an inherent difficulty in intervention: The authorities must determine whether the disturbance to be counteracted is associated with a change in the fundamental value of the exchange rate or represents a deviation from fundamentals. Given the presumption that, at the present, such a differentiation cannot be made with any degree of accuracy casts dark shadows on the ability of intervention to be predominantly stabilizing.

Even if the source of a disturbance is known, however, and intervention is called for, this does not mean that intervention can, in effect, prevent exchange rate changes from occurring. In other words, there is the further question of whether intervention could prevent exchange rate bubbles or extraneous beliefs in the foreign exchange market from influencing currency values. As discussed earlier in this chapter, nonsterilized intervention tends to be more effective than sterilized intervention in influencing exchange rates because it is associated with changes in the domestic money supply. Available evidence indeed suggests the relative ineffectiveness of sterilized intervention—and the effectiveness of nonsterilized intervention—in affecting exchange rates.[35]

15−10. THE DOLLAR, HYSTERESIS, AND THE U.S. TRADE BALANCE DEFICIT

Both the overshooting and Mundell–Fleming models conclude that, over the long run, the impact of currency appreciation associated with either monetary contraction or fiscal expansion is to deteriorate the trade balance. Similarly, the effect of currency depreciation is to improve the trade balance. According to this approach, then, the ups and downs in the value of the dollar in the decade of the 1980s implied that the U.S. trade deficit first would deteriorate and then improve. Figure 15−7 shows the behavior of the trade deficit in the 1980s and early 1990s jointly with an index of the value of the dollar. Although the deficit worsens in the period when the value of the dollar was rising, the depreciation occurring since 1985 does not seem to have generated an equally responsive improvement

[33]M. Friedman, "The Case for Flexible Exchange Rates," *Essays in Positive Economics* (Chicago: University of Chicago Press, 1953).

[34]Evidence of losses from official intervention is provided by A. J. Schwartz, "The Fed's Costly Trips to the Market," *The Wall Street Journal,* October 6, 1989; and D. Taylor, "The Mismanaged Float: Official Intervention by the Industrialized Countries," in M. Connolly, ed., *The International Monetary System* (New York: Praeger, 1982). Evidence on profits is provided by J. Williamson, *The Exchange Rate System* (Washington, D.C.: Institute for International Economics, 1983). See also V. Argy, "Exchange Rate Management in Theory and Practice," *Princeton Studies in International Finance* (October 1982).

[35]As already noted, sterilized intervention can work in the presence of expectational, or signaling, effects; for the evidence, see the work of Dominguez, Obstfeld, and Frankel cited earlier in the text. See also K. Rogoff, "On the Effects of Sterilized Intervention: An Analysis of Weekly Data," IMF Working Paper (May 1983).

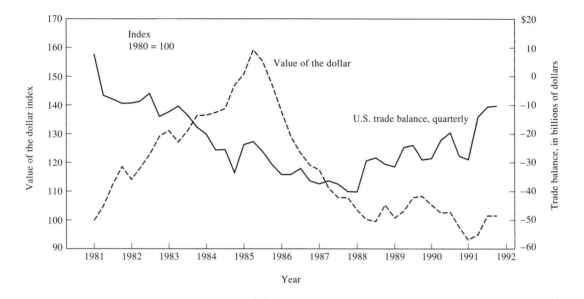

FIGURE 15–7.   The Value of the Dollar and U.S. Trade Balance Deficits, 1980–1992 (in billions of dollars)

SOURCE: International Monetary Fund, *International Financial Statistics* (various issues).

in the trade balance. First of all, the dollar depreciated dramatically between 1985 and 1987, yet the trade deficit continued to rise during the period. Only in 1988 was there finally an extended trade balance improvement.

Several hypotheses have been postulated to explain why the U.S. trade deficit continued to grow for so long after the depreciation of the dollar. First of all, this behavior can represent classic J-curve behavior.[36] As discussed earlier in

this chapter, the J curve suggests that the trade balance will first deteriorate and only later improve in response to a currency depreciation. This is because the short-run price elasticities of exports and imports are small. The quantities of goods exported and imported do not rise much in the short run in response to the currency depreciation; however, the relative prices of the foreign goods do, thus raising the *value* of imports relative to exports. After an extended period of time, exports and imports will respond to the exchange rate increase, and the trade balance then improves. Historical estimates of the responsiveness of U.S. exports and imports to currency depreciation suggest that the improvement in the trade balance may take as long as one or two years, which was precisely the amount of time it took in the late 1980s.

A second group of authors has suggested that the sluggish improvement of the trade balance, especially after 1987, may be the result of

---

[36]See W. R. Cline, "U.S. External Adjustment: Progress, Prognosis and Interpretation," in C. Fred Bergsten, ed., *International Adjustment and Financing: The Lessons of 1985–1991* (Washington, D.C.: Institute for International Economics, 1991). Some economists, though, have recently questioned whether the J curve has been exhibited by the long-term data for the U.S. See A. K. Rose and J. Yellen, "Is There a J-Curve?" *Journal of Monetary Economics* (1989); and M. Moeffett, "The J-Curve Revisited: An Empirical Examination for the United States," *Journal of International Money and Finance* (September 1989).

anomalies in the data and to circumstances associated with particular sectors unrelated to the value of the dollar. Computer trade volumes, for instance, have had measurement difficulties linked to the rapid technological and quality changes in the products sold in that industry. It has been extremely difficult for the U.S. Department of Commerce to construct price indices for computers. The behavior of trade values in computers is affected by the reliability of such indices. At the same time, petroleum imports increased in the late 1980s because of the relative price reduction in the price of crude oil during those years—a trend more related to events in world petroleum markets and OPEC behavior than the value of the dollar. Excluding computers and petroleum products from the analysis uncovers a stronger trade balance improvement associated with the dollar depreciation. As Brookings Institution economist Robert Z. Lawrence has noted, "the trade balance has increased in virtually all major end-use categories except for petroleum products and computers."[37]

A third explanation for the behavior of the trade deficit in the late 1980s and early 1990s is associated with the phenomenon of hysteresis. *Hysteresis* is defined in the *American Heritage Dictionary* as "failure of a property change by an external agent to return to its original value when the cause of the change has been removed."[38] According to this perspective, the appreciation of the dollar in the first half of the 1980s induced a variety of foreign firms to set up vast distribution, marketing, and R&D facilities in the United States, often referred to as beachheads.[39] Given the extensive

setup, or sunk, costs involved in these activities, when the dollar depreciated in the second half of the 1980s and early 1990s, foreign firms found it profitable to remain in their beachheads, lowering their profit margins but unwilling to abandon the U.S. market. A *New York Times* article at the time remarked: "The industries of countries that established big stakes in the American market appear unwilling to give them up. In the past they would raise their prices in line with the decline of the dollar, but no longer. Now they are willing to shave profits to remain competitive here."[40]

As a consequence, even though, by the late 1980s, the value of the dollar had returned to the levels prevailing in the early 1980s, imports had not declined proportionately. Hysteretic (not hysterical) behavior resulted. Evidence of hysteresis for the United States in the dollar cycle of the 1980s and for the 1979–1981 sterling exchange rate swing is supplied by economists Richard Baldwin and Charles Bean.[41]

Note that hysteresis occurs in the presence of large exchange rate shocks, which make the large investments in foreign distribution and marketing profitable during the entry phase. Small, short-term exchange rate changes are unlikely to generate the major entry-exit decisions that are involved in this phenomenon. This is particularly so in the environment of increased uncertainty in currency values since 1973. In order to make major entry and exit decisions in this environment, firms must be convinced that changes in exchange rates are not just temporary but will be sustained over the long run. As Krugman concludes: "the idea that market responses to exchange rates are limited

[37]R. Z. Lawrence, "U.S. Current Account Adjustment: An Appraisal," *Brookings Papers on Economic Activity* (1990), p. 347.

[38]See R. Baldwin, "Some Empirical Evidence on Hysteresis in Aggregate U.S. Import Prices," in S. Gerlach and P. Petri, eds., *The Economics of the Dollar Cycle* (Cambridge, Mass.: The MIT Press, 1990), p. 235.

[39]As developed by P. Krugman and R. Baldwin, "The Persistence of the U.S. Trade Deficit," *Brookings Papers on Economic Activity* (1987); R. Baldwin, "Hysteresis in Import Prices: The Beachhead Effect," *American Economic Review*

(September 1988); and A. Dixit, "Hysteresis, Import Penetration and Exchange Rate Pass-Through," *Quarterly Journal of Economics* (May 1989).

[40]*The New York Times,* July 14, 1986, as quoted by R. Baldwin, "Hysteresis in Trade," *Empirical Economics* (January 1990).

[41]C. Bean, "Sterling Misalignment and British Trade Performance," London School of Economics, Centre for Labor Economics, Discussion Paper no. 288 (July 1987); and Baldwin, cited in Footnotes 38 and 39.

by regressive expectations is helpful in understanding why the responses to exchange rates have been more limited in the 1980s than in the past."[42]

Summary

1. The introduction of exchange rate expectations into the analysis implies that interest rates do not always equalize internationally and that the equalization of net expected rates of return among domestic and foreign assets means that domestic interest rates have to equal foreign interest rates plus the expected rate of depreciation of domestic currency.

2. Dynamic adjustments in the open economy are shaped by two basic conditions: (a) organized asset markets clear relatively quickly, compared with the goods markets; and (b) any sudden excess demand for (or supply of) domestic goods tends to give rise to increases (or reductions) of domestic output, but only gradually over time. The implication is that the economy can remain out of equilibrium—that is, in disequilibrium—for extended periods of time, as long as the goods market adjusts sluggishly.

3. The full equilibrium of the economy is that equilibrium toward which the economy moves after all the disequilibrium adjustments connected to sluggish output response are over. It corresponds to the equilibrium established within the Mundell-Fleming framework studied in Chapter 13. In the absence of disturbances, full equilibrium does not entail anticipated changes in exchange rates and other economic variables.

4. The recent experience of most industrial countries with flexible exchange rates has been characterized by frequent and drastic exchange rate movements. These movements can be explained within the framework developed in this chapter. For instance, an unexpected shock to the economy in the form of an unanticipated money supply increase will be associated with an overshooting of the exchange rate. This means that the short-run response of the exchange rate exceeds the change that would occur if the economy's full equilibrium were attained immediately. This choppy, short-run adjustment is caused by the fact that, with output and income fixed in the short run, a money supply increase must be associated with a reduction of domestic interest rates in order to maintain money market equilibrium. Given world interest rates, however, the only means by which domestic interest rates can decline under perfect capital mobility is if an expected appreciation of the domestic currency arises. Such an expectation implies that the exchange rate must immediately rise above its anticipated longer-run value.

5. The case of the dollar in the 1980s and 1990s serves well to illustrate some of the basic issues relating to exchange rate dynamics. The dollar appreciated sharply in the first half of the 1980s and then depreciated equally sharply in the second half of the decade; it has remained in a narrower range of fluctuation since 1987. The appreciation of the dollar in the initial period of this dollar cycle could be attached to an overshooting effect related to the sudden introduction of a contractionary monetary policy regime in the Federal Reserve. This does not explain, however, the persistence of the dollar appreciation, which lasted from 1980 through February 1985. The latter could be accounted for by the unexpectedly staunch pursuit of monetary tightness on the part of the Federal Reserve. It could also be the result of the expansionary fiscal policy followed by the Reagan administration.

6. An alternative view for the failure of the dollar to depreciate to any significant extent in 1984 and early 1985 involves the presence of speculative effects embodied in a so-called

[42]P. Krugman, *Exchange Rate Instability* (Cambridge, Mass.: The MIT Press, 1989), p. 47. See also, L. S. Goldberg, "Exchange Rates and Entry, Exit and Investment in U.S. Industry," Working Paper, New York University Starr Center for Applied Economics (January 1991).

exchange rate bubble. A bubble involves a situation in which a given economic variable progressively or cumulatively deviates from the path consistent with its fundamental, long-run value. Bubbles can be explained by the presence of extraneous beliefs or misperceptions in the foreign exchange market, lack of information and general uncertainty regarding future exchange rate values, and/or a growing presence of chartists, as opposed to fundamentalists, in the foreign exchange market.

7. The dollar depreciated sharply after February 1985. This depreciation responded to shifting monetary and fiscal policies. Some authors have also assigned an important role to official intervention in foreign exchange markets.

8. Although the first Reagan administration constrained its foreign exchange market operations, the second Reagan administration jointly plunged into official intervention with other industrialized nations. In September 1985, the Plaza Agreement formalized coordinated intervention by a group of five industrialized nations (the G–5)—a group that eventually included seven (the G–7).

9. Central bank intervention can be of two types: sterilized and nonsterilized. Sterilized intervention occurs when the central bank buys or sells foreign exchange reserves but does not allow these changes in reserves to affect the domestic money supply. Nonsterilized intervention, on the other hand, means that the central bank allows its purchases and sales of foreign exchange to alter the domestic money supply. In general, nonsterilized intervention tends to be more effective than sterilized intervention in influencing exchange rates because it is associated with changes in the domestic money supply. Even then, sterilized intervention can affect exchange rates if it influences agent expectations by signaling the course of future monetary policies.

10. Anticipated disturbances, such as an expected money-supply expansion, can have immediate, real consequences. In this chapter, the mecha-

nism through which expectations affect the economy is by altering exchange rate expectations and, therefore, interest rates (through the uncovered interest parity condition).

11. Central bank intervention in foreign exchange markets can, in principle, be called for in situations where exchange rates tend to diverge considerably from fundamentals. In practice, however, it is difficult to discern the sources of sudden changes in exchange rates, making central bank intervention more difficult to justify.

12. Although the U.S. trade deficit worsened rapidly in response to the dollar appreciation of the early 1980s, the deficit did not improve quickly when the dollar depreciated beginning in early 1985. Only during 1988 was there a sustained improvement in the trade balance. This behavior can be interpreted as the result of a J-curve effect, sectoral trends, and measurement problems unrelated to the value of the dollar, or because of hysteresis.

13. Hysteresis represents the failure of U.S. imports to decline as a result of the dollar depreciation back to values prevailing in the early 1980s. Hysteresis may be associated with the massive sunk costs invested by foreign firms in the first half of the 1980s. These firms set up a vast distribution, marketing, and R&D network to sell in America based on the appreciation of the dollar. When the dollar depreciated, the firms found it unprofitable to exit the market, reducing their profit margins instead. As a consequence, U.S. imports did not decline in proportion to the dollar depreciation.

Problems

1. You are examining a country whose economic relationships are confined to trading with the United States exclusively. The country's currency is the peso, which freely floats against the U.S. dollar. Suppose that the country's real money demand has been estimated to be

$$L = 0.20\,Y - 3,000\,i,$$

where Y is income and i is the interest rate prevailing on three-month CDs in the economy's financial markets. The country faces perfect capital mobility and is initially in equilibrium, with its interest rate equal to the fixed 10 percent U.S. interest rate ($i* = 0.10$). The money supply is equal to 300 billion pesos and the price of the country's products is, on average, $P = 1$ peso. Suppose that the country's central bank unexpectedly reduces the money supply by 20 billion pesos. Assuming that the country's income is fixed over the short run and that investors form rational expectations, would the monetary contraction increase or decrease the peso's exchange rate against the dollar? What would be the change in the country's interest rate? Would investors anticipate further changes in the value of the peso? If the answer is positive, determine the numerical value of the anticipated rate of change of the currency over the next three months.

2. In the text, we saw how the exchange rate overshoots its long-run equilibrium value in response to an unanticipated money-supply expansion. This result was derived, however, under the assumption of perfect capital mobility. Assume instead that the economy does not trade in assets with the rest of the world, so that it faces zero capital mobility. Will overshooting still occur? What happens as the degree of capital mobility increases?

3. Estimates are that Europe's major central banks lost between $4 billion to $6 billion from their intervention in foreign exchange markets in September 1992 during their attempt to avoid realignments within the ERM. What do these losses imply about the effectiveness of exchange market intervention and the nature of the forces altering exchange rates in Europe at the time?

4. Assume that the expectations investors form about the exchange rate are described by

$$x = 0.50 \left(\frac{\bar{e} - e}{e} \right),$$

with all symbols as described in the text. The U.S. three-month interest rate is 15 percent, while the comparable U.K. interest rate is 10 percent. If the current exchange rate between the dollar and the pound is $2.00/£, what would be the implied full-equilibrium exchange rate, on the assumption that there are no anticipated economic disturbances in the foreseeable future? What would be the ninety-day dollar–pound forward exchange rate? Assuming perfect foresight, what would be the exchange rate three months from now, and what would be the numerical value of the forward rate at that time? (You can assume that uncovered interest parity holds in this question.)

5. During the first half of 1993, the value of the yen rose to post-World War II record highs against the dollar. Some American economists welcomed this adjustment since, they argued, Japan's trade success vis-à-vis the U.S. in recent years had been due partly to keeping the yen undervalued. Do you agree with this statement? How do you go about measuring whether the yen is undervalued against the dollar?

6. According to economic historian Anna J. Schwartz, "Sterilized intervention has only temporary effects on exchange rates." See "The Fed's Costly Trips to the Market," *The Wall Street Journal*, October 6, 1989. Do you agree or disagree with this statement? Explain your answer.

7. During the latter part of 1990 and the early months of 1991, the money-supply growth in Japan slowed to a record-low pace, dropping from more than 13 percent in 1990 to 4.9 percent in March 1991. Assuming that this change in monetary policy was unanticipated, what would the overshooting model predict for the value of the yen-dollar exchange rate? Explain your answer and test whether, during this episode, the overshooting hypothesis held, by looking at the behavior of the yen-dollar exchange rate in 1990 and 1991.

PART V

Inflation, Unemployment, and Economic Policy in the Open Economy

CHAPTER 16

Production, Prices, and Unemployment in the Open Economy

Throughout Part IV, we examined how domestic output, interest rates, the money supply, and other important economic variables are determined in open economies. The determination of domestic prices, however, has not been on our agenda up to this point. It is the purpose of Chapters 16 and 17 to study how the domestic price level is determined in an open economy and to inquire about how various economic policies affect it. Our everyday experience reminds us, in an often uncomfortable way, that the general price level is indeed rising over time. Figure 16–1 illustrates this tendency by plotting the behavior of the U.S. consumer price index (CPI). The generally rising trend of the price level can be detected, as well as the significant price deflation in the 1930s. What causes prices to change, and how is output altered by such changes? In order to answer these questions, we have to modify in a significant way the analytical framework developed in earlier chapters.

We have so far carried out the analysis on the basis of the simple Keynesian assumptions that the

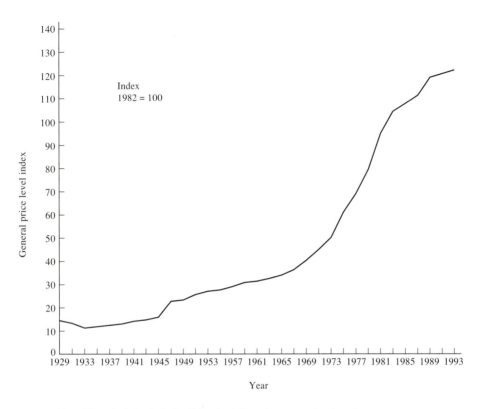

Note: The price index is the implicit price deflator for gross national product.

FIGURE 16–1.   Prices in the United States in the Twentieth Century.

SOURCE: Council of Economic Advisors. *The Economic Report of the President* (Washington, D.C.: U.S. Government Printing Office, January 1993).

prices of domestic goods are fixed and that the firms producing those goods supply all the output that is demanded of them at the given prices. In general, however, prices do change over time (i.e., inflation and deflation occur), and firms often find that they cannot supply all the output demanded of them without running into full-employment and capacity constraints. To take account of these situations, one has to modify the simple Keynesian framework, whereby changes in output are brought about solely by changes in aggregate demand, without any consequent effects on prices.

The following chapters show how both prices and output are determined by the interaction of aggregate demand for and aggregate supply of domestic goods, in much the same way that price and output of a given commodity are determined by its demand and supply. Chapter 16 focuses on output and price determination under fixed exchange rates; Chapter 17 extends the discussion to flexible exchange rate regimes; Chapter 18 then broadens the discussion by considering the role of expectations in macroeconomic equilibrium and by examining how international variables influence business cycles.

In Chapter 16 first we shall derive in detail the concepts of aggregate demand and aggregate supply within the context of an open economy, and then we shall show how their interaction determines the dynamic behavior of output and prices. This approach will involve analyzing the short-run and long-run equilibria of the economy as well as the process of adjustment of prices and output over time. Then the effects of fiscal, monetary, and exchange rate policies are reexamined, including their short-range and long-range impacts.

Let us start by considering an economy that faces no international capital movements and then move on to discuss capital mobility.

16–1 AGGREGATE DEMAND IN AN OPEN ECONOMY UNDER FIXED EXCHANGE RATES

The *aggregate demand* curve depicted in Figure 16–2(b) represents the economy's desired spending as a function of the price level. That is, it represents a relationship between the *aggregate quantity demanded* of domestic goods and the *price level* of domestic goods, at given levels of the domestic money supply, the exchange rate, and fiscal parameters such as the level of government spending and tax rates. It must be stressed that, in contrast to our analysis in previous chapters, in the

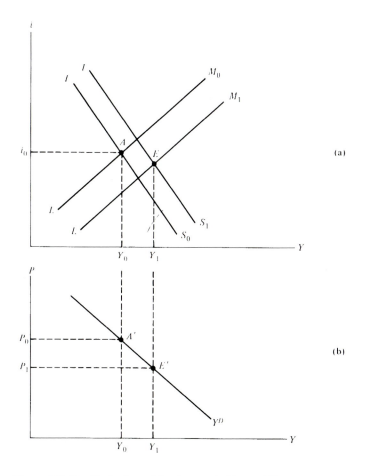

FIGURE 16–2. Derivation of the Aggregate Demand Curve

present framework aggregate demand does not completely determine the level of output of domestic goods. The equilibrium level of output is established by the interaction of the aggregate demand and aggregate supply functions and not solely by aggregate demand. Aggregate demand simply establishes a relationship specifying the quantity demanded of domestic goods at different prices. Which of these combinations of price and quantity demanded is actually chosen as the economy's price and equilibrium output will depend on the aggregate supply function, which shows the relationship between price and quantity supplied of domestic goods. As discussed subsequently, the equilibrium level of output and the price of domestic goods will be determined by the equality of quantity demanded and quantity supplied of domestic goods—that is, by the point at which the aggregate demand and aggregate supply curves intersect in Figure 16–5 (see p. 471). In this section, we are concerned exclusively with deriving the aggregate demand curve; in later sections, we will derive aggregate supply and then join the two to determine equilibrium prices and output in the economy.

In chapters 13 through 15, we addressed the problem of determining the equilibrium level of aggregate demand in the economy on the assumption that the prices of domestic goods were fixed. We proceed now to examine how this equilibrium level of aggregate demand changes when the prices of domestic goods are varied. This will provide us with a relationship between the quantity demanded of domestic goods and their prices, which is what the aggregate demand function represents.

To summarize our earlier work on the determination of the equilibrium level of aggregate demand, let us restate our two basic equilibrium relationships. First, the money market equilibrium condition equates real money supply with real money demand. Algebraically,

$$\frac{M_0}{P_0} = kY - hi, \qquad (16\text{--}1)$$

where real money demand is positively related to income, Y, and negatively related to the interest rate, i; and the real money supply is M_0/P_0, with P_0 the price of domestic goods and M_0 the level of money supply at any given moment. The level of the money supply can change over time if the central bank engages in monetary policy and/or depending on the economy's balance-of-payments situation. For the purposes of deriving the aggregate demand function, however, the level of the money supply is assumed fixed—a context referred to as the short run. We will later examine how changes in the money supply affect aggregate demand.

The money market equilibrium condition determines the LM curve—that is, the combinations of the interest rate and income that keep the money market in equilibrium, given the money supply, M_0, and the price level, P_0. A particular case is represented by the LM_0 curve in Figure 16–2(a).

Desired spending on domestic goods, Y, can be represented by

$$Y = A + T$$
$$= \bar{A} + \bar{T} + \phi q + (a - m)Y - bi. \qquad (16\text{--}2)$$

Simplifying, we obtain

$$Y = \alpha\left[\bar{A} - bi + \bar{T} + \phi\frac{eP^*}{P}\right], \quad (16\text{--}2a)$$

where $\alpha = 1/(s + m)$ and all symbols remain as defined in earlier chapters. (For further details, see Equations 14–10 and 14–11.) If the price of domestic goods is fixed at P_0, Equation 16–2(a) yields a negative relationship between desired spending and interest rates, given fixed fiscal policy parameters, the exchange rate, e, and the price of foreign goods, P^*. This is the basis of the IS curve represented in Figure 16–2(a) by IS_0.

The short-run level of aggregate demand (desired real spending) in the economy is Y_0, determined by the intersection of the IS_0 and LM_0 curves in Figure 16–2(a). This equilibrium point is established on the basis of a given level of the money supply, M_0 (so that it represents a given short-run equilibrium), a fixed level of government spending, and a *given price of domestic goods, P_0*.

What happens when we vary the price of domestic goods, *P?* Suppose that we decrease *P* from P_0 to P_1. What are the consequences for aggregate demand? Two effects exist. First, there is a *real money balances* effect: As the price of domestic goods decreases, real money balances increase (from M_0/P_0 to M_0/P_1). As a consequence, domestic interest rates decline and investment and aggregate demand increase. This effect is analogous to the effect of an exogenous increase in the *nominal* money supply (an increase in *M*) because both tend to increase *real* money balances. In geometric terms, a decrease in the price of domestic goods would be represented by a rightward shift of the *LM* curve: At any given level of the interest rate, aggregate real income and spending would have to increase to eliminate the excess supply of real balances arising from the decline in *P*. In terms of Figure 16–2(a), the *LM* curve would shift from LM_0 to LM_1, tending to raise desired spending.

The second effect of a reduction in the price of domestic goods, *P,* is the *foreign trade effect:* A decrease in the price of domestic goods tends to switch demand out of foreign and toward domestic goods, raising aggregate desired spending on domestic goods.[1] This effect is analogous to that of a devaluation on aggregate demand in the sense that it operates by affecting the relative price of foreign goods in terms of domestic goods, $q \equiv eP^*/P$. A devaluation, at fixed prices of foreign and domestic goods, would tend to raise *q*. A decrease in the price of domestic goods, at a fixed exchange rate and fixed prices of foreign goods, would raise *q,*

tending to improve the trade balance through the term ϕq. Geometrically, the positive effect of a reduction in *P* on the aggregate demand for domestic goods is reflected by an upward shift of the *IS* curve: At a given level of the interest rate, the decrease in *P* shifts demand toward domestic goods and tends to raise desired spending and real income. In Figure 16–2(a), this is depicted by the upward shift of the *IS* curve from IS_0 to IS_1.

Both the real money balances and the foreign trade effects imply that decreases in the price of domestic goods generate increases in the short-run quantity demanded of domestic goods; this suggests that the aggregate demand function has a negative slope: As the price of domestic goods decreases, desired spending increases. This is shown in Figure 16–2. At the initial price level, P_0, the IS_0 and LM_0 curves determine the initial level of quantity demanded of domestic goods at Y_0. When the price level decreases to P_1, with everything else constant (given the money supply and given fixed fiscal parameters), the *IS* curve shifts upward from IS_0 to IS_1 and the *LM* curve shifts rightward from LM_0 to LM_1. The new short-run quantity demanded would then be determined by the intersection of the IS_1 and LM_1 curves— point *E*— at an income level of Y_1, which is larger than Y_0. This relationship is illustrated in Figure 16–2(b) by the curve Y^D, which simply plots the pairs of price and aggregate quantity demanded of domestic goods corresponding to points *A* and *E* in Figure 16–2(a). The curve Y^D is the aggregate demand curve for domestic goods.

The aggregate demand curve is derived on the basis of a given level of the money supply, the exchange rate, and fiscal policy parameters. Changes in any of these will tend to shift the aggregate demand curve. Suppose, for instance, that the domestic nominal money supply increases (with fiscal parameters still fixed). This increase can arise mainly from two sources: through an open-market purchase of bonds by the central bank or through a balance of payments surplus in the economy. The rise in the nominal money supply, say from M_0 to M_1, increases real money

---

[1]This assumes that the Marshall-Lerner condition is satisfied (the parameter $\phi > 0$). Just as devaluation could worsen the trade balance and reduce the aggregate demand for domestic goods, a decrease in the price of domestic goods could also have the same consequences. Refer to the economic intuition of this result derived in chaps. 13 and 14.

balances, at a given level of the price of domestic goods. As domestic interest rates decline, investment and aggregate demand for domestic goods increase, at a given price level, P_0. This is represented in Figure 16–3 by the movement from point A to point B. The implication is that the aggregate demand curve, Y^D, would shift to the right, from Y^D_0 to Y^D_1. If the money supply decreases, exactly the opposite occurs. When real balances decline, the aggregate demand for domestic goods decreases, at any given price level. In other words, the aggregate demand curve shifts to the left.

Changes in the exchange rate also tend to shift the aggregate demand schedule. A devaluation switches demand toward domestic goods, at any given level of domestic prices, thus shifting the aggregate demand curve to the right. Similarly, a revaluation, a decrease in the exchange rate, shifts the Y^D curve to the left. Finally, expansionary fiscal policy (say an increase in government spending) has a positive multiplier effect on the aggregate demand for domestic goods, at any given level of prices, shifting the aggregate demand curve to the right.

The effects of fiscal, monetary, and exchange rate changes on aggregate demand can be visualized more clearly by determining the algebraic expression for the aggregate demand curve. Solving for the interest rate in Equation 16–1 and substituting the result into Equation 16–2 yields

$$Y_0 = \tilde{\alpha}\left[\bar{A} + \bar{T} + \phi\frac{eP^*}{P_0}\right] + \tilde{\alpha}\gamma\frac{M_0}{P_0}, \quad (16\text{–}3)$$

where

$$\tilde{\alpha} = \frac{1}{s + m + \gamma k}$$

is the Keynesian fiscal multiplier, and $\gamma = b/h$ depends on investment and money demand parameters determining the effects of the real money supply on aggregate demand. For given levels of autonomous spending and the nominal money supply, Equation 16–3 shows that a reduction of domestic prices from P_0 to P_1 raises desired spending on domestic goods, Y, by raising real

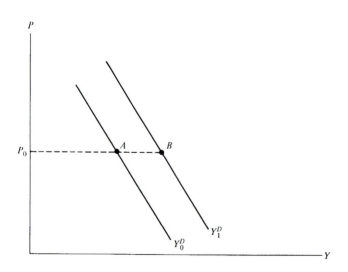

Figure 16–3. Shifts of Aggregate Demand

balances, M_0/P, and improving the trade balance through the term $\phi e P^*/P$. This is precisely what the aggregate demand curve, Y_0^D shows. In addition, by changing $A, M_0, \bar{T}$, and e in Equation 16–3, we can determine the effects of fiscal policy, money supply changes, exogenous foreign trade disturbances, and exchange rate changes on the aggregate demand curve in Figure 16–3. The rule to remember is that any exogenous factor increasing (or decreasing) the demand for domestic goods will cause the demand curve to shift to the right (or left) at any given level of prices.

16–2. EMPLOYMENT, CONTRACTS, AND THE THEORY OF AGGREGATE SUPPLY

The aggregate demand curve derived in Section 16–1 specifies combinations of desired spending and prices of domestic goods. Which of these combinations actually prevails in the economy depends on aggregate supply. The aggregate supply function represents a relationship between the aggregate quantity supplied of domestic goods and the price of domestic goods. The interaction of aggregate supply and aggregate demand then determines the equilibrium level of output (real income) and prices in the economy.

Our analysis of aggregate supply in previous chapters was limited to stating the assumption that domestic firms be capable of supplying the output demanded of them at fixed prices. In that situation, domestic output is determined by aggregate demand. For that reason, our emphasis was on the determinants of aggregate demand and on the possible effects of government policies on output and employment. This framework, a simple version of Keynes's paradigm, was widely used by macroeconomists in the post-World War II era but has been widely criticized in recent years. First, the assumption of fixed prices does not seem to hold in any modern industrial nation. In the case of the United States, the behavior of the price level in the nineteenth and early twentieth centuries exhib-

ited both extended periods of generally falling prices and sustained inflation. Recent experience, on the other hand, has been one of continuous—although variable—rises in prices. These price changes have sometimes been quite drastic, as in the period between 1973 and 1975 when the CPI increased by more than 36 percent, or almost 10 percent per year. Second, it is clear that firms cannot supply unlimited amounts of output; they will run into full-capacity constraints at some point. However, when such constraints are faced, increases in aggregate demand will not necessarily raise output; they may, rather, generate shortages and, as a consequence, rising prices. Any economy operating at close to its potential level of output cannot be expected to adjust supply without having some effect on prices.

In conclusion, the main problem with the analysis in previous chapters is that it can fully apply only to an economic environment in which price stability and conditions of high unemployment prevail—a situation that has existed only for short periods of time in the recent experience of most industrial economies. In the case of the United States, for example, high unemployment and relatively stable prices have coexisted only between 1938 and 1940 and 1970 and 1971. Periods of high unemployment have usually been associated with declining prices (deflation), as was the case during most of the Great Depression (when prices fell drastically), or with reduced inflation, as was the case during the 1982 recession, when U.S. inflation (as measured by the CPI) tumbled to about 6.1 percent—down from 13.5 and 10.4 percent in 1980 and 1981, respectively. Periods of moderate (or rising) unemployment and stagnation, however, have sometimes been associated with rising prices, a phenomenon that has been called *stagflation.*

This section initiates the study of the factors affecting the supply of goods in an open economy. Production in any economy requires the employment of some factors of production (e.g., capital and labor) that are combined by means of a certain

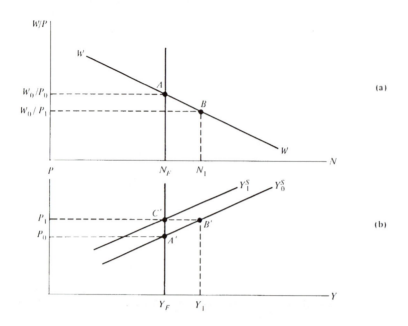

FIGURE 16-4. Derivation of the Aggregate Supply Curve

technology, such as an assembly line. Often, however, the blueprints of technology tend to be given over extended periods of time and the capital available to firms is more or less fixed. As a result, the economy can alter its output supply mostly through changes in labor employment.[2] Our task, then, is to show how employment (and thus output) changes when the price of domestic goods varies.

Employment Contracts and the Labor Market

Employment in a market economy is determined by the interaction of firms demanding the services of workers and households supplying those services through participation in the labor force. Figure 16–4(a) illustrates an economy's aggregate

[2]In general, firms can also alter production through a more intensive use of capital. In order to concentrate on unemployment changes, this factor will be bypassed.

labor market equilibrium. The vertical axis represents real wage rates, W/P, where W denotes nominal wage rates, and the horizonal axis represents employment, N. The downward-sloping WW locus depicts the demand for labor by firms in the economy. It represents the fact that a decrease in real wage rates reduces unit costs of production, increases profitability, and, therefore, induces firms to increase employment. Firms can raise employment along WW by hiring additional workers or by using their labor force more intensively through increased hours of work (overtime). All points along WW represent possible points of employment in the economy. Which of these points is actually prevalent in a given time period depends on the real wage rate employers face. The latter depends on the conditions, or terms, at which individuals are willing to supply their labor. Employment contracts explicitly or implicitly specify the conditions at which individuals are hired. These stipulate the nominal wage rates to be paid and the duration of the contract (two or three years). The hours of work the individual will be required to engage in, however, are not usually rigidly specified. These are frequently changed by firms on the basis of the fluctuations in demand they face, requiring extra hours under periods of high production and laying off workers when production is slack.[3]

The determination of the nominal wage rate at which contracts are settled is affected by a wide array of factors, including employer-employee bargaining and the search of employers and employees for alternative candidates and job opportunities, respectively. Suppose that all firms and individuals are bargaining over new employment contracts in an unregulated market in which no side enjoys monopoly power. The resulting equilibrium real wage rate would be determined at W_0/P_0 in Figure 16–4(a). This is the rate clearing the labor market, representing equality of the existing labor demand and supply. Consequently, at the wage rate W_0/P_0, employment would be equal to N_F, denoting full employment. That the labor market's equilibrium would be at full employment is easily visualized by noting that, if contracts were settled at wage rates above W_0/P_0, labor demand would be lower and as a result some workers would not find employment. In other words, there would be an excess supply of labor. The unemployed workers would then bid down

wages by offering to accept contracts with lower wage rates than those being offered to other workers. This labor market competition, involving thorough search and negotiation, would then move the labor market toward N_F and W_0/P_0. Similarly, low-wage contracts for which employment is above N_F imply some workers would have to labor more than the amount they desire to at those lower wages. Since they would not voluntarily accept such contracts, firms would have to bid up their wage offers. Again, the labor market would move to equilibrium at point A, which represents a fully employed economy.[4]

Prices, Employment, and the Aggregate Supply Curve

What happens to employment when the domestic price level increases? Suppose, for example, that the economy is initially at point A and that there is a sudden increase in the domestic price level. On the assumption that an important part of the economy's labor force is covered by existing contracts that fix nominal wage rates, real wages would decline. Symbolically, if the price level increases from P_0 to P_1, and the nominal wage rate is fixed at W_0 because of previously engaged labor

---

[3]The study of labor contracts in this context was pioneered by Costas Azariadis in his article, "Implicit Contracts and Underemployment Equilibria," *Journal of Political Economy* (December 1975) and has also been associated with the names of Martin N. Baily, Herschel Grossman, and Edmund S. Phelps, among many others. Labor contracts often specify extra compensation for overtime. This, however, does not basically alter the text's argument, since the employee will still be required to work extra hours at the predetermined overtime rate in periods of high demand. We should finally stress that the type of employment contract considered in this chapter—involving nominal wage rigidity in the short run—is part of an array of possible employment arrangements. Chapters 17 and 18 will undertake a fuller discussion of this topic, see also O. J. Blanchard, "Wage Bargaining and Unemployment Persistence," *Journal of Money, Credit and Banking* (August 1991).

[4]It should be stressed that full employment as defined here may be associated with some workers reported unemployed. Even if the aggregate labor market in the economy clears, with overall labor demand equal to supply, some unemployed workers can still exist. There are clearly some firms and sectors in the economy that are at any given time contracting while others expand. The labor released by the declining industries may take time to be absorbed by the expanding ones; thus, even though aggregate demand and supply for labor are equal, some unemployment would still arise. Because of its nature, this type of unemployment has been called *frictional* or *structural unemployment*. Given our present interest in analyzing how changes in the *aggregate* quantity demanded of labor generate unemployment (referred to as *cyclical unemployment*), we shall ignore structural unemployment. For informative purposes, some economists have calculated the frictional or structural component of unemployment (often referred to as the natural rate of unemployment) to have been between 4 and 5 percent during the 1960s and higher since the mid-1970s.

contracts, then real wages would decline from W_0/P_0 to W_0/P_1.[5] In this situation, employers will find it profitable to overemploy workers—that is, to employ workers above their full employment (by requiring extra hours of work or by delaying planned layoffs). In terms of Figure 16–4(a), employment, N_1, would move above full employment, N_F. Consequently, over the short run, increases in domestic prices will be associated with increases in employment. Over time, however, labor contracts will come up for renegotiation, and workers will try to regain their lost real wages by raising their nominal wage quotes and requesting upward adjustment of their wage rates. This means that, over the long run, labor market equilibrium would be restored to point A in Figure 16–4(a).

The rise of employment induced by an increase in the price of domestic goods is the consequence of the nominal wage rigidities in the economy over the short run. If nominal wage rates were fully flexible, the labor market would clear at its full-employment level. Given the labor market rigidities existing in most economies, however, this full-employment equilibrium of the labor market may not be attainable within a short-run time horizon.

In summary, as the price of domestic goods increases, employment will also tend to rise over the short run. The result is an increase in output. This positive relationship between changes in prices and quantity supplied of domestic goods in the short run is the *short-run aggregate supply curve of domestic goods*. It is represented in Figure 16–4(b) by means of the upward-sloping Y_0^S curve. As prices rise from P_0 to P_1, employment increases from N_F to N_1 in Figure 16–4(a), corresponding to an increase in output from Y_F to Y_1.

From the initial price-quantity supplied combination at point A', the economy thus moves to point B'. This movement corresponds to the switch from point A to point B in the labor market diagram in Figure 16–4(a).

The increase in output above full employment implied by the rise in prices, however, cannot persist. As noted earlier, the overemployment associated with the output expansion is the result of a reduction in real wages. Diagrammatically, at point B in Figure 16–4(a), workers face a lower real wage than at full employment at point A. As a consequence, when their employment contracts expire, they will demand higher nominal wage rates. As nominal wage rates increase, the real wage moves upward from W_0/P_1 back toward its original level. As this happens, firms will reduce employment and production back toward the initial (full-employment) level. This phenomenon is represented in Figure 16–4(b) by the leftward shift of the short-run aggregate supply curve from Y_0^S to Y_1^S. That is, at the price level P_1, the rise in wages forces firms to reduce their aggregate quantity supplied. This event brings about a leftward shift of the short-run aggregate supply curve.

Over the long run, production must return to its full-employment level because employment must return to N_F, the point at which the labor market is at long-run equilibrium. This suggests that the *long-run aggregate supply curve* is a vertical line lying, as drawn in Figure 16–4(b), at the full-employment level of output, Y_F. The long-run quantity supplied of domestic goods is, thus, unresponsive to changes in the price of domestic goods. Only over the short run will price changes have an effect on the aggregate quantity supplied in the economy; the output constraints imposed by the economy's limited labor force and other resources will surface over the long run.[6] Notice

---

[5]This assumes that workers do not expect the increase in prices from P_0 to P_1. Otherwise, they would make sure to bargain for cost-of-living increases. In the latter case, the price hike would be matched by an indexed increase in wage rates and the labor market equilibrium would not be disturbed away from full employment. This chapter does not include situations in which price increases are anticipated; that is a topic requiring separate, more detailed treatment. Chapter 18 examines the role of inflationary expectations.

[6]See the appendix to this chapter for the derivation of an explicit, algebraic expression of the aggregate supply curve. For a sophisticated exposition of aggregate supply within the aggregate supply–demand framework developed in this chapter, see M. Schmid, "Devaluation: Keynesian Trade Models

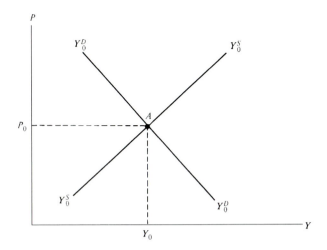

FIGURE 16–5.   The Economy's Short-Run Equilibrium

that, just as a rise in prices can generate short-run increases in output, a decrease in prices of domestic goods will result in a short-run decline in employment and output that is eliminated over the long run.

The aggregate supply curve, whether in the short or long run, specifies some combinations of aggregate quantity supplied and price of domestic goods. Which of these combinations is actually chosen as the equilibrium level of output and price in the economy is determined by the interaction of aggregate supply with aggregate demand, as will be shown in the next section.

16–3. The Short-Run Equilibrium of the Economy

We now proceed to integrate our analyses of aggregate demand and aggregate supply into an analysis of overall equilibrium in the open econ-

and the Monetary Approach," *European Economic Review* (January 1982); and J. Aizenman and J. A. Frenkel, "Wage Indexation, Supply Shocks, and Monetary Policy in a Small, Open Economy," in S. Edwards and L. Ahamed, eds., *Economic Adjustment and Exchange Rates in Developing Countries* (Chicago: University of Chicago Press, 1986).

omy. We start by circumscribing our attention first to a short time horizon. Over this *short run,* monetary parameters (mainly the domestic money supply), fiscal parameters (mainly government spending and taxation), and the exchange rate are all assumed to be given. This determines a particular aggregate demand curve, represented in Figure 16–5 by the $Y_0^D Y_0^D$ curve. In addition, over the short run, nominal wage rates are rigid because of binding employment contracts previously engaged in. This nominal wage rigidity determines a given short-run aggregate supply curve, shown by means of $Y_0^S Y_0^S$ in Figure 16–5.

The economy will be in *short-run equilibrium* when the quantity demanded of domestic goods equals the quantity supplied of domestic goods in the short run. This occurs at the point at which the aggregate demand curve intersects the short-run aggregate supply curve. There is then a simultaneous short-run equilibrium in the goods, money, and labor markets. The goods and money markets are in short-run equilibrium in the sense that they clear, given the money supply and other fiscal and exchange rate parameters. The labor market is also in short-run (or quasi-) equilibrium, in the sense that the quantity of workers employed is determined by the demand for labor, at the *given rigid nominal* wage rate in the short run.

Short-run equilibrium in the economy occurs at point *A* in Figure 16–5, where aggregate supply and aggregate demand intersect. The short-run equilibrium output of domestic goods is therefore Y_0 and the equilibrium level of the price of domestic goods is P_0. Policy disturbances—such as fiscal, monetary, and exchange rate changes—will alter the economy's short-run equilibrium by affecting the aggregate demand curve.

16–4. THE BALANCE OF PAYMENTS AND LONG-RUN EQUILIBRIUM

The short-run equilibrium of the economy represented by point *A* in Figure 16–5 is based on a given level of the money supply and a fixed nominal wage rate. It is clear, however, that the domestic stock of money will change over time in response to the country's balance-of-payments situation. In addition, nominal wages will be adjusting in response to the deviations of employment from its full-employment level and the consequent revision of employment contracts over time. Only when the economy is in balance-of-payments equilibrium will there be no change in the money supply, assuming that the central bank does not alter domestic credit and nominal wage rates will only stop adjusting at full employment. When the economy attains balance-of-payments equilibrium and full employment, given fixed policy parameters, it will be in *long-run equilibrium*. Long-run equilibrium exists, then, when the money market is in long-run equilibrium (when the money supply is not changing in response to the balance of payments) and when the labor market is at full-employment equilibrium (at which point, nominal wages stop changing in response to deviations from full employment). We will now characterize the long-run equilibrium of the economy and then describe the adjustment process involved in the movement from short-run to long-run equilibrium.

To carry out this analysis, however, we need to characterize the economy's balance of payments.

The balance of payments, *B*, is given by

$$B = T(q, Y) + K(i), \qquad (16-4)$$

where *T* represents the trade balance (which is a function of the relative price of domestic goods, *q*, and domestic real income, *Y*) and *K* the capital account (which depends on the domestic interest rate on the assumption that the foreign interest rate is fixed). For the sake of expository simplicity, we momentarily assume that the country faces no international capital movements. In that case, $K = 0$, and the balance of payments becomes the trade balance. Graphically, we illustrate the balance of payments by means of the trade balance equilibrium locus of the economy. This locus shows the combinations of real income, *Y*, and the price of domestic goods, *P*, which maintain a zero trade balance. Suppose that there is a reduction in the price of domestic goods. This will tend to improve the trade balance, as demand shifts from foreign to domestic goods. In order to maintain balanced trade, domestic real income would have to increase to raise imports and offset the improvement in the trade balance. This means that income and price are inversely related along the trade balance equilibrium locus. This is portrayed by the downward-sloping *TT* curve in Figure 16–6. Note that points above the *TT* curve depict points of trade deficit and points below it represent points of trade surplus. This is easy to visualize: Suppose that we are along *TT*. At any given level of *P*, if we increase real income, *Y*, this will raise imports causing the trade balance to go into deficit. Similarly, at a given *P*, a reduction in *Y* would decrease imports and create a trade surplus.

Figure 16–6 illustrates the long-run equilibrium of an open economy under capital immobility at point *E*, which corresponds to the intersection of the long-run aggregate supply curve (the vertical line at the full-employment level of output, Y_F) and the trade balance equilibrium curve *TT*. At

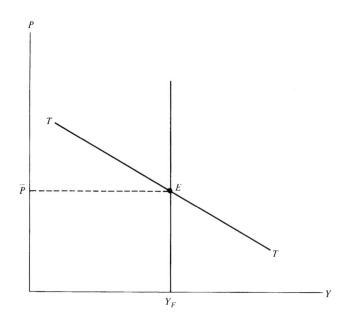

FIGURE 16–6. The Trade Balance Locus and Long-Run Equilibrium

point E, the economy is at full employment and balanced trade. The money, goods, and labor markets are all in long-run equilibrium.

16–5. THE MONETARY-PRICE ADJUSTMENT MECHANISM

How does the adjustment from the economy's current, or short-run, equilibrium to its long-run equilibrium occur? For example, suppose we have an economy facing a certain amount of unemployment and suffering from trade deficits. Starting from this point of short-run equilibrium, would there be any tendencies in the economy to move toward its long-run equilibrium (with full employment and external balance) without any need for policy intervention? The answer is yes. We represent the problem in Figure 16–7.

Point H in Figure 16–7 shows the short-run equilibrium of a given economy, as determined by the intersection of the short-run aggregate supply curve, $Y_0^S Y_0^S$, and the aggregate demand curve, $Y_0^D Y_0^D$. Short-run output is equal to Y_0, and the price of domestic goods is equal to P_0. Given that $Y_0 < Y_F$, the economy faces unemployment. Because point H lies above the TT curve, there is a trade balance deficit. What happens to the economy over time? Given that there is unemployment, nominal wages will decline, shifting the short-run aggregate supply curve to the right. In addition, the trade deficit implies that the central bank loses foreign exchange reserves; in the absence of sterilization, the money supply would shrink, shifting down the aggregate demand curve. As shown in Figure 16–7, even though these *price and monetary adjustments* may leave employment more or less unchanged (and may even increase unemployment) over short periods of time, both tend to reduce the price of domestic goods. This decrease in P tends to make domestic goods cheaper relative to foreign goods, stimulating net domestic

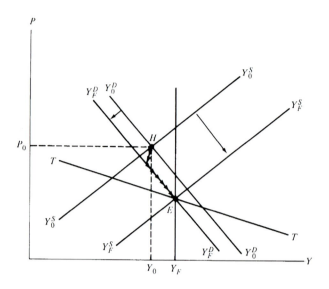

Figure 16–7.   The Monetary-Price Adjustment Mechanism

exports and improving the trade balance. In addition, in spite of the reduction in the price of domestic goods, real wages are generally declining, thus raising the profitability of production and eventually moving the economy toward full employment.

Over the long run (and if given enough time), the economy will move to point E. This is the result of monetary contractions associated with the balance-of-payments deficit at point H, which move the aggregate demand curve down from $Y_0^D Y_0^D$ to $Y_F^D Y_F^D$. It is also the result of reductions in nominal wages triggered by the unemployment associated with point H, which move the aggregate supply curve rightward from $Y_0^S Y_0^S$ to $Y_F^S Y_F^S$. At point E, there is full employment; the labor market is in long-run equilibrium with no incentive for nominal wages (and prices) to change. In addition, balanced trade has been achieved, with the money market in long-run equilibrium and no further changes in the domestic money supply. In conclusion, the unhampered functioning of the market economy leads to both internal and external bal-

ance over the long run. The big question, however, is how long it takes for the economy to adjust toward its long-run equilibrium. Given that the adjustment process just discussed involves a rather protracted recession, the problem arises as to whether the policymakers could speed it up by engaging in monetary, fiscal, and/or exchange rate policies. The answer to this question is explored in the next section.

16–6. Macroeconomic Adjustment Programs and Their Consequences

A broad array of situations can destabilize an economy, leading it to either balance-of-payments difficulties, recession, accelerated price increases (inflation), or to all them combined. This section examines the issue of macroeconomic adjustment to destabilization and the various alternative policy actions possible. We pay special attention to the adjustment policy alternatives open to developing countries and, in particular, those policy packages propounded by the IMF, whose aim is "the restoration and maintenance of viability to the balance of payments in an environment of price stability and sustainable rates of economic growth."[7] These are generally accepted goals of policy intervention in this context, and there is very little quarrel with them. The means by which they are to be attained, however, and the success of specific programs have bred deep disagreements. The IMF-supported adjustment programs followed by many developing countries in recent years, for example, are often perceived to rely heavily on the use of tools intended to correct balance-of-payments and inflation difficulties, with relatively little attention paid to their effects on output and employment. Also, it is clear that a wide array of policy strategies is possible, each with a different approach regarding the adjustment path the economy should follow. This section starts our examination of alternative adjustment programs and their effects.

Consider an economy whose initial condition is one of unemployment and balance-of-payments deficit, such as that represented by point H in Figure 16–8. A number of disturbances can bring an economy to that particular situation. An external shock in the form of increased raw material prices would raise the costs of imported inputs, inducing the aggregate supply curve to shift to the left, causing domestic prices to rise and output to fall.[8] Internal events in the economy may also

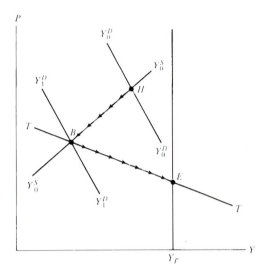

FIGURE 16–8. Simple Analytics of Macroeconomic Adjustment Programs

contribute to destabilization. Populist governments in Latin American countries, for example, are conspicuous in supporting (and maintaining) massive across-the-board wage hikes right after their takeovers.[9] These hikes shift the economy's aggregate supply leftward, increasing domestic prices, deteriorating the economy's international competitiveness, and worsening the trade balance. Whatever the background that leads the economy to a point like H in Figure 16–8, we can ask what adjustment policy alternatives can eliminate (or at least reduce) the economy's unemployment and balance-of-payments deficit and simultaneously

[7]M. Guitian, "Economic Management and International Monetary Fund Conditionality," in T. Killick, ed., *Adjustment and Financing in the Developing World: The Role of the International Monetary Fund* (Washington, D.C.: International Monetary Fund, 1982), p. 93.

[8]The role of external disturbances in destabilizing South American countries in the 1980s, and the macroeconomic policies followed in response, have been studied by V. Corbo and J. de Melo, "External Shocks and Policy Reforms in the Southern Cone," in G. Calvo et al., eds., *Debt, Stabilization and Development* (Oxford: Basil Blackwell, 1989). A similar analysis for some African countries is carried out by S. Devarajan and J. de Melo, "Adjustment with a Fixed Exchange Rate: Cameroon, Côte d'Ivoire, and Senegal," *The World Bank Economic Review* (May 1987).

[9]For a detailed description and an analysis of populist economic policies in Latin America and of adjustment policies in many of these countries, see E. Cardoso and A. Helwege, *Latin America's Economy: Diversity, Trends and Conflict* (Cambridge, Mass.: The MIT Press, 1992), chap. 8; R. Dornbusch and S. Edwards, *The Macroeconomics of Populism in Latin America* (Chicago: University of Chicago Press, 1991); and J. D. Sachs, "Social Conflict and Populist Policies in Latin America," National Bureau of Economic Research Working Paper no. 2897 (March 1989).

counteract upward pressures on domestic prices, reversing the economy's deteriorated competitiveness in world markets.

The laissez-faire adjustment process discussed in the last section is the most obvious alternative. Under this option, government authorities would dismantle any expansionary fiscal and monetary policies previously followed and would adopt a hands-off approach to the economy. The behavior of prices, output, and the balance of payments would then follow the time path we analyzed in Figure 16–7. With the central bank allowing its international reserves to decrease, the domestic money supply would contract and aggregate demand would shift down. With wages and prices free to vary, the aggregate supply curve would shift to the right over time. Eventually, equilibrium would be attained at point E, with balanced payments and full employment. Of course, when countries start at point H, facing dwindling foreign exchange reserves, the protracted payments deficit implied by this adjustment mechanism may be untenable. In these cases, a complementary government policy aimed at eliminating the balance-of-payments disequilibrium may lie in active contractionary monetary and fiscal policies. This shock-treatment approach to the economy's problems is represented in Figure 16–8 by the shift of the aggregate demand curve from $Y_0^D Y_0^D$ to $Y_1^D Y_1^D$. The aggregate demand contraction serves to attain the goal of external balance but leads to a short-run worsening of the recession. Only over time do recession and unemployment reduce real wages, stimulating the private sector and moving the economy toward full employment. A possible adjustment path is shown by the move from point H to point B and then to point E in Figure 16–8, highlighted by pointed arrows.

The shock-treatment type of macroeconomic program thus appears to be favorable in rapidly eliminating balance-of-payments deficits and in controlling inflation; however, it does not seem to have any positive short-run effects on output and employment and may actually intensify the economy's recession. Its social consequences are thus highly questionable and may not be acceptable to some governments. Of course, the whole question relies on how much unemployment may be created by the program over the short run, and by how much and how fast real wage rate reductions can drive a private sector's output expansion. The evidence available suggests that, over the short run, programs relying on sharp contractions of aggregate demand tend to increase unemployment and reduce output quite drastically. Using data from twenty-nine developing countries, IMF economists Mohsin S. Khan and Malcolm D. Knight have found that a program of contractionary monetary-fiscal policies intended to increase a country's level of foreign exchange reserves by 50 percent within a period of one year would lead to an average 5 percent increase in unemployment during that period, an increase that is, however, sharply reversed in the ensuing years. Less drastic plans instituting contractionary policies to improve the balance of payments more moderately over several years were also found to be recessionary, although less so than in the drastic program. They conclude: "Programs designed to achieve quick results on the balance of payments via sharp deflation are likely to have significant and undesirable effects on output, employment, and factor incomes, particularly in the short run."[10]

Is there an alternative adjustment program that would at least minimize the short-run output and employment effects on the economy? Our analysis in earlier chapters suggests that exchange rate changes can constitute an important part of a policy package intended to attain internal and external balance. What would be the effects of a devaluation in the present context?

Consider an economy that is originally at point H in Figure 16–9, at the intersection of the $Y_0^D Y_0^D$

---

[10]M. S. Khan and M. D. Knight, "Stabilization Programs in Developing Countries: A Formal Framework," *IMF Staff Papers* (March 1981), p. 43. This article provides a summary of the evidence on the issue and estimates the probable effects of various hypothetical policy measures.

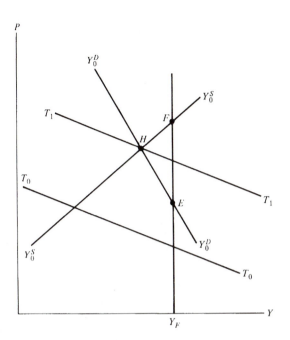

FIGURE 16–9. The Role of Devaluation in Macroeconomic Adjustment Programs

and $Y_0^S Y_0^S$ curves. The trade balance locus is given initially by $T_0 T_0$, implying that point H is a point of short-run balance-of-payments deficit. The impact effect of a devaluation is to switch demand toward domestic goods, shifting the aggregate demand curve upward and to the right. This would immediately tend to ignite increases in prices. In order to avoid such price hikes—in order to control inflation—the economy would have to follow contractionary policies to maintain the aggregate demand curve more or less unchanged. We assume that these policies are combined with the devaluation so that, in terms of Figure 16–9, the aggregate demand curve remains unchanged at $Y_0^D Y_0^D$. Note that if contractionary policies were not adopted, the devaluation could, in principle, move the economy to a high-employment point such as point F; however, that would clearly generate

rampant inflation. We assume that authorities in the economy avoid the inflation by means of contractionary demand policies, such as fiscal and monetary contractions, which maintain the short-run equilibrium of the economy at point H.

The devaluation also tends to shift the trade balance locus to the right because at any given domestic price level it would improve the trade balance (assuming that the Marshall-Lerner condition is satisfied). This shift of the trade balance curve is represented in Figure 16–9 by the shift from $T_0 T_0$ to $T_1 T_1$. We thus assume, for illustrative purposes, that the devaluation undertaken is large enough to completely wipe out the economy's balance-of-payments deficit. In terms of Figure 16–9, the new trade balance locus $T_1 T_1$ passes through point H. As a consequence, short-run equilibrium now occurs at balanced external payments. In conclusion, an adequatedevaluation-cum-contractionary demand policy could move the economy to balanced payments without sharp deflationary (or inflationary) effects. Therefore, exchange rate policy may serve an important role in macroeconomic adjustment programs not willing to tolerate widespread social costs; it is apparent, however, that it must be combined with other policy measures, as a package.

The stabilization programs supported by the IMF under its conditionality agreements (see our discussion of conditionality in Chapter 12, Section 12–5) embody both contractionary aggregate demand policies and currency devaluation. What has been the success of IMF-supported programs? The evidence at this time is ambivalent and inconclusive. Most studies find that IMF programs have been associated with improvements in the balance of payments and seem to have constrained price increases. That is, for instance, the conclusion obtained by Kahn in a study of sixty-nine developing countries with IMF programs between 1973 and 1988.[11] The effects on output, however, have been more modest. In fact, the programs have been

[11]M. S. Khan, "The Macroeconomic Effects of Fund-Supported Adjustment Programs," *IMF Staff Papers* (June 1990).

linked to output reductions in the short run.[12] In assessing these results, though, we need to compare the economy's behavior under an IMF-sponsored program with what it might have been *in the absence of the program*. It might, for instance, be the case that a deep recession spills over into the period in which the program is operating, giving the appearance that the IMF program caused it. In fact, the recession might have started as a result of the destabilization that precedes the program.

The issues that we have discussed in this section illustrate the inherent difficulties of attaining multiple objectives in an open economy. Contractionary monetary and fiscal policies oriented toward a rapid improvement in the balance of payments will generate a sharp recession and increased unemployment. Alternatively, if a devaluation is used to attain balanced payments and to raise output, prices will rapidly increase, fueling inflation. Finally, if contractionary demand policies are attached to devaluation as a package, price stability and balanced payments can in principle be attained, but unemployment will not be completely eliminated. The main reason for these conflicts of objectives lies in that, with an unchanged aggregate supply curve, the range of possible equilibria of the economy will lie along that curve, implying a short-run tradeoff between output and price increases. This suggests that policies oriented toward increasing aggregate supply (shifting the aggregate supply curve to the right) may have an important role in macroeconomic adjustment programs. This type of approach has been popularized by so-called supply-side economics, whose emphasis is on the use of tax cuts, labor market incentive policies, and other policies intended to manipulate aggregate supply.[13]

---

[12]See S. Edwards, "The International Monetary Fund and the Developing Countries: A Critical Evaluation," National Bureau of Economic Research Working Paper no. 2909 (March 1989), p. 47.

[13]See V. Canto, D. Joines, and A. Laffer, *Foundations of Supply-Side Economics* (New York: Academic Press, 1983) for an advanced exposition of this approach.

16–7 DEVALUATION IN THE SHORT AND LONG RUN

We have seen how devaluation combined with adequate contractionary aggregate demand policies can aid an economy with balance-of-payments deficits to adjust faster toward external balance. The use of devaluation as an economic policy, however, has been tarnished by long-standing controversies over its effects. In this section, we discuss some of the issues related to its short-run and long-run effects.

Consider an economy blessed with external and internal balance. In terms of Figure 16–10, the economy is initially at the long-run equilibrium corresponding to point A. Suppose that a devaluation of the domestic currency is undertaken. As was seen in Section 16–6, both the aggregate demand and the trade balance curves would shift upward and to the right. These changes are shown in Figure 16–10, where the aggregate demand curve shifts upward from $Y_0^D Y_0^D$ to $Y_1^D Y_1^D$ and the trade balance curve shifts from $T_0 T_0$ to $T_1 T_1$. The short-run equilibrium of the economy then moves from point A to point B, with a higher level for output and the price of domestic goods and an improvement in the trade balance reflected by the fact that point B lies below the $T_1 T_1$ locus.[14] However, as long as the trade balance moves into surplus, the domestic money supply will increase over time. As a result, over the long run, the aggregate demand curve for domestic goods will shift upward and to the right. In addition, because the economy has moved above full employment, nominal wages will rise and the short-run aggregate supply curve will shift to the left. Figure

---

[14]This assumes that the Marshall-Lerner condition holds. In addition, even though the exchange rate increase has a positive direct effect on the autonomous trade balance, the movement from point A to point B is also connected to increases in domestic income and prices, both of which tend to worsen the trade balance. Does a devaluation in the present case always improve the trade balance in the short run? As it turns out, it always does. The derivation is left to the reader as Problem 3 at the end of this chapter.

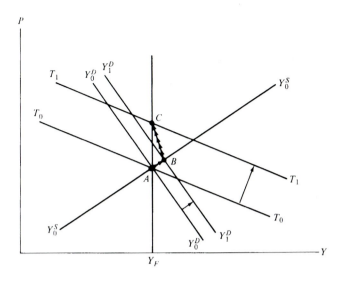

FIGURE 16–10. Short-Run and Long-Run Effects of Devaluation

16–10 does not show exactly how the aggregate demand and aggregate supply curves shift over time, but it does show one particular path of points. They reflect one possible path of their intersections over time, a path represented by the pointed arrows.

Full-employment equilibrium and balanced trade after the devaluation occur at point C, where the new trade balance curve, $T_1 T_1$, and the long-run aggregate supply curve, at Y_F, intersect. Point C, then, represents the new long-run equilibrium. No matter how the adjustment of the economy occurs from point B to point C, the latter must be the destination point. What has happened, compared with the initial equilibrium at point A? There has been no permanent increase in employment because output is back at its full-employment level. In addition, there has been no permanent effect on the trade balance because monetary adjustments in the economy have moved the trade balance back to its zero level. These monetary adjustments, however, imply that the central bank's foreign exchange reserves have increased

and that, as a result, the domestic nominal money supply has risen as well. Finally, the price of domestic goods has increased from P_0 to P_1. As a matter of fact, the price of domestic goods increases by exactly the same proportion as the exchange rate. Let us see why.

From the trade balance definition, we know that

$$B = T(q, Y)$$
$$= \bar{T} + \phi \frac{eP^*}{P} - mY, \qquad (16\text{–}5)$$

that is, the trade balance has a component that depends on domestic real income, Y, a part that is exogenous and a part that depends on the relative price of foreign goods in terms of domestic goods, q. Note, however, that in the long run the devaluation has no effect on real income. Therefore, Y in Equation 16–5 remains unchanged. In addition, the economy must return to balanced trade through the monetary adjustment mechanism; thus, a devaluation has no long-run effects on the overall trade balance, $T(q, Y)$, either. This implies that the trade balance component represented by $\phi(eP^*/P)$, cannot be permanently affected by a devaluation, meaning that eP^*/P cannot be permanently altered either. In other words, over the long run, the price of domestic goods increases in the same proportion as the increase in the exchange rate. It should be clear why this is so. The devaluation tends to make the economy relatively more competitive in the short run, by reducing real wages and inducing a decline in the relative price of domestic goods vis-à-vis foreign goods. As time transpires, however, labor contracts are revised and real wages increase to their level before the devaluation. The competitiveness and productivity of domestic production thus returns to previous levels, and so does the relative price of domestic goods, q. But, then, the price of domestic goods must rise in the same proportion as the devaluation to keep relative prices, $q = eP^*/P$, unchanged.

The hypothesis that a devaluation does not have any effects on the relative price of domestic goods is associated with the long-standing doctrine of *purchasing power parity*. The present analysis suggests that this hypothesis should tend to hold only over the long run and not over short periods of time. In addition, we must emphasize that our discussion has been carried out on the assumption that the economy starts from a position of long-run equilibrium, with external and internal balance. If the economy were out of long-run equilibrium instead, suffering perhaps from unemployment and balance-of-payments deficits, devaluation could very well induce changes in the relative price of domestic goods toward equilibrium. In this situation, the economy's initial employment and external payments difficulties may hinge heavily on a lack of international competitiveness, represented by high prices of domestic goods relative to foreign goods. A devaluation can then aid the economy in regaining its competitiveness by adjusting the relative price of domestic goods down toward its long-run equilibrium level.

16–8. DEVALUATION AND RELATIVE PRICES: THE EVIDENCE

What are the data regarding the effects of devaluation on relative prices? Available evidence suggests that devaluation generally has significant short-run effects on relative prices that disappear over the long run; the short-run increase in domestic competitiveness as a result of devaluation disappears at different rates of speed, depending on the country. In a recent analysis of thirty-nine devaluations in developing countries, Sebastian Edwards examined the erosion of nominal exchange rate increases through domestic price hikes. He found that in eight of the twenty-nine episodes, the devaluation led to an increase in the relative price of foreign goods during the year of the devaluation but was more than fully eroded after one year. In four cases, it took less than a year for the impact of the nominal devaluation on relative prices to be wiped out.[15] In twelve other episodes, the nominal exchange rate increase had been offset through price increases after three years. In the remaining cases, countries had been able to sustain real exchange rate increases, but only through additional devaluations. Periodic devaluations, as embodied in crawling peg regimes, were able to fight off the real exchange rate erosion caused by inflation through additional currency depreciation. The danger of this process is that it can generate a devaluation-inflation spiral. Devaluations generate rising prices that are followed by further devaluations, and so on. This inflationary proclivity of crawling peg regimes is evident in Edwards's data.

These results are also illustrated in the U.S.–U.K. data plotted in Figure 16–11. The figure shows the behavior of an index of the U.S. price level relative to an index of U.K. prices (converted

---

[15]S. Edwards, *Real Exchange Rates, Devaluation and Adjustment* (Cambridge, Mass.: The MIT Press, 1989). See also R. N. Cooper, "Currency Devaluation in Developing Countries," *Essays in International Finance* (Princeton, N.J.: Princeton University Press, June 1971), p. 23.

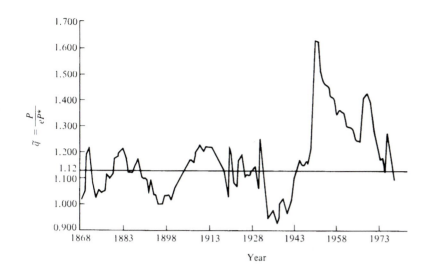

FIGURE 16–11. Behavior of the Ratio of the U.S. Price Index to the Dollar-Converted U.K. Price Index, 1868–1978

SOURCE: Milton Friedman, "Prices of Money and Goods Across Frontiers: The £ and $ Over a Century," *World Economy* (January 1979), p. 510.

to dollars) up to the advent of floating exchange rates in 1973. Symbolically, we are just plotting

$$\tilde{q} = \frac{P}{eP^*}$$

where P is the U.S. price level, e is the exchange rate ($/£), and P^* is the U.K. price level, so that $\tilde{q}$ is the reciprocal of q. As observed, $\tilde{q}$ varies significantly from period to period, even though, over the long run, it tends to return toward a level somewhere around 1.12. This is more evident for the period before 1932, when the fluctuations around $\tilde{q} = 1.12$ were only within a band of plus and minus 10 percent. After 1932, however, there appear to be persistent deviations from that level, associated quite closely with two quite major jumps (peaks) in 1949 and 1967. It may not be a coincidence that these two years corresponded to major devaluations of the pound. The picture suggested is one in which the government exchange rate policies appear to generate significant changes in $\tilde{q}$, giving rise to deviations from purchasing power parity. As Milton Friedman remarks, the ratio of relative prices, $\tilde{q}$, changes because

> every now and then, for whatever reason, the British government has stepped in and either devalued the currency deliberately or permitted it to depreciate. . . . Then market forces set in to correct it. The highest peak is for 1949–1950 and that corresponds to the immediate post-World War II devaluation of the pound in 1949. The market then gradually starts to bring the ratio back down toward about 1.2. Before it gets there, another devaluation occurs and the ratio shoots up again. The market again brings it down, the United States devaluation in 1971 speeding up the process.[16]

In summary, the evidence tends to indicate that devaluation has effects on relative prices, but only

---

[16]M. Friedman, "Prices of Money and Goods Across Frontiers: The £ and $ Over a Century," *World Economy* (January 1979), pp. 509–510.

over the short run. This ineffectiveness of devaluation in affecting relative prices may explain some findings that show a lack of any lasting effect of devaluation on the trade balance.[17]

16–9. FISCAL AND MONETARY POLICIES UNDER PERFECT CAPITAL MOBILITY

Up to this point, we have assumed that the economy faces no international capital mobility. It is clear, however, that this is not a realistic assumption for most industrial economies. Even among developing countries, the increased integration to international capital markets in recent years has greatly enhanced the degree of capital mobility.[18] It is thus time to consider capital flows. With perfect capital mobility, the aggregate demand function can be represented by

$$Y = \alpha \left[\bar{A} + \bar{T} + \phi \frac{eP^*}{P} - bi^* \right] \quad (16\text{–}6)$$

where $\alpha = 1/(s + m)$ is the open-economy Keynesian multiplier, b is the interest elasticity of investment spending, and i^* is the world interest rate. Note that Equations 16–2(a) and 16–6 are equivalent expressions, except that now the interest rate is exogenously given by i^*, as the environment of perfect capital mobility requires.[19]

[17]See M. Miles, *Devaluation, the Trade Balance and the Balance of Payments* (New York: Dekker, 1978). A general discussion of the linkages between nominal and real exchange rates is available in L. Rivera-Batiz, "Modeling the Role of the Real Exchange Rate in Macroeconomic Adjustment," and in M. Willumsen and R. Cruz, eds., *Modeling and Simulation* (Research Triangle Park, N.C.: Instrument Society of America, 1988).

[18]See N. U. Haque and P. Montiel, "Capital Mobility in Developing Countries: Some Empirical Tests," *IMF Working Paper* no. WP/90/117 (December 1990).

[19]The expression for aggregate demand represented in Equation 16–6 shows the combinations of aggregate quantity demanded and price of domestic goods consistent with full money market equilibrium, given fiscal policy, behavioral parameters, and the exchange rate. Equation 16–6 already

The conclusions reached in our earlier analysis of economic policy under perfect capital mobility (see Chapter 14) were that, for an economy under fixed exchange rates, fiscal policy would be highly effective in increasing domestic output and monetary policy would be ineffective. Even though the latter conclusion remains unscathed in the present context, the former is fundamentally altered. That monetary policy in the form of changes in central bank credit has no effect on output, whether in the short run or in the long run, is evident from Equation 16–6, which is independent of the domestic money supply. With no effect on aggregate demand, changes in central bank credit have no impact on the economy's equilibrium.

Changes in government spending, on the assumption that the economy is at full employment, have short-run effects on output but none over the long run. An increase in government spending, for instance, raises aggregate demand for domestic goods, increasing domestic output in the short run. With output above full employment, however, nominal wages start climbing, reducing employment and output back to their original full-employment levels. The chief impact of fiscal policy in this context is to raise domestic prices. Note that because domestic output remains unchanged over the long run, the increased aggregate spending associated with the fiscal expansion must be offset by a decline in another component of aggregate demand. It is spending on domestic exports and import-competing industries that worsens. Domestic price increases worsen domestic competitiveness in international markets, hurting domestic export and import-competing industries. In terms of Equation 16–6, as $\bar{A}$ rises in response to increased government spending,

embodies the instantaneous adjustments of the domestic money supply that occur in response to payments disequilibria under perfect capital mobility. Note that this differs from the aggregate demand expression in Equation 16–3, which represents the combination of the quantity demanded and the price of domestic goods that clears the money market, given fiscal and exchange rate parameters *and* a level of the domestic money supply.

the term $\phi eP^*/P$ declines in response to the reduction in $q \equiv eP^*/P$ associated with hikes in domestic prices. Increased government spending could have a permanent positive effect on output if the economy starts from a point of unemployment; at the same time, however, it will be inflationary if not combined with measures that shift aggregate supply.

Summary

1. The equilibrium level of prices and output of domestic goods is established by the equality of aggregate demand and aggregate supply. Geometrically, this equilibrium corresponds to the intersection of the aggregate demand and aggregate supply curves.

2. The aggregate demand curve represents a relationship between the aggregate quantity demanded of domestic goods and the price level of domestic goods, given a certain level of the domestic money supply, the exchange rate, and such fiscal parameters as tax rates and government expenditures.

3. The aggregate supply curve shows the relationship between price and quantity supplied of domestic goods. The short-run aggregate supply curve represents how quantity supplied responds to price changes over short periods of time, in the presence of nominal wage rigidities. The long-run aggregate supply curve is vertical at the full-employment level and represents how, in the absence of long-term rigidities, wage rates would adjust to clear the labor market.

4. The long-run equilibrium of an economy occurs at that point where there is full employment and balanced payments.

5. In the absence of disturbances generated by government intervention, an automatic adjustment mechanism tends to move the free-market economy over time toward its long-run equilibrium with full employment, balanced payments, and price stability.

6. Macroeconomic adjustment programs are intended to speed up the adjustment of an economy toward long-run equilibrium. Programs that rely on strong deflationary measures intended to obtain rapid improvement in the balance of payments will tend to generate sharp decreases in employment and output.

7. Devaluation used as a package with other policies can serve as an important tool in macroeconomic adjustment programs by generating improvements in the balance of payments without increasing unemployment in any significant way.

8. Policies oriented toward affecting aggregate supply can form a central part of macroeconomic programs whose goal is full employment and balanced payments without simultaneously igniting inflation in the short run.

9. For an economy close to or at full employment and balanced payments, devaluation will only generate a temporary improvement in the balance of trade. The long-run effects of a devaluation in this context are to increase domestic prices by the same proportion as the devaluation.

Problems

1. Consider the zero capital mobility framework developed in the text. If the economy is in long-run equilibrium, determine the equilibrium price of domestic goods as a function of the exchange rate, foreign prices, and full-employment income. Determine also the economy's equilibrium interest rate. (Hint: Note that in long-run equilibrium $Y = Y_F$ and $T = 0$; use the trade balance equation

$$T = \bar{T} + \phi \frac{eP^*}{P} - mY.$$

to solve for P as a function of exogenous variables.)

2. In April 1993, the Russian central bank—facing close to a 1,000 percent annual inflation rate—decided to restrain money supply growth. Some economists, such as Germany's Heiner Flassbeck, objected to the use of monetary restrictionism, arguing that the European experience was that the reductions in wages required for this policy to work would not be easily forthcoming: "Contemporary experience shows that even in the country which has shown to have the most flexible wages in the world, West Germany, it has taken three years to push the inflation rate down from 4 percent to 2 percent; and even this has been at the cost of a deep recession and a sharp rise in unemployment. How long will it take to free Russia from inflation in excess of 1,000 percent, and what will be the cost?" [H. Flassbeck, "The Brave Way to Banish Inflation," *The Financial Times* (May 17, 1993, p. 17)]. On the basis of the discussion in this chapter, (assume zero capital mobility) do you agree with this perspective?

3. Draw the aggregate demand curve described by Equation 16–6 in the text jointly with an aggregate supply curve.
   (a) Determine the short-run and long-run equilibria of an economy under perfect capital mobility and fixed exchange rates. Does long-run equilibrium require balanced trade?
   (b) Show diagrammatically the short-run and long-run effects of a reduction in domestic central bank credit, assuming that the economy is initially in long-run equilibrium.
   (c) Describe the short-run and long-run impact of a domestic currency depreciation.
   (d) Diagrammatically show the effects of an increase in government spending.
   Compare your results with those obtained under the assumption of zero capital mobility. Are there any differences? Explain your answer.

4. Banania is a small tropical country whose only item of production is bananas. The country only trades with the United States and has a fixed exchange rate equal to $\bar{e} = 2$ bananians/$\$$ (where a bananian is Banania's currency). The economy operates under perfect capital mobility. The following numerical expressions for absorption, A, the trade balance, T, and the world interest rate, i^*, have been determined:

$$A = 480 + 0.78\,Y - 900i^*$$

$$T = 100\,\frac{ep^*}{P} - 0.22\,Y$$

$$i^* = 0.10\ (10\%),$$

with absorption and the trade balance measured in terms of millions of Banania's output. Assume that Banania imports goods from the United States at an average price of one U.S. dollar per unit ($P^* = \$1.00$) and that the economy is producing at the full-employment level of output (440 million bananas).

   (a) Determine the price of a unit of Banania's output (the price of a banana in bananians). How much would a banana cost in U.S. dollars?
   (b) Suppose that Banania decides to devalue the bananian by 10 percent. What would be the long-run effect on the price of a banana in bananians?
   (c) Assume that the world interest rate faced by Banania rises to $i^* = 0.20$ (20 percent). What would be the effect on Banania's long-run equilibrium price level? Explain your results.
   (d) Suppose that Banania's government increases its expenditures by twenty million. What would be the impact on domestic prices and the trade balance?
   Questions (a) to (d) are independent of each other. Give numerical answers for each.

APPENDIX: AN ALGEBRAIC TREATMENT OF AGGREGATE SUPPLY

This appendix derives an analytical expression for the aggregate supply curve. This requires establishing relationships between changes in prices and changes in employment, and between employment and output.

The behavior of employment in response to changes in prices (described in the text in relation to Figure 16–4(a), can be depicted algebraically by

$$\frac{N - N_F}{N_F} = \theta \left(\frac{P - P_{-1}}{P_{-1}} \right), \qquad (16A-1)$$

where N is current employment, which can be above or below its long-run, full-employment level, N_F; P is the current price level, which can be above or below its previous level, P_{-1}, and θ is a positive parameter that will be interpreted subsequently. Equation 16A–1 suggests that if domestic prices rise above their previous level (as they did in our earlier example, from P_0 to P_1), employment will increase above its full-employment level (as it did in Figure 16–4, from N_F to N_1). Symbolically, if $(P - P_{-1})$ is positive, then $(N - N_F)$ is positive as well. Observe also that if the domestic price level were to stop increasing, at that point $P = P_{-1}$ and employment would return to full employment (N would again equal N_F).

The parameter θ represents how much a given percentage increase in domestic prices would tend to increase employment. The smaller (or larger) θ is, the smaller (or larger) will be the influence of an increase in the price of domestic goods on employment. The value of θ in any economy depends on the degree to which employment contracts pervade the economy. The less important these are, and the less rigid nominal wages are, the faster they will adjust to changes in prices. In this case, θ will be relatively small: Increases in price will have relatively little impact on real wages and

thus on employment. The opposite occurs if labor contracts are important in the economy.

Equation 16A–1 can be interpreted differently if it is transformed into

$$U = \frac{N_F - N}{N_F} = -\theta \left(\frac{P - P_{-1}}{P_{-1}} \right), \qquad (16A-2)$$

a so-called *Phillips curve*. It relates the rate of unemployment, $U = (N_F - N)/N_F$, to the rate of inflation, $(P - P_{-1})/P_{-1}$, suggesting a negative relationship between the two. A negative value of U in the present context means that employment is above full employment; it thus represents overemployment. The analysis in this chapter suggests the presence of a downward-sloping Phillips curve in the short run.

The next link in determining an analytical expression for aggregate supply is to specify how output is affected when employment changes. It is assumed that output behaves in the following way in relation to employment:

$$Y = Y_F + \beta \left(\frac{N - N_F}{N_F} \right), \qquad (16A-3)$$

where β is a positive parameter that measures how the output of domestic goods increases above its full-employment level when employment increases above full employment. The larger the parameter β is, the stronger the response of output to any given change in employment. When β is very small, changes in the use of labor will affect domestic output in a minor way.

The aggregate supply function of the economy can be derived by substituting Equation 16A–1 into Equation 16A–3, obtaining

$$Y = Y_F + \theta\beta \left(\frac{P - P_{-1}}{P_{-1}} \right). \qquad (16A-4)$$

Equation 16A-4 reflects algebraically the short-run, upward-sloping Y_0^S curve in Figure 16–4(b). Because θ and β are positive, if the current price level, P, increases above its previous level, P_{-1}, the supply of domestic goods, Y, increases above Y_F. Equation 16A-4 also reflects the behavior of aggregate supply over the long run. Once the labor market fully adjusts to a once-and-for-all disturbance, prices will stop increasing, so that P would equal P_{-1}, in that case $Y = Y_F$, and output returns to its full-employment level.

Prices, Output, and Economic Adjustment Under Flexible Exchange Rates

The 1970s saw a major shift in international monetary relations toward increased flexibility in the exchange rates of major industrial countries. They also saw a general increase in both the level and diversity of inflation rates among those countries. The inflation rates before and after the start of the recent period of floating exchange rates are compared in Table 17–1. In the United States, for example, the average annual inflation rate for the fixed exchange rate period from 1963 to 1972 was 3.5 percent; the corresponding rate for the floating exchange rate period from 1973 to 1992 was 8.0 percent. Table 17–1 also displays the increased variability of inflation after floating started, although by 1992 there was a substantial convergence of inflation rates. What explains this experience under the recent floating exchange rate regime? It is clear that the answer to this question must be related to the particular inflationary effects of economic policies under floating exchange rates, as well as to the massive oil price hikes of 1973 and 1979 and the role of floating exchange

TABLE 17–1. The Industrial Countries Before and After the Advent of Floating Exchange Rates (in percent)

	1963–1972	1973–1992	1983	1984	1985	1986	1987	1988	1989	1990	1991	1992
Real GNP growth (percentage change from previous year)												
United States	4.0%	2.0%	3.6%	6.8%	3.4%	2.7%	3.4%	4.5%	2.5%	1.0%	-0.3%	3.0%
European Countries	4.4	2.4	1.8	2.5	2.5	2.7	2.7	3.8	3.4	2.7	1.3	2.2
United Kingdom	2.8	1.4	3.7	2.2	3.6	3.9	4.8	4.3	2.3	0.8	-1.8	2.4
Germany	4.5	1.9	1.9	3.1	1.8	2.2	1.5	3.7	3.8	4.5	3.1	2.0
France	5.5	2.8	0.7	1.3	1.9	2.5	2.3	4.2	3.9	2.8	1.3	2.4
Japan	10.5	3.9	2.8	4.3	5.2	2.6	4.3	6.2	4.7	5.6	4.5	3.4
Canada	5.5	3.4	3.2	6.3	4.8	3.3	4.2	4.7	2.5	0.5	-0.9	3.8
Inflation (percentage change in GNP price deflator)												
United States	3.5%	8.0%	3.8%	3.8%	3.0%	2.6%	3.1%	3.3%	4.1%	4.1%	4.0%	3.7%
European Countries	5.0	10.5	7.7	6.3	5.5	5.1	3.8	4.1	4.7	5.2	5.0	4.1
United Kingdom	5.2	14.1	5.3	4.6	5.7	3.5	5.0	6.5	6.9	6.8	6.2	4.2
Germany	4.1	4.8	3.4	2.1	2.2	3.3	1.9	1.5	2.6	3.4	3.9	3.7
France	4.8	10.8	9.7	7.5	5.8	5.2	3.0	2.9	3.2	2.8	3.1	2.9
Japan	4.7	7.1	1.4	2.3	1.6	1.8	—	0.4	1.9	1.9	2.5	2.6
Canada	3.6	9.4	5.0	3.1	2.6	2.4	4.7	4.8	4.7	3.0	3.4	2.7
Unemployment rates												
United States	4.7%	7.0%	9.6%	7.5%	7.2%	7.0%	6.2%	5.5%	5.3%	5.5%	6.8%	6.3%
European Countries	—	5.2	9.7	10.1	10.4	10.3	10.1	9.5	8.7	8.1	8.7	9.0
United Kingdom	2.4	4.7	10.5	10.7	10.9	11.1	12.0	12.0	12.0	11.0	11.0	10.8
Germany	0.9	3.6	7.9	7.9	8.0	7.6	7.6	7.6	6.8	6.2	5.7	5.9
France	1.9	5.2	8.3	9.7	10.5	10.4	10.5	10.0	9.5	9.0	9.5	9.7
Japan	1.2	2.9	2.7	2.7	2.6	2.8	2.8	2.5	2.3	2.1	2.1	2.2
Canada	4.7	7.5	11.8	11.2	10.5	9.5	8.9	7.8	7.5	8.1	10.2	10.0

The average figures for 1963–1972 and 1973–1992 are compound annual rates of change.

The figures for Canada and France under the real GNP category are based on GDP; the data for the United Kingdom in this category are based on an average of expenditure, income and output estimates of GDP.

The numbers for 1992 are forecasts of the staff of the International Monetary Fund, based on past trends and expectations.

SOURCE: International Monetary Fund, *World Economic Outlook* (Washington, D.C.: IMF, October 1991 and October 1983).

rates on the adjustment of industrial economies to these shocks.

In this chapter we use the concepts of aggregate demand and aggregate supply to analyze the determination of the price level and unemployment in open economies under flexible exchange rates and to examine the effects of policy changes and external disturbances. The initial discussion sets aside the problem of the formation of expectations about the future, which is carefully studied in Chapter 18. The overall emphasis of the present chapter is on the longer-run effects of economic disturbances under flexible exchange rates, rather than the details of short-run exchange rate dynamics.

17–1. AGGREGATE DEMAND AND PRICES UNDER FLEXIBLE EXCHANGE RATES

This section discusses the concept of aggregate demand within the context of flexible exchange rate regimes. The aggregate demand function specifies how spending on domestic goods responds to the price of domestic goods. It is represented graphically in Figure 17–1(a) by the aggregate demand curve, $Y^D Y^{D.}$ We now examine the role played by exchange rate flexibility on the aggregate demand curve.

Figure 17–1(b) shows our now-standard diagram depicting the determination of aggregate spending on domestic goods by the intersection of the IS_0 and LM_0 curves. To simplify the exposition, our analysis assumes perfect capital mobility, in which case (ignoring exchange rate expectations and exchange risk) the domestic interest rate will be constrained to equal the world interest rate, that is, $i = i^*$. This constraint on domestic equilibrium is depicted by the horizontal BB curve in Figure 17–1(b).

The intersection of the IS_0, LM_0, and BB curves at point A in Figure 17–1(b) determines aggregate desired spending on domestic goods, given the money supply, the level of autonomous spending, and the domestic price level. At that point, the

spending decisions of domestic residents are consistent with assets market equilibrium and balanced payments.

Suppose now that we reduce the price of domestic goods, P, say from P_0 to P_1. What are the effects on desired aggregate spending? First, a reduction in the price of domestic goods increases real money balances—from M_0/P_0 to M_0/P_1—which, at a given interest rate, i^*, would require an increase in domestic spending to increase money demand and maintain money market equilibrium. This *real money balances effect* is represented by the rightward shift of the LM curve from LM_0 to LM_1 in Figure 17–1(b).

In addition, the reduction in domestic prices shifts the IS curve to the right. At a given level of the exchange rate, a reduction in domestic prices would raise the relative price of foreign goods in terms of domestic goods, $q = eP^*/P$, enhancing the price competitiveness of domestic goods relative to foreign goods in international markets and switching demand toward domestic goods. The stimulated spending on domestic goods then shifts the IS curve rightward, from IS_0 to IS_1 in Figure 17–1(b). This effect is called the *real exchange rate* effect, to stress that in the present context the relative price of foreign goods in terms of domestic goods, q, corresponds to the concept of real exchange rate. A real exchange rate is a price-adjusted nominal exchange rate, generally computed by multiplying the nominal exchange rate by the ratio of an index of the foreign and domestic price levels. Since we define the domestic price level in terms of domestically produced export goods, and the foreign price level in terms of import goods produced abroad, the real exchange rate would correspond to our concept of q. (For more details on the computation of real exchange rates, see Chapter 10.)

As depicted by point A', the net impact of the shifts in the IS and LM curves associated with a reduction in domestic prices—at a given level of the exchange rate—would be to increase spending and to lower domestic interest rates. Point A', however, cannot be a full-fledged equilibrium of

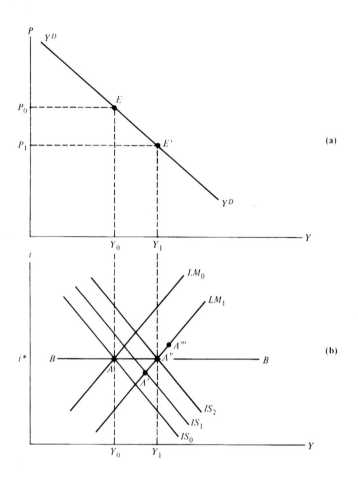

FIGURE 17–1.   Derivation of the Aggregate Demand Curve

the economy. Before the economy ever reaches that point, other changes will occur. The reason is that a reduction in domestic interest rates below world interest rates would immediately generate massive incipient capital outflows, inducing a domestic currency depreciation. The exchange rate increase then shifts the *IS* curve upward until a point like *A″* is reached. At that point, the domestic interest rate equals the world interest rate, and there are consequently no further capital outflows and no subsequent exchange rate changes. The equilibrium increase in aggregate spending in response to a reduction of the domestic price level is

thus from Y_0 to Y_1. This adjustment in desired spending takes into account both the direct effects of the decrease in the price of domestic goods on domestic spending as well as those of the associated depreciation of the domestic currency.[1]

---

[1] A decrease in the price of domestic goods will not necessarily be associated—everything else constant—with a currency depreciation. It all depends on how the initial shifts of the *IS* and *LM* curves compare. In the case we have described in the text, the initial shift of the *IS* curve is relatively small, compared with the shift of the *LM* curve. As a consequence, the resulting intersection of the curves occurs at a domestic interest

Our analysis has shown the negative connection existing between prices and spending on domestic goods, thereby establishing the downward-sloping nature of the aggregate demand curve, as shown by the $Y^D Y^D$ curve in Figure 17–1(a).

Points E and E' in that diagram lie along the aggregate demand curve and correspond to points A and A'' in Figure 17–1(b): A decrease in the price of domestic goods from P_0 to P_1 is associated with an increase in desired aggregate spending from Y_0 to Y_1. We should stress that the exchange rate is not constant along the aggregate demand curve; the latter incorporates those exchange rate adjustments that equilibrate the goods market and maintain balanced payments under flexible rates.

What are the effects of monetary disturbances and changes in government spending on the aggregate demand curve? Changes in the nominal money supply induce shifts of the aggregate demand curve. For instance, an open-market purchase of bonds by the central bank will tend to increase the money supply; at a given price level, the resulting increase in real money balances would then place downward pressure on domestic interest rates, inducing capital to flow out of the economy and depreciating domestic currency. The consequence would be an expenditure switch out of foreign and into domestic goods, with a resulting increase in spending on domestic goods. In other words, at a given price level, desired aggregate spending on domestic goods would increase.

rate below the world level. If the *IS* curve were to shift by a higher proportion—as if it intersected the LM_1 curve at point A''' instead of at point A'—there would be an *increase* in the domestic interest rate above its world level. Incipient capital inflows and an appreciating domestic currency would result. The full equilibrium of the economy would remain, however, at point A'': The appreciation of domestic currency would immediately shift the *IS* curve back from its hypothetical intersection with the LM_1 curve at point A''' to intersection at point A''. Finally, because the domestic interest rate has to return to its world level, the increase in domestic spending from Y_0 to Y_1 must be associated with a net increment of the real exchange rate: The decline of the exchange rate from point A''' to A'' is more than offset by the initial decline in the price of domestic goods, leaving $q = eP^*/P$ at a higher level.

This corresponds graphically to a shifting of the aggregate demand curve to the right. When the money supply decreases, exactly the opposite occurs: If real balances decline, aggregate demand for domestic goods will contract at any given price of domestic goods. Geometrically, the aggregate demand curve shifts to the left.

In contrast to monetary disturbances, changes in autonomous spending—such as may arise from variations in domestic fiscal policy regimes—will *not* induce any shifts in the aggregate demand curve in the present framework. The explanation is that the increased spending would at the same time raise money demand and place upward pressures on domestic interest rates. This would then be associated with incipient capital inflows and an immediate appreciation of domestic currency, which shifts aggregate spending back down toward its original level. Because, under perfect capital mobility, these changes occur instantaneously, the increased autonomous spending would not generate any perceptible shifts of aggregate demand; it would only change its composition among autonomous expenditures (that increase) and net exports (that decrease in response to the domestic currency appreciation).

The striking contrast between the effects of changes in the money supply and in autonomous expenditures on aggregate demand can be seen by transforming the money market equilibrium condition

$$\frac{M^S}{P} = kY - hi,$$

making use of the interest rate constraint $i = i^*$ and interchanging the dependent variable to show aggregate spending on domestic goods:

$$Y = \frac{M^S}{P}\frac{1}{k} + \frac{h}{k}i^*. \qquad (17\text{–}1)$$

This equation establishes a connection between aggregate spending, Y, and the price of domestic goods, P, at a given level of the world interest rate, i^*, and the money supply, M^S. Equation 17–1 can be interpreted as an equation of aggregate demand where—in the background—the exchange rate is being allowed to adjust in order to equilibrate the goods market. Increases in the money supply can be clearly seen to raise spending on domestic goods, at any given level of domestic prices. Changes in autonomous spending, on the other hand, do not affect in any perceptible way the relationship between price and spending shown by Equation 17–1 and would have no effect on aggregate demand; the presence of exchange rate changes in the background offsets the direct effects of changes in autonomous spending, leaving aggregate demand unchanged.

The lack of influence of changes in autonomous spending on overall spending in the economy can be more easily conceptualized by showing the components of aggregate desired spending. At a given price of domestic goods, P_0, and with the domestic interest rate constrained to equal world interest rates, desired spending on domestic goods is given by

$$Y = \alpha \left[\bar{A} + \bar{T} + \phi \frac{eP^*}{P_o} - bi^* \right]. \quad (17-2)$$

A rise in autonomous spending—an increase in $\bar{A}$—will lead to a reduction in the exchange rate, e. The currency appreciation lowers the real exchange rate, $q = eP^*/P_0$, deteriorating the international competitiveness of domestic products and worsening the trade balance component $\phi eP^*/P$. The declining net exports then offset the increased autonomous expenditures, leaving desired aggregate spending on domestic goods, Y, unchanged.

17–2. Determination of Prices and Output in the Short Run

The last section summarized the nature of demand behavior in the economy as portrayed by the aggregate demand curve. In order to determine the equilibrium levels of price and output of domestic goods, however, we have to join aggregate de-

mand with aggregate supply; that is, we have to examine the interaction of the aggregate supply *and* aggregate demand curves.

Following our discussion in Chapter 16, it is assumed that nominal wage rates are relatively rigid over the short run, as specified by binding employment contracts previously engaged in. This determines a certain short-run aggregate supply curve, shown by $Y_0^S Y_0^S$ in Figure 17–2(a), indicating how the quantity supplied of domestic goods changes over the short run when prices change. In addition, with fixed fiscal and monetary policy parameters, a certain aggregate demand curve will be given, showing how the quantity demanded of domestic goods changes when prices change. The curve $Y_0^D Y_0^D$ depicts this aggregate demand relationship in Figure 17–2(a).

The economy is in short-run equilibrium when the quantity demanded of domestic goods is equal to the short-run quantity supplied. This occurs at the point where the domestic aggregate demand curve intersects the given short-run aggregate supply curve. There is then a simultaneous short-run equilibrium of the goods and money markets in the sense that they all clear, given the rigid nominal wage existing in the short run and given fixed fiscal and monetary parameters. This short-run equilibrium of the economy is illustrated graphically by means of point A in Figure 17–2(a), which is the point of intersection of the aggregate demand curve, $Y_0^D Y_0^D$, with the short-run aggregate supply curve, $Y_0^S Y_0^S$. The resulting short-run equilibrium output of domestic goods is Y_0 and the short-run equilibrium price of domestic goods is P_0.

The economy's short-run equilibrium level of output can generally differ from its full-employment level. Such is the case depicted by point A in Figure 17–2(a), where short-run output, Y_0, is below its full-employment level, Y_F. This means that the economy suffers from unemployment. Is this a short-run phenomenon or does it remain permanently as a characteristic of the economy in the absence of economic policy or other disturbances? This question will be answered in the next section.

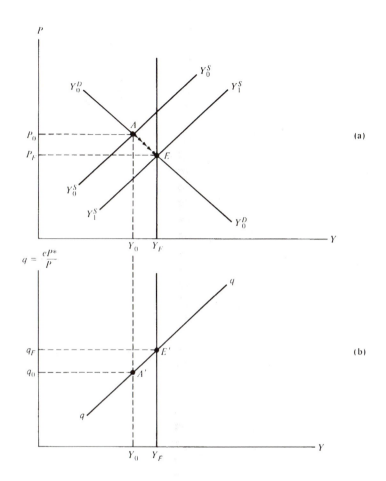

FIGURE 17-2. Short-Run Equilibrium and the Adjustment Toward Long-Run Equilibrium

17-3. THE ADJUSTMENT PROCESS, REAL WAGES, AND THE REAL EXCHANGE RATE

We now focus on the role played by the real wage rate and the real exchange rate in the adjustment of the economy toward long-run equilibrium.[2]

In Figure 17-2 we illustrate an economy's long-run process of recovery from a short-run aggregate demand curve and, consequently, the long-run behavior of the economy. For the moment, however, we are ignoring expectational considerations and assuming that the anticipated rate of inflation is zero. In this case, the domestic real interest rate becomes identical to the nominal interest rate; under perfect capital mobility, it is constrained to equal the world interest rate. With the latter assumed fixed, no changes in real interest rates would arise. The effect of expectations and changes in the real interest rate on the behavior of the economy will be examined in chaps. 18 and 19.

[2] A third basic variable is involved—the *real interest rate*. Domestic investment spending depends on nominal interest rates adjusted for anticipated inflation—that is, real interest rates. Changes in the latter over time could influence the

position of unemployment, depicted by point A. In the presence of unemployment, nominal wage rates tend to decline over time. As labor contracts come up for revision, the availability of unemployed workers and their effective competition with the employed bids down wage rates. At the initial prices, the nominal wage cuts reduce real wages. The resulting lower real unit labor costs induce producers to raise output and to pass on some of the cuts in real labor costs to consumers in the form of price reductions. Geometrically, a reduction in nominal wages at a given level of prices—a reduction in real wages—will shift the aggregate supply curve to the right. In terms of Figure 17–2(a), the economy would move along the pointed arrows, representing the intersection points of the shifting short-run aggregate supply curve with the unchanged aggregate demand curve. (Note that the latter remains fixed, as determined by monetary and fiscal policy parameters.) This *wage-price automatic adjustment mechanism* of a laissez-faire economy ends when full-employment output is reached, at which point (cyclical) unemployment has been eliminated and nominal—and real—wage rates stop declining. This is the long-run equilibrium of the economy, obtained when goods and money markets are in equilibrium *and* the labor market is at full-employment. It is depicted by point E in Figure 17–2(a), which shows the intersection of the long-run aggregate supply curve with the aggregate demand curve. The implication is that the economy's initial state of unemployment is eliminated over time. The declining nominal—and real—wage rates shift the aggregate supply curve all the way from its initial position at $Y_0^S Y_0^S$ to the one consistent with full employment at $Y_1^S Y_1^S$.

What is the behavior of the exchange rate over the adjustment process? In the present case, the path of the exchange rate cannot be pinned down exactly unless the specific structure of the economy is known. This is because the net effect on the exchange rate of the changes in income and prices involved is not completely determinate. Declining

domestic prices, at a given level of income, would raise the real money supply, place downward pressure on interest rates, and induce incipient capital outflows that tend to raise the exchange rate. On the other hand, at a fixed price level, rises in domestic income would have the opposite effect. They would raise money demand, place upward pressures on domestic interest rates, and induce capital inflows that tend to lower the exchange rate. The net balance of these two effects is not determinate and depends on such parameters as the income elasticity of money demand and the effects of exchange rate changes on the trade balance.

The variable that is indeed determinate in the adjustment process is the real exchange rate, which corresponds in our analysis to the relative price of foreign goods in terms of domestic goods, $q = eP*/P$. The real exchange rate rises over the process of adjustment toward full employment. In other words, the increase in output from Y_0 to Y_F in Figure 17–2(a) is directly associated with an increase in the real exchange rate, say from q_0 to q_F. What explains this connection between output of goods and the real exchange rate? With interest rates fixed at world levels and with aggregate autonomous spending fixed, changes in the demand for domestic goods can only be associated with changes in the trade balance, which are a direct function of the real exchange rate. This is best seen from the aggregate demand function

$$Y = \alpha [\bar{A} + \bar{T} + \phi q - bi*]. \quad (17–3)$$

With autonomous expenditures fixed at $\bar{A}$ and $\bar{T}$ the domestic interest rate equal to the—fixed—world rate, $i*$, the quantity demanded of domestic goods, Y, will be altered only when the real exchange rate, q, changes. An increase in the real exchange rate—an increase in q—is associated with an improvement in domestic competitiveness, inducing a switch in expenditure toward domestic goods and increasing its quantity demanded. Reductions of the real exchange rate—decreases in q—on the other hand, would deteriorate competitiveness, worsen the autonomous trade balance, and reduce the aggregate quantity demanded of domestic goods. This positive connection between the real exchange rate and domestic output is represented by means of the upward-sloping qq curve in Figure 17–2(b). The vertical axis in Figure 17–2(b) shows the values of the real exchange rate; the horizontal axis is the same as in Figure 17–2(a), displaying the level of domestic output.

The basic problem behind the unemployment existing at the short-run equilibrium of the economy at point A is the fact that real wages are too high for full employment to be attained. In other words, the short-run aggregate supply curve, $Y_0^S Y_0^S$, lies above the curve required to attain full employment, $Y_1^S Y_1^S$. The effect of the high real wage rates is to make domestic real labor costs high, compared with foreign firms; domestic production is thereby generated at prices that are not competitive in world markets. In other words, the real exchange rate at point A'—q_0 in Figure 17–2(b)—is below the level necessary to gain the access to international markets needed to attain the full-employment level of output (the required real exchange rate is denoted by q_F). The resulting slack demand for domestic goods is then associated with the shortfall of domestic output and employment below their full-employment levels at point E'.

As nominal and real wages decline over time, real labor costs also decline. This surfaces as an increase in the international competitiveness of domestic goods—an increase in q—eventually moving the economy to full employment. The output boom is spearheaded by rising net exports, reflected in an improvement of the trade balance. The increased real exchange rate is thus instrumental in transmitting the changes in real wages into changes in aggregate quantity demanded of domestic goods and increased output. In terms of Figure 17–2(b), the expansion in output from $Y_0 to Y_F$ is associated with an increase in the real exchange rate from $q_0 to q_F$. Note that this gain in international competitiveness is directly connected to the reduction of domestic prices from $P_0 to P_F$. It may also be associated, although not necessarily, with a rising nominal exchange rate, e.[3]

In summary, within the present framework, there appears to be an automatic wage-price adjustment mechanism that tends to move the laissez-faire flexible-rates economy toward full employment over time. This mechanism, which operates by influencing real wages and the real exchange rate, works when domestic output is above full employment just as well as it does when it is below. With overemployment, a rising wage-price spiral would raise real wages, reduce real exchange rates, and move the economy back to full employment. This suggests that, unless the full-employment level of output can be increased, the full utilization of the economy's limited resources will prevent permanent increases in output over the current level of full employment. The policy implications of this important point are examined in the next section. Note, finally, that the adjustment process under floating exchange rates does not rely on the nominal money supply changes that take place under fixed exchange rates. Under freely floating exchange rates, the economy's exchange rate will adjust to insure balance-of-payments equilibrium, and there will be no changes in the economy's monetary base except those initiated by the central bank in altering its credit.

---

[3] To understand that the increase in output from point A to point E is not necessarily associated with an increase in the nominal exchange rate, return to Figure 17–1 and, in particular, to the related discussion in Footnote 1 regarding the movement from point E to point E' along the aggregate demand curve $Y^D Y^D$. The exchange rate behavior behind this movement is similar to that relating to the movement from point A to point E along $Y_0^D Y_0^D$ in Figure 17–2(a).

17–4. AGGREGATE DEMAND POLICIES, EMPLOYMENT, AND INFLATION UNDER FLEXIBLE EXCHANGE RATES

This section examines the output and inflationary effects of government policies under floating exchange rates. In order for an aggregate demand policy disturbance to have perceptible effects on domestic output—whether in the short run or over time—it must be able to influence aggregate demand positively. As we concluded earlier, however, real disturbances in the form of changes in autonomous spending—such as fiscal policy disturbances—do not tend to be effective in altering aggregate demand under flexible exchange rates and perfect capital mobility. Any positive effects of the increased autonomous spending on aggregate demand are seriously hampered by the negative impact of the spending increase on the real exchange rate and, hence, on domestic exports. With no net effect on domestic spending, real disturbances would be powerless to shift aggregate demand or consequently to increase domestic output, whether in the short run or in the long run.

Monetary disturbances, on the other hand, tend to be more successful in altering the aggregate demand curve under flexible exchange rates. Consider the case of an expansionary monetary policy in the form of an open-market purchase of bonds by the central bank. The sudden injection of money into the banking system places downward pressure on domestic interest rates, causing incipient capital outflows and a depreciation of domestic currency. The consequence is a switch in expenditures toward domestic goods, shown by the shift of the aggregate demand curve from $Y_0^D Y_0^D$ to $Y_1^D Y_1^D$ in Figure 17–3(a). The economy thus moves from its initial equilibrium at point A to the short-run equilibrium depicted by point E, at the intersection of the aggregate demand curve $Y_1^D Y_1^D$ with the short-run aggregate supply curve $Y_0^S Y_0^S$. Domestic output rises above full employment—from Y_F to Y_1—but at the cost of domestic inflation—domestic prices rise from P_0 to P_1.

The short-run output boom induced by the increase in the money supply is closely linked to the decline in real labor costs associated with this disturbance. With nominal wage rates rigid over the short run, the inflationary spur associated with the monetary expansion will reduce real wage rates. These reduced real labor costs and the consequent stimulus to domestic production have, as a counterpart, a greater competitiveness of domestic goods in international markets, which is reflected in an increased real exchange rate. In terms of Figure 17–3(b), the equilibrium expansion of output above full employment—from Y_F to Y_1—is associated with an increase in the real exchange rate from q_F to q_1. This occurs in spite of the rising prices of domestic goods, which, by themselves, tend to cause a deterioration in the international competitiveness of domestic products. The nominal exchange rate depreciation associated with the monetary expansion more than offsets the effects of the domestic price hike, leaving a net positive impact on the real exchange rate. Symbolically, even though domestic prices, P, increase, the rise of the nominal exchange rate, e, more than compensates for it, leaving the real exchange rate, $q = eP^*/P$ at a higher level. The real depreciation of domestic currency improves the autonomous trade balance by switching demand away from foreign and toward domestic goods. In conclusion, the short-run expansionary impact of the monetary disturbance is closely linked to the decline of real wages, which spearheads an increase in net exports.

The reduction in real wages associated with output above full employment is reversed over the long run. As employment contracts come up for renewal, workers seeking to regain their lost real income will revise nominal—and real—wage rates upward. The outcome is an increase in real labor costs, partly passed on to consumers in the form of higher prices for domestic goods. This deteriorates domestic competitiveness in world goods markets, causing a loss of net exports, and reduces domestic output back toward its full-employment level. Diagrammatically, over the long run, inflationary

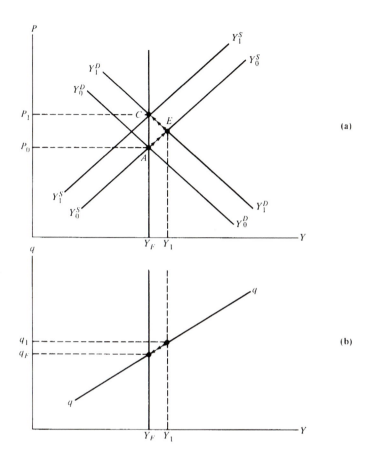

FIGURE 17–3. Short-Run and Long-Run Effects of Expansionary Monetary Policy

pressures result in a real appreciation of domestic currency from q_1 back to q_F and a leftward shift of aggregate supply from $Y_0^S Y_0^S$ to $Y_1^S Y_1^S$. The resulting long-run equilibrium is at point C, with output back at Y_F and domestic prices at a level equal to P_1. At this equilibrium point, domestic real wages will have returned to their original level with the labor market at full employment and no further wage adjustments required.[4] It appears that the

long-run effect of expansionary monetary policy is only inflation. The constraints imposed on the economy by full employment of limited resources cannot be permanently avoided and are directly associated with the lack of effectiveness of expansionary aggregate demand policies on output.

[4] Even though point C is the long-run equilibrium to which the economy would eventually move, the adjustment process toward that point may not be as direct and smooth as we have described. For instance, there may be an overshooting of the

shifting aggregate supply curve above point C, leading to a momentary shortfall of output below full employment. Over time, of course, the supply curve would shift precisely to $Y_1^S Y_1^S$ in response to the resulting unemployment. Similarly, real exchange rates generally will not necessarily approach long-run equilibrium in a smooth and direct way.

Monetary Policy, Prices, and Currency Depreciation

An implication of the analysis is that, in a fully employed economy, monetary disturbances do not have permanent effects on the real exchange rate. At points A and C, domestic output, interest rates, and autonomous spending are all the same. Consequently, from Equation 17–3, the term $\phi e P^*/P$ and, therefore, the real exchange rate will also have to be the same. However, note that the monetary expansion increases domestic prices. In order for the real exchange rate to remain unchanged, an exchange rate depreciation of the same proportion as the rise in prices has to occur. Symbolically, because the real exchange rate is $q = eP^*/P$, taking proportional changes on both sides implies that over the long run,

$$\hat{q} = \hat{e} + \hat{P}* - \hat{P} = 0, \qquad (17\text{–}4)$$

where $\hat{q}$, $\hat{e}$, $\hat{P}*$, and $\hat{P}$ are the proportional changes in the long-run equilibrium values of the real exchange rate, the nominal exchange rate, foreign prices, and domestic prices, respectively. Equation 17–4 states that, if the real exchange rate is to remain constant, the proportional changes in the nominal exchange rate and in foreign and domestic prices must add up to zero; that is, they must offset each other. Given that, for simplicity, we are assuming foreign inflation $\hat{P}*$ to be zero, the implication is that $\hat{e} = \hat{P}$: The proportional depreciation of the nominal exchange rate must equal the proportional increase in prices to leave the real exchange rate, q, unchanged.

The hypothesis that monetary disturbances do not affect the real exchange rate is associated with the doctrine of *purchasing power parity* (ppp). (ppp was discussed in Chapter 16 regarding an economy under fixed exchange rates and examined in the context of flexible exchange rates in Chapter 6.) Our present analysis suggests that, in the face of monetary disturbances, the hypothesis, in the version expressed by Equation 17–4, should tend

to hold only over the long run and not necessarily over short periods of time. Over the short run, sudden monetary disturbances can generate all kinds of changes in the real exchange rate, thereby causing deviations from ppp. In addition, the long-run real exchange rate may be altered by real disturbances, such as fiscal policy changes and changes in full-employment output, in which case Equation 17–4 may fail to hold even over the long run.

This section has examined the effects of aggregate demand policies within the context of an economy that operates initially at full employment and whose starting background is one of price stability. In this case, the full-employment constraint prevents expansionary aggregate demand policies from having any long-run effects on domestic output and leads them instead to fuel domestic inflation. Often, however, policies must be enacted in situations in which the economy is not characterized by full employment and price stability but is instead suffering initially from unemployment, chronic inflation, or both. What would be the effects of policy intervention within this context? For example, must expansionary monetary policy be associated only with price inflation over the long run? The following sections attempt to answer these questions.

17–5. SUPPLY SHOCKS IN THE OPEN ECONOMY: OIL PRICES AND STAGFLATION IN THE 1970s

A wide range of disturbances can destabilize an economy, leading it to stagnation, unemployment, inflation, or to all these problems combined. This section is concerned with the effects of a supply disturbance in the form of a sudden increase in the price of imported raw materials. This was the case facing most industrial economies in the 1970s, when oil prices spiraled, particularly from late 1973 to early 1974 and in 1979. From 1972 to 1974, for instance, the price of oil, according to Saudi Arabian quotes, increased from $1.90 per barrel to

$9.76, as spearheaded by the Arab oil embargo and the start of OPEC price hikes in the last quarter of 1973. In the United States, the price increase was rapidly translated into rising gasoline and motor oil prices, which soared by 39 percent in the period from September 1973 to May 1974 alone. The second massive oil price shock occurred in 1979; it was associated with political events in Iran and Iraq and resulted in an increase in the price of oil, from $12.70 to $28.67 per barrel between 1978 and 1980. Both of these sharp price hikes made big dents in the economies of most of the oil-importing industrial countries, significantly destablizing them. It is the purpose of this section to discuss these effects.

Table 17–2 shows the behavior of real GNP, inflation, and unemployment in the United States, Western Europe, and Japan in the 1970s and early 1980s. The immediate impact of the 1973–1974 and 1979 oil-price shocks on these countries was clearly recessionary, associated with falling real GNP and rising unemployment. In the case of the United States, for example, real GNP declined by 0.6 percent and 1.2 percent in 1974 and 1975 and by 0.4 percent in 1980; unemployment rose from a rate of 4.9 percent in 1973 to 8.5 percent in 1975 and from 5.8 percent in 1979 to 7.4 percent and then 7.6 percent in 1980 and 1981, respectively. Both episodes were also associated with rising inflation rates, although not in all countries. In the

TABLE 17–2. The Industrial Countries and Stagflation in the 1970s and Early 1980s

	1973	1974	1975	1976	1977	1978	1979	1980	1981	1982
Real GNP (percentage change from previous year)										
United States	5.8	−0.6	−1.2	5.4	5.5	5.0	2.8	−0.4	1.9	−1.7
European countries	5.8	2.0	−1.2	4.6	2.6	3.0	3.4	−1.5	−0.2	0.2
United Kingdom	7.2	−1.8	−1.1	3.4	1.6	3.9	2.0	−2.1	−2.2	0.7
Germany, FDR	4.6	0.5	−1.6	5.6	2.8	3.5	4.0	1.8	−0.2	−1.1
France	5.4	3.2	0.2	5.2	3.0	3.7	3.4	1.1	0.4	1.6
Japan	8.8	−1.2	2.4	5.3	5.3	5.1	5.2	4.8	3.8	3.0
Inflation (percentage change in GNP price deflator)										
United States	5.7	8.8	9.3	5.2	5.8	7.4	8.6	9.3	9.4	6.0
European countries	8.2	11.7	13.8	9.8	9.6	8.8	9.0	10.7	9.9	9.5
United Kingdom	7.0	14.9	26.9	14.6	14.1	10.9	15.0	19.2	12.2	8.0
Germany, FDR	6.5	6.8	6.1	3.4	3.7	4.2	4.0	4.4	4.2	4.8
France	7.8	11.2	13.3	9.9	9.0	9.5	10.3	11.8	12.0	12.1
Japan	11.7	20.6	8.1	6.4	5.7	4.6	2.6	2.8	2.6	2.0
Unemployment rates										
United States	4.9	5.6	8.5	7.7	7.1	6.1	5.8	7.2	7.6	11.0
United Kingdom	2.6	2.6	3.9	4.0	5.7	5.7	5.4	6.5	10.1	11.9
Germany, FDR	1.1	2.3	4.1	4.0	3.9	3.8	3.3	3.4	4.9	6.8
France	2.6	2.8	4.1	4.4	4.7	5.2	5.9	6.3	7.3	8.6
Japan	1.2	1.4	1.9	2.0	2.0	2.2	2.1	2.0	2.2	2.4

SOURCE: International Monetary Fund, *World Economic Outlook* (Washington, D.C.: IMF, 1983).

United States, inflation jumped from 5.7 percent in 1973 to 9.3 percent by 1975 and from 8.6 percent in 1979 to 9.4 percent in 1981. The term *stagflation,* a combination of recession (stagnation) and inflation, was coined to characterize the general features of the industrial world following the oil shocks of the 1970s.

Relatively large differences in the behavior of the various industrial economies in the aftermath of the oil shocks can be extrapolated from Table 17–2. For instance, economic recovery in the United States in the post-oil shock period of 1976 to 1978 was stronger than the European recovery; only the United States was able to achieve real GNP growth rates comparable to pre-oil shock levels. Even among the Western European countries, a wide variation of experience can be found. The recessionary period 1974 to 1975, for instance, appeared to be milder in France than in the other European countries, particularly the United Kingdom and West Germany. The experience in controlling inflation after the oil shock, on the other hand, seemed to be better for West Germany. The case of Japan stands out because of its steadily falling inflation rates from 1974 to 1982. What factors could give rise to these observed divergencies in the response of the industrial economies to the supply shocks of the 1970s? Differences in the policy actions of each country, combined with basic differences in their institutional wage-setting processes, clearly played an important role. The following sections describe these differences and their links to the relative economic performance of the industrial countries in the aftermath of the oil shocks.

17–6. STAGFLATION, MONETARY ACCOMMODATION, AND NOMINAL WAGE RIGIDITY

What are the economic mechanisms through which a supply shock gives rise to stagflation? This section examines in detail the various mechanisms through which an increase in the price of

imported raw materials, say oil, affects the economy. We begin by analyzing the effects of such a disturbance, using the standard aggregate demand-aggregate supply framework described earlier in this chapter. We then specify the policy options open, discussing in some detail the particular case of the United States and its experience in the period from 1973 to 1978.

Figure 17–4 shows the initial equilibrium of the economy at point E, corresponding to the intersection of the short-run aggregate demand and aggregate supply curves, $Y_0^D Y_0^D$ and $Y_0^S Y_0^S$, at the full-employment level of output, Y_F. Suppose there is a sudden increase in the price (real cost) of raw materials, everything else remaining constant, and that the economy considered is, for simplicity, wholly dependent on foreign supplies of these inputs. This disturbance will, first of all, increase the costs of production and raise the prices at which domestic producers are willing to supply any given quantity of domestic goods. This means that the short-run aggregate supply curve will shift in the northwest direction, as depicted by the shift from $Y_0^S Y_0^S$ to $Y_1^S Y_1^S$ in Figure 17–4. The impact effect of the rise in the price of imported raw materials is thus an increase in the prices of domestic goods and a reduction of domestic output. This is represented diagrammatically by the move of the economy from point E to point G. In other words, the supply shock is stagflationary, as it produces both recession and inflation.[5]

---

[5] It is possible for an increase in the price of imported inputs to shift aggregate demand downward, which would ameliorate the impact of the supply shock on inflation. According to the Laursen-Metzler-Harberger effect discussed in Chapter 14, increases in the prices of imported inputs shift the terms of trade against the domestic economy, reducing the standard of living of domestic residents. If the disturbance is expected to be permanent, domestic spending may decline in response to the anticipated drop in standard of living. For an overview of these issues within the context of the 1990 Iraq-Kuwait oil-price shock, see Council of Economic Advisors, *Economic Report of the President* (Washington, D.C.: GPO, February 1991). An analytical discussion of the consequences of supply shocks is provided by E. Buffie, "Input Price Shocks in the Small Open Economy," in P. J. N. Sinclair, ed., *Prices, Quantities and*

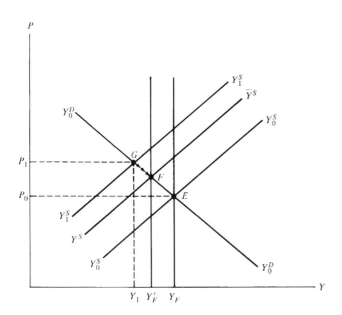

FIGURE 17-4. The Stagflationary Effects of a Supply Shock

Note that the leftward shift of the aggregate supply curve is exclusively associated with the rise in price of the imported raw materials and is drawn for a given level of the nominal wage rate. The assumption is that current nominal wage rates are stipulated and fixed by existing labor contracts and cannot therefore change over the short run. This is referred to, quite logically, as short-run *nominal wage rigidity*. It constitutes a significant attribute of the economy as long as long-term labor contracts—whether explicit or implicit—are an important feature of the domestic labor market. In the presence of nominal wage rigidity, the inflationary effects of a supply shock will reduce real wages in the short run. For instance, if the nominal wage rate was initially at W_0, the rise in prices from P_0 to P_1 lowers real wages from W_0/P_0 to W_0/P_1.

Expectations (Oxford: Clarendon, 1987); and R. C. Marston and S. Turnovsky, "Imported Material Prices, Wage Policy and Macroeconomic Stabilization," *Canadian Journal of Economics* (October 1985).

In the absence of government intervention, the short-run equilibrium of the economy at point G will not be sustained over time. Given the presence of a pool of unemployed workers, when labor contracts come up for renewal, nominal wages will be bid down. The short-run aggregate supply curve will be induced to shift in the southeastern direction, moving the economy toward full employment in the labor market. Note, however, that the supply shock reduces the full-employment level of output; as a result, the economy will not return to its initial level of income, Y_F; it will move instead to full employment at Y'_F. The reason for the decline in the level of domestic output at full employment lies in the fact that the rise in the real cost of oil implies a transfer of real income from oil-importing nations to the oil-producing countries. The implied reduction of real income in industrial oil-importing countries is reflected in a decrease in the output any of those economies can produce with their available labor force *net of the real cost of the imported oil input.* This is what the decrease in (net) full-employment output from Y_F to Y'_F in

Figure 17–4 depicts.[6] Therefore, when the economy adjusts to full employment in the labor market, a lower amount of net output will be produced. Note that the counterpart of this decline of domestic real income in oil-importing countries is an increase in the standard of living of the oil exporters. Similarly, note that over the long run, the price level does not return to its original level. The reason for this long-run increase in domestic prices in the present context lies in the shortage effect induced by a permanently reduced full-employment income. We should stress, however, that the effect of a supply shock on world inflation must be examined in order to specify its full implications for domestic inflation. The topic of world inflation will be covered in Chapter 22.

Monetary Accommodation

Up to this point, we have ruled out active government intervention in the form of monetary and/or fiscal policies, showing how full employment can be reestablished after a supply shock, but only in response to a protracted recession that reduces real wages over time. The alternative to laissez faire is for the authorities to engage in activist policies intended to counteract the unemployment effects of the supply shock in the short run and to ameliorate its consequent social disruption. Given the general impotence of autonomous fiscal policy actions followed independently by any single country[7] under flexible exchange rates, in the presence of a high degree of capital mobility, one possibility is to engage in an expansionary monetary policy.

An expansion of the money supply will tend to shift the aggregate demand curve upward; from $Y_0^D Y_0^D$ to $\hat{Y}^D \hat{Y}^D$ in Figure 17–5, which reproduces Figure 17–4 with less detail and depicts the economy's short-run equilibrium after the supply shock by means of point G. By increasing the money supply, policymakers could, in principle, move the economy to full employment, as depicted by point H. This, of course, does not prevent the loss of real income represented by the decline in the potential level of output from Y_F to Y'_F, but it serves to speed up the adjustment of the economy toward full employment in the labor market. It speeds it up by igniting inflation and therefore reducing real wages in the short run. In its absence, real wages would adjust, but only gradually over time, as the discipline imposed by unemployment is felt in the labor market and wage contracts embody lower nominal wages in response.

The effects of expansionary monetary policy in driving the economy to full employment operate by offsetting the negative impact of the supply

[6] John A. Tatom of the Federal Reserve Bank of St. Louis has estimated that the reduction in the potential full-employment level of output in the United States associated with the 1979–1980 oil-price hike was in the neighborhood of 5.7 percent: See J. A. Tatom, "Are the Macroeconomic Effects of Oil Price Changes Symmetric?" in K. Brunner and A. Meltzer, eds., *Carnegie-Rochester Series on Public Policy* (Spring 1988).

[7] As opposed to a coordinated fiscal expansion by the major industrial countries (which, as discussed in Chapter 13, may result in a worldwide economic recovery).

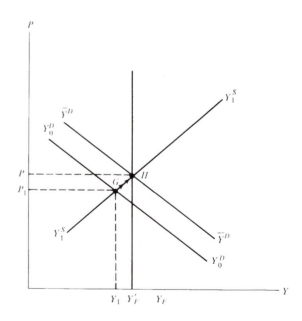

FIGURE 17–5. Supply Shocks and Monetary Accommodation

shock on the aggregate quantity demanded of domestic goods. The inflation associated with the shock shrinks real money balances, reducing economic activity. By increasing the nominal money supply, expansionary monetary policy acts to offset this recessionary effect, raising the quantity demanded of domestic goods and moving the economy to full employment. This type of policy is referred to as *monetary accommodation.*[8]

The expansionary monetary policy characterized by monetary accommodation will ignite domestic inflation. For those policymakers who are committed to controlling inflation, such an effect would be undesirable and anticlimactic. They would rather follow a restrictive or contractionary monetary policy, if necessary, to maintain or reduce the rate of domestic inflation. Clearly, depending on the specific policies followed by specific countries, different inflation rates will surface in the aftermath of a supply shock. Situations may consequently arise where inflation declines after the shock. Such appears to have been the situation in Japan and Germany in the aftermath of the oil-price shock of 1973 and 1974. In the case of Japan, the quantity of money grew at higher and higher rates from 1971 to early 1973. At that point, monetary policy was sharply reversed; the growth of the money supply declined from more than 25 percent per year in the spring of 1973 to about 10 percent by mid-1974.[9] Inflation in Japan, even though it increased in 1974, declined drastically in 1975, as recorded in Table 17–2. In the second oil-price shock of 1979, monetary growth was curtailed from 12.3 percent in the first quarter of 1979 to 8.4 percent by the third quarter of 1980. Japanese inflation declined from 4.6 to 2.8 percent from 1978 to 1980 and continued its downward movement in 1981 and 1982. In the

case of Germany, the rate of growth of the money supply was approximately halved between the first quarter of 1973 and mid-1974. The German inflation rate increased slightly from 6.5 percent in 1973 to 6.8 percent in 1974, but then declined to 6.1 and 3.4 percent in 1975 and 1976, respectively. Contractionary monetary policy in 1979 and 1980 was also drastic and was associated with controlled, or declining, German inflation in the aftermath of the oil shock.

Oil Shocks, the Current Account, and the Exchange Rate

One final aspect of supply shocks that has given rise to much confusion and misunderstanding is its effects on the CAB and the exchange rate. For instance, it is popularly believed that the increased U.S. oil imports resulting from the oil shock in 1973 and 1974 were the *cause* of CAB deficits and of the fall in the value of the dollar in its aftermath. Indeed, *everything else being constant,* an exogenous increase in the bill paid on oil imports that would tend to deteriorate the current account and—at the original exchange rate—generate a balance-of-payments deficit, would induce a currency depreciation. The problem, however, is that the everything-else-constant assumption does not generally hold. As Figure 17–4 illustrates, in addition to the increase in the price of oil, there will be changes in a number of other variables. In particular, the supply shock will tend to be recessionary. Therefore, as domestic income declines, imports of final goods will be reduced, tending to improve—rather than worsen—the current account. This appears to be part of the reason behind the very substantial *surplus* in the U.S. current account in 1975.[10] In any case, even if the situation

---

[8] An advanced analysis of the effects of accommodation is available in S. J. Turnovsky, "Supply Shocks and Optimal Monetary Policy," *Oxford Economic Papers* (September 1987); and in J. Aizenman and J. A. Frenkel, "Supply Shocks, Wage Indexation and Monetary Accommodation," *Journal of Money, Credit and Banking* (August 1986).

[9] Figures for the money supply in this section refer to currency and demand deposits plus large CDs.

[10] No statistically significant connection was found either between oil import bills and current account deficits in other OECD countries during this time period; see J. D. Sachs, "Aspects of the Current Account Behavior of OECD Economies," National Bureau of Economic Research Working Paper no. 859 (February 1982).

were one in which the CAB does deteriorate significantly as a result of the oil shock, this does not imply any definitive connection with short-run currency depreciation. Over the short run, the exchange rate adjusts to eliminate balance-of-payments disequilibria, not trade balance or CAB disequilibria. Because, in a world of high capital mobility, the capital account dominates the short-run behavior of the exchange rate, we must consider how the capital account reacts to a supply shock in any single country. There is no clear-cut pattern, but a key variable affecting the behavior of the capital account of any specific (oil-importing) country will be how the oil exporters (OPEC) invest their trade surpluses, which depends on their asset preferences. If OPEC investments in dollars are large enough, the consequent U.S. capital account improvement would tend to induce an exchange rate appreciation of the dollar—rather than a depreciation. With the portfolio of OPEC investors determined by a number of variables, such as interest rates and political risk, no a priori generalization can be made about the effects of a supply shock on either the current account or the exchange rate of any single country.

This conclusion appears to be supported by the wide variety in exchange rate behavior in the aftermath of the oil shock in 1973 and 1974. Even though the U.S. dollar did depreciate in effective terms from 1974 to 1975, the currencies of both Germany and Japan appreciated in effective terms during this period, in spite of the fact that both countries imported more oil as a percentage of GNP than the United States. On the other hand, the common wisdom that an oil price increase (decrease) is associated with a depreciation (appreciation) of the currencies of oil-importing economies has been found to be consistent with the substantial appreciation of the yen in 1986. From January to September of 1986, the yen appreciated by close to 70 percent relative to the dollar. During that time, the price of oil collapsed, with the spot price of a barrel of crude oil declining from $26 at the beginning of January to $9 in July. Although

other factors can explain part of the yen appreciation, Japanese economist Takatoshi Ito finds strong evidence that the oil price collapse had a lot to do with the yen appreciation.[11] It can be concluded that there is no simple causal connection between a supply shock and a domestic currency depreciation.

17−7. OIL PRICE SHOCKS AND THE U.S. ECONOMY: FROM THE 1970S TO THE 1990S

The general framework developed in this chapter and used up to this point to analyze the effects of supply shocks illustrates the impact of oil-price changes on the U.S. economy and how macroeconomic policies implemented simultaneously with those policies altered their impact. Figure 12−5 showed the upward jumps in the price of oil between 1973 and 1974 and 1979 and 1980, as well as its collapse in 1986; that collapse has continued uninterrupted, except during the Iraqui-Kuwait conflict (1990–1991). We will first consider the impact of the 1973–1974 oil-price shock on the U.S. economy. This is an appropriate starting point because our framework's basic assumptions—that the economy be initially at full employment and that nominal wage rigidity characterize labor market behavior in the short run—seem to be applicable to the United States at that time. By any measure, the U.S. economy was relatively close to, if not exactly at, its potential

---

[11] T. Ito, *The Japanese Economy* (Cambridge, Mass.: MIT Press, 1992), pp. 347–349. For a formal framework specifying the influence of oil imports, the current account and capital account behavior on the dollar exchange rate, see P. Krugman, "Oil and the Dollar," in J. S. Bhandari and B. H. Putnam, eds., *Economic Interdependence and Flexible Exchange Rates* (Cambridge, Mass.: The M.I.T. Press, 1983). For a less technical description of the connections (and lack of them) between oil shocks and the behavior of exchange rates, see D. R. Mudd and G. E. Wood, "Oil Imports and the Fall of the Dollar," *Federal Reserve Bank of St. Louis Review* (August 1978).

level of output in the period immediately preceding the oil shock. Furthermore, labor market practices in the United States, as embodied in the widespread presence of nonsynchronized, three-year labor contracts, do tend to generate a relatively high degree of nominal wage stickiness.

The strong recession suffered by the U.S. economy in 1974 and 1975—evident in the figures shown in Table 17–2—clearly reflected the recessionary impact of the sharp rise in the real cost of oil, as was described in the previous section. It also exhibited, however, the restrictive monetary and fiscal policies followed by the government in 1973 and the lack of any reversal of these policies during 1974. As Princeton economist—and Council of Economic Advisers member—Alan S. Blinder remarked:

> Both monetary and fiscal policy turned brusquely from stimulus to restraint in 1973. Anyone who has ever been in an automobile that was brought to an abrupt halt knows that, at best, this violent wrenching gives you an uneasy feeling in your stomach and, at worst, it puts you through the windshield. The economy got indigestion in 1973.[12]

In terms of Figure 17–4, the leftward shift of the aggregate supply curve was combined with a leftward shift of aggregate demand, thereby heightening the negative effects of the oil shock on U.S. output and employment.

The rising prices associated with the supply shock—documented in Table 17–2—were also connected to a reduction of U.S. real wages, as predicted by our framework. This is the picture obtained from Table 17–3, which shows U.S. real wages declining from 1973 to 1975. When combined with the gradual movement toward more expansionary policies between 1976 and 1978, this reduction of real wages laid the basis for a strong recovery in these later years. Still, the restrictive aggregate demand policies sustained in 1973 and

[12] A. S. Blinder, *Economic Policy and the Great Stagflation* (New York: Academic Press, 1979), p. 205.

TABLE **17–3.** **Real Wages in the United States, 1973–1990**

Year	Real Wage
1973	$103.4
1974	101.1
1975	101.2
1976	103.4
1977	105.7
1978	106.8
1979	104.0
1980	99.5
1981	99.2
1982	99.5
1983	100.0
1984	99.6
1985	100.0
1986	100.0
1987	98.3
1988	97.1
1989	95.3
1990	93.6

The real wage is equal to an index of hourly earnings in manufacturing divided by the CPI, with 1985 = 100.

SOURCE: International Monetary Fund, *International Financial Statistics Yearbook* (Washington, D.C.: IMF, 1991).

1974 clearly contributed to delaying the recovery. As a matter of fact, many economists have argued that the opposite policies should have been followed and that the oil shock should have been accommodated by means of expansionary monetary policy.

The behavior of the U.S. economy during and after the oil-price shock in 1979 and 1980 follows the pattern set by the 1973–1974 disturbance. As Table 17–2 depicts, the shock was associated with a slowdown of economic activity and an increase in unemployment from 5.8 percent in 1979 to 11.9 percent in 1982. Prices also rose rapidly and real wages dropped. (Table 17–3 documents the reduction in the real wage between 1979 and 1982.) Just as restrictive aggregate demand policies may have aggravated the impact of the 1973–1974 oil shock on U.S. output, the restrictive monetary policy followed by U.S. authorities beginning in 1979 and continuing into the early 1980s resulted in severe recession. The goal of the policies was to control inflation, which did drop substantially during the years following the shock, as Tables 17–1 and 17–2 illustrate.

A different type of oil shock occurred in 1986, when oil prices went spinning downward. In the framework developed in this chapter, a reduction in the price of imported inputs raises the potential level of output and shifts aggregate supply to the right, reducing inflation, increasing production, and raising real wages. The figures supplied by Table 17–1 show that the U.S. unemployment rate declined significantly in the years following the drop in oil prices. In fact, the economy maintained a comparatively high growth rate in the period from 1983 to 1988—a boom the recession of the early 1990s abruptly ended. It is thus clear that the increased output and reduced unemployment during the late 1980s was only partly linked to the favorable oil-price shock. It was more directly associated with the reversal of the policies adopted early in the administration of President Ronald Reagan—from fiscal and monetary restraint toward more expansionary aggregate demand policies—in the mid- and late 1980s.[13]

In 1990, the price of oil once again rose sharply in response to Iraq's invasion of Kuwait and the ensuing events. One difference between this disturbance and the previous oil shocks was its temporary nature: The oil hike occurred over a period of three months and was reversed in the following months. Although the shock coincided, and to some extent reinforced, the recession facing the U.S. economy in the early 1990s, this economic slowdown had begun earlier, in 1989.

As in previous oil shocks, some economists recommended that policymakers accelerate the rate of growth of the money supply in order to accommodate the oil shock. Others countered that higher money growth would ignite inflation and that what was needed was lower monetary expansion to reduce the risk of inflation. A third, middle-of-the-way approach was to keep the money supply growth unchanged in response to the shock.[14] In reality, money supply growth declined during the oil-price hike (from 4.8 percent during the three quarters before the shock in June 1990 to 3.6 percent during the shock) but then rose afterward (up to 6.8 percent during 1991).

It can be concluded that the role played by oil-price shocks in determining economic fluctuations in the U.S. in the 1970s, 1980s, and 1990s is difficult to disentangle from the simultaneous changes in macroeconomic policies being followed by policymakers. (This is particularly so when supply shocks also affect aggregate demand.) However, our analysis suggests that the data are broadly consistent with a substantial responsiveness of economic variables—such as output and employment—to supply shocks. Indeed, the available evidence for disentangling the effects of aggregate demand and aggregate supply disturbances indicates that shocks in the prices of imported inputs have been—to some extent or another—major determinants of economic activity in the United States.[15]

---

[13] For an analysis of the nature of the post-1983 recovery, see O. Blanchard, "Reaganomics," *Economic Policy* (1987). The links of the oil shock to economic activity in these years is examined by J. A. Tatom, "Macroeconomic Effects of the 1986 Oil Price Decline," *Contemporary Policy Issues* (July 1988).

[14] See M. Feldstein, "The Fed Must Not Accommodate Iraq," *The Wall Street Journal,* August 13, 1990; and J. A. Tatom, "The 1990 Oil Price Hike in Perspective," *Federal Reserve Bank of St. Louis* (November–December 1991).

[15] See R. C. Fair, "Sources of Economic Fluctuations in the United States," *Quarterly Journal of Economics* (May 1988); the different dynamic consequences of aggregate demand and supply disturbances have been identified by O. Blanchard and D. Quah, "The Dynamic Effects of Aggregate Demand and Supply Disturbances," *American Economic Review* (September 1989).

17–8. EFFECTS OF STABILIZATION POLICY WITH REAL WAGE RIGIDITY

One of the key concerns in European policy circles in recent years has been the relatively high unemployment rates prevailing in many European countries since the early 1970s. This is clear from the figures in Table 17–1. In 1990, for instance, the average unemployment rate in Europe was 8.1 percent, compared to 5.5 percent in the United States. In the United Kingdom, the unemployment rate persistently hovered above 10 percent and was equal to 11 percent in 1991; compare this to the period from 1945 to 1970, when the highest unemployment rate in that country was 3.3 percent. The persistence of unemployment in European countries spills over into skepticism over the use of expansionary monetary and fiscal policies to raise employment. European policymakers often make the argument that a rapid expansion of the money supply in their economies would only increase inflation without affecting output or employment to any significant extent. Is there any rationale for such a position? In this section we examine this question and the available evidence.

The discussion in the previous sections makes clear that in a situation of nominal wage rigidity, expansionary aggregate demand policies can, in principle, have an effective impact on output in the short run: They fuel domestic inflation and reduce real wage rates as a result. Faced with relatively lower real labor costs, employers will increase employment and output, spearheading a rapid recovery of the economy; however, it is precisely the connection between expansionary aggregate demand policies and declining real wages that European policymakers have questioned. Jeffrey Sachs notes, in relation to the debate in the 1970s:

There was widespread doubt, voiced by economists in West Germany in particular, that expansionary policies could moderate real wages and they rejected the Keynesian view that the stickiness of nominal wages

made it possible for policy-induced price inflation to reduce real wages.[16]

The alternative view propounded in European circles is that, because of the presence of automatic wage indexation or the existence of short-term labor contracts allowing workers to bargain in order to maintain undiminished their real earnings, the adjustment of nominal wages to changes in prices was consequently rapid and automatic in Europe. This led to the alleged lack of responsiveness of real wages to expansionary aggregate demand. This real wage rigidity makes it impossible for expansionary monetary policy to move the economy to full employment.[17]

The problems of economic policy in the presence of real wage rigidity are examined through the use of Figure 17–6, which shows an economy operating initially at the short-run equilibrium point E, with a level of output Y_0—below full employment—and an initial price level P_0. Given this situation, the policy debate regards the effectiveness of aggregate demand policies in increasing output in the presence of real wage rigidity.

Suppose that the central bank engages in expansionary monetary policy. This would shift the aggregate demand curve upward and, if large enough *and with rigid nominal wages,* it could move the economy to point F at full employment. This was exactly the argument made earlier, in

---

[16] J. D. Sachs, "Wages, Profits and Macroeconomic Adjustment: A Comparative Study," *Brookings Papers on Economic Activity,* (1979).

[17] See J. D. Sachs, "High Unemployment in Europe," National Bureau of Economic Research Working Paper no. 1830 (February 1986). For alternative views on the differences in labor market institutions among the United States, Western Europe, and Japan, as well as the implications, see T. Tachibanaki, "Labour Market Flexibility in Japan in Comparison with Europe and the U.S.," and R. J. Gordon, "Productivity, Wages and Prices Inside and Outside of Manufacturing in the U.S., Japan and Europe," in G. de Ménil and R. J. Gordon, eds., *International Volatility and Economic Growth* (Amsterdam: North Holland, 1991).

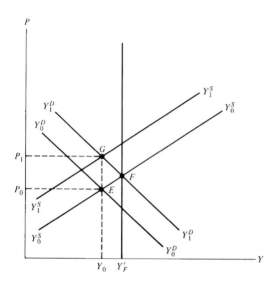

FIGURE 17–6. Economic Policy in the Presence of Real Wage Rigidity

reference to Figure 17–5. To derive this result, however, the assumption is made that long-term contracts fix the nominal wage rate to prevent it from rising in the short-run period of analysis. If, instead, we assume it is real wages that are rigid, in the sense that labor market institutions react immediately to the policy by raising nominal wages in response to the implied price inflation (from P_0 to P_1 in Figure 17–6), both aggregate demand and aggregate supply shift. In terms of Figure 17–6, if at the original output, Y_0, the aggregate demand shift implies an increase in prices from P_0 to P_1, real wage rigidity in the short run means that nominal wages would immediately rise to match the price hike. This is reflected by the leftward shift of the aggregate supply curve from $Y_0^S Y_0^S$ to $Y_1^S Y_1^S$. The resulting equilibrium occurs at point G, with an increase in prices from P_0 to P_1 but no increase in output. With real wage rates fixed in the short run, domestic producers do not have any incentive to increase employment and thus output. Therefore, the expansionary policy

would not be able to move the economy toward full employment. Eventually, of course, real wages would decline in response to unemployment. However, given real wage rigidity in the short run, expansionary monetary policy will not be able to speed up this process.

In conclusion, expansionary monetary policy in the presence of real wage rigidity appears to lack significant effects on output and to lead only to price inflation in the short run. Consequently, there is some basis for the Europeans lack of confidence vis-à-vis the United States in the use of expansionary aggregate demand policies to move their economies toward recovery in the aftermath of the oil shocks of 1973 and 1974 and 1979 and 1980. There are wide differences in the labor market institutions that set wage rates in the United States and Western European countries. Overlapping long-term wage contracts that are only partially indexed in the United States and a more indexed and synchronized system of wage setting in Europe generate significant differences in the effectiveness of macroeconomic policies.

The differences in the behavior of real wages in the aftermath of the oil shock of 1979 and 1980 in the industrial countries are shown in Table 17–4, which provides evidence supporting the hypothesis of the relative real wage rigidity faced by labor market institutions in Western Europe as compared with the United States.[18] In the United States, real wage rate growth declined drastically after the 1979 oil shock, while in Western Europe (with the possible exception of West Germany) real wage rate growth continued. These data also serve partially to explain the relative difficulty of Western Europe to recover from the oil shock, at least when compared with the United States. The decline of real labor costs in the United States served to boost production, leading the American economy

[18] For more evidence regarding the behavior of nominal and real wages in OECD countries in the aftermath of the 1973–1974 oil shock, see W. H. Branson and J. J. Rotemberg, "International Adjustment with Wage Rigidity," in de Ménil and Gordon, ibid.

TABLE 17−4. The Supply Shock of 1979−80 and Real Wages in the United States and Europe

Year	Real Wage				
	United States	France	Germany	Italy	United Kingdom
1977	$105.7	$83.1	$97.0	$85.8	$81.1
1978	106.8	86.4	98.7	89.1	85.9
1979	104.0	88.6	99.7	92.7	87.3
1980	99.5	89.3	99.1	93.2	87.8
1981	99.2	96.0	98.5	96.7	89.1
1982	99.5	97.7	98.4	97.6	91.2

Note: The real wage is equal to an index of labor compensation divided by the CPI; 1985 = 100.

SOURCE: International Monetary Fund, *International Financial Statistics* (Washington, D.C.: IMF, 1991).

to a stronger recovery in the 1980s relative to Western Europe's.

Just as short-run real wage rigidity makes it more difficult for expansionary monetary policy to stimulate output and employment within limited time contexts, it also makes it relatively easier for contractionary monetary policy to control inflation over short periods of time. When nominal wages respond immediately to offset changes in prices, a monetary contraction that reduces prices at any given level of output would immediately be associated with lower nominal wages. The reduced real labor costs would then serve as an incentive for domestic producers to increase aggregate supply. Both the aggregate demand contraction arising from the monetary shock and the associated aggregate supply expansion implied by the declining nominal wages tend to place downward pressure on domestic prices. Hence, there is some basis for expecting real wage rigidity to serve as an aid in controlling inflation. At the same time, the direct negative effects of restrictive aggregate demand policy on domestic output will be minimized by the positive impact of declining nominal wages on aggregate supply. In other words, with real wage rigidity, declining inflation will have a lesser impact on output than in the comparable situation with

nominal wage rigidity, where a monetary contraction lowers prices, raises real wages, and induces domestic production to decline in the short run. As Sachs summarizes the issues: "With sluggish nominal wages, monetary policy can affect output; with rigid real wages, monetary policy works on prices. Thus, in the latter case, monetary contraction is a powerful tool for controlling inflation."[19]

The persistence of European unemployment in the 1980s and early 1990s cannot be totally explained by the consequences of supply shocks in the presence of real wage rigidity. The contractionary aggregate demand policies adopted by the United States in the early 1980s, which resulted in a sharp worldwide recession and a global rise in real interest rates, also played a role.[20] In addition,

[19] J. D. Sachs, "Wages, Profits, and Macroeconomic Adjustment: A Comparative Study," *Brookings Papers on Economic Activity* (1979).

[20] The external constraints imposed by the repercussions of U.S. economic policies has been noted by J. P. Fitoussi, *The Slump in Europe* (Oxford: Basil Blackwell, 1988); see also G. S. Alogoskoufis and C. Martin, "External Constraints on European Unemployment," in G. Alogoskoufis, L. Papademos, and R. Portes, eds., *External Constraints on Macroeconomic Policy: The European Experience* (Cambridge: Cambridge University Press, 1991).

and in contrast to the United States, whose policies shifted from contractionary to expansionary in the 1980s, many European countries implemented sustained programs of fiscal austerity and contractionary monetary policies to control inflation in the 1980s (which did decline dramatically in some countries, as Table 17–1 exhibits). There is also some evidence that the full-employment rate of unemployment may have risen in Europe as a consequence of structural shifts from industry to services, regional dislocations and migration (spatial mismatch), shifts in skill requirements as a result of technological changes (skills mismatch), and demographic changes related to increased proportions of women and youth in the labor force.[21] Another hypothesis is that there has been *hysteresis* in unemployment. The idea here is that the increased unemployment associated with the oil shocks of 1973 and 1974 and 1979 and 1980 generated forces that sustained the unemployment rates at comparatively high levels in the 1980s. Several forces, or mechanisms, have been postulated for this self-sustained unemployment equilibrium. One theory is that unemployed workers suffer from a deterioration of human capital that makes them unemployable, particularly where skill requirements change over time in the economy. Another hypothesis is that those workers that remain employed—the "insiders," who are still in a bargaining position with employers—adopt strategies to maintain their employment while preventing the unemployed (the "outsiders") from competing effectively with them.[22]

[21] See F. P. Schioppa, ed., *Mismatch and Labour Mobility* (Cambridge: Cambridge University Press, 1991); and W. W. Lang, "Is There a Natural Rate of Unemployment?" *Federal Reserve Bank of Philadelphia Business Review* (March/April 1990).

[22] A discussion of the various hypotheses on the persistence of unemployment in European labor markets is supplied by O. J. Blanchard and L. Summers, "Hysteresis and the European Unemployment Problem," in S. Fischer, ed., *NBER Macroeconomics Annual, 1986* (Cambridge, Mass.: The MIT Press, 1986); and the articles in J. H. Dreze and C. R. Bean, eds., *Europe's Unemployment Problem* (Cambridge, Mass.: The MIT Press, 1990).

Summary

1. The equilibrium level of prices, output, and the exchange rate are established by the intersection of the economy's aggregate demand and aggregate supply curves.

2. Under a regime of flexible exchange rates, the aggregate demand curve depicts the relationship between the aggregate quantity demanded and the price of domestic goods, given the money supply and fiscal parameters, incorporating exchange rate adjustments.

3. The long-run equilibrium of the economy occurs at that point at which there is full employment. Exchange rate flexibility then guarantees balanced payments.

4. An automatic wage-price adjustment mechanism exists that operates by influencing real wages and real exchange rates and tends to move the laissez-faire economy toward full employment over time.

5. Supply shocks tend to destabilize the economy, shifting the short-run aggregate supply curve to the left and leading to short-run recession and to a reduction of the full-employment level of income.

6. Stagflation refers to episodes of stagnation and inflation like those that generally occurred in the industrial world in the aftermath of the massive oil-price hikes of 1973 to 1974 and 1979.

7. Stabilization policies are intended to speed up the adjustment of a destabilized economy toward its long-run equilibrium. However, fiscal policies pursued by a single country under flexible exchange rates will be ineffective in affecting the economy's output and employment both in the short run and in the long run. The expansionary effects of fiscal policy on aggregate demand, for instance, would be offset by a CAB deterioration arising from induced real exchange rate reductions.

8. A monetary accommodation policy can prevent the recessionary effects of reduced real liquidity resulting from sudden price hikes in

the economy. In the presence of nominal wage rigidity, the monetary expansion allows rising prices to speed up the adjustment of the economy by reducing real wages and encouraging output expansion.

9. Real wage rigidity exists in economies where labor market institutions guarantee the automatic indexing of nominal wages to cost-of-living increases over the short run. Under real wage rigidity, expansionary monetary policy is not significant in speeding up the adjustment of the economy toward full employment and will only result in inflation over the short run.

Problems

1. Consider an economy in long-run equilibrium with price stability and full employment. Suppose that, owing to increasing labor solidarity and militancy, unions are able to obtain a sudden 30 percent increase in nominal wage rates.
   (a) Describe verbally and diagrammatically the effects of this disturbance on domestic prices, output, trade balance, and nominal and real exchange rates. Distinguish between short-run and long-run effects.
   (b) What would be the impact of union-led wage hikes if the government decides to increase the money supply simultaneously? Would this ameliorate the impact of the wage disturbance on the economy? If so, in what sense?

2. The discussion in the text considered exclusively the case of perfect capital mobility. Consider the opposite extreme of an economy that does not trade in financial assets with the rest of the world. Would the results derived in Problem 1 regarding the ineffectiveness of policies on long-run output and the real exchange rate still hold? Would any conclusions be altered at all? Explain your answer.

3. It is the year 2001 and the moon and planets are populated by aliens who trade in goods, services, and assets with the countries of the Earth. The small lunar country of Selenia trades only with the United States, and its exchange rate, the selenian, freely fluctuates against the U.S. dollar. Selenia faces perfect capital mobility with a fixed interest rate $i^* = 0.10$. In addition, the lunar colony is at full employment, with a real level of output equal to 2000 units (in millions of Selenian goods). If we assume that the following real money demand function has been calculated for Selenia's residents,

$$L^D = 0.20Y - 2000i^*$$

(measured in millions of Selenian goods), and that Selenia's (nominal) money supply is currently equal to 600 million selenians:
   (a) What would be the current equilibrium price of Selenian goods?
   (b) Assume that you are provided with the following additional information regarding Selenia's absorption and trade balance relationships:

$$A = 480 + 0.78Y - 900i^*$$

$$T = 490 \frac{eP^*}{P} - 0.22Y,$$

where $\bar{T} = 0$, e is the selenian-dollar exchange rate (in selenians per dollar), P^* is the average price of U.S. goods imported by Selenia (in dollars), and P is the price of Selenian goods. Calculate the current value of the exchange rate on the assumption that $P^* = 6.00$.
   (c) Suppose that Selenia's central bank doubles the money supply from 600 to 1200 million selenians. What would be the long-run equilibrium impact on prices? How would the selenian exchange rate vis-à-vis the dollar be affected?

(d) Regarding the previous question, assume that, simultaneously with the doubling of Selenia's money supply, the United States decides to double its money supply. Assuming that the U.S. economy adjusts rapidly to long-run equilibrium, how would the U.S. monetary expansion affect Selenia? Would the U.S. policy alter in any way the effects of Selenia's policy? What does this suggest about interdependence in economies under flexible exchange rates?

(e) Consider the effects of a rise in the universe's interest rate from 10 to 15 percent. What would be the impact on lunar output, prices, and exchange rate?

(f) The Selenian government decides to reduce its expenditures on Selenian goods by 40 million units. Assuming the government expenditures form part of the 480 million autonomous absorption components in the absorption function A, what would be the inflationary, output, exchange rate, and trade balance effects of the reduced government spending over the long run? Would you expect the short-run effects of the policy to be any different?

4. In a controlled floating exchange rate regime, the central bank intervenes in foreign exchange markets at its discretion. Analyze, within the framework of this chapter, the impact of a Federal Reserve purchase of foreign exchange. What would be the effects of this operation on the U.S. money supply and on the dollar exchange rate? Explain your answer.

5. Consider an economy in long-run equilibrium under flexible exchange rates and perfect capital mobility. Assume that, because of disputes with a neighboring country, a war erupts with unfortunate long-term destruction of domestic industrial capacity. What would be the effects of these events on the country's output, prices, and nominal and real exchange rates? Would there be inflation or deflation, and by how much? Illustrate your answer diagrammatically and distinguish between the short run and the long run.

6. From February to August 1992, the U.S. money supply—measured by M2—declined in absolute terms, making 1992 the year with the slowest rate of monetary growth in the U.S. in three decades. Using the framework developed in this chapter, what would be your predictions as to the impact of the disturbance on: the dollar real and nominal exchange rate, U.S. output growth, and U.S. price level? Using data from publications such as *International Financial Statistics* and *The Federal Reserve Bulletin*, trace the behavior of the dollar real and nominal exchange rates during 1992 and 1993. Examine whether your predictions were actually realized, and, if not, provide an explanation why.

Expectations, Inflation, and Business Cycles

The often painful effects of the general ups and downs of aggregate economic activity usually referred to as business cycles, and the particularly traumatic experience of the Great Depression years of the 1930s, led to Keynesian economics and its emphasis on active government intervention to counteract or control these cycles. These so-called stabilization policies (also referred to as countercyclical policies) include both monetary and fiscal policies. They act as a package intended to restore the economy to the long-run trend from which business cycles have moved it. Actual experience, however, has shown the difficulties involved in fine tuning the economy. The relative stability of the U.S. economy in the 1950s and early 1960s, for instance, gave way to periods of rampant inflation and/or unemployment in the 1970s, 1980s, and 1990s. These events have raised serious questions about the effectiveness of stabilization policy, generating renewed study and controversy on the topic. This chapter will study the effectiveness of stabilization policies in open economies. The possibilities and problems of stabilization policies are closely related to how individuals react to those policies, both ex ante (when they try to anticipate policy changes), and ex post (when they respond to unanticipated policy changes). It is therefore of utmost importance to be able to assess the role of expectations, particularly inflationary expectations, in the effectiveness of stabilization policies.

513

The post-1970 global inflationary experience has led to increased awareness and anticipation of inflation. Inflation today seems to be viewed with serious concern by both the public and government. Such is the result obtained by public opinion polls asking individuals what they consider to be the most pressing economic problems. Inflation is usually among the top concerns, often outranking unemployment—although there is a marked difference among the responses of different groups in the population (high-income, educated white Republicans tend to worry the most about inflation). In cross-country studies, it appears that it is *unanticipated* inflation that worries most of the public. In countries where inflation has occurred for some extended period of time and is viewed as normal, individuals and firms devise instruments, such as cost-of-living provisions or other indexation schemes, to deal with inflation and do not appear to worry so much about it. The public's concern with inflation is also suggested by the observed negative association between the inflation rate in the year preceding an election and the likelihood of the re-election of a government administration. Inflation seems to be an effective way through which an administration can get toppled. It is thus not surprising that most governments assign a high priority to reducing, or at least to controlling, the rate of inflation in the economy.

Let us now introduce inflationary expectations into the aggregate demand and supply framework developed in Chapters 16 and 17. We begin with the simple analytics of flexible exchange rate regimes; later sections broaden the discussion to encompass economies under fixed exchange rates.

18–1. The Expectations-Augmented Aggregate Supply Curve

The role of inflationary expectations in the economy can best be introduced by determining their influence on aggregate supply, which depicts the relationship between prices and quantity supplied of domestic goods.

Suppose, for the sake of the argument, that the economy is initially at full employment and that there is an increase in the domestic price level. What effect would this have on the output domestic firms wish to supply? The answer to this question hinges crucially on whether the price level hike is anticipated by agents in the economy or it comes as a complete surprise to them. In an environment in which price changes occur frequently and workers and employers expect inflation to occur, labor contracts stipulating future wage rates will, in general, include escalating nominal wage rate clauses such as cost-of-living adjustments (COLAs). In their attempt to maintain desired standards of living in an inflationary environment, workers bargain with employers to keep nominal wage rate raises in parity with inflationary expectations for the duration of the contracts. As a consequence, anticipated price increases will have no effect on real wages: They are exactly matched by the nominal wage rate hikes stipulated in labor contracts. But with real labor costs unchanged, employers would have no incentive to change employment and, thus, output. In other words, if the increase in domestic prices is fully anticipated by agents in the economy, it will have no impact on either employment or output.

If the price rise is unanticipated, on the other hand, it would not be embodied in the nominal wage rate adjustments stipulated by labor contracts and would result in reduced real wages. The implied reduction of real labor costs would then induce domestic producers to increase employment and the output of domestic goods. The suggestion is that only unanticipated increases in price—that is, price surprises, have a positive effect on the aggregate quantity supplied of domestic goods. Similarly, unanticipated reductions in the price of domestic goods would be associated with a decrease in the output producers wish to supply.

The theoretical connection between changes in output and unanticipated (versus anticipated) price changes are summarized by the so-called expectations-augmented aggregate supply curve given by

$$Y = Y_F + \bar{\beta}\left(\frac{P - P^e}{P^e}\right), \qquad (18\text{--}1)$$

where Y denotes domestic output, Y_F is the full-employment level of output, and $(P - P^e)$ represents unanticipated price changes, equal to the difference between the current price level, P, and the price level agents in the economy anticipated would arise, P^e. Unanticipated price changes (price surprises) are expressed in proportional terms by dividing by the expected price level, P^e. Finally, $\bar{\beta}$ is a positive parameter representing the quantitative influence that unanticipated price changes have on domestic output. For instance, if output is measured in millions and $\bar{\beta} = 20$, then an unanticipated price increase equal to 5 percent—$(P - P^e)/P^e = 0.05$—would increase domestic output above full employment by one million, obtained by multiplying $(20)(0.05)$, which equals 1.

Equation 18–1 states that only unanticipated changes in domestic prices will generate deviations of domestic output from its potential level. For a given anticipated price of domestic goods—as determined by the information available to individuals in a previous time period—Equation 18–1 describes a positive relationship between domestic prices and output of domestic goods. This relationship is depicted by the upward–sloping expectations–augmented aggregate supply curve, AS, in Figure 18–1. If the domestic price level, P, is equal to its anticipated value, P_0^e, then output remains at full employment (when $P = P_0^e$, $Y = Y_F$). On the other hand, when the domestic price level rises above anticipated levels (such as in the case of $P_1 > P_0^e$), domestic output rises above full employment ($Y_1 > Y_F$ as depicted). Finally, when domestic prices are below their anticipated value (such as if $P' < P_0^e$), domestic output declines below full employment ($Y' < Y_F$).[1]

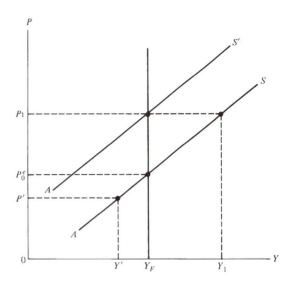

Figure 18–1. Expectations-Augmented Aggregate Supply Curve

As already described, the existence of labor contracts can explain the positive connection between unanticipated price changes and output of domestic goods. However, it is essential for the argument to get the timing correct. Inflation that is anticipated *at the start of* a given contract should have no impact on output because it is embodied in the nominal wage rate adjustments stipulated in advance. On the other hand, inflation that is perceived or anticipated *after the start of* a contract, so that it is unanticipated at the moment the contract is signed or agreed upon, could very well

---

[1]Note that the aggregate supply relationship established in Chapters 16 and 17 is just a special case of Equation 18–1. At that point in our analysis we assumed agents in the economy exhibited static expectations in the sense that they behaved on the presumption that prices would not change. The price level

expected to prevail today, P^e, was therefore equal to the price level in the previous time period, P_{-1}. In this case, Equation 18–1 becomes

$$Y = Y_F + \beta\left(\frac{P - P_{-1}}{P_{-1}}\right),$$

which is precisely the aggregate supply function we used in Chapters 16 and 17 (see the appendix to Chapter 16 and set $\bar{\beta} = \theta\beta$).

have an impact on domestic output because it is not embodied in the wage contracts previously signed.

Note, though, that what is unanticipated today becomes known tomorrow and, as a result, any unanticipated price changes that occur over the duration of a pre-existing labor contract will be embodied in new contracts when the existing ones expire. This suggests that, in the absence of additional disturbances, nominal wage rate raises matching unanticipated price hikes will eventually be incorporated into revised contracts. Real wage rates will thus be pressured upward, toward their original levels, and output will consequently return to its full-employment level. Algebraically, even though a rise in prices above previously anticipated levels ($P_1 > P_0^e$) may induce an expansion of output above full employment ($Y > Y_F$), when individuals revise their price expectations to conform with the realized increase in prices ($P_1 = P_1^e$), output must return to full employment ($Y = Y_F$). Geometrically, the revision in expectations embodied in new labor contracts tends to shift the aggregate supply curve to the left by raising real labor costs, thereby reducing employment and output at any given price level. In terms of Figure 18–1, the original aggregate supply curve AS would shift to the left toward AS'. This movement suggests that when the anticipated price level has been revised to equal the actual price level, P_1, and has correspondingly been embodied into negotiated wage contract raises, the domestic level of output would be at full employment ($Y = Y_F$). In other words, over the long run, the aggregate supply curve will become vertical. Exactly how much time is required for this to occur depends on the length of labor contracts and the particular labor market institutions existing in the economy, among other factors.

18–2. THE FORMATION OF EXPECTATIONS

The previous section has shown the key role inflationary expectations have in determining aggregate supply. This section examines how agents in the economy form expectations about inflation. Two basic types of expectations behavior have been widely examined in macroeconomics: *adaptive expectations* and *rational expectations* (see the discussion in Chapter 6). The basic concept behind the adaptive expectations mechanism is that individuals use information relating to past forecasting errors to revise expectations. For instance, if the expected domestic price level in a previous time period is denoted by P^e_{-1}, and the actual price level turns out to be P, then the expected level of domestic prices in the next period, P^e, will be revised according to

$$P^e - P^e_{-1} = \xi(P - P^e_{-1}),$$

where ξ is a positive coefficient between 0 and 1, to be interpreted momentarily. This equation states that if the actual price level observed in a given time period turns out to be above the expected price level for that period (if $P - P^e_{-1}$ is positive), the expected prices for the subsequent period are revised upward ($P^e - P^e_{-1}$ is positive). The parameter ξ indicates by how much the expected price level is adjusted in response to past mistakes. For example, if ξ is very small (close to zero), expectations are not adjusted in any significant way and P^e remains approximately equal to P^e_{-1}.

Adaptive expectations represent actual behavior in instances in which information is difficult or expensive to acquire. In these situations, it becomes easier to make predictions on the basis of rules concerning present and past values of the variables at stake. Such is the case of the person who looks out the window and assumes that the afternoon weather will be more or less like that of the morning. At the same time, however, we should recognize that adaptive expectational behavior can be consistently out of target. Its reliance on past values implies slow reactions to sudden changes. It is because of this problem that, in recent years, adaptive expectations has been increasingly discarded as forming the basis of any long-lasting expectations behavior in economic analysis. The alternative has become rational expectations.

In contrast to the person who relies on past values and arbitrary rules in deciding about the future, the person following rational expectations searches information and makes decisions on an informed basis. Under rational expectations behavior, people incorporate all the relevant systematic information available in forming their expectations of a given variable. Expectational errors are thus unsystematic; they arise from unanticipated, random disturbances about which the person had no information available or could not have made a prediction. The rational expectation of a given variable, X, is

$$X^e = E[X|I_t],$$

where $E[X|I_t]$ is the expected value of the variable X, given all the information available at time t, which is denoted by I_t. (The reader may want to review our discussion of rational expectations in Chapter 16.)[2] The rational expectation of the inflation rate—given the available information at time t—is

$$\Pi \equiv \hat{P}^e = E[\hat{P}|I_t],$$

where ˆ's represents proportional changes, $\hat{P}_e$ denotes anticipated inflation, $\hat{P}$ actual inflation, and so on.

In the case of predicting the weather, individuals rely heavily on information provided by weather bureau forecasts, which offers them the likely future weather as determined by the best meteorological models of climatic behavior. In the case of expectations regarding economic variables, what information can we assume that individuals have? The analogy to the weather case is to assume that individuals form expectations *as if* they knew the structure of the economic models under consideration. Thus, in our aggregate demand-aggregate

supply framework, the rational expectations approach would assume that individuals behave as if they knew the equations and parameters involved in the model (e.g., output, prices, the exchange rate, and money demand elasticities) and form expectations on the basis of that model and on the information they have about the likelihood of various possible disturbances to the economy in the future. Obviously, no one goes around every day calculating marginal propensities to consume or income elasticities of demand for money. Nevertheless, investors—and unions and firms, for that matter—do rely on the best information they have available about the future of the economy in making predictions. Thus, implicitly or explicitly they do make use of economic models when making predictions. Of course, they may not have the same model of the economy that we are using in this analysis. However, the arguments for using rational expectations to develop expectations formation in an economic model do not rely on whether individuals do know or actually believe in the economic framework under consideration. Every single economic model is a simplification of reality and clearly has to ignore factors occurring in the real world that, it is hoped, do not distort the model's conclusion or the problem considered in a significant way.

Although no economic model can be expected to consider all aspects of human behavior, and we cannot therefore assume that agents in the economy believe or act on its basis, the model must still be consistent with the way in which agents behave and process information. If individuals form rational expectations using their own models of the economic world, in our simplified economic model we must assume that individuals make rational expectations on the basis of their knowledge of that simplified economic world. Hence, the main question regarding rational expectations must be whether individuals actually do acquire information as postulated by the approach. The answer to this question is that in general they do, unless information costs are so high that rules of thumb and hunches become a more profitable (or least costly) way of making forecasts. Given the wide availability of economic statistics and the interest in acquiring information on the part of vital economic agents—unions, investors, firms, consumers—it has seemed more and more reasonable for economists to assume that rational expectations do actually mold expectations formation in their economic models. The following discussion, for the most part, assumes that rational expectations characterize the formation of expectations by agents in the economy.[3]

18–3. FLEXIBLE EXCHANGE RATES, ANTICIPATED REAL EXCHANGE RATE CHANGES, AND AGGREGATE DEMAND

This section examines the role played by expectations formation on aggregate demand. The incessant exchange rate changes arising under exchange rate flexibility add an important dimension to the analysis: They make the formation of exchange rate expectations a bread-and-butter aspect of that regime. In examining the behavior of the economy and government policy effectiveness, we must then incorporate as an integral part not only the role of inflationary expectations, but also that of exchange rate expectations. Because, in general, price and exchange rate changes are not independent of each other and may have common origins, we must closely examine their interrelationships. Therefore, we will analyze how price and exchange rate changes determine fluctuations in *real* exchange rates. By showing the ratio of the do-

mestic currency prices of foreign goods relative to the prices of domestic goods, real exchange rates are a basic measure of the relative competitiveness of domestic goods in foreign markets. Real exchange rates thus influence heavily the equilibrium and adjustment of the open economy. Figure 18–2 shows the considerable short-term variability of the U.S. real exchange rate in the period of increased exchange rate flexibility after 1973. What explains this real exchange rate variability? It is one of the purposes of the next sections to answer this question. We start the discussion by examining the connections between anticipated real exchange rate changes, real interest rates, and aggregate demand under floating exchange rates.

Anticipated Real Exchange Rate Changes and Real Interest Rate Differentials

We proceed to determine first how the links between domestic and foreign interest rates under perfect capital mobility affect the analysis of inflation and business cycles. One of the basic points to be made is the importance of differentiating between nominal and real interest rates in an inflationary environment.

When we buy an asset we are interested in how much it will earn us as a rate of return. The (domestic) *nominal interest rate* is the rate of return on any given asset in terms of domestic currency. The (domestic) *real interest rate,* on the other hand, is the rate of return on any given asset *in terms of its purchasing power in domestic goods* and is equal to the nominal interest rate adjusted for inflation. In general, however, when evaluating an investment opportunity, we do not know what the rate of inflation will be in the future and cannot therefore calculate the exact real rate of interest beforehand. We have to make an estimate of what the inflation rate will be. Consequently, the domestic anticipated (ex ante) real interest rate, r, can be defined as

$$r = i - \Pi \qquad (18–2)$$

---

[3]There is increasing recognition, though, that disturbances to the economy take time to be recognized as a result of the need to collect and process information. In addition, some researchers have observed that forming rational expectations may initially involve a trial-and-error learning process similar to adaptive expectations. See R. Lucas, "Adaptive Behavior and Economic Theory," *Journal of Business* (Spring 1986); and R. Marimon and S. Sundar, "Rational Expectations vs. Adaptive Expectations in a Hyperinflationary World: Experimental Evidence," Center for Economic Research Discussion Paper no. 247, University of Minnesota (July 1988).

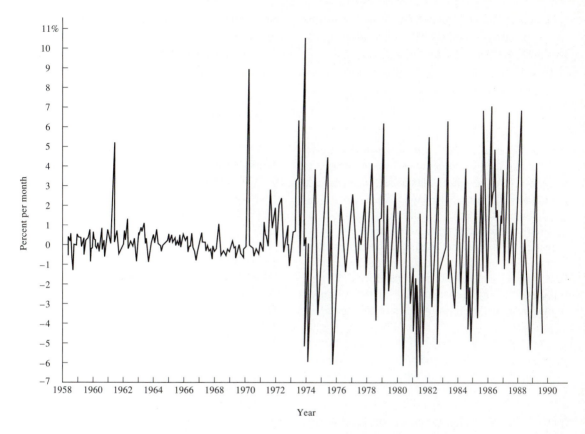

Note: The real exchange rate is equal to the bilateral dollar-deutsche mark exchange rate multiplied by an index of consumer prices in Germany divided by an index of consumer prices in the U.S.

FIGURE 18–2. The United States and Germany: Real Exchange Rate Variability, 1958–1989 (monthly percentage changes in the real exchange rate)

SOURCE: R. Dornbusch and S. Fischer, *Macroeconomics* (New York: McGraw-Hill, 1990), p. 775. Reprinted with permission of McGraw Hill Publishing Co.

where i is the (domestic) nominal interest rate and Π is the expected rate of inflation in the economy.

Exchange rate expectations are very closely linked to nominal interest rates. Under perfect capital mobility, the uncovered interest parity condition establishes the connection between domestic and world (nominal) interest rates, i and i^*, respec-tively, and exchange rate expectations. Algebra-ically (as derived in Chapter 5, with adequate caveats), we obtain

$$i = i^* + x, \qquad (18\text{--}3)$$

where x is the expected rate of depreciation of domestic currency.

By substituting Equation 18–3 into Equation 18–2, we obtain the following expression for the (ex ante) domestic real interest rate:

$$r = i - \Pi$$
$$= (i^* + x) - \Pi. \qquad (18\text{–}4)$$

Assuming that the world interest rate is fixed and cannot be significantly influenced by domestic forces, the domestic real interest rate will vary in response to expected exchange rate changes and anticipated inflation. The larger the expected depreciation of the domestic currency, the higher the domestic real interest rate will have to be to equalize domestic and foreign expected rates of return. The higher the anticipated domestic inflation rate, on the other hand, the lower the real interest rate—because the value of the return on domestic assets declines in terms of their purchasing power.

The domestic (ex ante) real interest rate expression in Equation 18–4 can be slightly modified by breaking down the nominal interest rate on foreign assets, i^*, into its components. We assume that $i^* = r^* + \Pi^*$; that is, the foreign nominal interest rate equals the foreign (ex ante) real interest rate, r^*, plus the anticipated rate of foreign inflation, Π^*. Substitution into Equation 18–4 yields

$$r = i^* + x - \Pi$$
$$= r^* + x + \Pi^* - \Pi$$
$$= r^* + \hat{q}^e, \qquad (18\text{–}5)$$

where $\hat{q}^e$ represents the anticipated proportional rate of change of the *real* exchange rate over a given time period and is equal to

$$\hat{q}^e = x + \Pi^* - \Pi. \qquad (18\text{–}6)$$

Observe that because the real exchange rate, $q = eP^*/P$, depends on the exchange rate, e, and the ratio of foreign to domestic prices, P^*/P, anticipated changes in the real exchange rate will

be determined by how these three variables are anticipated to change. With everything else constant, an anticipated domestic currency depreciation will increase the expected real exchange rate. This is what the first term on the right-hand side of Equation 18–6 shows, where the symbol x represents the anticipated domestic currency depreciation. Similarly, with domestic prices and the nominal exchange rate fixed, an anticipated foreign inflation equal to Π^* will also be anticipated to raise the real exchange rate. Finally, anticipated domestic inflation will—everything else being constant—be associated with an anticipated decline of the real exchange rate. How the real exchange rate is anticipated to change overall depends then on how each of these factors—anticipated nominal exchange rate changes and domestic and foreign inflation—fare against one another. If, for instance, the annual anticipated rate of depreciation of the domestic currency is equal to $x = 10$ percent, the foreign rate of inflation is anticipated to be $\Pi^* = 5$ percent and domestic inflationary expectations equal $\Pi = 8$ percent, the real exchange rate will be anticipated to increase by 7 percent over a year, or

$$\hat{q}^e = 10\% + 5\% - 8\% = 7\%.$$

Equation 18–5 suggests that a key factor generating deviations between domestic and foreign (ex ante) real interest rates involves anticipated real exchange rate changes.[4] To understand the economic reasoning behind this, recall that the domestic real interest rate is the rate of return on holding domestic assets in terms of its purchasing power over domestic goods, whereas the foreign real interest rate is the rate of return on holding foreign assets in terms of its purchasing power

---

[4]Our present discussion ignores risk considerations. The presence of an exchange risk premium, however, would also generate real interest rate differentials. A discussion of the macroeconomic role of exchange risk is provided in Chapter 19 (see also Chapter 5).

over foreign goods. An anticipated increase in the real exchange rate means that there is an expected increase in the relative price of foreign goods in terms of domestic goods. This suggests that a certain amount of purchasing power in foreign goods would have a higher value in terms of domestic goods. In order to compensate asset holders competitively for this expected increase in the foreign rate of return in terms of domestic goods, the domestic real interest rate would have to rise relative to its foreign counterpart. In other words, the anticipated increase of the real exchange rate would be associated with a positive differential between domestic and foreign (ex ante) real interest rates. Similarly, an anticipated real domestic currency appreciation would be associated with a reduction of domestic real interest rates relative to foreign real interest rates.

Aggregate Demand and the Real Interest Rate

The real interest rate is the relevant interest rate for investment decisions. When a firm, say a construction company, borrows to acquire capital or equipment, it calculates not only the nominal interest rate cost of the funds acquired, but also the real cost of borrowing, which is equal to the nominal interest rate adjusted for changes in the real value of the debt arising from increases in the general price level of the economy. Suppose, for example, that a firm borrows $100.00 at a 5 percent nominal rate of interest to finance the purchase of some equipment. The annual nominal interest cost of the investment is thus 5 percent. If the general price level is expected to increase by 5 percent, however, the real interest rate—and therefore the real cost of borrowing—is zero. The reason is that, although there is a 5 percent nominal interest cost, there is also a 5 percent gain arising from the decrease in the real value of the debt undertaken one year earlier. The increase in prices implies that the $100.00 the firm pays back one year later is worth 5 percent less in terms of its purchasing

power. Consequently, this gain to the borrower would exactly compensate the 5 percent nominal interest cost, leaving no net real interest cost on the borrowing.[5] Therefore, when firms undertake investments, they take into account the real cost of borrowing, which is the real rate of interest. Even though nominal rates may be very high, if the expected rate of inflation is also very high, the real cost of borrowing may be much smaller and investments more profitable. The higher the real interest rate, the more costly investing is; the lower the real rate, the less costly investment becomes.

By affecting investment, real interest rates are pivotal in the determination of aggregate demand.[6] Aggregate demand can be represented by

$$Y^D = \alpha[\bar{A} + \bar{T} + \phi q - br], \qquad (18\text{-}7)$$

where $\alpha = 1/(s + m)$ is the Keynesian open-economy multiplier, $\bar{A}$ is autonomous domestic spending, $\bar{T}$ is the autonomous trade balance, and r is the real interest rate.[7] Observe that b is a

---

[5]We are ignoring capital depreciation and taxes. In reality, the costs to the company of using the equipment purchased would have to include depreciation costs, in addition to the interest costs, and be adjusted for tax considerations.

[6]Real interest rates also affect capital accumulation by channeling investment toward real assets. They thus affect aggregate supply, too. In the presence of gestation lags in the actual process of capital accumulation, however, this would be a longer-term effect. Given our present concern with how actual output deviates from its potential, we will not consider this effect explicitly. It is clear, however, that when anticipated inflation reduces real interest rates, capital accumulation occurs and thus output increases. This is an often-neglected positive effect of (anticipated) monetary policy on the economy. For a detailed dicussion, see S. Fischer, "Anticipations and the Non-Neutrality of Money," *Journal of Political Economy* (April 1979).

[7]Equation 18–7 was derived in previous chapters. Note that the only difference between Equation 18–7 and Equation 17–2, for example, is that the domestic interest rate, r, is now equal to the *real* interest rate. In Chapter 17 we were not explicitly concerned with the role of inflationary expectations on macroeconomic equilibrium. Therefore, the nominal interest rate, i, was equated with the real rate.

positive parameter representing the sensitivity of investment spending to the real interest rate: the higher the real interest rate, the higher the real cost of capital. As a result, investment spending declines, shifting down aggregate demand. A declining real interest rate, on the other hand, would stimulate aggregate demand.

Substituting the expression for the real interest rate in Equation 18−5 into the aggregate demand function in Equation 18−7, we obtain

$$Y^D = \alpha[\bar{A} + \bar{T} + \phi q - b(r^* + \hat{q}^e)], \quad (18{-}8)$$

where the equation shows desired aggregate spending on domestic goods as a general function of autonomous expenditures, $\bar{A}$ and $\bar{T}$, the current value of the real exchange rate, q, the foreign real interest rate, r^*, and the anticipated proportional change of the real exchange rate, $\hat{q}^e$. This last factor illustrates that, by influencing domestic real interest rates, anticipated real exchange rate changes will tend to affect domestic investment and, therefore, aggregate desired spending on domestic goods.

Equation 18−8 is the algebraic counterpart of our now standard aggregate demand curve. Under floating exchange rates and perfect capital mobility, the curve shows the relationship between domestic prices and desired aggregate spending on domestic goods, given exchange rate flexibility and holding everything else constant. The aggregate demand curve in the present context is thus precisely the same as that derived in the last chapter, as shown in figures 17−1 and 17−2. The only caveat is that, now, the factors held constant along the demand curve include the anticipated change of the real exchange rate, $\hat{q}^e$. Variation in the latter will then generate shifts of the aggregate demand curve. Suppose, for instance, that $\hat{q}^e = 0$ initially and that suddenly agents in the economy anticipate the real exchange rate to decline ($\hat{q}^e < 0$). Other things being equal, we find that such an expectational disturbance will result in lower domestic real interest rates. Because there is

an anticipated increase in the value that any given amount of purchasing power in domestic goods has in terms of foreign goods, domestic asset holders will have to face a reduction in real interest rates to offset their relative gain of purchasing power in terms of foreign goods. Lower real interest rates, however, induce higher investment expenditures and, therefore, increase aggregate domestic spending, shifting the aggregate demand curve to the right.

18−4. RATIONAL EXPECTATIONS AND MONETARY POLICY IN THE OPEN ECONOMY

Expectational considerations force into the open the fact that the effectiveness of government policy intervention on the economy depends on whether the policy disturbance under consideration is anticipated by agents in the economy or is unanticipated. Let us consider the effects of a policy disturbance in the form of central bank credit creation. It is assumed that this is the only disturbance to the economy and that individuals form expectations following the rational expectations hypothesis. The latter implies that we can proceed as if agents in the economy determine their anticipated inflation rate by observing what inflation rate is predicted by the structural model of the economy described here—given, for example, their expectations about money supply changes. This is, as noted earlier, the weather forecaster's approach to forming expectations: Given some expected changes in atmospheric pressure, wind directions, and so on, the weather forecaster plugs all these variables into his or her meteorological model of weather determination, obtaining some forecasts of how climate conditions will be tomorrow. Individuals here are assumed to do so with regard to the aggregate supply-demand model of the economy utilized.

The issues are examined through the use of Figure 18−3, which shows the economy initially

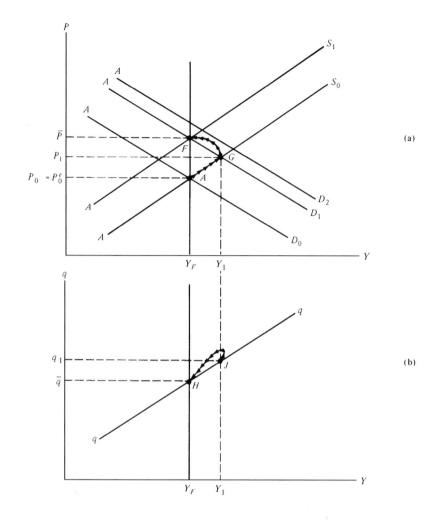

FIGURE 18–3. Unanticipated Monetary Policy Under Flexible Exchange Rates

in long-run equilibrium at point A, depicting the intersection of the aggregate demand AD_0 and aggregate supply AS_0 curves. With no anticipated disturbances, the economy would have price stability and full employment; no real exchange rate changes would be anticipated either ($\hat{q}^e = 0$). Figure 18–3(b) illustrates the determination of the real exchange rate. The curve qq depicts the positive connection between domestic output and the real exchange rate given no anticipated real

exchange rate changes. The economy's full employment output, Y_F, corresponds to a real exchange rate equal to $\bar{q}$.

The Impact of Unanticipated Monetary Policy Under Floating Exchange Rates

We examine first the impact of an unanticipated money supply increase. An unanticipated monetary expansion has no effects on the long-run aggregate supply curve, and no immediate impact on the anticipated real exchange rate and the (ex ante) real interest rate. Because the disturbance is unexpected, individuals presume the economy will remain at its initial, long-run equilibrium, as given by the intersection of the AD_0 and AS_0 curves. The domestic price level is expected to remain at $P_0^e = P_0$. This fixes the aggregate supply curve at its initial position. In addition, the real exchange rate is not anticipated to change so that $\hat{q}^e = 0$, implying that ex-ante real interest rates would remain unchanged at $r = r^*$ (from Equation 18–5).

What the money supply growth does is to place downward pressure on domestic nominal interest rates, inducing capital outflows and an increase of the nominal exchange rate. As a consequence, at the original price of domestic goods, the real exchange rate would increase, boosting domestic net exports and increasing aggregate spending on domestic goods: The aggregate demand curve shifts to the right from AD_0 to AD_1. The resulting short-run equilibrium of the economy in response to the unanticipated monetary expansion will occur at point G in Figure 18–3(a), where the aggregate demand curve AD_1 intersects the unchanged aggregate supply curve AS_0. The equilibrium level of output thus increases above full employment from Y_F to Y_1 and the domestic price level also rises, from P_0 to P_1. The explanation behind the short-run increase in domestic output lies in that the money supply growth is unanticipated. Its effects on domestic prices are consequently not embodied in the cost of living adjustments stipulated by previously bargained labor contracts and they reduce real wages. With lower real labor costs, employers are induced to raise employment and, thus, output.[8]

Point G is only a point of short-run equilibrium and will change as agents revise their expectations in response to new information about the economy. Consider the formation of inflationary expectations first. Once the central bank increases its credit, agents in the economy will observe the resulting domestic inflation (equal to $(P_1 - P_0)/P_0$ in Figure 18–3) and will thus adjust upward their expectations regarding the price level. By how much? In the presence of rational expectations, it will be recognized that, over the long run, and in the absence of other anticipated disturbances, the economy will return to full employment. The implied long-run equilibrium of the economy would then occur at the intersection of the aggregate demand curve, AD_1, with the vertical long-run aggregate supply curve lying at the full-employment level of output, Y_F. This is represented by point F in Figure 18–3(a). The long-run equilibrium price of domestic goods will then be given by $\bar{P}$, and individuals will consequently revise price expectations upward toward that level. As these inflationary expectations are embodied in labor contracts, real labor costs will rise, inducing producers to cut production. The short-run aggregate supply curve thus shifts left, stopping when it reaches the level consistent with long-run equilibrium.

In addition to inflationary expectations, the monetary disturbance influences real exchange rate expectations and ex ante real interest rates. The short-run movement of the economy from point A to point G generates a rise of the domestic real exchange rate. Individuals will recognize such a change and adjust their expectations regarding the future behavior of real exchange rates accordingly. In the presence of rational expectations, individuals would realize that, over the long run, and with no other anticipated disturbances, output will return to full employment and the real exchange rate must thus decline toward its original

---

[8]Workers whose labor contracts are about to be renegotiated will be able to revise their wages. Those whose labor contracts do not expire in the near future will be unable to revise their nominal wages; they will be stuck with (now obsolete) adjustments made when their contracts were negotiated. For an advanced exposition of this point, see S. Fischer, "Long-Term Contracts, Rational Expectations and the Optimal Money Sup-

ply Rule," and J. Taylor, "Staggered Wage Setting in a Macro Model," both in N. G. Mankiw and D. Romer, eds., *New Keynesian Economics* (Cambridge, Mass.: The MIT Press, 1991).

level at $\bar{q}$, which is the real exchange rate anticipated to prevail over the long run. Because the short-run real exchange rate is given by q_1, which exceeds its long-run level, individuals will anticipate a real exchange rate reduction over time. Symbolically, $\hat{q}^e$ becomes negative. But with agents in the economy anticipating their current purchasing power in domestic goods to increase in terms of foreign goods over the near future, the expected real return on domestic assets would tend to rise over its foreign counterpart and the domestic real interest rate would have to decline to offset this. The decline of the domestic real interest rate, r, will then raise investment spending and will immediately shift the aggregate demand curve to the right. This is depicted by the shift from AD_1 to AD_2 in Figure 18–3(a); it potentially increases the short-run expansionary impact of the monetary disturbance. Note, however, that as the real exchange rate declines over time back toward its initial level, the anticipated real currency appreciation disappears, raising the real interest rate back toward its original level. Graphically, the aggregate demand curve shifts leftward, back to AD_1, over the long run. The combination of the leftward shift of the aggregate supply curve with the described shifts of aggregate demand over time induces an adjustment path of the economy toward long-run equilibrium such as that depicted by the pointed arrows in Figure 18–3(a).

Even though over the short run, the unanticipated monetary policy has effects on output, over the long run the only effects are on domestic prices. In spite of the fact that rising real exchange rates and declining real interest rates push short-run output above full employment, both real exchange rates and real interest rates move back to their original levels. Figure 18–4 shows this result with regard to the behavior of the domestic real exchange rate. With the horizontal axis measuring time elapsed after the unanticipated disturbance, the short-run rise of the real exchange rate from $\bar{q}$ to q_1 is assumed to occur at t_0. As time continues to elapse—that is, as we move from t_0 to t_1 in Figure 18–4, the real exchange rate adjusts back

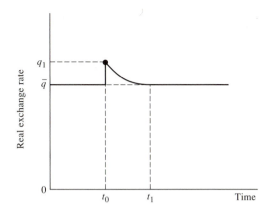

FIGURE 18–4. The Overshooting of the Real Exchange Rate

to its long-run value, $\bar{q}$. The fact that, in response to the unanticipated disturbance, the real exchange rate has temporarily jumped above its long-run equilibrium value is referred to as the overshooting of the real exchange rate.[9] In the present framework, real exchange rate overshooting is associated with the failure of the economy—and of the labor market in particular—to adjust completely and immediately to unanticipated disturbances. Note that, just as an unanticipated monetary increase moves the real exchange rate above its long-run value, an unanticipated *decline* of the money supply would induce the real exchange rate to move below its long-run value.

During the time the real exchange rate is above (below) its long-run value, individuals will expect domestic currency to appreciate (depreciate) in real terms. Algebraically, this can be expressed by

$$\hat{q}^e = -\mu(q_t - \bar{q})/q_t, \qquad (18\text{–}9)$$

[9]The term *real exchange rate overshooting* was coined by W. H. Buiter and M. Miller; see their "Real Exchange Rate Overshooting and the Output Cost of Bringing Down Inflation" in G. de Ménil and R. J. Gordon, eds., *International Volatility and Economic Growth* (Amsterdam: North Holland, 1991).

where $\bar{q}$ is the long-run exchange rate, $\hat{q}^e = (q^e_{t+1} - q_t)/q_t$ is the anticipated change in the real exchange rate from period t to period $t + 1$ (expressed in proportional terms), q_t is the real exchange rate at time t, and μ is a coefficient that reflects the proportion of the gap between the current and long-run exchange rate which is anticipated to be eliminated between period t and $t + 1$. Equation 18–9 states that, if the current real exchange rate is above its long-run value ($q_t - \bar{q} > 0$), there will an expected decrease in the exchange rate ($\hat{q}^e < 0$). Note that if agents in the economy expect the real exchange rate to revert to long-run equilibrium immediately, the parameter μ will be equal to 1. On the other hand, if the expectation is that the overshooting will last for a long period of time, then μ will be closer to zero. Equation 18–9 can be transformed into

$$(q_t - \bar{q})/q_t = -(1/\mu)\hat{q}^e. \qquad (18-10)$$

However, from Equation 18–5, anticipated real exchange rate changes, $\hat{q}^e$, are directly related to real interest rate differentials, $r - r^*$. Therefore,

$$(q_t - \bar{q})/q_t = -(1/\mu)(r - r^*). \qquad (18-11)$$

Equation 18–11 indicates that positive (negative) deviations of the real exchange rate from its long-run value will be associated with an interest rate differential favoring foreign (domestic) assets. The link between real interest rates and real exchange rates is related to the parameter μ. The larger μ is—that is, the faster the anticipated adjustments toward long-run equilibrium—the smaller and more transitory the role of real interest rate differentials in influencing deviations of real exchange rates from long-run values.

To summarize, instability in monetary policy, alternating between expansions and contractions of money-supply growth, leads to instability in real exchange rate behavior and provides one possible explanation for the real exchange rate turbulence shown in Figure 18–2.

What about the behavior of the nominal exchange rate? As we saw earlier in Chapter 15, in a disequilibrium framework, nominal exchange rate overshooting would be a natural outcome of unanticipated disturbances. Does this apply in the present framework? Not necessarily. In the case of an unanticipated increase of the money supply, the nominal exchange rate will increase, as in the analysis in Chapter 15; however, its short-run response will not necessarily be large enough to overshoot the new long-run value. There might be a relatively smooth rise of the exchange rate over time, unlike the abrupt exchange rate behavior obtained in Chapter 15. Whether overshooting of the nominal exchange rate occurs depends on, among other factors, how the exchange rate adjusts relative to domestic prices and aggregate income in the short run and on the income elasticity of demand for money.[10] Note that, if the overshooting of nominal exchange rates does occur, its nature in the present framework does not relate to disequilibria in the goods market of the economy, but to the informational imperfections and labor market rigidities present in any economy.

Insofar as the response of the nominal exchange rate to unanticipated monetary policy can be either to overshoot or undershoot its long-run equilibrium value, the monetary expansion can give rise either to an anticipated appreciation or depreciation of domestic currency. Because domestic nominal interest rates are equal to the world interest rate (assume fixed) plus the anticipated rate of change of the exchange rate, the implication is that unanticipated monetary growth can be associated with either a rise or a fall in domestic nominal interest rates. It then becomes apparent that, in contrast to usual practice, the level of domestic nominal interest rates cannot be effectively and unequivocally utilized as a measure of the govern-

---

[10]For an analysis of the exact conditions required for nominal exchange rate overshooting in a framework similar to the one developed in this chapter, see K. P. Kimbrough, "Price, Output and Exchange Rate Movements in the Open Economy," *Journal of Monetary Economics* (January 1983).

ment's monetary policy. An expansionary monetary policy might be associated with rising rather than declining nominal interest rates.

Monetary Policy and Real Exchange Rate Variability

The overshooting framework described in this section suggests that monetary shocks can explain the real exchange rate variability that has been characteristic of the floating exchange rate regime since 1973. What is the evidence for this? One line of research has examined whether particular episodes associated with sudden changes in monetary policy fit the general picture provided by the model. Another has tested the positive links between real interest rates and deviations from long-run real exchange rates established by the overshooting approach, as reflected in Equation 18–11.

One example of real exchange rate overshooting may have occurred in the United States in the early 1980s. In response to a sudden shift in the policy regime of U.S. monetary authorities in the first administration of Ronald Reagan, when Paul Volcker was the Federal Reserve chairman, U.S. real exchange rates tumbled sharply. The shift reduced U.S. competitiveness in international markets and threw the economy into recession. Insofar as this movement was perceived as an overshooting of the real exchange rate below its long-run equilibrium level, an expected real exchange rate increase resulted; real interest rates were pushed up in the United States and the economy sank deeper into recession.

According to Rudiger Dornbusch and Jeffrey Frankel, from 1980 through mid-1984, the long-term real interest rate differential between the United States and its trading partners increased by about five points (algebraically, $r - r^* = 0.05$). These authors also estimate that the real exchange rate regresses about 14 percent of the way to long-run equilibrium in a year (in terms of the symbols in this section: $\mu = 0.14$). They conclude that, "if this estimate is right, and if the real interest rate differential is assumed equal to the

expected rate of real depreciation (no risk premium), then it follows that between 1980 and 1984 the dollar appreciated by about 35 percent [= 0.05/0.14, as can be determined by substituting the values of μ and $r - r^*$ into Equation 18–11] relative to its perceived long-run equilibrium. This matches fairly well the real appreciation of the dollar between 1980 and 1984. . . . No large shift in the long-run equilibrium real exchange rate need necessarily have taken place. Subsequently, in 1985–1987, the real interest differential fell, and the dollar followed suit."[11]

Although major swings in monetary policy may very well explain some real exchange rate changes, there is a lack of evidence suggesting that the overshooting model in this section explains a significant part of short-term real exchange rate variability. For instance, in a study using data for real exchange rates between the United States, Germany, Japan, and the United Kingdom, University of California (Berkeley) economists Richard Meese and Kenneth Rogoff conclude that "the strongest prediction of those [overshooting] models—that real interest differentials will be highly correlated with real exchange rate movements—simply does not appear in the data."[12]

There are several explanations for the apparent difficulties of the overshooting model to account for real exchange rate variability. We postulated one possibility in Chapter 15: the presence of "exchange rate bubbles." It is, for example, difficult for the overshooting model to account for the real appreciation of the dollar from July 1984 to February 1985, when the real interest rate differential between the United States and its trading partners was declining (which, according to Equation 18–11, should be linked to a real depreciation of the dollar). The exchange rate bubbles

---

[11] See R. Dornbusch and J. Frankel, "The Flexible Exchange Rate System: Experience and Alternatives," in S. Boner, ed., *International Finance and Trade in a Polycentric World* (London: Macmillan, 1988), p. 163.

[12] R. Meese and K. Rogoff, "Was it Real? The Exchange Rate–Interest Differential Relation Over the Modern Floating-Rate Period," *Journal of Finance* (September 1988), p. 940.

hypothesis suggests that the sustained dollar exchange rate reduction generated further expectations of dollar appreciation in value. This in turn sustained an increase in the demand for dollars and led to the continued dollar appreciation. Even though the gap between the actual exchange rate and the fundamental long-run exchange rate ($q_t - \bar{q}_t$ in our earlier discussion) may have suggested that the dollar was due to depreciate, agents may have not expected such a depreciation to occur immediately, believing instead that the dollar would continue to appreciate, at least temporarily. This is an example of self-fulfilling expectations, in which an aggregate demand disturbance generates expectations that deviate from long-run fundamentals. They lead the economy to fluctuations in economic activity unrelated to "real" or long-run forces.[13]

The failure of monetary shocks of the type described in this section—and of the overshooting model—to explain fluctuations in real exchange rate changes could be the result of the fact that we have considered only unanticipated monetary policy. What is the impact of monetary policy changes that have been anticipated by agents in the economy? The next section shows that when monetary policies are anticipated they lose their power to affect output and real exchange rates, even temporarily.

The Ineffectiveness of Anticipated Monetary Policy

In contrast to the case of unanticipated monetary policy, an anticipated increase in the money supply has no effects on domestic output or the real

exchange rate, not even momentarily. The explanation is that as long as individuals form rational expectations, they will realize that the increased money supply will generate short-run inflation and will therefore embody the expected increased prices in the cost-of-living adjustments of their employment contracts. When the money supply increases and inflation ignites, employment contracts will call for scheduled nominal wage increases matching the rising prices. Real wages would thus remain unaltered, in spite of the inflation, and production changes would not be made. In terms of Figure 18–3, the anticipated central bank credit creation shifts both the AD and AS curves simultaneously. The aggregate demand curve shifts from AD_0 to AD_1 in response to the increased money supply associated with the credit creation. The aggregate supply curve also shifts—from AS_0 to AS_1—in response to the rising nominal wage adjustments previously negotiated by workers in anticipation of the current inflation. As a result, the anticipated monetary expansion moves the economy's short-run equilibrium from point A to point F. Note that these adjustments take place at full employment: If the inflationary effects of monetary policy are anticipated, the policy has no impact on output. Similarly, the economy would remain at point H in Figure 18–3(b), with no changes in real exchange rates.

This analysis suggests that anticipated money growth should not have systematic effects on output, whereas unanticipated money growth may have effects over the short run, but none over the long run. What do the data say? Empirical evidence has yielded mixed results, with some early work supporting the preceding conclusions and other studies unable to confirm it.[14] A major

---

[13]Some economists are reluctant to consider economic models that can, in essence, account for many possible economic equilibria, so-called sunspot equilibria, because they leave the outcome undetermined (there are many possible multiple equilibria). Others have argued that such models are still useful and have very specific implications because sunspot equilibria are possible only under certain conditions. See M. Woodford, "Self-Fulfilling Expectations and Fluctuations in Aggregate Demand," in N. Gregory Mankiw and D. Romer, *New Keynesian Economics* (Cambridge: The MIT Press, 1991).

[14]A survey of this research is available in C. L. F. Attfield; D. Demery, and N. W. Duck, *Rational Expectations in Macroeconomics* (Cambridge, Mass.: Basil Blackwell, 1991), chap. 7. For evidence confirming that it is unanticipated money growth that matters for policy effectiveness, see R. J. Barro, "Unanticipated Money Growth and Unemployment in the United States," *American Economic Review* (March 1977). For a critical re-examination of Barro's results, see F. Mishkin,

stumbling block for the empirical work in this area lies in the problems associated with breaking down money growth into its anticipated and unanticipated components. Because these are not observed variables, they have to be estimated. This turns out to be a difficult statistical problem, as assumptions have to be made regarding the information individuals have available in forming their expectations, the government's behavior, and so forth.

Given the difficulties in determining the linkages between monetary policy and output changes through statistical means, some authors have recurred to the use of case studies. This historical and narrative analysis was pioneered by Milton Friedman and Anna Schwartz in their *Monetary History of the United States* and supports the view that unanticipated monetary policy has significant effects on output.[15] Recent evidence on a number of post-World War II monetary shocks intended to reduce U.S. inflation has been provided by Christina and David Romer of the University of California at Berkeley. They conclude that "economic developments following these shifts in Federal Reserve policy provide decisive evidence on the importance of monetary policy. In every case, output fell substantially below what one would otherwise have expected. A shift to antiinflationary monetary policy led, on average, to an ultimate reduction in industrial production of 12 percent and an ultimate rise in the unemployment rate of two percentage points."[16]

Evidence that sudden monetary policy shifts are the ultimate *cause* of economic fluctuations and business cycles has been questioned by a relatively new school of thought in macroeconomics: the real business cycles approach. According to this framework, monetary policy shifts, such as those investigated by the Romers, are not themselves exogenous but are rather endogenous to the economy. They embody the reactions of the policymakers to other "real," or supply-side, disturbances in the economy, such as the oil-price shocks of 1973, 1979, and 1990. In a sense, then, the underlying determinants of business cycles are the real supply-side shocks and not the monetary demand-side disturbances emphasized earlier in this section. For instance, according to this view, monetary expansions are not an exogenous shock; they are a consequence of the monetary policies followed by U.S. authorities who respond to a boom in output by accommodating the associated increase in money demand through higher monetary growth. Recession, caused perhaps by an adverse supply shock in the form of an increase in the price of imported materials, is associated with contractionary monetary policy: Authorities reduce money supply to match the reduction in money demand while keeping inflation under control. In all these cases, the underlying disturbances to the economy are supply shocks, not demand shocks. In effect, in these examples, money supply is adjusted by policymakers to respond to output fluctuations, not the other way around.[17]

Are production fluctuations caused mainly by supply disturbances, as the real business cycles

"Does Anticipated Monetary Policy Matter? An Econometric Investigation," *Journal of Political Economy* (February 1982); R. J. Gordon, "Price Inertia and Policy Ineffectiveness in the United States, 1890–1980," *Journal of Political Economy* (December 1982); and R. Frydman and P. Rappoport, "Is the Distinction Between Anticipated and Unanticipated Money Growth Relevant in Explaining Aggregate Output?" *American Economic Review* (September 1987).

[15]M. Friedman and A. Schwartz, *A Monetary History of the United States, 1867–1960* (Princeton: N.J.: Princeton University Press, 1963).

[16]C. Romer and D. Romer, "Does Monetary Policy Matter?" in O. J. Blanchard and S. Fischer, eds., *NBER Macroeconomics Annual* (Cambridge, Mass.: The MIT Press, 1989), p. 168. The significance of monetary shocks in influencing output has also

been documented by C. M. Reinhart and V. R. Reinhart, "Output Fluctuations and Monetary Shocks," *IMF Staff Papers* (December 1991).

[17]This point was originally made by R. King and C. I. Plosser, "Money, Credit and Prices in a Real Business Cycle," *American Economic Review* (June 1984). The theory and evidence on the presence of monetary rules intended to stabilize output or prices in the United States in the current floating exchange rates regime has been examined by D. H. Papell, "Monetary Policy in the United States Under Flexible Exchange Rates," *American Economic Review* (December 1989).

hypothesis suggests, or by demand-side shocks—such as unanticipated monetary disturbances—or both? The next section discusses the nature of, the controversy over, and evidence for the real business cycles approach.

18–5. REAL BUSINESS CYCLES AND THE SOURCES OF ECONOMIC FLUCTUATIONS

One of the major new developments in macroeconomics in the 1980s and 1990s has been real business cycle theory, which views business cycles as determined by "real" shocks to the economy.[18] Real shocks mean such disturbances as technological changes, tax code and regulatory changes, the terms of trade fluctuations, good or bad weather, and any others that impinge on the production process. For instance, the oil-price shocks of 1973, 1979, and 1990 generated terms of trade disturbances that constituted adverse supply shocks to oil-importing countries. The slowdown of output growth among some oil-importing countries has been linked to the effects of these supply-side shocks. In the same vein, tax code and regulatory changes affect production incentives for firms and workers and, hence, the business cycle.

The underlying sources of macroeconomic fluctuations in the real business cycle approach are supply-side disturbances rather than aggregate demand fluctuations, as stressed in Keynesian and demand-side rational expectations business cycle models. The approach also differs from Keynesian theory in that it considers macroeconomic equilibrium to be achieved under conditions of price and wage flexibility, in contrast to the basic Keynesian tenet of price or wage rigidity. The name *equilib-*

rium real business cycle theory is frequently used to allude to the fact that, in this approach, fluctuations occur as a result of movements in output and prices that equilibrate aggregate demand and supply at all times. The distinction between short-run and long-run equilibria present in Keynesian macroeconomics (as described in the last section) does not exist in this approach; neither does the Keynesian feature of long-run "disequilibrium," in which the economy is away from long-run equilibrium as a result of sudden disturbances in the presence of prices or wages that are rigid and take time to adjust fully.

To illustrate how real business cycles occur, we make use of our aggregate demand-aggregate supply framework, reproduced in Figure 18–5. Because equilibrium real business cycle theory ignores price and wage rigidities, the aggregate supply curve is vertical at an initial value given by Y_F, the full-employment level of output. Aggregate demand is as given before, depicted by the curve AD in Figure 18–5. The initial equilibrium is at point E, with the price level equal to P_0. According to real business cycle theory, real shocks determine economic fluctuations. Such is the case, for example, if aggregate supply shifts over time first

[18]For a survey of real business cycle theory, see C. I. Plosser, "Understanding Real Business Cycles," *Journal of Economic Perspectives* (Summer 1989); see also the original contributions by J. B. Long and C. I. Plosser, "Real Business Cycles," *Journal of Political Economy* (February 1983); and F. E. Kydland and E. C. Prescott, "Time to Build and Aggregate Fluctuations," *Econometrica* (November 1982).

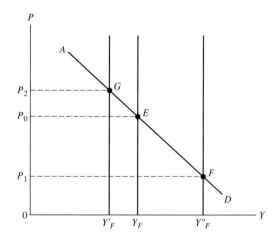

FIGURE 18–5. Supply Shocks and Output Fluctuations

to Y'_F and then to Y'_F. These supply shocks cause changes in output and prices that are negatively correlated with each other. For instance, the shift in the supply curve to the right, from Y_F to Y'_F moves equilibrium to point F and generates an increase in output and a reduction in prices; on the other hand, the shift to Y'_F reduces output and fuels inflation, raising prices from P_0 to P_2.

The real business cycle approach suggests that prices are countercyclical, dropping with higher output and rising with reduction in production. Indeed, the development and popularity of the approach is related to relatively recent empirical observations regarding the link between output and prices in the business cycle—observations that are not easy to reconcile with simple Keynesian models relying on aggregate demand fluctuations to explain them. Until the 1980s, approaches that stressed the demand side monopolized macroeconomic analysis. The most frequently voiced argument against supply-side approaches was based on a widely accepted empirical regularity that booms were associated with increased inflation and busts with reduced inflation. For instance, the Great Depression was accompanied by substantial price deflation in the United States and elsewhere. This suggests that reduced demand was the main shock involved in the 1930s' economic collapse. A supply shock would have led to price increases, not reductions. Evidence on the positive relationship between short-term price increases and output was found in various contexts and became embodied in the so-called Phillips curve (see Chapter 16). Because prices were taken to be procyclical, demand side theories appeared to be more relevant in explaining the data and dominated macroeconomics in the 1960s and 1970s. More recently, real business cycles researchers have noted that since the early 1950s there have been many instances in which prices have behaved procyclically—that is, the rate of inflation has slowed down during booms and has picked up during recessions. The most obvious cases are the oil crises of 1973 and 1979, when stagflation (recession combined with inflation) became prevalent (see our discussion in

Chapter 17). The finding of procyclical wages suggests that supply shocks have been influencing business cycles since World War II; it contradicts views that focus exclusively on demand-oriented explanations.

The empirical evidence presented by real business cycle researchers also suggests some inconsistencies in the behavior of real wages if economic fluctuations were totally determined by aggregate demand shocks. Keynesian and demand-side models tend to imply a negative relationship between real wages and output over the business cycle because higher levels of expected or unexpected demand raise product prices faster than nominal wages. On the other hand, the equilibrium business cycles approach can be made consistent with a positive relation between real wages and production upswings: The boom could be the result of increases in productivity that raise output and real wages at the same time.

A large body of research has failed to produce agreement about the cyclicality of wages. Researchers have sometimes found procyclical real wages, but at other times they appear to be countercyclical or neutral.[19] This ambiguity may suggest that some business cycle movements have their source in supply shocks, whereas others are the result of demand shocks. Still, proponents of real business cycles theories are currently challenging this traditional, ambiguous stance toward the cyclicality of wages. They have presented evidence suggesting that wages have behaved procyclically since the World War II. Economists Robert Barsky and Gary Solon, for instance, have examined data on individual firms that show procyclical behavior of real wages in the post-World War II era. They argue that the way in which data are aggregated obscures the cyclicality of real wages in industrywide data, but that firm-level data are not subject to this bias. Using firm-level data, Solon and Barsky conclude that postwar cyclical fluctuations have mostly been the

---

[19]See M. Bils, "Real Wages Over the Business Cycle," *Journal of Political Economy* (August 1985).

result of shifts in labor demand.[20] This and other recent research are leading to a re-examination of the controversy concerning the cyclical behavior of the real wage.

The 1990s are seeing a proliferation of scholarship on real business cycles. However, it remains a controversial approach that faces many critics. Although most economists would agree that supply shocks in the form of oil-price changes have been a major cause of economic fluctuations since World War II, they are more skeptical of the notion that output variability is being constantly generated by technological changes and productivity shocks. Real business cycle proponents have indeed tried to relate production swings to long-term technological change. One problem with this approach is the difficulty of measuring technological change. Most of the literature measures it indirectly by imputing that the portion of any increase in production over any given period that cannot be explained by factor accumulation (the use of additional capital, labor, raw materials, etc.) must be

accounted for by technological improvements. This unexplained component of output growth, called the Solow residual, in honor of its originator, MIT Nobel Prize winner Robert Solow, is interpreted as an index of technological change. Some authors have used it to explain business cycles. Critics reject the Solow residual as an adequate measure of technological change over short time horizons. They indicate that the residuals may themselves be a reflection of booms and busts, responding to variations in capacity utilization over the business cycle. It is thus suggested that the use of Solow residuals as a measure of technological change to explain business cycles may be a tautology: The residuals themselves could be explained by business cycles. One of the critics, Harvard's N. Gregory Mankiw, argues:

> Once the Solow residual is rejected as a measure of year-to-year technological change, there is no longer any evidence for substantial technological disturbances. Yet, to generate fluctuations that mimic observed fluctuations, real business cycle models require such disturbances. The existence of large fluctuations in the available technology is a crucial but unjustified assumption of real business cycle theory.[21]

If relating business cycles to technical changes and productivity shocks has been controversial, the international implications of real business cycles theory have been an even bigger item of debate. We proceed to examine real business cycle theory in an international context.

18–6. BUSINESS CYCLES AND REAL EXCHANGE RATES

We have so far examined real business cycles theory in terms of its implications for the cyclical behavior of output, prices, and real wages. Another

---

[20]From R. Barsky and G. Solon, "Real Wages Over the Business Cycle," National Bureau of Economic Research Working Paper no. 2888 (March 1989). Barsky and Solon also find lack of cyclicality in industrywide data. However, the industrywide lack of cyclicality is explained away as an artifact of the way data on aggregate real wages are constructed. When the economy slows down, the rising unemployment tends to affect low-wage workers more seriously than high-income workers. For this reason, the number of low-income workers declines in relation to the number of high-income ones. The opposite happens in an upswing. Hence, low-wage workers receive a relatively low weight in the computation of average wages during recessions and a relatively larger weight during upswings. The effect of the relative neglect of unemployed low-income workers in a recession leads to average wages that exhibit an upward bias in recession and a downward bias during recovery. This composition effect creates the impression that wages are countercyclical, even though they are not. The effect disappears when the authors analyze firm data that are not biased by this compositional effect. For a different view on the data, but for conclusions that still support procyclical real wages, see M. Keane, R. Moffitt, and D. Runkle, "Real Wages Over the Business Cycle: Estimating the Impact of Heterogeneity with Micro Data," *Journal of Political Economy* (December 1988).

[21]N. Gregory Mankiw, "Real Business Cycle Theory: A New Keynesian Perspective," *Journal of Economic Perspectives* (Summer 1989).

set of variables that is usually examined in this context is international. It involves the behavior of real exchange rates, trade flows, and the international transmission of business cycles.

The discussion of real exchange rates in the context of business cycle theories should start with a forewarning. At the present time, no general model of exchange rate behavior has been successfully able to pass the challenge of empirical testing. It could be said in humility (or humiliation) that in one way or another all models that have been tested have failed. Even the basic description of the statistical properties of exchange rate behavior is bitterly argued by the experts. To the demoralization (and sometimes deep anxiety) of countless students expecting to find a clear-cut exposition of the subject, what we can supply is a research mongrel, an odd mixture of results. Exchange rate economics brings more controversy than consensus.

The real business cycles approach advances the notion that the real exchange rate is mostly influenced by real, supply-side shocks, rather than by the monetary disturbances emphasized by the overshooting model and other approaches. The key matter of debate among the different perspectives narrows down to whether real exchange rate changes are permanent or transitory. Remember from our analysis of overshooting earlier in this chapter that real exchange rates can be dislodged from long-run equilibrium by monetary disturbances, but only temporarily. Furthermore, as we noted in Section 18–4 (see Equation 18–11), temporary disturbances in real exchange rates will be associated with (ex ante) real interest rate differentials. Therefore, if monetary disturbances explain the brusque real exchange rate variability present under the current floating exchange rate regime, then (ex ante) real interest rate differentials must account for real exchange rate fluctuations.

Equilibrium real business cycles models suggest that permanent changes in real currency values—not temporary changes—explain most of the variability of real exchange rates. What factors determine permanent disturbances in real currency values? The approach usually emphasizes supply shocks (prices of imported inputs and productivity shocks)—although it is also recognized that fiscal policies can alter equilibrium real exchange rates. We can specify algebraically the determinants of the long-run equilibrium real exchange rate in terms of the framework developed in this chapter. If aggregate demand-aggregate supply long-run equilibrium is instantaneously achieved (so that there are no rigidities in wages or prices), as real business cycles theory suggests, then the economy is always in short-run *and* long-run equilibrium. From Equation 18–7, such equilibrium is determined by

$$Y_F = \alpha[\bar{A} + \bar{T} + \phi q - br^*],$$

which can be transformed into

$$q = (1/\alpha\phi)Y_F - (1/\phi)[\bar{A} + \bar{T} - br^*]. \quad (18\text{–}12)$$

Equation 18–12 indicates that fluctuations in the permanent (full-employment) level of output, as well as fiscal policy shocks (which may affect $\bar{A}$), terms of trade disturbances (which may alter $\bar{T}$ and $\bar{A}$), and world real interest rate shocks (changes in r^*), could all cause permanent changes in real exchange rates. Note that in this equilibrium framework, ex ante real interest rate differentials would have no role in explaining real exchange rate changes because, in contrast to the overshooting model, there are no temporary exchange rate movements that could be anticipated to be reversed over time.

What is the evidence for whether real interest rate differentials (reflecting temporary changes in real exchange rates) or permanent shifts in real currency values explain real exchange rate variability? Economists John Y. Campbell and Richard H. Clarida have examined this question, and a sample of their results can be found in Table 18–1. The real exchange rates examined are for the United States with Canada, the United Kingdom, West Germany, and Japan. The first column depicts the fraction of the real exchange rate variability

TABLE 18–1. **Accounting for Real Exchange Rate Variability**

	Fraction of the Real Exchange Rate Variability Explained by	
Exchange Rate	*Changes in Ex-Ante Real Interest Rate Differential (percent) (a)*	*Changes in Long-Run Equilibrium Exchange Rate (percent) (b)*
United States–Canada	9%	85%
United States–United Kingdom	8	79
United States–West Germany	4	98
United States–Japan	4	81

SOURCE: J. Y. Campbell and R. H. Clarida, "The Dollar and Real Interest Rates," in K. Brunner and A. H. Metzler, eds., *Empirical Studies of Velocity, Real Exchange Rates, Unemployment, and Productivity* (Amsterdam: North Holland, 1987). These numbers are meant to be representative. Campbell and Clarida obtained more than one set of results, based on alternative assumptions about the risk premium on foreign exchange. The percentages for each row do not add up to 100 percent because of a nonzero covariance between real interest rate differentials and long-run equilibrium exchange rates.

that is accounted for by changes in ex ante real interest rate differentials; the second column shows the portion explained by changes in the long-run equilibrium exchange rate. The table shows that between 79 and 98 percent of real exchange rate fluctuations can be explained by changes in long-run equilibrium exchange rates. Other studies by University of Chicago's John Huizinga and the University of California's (San Diego) Graciela Kaminsky also find that a substantial portion of the real exchange rate variability of the U.S. dollar can be explained by permanent rather than temporary disturbances.[22]

[22]See the survey by A. C. Stockman, "Exchange Rates, the Current Account, and Monetary Policy," in W. S. Haraf and T. D. Willett, eds., *Monetary Policy for a Volatile Global Economy* (Washington, D.C.: American Enterprise Institute, 1990); J. Huizinga, "An Empirical Investigation of the Long-Run Behavior of Real Exchange Rates," in K. Brunner and A. H. Meltzer, eds., *Empirical Studies of Velocity, Real Exchange Rates, Unemployment and Productivity* (Amsterdam: North Holland, 1987); and G. Kaminsky, "The Real Exchange Rate in the Short and in the Long Run," Working Paper no. 88–11, Department of Economics, University of California (San Diego), 1987.

The studies just quoted focus on flexible exchange rates since 1973. It has been argued, though, that if the real exchange rate moves very slowly toward long-run equilibrium, then the post-1973 period is still too short a period in which to discern whether the real exchange rate has exhibited temporary disturbances or a tendency to return to a long-run equilibrium level.[23] The crux of the continuing controversy on this issue can be understood through the use of Figure 18–6, which shows the dollar-pound real exchange rate between 1869 and 1987. This period represents a long data set, especially by the standards of the empirical analysis of exchange rates. What we observe is a tendency of the real value of the pound to wander around a value near to $5.00/£ (at 1929 prices). There is no secular trend in the real exchange rate. There are deviations around the

[23]This point has been forcefully made by J. A. Frankel, "Zen and the Art of Modern Macroeconomics," in W. S. Haraf and T. D. Willett, eds., *Monetary Policy for a Volatile Global Economy* (Washington, D.C.: American Enterprise Institute, 1990).

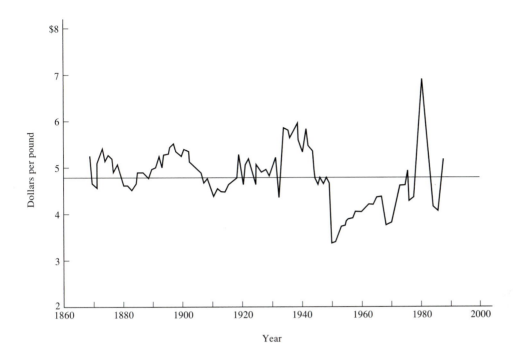

FIGURE 18–6. Dollar-Pound Real Exchange Rate, 1869–1987 (dollars per pound at 1929 prices)

SOURCE: J. Frankel, "Zen and the Art of Modern Macroeconomics," in W. S. Haraf and T. D. Willett, eds., *Monetary Policy for a Volatile Global Economy* (Washington, D.C.: American Enterprise Institute, 1990), p. 121. Reprinted with permission of the American Enterprise Institute.

value of $5.00 for extended periods of time. For instance, the Great Depression of the 1930s was associated with a real depreciation of the dollar vis-à-vis the pound. The 1940s brought a real dollar appreciation, partly reflecting a devaluation of the pound. The late 1970s brought a sharp real depreciation of the dollar. Yet, in all of these cases we observe a tendency for real currency values to return to the near-five real exchange rate. In fact, most of the time, the real exchange rate stays within a relatively narrow band. If we look at recent data only, on the other hand, we obtain a completely different picture. Since 1973, the real exchange rate has fluctuated more widely then in all peacetime periods. There is neither a detectable

trend nor a clear central value around which the exchange rate fluctuates. Actually, even if we go back to the 1950s, it is still difficult to detect either trend or central values.

What do we make of this evidence? On one point the evidence is clear: There is substantial variation in real exchange rates in the short term. However, on the question about the tendency for real currency values to return to their trend or central values, the answer is fuzzy. It could take one, five, or ten years before we see a steadfast reversion in some exchange rate movements. Evidence of a lack of immediate adjustment to a long-run central value does not preclude the possibility that adjustments toward long-run, fundamental values will occur later. Transitory shocks may just be very persistent. At the same time, the case can be made that if the tendency for real currency values to return to some central value is so weak it takes decades to discern, why not just assume that such a tendency is really insignificant in affecting short-run currency movements? According to this alternative view, the immediate behavior of real exchange rates is better explained not by temporary shocks, but by permanent shocks that move real currency values around without a perceptible tendency for them to return to a past position. Which of these two views prevails over the other cannot be determined with the inconclusive evidence available at this time. On balance, it can be assumed that real exchange rates are influenced by both supply-side disturbances and monetary shocks.

Exchange Rate Policy and the Equilibrium Approach

The equilibrium approach to real exchange rates, stressing the "real" determinants of real currency values, challenges various common notions about the macroeconomics of exchange rate changes. One of them is the view that trade or current account deficits can be suppressed by simply engineering a real currency depreciation.

In a real equilibrium model, trade balance deficits are the result of optimal spending patterns that engender planned external borrowing or of real shocks to the economy that generate a previously unplanned deficit. The elimination of a trade deficit sometimes requires a real depreciation and sometimes a real appreciation—it all depends on the source of the shock that causes the deficit. To illustrate this point, suppose that the demand for foreign goods experiences a temporary abnormally high level, while the demand for domestic goods goes down. Then the trade and current account balances would tend to move into a deficit position. The corresponding response of the exchange rate would be to rise. The domestic currency

depreciation would then turn into an appreciation as soon as the abnormally high demand fell and the trade deficit corrected itself. This appreciation-cum-deficit-reduction process is the one usually focused on in the literature. However, alternative scenarios lead to a different relationship between the deficit reduction and the associated exchange rate movement. Let us examine an example.

Consider the case of temporarily low domestic savings and high spending associated with current and trade account deficits. If the high spending is biased toward domestic goods, the domestic currency will appreciate. When the temporarily high spending falls back to normal levels, the trade and current account deficits will shrink and the currency will depreciate. This seems counter to the usual reasoning linking the elimination of the deficit with a domestic currency appreciation (or reductions in output). The apparent paradox is solved by noticing that the deficits are eliminated by reduced spending on domestic goods. This reduced spending occurs not because the currency depreciates, but as a result of household decisions concerning intertemporal spending. In the Keynesian framework, this would look similar to an autonomous reduction in spending on domestic goods.

Are Real Exchange Rates More Variable Under Flexible Exchange Rates?

The real business cycles approach takes the Keynesian, sticky-price model and turns it around 180 degrees. The sticky-price model views real exchange rate variability as being determined by nominal exchange rate variability, with the ratio of foreign to domestic price levels relatively unchanged. Algebraically, with real exchange rates defined by $q = eP^*/P$, the Keynesian model assumes that P^*/P is fixed and that fluctuations in e cause changes in q (see, for instance, our discussion at the beginning of Chapter 13). By contrast, the real business cycles approach assumes that real shocks affect the real exchange rate, q, and that this causes the nominal exchange rate to change. Algebraically, from their vantage point, the exchange rate is given by $e = qP/P^*$, and fluctuations in q then directly affect e, with P/P^* relatively unchanged. From this perspective, the variability of currency values reflects the role of the exchange rate in adjusting the economy to the relative price changes required by supply disturbances.

The issue of causality—whether nominal exchange rate changes cause real exchange rate changes or whether disturbances to real currency values cause shifts in nominal currency values—is a difficult one to determine statistically. Proponents of the Keynesian sticky-price model have instead argued that it is unlikely that supply shocks can explain the astounding volatility of nominal exchange rates. For instance, MIT's Paul Krugman queries: "What were the real shocks that raised the equilibrium relative price of U.S. labor by 15 percent from the second quarter of 1984 to the first quarter of 1985, then drove it down by 22 percent over the following year?"[24]

Another argument made against the direction of the causality of nominal and real exchange rates implied by real business cycles theories relates to the shift from fixed to flexible exchange rates in 1973. If nominal exchange rates reflect real phenomena, we would expect that a switch from fixed to flexible exchange rate regimes would not have much impact on real exchange rate volatility—which is a function of real forces that are unrelated to the exchange rate regime. Yet, as observed earlier, real exchange rates have been much more volatile since the industrialized countries moved to floating rates in 1973. It is thus concluded by critics of real business cycles that the volatility of nominal exchange rates since 1973 is related to monetary and asset market (expectational) forces that move them around brusquely; this movement has caused real exchange rate variability as a result

of the presence of price stickiness. From this perspective, it is frequently heard in policy circles that there has been "excessive" nominal and real exchange rate variability under the post-1973 floating rate regime, and that this variability should be corrected by foreign exchange market intervention. Real business cycles theory challenges this view. First of all, the approach vehemently negates that real exchange rates are inherently more variable under floating than under fixed exchange rates.

The year 1973 marks the dividing line between the dominance of fixed exchange rates under Bretton Woods and the beginning of floating rates among the industrialized countries. What effect did this change in the exchange rate regime have on business cycles and their international transmission? The post-1973 period differs significantly from its predecessor. First, it is absolutely true that real exchange rates, exports, and imports have become more volatile since 1973. Second, outputs have been less correlated across countries in the post-1973 period. Within each country, the association between national consumption, investment, and total output has increased. These findings suggest that business cycles are more country-specific under flexible exchange rates.[25]

The evidence for the greater volatility of the real exchange rate since 1973 appears to be consistent with the hypothesis that fixed exchange rates provide greater stability in real currency values

---

[24]P. Krugman, *Exchange Rate Instability* (Cambridge, Mass.: The MIT Press, 1989), p. 17.

[25]The high positive correlation between consumption, investment, and output fluctuations (their procyclicality) implies that savings and investment changes are also highly related, a phenomenon first noted by C. Horioka and M. Feldstein (and discussed in Chapter 11). For an analysis of how consumption, investment, and output relate over the business cycle, and the evidence for it, see E. G. Mendoza, "Real Business Cycles in a Small Open Economy," *American Economic Review* (September 1991); M. G. Finn, "On Savings and Investment Dynamics in a Small Open Economy," *Journal of International Economics* (August 1990); and D. K. Backus and P. J. Kehoe, "International Evidence on the Historical Properties of Business Cycles," Working Paper no. 402R, Federal Reserve Bank of Minneapolis Research Department, 1989.

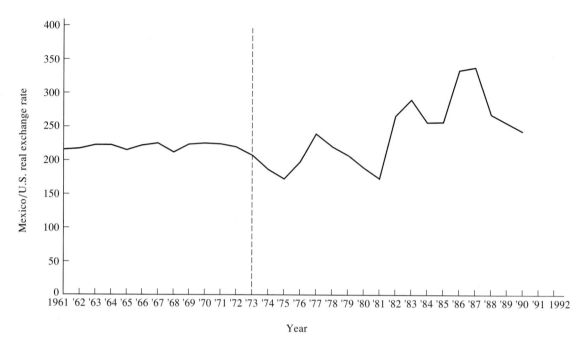

Note: The Mexican real exchange rate, q, is equal to the Mexico-U.S. bilateral exchange rate (in pesos per dollar), e, multiplied by the consumer price index in the United States, P^*, and divided by the consumer price index in Mexico, P. The base year for the consumer price indices is 1985 = 100.

FIGURE 18–7.   Mexico's Real Exchange Rate, 1961–1991

SOURCE: The data are from International Monetary Fund, *International Financial Statistics Yearbook* (Washington, D.C.: IMF, 1991).

when compared to flexible rates. This supports the Keynesian, sticky-price approach, which predicts that monetary disturbances under flexible exchange rates will continuously alter real currency values. However, this interpretation of the data has been brought into question by a number of economists.[26]

The issue lies in that the greater turbulence of real exchange rates after 1973 has been found both in countries that adopted fixed and those that

adopted flexible exchange rate regimes. For instance, consider Figure 18–7, which shows the behavior of Mexico's real exchange rate from 1961 to 1991. With some sporadic interruptions, Mexico was operating under fixed exchange rate regimes during the entire period. Yet, its real exchange rate shows much greater variability after 1973. The increase in volatility across many countries might then be the consequence of changed global circumstances in the post-1973 period, but not necessarily of the exchange rate regime. The changed circumstances that might explain the increase in the volatility of real exchange rates after 1973 include the oil shocks in 1973, 1979, and

[26]See, for example, M. Baxter and A. C. Stockman, "Business Cycles and the Exchange Rate Regime: Some International Evidence," *Journal of Monetary Economics* (1989).

1990; the "global recessions" between 1980 and 1982 and 1990 and 1992; and swings in world real interest rates, among others.

A failure to detect differences in the volatility of real exchange rates between those countries that chose fixed exchange rates and those that chose flexible systems after 1973 can be interpreted to mean that the exchange rate regime does not explain the increase in volatility. This is what Vittorio Grilli and Graciela Kaminsky conclude in their comprehensive study of real exchange rate changes in industrialized countries from January 1885 to December 1986: "The main lesson to be drawn from our results is that the behavior of the real exchange rate varies substantially across historical periods, but not necessarily across nominal exchange rate arrangements. . . . In particular, the high volatility of the real exchange rate since the breakdown of the Bretton Woods system in the early 1970s may have arisen as a consequence of factors unrelated to the nominal exchange rate regime—such as the two oil-price shocks of the 1970s or the wild fluctuations in interest rates in the late 1970s and early 1980s."[27]

Even if real exchange rate variability had been greater under floating exchange rates, real business cycles theories would still object to government policy intervention intended to reduce such variability. According to real business cycles theory, the exchange rate is an equilibrium rate, determined by "fundamentals." The variability of real and nominal rates thus represents an equilibrium response to basic economic forces. Unless specific market imperfections can be pointed out, the presumption is that this response is an optimal response to economic shocks. Consequently, according to this perspective, we cannot deduce that the increased variability under flexible rates is excessive in any sense. There is, therefore, no benefit from intervening in foreign exchange markets to stabilize the exchange rate. On the contrary, exchange market intervention may work to impede the adjustment of the exchange rate to economic change. This policy position stands in direct contradiction to the view that there is "excessive turbulence" in exchange rate markets, turbulence that can be corrected with foreign exchange market intervention.

18–7. MONETARY GROWTH AND DOMESTIC INFLATION

Up to this point, we have examined the effects of once-and-for-all changes in the money supply. Suppose, on the other hand, that the central bank engages in repeated credit expansions, in order to give rise to sustained growth of the domestic money supply. What effects would such a persistent central bank credit creation have on the economy? It is assumed, for expository purposes, that this is the only economic disturbance and that agents in the economy form expectations following the rational expectations hypothesis.

Once the central bank steps on the monetary machine, individuals will not only observe the credit growth, but also the consequent inflation. They will thus adjust their price expectations upward. In terms of Figure 18–8, the upward shifts of the aggregate demand curve implied by a sustained increase of the domestic money supply will be associated with equal leftward shifts of the aggregate supply. As long as individuals recognize the commitment of the central bank to maintain credit growing at a certain rate, they will embody the resulting anticipated inflation in the nominal wage adjustments stipulated in their labor contracts. Real labor costs will remain unchanged and production will be maintained at full employment.

Domestic prices, however, will be rising continuously. Will this hurt domestic competitiveness in world goods markets? Not if the domestic inflation is matched by an equal rate of increase of the nominal exchange rate. In that case, the domestic currency depreciation and inflation offset each other, leaving the relative price of foreign goods in

[27]V. Grilli and G. Kaminsky, "Nominal Exchange Rate Regimes and the Real Exchange Rate," *Journal of Monetary Economics* (April 1991).

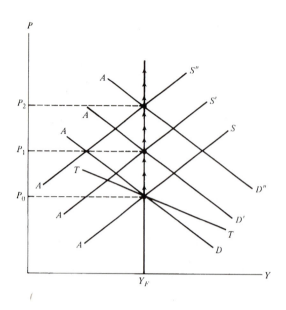

Figure 18-8. Monetary Growth and Domestic Inflation

terms of domestic goods unchanged. Algebraically, the relative price of foreign goods in terms of domestic goods, $q = eP^*/P$ would be fixed if the exchange rate and domestic prices (e and P, respectively) rise at the same rate. Hence, there would be no deleterious effects on domestic competitiveness and the trade balance.

The implication of this analysis is that in economies under flexible exchange rates, systematic monetary growth will be closely linked to inflation. This inflation does not hurt domestic competitiveness because of the currency depreciation associated with the monetary expansion. The issue of the impact of monetary growth in economies under fixed exchange rates may arise at this point. Assuming that the exchange rate is kept fixed, if monetary growth generates a domestic rate of inflation that exceeds world inflation, the real exchange rate will decline. This real appreciation of domestic currency would hurt domestic competitiveness and worsen the trade balance. If, as a

consequence, the trade balance moves into deficit, the country will have to finance this deficit, either through capital inflows—which may raise external debt—or through a loss of foreign exchange reserves. Of course, both the growth of external debt and losses of international reserves cannot go on for extended periods of time without foreign exchange and/or external debt crises emerging. The government could then devalue the currency. A devaluation alleviates the loss of reserves but, with domestic inflation exceeding world inflation, trade deficits will eventually grow again, requiring further devaluations.

The bottom line here is that openness of the economy under fixed exchange rates and the requirement that domestic products do not persistently become less price-competitive relative to foreign products—which would wipe out the exports sector—impose a strict constraint on what the rate of domestic inflation can be over the long run. Still, it is apparent that central bank credit growth can induce rates of domestic inflation well above the world rate for extended periods of time. As a matter of fact, when governments realize the need for domestic inflation to realign with world inflation and alter their monetary policy toward a contractionary one, they often find that domestic inflation does not simmer down over the short run.

18-8. The Effects of Devaluation Under Rational Expectations

This section discusses the effects of economic policymaking in economies under fixed exchange rates in the presence of rational expectations. We first review the aggregate demand-aggregate supply framework developed earlier in the chapter, applying it to a fixed exchange rate regime. We then discuss the impact of economic policies, focusing on the effects of currency devaluation.

Aggregate demand was expressed by Equation 18-7 as

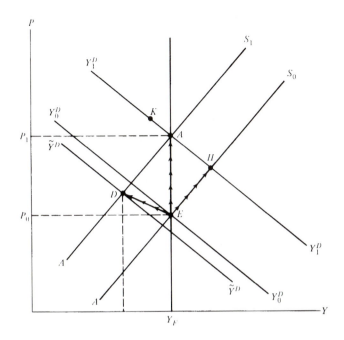

FIGURE 18–9. Effects of Devaluation Under Rational Expectations

$$Y^D = \alpha[\bar{A} + \bar{T} + \phi q - br]$$

$$= \alpha\left[\bar{A} + \bar{T} + \phi\frac{eP^*}{P}\right.$$

$$\left. - b(i^* + x - \Pi)\right], \qquad (18\text{–}7a)$$

in which we have substituted the expression for the real interest rate, r, stated by Equation 18–4. This aggregate demand relationship, illustrated in Figure 18–9 by means of the downward-sloping $Y_0^D Y_0^D$ curve, shows how changes in the price of domestic goods affect the quantity demanded of domestic goods given autonomous spending, the exchange rate, foreign prices, and the real interest rate. It slopes downward because an increase in domestic prices induces consumers to switch demand from domestic to foreign goods. Increases in government spending and in the exchange rate, and reductions of the real interest rate, all tend to

shift the aggregate demand upward. The main difference between the aggregate demand curve under fixed and flexible rates, is that, for the latter, the curve reflects the exchange rate changes required to assure balance-of-payments equilibrium and, for the former, the exchange rate is fixed. Note that, under the assumption of perfect capital mobility adopted in this chapter, balance-of-payments equilibrium under fixed exchange rates is achieved immediately through capital flows and changes in the central bank's international reserves.

Aggregate supply in the economy is as given by Equation 18–1 and is represented in Figure 18–9 by means of the upward-sloping AS_0 curve. The economy's long-run equilibrium is then illustrated by point E, where aggregate demand and aggregate supply intersect and where full employment and price stability exist. Any point of short-run equilibrium away from full employment would imply that the domestic price level differs from its expected value, from Equation 18–1. As a result, individuals would keep adjusting their expected price level until it equates with the actual one. At that point, no subsequent adjustments would arise and full employment would occur. Symbolically, at point E, $P_0 = P^e$, and therefore $Y = Y_F$.

Observe that the long-run equilibrium at point E is not necessarily a point of balanced trade. With perfect capital mobility, trade deficits can be financed immediately through capital account deficits. Monetary equilibrium at point E must entail balanced payments and, hence, no further monetary adjustments, but not necessarily balanced trade. We assume, for the sake of simplicity, that the central bank does not engage in any active monetary policy that would generate continuous losses of international reserves. The present is not a context of balance-of-payments crisis, a topic that will be discussed in Chapter 20. Finally, we also assume the absence of world inflation, so that the long-run equilibrium at point E implies domestic price stability and the equality of nominal and real interest rates.

With the analytical framework set up, we consider the impact of a currency devaluation. Under rational expectations, individuals will form forecasts about variables in the economy on the basis of available information, including the structure of the economy. A number of variables can be used to assess the likelihood of devaluation, such as the stock of international reserves at the central bank—the lower the level of reserves, the more likely the devaluation—or the rate of change of those reserves, among others.[28] Whatever the variable or set of variables utilized to assess the likelihood of devaluation, it is clear that certain assumptions about the government's behavior will

have to be made. For instance, even though a central bank may be running out of reserves, there is always the possibility that, instead of devaluing, the government will seek loans or swap agreements with which to stock up foreign exchange reserves. It is, accordingly, not possible to predict with perfect foresight whether or when a devaluation will arise, even if individuals are rational and use all the information available. Uncertainty about government behavior would prevent such foresight. Consequently, although still under the assumption of rational expectations, there are three possible cases to consider. The first is when a devaluation is correctly anticipated. The most obvious example of this case is when a devaluation is announced before it occurs and is consequently anticipated with perfect foresight and expectations are fulfilled. We must stress, though, that devaluations do not have to be announced ahead of time in order to be correctly anticipated. Often, the proximity of a devaluation is quite obvious, even if the government does not announce it. The second alternative is when devaluation is anticipated, but the government stubbornly decides not to devalue, with the result that expectations go unfulfilled. The third case is when the devaluation is completely unanticipated.

Preannounced Devaluations

The case of an announced devaluation is the easiest to examine. Suppose, for instance, that the government suddenly announces it will devalue the currency in a period of one month. What happens immediately—that is, over the transition period? Let us assume that individuals form rational expectations so that they know the structure of the economy and the possible effects of the devaluation. Once the exchange rate change is announced, individuals will expect the demand for domestic goods to rise and inflation to increase. Because, over the long run, the devaluation would lead to an equiproportional rate of inflation of domestic prices, individuals will expect domestic

---

[28]One variable frequently used to assess the likelihood of devaluation is the deviation of the actual exchange rate from its purchasing power parity value. The concept of a PPP exchange rate was examined in Chapter 5.

prices to rise by the same proportion as the devaluation (once it occurs). Algebraically, $\Pi = x$, the rational expectation of inflation after the devaluation, Π, is equal to x, the announced rate of devaluation (assuming foreign prices stay fixed at P^* in terms of foreign currency). The domestic real interest rate would then remain unaltered. The explanation is that the expected devaluation induces an increase in the domestic nominal interest rate, to compensate investors in domestic assets for their expected losses from the announced devaluation, as can be realized from Equation 18–3. Consequently, the rate of inflation and the increased nominal interest rate exactly compensate each other in leaving the real interest rate unchanged, as seen from Equation 18–4.

With real interest rates unchanged, aggregate demand would also remain unaffected, as far as it regards investment. Because domestic prices and the exchange rate have not yet changed, however, the relative price of foreign vis-à-vis domestic goods is also unchanged, with no consequent effect on aggregate demand from the trade balance side either. To reiterate, in the absence of other disturbances, the announced devaluation will have no effect on the aggregate demand curve ($Y_0^D Y_0^D$ in Figure 18–9) during the transition period—that is, before the devaluation actually occurs. As a result, with the devaluation not yet in effect, domestic prices will remain at their original level and will be expected to remain so during the predevaluation period. With actual and expected prices equal, the aggregate supply curve also remains unaffected, and the economy's equilibrium would continue to be at point E in Figure 18–9. Within this framework, the most visible immediate effects of the devaluation announcement are some capital outflows and losses of international reserves and an increase in domestic nominal interest rates. In the background, however, workers and firms are bargaining over the nominal wage adjustments to be in effect after the devaluation. With inflation expected to jump at that time, employment contracts will embody corresponding cost-of-living adjustments.

After the devaluation is undertaken, domestic prices would increase in proportion. The devaluation shifts aggregate demand upward, from $Y_0^D Y_0^D$ to $Y_1^D Y_1^D$ in Figure 18–9. It also shifts the aggregate supply curve from AS_0 to AS_1 because the bargained wage increases obtained by workers during the transition period would be in effect. Consequently, there is no effect on output, employment, real interest rates, or real wages. The bottom line here is that an announced devaluation does not have any real effects under rational expectations. It appears to have adverse effects by inducing losses of international reserves and fueling domestic inflation.

The Stagflationary Effects of Delayed Devaluations

What would be the effects of a devaluation that is anticipated but not actually carried out? In other words, what would the effects be of a devaluation that individuals rationally expect but that—because of the uncertainty of government behavior—does not materialize, at least during the period of concern?[29] During the period preceding the point in time at which a devaluation is expected to occur, the economy behaves very much like it would under an announced devaluation: Workers rationally expect prices to increase proportionally to the devaluation and they bargain for cost-of-living increases to take effect the moment the devaluation is expected to arise; in addition,

[29]Many factors may prevent or delay devaluation or stabilization policies from being implemented. It may be unwise politically for an administration to engage in devaluation if there are elections in the near future. There may be political pressures from specific interest groups that fear devaluations will be larger than generally anticipated and dread the possibility of suffering cuts in real income. The process leading to policy implementation may thus involve strategic considerations that are difficult to anticipate. See A. Alesina and A. Drazen, "Why Are Stabilizations Delayed?", and R. Fernandez and D. Rodrik, "Resistance to Reform: Status Quo Bias in the Presence of Individual-Specific Uncertainty," both published in *American Economic Review* (December 1991).

nominal interest rates rise and the government loses international reserves.

What happens at the moment when the government is expected to devalue, but no action is actually undertaken by the central bank? Because labor contracts are already drawn with corresponding cost-of-living clauses embodied in them, real wage rates will increase, causing labor costs to rise and shifting the aggregate supply curve leftward, from AS_0 to AS_1, in Figure 18–9. As a result, inflationary pressures will ensue, in spite of the fact that an actual devaluation has not materialized. Now, if individuals retain their expectations that devaluation is imminent, they will continue to believe that inflation will be fueled by it. However, given that prices are already increasing, they will rationally expect the devaluation to generate a less-than-proportionate increase in prices when it occurs. In other words, the expected rate of devaluation will exceed the expected rate of inflation, causing an increase in real interest rates that reduces investment and aggregate demand (shown by the shift from $Y_0^D Y_0^D$ to $\bar{Y}^D \bar{Y}^D$ in Figure 18–9). The economy's path during this period would be along the pointed arrows between points E and D. The unfulfilled expected devaluation will then be highly contractionary and mildly inflationary. In modern terminology, the expected but unfulfilled devaluation is stagflationary.

Of course, the short-run equilibrium at point D would not be the end of the story. If investors and agents in the economy remain firm in their expectations and the government keeps finding increasingly innovative ways of avoiding devaluation, the stalemate would remain and the equilibrium would be sustained at point D. However, clearly, something must give: Either the government will run out of means to support the exchange rate or individuals will reverse their expectations. At that moment, the economy would return to full-employment equilibrium. We conclude this discussion by noting that some of the empirical evidence on the effects of devaluation shows that stagflation is often associated with devaluation. It is quite possible that these contractionary effects of deval-

uation may arise from long delayed, but obviously imminent and widely anticipated, devaluation.[30]

The Expansionary Effects of Unanticipated Devaluation

The third possible devaluation alternative involves an unanticipated devaluation. Suppose, for instance, that the government suddenly announces it is devaluing domestic currency. As a result, there will be an upward shift of the aggregate demand curve, which increases output and employment above its trend and generates domestic inflation. In terms of Figure 18–9, the $Y_0^D Y_0^D$ curve would shift upward to $Y_1^D Y_1^D$, with the new short-run equilibrium occurring at point H. Initially, the rise in domestic prices is less than proportional to the devaluation. Over the long run, however, inflationary expectations arise, which shift the aggregate supply curve up and to the left, increasing prices further and inducing a long-run equilibrium at point A. Note that the source of the short-run output increase is the unanticipated price increase resulting from the unanticipated devaluation. Being unexpected, the price hike is not embodied in labor contracts and results in reductions of real wages, making increased production profitable. As contracts are revised, however, the expected increase in prices is embodied in them and no long-run output expansion would be sustained.

Observe finally that if expectations were to be formed adaptively, instead of following the rational expectations hypothesis we have adopted, the

---

[30]Evidence of the contractionary and other macroeconomic effects of devaluation is supplied by W. M. Corden, "Exchange Rate Policy in Developing Countries," in J. de Melo and A. Sapir, eds., *Trade Theory and Economic Reform* (Oxford: Basil Blackwell, 1991). For a discussion of the causes and consequences of delayed devaluation in an economy suffering from real appreciations related to Dutch disease phenomena, see R. Hausmann, "Venezuela," in J. Williamson, ed., *Latin American Adjustment: How Much Has Happened?* (Washington, D.C.: Institute for International Economics, 1990); and L. Clemente, "Dutch Disease Symptoms and Venezuelan Therapy," *Review of the Central Bank of Venezuela* (March 1987).

expected rate of inflation would adjust only sluggishly; hence, the aggregate supply curve might overshoot the final equilibrium at point *A*, shifting to an intersection with the aggregate demand curve at a point such as *K* before it settled back into its long-run equilibrium at point *A*. The reason for this is that, under adaptive expectations, the inflationary episode involved in the movement from point *H* to point *A* builds up an expectation that prices will continue to rise. The result would be further increases in negotiated wages and prices and a consequent decline in output below full employment. Of course, with unemployment growing, individuals will eventually realize that the long-run equilibrium price level is below the one that exists at points like *K*. Nominal wages would then decline until point *A* is reached. The adjustment to devaluation will thus differ according to the expectational assumptions made.

In summary, comparing the overall performance of announced, anticipated-but-delayed, and unanticipated devaluation, the latter appears to be the most positive in terms of generating short-run increases in output; the second one is the most negative, being stagflationary. In all three cases, however, the long-run consequences of devaluation are that domestic prices increase proportionally to the devaluation.

Summary

1. This chapter has examined the role of expectations formation, particularly inflationary expectations, on the effectiveness of stabilization policies under fixed and flexible exchange rates.

2. The aggregate demand-aggregate supply framework developed in Chapters 16 and 17 is easily extended to take into account the influence of expectations on the economy. The aggregate supply curve, in particular, can be modified to become an expectations-augmented aggregate supply curve.

3. The expectations-augmented aggregate supply curve shows how the quantity supplied of domestic goods is related to the unanticipated rate of domestic inflation. Unanticipated inflation induces an increase in domestic output above its potential level. Anticipated inflation, on the other hand, has no effects on output. This is explained by the fact that, in an inflationary environment, employment contracts will embody nominal wage adjustments based on the anticipated inflation at the time the contract is drawn. As a result, inflation that is unanticipated when contracts are drawn (even if recognized or anticipated after the fact) will affect real wages and employment, and hence output. Inflation anticipated at the time labor contracts are drawn, on the other hand, will be taken into account in cost-of-living adjustments, generating no change in real wages, employment, and output.

4. The rational expectations hypothesis states that individuals incorporate all the relevant information available in forming their expectations regarding the future value of a given variable. Expectations errors are thus unsystematic, arising from unanticipated disturbances. This contrasts with adaptive expectations formation, in which individuals adopt rigid rules in revising their expectations and can therefore incur systematic forecasting errors.

5. Under rational expectations, an anticipated increase in central bank credit leaves output unaltered, even in the short run, because any price changes induced by the monetary disturbance are matched by cost-of-living adjustments, leaving real wages unchanged. Only unanticipated disturbances may affect output—and then only temporarily, until workers revise their labor contracts in response to the new economic scenario.

6. Under flexible exchange rates, in the presence of wage rigidity, an unanticipated central bank credit expansion will result in increased output and prices over the short run—but only in inflation over the long run. During the adjustment process, real exchange rates increase, but gradually return to their initial value. This

behavior is referred to as real exchange rate overshooting. Even though it is associated with lower (ex ante) real interest rates, the unanticipated monetary expansion is not necessarily connected to a reduction (or an increase, for that matter) of nominal interest rates. Nominal interest rates cannot, therefore, be used to reflect unequivocally the state of the economy's monetary policy.

7. Although major swings in monetary policy may very well affect real exchange rates, there is lack of evidence suggesting the overshooting model explains short-term real exchange rate variability. There appears to be a lack of correlation between real interest differentials and real exchange rate movements, as is predicted by the overshooting approach.

8. The real business cycles approach asserts that economic fluctuations are caused by "real" or supply-side shocks, such as technological or productivity improvements, oil-price shocks, and weather fluctuations. This model predicts that the variability of long-run real exchange rates as a result of real shocks—not monetary shocks—is what causes real exchange rate volatility. It is too early to assess whether the real business cycles approach is more consistent with the data than the overshooting theory.

9. The degree of real exchange rate volatility has increased since 1973. Given that this period coincides with the switch by the industrialized countries from the Bretton Woods system of fixed exchange rates to a regime of floating rates, it has been argued that flexible rates have been the cause of the greater real exchange rate variability. The overshooting model indeed predicts that monetary shocks would engender brusque movements in real exchange rates under a regime of flexible rates. On the other hand, the real business cycles approach suggests that the behavior of real currency values since 1973 is unrelated to the regime of floating rates. According to this framework, the variability in real exchange rates is more closely linked to real shocks—

such as the oil shocks of 1973, 1979, and 1990—as well as fluctuations in world real interest rates, and productivity shocks, for example. There is some evidence that economies under both fixed and flexible exchange rates have exhibited increased real currency value variability since 1973.

10. The announcement of a devaluation, or the public's anticipation of a devaluation, has no effects on output. However, it drives up interest rates, reducing money demand and inducing a loss of international reserves. Once the exchange rate increase occurs, domestic inflation is fueled, although there are still no output effects. If the devaluation does not occur, inflation will still be fueled because of prearranged cost-of-living raises, which shift the aggregate supply curve to the left. With labor costs rising, employment and output also decline. In addition, expected inflation will be revised downward, resulting in a rise of real interest rates and a deepening of the output contraction. The unfulfilled devaluation is therefore stagflationary. Unanticipated devaluations have an expansionary effect on output, but only temporarily, generating inflation over the long run.

Problems

1. During the early 1980s, the Federal Reserve of the United States followed contractionary monetary policies. Using the framework developed in the latter part of this chapter, determine the effects of U.S. monetary tightness on:
   (a) U.S. real and nominal interest rates.
   (b) The dollar real (effective) exchange rate.
   (c) The dollar nominal (effective) exchange rate.
   (d) Real income.
   (e) Inflation.
   Look at the data regarding the behavior of these variables between 1980 and 1986. Do your answers fit the data?

2. Consider an economy in long-run equilibrium under floating exchange rates and suppose that a massive military buildup has caused government expenditures to rise drastically, generating huge budget deficits. To finance these deficits, the government starts printing money (by drawing checks on itself). What would be the effects of this type of increased government spending on the following:
   (a) Domestic real interest rates?
   (b) The country's currency value, in nominal and real terms?
   (c) Domestic inflation?

3. In the 1980s and early 1990s, world real interest rates climbed, relative to the 1970s. What would be the consequence of a rise in world interest rates on a small economy under floating exchange rates? Using the aggregate demand-aggregate supply model developed in this chapter, examine the impact on nominal and real domestic currency values, output, and prices, both in the short run and in the long run. Do differences in the impact of the disturbance on output depend on whether the economy is under fixed or flexible exchange rates? Explain your answer.

4. The 1990–1991 Persian Gulf conflict led to a major unanticipated, but temporary, increase in oil prices. Consider an oil-importing economy under flexible exchange rates. What would be the impact of such a disturbance on output and prices in the short run and in the long run? Would the oil shock be associated with a domestic currency depreciation or appreciation? Japan is an oil-importing economy; examine the actual behavior of the exchange rate between the yen and the dollar between 1990 and 1992 (one source of data is the IMF's *International Financial Statistics*). Did the yen appreciate or depreciate during that period? Explain the movement of the yen-dollar exchange rate during that period.

5. Find the behavior of the real exchange rate for a developing country between 1961 and 1992 (use figures for the bilateral nominal exchange rate between the dollar and the country's currency, multiply by the U.S. CPI, and then divide by the country's CPI; use the IMF's *International Financial Statistics Yearbook*). Do you see differences in the pattern of real exchange rate volatility before and after 1973?

6. A third-party politician gets elected to the presidency of the United States. One of his campaign promises was that he would reinstate and expand a number of programs in aid to the poor. When asked about financing, his answer was "Easy: We will just print the money necessary to finance the increased expenditures and give them directly to the people." In spite of the new president's frantic efforts, it becomes clear, after a protracted two-year bargaining process by the new administration, that conflicts with Congress and with Federal Reserve authorities would prevent the president's policies from being implemented until some later time. Assume that agents in the economy had anticipated that the money supply would grow rapidly during the new president's administration. What would be the consequences of the delays in the implementation of the policy? Explain your answer.

7. Consider the short-run and long-run output and inflationary effects of an unanticipated increase in central bank credit or government spending in an economy under fixed exchange rates. Then determine the impact of an anticipated increase in central bank credit and government expenditures and compare with your results on the unanticipated disturbance. Does it matter whether you assume that individuals follow rational expectations or adaptive expectations? How do the present results differ from those derived in earlier chapters? Illustrate all your conclusions diagrammatically.

8. Evaluate the statement: "Expansionary monetary policy is inflationary" for the cases of fixed and flexible exchange rates. Do you see any differences? Consider the cases of perfect and zero capital mobility and differentiate between the short run and the long run.

PART VI

Asset Markets, the Balance of Payments, and the Exchange Rate

CHAPTER 19

Asset Markets and Exchange Rate Determination

Have you ever asked yourself why is it that in the last ten years it has always taken between $1.00 and $2.50 to purchase a British pound rather than $3.50 and $4.50? What induces the dollar-pound exchange rate to fluctuate around a value of $2.00 instead of $4.00, or $5.00 for that matter? This chapter examines the factors determining or influencing exchange rates and their behavior over time. It is clear that any adequate theory of exchange rate behavior must face the fact that the values of the major industrial countries' currencies have shown marked turbulence in the recent period of floating exchange rates, a turbulence that often looks perplexing. For instance, why was it that the value of the dollar vis-à-vis other currencies generally moved downward the day President Ronald Reagan was shot in 1982 or when President George Bush became ill from a thyroid condition during his presidency? Can you explain why the dollar brusquely depreciates in value when the Federal Reserve Board announces money supply growth figures below what were anticipated or when the Commerce Department announces unexpectedly large U.S. trade balance deficits? What accounts for the surge in the value of the dollar vis-à-vis the German mark in response to political turmoil in the former Soviet Union? All these situations involve either sudden events or new information unanticipated by agents in the economy. In this sense, they can all be catalogued as "news." A major task of this chapter is to explain why and how news relates to exchange rate turbulence.

When we observe the day-to-day fluctuations of exchange rates in response to news, we are reminded of the wild movements in the prices of assets traded on the stock exchange. The gyrations of the price of a share of IBM, General Motors, and the Tandy Corporation in large part reflect new information, rumors, or announcements made by these companies regarding present or future returns. An unanticipatedly dismal quarter in terms of sales or profits may prompt a rapid downfall of share prices. Growing expectations of economic recovery and increased sales, on the other hand, may start a sudden rise of share prices. Clearly, the bumbling behavior of stock market prices in response to news looks very similar to that of exchange rates, which suggests that exchange rates can be analyzed in a framework similar to the one for stock prices.

The asset market approach states that "the exchange rate must adjust instantly to equilibrate the international demand for stocks of national assets."[1] Exchange rate behavior is thus looked at from the point of view of its role in clearing relative demands for stocks of domestic and foreign assets, rather than in terms of clearing international trade flows of goods and services. The asset market approach to analyzing exchange rates sprouted in the late 1970s from a variety of

intellectual perspectives. As a result of that diversity of origins, there exists a whole range of alternative frameworks of analysis whose common underlying core in some way involves the asset market approach.

The simplest version of the asset market view is referred to as the *monetary approach to the exchange rate*. This approach looks at exchange rate adjustment as equilibrating the domestic and foreign markets for money. Factors affecting supplies and demands for domestic and foreign money—as might arise from the government's monetary policies or from changes in relative income growth among countries—will disturb equilibrium in money markets and will influence exchange rates. We will examine the various implications of the monetary approach with regard to exchange rate determination and variability. The phenomenon of currency substitution, occurring when residents of a given country hold money balances in foreign currencies in addition to domestic currency, is also examined and its implications for exchange rate determination stated.

In emphasizing the association between exchange rate adjustments and money market equilibrium, the monetary approach assumes that domestic and foreign bonds are perfect substitutes, freely interchangeable in investors' portfolios. On the other hand, the *portfolio balance* approach to the exchange rate relaxes precisely this assumption by focusing on the situation where domestic and foreign bonds are instead imperfect substitutes. This implies that in addition to considering equilibrium in the money market, we must also pay attention to the association between exchange rate behavior and changes in the relative demands and supplies of domestic and foreign bonds. Factors increasing the relative demand for domestic bonds, for instance, would disturb portfolio equilibrium among domestic and foreign assets; according to the portfolio balance approach, they will also influence the exchange rate. The details of these connections are examined later. We start at the beginning, by describing the monetary approach.

[1] J. A. Frankel, "Monetary and Portfolio-Balance Models of Exchange Rate Determination," in J. S. Bhandari and B. H. Putnam, *Economic Interdependence and Flexible Exchange Rates* (Cambridge, Mass.: The M.I.T. Press, 1983), p. 84.

19–1. THE MONETARY APPROACH TO THE EXCHANGE RATE

The monetary approach to the exchange rate was developed in the late 1970s in response to the increased exchange rate flexibility faced by most industrial countries after 1973 and the corresponding growth of academic interest in exchange rate determination. Its sources, though, go as far back as the early writings of Joan Robinson (in the 1930s), Lord Keynes (1924), Gustav Cassel (1916), and even David Ricardo in the early 1800s.[2]

The monetary approach to exchange rates begins at the most basic level, with the definition of an exchange rate. An *exchange rate* is the price at which foreign currency (foreign money) is sold in terms of domestic currency (domestic money). It is almost obvious in the monetary approach that, as any relative price, the exchange rate should be determined by the forces of demand and supply. Because the relative price involved is that between two monies, it should relate to the demands and supplies of the two.

More specifically, to sustain domestic money market equilibrium, the existing supply (stock) of money must be willingly held (demanded) or

$$\frac{M}{P} = L(i, Y), \qquad (19\text{–}1)$$

where M/P represents the domestic real money supply and $L(i, Y)$ depicts domestic (real) money demand as a function of domestic interest rates, i, and income, Y. Similarly, the foreign money market equilibrium condition is given by

$$\frac{M^*}{P^*} = L^*(i^*, Y^*), \qquad (19\text{–}2)$$

<hr/>

[2]For details on the origins of the monetary approach to the exchange rate, see J. Frenkel, "A Monetary Approach to the Exchange Rate: Doctrinal Aspects and Empirical Evidence," in J. Frenkel and H. Johnson, *The Economics of Exchange Rates: Selected Studies* (Reading, Mass.: Addison-Wesley, 1978).

where asterisks represent foreign variables (e.g., M^* is the foreign nominal money supply, L^* foreign real money demand). Observe that the money market equilibrium conditions in Equations 19–1 and 19–2 do not show explicitly how the equilibrium exchange rate is established. In order to do that, we have to specify an additional relationship determining explicitly how the exchange rate influences money market equilibria; that is, how do exchange rate changes contribute to equilibrate money demands and supplies?

To answer this question, one can utilize the so-called absolute purchasing power parity (PPP) relationship, stating the equality between domestic prices, P, and foreign prices converted into domestic currency, eP^*, or

$$P = eP^*, \qquad (19\text{–}3)$$

which can be transformed into an expression for the exchange rate:

$$e = \frac{P}{P^*}. \qquad (19\text{–}3a)$$

Equation 19–3(a) establishes a relationship between the exchange rate and the domestic price level. Its implication is that the higher the domestic price level relative to foreign prices, the higher the exchange rate must be in order to maintain PPP between domestic and foreign money. If, for instance, the U.S. price level is twice that in Britain $(P/P^* = 2)$, the exchange rate will have to reflect the lower relative purchasing power of U.S. money vis-à-vis British money by making U.S. money (the dollar) half as valuable in terms of British money (the pound). The dollar-pound exchange rate should thus equal \$2.00/£.

The PPP relationship in Equation 19–3 implies that exchange rates can influence money market equilibria through their connections to domestic and foreign prices. Transforming equations 19–1 and 19–2 to express them in terms of prices yields

$P = M/L(i,Y)$ and $P^* = M^*/L^*(i^*,Y^*)$, which can be substituted into Equation 19–3 to obtain

$$e = \frac{M}{M^*} \frac{L^*(i^*, Y^*)}{L(i, Y)}. \qquad (19\text{–}4)$$

This shows that the exchange rate is determined by the ratio of the domestic money supply to the foreign money supply, M/M^*, and the ratio of the demand for foreign money to the demand for domestic money, L^*/L. This version of the monetary approach to the exchange rate succinctly shows the economic interdependence involved in exchange rate determination. Being the relative price of two monies, the exchange rate depends not only on demand for and supply of domestic money, but also on demand for and supply of foreign money. Exchange rate adjustments are therefore dependent on changes in both domestic and foreign variables. Even though a given domestic money supply increase by itself tends to raise the exchange rate, if there is a simultaneously larger proportional increase in the foreign money supply, the result is an excess supply of foreign money relative to domestic money. This requires a reduction in the relative price of foreign money—that is, a lower exchange rate. Exchange rates cannot, therefore, be determined independently of the behavior of foreign economies or the actions of foreign governments. Questions related to the control of exchange rate changes or fluctuations must then be addressed within the context of a common dialogue among the countries involved. This serves well to illustrate that, in general, no single open economy can dissociate itself entirely from foreign influences.

Equation 19–4 shows that, given relative money supplies, factors increasing domestic money demand relative to foreign money demand will raise the value of domestic currency—that is, they will lower the exchange rate. An increase in domestic income relative to foreign income, Y/Y^*, for instance, will tend to increase relative domestic money demand and appreciate the value of domes-

tic currency. Similarly, lower domestic nominal interest rates relative to foreign nominal interest rates raise relative domestic money demand and will also appreciate the value of domestic currency.

These results stand squarely opposed to those derived from other perspectives on exchange rate determination. For example, it is often argued that higher domestic real incomes reduce rather than increase the value of domestic money. Because they tend to increase imports and worsen the current account, the exchange rate would have to increase to assure external balance. This positive connection between depreciation of domestic currency and higher domestic income is often voiced in official circles. The monetary approach to the exchange rate suggests an opposite view. The same dichotomy arises with regard to the effects of changes in nominal interest rates on the exchange rate. A popular view is that higher nominal interest rates strengthen the value of domestic currency because they induce incipient capital inflows reflected in a rising capital account surplus that requires a domestic currency appreciation to assure external balance. The Federal Reserve Board has frequently supported this perspective, arguing that in order to strengthen the dollar, higher U.S. nominal interest rates are required. The monetary approach suggests the opposite.

What is the evidence for the monetary approach to the exchange rate? Do equations such as Equation 19–4 explain accurately actual exchange rates? Are changes in relative money supplies, income, and interest rates related to exchange rate changes as predicted by the monetary approach? The next sections wrestle with these questions.

19–2. Empirical Evidence on the Monetary Approach: A First Look

This section introduces the data available on the monetary approach to exchange rate determination and, in particular, the question as to whether Equation 19–4 accurately explains actual exchange rates. In order to answer this question, it is apparent that one must deal with the problem of specifying, in a precise way, the form that the money demand functions, L^* and L, take. Even though the monetary approach clearly asserts that these money demands are stable functions of certain variables—income and interest rates—it still leaves open the question of exactly how money demands relate to those variables. In a simple version, money demands are assumed to be of the following multiplicative form:

$$L = YK(i)$$

and

$$L^* = Y^* K^* (i^*),$$

where the K functions reflect the particular influence of interest rates on money demand. These can be substituted into Equation 19–4 to obtain the following simplified exchange rate determination equation:

$$e = \frac{M}{M^*} \frac{Y^* K^*(i^*)}{Y K(i)}. \qquad (19\text{–}4a)$$

It is clear that how interest rates are related to money demands through the functions K and K^* must still be specified. This, however, need not concern us here, as different studies generally adopt different versions for K.

Table 19–1 displays the computation of the exchange rates implied by Equation 19–4(a) for the dollar vis-à-vis selected foreign monies using actual 1978 data for relative money supplies, income, and interest rates and the specific measures of these variables. The predicted exchange rates are compared with actual exchange rates prevailing then. Notice that in some cases the exchange rates implied by the monetary approach as given by Equation 19–4(a) are relatively close to the actual values of the exchange rates; how-

ever, there are clear substantial deviations in most cases. Other studies following the same or a similar strategy yield similar findings.

What causes these deviations? A major factor generating divergencies between the predictions of the monetary approach as embodied in equations 19–4 and 19–4(a) and actual exchange rates is the fact that, in order to derive these equations, the absolute version of PPP, as stated in Equation 19–3(a), is used. As a consequence, the predicted exchange rates quoted in Table 19–1 are the joint result not only of the monetary approach hypotheses regarding money market equilibrium, but also of the absolute PPP assumption.

The empirical evidence shows that the absolute PPP hypothesis fails to hold on a systematic basis over time. In the case of the United States, for example, Figure 19–1 shows how the dollar-pound exchange rate, e, has generally failed to equal the ratio of an index of United States to United Kingdom prices, P/P^*. Therefore, if the relationship between the exchange rate and relative prices used is to have any empirical basis, it must be modified from the one stated by Equation 19–3.

Let us denote the ratio of foreign prices (expressed in domestic currency) to domestic prices by $\tilde{q} = eP^*/P$. Absolute PPP assumes that $\tilde{q}$ is equal to 1 on a systematic basis, which is the basis for Equation 19–3. In general, however, $\tilde{q} > 1$ if domestic prices, P, are lower than comparable foreign prices, eP^*, and $\tilde{q} < 1$ if domestic prices exceed foreign prices converted into domestic currency. The relationship between the exchange rate and relative price levels can then be expressed by

$$e = \tilde{q} \frac{P}{P^*}. \qquad (19\text{–}5)$$

A modified version of the PPP hypothesis allows the exchange rate to diverge from relative price levels ($\tilde{q} \neq 1$), but by a fixed margin; this implies that $\tilde{q}$ is fixed over time.

TABLE 19–1. **The Fundamental Determinants of the Exchange Rate**

Country	M($)/M(*)	Y(*)/Y($)	K(*)/K($)	Exchange Rate Prediction	Exchange Rate Actual
Australia	1.47	0.78	1.09	$1.25	$1.15
Austria	0.05	0.85	1.19	0.05	0.07
Belgium	0.03	1.11	1.19	0.04	0.03
Canada	0.93	0.85	1.06	0.85	0.84
France	0.22	0.98	1.10	0.23	0.24
Germany	0.31	1.18	1.75	0.65	0.54
Italy	0.001	0.48	0.51	0.0003	0.0012
Japan	0.003	0.95	1.75	0.005	0.005
Netherlands	0.37	1.06	1.43	0.56	0.51
Norway	0.14	1.02	1.19	0.17	0.20
South Africa	8.33	0.16	0.88	1.18	1.15
Sweden	0.24	1.14	0.92	0.25	0.23
Switzerland	0.14	1.56	2.5	0.56	0.62
United Kingdom	4.55	0.60	0.66	1.79	2.04

Note: The predicted exchange rate is the product of the first three columns:

$M(\$)/M(*)$ = Quantity of money per capita in the United States relative to the quantity of money per capita in the sample country.

$Y(*)/Y(\$)$ = U.S. dollar value of GNP per capita in the sample country, relative to the U.S. GNP per capita.

$K(*)/K(\$)$ = 0.84 exp 0.13($i[*]$ − $i[\$]$), where $i(\$)$ is the long-term bond yield in the United States and $i(*)$ is the long-term bond yield in the sample country. The 0.84 adjustment insures that the geometric mean of the forecast errors is equal to zero.

SOURCE: Based on John Bilson, "Comment on Willet and Sweeney," in J. Dreyer, G. Haberler, and T. Willet, eds., *The International Monetary System: A Time of Turbulence* (Washington, D.C.: American Enterprise Institute, 1982).

Expressing Equation 19–5 in terms of percentage changes yields

$$\hat{e} = \hat{q} + \hat{P} - \hat{P}*, \qquad (19\text{–}6)$$

where $\hat{P} \equiv \Delta P/P$ is the rate of increase of domestic prices, $\hat{q} \equiv \Delta \bar{q}/\bar{q}$ represents proportional changes in the gap between domestic and foreign prices, $\hat{e}$ is the rate of domestic currency depreciation, and $\hat{P}*$ is the rate of increase of prices in world markets, over a given time period. Symbolically, the assumption that $\bar{q}$ remains fixed over time means $\hat{q} = 0$, in which case Equation 19–6 can be expressed as

$$\hat{e} = \hat{P} - \hat{P}*, \qquad (19\text{–}7)$$

referred to as the *relative purchasing power parity* hypothesis, to distinguish it from the *absolute* version of PPP embodied in Equation 19–3. Equation 19–7 asserts that the rate of domestic currency depreciation or appreciation is equal to the differential rates of inflation among countries. If domestic inflation exceeds foreign inflation, a do-

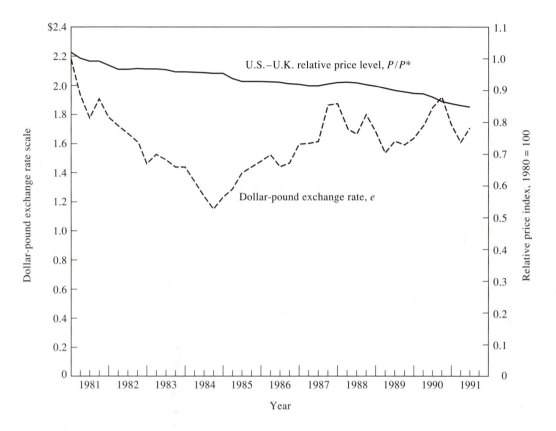

Note: The dollar exchange rate is the quarterly average rate; the U.S. and U.K. price levels are the consumer price indexes (1980 = 100).

FIGURE 19–1. Deviations from Absolute Purchasing Power Parity, 1981–1991.

SOURCE: Data are from the international Monetary Fund, *International Financial Statistics* (selected issues).

mestic currency depreciation is required to sustain PPP between domestic and foreign money. Similarly, if foreign inflation exceeds domestic inflation, this will be associated with a domestic currency appreciation. In summary, Equation 19–7 is less stringent than Equation 19–3 in allowing domestic and foreign prices (in domestic currency) to differ from each other; however, it still sustains the assumption that these deviations will not grow or diminish persistently over time.

The relative purchasing power of domestic money vis-à-vis foreign money will therefore be fixed over time, with exchange rate changes, $\hat{e}$, assuring such parity.

Most studies following the monetary approach have utilized the relative version of PPP in deriving an expression for the determinants of exchange rate changes. The following section derives the monetary approach to exchange rate adjustment on this basis.

19−3. EXCHANGE RATE CHANGES AND THE MONETARY APPROACH

The state of flux in which the world operates implies that economic variables will be changing constantly. Interest rates, income, prices, and so on, all change significantly over time. According to the monetary approach, changes in these variables will generally influence exchange rates by affecting money market equilibrium. Formally expressed, taking proportional changes in equations 19−1 and 19−2 yields

$$\hat{M} - \hat{P} = \hat{L} \text{ and } \hat{M}^* - \hat{P}^* = \hat{L}^*.$$

Expressing these relationships in terms of domestic and foreign inflation, $\hat{P} = \hat{M} - \hat{L}$ and $\hat{P}^* = \hat{M}^* - \hat{L}^*$, respectively, and substituting the resulting expression into Equation 19−7, we obtain

$$\hat{e} = \hat{P} - \hat{P}^*$$
$$= (\hat{M} - \hat{M}^*) + (\hat{L}^* - \hat{L}). \quad (19-7a)$$

Exchange rate changes, $\hat{e}$, are thus determined by changes in relative money supplies, $\hat{M} - \hat{M}^*$, and changes in relative money demands, $\hat{L}^* - \hat{L}$. Changes in relative money supplies reflect the countries' monetary policies. Changes in relative money demands, in turn, reflect differential changes in the variables affecting money demand, mainly income and interest rates. The specific way through which these variables influence relative money demands clearly depends on the form of the money demand functions and is therefore subject to a degree of discretion. Most studies following the monetary approach, however, assume that

$$\hat{L}^* - \hat{L} = \phi(\hat{Y}^* - \hat{Y}) + \lambda(i - i^*), \quad (19-8)$$

where ϕ and λ are both positive parameters. Equation 19−8 states, first, that higher foreign income growth relative to domestic growth results

in a higher proportional growth of foreign money demand relative to domestic money demand. This reflects the higher rate of increase of transactions abroad, which generates a relatively higher growth of foreign money demand. In addition, an increase in domestic interest rates above foreign interest rates—a positive $(i - i^*)$ term—will also result in a relatively higher growth of foreign money demand vis-à-vis domestic money demand. The relatively higher domestic interest rate puts a brake on domestic money demand growth relative to foreign demand by inducing domestic residents to shift out of money and into bonds.

Substitution of Equation 19−8 into 19−7(a) yields the following expression. It shows the determinants of exchange rate changes according to the monetary approach

$$\hat{e} = (\hat{M} - \hat{M}^*) + \phi(\hat{Y} - \hat{Y}^*)$$
$$+ \lambda(i - i^*). \quad (19-9)$$

This basic equation is used by the monetary approach to examine exchange rate changes. As shown next, it provides us with additional insights into the economics of exchange rate movements, particularly on how expectations influence exchange rates.

Interest Differentials, Expected Inflation, and the Exchange Rate

The role of expectations can be explicitly examined by modifying Equation 19−9 through the use of the uncovered interest rate parity condition:

$$i - i^* = x. \quad (19-10)$$

This condition establishes the equality of interest rate differentials with anticipated exchange rate changes, x, where exchange risk premia are being momentarily ignored (the role of the latter on exchange rate determination is examined in Section 19−6). In addition, on the assumption that relative PPP holds, agents in the economy would anticipate exchange rates to change according to the anticipated differential in the rates of domestic and foreign inflation, or

$$x = \pi - \pi^*, \qquad (19-11)$$

where π and π^* denote expected domestic and foreign inflation. Equation 19–11 is essentially the expectational counterpart of Equation 19–7 in the general situation where future inflation rates are not known.

Substituting Equation 19–11 into Equation 19–10 and then into Equation 19–9 yields

$$\hat{e} = (\hat{M} - \hat{M}^*) + \phi(\hat{Y}^* - \hat{Y})$$
$$+ \lambda(\pi - \pi^*). \qquad (19-9a)$$

The first two terms of Equation 19–9(a) have already been explained. The last term requires more attention. It states that, everything else being constant, higher domestic anticipated inflation tends to depreciate the value of domestic currency. The higher anticipated inflation will be associated with higher domestic nominal interest rates, which consequently reduce domestic real money demand and require a reduction in the value of domestic currency to sustain asset market equilibrium.

This point makes clear the important role that expectational considerations have according to the monetary approach; it illustrates the monetary approach's view of exchange rate variability. News relevant to the formation of expectations regarding future domestic and foreign inflation will be reflected immediately in spot exchange rate changes. Because such news are sudden and not known beforehand, the changes in exchange rates will also be sudden and unanticipated. Consequently, there is a significant component of exchange rate changes that is uncertain; it moves along the bumbling, unpredictable path that new events and information induce it to follow.

Evidence on the Monetary Approach to Exchange Rate Changes

Initial tests of the monetary approach using data for the 1970s supported the theory; more recent research, however, has led to a general rejection of the framework as an explanation for short-run exchange rate behavior. In the case of the U.S. dollar, for instance, studies using data for the period 1973 to 1978 yielded findings consistent with the monetary approach stated by Equation 19–9.[3] Research incorporating data since that time have not supported the model, however.[4]

A problem that has received considerable attention is shown by Figure 19–2, in which the U.S. dollar-pound sterling exchange rate is plotted against the U.S.-U.K. interest rate differential, $i - i^*$. According to the monetary approach, a lower U.S.-U.K. interest rate differential should be associated with an equivalent U.S. dollar appreciation, other things held equal. Such a relationship seems to hold for the period between 1981 and 1982, but in 1983 and 1984, an interest differential increasingly favoring the United States was associated with a continued appreciation of the dollar in terms of sterling. This development seemingly contradicts the presumption of the monetary approach. Another example occurs in 1989 and 1990 when the U.S.-U.K. interest differential moved sharply in favor of the United Kingdom but was accompanied by a dollar depreciation. Casting further doubts on the robustness of the monetary approach.

[3]See J. Bilson, "The Monetary Approach to the Exchange Rate: Some Evidence," *IMF Staff Papers* (March 1978); R. Hodrick, "An Empirical Analysis of the Monetary Approach to the Determination of the Exchange Rate," in Jacob Frenkel and Harry Johnson, eds., *The Economics of Exchange Rates: Selected Studies* (Reading, Mass.: Addison-Wesley Publishing Co., Inc., 1978).

[4]See the surveys by R. MacDonald, "Exchange Rate Economics: An Empirical Perspective," in G. Bird, ed., *The International Financial Regime* (London: Surrey University Press, 1990); and J. Boughton, "The Monetary Approach to Exchange Rates: What Now Remains?" *Princeton Essays in International Finance* (October 1988).

Note: Interest rates are for Treasury bills, annualized. The data is presented on a quarterly basis and shows the value of the dollar with respect to the pound.

FIGURE 19–2.   The U.S. Dollar–Pound Exchange Rate and the U.S.–U.K. Interest Rate Differential, 1981–1991

SOURCE: Data are from the International Monetary Fund, *International Financial Statistics* (various issues).

However, we must be very careful in evaluating this experience. First, just as the power of Equation 19–4(a) in explaining exchange rates is dependent on the accuracy of absolute PPP, the ability of Equation 19–9 to account for exchange rate changes is associated with whether the relative version of PPP holds. As a consequence, the failure of some studies to find results consistent with an equation such as 19–9 might very well be attributable to the breakdown of relative PPPs in the periods examined. This lack of consistency may not necessarily imply that the monetary approach should not be accepted. Second, additional issues must be considered when evaluating the monetary approach, such as the phenomenon of currency substitution and the presence of exchange risk, both of which drastically modify the predictions of the monetary approach. The evidence and role of each of these factors in explaining the data will be the subject of the following sections.

19–4. Deviations from Purchasing Power Parity and Exchange Rate Changes Pricing to Market and the Real Exchange Rate

The relative version of PPP does not appear to have held to any significant extent in the recent period of increased exchange rate flexibility. The dollar real exchange rate has not been constant over the last few decades, as relative PPP assumes. Figure 18–6 on page 535 illustrates this breakdown of relative PPPs since the 1970s for the U.S.-U.K. case. Similar data appear to hold for other currencies as well.[5] However, a close look at Figure 18–6 suggests that even though there are substantial and persistent short-run deviations from relative PPP, on average these deviations tend to even out over time. Thus, in the long run, the relative PPP hypothesis is much closer to being satisfied.[6] We could, consequently, think about Equation 19–9(a) as being a long-run relationship, toward which exchange rate changes move over time, but from which they deviate in the short run.

Why does relative PPP break down over certain periods of time? Relative PPP involves the assumption that the real exchange rate remains unchanged over time. Factors altering the real exchange rate, whether temporarily or permanently, will then generate deviations from relative PPP.

Algebraically, from Equation 19–6, exchange rate changes are given by

$$\hat{e} = \hat{P} - \hat{P}* + \hat{q}, \qquad (19\text{–}6)$$

where $\hat{q}$ represents changes in the real exchange rate. Relative PPP assumes $\hat{q} = 0$—that is, the absence of real exchange rate changes. But more generally, $\hat{q}$ will differ from zero.

Various factors generate changes in real exchange rates. Differential changes in taste, technology, factor supplies, and market structures between countries will generally affect their relative costs of production. Production cost thereby influence countries' relative price competitiveness and, therefore, real exchange rates. These long-term changes in real exchange rates appear as deviations from relative PPP.[7] However, even if the long-run real exchange rate is fixed, our analysis in previous chapters should have alerted us to the possibility that disturbances in the economy, particularly unanticipated disturbances, may lead to short-term fluctuations in real exchange rates. Labor and/or goods market rigidities facing the economy generally imply that the economy's adjustment to these disturbances will not occur instantaneously and will have short-run effects on real variables, such as real exchange rates.

To take an extreme example, when domestic and foreign prices are relatively rigid in how much

---

[5]For statistical evidence on the breakdown of PPP since the end of the Bretton Woods system, see J. Frenkel, "The Collapse of Purchasing Power Parities in the 1970s" in G. de Meñil and R. J. Gordon, eds., *International Volatility and Economic Growth* (Amsterdam: North Holland, 1991); and W. Enders, "ARIMA and Co-Integration Tests of Purchasing Power Parity," *Review of Economics and Statistics* (August 1988).

[6]This point has been forcefully made by R. Dornbusch and T. Vogelsang, "Real Exchange Rates and Purchasing Power Parity," in J. de Melo and A. Sapir, eds., *Trade Theory and Economic Reform: North, South and East* (Oxford: Basil Blackwell, 1991). See also C. S. Hakkio, "Is Purchasing Power Parity a Useful Guide to the Dollar?" *Federal Reserve Bank of Kansas City Economic Review* (Third Quarter, 1992).

[7]A wide variety of research has studied the long-run determinants of real exchange rates. For instance, the effects on real exchange rates of the generally higher industrial productivity growth in Japan relative to that of the United States in recent years has been investigated by C. Morrison and W. E. Diewert, "Productivity Growth and Changes in the Terms of Trade in Japan and the United States," in C. R. Hulten, ed., *Productivity Growth in Japan and the United States* (Chicago: University of Chicago Press, 1990); and R. C. Marston, "Systematic Movements in Real Exchange Rates in the G–5," National Bureau of Economic Research Working Paper no. 3332 (April 1990). See also our discussion of real exchange rate determination in Chapter 18.

they can change in the short run, domestic currency appreciation or depreciation over that time period will result in deviations from relative PPP. Such was the case analyzed in Chapter 15, where an (unanticipated) increase in the money supply was observed to require a short-run currency depreciation exceeding its longer-term equilibrium depreciation. This overshooting of the exchange rate in the presence of price rigidity is then associated with a short-run real exchange rate change and to deviations from PPP. Note, however, that prices and/or other economic variables will adjust over time in moving the economy to its long-run equilibrium. As a result, the deviations from relative PPP arising from an unanticipated monetary expansion would be gradually eliminated over time. The real exchange rate will therefore decline back toward its long-run value, above which it momentarily moved in response to the disturbance.

To reiterate, according to the overshooting approach, over the long run, exchange rate changes generally tend to reflect inflation rate differentials among countries. In the short run, however, fluctuations in real exchange rates give rise to substantial deviations from relative PPP. A number of studies testing the overshooting approach have incorporated deviations from relative PPP into the structure of the monetary approach to the exchange rate.[8] Still, even in this case, the data often do not seem to provide support for the hypothesized relationships connecting relative money growth and relative income to exchange rate changes, as stated by Equation 19–9(a), especially

when updated to take into account the events of the 1980s and 1990s. As Rudiger Dornbusch and Jeffrey Frankel conclude: "While the overshooting theory does seem to explain gross movements in the real exchange rate, better at least than competing theories, shorter-term movements remain completely unexplained."[9]

Pricing to Market and the Real Exchange Rate

One explanation for the failure of the overshooting approach in accounting for short-run exchange rate movements is that the model completely associates short-run nominal exchange rate variability with real exchange rate variability: It assumes that prices in local currencies are rigid over the short-run. In terms of Equation 19–6, $\hat{e} = \hat{q}$, because $\hat{P}$ and $\hat{P}^*$ are assumed to be equal to zero. However, there is some evidence to suggest that in some industries exchange rate changes are not matched exactly by real exchange rate changes because the prices of imports, P^*, change when exchange rates vary. In particular, evidence gathered in the 1980s and early 1990s indicates that when the dollar depreciates in value (when e rises), foreign producers selling in the United States often lower their export prices, P^*, denominated in foreign currency—a phenomenon described as "pricing to market."[10] For instance, University of Pennsylvania economist Richard C. Marston has found widespread evidence of pricing to market in the behavior of Japanese and Ameri-

[8]See, for example, A. Giovannini and J. Rotemberg, "Exchange Rate Dynamics with Sticky Wages: The Deutsche Mark, 1974–1982," *Journal of Business and Economics* (April 1989); J. Huizinga, "An Empirical Investigation of the Long-Run Behavior of Real Exchange Rates," in K. Brunner and A. Meltzer, eds., *Carnegie-Rochester Series on Public Policy* (Amsterdam: North Holland, 1987); and J. A. Frankel, "On the Mark: A Theory of Floating Exchange Rates Based on Real Interest Differentials," *American Economic Review* (September 1979).

[9]R. Dornbusch and J. Frankel, "The Flexible Exchange Rate System: Experience and Alternatives," in S. Borner, ed., *International Finance and Trade in a Polycentric World* (London: Macmillan, 1988), p. 163. See also, R. A. Meese and K. Rogoff, "Empirical Exchange Rate Models of the Seventies: Do They Fit Out of Sample?" *Journal of International Economics* (1983).

[10]See P. Krugman, "Pricing to Market when the Exchange Rate Changes," in S. W. Arndt and J. D. Richardson, eds., *Real-Financial Linkages Among Open Economies* (Cambridge, Mass.: The MIT Press, 1987).

can exporters. He concludes that "there is evidence that firms in both countries pursue such pricing to market, but Japanese firms appear to change their export prices more than American firms."[11]

What factors motivate firms to employ pricing to market? One hypothesis is that, when faced with an unexpected dollar depreciation, foreign exporters to the United States lower their price markups in order to keep their share of the domestic market.[12] They thus reduce their export price (denominated in foreign currency) and sustain a reduction in profit margins in order to sustain their price competitiveness temporarily. The expectation is that the exchange rate change would be reversed in the future and profit margins would then be restored. The uncertainty of currency values over the last two decades provides a basis for this cautious behavior by firms. An alternative explanation relies on the presence of a "beachhead effect," a theory which is based on the reaction of foreign firms to the dollar's behavior in the 1980s. Briefly, the beachhead effect is based on the observation that, as the dollar in the early 1980s appreciated in value, it made foreign goods relatively cheaper. This induced foreign firms to enter the U.S. market (establishing marketing beachheads); however, when the dollar depreciated after early 1985, those firms stayed in the market because they already had substantial "sunk" costs (fixed costs of entering the U.S. market, such as advertising, marketing costs). The lasting presence of the foreign firms in the U.S. market for imports then enhanced competition in those markets and lowered profit margins, which were then reflected in a drop in the prices charged by foreign produc-ers. The depreciation of the dollar in the second half of the 1980s was thus associated with a reduction in the foreign-currency prices of U.S. imports.[13]

In terms of Equation 19–6, when pricing to market is present, the one-to-one relationship between real and nominal exchange rates is broken. Suppose, for example, that pricing to market is being considered by foreign producers selling to the United States. To simplify the example, assume that U.S. firms keep their prices rigid, so that $\hat{P} = 0$. In this case, from Equation 19–6 we have $\hat{q} = \hat{e} + \hat{P}^*$. Consider, then, a 20 percent dollar depreciation, $\hat{e} = 0.20$. If there is pricing to market, foreign producers would lower their export prices in reaction to the dollar depreciation. Suppose that the drop in the price of foreign goods (in foreign currency) is $\hat{P}^* = -0.10$. Then the dollar real exchange rate changes by $\hat{q} = 0.10$—that is, there is a real dollar depreciation of 10 percent. The exchange rate increase is thus not fully *"passed through,"* into higher domestic import prices—it is partly offset by the lower foreign-currency prices. Similarly, if there were a dollar appreciation of 20 percent and pricing to market, the real exchange rate would drop by less than 20 percent because foreign-currency prices would rise by a certain percentage.

Beside pricing to market, a second explanation for the failure of the monetary and overshooting models to account for short-run exchange rate behavior is related to the so-called *safe-haven hypothesis*. This hypothesis incorporates risk considerations into the monetary and overshooting approaches. The main idea is that changes in the risk assessed by investors to national currencies and assets lead to shifts in the relative demands for monies, which then alter exchange rates. The following sections explore versions of this theory.

[11]R. C. Marston, "Price Behavior in Japanese and U.S. Manufacturing," in P. Krugman, ed., *Trade with Japan: Has the Door Opened Wider?* (Chicago: University of Chicago Press, 1991), p. 140.

[12]See P. Krugman, *Exchange Rate Instability* (Cambridge, Mass.: The MIT Press, 1989); and C. Mann, "Prices, Profit Margins, and Exchange Rates," *Federal Reserve Bulletin* (June 1986).

[13]This hypothesis has been developed by R. Baldwin, "Some Empirical Evidence on Hysteresis in Aggregate U.S. Import Prices," in S. Gerlach and P. A. Petri, eds., *The Economics of the Dollar Cycle* (Cambridge, Mass.: The MIT Press, 1990).

19–5. CURRENCY SUBSTITUTION AND THE EXCHANGE RATE

Up to this point, it has been assumed that each country's money is held only by its own residents. In other words, only U.S. residents hold dollars and only German residents demand marks. More generally, however, it appears that residents of major industrial countries do hold both domestic and foreign currencies. For example, U.S. multinational corporations engaging in frequent transactions abroad acquire foreign currency deposits to facilitate and reduce the costs of such transactions. Similarly, speculators and/or arbitrageurs seeking to profit from purchases and sales of currencies hold domestic and foreign money. These currencies are highly liquid funds that can be quickly transferred across borders or easily exchanged for other currencies. Finally, central banks also hold international reserves in the form of foreign currency balances that are often used to intervene in foreign exchange markets. Whatever the reason, when residents of different countries hold a portfolio of currencies, changes in economic variables may alter the desired share of each currency in that portfolio, leading to changes in relative money demands. This phenomenon is referred to as *currency substitution.*

What determines the proportion of total money balances that domestic and foreign residents wish to hold in domestic money relative to foreign money? A crucial factor here is the opportunity cost of holding domestic relative to foreign money, which is often represented by the anticipated rate of depreciation of domestic currency. An increase in the anticipated rate of depreciation of domestic currency raises the expected cost of holding domestic money vis-à-vis foreign currency and will result in an increase in the share of money balances held in foreign money, other things held constant. On the other hand, an expected domestic currency appreciation will raise the proportion of domestic money in currency portfolios.

Under flexible exchange rates, expected depreciations of domestic currency can induce money holders to switch their cash holdings from domestic to foreign currency. The concomitant drop in the demand for domestic money relative to foreign money would then induce a depreciation of domestic currency. Observe that this effect of anticipated exchange rate changes in shifting the demand for money out of the domestic and into *foreign currency* operates in addition to the effect of expected exchange rate changes in shifting the demand for money out of domestic currency and into *bonds.*[14] As specified earlier, by raising domestic nominal interest rates relative to foreign rates, a sudden expected depreciation of domestic currency reduces domestic money demand and increases the demand for bonds. The currency substitution effect adds an additional factor affecting relative demands for domestic and foreign money not considered earlier. Introducing currency substitution into the analysis may thus improve upon the ability of equations such as Equation 19–9(a) to explain exchange rate changes.

An unexplained shift in relative money demands could be partially accounted for by a currency portfolio shift arising from a heightened preference for foreign currencies relative to dollars. However, it could also be the result of a portfolio balance shift arising from an increased preference for holding bonds denominated in foreign currencies relative to bonds denominated in dollars. It is the purpose of the next section to examine the role of portfolio balance considerations on the exchange rate.

19–6. EXCHANGE RISK AND THE PORTFOLIO BALANCE APPROACH

In studying the connections between exchange rates and money market equilibrium, the monetary approach assumes that domestic and foreign bonds

---

[14]For a survey of the effects of expected exchange rate changes in generating shifts between money and bonds and among different moneys, see A. Giovannini and B. Turtelboom, "Currency Substitution," National Bureau of Economic Research Working Paper No. 4232 (December 1992); see also R. McKinnon, "Currency Substitution and Instability in the World Dollar Standard," *American Economic Review* (June 1982).

are perfect substitutes and therefore are freely interchangeable in investors' portfolios. However, there are reasons why domestic and foreign assets might not be perfect substitutes: differences in liquidity, government tax laws, default risk, political risk, and exchange risk. The portfolio balance approach to the exchange rate focuses on examining the case in which exchange risk makes domestic and foreign bonds imperfect substitutes.[15] Exchange risk is the particular risk associated with holding uncovered investments in foreign-currency-dominated assets relative to domestic investments. Risk-averse investors will generally diversify their asset holdings internationally. Diversification avoids "placing all the eggs in the same basket" and reduces the risks attached to holding only one type of asset. International portfolio diversification involves assessing the effect of uncovered foreign investments on the risk of the investors' portfolio. If, for example, adding the uncovered foreign investment results in an increase in the overall risk of the investors' portfolios, investors will have to be compensated for the hair-raising and heart-stopping effects of the increased risk. That is, risk-averse investors will require an exchange *risk premium* to compensate them for the increased risk of their uncovered undertakings. Similarly, if investors are already holding high-risk domestic currency-denominated asset portfolios and the uncovered foreign investments reduce their portfolios' overall riskiness, the foreign-currency-denominated assets will be associated with a negative risk premium (a discount). Investors would then be willing to pay a certain amount to obtain the reduced portfolio risk.[16]

An exchange risk premium (or discount) deeply influences international financial equilibrium and the determination of domestic-foreign interest rates. The existence of an exchange risk premium implies that the uncovered interest parity condition must be modified to

$$i = i^* + x - R, \qquad (19\text{–}12)$$

where R represents the risk premium or discount attached to the addition of foreign investments to asset portfolios in the absence of covering. This foreign exchange premium is positive if foreign investments increase investors' portfolio risk. In that case, the foreign rate of return, as represented by the foreign interest rate, i^*, plus the expected domestic currency depreciation, x, must exceed the domestic interest rate in order to compensate investors for their increased risk taking. Similarly, if the risk premium is negative, foreign investments reduce portfolio risk and domestic interest rates will have to exceed the foreign rate of return, $i^* + x$, to compensate for the relative riskiness of domestic currency-denominated assets.

Obviously, changes in the foreign exchange risk premium will generally influence domestic-foreign interest rate differentials, relative asset demands, and consequently the exchange rate. What factors, then, affect the exchange rate risk premium? One crucial factor is the relative variability of real returns on domestic vis-à-vis foreign investments.[17] Other things being equal, if foreign real returns become less variable relative to domestic

---

[15]For excellent, although somewhat advanced, expositions of the portfolio balance approach, see R. MacDonald, "Exchange Rate Economics: An Empirical Perspective," in G. Bird, ed., *The International Financial Regime* (London: Surrey University Press, 1990); M. Mussa, "Exchange Rates in Theory and in Reality," *Princeton Essays in International Finance* (December 1990); and J. Frankel, "Monetary and Portfolio-Balance Models of Exchange Rate Determination," in Bhandari and Putnam, op. cit.

[16]What is the source of real return variability in domestic assets when default-free short-term assets bearing a fixed

nominal interest rate are being evaluated? In this case, the source of domestic real return variability is inflation risk. This means that a highly uncertain domestic inflation contributing to portfolio real return variability could make domestic assets riskier than foreign assets. Hence, there is no a priori presumption regarding whether domestic assets bear a risk premium or discount. (See the discussion in chaps. 5 and 6.)

[17]Advanced treatments of the determinants of the risk premium are provided by R. Hodrick, "Risk, Uncertainty and Exchange Rates," *Journal of Monetary Economics* (1991); F. Diebold and P. Pauly, "Endogenous Risk in a Portfolio Balance Rational Expectations Model of the Deutsche mark-Dollar *(continued)*

real returns, the risk premium will tend to decline; if foreign real yields become relatively more variable, the risk premium will increase. Consider, for example, an appreciation of the German deutsche mark relative to the U.S. dollar. This appreciation could be a result of a portfolio diversification effect toward the deutsche mark induced by a reduction of real return variability in deutsche mark-denominated assets relative to U.S. dollar-denominated assets. In this situation, investors seeking to minimize risks would desire to increase the share of deutsche mark-denominated assets in their portfolios. The consequent capital flows would result in an increase in the demand for marks relative to U.S. dollars and a deutsche mark appreciation. Algebraically, this effect appears through a reduction of the exchange risk premium, R. Its influence on exchange rate changes can be seen in Equation 19–12, which implies $i - i^* = x - R$. This equation can be substituted into Equation 19–9 to yield

$$\hat{e} = (\hat{M} - \hat{M}^*) + \phi(\hat{Y}^* - \hat{Y})$$
$$+ \lambda(\pi - \pi^*) - \lambda R. \qquad (19\text{–}9b)$$

Equation 19–9(b) is identical to Equation 19–9(a) except for the additional final term involving the exchange risk premium, R. If Equation 19–9(b) is applied to our example using the U.S. dollar-deutsche mark exchange rate, the reduced risk premium, $R,$ associated with the decline of relative real yield variability in favor of deutsche mark-denominated assets results in an increased U.S. dollar depreciation ($\hat{e}$ increases). An inability of Equation 19–9(a) to explain the appreciation of the mark during this period could then be accounted for by the exclusion of the risk premium effect.

A second source of changes in exchange risk premia is the relative net supplies of domestic and foreign bonds. Suppose, for instance, that, perhaps because of relatively high real yield variability, foreign bonds have a positive risk premium attached to them. In this situation, an increase in the net supply of foreign bonds relative to domestic bonds means investors will have to be compensated in order to hold the larger supply of foreign bonds; this compensation will require a higher exchange risk premium. The changes in bond supplies influencing the risk premium involve changes in relative net supplies of bonds in the market. If one market participant issues a debt to another, the assets and liabilities will cancel each other out, leaving no net additional supply of bonds. What matters, therefore, is the additional relative supplies of outside assets in the market, such as government bonds.[18] In the preceding example, with foreign bonds bearing an exchange risk premium, an additional supply of foreign currency-denominated government bonds would raise the premium. This has crucial implications for the impact of government financing on the economy and, in particular, on the exchange rate. Suppose, for instance, that growing budget deficits have forced foreign authorities to borrow in the market by issuing foreign currency-denominated government bonds. The resulting rise in the relative net supply of foreign bonds increases the foreign exchange risk premium and therefore induces foreign interest rates to rise relative to

Rate," *European Economic Review* (September 1988); and R. Dornbusch, "Exchange Rate Risk and the Macroeconomics of Exchange Rate Determination," in R. Hawkins, R. Levich, and C. Wihlborg, eds., *Internationalization of Financial Markets* (Greenwich, Conn.: JAI Press, 1982).

[18]This assumes that government bonds are considered net wealth by the private sector. In addition, the mechanism relies on the assumption that exchange risk premia have a significant influence on exchange rates. It has been argued, however, that risk premia are too small in absolute value to explain the major exchange rate changes that occurred in the 1980s and continue in the 1990s. See J. Frankel, "The Dazzling Dollar," *Brookings Papers on Economic Activity* (1985). See also R.H. Thaler and K. Frost, "Foreign Exchange," in R.H. Thaler, *The Winner's Curse: Paradoxes and Anomalies of Economic Life* (New York: The Free Press, 1992).

domestic interest rates; that is, the term R in Equation 19–12 increases. Therefore, as Equation 19–9(b) shows, a domestic currency appreciation occurs. But, from an exchange risk perspective, bigger domestic budget deficits financed by increased borrowing will tend to lead to a depreciation of domestic currency.

A third way by which the risk premium can be influenced is through changes in relative wealth. In general, assuming that a larger fraction of domestic wealth is held in domestic assets relative to foreign assets, an increase in domestic wealth relative to foreign wealth will raise the demand for domestic securities relative to foreign securities. It will also increase the risk premium required by investors to hold foreign securities. Similarly, an increase in foreign wealth relative to domestic wealth will result in a decrease of the exchange risk premium. The implication is that rising (or declining) domestic wealth relative to foreign wealth will be associated with an appreciation (or depreciation) of domestic currency. In addition, whenever CAB surpluses (or deficits) are associated with rising (or declining) domestic wealth relative to foreign wealth, such surpluses (deficits) can be linked with domestic currency appreciation (depreciation).[19]

Some empirical studies examining the connection between the CAB and exchange rate changes find surpluses (or deficits) associated with currency appreciation (or depreciation). Others, however, have failed to find a significant linkage.[20] Apparently, it is only unexpected current account surpluses or deficits that influence the exchange rate. The impact of anticipated surpluses or deficits is already embodied in exchange rates. The next section examines the nature and evidence of the effect of unanticipated economic events on the exchange rate.

19–7. NEWS AND ANNOUNCEMENT EFFECTS IN THE FOREIGN EXCHANGE MARKET

The asset market approach asserts that new information affecting expectations regarding future exchange rate changes will immediately influence the current exchange rate. Political events provide a dramatic illustration of this proposition. When President Ronald Reagan was shot in 1982, for instance, the possibility of his death raised serious doubts about the success and continuation of the tough anti-inflation contractionary monetary policy stance at the time. These doubts sent the U.S. dollar tumbling in foreign exchange markets. In this particular case, later news eliminated any expectations of a possible reversal of the government's policies. It is apparent, however, that *lasting* political events, such as an administration shakeup, or a shift in foreign policy stances, will influence economic policy and will therefore have some bearing on the exchange rate.

Our analysis in this chapter—and in earlier discussions—suggests some leading economic variables that should be watched to determine possible changes in the economy and, particularly, in exchange rates. News of these variables can be expected to give rise to substantial action in foreign exchange markets. First of all, consider the CAB. As noted in the previous section, CAB surpluses

[19]As described in previous chapters, the exchange rate adjusts to eliminate balance-of-payments disequilibria. Because under a high degree of capital mobility, the current account will be swamped by international capital movements in the balance of payments, the standard short-run open-economy macroeconomics developed in the 1960s and 1970s emphasized the role of capital mobility in exchange rate adjustment. The role of the current account was consequently neglected. The asset market approach noted the association between the current account and wealth adjustments, returning the current account to the picture. See P. Kouri, "The Exchange Rate and the Balance of Payments in the Short-Run and in the Long-Run: A Monetary Approach," *Scandinavian Journal of Economics* (May 1976); R. Dornbusch and S. Fischer, "Exchange Rates and the Current Account," *American Economic Review* (December 1980).

[20]See S. Golub, "The Current Account Balance and the Dollar," *Princeton Studies in International Finance* (October 1986).

(deficits) associated with rising (declining) domestic wealth relative to foreign wealth will generally give rise to domestic currency appreciation (depreciation). Indeed, substantial foreign exchange market trading and significant exchange rate changes are frequently observed in response to the release by the government of figures on the U.S. CAB. Furthermore, it seem that it is the unanticipated component of the current account figures that is associated with the exchange rate changes. Unanticipatedly large announced current account deficits are observed to generate immediate U.S. dollar depreciation; unexpected surpluses are usually connected to U.S. dollar appreciation.[21]

A second factor influencing exchange rate changes involves budget deficits. Increased government borrowing to finance deficits can take the form of increased net supplies of domestic bonds relative to foreign bonds, which alters foreign exchange risk premia and induces changes in currency values. Indeed, U.S. budget deficit pronouncements tend to have a strong effect on exchange rates. Unanticipatedly large domestic budget deficits—relative to foreign budget deficits—tend to weaken the value of the dollar.[22]

A third variable whose announcements appear to generate substantial action in foreign exchange markets is the growth of the domestic money supply. The Federal Reserve announces on Friday afternoons the Fed's estimates of the money supply growth for the week ending nine days earlier. Usually, unexpectedly large money supply growth figures tend to be associated with dollar appreciation in foreign exchange markets and with increases of U.S. nominal interest rates. Conversely, unanticipatedly low money supply growth figures are usually connected to U.S. dollar depreciation and lower nominal interest rates. Notice that these figures appear to contradict the standard dictum that higher domestic monetary growth should lead to a dollar depreciation and to lower nominal interest rates. This apparent inconsistency has been referred to as the money supply announcements puzzle. Note, however, that the money supply growth figures reported by the Federal Reserve do not actually change the *current* rate of growth of the money supply; the figures refer to the past rate of money growth. In other words, the announcement must alter economic variables—exchange rates and interest rates—purely through its effects on the expectations that agents form about the future.

In one interpretation, an unexpectedly high rate of growth of the money supply pushes upward the agents' expectations regarding future inflation.[23] This is consistent with the observed rise of domestic nominal interest rates but appears to be inconsistent with the noted appreciation of the dollar: Rising domestic nominal interest rates reduce

---

[21]R. Dornbusch finds that an unanticipated current account surplus in the United States of $1 billion is worth half a percent of dollar appreciation; see his "Exchange Rate Economics: Where Do We Stand?" in Bhandari and Putnam, op. cit. More recent studies linking U.S. Department of Commerce announcements of trade balance deficits and the value of the dollar include K. Hogan, M. Melvin, and D. Roberts, "Trade Balance News and Exchange Rates: Is There a Policy Signal?" *Journal of International Money and Finance* (November 1991); and G. Hardouvelis, "Economic News, Exchange Rates and Interest Rates," *Journal of International Money and Finance* (March 1988).

[22]The presence of a clearcut connection between budget deficits and the exchange rate has been a matter of controversy, with economists such as Harvard's Martin Feldstein supporting it while others, such as Northwestern's Alan Stockman, denying it. See M. Feldstein, "The Budget Deficit and the Dollar," in S. Fischer, ed., *NBER Macroeconomics Annual, 1986* (Cambridge, Mass.: The MIT Press, 1986); A. C. Stockman, "Exchange Rates, the Current Account and Monetary Policy," in W. S. Haraf and T. D. Willett, eds., *Monetary Policy for a Volatile Global Economy* (Washington, D.C.: American Enter-

prise Institute, 1990); and P. Evans, "Is the Dollar High Because of Large Budget Deficits?" *Journal of Monetary Economics* (November 1986).

[23]For a discussion of the money supply announcements puzzle and alternative explanations, see D. H. Joines, "Money Supply Announcements and Real Economic Activity," *Journal of Monetary Economics* (December 1991); J. Huizinga and L. Leiderman, "The Signalling Role of Base and Money Supply Announcements and their Effects on Interest Rates," *Journal of Monetary Economics* (December 1987); and B. Cornell, "The Money Supply Announcements Puzzle: Review and Interpretations," *American Economic Review* (September 1983).

money demand and would depreciate domestic currency. An alternative explanation is that an unexpectedly high reported rate of growth of the past money supply generates expectations in investors that, in response, the Federal Reserve will tighten the future growth of the money supply. This tightening would maintain current target rates of monetary growth to which the Federal Reserve subscribes. Expectations of future monetary tightening then tend to raise domestic real interest rates. This view is consistent with both the observed rise of domestic nominal interest rates and the appreciation of the dollar in response to high money growth figures: A rise in real interest rates induces capital to flow into the economy, and the domestic currency then appreciates in value.

The role played by central bank foreign exchange market intervention in exchange rate determination is clearly specified by the asset market approach. Nonsterilized intervention generally affects relative money supplies and directly influences the exchange rate. Sterilized intervention, on the other hand, cannot utilize this mechanism. However, according to the asset market approach, sterilized intervention can influence exchange rates if it acts to signal future changes in domestic economic policy. For instance, a sterilized sale of dollars by the Federal Reserve—accompanied by statements from the Fed to the effect that U.S. authorities are committed to lowering the value of the dollar—may induce agents in the economy to anticipate future nonsterilized intervention intended to lower the value of the dollar. In this case, the anticipated depreciation of the dollar will raise domestic interest rates, lowering U.S. money demand and immediately depreciating the dollar.

19–8. IS THE EXCHANGE RATE A RANDOM WALK?

Section 19–7 makes it clear that exchange rates respond quickly to news and unanticipated events. Indeed, the asset market approach suggests that current and anticipated values of fundamental variables such as money supplies and income determine the exchange rate. Assuming that all the information available on fundamentals is already incorporated into existing currency values, exchange rate changes will be associated with unanticipated events. Unpredictable disturbances altering current or anticipated future values of fundamentals then move exchange rates. This unpredictability of exchange rates has led many to suggest that exchange rates follow a *random walk*. Formally, the exchange rate is a random walk if the future value of the exchange rate is its current value plus a disturbance term that is uncorrelated to past disturbances and whose expected value is zero.[24] Although this description seems to fit the unpredictability of the exchange rate changes observed in the foreign exchange market, it also has implications that do not coincide with reality.

If the exchange rate were to follow a random walk, there would always be a 50 percent chance that the exchange rate changes would move up or down. There is thus no tendency for exchange rate changes to be reversed to a central level or to a mean. In fact, there is nothing to prevent the exchange rate from moving to plus or minus infinity, if given enough time. This trait of random walks does not fit exchange rates. As Stanford economist David Robinson suggests: "with a couple of notable exceptions . . . exchange rates appear to remain within relatively close bounds in the long run, though period-to-period changes are quite erratic. . . . This long-run boundedness is inconsistent with the random walk characterization which would imply that, with a large enough sample size, the series will cross an arbitrary

[24]Technically, a random walk also assumes that the disturbances over time represent independent, identically distributed random variables with constant variance. Exchange rate changes could conceivably have a nonzero mean, in which case the process is called random walk with drift. For more details, see R. Baillie and P. McMahon, *The Foreign Exchange Market: Theory and Econometric Evidence* (Cambridge: Cambridge University Press, 1989).

bound with probability one."[25] This observation coincides with the evidence we presented earlier on the dollar-pound exchange rate.

What explains the fact that, even though short-run exchange rate changes appear to follow a random walk, long-term changes contradict the hypothesis? Recent research points to the role of central banks in imposing long-run bounds on exchange rate fluctuations. Explicitly, EEC members under the European Monetary System impose bounds on the flexibility of exchange rates. In addition, most other industrialized economies have also had implicit or explicit target zones in setting exchange rates, as will be discussed in the last chapter of this book. These target zones impose nonlinearities in the behavior of exchange rate changes and contradict the notion that currency values follow a random walk over the long run.[26]

19–9. Are Exchange Rate Changes Chaotic?

Although exchange rate changes appear to be uncertain in nature, some very recent research is studying the possibility that disturbances in currency values could be determined by underlying forces that are deterministic and not random. This research surrounds the concept called *deterministic chaos*. Although the word *chaos* suggests uncertainty, in the present context it describes the path of a variable that seems unpredictable but is in fact perfectly predictable once the rules governing its behavior are known.[27]

Suppose, for example, that the rule determining exchange rate behavior is given by

$$e_{t+1} = (1 + r)e_t - re_t^2.$$

This suggests that the exchange rate in period $t + 1$, e_{t+1}, is related to the exchange rate at time e_t, by the given rule.

Although it is very simple, this exchange rate rule (called the *Verhulst rule*) can lead to chaotic exchange rate behavior—that is, to exchange rate behavior that appears to be random if the rule is not known. To show this, Figure 19–3 gives the behavior of the exchange rate over time (for $t = 1, 2, 3$, etc.) when $r = 3.0$, on the assumption that the initial exchange rate is equal to $e_0 = 0.10$. Note that the exchange rate jumps up and down with no apparent pattern or trend. In fact, the exchange rate can take an infinite number of values; it would be impossible to distinguish them from a random series without knowing the rule that generated the series.

The suggestion made by chaos research is that the presence of simple—but unknown—rules can generate behavior that appears to be random but is deterministic. In the foreign exchange market, rules followed by market participants, whether chartists or fundamentalists or a combination of the two, could in theory generate deterministic chaos. It remains a matter for future research to determine which rule, if any, can actually explain exchange rate dynamics.

[25]D. Robinson, "Is the Exchange Rate a Random Walk?" (Department of Economics, Stanford University, November 1990), mimeo.

[26]See M. Chinn, "Some Linear and Nonlinear Thoughts on Exchange Rates," *Journal of International Money and Finance* (March 1991); C. Engle and J. Hamilton, "Long Swings in the Exchange Rate: Are They in the Data and Do Markets Know It?" *American Economic Review* (September 1990); and D. Hsieh, "Testing for Nonlinear Dependence in Foreign Exchange Rates," *Journal of Business* (July 1989).

[27]For applications of chaos to economic analysis, see J. Benhabib, ed., *Cycles and Chaos in Economic Equilibrium* (Princeton, N.J.: Princeton University Press, 1992); and P. De-Grauwe and K. Vansanten, "Speculative Dynamics and Chaos in the Foreign Exchange Market," (Department of Economics, University of Leuven, (June 1990), mimeo.

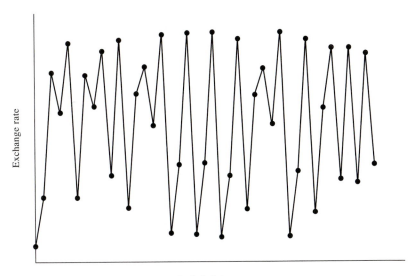

FIGURE 19–3.   Chaotic Exchange Rate Behavior

SOURCE: Based on H. O. Peitgen and P. M. Richter, *The Beauty of Fractals: Images of Complex Dynamical Systems* (Berlin: Soringer-Verlag, 1986), p. 24.

19–10. FITTING THE PIECES TOGETHER: THE ASSET MARKET APPROACH TO THE EXCHANGE RATE AND SHORT-RUN MACROECONOMIC THEORY

We have now dissected in some detail the nature, implications, and empirical evidence regarding the asset market approach to the exchange rate. In this section, we gain some perspective on how this approach fits into the overall scheme of open-economy macroeconomics and exchange rate theory. To simplify the exposition, we concentrate on examining how the monetary approach fits into the structural scheme of macroeconomics.[28]

How does the monetary approach relate to the analysis of exchange rate determination we learned in Part IV? In our general framework of analysis, the equilibrium exchange rate was determined jointly with equilibrium income, prices, interest rates, and so forth, by means of the following relationships: a money market equilibrium condition, an aggregate demand relationship, an aggregate supply equation, and a balance-of-payments equilibrium condition,

$$B = T(q, Y) + K(i) = 0, \qquad (19–13)$$

[28]An advanced exposition of the points made in this section is made by T. Gylfason and J. F. Helliwell, "A Synthesis of Keynesian, Monetary, and Portfolio Approaches to Flexible Exchange Rates," National Bureau of Economics Research,

Working Paper no. 949 (July 1982). For an integration of monetary and portfolio balance considerations into a comprehensive structural open-economy macroeconomics framework, see P. Allen and P. B. Kenen, *Asset Markets and Exchange Rates: Modelling an Open Economy* (Cambridge: Cambridge University Press, 1980).

which states that, under a free float, the exchange rate will adjust to guarantee balanced payments (see Equation 13–23). This last condition, however, provides a view of the relationship between, say, domestic income and the exchange rate that is very different from that stated by the monetary approach. From its perspective, an increase in domestic income, Y, raises imports and tends to deteriorate the trade balance, all else being constant. The exchange rate would then have to increase (by raising q) to assure external balance. Summarizing: higher U.S. income growth reduces the value of the dollar. The monetary approach to the exchange rate suggests the opposite view: An increase of domestic income raises domestic money demand and appreciates the dollar; higher U.S. income strengthens the U.S. dollar. Why is there this divergence in viewpoints?

It is apparent that what the monetary approach does is to select one relationship—the money market equilibrium condition—out of a set of relationships establishing the economy's equilibrium. It then proceeds to study in detail the connections between the exchange rate and other economic variables as determined by the money market equilibrium condition. The balance-of-payments equilibrium equation (19–13), on the other hand, singles out another particular relationship from the package of conditions required to establish equilibrium in the economy and examines its specific implications for the connections among exchange rates, income, and so forth. As it turns out, the implications obtained this way are the opposite of those yielded by looking at the money market equilibrium condition. This does not mean, however, that the two points of view are mutually exclusive. Just as in the simple demand and supply model of price, P, and output, Q, there is a demand curve (or an equation) that establishes a negative relationship between P and Q and a supply curve (or an equation) that establishes a positive connection between P and Q without their being mutually inconsistent. The two relationships between the exchange rate and income implied by the monetary approach as

given by Equation 19–4(a), and the balance-of-payments equilibrium equation (19–13) are not inconsistent with each other.

As a matter of fact, just as we can draw demand-and-supply curves showing the opposite connections between P and Q implied by the supply-and-demand relationships, we can also draw curves showing how the monetary approach and Equation 19–13 depict different relationships between income, Y, and the exchange rate, e. In Figure 19–4, the MM curve shows the negative connection between e and Y established by the money market equilibrium condition; the KK curve shows the positive association between e and Y implied by balance-of-payments equilibrium, Equation 19–13. Now, again utilizing the supply-demand analogy, just as the equilibrium price and output in a market are determined by the intersection of demand-and-supply curves, we can look at the intersection of the KK and MM curves as establishing the levels of the exchange rate and income consistent with the economy's general equilibrium. The equilibrium exchange rate, e^*, and income, Y^*, are consistent with both monetary equilibrium and the balance-of-payments equilibrium condition, Equation 19–13.

We can now see that stating that income and the exchange rate are negatively related, as given by the money market equilibrium condition, refers just to the relationship between the exchange rate and income along the MM curve. While this relationship provides us with information about the money market, it does not necessarily show us how equilibrium income and the exchange rate are related in the economy. To determine these relationships, we have to examine not only the money market equilibrium condition, but also the other conditions establishing equilibrium in the economy, which includes the balanced payments condition represented by Equation 19–13. Geometrically, the equilibrium e and Y are determined jointly by KK and MM and not by MM alone. Similarly, the positive relationship between income and the exchange rate postulated by Equation 19–13 corresponds

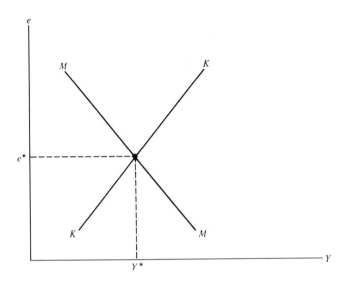

FIGURE 19–4. Simultaneous Determination of Income and the Exchange Rate

geometrically to how e and Y are related along the KK curve, again it does not tell us how the equilibrium income and the exchange rate are related in the economy.

In a broader context, it can be concluded that when evaluating the implications of, and the evidence regarding, the asset market approach,[29] the results can shed light on the asset market relationship between exchange rates and other variables but not necessarily on how equilibrium exchange rate changes and income are related in the economy.

Summary

1. Being the relative price of two monies, the exchange rate depends not only on the demand and supply of domestic money, but also on the demand and supply of foreign money. Exchange rate adjustments are therefore de-

[29]For further details on the statistical problems involved in estimating one relationship—the monetary or portfolio balance equilibrium—out of a whole structural set of relationships establishing the economy's equilibrium, see Section 20–9.

pendent on changes in both domestic and foreign variables and cannot be determined independently of the behavior of foreign economies or the actions of foreign governments.

2. The monetary approach adopts a point of view in which exchange rates adjust to assure money market equilibrium in the open economy. According to the monetary approach, given fixed relative money supplies, factors increasing (or decreasing) domestic money demand relative to foreign money demand will raise (or lower) the value of domestic currency. For instance, a reduction of domestic interest rates relative to foreign nominal rates raises relative domestic money demand and appreciates the value of domestic currency. Similarly, the higher domestic income is relative to foreign income, the higher the value of domestic currency, *ceteris paribus*.

3. A key factor accounting for divergencies in exchange rate predictions of the monetary approach from actual exchange rates is that predicted exchange rates are the joint result

not only of the monetary approach's hypothesis regarding money market equilibrium, but also of the PPP assumption used to relate exchange rates and prices. The empirical evidence available shows that both the absolute and the relative versions of PPP fail to hold systematically over time. If the relationship between the exchange rate and relative prices utilized is to have any empirical basis, its computation must be modified to allow for deviations from PPP. Evidence gathered in the 1980s and early 1990s suggests that when the dollar depreciates in value, foreign producers selling in the United States often lower their export prices denominated in foreign currency. This behavioral pattern is described as pricing to market.

4. "News" relevant to the formation of expectations regarding future domestic and foreign inflation will immediately be reflected in changes in the spot exchange rate. As a result, a significant component of exchange rate changes is uncertain, moving along the unpredictable path induced by new events and information. An event leading to higher anticipated inflation, for instance, will be associated with higher domestic interest rates, reduced domestic real money demand, and a reduced value of domestic currency in sustaining market equilibrium.

5. Currency substitution arises when residents of different countries hold a portfolio of currencies. Changes in economic variables may then alter the desired share of each currency in that portfolio, leading to changes in relative money demands. A crucial factor in determining the proportion of total money balances that domestic and foreign residents wish to hold in domestic money relative to foreign money is the opportunity cost of holding domestic money relative to foreign money, represented by the anticipated rate of depreciation of domestic currency.

6. Currency substitution has essential implications for the functioning of both fixed and flexible exchange rates. Under fixed exchange rates, growing expectations of domestic currency devaluation can generate massive currency substitution away from domestic money and could, in the process, wipe out the central bank's international reserves. Under flexible exchange rates, expected depreciations of domestic currency may induce domestic and foreign residents to switch their cash holdings form domestic to foreign currency. The resulting decline in the demand for domestic money relative to foreign money would then immediately depreciate domestic currency. This effect of anticipated exchange rate changes in shifting the demand for money out of domestic and into foreign currency operates in addition to the effect of expected currency depreciation in increasing domestic interest rates and shifting the demand for money out of domestic money and into bonds.

7. A currency will bear an exchange risk premium, or discount, depending on whether additional funds invested in assets denominated in that currency increase or decrease the risk of investors' portfolios. The exchange risk premium can change as a result of shifts in the distribution of asset returns, in relative supplies of assets denominated in different currencies, and in the relative wealth of domestic and foreign investors.

8. Overall, a currency's value is a random walk if the future value of the exchange rate is its current value plus a disturbance term that is uncorrelated to past or future disturbances and whose expected value is zero.

9. The monetary approach selects one relationship—the money market equilibrium condition—out of a set of relationships establishing the economy's equilibrium and analyzes the connections between the exchange rate and other economic variables as determined by that condition. This does not exclude alternative approaches to the exchange rate based on other equilibrium relationships in the economy.

Problems

1. Assess the evidence on alternative models of exchange rate behavior and on the monetary approach to the exchange rate in particular. Which factors can account for deviations from the predictions of these models? Support your analysis with specific real-world examples.

2. Royalia is a developing country that trades only with another developing country, Glutonia. Currently, Royalia had a wide range of exchange controls and uses various different exchange rates for different balance-of-payments transactions. The government is seeking to eliminate all of its controls and to fix an across-the-board exchange rate for all international transactions. Royalia's governor asks you to tell him at which exchange rate the country should fix the value of the royalian (Royalia's currency) vis-à-vis the glutonian (Glutonia's currency). You decide, based on your reading of Chapter 19, to calculate the exchange rate predicted by the monetary approach. The following information is provided by the governor's statistical office regarding Royalia's real money demand relative to Glutonia's (Glutonia's variables are in asterisks):

$$\frac{L}{L^*} = \frac{Y}{Y^*} 1.5 \, (i - i^*).$$

These symbols are as used in the text. You also find out the following information:
   (a) Royalia's money supply consists of 500 million royalians.
   (b) Glutonia's money supply consists of 250 million glutonians.
   (c) Royalia's real income is five times that of Glutonia's.
   (d) Royalia's interest rate is 10 percent; Glutonia's is 5 percent.

What exchange rate (in royalians per glutonian) would you recommend be set? With what caveats?

3. You are forecasting exchange rate changes between the dollar and the German deutsche mark over the next year. You are told that, for the period of concern, relative money demand between Germany and the United States will change according to:

$$\hat{L}^* - \hat{L} = 0.75 \, (\hat{Y}^* - \hat{Y}) + 0.10 \, (i - i^*).$$

All these variables are defined in the text. Asterisks denote the German variables. The following forecasts for next year are available:
   U.S. money supply growth: 10 percent.
   German money supply growth: 5 percent.
   U.S. real income growth: 2 percent.
   German real income growth: 5 percent.
   U.S. nominal interest rate: 12 percent.
   German nominal interest rate: 10 percent.
   (a) By how much, in percentage terms, do you forecast that the U.S. dollar–deutsche mark exchange rate will change during the next year? Will the mark depreciate or appreciate? (Hint: Assume that you are a hardened monetarist.)

4. Consider a small country that faces exogenously given external prices, P^*. Assuming that $M/P = L(i,Y)$, obtain the exchange rate as a function of P^* and the values of the domestic money supply, income, and interest rate. (Hint: Assume that $P = eP^*$.) What is the role of foreign price disturbances, foreign monetary policies, and changes in the levels of foreign income and interest rates on the determination of the exchange rate?

5. "Because exchange rates reflect anticipated future events, they can only change as a consequence of "news"—that is, of new developments and information not already available and incorporated in the exchange rate. Consequently, exchange rates follow a random walk. Algebraically, $P_{t+1} = P_t + U_t$, where U_t reflects new information and is statistically independent of P_t and of its own past values." Do you agree with this statement?

6. Private forecasters and government agencies are predicting large and persistent U.S. budget deficits for the next five years. What is the implication of this prediction for the value of the dollar in foreign exchange markets? In answering the question, consider alternative scenarios regarding the monetization of the debt and foreign monetary policies.

7. "If foreign real returns become less variable relative to domestic real returns, the exchange risk premium for foreign assets will tend to decline; if foreign real yields become relatively more variable, then the risk premium will increase." Evaluate this statement.

8. It is often stated that wealth influences money demand. Assuming that it does, in what way would including wealth in money demand functions affect exchange rate determination? In other words, what effects would changes in domestic and foreign wealth have on the exchange rate, holding everything else constant? Develop a monetary model of exchange rate determination. Derive an equation that determines the effects of relative wealth on the exchange rate.

9. In previous chapters we have discussed exchange rate bubbles, which tend to deviate currency values from fundamentals. How would you introduce bubbles into the asset market approach to exchange rates? Could bubbles account for the failure of the monetary and overshooting models to explain the behavior of short-run exchange rates in the 1980s and 1990s?

10. Consider this clipping from *The Wall Street Journal* (October 14, 1988) describing the immediate behavior of the U.S. dollar exchange rate in response to the trade balance announcement made by the U.S. Department of Commerce. Explain it in detail and give alternative explanations, if possible, including the one you favor the most.

TRADE NEWS
SENDS DOLLAR
LOWER AGAIN

Thursday's

Markets

By Tom Herman
Staff Reporter of THE WALL STREET JOURNAL.
   New York—The dollar tumbled again yesterday, but stocks posted small gains and bonds finished with small losses.
   Trading began on an ominous note. The government reported an unexpectedly large $12.18 billion trade deficit for August, up from $9.47 billion in July. The dollar immediately plummeted, depressing bond prices, too.

---

11. During the first half of 1993, the yen appreciated sharply in value. As a result, many economists expected that the prices of U.S. products sold in Japan (expressed in yen) would decline. Yet, this didn't seem to happen. For example, on May 5, 1993, *The Wall Street Journal* (on p. D1) noted the comments of S. Taguchi, an official at Japan's Ministry of International Trade and Industry, who said that "Unfortunately at present we don't have any examples of the lowering of prices by U.S. companies." Is this behavior pricing to market? Can you explain it?

CHAPTER 20

The Monetary and Asset Market Approach to the Balance of Payments

The asset market approach to fixed exchange rate regimes views the balance of payments as reflecting essential asset market adjustments in the economy. The focus of the approach is on how the international transactions in goods and assets that constitute the balance of payments embody to some extent or another the decisions of individuals, firms, and governments regarding their economic wealth and asset holdings. Imports of foreign goods, for instance, may be connected to increases in the wealth owned—or the value of assets held—by domestic residents. In addition, in financially open economies, international capital flows are directly linked to portfolio readjustments involving domestic and foreign assets.

The asset market approach emphasizes that portfolio and wealth adjustments are extremely sensitive to expectational considerations and that they sometimes can have overwhelming effects on the balance of payments. An expected currency devaluation, for instance, may trigger massive capital outflows that can completely wipe out a central bank's foreign exchange reserves in a matter of weeks, days, or even hours. In most of such cases, a financial and external payments crisis is precipitated by the outflow of funds caused by the speculative run on the currency. The case of Mexico in 1982 is one case in point. Under massive dollar outflows encouraged by an expected peso devaluation, the government was forced to let the currency float (and effectively depreciate) and to impose restrictions on dollar outflows.[1] Another example is that of the British pound in September 1992, when a speculative run on the pound forced the administration of Prime Minister John Major to withdraw the pound from the exchange rate mechanism of the EMS, letting the currency float freely versus other European Community currencies.

It is not only speculative capital *outflows* that may precipitate a foreign exchange crisis: Speculative capital *inflows* may also lead to intolerable consequences. The classic case is the German expected revaluation of the mark in early 1973. In the face of Germany's continued trade surplus with the United States, there was widespread speculation that the deutsche mark would have to be revalued vis-à-vis the dollar. The expected revaluation led to sharp increases in the expected rate of return on deutsche mark-denominated assets relative to U.S. dollar assets. As a result, a massive shift of funds from dollars into marks

occurred. Under the pegged exchange rate system at the time, the West German central bank was committed to purchasing dollars and exchanging them for marks. The result was a huge accumulation of foreign exchange (dollar) reserves on the part of the Bundesbank, which led to a tremendous money supply expansion. In little more than one month (January to February 1973), the Bundesbank acquired $10 billion of international reserves, which amounted to about 20 percent of the German money supply at the time. With the inability to sterilize such massive capital inflows—and without intending to let the economy's money supply explode, with its obvious inflationary and destabilizing impact—the Bundesbank abandoned its intervention in foreign exchange markets by letting the mark float freely. It is apparent, then, that expectations concerning the exchange rate and associated capital flows can have a powerful effect on the economy. It is the purpose of this chapter to consider these issues fully in analyzing the economics of fixed exchange rates.

The asset market approach states that the balance of payments reflects essential equilibrium adjustments in the domestic and foreign demand for stocks of national assets. Changes in the balance of payments are understood to reflect the choices that agents in the economy make in clearing relative demands for domestic and foreign assets. The framework of the asset market approach has become very popular in recent years, with many young economists writing about speculative attacks, balance-of-payments crises, and self-fulfilling expectations. The asset market approach has its origins in the *monetary approach to the balance of payments,* with which we begin our discussion.

20–1. THE MONETARY APPROACH TO THE BALANCE OF PAYMENTS

The development of the monetary approach to the balance of payments in the early 1970s set afire discussions of open-economy macroeconomics for

---

[1]For a discussion of the speculative attack on the peso, see H. Blanco and P. M. Garber, "Recurrent Devaluation and Speculative Attacks on the Mexican Peso," *Journal of Political Economy* (February 1986).

years to come. Academic journals, the financial press, and professional conferences addressed the issues for and against. Influential international organizations, such as the IMF have evaluated and repeatedly used the monetary approach to derive policy prescriptions considered highly questionable by economists unfriendly to the approach. If there is anything on which everyone can agree, it is the controversial nature of the approach and the heat it has generated. Notwithstanding the intensity of the debate (and sometimes because of it), much confusion remains about the nature of the monetary approach and what it does and does not assert. The discussion in the following sections presents a detailed view of the approach.

The intellectual origins of the approach can be traced back to David Hume's writings on money; however, its modern form evolved in the 1950s and 1960s out of the work of economists associated mostly with the IMF, the University of Chicago, and the London School of Economics. Its sources include the original writings of Robert Mundell, the late Harry Johnson, and J. J. Polak. In the following generation its proponents include Rudiger Dornbusch, Jacob Frenkel, Arthur B. Laffer, and Michael Mussa, among many others. The strength of their writings and the solidity of their analysis can account for much of the widespread diffusion and influence of the approach in the last decade.[2]

What is the essence of the monetary approach to the balance of payments? The monetary approach stresses that the balance of payments involves essential monetary phenomena. We will explain in detail what this means in the next sections, but we will now discuss what it does not say. First, it does not say that the balance of payments is only a monetary phenomenon; rather it says that money plays a vital role (is essential) in understanding the balance of payments. The approach, as such, does not deny the importance of nonmonetary factors (such as productivity changes, tariffs, government spending, and taxation) on the balance of payments. If anything, it stresses the links between these aspects and the money market (the demand and supply of money); it certainly does not reject them as unimportant.

A second misinterpretation of the monetary approach is that it implies a *monetarist* point of view on the economy. The confusion probably arises because most of the developers of the approach have been closely associated with monetarist centers, such as the University of Chicago, and/or strongly influenced by monetarist thought. Hence their identification with monetarism, an identification that is misleading and, strictly speaking, incorrect. As stated, the monetary approach emphasizes monetary considerations in the study of open economies and the balance of payments. It also pays special attention to the behavior of the open economy over time, particularly to the monetary adjustment mechanisms involved. Both in principle and in practice, these concerns can be incorporated into diverse theories of the economy: monetarist, Keynesian, supply-side, and others. The monetary approach, then, is *not* a theory; as its name clearly indicates, it is a general approach to (a way of looking at) the balance of payments. It is consistent with a variety of economic environments, including inflation and recession, unemployment and full employment, stagflation, and so on. It is also as relevant to the problems in world markets faced by a small country as it is to those faced by a large country.

There is particular confusion about the monetary approach's policy implications: it is believed that its proponents think that "only money matters when it comes to balance-of-payments policy."

---

[2]A survey of the monetary approach appears in M. I. Blejer and J. A. Frenkel, "Monetary Approach to the Balance of Payments," in J. Eatwell, M. Milgate, and P. Newman, eds., *The New Palgrave: A Dictionary of Economics* (London: Mamillan, 1987). The classic collection of papers on the subject is *The Monetary Approach to the Balance of Payments*, edited by J. A. Frenkel and H. Johnson (Toronto: University of Toronto Press, 1976). The important research conducted under the auspices of the IMF is gathered in *The Monetary Approach to the Balance of Payments* (Washington, D.C.: IMF, 1977).

This is, again, a misinterpretation. As Frenkel and Johnson state,

> The monetary approach to the balance of payments asserts neither that monetary mismanagement is the only cause nor that monetary policy change is the only possible cure, for balance-of-payments problems; it does suggest, however, that monetary processes will bring about a cure of some kind—not necessarily very attractive—unless frustrated by deliberate monetary policy action, and that policies that neglect or aggravate the monetary implications of deficits and surpluses will not be successful in their declared objectives.[3]

The approach does stress the important role that overall government policies have in the economy, especially in the balance of payments. Careful examination of the government sector is thus standard, including both its central bank and budgetary functions.

Having now clarified some common misconceptions about the monetary approach, we now proceed to examine its basic features in detail. The following section reviews some balance-of-payments and monetary concepts relevant to understanding the approach. In later sections we will analyze the implications of the monetary approach for a variety of different economic situations. We will give special attention in this chapter to the study of the open-economy macroeconomics and policy problems of small economies under fixed exchange rates. These rates are of particular relevance to developing countries and to some of the European countries participating in the EMS.

20−2. THE BALANCE OF PAYMENTS AND THE ECONOMY'S MONETARY SECTOR

The environment characterizing any modern economy is one of flux. Interest rates, prices, income, central bank credit, and many other economic

variables change with a frequency that is sometimes astonishing, sometimes horrifying. Goods and assets markets reflect all these changes and have to respond accordingly. In the market for money, for example, changes in income, prices, central bank credit, and so on, all tend to affect the demand and/or supply of money. As a result, equilibrium in the market is often disturbed, and adjustments have to take place to maintain or restore market equilibrium. The monetary approach stresses these adjustments and how they are related to the balance of payments.

The market for money will be maintained in equilibrium when the changes in money demand occurring over any given time period are equal to the changes in the money supply forthcoming from the economy. Symbolically, we obtain

$$\Delta M^D = \Delta M^S \qquad (20-1)$$

where ΔM^D represents changes in the demand for nominal money balances (demand for dollars, in terms of the United States), and ΔM^S represents changes in the domestic money supply.

What induces individuals to change their demand for money—that is, what factors give rise to ΔM^D? Changes in income and interest rates (among others) tend to generate changes in the amount of money individuals wish to hold. If individuals get richer, for instance, their bank accounts tend to swell, reflecting a desired increase in monetary assets. Similarly, increases in interest rates induce people to shift toward holding interest-earning assets and reducing their desired money balances—and, therefore, their demand for money.

The factors determining money supply changes in an open economy were discussed in Section 14−1: Changes in the money supply, ΔM^S, are proportional to changes in high-powered money, ΔH, which, in turn, can be represented as the sum of changes in the international reserves of the central bank, ΔIR, plus changes in central bank credit, ΔCBC. Algebraically, we find that

[3]Ibid., p. 24.

$$\Delta M^S = \mu \Delta H = \mu(\Delta IR + \Delta CBC)$$
$$= \Delta IR + \Delta CBC, \qquad (20-2)$$

Note that Equation 20–2 corresponds to Equation 14–7, but in which, for expositional convenience, we have assumed that the money market multiplier is a fixed constant equal to $1(\mu = 1)$. As before, the concept of the balance payments we utilize, and the relevant one for the money supply process, is the money account of the balance of payments, B_N, which, in our simplified framework, is equal to ΔIR.[4] It follows that

$$\Delta M^S = B_N + \Delta CBC. \qquad (20-2a)$$

The money account surplus or deficit in conjunction with central bank credit creation emerge as the sources of change in the domestic money supply. Substituting Equation 20–2(a) into Equation 20–1, we obtain the following relationship between monetary variables and the balance of payments:

$$\Delta M^D = B_N + \Delta CBC, \qquad (20-1a)$$

which suggests the following representation of the balance of payments:

$$B_N = \Delta M^D - \Delta CBC. \qquad (20-3)$$

Equation 20–3 states that the balance of payments corresponds to those additions to (or subtractions from) money balances that domestic residents demand but are not provided by the central bank in the form of changes in credit. For example, a balance of payments surplus $(B_N > 0)$ represents a situation in which domestic residents increase their demand for money balances by more than the central bank in-

[4]The balance-of-payments expression B_N is in nominal terms (in dollars, for the United States), not in real terms (in terms of domestic goods). In earlier chapters, we denoted the balance of payments in real terms simply as B. Recall that a real variable is always obtained by dividing the nominal variable by a corresponding price.

creases its supply $(\Delta M^D > \Delta CBC)$. A balance-of-payments deficit $(B_N < 0)$, on the other hand, represents a situation in which credit creation by the central bank outpaces the growth of money demand $(\Delta CBC > \Delta M^D)$. What is the meaning of this in terms of the actions of agents in the economy? Suppose that there is a balance-of-payments deficit $(B_N < 0)$. Equation 20–3 suggests that part of the money supply created by the central bank in the period of concern is not being demanded by domestic residents—who thus find themselves holding excess money balances. How does this come to be reflected in a balance-of-payments deficit?

An analogy here with the case of an individual may be illuminating. What would you do, for example, if you found yourself holding excess cash? Spend it, of course! You might buy some interest-earning assets (like some bonds) or some goods you want (like an open-economy macroeconomics textbook). What is the counterpart of your actions in an overall economy? In other words, what do domestic residents do when they as an entity have excess balances of domestic money? They spend it on *foreign* goods and/or assets. But these purchases require the use of foreign exchange. As domestic residents sell their money (local currency) in exchange for these foreign currencies, the central bank loses international reserves and the money account moves into a deficit. The balance-of-payments deficit thus measures the amount of money domestic residents want to "get rid of," or spend, which they do through net purchases of foreign goods and/or assets. Note that the deficit may continue over an extended period. Individuals do not generally adjust their money holdings instantaneously but make the corrections gradually over time. Observe also that the excess money can be used to purchase either foreign goods or foreign financial assets. Because the trade balance measures the economy's overall net purchases of foreign goods, and the capital account measures its net purchases of foreign financial assets,

$$B_N = \Delta M^D - \Delta CBC = T_N + K_N, \qquad (20-4)$$

where T_N represents the trade balance (expressed in nominal terms, i.e., in dollars for the United States) and K_N the capital account.[5]

In summary, Equation 20–3 is the basis for the emphasis of the monetary approach on the balance of payments involving essential monetary phenomena. As represented, the balance of payments corresponds to an excess of changes in money demand over the credit created by the central bank in the economy. It should be clear, though, that to look at the balance of payments in terms of money demand and supply (even if particularly illuminating, as we will see), does not exclude other ways of looking at (other approaches to) the balance of payments. We expand this idea in later sections.

Equation 20–3, simple as it is, already suggests some policy implications difficult to visualize otherwise. Because a balance-of-payments deficit represents an excess of central bank credit creation over the increases in money demanded by domestic residents, one obvious way of eliminating it—and the corresponding loss of international reserves—is to limit the amount of central bank credit creation—that is, through some sort of *domestic credit ceiling*. Such a policy may also be combined with *financial programming* of government activities, which involves forecasting money demand changes and gearing central bank credit creation to fulfill those demands. Actually, this type of policy recommendation has frequently been advocated by the IMF.

It may seem disconcerting, at first, to think about the balance of payments in terms of money demand and supply. The next section presents a simple exposition highlighting the basic mechanism relating the balance of payments and the monetary sector.

---

[5]Recall that variables with the subscript N always represent nominal variables. In earlier chapters, we more often utilized the trade balance and the capital account as expressed in terms of domestic goods (or the *real* trade and capital accounts, T and K). It is more convenient here to utilize these concepts by means of their nominal representations.

20–3. A MONETARY MECHANISM OF BALANCE-OF-PAYMENTS ADJUSTMENT

One of the main features of the monetary approach is its concern with the long-run effects of disturbances on the economy and the influence of monetary factors on the response of the balance of payments to such disturbances. It therefore tries to answer the question: If equilibrium in an open economy is lost, are there any tendencies for equilibrium to be restored, and how is that long-run equilibrium reached? This concern of the monetary approach with how adjustments are made over time is a dynamic concern. It was apparently neglected in most conventional analyses of the balance of payments at the time the approach appeared in the 1950s and 1960s.

Basic Setup

The dynamic processes involved in any modern economy are disturbingly complicated. They involve changes in prices, interest rates, employment, output, and a wide array of interrelated factors. To simplify the present exposition, we concentrate our attention on the case of a small open economy perfectly integrated in world markets and producing at its potential level of output. The small-country assumption implies that the prices of goods bought and/or sold in international markets are determined completely by prevailing prices in those markets and cannot be affected by any changes in domestic production or consumption. This means that the country is a price taker in international goods markets. As a consequence, the domestic prices of these goods must be equal to the domestic currency equivalent of world prices (which are usually denominated in foreign currencies). In addition, the small-country assumption implies that the rate of interest at which the country borrows or lends is externally determined and cannot be affected by domestic economic conditions. In other words, the country is a price taker in international capital markets. Finally, in assuming that the economy produces at its potential level of output, the implication is that domestic output, and real income, are not affected by changes in aggregate demand but depend on long-run factors—such as population growth, changes in labor force participation, and technical change. (This determination is outside the purview of the present discussion.) In contrast to the analysis in previous chapters, output is thus assumed not to deviate from its potential level, not even in the short run.

We start by restating our earlier expression for absorption, A (equal to the expenditures of domestic residents on both domestic and foreign goods), but emphasizing something overlooked before, which is the influence of asset holdings (wealth) on expenditure:

$$A = \bar{A} + aY - bi + \rho \frac{W}{P}, \qquad (20\text{--}5)$$

where $\bar{A}$ refers to autonomous absorption, P is the domestic price level, W represents the value of the nominal wealth holdings of domestic residents (and W/P represents their *real* wealth), and a, ρ, and b are all positive parameters, suggesting that higher levels of income and wealth, and lower interest rates, lead to higher levels of domestic spending. For purposes of comparison, Equation 20–5 is identical to Equation 13–9, except that the wealth effect on domestic absorption has been added.

The hypothesis that wealth is a determinant of expenditure was stressed by the economist A. C. Pigou and is sometimes referred to as the Pigou effect. It relies on the influence of wealth on consumption, derived from the fact that a part of consumer spending is financed out of wealth holdings. The consumption expenditures of retired citizens, for example, are financed essentially out of assets they have accumulated over their lifetime. Hence, a rise in the level of wealth will support higher levels of spending. This type of effect is what the variable W/P in Equation 20–5 intends to represent.

Monetary Assets and Absorption

In order to simplify the present exposition, we will ignore nonmonetary assets for the moment and assume that domestic residents hold only domestic money as wealth. Symbolically, $W/P = M/P$. In this case, because international trade in nonmonetary assets is ignored, the capital account disappears and the balance of payments equals the trade balance. As a result, the present discussion can be understood as examining the role of the trade balance in balance-of-payments adjustments. Balance-of-payments adjustments, however, may involve capital flows in addition to the trade balance adjustments stressed in this and the following sections. The role of portfolio choice and capital movements in the balance of payments will be examined later in this chapter.

With no assets other than money, the interest rate loses importance (because there is no possible substitution between money and bonds) and, for our purposes, it can be ignored. Equation 20–5 then becomes

$$A = \bar{A} + aY + \rho \frac{M}{P}$$

$$= \bar{A} + aY_F + \rho \frac{M}{\bar{P}}, \qquad (20\text{--}5a)$$

where we have made use of the assumption that the economy produces at its potential level of output, Y_F (implying $Y = Y_F$), and the small-country assumption indicating that the domestic price level, P, is determined by world markets at a level denoted by $\bar{P}$.[6]

Equation 20–5(a) is represented graphically by means of the AA curve in Figure 20–1. Note that

---

[6] We are ignoring goods that are not traded internationally, so-called nontraded goods. The prices of nontraded goods are determined in local markets and are not, therefore, exogenously given by world market conditions. The appendix to this chapter examines the implications of incorporating nontraded goods into the analysis.

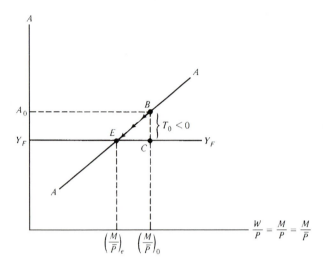

FIGURE 20–1.   The Purely Monetary Adjustment Mechanism

AA is upward sloping because of the positive association of wealth and expenditure: An increase in the real money balances held by domestic residents will increase their expenditures, holding everything else constant. The horizontal line $Y_F Y_F$ shows the level of absorption corresponding to the full-employment level of income.

The economy's trade balance deficit or surplus at any given point in time is represented by the vertical distance between the *AA* curve and the $Y_F Y_F$ line in Figure 20–1. Suppose, for example, that the quantity of money in the economy is $(M/\bar{P})_0$. At that level of monetary wealth, the expenditures of domestic residents would be given by Equation 20–5(a) as $A_0 \equiv \bar{A} + aY_F + \rho\left(\dfrac{M}{\bar{P}}\right)_0$, which, as shown in Figure 20–1, exceeds the full-employment level of income, Y_F. Domestic residents would be spending more than their income. Because the trade balance is equal to the excess of income over absorption ($T = Y - A$), in this case there is a deficit ($T_0 = Y_F - A_0 < 0$). Indeed, any level of monetary wealth above that of $(M/\bar{P})_e$ would give rise to an excess of domestic expenditure over income, inducing trade deficits. Similarly, any level of monetary wealth *below* that of $(M/\bar{P})_e$ would give rise to an excess of income over expenditure and a trade balance surplus. Only at a level of monetary wealth equal to $(M/\bar{P})_e$ will income and expenditure be the same, at which point there would be balanced trade and payments. This external balance point is shown by point *E* in Figure 20–1. It can be represented algebraically by the equality of full-employment income and absorption:

$$Y_F = A^e \equiv \bar{A} + aY_F + \rho\left(\frac{M}{\bar{P}}\right)_{e,} \qquad (20\text{–}6)$$

where A^e is the level of domestic absorption associated with monetary holdings of $(M/\bar{P})_e$. By solving this equation for $(M/\bar{P})_e$, we can find the exact level of the monetary stock consistent with external balance:

$$\left(\frac{M}{\bar{P}}\right)_e = \frac{1}{\rho}[(1 - a)Y_F - \bar{A}], \qquad (20\text{–}7)$$

which is a function of full-employment income and various parameters. The expression in Equation 20–7 can also be seen as specifying the long-run demand for money or the target amount of money toward which individuals strive.

Having specified the external balance equilibrium of the economy, the question still remains of whether (and how) that balance can be reached. The monetary approach suggests that there are tendencies in a laissez-faire open economy inducing it to move toward balanced payments, toward point E in Figure 20–1. These tendencies arise from the changes in monetary holdings implied by payments (trade) deficits and surpluses. Consider the case of a deficit, represented by the gap between points B and C in Figure 20–1. The deficit implies that domestic residents are spending more than their income $(A_0 > Y_F)$. In order to finance these "excess" expenditures, they have to draw upon their asset holdings—which, in this simplified context are in the form of monetary balances. If we assume the central bank acts passively (does not inject new money into the economy), there would then be a reduction in the money supply. In other words, domestic residents would be disposing of some of their money balances by buying a net amount of foreign goods.

What happens over time? As domestic residents reduce their money holdings, domestic absorption starts to decline; given the full-employment level of income, the trade deficit also tends to decrease $(T \equiv Y_F - A$ becomes less negative.). This is represented Figure 20–1 by the pointed arrows, which show the economy's leftward move along the AA line. Only when the trade and payments deficit is eliminated will the monetary adjustments stop occurring. At that point, point E in Figure 20–1, domestic income will equal absorption and wealth will stop changing. The adjustment process has generated a reduction in money holdings, from their original level at $(M/\bar{P})_0$, to their long-run level at $(M/\bar{P})_e$. Domestic residents reach their desired (target) amount of money and have no need to adjust their money balances any further.

Observe that the trade and payments deficits have been eliminated without any changes in prices, income, and interest rates occurring. This is a *purely monetary automatic adjustment mechanism,* moving the economy toward balanced trade on the basis of changes in monetary wealth holdings. It is one of the key suggestions of the monetary approach that external balance can be reached without any need for a change in prices, income, or interest rates in the process. In particular, attaining external balance *does not have to* involve the painful deflationary adjustments in the economy discussed in previous chapters. This does not mean, of course, that such adjustments cannot occur. The presence of short-run rigidities in the economy, for example, may make impossible the monetary adjustments just mentioned without concurrent increases in unemployment. This was the point made in Chapter 16. In any case, whether alone or combined with changes in other basic economic variables, the monetary mechanism of adjustment represents one force tending to move the economy toward external balance.

An important aspect is the time factor. How long does it take monetary wealth adjustments to move the economy toward external balance? The answer to this question depends on how quickly domestic residents adjust their money balances. If the central bank acts passively, domestic monetary holdings will change only through the trade balance; however, the trade balance is the excess of income, Y_F in the present case, over absorption, A, as given by Equation 20–5(a), or

$$T = Y_F - A$$
$$= (1 - a)Y_F - \bar{A} - \rho \frac{M}{\bar{P}}. \qquad (20–8)$$

Because Equation 20–7 tells us that

$$(1 - a)Y_F - \bar{A} = \rho \left(\frac{M}{\bar{P}} \right)_e,$$

we can substitute this expression into Equation 20–8 and obtain

$$T = \rho\left[\left(\frac{M}{P}\right)_e - \left(\frac{M}{P}\right)\right]. \qquad (20\text{–}8a)$$

Equation 20–8(a) states that adjustments in monetary wealth (represented in this case by the trade balance) are made in proportion to the gap between the long-run equilibrium stock of money holdings, $(M/\bar{P})_e$ and the actual stock of money at any given point in time, $(M/\bar{P})$. This formulation of monetary wealth adjustments over time represents a so-called *stock adjustment mechanism;* in this case, it describes how domestic residents respond to temporary disequilibria in the monetary sector. Equation 20–8(a) shows that two factors determine the speed at which changes in monetary wealth occur:

1. The gap between the existing stock of money $(M/\bar{P})$ and its desired level $(M/\bar{P})_e$. The larger this gap, the farther away the economy is from its long-run, desired state and, everything else being constant, the larger the changes in money balances over any given time period. As a result, the economy moves faster toward long-run equilibrium.
2. The value of the parameter ρ. From Equation 20–8(a), ρ represents the fraction of the gap between desired and actual money holdings that is eliminated in any given time period. The larger ρ is, the larger the proportion of excess money balances spent and, consequently, the faster the adjustment toward long-run equilibrium.

The empirical evidence yields a low value of ρ, indicating a slow monetary adjustment. Studies by economists K. N. Clements, G. Craig, and P. D. Jonson, among others, tend to show that the time required to dispose of excess money balances through trade balance deficits may be at the level

of years, perhaps as long as seven years.[7] In general, consumers dislike sharply fluctuating patterns of spending and try to smooth out any desired changes so that they occur gradually. As a consequence, monetary adjustments that require changes in wealth usually take a long time. This, however, should not be taken to imply that monetary adjustments are always slow. As we will see later, rapid changes in money holdings can take place by means of capital flows.

We have shown how monetary adjustments tend to eliminate external payments imbalances automatically. One important qualification is necessary. The monetary mechanism of adjustment can be interrupted by sterilization operations. Sterilization operations refer to operations carried out by the central bank to neutralize the effects of the balance of payments on the monetary base. For instance, the central bank may prevent a payments deficit from decreasing the domestic money supply by injecting money into the economy at the same time. The monetary approach asserts that sterilization operations can indeed interrupt the automatic monetary mechanism. At the same time, it stresses that by injecting money into the economy, the central bank may really be perpetuating the monetary disequilibrium the deficit was trying to correct. Individuals find themselves trying to get rid of money while the central bank keeps pumping it into the economy, accentuating the disequilibrium and perhaps causing larger deficits subsequently.

In the absence of sterilization, monetary wealth adjustments tend to move an economy with payments imbalances back toward external balance.

---

[7]For more details, see P. D. Jonson, "Money and Economic Activity in the Open Economy: The United Kingdom, 1880–1970," *Journal of Political Economy* (October 1976); G. Craig, "*A Monetary Approach to the Balance of Trade.*" Ph.D. diss. (Department of Economics, University of Chicago, 1979); and K. W. Clements, "*The Trade Balance in Monetary General Equilibrium,*" Ph.D. diss. (Department of Economics, University of Chicago, 1977).

What are the factors that may disturb that balance in the first place? Equation 20–8 shows that factors affecting potential output, Y_F, autonomous absorption, $\bar{A}$, and/or the real money supply, $M/\bar{P}$, will disturb the balance of trade and payments of the economy. The next sections examine the role of government policies, beginning with the effects of exchange rate changes. Other factors are considered in exercises at the end of this chapter.

20–4. DEVALUATION: A MONETARY APPROACH

To study the effects of a devaluation, we will first analyze the determinants of the price level in the case of a small open economy closely integrated to world markets.

The domestic price level represents the cost of a given basket of goods purchased by a representative domestic consumer. If we consider only the consumer's purchases of traded goods (exportables and importables), the domestic price level, $\bar{P}$, can be expressed as an index of the prices of these goods:

$$\bar{P} = \theta P_{\hat{x}} + (1 - \theta)P_M, \qquad (20\text{–}9)$$

where $P_{\hat{x}}$ is the domestic price of exportable commodities, P_M is the domestic price of importable commodities, and θ is the share of exportables in the consumption bundle of a domestic consumer (so that $1 - \theta$ is the importables' share).[8]

For a small economy, the domestic prices of traded goods are determined by their prices in world markets (the economy is a price taker). Hence, to calculate domestic prices, we convert world prices into their domestic currency values. If, for example, the price of importables in world

markets is P_M^* (in foreign currency), the domestic price, faced by local consumers, would be

$$P_M = eP_M^*, \qquad (20\text{–}10)$$

where e is the exchange rate converting the foreign currency price into domestic currency. Similarly, the domestic price of an exportable commodity would be

$$P_x = eP_x^*, \qquad (20\text{–}11)$$

given the foreign-currency price, P_x^*, available in world markets.

Substituting the expressions for P_M and P_x in Equations 20–10 and 20–11 into Equation 20–9, we find that the domestic price level is equal to

$$\begin{aligned} \bar{P} &= \theta e P_x^* + (1 - \theta)eP_M^* \\ &= e(\theta P_x^* + (1 - \theta)P_M^*) \\ &= e\bar{P}*, \end{aligned} \qquad (20\text{–}9a)$$

where $\bar{P}* \equiv \theta P_x^* + (1 - \theta)P_M^*$ is the world price (foreign currency price) of the typical consumption basket of a domestic resident.

Having established the determinants of the domestic price level, we can see how a devaluation affects domestic residents. As Equation 20–9(a) shows, an increase in the exchange rate, e, will raise the domestic price level, $\bar{P}$, because it immediately increases the prices of traded goods purchased locally. As a consequence, the real value of the money balances held in the economy declines below their initial equilibrium level. This is illustrated in Figure 20–2 by the reduction in real monetary wealth from its initial (long-run) level at $(M/P)_e$ to the lower level at $(M/P)_1$. The monetary process of adjustment is then triggered: Domestic residents will reduce spending below income to accumulate money balances with which to replenish their reduced real money stock. As a

---

[8]It would be useful to refer now to the brief introduction to exchange rate and price indices in Chapter 10.

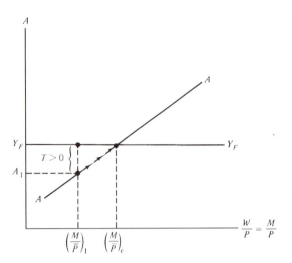

FIGURE 20–2.   The Monetary Approach to Devaluation

consequence, the immediate effect of the devaluation is to create a trade surplus, which is shown in Figure 20–2 by $T = Y_F - A_1$, the gap between the AA curve and the $Y_F Y_F$ line. This impact effect of a devaluation can be better visualized by looking back at Equation 20–8. A devaluation, by increasing the price level, $\bar{P}$, induces a reduction in real money balances, $M/\bar{P}$, which reduces absorption and improves the trade balance.

The payments surplus will generate additions to the economy's money supply over time, however. The economy's equilibrium should then move along the pointed arrows in Figure 20–2 until the desired long-run level of monetary wealth $(M/P)_e$ is reached. At that point, absorption will again equal income, and the trade imbalances will disappear. The devaluation improves the trade balance only temporarily. Its long-run effects are to increase the domestic price level and the *nominal* money supply by the same proportion, leaving *real* money balances unchanged. The level of international reserves at the central bank also increases, as a result of the temporary trade surpluses arising during the adjustment process.

Observe that, even though the *absolute* price level of the economy, $\bar{P}$, has increased, the *relative* price of imports in terms of exports, P_M/P_x, is not affected. The reason for this is that, in a small open economy, devaluation increases P_M and P_x by the same proportion. From equations 20–10 and 20–11:

$$\frac{P_M}{P_x} = \frac{eP^*_M}{eP^*_x} = \frac{P^*_M}{P^*_x}.$$

Because world prices, P^*_x and P^*_M, are unaffected by the devaluation (the country is too small to affect world prices in any noticeable way), P_M/P_x remains unchanged during the entire process. It is one of the outcomes of the monetary approach that devaluation can affect the trade balance (at least temporarily) without changing relative prices. This does not mean that such changes cannot occur. In previous chapters we saw how a country that faces rigidities in the prices of the goods it produces and exports can affect the relative price of those goods relative to the prices of imports. In this context, an increase in the exchange rate raises the domestic prices of imports but not those of domestically produced export goods (or at least not immediately). As a result, the relative price of imports in terms of exports increases, inducing a shift in spending away from foreign and toward domestic goods, and improving the trade balance. Chapters 14 and 16 analyzed devaluation in such an environment; Chapter 16 acknowledged the effects of a devaluation on the prices of domestic exports and viewed changes in relative prices only as a temporary phenomenon that is eliminated over the long run. The point made by the monetary approach is that, whether or not relative price changes occur, devaluation has a positive effect on the trade (and payments) balance by reducing real money balances and, therefore, domestic spending.

Finally, observe that devaluation is not the only factor impinging on the domestic price level in a small open economy. Increases in the world price level, $\bar{P}*$, for example, will tend to raise domestic prices and have effects similar to a devaluation. Commercial policies, such as tariffs and quotas, will also affect prices. Many governments respond to balance-of-payments difficulties by trying to reduce imports through tariffs and quotas. A tariff on imports will increase the price of foreign goods faced by domestic residents and reduce real money balances, which tends to improve the trade balance. At the same time, a tax on imports distorts resource allocation, artificially raising the price of foreign goods to domestic consumers. This can reduce real income and, therefore, money demand, worsening the trade balance. In addition, whether the balance of exports over imports improves or not depends on how much revenue the government obtains from the tariff and how it is spent. Whatever the case, the monetary approach suggests that the monetary effects of commercial policies will be temporary.[9]

20–5. Money, Budget Deficits, and the Balance of Payments

Monetary policy in the form of open-market operations, in which the central bank buys or sells securities in the open market, is an essential tool in

[9]The impact of tariffs is also related to whether they are anticipated to be temporary or permanent changes in policy. This issue is particularly important in examining the effects of trade liberalization. Governments liberalizing the economy may not have credibility in their actions, and agents in the economy may predict that the tariff reductions will be reversed. For theoretical and empirical evidence on this issue, see J. D. Ostry and A. K. Rose, "An Empirical Evaluation of the Macroeconomic Effects of Tariffs," *Journal of International Money and Finance* (February 1992); G. W. Gardner and K. P. Kimbrough, "The Behavior of U.S. Tariff Rates," *American Economic Review* (March 1989); J. Traslosheros, "Trade Liberalization, Structural Adjustment and Change in Mexico During the 1980s," Ph.D. diss. (Department of Economics, Rutgers University, 1991), and M. Gavin, "The Effects of Trade Liberalization on the Trade Balance," *Journal of International Economics* (November 1990).

modern industrial economies. As such, previous chapters have emphasized its workings and possible effects. A second expression of monetary policy often appears as "printing money:" The government in effect prints money and distributes it to the public. Economists refer to this operation as a helicopter operation, which evokes a picture of a government (or politician) throwing money from a helicopter. Of course, although some kings and dictators have been known to run through the streets tossing money into the hands of their subjects, helicopter operations do not literally take place. However, the same type of operation is involved when a government has expenditures it pays for simply by printing money. Budget deficits—the excess of government spending over its revenues—are often financed by printing money. Politicians sometimes find it distressing to raise taxes (especially in election years) and may also prefer, or find it easier, to print money than to engage in government borrowing to finance the deficit. Accordingly, government fiscal and monetary policies are often interconnected, with deficits linked to corresponding increases in the money supply.

Suppose there is an increase of the domestic money supply because money has been issued. As a consequence, domestic residents will find themselves holding excess money balances they will try to get rid of through trade deficits. This can be seen in Equation 20–8: An increase in monetary wealth (an increase in $M/\bar{P}$) induces an increase in absorption relative to income, worsening the trade balance (bringing down T). Graphically, if the economy starts from a point of external balance at point E in Figure 20–1, an increased money supply—from, say $(M/P)_e$ to $(M/P)_0$—would result in a trade deficit equal to $T_0 < 0$.

The economy will adjust to the monetary disturbance over time. The monetary process of adjustment described in Section 20–3 operates to eliminate the excess money balances that the money printing spree has generated. Only when the economy has moved back to external balance will the mechanism stop. This is illustrated in Figure 20–1 by the pointed arrows, indicating the motion of the economy after the monetary injection.

The implication here is that government deficits financed by printing money will tend to generate balance-of-payments deficits, everything else being constant. If the budget deficit is only temporary (say, a one-year event), the central bank just pumps a fixed amount of money into the economy. As a consequence, the external deficit will be temporary, as domestic residents get rid of the fixed amount of money printed by the government. Because the money supply returns again to its initial level, the increased central bank credit is matched exactly by a loss of international reserves. In other words, the government, which initially tries to finance its deficit by creating more money, finds out that the deficit is really being financed out of foreign exchange reserves.

If budget deficits are sustained over time, and everything else is constant, the economy's balance-of-payments deficits (brought about by deficit finance through printing money) would also tend to be persistent. The central bank would face continuous losses of international reserves. This process, of course, cannot continue forever because foreign exchange reserves are limited in amount. Observing its international reserves dwindle, what could the central bank do? Clearly, it could devalue its currency. As we saw earlier in Section 20–4, devaluation tends to improve the balance of payments by increasing domestic prices and reducing the real value of the money balances the government keeps pumping into the economy. This will ameliorate, if not eliminate, the loss of reserves. It is, however, only a temporary palliative. As domestic prices settle at their new (higher) levels, the sustained money creation will again move the balance of payments into deficit, renewing the loss of international reserves. Eventually, another devaluation will be required. This spiral in which balance-of-payments deficits and relative price stability are followed by devaluation and soaring inflation, to be followed by periods of

payments deficit and renewed price stability, and so on, has been called the "devaluation-inflation spiral."[10] It points out that the ultimate source of rising prices (inflation) in developing countries with deficit government spending may not be devaluation per se—in cases where the country frequently devalues—but rather the government deficits and their monetization, which give rise to payments deficits and the need for devaluation. Actually, ample evidence does exist associating devaluation with the presence of relatively large, monetized budget deficits.[11]

In this section, we have focused on analyzing the effects of an increase in the money supply through printing money and particularly on the long-run monetary adjustments it fosters. In the next section, we analyze the role of nonmonetary financial assets in balance-of-payments adjustments.

20–6. PORTFOLIO CHOICE IN THE OPEN ECONOMY

Real-world investors diversify their portfolios among a variety of assets that include not only monetary, but also domestic and foreign nonmonetary assets.[12] This is recognized here by observing that domestic residents can hold their wealth in the form of financial assets, represented by bonds, V, in addition to money, M/P:

---

[10]For an advanced exposition of this phenomenon, see M. Khan and J. S. Lizondo, "Devaluation, Fiscal Deficits and the Real Exchange Rate," *World Bank Economic Review* (January 1987); and C. Rodriguez, "A Stylized Model of the Devaluation–Inflation Spiral," *IMF Staff Papers* (March 1978).

[11]See S. Edwards, *Real Exchange Rates, Devaluation and Adjustment: Exchange Rate Policy in Developing Countries* (Cambridge, Mass.: The MIT Press, 1989), chap. 6.

[12]For a full (but advanced) treatment of the portfolio models discussed here, see R. Dornbusch, *Open Economy Macroeconomics* (New York: Basic Books, 1980), pt. 5; and J. Frenkel and C. Rodriguez, "Portfolio Equilibrium and the Balance of Payments," *American Economic Review* (September 1975).

$$\frac{W}{P} = \frac{M}{P} + V. \qquad (20\text{--}12)$$

This means that two main decisions have to be made: what the *size* of the portfolio is going to be (how much wealth is going to be held), and what its *composition* will look like (what type of assets are going to be held).[13]

Determining Portfolio Size and Composition

Figure 20–3(a) shows our familiar absorption and full-employment loci, where wealth now includes nonmonetary as well as monetary holdings. The desired portfolio size of domestic residents is represented by $(W/P)_e$. At that level of wealth, income equals absorption, as shown by point $E;$ thus, there is balanced trade. Figure 20–3(b) describes, on the other hand, the portfolio composition decision. If the total wealth to be invested is given by $(W/P)_e$, the possible combinations of bonds and money that can be held is represented by the downward-sloping line in Figure 20–3(b) called the *wealth constraint line*. The equation for this line is determined by noting that $(W/P)_e = (M/P) + V$, or

$$V = \left(\frac{W}{P}\right)_e - \frac{M}{P}, \qquad (20\text{--}13)$$

indicating that, given a certain amount of wealth, additional bonds can be acquired only by sacrificing some money holdings. If the entire portfolio is held as money—if $(W/P)_e = M/P$—no bonds will be held $(V = 0)$; we obtain the horizontal intercept of the wealth constraint line. If, on the other hand, all of the portfolio is invested in bonds—if $V = (W/P)_e$—no money can be held and the vertical

intercept shown in Figure 20–3(b) results. Other intermediate combinations, with both bonds and money held, are depicted by the wealth constraint line. Which of these combinations is actually chosen in the economy? In other words: How do individuals prefer to divide or distribute a given amount of wealth between money and bonds?

The theory of portfolio choice discussed in Part I shows how investors diversify their asset holdings on the basis of risks, returns, and other characteristics. Given these characteristics, investors decide which proportion of their portfolio to hold in bonds versus money. We denote the ratio of bonds to money individuals wish to hold by the parameter l so that

$$V = l\frac{M}{P} \qquad (20\text{--}14)$$

For example, if $l = 2$, for every dollar held in monetary assets, two dollars' worth of bonds would be held $(V = 2M/P)$. Even though we assume that l is fixed, its value is not an absolute constant and will be affected by various factors, the most obvious of which is interest rates. The higher the interest rate, the larger the value of l, as investors shift toward holding more bonds and less money. Equation 20–14 is the equation of a straight line, with slope l, and is represented in Figure 20–3(b) by an upward-sloping line called the *portfolio-diversification line*.

Desired portfolio composition is obtained at point C, at the intersection of the wealth-constraint and portfolio-diversification lines. At that point, the relative amounts of bonds and money desired by domestic residents will be satisfied (the point lies along the portfolio-diversification line), given the boundary imposed by the amount of wealth to be invested (represented by the wealth constraint line).

In general, domestic residents will hold both money and bonds. Bonds, of course, can be domestic or foreign because in open economies domestic residents can certainly purchase foreign

---

[13]We are assuming that domestic and foreign bonds are perfect substitutes, in which case they can be aggregated into the general category of *V*. For a general discussion of cases in which they are not perfect substitutes, see chap. 21.

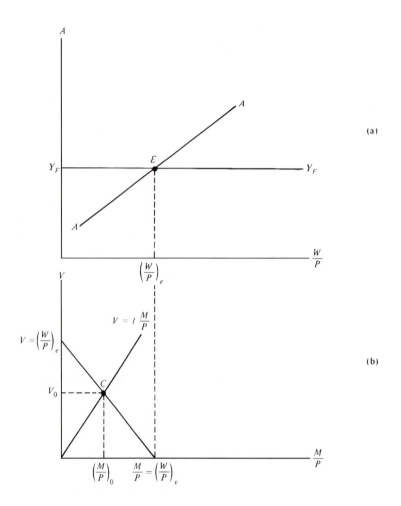

FIGURE 20–3.   Portfolio Choice in the Open Economy

assets. In this section, we thus return to our conception of the balance of payments as

$$B_N = \Delta M^D - \Delta CBC$$
$$= T_N + K_N, \qquad (20\text{-}4)$$

whereas in the last few sections we ignored the capital account, K_N. What main differences arise now in terms of our analysis?

Money, Capital Flows, and Balance-of-Payments Adjustment

Consider the effects of a sudden increase in the money supply through the "printing of money." This gives rise to an excess supply of money, which domestic residents will try to get rid of. They have two possible mechanisms to change their money holdings. First, as discussed in detail in the previous sections, they can spend it by buying foreign goods. This mechanism operates through a trade balance deficit and, by itself, is associated with a reduction in the total size of the portfolio—that is, the decline of money balances by means of a trade deficit causes a reduction of total domestic assets, constituting a *portfolio-size* adjustment mechanism. The second mechanism to dispose of excess money is to spend it on the purchase of foreign assets, which is recorded as a capital account deficit. This exchange of money to acquire foreign assets involves no change in the size of the total portfolio, only a change in its composition (less money and more bonds). It is called a *portfolio-composition* adjustment mechanism. Both mechanisms can be used to eliminate excess money balances. There is, however, a general difference between them.

Portfolio-composition adjustments are usually carried out instantaneously or over short periods of time. Portfolio-size adjustments generally take longer because they can occur only through changes in spending relative to income. Given that individuals do not in general like sudden changes in spending or standard of living, they will adjust only gradually in response to desired changes in asset holdings. To illustrate this basic difference between portfolio-size and portfolio-changing mechanisms, we will carry out explicitly all the effects of our printing money example. See the graphic representation in Figure 20–4.

Figure 20–4(a) shows the initial full equilibrium of the economy at point E, with a portfolio size equal to $(W/P)_e$. With that amount of wealth, the desired amounts of bonds and money are V_e and $(M/P)_e$, respectively, shown by point C in Figure 20–4(b). When the government prints money, implying a rise in real balances from $(M/P)_e$ to $(M/P)_1$, the stock of financial assets increases, as shown by the movement from $(W/P)_e$ to $(W/P)_1$ in Figure 20–4(a). In terms of portfolio composition, the effect of printing money is to create excess money holdings, represented by the movement from point C to point D in Figure 20–4(b). Point D is a point of portfolio disequilib-

rium because it lies away from the portfolio diversification line.

In order to attain their desired portfolio composition, domestic residents will exchange money for bonds, generating a capital account deficit. This is shown in Figure 20–4(b) by the adjustment from point D to point F. The balance of payments will instantaneously move into deficit. This adjustment of money balances through the capital account, although moving the composition of domestic portfolios back to their desired level, along the portfolio diversification line does not move the economy to its desired total holdings of financial assets—that is, to its desired portfolio size. The excess money that has been disposed of has been supplanted by acquisitions of foreign bonds; therefore, total asset holdings are still higher than they were at their initial level. This is represented in Figure 20–4 by the fact that the portfolio composition adjustment leaves the economy at a level of wealth equal to $(W/P)_1$, above its long-run level $(W/P)_e$.

The adjustment of total portfolio size toward its original level—toward points E and C in Figure 20–4—must occur over time, by means of net purchases of foreign goods, which get rid of (deplete) asset holdings overall. This slower adjustment is reflected by trade balance deficits. It is shown by the pointed arrows in Figure 20–4(a) and by the movement from point F to point C in Figure 20–4(b).

Once the economy moves back to its desired portfolio size—once asset holdings overall, both monetary and nonmonetary, have been adjusted to long-run equilibrium levels—absorption will equal income and the trade balance deficit is eliminated. At that point, the balance-of-payments deficit will also have been eliminated: All excess money balances will have been spent. In conclusion, an increase in the money supply through printing money will induce both the balance of trade and the balance of payments to worsen over the short run. If no other disturbances occur, however, these payments and trade deficits will be eliminated over

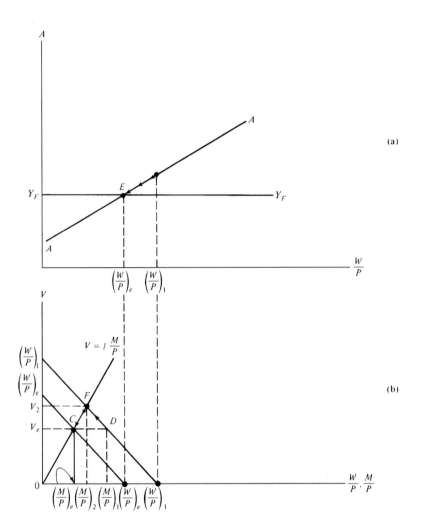

FIGURE 20–4. Printing Money and the Economy's Adjustment

time. The monetary injection then only reduces international reserves, without any other major real consequence. We must stress that the initial adjustment of the balance of payments represents mostly a portfolio-composition move, operating through the capital account; the subsequent adjustment represents mostly a move to reduce portfolio size, operating through the trade balance.

20–7. GROWTH, INFLATION, AND THE MONEY ACCOUNT

Persistent and continuous changes in economic variables are a fact of life in any modern economy. Output grows and prices rise (or fall) for extended periods of time—even the monetary policy of the central bank acquires a dynamic flavor, indicating target levels for the *rate of growth* of the money supply, instead of just stating increases in the *level* of the money supply. In this environment, economic changes occur in the form of disturbances in the rate of growth of some variable, such as an increase in the rate of growth of output or a reduction in the rate of growth of central bank credit. This differs from the analysis of a stationary (nongrowing) economy, focusing on the impact of once-and-for-all changes in the level of several variables, such as an increase in central bank credit or an increase in the exchange rate.

This section shows how the asset market approach links growth in basic economic variables to the behavior of the money account of the balance of payments. Our attention is thus focused on the overall external payments situation of the economy and not on specific accounts, such as the trade or capital accounts.

The growth of various economic variables (such as income and central bank credit) gives rise to changes in money demand and/or changes in the money supply. As discussed in Section 20–2, equilibrium in the market for money will be maintained when the changes in the nominal demand for money occurring over any given period are equal to the changes in the money supply forthcoming over that same period. From Equation 20–1, $\Delta M^D = \Delta M^S$. We find it very convenient to express equilibrium in terms of growth rates, or as

$$\hat{M}^D = \hat{M}^S, \qquad (20\text{–}15)$$

where $\hat{M}^D \equiv \Delta M^D / M^D$ represents the rate of growth (the proportional change) of money demand, and $\hat{M}^S = \Delta M^S / M^S$ is the rate of growth of money supply over a given period. What Equation 20–15 says is that the market for money will remain in equilibrium, $M^D = M^S$, when money demand and money supply grow at the same rate.

We have already studied the money supply process in some detail. We have seen that changes in the money multiplier, external payments imbalances, and central bank credit creation can all act

upon the money supply. The effects of these variables on the rate of growth of the money supply can be expressed algebraically as

$$\hat{M}^S = \hat{\mu} + \frac{B_N}{H} + \frac{CBC}{H}\,\widehat{CBC}, \qquad (20\text{–}16)$$

where $\hat{\mu}$ represents the rate of change of the money multiplier ($\hat{\mu} = \Delta\mu/\mu$), B_N is, as before, the balance of payments (so that B_N/H expresses it as a proportion of the monetary base), and $\widehat{CBC}$ represents the proportional rate of change of central bank credit ($\widehat{CBC} = \Delta CBC/CBC$).[14] Equation 20–16 is similar to Equation 20–2(a) in Section 20–1. The difference is that we are now allowing for changes in the money multiplier, which were ignored before, and that all variables appear in proportional terms.

Equation 20–16 can be rewritten as

$$\frac{B_N}{H} = \hat{M}^D - \hat{\mu} - \frac{CBC}{H}\,\widehat{CBC}, \qquad (20\text{–}17)$$

where we have substituted the condition of equality of money demand and money supply growth ($\hat{M}^D = \hat{M}^S$). Equation 20–17 shows the balance of payments (measured as a proportion of high-powered money) as being affected by changes in money demand ($\hat{M}^D$), changes in the money supply multiplier ($\hat{\mu}$), and by changes in central bank credit ($\widehat{CBC}$). Observe that factors augmenting the

---

[14]From $M^S = \mu H$ we obtain

$$\hat{M}^S = \hat{\mu} + \hat{H} = \hat{\mu} + \frac{B_N + \Delta CBC}{H}$$

$$= \hat{\mu} + \frac{B_N}{H} + \frac{CBC}{H}\frac{\Delta CBC}{CBC}$$

$$= \hat{\mu} + \frac{B_N}{H} + \frac{CBC}{H}\,\widehat{CBC}$$

where $\hat{\mu}$, $\hat{H}$, and $\widehat{CBC}$ represent proportional changes in the respective variables (e.g., $\hat{H} = \Delta H/H$).

money supply—that is, growth of the money multiplier and central bank credit creation—deteriorate the balance of payments (the money account), while factors increasing money demand improve it. What factors affect the nominal demand for money?

The *nominal* demand for money balances, M^D, should be distinguished from the *real* demand for money, L^D. The nominal demand is the demand individuals have for domestic money (dollars if a U.S. resident). The real demand for money represents how much the money you demand—your nominal money balances—is worth in terms of its purchasing power. Symbolically, we find that

$$L^D = M^D / \bar{P},$$

where $\bar{P}$ is the domestic price level used to express the nominal demand for money, M^D, in terms of its purchasing power value. Of course, you demand money for what it buys and so the demand for money is a demand for real money balances. As we saw earlier, the demand for real balances depends on income and on interest rates. Changes in the price level will then give rise to changes in the nominal demand for money. For example, if the price level doubles ($\bar{P}$ doubles), you will have to pay twice as much for everything you buy; therefore, you will have to double your holdings of nominal balances to be able to buy the same amount of goods as before (M^D doubles). This relationship between the price level and the nominal demand for money can be seen more clearly by observing that

$$M^D = \bar{P} L^D. \qquad (20\text{--}18)$$

The higher the price level, the more domestic money (dollars if a U.S. resident) you will need to purchase your consumption basket and the larger the amount of nominal money balances you will demand. Similarly, the higher the demand for real balances, the larger the demand for nominal balances, everything else being constant. Taking percentage changes in Equation 20–18 yields

$$\hat{M}^D = \hat{\bar{P}} + \hat{L}^D, \qquad (20\text{--}19)$$

where $\hat{\bar{P}} = \Delta \bar{P}/\bar{P}$ is the rate of increase of the domestic price level (domestic inflation), and $\hat{L}^D \equiv \Delta L^D/L^D$ is the rate of growth of real money demand. Desired growth of nominal money balances thus arises from inflation and from growth in real money demand.

The demand for real money balances, L^D, is a function of income, Y, and the interest rate, i, or

$$L^D = L(Y, i).$$

If income rises, holding interest rates constant, transactions increase and so does the demand for money. Increases in interest rates, on the other hand, with income constant, induce a shift toward interest-earning assets, reducing the real demand for money. The effects of changes in income and interest rates on the *growth* of real money demand can be expressed algebraically by

$$\hat{L}^D = \eta_Y \hat{Y} + \eta_r \hat{i}, \qquad (20\text{--}20)$$

where $\hat{L}^D, \hat{Y}$, and $\hat{i}$ are the growth rates of money demand, income, and interest rate, and with

$$\eta_Y = \frac{\Delta L^D/L^D}{\Delta Y/Y}\Big|_{i = i_0} > 0 \text{ and}$$

$$\eta_r = \frac{\Delta L^D/L^D}{\Delta i/i}\Big|_{Y = Y_0} < 0.$$

The parameter η_Y is the *income elasticity* of the demand for money and represents how responsive money demand is to percentage changes in income, given a fixed level of the interest rate (at $i = i_0$). For example, a value of 2 for this elasticity ($\eta_Y = 2.0$) means that, keeping interest rates constant, a 1 percent increase in income raises money demand by 2 percent.

The parameter η_r, on the other hand, is the *interest rate elasticity* of demand for money and measures the responsiveness of money demand to changes in the interest rate, keeping income constant (at $Y = Y_0$). A value of $\eta_r = -0.5$ means that, keeping income constant, a 1 percent increase in the interest rate would decrease money demand by one-half a percentage point.

Given these definitions, it is easy to see that the first term in Equation 20–20 represents the particular (partial) influence of income growth on money demand (holding fixed interest rates), and the second term represents the partial influence of changes in interest rates on money demand (holding constant the level of income). Combining the effects of these two variables must then give us the overall changes in money demand, $\hat{L}^D$.

Substituting Equation 20–20 into Equation 20–19, and placing the resulting expression into Equation 20–17, we finally obtain

$$\frac{B_N}{H} = \hat{P} + \eta_Y \hat{Y} + \eta_r \hat{i} - \hat{\mu}$$

$$- \frac{CBC}{H} \widehat{CBC}. \qquad (20\text{--}21)$$

Equation 20–21 is extremely useful for various reasons. First, it conveniently summarizes the influence of growth in various economic variables on the balance of payments; it therefore helps us in reviewing and pulling together many of the points discussed earlier. Second, it can be used as a basic tool of central bank financial programming, aiding policymakers in evaluating the balance-of-payments implications of various policies.[15] Finally,

[15]The IMF utilizes versions of the monetary approach in its examination of the sources of—and the policies to deal with—balance-of-payments difficulties. See IMF, *Theoretical Aspects of the Design of Fund-Supported Adjustment Programs*, Occasional Paper no. 55 (September 1987).

Equation 20–21 has served as a basis for much of the empirical evidence on the monetary approach. Virtually identical equations have been estimated for many countries, providing information on how the monetary approach fares in explaining the balance-of-payments behavior of actual economies. Each of these facets of Equation 20–21 will now be examined in detail.

Equation 20–21 provides a concise statement of the influence of growth in various variables on the balance of payments, B_N. As observed, higher inflation, higher income growth rates, and greater reductions in interest rates are all positively associated with the balance of payments. These factors increase the rate of growth of (nominal) money demand, inducing higher inflows of international reserves. Similarly, the higher the growth in the money multiplier and in central bank credit, the more likely a payments deficit will arise. This reflects the negative relationship between factors leading to excess money supply growth and the balance of payments.

A key aspect of central bank financial programming involves the evaluation of the balance-of-payments impact of central bank policies. Equation 20–21 can serve as a basic tool for such endeavors. If forecasts of inflation, output growth, interest rate changes, and money market multiplier trends exist, Equation 20–21 will tell us what various central bank credit growth targets will do to the balance of payments. Suppose, for example, that you were given the figures shown in Table 20–1, and you were asked about the balance-of-payments impact of a 4 percent target on the rate of growth of central bank credit (i.e., $\widehat{CBC} = 0.04$). Plugging all the numbers quoted into Equation 20–21, you would obtain that $B_N/H = 0.089$; if the monetary base is $H = \$100$ billion, then $B_N = (0.089)(100) = \$8.9$ billion, which would increase the central bank's international reserves by that amount. A 20 percent target on the rate of growth of central bank credit, however, would lead to a deficit in the balance of payments equal to $B_N = -\$3.1$ billion.

TABLE 20–1.   **Hypothetical Values of Crucial Economic Parameters**

$\hat{P}$	$\hat{Y}_F$	η_Y	η_r	$\hat{i}$	$\hat{\mu}$	CBC/H
0.10 (10%)	0.04 (4%)	0.50	−0.10	−0.09 (9%)	0.01 (1%)	0.75

Economic Growth and the Money Supply Rule Under Fixed Exchange Rates

In sections 20–4 and 20–5, we suggested that monetary policy, in the form of a once-and-for-all increase in central bank credit, gives rise to a loss of reserves of exactly the same amount. Expansionary monetary policy was consequently associated with balance-of-payments deficits. The analysis at that point was carried out under the assumption that prices, income, and interest rates were fixed so that money demand was not changing. In this situation, increased central bank credit leads to an excessive increase in money balances that is eliminated from the economy by means of payments deficits. When the economy grows, however, expansionary monetary policy may not necessarily lead to balance-of-payments deficits, but it may actually work to maintain external balance. For example, as income grows, so does the demand for money. As a result, central bank credit growth could be used to satisfy these desired increases in money holdings without causing any excess accumulation of money balances. No payments deficit would arise. Just as we saw in the previous subsection—that varying rates of central bank credit creation can generate persistent balance-of-payments disequilibria—adequate monetary policy can potentially be used to attain external balance in a growing economy.

What determines the target rate of credit creation that produces external balance in the economy? Setting Equation 20–21 equal to zero, and solving for $\widehat{CBC}$, implies that

$$\widehat{CBC}_0 = \frac{H}{CBC}[\hat{P} + \eta_Y\hat{Y} + \eta_r\hat{i} - \hat{\mu}]. \quad (20\text{–}22)$$

This expression gives us the central bank credit growth required to maintain balanced payments over time. A higher rate of credit creation would lead to persistent balance-of-payments deficits; a lower rate would lead to persistent surpluses. With the hypothetical values of basic economic parameters given in Table 20–1, the rate of growth that the central bank should target for is

$$\widehat{CBC}_0 = \frac{1}{0.75}[0.10 + (0.5)(0.04)$$
$$+ (-0.10)(-0.09) - 0.01]$$
$$\cong .135.$$

With a 13.5 percent rate of growth of central bank credit, the balance of payments would net out to zero and the central bank would avoid any loss (or gain) of international reserves. A rate of growth of central bank credit higher than 13.5 percent would lead to persistent payments deficits, as a 20 percent target did in the examples of the last subsection. A smaller rate of growth of central bank credit, on the other hand, would cause persistent surpluses, as the 4 percent target experimented with in the last subsection did.

The main point made here is that, in a growing economy, expansionary monetary policy in the form of positive targets for the rate of growth of central bank credit does not necessarily disturb (or perpetuate) external balance but can potentially help attain it. Of course, in reality, the monetary authorities would have to know exactly how prices, output, and interest rates change over time; they would also have to determine the values of income and interest rate elasticities of money demand, as well as of money multipliers. Because all the actual values of these variables fluctuate significantly, it may be extremely difficult for the monetary authorities to attain external balance; if the estimates used are grossly off target, the central bank may even move the economy away from balanced payments. In this situation, the best the monetary authorities may be able to do is to follow long-term trends in prices, income, and so on, and set a central bank credit growth target consistent with those trends, no matter what happens over the short run. Nobel laureate Milton Friedman has advocated such a monetary policy, called a *monetary rule,* for a long time. We should stress, however, that even though the spirit is the same, the nature and goals of the monetary rule discussed here differ from Friedman's. Actually, a discussion of the differences between the two reveals the divergencies between open-economy and closed-economy macroeconomics.

The monetary rule proposed by Friedman is that "the *stock of money* be increased at a fixed rate year-in and year-out without any variation in the rate of increase to meet cyclical needs."[16] This differs from the monetary rule discussed here, suggesting *central bank credit* expansion be maintained at a fixed rate. In an open economy under fixed exchange rates, the central bank does not have complete control over the growth of the stock of money. Changes in international reserves are not under the (direct) handle of the central bank but are in the hands of individuals buying or selling domestic money for foreign exchange. What the central bank does control is credit creation, which is the tool the monetary rule should refer to in such economies.

One of the goals of Friedman's monetary rule is to control the rate of increase of prices in the economy. In his framework, money supply growth causes inflation. Accordingly, "the rate of increase [of the money stock] should be chosen so that on the average it could be expected to correspond

with a roughly stable, long-run level of final product prices."[17] The monetary rule represented by Equation 20–22, on the other hand, has the goal of maintaining the economy as close as possible to external balance. It has nothing to do with controlling domestic inflation. In an open economy under fixed exchange rates, money supply growth has no clear-cut causal effect on domestic inflation.

A central bank credit rule that is oriented to sustaining external balances may allow a reform-minded government that has the means to reduce domestic inflation by providing credibility to its policies. In countries where discretion in monetary policy exists, past periods of reckless monetary growth (and previous balance-of-payments crises) will remain in the memories of investors for many years. In such circumstances, agents in the economy may attach a low probability of success to the current policies, no matter how prudent those policies are. This lack of credibility can be self-fulfilling because expectations of a future reversal of current policies may lead to the belief that a devaluation is likely to occur. As will be discussed in detail in the next section, an anticipated devaluation can cause a drain of international reserves and balance-of-payments deficits; it may eventually force the central bank to devalue domestic currency, even if the country's current credit policies are trying to match money supply growth with changes in money demand. Lack of private sector credibility on discretionary government policies may thus inevitably be linked to devaluation and inflation, despite the attempts of reform-minded governments. An alternative route is for the authorities to break with the past by adopting a strict

---

[16]M. Friedman, *A Program for Monetary Stability* (New York: Fordham University Press, 1960), p. 90 (italics added).

[17]Ibid., p. 91. In all fairness to Friedman, his monetary rule is really tailored to a flexible exchange rate regime, to which it applies much better. Within the case of fixed exchange rates, it would also be relevant to large countries whose price level partially determines (rather than is determined by) world inflation; as we show, however, it is not relevant for small countries lacking control of their money supply and for which domestic inflation is heavily determined by world inflation. This point is not often recognized.

rule restricting central bank credit growth to a certain level. Assuming that the rule is enforceable, the reputational baggage of the previous economic policies are disposed of. The economy would then be free to settle at an equilibrium with no anticipated devaluation, no actual devaluations, and lower inflation.[18]

As the discussion in this section makes clear, expectational considerations can have an enormous effect on the behavior of the balance of payments and the outcome of economic policies oriented toward external balance. The next section focuses our analysis on how expectations of devaluation and inflation can disturb the balance of payments and generate balance-of-payments crises.

20–8. EXPECTED EXCHANGE RATE CHANGES, INTEREST RATES, AND FOREIGN EXCHANGE CRISES

Expectational considerations are intimately linked to portfolio adjustments and, thus, to the balance of payments. Exchange rate expectations enter the analysis directly through their role in the determination of domestic interest rates. This is formally embodied in the uncovered interest parity condition

$$i = i^* + x,$$

where i is the domestic interest rate, i^* is the world interest rate, and x is the expected rate of domestic currency depreciation.

Recognizing the role played by expected exchange rate changes in interest rate determination and, therefore, in the money market, is essential to understanding foreign exchange crises.[19] Suppose, for example, that we are considering an economy in which the central bank increases its credit at such a high rate that it exceeds the desired money holdings of domestic residents. As has been explained earlier in the chapter, such monetary injections cause the central bank to lose foreign exchange reserves year in and year out. The bank's stock of international reserves would eventually dry out. At that point, a devaluation, or a series of currency depreciations, would be required.

Suppose, then, that investors in the economy predict that the central bank will devalue the currency within a few days. What happens? Initially, before the devaluation is expected, the domestic interest rate would equal the world rate, that is, $i_0 = i^*$. At that transitional moment when the devaluation is expected to occur but has not yet taken place, however, there would be a rise in the domestic (nominal) interest rate above the world rate. From the uncovered interest parity condition, the domestic interest rate would increase to $i_1 = i^* + x$, to reflect the expected devaluation. In other words, the information about the expected depreciation of the exchange rate is immediately embodied in the domestic interest rate. The rise in the interest rate compensates for the expected capital loss in holding domestic currency vis-à-vis foreign currency. What is the consequence of the increase in domestic interest rates?

The economy's money market equilibrium can be depicted by

$$\frac{M}{P} = kY_F - hi,$$

---

[18]A survey of the issues regarding the economics of rules and discretion is supplied by R. Barro, "Developments in the Theory of Rules and Discretion," *Macroeconomic Policy* (Cambridge, Mass.: Harvard University Press, 1990); see also F. W. Kydland and E. C. Prescott, "Rules Rather than Discretion: The Inconsistency of Optimal Plans," *Journal of Political Economy* (June 1977).

[19]Expositions of the various analytical aspects of external financial crises are supplied by S. van Wijnbergen, "Fiscal Deficits, Exchange Rate Crises and Inflation," *Review of Economic Studies* (January 1991); M. Obstfeld, "Balance of Payments Crises and Devaluation," *Journal of Money, Credit and Banking* (May 1984); and P. Krugman, "A Model of Balance of Payments Crises," *Journal of Money, Credit and Banking* (August 1979).

with Y_F equal to the economy's potential output, at which production will remain in the absence of unanticipated disturbances, i is the domestic nominal interest rate, and k and h are positive parameters measuring income and interest rate responsiveness of the demand for money. Originally, $i = i^*$, but after the expected devaluation the interest rate becomes $i_1 = i^* + x$. As a result, the demand for money declines, making necessary a decrease in the real money supply, M/P. With the devaluation anticipated, but not yet undertaken, domestic inflation remains unchanged at its current world inflation level. If the central bank continues to create credit, in order for the domestic money supply to decline, a sudden run on the central bank's international reserves would be required. With declining money demand and the central bank pumping out more money, a massive capital outflow would emerge, resulting in a critical loss of international reserves. A balance-of-payments crisis would then develop.

Another way of visualizing the crisis is to note that the immediate impact of an expected devaluation is to make domestic assets relatively unattractive at their initial interest rates. Hence, investors shift to other currencies *en masse,* leading to huge capital outflows and a corresponding loss of international reserves. The outflows stop only when domestic interest rates rise by an amount sufficient to compensate investors for their anticipated loss from holding domestic currency.

Balance-of-payments crises are troublesome for bankers and finance ministers because the crises recur. In order to deal with them and avoid future crises, it is important to recognize that speculative capital flows generally arise from the decisions of rational investors making forecasts on the basis of real conditions and available information. In order to reverse a draining run on a currency, the conditions that give rise to the speculative flow must be reversed. In the preceding example, stepping on the monetary brakes would be a possible solution; however, only a committed policy would change investors' expectations. A casual, tempo-rary, once-and-for-all decline in the money supply would have no effect on agents' expectations and would not prevent the crisis. Long-term commitments to policy changes would be required.

Balance-of-payments crises can be the outcome of purely speculative disturbances that are not based on the current macroeconomic policies of domestic authorities but on anticipations of future policies. These speculative outbursts may be based on bad experiences with previous administrations. They may be linked to a lack of private sector credibility about the government's resolve to stick with prudent economic policies. Whatever the origin, the impact of the expectations is self-fulfillment: anticipation of a balance-of-payments crisis does eventually result in one.[20] Consider, for example, a central bank that is currently tightly controlling its credit creation in order to stabilize the level of international reserves. If agents in the economy believed that such a policy would continue over time, there would be no anticipated loss of international reserves and no rational basis for a balance-of-payments crisis. However, suppose that as a result of a lack of reputation, investors believe that monetary authorities will soon step on the monetary accelerator. Then there will be an anticipation of a balance-of-payments crisis. Such a crisis would very likely be associated with domestic currency devaluation. The expected devaluation would then raise domestic interest rates and reduce money demand, which results in a loss of international reserves. If the speculative run on the domestic currency gathers momentum, the central bank may lose enough international reserves and a foreign exchange crisis may be precipitated. The anticipations of a crisis are thus self-fulfilling.

To avoid or stop a drain of international reserves, governments often threaten to impose capital controls. The assets market approach to the balance of payments suggests that such a threat

---

[20]This point has been made by M. Obstfeld, "Rational and Self-fulfilling Balance-of-Payments Crises," *American Economic Review* (March 1986).

may act to further precipitate a foreign exchange crisis. The culprit at hand here is again self-fulfilling expectations. Given a certain probability that the crisis will occur, capital controls raise the cost of holding domestic currency in that state of the world. Domestic interest rates thus rise, which reduces money demand and leads to a loss of international reserves. Such a loss of reserves may trigger a run on the currency, leading in effect to a balance-of-payments crisis. Note that all of this may occur even if the government is pursuing prudent monetary policy. The crisis is generated by self-fulfilling speculation, not inadequate current macro policies.[21]

Up to this point, we have assumed that foreign exchange crises are related to speculative capital outflows that exhaust the central bank's foreign exchange reserves. In fact, persistent capital inflows can also generate a foreign exchange crisis. Consider the following scenario. Countries with balance of trade surpluses and strong currencies often face substantial capital inflows as a result of expectations that the currency will be revalued. To avoid having an explosion in the domestic money supply, monetary authorities sterilize the effects of balance-of-payments surpluses on the monetary base by means of open-market operations. However, if these open-market operations involve the sale of government debt (say, government bonds), the accumulation of public debt may in fact generate fears of high debt-service payments. The high debt service may then lead to expectations of budget deficits and future monetary expansion. The capital inflows may then turn to capital outflows, losses of reserves, and a foreign exchange crisis.[22]

20−9. FITTING THE PIECES TOGETHER: THE ASSET MARKET APPROACH AND SHORT-RUN BALANCE-OF-PAYMENTS THEORY

We have now examined in detail the nature and implications of the monetary and assets market approach to the balance of payments. It is time to steer the discussion away from the specifics of the approach and seek some perspective on how it fits into the overall scheme of open-economy macroeconomics and balance-of-payments theory. As the parable goes, we must stop looking at the trees and glance at the forest.[23]

How does the assets market approach relate to our analysis of the balance of payments in previous chapters? Our general framework of analysis in Chapter 16 included the following relationships, which we have related to equations in that chapter:

$$\frac{M^S}{P} = L(Y, i) \quad \begin{array}{l} \textit{(money market} \\ \textit{equilibrium} \\ \textit{condition)} \end{array} \quad (16\text{--}1)$$

$$\begin{array}{l} Y^D = \alpha[\bar{A} + \bar{T} \\ \qquad + \phi q - bi] \end{array} \quad \begin{array}{l} \textit{(aggregate} \\ \textit{demand} \\ \textit{function)} \end{array} \quad (16\text{--}2\text{a})$$

$$\begin{array}{l} Y^S = Y_F \\ + \theta\beta\left(\dfrac{P - P_{-1}}{P_{-1}}\right) \end{array} \quad \begin{array}{l} \textit{(short-run} \\ \textit{aggregate} \\ \textit{supply equation)} \end{array} \quad (16\text{--}4)$$

and

$$B = T(q, Y) + K(i) \quad \begin{array}{l} \textit{(balance-of-} \\ \textit{payments} \\ \textit{equation)} \end{array} \quad (16\text{--}4)$$

---

[21]See H. Dellas and A. C. Stockman, "Self-fulfilling Expectations, Speculative Attacks and Capital Controls," National Bureau of Economic Research Working Paper no. 2625 (June 1988).

[22]This argument especially applies to the case of developing countries that pursue capital account liberalization but sterilize the effects of the subsequent capital inflows on the monetary base by issuing debt; see G. Calvo, "The Perils of Sterilization," *IMF Staff Papers* (December 1991).

[23]Studies indicating how the monetary and asset market approach fit into a broad perspective of the open economy include S. Edwards, *Exchange Rate Misalignment in Developing Countries* (Baltimore: Johns Hopkins University Press, 1988), appendix; and J. Frenkel, T. Gylfason, and J. F. Helliwel, "A Synthesis of Monetary and Keynesian Approaches to Short-Run Balance of Payments Theory," *Economic Journal* (September 1980).

Equations 16–1 and 16–2(a) were combined into what we referred to as an aggregate demand equation. The economy's short-run equilibrium was then determined by that point at which aggregate demand equaled aggregate supply. This condition gave rise to a certain short-run balance-of-payments deficit or surplus, as represented by Equation 16–4. In other words, the system of equations 16–1 to 16–4 was used to represent the economy's equilibrium, determining the basic variables of concern (domestic prices, output, interest rates, and the balance of payments).

How does the monetary approach fit into this framework? The monetary approach singles out the money market equilibrium equation (16–1) and focuses its attention on analyzing it. By noting that money market equilibrium is maintained when $\Delta M^D = \Delta M^S$, the monetary approach establishes its basic representation of the balance of payments as follows:

$$B = \frac{B_N}{P} = \frac{1}{P}(\Delta M^D - \Delta CBC). \quad (20\text{–}3a)$$

The interpretation of Equation 20–3(a), a variant of Equation 20–3, has been the main point of this chapter; its cousin, Equation 20–21, is the basis for most of the empirical work on the monetary approach. Note, however, that the balance-of-payments expression derived by the monetary approach appears to differ from the explicit representation of the balance of payments stated in Equation 16–4. Does this mean that these two balance-of-payments equations are inconsistent? Take the following example. According to Equation 20–3(a), increases in income imply that the balance of payments improves because the demand for money rises. The balance-of-payments expression in Equation 16–4, however, associates increases in income with increased imports and a deteriorating balance of payments. Does this mean that the two equations provide conflicting views on the balance of payments? Surprisingly, no.

To visualize the fallacy involved, think in terms of the standard demand and supply model of determination of market output, Q, and price, P. In this system, there is a demand curve (or equation) that establishes a negative relationship between P and Q, and a supply curve that establishes a positive relation between P and Q. Clearly, the fact that P and Q are related differently by each curve does not imply that the demand and supply curves are inconsistent. It just suggests that demand and supply curves embody the behavior of different sectors of the market (consumers and producers), and that only their interaction will simultaneously determine the market's *equilibrium* price and output (at that point at which demand and supply meet). Analogously, in our balance-of-payments example, even though equations 20–3(a) and 16–4 represent two different responses of the balance of payments with respect to income, they are not inconsistent. The two form part of the aggregate demand and supply model shown by equations 16–1 to 16–4, just as demand and supply curves form part of a market model.

Figure 20–5 illustrates the issue. Curve *MM* represents the positive relationship between the balance of payments, B, and income, Y, established by the monetary equation (20–3a). The *KK* curve, on the other hand, represents the negative

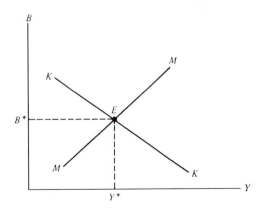

FIGURE 20–5. Simultaneous Determination of Income and the Balance of Payments

association between income and the balance of payments shown by Equation 16–4. In equilibrium, both equations must be satisfied and point E would be established, with a short-run *equilibrium* level of income Y^* and a short-run balance-of-payments surplus equal to B^*. Note that MM and KK are consistent with each other, even though, when considered in isolation, they appear to be in conflict. This has been the source of enormous controversy regarding the monetary approach. Economists emphasizing an equation such as 16–4 would, for example, point to curve KK and stress that Y and B are negatively related. Monetary economists concentrating on Equation 20–3(a), however, would angrily disagree, indicating that the unavoidable monetary equilibrium of the economy implies that income and the balance of payments are positively related, as curve MM illustrates. In a sense, both statements are correct, and in another both are incorrect. They are both correct because they are consistent with a general model of how the economy behaves (both form an integral part of equations 16–1 to 16–4). They are both wrong, however, because each equation is part of a broader system describing the economy. It would be misleading to analyze the actual behavior of the economy (its equilibrium paths of Y^* and B^*) on the basis of one equation alone (i.e., on the basis of either KK or MM alone). Stating that income and the balance of payments are positively related through their monetary implications says as much as that price and output are positively related through a supply curve. It provides us with information about the money market, but it does not tell us about how the short-run equilibrium income and balance of payments of the economy are related—just as a supply curve alone cannot tell us how the equilibrium price and output of a market are related. We therefore must be very careful in evaluating the results of an equation such as 20–22, which really forms part of a broader system.

20–10. ELASTICITIES, ABSORPTION, AND MONETARY APPROACHES TO THE BALANCE OF PAYMENTS

The last section showed that different conceptions of the balance of payments are not necessarily inconsistent with each other. Differences in their appearance, however, have given rise to intense controversy and the consequent emergence of competing approaches to the balance of payments. In this section we provide some perspective on these views from a contemporary vantage point.

In the analysis of the balance of payments, we often observe studies that concentrate on discussing either the trade balance or the capital account. Two of the best-known approaches to the balance of payments, the so-called elasticities and absorption approaches, pay special attention to the trade balance.

The *elasticities approach* stresses the need for an explicit analysis of a country's exports and imports in dissecting the balance of payments. It thus emphasizes the conception of the trade balance as the difference between exports and imports:

$$T = X - M.$$

The elasticities approach, for instance, addresses the problem of the impact of devaluation by discerning how exchange rate changes disturb the terms of trade and how these changes affect exports, imports, and the trade balance. In so doing, many of the initial practitioners of the approach ignored the income effects of a devaluation as well as its monetary implications. The discussion encompassed what, in our own treatment, we have referred to as the effects of devaluation on the trade balance. As may be recalled from chapters 13 and 14, the answer to this question involves the specification of the values of the price elasticities of demand for domestic imports and exports. This is the basis, of course, for the name of the approach.

The income effects of a devaluation were emphasized by the *absorption approach,* which looked at the trade balance as the difference between income and absorption:

$$T = Y - A.$$

In this conception, a devaluation tends to improve the trade balance only insofar as it reduces the level of spending relative to income. In practice, the absorption approach overlooked the long-run monetary adjustments that the monetary approach suggests will prevent a devaluation from having any lasting effect on the trade balance. In addition, many of the initial practitioners of the approach disregarded the relative price effect of a devaluation (its impact by altering the real exchange rate); its results appeared to be opposed to those of the elasticities approach. In reality, a devaluation involves both income and relative price effects, implying that the elasticities and absorption approaches can be integrated into an overall analysis of devaluation. That was our own approach in chapters 13 and 14 and the one implicit in Equation 16–4, in which both income, Y, and relative prices, q, affect the trade balance, T. We must thus stress that, in a well-specified framework, it should not matter if the trade balance is analyzed as the difference between exports and imports or as the gap between income and spending; symbolically,

$$T = X - M = Y - A = T(q, Y). \qquad (20\text{–}23)$$

To study the overall balance of payments, we must consider the capital account in addition to the trade balance. Because the elasticities and absorption approaches essentially look at the *trade balance,* we have to add the capital account to the expression in Equation 20–23 to obtain their representation of the *balance of payments.* Using Equation 20–3(a) also, we obtain

$$B = (X - M) + K$$
$$= (Y - A) + K$$
$$= \frac{1}{P}(\Delta M^D - \Delta CBC),$$

stating that, no matter what the approach to the balance of payments is—elasticities, absorption, or monetary—it should be consistent with the other approaches. The difference between them lies in the way the balance of payments is looked at.

As a practical matter, however, adopting a particular point of view, even though it provides particular insights, may obscure other possible insights from other points of view. Furthermore, in the case in point, many of the supporters of each approach have been associated with different theories and schools of thought about the behavior of the open economy. All of this has generated intense, and often wasteful, disputes and controversy over balance-of-payments policy. In this book, enjoying the benefits of hindsight, we have synthesized the approaches and studied each of their insights.

Summary

1. The asset market approach to fixed exchange rates states that the balance of payments reflects essential equilibrium adjustments in the domestic and foreign demand for stocks of national assets. Changes in the balance of payments are visualized as reflecting the choices that agents in the economy make in clearing relative demands for foreign and domestic assets.

2. The simplest version of the asset market approach is the monetary approach. The monetary approach to the balance of payments asserts that the balance of payments involves *essential monetary phenomena.* This does not imply that the balance of payments is uniquely a monetary phenomenon, nor does it propose a *monetarist* view of the economy.

3. In equilibrium, the money account of the balance of payments represents a gap between people's desired accumulation of money and the money forthcoming from monetary injections by the central bank or from changes in the money multiplier.

4. In the absence of government meddling with the economy, a purely monetary mechanism exists that can correct payments imbalances automatically, without requiring changes in output, prices, or interest rates.

5. Devaluation tends to increase the domestic price level, reducing the real value of the money stock and triggering a temporary improvement in the money account.

6. Printing money (or its equivalent) leads to a worsening of both the trade and money accounts and a consequent loss of international reserves. If the government continuously prints money, the balance-of-payments deficits will be persistent; otherwise, they will subside as domestic residents return their money holdings to their desired level.

7. The monetary effects of higher inflation, higher income growth rates, and greater reductions in interest rates are all positively associated with the balance of payments. These factors increase the rate of growth of (nominal) money demand, inducing larger inflows of international reserves. Similarly, the higher the growth of the money multiplier and central bank credit, the worse the balance of payments will turn. This reflects the negative relationship between factors leading to excess money supply growth and the balance of payments.

8. The formulation of monetary rules for open economies should recognize that neither the price level nor the money supply may be controllable by domestic monetary authorities under a fixed exchange rate regime. Still, a monetary rule specifying a target rate of growth of central bank credit can be formulated with the purpose of keeping external balance in the economy.

9. Expectations play a critical role in the asset market approach to the balance of payments. Expectations of a devaluation can generate capital outflows that can drain the central bank's international reserves in a very short time. The asset market approach suggests that the portfolio choices of agents in the economy, based on anticipated future economic outcomes and the credibility of current economic policies, are an essential determinant of balance-of-payments crises.

Problems

1. In 1987, Taiwan's central bank controlled the world's third largest supply of foreign exchange reserves, after Japan and West Germany. According to Claudia Rosett, the basic reason for these unusually high international reserves was that the central bank of Taiwan was following "a process known as sterilization" ("Taiwan's Perilous Midas Touch," *The Wall Street Journal,* June 2, 1987). What is sterilization? What phenomena may have occurred in the Taiwanese balance of payments that could explain the massive growth of foreign exchange reserves in Taiwan? (Hint: Return to previous chapters to review the monetary operations relating to sterilization; then specify which type of capital flow or trade balance disturbance may have generated the balance-of-payments changes required for the central bank to absorb increased foreign exchange reserves.)

2. The government of a small Latin American country announces it will devalue its currency by 5 percent in twenty days. The interest rate on the economy's one-month Treasury bills, i, is initially equal to the world interest rate $i^* = 10$ (10%). The country's money supply is currently equal to 600 million pesos, with the monetary base composed of 400 million pesos worth of central bank credit and 200 million pesos worth of international reserves (and a money supply multiplier equal to $\mu = 1$). You

are told that real money demand in the economy is given by

$$L = 0.25Y - 2000i$$

and the country's output is $Y = 2000$ million units with the price of each unit of output equal to $P = 2$ pesos. Assuming that there is no change in central bank credit, what would be the effect of the peso devaluation announcement on the country's level of international reserves? Provide a numerical answer and speculate on what the government might be forced to do before the twenty days pass. (Hint: Assume that uncovered interest parity holds, with $x = 0.05$, and substitute it into the real money demand equation.)

3. Within the simple monetary wealth framework examined in sections 20–2 through 20–5, describe the effects of an increase in full-employment income, Y_F, on the desired real money balances of individuals in the economy. Then trace the short-run and long-run behavior of the trade balance in response to the increase in real income. Does the trade balance worsen or improve over the short run? Is the short-run relationship between income and the trade balance obtained in any way different from that obtained in earlier chapters? If it is, explain the reason for the differences. Explain your results using the diagrammatic tools developed in the text.

4. Consider the simple model of monetary wealth examined in sections 20–2 through 20–5. Suppose that you are given the following numerical parameters: $Y_F = 800$ billion, $\rho = 0.25, \bar{A} = 110$ billion, $\alpha = 0.80$, with all variables as defined in the text and with income and absorption measured in terms of units of domestic goods (over a period of a year).

(a) Calculate the desired real money balances $(M/P)_e$ of residents in this economy. The income velocity of money, V, is defined as the ratio of real income to real money balances—that is, $V = Y_F/(M/P)$. How

much is the value of money velocity in the present case?

(b) You are told that the country considered is a small open economy producing and consuming only goods traded in world markets. The country faces prices of exportables and importables in world markets equal to $P_x = £5$ and $P_m = £5$, where world prices are expressed in pounds. Assuming that the share of exportables in a domestic resident's consumption basket is 20 percent and that the exchange rate is currently fixed at $e = \$2.00/£$:

(1) Calculate the domestic price level and the level of nominal money balances (in dollars), using your results in part (a). Assume that the economy is in long-run equilibrium.

(2) Suppose that the exchange rate increases from $\$2/£$ to $\$4/£$. What would be the effects on the world prices of exportables and importables? On the prices faced by domestic consumers? On the domestic price level? Assuming that the economy is initially in long-run equilibrium, what would be the impact effect of the devaluation on the level of real money balances (at the original level of nominal balances)? Would money balances be disturbed? If so, by how much? What would be the "new" long-run value of desired nominal money balances in view of the devaluation? Would money velocity change in the short run? All your answers should be numerical and the economic intuition behind the results explained in detail.

5. Utilizing the framework of sections 20–2 through 20–5, determine what the effects of a halving of world market prices on:

(a) Domestic prices.

(b) Short-run and long-run desired real money balances.

(c) The trade balance in the short run and the long run.

Use diagrams if possible.

6. Open-market operations are the bread and butter of central bank actions in many of the industrial economies. Suppose that the central bank engages in an open-market purchase of bonds. Utilizing the monetary approach, what would be the impact of this disturbance on the trade balance, capital flows, and the balance of payments in the short run and in the long run? How does this policy differ from the printing money (so-called helicopter operation) examined in Section 20–5? Use diagrams if possible.

7. What would be the effects of a government budget deficit financed by printing money on the capital account, the trade balance, and the balance of payments? Suppose that the budget deficit is financed by external borrowing (say, selling government bonds to the rest of the world), would your answers change? Explain.

8. You are in charge of the financial programming of a central bank in a small developing country. The following public forecasts for the next year are available: $\hat{P} = 5\%$, $\hat{Y} = 2\%$, $\eta_Y = 0.50$, $\eta_r = -0.10$, $\hat{\mu} = 0$, $\hat{i} = 0$, $CBC = 200$ million pesos, $IR = 10$ million pesos, with all symbols as defined in the text. In addition, the president of the central bank tells you (in secrecy) that domestic currency will be devalued by 10 percent in a few months. Your task is to find next year's CBC growth consistent with balanced payments, for which you use the monetary approach. What would be your recommendation? Would you give any warnings regarding its adoption?

APPENDIX: NONTRADED GOODS AND ECONOMIC POLICY

In this appendix we discuss the analytical aspects of modeling nontraded goods in the open economy and explore some of the consequent policy implications. To simplify matters, it is assumed that the economy of concern is a small open economy that takes the prices of traded goods as given by world markets and thus faces fixed terms of trade. This type of economy has been referred to as a *dependent economy*, to stress its inability to influence the prices of its export and import products in world markets. The pioneering work in examining the economics of dependent economies was carried out initially by James Meade, W. E. Salter, T. Swan, and W. Corden, among others. It has been developed and popularized by Rudiger Dornbusch and Sebastian Edwards in various articles.[A1]

First of all, for expositional purposes, let us lump together exportables and importables into a category called internationally traded goods, or, for short, *traded goods*. When we refer to the price of traded goods, P_T, we will then refer to an index of the prices of exportables, P_X, and importables, P_M. If we let θ be the symbol representing the share of expenditure allocated to exportables, then the price of traded goods is

$$P_T = \theta P_X + (1 - \theta)P_M,$$

and assuming, for present purposes, that the domestic prices of importables and exportables are equal to their world prices, translated to domestic currency ($P_X = eP_X^*$ and $P_M = eP_M^*$, where P_X^* and P_M^* are world prices), then

$$P_T = \theta eP_M^* + (1 - \theta)eP_M^*$$
$$= e(\theta P_X^* + (1 - \theta)P_M^*)$$
$$= eP_T^*.$$

[A1] See S. Edwards, *Real Exchange Rates, Devaluation and Adjustment* (Cambridge, Mass.: The MIT Press, 1989); and R. Dornbusch, *Open Economy Macroeconomics* (New York: Basic Books, 1980).

where P_T^* is the world price (foreign currency price) of the typical basket of traded goods consumed by a domestic resident. For a small economy that takes P_T^* as given, the domestic prices of traded goods would then be solely determined by prices in world markets, assuming a fixed exchange rate. This does not imply, however, that domestic prices will be completely determined by world prices. Because they are not traded internationally, the prices of nontraded goods are determined by local demand and supply in the country in which they are both produced and consumed. With domestic consumers purchasing both traded and nontraded goods, the domestic price level will then be affected by the prices of both of these types of commodities, with the relative importance of each determined by the share of each commodity in the consumers' expenditures. Accordingly, if σ represents the fraction of expenditure on nontraded goods, the domestic price level is given by

$$P = \sigma P_N + (1 - \sigma)P_T$$
$$= \sigma P_N + (1 - \sigma)eP_T^*.$$

Observe that if nontraded goods were unimportant in the consumption patterns of domestic residents, their share of domestic expenditures would be insignificant, $\sigma = 0$, and the domestic price level would be completely determined by the prices of traded goods in world markets (converted to domestic currency). With nontraded goods an important part of expenditure, however, the prices of nontraded goods form an integral part of the domestic price level. Different countries will have different inflation rates, depending on how the prices of nontraded goods behave in each.

Actually, it appears that, for most countries, there has been a systematic tendency over the years for increases in the prices of nontraded goods to exceed increases in the prices of traded goods. The result is an observed increase in the prices of nontraded goods relative to those of

traded goods.[A2] That is the picture we obtain from Figure 20A–1, in which the ratio of a price index of nontraded goods to a price index of traded goods is presented for various countries for the period 1950 to 1972. What explains this clear trend? One of the main hypotheses is that postulated by the late economist Bela Balassa,[A3] who convincingly argued that the rate of productivity change in the traded goods sector has systematically exceeded that in the nontraded goods sector over the years. Lagging productivity growth in the nontraded goods sector will result in higher relative nontraded goods prices. The upward trend in the prices of nontraded goods will then remain so long as the differential productivity growth persists. A second explanation offered regards the behavior of the demand for nontraded goods as income increases. The hypothesis is that the income elasticity of the demand for nontraded goods exceeds unity. As a consequence, as income grows, the demand for nontraded goods grows at a higher rate, generating the observed increase in the relative price of nontraded goods.

Subsequently, we will refer in more detail to this systematic tendency regarding the prices of traded and nontraded goods and its implications. For the moment, however, let us discuss more fully the implications of the presence of nontraded goods with respect to policymaking. The effects of government policies will be affected by how the nontraded goods sector responds to those policies. Consider the case of monetary policy.

As noted earlier in the chapter, a small open economy under fixed exchange rates has a limited scope in using monetary policy to affect domestic prices. This will be true provided that the nontraded goods sector is not significant and the

---

[A2]Recent evidence of this trend is provided by I. B. Kravis and R. E. Lipsey, "National Price Levels and the Prices of Tradables and Nontradables," *American Economic Review* (May 1988).

[A3]B. Balassa, "The Purchasing Power Parity Doctrine: A Reappraisal," *Journal of Political Economy* (December 1964).

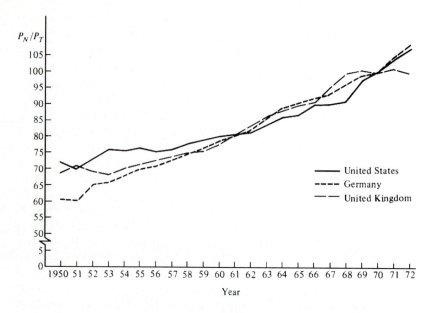

FIGURE 20 A–1. Ratio of the Price Index of Nontraded Goods to the Price Index of Traded Goods (1970 = 100).

SOURCE: M. Goldstein and L. Officer, "New Measures of Prices and Productivity of Tradable and Nontradable Goods," *Review of Income and Wealth* (1976), p. 173.

economy is closely integrated to world markets. In economies in which the nontraded goods sector is important, however, domestic monetary authorities may affect domestic prices by altering the prices of nontraded goods. The impact effect of a reduction in central bank credit on the economy, for instance, will be to reduce real money balances and, consequently, expenditure relative to income. This reduction in expenditure decreases the demand for both traded and nontraded goods, inducing a decline in the prices of nontraded goods relative to traded goods. (A decrease in the demand for nontraded goods results in lower non-traded goods prices, but a decrease in the demand for traded goods does not affect the externally given traded goods prices). Similarly, the impact of a monetary expansion will be to increase the prices of nontraded goods relative to the prices of

traded goods. Of course, over longer periods of time, decreases in the domestic money supply below the desired level would be eliminated through the hoarding actions of domestic residents. Conversely, increases in the money supply above the desired level would be gradually "dishoarded" over time until they were eliminated. These adjustments return the domestic money supply to its original, desired level, inducing the relative price of nontraded goods to revert to its initial level also. The economy's monetary adjustment mechanism makes the effects of monetary policy only temporary. This is a result we have found many times before in other contexts; it is not altered by considering nontraded goods.

The analysis of the effects of devaluation is also affected by the presence of nontraded goods. Devaluation tends to increase the prices of traded goods, thereby reducing real money balances at a given level of the nominal money supply. However, a reduction in real money balances decreases expenditure, causing a decrease in the relative price of nontraded goods. This has two effects: It switches domestic consumption toward the now relatively cheaper nontraded goods and away from traded goods (like imports), and it shifts production toward the now relatively more profitable traded goods (such as export and import competing products). Both of these effects improve the balance of trade. The suggestion is that devaluation can affect the balance of trade, even if it cannot influence the terms of trade (i.e., even if the prices of traded goods—exports and imports—all increase in the same proportion). This additional effect of devaluation results from its expenditure-reducing effects and from the decrease in the relative price of nontraded goods it causes—an effect not discussed before. Note that this influence of devaluation on the trade balance would only be temporary. Over time, domestic residents will replenish their depleted real money balances, increasing expenditure in the process and returning the relative price of nontraded goods to its predevaluation level.[A4]

The empirical work focusing on the responsiveness of the prices of nontraded goods to devaluation and the consequent effects on the trade balance remains in its infancy but is a current topic of research in the field. The evidence available, suggests, however, that devaluation has a negative impact on the prices of nontraded goods relative to traded goods. This discovery makes the adjustments mentioned earlier potentially important.[A5]

In conclusion, we have seen how the domestic price level can deviate and be made to deviate, by various policies, from world-determined prices in the presence of a significant nontraded goods sector.

[A4]I. B. Kravis and R. E. Lipsey provide such evidence on devaluations and revaluations in various industrial countries between 1970 and 1973: "Price Behavior in the Light of Balance of Payments Theories," *Journal of International Economics* (May 1978).

[A5]Empirical analysis of the impact of devaluation on the relative price of nontraded goods has been carried out by G. R. LeFort, "The Relative Price of Nontraded Goods, Absorption, and Exchange Rate Policy in Chile," *IMF Staff Papers* (June 1988).

PART **VII**

Interdependence in the World Economy

CHAPTER 21

The International Monetary System: History and Controversies

Economic transactions between residents of different countries require some sort of arrangement to effectuate payments and settle the trade or exchange involved. This is not a trivial task because the required arrangements have to cut across diverse political regimes, legal systems, and customary ways of doing business. In antiquity, trade among reigns was settled in kind through barter. Sovereigns would exchange cattle for wheat or send a shipment of timber for oil or grain. Direct barter of goods gave way to monetary arrangements when some commodities, particularly metals, began to command a general acceptability as a form of payment in different regions, assuming the role of commodity monies. In modern times, the inconvenience of international barter has been avoided by a wide array of monetary arrangements ranging from black markets in foreign exchange (operating at the margin of the official or legal framework) to multilateral agreements embracing dozens of countries and supervised by international organizations.

It has been said that the international monetary system is like a traffic light network, in that it is usually taken for granted until it breaks down. The analogy is appropriate because the international monetary system—the collection of conventions, rules, procedures, and institutions that govern financial relations among nations—usually remains in the background of international affairs, with banks, investors, speculators, and other international traders in full control of its day-to-day activities. It is when international monetary arrangements are in disarray that we suddenly become aware of them. On these occasions, as in the period from 1971 to 1973, when the Bretton Woods regime collapsed and was replaced with a new set of international monetary procedures, or in September 1992 when the European Monetary System was at the verge of total breakdown; the international monetary system suddenly becomes visible and makes headlines. Perhaps because the international monetary system is indeed crisis prone and subject to violent shakedowns from time to time it is a recurrent subject in economic history.

Our previous analysis has dealt with specific facets of the international monetary system. Witness our discussion of foreign exchange markets in Chapters 1 and 2, of international banking and Eurodollars in Chapter 8, and our examination of macroeconomic adjustment under alternative exchange rate regimes in parts IV and V. Most of the time, however, we treated the international monetary system as exogenously given, focusing our attention on specific aspects of its operation. In this and the following chapter we change gear: The international monetary system finally gets to the center of the stage and becomes the endogenous variable to be explained. We offer a broad comparative perspective on alternative monetary regimes that stresses the historical evolution of international monetary arrangements, critically evaluates alternative views on the proper design of an international monetary system, and discusses specific reform proposals regarding the current regime. We also examine the roles of the main international organizations and agencies facilitating the global operation of the system. We begin this chapter by going back to the early history of

monetary arrangements and up to the final collapse of the Bretton Woods system in early 1973. In Chapter 22 we will focus on the current set of international monetary arrangements and future prospects.

21–1. COMMODITY STANDARDS AND THE PLIGHT OF BIMETALLISM

From antiquity to modern times, city-states and countries generally operated on a *specie commodity standard,* in which metals—predominantly gold and silver—made up the bulk of an economy's circulating media. Although gold and silver initially circulated mostly in raw form or in bars and rings, the monetary innovation of standardization and certification by means of official coinage was introduced by 600 B.C. Coinage facilitated transactions and saved traders the time and effort of weighing and assessing metal values, substituting instead the simple task of counting stamped coins. Coins were stamped according to their metal worth in weight and fineness, and these qualities were guaranteed by the sovereign.[1]

That gold and silver have been particularly favored relative to other metals throughout history is not surprising if we take into account the many attributes that make them suitable as commodity money: their scarcity, durability, transportability, divisibility, homogeneity, and consistency of quality. The acceptability of these metals as money was also aided by the fact that they were widely recognized as having value in nonmonetary uses (e.g., industrially and as jewelry). They also enjoyed a relatively stable value in terms of other

---

[1] An etymological note is that weight is associated with the names of many of today's currencies. The British *pound sterling* originally denoted a pound of silver of a certain fineness. Similarly, the *mark* was originally a unit of weight, the Italian *lira* derives from the Latin term for pound, and *peso* means weight in Spanish. The word *dollar* is a corruption of the Germanic *thaler,* first coined in Joachims*thal* (Valley of Joachim) in the sixteenth century.

commodities, and their quality could be verified or certified by a qualified expert or by biting them in the absence of better means.

In their purest form, specie commodity standards operated on the basis of full-bodied coins whose monetary value equaled the value of the metals they contained.[2] This generally meant that, when the price of gold changed relative to the price of silver, so would the rate at which silver and gold coins were exchanged for each other. Even though sovereigns minted their own coins bearing a particular stamp as evidence of their metallic content, the counterfeiting of coins was frequently undertaken by mixing gold or silver with other, less valuable, metals. Sovereigns themselves frequently reduced the gold (or silver) content of the coins they minted, a practice called *debasement*. Coin debasement, the predecessor of the modern devaluation of a currency, usually led to a loss of a coin's value.

What was the effect, in a monetary system based on commodity monies, of the simultaneous circulation of full-bodied money and debased coins of the same denomination, both often similarly stamped? The British series of debasements between 1540 and 1560 clearly illustrates the result: Debased coins drove the fuller-bodied ones out of circulation.[3] The reason for this outcome stemmed directly from the official imposition of the same nominal value to debased and full-bodied coins, even if they differed in metallic content. Debased money was overvalued as a medium of exchange because it was assigned a higher face

value than its metal content justified. Conversely, fuller-bodied money was relatively undervalued as a medium of exchange. For that reason, people holding both types of coins would effectuate payments by means of debased coins, retaining for their own accumulation the fuller-bodied ones, whose greater value in metal made them a better store of value. Fuller-bodied coins could also be melted to be sold as metal, exported, or even sent to the coinage to be exchanged or coined into new, debased coins.[4] The end product was that debased money—overvalued as a medium of exchange—would remain in circulation, while full-bodied coins—undervalued as a medium of exchange—would disappear.

The notion that overvalued money drives undervalued money out of circulation when they bear the same face value, popularly expressed as "bad money drives out good," has come to us under the heading of *Gresham's law*. This was precisely the reasoning followed by Thomas Gresham (1529–1579) to explain why British circulating media had been reduced to debased money by 1560 (following substantial coin debasements from 1542 to 1551), and to convince Queen Elizabeth I to replace all those debased coins with newly minted full-bodied coins. Actually, a coin reform in which debased coins were retired from circulation and substituted by newly minted full-bodied coins did take effect in 1560 and 1561.

On a quite different front, the U.S. experience under bimetallism from 1792 to 1861 also sheds light on Gresham's law. The Coinage Act of 1792 adopted the dollar as the U.S. monetary unit and

[2]In practice (specie) commodity standards functioned as a combination of full-bodied and token coins, whose monetary value exceeds their value as metals. Token coins, often made from copper, bronze, or iron, facilitated everyday transactions in small sums and were a preferred choice for small change. Currently, only the U.S. government issues token coins. The American quarter, for instance, is worth 25 cents as a medium of exchange, but its metallic value is far less than that.

[3]Similar to the effects of a devaluation, the debasements over this period were accompanied by substantial price inflation. For more details, see J. D. Gould, *The Great Debasement* (New York: Oxford University Press, 1970).

[4]Official mints stood ready to accept metals—either bullion or old coins—to be minted or reminted into new, debased coins. Old coins could then be exchanged for a higher number of debased coins, with the precise quantity determined by the metallic content of the old coins vis-à-vis the new coins. People could therefore exchange their old coins to acquire the new coins, with which they could then carry out transactions. Note, however, that the sovereign would charge a seignorage fee on the creation of the new coins. The revenues so obtained were a gain for the sovereign, a side product of its monopoly over money creation.

gave it a fixed value in terms of both gold and silver, thus officially establishing a *bimetallic standard* in the United States. The dollar was set equal to 24.75 grains of fine gold and 371.25 grains of fine silver, implying that a troy ounce (480 grains) of gold was worth $19.394 and a troy ounce of silver $1.293.[5] Under this system, the U.S. mint stood ready to convert, at a nil seignorage charge, each ounce of gold it was offered into $19.394. Similarly, each ounce of silver would command $1.293 at the mint. This established a mint price of gold in the United States fifteen times that of an equivalent amount of silver. The mint ratio of 15 to 1 was approximately equal to the prevailing ratio of the market values of gold and silver bullion at the time; however, toward the end of the century the market price of silver fell. Furthermore, other countries, such as France in 1803, established a bimetallic standard with a mint ratio of 15.5 to 1. As a result, gold could command more silver abroad than in the United States. One could then gather 15 ounces of silver in the United States, exchange them locally for an ounce of gold, and export the gold so obtained to get $15\frac{1}{2}$ ounces of silver abroad. This operation could yield a net profit of $\frac{1}{2}$ ounce of silver, transaction costs aside, and created an incentive to ship silver into the United States and export gold abroad. Furthermore, Americans effectuating payments abroad found it cheaper to pay in gold (which had a higher relative value abroad), whereas foreigners found it cheaper to pay in silver for their spending in the United States. In effect, gold was undervalued, and silver overvalued, as means of payment in the United States. Under these conditions Gresham's law operated quite efficiently. Gold disappeared from circulation and the United States, while officially on a bimetallic standard, effectively ended up on a monometallic silver standard.

Overvalued silver thus drove gold out of circulation in the United States.

These were the conditions prevailing until 1834, when Congress raised the mint price of gold from $19.394 to $20.67 per ounce, leaving the mint price of silver unchanged, in an attempt to reestablish the bimetallic standard. This altered the U.S. mint ratio up to 16 to 1, but the mint ratios abroad remained at 15.5 to 1. This time, Gresham's law operated in reverse. Gold was now overvalued in the United States and drove silver out of circulation, placing the United States on a de facto monometallic gold standard.

The United States continued to operate on a de jure bimetallic but de facto monometallic standard until 1861. Throughout this period, paper money and bank deposits gradually increased in importance relative to coins in the U.S. money supply. The rigid link of the monetary system to metals, however, remained untainted as the dollar was defined in terms of, and freely convertible into, gold and silver. If, for instance, you were holding $20.67 in currency, the U.S. government would freely convert that amount into an ounce of gold. This convertibility, however, was suspended in 1861 at the start of the Civil War. After the Civil War, there was a return to gold convertibility but not to silver, effectively obstructing an eventual return to a bimetallic standard in the United States. The decision taken in 1879 to resume convertibility of the U.S. dollar into gold, but not silver, was the major single step in establishing a gold standard in the United States. This move was fraught with great quarrels and intrigue and did not go without the strong opposition of vocal silver proponents. Bimetallism represented a price-support scheme for silver, and its replacement by a single gold standard had an obvious negative impact on the powerful silver-mining interests (particularly mine owners) profiting from the scheme. As a result, the issue of bimetallism became a political battleground, partly explaining why, in spite of being de facto on a gold standard, the United States did not legally sanction the system until the Gold Standard Act of 1900.

[5]A troy ounce equals 480 grains, or one-twelfth of a pound. Troy weights are commonly used for gold, silver, and other metals and should not be confused with the usual avoirdupois ounce, which equals 437.5 grains, or one-sixteenth of a pound.

21–2. THE GOLD STANDARD AND ITS RULES

Although Britain operated under a gold standard for most of the nineteenth century, it was not until the 1870s that the gold standard achieved widespread adoption. Most European countries, led by Germany in 1871, moved toward the gold standard during that decade, and the United States followed suit in 1879. By 1880, the gold standard had developed from a domestic standard adopted by a few nations to a full-fledged international monetary system adopted by major countries. For the next thirty years, until its abandonment after the outbreak of World War I in 1914, the international gold standard reigned supreme. It came to incorporate the major trading countries and colonial territories of the time.

The essential features of the operation of a "pure" gold standard can be characterized in terms of three basic rules of the game. First, a country on the gold standard fixes the value of its currency in terms of gold. The government accomplishes this by setting a fixed price for gold in terms of its currency; a government stands ready to buy or sell gold at that price. This establishes a two-way convertibility between domestic currency or coin and gold. In the case of the United States, for instance, the value of a troy ounce of pure gold was set at $20.67, with the U.S. mint ready to buy or sell gold on demand at that price. With various countries operating under a gold standard, the gold values of any two currencies as set by each country's mints implicitly specify their relative value, referred to as *mint parity* or *mint exchange rate*. Consider, for example, the case of the U.S. dollar and the pound sterling. In the United Kingdom, an ounce of pure gold was set at a value of approximately £4.24. Because the value of an equivalent ounce of gold in the United States was $20.67, the implicit relative value of the dollar in terms of the pound was approximately $4.87/£ ($20.67/£4.24). In other words, the mint parity between the U.S. dollar and the pound was $4.87

per pound, which remained so from 1880 to 1914. Observe that the mint parity exchange rate is an implicit, or imputed, rate of exchange (or relative value) between two currencies. The direct market exchange rate between dollars and pounds, however, did not deviate significantly from mint parities. This was guaranteed by the free flow of gold among countries, as we will now see.

The second basic rule of a pure gold standard is that imports and exports of gold be allowed to flow unrestricted among countries. Free trade in gold insured that market exchange rates would not deviate much from the mint exchange rates implied by the gold values of currencies. To illustrate why, let us suppose that the U.S. dollar–pound market exchange rate was equal to $5.00 per pound, which deviates significantly from the mint parity of $4.87 established earlier and determined by a U.S. gold price of $20.67 and a U.K. gold price of £4.24. In this situation, an ounce of gold could be bought in the United States for $20.67, sold in the United Kingdom for £4.24, and then the pounds could be exchanged for U.S. dollars in the free market, which would yield $21.20. (Multiply £4.24 by the market exchange rate of $5.00 per pound.) In other words, a profit of $1.20 could be made by freely buying and selling an ounce of gold across countries. Of course, such a situation would not be sustainable, as the market exchange rate would decline in response to the flood of profit-seeking arbitrageurs willing to sell pounds in exchange for U.S. dollars. Although the presence of transaction costs, particularly in the shipment of gold, prevented mint parities from precisely fixing market exchange rates, the rates were nevertheless confined within narrow limits—the so-called *gold points*—around mint parities.

The third rule of the pure gold standard specifies that the central bank or the monetary authority in charge has to hold gold reserves in a direct relationship to the money notes it issues. These gold reserves allow central banks to engage smoothly in their purchases and sales of gold without running into the embarrassing situation of not being able to fulfill a sudden demand for gold on the part of the public. The gold backing provides for a certain amount of gold behind the currency issued, thereby assuring the convertibility of the currency into gold. In its extreme, this rule could take the form of 100 percent gold backing, in which gold reserves of an amount equal to the domestic currency's worth in gold are held in the monetary authorities' coffers.

The presence of a strict rule connecting gold reserves and money note issues imposes some discipline on monetary expansion in the economy: The central bank can issue domestic currency only by acquiring gold from the public. Consequently, the main source of changes in the domestic money supply is given by changes in the amount of gold available to domestic residents. The amount available can be determined by gold production—the amount supplied by the domestic mining industry, some of which would be sold directly for the private use of citizens and the rest to the government. In addition, when there is a balance-of-payments surplus and domestic residents receive gold for their net sales to foreigners, the domestic money supply would also increase. Note that the role of the central bank under a pure gold standard is limited to purchasing gold acquired by domestic residents and issuing notes in exchange. The pure gold standard thus constrains the discretion of domestic monetary authorities in altering the money supply, and it can be seen as a form of monetary rule.

Credible monetary rules—rules that are followed by those playing the game—can be very significant in controlling inflation; through this mechanism, the pure gold standard has been seen as a system that can promote price stability. How can a monetary rule promote price stability, as compared to discretionary actions by the authorities? The tendency is to think that discretion allows *greater* price stability by permitting the central bank to cut money supply growth when the economy is suffering from inflation (thus acting to ameliorate price increases), and to expand the

money supply under conditions of deflation (counteracting the dropping price level). Such actions would indeed stabilize prices. What this view ignores is that price stability is not the only goal of monetary authorities. Policymakers tend frequently to break their commitment to price stability in order to pursue these other goals. For instance, governments face financial constraints. The need to finance budget deficits may lead them to use inflation as a tax. Recall from our discussion of currency devaluation (see Chapter 20) that devaluation constitutes a tax on domestic residents because it raises domestic prices and decreases real money balances. The inflationary outburst represents, in effect, a confiscation of real money balances from citizens by monetary authorities. Inflation has been used to generate government revenue from time immemorial, and when governments find themselves with budget deficits, they are tempted to abandon the goal of price stability to pursue their financing needs. Because individuals in the economy cannot predict future budget deficits accurately, the possibility that inflation will emerge is always present, even if current government policies are prudent.[6] Another goal that governments pursue, in addition to price stability, is to stimulate the economy. As discussed in Chapter 18, output increases can be generated by unanticipated monetary growth. An unanticipated money supply increase is associated with a temporary economic expansion by inducing unanticipated inflation and lowering real wages. This means that central banks have the incentive to "surprise" domestic residents with unanticipated inflation. Even if authorities declare: "Read my lips: no higher prices," citizens suspect the government will break the promise if it is apparent that the administration needs an economic expansion to gain re-election.

---

[6] A comprehensive survey of the many aspects of inflation is provided by J. Fender, *Inflation: Welfare Costs, Positive Theory and Policy Options* (Ann Arbor: University of Michigan Press, 1990).

Given that governments have incentives to break promises made about price stability, domestic residents can expect inflation to occur to a certain extent, independent of government pronouncements. On the basis of such expectations, they will then embody inflationary expectations into the cost-of-living clauses of nominal wage contracts. This is inflationary itself. It also motivates policymakers to engage in expansionary monetary policy to accommodate the wage growth without negative effects on output. The anticipated inflation is thus self-fulfilling, and the stated government policy of price stability becomes inconsistent over time. This problem of governmental policy statements that lack credibility and are inconsistent with eventual outcomes falls under the terminological aegis of *time consistency*.[7]

It can be concluded that lack of credibility and reputation may cause monetary discretion to be inflationary even in the presence of statements by government authorities that their goal is price stability. On the other hand, under the pure gold standard, so long as the rules of the system are followed, central banks will be limited in their ability to engage in inflationary surprises. Agents in the economy will not form expectations of inflation on this account and the outcome will be greater price stability.[8] It is the discipline imposed on the government by the pure gold standard that has attracted the favor (and candor) of many economists and politicians.[9] At the same time, and

for the same reasons, other economists and politicians also oppose the gold standard. Their argument is that to combat the maladies of unemployment and recession, and the ups and downs of the business cycle, an active monetary policy is required—not one that has its hands tied. In spite of all this controversy, when evaluating the real possibility of the re-establishment of the gold standard—or in assessing the actual experience with that regime—we need to be aware that the way in which international monetary systems actually operate can differ substantially from the image given by rules or dictums that are never followed in practice. This will be a critical point when we evaluate the performance of the gold standard in the next section.

21–3. The Heyday of the Gold Standard (1880–1914)

The gold standard regime between 1880 and 1914 is often presented as a smoothly operating system in which countries abided by the key rules of the game mentioned in the previous section. That this was so to a large extent should not be taken to mean that there were no significant exceptions. First, even though the major European countries

---

[7]Economists Guillermo Calvo, Finn E. Kydland, and Edward C. Prescott formalized the problem of time consistency in economic theory in the late 1970s. The topic has been a continuing source of economic research since. A recent survey of the political aspects of credibility is supplied by T. Persson and G. Tabellini, *Macroeconomic Policy, Credibility and Politics* (Chur, Switzerland: Harwood Academic Publishers, 1990).

[8]The view of the gold standard as a rule is discussed by M. D. Bordo and F. E. Kydland, "The Gold Standard as a Rule," National Bureau of Economic Research Working paper no. 3367 (May 1990).

[9]The return to a gold standard has been a recurrent theme in discussions in both the academic arena and in political circles. See, for instance, D. B. Bostian, "Conduct a Test of a Gold

Standard," *The New York Times,* November 19, 1989; R. N. Cooper, "Gold: Does It Provide a Viable Basis for a Monetary System?" in R. Z. Aliber, ed., *The Reconstruction of International Monetary Arrangements* (New York: St. Martin's, 1987); and L. B. Yeager, *In Search of a Monetary Constitution* (Cambridge, Mass.: Harvard University Press, 1962). In the 1980s, the interest in the gold standard in political circles was reflected in the appointment of a commission by the president of the United States to study the possibility of re-establishing, to some degree, the basic characteristics of a gold standard. The commission's recommendations were in the negative, although it has been alleged that the members appointed to the commission might have been stacked against the idea. The report is available from the U.S. Department of Treasury, *Report of the Gold Commission* (1982). See also, Rep. R. Paul Lehrman and L. Lehrman, *The Case for Gold* (Washington, D.C.: Cato Institute, 1982).

and the United States adopted and remained on the gold standard during the period, a number of other countries either abandoned the system or otherwise avoided adopting the regime altogether. The turbulent monetary history of Argentina, Mexico, and other Latin American countries at the time—involving shifts in and out of the gold standard with accompanying monetary crises, exchange controls, and exchange rate instability—presents a very different picture from the ideal image so often offered of the gold standard regime from 1880 to 1914.

If we take a world perspective, the period was actually characterized by a whole range of international monetary arrangements, all functioning alongside each other. Some countries, for instance, pegged the value of their currencies directly to sterling and held foreign exchange (mostly sterling) reserves to support their parity. Such an arrangement, referred to as a *gold exchange standard,* was based on the convertibility of sterling into gold and the confidence traders had in the use of sterling as an international means of payment. At the time, Great Britain was extremely influential in the world economy (accounting for roughly 10 percent of world income) and had an even greater role in world trade and investment (e.g., British capital was crucial in financing railroads and industrial development in places as far apart as the United States, Argentina, and India). It is not surprising, then, that sterling became a widely diffused means of payment and the main international reserve of central banks in many countries. It was actually possible for Phineas Fogg, Jules Verne's character in *Around the World in Eighty Days,* to pay his expenses with Bank of England notes, which were accepted almost everywhere.

Did countries adhering to the gold standard abide by the rules discussed in the previous section? Consider the fixing of the value of currency in terms of gold. It is impressive that there were no devaluations or revaluations (no changes in mint parities) between the currencies of the United States, United Kingdom, France, and Germany during the entire period. This remarkable feat credits the gold standard as being the closest example of a truly fixed exchange rate regime among major countries.[10] As far as the first rule of the gold standard is concerned, the record for these countries shows it was indeed strictly followed. The second basic rule of a pure gold standard involves the free flow of gold among the participating countries. As far as the period 1880 to 1914 goes, the rule appears to have been followed very closely. Barriers to trade in gold were generally dismantled and exchange or capital controls seldom used. As a matter of fact, a thriving international capital market operated, with its nerve center in London, shifting funds across borders quite actively in search of profits. The commitment of policymakers, particularly British authorities, to sustain gold convertibility at fixed values provided credibility for the system. This is consistent with data suggesting that speculative capital flows were mostly stabilizing.[11]

Contrary to the evidence showing that the first two rules of a pure gold standard were mostly satisfied between 1880 and 1914, the third rule bearing on the connection between gold reserves and the supply of domestic currency does not appear to have been closely followed. Although laws were passed requiring a certain proportion of gold reserves be held to back issues of notes—such as the Bank Act of 1844 in the United States—waivers to the law were frequently drawn. Central banks often tried to offset the effects of

---

[10]Although market exchange rates were not fixed directly by these countries and did fluctuate within a narrow band, the efficient operation of the system, as well as the numerous improvements in information and communications networks (such as the telegraphic cable) and reductions in transport costs, systematically shrank the spread between gold points during the period. The U.S. dollar–sterling market exchange rate, for instance, stayed mostly within the range of $4.84 and $4.90/£.

[11]See B. Eichengreen, "The Gold Standard Since Alec Ford" (Department of Economics, University of California at Berkeley, April 1989), mimeo.

gold flows on the domestic money supply, a venture precisely opposite the purpose of the laws; when necessary, governments would sidestep them in some way. The next section examines the theory of, and evidence for, the connections between gold flows and money supply changes under the gold standard, in addition to relevant macroeconomic issues.

21-4. THE MACROECONOMIC PERFORMANCE OF THE GOLD STANDARD

Proponents of the gold standard argue that, under this regime, the economy has an inherent tendency toward price stability and external balance. First, the requirement that the money created be backed with gold reserves limits the ability of the monetary authorities to print money and puts a brake on the inflationary sprees that undisciplined central banks can impose on the economy. As a result, price stability would be more likely. In addition, it is argued, gold flows among countries imply that the system provides an automatic mechanism through which external payments disequilibria can be eliminated. How does this occur?

One of the most discussed aspects of the gold standard is the so-called *price-specie-flow* mechanism proposed by David Hume as a description of the automatic balance-of-payments adjustment mechanism implicit in the system. Hume's argument rests on the third rule of the pure gold standard in assuming that gold flows are strictly linked to changes in the domestic money supply. Balance-of-payments deficits associated with net gold payments to foreigners would then reduce the domestic money supply and lead to deflation. With domestic prices declining, the increased competitiveness of domestic products in international markets would result in an improvement of the current account balance (CAB) and in an eventual elimination of the balance-of-payments deficit. In other words, the external disequilibrium would be automatically corrected. Similarly, the gold inflows linked to a balance-of-payments surplus would raise the domestic money supply and lead to inflation. The rising prices of domestic goods would then reduce domestic competitiveness in international markets, deteriorating the current account and eliminating the surplus. Again, the external disequilibria would self-correct.

Hume's price-specie-flow mechanism has the problem of associating balance-of-payments adjustment with CAB adjustment. As we have seen many times before, however, the balance of payments is composed of the current account *and* the capital account. As a result, depending on how capital flows behave, the effects of gold flows in adjusting the current account would not necessarily be associated with the elimination of balance-of-payments disequilibria. Subsidiary mechanisms of capital account adjustment are necessary. One alternative is to connect the changes in the money supply implied by gold flows with interest rate changes. A gold outflow connected to a payments deficit would lower the domestic money supply, pressuring domestic interest rates to rise above world levels and inducing incipient capital inflows that offset the initial gold outflows. Similarly, balance-of-payments surpluses linked to gold inflows would raise the money supply and lower domestic interest rates relative to foreign rates. The consequent capital outflows—and the associated shipment of gold abroad—would then offset the initial inflow of gold.

Clearly, there are various mechanisms through which balance-of-payments disequilibria under a pure gold standard could be automatically eliminated. Unfortunately, the crucial link in these mechanisms—the link between gold flows and money supplies—does not appear to have held during the actual practice of the gold standard between 1880 and 1914. Laws requiring the backing of currency creation with gold reserves were often waived or not extended to bank deposits, which reduced their effectiveness in controlling money creation. As a matter of fact, the evidence suggests that monetary authorities frequently and actively attempted to offset the contractionary (or expansionary) effect of a gold outflow (or inflow) on the money supply.[12] One way this occurred was through sterilization operations in which the central bank would decrease its domestic asset holdings in response to acquisitions of gold and increase its domestic assets when gold withdrawals occurred. In general, though, these operations resulted only in a partial offset of the effects of gold flows on the money supply. In addition to sterilization, monetary authorities would frequently use their discount rate—the interest rate charged on loans to private banks or private citizens—to influence domestic credit in the face of the monetary changes associated with gold flows. In conclusion, even though, on paper, a pure gold standard implies monetary discipline, in actual practice such discipline did not completely materialize between 1880 and 1914. Monetary authorities frequently broke the third rule of the gold standard and engaged in active monetary policy.

It remains true, though, that under the gold standard, changes in the supply of gold constituted a major source of variation in the U.S. money supply. The increased domestic production of gold above the level privately demanded was purchased by the monetary authorities and directly increased the money supply. Increased foreign production of gold would also spill over into an increase in the U.S. money supply since some of the increased expenditures of foreigners in response to their rise in wealth would be spent on domestic goods, resulting in an improvement of the balance of pay-

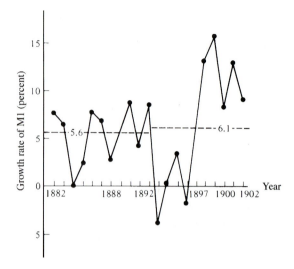

FIGURE 21–1. Money Growth (M1, as currently defined) Under the Gold Standard, 1881–1902.

SOURCE: U.S. Department of Commerce, *Historical Statistics of the World States,* (Washington, D.C.: G.P.O., 1976), pp. 992–993.

ments. In addition, some of the foreign wealth would end up being invested in the United States, again bringing about an inflow of gold.

The connection between the domestic money supply and the vagaries of gold production under the gold standard means money supply changes are subject to a high degree of uncertainty. Figure 21–1 shows the behavior of the U.S. money supply (M1, as currently defined) growth between 1880 and 1902. There is a high variability for money supply growth in those years, much of which can be associated with changes in the supply of gold. For instance, the relatively low— even negative—rates of U.S. money growth in the 1890s have been associated with a slow growth rate for world gold production then. The higher growth rates after 1896 are associated with the discovery of new gold mines in South Africa in

---

[12]See A. Bloomfield, *Monetary Policy Under the International Gold Standard: 1880–1914* (New York: Arno Press, 1978). In the case of Latin American countries, such as Argentina, domestic failure to adhere to the rules of the game was combined with severe external shocks in the form of commodity price fluctuations in generating instability during the gold standard era. See A. Fishlow, "Lessons of the 1890s for the 1980s," in G. Calvo et al., *Debt, Stabilization and Development* (Oxford: Basil Blackwell, 1989); and A. G. Ford, *The Gold Standard, 1880–1914: Britain and Argentina* (Oxford: Clarendon, 1962).

1895 and the development of new processes for working old gold mines.[13]

The variability of U.S. money supply growth shown in Figure 21–1 suggests that U.S. inflation might also have been highly variable. Still, the picture we obtain from many studies of the gold standard is that it was a period of price stability. Indeed, wholesale commodity prices in Britain and the United States in 1914 were actually slightly lower than those in 1880. Does this mean that, in spite of money growth variability, there was price stability during the period? The answer to this question is obtained by looking at Figure 21–2, which shows the behavior of an index of U.S. and U.K. wholesale price levels from 1880 to 1935. What is observed is a year-to-year instability of price changes—consistent with the U.S. money growth variability noted earlier—but the absence of a general trend (whether upward or downward) in prices between 1880 and 1914. What can be concluded is that, on the average, the gold standard period of 1880 to 1914 was one of relatively low, but highly variable, inflation in the United States and the United Kingdom.[14]

Perhaps the strongest case against the popular view on the economic stability of the gold standard period regards the behavior of output growth and employment. On average, the period between 1880 and 1914 was one of respectable growth worldwide. In the United States, for example, the average annual growth rate of the GNP was close to 4 percent. On a per capita basis, though, growth

rates were between 1 and 2 percent. Furthermore, large year-to-year fluctuations were observed. Figure 21–3 shows the striking variability of U.S. unemployment between 1880 and 1914, sinking below 5 percent in the early 1890s and the mid-1900s, yet rising above 15 percent in between, in the late 1890s.

The data we have presented on the macroeconomic performance of the gold standard disprove claims that the system was one of remarkable stability. In certain essential economic variables, substantial variability was indeed observed. Still, when assessing the performance of the gold standard as compared to other international monetary systems, what we must evaluate is whether the gold standard performed "better" or "worse" than these other systems.

This task is a difficult one. First, we must determine which aspects of the economy are more crucial. The gold standard, for example, generally showed low inflation rates, on average, as compared with the Bretton Woods system or the current regime of dirty floating. The high unemployment rates of the late 1890s, however, mean the gold standard performed worse on average than the Bretton Woods system in this respect. How does one go about evaluating the relative merits of these accomplishments or failures? Furthermore, undertaking comparisons of this sort makes the mistake of comparing economies whose structure varies significantly among regimes. It is apparent, for example, that the increased role of the government through regulation of the banking system and through government expenditures in the aftermath of the Great Depression made the wild fluctuations in unemployment to which the gold standard was subject less likely.[15] Fiscal policy, as it is known today, was virtually unknown in most of the period of the gold standard

---

[13]Ibid., p. 21. See also H. Rockoff, "Some Evidence on the Real Price of Gold, Its Costs of Production, and Commodity Prices," in M. Bordo and A. Schwartz, eds., *Retrospective on the Classical Gold Standard, 1821–1931* (Chicago: University of Chicago Press, 1984).

[14]For more details on these and other aspects of the classic gold standard, see A. H. Meltzer and S. Robinson, "Stability Under the Gold Standard in Practice," in M. D. Bordo, *Money, History and International Finance: Essays in Honor of Anna J. Schwartz* (Chicago: University of Chicago Press, 1989); and R. N. Cooper, "The Gold Standard: Historical Facts and Future Prospects," *Brookings Papers on Economic Activity* (1982).

[15]See M. Bordo, "The Classical Gold Standard: Lessons from the Past," in M. B. Connolly, ed., *The International Monetary System: Choices for the Future* (New York: Praeger, 1982).

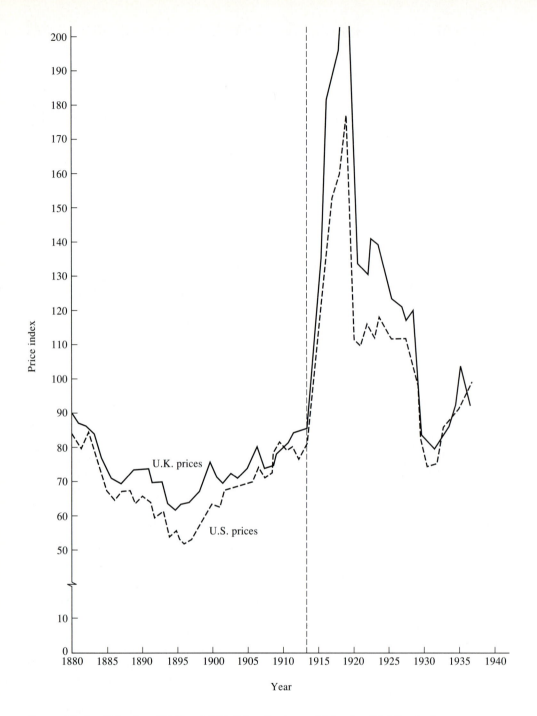

FIGURE 21–2. Behavior of U.S. and U.K. Prices During and After the Gold Standard of 1880–1914 (wholesale price levels)

SOURCE: R. W. Jastram, *The Golden Constant: The English and American Experience* (New York: John Wiley & Sons, Inc., 1977). Reprinted by permission.

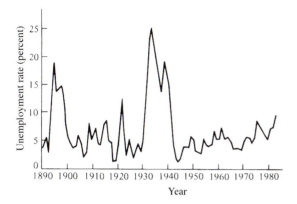

FIGURE 21–3. U.S. Unemployment Rate, 1890–1983

SOURCE: U.S. Department of Commerce, *Historical Statistics of the United States* (Washington, D.C.: GPO, 1978), p. 135; and *Economic Report of the President* (1984.)

(1880–1914). The present fractional reserve banking system was also unknown; even the U.S. Federal Reserve Board was nonexistent for most of the period, being created only in 1913. It is, therefore, not totally appropriate to compare the gold standard with other regimes using such incomparable situations. Furthermore, in political terms, the period from 1880 to 1914 was rather remarkably—and unusually—peaceful, forming part of the so-called Pax Britannica. Comparing the gold standard with other regimes operating in periods of political instability would again involve inappropriate comparisons.

21–5. THE INTERNATIONAL MONETARY SYSTEM DURING THE INTERWAR PERIOD

The outbreak of World War I in 1914 struck a fatal blow to the gold standard, as country after country suspended the convertibility of currency into gold. The system of fixed exchange rates that had operated for almost thirty-five years gave way to floating exchange rates. The United States maintained gold convertibility of the dollar, but because other currencies were no longer convertible into dollars, the U.S. dollar in effect floated in value against them.

The World War I period saw rising inflation rates as governments oriented their monetary policies toward financing war expenditures. The inflation in Europe, however, was higher than that in the United States, partly because of the latter's delayed formal entrance into the war (in 1917) and partly because the war was being physically fought in Europe, with obvious disruptive effects on production. The result was the increased competitiveness of U.S. products abroad and the rapid growth of U.S. international trade. In addition, the convertibility of the dollar into gold, together with the inconvertibility of the European currencies, resulted in a growing attractiveness of dollar-dominated assets as a haven for investment purposes. The dollar became increasingly involved in international transactions. Because gold remained at the heart of the system, the growing demand for dollars resulted in rising gold inflows to the United States and ballooning U.S. gold reserves.

After World War I, the European countries continued to allow their currencies to float in value; most of the currencies depreciated sharply against the dollar. The float was seen, however, only as a temporary situation. The main question pondered at the time was at which value to re-establish the price of gold in terms of each currency—that is, gold parities. The return to a gold standard at prewar gold prices became a subject of much debate. A number of economists, and prominently Gustav Cassell, made use of the idea of purchasing power parity to advocate a return to a price of gold above that prevailing under the prewar (classical) gold standard. They argued that in order to maintain the prewar relationship between gold prices, P_G, and other goods' prices, P, a substantial deflation was necessary. Given that the inflation of the 1910s substantially lowered the price of gold relative to that of other goods' prices (P_G/P declined), an equivalent deflation was necessary to re-establish parity. Otherwise, to spare deflation, the price of gold would have to be reset at a higher level, consistent with the hike in goods market prices.

Contrary to countries that had rapid inflation rates (hyperinflation) in the 1920s—such as Germany and Austria—and eventually set parities of their currencies with gold higher than the prewar levels, the United Kingdom did face some deflation in the early 1920s. When the U.K.'s gold parity was re-established in the mid-1920s, it was set at its 1913 level. This meant that, in spite of most currencies having been devalued vis-à-vis the dollar, the pound sterling–U.S. dollar exchange rate remained what it was before the war, $4.8065/£.

The re-establishment of gold parities in the mid-1920s led to a rebirth of the gold standard. This version of the gold standard (1925–1931), however, was fraught with difficulties; it was, in many ways, dissimilar to the classic gold standard. First, goods market prices in the United Kingdom had not returned to prewar levels by 1925; as a result, the setting of the prewar gold–sterling parity resulted in an overvalued sterling. By contrast, other countries, such as France, had gone too far in devaluating their currency, resulting in undervalued currencies. The established gold parity levels, therefore, did not have the expected stability of those under the classic gold standard. Secondly, the gold standard from 1925 to 1931 moved much closer to becoming a gold-exchange standard. Many central banks no longer maintained the bulk of their international reserves in gold but kept them in currencies convertible to gold, especially sterling and, increasingly, dollars. This shift was partly a result of the continued growth of U.S. international trade and investment and the increased use of the dollar in international transactions. It was also associated with a scarcity of gold production relative to demand.

The return to a gold standard in the 1920s turned out to be short lived. The Great Depression of 1929 brought a collapse of banking systems around the world—bankruptcies, panics, and bank closings proliferated—and a grave crisis of confidence in the ability of countries to maintain the convertibility of their currencies into gold.[16] The burden fell especially heavily on the United Kingdom, which went off gold on September 21, 1931. Fixed exchange rates were finally abandoned as other major countries followed suit (the United States in 1933) in suspending gold convertibility. The world monetary system then disintegrated into currency blocs, such as the sterling bloc, dollar bloc, and a bloc of currencies still based on gold, with floating exchange rates among them. What followed was indeed monetary chaos. Dirty floating, nominally pegged exchange rates accompanied by frequent devaluations to improve competitive positions, collapsing currency blocks, multiple agreements directed to re-establish some order to monetary arrangements that were then broken, and so forth, all coexisted. Furthermore, exchange controls, tariffs, and other trade restrictions proliferated. The result was a collapse of international trade and finance that left a deep impression on subsequent generations and established the prevention of such a situation as a main objective of the international monetary system.

---

[16]Shocks to countries in a gold exchange standard system, such as a global recession, have the propensity to generate crises of confidence on the future value of national currencies. These can lead (following Gresham's law) to a shift out of foreign exchange reserves and into gold. The resulting reduction in worldwide reserves reinforces the global recession. This is compounded by the gold exchange standard being very effective in transmitting income contractions from one country to another. Under such a system, an output reduction in one country can be rapidly transmitted to other countries through capital flows that affect money supplies. (See the discussion of the international transmission mechanism under fixed exchange rates in Chapter 14.) For a discussion of the evidence on the links between the gold standard and the Great Depression, see M. D. Bordo, "The Contribution of 'A Monetary History of the United States' to Monetary History," in Bordo, *Money, History and International Finance*, op. cit., pp. 55–56; and B. Eichengreen, *Golden Fetters: The Gold Standard and the Great Depression 1919–1939* (Oxford: Oxford University Press, 1992).

21–6. THE BRETTON WOODS SYSTEM (1946–1971)

World War II was still raging in 1941 when the United States and the United Kingdom began a series of bilateral conversations and negotiations that laid the basis for the postwar international monetary order. Alternative plans for re-establishing a workable monetary system were presented and discussed, and differences were gradually settled. The negotiation process culminated in an international monetary conference held in July 1944 at the resort town of Bretton Woods, New Hampshire. This conference, which gathered representatives from forty-four countries, turned out to be a major international economic event. It created the International Monetary Fund (IMF), the chief organization in charge of overseeing and monitoring the operation of a new monetary order. The conference drafted the Articles of Agreement for the IMF, which specified the basic structure and rules of the game of the new regime. The international monetary system so created came to be known as the Bretton Woods system. It was to maintain its basic structure until 1971, for almost a quarter of a century after the IMF was organized in 1947.

The IMF's Articles of Agreement stipulated that each participating country would set a fixed value—called *par value*—for its currency in terms of gold (or the U.S. dollar). The *par values* of two currencies determined the official exchange rate (also called parity) between them. Exchange rate fluctuations were to be limited to a narrow band around the official exchange rate. In other words, participating countries had to adopt a pegged exchange rate regime. However, the Bretton Woods system was not conceived in terms of fixed, immutable exchange rates in the manner in which the gold standard had operated among major countries from 1880 to 1914. Instead, it was an adjustable peg system, allowing alterations in official exchange rates—subject to the approval of the IMF—to correct a *fundamental disequilibrium*

in the balance of payments. Although the term *fundamental disequilibrium* was never formally defined by the IMF, what was meant in practice was that countries facing chronic payments deficits (or surpluses) and heavy reserve losses (or gains) could alter their exchange rates. The purpose of establishing an adjustable peg system was to attain a balance between the objective of stable exchange rates and the concerns of participating countries with domestic macroeconomic goals. For instance, the expedient of devaluation was left open to correct chronic payments deficits. This option, it was hoped, would smooth out the high cost of adjustment toward payments equilibrium in the form of unemployment and recession. The availability of devaluation as a policy tool also had the benefit of reducing the likelihood that exchange controls and other restrictions on trade would be imposed to suppress a payments imbalance, deemed an important objective in light of the experience of the 1930s. Supervision and scrutiny over desired exchange rate changes, on the other hand, tried to prevent competitive devaluations; by means of competitive devaluations, some countries can attempt to obtain an advantage in international markets at the expense of others.

The key role of gold in the Bretton Woods system was connected to the convertibility of the U.S. dollar into gold at a fixed price. This meant that the United States stood ready to sell gold to foreign central banks, but not to private citizens, in exchange for U.S. dollars at a fixed price of $35 per ounce. Aside from the United States, however, countries were not committed to exchanging their money into gold (i.e., their currencies were not convertible into gold). The Bretton Woods system operated on the basis of a *gold exchange standard.* Under a gold exchange standard, countries are expected to redeem their currencies into gold-convertible currencies (but not necessarily into gold directly), and central bank reserves are held in convertible currencies (but not necessarily in the form of gold itself). Under Bretton Woods, most central banks kept a large part of their international reserves in the form of dollar-denominated assets, such as dollar deposits or U.S. Treasury bills. The dollar became the system's main reserve currency, a role it had been chipping away from the pound sterling ever since World War I.

Exchange rates were maintained within the narrow limits allowed by the IMF by means of central bank intervention in foreign exchange markets. The U.S. dollar played a predominant role here because it was used as an intervention currency by foreign central banks. For instance, when a depreciating French franc reached the limit allowed by the IMF, the Bank of France would buy francs and sell dollars in exchange to support the value of the franc. Conversely, when the franc appreciated relative to the dollar, the Bank of France would sell francs and buy dollars in the foreign exchange markets, supporting the value of the dollar in the process. In effect, France was in charge of determining the French franc–U.S. dollar exchange rate. The same pattern applied to other foreign countries. The United States, therefore, could not devalue or revalue the dollar vis-à-vis other currencies by itself—that is, the United States was spared the need to intervene in foreign exchange markets in order to keep its exchange rate fixed. Other countries fulfilled that function.

In a nutshell, the Bretton Woods system was an adjustable peg regime operating under a gold exchange standard in which most currencies were convertible into the U.S. dollar and the dollar, in turn, was convertible into gold.

21–7. THE ECONOMIC EXPERIENCE UNDER BRETTON WOODS

The aftermath of World War II left the European countries and Japan with both a shortage of international reserves and the need to finance large trade deficits to reconstruct their war-ravaged economies. In 1948, the United States offered the European Recovery Program (ERP)—usually called the Marshall Plan, in honor of George C. Marshall, then U.S. secretary of state—to aid in financing infrastructure, food, basic needs, and the large net exports that the United States incurred abroad (U.S. trade surpluses climbed to 4 percent of GNP in the late 1940s).

The generally low levels of international reserves held by the major foreign industrial countries after the war and their large trade deficits with the United States became associated with a massive dollar shortage abroad and with acute balance-of-payments difficulties for those countries in the late 1940s and 1950s. As a result, most European countries maintained a range of capital controls throughout the 1950s. It was not until 1958 that their currencies really became fully convertible to the dollar.[17] Hence, the Bretton Woods system became fully operational—in the sense that major countries featured full convertibility of their currencies into others, particularly into U.S. dollars—only in the late 1950s.

In the 1950s, the United States began to show substantial deficits on an official reserve settlements basis, a pattern that persisted and deteriorated during the next decade. For most of the 1950s, U.S. deficits were not generally regarded as a problem because foreign central banks desired to accumulate dollar reserves. In the 1960s, however, the previous decade's dollar shortage turned into a dollar glut. Between 1950 and 1970, foreign hold-

---

[17]The term *convertibility* is used in two different contexts: convertibility into gold and convertibility into other currencies. Only the United States maintained gold convertibility during Bretton Woods. Convertibility into other currencies essentially means that foreign currencies can be freely obtained from central banks on demand, at the established exchange rate parities. Convertibility into other currencies for current account transaction purposes was a main goal of Bretton Woods and was reached, to a large extent, early on in the system; however, the agreements of the IMF allowed more flexibility with regard to the imposition of exchange controls on capital account transactions. This flexibility was partly a result of a prevailing feeling that short-run speculative capital flows could be potentially destabilizing and governments should therefore have the freedom to restrict them.

ings of dollars rose by $39 billion. The increasing supply of dollars abroad was accompanied by a rapidly shrinking stock of U.S. gold reserves. The gold holdings of the U.S. Treasury declined by $8 billion between 1949 and 1960, a loss whose rate picked up even more in the mid- and late 1960s.

The growth of gold-convertible dollars abroad combined with the depletion of U.S. gold reserves gradually eroded confidence in the ability of the United States to sustain sales of gold for dollars. In the face of growing purchases of gold on the part of foreign central banks and private citizens, the gold convertibility of the U.S. dollar was threatened. Various solutions were proposed, and some actually implemented, to solve this problem. One of them involved restricting the private demand for gold. In general, the post–World War II period saw the rising private demand for gold combined with sagging production. If the price of gold had been set in a free market, such events would have led to a rise in the price of gold. With the United States fixing the price of gold at $35, however, the increased demand for gold by the private sector was filled by sales of gold by central banks and, in particular, the U.S. Treasury. In order to prevent the continuation of this situation, the U.S. government barred U.S. citizens from buying gold, whether from the U.S. Treasury or from foreign central banks. Unfortunately, the same regulations were not adopted by foreign central banks, which continued to sell gold to their citizens. The impact of the policy on gold outflows was thus minimal.

An alternative approach would have been to induce an increase in the quantity of gold supplied. To do that, however, a higher price of gold relative to the general price level would have been required. With the price of gold fixed at $35, only a deflation—à la gold standard—would have been able to manage a rise in the relative price of gold. Another dead end was reached.

Another experiment was tried in 1968: The so-called *two-tier gold market*. The two-tier gold market consisted of a segmentation of the private and the central bank markets for gold. The private

market, where the purchases of private citizens and most of the sales of newly mined gold were to be settled, was left free to clear through a flexible price. The central bank market for gold, where foreign central banks would buy and sell gold from the U.S. Treasury, was to remain transacting at the official $35 price per ounce of gold. The result was that the dollar remained convertible into gold for foreign central banks at $35 per ounce, but the private market price rose above that level. Again, the experiment did not stop the outflow of gold from the U.S. Treasury's coffers.

The difficulties faced in controlling the gold shortage and the questions raised by the dollar glut regarding the role of the dollar as an international reserve asset crystallized a movement on the part of some European countries—with France at the helm—to create an alternative international reserve asset that could serve the functions of the dollar and be as good as gold in international transactions among central banks. As early as 1964, France had publicly supported the idea of the creation of a so-called Composite Reserve Unit, which would be made up of major currencies and be issued by the IMF. The original French proposal called for the Composite Reserve Unit to replace the U.S. dollar and sterling as international reserve assets, which was clearly unacceptable to the United States and the United Kingdom. As a result, the proposal was substantially modified before the IMF accepted to create *special drawing rights* (SDRs). When it was created in 1967, an SDR was worth one U.S. dollar and one thirty-fifth of an ounce of gold. Later on, in the 1970s, the IMF reverted to the original French proposal and assigned a value to the SDR in terms of the currencies of major member countries. The value of SDRs created initially in 1970 was worth $3.1 billion. These were distributed among the central banks of member countries, which could use them in their transactions with other central banks. (SDRs, therefore, did not circulate among the public.) Unfortunately, the possible role of SDRs under Bretton Woods could not be determined: the system collapsed under its feet before SDRs were created to any significant extent.

Even though, in 1968 and 1969, the U.S. Official Reserve Settlements (ORS) balance had been in surplus, the situation brusquely reversed between 1970 and 1971. The ORS went into deep deficits then, including an unheard-of $30 billion in 1971. The Bretton Woods system literally collapsed in 1971. With rampant expectations that an increase in the dollar price of gold was imminent and that a major devaluation of the dollar vis-à-vis most other major currencies was soon forthcoming, the resulting speculative run on the dollar became unsustainable. In May 1971, in the face of massive short-term capital inflows associated with speculation against the dollar, Germany decided to let its currency float vis-à-vis the dollar. The Netherlands followed suit, and Switzerland and Austria also both revalued their currencies. Still, the speculative run on the dollar was not abated. On August 15, 1971, President Richard Nixon went on television to announce the closing of the *gold window*—that is, the end of the U.S. Treasury's sales and purchases of gold, in addition to a package of policies referred to as the New Economic Policy. In response, the major European countries and Japan decided to let their currencies float in terms of the dollar. The dollar "took it on the chin" through declining values vis-à-vis other currencies.

In the months following the closing of the gold window in August 1971, a substantial amount of discussion and negotiation took place about how exchange rates were to be realigned and about what the role changes in the official price of gold would play. In December, the so-called *Smithsonian Agreement* established a currency realignment with the official dollar price of gold rising to $38 and the exchange rate of the dollar vis-à-vis foreign currencies pegged at a higher level in terms of the major European currencies and the yen. Gold convertibility, however, was not re-established. The Smithsonian Agreement did not last long. Renewed speculation and capital movements forced foreign central banks to abandon any intent to fix exchange rates. Early in 1973, the major European currencies and the Japanese yen started floating vis-à-vis the dollar. They have been bumbling ever after.

The Bretton Woods system operated well while it lasted. It supported a flourishing regime of international trade and finance, with stable and relatively high growth rates, by historical standards, and with relatively low unemployment and inflation rates. Given this record, and taking into account that the period from 1971 to 1973 was not directly connected to any major war involving the European industrial countries, the collapse of the Bretton Woods system appears paradoxical. Nevertheless, its history shows a number of basic problems.

21–8. THE BRETTON WOODS SYSTEM: WHY DID IT FAIL?

Under Bretton Woods, the United States effectively acquired two essential roles in the international monetary system. The first was to keep the U.S. dollar convertible to gold at a fixed price and to maintain confidence in its ability to do so. This required the United States to hold gold reserves in a high enough proportion to confidently back its convertibility commitment. The second role was to provide adequate supplies of what became the main international reserve asset of the system: the dollar. The United States, as a reserve currency country, was supposed to supply international *liquidity* at an adequate rate.[18] As it turns out, in its second role, as supplier of liquidity to the world

---

[18]The role of the United States in supplying international liquidity was linked to its role as a world banker, accepting liquid dollar-denominated deposits from foreign central banks and lending to foreign countries in the form of long-term investments abroad. See C. P. Kindleberger, "Balance of Payments Deficits and the International Market for Liquidity," in his *Europe and the Dollar* (Cambridge, Mass.: The M.I.T. Press, 1965).

economy—and to foreign central banks in particular—the United States was in conflict with its role of maintaining confidence in the gold convertibility of the dollar at a fixed price of $35 per ounce. The need to incur higher and higher liabilities to foreign central banks would gradually reduce U.S. gold reserves as a proportion of total liabilities to foreign central banks. This eventually undermined confidence in the ability of the United States to convert dollars into gold on demand: The United States could not fulfill its role in sustaining confidence in the dollar as an international reserve asset. Of course, policy measures could be taken to avoid U.S. external payments deficits and maintain the ratio of U.S. gold reserves to foreign official liabilities at safe levels. In this event, the confidence problem would be solved but not the liquidity problem.

In short, the Bretton Woods system faced a dilemma, the so-called *Triffin Dilemma,* between the role of the United States in solving the world liquidity problem by incurring liabilities to foreigners and its role in maintaining the confidence in the dollar.[19] A major crisis was then bound to arise at some point, whose timing was dependent on historical circumstances. At that juncture, the confidence crisis would not only give rise to destabilizing speculation, but would also undermine the U.S.'s role as a supplier of liquidity. As soon as central banks lost their confidence in the dollar, they would begin to exchange their dollar assets for gold. For them, this would just represent a shift in the composition of international reserves, reducing dollar assets and increasing gold holdings. World international reserves would shrink, however, because U.S. international reserves are in

the form of gold holdings and these would decline. The confidence problem would then be compounded by a liquidity problem because world international reserves contract in the face of dollar conversions into gold.

The Triffin dilemma is depicted in Figure 21–4. As shown, the ratio of U.S. gold reserves to U.S. liabilities to foreign officials declined rapidly in the late 1950s and 1960s, undermining confidence in the dollar's gold convertibility. This inherent conflict between the role of the United States as a supplier of liquidity and its role in maintaining gold convertibility was heightened by the massive explosion of international liquidity provided by the United States in 1970 and 1971. The dollar glut in these years was associated with huge U.S. balance-of-payments deficits and resulted in a drastic increase of world inflation. This episode, a prelude to the breakdown of Bretton Woods, serves to illustrate some of the other problems of this fixed exchange rate regime.

Given that, by any standards, the liquidity explosion of 1970 and 1971 was excessive, on whom—and by what means—does the burden of correcting the U.S. balance-of-payments deficits fall? As far as the United States was concerned at the time, the policy was one of benign neglect—that is, of ignoring the effects of external imbalance in the hope that the balance-of-payments deficits would be accepted in the form of increased dollar holdings by foreign central banks. This meant that the United States could worry about its internal economic policy matters without any external balance objectives in mind. As a matter of fact, the growth of defense spending in the United States as a result of the Vietnam War was connected to the balance-of-payments deficits of 1970 and 1971. The growing budget deficits were associated with rising U.S. inflation, which jumped from 1.9 percent in 1965 to 4.7 percent by 1968. The United States was suffering increased competition in world trade—particularly at the hands of West Germany and Japan. This deteriorating competitiveness in response to the rising relative U.S.

---

[19]In honor of Robert Triffin, who spelled it out in the late 1950s. See his *Europe and the Money Muddle: From Bilateralism to Near-Convertibility, 1947–56,* and *Gold and the Dollar Crisis: The Future of Convertibility* (New Haven, Conn.: Yale University Press, 1957 and 1960, respectively). See also M. Bordo and B. Eichengreen, eds., *A Retrospective on the Bretton Woods System: Lessons for International Monetary Reform* (Chicago: University of Chicago Press, 1993).

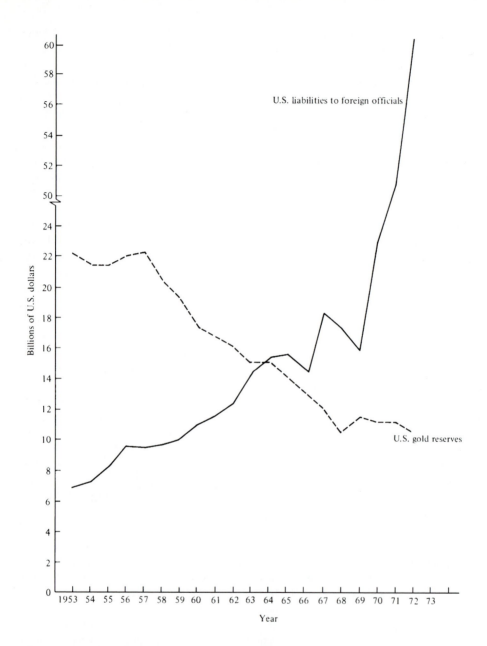

Figure 21–4. The Triffin Dilemma: Growing Dollar World Liquidity and Dwindling U.S. Gold Reserves.

source: International Monetary Fund, *International Financial Statistics* (December 1972).

inflation rate resulted in a drastic worsening of the CAB, giving impetus to the payments deficits of 1971 and 1972.

From the U.S. viewpoint, the problem of adjustment to an "excessive" U.S. balance-of-payments deficit lay in the hands of foreign countries. It was indeed true that adequate policies on the part of foreign governments and/or the automatic adjustment mechanisms inherent in a fixed exchange rate regime would have moved foreign economies toward readjustment. The West German external payments surpluses, for example, would have increased Germany's money supply—under laissez-faire—and consequently its inflation rate. The resulting worsening of West Germany's competitiveness in international markets would then have reduced the U.S. current account deterioration vis-à-vis Germany. A West German policy of increased credit growth would have accelerated this process. The key assumption made, however, was that West German authorities would have tolerated the Bundesbank support of inflationary policies, just for the sake of sustaining external balance. As the years passed after the beginning of the Bretton Woods system, the European countries and Japan became increasingly reluctant to accept the asymmetry of bearing the burden of adjustment regarding external payments disequilibria vis-à-vis the United States. It was felt that the reserve currency country—the United States—had as much responsibility in controlling is external payments situation as nonreserve currency countries.

As early as 1965, Charles de Gaulle protested and challenged U.S. hegemony by refusing to accept $2 billion in reserves and exchanging them for gold while clamoring for a return to a pure gold standard.[20] The gold standard provides a good basis for comparison with the Bretton Woods system of the late 1960s. Under a pure gold standard, a country like the United States, with growing inflation, current account deficits, and losses of international reserves (gold), would have been forced to reduce its money supply in proportion to the losses of gold. The resulting U.S. deflation would have then increased U.S. competitiveness abroad, reduced net imports, and therefore improved the CAB. In addition, the inflow of gold into the surplus countries would have resulted in an increase in their inflation rates and in the further adjustment of their economies and external payments surpluses. In this situation, adjustment would have been more symmetric than that under Bretton Woods.[21] It must be realized, though, that the link between world liquidity and gold production established by a pure gold standard cuts both ways. It also implies that world liquidity is costly to acquire because it takes resources (e.g., labor and machinery) to mine gold out of the ground. On the other hand, the creation of dollars, or any other paper money, is virtually costless. In addition, world liquidity under a gold standard would be

---

[20]The case of France against the accumulation of dollar reserves at the time also involved the view that the United States was extracting a seignorage gain from its creation of international liquidity at the expense of the nonreserve currency countries. Because, in order to acquire dollar-denominated reserves, foreign countries had to release real resources—such as those involved in net exports to the United States—the idea was that the United States was benefiting from its almost costless creation of international money. Nevertheless, a large share of the international reserves acquired by foreign countries were invested in interest-yielding dollar-denominated assets or were exchanged for gold. As a result, even though a seignorage gain was most likely being earned, its absolute magnitude and importance are not easily discernable. See H. G. Grubel, "The Distribution of Seignorage from International Liquidity Creation," in R. A. Mundell and A. K. Swoboda, eds., *Monetary Problems of the International Economy* (Chicago: University of Chicago Press, 1969).

[21]For a discussion of the impact of establishing a gold reserves–money supply rule within a Bretton Woods regime in order to discipline (anchor) both reserve and nonreserve currency countries in their national and international money creation, see R. A. Mundell, "The Case for a Managed International Gold Standard," in M. B. Connolly, ed., *The International Monetary System: Choices for the Future* (New York: Praeger, 1982). For a general examination of the issue of asymmetry in external payments adjustment under Bretton Woods and other fixed exchange rate regimes, see A. Giovannini, "How Do Fixed Exchange Rate Regimes Work? Evidence from the Gold Standard, Bretton Woods and the EMS," in M. Miller, B. Eichengreen, and R. Portes, eds., *Blueprints for Exchange Rate Management* (London: Academic Press, 1989).

subject to the vagaries of gold discoveries, which may or may not be superior to the vagaries of U.S. balance-of-payments deficits.

In summary, the absence of external payments adjustment steps on the part of the United States meant that nonreserve currency countries had the burden of adjustment under Bretton Woods. Whether through internal adjustment involving monetary, price, output, and/or interest rate changes, or through external adjustments involving devaluations or revaluations of their currencies, European countries and Japan had to subjugate their policy attention toward external balance. Even though in the environment of the immediate post-World War II period such a scheme of things was tolerable, it could not be sustained permanently. When the supply of dollars in 1970 and 1971 exploded, straining to its limits the internal goals of price stability in nonreserve currency countries, the latter reacted by converting dollars into gold, sterilizing increases in reserves and, finally, by letting their currencies float vis-à-vis the dollar. The inconsistency of the explosion in international liquidity with the national policy autonomy and goals of nonreserve currency countries finally pushed the Bretton Woods system into collapse. Chapter 22 deals with the international monetary arrangements that gradually emerged after March 1973 and are currently operating in the world economy.

Summary

1. Since antiquity, countries generally have operated on a specie commodity standard, in which metals—predominantly gold and silver—compose the bulk of the circulating media of the economy.

2. In their purest form, specie commodity standards operated on the basis of full-bodied coins, whose monetary value equaled the value of the metals they contained. Sovereigns could reduce the metallic (say, gold) content of the coins they minted, a practice called debasement.

3. In a monetary system based on commodity monies, the simultaneous circulation of full-bodied and debased coins of the same denomination would lead to the operation of Gresham's law, which states that overvalued money drives undervalued money out of circulation.

4. By 1880, the gold standard had developed into a full-fledged international monetary system, having been adopted by a range of major countries. The essential features of the operation of a pure gold standard can be characterized in terms of three basic rules: (1) A country on the gold standard fixes the value of its currency in terms of gold; the gold values of any two countries' currencies then specify their relative value, referred to as mint parity or mint exchange rate; (2) under the pure gold standard, imports and exports of gold among countries are freely allowed; and (3) central banks or appropriate monetary authorities have to hold gold reserves in relation to paper money in order to assure the gold convertibility of paper money and fulfill the public's demand for gold; the amount of gold reserves then controls the economy's amount of money growth. Even though the first two rules of a pure gold standard were satisfied to a large extent in the heyday of the gold standard (1880–1914), the third rule does not appear to have been closely followed.

5. The outbreak of World War I in 1914 struck a fatal blow to the gold standard. Attempts to re-establish it in the interwar period were unsuccessful.

6. The Bretton Woods system was organized in 1947 with the creation of the International Monetary Fund, which was to oversee and monitor the operations of the new international monetary system. The IMF's agreements stipulated that member countries would set a fixed value for their currency in terms of gold (or U.S. dollars). The par value of two currencies then determined the official exchange rate, or parity. Exchange rate fluctua-

tions were to be limited to a narrow band around the official exchange rate.

7. Under Bretton Woods, the United States was the reserve currency country, providing world liquidity through a supply of dollars and guaranteeing the convertibility of dollars into gold. A major reason for the collapse of Bretton Woods was the so-called Triffin dilemma: The role of the United States in solving world liquidity problems required it to incur liabilities to foreigners, but its role in maintaining the confidence in the convertibility of the dollar into gold was undermined as a result of the expansion of dollar liabilities.

8. The Bretton Woods system was an adjustable peg regime, allowing exchange rate changes to correct fundamental disequilibria in the balance of payments, subject to IMF approval. The absence of external payments adjustment constraints on the part of the United States—the reserve currency country—meant that nonreserve currency countries had the burden of adjustment under Bretton Woods. Whether through internal adjustments involving monetary, price, output, and interest rate changes, or through devaluations or revaluations of their currencies, European countries and Japan had to subjugate their policy attention toward external balance.

9. The massive U.S. balance-of-payments deficits of 1970 and 1971 strained to the limit the ability of European countries and Japan to absorb the increased dollar supply without compromising domestic goals of price stability. As a result, in 1971, these countries finally allowed their currencies to fluctuate vis-à-vis the dollar. Later attempts to realign fixed exchange rates failed, and in March 1973 all serious efforts to sustain fixed exchange rates among the industrial countries ended.

Problems

1. Suppose that you were living in London in the 1540s. What effects would you most likely observe on prices, real income, and trade in response to a coin debasement? Assuming that you adopt a monetary approach to the debasement, what would you emphasize as being the effects of the disturbance?

2. Based on the considerations noted in the text, would you make any particular adjustments or qualifications in the official reserve settlements balance to measure fundamental disequilibria in the "balance of payments" of a reserve currency country? If you have any suggestions, how would they alter the popular view that the United States was in fundamental balance-of-payments disequilibrium in the late 1960s?

3. Evaluate the following statement: "SDRs would have never been widely utilized as an international means of transaction among central banks during Bretton Woods because of Gresham's law."

4. Evaluate or comment on the statement: "The collapse of Bretton Woods was a reflection of the decline in the economic and political power of the United States over West European countries and Japan obtained during World War II but no longer sustainable."

5. At a conference on international monetary economics, an economist assails the monetary approach to the balance of payments as adding nothing new to the adjustment process operating through Hume's price-specie-flow mechanism. Is this correct? Explain your answer.

6. According to Carnegie Mellon University economist Allan H. Meltzer: "By far the major flaw of U.S. policy, and the most damaging feature of the Bretton Woods system, was the failure to prevent U.S. inflation" (From A. H. Meltzer, "U.S. Policy in the Bretton Woods Era," *Review of the Federal Reserve Bank of St. Louis* [May-June 1991], p. 82). Do you agree with this statement? Explain why or why not.

7. This exercise compares the equilibrium inflation rate in an international monetary system that allows discretion to monetary authorities

versus a system—like the pure gold standard—that does not permit any discretion. Suppose that domestic monetary authorities value output positively and inflation negatively. Under this assumption, we can postulate that the economy's policymakers have the following utility function:

$$U = Y - \alpha\pi^2, \qquad (1)$$

where U denotes utility, Y is domestic production, π is domestic inflation, and α is a positive parameter. Equation 1 implies that higher income (larger values of Y) and lower inflation (smaller values of π) raise the policymakers' utility. The parameter α is a measure of how much the authorities dislike inflation. The larger the value of α, the stronger the dislike for inflation.

Suppose now that the economy's aggregate supply curve is represented by

$$Y = Y_F + \beta(\pi - \pi^e), \qquad (2)$$

where $\pi = (P - P_{-1})/P_{-1}$ is the actual rate of inflation and $\pi^e = (P^e - P_{-1})/P_{-1}$ is the expected inflation rate, with P^e denoting the anticipated price level by agents in the economy. Equation 2 is a variant of the expectations-augmented aggregate supply curve shown by Equation 18–1. It suggests that unanticipated inflation has positive effects on output.

(1) Suppose that the monetary authorities have the discretion to choose the money supply (and thus domestic inflation) to maximize their utility. Assuming that there are no other disturbances to the economy, what would be the equilibrium inflation in this case? (*Hint:* substitute Equation 2 into Equation 1 and maximize the resulting utility with respect to inflation.)

(2) Assume that monetary authorities do not really have control over the money supply. What would be the equilibrium inflation? How does this compare with the inflation in the preceding question?

8. In a *Newsweek* article (September 30, 1991, p. 32), Robert J. Samuelson states: "Paradoxically, the gold standard's virtues and vices were intertwined. Its rigidity fostered the Great Depression while also checking inflation." Explain the rationale behind this statement.

9. Using an aggregate demand–aggregate supply framework, economists Tamim Bayoumi and Barry Eichengreen have examined whether exchange rate regimes aid in stabilizing output in response to sudden economic policy shifts. In this respect, Professor Eichengreen concludes of the Bretton Woods period: "Agents perceived that countries could not pursue consistently inflationary policies given their commitment to the maintenance of Bretton Woods. Hence, one-time policy initiatives affecting the price level were more likely to stabalize output and employment and less likely to be neutralized by offsetting changes in wages and costs" [(from: "Epilogue," in M. Bordo and B. Eichengreen, *A Retrospective on the Bretton Woods System* (Chicago: University of Chicago Press, 1993), p. 634]. Using the framework developed in chapters 16 to 18, explain the economic mechanisms behind Eichengreen's point.

CHAPTER 22

Interdependence, Monetary Regimes, and the Current State of the World Economy

639

In July 1991, the Bank of Japan reduced its discount rate, the rate it charges on its loans to financial institutions. This lowering of Japanese interest rates followed two years of rate increases in that country and sharp pressures by other industrial countries for Japan to follow a looser monetary policy and to lower interest rates. The move was viewed by many as a step in stimulating the world economy out of the 1990–1991 recession. This recession had hit the American economy hard. The economy had suffered a rise in unemployment from 5.2 percent in January 1990 to 6.8 percent in June 1991. To compound matters, the recession was coupled with a revival of inflationary pressures (the U.S. inflation rate in 1990 was 6.1 percent, the highest since 1981), generating fears of stagflation. Other industrialized countries were also suffering from economic stress. Germany, for instance, faced rising inflation and unemployment partly associated with the 1990 reunification of the former East and West German economies. These conditions, combined with the continuing growth of the Japanese economy in the midst of global recession, made Japan the country of last recourse in efforts to find a way out of stagnation.

The host of pressures and international discussions associated with the Japanese move has become a trademark of the post-1985 global economy. There is growing recognition everywhere of the high degree of worldwide economic interdependence. Governments are now increasingly coordinating economic policymaking and even forming economic blocks to pursue joint policies. The member countries of the European Monetary System, for instance, are continuously engaged in joint policymaking through a variety of means. Consultation and the coordination of policies among industrial countries have become a feature of international macroeconomics.

The changed environment poses a number of questions and problems. How are national economic policies determined in an interdependent world economic environment? Is the brand of international pressure and ad hoc coordination we

witnessed recently useful, or might it be counterproductive in terms of greater macroeconomic stability and growth? How successful has been the macroeconomic experience of the EMS? Should we attribute the results, whatever they are, to the EMS or to other factors?

This chapter analyzes the economics of coordination and strategic decision making in an interdependent world, as well as the state and prospects of present international monetary arrangements. We begin by reviewing the historical evolution of the post-Bretton Woods international arrangements, focusing on macroeconomic interaction and coordination. We then examine the economic theory of the international coordination of policies. We distinguish between the ad hoc, loose coordination of the major industrial countries and the interaction through rules and institutional arrangements that characterizes the EMS. Finally, we analyze current monetary arrangements and procedures such as the economics of target zones and the crawling peg system adopted by many developing countries.

22–1. FROM RAMBOUILLET TO THE LOUVRE: COOPERATION AMONG INDUSTRIAL COUNTRIES

Following the demise of the Bretton Woods system in 1973, a series of policy discussions took place among the countries forming part of the Organization for Economic Co-operation and Development (OECD).[1] The current regime of formal international consultation and coordination developed as a by-product of those discussions.

The mechanism of periodic "summits" that have regularly gathered the economic policy au-

---

[1] The OECD was set up in 1960. It represented a membership expansion of the all-European Organization for European Economic Co-operation, established in 1948 to promote growth and trade in Europe on the eve of the post-World War II reconstruction.

thorities of major countries was born with the summit held at Rambouillet, outside Paris, in 1975. The Rambouillet summit formally established the current floating exchange rate regime and allowed exchange market intervention to keep orderly markets. Coordination of macroeconomic policies became an issue at the 1977 London summit, when Japan agreed to undertake expansionary fiscal measures whose goal was to stimulate world economic recovery out of the recession associated with the 1974 oil-price shock. At the 1978 Bonn summit, Germany agreed to increase government spending. The United States, in turn, promised to introduce inflation-reducing measures and gave in to mounting external pressures to decontrol oil prices. This last measure was to reduce U.S. oil imports and move U.S. prices toward those prevailing internationally. The coordinated policy package was intended to stop the dollar depreciation of 1978 and to restrain the then expansionary U.S. monetary and fiscal policies that had led to a strong American recovery but to rising inflation, as well. Germany's expansionary stance was supposed to compensate for the restrictive measures by the United States. In the language of the time, the German economy would be the locomotive that would lead the economic recovery.

The coordinated exercises of the 1977–1978 summits paved the way for further consultation and periodic policy review by the major industrial countries. Coordinated policymaking did not come into its own until 1985, however. From 1975 to 1985, a largely uncoordinated managed floating regime prevailed. To a large extent, countries formulated their macroeconomic policies and foreign exchange market intervention operations independently of each other. For this reason, we can characterize that period as dominated by a noncooperative macroeconomic policy formulation. For instance, the Reagan administration followed high-deficit, low-tax, high government expenditure policies, coupled with restrictive but unstable monetary policies. This package differed from those of its major industrial partners and was

accompanied by a five-year dollar appreciation. The United States called for other countries to assume the burden of adjustment to the dollar appreciation. Its trading partners refused, calling instead for a shift in U.S. policies. An agreement was not reached until 1985.

In September 1985, a meeting of the finance ministers of the Group of Five (G–5)[2] agreed to undertake a cooperative effort to generate a depreciation of the then strongly appreciating U.S. dollar. The Plaza Accord, which took its name from the Plaza Hotel in New York City where the meeting took place, gave way to coordinated actions on the matter. The accord is often assigned a significant role in the depreciation of the dollar after 1985. It also began a process whose goal was to formalize regular consultation and joint actions by the largest economies worldwide.

In 1986, the G–5 group was expanded to include Italy and Canada, becoming the Group of Seven (G–7). At the Tokyo meetings held that year, it was decided that the finance ministers of the G–7 countries would meet at least once a year for economic policy consultation and a review of their countries' economic policies. The goals of those meetings would be to achieve a set of mutually consistent policies. In addition, the G–7 ministers decided to introduce a greater degree of formalization in the macroeconomic consultation and coordination process. The group's ministers agreed to focus on a set of ten economic variables, which were reduced to seven indicators at the 1987 meetings at the Louvre in Paris. These seven indicators were growth, inflation, current and trade account balances, exchange rates, monetary conditions, and government budgets. Since that time, other variables have been discussed, and a commodity price index has been added to the list. The variables are supervised by the member countries and serve as the basis for the formulation of individual countries' targets.

---

[2]See the discussion in Chapter 15 on the role of the G–5 in foreign exchange market intervention.

The post-1985 period has been one of partial coordination in macroeconomic policies and concerted exchange market intervention.[3] The results have been mixed: Agreements have been difficult to reach and countries have not always abided by them. According to research carried out by Indiana University economist George M. von Furstenberg and Marquette University's Joseph P. Daniels, the nations participating in economic summits follow only a small fraction of the promises made at the meetings.[4] For the group as a whole, only about one-quarter of the agreements made between 1975 and 1989 were kept. The country with the best record is Great Britain, which has a 41.3 percent fraction of promises kept; the worst performers have been France and the United States, with a record of 26 percent each.

The behavior of economic policies after 1987 illustrates the difficulties involved in sustaining long-term economic policy coordination. The Louvre Accord of February 1987 gave shape to a system of exchange rate coordination based on target zones for exchange rates. Monetary and fiscal policies were also targeted for coordination: The U.S. promised to reduce its budget deficit, Germany agreed to reduce taxes, and Japan agreed to lower interest rates through easy monetary policy and to expand its government's budget. The idea was to stimulate growth while reducing the Japanese current account surplus. From 1987 to

1989, the U.S. budget deficit gradually declined to about 3 percent of the GNP, which its lower-deficit partners in the G-7 group still considered large. Exchange rate coordination was utilized and interest rates were reduced in the aftermath of the October 1987 stock market collapse, to prevent secondary effects on the financial and real sectors of the economy. By 1990, U.S. trading partners had mounted pressures on the United States to further reduce its budget deficit, which exceeded that of all the other G-7 countries. However, the recession that took hold in mid-1990 and the invasion of Kuwait by Iraq in August 1990 drastically changed the panorama. U.S. deficits surged to more than 5 percent of its output in 1991. In the spring of 1990, the U.S. and Japan's trading partners rejected a request by Japan to reduce interest rates. However, by the following year, they had turned around and were asking for interest rate reductions. In July 1991, Japan proceeded to reduce its interest rates to promote the recovery from the 1990–1991 recession and to avoid the potentially harmful secondary effects of its own stock market decline. During 1992 and 1993, additional pressures from the United States and other industrialized countries led to further interest rate cuts in Japan. To this was added enormous pressure on Germany to lower its own interest rates, which had more than doubled between 1988 and 1992. To summarize, the outcome of the process of coordination since the Louvre Accord was to move in the direction suggested by the accord—but only loosely.

22–2. SHOULD NATIONS COORDINATE THEIR ECONOMIC POLICIES?

The introduction of mechanisms for policy coordination poses a set of difficult questions. To what extent should countries design their policies based on international accords or a negotiated consensus? If coordination beats independent policymaking by each country, how should coordination be

[3]For an account of the 1975–1982 summits, see G. de Ménil and A. M. Solomon, *Economic Summitry* (New York: Council on Foreign Relations, 1983). The more recent experience is discussed in R. D. Putnam and N. Bayne, *Hanging Together: Cooperation and Conflict in the Seven Power Summits* (London: Sage, 1987); and Y. Funabashi, *Managing the Dollar: From the Plaza to the Louvre* (Washington D.C.: Institute for International Economics, 1988). For a study of the G-7 in the period from 1985 to 1990, see W. Dobson, *Economic Policy Coordination: Requiem or Prologue?* (Washington D.C., Institute for International Economics, 1991).

[4]G. M. von Furstenberg and J. P. Daniels, "Economic Summit Declarations; 1979—1989: Examining the Written Record of International Cooperation," *Princeton Studies in International Finance* (February 1992).

implemented and by which means is compliance with the agreements going to be verified and enforced?[5]

In order to analyze the coordinated interaction between the major world economies, we must explicitly examine the way by which countries take into account the actions of others in deciding on policies.[6] Coordination is considered to be a significant alternative to independent policymaking because there are potential gains to be made from coordination. The following example illustrates the main issues involved.

Consider a situation of generalized recession under fixed exchange rates. A large country that follows expansionary fiscal policy will expand internally. It will also generate demand for other countries' output, stimulating recovery abroad. However, this positive external effect on others is matched by increased domestic trade deficits caused by an expansion in the demand for foreign goods. Because the trade deficits may involve the accumulation of external debt, some domestic policymakers may not want them. This will reduce the incentives for a single country to expand: The country that expands alone generates some benefits to others, but at a cost to itself. In this example,

independent policymaking can be improved by coordination. Let us see why.

When all countries follow expansionary policies simultaneously, the trade deficit problem disappears. The reason is that the world as a whole cannot have a trade deficit. When all countries expand at the same time, national incomes increase without the adverse effects on the trade deficit that follows from a single country's expansion. Consequently, countries will be willing to follow a coordinated expansion even if they were not willing to expand on their own. This is the basis for the international coordination of policies.[7]

A similar analysis applies under flexible exchange rates. A fiscal expansion taken by one country attracts capital inflows and is associated with a reduction of the exchange rate. This domestic currency appreciation has an attached cost, in the form of a loss of international competitiveness, which will tend to offset the positive effects of the expansion, assuming rigid prices. However, as discussed in Chapter 13, if countries expand simultaneously, the exchange rate appreciation will not return output to its initial level. This would allow all the countries to expand. The fiscal expansion has a positive output effect with no loss (or no major loss) of competitiveness. In this case, countries will have an incentive to expand less when they do it alone than when they engage in a coordinated expansion. This creates gains from a coordinated expansion when the dominant goal is to get out of a generalized recessionary situation.

---

[5]For an analysis of coordination within the European Monetary System, see M. Guitian, M. Russo, and G. Tullio, *Policy Coordination in the European Monetary System* (Washington D.C.: IMF, September 1988).

[6]*Coordination* and *cooperation* are terms used loosely in the economic literature. Strictly speaking, international policy coordination means that countries follow mutually agreed-on policies. Each country is assigned a policy package designed or negotiated within the coordinating group or organization. International coordination is designed to move policymaking from the arena of noncooperative actions to the realm of cooperative solutions to the policymaking problem. We need to be aware that this definition entails the establishment of a common policy package, which represents a high degree of cooperation. Loosely speaking, policy cooperation or coordination can take the form of consultation, exchange of information, informal or partial policy coordination, and other activities that do not require a coordinating group to relinquish the power to make policy.

[7]The example considers a situation of general recession in which expansionary policies are not expected to ignite inflation. Another case would be one where expansion by one country generates inflation in others, shifting part of the inflation costs of expansionary policies to foreign countries. This alternative case leads to perverse incentives for overexpansion; coordination should be geared to avoid the inflationary outcome. In practice, of course, observers might not agree about which situation is the relevant one. The simplicity of our examples should not mislead the reader into believing that the international coordination of macroeconomic policies is a straightforward exercise.

In the absence of coordination, countries will be too timid in the use of expansive macropolicies.

The justification of coordination policies seems straightforward at first glance. In practice, however, the implementation of coordinated policy initiatives faces a series of obstacles.[8] One of them is the problem of securing countries' compliance with the policies adopted. Even if coordinated policymaking benefits the group of countries undertaking them, each country gains individually if it lets the others follow the right policy while abstaining from doing its part. This is the so-called free rider issue that makes voluntary compliance problematic. An informal coordination system fails in this instance because it lacks mechanisms to enforce or encourage compliance.

Although the G–7 has not yet established an enforcement mechanism, remedial action might be taken if a country deviates from the targets set. However, whether the targets should be interpreted as forecasts, guides, or commitments by the G–7 countries is not specified. Furthermore, the way in which the indicator variables are put together to formulate policy is not determined at all; it is only understood that the indicators will be supervised. Assigning weights to different targets is a knotty technical and negotiation problem. In addition, because the targets are secret, it is difficult for the public to know whether a target is being violated. Even if the information were available, it would still be difficult to determine whether the target in place is an optimal target and whether a country violated it as a result of unanticipated disturbances (such as an armed conflict).

We have spelled out some initial difficulties in implementing international policy coordination. However, these do not exhaust the obstacles that must be faced. Coordination can, in fact, be counterproductive. We examine next a case of potentially counterproductive monetary policy coordination.[9]

Can Monetary Policy Coordination Be Counterproductive?

The coordination of policy actions by different countries can severely undermine the credibility of each nation's central bank. Actually, the mere fact that the central bank is perceived as responding to foreign policy pressures and subjecting its policymaking to foreign approval could be enough to undermine its credibility in setting commitments involving domestic fiscal and monetary policy. The public will view these commitments as subject to the coordinated mechanism and, hence, as uncertain. As Martin Feldstein has noted: "It is frightening to the American public and upsetting to our financial markets to believe that the fate of our economy depends on the decisions made in Bonn and Tokyo. Portfolio investors, business managers, and the public in general need to be reassured that we are not hostages to foreign economic policies, that the U.S. is the master of its own destiny, and that our government can and will do what is needed to maintain healthy economic growth."[10]

The view that credibility is undermined by coordinated mechanisms has been formalized by Princeton University economist Kenneth Rogoff.[11] He argues that a basic element in inflation policy is establishing the credibility that central banks will

---

[8]A detailed analysis of the many practical problems coordination poses is found in J. A. Frankel, "Obstacles to International Policy Coordination," *Princeton Studies in International Finance* (December 1988).

[9]For an example of counterproductive fiscal policy coordination, see P. J. Kehoe, "Coordination of Fiscal Policies in a World Economy," *Journal of Monetary Economics* (May 1987).

[10]M. Feldstein, "The End of Policy Coordination," *The Wall Street Journal,* November 9, 1987, p. A21.

[11]See K. Rogoff, "International Macroeconomic Policy Coordination May Be Counterproductive," *Journal of International Economics* (November 1985). A similar point is formalized in a flexible price model by F. van der Ploeg, "International Policy Coordination in Interdependent Monetary Economies," *Journal of Monetary Economics* (September 1988).

actually follow announced anti-inflation programs. One credible way for a central bank to establish the precommitment to a given inflation path is to renounce explicitly engaging in internationally co-ordinated exercises that may involve higher infla-tion. Under the surface, the international coordina-tion exemplified by the accords and agreements of the 1980s is a form of activist policy that under-mines any previous policy announcements and commitments made by domestic authorities.

A question that arises immediately from Rogoff's analysis concerns why cooperation fails. In principle, the parties to a cooperative agreement can agree to choose the noncooperative solution to their problem. If the noncooperative solution is better, why not agree on it? The apparent paradox of obtaining a coordinated equilibrium that is suboptimal, compared to an uncoordinated one, arises because there is another player that does not participate in the coordinated arrangement among governmental authorities but that can undermine the arrangements. This third player is the domestic private sector. The interaction of domestic author-ities with the domestic private sector and foreign governments is a three-player game. The coordi-nated arrangements authorities arrive at will touch off changes in private sector behavior that can make a country worse off than in the absence of coordination.

The following example is an illustration of the mechanisms involved. Consider the effects of international coordination under flexible exchange rates, ignoring the private sector's response to it. Assume that the economy is producing at its potential level of output and that domestic fiscal authorities are in the process of deciding whether to (unexpectedly) raise government spending, which may supply needed voter goodwill in an election year. In the absence of coordination, government authorities would not have an incen-tive to engage in fiscal expansion since the resulting domestic currency appreciation would offset any positive output effects. However, coor-dination provides an incentive to expand fiscal

expenditures jointly because the coordinated in-crease can raise output in the short run. Of course, the increase in aggregate demand will lead only to a temporary output expansion, and it will raise prices. This means that there is a greater inflation-ary bias under coordination than in its absence. How does the private sector react to the coordi-nated arrangement under these circumstances? The private sector response to the inflationary bias is to attach low credibility to anti-inflationary programs in the presence of a coordinated regime. Such a lack of credibility can have disastrous consequences if governments do attempt to lower inflation in such an environment, as the next section shows.

Credibility and the Success of Anti-Inflationary Stabilization Programs

We use the aggregate demand-aggregate supply framework developed in chapters 16 through 18 to show the difficulties faced by anti-inflationary stabilization programs that lack credibility. One of the basic problems faced by stabilization programs in reducing inflation is the inelasticity, or sticki-ness, of inflationary expectations to changes envi-sioned by agents in the economy to be only temporary. We illustrate the issues involved in Figure 22–1, which shows the economy's initial equilibrium at point E, at the intersection of the now-standard aggregate demand and supply curves AD and AS, respectively. (For more details, see sections 16–1 through 16–2.) It is assumed that the central bank has been injecting credit into the economy for an extended period of time and that individuals expect prices to increase from P_0 to P^e in the following time period. The antici-pation of agents in the economy is thus that equilibrium will be achieved at point E'—where the shift in aggregate demand from AD to AD' is what individuals expect based on the past and present behavior of the economy's central bank— and the shift in aggregate supply from AS to AS' is

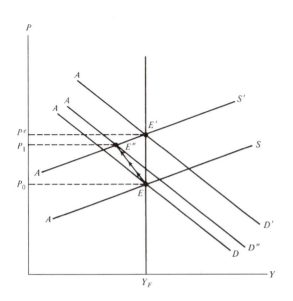

FIGURE 22–1. The Problem of Disinflation in the Open Economy

a result of the inflationary expectations associated with the anticipated monetary growth.

Suppose now that the government engages in a sudden, unanticipatedly restrictive aggregate demand policy (through reduced government spending and/or reduced credit creation). This change means that the aggregate demand curve actually shifts to AD'', instead of shifting to AD' as anticipated by individuals in the economy. Does this unanticipated policy shift reduce domestic inflation? As observed in Figure 22–1, the economy's equilibrium would occur at point E'', determined by the intersection of the aggregate demand curve prevailing under the restrictionist government policy regime, AD'', with the aggregate supply curve associated with the inflationary anticipations of agents in the economy, AS'. The economy, therefore, still faces unyielding inflation (equal to $\hat{P} = (P_1 - P_0)/P_0$), but there is, in addition, a decline in production, throwing the economy into recession. What are the basic factors behind this result? First

of all, given the unexpected nature of the policy shock, individuals mistakenly anticipated that inflation would remain at the level $\Pi = (P^e - P_0)/P_0$; as a result, nominal wage rate hikes of the same proportion were embodied in labor contracts. These adjustments keep fueling inflation, in spite of the relative contraction of monetary growth. Diagrammatically, even though the aggregate demand only shifts from AD to AD'', aggregate supply, as determined by inflationary expectations, shifts upward more than proportionally, from AS to AS'. The restrictive aggregate demand policy shift, combined with the real wage growth sustained through pre-established cost-of-living adjustments, throws the economy into recession while it keeps inflation going. Note that the decline of output relative to price increases depends on the steepness of the aggregate supply curve, AS'. The flatness of AS' shown in Figure 22–1 means that output is highly influenced by the expectational errors of agents in the economy, while inflation deviates relatively little from its anticipated rate. This may be attributable to a large share of labor contracts being indexed in previous periods and, thus, to a relative insensitivity of current labor contracts to the unemployment arising from negative deviations of output from its potential level.

What happens to inflationary expectations over time in the present situation? Depending on whether individuals believe the restrictive aggregate demand policy is permanent or not, they may or may not adjust their inflationary expectations downward. If the government sticks to its stabilization program, it may eventually become credible; at that moment, inflation expectations would decline, causing the aggregate supply curve to shift to the right. On the other hand, it is highly likely that agents in the economy will lack confidence in the government's willingness to maintain a restrictive aggregate demand policy. In this situation, inflationary expectations would not diminish. Wage settlements would continue to embody high nominal wage adjustments, which are then passed on to consumers as price increases.

Inflation would therefore continue unabatedly, with a stalemate between the stubborn sticky downward inflationary expectations of agents in the economy and the government's continued policy of restrictive aggregate demand.

22–3. GOVERNMENT CREDIBILITY, LEGAL CONSTRAINTS, AND REPUTATION: COORDINATING BY RULES

Governments fall into credibility problems in large part because they do not abide by their previous promises. Unexpected shocks may, of course, force a government to deviate from policies it adopted. A worldwide collapse in the price of an important export crop may force a developing economy to engage in currency devaluation, even if such a policy was not originally contemplated as an option. However, governments are expected to alter their policies in the face of misfortunes and, as long as such misfortunes are unlikely, no lack of credibility is generated. The problem of government credibility thus goes beyond the appearance of surprises or unanticipated events that alter policy.

Governments run into serious credibility problems when their policies are *time inconsistent.* Policies are subject to a time inconsistency problem when authorities have an *inherent incentive* to renege on established policies and follow new policy packages. Such an incentive is independent of the surprises or unusual circumstances the future can bring; it can be anticipated even if circumstances remain what they were expected to be when policies were initially formulated. For instance, when there is a large government debt, incentives arise for the government to inflate and reduce its real value. Inflation lowers the real value of government debt, and this acts in effect as a tax on the holders of the debt (a confiscation of the money they were owed). Agents in the economy may thus anticipate that, whatever the governmental stance, high public indebtedness will be

associated with future inflation. Any statements by the authorities to the effect that they will engage in a battle to reduce inflation would not be credible in these circumstances. Note that both noncooperative and cooperative regimes are subject to time inconsistency problems. If countries want to reduce the real value of their debt, it does not matter whether they act independently or jointly. The incentive to inflate is there in both cases.

In order to solve the time consistency problem, the authorities must offer some precommitment. This means that the government commits itself to follow certain policies no matter what happens. Because there are costs involved in keeping the precommitments, how can they be enforced? There are various mechanisms to enforce a government's commitments.[12] All of them work by effectively limiting governmental action in practice. One way to ensure that the authorities will keep their promises is by establishing a system of rules that impose discipline in policy formation. Legal constraints, like constitutional rules, impose limits on a government's actions. However, the consensus required to agree on them is difficult to reach, partly because authorities do not wish to tie their hands too much. Reputation can also be a force in limiting a government's breaking of promises, but usually it is not enough. Another mechanism involves setting rules to be maintained on the basis of a collective system of monitoring and rewards. Such rules can form part of a system such as the gold standard (see our discussion in Chapter 21), or a fixed exchange rate regime, such as the Bretton Woods system or the EMS. We proceed to discuss how governments in countries under these regimes may be forced towards inflation rates that are heavily influenced by systemic-wide forces.

---

[12]For further discussion and a survey of these issues, see the articles by K. Rogoff, "Reputation, Coordination, and Monetary Policy," and V. V. Chari, P. J. Kehoe, and E. C. Prescott, "Time Consistency and Policy," in *Modern Business Cycle Theory,* ed. R. J. Barro (Cambridge, Mass.: Harvard University Press, 1989).

Bretton Woods and the Anatomy of Inflation Under Fixed Exchange Rates

In economies operating under a regime of truly fixed exchange rates, the domestic rate of inflation is constrained to approach the world rate of inflation over the long-run. There is no way around the fact that long-term deviations of domestic from world inflation would, *ceteris paribus,* generate significant downward or upward trends in a country's international competitiveness. That lack of competiveness would eventually wipe out or over-extend the production of traded goods. Before that happens, however, the forces of adjustment we have discussed many times before (such as wage-price deflation, the monetary mechanism of payments adjustments, and international goods arbitrage) would tend to realign domestic and foreign inflation. As UCLA economist Arnold Harberger remarks,

> If a country initially does not fully share in an ongoing world inflation, it is only a matter of time before it will, so long as it maintains its fixed exchange rate, . . . in much the same way that water finds its own level in the different parts of an interconnected hydraulic system.[13]

This view of domestic inflation as closely linked to world inflation is supported by the experience of industrial countries during the Bretton Woods period, as shown in Table 22–1. It appears that 80 percent of the countries listed had inflation rates within a range of 1.7 and 3.7 percent between 1952 and 1967, and within a range of 3.9 to 6.1 percent between 1967 and 1972. Hence, there is a remarkably similar inflation experience in these countries, all of them clustering around the median rates of inflation of 3.0 percent and 4.6 percent for each period.

Even though, over the long run and when countries abstain from regulating international

[13]A. Harberger, "A Primer on Inflation," *Journal of Money, Credit, and Banking* (November 1978), p. 516.

TABLE 22–1. Industrial Countries, Average Annual Inflation Rates (percent per annum)

	1952–1967	*1967–1972*
United States	1.5%	4.6%
Canada	1.7	3.9
Japan	4.3	5.9
Australia	2.5	4.3
New Zealand	3.2	6.6
Austria	3.1	4.3
Belgium	1.9	4.0
Denmark	3.9	6.1
France	3.7	4.7
Germany	1.9	3.5
Italy	3.1	3.9
Netherlands	3.0	6.0
Norway	3.3	6.1
Sweden	3.5	5.1
Switzerland	2.1	4.3
United Kingdom	2.8	6.6
Median	3.0	4.6
Range encompassing 80% of observations	1.7–3.7	3.9–6.1

SOURCE: Reprinted, with permission from Arnold C. Harberger, "A Primer on Inflation," *Journal of Money, Credit, and Banking,* 10 (November 1978), p. 508. Copyright © 1978 by the Ohio State University Press.

trade, domestic inflation is predominantly determined by world inflation, it is clear that, over the short run and when countries impose exchange controls and other means of interfering with international transactions, substantial deviations may arise. Table 22–2 shows a selected group of countries exhibiting chronically high inflation rates during, or immediately following, the Bretton Woods regime. For these countries, domestic inflation dramatically exceeded world inflation, in some cases for quite sustained periods. What factors can cause domestic inflation to exceed world inflation? A number of variables has been postulated along the path of our discussion in earlier chapters. These include money supply growth, devaluation of the currency, budget deficits and their monetization,

TABLE 22–2. **Examples of Acute Inflation**

Country	Period	*In Prices*[a]	*In Money Supply*[b]
		Average Annual Percentage Increase	
Argentina	1974–1976	$293	$262
Bolivia	1952–1959	117	100
Chile	1971–1976	273	231
Indonesia	1965–1968	306	223
Paraguay	1951–1953	81	54
South Korea	1950–1955	102	101
Uruguay }	1965–1968	95	66
	1971–1974	83	63

[a]Basic data were yearly averages of monthly price levels.
[b]Basic data were end-of-year money supply figures.

SOURCE: Reprinted with permission from Arnold C. Harberger, "A Primer on Inflation," *Journal of Money, Credit and Banking,* 10 (November 1978), p. 507. Copyright © 1978 by the Ohio State University Press.

and aggregate supply shocks (such as bad weather or climate), to name a few. Obviously, each country would have to be closely examined to discern the details of its inflation. The conclusion is clear, however, that, in a fixed exchange rate regime, domestic inflation can get quite out of line with world inflation. This means that a fixed exchange rate regime alone cannot afford credibility to a governmental anti-inflationary program. Additional disciplinary rules and mechanisms must exist to constrain authorities from imposing exchange controls and devaluing currencies at will, for example. Some economists allege that the EMS provides such a regime.

The EMS as a Disciplinary Mechanism

Can joining the EMS provide a mechanism for imposing discipline on a country's policymakers? By joining the EMS a country agrees to a set of rules that change the costs and benefits of engaging in expansionary policies. If the costs of being expansionary are raised, monetary policies will become more restrictive than in the absence of membership. Countries that do not desire constraints on their monetary policy may not wish to join such a union. However, governments engaged in serious anti-inflation efforts, but that have a bad reputation and low credibility, may derive positive effects from joining a system like the EMS. The credibility that comes from adhering to a set of disciplinary rules may prove essential in the government's anti-inflation policy.

From the point of view of the potential EMS member, a key requirement leading to a positive disciplinary effect from membership is that the joining country be more inflation-prone than the countries it joins. In that case, the rules and exchange rate setting mechanisms of the EMS work to impose macroeconomic discipline. There are a number of ways through which the rules of operation tend to force lower inflation rates. The EMS requires the approval of exchange rate changes before the changes are made. It also limits the extent and frequency of the adjustments. The consequence is that the joining country loses control over the extent, as well as the timing and frequency, of devaluations. Limiting the use of devaluation as a policy, imposes steep costs on governments that pursue inflationary policies. As noted earlier in relation to the Bretton Woods system, a country that joins low-inflation economies in a truly fixed exchange rate regime but keeps inflationary policies will suffer a real domestic currency appreciation. The real appreciation reduces the international competitiveness of the inflation-prone country vis-à-vis its lower-inflation partners. The loss in competitiveness entails a palpable cost of inflation. This cost would not be present if the currency were allowed to be devalued easily as the inflation occurs. Under the EMS, exchange rate realignments take place sporadically and are always delayed in relation to ongoing inflation; the delay causes the inflating country to experience a temporary loss of competitiveness. It is this additional cost imposed by the exchange rate regime that induces the joining member to restrict its monetary policies and control inflation.

A second cost from inflationary policies derives from the EMS practice of devaluing by less than what is required to offset the previous real currency appreciation of the devaluing country. This means that an inflationary country is forced to bear the costs of overvaluation, even after exchange rates are adjusted. These procedures for realigning exchange rates reduce inflationary incentives. At the same time, they could threaten the system's long-term sustainability. The sustainability problem arises if the full adjustment of exchange rates to inflation is not allowed: Each inflation episode will be followed by a growingly overvalued domestic currency. The extent of the overvaluation will increase over time as the currency becomes increasingly overvalued in response to the inability to devalue. Reserve loses will continue until the inflating country runs out of them and is thrown into a foreign exchange crisis. At that point, membership will be unsustainable. A solution to the problem is to allow for periodic adjustments that more than fully offset for past inflation. However, this would undermine the incentive to reduce inflation.

In short, under EMS rules, inflation-prone countries are limited in the timing, frequency, and extent of exchange rate adjustments. As long as they inflate more than other member countries, they will face real currency appreciations. The presumed effect is to reduce the incentives to inflate. The benefits of this system of "tying one's hand" derive from the credibility-enhancing effects it induces. The enhanced credibility of the central bank and the policymaking authorities makes up for the loss of policy autonomy involved in accepting the EMS rules.[14] At the same time,

[14] See F. Giavazzi and M. Pagano, "The Advantage of Tying One's Hands: EMS Discipline and Central Bank Credibility," *European Economic Review* (November 1988); and S. Collins and F. Giavazzi, "Attitudes Toward Inflation and the Viability of Fixed Exchange Rates: Evidence from the EMS," in M. Bordo and B. Eichengreen, eds., *A Retrospective on the Bretton Woods System* (Chicago: University of Chicago Press, 1993).

the loss of policy autonomy may make the system unsustainable for countries with governments that have a persistent tendency to inflate the economy.

An issue remains as to why a low-inflation country like Germany would like to join a system of inflation-prone countries. The advantages to Germany, however, come from the reserve currency role played by a low-inflation country. The country loses the ability to determine its exchange rate, but the reserve currency role consolidates the autonomy of its monetary policies.

The limits of the rigidities inherent in the EMS's reluctance to engage in exchange rate realignments and the Bundesbank adherence to conservative monetary policies were reached in September 1992 (so-called Black September) when the EMS suffered its worst crisis since its inception. The crisis had, in a sense, been bubbling for months. A number of EMS members had been having difficulties sustaining their exchange rates within the limits prescribed by the ERM. Central banks in France, Italy, the United Kingdom, and others had been frantically intervening to keep their currencies from depreciating against the deutsche mark. Massive capital flows into Germany associated with relatively high (and rising) German interest rates and speculation of a major realignment of EMS currencies led, in turn, to growing central bank intervention and to shifts in domestic monetary policies intended to prevent currency depreciation vis-à-vis the mark.

On September 17th, the Bank of England desperately raised interest rates, first by two percentage points and then by three more percentage points, in a last ditch effort to prevent further capital outflows. Having failed with these extreme measures, a decision was finally made to let the pound float freely in value relative to other EMS currencies and, therefore, to move the pound out of the ERM. Italy followed later, also leaving the EMS, and a number of major EMS realignments, of the Spanish peseta, the Portuguese escudo, and others were undertaken in the following months.

Although the EMS survived the crisis (Germany eventually lowered interest rates and speculation subsided), the bruises left by the Italian and British abandonment of the ERM were deep. Questions were raised as to the inherent stability of the EMS. Bundesbank President Helmut Schlesinger remarked that the EMS was indeed inherently unstable, subject to speculative attacks. Even Milton Friedman, the Nobel Laureate in Economics, commented that the fixed exchange rate system followed by the EMS was not a satisfactory financial arrangement for a group of large countries with independent political systems and independent national policies.[15]

What had been the performance of the EMS *before* Black September? The next section looks at the evidence on this score.

22–4. THE MACROECONOMIC PERFORMANCE OF THE EUROPEAN MONETARY SYSTEM

Let us now examine the macroeconomic performance of the EMS, a performance that some researchers have hailed for reducing European inflation since 1979 and for leading to the convergence of inflation rates among member countries. Other researchers, however, have argued that the EMS experience with real exchange rate variability has been disappointing. What is the answer? As we will show, both views seem overblown when we compare the performance of EMS countries with that of other industrial countries for the same period.

Figure 22–2 shows the bilateral exchange rates between the European currencies and the deutsche mark (in marks per unit of each European currency). The Netherlands' guilder has gravitated toward the German mark, but the currencies of Belgium, Denmark, France, Ireland, and Italy have depreciated together, leading some analysts to talk of a bipolar standard in which some countries peg to the German currency and others to the French franc. At the same time, the depreciating tendency of the currencies moving with the French franc did

gradually phase itself out by the late 1980s. This phenomenon is depicted in Figure 22–2 by the achievement of a plateau in the gently sloping curve characterizing the depreciating currencies. The decade-long depreciation of the French franc and other currencies fizzled out as more stable values were achieved vis-à-vis the mark. The stability of these currencies' values in terms of the German mark could be alleged to signal the establishment of a mark currency zone in Europe.

The increased stability of nominal exchange rates in Europe has been associated with the gradual convergence of inflation rates within the EMS, except for the recent entrants, Greece and Portugal. In the early 1990s, two-digit inflation rates continued in Portugal and Greece. The inflation rates of all the other EMS members varied between 2 and 7 percent. This 5 percent range in the intercountry variability of inflation within the EMS contrasted with the over 10 percent range prevailing among the original members when the system was established. For instance, in 1979 Germany's 3 percent inflation fell well below Ireland's 13 percent. The inflation range among the EMS countries was equal to about 20 percent in the early 1980s. The ensuing narrowing of the range of inflation rates has been impressive indeed.

Increased exchange rate stability and convergence of inflation rates within the EMS was accompanied by a third pattern: the gradual disinflation after 1982. Figure 22–3 shows the inflation rates for some EMS and non-EMS European countries from 1979 until 1990.[16] The disinflation among the EMS countries is clear. However, this disinflation was mirrored by the experience of the

---

[15]M. Friedman, "Déjà Vu in Currency Markets," *The Wall Street Journal* (September 22, 1992, p. A21).

[16]A full discussion of the EMS experience appears in R. Dornbusch, "Problems of European Monetary Integration," in A. Giovannini and C. Mayer, eds., *European Financial Integration* (Cambridge: Cambridge University Press, 1991); M. Fratianni and J. von Hagen, "The European Monetary System Ten Years After," in A. H. Meltzer and C. Plosser, eds., *Carnegie-Rochester Conference Series on Public Policy* (Amsterdam: North Holland, 1990); and A. Weber, "Reputation and Credibility in the European Monetary System," *Economic Policy* (April, 1991).

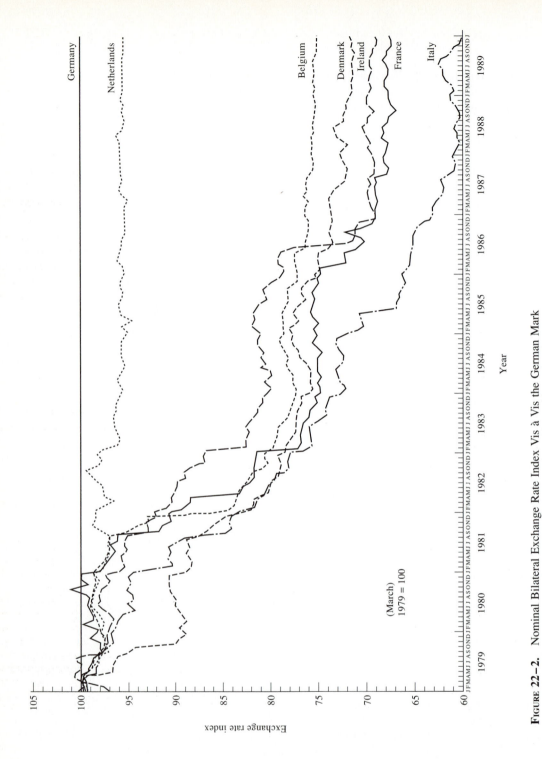

FIGURE 22-2. Nominal Bilateral Exchange Rate Index Vis à Vis the German Mark

SOURCE: A. A. Weber, "Reputation and Credibility in the European Monetary System," *Economic Policy* (April 1991), p. 60.

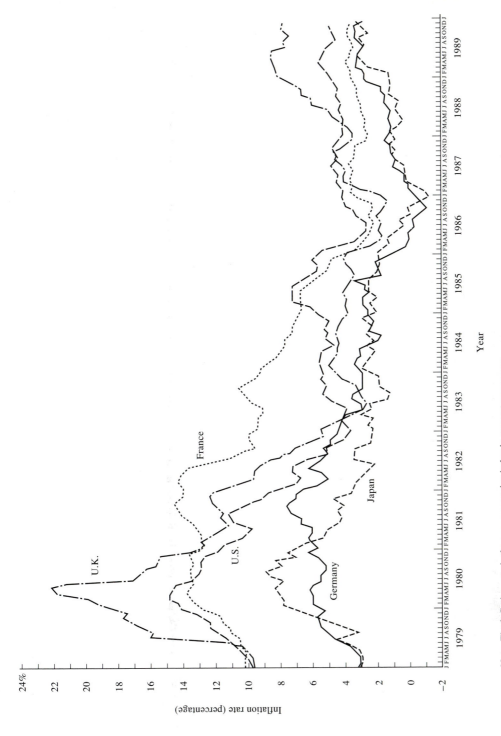

FIGURE 22–3. Inflation Rates in Some EMS and Non-EMS Countries

Note: The inflation rate is the consumer price index in percent per annum.

SOURCE: A. A. Weber, "Reputation and Credibility in the European Monetary System," *Economic Policy* (April 1991), p. 63.

non-EMS group. It is thus difficult to attribute the disinflation—as well as the convergence of inflation—to the EMS regime as such. This is especially so once we recall—from earlier discussions—that those countries joining the EMS are predisposed toward disinflation. The EMS experience can then be interpreted as resulting from the system attracting disinflation-prone countries to begin with. Finally, the capabilities of the EMS to lead to low inflation rates are challenged by the renewal of inflation after 1986—an experience shared with the non-EMS countries.

Underlying the behavior of the EMS are Germany's low inflation and conservative monetary policies. Whatever the credibility aspects involved in the system, they must rely heavily on the low inflationary expectations generated by Bundesbank policies. If the German central bank, for instance, were to follow inflationary policies, such inflation would be transmitted to other EMS member countries and the whole system would break down. As Princeton University economist Kenneth Rogoff observes: "The German central bank's main concern is simply to hold down Germany's inflation rate. . . . Naturally there are many periods when soft inflation countries complain that the Germans are being insensitive to Europe's fiscal and employment woes. But, of course, if Germany were consistently to yield to such pressures, inflationary expectations would rise throughout Europe."[17] The next section discusses how inflation is transmitted from country to country under fixed exchange rates.

22–5. THE INTERNATIONAL TRANSMISSION OF INFLATION UNDER FIXED EXCHANGE RATES

We have so far examined the nature and possible cures of inflation on the assumption that world inflation is fixed. A key aspect of domestic infla-

tion in economies under fixed exchange rates is, however, that it can be imported from abroad. This section examines the nature of *imported inflation* and ways to control it in interdependent economies. To concentrate on analyzing inflation, the framework utilized is simplified by assuming that domestic and foreign output stay fixed in the period concerned. In addition, only two (interdependent) economies are considered, domestic and foreign (or rest of the world) economies. Asterisks denote variables associated with the foreign country.

Domestic and foreign real money demand functions are assumed to be given by

$$L = kY \qquad \text{and} \qquad L^* = k^*Y^*,$$

where k and k^* are assumed constant. In other words, real money demands depend exclusively on income, with the effect of interest rates assumed to be negligible. Note that nominal money demands can be easily obtained by multiplying real money demands by the corresponding price levels. The equality of world money supply and demand is then given by

$$M + M^* = kPY + k^*P^*Y^*, \qquad (22\text{–}1)$$

with M and M^* equal to the domestic and foreign nominal money supplies, respectively, and where the exchange rate is, for simplicity, normalized to equal $e = 1$. Observe that, given nominal money supplies in each country, if the price of domestic goods rises, there is an increase in nominal money demand; this increase requires a decrease in the price of foreign goods, to eliminate the excess world demand for money. This negative relationship between domestic and foreign prices in maintaining world money market equilibrium is shown by the downward-sloping *MM* curve in Figure 22–4.

If we assume capital immobility, balanced payments will occur when the trade balance is equal to zero—that is,

$$T = \bar{T}\left(\frac{eP^*}{P}\right) - mY = 0. \qquad (22\text{–}2)$$

[17]K. Rogoff, "Strategic Perspectives on Economic Policy," in D. Vines and A. Stevenson, eds., *Information, Strategy and Public Policy* (Oxford: Basil Blackwell, 1991), p. 133.

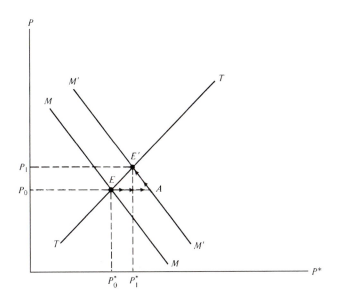

FIGURE 22–4.   International Transmission of Inflation

With domestic and foreign income fixed, Equation 22–2 expresses an implicit relationship between domestic and foreign price levels: An increase in domestic prices, P, requires an offsetting rise of foreign prices, P^*, to sustain domestic competitiveness in international markets and, therefore, balanced trade. This positive connection between domestic and foreign prices in maintaining external balance is depicted by the TT curve in Figure 22–4. Observe that domestic trade balance deficits or surpluses correspond to rest-of-the-world trade surpluses or deficits ($T = -T^*$). Points to the right of the TT curve depict domestic trade surpluses (foreign deficits), easily visualized by realizing that a movement to the right of TT implies a rise in the price of foreign goods at any given price of domestic goods. The gain in domestic price competitiveness improves the domestic trade balance. Similarly, points to the left of TT represent domestic trade balance deficits (foreign surpluses).

Long-run equilibrium is achieved when equations 22–1 and 22–2 are simultaneously satisfied, as illustrated by point E in Figure 22–4. We

assume the economies considered are initially at that point.

Consider now the effects of a foreign central bank credit expansion. At a given level of domestic prices, the foreign price level would have to rise in proportion to the monetary expansion in order to sustain world money market equilibrium. This is illustrated by the move from point E to point A in Figure 22–4, a result of the shift of the MM curve to $M'M'$ following the expansion of the world money supply implied by the foreign credit creation. At point A, however, there is a domestic trade balance surplus (and a deficit abroad). Consequently, the domestic money supply will rise while the foreign money supply shrinks. This redistribution of the world money supply fuels domestic inflation while diminishing foreign inflation. Diagrammatically, this is shown by the move from point A to point E' along the $M'M'$ locus. Only when balanced trade occurs—at point E'— will the money supply redistribution stop. At that point, a new world long-run equilibrium has been reached. Note, however, that the foreign credit creation and inflation spill over into the domestic economy, causing domestic inflation of $\hat{P} = (P_1 - P_0)/P_0$; this represents imported inflation. At the same time, because the foreign price level at point A exceeds that at point E, the repercussion effects of the foreign monetary expansion act to ameliorate the inflationary impact in the foreign economy. In a sense, foreign monetary authorities export part of their inflationary problem.

Assuming that domestic policymakers do not wish to tolerate imported inflation, what action, if any, could they take? One possibility is sterilization. The domestic central bank can engage in open-market operations (selling bonds in the open market) to offset the effects of trade surpluses in raising the domestic money supply. In doing this, the domestic nominal money supply is kept at its initial level and the foreign disturbance cannot, therefore, influence domestic prices. Note that the reduction in the international reserves of the foreign central bank in response to the foreign payments deficit decreases the world money supply, shifting the $M'M'$ curve back to its original level at MM. The domestic sterilization operations thus offset the foreign central bank credit expansion. The expansion leaves the long-run world money supply unchanged and eliminates upward pressures on foreign, as well as domestic, prices. Thus, under fixed exchange rates, the United States could insulate itself from European monetary policy by sterilization. At the same time, this type of action keeps European monetary policy from affecting European inflation or other variables. This point illustrates the drastic, but sometimes subtle, interdependence to which open economies under fixed exchange rates are subject.[18]

World Inflation and Global Monetarism

The previous discussion can be expanded to describe the potentially close relationship between domestic and world inflation in open economies. This link is one of the benchmarks of so-called global monetarism; *global monetarism* argues that in a fixed exchange rate regime, it is the *world* rate of growth of the money supply (an aggregate of all countries' money supply growth) that determines the world rate of inflation and is thus closely related to domestic inflation.[19] This is opposed to *local (domestic) monetarism,* which argues that it is the *domestic* rate of growth of the money supply that determines domestic inflation. The present discussion should help us understand the pros and cons of a fixed exchange rate regime with respect to the goal of controlling inflation. On the one hand, fixed exchange rates tend to constrain the inflationary impact of government policies, limiting domestic inflation from going above the world inflation rate. On the other hand, countries that desire inflation rates below the world level may not be able to attain that goal, particularly if they are small economies with relatively little power over prices set in world markets.

22−6. ACCOUNTING FOR INFLATION UNDER EXCHANGE RATE FLEXIBILITY

One of the essential differences between fixed and flexible exchange rate regimes lies in the greater degree of monetary control facilitated by exchange rate flexibility. It is often asserted, however, that such control might not be a blessing but a curse. The fear is that expansionary monetary policy will

---

[18]For more details on the complexities of interdependence and strategic policy formulation under fixed and flexible exchange rates, see M. B. Canzoneri and D. W. Henderson, *Monetary Policy in Interdependent Economies* (Cambridge, Mass.: The MIT Press, 1991); and M. Mussa, "Macroeconomic Interdependence and the Exchange Rate Regime," in J. Frenkel and R. Dornbusch, eds., *International Economic Policy* (Baltimore: Johns Hopkins University Press, 1979).

[19]For studies developing and evaluating the global monetarism doctrine see M. V. N. Whitman, "Global Monetarism and the Monetary Approach to the Balance of Payments," *Brookings Papers on Economic Activity* (1975); and D. I. Meiselman, "Worldwide Inflation: A Monetarist View, in D. A. Meiselman and A. B. Laffer, eds., *The Phenomenon of Worldwide Inflation* (Washington D.C.: American Enterprise Institute, 1975).

be used indiscriminately, leading to skyrocketing inflation. What is the connection between monetary growth and inflation? We start by examining how inflation and once-and-for-all changes in the money supply are related.

The initial step is to recall the money market equilibrium condition given by

$$\frac{M^S}{P} = L^D (i, Y), \qquad (22\text{–}3)$$

stating the equality of the domestic real money supply, M^S/P, with the real demand for money, $L^D(i, Y)$, which is itself a function of the domestic nominal interest rate, i, and domestic income, Y. For an economy initially at full employment, with a given money supply $M^S = M_0$ and price level $P = P_0$, and facing perfect capital mobility so that the domestic nominal interest rate aligns itself with the foreign interest rate, i^*, Equation 22–3 becomes

$$\frac{M_0}{P_0} = L^D (i^*, Y_F). \qquad (22\text{–}3a)$$

Within this context, a once-and-for-all increase in the domestic money supply will generally tend to change output, interest rates, and/or prices over the short run but will be associated only with an increase in prices over the long run. This is so because in the absence of other disturbances—anticipated and unanticipated—the economy would return in time to full employment and the domestic interest rate would align itself back with the world interest rate. If the money supply expansion is not linked to any long-run effects on output and nominal interest rates, however, money demand would remain unchanged at $L^D(i^*, Y_F)$. Therefore, the real money supply would also remain unaltered.

If we denote the economy's long-run price level after the monetary expansion by P_1, then M_1/P_1 must be equal to M_0/P_0—that is, the domestic price increase must exactly match the money supply increase. This is indeed a remarkable result, suggesting that a close quantitative connection may exist between changes in the money supply and changes in the domestic price level. Notice, however, that this does not mean that inflation is determined by money supply changes.

First of all, the strict one-to-one relationship between changes in the money supply and changes in price level is really relevant within a long-run time context. In the short run, changes in the money supply will generally be associated with changes in output and interest rates in addition to inflation. An output expansion in response to a given unanticipated jump in the money supply, for example, will tend to boost real money demand, requiring a short-run increase in the real money supply to sustain money market equilibrium. As a consequence, in this short-run context, domestic prices will rise by a smaller proportion than the money supply. How much inflation actually occurs vis-à-vis output expansion in the short run is then a matter that relates to the short-run aggregate demand-aggregate supply structure establishing short-run changes in prices and output in the economy. The particular type of labor market institutions present, the nature of the transmission and acquisition of information by agents in the economy, the responsiveness of real interest rates and real exchange rates to the unanticipated monetary disturbance, and a whole range of other factors will influence the determination of short-run changes in prices.

Moving away from the analysis of once-and-for-all changes in the money supply and toward a more dynamic analysis, what is the relationship between money growth and inflation? Even if domestic output does not change in response to the monetary expansion, divergencies will arise between the rate of monetary growth and the associated short-run inflation. The explanation lies in that increased monetary growth will in general be associated not only with spiraling prices, but also, in order to sustain domestic competitiveness, with domestic currency depreciation. Increased monetary growth will give rise to a given anticipated rate of increase of the exchange rate that, following the uncovered parity condition, will raise domestic nominal interest rates and reduce money demand. In order to sustain money market equilibrium, the real money supply would have to decline. In other words, money supply growth would have to fall short of the short-run inflation rate.

This process is illustrated in Figure 22–5, which shows the paths of the real money supply (Figure 22–5[a]) and nominal money growth and inflation (Figure 22–5[b]) before and after an increase in money supply growth from M_0 to M_1 at time t_0. Notice that because nominal interest rate rises reduce money demand, the real money supply has to decline from $(M/P)_0$ to $(M/P)_1$. In order for this to occur, domestic prices will have to rise

at a higher pace than the nominal money supply over a certain period of time. This is represented in Figure 22–5(b) by the faster rate of growth of prices, depicted by the PP curve, as compared to the money supply growth of $\hat{M}_1$. In the time period from t_0 to t_1, the real money supply then adjusts downward to its new equilibrium level. Note, however, the lack of coincidence of monetary growth and domestic inflation in this time period in Figure 22–5(b). Once again, the one-to-one relation between money growth and inflation breaks down in the short run.

The breakdown is especially apparent if the economy is being subject not only to money supply changes, but to other disturbances as well. The economy's adjustment to real disturbances, such as oil-price shocks, will generally give rise to

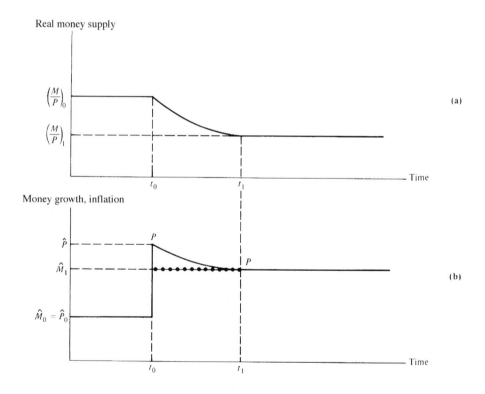

FIGURE 22–5. Changes in Money Growth and Inflation

short-run price level changes, even if the domestic money supply is being held fixed. The reduction in the level of potential output associated with a sudden rise in the price of imported materials, for instance, could in principle generate substantial short-run domestic inflation in the absence of domestic money supply changes, as explained in Chapter 17. Capital accumulation and increased growth of potential output, on the other hand, will tend to make possible a lower short-run rate of inflation consistent with any given rate of monetary growth.

In conclusion, there appear to be strong reasons to expect changes in the rate of inflation, in a country under flexible exchange rates, to be highly correlated with changes in money supply growth over the long run. The connection is more tenuous in the short run, leaving domestic inflation subject to the wide array of real and monetary factors that affect aggregate supply and demand in the short run.

22–7. VICIOUS CIRCLES AND EXCHANGE RATE FLEXIBILITY

The relative autonomy of monetary policy under flexible exchange rates has given rise to the frequent argument that flexible exchange rates is a regime that lacks monetary discipline and will consequently be more inflationary than a fixed exchange rate regime. Consider the case, for instance, when a sudden pressure for higher nominal wages in the labor market—linked perhaps to expectations of future inflation or to an increased relative bargaining power of unions vis-à-vis employers—serves to raise real labor costs and places upward pressures on prices and downward pressures on employment. If the central bank follows a completely accommodating monetary policy, it will increase the money supply to offset any negative effects of rising prices on real money balances and, hence, on output. The monetary expansion validates the price increase, however; it

is correspondingly associated with an exchange rate depreciation that sustains domestic competitiveness in international markets and, thus, employment and output. Note, however, that the rising prices may, in turn, induce workers to bargain for further nominal wage increases in order to sustain their newly gained standard-of-living raise. This is especially so if labor contracts are subject to indexation schemes automatically adjusting nominal wages upward in response to cost-of-living increases. A wage-price-currency depreciation spiral will then arise; workers will continue to demand nominal wage hikes and monetary authorities validating them through money supply increases that further fuel inflation, renewing nominal wage hikes, and so on. This *vicious circle hypothesis,* as it is usually referred to, is based on the relative control over the money supply that domestic monetary authorities have under exchange rate flexibility; it is also based on currency depreciation preventing rising prices from deteriorating domestic competitiveness in international markets.[20] The notion of a vicious circle has often been used as an argument by opponents of flexible exchange rate regimes.

The key point to bear in mind is that the vicious circle can be sustained only if the monetary authorities create the additional money to finance the initial increase in nominal wages and prices.[21] In other words, it requires a central bank that lacks discipline in this respect. Consequently, vicious circles are not an inherent aspect of a regime of flexible exchange rates but the result of the particular policies of central banks in such a regime. Furthermore, it is well known that central banks operating under fixed exchange rates do have their money-printing mania and can also generate high

---

[20]For a detailed presentation of the vicious circle phenomenon, see J. F. O. Bilson, "The Vicious Circle Hypothesis," *IMF Staff Papers* (March 1979).

[21]This point has been made forcefully by Milton Friedman in "The Case for Flexible Exchange Rates," in his *Essays in Positive Economics* (Chicago: University of Chicago Press, 1953).

inflation within the context of that regime. The use of exchange controls, trade barriers, and a whole range of other instruments; the existence of black markets operating at the margin of legality; and reliance on repeated devaluations make possible domestic rates of inflation above world inflation for extended periods under a regime of fixed (but adjustable) exchange rates. The high rates of inflation of many Latin American countries in the recent past substantiate this point.

It must be concluded, then, that even though higher inflation rates may be associated with exchange rate flexibility—and, in particular, with depreciating currencies—there is no necessary causal influence of exchange rate flexibility on inflation. Rather, both the inflation and the depreciating currency may be the result of other factors, key among which is increased monetary growth.

22−8. PERFORMANCE OF THE MANAGED FLOAT IN PERSPECTIVE

The managed floating regime currently being followed by the major industrial countries is unique. It provides a case in which major currencies have been floating in value against each other over a substantial time interval. Before this experience, most analyses of floating regimes were based either on theoretical speculation or on the analysis of limited experiences with floating rates, such as the Canadian float of 1952 to 1961 and the interwar experience between 1918 and 1925. The present regime of managed floating provides us with a richer basis on which to evaluate alternative exchange rate regimes. Unfortunately, just as comparisons between the classic gold standard and Bretton Woods could be highly inappropriate, so comparisons between the fixed exchange rate regime of Bretton Woods and the current managed floating regime can be inadequate. For instance, the post-1973 time interval has been characterized by inflation and unemployment rates that, on average, have been well above those under Bretton

Woods. Output growth after 1973 has also been slower than the Bretton Woods average. These data, however, should not be taken to indicate superiority of the performance of Bretton Woods over that of managed floating. The explanation is that, in contrast to the relative global economic stability of Bretton Woods, the post-1973 period has involved massive external shocks to the economies of the industrial countries. The oil crises of 1973 and 1979 were major exogenous disturbances to the world economy; there were no comparable shocks under Bretton Woods. The external debt crisis of developing countries in the 1980s and early 1990 was another major disturbance which Bretton Woods was spared. Ideally, comparing the performance of alternative international monetary regimes requires controlled comparisons. For that reason, evaluations based on a casual look at the behavior of the industrial economies are not appropriate. It may be that exchange rate flexibility has not contributed to accentuating economic instability, but that the apparent massive global economic disturbances that occurred in the 1970s and 1980s contributed to accentuating exchange rate instability. The question of the relative economic performance of Bretton Woods and managed floating must for now remain an open question.

In addition to giving rise to a few "I told you so" comments, the significance of the performance of the current regime of floating dollar exchange rates to the debate on fixed versus flexible exchange rates is greatly eclipsed by the extent of central bank intervention. The current regime is one of managed floating; as such, it cannot be considered to be either free floating or fixed exchange rates but a hybrid regime. Indeed, the nature of the present system has led to recasting the debate between fixed and flexible exchange rates from one involving irreconcilable adversaries to one involving what is the desirable or optimal degree of exchange rate flexibility. The point has been made that whether the economy should peg or float exchange rates depends on the particular economic environment or the specific economic disturbance facing a country.[22] As a matter of fact, an economy could find it optimal to adopt a fixed exchange rate vis-à-vis some countries and a flexible exchange rate against others. This type of regime is what European countries are trying to achieve through European monetary unification. Through unification, EMS member countries are, in effect, seeking the ultimate fixed exchange rate among themselves: the presence of one currency. At the same time, this currency—the ECU perhaps—would fluctuate relative to the dollar, the yen, and other currencies. The next section examines the economic issues behind unification.

22–9. MONETARY UNIFICATION AND THE EUROPEAN MONETARY UNION

In May 1989, the EMS Council of Ministers endorsed the recommendation toward economic and monetary union incorporated in the Delors Report.[23] The goal of moving toward a monetary union sketched out in the Delors Report has required enormous effort. The Maastricht Treaty of December 1991 set the year 1994 for the creation of an embryonic European central bank. Eventually, the central bank will be in charge of monetary policy for the EMS as a whole. The ultimate goal is to create a single currency for Europe and to create a European Monetary Union (EMU) to replace the EMS.

The EMU will differ from current arrangements because it will entail establishing permanent, fixed exchange rates and the abandonment of the present realignment system. The European central bank will establish a centralized monetary policy for the union as a whole.[24] Monetary policy will be determined by negotiation within the union's central bank. Some rules or procedures would thus have to be established to determine member countries' representation in setting monetary policy. Depending on the procedures followed, the monetary policy process could entail economic incentives to individual countries unlike those under the EMS. For one, the members of a monetary union would not be able to set their own money supplies. There would therefore have to be a bargaining process in the formation of the union to determine how the monetary policies of the Eurocentral bank would be governed and how seigniorage revenues would be allocated.[25] The credibility the union lends to the European central bank would depend on how these decisions are made. Another aspect that would have to be specified is the role of fiscal policies in the union and whether restrictions on individual countries need to be or should not be imposed.

The Determination of Monetary and Fiscal Policies Under Unification

As discussed earlier in this chapter, the arrangements and commitments attached to EMS membership have provided an anti-inflation anchor linked to the German mark. The arrangement can

---

[22]See, for instance, J. Frenkel and J. Aizenman, "Aspects of the Optimal Management of Exchange Rates," *Journal of International Economics* (November 1982); D. Henderson, "The Role of Intervention Policy in Open Economy Financial Policy: A Macroeconomic Perspective," International Finance Discussion Paper no. 202 (Washington, D.C.: Federal Reserve Bank, February 1982); and E. Helpman and M. June Flanders, "On Exchange Rate Policies for a Small Country," *The Economic Journal* (March 1978).

[23]The details of the European unification drive are spelled out in Chapter 2.

[24]Some limited leeway on monetary policy could be left to individual countries. A government could buy back or augment its debt, with monetary implications similar to those of central bank open-market operations. Also, reserve requirements could be used to implement monetary policy, albeit on a very restricted basis.

[25]See A. Casella, "Voting on the Adoption of a Common Currency," in M. B. Canzoneri et.al., *Establishing a Central Bank: Issues in Europe and Lessons from the U.S.* (Cambridge: Cambridge University Press, 1992), and R. Chang, "Bargaining a Monetary Union," (Department of Economics, New York University, February 1991), mimeo.

be seen as a mechanism that relinquishes the power to engage in monetary policy to the German Bundesbank, a certified, low-inflation-prone central bank. Germany's low-inflation preferences are then imposed on all members of the EMS. Monetary unification changes these conditions because the new European central bank replaces the Bundesbank as the center of policy formation. The determination of the EMU monetary policies is then a function of the internal decision-making procedures of the "Euro-Fed" and the incentives it faces under unification.

The new central bank's credibility problem under unification is in principle different from that under the EMS. Under the EMS, member central banks in a sense "borrow" the Bundesbank's credibility. Membership in a system dominated by a low-inflation country acts as a precommitment to a low-inflation policy. Under monetary unification, monetary policy is delegated to the European central bank. The Bundesbank's credibility can no longer be borrowed.

Which alternative arrangement, the EMS or the EMU, is likely to yield greater credibility? Which one should produce a lower inflation rate? Consider the move from a system of independent monetary policymaking to an EMS-styled adjustable fixed exchange rate regime. High-inflation countries joining the EMS would tend to achieve a lower inflation rate determined by dominant Germany. However, Germany has an incentive to export inflation to other members. It receives the seigniorage and inflation tax benefits from money creation, but the inflation costs are shared with the other EMS members. This situation provides incentives to choose an inflation rate higher than the low, conservative one that made Germany the leader of the EMS to begin with. In short, one should have expected convergence of inflation under the EMS—but not necessarily a reduction in average inflation: Under an EMS-type system, the dominant central bank can choose a higher inflation as a result of the changed incentives derived from its leadership position.

What happens when the monetary union is formed? In this case, the new, EC-wide monetary authority would share the concerns not only of the German central bank, but also those of the other countries seeking a low-inflation, credible policy. As a result, the incentives that promote increased inflation under a system like the EMS disappear. This effect suggests that the EMU could even have a lower inflation rate than the EMS. However, how the member countries' voting power is distributed within the central bank affects the final inflation outcome. This decision-making process could offset the internalization effect. For instance, a coalition of countries that desire high inflation can block the preferences of low-inflation prone countries within the union. The coalition would then force a higher average inflation rate than would be obtained under a regime dominated by a low-inflation prone country. Because the internalization and the coalition effects can go in different directions, there is no clear presumption about whether a monetary union would experience more or less inflation than the EMS.

Fiscal Policy in a Monetary Union

Although it is clear that in a monetary union there is no independent domestic monetary policymaking, the possibility of independent fiscal policies remains. Countries can run budget deficits financed through the accumulation of debt. The size of the deficit depends on the deficit country's ability to borrow. Unless the monetary union limits them directly, member countries can run as large a deficit as the financial markets can tolerate.

The Delors Report proposed to restrict the size of the member countries' government budget deficits. Many economists have raised questions about, first, whether these restrictions are necessary for the success of the union and, second, whether they are wise. The experience with existing monetary unions is that the central authority does not tend to impose limits on the budget deficits that the members can incur. Looking at the

U.S. as a monetary union composed of American states, we find that the federal government imposes no limits on state debt. The limits that exist in some states are self-imposed. Within the EMS, the fact that the Netherlands managed to have 10 percent fiscal deficit to GDP ratios in combination with a stable guilder-deutsche mark exchange rate in the 1980s, suggests that relatively large government deficits are consistent with a stable exchange rate. In the Netherlands, the stable exchange rate was feasible because budget deficits were not heavily monetized. Nonmonetization of budget deficits is precisely what a monetary union can insure as a way to keep fiscal policy independence consistent with a fixed exchange rate. By making monetary policy a collective decision, a monetary union cuts loose the link between fiscal deficits and their monetization by domestic monetary authorities.[26]

In general, so long as the financial situation of an individual country does not compromise the health of the system as a whole, there is no need to restrict fiscal policies for the success of a monetary union. However, if there is no need to restrict or coordinate member countries' fiscal policies in a monetary union, the issue as to whether it is wise to do so remains. Because fiscal deficits are a mechanism to smooth out adjustment to changed circumstances, placing effective restrictions on them can make adjustments to recessions and supply shocks more difficult. Furthermore, as U.S. attempts to impose legal constraints on budget deficits in the 1980s show, these restrictions are not always effective.

Assuming the absence of legal restrictions on budget deficits, does a monetary union affect, by itself, the incentives to incur such deficits? The main factor here is that domestic fiscal deficits cannot be monetized by domestic authorities in a monetary union. A government that is running a deficit does not have a domestic central bank to monetize its debt. In a monetary union, the government would have to convince the union's central bank to promote a more expansionary monetary policy. Even if the government were to achieve this, it would only benefit according to the share it has in seigniorage and inflation tax proceeds. Because of this, individual governments face a more difficult budget constraint under a monetary union than if they were to conduct their own independent monetary policy.[27] The presumption is that the nonmonetization of debt and the consequent "harder budget constraint" create incentives for lower budget deficits than under either the EMS or exchange rate flexibility.

22–10. OPTIMUM CURRENCY AREAS

Because exchange rate adjustments are truly ruled out, the preconditions for the success of an EMU are more stringent than those for the existing system of adjustable exchange rates. The required precondition is that exchange rate adjustments not be a key to successful macroeconomic performance. If the right preconditions are not met, a monetary union will either fail to be negotiated or will produce poor macroeconomic performance. This section investigates the conditions under which fixed exchange rates dominate exchange rate flexibility as a currency regime for a particular group of countries.

---

[26]In principle, a central bank that acts independently of the fiscal authorities can play the same role in ensuring the nonmonetization of deficits. See M. Fratianni and J. von Hagen, "Monetary Union and Central Bank Independence," in F. Rivera-Batiz and R. Ginsberg, eds., *The European Regional Economic Integration of 1992*, published as a Special Issue of the journal *Regional Science and Urban Economics* (Summer 1993).

[27]This point has been made by P. De Grauwe, "Fiscal Discipline in Monetary Unions," in F. Rivera-Batiz, ed., *The European Economic Integration of 1992*, appearing as a Special Issue of *International Economic Journal* (Spring 1992). The argument assumes that the monetary union is not financially supporting the governments directly. In the United States, for example, there is a system by means of which the federal government finances some state expenditures. This effect can undo difficult budget constraints.

Factors Promoting Monetary Unions

What are the conditions for a well-functioning monetary union? A well-functioning monetary union should contribute to stabilizing income and prices and facilitating payments adjustment among participating countries. Columbia University economist Robert Mundell has stressed the need for substantial factor (capital and labor) mobility as a precondition for a successful monetary union.[28] He has argued that regions or countries featuring high factor mobility should join in a single currency area or a multicurrency area with fixed exchange rates (to which he referred as an optimum currency area); those regions or countries whose factors are relatively immobile should adopt flexible exchange rates vis-à-vis each other. The issues can best be appreciated by analyzing how two regions, say West and East, react to an exogenous shift in demand away from Western and toward Eastern goods. This disturbance, would—everything else being constant—tend to generate a trade surplus and inflationary pressures in the East and a trade deficit and stagnation in the West. A depreciation of Western currency in terms of Eastern currency, however, could switch demand back to the West, offsetting the aggregate demand effects of the initial disturbance. This stabilizing property is one of the main arguments for exchange rate flexibility. Exchange rate changes, however, will not always be necessary for adjustment to occur. A high degree of factor mobility would result in migration from West to East. This mobility would increase the supply of factors of production and output and alleviate inflationary pressures in the East, while relieving

unemployment in the West. Factor mobility, then, acts as a substitute for exchange rate changes in achieving equilibrium and improving welfare in both regions, suggesting that it is an important condition in the success of monetary union. Indeed, the considerable promotion of European factor market integration after World War II must have paved the way for the monetary union experiments in that region.

Factor mobility is not, though, a necessary or sufficient condition for a successful monetary union. Stanford University economist Ronald McKinnon has argued, for example, that small open economies will not be able to use exchange rate flexibility effectively: In such economies domestic prices would react quickly to exchange rate changes, nullifying any impact the exchange rate changes would otherwise have on the relative price of domestic and foreign goods.[29] A high share of traded goods relative to nontraded goods in the economy would then essentially mean that the country faces externally given prices and cannot alter relative prices through exchange rate changes. It is in countries with a significant nontraded goods sector that exchange rate changes can have a substantial impact on the economy by altering the relative price of traded and nontraded goods. In conclusion, even if there is zero factor mobility, countries might be advised to peg their currencies if they are small and open and produce an insignificant amount of nontraded goods.

Other factors can affect the choice of a monetary union. When different countries join under the head of a single monetary authority, complications may arise regarding the financing of fiscal deficits. The usual interaction between the economy's central bank and treasury in financing the government is now subordinated to the jurisdiction of the currency area's monetary authorities—something that might be objectionable to domestic policymakers. As a matter of fact, the nature of a

---

[28]R. Mundell, "A Theory of Optimum Currency Areas" *American Economic Review* (September 1961). For surveys of the literature on the subject, see the articles in M. de Cecco and A. Giovannini, eds., *A European Central Bank? Perspectives on Monetary Unification After Ten Years of the EMS* (Cambridge: Cambridge University Press, 1988), and P. De Grauwe, *The Economics of Monetary Integration* (Oxford: Oxford University Press, 1992).

[29]R. I. McKinnon, "Optimum Currency Areas," *American Economic Review* (September 1963).

monetary union strongly suggests that the regions or countries involved must have some common political interests and/or a willingness to adopt fiscal and monetary policies consistent with those of the other countries in the union. This requires close similarity of political and/or economic interests. It would be naive to assume that countries with long-standing sociopolitical conflicts, such as Greece and Turkey or Iran and Iraq, would convene to form a monetary union. Similarly, countries desiring different policy mixes would have difficulty agreeing on a common monetary policy. If countries A and B form a common currency area, but country A feels that a 15 percent growth of the money supply is more consistent with its booming, developing economy, and country B considers a 5 percent money growth more appropriate to contain its high inflation rate, there is little chance a consensus will be reached on the growth of the common currency supply. Similarity and/or affinity in sociopolitical and economic spheres may be the deciding factor contributing to the success of a monetary union.

22−11. THE INTERNATIONAL ECONOMICS OF REFORM IN EASTERN EUROPE AND THE FORMER SOVIET UNION

The late 1980s and early 1990s saw anti-communist revolutions in Eastern Europe and the breakdown of the Union of Soviet Socialist Republics (USSR) into a group of fifteen independent republics, most of which have remained part of a much looser Commonwealth of Independent States. As many of these countries moved toward creating market economies, the wide array of international issues examined in this book have been prominent. Key among them is the question of whether the now-independent republics should form part of an economic union with other countries.

Monetary Integration or Disintegration?

Eastern European countries have expressed acute interest in forming part of the EEC. In fact, they perceive the distinction between Eastern and Western Europe as being the artificial result of the communist–non–communist separation after World War II. Many of the intellectual leaders of the revolutions in these countries saw the dismantling of the Berlin Wall as a dissolution of the East-West division as well. They refer to the region as East Central, or Middle, Europe to stress the artificiality of the distinction. Although in the case of East Germany, the East-West differentiation has indeed collapsed into unification, the prospects for other countries to join the EC in the near future are not so good. There are, first of all, major changes occurring every day in the region's fundamental political and economic institutions. Some countries, such as Poland, Czechoslovakia, and Hungary, appear to be moving quickly to multiparty parliamentary democracies with full-fledged market economies and private property. Others are moving more slowly or not at all. Whatever the country, the transition from economies in which the state sector dominated most activities to economies with a more limited governmental role will take many years. Because the economic links between the EC and most Eastern European countries have been minimal in the last few decades, we can expect their integration into the EC to be slow.

The case of the former Soviet republics is altogether different. Before the breakup of the USSR in the early 1990s, the republics operated under a monetary union, with the Russian ruble as the single currency. The ruble was not a convertible currency: Local residents were not permitted to purchase or sell foreign currencies in exchange for rubles. Until the late 1980s, the state officially exchanged rubles through a set of multiple fixed rates; for instance, in 1988, the exchange rate for trade and investment transactions was equal to R1.8 per dollar. In response to the emergence of a thriving black market in dollars in the late 1980s (in which the dollar could fetch as much as R25), the Soviet government experimented with selling some foreign currencies through auctions, a practice that continues.

With the political turmoil, economic crisis, and eventual dissolution of the central government of the Soviet Union, a huge budget deficit emerged. In 1991, the consolidated budget deficit became more than 15 percent of the GDP, having been on the order of 9 percent in 1990.[30] The deficit was financed mostly through monetization. As a result, when control over the printing of the Soviet currency was shifted to Russia's President Boris Yeltsin in November 1991, the central government was running its printing presses twenty-four hours a day to finance the deficit expenditures. (In June 1992, the Russian government owed workers one trillion rubles in back payments.) By May 1993, the ruble was worth close to R940 per dollar in the black market and in weekly bank auctions. This rapid depreciation of the currency was in response to soaring prices (the inflation rate in mid-1993 was running at an annual rate of 200 percent).

The choice facing the budding former Soviet republics was either to continue the use of the ruble or create new currencies of their own. The IMF—which became involved in lending to the republics after their entry as members of the fund—favored the formation of a central bank, based on the existing Russian central bank. The central bank would govern the supply of rubles and monetary policy all over the Commonwealth (the Commonwealth excludes four former Soviet republics: Estonia, Latvia, Lithuania, and Georgia). However, some republics were reluctant to maintain a Russian-based central bank. Because of

the serious political, cultural, and economic tensions with Russia, some republics have reacted by organizing their own central banks and creating their own currencies. The Ukraine, for instance, has moved to create a national currency, the *grivna,* although rubles, dollars, and other temporary currencies (called coupons) circulate more or less freely in Kiev. The outcome of this process is that, while Western Europe is engaged in a historical move toward monetary unification, the former Soviet republics are approaching monetary disintegration.

Exchange Rate Policy in Emerging Market Economies

Lack of confidence in the ruble has been one of the key difficulties faced by President Boris Yeltsin, the IMF, and others in their quest to keep the ruble the common currency of the confederation of former Soviet republics. To solve this difficult problem, the IMF promised a $24-billion aid package in 1993, out of which $6 billion would be used as a reserve fund to buy rubles to prevent the currency from depreciating in value. Under the conditionality terms of IMF lending ("stand-by agreement"), however, the fund requested that Russia commit to a plan of economic reforms involving, as a prime component, the balancing of the budget. As part of this plan, Russia promised to seek ruble convertibility by allowing the ruble to float freely and by allowing Russian residents to buy and sell dollars for rubles. There have been alternative proposals. One would set a dual exchange rate system, with one exchange rate floating and the other under a controlled floating regime. Others have suggested that, although the ruble should depreciate in line with inflation, once the Russian government "puts its house in order" through economic reform, the value of the ruble should be fixed vis-à-vis a "hard" currency like the dollar.[31]

---

[30]For a discussion of events in the republics forming part of the former Soviet Union and the economics of reform in the "new" countries, see D. Lipton an J. Sachs, "Prospects for Russia's Economic Reforms," *Brookings Papers on Economic Activity* (1992); S. Fischer, "Stabilization and Economic Reform in Russia," *Brookings Papers on Economic Activity* (1992); and IMF, *The Economy of the U.S.S.R.: Summary and Recommendations* (December 1990).

[31]See S. H. Hanke, "Soviets Need Honest Money, Not Aid," *The Wall Street Journal,* June 1991.

The issues surrounding the ruble are typical of those facing other former communist countries. Early in the economic reform process started by countries like Poland and Czechoslovakia, a choice between a flexible or a pegged exchange rate (or a mix) had to be made. Often, the debate centers on two issues. If the currency is allowed to float, policymakers worry about possible speculative outbursts that may cause the exchange rate to lose value not based on fundamentals. On the other hand, there are difficulties involved in setting a fixed exchange rate that is not overvalued; it is feared that, if unaccompanied by restrictive monetary and fiscal policies, a fixed rate in these countries would soon become overvalued, disrupting international trade and investment.

Given these conflicting considerations, many developing countries have chosen a middle way in the form of a *crawling peg* regime. Under this regime, the country sets a peg, or par, value for its currency; at the same time, it allows the peg to change gradually, in small steps, over time. The crawling peg is therefore an adjustable peg regime, as the Bretton Woods system was. The main difference between them lies in the exchange rate adjustments, which under Bretton Woods were supposed to be less frequent and of larger magnitude. In a sense, the crawling peg is another hybrid between fixed and flexible exchange rates because it embodies aspects of both regimes: External balance adjustments now involve both changes in international reserves as well as exchange rate changes.[32]

Key aspects in setting up a crawling peg regard the currency (or basket of currencies) selected to peg and which rule, if any, to follow in making exchange rate adjustments—that is, by how much and how fast exchange rates will change. For instance, a possible exchange rate rule is to set monthly changes in the exchange rate based on the differential between domestic and foreign inflation rates in previous months. Such a ppp rule would allow domestic inflation to diverge from world inflation without major effects on real exchange rates and, therefore, on domestic competitiveness. One disadvantage of such a rule is that because future exchange rate changes are not determined much in advance, speculation based on inflationary expectations might arise as to future exchange rate adjustments, generating instability.[33] An alternative rule would be to set a preannounced path of exchange rate changes, such as Chile instituted by means of its *tablita* (a table of preset exchange rate changes) in the late 1970s, which other Latin American countries have followed recently. One of the possible advantages of this type of crawling is that it tends to reduce the instability surrounding speculation about exchange rate changes and thereby the possibility of exchange crises. At the same time, in practice, governments also alter exchange rate rules by reducing, say, the rate of devaluation of domestic currency; therefore, destabilizing speculation may still arise.

Another postulated advantage of the crawling peg lies in the possibility that central banks may be able to hold a smaller volume of international reserves as a buffer to finance balance-of-payments deficits. The explanation lies in that, everything else being constant, the heightened use of exchange rate changes as a device for external balance under a crawling peg regime might reduce the level of reserves below those required in a regime where only expenditure-changing policies are used to solve balance-of-payments problems.

Whatever the relative costs and benefits of fixed, flexible, and crawling peg regimes, several of the postrevolutionary governments have already followed pegged exchange rate regimes. In Czechoslovakia, the local currency, the koruna, was pegged to a basket of currencies of major Western

---

[32]For an economic analysis of the simultaneous determination of the balance of payments (or changes in international reserves) and the exchange rate under a crawling peg applied to the case of Brazil, see M. Blejer and L. Leiderman, "A Monetary Approach to the Crawling Peg System: Theory and Evidence," *Journal of Political Economy* (February 1981).

[33]Arguments for and against the crawling peg and various exchange rate rules can be found in J. Williamson, *Exchange Rate Rules: The Theory, Performance, and Prospects of the Crawling Peg* (New York: St. Martin's, 1981).

trading partners. In Poland, the foreign exchange market consists of a dual market, with an officially pegged exchange rate for current account transactions and a parallel market for other transactions. Before this system was implemented, though, the Polish currency (the zloty) was sharply devalued to align it with the black market exchange rate. The argument made was that this reflected the equilibrium exchange rate.[34]

One of the major aspirins for the headaches faced by Eastern European countries (countries that have suffered from a serious case of stagflation, with sharp contractions of economic activity combined with rapidly rising prices) has been the foreign aid supplied by the world community. In April 1992, for instance, a $44-billion package of aid to Russia and fourteen other former Soviet republics was constructed. It included bilateral aid from the EC, the United States, and other countries, deferred debt payments, and World Bank and IMF loans. One of the concerns raised by the resources flowing into the region is the impact that they may have on the world capital market. Fears of a global shortage of capital have emerged, given low or declining savings rates in the industrialized nations and the higher demands for funds in Eastern Europe and the former Soviet Union. As Michael Camdessus, managing director of the IMF has noted: "In the absence of concerted and decisive action, the potential imbalance between projected saving and intended investment can only be resolved by crowding out some investment, probably to the detriment of the developing and reforming countries."[35] Indeed, Harvard economist Susan M. Collins and Columbia's Dani Rodrik estimate that the increase in capital flows to Eastern Europe and the former Soviet Union could raise world interest rates between roughly one and three percentage points or reduce net transfers of resources to developing countries in the range of 1 to 3 percent of developing-country income.[36]

The role of the IMF in the economic reforms and aid packages to republics from Eastern Europe and the former Soviet Union has been key. The next section discusses the history of the IMF's involvement in world affairs.

22–12. THE INTERNATIONAL MONETARY FUND AND ITS CURRENT ROLE IN THE WORLD ECONOMY

The IMF is a membership organization of nations.[37] It is open to countries that consent to abide by its Articles of Agreement—the IMF's basic constitution—and agree to contribute an assigned *subscription, or quota,* a sort of entry fee, 75 percent of which is to be paid in the currency of the member country and the remaining 25 percent in SDRs or a currency acceptable to the IMF (originally this portion was payable in gold). The quotas are determined by a formula that takes into account the size of the country and its importance in international trade. The voting power of a member country is directly related to its quota and is thus unevenly distributed among countries. For instance, the United States commands about 20 percent of the total number of votes, whereas the smaller countries' voting power is indeed negligible.

The board of governors, in which every member has a representative casting the votes assigned to the country, is the senior IMF decision-making body. It approves all amendments to the Articles of Agreement and decides on such matters as the acceptance of new members and the allocation of SDRs. The board of governors only meets from

[34]See D. Lipton and J. D. Sachs, "Creating a Market Economy in Eastern Europe: The Case of Poland," *Brookings Papers on Economic Activity* (1990).

[35]M. Camdessus, "Momentous Changes in the Global Economy Raise Difficult Transitional Problems," *IMF Survey* (March 1992), p. 83.

[36]S. M. Collins and D. Rodrik, *Eastern Europe and the Soviet Union in the World Economy* (Washington, D.C.: Institute for International Economics, 1991).

[37]A full description of the IMF can be obtained from A. W. Hooke, *The International Monetary Fund: Its Evolution, Organization, and Activities,* 2nd ed., Pamphlet Series no. 37 (Washington, D.C.: IMF, 1982).

time to time; actually, a governor is typically a minister of finance or the head of the central bank of a member country, having a full set of commitments besides being on the board. Responsibility for the IMF's day-to-day operation belongs to the executive board, consisting of executive directors representing member countries and headed by a managing director, the IMF's chief executive officer.

Created originally to monitor and oversee the operation of the Bretton Woods system, the IMF has proved to be a survivor in international monetary affairs. More than a decade after Bretton Woods passed away, it operates in full capacity and remains a pivotal international financial institution. From an original membership of fewer than fifty countries, the IMF currently embraces more than 156 countries (a substantial number of them excolonial territories that did not exist as independent nations when the IMF was created). These comprise most countries in the world, except China, which has never joined the fund, and a few others—mostly communist—countries. In April 1992, the IMF announced that its members had voted to allow Russia and the other republics of the former Soviet Union to become members.

Although the fund's rules and operations have changed over time to adapt to drastically altered circumstances, its basic objectives have remained unchanged: to contribute to maintaining a stable and workable international payments system that stimulates international trade and promotes worldwide economic growth. How the fund works toward attaining these objectives is best shown by examining its current functions in international monetary affairs.

Perhaps the IMF's foremost current role, and the main reason it has been in the headlines lately, is its lending to member countries. Counting with huge financial assets, the IMF is a major leaguer among financial institutions and an important supplier of funds to member countries. The main source of funds the IMF itself has available is provided by its member countries in the form of subscriptions, or quotas, but also through their lending to the IMF.

The IMF provides last-resort financing to those countries with short-term balance-of-payments difficulties. In doing so, it contributes toward speeding up the balance-of-payments adjustment process in those countries and prevents disruptive monetary crises. The loans usually serve to finance directly the replenishing of international reserves, external debt repayments, and so on. Most fund lending is made on a conditional basis—that is, the fund imposes conditions on the countries to which it lends. These include restrictions on economic policies—such as reductions in government budget deficits or monetary contractionism—that are deemed by many to be undue foreign intervention in the countries involved, particularly in the less developed countries, which represent a substantial portion of the fund's clientele. The issue of conditionality has strong political connotations, especially in light of the fund's being effectively controlled by a few large industrial countries. The restrictions on economic policies imposed by IMF conditions are themselves the subject of controversy, as we have repeatedly shown in previous chapters (particularly chapters 12 and 16).

The IMF's role in the international monetary system was at the forefront in the debt crisis of the 1980s, when the IMF emerged as a main negotiator, collaborator, and intermediary in the negotiations between creditor and debtor countries. Its coordinating role is generally considered to have been crucial in the successful completion of many negotiations.

Finally, the IMF is the organism in charge of creating SDRs, an international reserve asset. In this respect, it fulfills some of the functions of a world central bank, but only partially, because SDRs comprise less than 5 percent of world international reserves. Furthermore, the SDR does not generally circulate as a currency and has a limited commercial use. Other IMF functions include providing a code of conduct in international trade and financial matters (it condemns competitive devaluations and other beggar-thy-neighbor policies) and surveillance over member exchange controls and other restrictions that obstruct international trade (although countries no longer have any commitment or obligation to follow IMF guidelines).

22−13. THE REFORM AND EVOLUTION OF INTERNATIONAL MONETARY ARRANGEMENTS: A SUMMING UP AND A LOOK AHEAD

We have now completed an overview of the main international monetary arrangements currently prevailing in the world economy. We conclude by venturing some comments on where we stand and on where to go in terms of international monetary reform.

In the present context, there are three major international economic developments associated predominantly with the post-Bretton Woods era that have drastically modified the world economy. The first one regards the higher degree of exchange rate flexibility faced by the industrial countries; the second is the growth of international financial markets—including the Eurocurrency market—and the enhanced degree of international capital mobility; and the third is the decline in the role of gold and the dollar in international reserve transactions among central banks. In addition, there is a common thread running through the many events of the post-Bretton Woods era: the substantial variability observed of certain fundamental economic variables. Although not a general rule, it is widely recognized—as documented in this and previous chapters—that the last decade has witnessed substantial variability of real exchange rates, nominal and real interest rates, and inflation rates. There are two schools of thought interpreting these observations. One argues that the marked turbulence of economic variables has been the product of the inherent uncertainty connected with recent economic and political events and that the current set of international monetary arrangements, if anything, has contributed to ameliorating the effects of such exogenous shocks. In

an extreme version of this viewpoint, there is no major problem with the state of current international monetary affairs.[38]

An alternative approach postulates that, in spite of the shocks to the system, the turbulence of economic variables has been excessive by any measure, and therefore the current state of international monetary arrangements requires some basic modifications to promote greater stability.[39] From this point of view, for instance, the greater degree of capital mobility since the 1970s has been associated with destabilizing speculative movements, generating sustained deviations of real exchange rates from fundamentals and resulting in distortionary effects on domestic inflation, output, and employment. It is implied that capital mobility has resulted in a system that is too greased, too easily and drastically influenced by purely speculative disturbances. It is from this vantage point that Nobel Prize winner James Tobin has argued that controls or disincentives on capital movements should be imposed—in the form of, say, interest rate equalization taxes—to "throw some sand on the wheels" of the system and stabilize its response to disturbances.[40] Opponents of such a proposal have noted its potentially distortionary effects if it channels capital to areas of low marginal productivity and out of higher productivity regions. Still, the proposal could be advocated as a second-best policy: Its stabilization benefits might more than offset the efficiency costs.

---

[38]See, for instance, M. Feldstein, "The Case Against Trying to Stabilize the Dollar," *American Economic Review* (May 1989), or A. C. Stockman, "Exchange Rates, the Current Account, and Monetary Policy," in W. S. Haraf and T. D. Willett, eds., *Monetary Policy for a Volatile Global Economy* (Washington, D.C.: American Enterprise Institute, 1990).

[39]This view has been exposed by P. Krugman, "The Case for Stabilizing Exchange Rates," *Oxford Review of Economic Policy* (February 1989); R. McKinnon, "Monetary and Exchange Rate Policies for International Financial Stability: A Proposal," *Journal of Economic Perspectives* (Winter 1988); and J. Williamson, "The Case for Roughly Stabilizing the Real Value of the Dollar," *American Economic Review* (May 1989).

[40]See J. Tobin, "A Proposal for International Monetary Reform," *Eastern Economic Journal* (July-October 1978).

The future of the international monetary system seems uncertain at this point. Recent proposals for modifying or reforming international monetary arrangements are baffling in their diversity. Each politician or economist seems to have his or her own pet proposal, whether it is a return to the gold standard, a pegged exchange rate regime, full flexibility of currency values, managed floating, managed floating with cooperation and coordination among countries, target zones of exchange rate stability, or other hybrid systems. Behind these proposals is a whole range of arguments for or against alternative exchange rate regimes, arguments that have a long history of debate.

For many years, the controversies centered on the relative merits of fixed and flexible exchange rate regimes in leading to economic stability and an efficient use of money in society. On the one hand, fixed rates were hailed by some because, under free currency convertibility, they mimic a single world currency—promoting monetary efficiency—and impose some discipline on the use of economic policy instruments. On the other hand, it was recognized that fixed rates could impose a severe constraint on the ability of a country to choose its inflation rate because the latter was closely linked to world inflationary conditions. Individual countries could thus be prevented from attaining their optimal inflation rate as determined by their particular circumstances. In addition, pro-free-market economists claimed that a fixed exchange rate regime, as a price- (exchange rate) fixing mechanism, interferes with market determination of exchange rates and forces domestic economic policy, particularly monetary policy, to be geared toward keeping the exchange rate fixed. The business cycle insulation properties of a flexible exchange rate regime were stressed by pro-flexible-rates economists. Opponents pointed out the possibility of wildly fluctuating exchange rates and the likelihood that destabilizing speculation would move exchange rates away from their fundamental equilibrium values, with a deleterious effect on world trade and income.

In spite of some misgivings, most academic experts in the late 1960s were inclined to favor floating exchange rates as an international payments system. There were prominent exceptions, such as C. P. Kindleberger, A. B. Laffer, and R. A. Mundell, however. The experience since 1973 has shattered the belief in the insulating properties of exchange rate flexibility, as well as the hope that real exchange rate variability would not be much higher than under Bretton Woods. As a matter of fact, the increased awareness of interdependence in the world economy and the absence of rules governing central bank intervention in foreign exchange markets have led to a reformulation of the controversies on exchange rate regimes. The emphasis has shifted to other questions: the optimal degree of foreign exchange market intervention, the setting of exchange rate targets and currency bands[41], and, more recently, policy coordination among countries. Some economists currently propose a coordinated, managed floating regime as a better alternative to fixed and floating regimes, as well as to the current managed floating regime, which lacks a coordinating authority or general rules of intervention.

Inconsistent policy goals in a world lacking coordination can indeed be a source of difficulty for the current regime of managed floating. For instance, if the intervention of the United States in exchange markets tries to keep the dollar from appreciating while that of other countries is aimed at encouraging a depreciation of their currencies against the dollar, inconsistency and conflict will arise globally. These objectives cannot be realized simultaneously. Similarly, conflict arises if all countries try to achieve trade surpluses. Because

---

[41]A target zone establishes a broad band within which the exchange rate is allowed to fluctuate. Central banks are committed to intervene when the exchange rate reaches the margins of the band. For an analysis of the economics of target zones, see P. Krugman, "Target Zones and Exchange Rate Dynamics," *Quarterly Journal of Economics* (August 1991); and L.E.O. Svensson, "An Interpretation of Recent Research on Exchange Rate Target Zones," *Journal of Economic Perspectives* (Fall 1992).

the world trade surplus has to be zero, at least one country will find its effects frustrated. The problems connected to the presence of global constraints on national economic policies are often referred to collectively as the consistency, or $n-1$, problem: Once $n-1$ national authorities, in a set of n countries, have attained a certain trade balance or exchange rate target, the remaining country's trade balance or exchange rate is automatically determined. This last country's goal is redundant because it cannot be attained without frustrating other countries' targets. Because n independent goals may conflict and be impossible to attain, either one country abandons its targets, or some agreement is made by all countries to coordinate their policies and make them consistent. If countries try to pursue their own policies, the ensuing conflict might lead to losses for all—such as when the attempt to improve the trade balance in one country through protection results in reduced world trade but no improvement in each country's trade balance. The same type of issue arises with respect to exchange rate determination and the intervention policies of n countries trying to achieve targets regarding the value of their currencies.

Still, the issue of policy coordination and harmonization is not yet settled. There are enormous practical difficulties in implementing coordinated intervention policies. Two specific proposals that have been widely discussed recently are a return to a classic gold standard and the expansion of the SDR as an international reserve currency. In our discussion of the gold standard in Chapter 16, we noted the advantages and disadvantages of such a regime. Still, a basic problem with such a proposal is its political infeasibility. Rearranging international monetary arrangements at the present time would require the consent and coordination of the major industrial countries. Unilateral moves seem doomed to failure. The gold standard, however, imposes substantial constraints on the autonomy of domestic monetary authorities, something most industrial countries would probably be unwilling to accept. Besides, in a world in which gold supplies are largely monopolized by Russia and the Republic of South Africa, the return to a gold-determined world money supply seems politically infeasible.

An alternative set of proposals encourages the expansion of the SDR as an international reserve currency.[42] The proposals here include making the SDR more prominent by trying to induce voluntary substitution from dollars to SDRs. One possibility is for the IMF to issue a so-called substitution account by means of which the fund would accept dollar deposits owned by central banks and issue in exchange an equivalent amount in SDRs. The payment of interest on such an account would then encourage the substitution. Although it has been discussed at IMF meetings, the future of this proposal is still an open question.

It appears that the international monetary system is slowly moving toward multiple reserve currencies, with a decline in the role of gold and the dollar as international reserves. Even though the dollar continues to be a major reserve currency (see our discussion in Chapter 2), the fact that central banks keep diversified currency portfolios—holding ECUs, deutsche marks, yen, and Swiss francs as reserve currencies—is seen by some as a destabilizing force. The fear is that, in such a multiple reserve currency regime, central banks will shift among reserve currencies in response to actual or anticipated changes in economic variables, amplifying exchange rate movements in much the same manner as private speculators would (in the presence of currency substitution).[43] Proposals in this area usually promote a single reserve currency asset as international money, such as the SDR or a

---

[42]See P. B. Kenen, "The Use of the SDR to Supplement or Substitute for Other Means of Finance" in G. M. von Furstenberg, ed., *International Money and Credit: The Policy Roles* (Washington, D.C.: IMF, 1983); and D. M. Sobol, "A Substitution Account: Precedents and Issues," *Federal Reserve Bank of New York Quarterly Review* (Summer 1979).

[43]This is suggested by the evidence provided by C. F. Bergsten and J. Williamson, *The Multiple Reserve Currency System: Evolution, Consequences and Alternatives* (Washington, D.C.: Institute for International Economics, 1983).

composite currency involving the dollar, the German mark, and other currencies.

This chapter has surveyed a substantial number of proposals for reform of the international monetary system, most of them—as can be expected—plagued by controversy. As long as they continue to generate heat, it is clear that international monetary reform will continue to be in the headlines and remain at the center of the current international dialogue.

Summary

1. The mechanism of periodic political summits that has regularly gathered the top financial and monetary ministers and secretaries of major countries was born in the Rambouillet summit of 1975. This summit formally established the current regime of floating exchange rates and allowed exchange market intervention to keep orderly markets.

2. The floating exchange rate regime followed after 1973 by most industrial countries vis-à-vis the dollar has been characterized by active intervention of central banks in foreign exchange markets. The system has thus been one of managed floating. In September 1985, the G–5 finance ministers met and agreed to undertake a cooperative effort to generate a depreciation of the then strongly appreciating U.S. dollar. Since then, a system of central bank coordinated intervention has been developed by the major industrial countries. Regular consultation and joint actions were formalized by the G–7, which includes France, Germany, Great Britain, Japan, the United States, Italy, and Canada.

3. In theory, the coordination of economic policies can provide net benefits for the participating economies. The joint actions of countries can generate externalities or spillover effects absent when policies are undertaken noncooperatively. In practice, the implementation of coordinated policy initiatives faces many obstacles and could, in fact, be counterproductive by undermining the credibility of national economic policies.

4. Governments run into serious credibility problems when their policies are time inconsistent. Policies are subject to a time inconsistency problem when governments have an incentive to renege on previous policies and follow new policy packages even in the absence of unexpected events or surprises. Such is the case when there is a large government debt. In this instance, incentives exist for the government to inflate and reduce the real value of its debt. Inflation reduces the real value of public debt at the expense of money holders. Both noncooperative and cooperative regimes are subject to time inconsistency problems.

5. There are various possible mechanisms to enforce governments' commitments. All of them work by effectively limiting government action in practice. One way to insure that governments will keep their promises is by establishing a system of rules that impose a discipline in policy formation. Legal constraints, such as constitutional rules, impose limits on governments' actions. However, the consensus required to achieve them is often not feasible, partly because governments do not wish to tie their hands too much. Reputation can be a force in limiting governmental deviation from promised policies, but usually it is not enough. Another mechanism involves setting up rules to be maintained on the basis of a collective system of monitoring and rewards. The European Monetary System (EMS) has been alleged to fulfill that role.

6. Under EMS rules, inflation-prone countries are limited in the timing, frequency, and extent of exchange rate adjustments. As long as they inflate more than other member countries, they will face sustained currency appreciations. In practice, exchange rate realignments take place sporadically, are delayed in relation to ongoing domestic inflation, and when they occur they fail to compensate for past inflation. These

mechanisms limit exchange rate adjustments and force inflation-prone countries to bear the costs of their policies. The presumed effect is to reduce the incentives to inflate. The benefits of this system of "tying one's hand" derive from the credibility-enhancing effects it induces. The enhanced credibility of the central bank and the policymaking authorities makes up for the loss of policy autonomy involved in accepting EMS rules.

7. A target zone establishes a broad band within which the exchange rate is allowed to fluctuate. Central banks are committed to intervene when the exchange rate reaches the margins of the band. A nominal target zone keeps the nominal rate within predetermined bounds. A real target zone maintains the real exchange rates within set limits. Target zones reduce the responsiveness of the market exchange rate to changes in their fundamental determinants and stabilize the fluctuations of the exchange rates within the band. However, target zones are subject to attack and credibility problems when the central bank has low levels of reserves. Speculative attacks and credibility problems arise from a loss of confidence in the countries' ability to maintain the band.

8. Whether an economy should peg or float the exchange rate depends on its particular environment or the specific economic disturbances facing it. A country might find it optimal to adopt a fixed exchange rate against some currency and a flexible exchange rate against others.

9. A monetary union represents a group of countries that fix their exchange rates vis-à-vis each other and abdicate the active use of monetary policy. If a country is a small open economy with a minor nontraded goods sector and faces a high degree of factor mobility with another country, it will be more likely that a monetary union with that country will be successful.

10. In a world of fixed exchange rates, world inflation is determined by the world money supply, a major proposition of global monetarism. In the absence of government intervention, world inflation will be transmitted among the countries in the system, tending to push single-country rates toward world levels.

11. There is a close connection between changes in monetary growth and changes in domestic inflation in economies under flexible exchange rates, though this connection is a long-run one and arises only in the absence of real disturbances in the economy.

12. Under exchange rate flexibility, the monetary authorities have tighter control over the money supply and can generate deviations of domestic inflation from world levels. In order to prevent systematic changes in international competitiveness, however, countries with relatively high inflation will have depreciating currencies, whereas countries with low inflation will have appreciating currencies.

13. Increased exchange rate flexibility could lead to higher inflation rates if central banks adopt a purely accommodating monetary policy posture, automatically raising the money supply in response to deflationary disturbances, and tending to increase domestic prices.

14. Floating exchange rates can generate as much—if not more—interdependence as fixed exchange rates. A money supply expansion linked to a domestic nominal and real exchange rate increase will be associated with foreign nominal and real exchange rate reductions, having contractionary effects abroad.

Problems

1. In 1991, the Canadian government proposed amending the constitution of the Bank of Canada, Canada's central bank, to state that the bank's goal was "to achieve and preserve price stability." Do mandates and rules such as the one debated in Canada help central

banks achieve price stability or are they useless?

2. Compare pegging as followed in most developing countries with the mechanisms established by the EMS. Which system is more credible? Why? Examine the costs and benefits of each type of arrangement. Support your answer to this question with relevant empirical evidence on developing countries and the experience of the EMS. In particular, consider the frequency and extent of exchange rate readjustments, inflation levels, and real exchange rate stability.

3. In the discussions during 1990 to set a timetable for monetary unification among EMS members, the German central bank opposed the unification process. However, the German government voted in favor of the plan that would establish an embryonic European central bank by 1994. Why do you think the German government and central bank differed on this issue? Consider the costs and benefits of the plan, as well as the incentives faced by the government and the central bank.

4. The so-called Delors Report recommended imposing limits on the size of the budget deficits for the members of a future European Monetary Union. What does the experience of the United States and other countries suggest about the effectiveness of such measures?

5. Monetary integration is typically established in stages. Some experts suggest that a system of fixed exchange rates among participating countries should be introduced even before factor mobility and effective policy coordination and harmonization have been promoted. Others argue for the opposite path—that is, attaining the freer movement of labor and capital and coordinating policies before establishing fixed exchange rates and consummating the union. Discuss the arguments for and against each position and evaluate them. Provide, if possible, historical examples of how monetary integration has proceeded in practice.

6. Consider the following statement by Nobel Prize-winning economist Milton Friedman: "I think that international coordination does a great deal of harm, that it never does any good, and that there ought not to be any. If each country behaves properly in terms of its own interests, you will get the most effective kind of international coordination, which is through the market," [as stated in R. Hinshaw, ed., *International Monetary Issues After the Cold War, A Conversation among Leading Economists* (Baltimore: The Johns Hopkins University Press, 1993), p. 65)]. Do you agree or disagree with this statement. Why?

7. Would it aid Pennsylvania to be endowed with a separate currency, with a floating exchange rate against the dollar, in solving the problems of unemployed steelworkers?

8. Suppose that the U.S. government wants the world to return to a classic gold standard.
(a) Could it do so without coordination with other industrial countries?
(b) Assuming that all countries concerned agreed to belong to the system, would it be feasible—that is, would the regime be able to operate at all?

9. Some economists have suggested that industrial countries return to a gold exchange standard as an alternative to the current regime of floating exchange rates. Assume that the United States decided to fix the dollar price of gold. What problems, if any, economic and political, do you foresee arising from such a move?

10. Examine the advantages and disadvantages of a group of countries fixing their currency values in terms of each other, versus setting up a single currency area.

11. Could the state of Illinois suffer from balance-of-payments deficits? Could Illinois face an external debt crisis? Explain your answer.

12. Using the framework developed in chapters 16 and 17, analyze the short-run and long-run effects of a central bank credit expansion in an

economy under a crawling peg. Assume that the exchange rate rule followed is to raise the exchange rate in the same proportion as the last period's increase in domestic prices. For the sake of simplicity, assume no capital mobility and fixed foreign prices.

13. Consider the economics of exchange rate target zones. Proponents of target zones argue that such zones stabilize exchange rates and reduce the costs associated with exchange rate uncertainty. Other economists have been more skeptical, noting that target zones could be counterproductive, generating instead speculative activity and economic instability. In what ways could target zones give rise to speculative outbursts and instability? (*Hint:* Refer to Problem 6 in Chapter 1.)

14. Recent research suggests that macroeconomic crises could have great long-run benefits for the economies involved [see A. Drazen and V. Grilli, "The Benefit of Crises for Economic Reforms," *American Economic Review* (June 1993) and A. Alessina and A. Drazen, "Why are Stabilizations Delayed?" *American Economic Review* (December 1991)]. By accelerating necessary reforms, a crises leads to otherwise difficult policy reversals, which in the long-run provide a net gain to the country. Available evidence supports this perspective on crises. However, the evidence also suggests that successful stabilizations induced by crises

also lead to greater central bank independence from fiscal authorities [A. Cukierman, *Central Bank Strategy, Credibility and Independence* (Cambridge, Mass.: The MIT Press, 1992)]. Explain why central bank independence may be spurred by balance-of-payments crises.

15. Some economists suggest that a *currency board* represents a system which is superior to traditional fixed and flexible exchange rate regimes and could be a system of interest to Eastern European and former Soviet Republics seeking macroeconomic stability. Such a system has been used recently by only a few small countries, including Hong Kong and Singapore. Under currency boards, a Board exchanges domestic currency (say, zlotys) for a foreign reserve currency, say the dollar, at a specified, fixed rate (say, one to one). To perform this function, the Board is required to hold financial assets in the reserve currency at least equal to the value of the domestic currency outstanding [see A. Walters, "Currency Boards," in J. Eatwell, M. Milgate and P. Newman, eds., *The New Palgrave: A Dictionary of Economics* (London: Macmillan, 1987)]. Do you think currency boards are superior to traditional fixed exchange rate regimes? Why? Would you recommend it as a system to be adopted by the newly-created Republics of the former Soviet Union?

Author Index

Country Index

Subject Index